FUNDAMENTAL METHODS
OF MATHEMATICAL ECONOMICS

ALPHA C. CHIANG

Professor of Economics
The University of Connecticut

SECOND EDITION

McGRAW-HILL BOOK COMPANY

New York   St. Louis   San Francisco   Düsseldorf
Johannesburg   Kuala Lumpur   London   Mexico
Montreal   New Delhi   Panama   Paris
São Paulo   Singapore   Sydney   Tokyo   Toronto

Library of Congress Cataloging in Publication Data
Chiang, Alpha C   date

    Fundamental methods of mathematical economics.
    Bibliography: p.
    1.   Economics, Mathematical.   I.   Title.
HB135.C47   1974   330'.01'51   74-1214
ISBN 0-07-010780-7

**FUNDAMENTAL METHODS
OF MATHEMATICAL ECONOMICS**

1213141516 HDHD 898765432

This book was set in Modern.
The editors were Jack R. Crutchfield and Claudia A. Hepburn;
the designer was Nicholas Krenitsky;
the production supervisor was Sam Ratkewitch.
New drawings were done by Eric G. Hieber Associates Inc.

TO EMILY

CONTENTS

PREFACE
TO THE SECOND EDITION

Since the publication of the first edition, numerous economists have favored me with their generous comments and thoughtful suggestions. It is to find embodiment for many of these suggestions, as well as for certain ideas that have crystallized in my own mind in the meantime, that I am bringing out a new edition. With quite a few sections now duly amplified, and some others duly simplified, it is hoped that the present version will prove more useful than the previous one.

The most important change in this edition consists of an all-new chapter on nonlinear programming (Chap. 20), where I introduce the famous Kuhn-Tucker theorem (concave programming), as well as the subsequent Arrow-Enthoven generalization (quasiconcave programming). Substantial attention is paid in that discussion to the clarification of the important but tricky concept of the so-called "constraint qualification." The second major change is the explicit use of the implicit-function theorem as the analytical foundation for the entire discussion of the comparative statics of general-function models (Chap. 8). In the latter chapter, I now emphasize the total-differential method rather than the total-derivative method of obtaining the comparative-static derivatives.

Other changes are widely scattered in the various chapters. Among other things, I have adopted as standard terminology the names of *concave* and *convex functions* (Chap. 9 and thereafter), and also included new materials on quasiconcave and quasiconvex functions (Chaps. 12, 20). As an alternative means of testing the sign-definiteness of a quadratic form, the notion of the characteristic equation of a matrix has been introduced (Chap. 11), which is later compared with the characteristic equation of differential equations and difference equations (Chap. 17). There is in this edition also a discussion of L'Hôpital's rule (Chap. 12) and integration by parts (Chap. 13). The Lagrange multiplier is now given a full economic interpretation (Chap. 12), and this is later tied to the dual choice variable in linear programming (Chap. 19). Exact differential equations are now tackled by a simpler method (Chap. 14). In the dynamic models (Chaps. 14 to 17), a careful distinction is now made between the *intertemporal* and the *market-clearing* senses of equilibrium. New exercises have been added in many chapters. Also, in response to a suggestion by several people, I have attempted to "toughen" the exercises somewhat. But I have by no means abandoned my original intention of letting the exercises serve as drills to firm up the student's grasp and bolster his or her confidence, rather than as intellectual challenges that could unwittingly frustrate or intimidate the novice.

Despite the multitude of changes, the basic format and approach of the book has been kept intact. However, I have come to the realization that the book permits much more flexibility in its use than was suggested in the preface to the first edition. Upon completing the study of matrix algebra (Chap. 5), for instance, the reader may proceed directly to linear programming (Chaps. 18 and 19) and game theory (Chap. 21) without difficulty. Similarly, after finishing the topic of constrained optimization (Chap. 12), it is possible to proceed to nonlinear programming (Chap. 20) with or without the background of linear programming. Readers who are primarily interested in optimization problems may also omit the comparative-static analysis of general-function models (Chap. 8) and go from Chap. 7 directly to Chap. 9. In that case, though, it may be necessary also to omit Sec. 11.6 and the comparative-static portion of Sec. 12.4.

In one way or another, the following persons have influenced the final shape of this edition, and I wish to thank them all: Professors Nancy S. Barrett (The American University), Thomas Birnberg (Yale University), E. J. R. Booth (The University of Connecticut), Harald Dickson (University of Gothenburg, Sweden), Roger N. Folsom (Naval Postgraduate School), Jack Hirshleifer (University of California, Los Angeles), James C. Hsiao (Southern Connecticut State College), Ki-Jun Jeong (Seoul National University, Korea), J. Frank Sharp (New York University Graduate School of Business Administration), Dennis R. Starleaf (Iowa State University), and Mr. Chiou-Nan Yeh (University of Massachusetts). Since not all of their recommendations have been accepted, however, I alone must remain responsible for the finished product. In particular, I have regretfully decided to discard the suggestion to include in this edition an introduction to dynamic optimization. This topic cannot possibly be treated adequately without an extended excursion into the mathematical methods of calculus of variations, optimal control theory, and dynamic programming, but to undertake such an excursion would likely cause this book to burst at the seams. A better alternative is, therefore, to relegate the topic to a separate volume where it can be presented free from a stringent space constraint.

ALPHA C. CHIANG

PREFACE
TO THE FIRST EDITION

This book is written for economists. Its chief purpose is twofold: (1) to render a systematic exposition of certain basic mathematical methods, and (2) to relate these mathematical techniques to the various types of economic analysis in such a way that the mutual relevance of the two disciplines is clearly brought out. Two types of readers may therefore find it useful: first, those who possess the mathematical background but are looking for a bridge to link it to economics, and secondly, those who have yet to learn the mathematics. Since most readers will probably fall into the latter category, I have endeavored to develop the technical materials with considerable patience—assuming very little fore-knowledge and proceeding in a step-by-step manner designed to minimize the likelihood of the reader getting lost along the way. Moreover, I have resorted to a much greater degree of informality in the presentation than would please the mathematical purist in the belief that, especially in a book of this type, *readability* should be an overriding consideration.

In order to equip the reader with sufficient mathematics to wade through the current economic literature with confidence rather than trepidation, a wide range of mathematical topics is covered in the ensuing pages. Even though the treatment of each topic is of necessity limited to an elementary level, the reader who faithfully ploughs his way through the volume should acquire at least a reading knowledge, or even a working knowledge, of the concepts of sets, set operations, relations and functions, matrix algebra, differential and integral calculus, simple differential equations and difference equations, and the rudimentary notions of convex sets.

To integrate these mathematical subjects with economic analysis, numerous illustrations of mathematically formulated economic models are given in the text. Better yet, the entire book has actually been organized along *economic* rather than mathematical lines. After a brief introduction (Part 1), discussing the nature and structure of mathematical models, the remainder of the book is divided into five parts, each dealing with a distinct type of economic study:

Part 2: Static (or Equilibrium) Analysis

Part 3: Comparative-Static Analysis

Part 4: Optimization Problems
(a special case of equilibrium analysis)

Part 5: Dynamic Analysis

Part 6: Mathematical Programming and Game Theory
(a different framework of optimization)

The mathematical tools appropriate for each are then introduced in due order within the economic framework. By fitting the mathematics into the economic context, rather than the reverse, I believe the reader can gain a better perspective of the interrelation between the two disciplines, as well as a better motivation in the reading of the technical materials.

The arrangement of the economic topics, as outlined above, follows a natural order—from statics to comparative statics to dynamics. As it turns out, this arrangement leads also to a meaningful and convenient order of presentation for the relevant mathematical materials. The discussion of equilibrium analysis in Part 2 provides the setting for the introduction of elementary matrix algebra, because equilibrium analysis often involves the solving of a simultaneous linear-equation system. This early introduction of matrix algebra, a feature not usually found in the other books in the field, proves extremely desirable, since it permits the explicit use of vectors, matrices, and determinants throughout the remaining parts of the volume. In Part 3, the study of comparative statics leads to the notion of rate of change and of derivatives, including partial and total derivatives; these are then applied, in Part 4, to problems of optimization. In Parts 3 and 4, however, use is made of the matrix algebra learned earlier. When we proceed to dynamics in Part 5, the mathematics moves from the realm of differential calculus into that of integral calculus and differential equations, followed by a parallel discussion of difference equations. Here again, the reader will find matrix algebra of service. And finally, in mathematical programming and game theory, Part 6, matrix algebra again figures prominently, although elementary concepts of convex sets are also discussed there. In short, there is a systematic buildup of the "tool kit" in the text. For this reason, the reader is advised to read the first four parts (the first twelve chapters) in the exact order given. Part 5 and Part 6, on the other hand, may be read in reverse sequence. Mathematically, it is more desirable to let differential equations (Part 5) follow differential calculus (Part 4) directly, but in terms of economics, mathematical programming and game theory (Part 6) should follow optimization (Part 4) before tackling dynamics. The reader can take his choice.

The major guiding principle in the writing of this book is to make it readable and teachable. To this end, graphs are employed, wherever needed, to elucidate the mathematical discussion. Also, a liberal quantity of cross references are supplied so that the reader may review, compare, and integrate the various subjects presented at different points in the volume. Toward the same goal, intuitive and economic explanations are frequently given to clarify the *why* of a particular mathematical operation. Exercises are presented at the end of almost every section; for maximum benefit, the reader should work out as many of these exercises as possible, if indeed not all.

Although the emphasis within the book falls primarily on methodology, the text does contain detailed discussions of numerous economic models, including several models of the market, models of the firm and of the consumer, national-income models, input-output models, as well as models of economic growth. Consequently, aside from its obvious relevance to the standard courses of mathematics for economists and mathematical economics, it should also be helpful as a supplementary text in such courses as price theory, national-income analysis, business cycles, economic development, and economic growth.

The materials presented herein have been used by my students during the years past. Their questions and comments, especially those of Mrs. Roberta Grower Carey, often provided valuable guidance in the revisions which culminated in the present version. In addition, Professor Marc Nerlove of Northwestern University was kind enough to read the entire manuscript and to provide me with detailed suggestions that have led to substantial improvement. Professor John C. H. Fei of Yale University also read portions of the manuscript and made useful comments. To all of them, I am deeply grateful. My thanks go also to The University of Connecticut for lightening my teaching load while the book was under way. Last, but not least, I must express my profound appreciation to my wife, who not only had to relinquish countless hours of my time that rightfully belonged to her, but also cheerfully contributed her talent as a critic and as a typist to this undertaking.

ALPHA C. CHIANG

ONE

INTRODUCTION

1

THE NATURE OF MATHEMATICAL ECONOMICS

Mathematical economics is not a distinct branch of economics in the sense that public finance or international trade is. Rather, it is an *approach* to economic analysis, in which the economist makes use of mathematical symbols in the statement of his problem and also draws upon known mathematical theorems to aid in his reasoning. As far as the specific subject matter of analysis goes, it can be micro- or macroeconomic theory, or public finance, or the economics of underdeveloped countries, or what not.

Using the term *mathematical economics* in the broadest possible sense, one may very well say that every elementary textbook of economics today exemplifies mathematical economics insofar as geometrical methods are frequently utilized to derive theoretical results. Such a usage of the term is obviously too general. Conventionally, mathematical economics is reserved to describe cases employing mathematical techniques beyond simple geometry, such as matrix algebra, differential and integral calculus, differential equations, difference equations, and set theory. It is the purpose of this book to introduce the reader to the most fundamental aspects of these mathematical methods—those encountered daily in the current economic literature.

1.1   Mathematical versus Nonmathematical Economics

Since mathematical economics is merely an approach to economic analysis, it should not and does not differ from the *non*mathematical approach to economic analysis in any fundamental way. The purpose of any theoretical analysis, regardless of the approach, is always to derive a set of conclusions or theorems from a given set of assumptions or postulates via a process of reasoning. The major difference between "mathematical economics" and so-called "literary economics" lies principally in the fact that, in the former, the assumptions and conclusions are stated in mathematical symbols rather than words and in equations rather than sentences; moreover, in place of literary logic, use is made of mathematical theorems—of which there exists an abundance to draw upon—in the reasoning process. Inasmuch as symbols and words are really equivalents (witness the fact that symbols are usually defined in words), it matters little which is chosen over the other. But it is perhaps beyond dispute that symbols are more convenient to use in deductive reasoning, and certainly are more conducive to conciseness and preciseness of statement.

The choice between literary logic and mathematical logic, again, is a matter of little import, but mathematics has the advantage of forcing the analyst to make his assumptions explicit at every stage of reasoning. This is because mathematical theorems are usually stated in the "if-then" form, so that in order to tap the "then" (result) part of the theorem for his benefit, the analyst must assure that the "if" (condition) part does conform to the explicit assumptions adopted.

What about geometrical methods as a tool of analysis? Geometry is, of course, a branch of mathematics itself, and whenever it is utilized, we have categorically left the realm of literary economics. One decided advantage of geometrical analysis is its visual character, which makes it relatively easy to perceive and grasp. This advantage is, unfortunately, more than offset by its serious dimensional limitations. The reader may recall that in the usual graphical discussion of indifference curves, for instance, the standard assumption is that only *two* commodities are available to the consumer. Such a simplifying assumption is not willingly adopted but is forced upon us because the task of drawing a three-dimensional graph is exceedingly difficult and the construction of a four- (or higher) dimensional graph is actually a physical impossibility. To deal with the more general case of 3, 4, or n goods, we must instead resort to the more flexible tool of equations. This reason alone should provide sufficient motivation for the study of mathematical methods beyond geometry.

In short, we see that the mathematical approach has claim to the following advantages: (1) The "language" used is more concise and precise. (2) There exists a wealth of mathematical theorems at our service. (3) In forcing us to state explicitly all our assumptions as a prerequisite to the use of the mathematical theorems, it keeps us from the pitfall of an unintentional adoption of unwanted implicit assumptions. (4) It allows us to treat the general n-variable case.

These considerations comprise a substantial list of advantages. In fairness, however, we must grant equal time to the other side of the argument. The principal disadvantages of the mathematical approach are two: First, the language of mathematics is not the vernacular of all economists, and as a result there exist difficulties of communication between mathematical and nonmathematical economists. This means, on the one hand, that the nonmathematical economists cannot benefit from the findings of the mathematical economists (unless they take the trouble to translate their findings into the literary language). On the other hand, and perhaps more importantly, the mathematical economists cannot benefit from the critical reaction of the nonmathematical economists. Strictly speaking, this is not really a shortcoming of the mathematical approach itself but is rather a problem inherent in, and peculiar to, a particular period of transition—a phase in which there do exist two "camps" of economists. All the same, an economic theorist using the mathematical approach does run the risk of having a more limited audience for his research findings.

Second, an economist with mathematical training is subject to the dual temptations of (1) limiting himself to problems that *can* be solved mathematically and (2) adopting inappropriate economic assumptions for the sake of mathematical convenience. Unless he is careful, therefore, he may become preoccupied with, and engulfed in, *mathematical techniques* instead of *economic principles*. In other words, one may unwittingly let mathematics assume the status of master rather than servant. Should this happen, though, it represents the failing not so much of mathematical economics as of the economist himself.

The reader may notice that we have failed to list a frequently encountered criticism of the mathematical approach: namely, that mathematically stated theory is unrealistic. The reason we exclude this from the list is simply that such criticism is invalid. In fact, the epithet "unrealistic" cannot even be used in criticizing economic theory in general, whether or not the approach is mathematical. Theory is by its very nature an abstraction from the real world. It is a device for singling out only the most essential factors and discerning their interrelationships, so that we can study the essence of the problem at hand—free of the numerous specific complications that do exist in the actual world. Thus the statement "theory lacks realism" is merely a truism that cannot be accepted as valid criticism of theory. It then follows logically that it is quite meaningless to pick out any one approach to theory as unrealistic. For example, the theory of firm under pure competition is unrealistic, as is the theory of firm under imperfect competition, but whether these theories are derived mathematically or not is irrelevant and immaterial.

In sum, we might consider the mathematical approach as a "mode of transportation" that can take us from a set of postulates (point of departure) to a set of conclusions (destination) at a good speed. Common sense would tell us that, if a person intends to go to a place two miles away, he will very likely prefer driving to walking, unless he has time to kill or wants to exercise his legs. Similarly, a theorist who wishes to get to his conclusions more rapidly will find it convenient to "drive" the vehicle of mathematical techniques appropriate for his particular purpose. He will, of course, have to take "driving lessons" first; but since the skill thus acquired tends to be of service for a long, long while, the time and effort required would normally be well-spent indeed.

For a serious "driver"—to continue with the metaphor—some solid lessons in mathematics are imperative. According to a recommendation of the Social Sciences Research Council,[1] social scientists should be exposed to the following areas in mathematics: set theory, relations, functions, calculus, probability, matrix theory, finite differences, difference equations, differential equations, partial differentiation, and multiple integration. It is, of course, impossible to treat all these topics in detail in this volume, but most of them will find their way—if only at an elementary level—into the ensuing pages. Therefore, the reader who works through this book conscientiously should at least become proficient enough to comprehend most of the professional articles he will come across in such periodicals as the *American Economic Review, Quarterly Journal of Economics, Journal of Political Economy, Review of Economics and Statistics*, and *Economic Journal*. Those who, through this exposure, develop a serious interest in mathematical economics can then proceed to a more rigorous and advanced study of mathematics.

1.2   Mathematical Economics versus Econometrics

Many words in economics have been used in different senses by different writers, at different times, and in different contexts. The word *econometrics* is a case in point. According to one definition,[2] econometrics is "a special type of economic analysis in which the general theoretical approach—often formulated in explicitly mathematical terms—is combined—frequently through the medium of intricate statistical procedures—with empirical measurement of economic phenomena." In

---

[1] "Recommended Policies for the Mathematical Training of Social Scientists: Statement by a Committee of the Social Sciences Research Council," *Econometrica*, January 1956, pp. 82–86.
[2] Wassily Leontief, "Econometrics," in H. S. Ellis (ed.), *A Survey of Contemporary Economics*, Richard D. Irwin, Inc., Homewood, Ill., 1948, p. 388 (footnote).

this sense, econometrics is a general term encompassing both *theoretical* and *statistical* aspects of economic analysis.

In more recent usage, however, this word has acquired a narrower connotation, and it now refers almost exclusively to the study of empirical data by *statistical* methods of estimation and hypothesis testing. The application of mathematics to the purely *theoretical* aspects of economic analysis, on the other hand, has come to be referred to as mathematical economics. Consequently, econometrics and mathematical economics have become coordinate terms (instead of one being subordinate to the other), each denoting a distinct area of application of mathematical techniques in the study of economic problems.

In the present volume, we shall confine ourselves to mathematical economics. That is, we shall concentrate on the application of mathematics to deductive reasoning rather than inductive study, and as a result we shall be dealing primarily with theoretical rather than empirical material. This is, of course, solely a matter of choice of the scope of discussion, and it is by no means implied that econometrics is less important.

Indeed, empirical studies and theoretical analyses are often complementary and mutually reinforcing. On the one hand, theories must be tested against empirical data for validity before they can be applied with confidence. On the other, statistical work needs economic theory as a guide, in order to determine the most relevant and fruitful direction of research. A very good illustration of the complementary nature of theoretical and empirical studies is found in the study of the aggregate consumption function. The theoretical work of Keynes on the consumption function led to the statistical estimation of the propensity to consume, but the statistical findings of Kuznets and Goldsmith regarding the relative long-run constancy of the propensity to consume (in contradiction to what might be expected from the Keynesian theory), in turn, stimulated the refinement of aggregate consumption theory by Duesenberry, Friedman, and others.[1]

In one sense, however, mathematical economics may be considered as the more basic of the two: for, to have a meaningful statistical and econometric study, a good theoretical framework—preferably in a mathematical formulation —is indispensable. Hence the subject matter of the present volume should be useful not only for those interested in theoretical economics but also for those seeking a foundation for the pursuit of econometric studies.

[1] John M. Keynes, *The General Theory of Employment, Interest and Money*, Harcourt, Brace and Company, Inc., New York, 1936, Book III; Simon Kuznets, *National Income: A Summary of Findings*, National Bureau of Economic Research, 1946, p. 53; Raymond Goldsmith, *A Study of Saving in the United States*, vol. I, Princeton University Press, Princeton, N.J., 1955, chap. 3; James S. Duesenberry, *Income, Saving, and the Theory of Consumer Behavior*, Harvard University Press, Cambridge, Mass., 1949; Milton Friedman, *A Theory of the Consumption Function*, National Bureau of Economic Research, Princeton University Press, Princeton, N.J., 1957.

2

ECONOMIC MODELS

As mentioned before, any economic theory is necessarily an abstraction from the real world. For one thing, the immense complexity of the real economy makes it impossible for us to understand all the interrelationships at once; nor, for that matter, are all these interrelationships of equal importance for the understanding of the particular economic phenomenon under study. The sensible procedure is, therefore, to pick out what appeal to our reason to be the primary factors and relationships relevant to our problem and to focus our attention on these alone. Such a deliberately simplified analytical framework is called an *economic model*, since it is only a skeletal and rough representation of the actual economy.

2.1 Ingredients of a Mathematical Model

An economic model is merely a theoretical framework, and there is no inherent reason why it must be mathematical. If the model *is* mathematical, however, it will usually consist of a set of *equations* designed to describe the structure of the model. By relating a number of *variables* to one another in certain ways, these equations give mathematical form to the set of analytical assumptions adopted. Then, through application of the relevant mathematical operations to these equations, we may seek to derive a set of conclusions which logically follow from those assumptions.

variables, constants, and parameters   A *variable* is something whose magnitude can change, i.e., something that can take on different values. Variables frequently used in economics include price, profit, revenue, cost, national income, consumption, investment, imports, exports, and so on. Since each variable can assume various values, it must be represented by a symbol instead of a specific number. For example, we may represent price by P, profit by π, revenue by R, cost by C, national income by Y, and so forth. When we write $P = 3$ or $C = 18$, however, we are "freezing" these variables at specific values (in appropriately chosen units).

Properly constructed, an economic model can be solved to give us the *solution values* of a certain set of variables, such as the market-clearing level of price, or the profit-maximizing level of output. Such variables, whose solution values we seek from the model, are known as *endogenous variables* (originating from within). However, the model may also contain variables which are assumed to be determined by forces external to the model, and whose magnitudes are accepted as given data only; such variables are called *exogenous variables* (originating from without). It should be noted that a variable that is endogenous to one model may very well be exogenous to another. In an analysis of the market determination of wheat price (P), for instance, the variable P should definitely be endogenous; but in the framework of a theory of consumer expenditure, P would become instead a datum to the individual consumer, and must therefore be considered exogenous.

Variables frequently appear in combination with fixed numbers or constants, such as in the expressions $7P$ or $0.5R$. A *constant* is a magnitude that does not change and is therefore the antithesis of a variable. When a constant is joined to a variable, it is often referred to as the *coefficient* of that variable. However, a coefficient may be symbolic rather than numerical. We can, for instance, let the symbol a stand for a given constant and use the expression aP in lieu of $7P$ in a model, in order to attain a higher level of generality (see Sec. 2.7). This symbol a is a rather peculiar case—it is supposed to represent a given constant, and yet, since we have not assigned to it a specific number, it can take virtually any value. In short, it is a *constant* that is *variable*! To identify its special status, we give it the distinctive name *parametric constant* (or simply *parameter*).

It must be duly emphasized that, although different values can be assigned to a parameter, it is nevertheless to be regarded as a datum in the model. It is for this reason that people sometimes use "constant" even when the constant is parametric. In this respect, parameters closely resemble exogenous variables, for both are to be treated as "givens" in a model. This explains why many writers, for simplicity, refer to both collectively with the single designation "parameters."

As a matter of convention, parametric constants are normally represented by the symbols a, b, c, or their counterparts in the Greek alphabet: α, β, and γ. But other symbols naturally are also permissible. As for exogenous variables, in order that they can be instantly distinguished from their endogenous cousins, we shall follow the practice of attaching a subscript 0 to the chosen symbol. For example, if P symbolizes price, then P_0 signifies an exogenously determined price.

equations and identities   Variables may exist independently, but they do not really become interesting until they are related to one another by equations or by inequalities. At this juncture we shall discuss equations only.

For our purposes, we may distinguish between three types of equations: definitional equations, behavioral equations, and equilibrium conditions.

A *definitional equation* sets up an identity between two alternate expressions that have exactly the same meaning. For such an equation, the identical-equality sign $\equiv$ (read: is identically equal to) is often employed in place of the regular equals sign $=$, although the latter is also acceptable. As an example, total profit is defined as the excess of total revenue over total cost; we can therefore write

$$\pi \equiv R - C$$

A *behavioral equation*, on the other hand, specifies the manner in which a variable behaves in response to changes in other variables. This may involve either human behavior (such as the aggregate consumption pattern in relation to national income) or nonhuman behavior (such as how total cost of a firm reacts to output changes). Broadly defined, behavioral equations can be used to describe the general institutional setting of a model, including the technological (e.g., production function) and legal (e.g., tax structure) aspects. Before a behavioral equation can be written, however, it is always necessary to adopt definite assumptions regarding the behavior pattern of the variable in question. Consider the two cost functions

(2.1) $C = 75 + 10Q$

(2.2) $C = 110 + Q^2$

where Q denotes the quantity of output. Since the two equations have different forms, the production condition assumed in each is obviously different from the other. In (2.1), the fixed cost (the value of C when $Q = 0$) is 75, whereas in (2.2) it is 110. The variation in cost is also different. In (2.1), for each unit increase in Q, there is a constant increase of 10 in C. But in (2.2), as Q increases unit after unit, C will increase by progressively larger amounts. Clearly, it is primarily through the specification of the form of the behavioral equations that we give mathematical expression to the assumptions adopted for a model.

The third type of equations, *equilibrium conditions*, have relevance only if our model involves the notion of equilibrium. If so, then the equilibrium condition is an equation that describes the prerequisite for the attainment of equilibrium. Two of the most familiar equilibrium conditions in economics are

$$Q_d = Q_s \qquad \text{[quantity demanded = quantity supplied]}$$
$$\text{and} \qquad S = I \qquad \text{[intended saving = intended investment]}$$

which pertain, respectively, to the equilibrium of a market model and the equilibrium of the Keynesian national-income model in its simplest form. Being neither definitional nor behavioral, equations of this type constitute a class by themselves.

2.2   The Real-Number System

Equations and variables are the essential ingredients of a mathematical model. But since the values that an economic variable takes are usually numerical, a few words should be said about the number system. Here, we shall deal only with so-called "real numbers."

Whole numbers such as $1, 2, 3, \ldots$ are called *positive integers*; these are the numbers most frequently used in counting. Their negative counterparts $-1, -2, -3, \ldots$ are called *negative integers*; these can be employed, for example, to indicate subzero temperatures (in degrees). The number 0 (zero), on the other hand, is neither positive nor negative, and is in that sense unique. Let us lump all the positive and negative integers and the number zero into a single category, referring to them collectively as the *set of all integers*.

Integers, of course, do not exhaust all the possible numbers, for we have *fractions*, such as $\frac{2}{3}, \frac{5}{4}$, and $\frac{7}{3}$, which—if placed on a ruler—would fall between the integers. Also, we have negative fractions, such as $-\frac{1}{2}$ and $-\frac{2}{5}$. Together, these make up the *set of all fractions*.

The common property of all fractional numbers is that each is expressible as a ratio of two integers; thus fractions qualify for the designation *rational numbers* (in this usage, rational means *ratio*-nal and does not carry any implications of "sensibility"). But integers are also rational, because any integer n can be considered as the ratio $n/1$. The set of all integers and the set of all fractions together form the *set of all rational numbers*.

Once the notion of rational numbers is used, however, there naturally arises the concept of *irrational numbers*—numbers that *cannot* be expressed as ratios of a pair of integers. One example is the number $\sqrt{2} = 1.4142 \ldots$, which

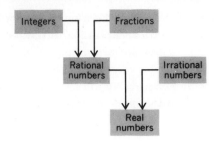

FIGURE 2.1

is a nonrepeating, nonterminating decimal. Another is the special constant $\pi = 3.1415\ldots$ (representing the ratio of the circumference of any circle to its diameter), which is again a nonrepeating, nonterminating decimal, as is characteristic of all irrational numbers.

Each irrational number, if placed on a ruler, would fall between two rational numbers, so that, just as the fractions fill in the gaps between the integers on a ruler, the irrational numbers fill in the gaps between rational numbers. The result of this filling-in process is a continuum of numbers, all of which are so-called "real numbers." In fact, this continuum constitutes the *set of all real numbers*.

In Fig. 2.1 are listed (in the order discussed) all the number sets, arranged in relationship to one another. If we read from bottom to top, however, we find in effect a classificatory scheme in which the set of real numbers is broken down into its component and subcomponent number sets. This figure therefore is a summary of the structure of the real-number system.

Real numbers are all we need for the first fourteen chapters of this book, but they are not the only numbers used in mathematics. In fact, the reason for the term "real" is that there are also "imaginary" numbers, which have to do with the square roots of negative numbers. That concept will be discussed later, in Chap. 15.

2.3   The Concept of Sets

We have already employed the word "set" several times. Inasmuch as the concept of sets underlies every branch of modern mathematics, it is desirable to familiarize ourselves at least with its more basic aspects.

set notation   A *set* is simply a collection of distinct objects. These objects may be a group of (distinct) numbers, or something else. Thus, all the students enrolled in a particular economics course can be considered a set, just as the three integers 2, 3, and 4 can form a set. The objects in a set are called the *elements* of the set.

There are two alternative ways of writing a set: by *enumeration* and by *description*. If we let S represent the set of three numbers 2, 3, and 4, then we can write, by enumeration of the elements,

$$S = \{2,3,4\}$$

But if we let I denote the set of *all* positive integers, then enumeration becomes difficult, and we may instead simply describe the elements and write

$$I = \{x \mid x \text{ a positive integer}\}$$

which is read as follows: I is the set of all (numbers) x, such that x is a positive integer. Note that braces are used to enclose the set in both cases. In the descriptive approach, a vertical bar (or a colon) is always inserted to separate the general symbol for the elements from the description of the elements. As another example, the set of all real numbers greater than 2 but less than 5 (call it J) can be expressed symbolically as

$$J = \{x \mid 2 < x < 5\}$$

Here, even the descriptive statement is symbolically expressed.

A set with a finite number of elements, exemplified by set S above, is called a *finite set*. Set I and set J, each with an infinite number of elements, are on the other hand examples of an *infinite set*. Finite sets are always *denumerable* (or *countable*), i.e., their elements can be counted one by one in the sequence 1, 2, 3, ... Infinite sets may, however, be either denumerable (set I), or *nondenumerable* (set J). In the latter case, there is no way to associate the elements of the set with the natural counting numbers 1, 2, 3, . . . , and thus the set is not countable.

Membership in a set is indicated by the symbol $\in$ (a variant of the Greek letter epsilon, ϵ, for "element"), which is read: is an element of. Thus, for the two sets S and I defined above, we may write

$$2 \in S \qquad 3 \in S \qquad 8 \in I \qquad 9 \in I \qquad \text{(etc.)}$$

but obviously $8 \notin S$ (read: 8 is not an element of set S).

relationships between sets   When two sets are compared with each other, several possible kinds of relationship may be observed. If two sets S_1 and

S_2 happen to contain identical elements,

$$S_1 = \{2,7,a,f\} \quad \text{and} \quad S_2 = \{2,a,7,f\}$$

then S_1 and S_2 are said to be *equal* ($S_1 = S_2$). Note that the order of appearance of the elements in a set is immaterial. Whenever even one element is different, however, two sets are not equal.

Another kind of relationship is that one set may be a *subset* of another set. If we have two sets

$$S = \{1,3,5,7,9\} \quad \text{and} \quad T = \{3,7\}$$

then T is a subset of S, because every element of T is also an element of S. A more formal statement of this is: T is a subset of S if and only if "$x \in T$" implies "$x \in S$." Using the set inclusion symbols $\subset$ (is contained in) and $\supset$ (includes), we may then write

$$T \subset S \quad \text{or} \quad S \supset T$$

It is possible that two given sets happen to be subsets of each other. When this occurs, however, we can be sure that these two sets are equal. To state this formally: we can have $S_1 \subset S_2$ and $S_2 \subset S_1$ if and only if $S_1 = S_2$.

Note that, whereas the $\in$ symbol relates an individual *element* to a *set*, the $\subset$ symbol relates a *subset* to a *set*. As an application of this idea, we may state on the basis of Fig. 2.1 that the set of all integers is a subset of the set of all rational numbers. Similarly, the set of all rational numbers is a subset of the set of all real numbers.

How many subsets can be formed from the five elements in the set $S = \{1,3,5,7,9\}$? First of all, each individual element of S can count as a distinct subset of S, such as $\{1\}$, $\{3\}$, etc. But so can any pair, triple, or quadruple of these elements, such as $\{1,3\}$, $\{1,5\}$, . . . , $\{3,7,9\}$, etc. For that matter, the set S itself (with all its five elements) can be considered as one of its own subsets—every element of S is an element of S, and thus the set S itself fulfills the definition of a subset. This is, of course, a limiting case, that from which we get the "largest" possible subset of S, namely, S itself.

At the other extreme, the "smallest" possible subset of S is a set that contains no element at all. Such a set is called the *null set*, or *empty set*, denoted by the symbol $\varnothing$. The reason for considering the null set as a subset of S is quite interesting: If the null set is not a subset of S ($\varnothing \not\subset S$), then $\varnothing$ must contain at least one element x such that $x \notin S$. But since by definition the null set has no element whatsoever, we cannot say that $\varnothing \not\subset S$; hence the null set is a subset of S.

Counting all the subsets of S, including the two limiting cases S and $\varnothing$, we find a total of $2^5 = 32$ subsets. In general, if a set has n elements, then a total of 2^n subsets can be formed from those elements.[1]

It is extremely important to distinguish the symbol $\varnothing$ clearly from the notation $\{0\}$; the former is devoid of elements, but the latter does contain an element, zero. The null set is unique; there is only one such set in the whole world, and it is considered a subset of *any* set that can be conceived.

As a third possible type of relationship, two sets may have no elements in common at all. In that case, the two sets are said to be *disjoint*. For example, the set of all positive integers and the set of all negative integers are disjoint sets. A fourth type of relationship occurs when two sets have some elements in common but some elements peculiar to each. In that event, the two sets are neither equal nor disjoint; also, neither set is a subset of the other.

operations on sets   When we add, subtract, multiply, divide, or take the square root of some numbers, we are performing mathematical operations. Sets are different from numbers, but one can similarly perform certain mathematical operations on them. Three principal operations to be discussed here involve the union, intersection, and complement of sets.

To take the *union* of two sets A and B means to form a new set containing those elements (and only those elements) belonging to A, or to B, or to both A and B. The union set is symbolized by $A \cup B$ (read: A union B).

Example 1   If $A = \{3,5,7\}$ and $B = \{2,3,4,8\}$, then

$$A \cup B = \{2,3,4,5,7,8\}$$

This example illustrates the case in which two sets A and B are neither equal nor disjoint and in which neither is a subset of the other.

Example 2   Again referring to Fig. 2.1, we see that the union of the set of all integers and the set of all fractions is the set of all rational numbers. Similarly, the union of the rational-number set and the irrational-number set yields the set of all real numbers.

The *intersection* of two sets A and B, on the other hand, is a new set which contains those elements (and only those elements) belonging to *both A and B*. The intersection set is symbolized by $A \cap B$ (read: A intersection B).

---

[1] Given a set with n elements $\{a,b,c, \ldots ,n\}$ we may first classify its subsets into two categories: one with the element a in it, and one without. Each of these two can be further classified into two subcategories: one with the element b in it, and one without. Note that by considering the second element b, we double the number of categories in the classification from 2 to 4 ($=2^2$). By the same token, the consideration of the element c will increase the total number of categories to 8 ($=2^3$). When all n elements are considered, the total number of categories will become the total number of subsets, and that number is 2^n.

Example 3   From the sets A and B in Example 1, we can write

$$A \cap B = \{3\}$$

Example 4   If $A = \{-3,6,10\}$ and $B = \{9,2,7,4\}$, then $A \cap B = \emptyset$. Set A and set B are disjoint; therefore their intersection is the empty set—no element is common to A and B.

It is obvious that intersection is a more restrictive concept than union. In the former, only the elements *common to A and B* are acceptable; whereas in the latter, membership in either A or B is sufficient to establish membership in the union set. The operator symbols $\cap$ and $\cup$—which, incidentally, have the same kind of general status as the symbols $\sqrt{}$, $+$, $\div$, etc.—therefore have the connotations "and" and "or," respectively. This point can be better appreciated by comparing the following formal definitions of intersection and union:

Intersection: $A \cap B = \{x \mid x \in A \text{ and } x \in B\}$
Union: $A \cup B = \{x \mid x \in A \text{ or } x \in B\}$

Before explaining the *complement* of a set, let us first introduce the concept of *universal set*. In a particular context of discussion, if the only numbers used are the set of the first seven positive integers, we may refer to it as the universal set, U. Then, with a given set, say, $A = \{3,6,7\}$, we can define another set $\tilde{A}$ (read: the complement of A) as the set that contains all the numbers in the universal set U which are not in the set A. That is,

$$\tilde{A} = \{x \mid x \in U \text{ and } x \notin A\} = \{1,2,4,5\}$$

Note that, whereas the symbol $\cup$ has the connotation "or" and the symbol $\cap$ means "and," the complement symbol $\sim$ carries the implication of "not."

Example 5   If $U = \{5,6,7,8,9\}$ and $A = \{5,6\}$, then $\tilde{A} = \{7,8,9\}$.

Example 6   What is the complement of U? Since every object (number) under consideration is included in the universal set, the complement of U must be empty. Thus $\tilde{U} = \emptyset$.

The three types of set operations can be visualized in the three diagrams of Fig. 2.2, known as *Venn diagrams*. In diagram *a*, the points in the upper circle form a set A, and the points in the lower circle form a set B. The union of A and B then consists of the shaded area covering both circles. In diagram *b* are shown the same two sets (circles). Since their intersection should comprise only the points common to both sets, only the (shaded) overlapping portion of the

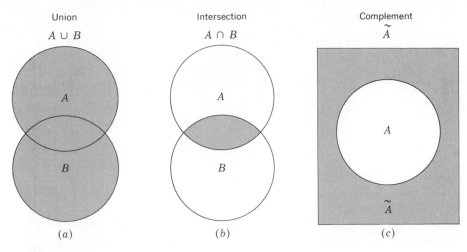

Union	Intersection	Complement
$A \cup B$	$A \cap B$	$\tilde{A}$

(a)   (b)   (c)

FIGURE 2.2

two circles satisfies the definition. In diagram c, let the points in the rectangle be the universal set and let A be the set of points in the circle; then the complement set $\tilde{A}$ will be the (shaded) area outside the circle.

laws of set operations   From Fig. 2.2, it may be noted that the shaded area in diagram a represents not only $A \cup B$ but also $B \cup A$. Analogously, in diagram b the small shaded area is the visual representation not only of $A \cap B$ but also of $B \cap A$. When formalized, this result is known as the *commutative law* (of unions and intersections):

$$A \cup B = B \cup A \qquad A \cap B = B \cap A$$

The reader will observe that these relations are very similar to the algebraic laws $a + b = b + a$ and $a \times b = b \times a$.

To take the union of three sets A, B, and C, we first take the union of any two sets and then "union" the resulting set with the third; a similar procedure is applicable to the intersection operation. The results of such operations are illustrated in Fig. 2.3. It is interesting that the order in which the sets are selected for the operation is immaterial. This fact gives rise to the *associative law* (of unions and intersections):

$$A \cup (B \cup C) = (A \cup B) \cup C$$
$$A \cap (B \cap C) = (A \cap B) \cap C$$

These equations are strongly reminiscent of the algebraic laws $a + (b + c) = (a + b) + c$ and $a \times (b \times c) = (a \times b) \times c$.

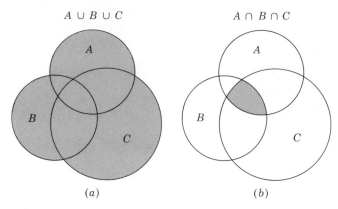

$A \cup B \cup C$ $A \cap B \cap C$

(a)   (b)

FIGURE 2.3

There is also a law of operation that applies when unions and intersections are used in combination. This is the *distributive law* (of unions and intersections):

$$A \cup (B \cap C) = (A \cup B) \cap (A \cup C)$$
$$A \cap (B \cup C) = (A \cap B) \cup (A \cap C)$$

These resemble the algebraic law $a \times (b + c) = (a \times b) + (a \times c)$.

Example 7   Verify the distributive law, given $A = \{4,5\}$, $B = \{3,6,7\}$, and $C = \{2,3\}$. To verify the first part of the law, we find the left- and right-hand expressions separately:

Left: $A \cup (B \cap C) = \{4,5\} \cup \{3\} = \{3,4,5\}$
Right: $(A \cup B) \cap (A \cup C) = \{3,4,5,6,7\} \cap \{2,3,4,5\} = \{3,4,5\}$

Since the two sides yield the same result, the law is verified. Repeating the procedure for the second part of the law, we have

Left: $A \cap (B \cup C) = \{4,5\} \cap \{2,3,6,7\} = \emptyset$
Right: $(A \cap B) \cup (A \cap C) = \emptyset \cup \emptyset = \emptyset$

Thus the law is again verified.

EXERCISE 2.3

1   Write the following in set notation:

(a)   The set of all real numbers greater than 14.
(b)   The set of all real numbers greater than 2 but less than 17.

Introduction

2   Given the sets $S_1 = \{2,4,6\}$, $S_2 = \{1,2,6\}$, $S_3 = \{4,2,6\}$, and $S_4 = \{2,6\}$, which of the following statements are true?

(a) $S_1 = S_2$ (d) $3 \notin S_2$ (g) $S_1 \supset S_4$

(b) $S_1 = S_3$ (e) $4 \notin S_4$ (h) $\varnothing \subset S_2$

(c) $5 \in S_2$ (f) $S_4 \subset S_2$ (i) $S_3 \supset \{1,2\}$

3   Referring to the four sets given in the preceding problem, find:

(a) $S_1 \cup S_2$ (c) $S_2 \cap S_3$ (e) $S_4 \cap S_2 \cap S_1$

(b) $S_1 \cup S_3$ (d) $S_2 \cap S_4$ (f) $S_3 \cup S_1 \cup S_4$

4   Which of the following statements are valid?

(a) $A \cup A = A$ (e) $A \cap \varnothing = \varnothing$

(b) $A \cap A = A$ (f) $A \cap U = A$

(c) $A \cup \varnothing = A$ (g) The complement of $\tilde{A}$ is A.

(d) $A \cup U = U$

5   Given $A = \{4,5,6\}$, $B = \{3,4,6,7\}$, and $C = \{2,3,6\}$, verify the distributive law.

6   Verify the distributive law by means of Venn diagrams, with different orders of successive shading.

7   Enumerate all the subsets of the set $\{a,b,c\}$.

8   Enumerate all the subsets of the set $S = \{1,3,5,7\}$. How many subsets are there altogether?

9   Example 6 shows that $\varnothing$ is the complement of U. But since the null set is a subset of *any* set, $\varnothing$ must be a subset of U. Inasmuch as the term "complement of U" implies the notion of being *not in* U, whereas the term "subset of U" implies the notion of being *in* U, it seems paradoxical for $\varnothing$ to be both of these. How do you resolve this paradox?

2.4   Relations and Functions

Our discussion of sets was prompted by the usage of that term in connection with the various kinds of numbers in our number system. However, sets can refer as well to objects other than numbers. In particular, we can speak of sets of "ordered pairs"—to be defined presently—which will lead us to the important concepts of relations and functions.

ordered pairs   In writing a set $\{a,b\}$, we do not care about the order in which the elements a and b appear, because by definition $\{a,b\} = \{b,a\}$. The pair of elements a and b is in this case an *unordered pair*. When the ordering of a and b does carry a significance, however, we can write two different *ordered pairs* denoted by (a,b) and (b,a), which have the property that $(a,b) \neq (b,a)$ unless $a = b$. Similar concepts apply to a set with more than two elements, in which case we can distinguish between ordered and unordered triples, quadruples, quintuples, and so forth. Ordered pairs, triples, etc., collectively can be called *ordered sets*.

Example 1   To show the age and weight of each student in a class, we can form ordered pairs (a,w), in which the first element indicates the age (in years) and the second element indicates the weight (in pounds). Then (19,127) and (127,19) would obviously mean different things. Moreover, the latter ordered pair would hardly fit any student anywhere.

Example 2   When we speak of the set of the five finalists in the Miss America contest, the order in which they are listed is of no consequence and we have an unordered quintuple. But after they are judged, respectively, as Miss America, first runner-up, etc., the list becomes an ordered quintuple.

Ordered pairs, like other objects, can be elements of a set. Consider the rectangular (cartesian) coordinate plane in Fig. 2.4, where an x axis and a y axis cross each other at a right angle, dividing the plane into four quadrants. This xy plane is an infinite set of points, each of which represents an ordered pair whose first element is an x value and the second element a y value. Clearly, the point labeled (4,2) is different from the point (2,4); thus ordering is significant here.

With this visual understanding, we are ready to consider the process of generation of ordered pairs. Suppose, from two given sets, $x = \{1,2\}$ and $y = \{3,4\}$, we wish to form all the possible ordered pairs with the first element taken from set x and the second element taken from set y. The result will, of course, be the set of four ordered pairs (1,3), (1,4), (2,3), and (2,4). This set is called the *cartesian product* (named after Des Cartes), or *direct product*, of the sets x and y and is denoted by $x \times y$ (read: x cross y). It is important to remember that, while x and y are sets of numbers, the cartesian product is a set of ordered pairs. By enumeration, or by description, we may express the cartesian product alternatively as

$$x \times y = \{(1,3), (1,4), (2,3), (2,4)\}$$
$$\text{or} \quad x \times y = \{(a,b) \mid a \in x \text{ and } b \in y\}$$

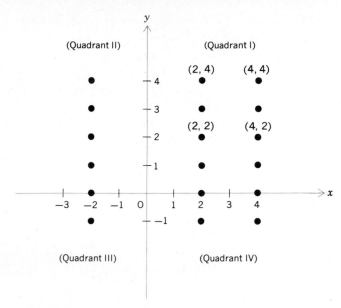

FIGURE 2.4

The latter expression may in fact be taken as the general definition of cartesian product for any given sets x and y.

To broaden our horizon, now let both x and y include all the real numbers. Then the resulting cartesian product

(2.3) $x \times y = \{(a,b) \mid a \text{ and } b \text{ are both real numbers}\}$

will represent the set of all ordered pairs with real-valued elements. Besides, each ordered pair corresponds to a *unique* point in the cartesian coordinate plane of Fig. 2.4, and, conversely, each point in the coordinate plane also corresponds to a *unique* ordered pair in the set $x \times y$. In view of this double uniqueness, a *one-to-one correspondence* is said to exist between the set of ordered pairs in the cartesian product (2.3) and the set of points in the rectangular coordinate plane. The rationale for the notation $x \times y$ is now easy to perceive; we may associate it with the crossing of the x axis and the y axis in Fig. 2.4.

Extending this idea, we may also define the cartesian product of three sets x, y, and z as follows:

$x \times y \times z = \{(a,b,c) \mid a \in x, b \in y, c \in z\}$

which is a set of ordered triples. Furthermore, if the sets x, y, and z each consist of all the real numbers, then the cartesian product will correspond to the set of all points in a three-dimensional space.

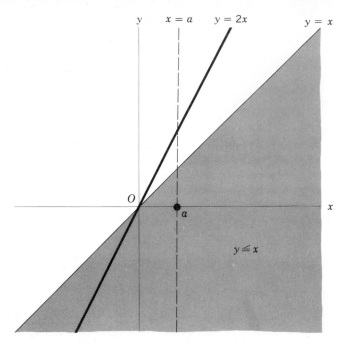

FIGURE 2.5

relations and functions   Since any ordered pair associates a y value with an x value, any collection of ordered pairs—any subset of the cartesian product (2.3)—will constitute a *relation* between y and x. Given an x value, one or more y values will be specified by that relation. For convenience, we shall now write the elements of $x \times y$ generally as (x,y)—rather than as (a,b), as was done in (2.3)—where both x and y are variables.

Example 3   The set $\{(x,y) \mid y = 2x\}$ is a set of ordered pairs including, for example, $(1,2)$, $(0,0)$, and $(-1,-2)$. It constitutes a relation, and its graphical counterpart is the set of points lying on the straight line $y = 2x$, as seen in Fig. 2.5.

Example 4   The set $\{(x,y) \mid y \leq x\}$, which consists of such ordered pairs as $(1,0)$, $(1,1)$, and $(1,-4)$, constitutes another relation. In Fig. 2.5, this set corresponds to the set of all points in the shaded area which fulfill the inequality $y \leq x$.

Observe that, when the x value is given, it may not always be possible to determine a *unique* y value from a relation. In Example 4, the three exemplary ordered pairs show that if $x = 1$, y can take various values, such as 0, 1, or -4,

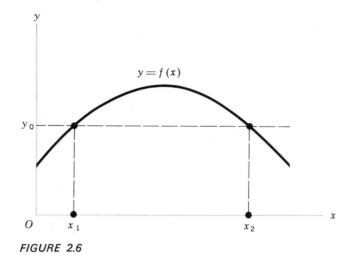

FIGURE 2.6

and yet in each case fulfill the stated relation. Graphically, two or more points of a relation may fall on a single vertical line in the xy plane. This is exemplified in Fig. 2.5, where many points in the shaded area (representing the relation $y \leq x$) fall on the broken vertical line labelled $x = a$.

As a special case, however, a relation may be such that for each x value there exists only *one* corresponding y value. The relation in Example 3 is a case in point. In that case, y is said to be a *function* of x, and this is denoted by $y = f(x)$, which is read: y equals f of x. [*Note*: $f(x)$ does *not* mean f times x.] A function is therefore a set of ordered pairs with the property that any x value *uniquely* determines a y value.[1] It should be clear that a function must be a relation, but a relation may not be a function.

Although the definition of a function stipulates a unique y for each x, the converse is not required. In other words, more than one x value may legitimately be associated with the same y value. This possibility is illustrated in Fig. 2.6, where the values x_1 and x_2 in the x set are both associated with the same value (y_0) in the y set by the function $y = f(x)$.

A function is also called a *mapping*, or *transformation*; both words connote the action of associating one thing with another. In the statement $y = f(x)$, the functional notation f may thus be interpreted to mean a rule by which the set x is "mapped" ("transformed") into the set y. Thus we may write

$$f: x \rightarrow y$$

where the arrow indicates a mapping, and the letter f symbolically specifies a

---

[1] Our definition of "function" follows the current usage. It corresponds to what would be called a *single-valued function* in the older terminology. What was formerly called a *multivalued function* is now referred to as a *relation*.

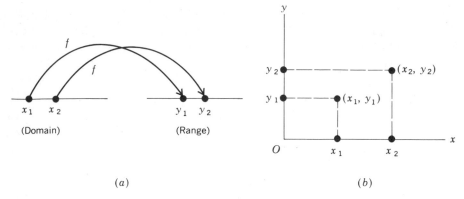

(a)   (b)

FIGURE 2.7

rule of mapping. Since f represents a *particular* rule of mapping, a different functional notation must be employed to denote another function that may appear in the same model. The customary symbols (besides f) used for this purpose are g, F, G, the Greek letters ϕ and ψ, and their capitals, Φ and Ψ. For instance, two variables y and z may both be functions of x, but if one function is written as $y = f(x)$, then the other should be written as $z = g(x)$, or $z = \phi(x)$. It is also permissible, however, to write $y = y(x)$ and $z = z(x)$, thereby dispensing with the symbols f and g entirely.

In the function $y = f(x)$, x is referred to as the *argument* of the function, and y is called the *value* of the function. We shall also alternatively refer to x as the *independent variable* and y as the *dependent variable*. The set of all permissible values that x can take in a given context is known as the *domain* of the function, which may be a subset of the set of all real numbers. The y value into which an x value is mapped is called the *image* of that x value. The set of all images is called the *range* of the function, which is the set of all values that the y variable will take. Thus the domain pertains to the independent variable x, and the range has to do with the dependent variable y.

As illustrated in Fig. 2.7a, we may regard the function f as a rule for mapping each point on some line segment (the domain) into some point on another line segment (the range). By placing the domain on the x axis and the range on the y axis, as in diagram b, however, we immediately obtain the familiar two-dimensional graph, in which the association between x values and y values is specified by a set of ordered pairs such as (x_1, y_1) and (x_2, y_2).

In economic models, behavioral equations usually enter as functions. Since most variables in economic models are by their nature restricted to being nonnegative real numbers,[1] their domains are also so restricted. This is why most

[1] We say "nonnegative" rather than "positive" when zero values are permissible.

geometric representations in economics are drawn only in the first quadrant. In general, we shall not bother to specify the domain of every function in every economic model. When no specification is given, it is to be understood that the domain (and the range) will only include numbers for which a function makes economic sense.

Example 5   The total cost C of a firm per day is a function of its daily output Q: $C = 150 + 7Q$. The firm has a capacity limit of 100 units of output per day. What are the domain and the range of the cost function? Inasmuch as Q can vary only between 0 and 100, the domain is the set of values $0 \leq Q \leq 100$; or more formally,

$$\text{Domain} = \{Q \,|\, 0 \leq Q \leq 100\}$$

As for the range, since the function plots as a straight line, with the minimum C value at 150 (when $Q = 0$) and the maximum C value at 850 (when $Q = 100$), we have

$$\text{Range} = \{C \,|\, 150 \leq C \leq 850\}$$

Beware, however, that the extreme values of the range may not always occur where the extreme values of the domain are attained.

EXERCISE 2.4

1   Given $S_1 = \{1,3,5\}$, $S_2 = \{a,b\}$, and $S_3 = \{m,n\}$, find the cartesian products:

(a) $S_1 \times S_2$ (b) $S_2 \times S_3$ (c) $S_1 \times S_3$

2   From the information in the preceding problem, find the cartesian product $S_1 \times S_2 \times S_3$.

3   In general, is it true that $S_1 \times S_2 = S_2 \times S_1$? Under what conditions will these two cartesian products be equal?

4   Does each of the following, drawn in a rectangular coordinate plane, represent a function?

(a)   A circle   (b)   A triangle   (c)   A rectangle

5   If the domain of the function $y = 5 + 3x$ is the set $\{x \,|\, 1 \leq x \leq 4\}$, find the range of the function and express it as a set.

6   For the function $y = x^2$, if the domain is the set of all nonnegative real numbers, what will its range be?

2.5 Types of Functions

The functional expression $y = f(x)$ is a general statement to the effect that a mapping is possible, but the actual rule of mapping is not thereby made explicit. Now let us consider several specific types of functions, each representing a different rule of mapping.

constant functions   A function whose range consists of only one element is called a *constant function*. As an example, we cite the function

$$y = f(x) = 7$$

which is alternatively expressible as $y = 7$ or $f(x) = 7$, whose value stays the same regardless of the value of x. In the coordinate plane, such a function will appear as a horizontal straight line. In national-income models, when investment (I) is exogenously determined, we may have an investment function of the form $I = \$100$ million, or $I = I_0$, which exemplifies the constant function.

polynomial functions   The constant function is actually a "degenerate" case of what are known as *polynomial functions*. The word polynomial means "multiterm," and a polynomial function has the general form

$$(2.4) \qquad y = a_0 + a_1x + a_2x^2 + \cdots + a_nx^n$$

in which each term contains a coefficient as well as a nonnegative-integer power of the variable x. (As will be explained later in this section, we can write $x^1 = x$ and $x^0 = 1$ in general; thus the first two terms may be taken to be a_0x^0 and a_1x^1, respectively.) Note that, instead of the symbols a, b, c, $\ldots$, we have employed the subscripted symbols a_0, a_1, $\ldots$, a_n for the coefficients. This is motivated by two considerations: (1) We can economize on symbols, since only the letter a is "used up" in this way. (2) The subscript helps to pinpoint the location of a particular coefficient in the entire equation. For instance, in (2.4), a_2 is the coefficient of x^2, and so forth.

Depending on the value of the integer n (which specifies the highest power of x), we have several subclasses of polynomial functions:

Case of $n = 0$:	$y = a_0$	[*constant* function]
Case of $n = 1$:	$y = a_0 + a_1x$	[*linear* function]
Case of $n = 2$:	$y = a_0 + a_1x + a_2x^2$	[*quadratic* function]
Case of $n = 3$:	$y = a_0 + a_1x + a_2x^2 + a_3x^3$	[*cubic* function]

and so forth. The superscript indicators of the powers of x are called *exponents*. The highest power involved, i.e., the value of n, is often called the *degree* of the polynomial function; a quadratic function, for instance, is a second-degree polynomial, and a cubic function is a third-degree polynomial.[1] The order in which the several terms appear to the right of the equals sign is inconsequential; they may be arranged in descending order of power instead. Also, even though we have put the symbol y on the left, it is also acceptable to write $f(x)$ in its place.

When plotted in the coordinate plane, a linear function will appear as a straight line, as illustrated in Fig. 2.8a. When $x = 0$, the linear function yields $y = a_0$; thus the ordered pair $(0, a_0)$ is on the line. This gives us the so-called "y intercept" (or *vertical intercept*), because it is at this point that the vertical axis intersects the line. The other coefficient, a_1, measures the *slope* (the steepness of incline) of our line. This means that a unit increase in x will result in an increment in y in the amount of a_1. What Fig. 2.8a illustrates is the case of $a_1 > 0$, involving a positive slope and thus an upward-sloping line; if $a_1 < 0$, the line will be downward-sloping.

A quadratic function, on the other hand, plots as a *parabola*—or roughly, a curve with a single built-in bump or wiggle. The particular illustration in Fig. 2.8b implies a negative a_2; in the case $a_2 > 0$, the curve will "open" the other way, displaying a valley rather than a hill. The graph of a cubic function will, in general, manifest two wiggles, as illustrated in Fig. 2.8c. These functions will be used quite frequently in the economic models discussed below.

rational functions   A function such as

$$y = \frac{x - 1}{x^2 + 2x + 4}$$

in which y is expressed as a ratio of two polynomials in the variable x, is known as a *rational function* (again, meaning *ratio*-nal). According to this definition, any polynomial function must itself be a rational function, because it can always be expressed as a ratio to 1, which is a constant function.

A special rational function that has interesting applications in economics is the function

$$y = \frac{a}{x} \quad \text{or} \quad xy = a$$

which plots as a *rectangular hyperbola*, as in Fig. 2.8d. Since the product of the two variables is always a fixed constant in this case, this function may be used to represent the special demand curve—with price P and quantity Q on the two

---

[1] In the several equations just cited, the last coefficient (a_n) is always assumed to be nonzero; otherwise the function would degenerate into a lower-degree polynomial.

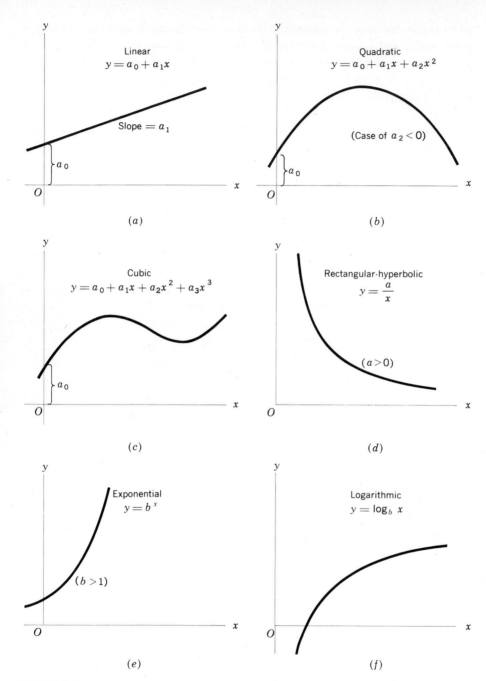

FIGURE 2.8

axes—for which the total expenditure PQ is constant at all levels of price. (The reader will recall that such a demand curve is the one with a unitary elasticity at each point on the curve.) Another application is to the average fixed cost (AFC) curve. With AFC on one axis and output Q on the other, the AFC curve must be rectangular-hyperbolic because AFC $\times$ Q ($=$ total fixed cost) is a fixed constant.

The rectangular hyperbola drawn from $xy = a$ never meets the axes, even if extended indefinitely upward and to the right. Rather, the curve approaches the axes *asymptotically*: as y becomes very large, the curve will come ever closer to the y axis but never actually reach it, and similarly for the x axis. The axes constitute the *asymptotes* of this function.

nonalgebraic functions   Any function expressed in terms of polynomials and/or roots (such as square root) of polynomials is an *algebraic function*. Accordingly, the functions discussed thus far are all algebraic. A function such as $y = \sqrt{x^2 + 3}$ is not rational, yet it is algebraic.

However, *exponential functions* such as $y = b^x$, in which the independent variable appears in the exponent, are *nonalgebraic*. The closely related *logarithmic functions*, such as $y = \log_b x$, are also nonalgebraic. These two types of functions will be explained in detail in Chap. 10, but their general graphic shapes are indicated in Fig. 2.8e and f. Another type of nonalgebraic functions are the *trigonometric* (or *circular*) *functions*, which we shall discuss in Chap. 15 in connection with dynamic analysis. The reader may note that nonalgebraic functions are also known by the more esoteric name of *transcendental functions*.

a digression on exponents   In discussing polynomial functions, we introduced the term *exponents* as indicators of the power to which a variable (or number) is to be raised. The expression 6^2 means that 6 is to be raised to the second power; that is, 6 is to be multiplied by itself, or $6^2 \equiv 6 \times 6 = 36$. In general, we define

$$x^n \equiv \underbrace{x \times x \times \cdots \times x}_{n \text{ terms}}$$

and as a special case, we note that $x^1 = x$. From the general definition, it follows that exponents obey the following rules:

RULE I $x^m \times x^n = x^{m+n}$ (for example, $x^3 \times x^4 = x^7$)

Proof
$$x^m \times x^n = \underbrace{(x \times x \times \cdots \times x)}_{m \text{ terms}}\underbrace{(x \times x \times \cdots \times x)}_{n \text{ terms}}$$

$$= \underbrace{x \times x \times \cdots \times x \, x}_{m+n \text{ terms}} = x^{m+n}$$

RULE II $\quad \dfrac{x^m}{x^n} = x^{m-n} \quad (x \neq 0) \quad \left(\text{for example, } \dfrac{x^4}{x^3} = x\right)$

Proof $\quad \dfrac{x^m}{x^n} = \dfrac{\overbrace{x \times x \times \cdots \times x}^{m \text{ terms}}}{\underbrace{x \times x \times \cdots \times x}_{n \text{ terms}}} = \underbrace{x \times x \times \cdots \times x \, x}_{m-n \text{ terms}} = x^{m-n}$

because the n terms in the denominator cancel out n of the m terms in the numerator. Note that the case of $x = 0$ is ruled out in the statement of this rule. This is because when $x = 0$, the expression x^m/x^n would involve division by zero, which is undefined.

What if $m < n$: say, $m = 2$ and $n = 5$? In that case we get, according to Rule II, $x^{m-n} = x^{-3}$, a *negative power* of x. What does this mean? The answer is actually supplied by Rule II itself: When $m = 2$ and $n = 5$, we have

$$\frac{x^2}{x^5} = \frac{x \times x}{x \times x \times x \times x \times x} = \frac{1}{x \times x \times x} = \frac{1}{x^3}$$

Thus $x^{-3} = 1/x^3$, and this may be generalized into another rule:

RULE III $\quad x^{-n} = \dfrac{1}{x^n} \quad (x \neq 0)$

To raise a (nonzero) number to a power of *minus n* is to take the *reciprocal* of its *n*th power.

Another special case in the application of Rule II is when $m = n$, which yields the expression $x^{m-n} = x^{m-m} = x^0$. To interpret the meaning of raising a number x to the zeroth power, we can write out the term x^{m-m} in accordance with Rule II above, with the result that $x^m/x^m = 1$. Thus we may conclude that any (nonzero) number raised to the zeroth power is equal to 1. (The expression 0^0 is undefined.) This may be expressed as another rule:

RULE IV $\quad x^0 = 1 \quad (x \neq 0)$

As long as we are concerned only with polynomial functions, only (non-negative) integer powers are required. In exponential functions, however, the exponent is a variable that can take noninteger values as well. In order to interpret a number such as $x^{1/2}$, let us consider the fact that, by Rule I above, we have

$$x^{1/2} \times x^{1/2} = x^1 = x$$

Since $x^{1/2}$ multiplied by itself is x, $x^{1/2}$ must be the square root of x. Similarly, $x^{1/3}$ can be shown to be the cube root of x. In general, therefore, we can state the following rule:

RULE V $\qquad x^{1/n} = \sqrt[n]{x}$

Two other rules obeyed by exponents are:

RULE VI $\qquad (x^m)^n = x^{mn}$

RULE VII $\qquad x^m \times y^m = (xy)^m$

EXERCISE 2.5

1 Graph the functions

(a) $y = 5 + 3x$ (b) $y = 5 - 3x$ (c) $y = 3x + 7$

(In each case, consider the domain as consisting of nonnegative real numbers only.)

2 What is the major difference between (a) and (b) above? How is this difference reflected in the graphs? What is the major difference between (a) and (c)? How do their graphs reflect it?

3 Graph the functions

(a) $y = -x^2 + 4x - 2$ (b) $y = x^2 + 4x - 2$

with the set of values $-5 \leq x \leq 5$ as the domain. It is well known that the sign of the coefficient of the x^2 term determines whether the graph of a quadratic function will have a "hill" or a "valley." On the basis of the present problem, which sign is associated with the hill? Supply an intuitive explanation for this.

4 Graph the function $y = 24/x$, assuming that x and y can take positive values only. Next, suppose that both variables can take negative values as well; how must the graph be modified to reflect this change in assumption?

5   Condense the following expressions:

    (a) $x^{15} \times x^4$ (b) $x^a \times x^b \times x^c$ (c) $x^3 \times y^3 \times z^3$

6   Find: (a) x^3/x^{-2} (b) $(x^{1/2} \times x^{1/3})/x^{2/3}$

7   Show that $x^{m/n} = \sqrt[n]{x^m} = (\sqrt[n]{x})^m$. Specify the rules applied in each step.

8   Prove Rule VI and Rule VII.

2.6   Functions of Two or More Independent Variables

Thus far, we have considered only functions of a single independent variable, $y = f(x)$. But the concept of a function can be readily extended to the case of two or more independent variables. Given a function

$$z = g(x,y)$$

a given pair of x and y values will uniquely determine a value of the dependent variable z. Such a function is exemplified by equations like

$$z = ax + by \qquad \text{or} \qquad z = a_0 + a_1 x + a_2 x^2 + b_1 y + b_2 y^2$$

Just as the function $y = f(x)$ maps a point in the domain into a point in the range, the function g will do precisely the same. However, the domain is in this case no longer a set of numbers but a set of ordered pairs (x,y), because we can determine z only when *both* x *and* y are specified. The function g is thus a mapping from a point in a two-dimensional space into a point on a line segment (i.e., a point in a one-dimensional space), such as from the point (x_1,y_1) into the point z_1 or from (x_2,y_2) into z_2 in Fig. 2.9a.

If a vertical z axis is erected perpendicular to the xy plane, as is done in diagram b, however, there will result a three-dimensional space in which the function g can be given a graphical representation as follows. The domain of the function will be some subset of the points in the xy plane, and the value of the function (value of z) for a given point in the domain—say, (x_1,y_1)—can be indicated by the height of a vertical line planted on that point. The association between the three variables is thus summarized by the ordered triple (x_1,y_1,z_1), which is a specific point in the three-dimensional space. The locus of such ordered triples, which will take the form of a *surface*, then constitutes the graph of the function g. Whereas the function $y = f(x)$ is a set of ordered *pairs*, the function $z = g(x,y)$ will be a set of ordered *triples*. We shall have many occasions to use functions of this type in economic models. One ready application is in the area

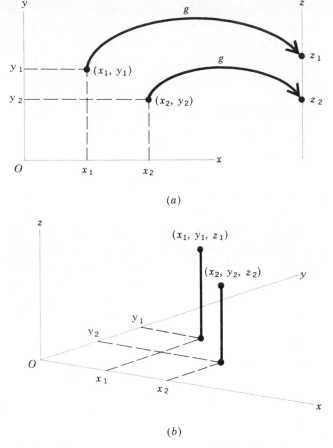

FIGURE 2.9

of production functions: Suppose that output is determined by the amounts of capital (K) and labor (L) employed; then we can write a production function in the general form $Q = Q(K,L)$.

The possibility of further extension to the cases of three or more independent variables is now self-evident. With the function $y = h(u,v,w)$, for example, we can map a point in the three-dimensional space, (u_1,v_1,w_1), into a point in a one-dimensional space (y_1). Such a function might be used to indicate that a consumer's utility is a function of his consumption of three different commodities, and the mapping is from a three-dimensional commodity space into a one-dimensional utility space. But this time it will be physically impossible to graph the function, because for that task a four-dimensional diagram is needed to picture the ordered quadruples, which presents a task we cannot manage.

Nonetheless, in view of the intuitive appeal of geometric analogy, we can continue to refer to an ordered quadruple (u_1,v_1,w_1,y_1) as a "point" in the four-dimensional space. The locus of such points will give the (nongraphable) graph of the function $y = h(u,v,w)$, which is called a *hypersurface*. These terms, viz., point and hypersurface, are also carried over to the general case of the n-dimensional space.

Functions of more than one variable can be classified into various types, too. For instance, a function of the form

$$y = a_1 x_1 + a_2 x_2 + \cdots + a_n x_n$$

is a *linear* function, whose characteristic is that every variable is raised to the first power only. A *quadratic* function, on the other hand, involves first and second powers of one or more independent variables, but the sum of exponents of the variables appearing in any single term must not exceed two.

Note that instead of denoting the independent variables by x, u, v, w, etc., we have switched to the symbols x_1, x_2, ..., x_n. The latter notation, like the system of subscripted coefficients, has the merit of economy of alphabet, as well as of an easier accounting of the number of variables involved in a function.

2.7　The Level of Generality

In discussing the various types of functions, we have without explicit notice introduced examples of functions that pertain to varying levels of generality. In certain instances, we have written functions in the form

$$y = 7 \qquad y = 6x + 4 \qquad y = x^2 - 3x + 1 \qquad \text{(etc.)}$$

Not only are these expressed in terms of numerical coefficients, but they also indicate specifically whether each function is constant, linear, or quadratic. In terms of graphs, each such function will give rise to a well-defined unique curve. In view of the numerical nature of these functions, the solutions of the model based on them will emerge as numerical values also. The drawback is that, if we wish to know how our analytical conclusion will change when a different set of numerical coefficients comes into effect, we must go through the reasoning process afresh each time. Thus, the results obtained from specific functions have very little generality.

On a more general level of discussion and analysis, there are functions in the form

$$y = a \qquad y = a + bx \qquad y = a + bx + cx^2 \qquad \text{(etc.)}$$

By using parameters, each function will represent not a single curve but a whole family of curves. The function $y = a$, for instance, encompasses not only the specific cases $y = 0$, $y = 1$, and $y = 2$ but also $y = \frac{1}{3}$, $y = -5, \ldots$, ad infinitum. With parametric functions, the outcome of mathematical operations will also be in terms of parameters. These results are more general in the sense that, by assigning various values to the parameters appearing in the solution of the model, a whole family of specific answers may be obtained without having to repeat the reasoning process anew.

In order to attain an even higher level of generality, we may resort to the general functional statement $y = f(x)$, or $z = g(x,y)$. When expressed in this form, the function is not restricted to being either linear, quadratic, exponential, or trigonometric—all of which are subsumed under the notation. The analytical result based on such a general formulation will therefore have the most general applicability. As will be found below, however, in order to obtain economically meaningful results, it is often necessary to impose certain qualitative restrictions on the functions built into an economic model, such as the restriction that a demand function have a negatively sloped graph or that a consumption function have a graph with a positive slope of less than 1.

To sum up the present chapter: The structure of a mathematical economic model is now clear. In general, it will consist of a system of equations, which may be definitional, behavioral, or in the nature of equilibrium conditions.[1] The behavioral equations are usually in the form of functions, which may be linear or nonlinear, numerical or parametric, and with one independent variable or many. It is through these that the analytical assumptions adopted in the model are given mathematical expression.

In attacking an analytical problem, therefore, the first step is to select the appropriate variables—exogenous as well as endogenous—for inclusion in the model. Next, we must translate into equations the set of chosen analytical assumptions regarding the human, institutional, technological, legal, and other behavioral aspects of the environment affecting the working of the variables. Only then can an attempt be made to derive a set of conclusions through relevant mathematical operations and manipulations and to give them appropriate economic interpretations.

---

[1] Inequalities may also enter as an important ingredient of a model, but we shall not worry about them for the time being.

TWO

STATIC (OR EQUILIBRIUM) ANALYSIS

3

EQUILIBRIUM ANALYSIS IN ECONOMICS

The analytical procedure outlined in the preceding chapter will first be applied to what is known as *static analysis*, or *equilibrium analysis*. For this purpose, it is imperative first to have a clear understanding of what "equilibrium" means.

3.1   The Meaning of Equilibrium

Like any economic term, *equilibrium* can be defined in various ways. According to Professor Machlup, an equilibrium is "a constellation of selected interrelated variables so adjusted to one another that no inherent tendency to change prevails in the model which they constitute."[1] Several words in this definition deserve special attention. First, the word "selected" underscores the fact that there do exist variables which, by the analyst's choice, have not been included in the model. Hence the equilibrium under discussion can have relevance only in the context of the particular set of variables chosen, and if the model is enlarged to include additional variables, the equilibrium state pertaining to the smaller model will no longer apply.

Second, the word "interrelated" suggests that, in order for equilibrium to obtain, all variables in the model must simultaneously be in a state of rest. Moreover, the state of rest of each variable must be compatible with that of every

[1] Fritz Machlup, "Equilibrium and Disequilibrium: Misplaced Concreteness and Disguised Politics," *Economic Journal*, March 1958, p. 9. (Reprinted in F. Machlup, *Essays on Economic Semantics*, Prentice-Hall, Inc., Englewood Cliffs, N.J., 1963.)

other variable; otherwise some variable(s) will be changing, thereby also causing the others to change in a chain reaction, and no equilibrium can be said to exist.

Third, the word "inherent" implies that, in defining an equilibrium, the state of rest involved is only based on the balancing of the internal forces of the model, while the external factors are assumed fixed. Operationally, this means that parameters and exogenous variables are treated as constants. When the external factors do actually change, there may result a new equilibrium defined on the basis of the new parameter values, but in defining the new equilibrium, the new parameter values are again assumed to persist and stay unchanged.

In essence, an equilibrium for a specified model is a situation that is characterized by a lack of tendency to change. It is for this reason that the analysis of equilibrium (more specifically, the study of what the equilibrium state is like) is referred to as *statics*. The fact that an equilibrium implies no tendency to change may tempt one to conclude that an equilibrium necessarily constitutes a desirable or ideal state of affairs, on the ground that only in the ideal state would there be a lack of motivation for change. Such a conclusion is unwarranted. Even though a certain equilibrium position may represent a desirable state and something to be striven for—such as a profit-maximizing situation, from the firm's point of view—another equilibrium position may be quite undesirable and therefore something to be avoided, such as an under-employment equilibrium level of national income. The only warranted interpretation is that an equilibrium is a situation which, if attained, would tend to perpetuate itself, barring any changes in the external forces.

The desirable variety of equilibrium, which we shall refer to as *goal equilibrium*, will be treated later in Parts 4 and 6 as optimization problems. In the present chapter, the discussion will be confined to the *nongoal* type of equilibrium, resulting not from any conscious aiming at a particular objective but from an impersonal or suprapersonal process of interaction and adjustment of economic forces. Examples of this are the equilibrium attained by a market under given demand and supply conditions and the equilibrium of national income under given conditions of consumption and investment patterns.

3.2   Partial Market Equilibrium—A Linear Model

In a static-equilibrium model, the standard problem is that of finding the set of values of the endogenous variables which will satisfy the equilibrium condition of the model. This is because once we have identified those values, we have in effect identified the equilibrium state. Let us illustrate with a so-called "partial-equilibrium market model," i.e., a model of price determination in an isolated market.

constructing the model   Since only one commodity is being considered, it is necessary to include only three variables in the model: the quantity demanded of the commodity (Q_d), the quantity supplied of the commodity (Q_s), and its price (P). The quantity is measured, say, in pounds per week, and the price in dollars. Having chosen the variables, our next order of business is to make certain assumptions regarding the working of the market. First, we must specify an equilibrium condition—something indispensable in an equilibrium model. The standard assumption is that equilibrium obtains in the market if and only if the excess demand is zero ($Q_d - Q_s = 0$), that is, if and only if the market is cleared. But this immediately raises the question of how Q_d and Q_s themselves are determined. To answer this, we assume that Q_d is a decreasing linear function of P (as P increases, Q_d decreases). On the other hand, Q_s is postulated to be an increasing linear function of P (as P increases, so does Q_s), with the proviso that no quantity is supplied unless the price exceeds a particular positive level. In all, then, the model will contain one equilibrium condition plus two behavioral equations which govern the demand and supply sides of the market, respectively.

Translated into mathematical statements, the model can be written as:

$$(3.1) \quad \begin{aligned} Q_d &= Q_s \\ Q_d &= a - bP \qquad (a,\ b > 0) \\ Q_s &= -c + dP \qquad (c,\ d > 0) \end{aligned}$$

Four parameters, a, b, c, and d, appear in the two linear functions, and all of them are specified to be positive. When the demand function is graphed, as in Fig. 3.1, its vertical intercept is at a and its slope is $-b$, which is negative, as required. The supply function also has the required type of slope, d being positive, but its vertical intercept is seen to be negative, at $-c$. Why did we want to specify such a negative vertical intercept? The answer is that, in so doing, we force the supply curve to have a positive horizontal intercept at P_1, thereby satisfying the proviso stated earlier that supply will not be forthcoming unless the price is positive and sufficiently high.

The reader should observe that, contrary to the usual practice, quantity rather than price has been plotted vertically in Fig. 3.1. This, however, is in line with the mathematical convention of placing the *dependent* variable on the vertical axis. In a different context below, in which the demand curve is viewed from the standpoint of a business firm as describing the average-revenue curve, $\text{AR} \equiv P = f(Q_d)$, we shall reverse the axes and plot P vertically.

With the model thus constructed, the next step is to solve it, i.e., to obtain the solution values of the three endogenous variables, Q_d, Q_s, and P. The solution values, to be denoted $\bar{Q}_d$, $\bar{Q}_s$, and $\bar{P}$, are those values that satisfy the three equations in (3.1) simultaneously. In the context of an equilibrium model, those values may also be referred to as the *equilibrium values* of the said variables.

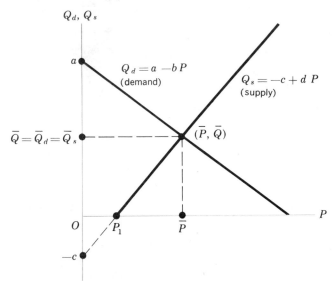

FIGURE 3.1

Since $\bar{Q}_d = \bar{Q}_s$, however, they can be replaced by a single symbol $\bar{Q}$. Hence, an equilibrium solution of the model may simply be denoted by an ordered pair $(\bar{P},\bar{Q})$. In case the solution is not unique, several ordered pairs may each satisfy the system of simultaneous equations; there will then be a solution set with more than one element in it. However, the multiple-equilibrium situation cannot arise in a linear model such as the present one.

solution by elimination of variables   One way of finding a solution to an equation system is by successive elimination of variables and equations through substitution. In (3.1), the model contains three equations in three variables. However, in view of the equating of Q_d and Q_s by the equilibrium condition, we can let $Q = Q_d = Q_s$ and rewrite the model equivalently as follows:

$$(3.2) \quad \begin{aligned} Q &= a - bP \\ Q &= -c + dP \end{aligned}$$

thereby reducing the model to two equations in two variables. Moreover, by substituting the first equation into the second in (3.2), the model can be further reduced to a single equation in a single variable:

$$a - bP = -c + dP$$

or

$$(3.3) \quad (b + d)P = a + c$$

Static (or Equilibrium) Analysis

This result is also obtainable directly from (3.1) by substituting the second and third equations into the first.

Since $b + d \neq 0$, it is permissible to divide both sides of (3.3) by $(b + d)$. The result is the solution value of P:

$$(3.4) \qquad \bar{P} = \frac{a + c}{b + d}$$

Note that $\bar{P}$ is expressed entirely in terms of the parameters. Since the latter represent given data for the model, $\bar{P}$ is a determinate value. Also note that $\bar{P}$ is positive—as a price should be—because all the four parameters are positive by model specification.

To find the equilibrium quantity $\bar{Q}$ ($= \bar{Q}_d = \bar{Q}_s$) that corresponds to the value $\bar{P}$, simply substitute (3.4) into *either* equation of (3.2), and then solve the resulting equation. Substituting (3.4) into the demand function, for instance, we can get

$$(3.5) \qquad \bar{Q} = a - \frac{b(a + c)}{b + d} = \frac{a(b + d) - b(a + c)}{b + d} = \frac{ad - bc}{b + d}$$

which is again an expression in terms of parameters only. Since the denominator $(b + d)$ is positive, the positivity of $\bar{Q}$ requires that the numerator $(ad - bc)$ be positive as well. Hence, to be economically meaningful, the present model should contain the additional restriction that $ad > bc$.

The meaning of this restriction can be seen in Fig. 3.1. It is well known that the $\bar{P}$ and $\bar{Q}$ of a market model may be determined graphically at the intersection of the demand and supply curves. To have $\bar{Q} > 0$ is to require the intersection point to be located above the horizontal axis in Fig. 3.1, which in turn requires the slopes and vertical intercepts of the two curves to fulfill a certain restriction on their relative magnitudes. That restriction, according to (3.5), is $ad > bc$, given that both b and d are positive.

The intersection of the demand and supply curves in Fig. 3.1, incidentally, is in concept no different from the intersection shown in the Venn diagram of Fig. 2.2b. There is one difference only: instead of the points lying within two circles, the present case involves the points that lie on two lines. Let the set of points on the demand and supply curves be denoted, respectively, by D and S. Then, by utilizing the symbol Q ($= Q_d = Q_s$), the two sets and their intersection can be written

$$D = \{(P,Q) \mid Q = a - bP\}$$
$$S = \{(P,Q) \mid Q = -c + dP\}$$
$$\text{and} \qquad D \cap S = (\bar{P},\bar{Q})$$

The intersection set contains in this instance only a single element, the ordered pair $(\bar{P},\bar{Q})$. The market equilibrium is unique.

EXERCISE 3.2

1 Given the market model

$$Q_d = Q_s$$
$$Q_d = 18 - 2P$$
$$Q_s = -6 + 6P$$

find $\bar{P}$ and $\bar{Q}$: (a) by elimination of variables; (b) by formulas (3.4) and (3.5); and (c) graphically.

2 Solve the market model

$$Q_d = Q_s$$
$$Q_d = 15 - 4P$$
$$Q_s = 6P - 1$$

by the three methods cited in the preceding problem.

3 If $b + d = 0$ in the linear market model, no equilibrium solution can be found. Supply a *mathematical* explanation as well as an *economic* explanation for this. [*Hint:* For the mathematical explanation, examine (3.4) and (3.5); for the economic one, examine the demand and supply functions in (3.1) along with Fig. 3.1.]

3.3 Partial Market Equilibrium—A Nonlinear Model

Let the linear demand in the isolated market model be replaced by a quadratic demand function, while the supply function remains linear. Then, if numerical coefficients are employed rather than parameters, a model such as the following may emerge:

$$Q_d = Q_s$$
(3.6) $$Q_d = 4 - P^2$$
$$Q_s = 4P - 1$$

As previously, this system of three equations can be reduced to a single equation by elimination of variables (by substitution):

$$4 - P^2 = 4P - 1$$

or

(3.7) $$P^2 + 4P - 5 = 0$$

This is a quadratic equation because the left-hand expression is a quadratic function of variable P. The major difference between a quadratic equation and a linear one is that, in general, the former will yield two solution values.

quadratic equation versus quadratic function   Before discussing the method of solution, a clear distinction should be made between the two terms *quadratic equation* and *quadratic function*. According to the earlier discussion, the expression $P^2 + 4P - 5$ constitutes a quadratic *function*, say, $f(P)$. Hence we may write

(3.8) $f(P) = P^2 + 4P - 5$

Even though this appears as an equation, it does not possess—nor does it call for—any "solution." What function (3.8) does is to specify a rule of mapping from P to $f(P)$, such as

P	$\cdots$	-6	-5	-4	-3	-2	-1	0	1	2	$\cdots$
$f(P)$	$\cdots$	7	0	-5	-8	-9	-8	-5	0	7	$\cdots$

which yields the parabola in Fig. 3.2. Hence it is quite pointless to ask: Which value(s) of P will satisfy (be solutions to) the equation (3.8)?

When $f(P)$ is set equal to zero, as in (3.7), however, a quadratic *equation* in one variable results. It is then meaningful to speak of solutions to the equation. Since (3.7) means $f(P) = 0$, to find its solutions means to locate particular P values at which the parabola in Fig. 3.2 intersects the horizontal axis where $f(P)$ is zero. For this reason, solving a quadratic equation is sometimes referred to as "finding the zeros of the (corresponding) quadratic function."[1]

There are two such intersection points in Fig. 3.2, namely, $(1,0)$ and $(-5,0)$. Note that the second element of each of these ordered pairs (the *ordinate* of the corresponding point) shows $f(P) = 0$ in both cases. The first element of each ordered pair (the *abscissa* of the point), on the other hand, gives the solution value of P. Here we get two solutions,

$$\bar{P}_1 = 1 \qquad \text{and} \qquad \bar{P}_2 = -5$$

although only the first is economically admissible, negative prices being ruled out. The solution values $\bar{P}_1$ and $\bar{P}_2$ are often called the *roots* of the quadratic equation.

[1] The distinction between quadratic function and quadratic equation just discussed can be extended also to cases of polynomials other than quadratic. Thus, a cubic equation results when a cubic function is set equal to zero.

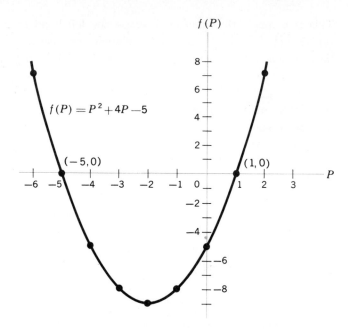

$f(P) = P^2 + 4P - 5$

$(-5, 0)$

$(1, 0)$

P

FIGURE 3.2

the quadratic formula   Equation (3.7) has been solved graphically, but an algebraic method is also available. In general, given a quadratic equation in the form

(3.9) $ax^2 + bx + c = 0$ $(a \neq 0)$

its two roots can be obtained from the *quadratic formula*:

(3.10) $\bar{x}_1, \bar{x}_2 = \dfrac{-b \pm (b^2 - 4ac)^{1/2}}{2a}$

where the $+$ part of the $\pm$ sign yields $\bar{x}_1$, and the $-$ part yields $\bar{x}_2$.

This widely used formula is derived by means of a process known as "completing the square." First, dividing each term of (3.9) by a results in the equation

$$x^2 + \frac{b}{a}x + \frac{c}{a} = 0$$

Transposing c/a and adding $b^2/4a^2$ to both sides of the equation, we get

$$x^2 + \frac{b}{a}x + \frac{b^2}{4a^2} = \frac{b^2}{4a^2} - \frac{c}{a}$$

The left side is now a "perfect square," and thus the equation can be expressed as

$$\left(x + \frac{b}{2a}\right)^2 = \frac{b^2 - 4ac}{4a^2}$$

or, after taking the square root on both sides,

$$x + \frac{b}{2a} = \pm \frac{(b^2 - 4ac)^{1/2}}{2a}$$

Finally, by transposing $b/2a$, the result in (3.10) is evolved.

Applying the formula to (3.7), where $a = 1$, $b = 4$, $c = -5$, and $x = P$, the roots are found to be

$$\bar{P}_1, \bar{P}_2 = \frac{-4 \pm (16 + 20)^{1/2}}{2} = \frac{-4 \pm 6}{2} = 1, -5$$

which check with the graphical solutions in Fig. 3.2. Again, we reject $\bar{P}_2 = -5$ on economic grounds and, after omitting the subscript 1, write simply $\bar{P} = 1$.

With this information in hand, the equilibrium quantity $\bar{Q}$ can readily be found from either the second or the third equation of (3.6) to be $\bar{Q} = 3$.

another graphical solution   One method of graphical solution of the present model has been presented in Fig. 3.2. However, since the quantity variable has been eliminated in deriving the quadratic equation, only $\bar{P}$ can be found from that figure. If we are interested in finding $\bar{P}$ and $\bar{Q}$ simultaneously from a graph, we must instead use a diagram with Q on one axis and P on the other, similar in construction to Fig. 3.1. This is illustrated in Fig. 3.3. Our problem is of course again to find the intersection of two sets of points, namely,

$$D = \{(P,Q) \mid Q = 4 - P^2\}$$
$$\text{and} \quad S = \{(P,Q) \mid Q = 4P - 1\}$$

If no restriction is placed on the domain and the range, the intersection set will contain two elements, namely,

$$D \cap S = \{(1,3),(-5,-21)\}$$

The former is located in quadrant I, and the latter (not drawn) in quadrant III. If the domain and range are restricted to being nonnegative, however, only the first ordered pair (1,3) can be accepted. Then the equilibrium is again unique.

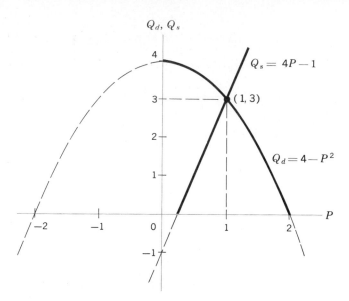

FIGURE 3.3

higher-degree polynomial equations If a system of simultaneous equations reduces not to a linear equation such as (3.3)† or to a quadratic equation such as (3.7) but to a cubic (third-degree polynomial) equation or quartic (fourth-degree polynomial) equation, the roots will be more difficult to find. One useful method which may work is that of *factoring* the function. For example, the expression $x^3 - x^2 - 4x + 4$ can be written as the product of three factors $(x - 1)$, $(x + 2)$, and $(x - 2)$. Thus the cubic equation

$$x^3 - x^2 - 4x + 4 = 0$$

can be written after factoring as

$$(x - 1)(x + 2)(x - 2) = 0$$

In order for the left-hand product to be zero, one of the three terms in the product must be zero. Setting each term equal to zero in turn, we get

$$x - 1 = 0 \quad \text{or} \quad x + 2 = 0 \quad \text{or} \quad x - 2 = 0$$

These three equations will supply the three roots of the cubic equation, namely,

$$\bar{x}_1 = 1 \quad \bar{x}_2 = -2 \quad \text{and} \quad \bar{x}_3 = 2$$

The trick is, of course, to discover the appropriate way of factoring. Unfortunately, no general rule exists, and it must therefore remain a matter of

† Equation (3.3) can be viewed as the result of setting the linear function $(b + d)P - (a + c)$ equal to zero.

Static (or Equilibrium) Analysis

trial and error. Generally speaking, however, given an nth-degree polynomial equation $f(x) = 0$, we can expect exactly n roots, which may be found as follows. First, try to find a constant c_1 such that $f(x)$ is divisible by $(x + c_1)$. The quotient $f(x)/(x + c_1)$ will be a polynomial function of a lesser—$(n - 1)$st—degree; let us call it $g(x)$. It follows then that

$$f(x) = (x + c_1)g(x)$$

Now, try to find a constant c_2 such that $g(x)$ is divisible by $(x + c_2)$. The quotient $g(x)/(x + c_2)$ will again be a polynomial function of a lesser—this time $(n - 2)$nd —degree, say, $h(x)$. Since $g(x) = (x + c_2)h(x)$, it follows that

$$f(x) = (x + c_1)g(x) = (x + c_1)(x + c_2)h(x)$$

By repeating the process, it will be possible to reduce the original nth-degree polynomial $f(x)$ to a product of exactly n terms:

$$f(x) = (x + c_1)(x + c_2) \cdots (x + c_n)$$

which, when set equal to zero, will yield n roots. Setting the first factor equal to zero, for example, one gets $\bar{x}_1 = -c_1$. Similarly, the other factors will yield $\bar{x}_2 = -c_2$, $\bar{x}_3 = -c_3$, etc. These results can be more succinctly expressed by employing an *index subscript* i:

$$\bar{x}_i = -c_i \qquad (i = 1, 2, \ldots, n)$$

Even though only one equation is written, the fact that the subscript i can take n different values means that in all there are n equations involved. Thus the index subscript provides a very concise way of statement.

EXERCISE 3.3

1   Find the zeros of the following functions graphically:

    (a) $f(x) = x^2 - 7x + 10$ (b) $g(x) = x^2 - 3x - 10$

    Check your results with the quadratic formula.

2   Solve the cubic equation $x^3 - 2x^2 - 5x + 6 = 0$ graphically.

3   Solve the following polynomial equations by factoring:

    (a) $P^2 + 4P - 5 = 0$ [see (3.7)]   (c) $x^3 - 3x^2 - 6x + 8 = 0$
    (b) $x^3 + 3x^2 - 4 = 0$ (d) $x^3 - 5x^2 + 4x = 0$

④ Find a cubic equation with roots 4, -2, and 3.

⑤ Find the equilibrium solution for each of the following models:

(a) $Q_d = Q_s$
$Q_d = 5 - P^2$
$Q_s = 2P - 3$

(b) $Q_d = Q_s$
$Q_d = 5 - P^2$
$Q_s = P^2 - 3$

6 Solve the market models of the preceding problem graphically as in Fig. 3.3.

3.4   General Market Equilibrium

The last two sections dealt with models of an isolated market, wherein the Q_d and Q_s of a commodity are functions of the price of that commodity alone. In the actual world, though, no commodity ever enjoys (or suffers) such a hermitic existence; for every commodity, there would normally exist many substitutes and complementary goods. Thus a more realistic depiction of the demand function of a commodity should take into account the effect not only of the price of the commodity itself but also of the prices of most, if not all, of the related commodities. The same also holds true for the supply function. Once the prices of other commodities are brought into the picture, however, the structure of the model itself must be broadened so as to be able to yield the equilibrium values of these other prices as well. As a result, the price and quantity variables of multiple commodities must enter endogenously into the model en masse.

In an isolated-market model, the equilibrium condition consists of only one equation, $Q_d = Q_s$, or $E \equiv Q_d - Q_s = 0$, where E stands for excess demand. When several interdependent commodities are simultaneously considered, equilibrium would require the absence of excess demand for each and every commodity included in the model, for if so much as *one* commodity is faced with an excess demand the price adjustment of that commodity will necessarily affect the quantities demanded and quantities supplied of the remaining commodities, thereby causing price changes all around. Consequently, the equilibrium condition of an n-commodity market model will involve n equations, one for each commodity, in the form

(3.11) $E_i \equiv Q_{di} - Q_{si} = 0$ $(i = 1, 2, \ldots, n)$

If a solution exists, there will be a set of prices $\bar{P}_i$ and corresponding quantities $\bar{Q}_i$ such that all the n equations in the equilibrium condition will be simultaneously satisfied.

two-commodity market model   To illustrate the problem, let us discuss a simple model in which only two commodities are related to each other. For simplicity, the demand and supply functions of both commodities are assumed to be linear. In parametric terms, such a model can be written as

$$
\begin{aligned}
Q_{d1} - Q_{s1} &= 0 \\
Q_{d1} &= a_0 + a_1 P_1 + a_2 P_2 \\
Q_{s1} &= b_0 + b_1 P_1 + b_2 P_2 \\
Q_{d2} - Q_{s2} &= 0 \\
Q_{d2} &= \alpha_0 + \alpha_1 P_1 + \alpha_2 P_2 \\
Q_{s2} &= \beta_0 + \beta_1 P_1 + \beta_2 P_2
\end{aligned}
$$

(3.12)

where the a and b coefficients pertain to the demand and supply functions of the first commodity, and the α and β coefficients are assigned to those of the second. We have not bothered to specify the signs of the coefficients, but in the course of analysis certain restrictions will emerge as a prerequisite to economically sensible results. Also, in a subsequent numerical example, some comments will be made on the specific signs to be given the coefficients.

As a first step toward the solution of this model, we can again resort to elimination of variables. By substituting the second and third equations into the first (for the first commodity), and the fifth and sixth equations into the fourth (for the second commodity), the model is reduced to two equations in two variables:

(3.13)
$$
\begin{aligned}
(a_0 - b_0) + (a_1 - b_1)P_1 + (a_2 - b_2)P_2 &= 0 \\
(\alpha_0 - \beta_0) + (\alpha_1 - \beta_1)P_1 + (\alpha_2 - \beta_2)P_2 &= 0
\end{aligned}
$$

These represent the two-commodity version of (3.11), after the demand and supply functions have been substituted into the two equilibrium-condition equations.

Although this is but a simple system of only two equations, as many as twelve parameters are involved, and algebraic manipulations will prove unwieldy unless some sort of shorthand is introduced. Let us therefore define the shorthand symbols

$$
\begin{aligned}
c_i &\equiv a_i - b_i \\
\gamma_i &\equiv \alpha_i - \beta_i
\end{aligned}
\qquad (i = 0, 1, 2)
$$

Then (3.13) becomes—after transposing the c_0 and γ_0 terms to the right-hand side of the equals sign:

(3.13')
$$
\begin{aligned}
c_1 P_1 + c_2 P_2 &= -c_0 \\
\gamma_1 P_1 + \gamma_2 P_2 &= -\gamma_0
\end{aligned}
$$

which may be solved by further elimination of variables. From the first equation, it can be found that $P_2 = -(c_0 + c_1 P_1)/c_2$. Substituting this into the second equation and solving, we get

$$(3.14) \qquad \bar{P}_1 = \frac{c_2 \gamma_0 - c_0 \gamma_2}{c_1 \gamma_2 - c_2 \gamma_1}$$

Note that $\bar{P}_1$ is entirely expressed, as a solution value should be, in terms of the data (parameters) of the model. By a similar process, the equilibrium price of the second commodity is found to be

$$(3.15) \qquad \bar{P}_2 = \frac{c_0 \gamma_1 - c_1 \gamma_0}{c_1 \gamma_2 - c_2 \gamma_1}$$

For these two values to make sense, however, certain restrictions should be imposed on the model. First, since division by zero is undefined, we must require the common denominator of (3.14) and (3.15) to be nonzero, that is, $c_1 \gamma_2 \neq c_2 \gamma_1$. Second, to assure positivity, the numerator must have the same sign as the denominator.

The equilibrium prices having been found, the equilibrium quantities $\bar{Q}_1$ and $\bar{Q}_2$ can readily be calculated by substituting (3.14) and (3.15) into the second (or third) equation and the fifth (or sixth) equation of (3.12). These solution values will naturally also be expressed in parameters. (Their actual calculation is left to the reader as an exercise.)

numerical example   Suppose that the demand and supply functions are numerically as follows:

$$(3.16) \qquad \begin{aligned} Q_{d1} &= 10 - 2P_1 + P_2 \\ Q_{s1} &= -2 + 3P_1 \\ Q_{d2} &= 15 + P_1 - P_2 \\ Q_{s2} &= -1 \qquad\quad + 2P_2 \end{aligned}$$

What will be the equilibrium solution?

Before answering the question, let us take a look at the numerical coefficients. For each commodity, Q_{si} is seen to depend on P_i alone, but Q_{di} is shown as a function of both prices. Note that while P_1 has a negative coefficient in Q_{d1}, as we would expect, the coefficient of P_2 is positive. The fact that a rise in P_2 tends to raise Q_{d1} suggests that the two commodities bear a substitute relationship to each other. The role of P_1 in the Q_{d2} function has a similar interpretation.

With these coefficients, the shorthand symbols c_i and γ_i will take the following values:

$$c_0 = 10 - (-2) = 12 \qquad c_1 = -2 - 3 = -5 \qquad c_2 = 1 - 0 = 1$$
$$\gamma_0 = 15 - (-1) = 16 \qquad \gamma_1 = 1 - 0 = 1 \qquad \gamma_2 = -1 - 2 = -3$$

By direct substitution of these into (3.14) and (3.15), we obtain

$$\bar{P}_1 = \tfrac{52}{14} = 3\tfrac{5}{7} \qquad \text{and} \qquad \bar{P}_2 = \tfrac{92}{14} = 6\tfrac{4}{7}$$

And the further substitution of $\bar{P}_1$ and $\bar{P}_2$ into (3.16) will yield

$$\bar{Q}_1 = \tfrac{64}{7} = 9\tfrac{1}{7} \qquad \text{and} \qquad \bar{Q}_2 = \tfrac{85}{7} = 12\tfrac{1}{7}$$

Thus all the equilibrium values turn out positive, as required. The reader should observe that, in order to preserve the exact values of $\bar{P}_1$ and $\bar{P}_2$ to be used in the further calculation of $\bar{Q}_1$ and $\bar{Q}_2$, it is advisable to express them as fractions rather than decimals.

Could we have obtained the equilibrium prices graphically? The answer is yes. From (3.13), it is clear that a two-commodity model can be summarized by two equations in two variables P_1 and P_2. With known numerical coefficients, both equations can be plotted in the P_1P_2 coordinate plane, and the intersection of the two curves will then pinpoint $\bar{P}_1$ and $\bar{P}_2$.

n-commodity case   The above discussion of the multicommodity market has been limited to the case of two commodities, but it should be apparent that we are already moving from *partial-equilibrium* analysis in the direction of *general-equilibrium* analysis. As more commodities enter into a model, there will be more variables and more equations, and the equations will get longer and more complicated. If all the commodities in an economy are included in a comprehensive market model, the result will be a Walrasian type of general-equilibrium model, in which the excess demand for every commodity is considered to be a function of the prices of all the commodities in the economy.

Some of the prices may, of course, carry zero coefficients when they play no role in the determination of the excess demand of a particular commodity, e.g., in the excess-demand function of pianos the price of peanuts may well have a zero coefficient. In general, however, with n commodities in all, we may express the demand and supply functions as follows (using Q_{di} and Q_{si} as function symbols in place of f and g):

$$(3.17) \qquad \begin{array}{l} Q_{di} = Q_{di}(P_1, P_2, \ldots, P_n) \\ Q_{si} = Q_{si}(P_1, P_2, \ldots, P_n) \end{array} \qquad (i = 1, 2, \ldots, n)$$

In view of the index subscript, these two equations represent the totality of the $2n$ functions which the model contains. (These functions are not necessarily linear.) Moreover, the equilibrium condition is itself composed of a set of n equations,

$$(3.18) \qquad Q_{di} - Q_{si} = 0 \qquad (i = 1, 2, \ldots, n)$$

When (3.18) is added to (3.17), the model becomes complete. The reader should therefore count a total of $3n$ equations.

Upon substitution of (3.17) into (3.18), however, the model can be reduced to a set of n simultaneous equations only:

$$Q_{di}(P_1, P_2, \ldots, P_n) - Q_{si}(P_1, P_2, \ldots, P_n) = 0 \qquad (i = 1, 2, \ldots, n)$$

Besides, inasmuch as $E_i \equiv Q_{di} - Q_{si}$, where E_i is necessarily also a function of all the n prices, the above set of equations may be written alternatively as

$$E_i(P_1, P_2, \ldots, P_n) = 0 \qquad (i = 1, 2, \ldots, n)$$

Solved simultaneously, these n equations will determine the n equilibrium prices $\bar{P}_i$—if a solution does indeed exist. And then the $\bar{Q}_i$ may be derived from the demand or supply functions.

solution of a general-equation system   If a model comes equipped with numerical coefficients, as in (3.16), the equilibrium values of the variables will be in numerical terms, too. On a more general level, if a model is expressed in terms of parametric constants, as in (3.12), the equilibrium values will also involve parameters and will hence appear as "formulas," as exemplified by (3.14) and (3.15). If, for greater generality, even the function forms are left unspecified in a model, however, as in (3.17), then the manner of expressing the solution values will of necessity be exceedingly general as well.

Drawing upon our experience in parametric models, we know that a solution value is always an expression in terms of parameters. For a general-function model containing, say, a total of m parameters $(a_1, a_2, \ldots, a_m)$—where m is not necessarily equal to n—the n equilibrium prices can therefore be expected to take the general analytical form of

$$(3.19) \qquad \bar{P}_i = \bar{P}_i(a_1, a_2, \ldots, a_m) \qquad (i = 1, 2, \ldots, n)$$

This is a symbolic statement to the effect that the solution value of *each* variable (here, price) is a function of the set of all parameters of the model. Being a very general statement, this really does not give much detailed information about the solution. But in the general analytical treatment of some types of problem, even this seemingly uninformative way of expressing a solution will prove of use, as will be seen in a later chapter.

Writing such a solution is an easy task. But an important catch exists: the expression in (3.19) can be justified if and only if a *unique* solution does indeed exist, for then and only then can we map the ordered m-tuple $(a_1, a_2, \ldots, a_m)$ into a determinate value for each price $\bar{P}_i$. Yet, unfortunately for us, there is no a priori reason to presume that every model will automatically yield a unique solution. In this connection, it needs to be emphasized that the process of "counting equations and unknowns" does not suffice as a test. Some very simple examples should convince us that an equal number of equations and unknowns (endogenous variables) does not necessarily guarantee the existence of a unique solution.

Consider the simultaneous-equation systems

$$(3.20) \quad \begin{aligned} x + y &= 8 \\ x + y &= 9 \end{aligned}$$

$$(3.21) \quad \begin{aligned} 2x + y &= 12 \\ 4x + 2y &= 24 \end{aligned}$$

$$(3.22) \quad \begin{aligned} 2x + 3y &= 58 \\ y &= 18 \\ x + y &= 20 \end{aligned}$$

In (3.20), despite the fact that two unknowns are linked together by exactly two equations, there is nevertheless no solution. These two equations happen to be *inconsistent*, for if the sum of x and y is 8 then it cannot possibly be 9 at the same time. In (3.21), another case of two equations in two variables, the two equations are *functionally dependent*, which means that one can be derived from (and is implied by) the other. (Here, the second equation is equal to two times the first equation.) Consequently, one equation is redundant and may be dropped from the system, leaving in effect only one equation in two unknowns. The solution will then be the equation $y = 12 - 2x$, which yields not a unique ordered pair $(\bar{x}, \bar{y})$ but an infinite number of them, including (0,12), (1,10), (2,8), etc., all of which fulfill that equation. Lastly, the case of (3.22) involves more equations than unknowns, yet the ordered pair (2,18) does constitute the unique solution to it. The reason is that, in view of the existence of functional dependence among the equations (the first is equal to the second plus twice the third), we have in effect only two independent, consistent equations in two variables.

These simple examples should suffice to convey to the reader the importance of *consistency* and *functional independence* as the two prerequisites for application of the process of counting equations and unknowns. In general, in order to apply that process, one should make sure that (1) the satisfaction of any one equation in the model will not preclude the satisfaction of another and (2) no equation is redundant. In (3.17), for example, the n demand and n supply functions may safely be assumed to be independent of one another, each being derived from a different source—each demand from the decisions of a group of consumers, and each supply from the decisions of a group of firms. Thus each function serves to describe one facet of the market situation, and none is redundant. Mutual consistency may perhaps also be assumed. In addition, the equilibrium-condition equations in (3.18) are also independent and presumably consistent. Therefore the analytical solution as written in (3.19) can in general be considered justifiable.[1]

For simultaneous-equation models, there exist systematic methods of testing the existence of a unique (or determinate) solution. These would involve, for linear models, an application of the concept of *determinants*, to be introduced in Chap. 5. In the case of nonlinear models, such a test would also require a knowledge of so-called "partial derivatives" and a special type of determinant called the *Jacobian determinant*, which will be discussed in Chaps. 7 and 8.

EXERCISE 3.4

1. Work out the step-by-step solution of (3.13′), thereby verifying the results in (3.14) and (3.15). find $\bar{Q}_1$ & $\bar{Q}_2$

2. Rewrite (3.14) and (3.15) in terms of the original parameters of the model in (3.12).

3. The demand and supply functions of a two-commodity market model are as follows:

$$Q_{d1} = 18 - 3P_1 + P_2 \qquad Q_{d2} = 12 + P_1 - 2P_2$$
$$Q_{s1} = -2 + 4P_1 \qquad Q_{s2} = -2 \qquad + 3P_2$$

Find $\bar{P}_i$ and $\bar{Q}_i$ ($i = 1, 2$). (Use fractions rather than decimals.)

3.5   Equilibrium in National-Income Analysis

Even though the discussion of static analysis has hitherto been restricted to *market models* in various guises—linear and nonlinear, one-commodity and multicommodity, specific and general—it, of course, has applications in other areas of economics also. As a simple example, we may cite the familiar Keynesian national-income model,

$$(3.23) \qquad \begin{aligned} Y &= C + I_0 + G_0 \\ C &= a + bY \end{aligned}$$

---

[1] This is essentially the way that Léon Walras approached the problem of the existence of a general market equilibrium. In the modern literature, there can be found a number of sophisticated mathematical proofs of the existence of a competitive market equilibrium under certain postulated economic conditions. But the mathematics used is advanced. The easiest one to understand is perhaps the proof given in Robert Dorfman, Paul A. Samuelson, and Robert M. Solow, *Linear Programming and Economic Analysis*, McGraw-Hill Book Company, New York, 1958, chap. 13, which the reader should read *after* having studied Part 6 of the present volume.

where Y and C stand for the endogenous variables national income and consumption expenditure, respectively, and I_0 and G_0 represent the exogenously determined investment and government expenditures. The first equation is an equilibrium condition (national income = total expenditure). The second, the consumption function, is behavioral.

It is quite clear that these two equations in two endogenous variables are neither functionally dependent upon, nor inconsistent with, each other. Thus we would be able to find the equilibrium values of income and consumption expenditure, $\bar{Y}$ and $\bar{C}$, in terms of the given data: the parameters a and b and the exogenous variables I_0 and G_0.

Substitution of the second equation into the first will reduce (3.23) to a single equation in one variable, Y:

$$Y = a + bY + I_0 + G_0$$
$$\text{or} \quad (1 - b)Y = a + I_0 + G_0$$

Thus the solution value of Y (equilibrium national income) is

$$(3.24) \qquad \bar{Y} = \frac{a + I_0 + G_0}{1 - b}$$

which, it should be noted, is expressed entirely in terms of the parameters and exogenous variables, the given data of the model. Putting (3.24) into the second equation of (3.23) will then yield the equilibrium level of consumption expenditure:

$$(3.25) \qquad \bar{C} = a + b\bar{Y} = a + \frac{b(a + I_0 + G_0)}{1 - b}$$

$$= \frac{a(1 - b) + b(a + I_0 + G_0)}{1 - b} = \frac{a + b(I_0 + G_0)}{1 - b}$$

which is again expressed entirely in terms of the given data.

Both $\bar{Y}$ and $\bar{C}$ have the expression $(1 - b)$ in the denominator; thus a restriction $b \neq 1$ is necessary. Since b represents the marginal propensity to consume, which is normally taken to be a positive fraction $(0 < b < 1)$, this restriction is automatically satisfied. For $\bar{Y}$ and $\bar{C}$ to be positive, moreover, the numerators in (3.24) and (3.25) must be positive. Since the exogenous expenditures I_0 and G_0 are normally positive, as is the parameter a (the vertical intercept of the consumption function), the sign of the numerator expressions will work out, too.

As a check on our calculation, we can add the $\bar{C}$ expression in (3.25) to $(I_0 + G_0)$ and see whether the sum is equal to the $\bar{Y}$ expression in (3.24). If so, the $\bar{C}$ and $\bar{Y}$ values do fulfill the equilibrium condition, and the solution is valid.

This model is obviously one of extreme simplicity and crudity, but other models of national-income determination, in varying degrees of complexity and sophistication, can be constructed as well. In each case, however, the principles involved in the construction and analysis of the model are identical with those already discussed. For this reason, we shall not go into further illustrations here. A more comprehensive national-income model, involving the simultaneous equilibrium of the money market and the goods market, will be discussed in Sec. 8.6 below.

EXERCISE 3.5

1 Given the following model:

$$Y = C + I_0 + G_0$$
$$C = a + b(Y - T) \qquad [T: \text{tax collection}]$$
$$T = d + tY \qquad [t: \text{given income tax rate}]$$

(a) How many endogenous variables are there?

(b) Find $\bar{Y}$, $\bar{T}$, and $\bar{C}$.

2 Find $\bar{Y}$ and $\bar{C}$ from the following:

$$Y = C + I_0 + G_0$$
$$C = 20 + 5Y^{1/2}$$
$$I_0 + G_0 = 30$$

(Hint: After substituting the last two equations into the first, consider the resulting equation as a quadratic equation in the variable $w \equiv Y^{1/2}$.)

4

LINEAR MODELS AND MATRIX ALGEBRA

For the one-commodity model (3.1), the solutions $\bar{P}$ and $\bar{Q}$ as expressed in (3.4) and (3.5) are relatively simple, even though a number of parameters are involved. As more and more commodities are incorporated into the model, such solution formulas quickly become cumbersome and unwieldy. That was why we had to resort to a little shorthand, even for the two-commodity case—in order that the solutions (3.14) and (3.15) can still be written in a relatively concise fashion. We did not attempt to tackle any three- or four-commodity models, even in the linear version, primarily because we did not yet have at our disposal a method suitable for handling a large system of simultaneous equations. Such a method is found in *matrix algebra*, the subject of this chapter and the next.

Matrix algebra can enable us to do many things. In the first place, it provides a compact way of writing an equation system, even an extremely large one. Second, it leads to a way of testing the existence of a solution by evaluation of a *determinant*—a concept closely related to that of a matrix. Third, it gives a method of finding that solution (if it exists). Since equation systems are encountered not only in static analysis but also in comparative-static and dynamic analyses and in optimization problems, the reader will find ample application of matrix algebra in almost every chapter that is to follow.

However, one slight "catch" should be mentioned at the outset. Matrix algebra is applicable only to *linear*-equation systems. How realistically linear equations can describe actual economic relationships depends, of course, on the

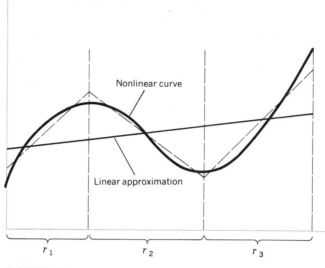

FIGURE 4.1

nature of the relationships in question. In many cases, even if some sacrifice of realism is entailed by the assumption of linearity, an assumed linear relationship can produce a sufficiently close approximation to an actual nonlinear relationship to warrant its use. In other cases, the closeness of approximation may also be improved by having a separate linear approximation for each segment of a nonlinear relationship, as is illustrated in Fig. 4.1. If the solid curve is taken as the actual nonlinear relationship, a single linear approximation might take the form of the solid straight line, which shows substantial deviation from the curve at certain points. But if the domain is divided into three regions r_1, r_2, and r_3, we can have a much closer linear approximation (broken straight line) in each region.

In yet other cases, while preserving the nonlinearity in the model, we can effect a transformation of variables so as to obtain a linear relation to work with. For example, the nonlinear function

$$y = ax^b$$

can be readily transformed, by taking the logarithm on both sides, into the function

$$\log y = \log a + b \log x$$

which is linear in the two variables ($\log y$) and ($\log x$). (Logarithms will be discussed in detail in Chap. 10.)

In short, the linearity assumption frequently adopted in economics may in certain cases be quite reasonable and justified. On this note, then, let us proceed to the study of matrix algebra.

4.1   Matrices and Vectors

The two-commodity market model (3.12) can be written—after eliminating the quantity variables—as a system of two linear equations, as in (3.13′),

$$c_1 P_1 + c_2 P_2 = -c_0$$
$$\gamma_1 P_1 + \gamma_2 P_2 = -\gamma_0$$

where the parameters c_0 and γ_0 appear to the right of the equals sign. In general, a system of m linear equations in n variables $(x_1, x_2, \ldots, x_n)$ can also be arranged into such a format:

$$
(4.1) \qquad
\begin{aligned}
a_{11}x_1 + a_{12}x_2 + \cdots + a_{1n}x_n &= d_1 \\
a_{21}x_1 + a_{22}x_2 + \cdots + a_{2n}x_n &= d_2 \\
&\cdots \cdots \cdots \cdots \cdots \cdots \\
a_{m1}x_1 + a_{m2}x_2 + \cdots + a_{mn}x_n &= d_m
\end{aligned}
$$

In (4.1), the variable x_1 appears only within the leftmost column, and in general the variable x_j appears only in the jth column on the left side of the equals sign. The double-subscripted parameter symbol a_{ij} represents the coefficient appearing in the ith equation and attached to the jth variable. For example, a_{21} is the coefficient in the second equation, attached to the variable x_1. The parameter d_i which is unattached to any variable, on the other hand, represents the constant term in the ith equation. For instance, d_1 is the constant term in the first equation. All subscripts are therefore keyed to the specific locations of the variables and parameters in (4.1).

matrices as arrays   There are essentially three types of ingredients in the equation system (4.1). The first is the set of coefficients a_{ij}; the second is the set of variables $x_1, \ldots, x_n$; and the last is the set of constant terms $d_1, \ldots, d_m$. If we arrange the three sets as three arrays and label them, respectively, as A, x, and d (without subscripts), then we have

$$
(4.2) \qquad
A =
\begin{bmatrix}
a_{11} & a_{12} & \cdots & a_{1n} \\
a_{21} & a_{22} & \cdots & a_{2n} \\
\multicolumn{4}{c}{\cdots\cdots\cdots\cdots} \\
a_{m1} & a_{m2} & \cdots & a_{mn}
\end{bmatrix}
\qquad
x =
\begin{bmatrix}
x_1 \\
x_2 \\
\vdots \\
x_n
\end{bmatrix}
\qquad
d =
\begin{bmatrix}
d_1 \\
d_2 \\
\vdots \\
d_m
\end{bmatrix}
$$

As a simple example, given the linear-equation system

$$
\begin{aligned}
6x_1 + 3x_2 + x_3 &= 22 \\
x_1 + 4x_2 - 2x_3 &= 12 \\
4x_1 - x_2 + 5x_3 &= 10
\end{aligned}
\tag{4.3}
$$

we can write

$$
A = \begin{bmatrix} 6 & 3 & 1 \\ 1 & 4 & -2 \\ 4 & -1 & 5 \end{bmatrix} \qquad x = \begin{bmatrix} x_1 \\ x_2 \\ x_3 \end{bmatrix} \qquad d = \begin{bmatrix} 22 \\ 12 \\ 10 \end{bmatrix}
\tag{4.4}
$$

Each of the three arrays in (4.2) or (4.4) constitutes a *matrix*.

A matrix is defined as a rectangular array of numbers, parameters, or variables. The members of the array, referred to as the *elements* of the matrix, are usually enclosed in brackets, as in (4.2), or sometimes in parentheses or with double vertical lines: $\|\ \ \|$. Note that in matrix A (the *coefficient matrix* of the equation system), the elements are separated not by commas but by blank spaces only. As a shorthand device, the array in matrix A can be written more simply as

$$
A = [a_{ij}] \qquad \begin{pmatrix} i = 1, 2, \ldots, m \\ j = 1, 2, \ldots, n \end{pmatrix}
$$

Inasmuch as the location of each element in a matrix is unequivocally fixed by the subscript, every matrix is an ordered set.

vectors as special matrices   The number of rows and the number of columns in a matrix together define the *dimension* of the matrix. Since matrix A in (4.2) contains m rows and n columns, it is said to be of dimension $m \times n$ (read: m by n). It is important to remember that the row number always precedes the column number; this is in line with the way the two subscripts in a_{ij} are ordered. In the special case where $m = n$, the matrix is called a *square matrix*; thus the matrix A in (4.4) is a 3×3 square matrix.

Some matrices may contain only one column, such as x and d in (4.2) or (4.4). Such matrices are given the special name *column vectors*. In (4.2), the dimension of x is $n \times 1$, and that of d is $m \times 1$; in (4.4) both x and d are 3×1. If we arranged the variables x_j in a horizontal array, though, there would result a $1 \times n$ matrix, which is called a *row vector*. For notation purposes, a row vector is usually distinguished from a column vector by the use of a primed symbol:

$$
x' = [x_1 \quad x_2 \quad \cdots \quad x_n]
$$

The reader may observe that a vector (whether row or column) is merely an ordered n-tuple, and as such it may be interpreted as a point in an n-dimensional space. In turn, the $m \times n$ matrix A can be interpreted as an ordered set of m row vectors or as an ordered set of n column vectors. These ideas will be followed up later.

A question of more immediate interest is: How can the matrix notation enable us, as promised, to express an equation system in a compact way? The answer is that, with the matrices defined in (4.4), we can express the equation system (4.3) simply as

$$Ax = d$$

In fact, if A, x, and d are given the meanings in (4.2), then even the general-equation system in (4.1) can be written as $Ax = d$. The compactness of this notation is thus unmistakable.

However, the equation $Ax = d$ prompts at least two questions: How do we multiply two matrices A and x? And, what is meant by the equality of Ax and d? Since matrices involve whole blocks of numbers, the familiar algebraic operations defined for single numbers are not directly applicable, and there is need for a new kind of algebra.

EXERCISE 4.1

1 Rewrite the equation system (3.1) in the format of (4.1), and show that, if the three variables are arranged in the order Q_d, Q_s, and P, the coefficient matrix will be

$$\begin{bmatrix} 1 & -1 & 0 \\ 1 & 0 & b \\ 0 & 1 & -d \end{bmatrix}$$

How would you write the vector of constants?

2 Rewrite the equation system (3.12) in the format of (4.1) with the variables arranged in the following order: Q_{d1}, Q_{s1}, Q_{d2}, Q_{s2}, P_1, P_2. Write out the coefficient matrix, the variable vector, and the constant vector.

4.2   The Algebra of Matrices

As a preliminary, let us first define the word *equality*. Two matrices $A = [a_{ij}]$ and $B = [b_{ij}]$ are said to be *equal* if and only if they have the same dimension and have identical elements in the corresponding locations in the array. In other words, $A = B$ if and only if $a_{ij} = b_{ij}$ for all values of i and j. Thus, for example, we find

$$\begin{bmatrix} 4 & 3 \\ 2 & 0 \end{bmatrix} = \begin{bmatrix} 4 & 3 \\ 2 & 0 \end{bmatrix} \neq \begin{bmatrix} 2 & 0 \\ 4 & 3 \end{bmatrix}$$

As another example, if $\begin{bmatrix} x \\ y \end{bmatrix} = \begin{bmatrix} 7 \\ 4 \end{bmatrix}$, this will mean that $x = 7$ and $y = 4$.

addition and subtraction of matrices   Two matrices can be added if and only if they have the same dimension. When this dimensional requirement is met, the matrices are said to be *conformable for addition*. In that case, the addition of $A = [a_{ij}]$ and $B = [b_{ij}]$ is defined as the addition of each pair of corresponding elements.

Example 1

$$\begin{bmatrix} 4 & 9 \\ 2 & 1 \end{bmatrix} + \begin{bmatrix} 2 & 0 \\ 0 & 7 \end{bmatrix} = \begin{bmatrix} 4+2 & 9+0 \\ 2+0 & 1+7 \end{bmatrix} = \begin{bmatrix} 6 & 9 \\ 2 & 8 \end{bmatrix}$$

Example 2

$$\begin{bmatrix} a_{11} & a_{12} \\ a_{21} & a_{22} \\ a_{31} & a_{32} \end{bmatrix} + \begin{bmatrix} b_{11} & b_{12} \\ b_{21} & b_{22} \\ b_{31} & b_{32} \end{bmatrix} = \begin{bmatrix} a_{11}+b_{11} & a_{12}+b_{12} \\ a_{21}+b_{21} & a_{22}+b_{22} \\ a_{31}+b_{31} & a_{32}+b_{32} \end{bmatrix}$$

In general, we may state the rule thus:

$$[a_{ij}] + [b_{ij}] = [c_{ij}] \qquad \text{where } c_{ij} = a_{ij} + b_{ij}$$

Note that the sum matrix $[c_{ij}]$ must have the same dimension as the component matrices $[a_{ij}]$ and $[b_{ij}]$.

The subtraction operation $A - B$ can be similarly defined if and only if A and B have the same dimension. The operation entails the result

$$[a_{ij}] - [b_{ij}] = [d_{ij}] \qquad \text{where } d_{ij} = a_{ij} - b_{ij}$$

Example 3

$$\begin{bmatrix} 19 & 3 \\ 2 & 0 \end{bmatrix} - \begin{bmatrix} 6 & 8 \\ 1 & 3 \end{bmatrix} = \begin{bmatrix} 19-6 & 3-8 \\ 2-1 & 0-3 \end{bmatrix} = \begin{bmatrix} 13 & -5 \\ 1 & -3 \end{bmatrix}$$

The subtraction operation $A - B$ may be considered alternatively as an addition operation involving a matrix A and another matrix $(-1)B$. This, however, raises the question of what is meant by the multiplication of a matrix by a single number (here, -1).

scalar multiplication   To multiply a matrix by a number—or in matrix-algebra terminology, by a *scalar*—is to multiply *every* element of that matrix by the given scalar.

Example 4

$$7\begin{bmatrix} 3 & -1 \\ 0 & 5 \end{bmatrix} = \begin{bmatrix} 21 & -7 \\ 0 & 35 \end{bmatrix}$$

Example 5

$$\frac{1}{2}\begin{bmatrix} a_{11} & a_{12} \\ a_{21} & a_{22} \end{bmatrix} = \begin{bmatrix} \frac{1}{2}a_{11} & \frac{1}{2}a_{12} \\ \frac{1}{2}a_{21} & \frac{1}{2}a_{22} \end{bmatrix}$$

From these examples, the rationale of the name scalar should become clear, for it "scales up (or down)" the matrix by a certain multiple. The scalar can, of course, be a negative number as well.

Example 6

$$-1\begin{bmatrix} a_{11} & a_{12} & d_1 \\ a_{21} & a_{22} & d_2 \end{bmatrix} = \begin{bmatrix} -a_{11} & -a_{12} & -d_1 \\ -a_{21} & -a_{22} & -d_2 \end{bmatrix}$$

Note that if the matrix on the left represents the coefficients *and* the constant terms in the simultaneous equations

$$a_{11}x_1 + a_{12}x_2 = d_1$$
$$a_{21}x_1 + a_{22}x_2 = d_2$$

then multiplication by the scalar -1 will amount to multiplying both sides of both equations by -1, thereby changing the sign of every term in the system.

multiplication of matrices   Whereas a scalar can be used to multiply a matrix of any dimension, the multiplication of two matrices is contingent upon the satisfaction of another dimensional requirement.

Suppose, given two matrices A and B, we want to find the product AB. The conformability condition for multiplication is that the *column* dimension of A (the "lead" matrix in the expression AB) must be equal to the row dimension of B (the "lag" matrix). For instance, if

$$(4.5) \qquad \underset{(1 \times 2)}{A} = [a_{11} \quad a_{12}] \qquad \underset{(2 \times 3)}{B} = \begin{bmatrix} b_{11} & b_{12} & b_{13} \\ b_{21} & b_{22} & b_{23} \end{bmatrix}$$

the product AB then *is* defined, since A has *two columns* and B has *two rows*— precisely the same number.[1] This can be checked at a glance by comparing the *second* number in the dimension indicator for A, which is (1×2), with the *first* number in the dimension indicator for B, (2×3). On the other hand, the reverse product BA is *not* defined in this case, because B (now the lead matrix) has *three* columns while A (the lag matrix) has only *one* row; hence the conformability condition is violated.

In general, if A is of dimension $m \times n$ and B is of dimension $p \times q$, the matrix product AB will be defined if and only if $n = p$. If defined, moreover, the product matrix AB will have the dimension $m \times q$—the same number of *rows* as the lead matrix A and the same number of *columns* as the lag matrix B. For the matrices given in (4.5), AB will be 1×3.

It remains to define the exact procedure of multiplication. For this purpose, let us take the matrices A and B in (4.5) as illustration. Since the product AB is defined and is expected to be of dimension 1×3, we may write (using the symbol C rather than c' for the row vector)

$$AB = C = [c_{11} \quad c_{12} \quad c_{13}]$$

Each of the three elements of C is defined as a sum of products of the elements of a particular row in A and a particular column in B. Specifically, we have

$$(4.6) \quad \begin{aligned} c_{11} &= a_{11}b_{11} + a_{12}b_{21} && \text{[from row 1 in } A\text{, column 1 in } B\text{]} \\ c_{12} &= a_{11}b_{12} + a_{12}b_{22} && \text{[from row 1 in } A\text{, column 2 in } B\text{]} \\ c_{13} &= a_{11}b_{13} + a_{12}b_{23} && \text{[from row 1 in } A\text{, column 3 in } B\text{]} \end{aligned}$$

Note that the first subscript in the symbol c_{ij} tells us which row of the lead matrix A to use to form the sum of products, whereas the second subscript points to the appropriate column in the lag matrix B. Once the row and column are properly picked, the elements therein are to be paired sequentially, as in Fig. 4.2, and the two elements in each pair are then multiplied together, and the sum of such products taken. The reader may observe that it is this pairing rule which necessitates the matching of the column dimension of the lead matrix and the row dimension of the lag matrix before multiplication can be performed.

The multiplication procedure illustrated in Fig. 4.2 can also be described by using the concept of the *inner product* of two vectors. Given two vectors u and v with n elements each, say, $(u_1, u_2, \ldots, u_n)$ and $(v_1, v_2, \ldots, v_n)$, arranged *either* as two rows *or* as two columns *or* as one row and one column, their inner product, written as $u \cdot v$, is defined as

$$u \cdot v = u_1 v_1 + u_2 v_2 + \cdots + u_n v_n$$

---

[1] The matrix A, being a row vector, would normally be denoted by a'. We use the symbol A here to stress the fact that the multiplication rule being explained applies to matrices in general, not only to the product of one vector and one matrix.

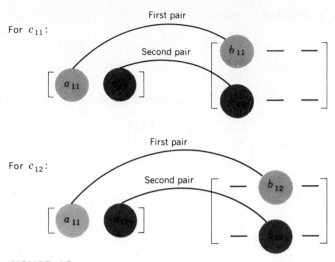

For c_{11}:

First pair

Second pair

b_{11}

a_{11}

For c_{12}:

First pair

Second pair

b_{12}

a_{11}

FIGURE 4.2

This is a sum of products of corresponding elements, and hence the inner product of two vectors is a scalar. If, for instance, we prepare after a shopping trip a vector of quantities purchased of n goods and a vector of their prices (listed in the corresponding order), then their inner product will give the total purchase cost. Note that the inner-product concept is exempted from the conformability condition, since the arrangement of the two vectors in rows or columns is immaterial.

Using this concept, the element c_{ij} in the product matrix $C = AB$ can simply be described as the inner product of the ith row of the lead matrix A and the jth column of the lag matrix B. By examining (4.6), the reader can easily verify the validity of this description.

The rule of multiplication outlined above applies with equal validity when the dimensions of A and B are other than those illustrated above; the only prerequisite is that the conformability condition be met.

Example 7   Given

$$\underset{(2 \times 2)}{A} = \begin{bmatrix} 3 & 5 \\ 4 & 6 \end{bmatrix} \quad \text{and} \quad \underset{(2 \times 2)}{B} = \begin{bmatrix} -1 & 0 \\ 4 & 7 \end{bmatrix}$$

find AB. The product AB is obviously defined, and will be 2×2:

$$AB = \begin{bmatrix} 3(-1) + 5(4) & 3(0) + 5(7) \\ 4(-1) + 6(4) & 4(0) + 6(7) \end{bmatrix} = \begin{bmatrix} 17 & 35 \\ 20 & 42 \end{bmatrix}$$

Example 8   Given

$$
\underset{(3\times 2)}{A} = \begin{bmatrix} 1 & 3 \\ 2 & 8 \\ 4 & 0 \end{bmatrix} \quad \text{and} \quad \underset{(2\times 1)}{b} = \begin{bmatrix} 5 \\ 9 \end{bmatrix}
$$

find Ab. This time the product matrix should be 3×1, that is, a column vector:

$$
Ab = \begin{bmatrix} 1(5) + 3(9) \\ 2(5) + 8(9) \\ 4(5) + 0(9) \end{bmatrix} = \begin{bmatrix} 32 \\ 82 \\ 20 \end{bmatrix}
$$

Example 9   Given

$$
\underset{(3\times 3)}{A} = \begin{bmatrix} 3 & -1 & 2 \\ 1 & 0 & 3 \\ 4 & 0 & 2 \end{bmatrix} \quad \text{and} \quad \underset{(3\times 3)}{B} = \begin{bmatrix} 0 & -\frac{1}{5} & \frac{3}{10} \\ -1 & \frac{1}{5} & \frac{7}{10} \\ 0 & \frac{2}{5} & -\frac{1}{10} \end{bmatrix}
$$

find AB. The same rule of multiplication now yields a very special product matrix:

$$
AB = \begin{bmatrix} 0+1+0 & -\frac{3}{5} - \frac{1}{5} + \frac{4}{5} & \frac{9}{10} - \frac{7}{10} - \frac{2}{10} \\ 0+0+0 & -\frac{1}{5} + 0 + \frac{6}{5} & \frac{3}{10} + 0 - \frac{3}{10} \\ 0+0+0 & -\frac{4}{5} + 0 + \frac{4}{5} & \frac{12}{10} + 0 - \frac{2}{10} \end{bmatrix} = \begin{bmatrix} 1 & 0 & 0 \\ 0 & 1 & 0 \\ 0 & 0 & 1 \end{bmatrix}
$$

This last matrix—a square matrix with 1s in its *principal diagonal* (the diagonal running from northwest to southeast) and 0s everywhere else—exemplifies the important type of matrices known as *identity matrices*. These shall be further discussed below.

Example 10   Let us now take the matrix A and the vector x as defined in (4.4) and find Ax. The product matrix is a 3×1 column vector:

$$
Ax = \underset{(3\times 3)}{\begin{bmatrix} 6 & 3 & 1 \\ 1 & 4 & -2 \\ 4 & -1 & 5 \end{bmatrix}} \underset{(3\times 1)}{\begin{bmatrix} x_1 \\ x_2 \\ x_3 \end{bmatrix}} = \underset{(3\times 1)}{\begin{bmatrix} 6x_1 + 3x_2 + x_3 \\ x_1 + 4x_2 - 2x_3 \\ 4x_1 - x_2 + 5x_3 \end{bmatrix}}
$$

Repeat: The product on the right is a *column* vector, its corpulent appearance notwithstanding! When we write $Ax = d$, therefore, we have

$$
\begin{bmatrix} 6x_1 + 3x_2 + x_3 \\ x_1 + 4x_2 - 2x_3 \\ 4x_1 - x_2 + 5x_3 \end{bmatrix} = \begin{bmatrix} 22 \\ 12 \\ 10 \end{bmatrix}
$$

which, according to the definition of matrix equality, is equivalent to the statement of the entire equation system in (4.3).

Note that, to use the matrix notation $Ax = d$, it is necessary, because of the conformability condition, to arrange the variables x_j into a column vector rather than a row vector, even though these variables are listed in a horizontal order in the original equation system.

the question of division   While matrices, like numbers, can undergo the operations of addition, subtraction, and multiplication—subject to the conformability conditions—it is not possible to divide one matrix by another. That is, we cannot write A/B.

For two numbers a and b, the quotient a/b (with $b \neq 0$) can be written alternatively as ab^{-1} or $b^{-1}a$, where b^{-1} represents the *inverse* or *reciprocal* of b. Since $ab^{-1} = b^{-1}a$, the quotient expression a/b can be used to represent both ab^{-1} and $b^{-1}a$. The case of matrices is different. Applying the concept of inverses to matrices, we may in certain cases (discussed below) define a matrix B^{-1} that is the inverse of matrix B. But from the discussion of conformability condition it follows that, if AB^{-1} is defined, there can be no assurance that $B^{-1}A$ is also defined. Even if AB^{-1} and $B^{-1}A$ are indeed both defined, they still may not represent the same product. Hence the expression A/B cannot be used without ambiguity, and it must be avoided. Instead, one must specify whether he is referring to AB^{-1} or $B^{-1}A$—provided that the inverse B^{-1} does exist and that the matrix product in question is defined. Inverse matrices will be further discussed below.

digression on $\sum$ notation   The use of subscripted symbols not only helps in designating the locations of parameters and variables but also lends itself to a flexible shorthand for denoting sums of terms, such as those which arose during the process of matrix multiplication.

The summation shorthand makes use of the Greek letter $\sum$ (sigma, for "sum"). To express the sum of x_1, x_2, and x_3, for instance, we may write

$$x_1 + x_2 + x_3 = \sum_{j=1}^{3} x_j$$

which is read: the sum of x_j as j ranges from 1 to 3. The symbol j, called the *summation index*, takes only integer values. The expression x_j represents the *summand* (that which is to be summed), and it is in effect a function of j. Aside from the letter j, summation indices are also commonly denoted by i or k, such as

$$\sum_{i=3}^{7} x_i = x_3 + x_4 + x_5 + x_6 + x_7$$

$$\sum_{k=0}^{n} x_k = x_0 + x_1 + \cdots + x_n$$

The application of $\sum$ notation can be readily extended to cases in which the x term is prefixed with a coefficient or in which each term in the sum is raised to some integer power. For instance, we may write:

$$\sum_{j=1}^{3} ax_j = ax_1 + ax_2 + ax_3 = a(x_1 + x_2 + x_3) = a \sum_{j=1}^{3} x_j$$

$$\sum_{j=1}^{3} a_j x_j = a_1 x_1 + a_2 x_2 + a_3 x_3$$

$$\sum_{i=0}^{n} a_i x^i = a_0 x^0 + a_1 x^1 + a_2 x^2 + \cdots + a_n x^n$$

$$= a_0 \quad + a_1 x \ + a_2 x^2 + \cdots + a_n x^n$$

The last example, in particular, shows that the expression $\sum_{i=0}^{n} a_i x^i$ can in fact be used as a shorthand form of the general polynomial function of (2.4).

It may be mentioned in passing that, whenever the context of the discussion leaves no ambiguity as to the range of summation, the symbol $\sum$ can be used alone, without an index attached (such as $\sum x_i$), or with only the index letter underneath (such as $\sum_i x_i$).

Let us apply the $\sum$ shorthand to matrix multiplication. In (4.6), each element of the product matrix $C = AB$ is defined as a sum of terms, which may now be rewritten as follows:

$$c_{11} = a_{11}b_{11} + a_{12}b_{21} = \sum_{k=1}^{2} a_{1k}b_{k1}$$

$$c_{12} = a_{11}b_{12} + a_{12}b_{22} = \sum_{k=1}^{2} a_{1k}b_{k2}$$

$$c_{13} = a_{11}b_{13} + a_{12}b_{23} = \sum_{k=1}^{2} a_{1k}b_{k3}$$

In each case, the first subscript of c_{1j} is reflected in the first subscript of a_{1k}, and the second subscript of c_{1j}, in the second subscript of b_{kj} in the $\sum$ expression. The index k, on the other hand, is a "dummy" subscript; it serves to indicate which particular pair of elements is being multiplied, but it does not show up in the symbol c_{1j}.

Extending this to the multiplication of an $m \times n$ matrix $A = [a_{ik}]$ and an $n \times p$ matrix $B = [b_{kj}]$, the elements of the $m \times p$ product matrix $AB = C = [c_{ij}]$ may now be written as

$$c_{11} = \sum_{k=1}^{n} a_{1k}b_{k1} \qquad c_{12} = \sum_{k=1}^{n} a_{1k}b_{k2} \qquad \cdots$$

or more generally,

$$c_{ij} = \sum_{k=1}^{n} a_{ik}b_{kj} \qquad \begin{pmatrix} i = 1, 2, \ldots, m \\ j = 1, 2, \ldots, p \end{pmatrix}$$

This last equation represents yet another way of stating the rule of multiplication for the matrices defined above.

EXERCISE 4.2

1   Given $A = \begin{bmatrix} 3 & -7 \\ 6 & 9 \end{bmatrix}$, $B = \begin{bmatrix} 0 & 8 \\ 3 & -2 \end{bmatrix}$, and $C = \begin{bmatrix} 7 & 3 \\ 6 & 1 \end{bmatrix}$, find:

(a) $A + B$ (b) $C - A$ (c) $3A$ (d) $4B + 2C$

2   Given $A = \begin{bmatrix} 2 & 1 \\ 3 & 0 \\ 5 & 1 \end{bmatrix}$, $B = \begin{bmatrix} 4 & 0 \\ 3 & 8 \end{bmatrix}$, and $C = \begin{bmatrix} 1 & 2 \\ 6 & 3 \end{bmatrix}$:

(a) Is AB defined? Calculate AB. Can you calculate BA? Why?
(b) Is BC defined? Calculate BC. Is CB defined? If so, calculate CB. Is it true that $BC = CB$?

3   On the basis of the matrices given in Example 9, is the product BA defined? If so, calculate the product. In this case do we have $AB = BA$?

4   Find the product matrices in the following (in each case, append beneath every matrix a dimension indicator):

(a) $\begin{bmatrix} 9 & 7 & 0 \\ 3 & 0 & 4 \\ 2 & 3 & 0 \end{bmatrix} \begin{bmatrix} 2 & 0 \\ 0 & 1 \\ 3 & 5 \end{bmatrix}$

(c) $\begin{bmatrix} 3 & 6 & 0 \\ 4 & 2 & -7 \end{bmatrix} \begin{bmatrix} x \\ y \\ z \end{bmatrix}$

(b) $\begin{bmatrix} 4 & 5 & 0 \\ 3 & 0 & 1 \end{bmatrix} \begin{bmatrix} 4 & -1 \\ 5 & 2 \\ 0 & 1 \end{bmatrix}$

(d) $\begin{bmatrix} -9 & 5 & 1 \end{bmatrix} \begin{bmatrix} 7 & 0 \\ 0 & 2 \\ 1 & 4 \end{bmatrix}$

5   Expand the following summation expressions:

(a) $\sum_{i=2}^{5} x_i$ (c) $\sum_{i=1}^{4} bx_i$ (e) $\sum_{i=0}^{3} (x + i)^2$

(b) $\sum_{i=5}^{8} a_i x_i$ (d) $\sum_{i=1}^{n} a_i x^{i-1}$

6   Rewrite the following in $\sum$ notation:

(a) $x_1(x_1 - 1) + x_2(x_2 - 1) + x_3(x_3 - 1)$

(b) $a_2(x_3 + 2) + a_3(x_4 + 3) + a_4(x_5 + 4)$

(c) $\dfrac{1}{x} + \dfrac{1}{x^2} + \cdots + \dfrac{1}{x^n}$ $(x \neq 0)$

(d) $1 + \dfrac{1}{x} + \dfrac{1}{x^2} + \cdots + \dfrac{1}{x^n}$ $(x \neq 0)$ $(Hint:\ x^0 = 1)$

7   Show that the following are true:

(a) $\left(\displaystyle\sum_{i=0}^{n} x_i \right) + x_{n+1} = \displaystyle\sum_{i=0}^{n+1} x_i$

(b) $\displaystyle\sum_{j=1}^{n} ab_j y_j = a \displaystyle\sum_{j=1}^{n} b_j y_j$

(c) $\displaystyle\sum_{j=1}^{n} (x_j + y_j) = \displaystyle\sum_{j=1}^{n} x_j + \displaystyle\sum_{j=1}^{n} y_j$

4.3   Notes on the Algebra of Vectors

In the above, vectors are considered as special types of matrices. As such, they qualify for application of all the algebraic operations discussed. Owing to their dimensional peculiarities, however, some additional comments on vector operations are useful.

multiplication of vectors   An $m \times 1$ column vector u and a $1 \times n$ row vector v' yield a product matrix uv' of dimension $m \times n$.

Example 1   Given $u = \begin{bmatrix} 3 \\ 2 \end{bmatrix}$ and $v' = [1 \quad 4 \quad 5]$, we can get

$$uv' = \begin{bmatrix} 3(1) & 3(4) & 3(5) \\ 2(1) & 2(4) & 2(5) \end{bmatrix} = \begin{bmatrix} 3 & 12 & 15 \\ 2 & 8 & 10 \end{bmatrix}$$

Since each row in u consists of one element only, as does each column in v', each element of uv' turns out to be a single product instead of a sum of products. The product is a 2×3 matrix, even though we started out only with two vectors.

On the other hand, given a $1 \times n$ row vector u' and an $n \times 1$ column vector v, the product $u'v$ will be of dimension 1×1.

Example 2   Given $u' = [3 \quad 4]$ and $v = \begin{bmatrix} 9 \\ 7 \end{bmatrix}$, we have

$$u'v = [3(9) + 4(7)] = [55]$$

As written, $u'v$ is a matrix, despite the fact that only a single element is present. However, 1×1 matrices behave exactly like scalars with respect to addition and multiplication: $[4] + [8] = [12]$, just as $4 + 8 = 12$; and $[3][7] = [21]$, just as $3(7) = 21$. Moreover, 1×1 matrices possess no major properties that scalars do not have. In fact, there is a one-to-one correspondence between the set of all scalars and the set of all 1×1 matrices whose elements are scalars. For this reason, we may redefine $u'v$ to be the *scalar* corresponding to the 1×1 product matrix. For the above example, we can accordingly write $u'v = 55$. Such a product is called a *scalar product*.[1] Remember, however, that while a 1×1 matrix can be treated as a scalar, a scalar cannot be replaced by a 1×1 matrix at will if further calculation is to be carried out, unless conformability conditions are fulfilled.

Example 3   Given a row vector $u' = [3 \quad 6 \quad 9]$, find $u'u$. Since u is merely the column vector with the elements of u' arranged vertically, we have

$$u'u = [3 \quad 6 \quad 9] \begin{bmatrix} 3 \\ 6 \\ 9 \end{bmatrix} = (3)^2 + (6)^2 + (9)^2$$

where we have omitted the brackets from the 1×1 product matrix on the right. Note that the product $u'u$ gives the sum of squares of the elements of u.

In general, if $u' = [u_1 \quad u_2 \quad \cdots \quad u_n]$, then $u'u$ will be the sum of squares (a scalar) of the elements u_j:

$$u'u = u_1{}^2 + u_2{}^2 + \cdots + u_n{}^2 = \sum_{j=1}^{n} u_j{}^2$$

Had we calculated the inner product $u \cdot u$ (or $u' \cdot u'$), we would have, of course, obtained exactly the same result.

To conclude, the reader must clearly distinguish between the meanings of uv' (a matrix larger than 1×1) and $u'v$ (a 1×1 matrix, or a scalar). Observe, in particular, that a scalar product must have a *row* vector as the lead matrix and a *column* vector as the lag matrix; otherwise the product cannot be 1×1.

geometric interpretation of vector operations   It was mentioned earlier that a column or row vector with n elements (referred to hereafter as an

---

[1] The concept of scalar product is thus akin to the concept of inner product of two vectors with the same number of elements in each, which also yields a scalar. Recall, however, that the inner product is exempted from the conformability condition for multiplication, so that we may write it as $u \cdot v$. In the case of scalar product (denoted without a dot between the two vector symbols), on the other hand, we can only express it as a row vector multiplied by a column vector, with the row vector in the lead.

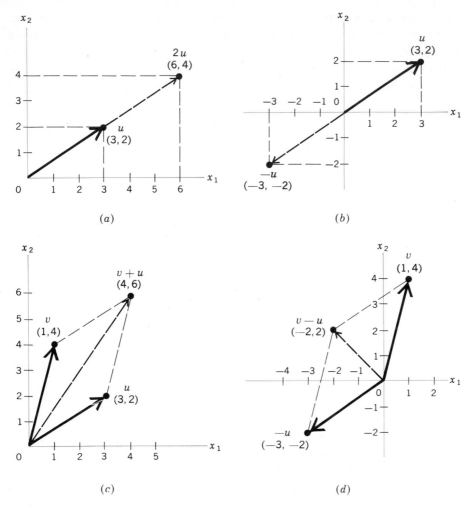

FIGURE 4.3

n-vector) can be viewed as an n-tuple, and hence as a point in an n-dimensional space (referred to hereafter as an n-space). Let us elaborate on this idea. In Fig. 4.3a, a point (3,2) is plotted in a 2-space and is labeled u. This is the geometric counterpart of the vector $u = \begin{bmatrix} 3 \\ 2 \end{bmatrix}$ or the vector $u' = [3 \quad 2]$, both of which indicate in this context one and the same ordered pair. If an arrow (a directed-line segment) is drawn from the point of origin (0,0) to the point u, it will specify the unique straight route by which to reach the destination point u from the point of origin. Since a unique arrow exists for each point, we can regard the

Static (or Equilibrium) Analysis

vector u as graphically represented *either* by the point (3,2), *or* by the corresponding arrow. Such an arrow, which emanates from the origin (0,0) like the hand of a clock, with a definite length and a definite direction, is sometimes referred to as a *radius vector*.

Following this new interpretation of a vector, it becomes possible to give geometric meanings to: (*a*) the scalar multiplication of a vector; (*b*) the addition and subtraction of vectors; and more generally, (*c*) the so-called "linear combination" of vectors.

First, if we plot the vector $\begin{bmatrix} 6 \\ 4 \end{bmatrix} = 2u$ in Fig. 4.3*a*, the resulting arrow will overlap the old one but will be twice as long. In fact, the multiplication of vector u by any scalar k will produce an overlapping arrow, but the arrowhead will be relocated, unless $k = 1$. If the scalar multiplier is $k > 1$, the arrow will be extended out (scaled up); if $0 < k < 1$, the arrow will be shortened (scaled down); if $k = 0$, the arrow will shrink into the point of origin—which represents a *null vector*, $\begin{bmatrix} 0 \\ 0 \end{bmatrix}$. A negative scalar multiplier will even reverse the direction of the arrow. If the vector u is multiplied by -1, for instance, we get $-u = \begin{bmatrix} -3 \\ -2 \end{bmatrix}$, and this plots in Fig. 4.3*b* as an arrow of the same length as u but diametrically opposite in direction.

Next, consider the addition of two vectors, $v = \begin{bmatrix} 1 \\ 4 \end{bmatrix}$ and $u = \begin{bmatrix} 3 \\ 2 \end{bmatrix}$. The sum $v + u = \begin{bmatrix} 4 \\ 6 \end{bmatrix}$ can be directly plotted as the broken arrow in Fig. 4.3*c*. If we construct a parallelogram with the two vectors u and v (solid arrows) as two of its sides, however, the diagonal of the parallelogram will turn out exactly to be the arrow representing the vector sum $v + u$. In general, a vector sum can be obtained geometrically from a parallelogram. Moreover, this method can also give us the *vector difference* $v - u$, since the latter is equivalent to the *sum* of v and $(-1)u$. In Fig. 4.3*d*, we first reproduce the vector v and the negative vector $-u$ from diagrams c and b, respectively, and then construct a parallelogram. The resulting diagonal represents the vector difference $v - u$.

It takes only a simple extension of the above results to interpret geometrically a linear combination (i.e., a linear sum or difference) of vectors. Consider the simple case of

$$3v + 2u = 3 \begin{bmatrix} 1 \\ 4 \end{bmatrix} + 2 \begin{bmatrix} 3 \\ 2 \end{bmatrix} = \begin{bmatrix} 9 \\ 16 \end{bmatrix}$$

The scalar multiplication aspect of this operation involves the relocation of the respective arrowheads of the two vectors v and u, and the addition aspect calls for the construction of a parallelogram. Beyond these two basic graphical operations, there is nothing new in a linear combination of vectors. This is true even if there are more terms in the linear combination, as in

$$\sum_{i=1}^{n} k_i v_i = k_1 v_1 + k_2 v_2 + \cdots + k_n v_n$$

where k_i are a set of scalars but the subscripted symbols v_i now denote a set of vectors. To form this sum, the first two terms may be added first, and then the resulting sum is added to the third, and so forth, till all terms are included.

linear dependence   A set of vectors $v_1, \ldots, v_n$ is said to be *linearly dependent* if (and only if) one of them can be expressed as a linear combination of the remaining vectors; otherwise they are *linearly independent*.

Example 4   The three vectors $v_1 = \begin{bmatrix} 2 \\ 7 \end{bmatrix}$, $v_2 = \begin{bmatrix} 1 \\ 8 \end{bmatrix}$, and $v_3 = \begin{bmatrix} 4 \\ 5 \end{bmatrix}$ are linearly dependent because v_3 is a linear combination of v_1 and v_2:

$$3v_1 - 2v_2 = \begin{bmatrix} 6 \\ 21 \end{bmatrix} - \begin{bmatrix} 2 \\ 16 \end{bmatrix} = \begin{bmatrix} 4 \\ 5 \end{bmatrix} = v_3$$

Note that this last equation is alternatively expressible as

$$3v_1 - 2v_2 - v_3 = 0$$

where $0 \equiv \begin{bmatrix} 0 \\ 0 \end{bmatrix}$ represents a null vector (also called *zero vector*).

Example 5   The two row vectors $v_1' = \begin{bmatrix} 5 & 12 \end{bmatrix}$ and $v_2' = \begin{bmatrix} 10 & 24 \end{bmatrix}$ are linearly dependent because

$$2v_1' = 2\begin{bmatrix} 5 & 12 \end{bmatrix} = \begin{bmatrix} 10 & 24 \end{bmatrix} = v_2'$$

The fact that one vector is a multiple of another vector illustrates the simplest case of linear combination. Note again that this last equation may be written equivalently as

$$2v_1' - v_2' = 0'$$

where $0'$ represents the null row vector $\begin{bmatrix} 0 & 0 \end{bmatrix}$.

With the introduction of null vectors, linear dependence may be redefined as follows: A set of m-vectors $v_1, \ldots, v_n$ is *linearly dependent* if and only if there exists a set of scalars $k_1, \ldots, k_n$ (not all zero) such that

$$\sum_{i=1}^{n} k_i v_i = \underset{(m \times 1)}{0}$$

If this equation can be satisfied only when $k_i = 0$ for all i, on the other hand, these vectors are linearly independent.

The concept of linear dependence admits of an easy geometric interpretation also. Two vectors u and $2u$—one being a multiple of the other—are obviously dependent. Geometrically, in Fig. 4.3*a*, their arrows lie on a single straight line. The same is true of the two dependent vectors u and $-u$ in Fig. 4.3*b*. In contrast, the two vectors u and v of Fig. 4.3*c* are linearly *independent*, because it is impossible to express one as a multiple of the other. Geometrically, their arrows do not lie on a single straight line.

When more than two vectors in the 2-space are considered, there emerges this significant conclusion: Once we have found two linearly *independent* vectors in the 2-space (say, u and v), all the other vectors in that space will be expressible as a linear combination of these (u and v). In Fig. 4.3*c* and *d*, it has already been illustrated how the two simple linear combinations $v + u$ and $v - u$ can be found. Furthermore, by extending, shortening, and reversing the given vectors u and v and by combining these into various parallelograms, we can generate an infinite number of new vectors, which will exhaust the set of all 2-vectors. Because of this, any set of three or more 2-vectors (three or more vectors in a 2-space) must be linearly dependent. Two of them can be independent, but then the third must be a linear combination of the first two.

vector space   The totality of the 2-vectors generated by the various linear combinations of two independent vectors u and v is called a two-dimensional *vector space*. This is precisely the 2-space we have been referring to all along. A 2-space cannot be generated by a single 2-vector, because "linear combinations" of the latter can only give rise to the set of vectors lying on a single straight line. Nor does the generation of a 2-space require more than two linearly independent 2-vectors—at any rate, it would be impossible to find more than two.

The two linearly independent vectors u and v are said to *span* the 2-space. They are also said to constitute a *basis* for the 2-space. Note that we said *a* basis, not *the* basis, because any pair of 2-vectors can serve in that capacity as long as they are linearly independent. In particular, consider the two vectors [1 0] and [0 1], which are called *unit vectors*. The first one plots as an arrow lying along the horizontal axis, and the second represents an arrow lying along the vertical axis. Being linearly independent, they can serve as a basis for the 2-space, and we do in fact ordinarily think of a 2-space as spanned by its two axes, which are nothing but the extended versions of the two unit vectors.

By analogy, a three-dimensional vector space is the totality of 3-vectors, and it must be spanned by exactly three linearly independent 3-vectors. As an

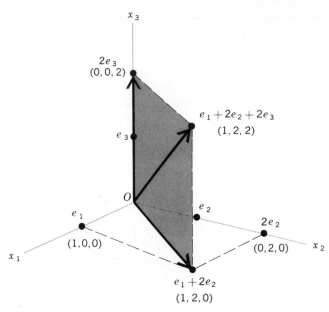

FIGURE 4.4

illustration, consider the set of three unit vectors

$$(4.7) \qquad e_1 \equiv \begin{bmatrix} 1 \\ 0 \\ 0 \end{bmatrix} \qquad e_2 \equiv \begin{bmatrix} 0 \\ 1 \\ 0 \end{bmatrix} \qquad e_3 \equiv \begin{bmatrix} 0 \\ 0 \\ 1 \end{bmatrix}$$

where each e_i is a vector with 1 as its ith element and with zeros elsewhere. These three vectors are obviously linearly independent; in fact, their arrows lie on the three axes of the 3-space in Fig. 4.4. Thus they span the 3-space, which implies that the entire 3-space can be generated from these unit vectors. For example, the vector $\begin{bmatrix} 1 \\ 2 \\ 2 \end{bmatrix}$ can be considered as the linear combination $e_1 + 2e_2 + 2e_3$.

Geometrically, we can first add the vectors e_1 and $2e_2$ in Fig. 4.4 by the parallelogram method, in order to get the vector represented by the point (1,2,0) in the x_1x_2 plane, and then add the latter vector to $2e_3$—via the parallelogram constructed in the shaded vertical plane—to obtain the desired final result, at the point (1,2,2).

The further extension to n-space should be obvious. An n-space can be defined as the totality of n-vectors. Though nongraphable, we can still think of

Static (or Equilibrium) Analysis

an n-space as being spanned by a total of n (n-element) unit vectors that are all linearly independent. Each n-vector, being an ordered n-tuple, represents a *point* in the n-space, or an arrow extending from the point of origin (i.e., the n-element null vector) to said point. And any given set of n linearly independent n-vectors is, in fact, capable of generating the entire n-space.

The n-space referred to above is usually taken to be a so-called "euclidean n-space" (named after Euclid, and often denoted by E^n). To explain this latter concept, we must first comment briefly on the concept of *distance* between two vector points. For any pair of vector points u and v in a given space, the distance from u to v is some real-valued function

$$d = d(u,v)$$

with the following properties: (1) When u and v coincide, the distance is zero; (2) when the two points are distinct, the distance from u to v and the distance from v to u are represented by an identical positive real number; (3) the distance between u and v is never longer than the distance from u to w (a point distinct from u and v) plus the distance from w to v. Expressed symbolically,

$$d(u,v) = 0 \qquad \qquad \text{(for } u = v)$$
$$d(u,v) = d(v,u) > 0 \qquad \text{(for } u \neq v)$$
$$d(u,v) \leq d(u,w) + d(w,v) \qquad \text{(for } w \neq u,v)$$

The last property is known as the *triangular inequality*, because the three points u, v, and w together will usually define a triangle.

When a vector space has a distance function defined that fulfills the above three properties, it is called a *metric space*. However, note that the distance $d(u,v)$ has been discussed above only in general terms. Depending on the specific form assigned to the d function, there may result a variety of metric spaces. The so-called "euclidean space" is one specific type of metric space, with a distance function defined as follows: Let point u be the n-tuple $(a_1, a_2, \ldots, a_n)$ and point v be the n-tuple $(b_1, b_2, \ldots, b_n)$; then the euclidean distance function is

$$d(u,v) = \sqrt{(a_1 - b_1)^2 + (a_2 - b_2)^2 + \cdots + (a_n - b_n)^2}$$

where the square root is taken to be positive. As can be easily verified, this specific distance function satisfies all three properties enumerated above. Applied to the two-dimensional space (E^2) in Fig. 4.3a, the distance between the two points $(6,4)$ and $(3,2)$ is found to be

$$\sqrt{(6 - 3)^2 + (4 - 2)^2} = \sqrt{3^2 + 2^2} = \sqrt{13}$$

This result is seen to be consistent with *Pythagoras' theorem*, which states that the length of the hypotenuse of a right-angled triangle is equal to the (positive) square root of the sum of the squares of the lengths of the other two sides. For if we take (6,4) and (3,2) to be u and v, and plot a new point w at (6,2), then we shall indeed have a right-angled triangle with the lengths of its horizontal and vertical sides equal to 3 and 2, respectively, and the length of the hypotenuse (the distance between u and v) equal to $\sqrt{3^2 + 2^2} = \sqrt{13}$.

The euclidean distance function can also be expressed in terms of the square root of a scalar product of two vectors. Since u and v denote the two n-tuples $(a_1, \ldots, a_n)$ and $(b_1, \ldots, b_n)$, we can write a column vector $u - v$, with elements $a_1 - b_1, a_2 - b_2, \ldots, a_n - b_n$. What goes under the square-root sign in the euclidean distance function is, of course, simply the sum of squares of these n elements, which, in view of Example 3 above, can be written as the scalar product $(u - v)'(u - v)$. Hence we have

$$d(u,v) = \sqrt{(u - v)'(u - v)}$$

EXERCISE 4.3

1   Having bought n items of merchandise at quantities $Q_1, \ldots, Q_n$ and prices $P_1, \ldots, P_n$, how would you express the total cost of purchase in (a) $\sum$ notation and (b) vector notation?

2   Given $u' = [5\ \ 6\ \ 2]$, $v' = [3\ \ 1\ \ 9]$, $w' = [7\ \ 4\ \ 8]$, and $x' = [x_1\ \ x_2\ \ x_3]$, write out the column vectors u, v, w, and x, and find

   (a) uv' (c) xx' (e) $u'v$ (g) $u'u$
   (b) uw' (d) $v'u$ (f) $w'x$ (h) $x'x$

3   Given $w = \begin{bmatrix} 5 \\ 2 \\ 16 \end{bmatrix}$, $x = \begin{bmatrix} x_1 \\ x_2 \end{bmatrix}$, $y = \begin{bmatrix} y_1 \\ y_2 \end{bmatrix}$, and $z = \begin{bmatrix} z_1 \\ z_2 \end{bmatrix}$:

   (a) Which of the following are defined: $w'x$, $x'y'$, xy', $y'y$, zz', yw', $x \cdot y$?
   (b) Find all the products that are defined.

4   Given $u = \begin{bmatrix} 3 \\ 1 \end{bmatrix}$ and $v = \begin{bmatrix} 0 \\ 3 \end{bmatrix}$, find the following graphically:

   (a) $2v$ (c) $u - v$ (e) $2u + 3v$
   (b) $u + v$ (d) $v - u$ (f) $4u - 2v$

5   Given $u = \begin{bmatrix} 3 \\ 1 \end{bmatrix}$, $v = \begin{bmatrix} 2 \\ 0 \end{bmatrix}$, and $w = \begin{bmatrix} 1 \\ 4 \end{bmatrix}$:

   (a) Use the parallelogram method to find $u + v$, and then find $(u + v) + w$.
   (b) Use the same method to find $v + w$, and then $u + (v + w)$.

(c)   Do you obtain the same answer in both cases? What kind of law of operation does this suggest?

6   Since a 3-space is spanned by the three unit vectors defined in (4.7), any other 3-vector should be expressible as a linear combination of e_1, e_2, and e_3. Show that the following 3-vectors can be so expressed:

(a) $\begin{bmatrix} 1 \\ 7 \\ 0 \end{bmatrix}$
(b) $\begin{bmatrix} 5 \\ -2 \\ 1 \end{bmatrix}$
(c) $\begin{bmatrix} -1 \\ 3 \\ 9 \end{bmatrix}$
(d) $\begin{bmatrix} 2 \\ 0 \\ 8 \end{bmatrix}$

7   In a three-dimensional euclidean space, what is the distance between the following points?

(a)   (3,2,4) and (0, −1,5)   (b)   (7,0,4) and (2,0, −4)

8   The triangular inequality is written with the *weak* inequality sign $\leq$, rather than the strict inequality sign $<$. Under what circumstances would the "$=$" part of the inequality apply?

9   Express the length of a radius vector v in the euclidean n-space (i.e., the distance from the origin to point v) in terms of:

(a)   scalars   (b)   a scalar product   (c)   an inner product

4.4   Commutative, Associative, and Distributive Laws

In the algebra of numbers (say, a, b, and c), the additive and multiplicative operations obey the commutative, associative, and distributive laws as follows:

Commutative law of addition:	$a + b = b + a$
Commutative law of multiplication:	$ab = ba$
Associative law of addition:	$(a + b) + c = a + (b + c)$
Associative law of multiplication:	$(ab)c = a(bc)$
Distributive law:	$a(b + c) = ab + ac$

These have been referred to during the discussion of the similarly named laws applicable to the union and intersection of sets. Most, but not all, of these laws also apply to matrix operations—the significant exception being the commutative law of multiplication.

matrix addition   Matrix addition is commutative as well as associative. This follows from the fact that matrix addition calls only for the addition of the corresponding elements of two matrices, and that the order in which each pair of corresponding elements is added is immaterial. In this context, incidentally, the subtraction operation $A - B$ can simply be regarded as the addition operation $A + (-B)$, and thus no separate discussion is necessary.

The commutative and associative laws can be stated as follows:

COMMUTATIVE LAW $A + B = B + A$

Proof $A + B = [a_{ij}] + [b_{ij}] = [a_{ij} + b_{ij}] = [b_{ij} + a_{ij}] = B + A$

Example 1   Given $A = \begin{bmatrix} 3 & 1 \\ 0 & 2 \end{bmatrix}$ and $B = \begin{bmatrix} 6 & 2 \\ 3 & 4 \end{bmatrix}$, we find that

$$A + B = B + A = \begin{bmatrix} 9 & 3 \\ 3 & 6 \end{bmatrix}$$

ASSOCIATIVE LAW $(A + B) + C = A + (B + C)$

Proof $(A + B) + C = [a_{ij} + b_{ij}] + [c_{ij}] = [a_{ij} + b_{ij} + c_{ij}]$
$$= [a_{ij}] + [b_{ij} + c_{ij}] = A + (B + C)$$

Example 2   Given $v_1 = \begin{bmatrix} 3 \\ 4 \end{bmatrix}$, $v_2 = \begin{bmatrix} 9 \\ 1 \end{bmatrix}$, and $v_3 = \begin{bmatrix} 2 \\ 5 \end{bmatrix}$, we find that

$$(v_1 + v_2) - v_3 = \begin{bmatrix} 12 \\ 5 \end{bmatrix} - \begin{bmatrix} 2 \\ 5 \end{bmatrix} = \begin{bmatrix} 10 \\ 0 \end{bmatrix}$$

which is equal to

$$v_1 + (v_2 - v_3) = \begin{bmatrix} 3 \\ 4 \end{bmatrix} + \begin{bmatrix} 7 \\ -4 \end{bmatrix} = \begin{bmatrix} 10 \\ 0 \end{bmatrix}$$

Applied to the linear combination of vectors $k_1 v_1 + \cdots + k_n v_n$, this law permits us to select any pair of terms for addition (or subtraction) first, instead of having to follow the sequence in which the n terms are listed.

matrix multiplication   Matrix multiplication is *not* commutative, that is,

$$AB \neq BA$$

As explained previously, even when AB is defined, BA may not be; but even if both products are defined, the general rule is still $AB \neq BA$.

Example 3   Let $A = \begin{bmatrix} 1 & 2 \\ 3 & 4 \end{bmatrix}$ and $B = \begin{bmatrix} 0 & -1 \\ 6 & 7 \end{bmatrix}$; then

$$AB = \begin{bmatrix} 1(0) + 2(6) & 1(-1) + 2(7) \\ 3(0) + 4(6) & 3(-1) + 4(7) \end{bmatrix} = \begin{bmatrix} 12 & 13 \\ 24 & 25 \end{bmatrix}$$

but $$BA = \begin{bmatrix} 0(1) - 1(3) & 0(2) - 1(4) \\ 6(1) + 7(3) & 6(2) + 7(4) \end{bmatrix} = \begin{bmatrix} -3 & -4 \\ 27 & 40 \end{bmatrix}$$

Example 4   Let u' be 1×3 (a row vector); then the corresponding column vector u must be 3×1. The product $u'u$ will be 1×1, but the product uu' will be 3×3. Thus, obviously, $u'u \neq uu'$.

In view of the general rule $AB \neq BA$, the terms *premultiply* and *post-multiply* are often used to specify the order of multiplication. In the product AB, the matrix B is said to be *premultiplied* by A, and A to be *post*multiplied by B.

There do exist interesting exceptions to the rule $AB \neq BA$, however. One such case is when A is a square matrix and B is an identity matrix. Another is when A is the inverse of B, that is, when $A = B^{-1}$. Both of these will be taken up again later. It should also be remarked here that the scalar multiplication of a matrix does obey the commutative law; thus

$$kA = Ak$$

if k is a scalar.

Though it is not in general commutative, matrix multiplication *is* associative.

ASSOCIATIVE LAW $(AB)C = A(BC) = ABC$

In forming the product ABC, the conformability condition must naturally be satisfied by each *adjacent* pair of matrices. If A is $m \times n$ and if C is $p \times q$, then conformability requires that B be $n \times p$:

$$\underset{(m \times n)\,(n \times p)\,(p \times q)}{A \quad B \quad C}$$

The reader should note the dual appearance of n and p in the dimension indicators. If conformability is met, the associative law states that any *adjacent* pair of matrices may be multiplied out first, provided that the product is duly inserted in the exact place of the original pair.

Example 5   If $x = \begin{bmatrix} x_1 \\ x_2 \end{bmatrix}$ and $A = \begin{bmatrix} a_{11} & 0 \\ 0 & a_{22} \end{bmatrix}$, then

$$x'Ax = x'(Ax) = \begin{bmatrix} x_1 & x_2 \end{bmatrix} \begin{bmatrix} a_{11}x_1 \\ a_{22}x_2 \end{bmatrix} = a_{11}x_1{}^2 + a_{22}x_2{}^2$$

which is a "weighted" sum of squares, in contrast to the simple sum of squares given by $x'x$. Exactly the same result comes from

$$(x'A)x = [a_{11}x_1 \quad a_{22}x_2] \begin{bmatrix} x_1 \\ x_2 \end{bmatrix} = a_{11}x_1{}^2 + a_{22}x_2{}^2$$

Matrix multiplication is also distributive.

DISTRIBUTIVE LAW $A(B + C) = AB + AC$ [premultiplication by A]
$\qquad\qquad\qquad\qquad (B + C)A = BA + CA$ [postmultiplication by A]

In each case, the conformability conditions for addition as well as for multiplication must, of course, be observed.

EXERCISE 4.4

1 Given $A = \begin{bmatrix} 3 & 6 \\ 7 & 0 \end{bmatrix}$, $B = \begin{bmatrix} -1 & 7 \\ 8 & 4 \end{bmatrix}$, and $C = \begin{bmatrix} 5 & 4 \\ 1 & 9 \end{bmatrix}$, verify that

    (a) $(A + B) + C = A + (B + C)$
    (b) $(A + B) - C = A + (B - C)$

2 The subtraction of a matrix B may be considered as the addition of the matrix $(-1)B$. Does the commutative law of addition permit us to state that $A - B = B - A$? If not, how would you correct the statement?

3 Test the associative law of multiplication with the following matrices:

$$A = \begin{bmatrix} 5 & 3 \\ 0 & 5 \end{bmatrix} \qquad B = \begin{bmatrix} -8 & 0 & 7 \\ 1 & 3 & 2 \end{bmatrix} \qquad C = \begin{bmatrix} 1 & 0 \\ 0 & 3 \\ 7 & 1 \end{bmatrix}$$

4 Prove that for any two scalars j and k

    (a) $k(A + B) = kA + kB$
    (b) $(j + k)A = jA + kA$

5 Prove that $(A + B)(C + D) = AC + AD + BC + BD$. (*Hint:* Use the two statements in the distributive law in succession.)

6 If the matrix A in Example 5 had all its four elements nonzero, would $x'Ax$ still give a weighted sum of squares? Would the associative law still apply?

4.5   Identity Matrices and Null Matrices

identity matrices   Reference has been made earlier to the term *identity matrix*. Such a matrix is defined as a *square* (repeat: square) matrix with 1s in its principal diagonal and 0s everywhere else. It is denoted by the symbol I, or I_n, in which the subscript n serves to indicate its row (as well as column) dimension. Thus,

$$I_2 = \begin{bmatrix} 1 & 0 \\ 0 & 1 \end{bmatrix} \qquad I_3 = \begin{bmatrix} 1 & 0 & 0 \\ 0 & 1 & 0 \\ 0 & 0 & 1 \end{bmatrix}$$

But both of these can also be denoted by I.

The importance of this special type of matrix lies in the fact that it plays a role similar to that of the number 1 in the algebra of numbers. For any number a, we have $1(a) = a(1) = a$. Similarly, for any matrix A, we have

(4.8) $IA = AI = A$

Example 1   Let $A = \begin{bmatrix} 1 & 2 & 3 \\ 2 & 0 & 3 \end{bmatrix}$, then

$$IA = \begin{bmatrix} 1 & 0 \\ 0 & 1 \end{bmatrix} \begin{bmatrix} 1 & 2 & 3 \\ 2 & 0 & 3 \end{bmatrix} = \begin{bmatrix} 1 & 2 & 3 \\ 2 & 0 & 3 \end{bmatrix} = A$$

$$AI = \begin{bmatrix} 1 & 2 & 3 \\ 2 & 0 & 3 \end{bmatrix} \begin{bmatrix} 1 & 0 & 0 \\ 0 & 1 & 0 \\ 0 & 0 & 1 \end{bmatrix} = \begin{bmatrix} 1 & 2 & 3 \\ 2 & 0 & 3 \end{bmatrix} = A$$

Because A is 2×3, the premultiplication and postmultiplication of A by I call for identity matrices of different dimensions, namely, I_2 and I_3, respectively. But in case A is $n \times n$, then the same identity matrix I_n can be used, so that (4.8) becomes $I_n A = A I_n$, thus illustrating an exception to the rule that matrix multiplication is not commutative.

The special nature of identity matrices makes it possible, during the multiplication process, to *insert* or *delete* an identity matrix without affecting the matrix product. This follows directly from (4.8). Recalling the associative law, we have, for instance,

$$\underset{(m \times n)\,(n \times n)\,(n \times p)}{A \quad I \quad B} = (AI)B = \underset{(m \times n)\,(n \times p)}{A \quad B}$$

which shows that the presence or absence of I does not affect the product. Observe that dimension conformability is preserved whether or not I appears in the product.

An interesting case of (4.8) occurs when $A = I_n$ for then we have

$$AI_n = (I_n)^2 = I_n$$

which states that an identity matrix squared is equal to itself. A generalization of this result is that

$$(I_n)^k = I_n \qquad (k = 1, 2, \ldots)$$

An identity matrix remains unchanged when it is multiplied by itself any number of times. Any matrix with such a property (namely, $AA = A$) is referred to as an *idempotent matrix*.

null matrices   Just as an identity matrix I plays the role of the number 1, a *null matrix*—or *zero matrix*—denoted by 0, plays the role of the number 0. A null matrix is simply a matrix whose elements are all zero. Unlike I, the zero matrix is not restricted to being square. Thus it is possible to write

$$\underset{(2 \times 2)}{0} = \begin{bmatrix} 0 & 0 \\ 0 & 0 \end{bmatrix} \qquad \text{and} \qquad \underset{(2 \times 3)}{0} = \begin{bmatrix} 0 & 0 & 0 \\ 0 & 0 & 0 \end{bmatrix}$$

and so forth. A square null matrix is idempotent, but a nonsquare one is not. (Why?)

As the counterpart of the number 0, null matrices obey the following rules of operation (subject to conformability) with regard to addition and multiplication:

$$\underset{(m \times n)}{A} + \underset{(m \times n)}{0} = \underset{(m \times n)}{0} + \underset{(m \times n)}{A} = \underset{(m \times n)}{A}$$

$$\underset{(m \times n)(n \times p)}{A \quad 0} = \underset{(m \times p)}{0} \qquad \text{and} \qquad \underset{(q \times m)(m \times n)}{0 \quad A} = \underset{(q \times n)}{0}$$

Note that, in multiplication, the null matrix to the left of the equals sign and the one to the right may be of different dimensions.

Example 2

$$A + 0 = \begin{bmatrix} a_{11} & a_{12} \\ a_{21} & a_{22} \end{bmatrix} + \begin{bmatrix} 0 & 0 \\ 0 & 0 \end{bmatrix} = \begin{bmatrix} a_{11} & a_{12} \\ a_{21} & a_{22} \end{bmatrix} = A$$

Example 3

$$\underset{(2 \times 3)(3 \times 1)}{A \quad 0} = \begin{bmatrix} a_{11} & a_{12} & a_{13} \\ a_{21} & a_{22} & a_{23} \end{bmatrix} \begin{bmatrix} 0 \\ 0 \\ 0 \end{bmatrix} = \begin{bmatrix} 0 \\ 0 \end{bmatrix} = \underset{(2 \times 1)}{0}$$

To the left, the null matrix is a 3×1 null vector; to the right, it is a 2×1 null vector.

idiosyncracies of matrix algebra   Despite the apparent similarities between matrix algebra and the algebra of numbers, the case of matrices does display certain idiosyncracies that serve to warn us not to "borrow" from the algebra of numbers too unquestioningly. We have already seen that, in general, $AB \neq BA$ in matrix algebra. Let us look at two more such idiosyncracies of matrix algebra.

For one thing, in the case of numbers, the equation $ab = 0$ always implies that either a or b is zero, but this is not so in matrix multiplication. Thus, we have

$$AB = \begin{bmatrix} 2 & 4 \\ 1 & 2 \end{bmatrix} \begin{bmatrix} -2 & 4 \\ 1 & -2 \end{bmatrix} = \begin{bmatrix} 0 & 0 \\ 0 & 0 \end{bmatrix} = 0$$

although neither A nor B is itself a zero matrix.

As another illustration, for numbers, the equation $cd = ce$ (with $c \neq 0$) implies that $d = e$. The same does not hold for matrices. Thus, given

$$C = \begin{bmatrix} 2 & 3 \\ 6 & 9 \end{bmatrix} \qquad D = \begin{bmatrix} 1 & 1 \\ 1 & 2 \end{bmatrix} \qquad E = \begin{bmatrix} -2 & 1 \\ 3 & 2 \end{bmatrix}$$

we find that

$$CD = CE = \begin{bmatrix} 5 & 8 \\ 15 & 24 \end{bmatrix}$$

even though $D \neq E$.

These strange results actually pertain only to the special class of matrices known as *singular matrices*, of which the matrices A, B, and C are examples. (Roughly, these matrices contain a row which is a multiple of another row.) Nevertheless, such examples do reveal the pitfalls of unwarranted extension of algebraic theorems to matrix operations.

EXERCISE 4.5

Given $A = \begin{bmatrix} -1 & 3 & 1 \\ 0 & -2 & 4 \end{bmatrix}$, $B = \begin{bmatrix} 7 \\ 6 \\ 0 \end{bmatrix}$, and $x = \begin{bmatrix} x_1 \\ x_2 \end{bmatrix}$:

1   Calculate: (a) AI (b) IA (c) Ix (d) $x'I$
Indicate the dimension of the identity matrix used in each case.

2   Calculate: (a) AB (b) AIB (c) $x'IA$ (d) $x'A$
Does the insertion of I in (b) affect the result in (a)? Does the deletion of I in (d) affect the result in (c)?

3   What is the dimension of the null matrix resulting from each of the following?

(a)   Premultiply A by a 3×2 null matrix.
(b)   Postmultiply A by a 3×5 null matrix.
(c)   Premultiply B by a 3×3 null matrix.
(d)   Postmultiply x by a 1×3 null matrix.

4   Show that a *diagonal matrix*, i.e., a matrix of the form

$$\begin{bmatrix} a_{11} & 0 & \cdots & 0 \\ 0 & a_{22} & \cdots & 0 \\ \cdots & \cdots & \cdots & \cdots \\ 0 & 0 & \cdots & a_{nn} \end{bmatrix}$$

can be idempotent only if each diagonal element is either 1 or 0. How many different numerical idempotent diagonal matrices of dimension $n \times n$ can be constructed altogether?

4.6   Transposes and Inverses

When the rows and columns of a matrix A are interchanged—so that its first row becomes the first column, and vice versa—we obtain the *transpose* of A, which is denoted by A' or A^T. The prime symbol is by no means new to us; it was used earlier to distinguish a row vector from a column vector. In the newly introduced terminology, a row vector x' constitutes the transpose of the column vector x. The superscript T in the alternative symbol is obviously shorthand for the word transpose.

Example 1   Given $\underset{(2 \times 3)}{A} = \begin{bmatrix} 3 & 8 & -9 \\ 1 & 0 & 4 \end{bmatrix}$ and $\underset{(2 \times 2)}{B} = \begin{bmatrix} 3 & 4 \\ 1 & 7 \end{bmatrix}$, we can inter-

change the rows and columns and write

$$\underset{(3 \times 2)}{A'} = \begin{bmatrix} 3 & 1 \\ 8 & 0 \\ -9 & 4 \end{bmatrix} \quad \text{and} \quad \underset{(2 \times 2)}{B'} = \begin{bmatrix} 3 & 1 \\ 4 & 7 \end{bmatrix}$$

By definition, if a matrix A is $m \times n$, then its transpose A' must be $n \times m$. An $n \times n$ square matrix, however, possesses a transpose of the same dimension.

Example 2 If $C = \begin{bmatrix} 9 & -1 \\ 2 & 0 \end{bmatrix}$ and $D = \begin{bmatrix} 1 & 0 & 4 \\ 0 & 3 & 7 \\ 4 & 7 & 2 \end{bmatrix}$, then

$$C' = \begin{bmatrix} 9 & 2 \\ -1 & 0 \end{bmatrix} \quad \text{and} \quad D' = \begin{bmatrix} 1 & 0 & 4 \\ 0 & 3 & 7 \\ 4 & 7 & 2 \end{bmatrix}$$

Here, the dimension of each transpose is identical with that of the original matrix.

In D', we also note the remarkable result that D' inherits not only the dimension of D but also the original array of elements! The fact that $D' = D$ is the consequence of the symmetry of the elements with respect to the principal diagonal. Considering the principal diagonal in D as a mirror, the elements located to its northeast are exact images of the elements to its southwest; hence the first row reads identically with the first column, and so forth. The matrix D exemplifies the special class of square matrices known as *symmetric matrices*. Another example of such a matrix is the identity matrix I, which, as a symmetric matrix, has the transpose $I' = I$.

properties of transposes   The following properties characterize transposes:

(4.9) $(A')' = A$

(4.10) $(A + B)' = A' + B'$

(4.11) $(AB)' = B'A'$

The first says that the transpose of the transpose is the original matrix—a rather self-evident conclusion.

The second property may be verbally stated thus: The transpose of a sum is the sum of the transposes.

Example 3   If $A = \begin{bmatrix} 4 & 1 \\ 9 & 0 \end{bmatrix}$ and $B = \begin{bmatrix} 2 & 0 \\ 7 & 1 \end{bmatrix}$, then

$$(A + B)' = \begin{bmatrix} 6 & 1 \\ 16 & 1 \end{bmatrix}' = \begin{bmatrix} 6 & 16 \\ 1 & 1 \end{bmatrix}$$

and $A' + B' = \begin{bmatrix} 4 & 9 \\ 1 & 0 \end{bmatrix} + \begin{bmatrix} 2 & 7 \\ 0 & 1 \end{bmatrix} = \begin{bmatrix} 6 & 16 \\ 1 & 1 \end{bmatrix}$

The third property is that the transpose of a product is the product of the transposes *in reverse order*. To understand the necessity of the reversed order, let us examine the dimension conformability of the two products on the two sides of (4.11). If we let A be $m \times n$ and B be $n \times p$, then AB will be $m \times p$, and $(AB)'$ will be $p \times m$. For equality to hold, it is necessary that the right-hand expression $B'A'$ be of an identical dimension. Since B' is $p \times n$ and A' is $n \times m$, the product $B'A'$ is indeed $p \times m$, as required. The dimension of $B'A'$ thus works out. Note that, on the other hand, the product $A'B'$ is not even defined unless $m = p$.

Example 4   Given $A = \begin{bmatrix} 1 & 2 \\ 3 & 4 \end{bmatrix}$ and $B = \begin{bmatrix} 0 & -1 \\ 6 & 7 \end{bmatrix}$, we have

$$(AB)' = \begin{bmatrix} 12 & 13 \\ 24 & 25 \end{bmatrix}' = \begin{bmatrix} 12 & 24 \\ 13 & 25 \end{bmatrix}$$

and $B'A' = \begin{bmatrix} 0 & 6 \\ -1 & 7 \end{bmatrix} \begin{bmatrix} 1 & 3 \\ 2 & 4 \end{bmatrix} = \begin{bmatrix} 12 & 24 \\ 13 & 25 \end{bmatrix}$

This verifies the property.

inverses and their properties   For a given matrix A, the transpose A' is always derivable. On the other hand, its *inverse* matrix—another type of "derived" matrix—may or may not exist. The inverse of matrix A, denoted by A^{-1}, is defined only if A is a square matrix, in which case the inverse is the matrix that satisfies the condition

(4.12) $AA^{-1} = A^{-1}A = I$

That is, whether A is pre- or postmultiplied by A^{-1}, the product will be the same identity matrix. This is another exception to the rule that matrix multiplication is not commutative.

The following points are worth noting: (1) Not every square matrix has an inverse—squareness is a *necessary* condition, but *not* a *sufficient* condition, for the existence of an inverse. If a square matrix A has an inverse, A is said to be *nonsingular*; if A possesses no inverse, it is called a *singular* matrix. (2) If A^{-1} does exist, then the matrix A can be regarded as the inverse of A^{-1}, just as A^{-1} is the inverse of A. In short, A and A^{-1} are inverses of each other. (3) If A is $n \times n$, then A^{-1} must also be $n \times n$; otherwise it cannot be conformable for *both* pre- and postmultiplication. The identity matrix produced by the multiplication will also be $n \times n$. (4) If an inverse exists, then it is unique. To prove its uniqueness, let us suppose that B has been found to be an inverse for A, so that

$AB - BA = I$

Now assume that there is another matrix C such that $AC = CA = I$. By premultiplying both sides of $AB = I$ by C, we find that

$$CAB = CI \; (=C) \qquad \text{[by (4.8)]}$$

Since $CA = I$ by assumption, the preceding equation is reducible to

$$IB = C \qquad \text{or} \qquad B = C$$

That is, B and C must be one and the same inverse matrix. For this reason, we can speak of *the* (as against *an*) inverse of A. (5) The two parts of condition (4.12)—namely, $AA^{-1} = I$ and $A^{-1}A = I$—actually imply each other, so that satisfying either equation is sufficient to establish the inverse relationship between A and A^{-1}. To prove this, we should show that if $AA^{-1} = I$, and if there is a matrix B such that $BA = I$, then $B = A^{-1}$ (so that $BA = I$ must in effect be the equation $A^{-1}A = I$). Let us postmultiply both sides of the given equation $BA = I$ by A^{-1}; then

$$(BA)A^{-1} = IA^{-1}$$

$$B(AA^{-1}) = IA^{-1} \qquad \text{[associative law]}$$

$$BI = IA^{-1} \qquad \text{[}AA^{-1} = I \text{ by assumption]}$$

Therefore, as required,

$$B = A^{-1} \qquad \text{[by (4.8)]}$$

Analogously, it can be demonstrated that, if $A^{-1}A = I$, then the only matrix C which yields $CA^{-1} = I$ is $C = A$.

Example 5   Let $A = \begin{bmatrix} 3 & 1 \\ 0 & 2 \end{bmatrix}$ and $B = \dfrac{1}{6}\begin{bmatrix} 2 & -1 \\ 0 & 3 \end{bmatrix}$; then, since the scalar multiplier ($\frac{1}{6}$) in B can be moved to the rear (commutative law), we can write

$$AB = \begin{bmatrix} 3 & 1 \\ 0 & 2 \end{bmatrix}\begin{bmatrix} 2 & -1 \\ 0 & 3 \end{bmatrix}\frac{1}{6} = \begin{bmatrix} 6 & 0 \\ 0 & 6 \end{bmatrix}\frac{1}{6} = \begin{bmatrix} 1 & 0 \\ 0 & 1 \end{bmatrix}$$

This establishes B as the inverse of A, and vice versa. The reverse multiplication, as expected, also yields the same identity matrix:

$$BA = \frac{1}{6}\begin{bmatrix} 2 & -1 \\ 0 & 3 \end{bmatrix}\begin{bmatrix} 3 & 1 \\ 0 & 2 \end{bmatrix} = \frac{1}{6}\begin{bmatrix} 6 & 0 \\ 0 & 6 \end{bmatrix} = \begin{bmatrix} 1 & 0 \\ 0 & 1 \end{bmatrix}$$

The following three properties of inverse matrices are of interest:

(4.13) $(A^{-1})^{-1} = A$

(4.14) $(AB)^{-1} = B^{-1}A^{-1}$

(4.15) $(A')^{-1} = (A^{-1})'$

The first says that the inverse of an inverse is the original matrix. The second states that the inverse of a product is the product of the inverses *in reverse order*. And the last one may be stated thus: The inverse of the transpose is the transpose of the inverse. It should be understood that in these statements the existence of the inverses and the satisfaction of the conformability condition are presupposed.

The validity of (4.13) is fairly obvious, but let us prove (4.14) and (4.15). Given the product AB, let us find its inverse—call it C. From (4.12) we know that $CAB = I$; thus, postmultiplication of both sides by $B^{-1}A^{-1}$ will yield

$$(4.16) \qquad CABB^{-1}A^{-1} = IB^{-1}A^{-1} \, (=B^{-1}A^{-1})$$

But the left side is reducible to

$$CA(BB^{-1})A^{-1} = CAIA^{-1} \qquad \qquad \text{[by (4.12)]}$$
$$= CAA^{-1} = CI = C \quad \text{[by (4.12) and (4.8)]}$$

Substitution of this into (4.16) then tells us that $C = B^{-1}A^{-1}$ or, in other words, that the inverse of AB is equal to $B^{-1}A^{-1}$, as alleged. Note that the existence of $(AB)^{-1}$ is contingent upon the existence of A^{-1} and B^{-1}. That is, AB is nonsingular only if A and B are. In this proof, the equation $AA^{-1} = A^{-1}A = I$ was utilized twice. The reader should take notice that the application of this equation is permissible if and only if a matrix and its inverse are strictly adjacent to each other in a product. We may write $AA^{-1}B = IB = B$, but *never* $ABA^{-1} = B$.

The proof of (4.15) is as follows. Given A', let us find its inverse—call it D. By definition, we have $DA' = I$. But we know that

$$(AA^{-1})' = I' = I$$

produces the same identity matrix. Thus we may write

$$DA' = (AA^{-1})'$$
$$= (A^{-1})'A' \qquad \text{[by (4.11)]}$$

Postmultiplying both sides by $(A')^{-1}$, we obtain

$$DA'(A')^{-1} = (A^{-1})'A'(A')^{-1}$$

or $\qquad \qquad \qquad D = (A^{-1})' \qquad \qquad \qquad \text{[by (4.12)]}$

Thus, the inverse of A' is equal to $(A^{-1})'$, as alleged.

In the proofs just presented, mathematical operations were performed on whole blocks of numbers. If those blocks of numbers had not been treated as mathematical entities (matrices), the same operations would have been much more lengthy and involved. The beauty of matrix algebra lies precisely in its simplification of such operations.

inverse matrix and solution of linear-equation system   The application of the concept of inverse matrix to the solution of a simultaneous-equation
system is immediate and direct. Referring to the equation system in (4.3), we
pointed out earlier that it can be written in matrix notation as

$$(4.17) \qquad \underset{(3\times3)}{A} \underset{(3\times1)}{x} = \underset{(3\times1)}{d}$$

where A, x, and d are as defined in (4.4). Now if the inverse matrix A^{-1} exists,
the premultiplication of both sides of the equation (4.17) by A^{-1} will yield

$$A^{-1}Ax = A^{-1}d$$

or

$$(4.18) \qquad \underset{(3\times1)}{x} = \underset{(3\times3)(3\times1)}{A^{-1}\ d}$$

The left side of (4.18) is a column vector of variables, whereas the right-hand
product is a column vector of certain known numbers. Thus, by definition of the
equality of matrices or vectors, (4.18) is a statement of a set of values of the
variables that satisfy the equation system, i.e., solution values. Furthermore,
since A^{-1} is unique if it exists, $A^{-1}d$ must be a unique vector of solution values.
We shall therefore write the x vector in (4.18) as $\bar{x}$, to indicate its status as a
(unique) solution.

Methods of testing the existence of the inverse and of its calculation will
be discussed in the next chapter. It may be stated here, however, that the
inverse of the matrix A in (4.4) is

$$A^{-1} = \frac{1}{52}\begin{bmatrix} 18 & -16 & -10 \\ -13 & 26 & 13 \\ -17 & 18 & 21 \end{bmatrix}$$

Thus (4.18) will turn out to be

$$\begin{bmatrix} \bar{x}_1 \\ \bar{x}_2 \\ \bar{x}_3 \end{bmatrix} = \frac{1}{52}\begin{bmatrix} 18 & -16 & -10 \\ -13 & 26 & 13 \\ -17 & 18 & 21 \end{bmatrix}\begin{bmatrix} 22 \\ 12 \\ 10 \end{bmatrix} = \begin{bmatrix} 2 \\ 3 \\ 1 \end{bmatrix}$$

which gives the solution: $\bar{x}_1 = 2$, $\bar{x}_2 = 3$, and $\bar{x}_3 = 1$.

The upshot is that, to find the solution of a linear-equation system $Ax = d$,
where the coefficient matrix A is nonsingular, we can first find the inverse A^{-1},
and then postmultiply A^{-1} by the constant vector d. The product $A^{-1}d$ will
then give the solution values of the variables.

EXERCISE 4.6

1   Given $A = \begin{bmatrix} 2 & 4 \\ -1 & 5 \end{bmatrix}$, $B = \begin{bmatrix} 3 & 7 \\ 0 & 4 \end{bmatrix}$, and $C = \begin{bmatrix} 1 & 2 & 3 \\ 0 & 1 & 1 \end{bmatrix}$, find A', B',
    and C'.

2   Use the matrices given in the preceding problem to verify that

(a) $(A + B)' = A' + B'$ (b) $(AC)' = C'A'$

3   Generalize the result (4.11) to the case of a product of three matrices by proving that, for any conformable matrices A, B, and C, the equation $(ABC)' = C'B'A'$ holds. [*Hint:* Let $D \equiv AB$, and apply (4.11).]

4   Given $D = \begin{bmatrix} 2 & 6 \\ 0 & 3 \end{bmatrix}$, $E = \begin{bmatrix} \frac{1}{2} & -1 \\ 0 & \frac{1}{3} \end{bmatrix}$, $F = \begin{bmatrix} 1 & 4 \\ 6 & 8 \end{bmatrix}$, and $G = \begin{bmatrix} -\frac{1}{2} & \frac{1}{4} \\ \frac{3}{8} & -\frac{1}{16} \end{bmatrix}$,

show that E is the inverse of D and that G is the inverse of F.

5   Generalize the result (4.14) by proving that, for any conformable matrices A, B, and C, the equation $(ABC)^{-1} = C^{-1}B^{-1}A^{-1}$ holds. [*Hint:* Let $D \equiv AB$, and apply (4.14).]

6   Prove that, if $A^{-1}A = I$ and if $CA^{-1} = I$, then $C = A$.

7   Let $A = I - X(X'X)^{-1}X'$.

(a)   If I is $n \times n$, what must be the dimension of X and A?
(b)   Show that matrix A is idempotent.

5

LINEAR MODELS
AND MATRIX ALGEBRA (continued)

In the last chapter, it was shown that a linear-equation system, however large, may be written in a compact matrix notation. Furthermore, such an equation system can be solved by finding the inverse of the coefficient matrix, provided the inverse exists. Now we must address ourselves to the questions of how to test for the existence of the inverse and how to find the inverse. Only after we have answered these questions will it be possible to apply matrix algebra effectively to economic models.

5.1 Conditions for Nonsingularity of a Matrix

A given coefficient matrix A can have an inverse (i.e., can be "nonsingular") only if it is square. As was pointed out earlier, however, the squareness condition is necessary but not sufficient for the existence of the inverse A^{-1}. A matrix can be square, but singular (without an inverse) nonetheless.

necessary versus sufficient conditions The concepts of "necessary condition" and "sufficient condition" are used frequently in economics. It is important that we understand their precise meanings before proceeding further.

A necessary condition is in the nature of a prerequisite: Suppose that a statement p is true *only if* another statement q is true; then q constitutes a necessary condition for p. Symbolically, we express this as follows:

$$(5.1) \qquad p \Rightarrow q$$

which is read: *p only if q*—or alternatively, if p, then q. It is also logically correct to interpret (5.1) to mean p *implies* q. It may happen, of course, that we also have $p \Rightarrow w$ at the same time. Then both q and w are necessary conditions for p.

Example 1   If we let p be the statement "a person is a father" and q be the statement "a person is male," then the logical statement $p \Rightarrow q$ applies. A person is a father *only if* he is male, and to be male is a necessary condition for fatherhood. Note, however, that the converse is not true: fatherhood is not a necessary condition for maleness.

A different type of situation is that in which a statement p is true if q is true, but where p can also be true when q is not true. In this case, q is said to be a sufficient condition for p. The truth of q suffices for the establishment of the truth of p, but it is not a necessary condition for p. This case is expressed symbolically by

$$(5.2) \qquad p \Leftarrow q$$

which is read: *p if q* (without the word "only")—or alternatively, if q, then p, as if reading (5.2) backwards. It can also be interpreted to mean "q implies p."

Example 2   If we let p be the statement "one can get to Europe" and q be the statement "one takes a plane to Europe," then $p \Leftarrow q$. Flying can serve to get one to Europe, but since ocean transportation is also feasible, flying is not a prerequisite. We can write $p \Leftarrow q$, but not $p \Rightarrow q$.

In a third possible situation, q is *both* necessary and sufficient for p. In such an event, we write

$$(5.3) \qquad p \Leftrightarrow q$$

which is read: *p if and only if q* (also written as p iff q). The double-headed arrow is really a combination of the two types of arrows of (5.1) and (5.2); hence the joint use of the two terms "if" and "only if." Note that (5.3) states not only that p implies q but also that q implies p.

Example 3   If we let p be the statement "there are less than 30 days in the month" and q be the statement "it is the month of February," then $p \Leftrightarrow q$. To have less than 30 days in the month, it is necessary that it be February. Conversely, the specification of February is sufficient to establish that there are less than 30 days in the month. Thus q is a necessary-and-sufficient condition for p.

In order to prove $p \Rightarrow q$, it needs to be shown that q follows logically from p. Similarly, to prove $p \Leftarrow q$ requires a demonstration that p follows logically from q. But to prove $p \Leftrightarrow q$ necessitates a demonstration that p and q follow from each other.

conditions for nonsingularity   When the squareness condition is already met, a sufficient condition for the nonsingularity of a matrix is that its rows be linearly independent (or, what amounts to the same thing, that its *columns* be linearly independent). When the dual conditions of squareness and linear independence are taken together, they constitute the necessary-and-sufficient condition for nonsingularity (nonsingularity $\Leftrightarrow$ squareness *and* linear independence).

An $n \times n$ coefficient matrix A can be considered as an ordered set of row vectors, i.e., as a column vector whose elements are themselves row vectors:

$$A = \begin{bmatrix} a_{11} & a_{12} & \cdots & a_{1n} \\ a_{21} & a_{22} & \cdots & a_{2n} \\ \cdots & \cdots & \cdots & \cdots \\ a_{n1} & a_{n2} & \cdots & a_{nn} \end{bmatrix} = \begin{bmatrix} v_1' \\ v_2' \\ \vdots \\ v_n' \end{bmatrix}$$

where $v_i' = [a_{i1} \quad a_{i2} \quad \cdots \quad a_{in}]$, $i = 1, 2, \ldots, n$. For the rows (row vectors) to be linearly independent, none must be a linear combination of the rest. More formally, as was mentioned in Sec. 4.3, linear row independence requires that the only set of scalars k_i which can satisfy the vector equation

$$(5.4) \qquad \sum_{i=1}^{n} k_i v_i' = \underset{(1 \times n)}{0}$$

be $k_i = 0$ for all i.

Example 4   If the coefficient matrix is

$$A = \begin{bmatrix} 3 & 4 & 5 \\ 0 & 1 & 2 \\ 6 & 8 & 10 \end{bmatrix} = \begin{bmatrix} v_1' \\ v_2' \\ v_3' \end{bmatrix}$$

then, since $[6 \quad 8 \quad 10] = 2[3 \quad 4 \quad 5]$, we have $v_3' = 2v_1' = 2v_1' + 0v_2'$. Thus the third row is expressible as a linear combination of the first two, and the rows are *not* linearly independent. Alternatively, we may write

$$2v_1' + 0v_2' - v_3' = [6 \quad 8 \quad 10] + [0 \quad 0 \quad 0] - [6 \quad 8 \quad 10] = [0 \quad 0 \quad 0]$$

where the set of scalars that led to the zero vector of (5.4) is not $k_i = 0$ for all i. Consequently, the rows are linearly dependent.

Unlike the squareness condition, the linear-independence condition cannot normally be ascertained at a glance. Thus a method of testing linear independence among rows (or columns) needs to be developed. Before we concern ourselves with that task, however, it would strengthen our motivation first to have an intuitive understanding of why the linear-independence condition is heaped together with the squareness condition at all. From the discussion of counting equations and unknowns in Sec. 3.4, we recall the general conclusion that, for a system of equations to possess a unique solution, it is not sufficient to have the same number of equations as unknowns. In addition, the *equations* must be consistent with and functionally independent (meaning, in the present context of linear systems, *linearly* independent) of one another. There is a fairly obvious tie-in between the "same number of equations as unknowns" criterion and the *squareness* (same number of rows and columns) of the coefficient matrix. What the "linear independence among the rows" requirement does is to preclude the inconsistency and the linear dependence *among the equations* as well. Taken together, therefore, the dual requirement of squareness and row independence in the coefficient matrix is tantamount to the conditions for the existence of a unique solution enunciated in Sec. 3.4.

Let us illustrate how the linear dependence *among the rows* of the coefficient matrix can cause inconsistency or linear dependence *among the equations* themselves. Let the equation system $Ax = d$ take the form

$$\begin{bmatrix} 10 & 4 \\ 5 & 2 \end{bmatrix} \begin{bmatrix} x_1 \\ x_2 \end{bmatrix} = \begin{bmatrix} d_1 \\ d_2 \end{bmatrix}$$

where the coefficient matrix A contains linearly dependent rows: $v_1' = 2v_2'$. (Note that its columns are also dependent, the first being $\frac{5}{2}$ of the second.) We have not specified the values of the constant terms d_1 and d_2, but there are only *two* distinct possibilities regarding their relative values: (1) $d_1 = 2d_2$ and (2) $d_1 \neq 2d_2$. Under the first—with, say, $d_1 = 12$ and $d_2 = 6$—the two equations are consistent but *linearly dependent* (just as the two rows of matrix A are), for the first equation is merely the second equation times 2. One equation is redundant, and the system reduces in effect to a single equation, $5x_1 + 2x_2 = 6$, with an infinite number of solutions. For the second possibility—with say, $d_1 = 12$ but $d_2 = 0$—the two equations are *inconsistent*, because if the first equation ($10x_1 + 4x_2 = 12$) is true, then, by halving each term, we can deduce that $5x_1 + 2x_2 = 6$; consequently the second equation ($5x_1 + 2x_2 = 0$) cannot possibly be true also. Thus no solution exists.

The upshot is that no unique solution will be available (under either possibility) so long as the rows in the coefficient matrix A are linearly dependent. In fact, the only way to have a unique solution is to have linearly independent rows (or columns) in the coefficient matrix. In that case, matrix A will be nonsingular, which means that the inverse A^{-1} will exist, and that a unique solution $\bar{x} = A^{-1}d$ can be found.

rank of a matrix   Even though the concept of row independence has been discussed only with regard to square matrices, it is equally applicable to any $m \times n$ rectangular matrix. If the maximum number of linearly independent rows that can be found in such a matrix is r, the matrix is said to be of *rank r*. (This number must also be equal to the maximum number of linearly independent *columns* in the said matrix.) The rank of an $m \times n$ matrix can be at most m or n, whichever is smaller.

By definition, an $n \times n$ nonsingular matrix A has n linearly independent rows (or columns); consequently it must be of rank n. Conversely, an $n \times n$ matrix having rank n must be nonsingular.

EXERCISE 5.1

1   In the following paired statements, let p be the first statement and q the second. Indicate for each case whether (5.1) or (5.2) or (5.3) applies.

(a)   It is a holiday; it is Thanksgiving Day.
(b)   A geometric figure has four sides; it is a rectangle.
(c)   Two ordered pairs (a,b) and (b,a) are equal; a is equal to b.
(d)   A number is rational; it can be expressed as a ratio of two integers.
(e)   A 4×4 matrix is nonsingular; the rank of the matrix is 4.

2   Let p be the statement "a geometric figure is a square," and let q be as follows:

(a)   It has four sides.
(b)   It has four equal sides.
(c)   It has four equal sides each perpendicular to the adjacent one.

Which is true for each case: $p \Rightarrow q$, $p \Leftarrow q$, or $p \Leftrightarrow q$?

3   Are the rows linearly independent in each of the following?

(a) $\begin{bmatrix} 6 & 2 \\ 9 & 3 \end{bmatrix}$ (b) $\begin{bmatrix} 1 & 0 \\ 0 & 1 \end{bmatrix}$ (c) $\begin{bmatrix} 0 & 1 \\ 3 & 2 \end{bmatrix}$ (d) $\begin{bmatrix} -1 & 3 \\ 2 & -6 \end{bmatrix}$

4 Check whether the columns of each matrix in the preceding problem are also linearly independent. Do you get the same answer as for row independence?

5.2 Test of Nonsingularity by Use of Determinant

To ascertain whether a square matrix is nonsingular, we can make use of the concept of the determinant.

determinants and nonsingularity   The determinant of a square matrix A, denoted by $|A|$, is a uniquely defined scalar (number) associated with that matrix. Determinants are defined only for *square* matrices. For a 2×2 matrix $A = \begin{bmatrix} a_{11} & a_{12} \\ a_{21} & a_{22} \end{bmatrix}$, its determinant is defined to be the sum of two terms as follows:

$$(5.5) \qquad |A| = \begin{vmatrix} a_{11} & a_{12} \\ a_{21} & a_{22} \end{vmatrix} = a_{11}a_{22} - a_{21}a_{12} \; [= \text{ a scalar}]$$

which is obtained by multiplying the two elements in the principal diagonal of A and then subtracting the product of the two remaining elements. In view of the dimension of matrix A, $|A|$ as defined in (5.5) is called a *second-order determinant*.

Example 1   Given $A = \begin{bmatrix} 10 & 4 \\ 8 & 5 \end{bmatrix}$ and $B = \begin{bmatrix} 3 & 5 \\ 0 & -1 \end{bmatrix}$, their determinants are:

$$|A| = \begin{vmatrix} 10 & 4 \\ 8 & 5 \end{vmatrix} = 10(5) - 8(4) = 18$$

and $\quad |B| = \begin{vmatrix} 3 & 5 \\ 0 & -1 \end{vmatrix} = 3(-1) - 0(5) = -3$

The reader should note that, while a determinant (enclosed by vertical lines rather than brackets) is by definition a scalar, a matrix as such does not have a numerical value. In other words, a determinant is reducible to a number, but a matrix is, in contrast, a whole block of numbers. It should also be emphasized that a determinant is defined only for a square matrix, whereas a matrix as such does not have to be square.

Even at this early stage of discussion, it is possible to have an inkling of the relationship between the linear dependence of the rows in a matrix A, on the one hand, and its determinant $|A|$, on the other. The two matrices

$$C = \begin{bmatrix} c_1' \\ c_2' \end{bmatrix} = \begin{bmatrix} 3 & 8 \\ 3 & 8 \end{bmatrix} \quad \text{and} \quad D = \begin{bmatrix} d_1' \\ d_2' \end{bmatrix} = \begin{bmatrix} 2 & 6 \\ 8 & 24 \end{bmatrix}$$

both have linearly dependent rows, because $c_1' = c_2'$ and $d_2' = 4d_1'$. Both of their determinants also turn out to be equal to zero:

$$|C| = \begin{vmatrix} 3 & 8 \\ 3 & 8 \end{vmatrix} = 3(8) - 3(8) = 0$$

$$|D| = \begin{vmatrix} 2 & 6 \\ 8 & 24 \end{vmatrix} = 2(24) - 8(6) = 0$$

This result strongly suggests that a "vanishing" determinant (a zero-value determinant) may have something to do with linear dependence. We shall see that this is indeed the case. Furthermore, the value of a determinant $|A|$ can not only serve as a criterion for testing the linear independence of the rows (hence the nonsingularity) of matrix A, but also aid in the calculation of the inverse A^{-1}, if it exists.

First, however, we must widen our vista by a discussion of higher-order determinants.

evaluating a third-order determinant   A determinant of order 3 is associated with a 3×3 matrix. Given

$$A = \begin{bmatrix} a_{11} & a_{12} & a_{13} \\ a_{21} & a_{22} & a_{23} \\ a_{31} & a_{32} & a_{33} \end{bmatrix}$$

its determinant has the value

$$(5.6) \quad |A| = \begin{vmatrix} a_{11} & a_{12} & a_{13} \\ a_{21} & a_{22} & a_{23} \\ a_{31} & a_{32} & a_{33} \end{vmatrix} = a_{11} \begin{vmatrix} a_{22} & a_{23} \\ a_{32} & a_{33} \end{vmatrix} - a_{12} \begin{vmatrix} a_{21} & a_{23} \\ a_{31} & a_{33} \end{vmatrix}$$

$$+ a_{13} \begin{vmatrix} a_{21} & a_{22} \\ a_{31} & a_{32} \end{vmatrix}$$

$$= a_{11}a_{22}a_{33} - a_{11}a_{23}a_{32} + a_{12}a_{23}a_{31} - a_{12}a_{21}a_{33}$$
$$+ a_{13}a_{21}a_{32} - a_{13}a_{22}a_{31} \qquad [= \text{a scalar}]$$

Looking first at the lower line of (5.6), we see the value of $|A|$ expressed as a sum of six product terms, three of which are prefixed by minus signs and three by plus signs. Complicated as this sum may appear, there is nonetheless a very easy way of "catching" all these six terms from a given third-order determinant. This is best explained diagrammatically (Fig. 5.1). In the determinant shown in Fig. 5.1, each element in the top row has been linked with two

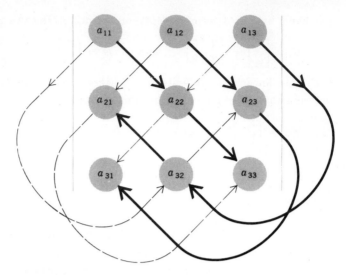

FIGURE 5.1

other elements via two *solid* arrows as follows: $a_{11} \to a_{22} \to a_{33}, a_{12} \to a_{23} \to a_{31}$, and $a_{13} \to a_{32} \to a_{21}$. Each triplet of elements so linked can be multiplied out, and their product be taken as one of the six product terms in (5.6). The solid-arrow product terms are to be prefixed with plus signs.

On the other hand, each top-row element has also been connected with two other elements via two *broken* arrows as follows: $a_{11} \to a_{32} \to a_{23}, a_{12} \to a_{21} \to a_{33}$, and $a_{13} \to a_{22} \to a_{31}$. Each triplet of elements so connected can also be multiplied out, and their product taken as one of the six terms in (5.6). Such products are prefixed by minus signs. The sum of all the six products will then be the value of the determinant.

Example 2

$$\begin{vmatrix} 2 & 1 & 3 \\ 4 & 5 & 6 \\ 7 & 8 & 9 \end{vmatrix} = (2)(5)(9) + (1)(6)(7) + (3)(8)(4) - (2)(8)(6) \\ - (1)(4)(9) - (3)(5)(7) = -9$$

Example 3

$$\begin{vmatrix} -7 & 0 & 3 \\ 9 & 1 & 4 \\ 0 & 6 & 5 \end{vmatrix} = (-7)(1)(5) + (0)(4)(0) + (3)(6)(9) - (-7)(6)(4) \\ - (0)(9)(5) - (3)(1)(0) = 295$$

This method of cross-diagonal multiplication provides a handy way of evaluating a third-order determinant, but unfortunately it is *not* applicable to

Static (or Equilibrium) Analysis

determinants of orders higher than 3. For the latter, we must resort to the so-called "Laplace expansion" of the determinant.

evaluating an nth-order determinant by Laplace expansion   Let us first explain the *Laplace-expansion* process of a third-order determinant. Returning to the first line of (5.6), we see that the value of $|A|$ can also be regarded as a sum of *three* terms, each of which is a product of a first-row element and a particular *second*-order determinant. This latter process of evaluating $|A|$—by means of certain lower-order determinants—illustrates the Laplace expansion of the determinant.

The three second-order determinants in (5.6) are not arbitrarily determined, but are specified by means of a definite rule. The first one, $\begin{vmatrix} a_{22} & a_{23} \\ a_{32} & a_{33} \end{vmatrix}$, is a *sub*-determinant of $|A|$ obtained by deleting the *first* row and *first* column of $|A|$. This is called the *minor* of the element a_{11} (the element at the intersection of the deleted row and column) and is denoted by $|M_{11}|$. In general, the symbol $|M_{ij}|$ can be used to represent the minor obtained by deleting the ith row and jth column of a given determinant. Since a minor is itself a determinant, it has a value. As the reader can verify, the other two second-order determinants in (5.6) are, respectively, the minors $|M_{12}|$ and $|M_{13}|$; that is,

$$|M_{11}| \equiv \begin{vmatrix} a_{22} & a_{23} \\ a_{32} & a_{33} \end{vmatrix} \qquad |M_{12}| \equiv \begin{vmatrix} a_{21} & a_{23} \\ a_{31} & a_{33} \end{vmatrix} \qquad |M_{13}| \equiv \begin{vmatrix} a_{21} & a_{22} \\ a_{31} & a_{32} \end{vmatrix}$$

A concept closely related to the minor is that of the *cofactor*. A cofactor, denoted by $|C_{ij}|$, is a minor with a prescribed algebraic sign attached to it.[1] The rule of sign is as follows: If the sum of the two subscripts i and j in the minor $|M_{ij}|$ is even, then the cofactor takes the same sign as the minor; that is, $|C_{ij}| \equiv |M_{ij}|$. If it is odd, then the cofactor takes the opposite sign to the minor; that is, $|C_{ij}| \equiv -|M_{ij}|$. In short, we have

$$|C_{ij}| \equiv (-1)^{i+j}|M_{ij}|$$

where it is obvious that the expression $(-1)^{i+j}$ can be positive if and only if $(i + j)$ is even. The fact that a cofactor has a specific sign is of extreme importance and should always be borne in mind.

Example 4   In the determinant $\begin{vmatrix} 9 & 8 & 7 \\ 6 & 5 & 4 \\ 3 & 2 & 1 \end{vmatrix}$, the minor of the element 8 is

---

[1] Many writers use the symbols M_{ij} and C_{ij} (without the vertical bars) for minors and cofactors. We add the vertical bars to give visual emphasis to the fact that minors and cofactors are in the nature of determinants and, as such, have scalar values.

$$|M_{12}| = \begin{vmatrix} 6 & 4 \\ 3 & 1 \end{vmatrix} = -6; \text{ but the cofactor of the same element is}$$

$$|C_{12}| = -|M_{12}| = 6$$

because $i + j = 1 + 2 = 3$ is odd. Similarly, the cofactor of the element 4 is

$$|C_{23}| = -|M_{23}| = - \begin{vmatrix} 9 & 8 \\ 3 & 2 \end{vmatrix} = 6$$

Using these new concepts, we can express a third-order determinant as

$$(5.7) \qquad |A| = a_{11}|M_{11}| - a_{12}|M_{12}| + a_{13}|M_{13}|$$
$$= a_{11}|C_{11}| + a_{12}|C_{12}| + a_{13}|C_{13}| = \sum_{j=1}^{3} a_{1j}|C_{1j}|$$

i.e., as a sum of three terms, each of which is the product of a first-row element and its corresponding cofactor. Note the difference in the signs of the $a_{12}|M_{12}|$ and $a_{12}|C_{12}|$ terms in (5.7). This is because $1 + 2$ gives an odd number.

The Laplace expansion of a *third*-order determinant serves to reduce the evaluation problem to one of evaluating only certain *second*-order determinants. A similar reduction is achieved in the Laplace expansion of higher-order determinants. In a fourth-order determinant $|B|$, for instance, the top row will contain four elements, $b_{11} \ldots b_{14}$; thus, in the spirit of (5.7), we may write

$$|B| = \sum_{j=1}^{4} b_{1j}|C_{1j}|$$

where the cofactors $|C_{1j}|$ are of order 3. Each third-order cofactor can then be evaluated as in (5.6). In general, the Laplace expansion of an nth-order determinant will reduce the problem to one of evaluating n cofactors, each of which is of the $(n - 1)$st order, and the repeated application of the process will methodically lead to lower and lower orders of determinants, eventually culminating in the basic second-order determinants as defined in (5.5). Then the value of the original determinant can be easily calculated.

Although the process of Laplace expansion has been couched in terms of the cofactors of the first-row elements, it is also feasible to expand a determinant by the cofactor of any row or, for that matter, of any column. For instance, if the first column of a third-order determinant $|A|$ consists of the elements $a_{11}, a_{21},$ and a_{31}, expansion by the cofactors of these elements will also yield the value of $|A|$:

$$|A| = a_{11}|C_{11}| + a_{21}|C_{21}| + a_{31}|C_{31}| = \sum_{i=1}^{3} a_{i1}|C_{i1}|$$

Example 5   Given $|A| = \begin{vmatrix} 5 & 6 & 1 \\ 2 & 3 & 0 \\ 7 & -3 & 0 \end{vmatrix}$, expansion by the first *row* produces

the result

$$|A| = 5 \begin{vmatrix} 3 & 0 \\ -3 & 0 \end{vmatrix} - 6 \begin{vmatrix} 2 & 0 \\ 7 & 0 \end{vmatrix} + \begin{vmatrix} 2 & 3 \\ 7 & -3 \end{vmatrix} = 0 + 0 - 27 = -27$$

But expansion by the first *column* yields the identical answer:

$$|A| = 5 \begin{vmatrix} 3 & 0 \\ -3 & 0 \end{vmatrix} - 2 \begin{vmatrix} 6 & 1 \\ -3 & 0 \end{vmatrix} + 7 \begin{vmatrix} 6 & 1 \\ 3 & 0 \end{vmatrix} = 0 - 6 - 21 = -27$$

Insofar as numerical calculation is concerned, this fact affords us an opportunity to choose some "easy" row or column for expansion. A row or column with the largest number of 0s or 1s is always preferable for this purpose, because a 0 times its cofactor will equal 0, so that the term will drop out, and a 1 times its cofactor is simply the cofactor itself, so that at least one multiplication step can be saved. In Example 5, the easiest way to expand the determinant is by the third column, which consists of the elements 1, 0, and 0. We could have evaluated it thus:

$$|A| = 1 \begin{vmatrix} 2 & 3 \\ 7 & -3 \end{vmatrix} - 0 + 0 = -27$$

To sum up, the value of a determinant $|A|$ of order n can be found by the Laplace expansion of *any row* or *any column* as follows:

$$(5.8) \qquad |A| = \sum_{j=1}^{n} a_{ij}|C_{ij}| \qquad \text{[expansion by the } i\text{th row]}$$

$$= \sum_{i=1}^{n} a_{ij}|C_{ij}| \qquad \text{[expansion by the } j\text{th column]}$$

EXERCISE 5.2

1   Evaluate the following determinants:

(a) $\begin{vmatrix} 1 & 1 & 1 \\ 1 & 2 & 3 \\ 1 & 3 & 6 \end{vmatrix}$

(c) $\begin{vmatrix} 8 & 1 & 3 \\ 4 & 0 & 1 \\ 6 & 0 & 3 \end{vmatrix}$

(e) $\begin{vmatrix} a & b & c \\ b & c & a \\ c & a & b \end{vmatrix}$

(b) $\begin{vmatrix} 1 & 2 & 3 \\ 3 & 6 & 9 \\ 4 & 5 & 7 \end{vmatrix}$

(d) $\begin{vmatrix} a & b & c \\ a & b & c \\ d & e & d \end{vmatrix}$

2   Determine the signs to be attached to the relevant minors in order to get the following cofactors of a determinant: $|C_{13}|$, $|C_{23}|$, $|C_{33}|$, $|C_{41}|$, and $|C_{34}|$.

3   Given $\begin{vmatrix} a & b & c \\ d & e & f \\ g & h & i \end{vmatrix}$, find the minors and cofactors of the elements a, b, and h.

4   Evaluate the following determinants:

(a) $\begin{vmatrix} 1 & 8 & 0 & 7 \\ 2 & 3 & 4 & 6 \\ 1 & 6 & 0 & -1 \\ 0 & -5 & 0 & 8 \end{vmatrix}$ (b) $\begin{vmatrix} 4 & 7 & 0 & 4 \\ 5 & 6 & 1 & 8 \\ 0 & 0 & 9 & 0 \\ 1 & -3 & 1 & 4 \end{vmatrix}$

5   In the first determinant of the preceding problem, find the value of the cofactor of the element 7.

5.3   Basic Properties of Determinants

We can now discuss some properties of determinants which will enable us to "discover" the connection between linear dependence among the rows of a square matrix and the vanishing of the determinant of that matrix.

Five basic properties will be discussed here. These are properties common to determinants of all orders, though we shall illustrate mostly with second-order determinants:

PROPERTY I   The interchange of rows and columns does not affect the value of a determinant. In other words, the determinant of a matrix A has the same value as that of its transpose A', that is, $|A| = |A'|$.

Example 1 $\begin{vmatrix} 4 & 3 \\ 5 & 6 \end{vmatrix} = \begin{vmatrix} 4 & 5 \\ 3 & 6 \end{vmatrix} = 9$

Example 2 $\begin{vmatrix} a & b \\ c & d \end{vmatrix} = \begin{vmatrix} a & c \\ b & d \end{vmatrix} = ad - bc$

PROPERTY II   The interchange of any two rows (or any two columns) will alter the sign, but not the numerical value, of the determinant.

Example 3

$$\begin{vmatrix} a & b \\ c & d \end{vmatrix} = ad - bc,$$ but the interchange of the two rows yields

$$\begin{vmatrix} c & d \\ a & b \end{vmatrix} = cb - ad = -(ad - bc)$$

Example 4

$$\begin{vmatrix} 0 & 1 & 3 \\ 2 & 5 & 7 \\ 3 & 0 & 1 \end{vmatrix} = -26,$$ but the interchange of the first and third

columns yields $$\begin{vmatrix} 3 & 1 & 0 \\ 7 & 5 & 2 \\ 1 & 0 & 3 \end{vmatrix} = 26.$$

PROPERTY III   The multiplication of any *one* row (or *one* column) by a scalar k will change the value of the determinant k-fold.

Example 5   By multiplying the top row of the determinant in Example 3 by k, we get

$$\begin{vmatrix} ka & kb \\ c & d \end{vmatrix} = kad - kbc = k(ad - bc) = k\begin{vmatrix} a & b \\ c & d \end{vmatrix}$$

It is important to distinguish between the two expressions kA and $k|A|$. In multiplying a *matrix* A by a scalar k, all the elements in A are to be multiplied by k. But, if we read the equation in the present example from right to left, it should be clear that, in multiplying a *determinant* $|A|$ by k, only a single row (or column) should be multiplied by k. This equation, therefore, in effect gives us a rule for factoring a determinant: Whenever any single row or column contains a common divisor, it may be factored out of the determinant.

Example 6   Factoring the first column and the second row in turn, we have

$$\begin{vmatrix} 15a & 7b \\ 12c & 2d \end{vmatrix} = 3\begin{vmatrix} 5a & 7b \\ 4c & 2d \end{vmatrix} = 3(2)\begin{vmatrix} 5a & 7b \\ 2c & d \end{vmatrix} = 6(5ad - 14bc)$$

The direct evaluation of the original determinant will of course produce the same answer.

In contrast, the factoring of a *matrix* requires the presence of a common divisor for *all* its elements, as in

$$\begin{bmatrix} ka & kb \\ kc & kd \end{bmatrix} = k\begin{bmatrix} a & b \\ c & d \end{bmatrix}$$

PROPERTY IV   The addition (subtraction) of a multiple of any row to (from) another row will leave the value of the determinant unaltered. The same holds true if we replace the word *row* by *column* in the above statement.

Example 7   Adding k times the top row of the determinant in Example 3 to its second row, we end up with the original determinant:

$$\begin{vmatrix} a & b \\ c + ka & d + kb \end{vmatrix} = a(d + kb) - b(c + ka) = ad - bc = \begin{vmatrix} a & b \\ c & d \end{vmatrix}$$

PROPERTY V   If one row (or column) is a multiple of another row (or column), the value of the determinant will be zero. As a special case of this, when two rows (or two columns) are *identical*, the determinant will vanish.

Example 8

$$\begin{vmatrix} 2a & 2b \\ a & b \end{vmatrix} = 2ab - 2ab = 0 \qquad \begin{vmatrix} c & c \\ d & d \end{vmatrix} = cd - cd = 0$$

Additional examples of this type of "vanishing" determinants can be found in Exercise 5.2-1.

This important property is, in fact, a logical consequence of Property IV. To understand this, let us apply Property IV to the two determinants in Example 8 and watch the outcome. For the first one, try to subtract twice the second row from the top row; for the second determinant, subtract the second column from the first column. Since these operations do not alter the values of the determinants, we can write

$$\begin{vmatrix} 2a & 2b \\ a & b \end{vmatrix} = \begin{vmatrix} 0 & 0 \\ a & b \end{vmatrix} \qquad \begin{vmatrix} c & c \\ d & d \end{vmatrix} = \begin{vmatrix} 0 & c \\ 0 & d \end{vmatrix}$$

The new (reduced) determinants now contain, respectively, a row and a column of zeros; thus their Laplace expansion must yield a value of zero in both cases. In general, when one row (column) is a multiple of another row (column), the application of Property IV can always reduce all elements of that row (column) to zero, and Property V therefore follows.

The basic properties just discussed are useful in several ways. For one thing, they can be of great help in simplifying the task of evaluating determinants. By subtracting multiples of one row (or column) from another, for instance, the elements of the determinant may be reduced to much smaller and simpler numbers. Factoring, if feasible, can also accomplish the same. If we can indeed apply these properties to transform some row or column into a form containing mostly 0s or 1s, Laplace expansion of the determinant will become a much more manageable task.

determinantal criterion of nonsingularity   Our present concern, however, is primarily to link the linear dependence of rows with the vanishing of a determinant. For this purpose, property V can be invoked. Consider an equation system $Ax = d$:

$$\begin{bmatrix} 3 & 4 & 2 \\ 15 & 20 & 10 \\ 4 & 0 & 1 \end{bmatrix} \begin{bmatrix} x_1 \\ x_2 \\ x_3 \end{bmatrix} = \begin{bmatrix} d_1 \\ d_2 \\ d_3 \end{bmatrix}$$

This system can have a unique solution if and only if the rows in the coefficient matrix A are linearly independent, so that A is nonsingular. But the second row is five times the first; the rows are indeed *dependent*, and hence no unique solution exists. The detection of this row dependence was by visual inspection, but by virtue of Property V we could also have discovered it through the fact that $|A| = 0$.

The row dependence in a matrix may, of course, assume a more intricate and secretive pattern. For instance, in the matrix

$$B = \begin{bmatrix} 4 & 1 & 2 \\ 5 & 2 & 1 \\ 1 & 0 & 1 \end{bmatrix} \equiv \begin{bmatrix} v_1' \\ v_2' \\ v_3' \end{bmatrix}$$

there exists row dependence because $2v_1' - v_2' - 3v_3' = 0$; yet this fact defies visual detection. Even in this case, however, Property V will give us a vanishing determinant, $|B| = 0$, since by adding three times v_3' to v_2' and subtracting twice v_1' from it, the second row can be reduced to a zero vector. In general, *any* pattern of linear dependence among rows will be reflected in a vanishing determinant— and herein lies the beauty of Property V! Conversely, if the rows are linearly independent, the determinant must have a nonzero value.

We have, in the above, identified the property of nonsingularity of a matrix principally with the concept of linear independence among *rows*. But, on occasion, we have made the claim that, for a *square* matrix A, row independence $\Leftrightarrow$ column independence. We are now equipped to prove that claim:

According to Property I, we know that $|A| = |A'|$. Since row independence in $A \Leftrightarrow |A| \neq 0$, we may also state that row independence in $A \Leftrightarrow |A'| \neq 0$. But $|A'| \neq 0 \Leftrightarrow$ row independence in the transpose $A' \Leftrightarrow$ column independence in A (rows of A' are by definition the columns of A). Therefore, *row* independence in $A \Leftrightarrow$ *column* independence in A.

Our discussion of the test of nonsingularity can now be summarized. Given a linear-equation system $Ax = d$, where A is an $n \times n$ coefficient matrix,

$|A| \neq 0 \Leftrightarrow$ there is row (column) independence in matrix A

$\Leftrightarrow A$ is nonsingular

$\Leftrightarrow A^{-1}$ exists

$\Leftrightarrow$ a unique solution $\bar{x} = A^{-1}d$ exists

Thus the value of the determinant of the coefficient matrix, $|A|$, provides a convenient criterion for the testing of nonsingularity of matrix A and of the existence of a unique solution to the equation system $Ax = d$. Note, however, that the determinant criterion says nothing about the algebraic signs of the solution values, i.e., even though we are assured of a unique solution when $|A| \neq 0$, we may sometimes get negative solution values that are economically inadmissible.

Example 9   Does the equation system

$$7x_1 - 3x_2 - 3x_3 = 7$$
$$2x_1 + 4x_2 + x_3 = 0$$
$$ - 2x_2 - x_3 = 2$$

possess a unique solution? The determinant $|A|$ is

$$\begin{vmatrix} 7 & -3 & -3 \\ 2 & 4 & 1 \\ 0 & -2 & -1 \end{vmatrix} = -8 \neq 0$$

Therefore a unique solution does exist.

rank of a matrix redefined   The rank of a matrix A was earlier defined to be the maximum number of linearly independent rows in A. In view of the link between row independence and the nonvanishing of the determinant, we can redefine the rank of an $m \times n$ matrix as the maximum order of a nonvanishing determinant that can be constructed from the rows and columns of that matrix. The rank of any matrix is a unique number.

Obviously, the rank can at most be m or n, whichever is smaller, because a determinant is defined only for a square matrix, and from a matrix of dimension, say, 3×5, the largest possible determinants (vanishing or not) will be of order 3. Symbolically, this fact may be expressed as follows:

$$r(A) \leq \min \{m,n\}$$

which is read: The rank of A is less than or equal to the minimum of the set of two numbers m and n. The rank of an $n \times n$ nonsingular matrix A must be n; in that case, we may write $r(A) = n$.

Sometimes, one may be interested in the rank of the product of two matrices. In that case, the following rule is of use:

$$r(AB) = \min \{r(A),r(B)\}$$

EXERCISE 5.3

1   Use the determinant $\begin{vmatrix} 1 & 0 & -1 \\ 1 & 5 & 7 \\ 3 & 3 & 9 \end{vmatrix}$ to verify the first four properties of determinants.

2   Show that, when all the elements of an nth-order determinant $|A|$ are multiplied by a number k, the result will be $k^n|A|$.

3   Which properties of determinants enable us to write the following?

(a) $\begin{vmatrix} 9 & 18 \\ 27 & 56 \end{vmatrix} = \begin{vmatrix} 9 & 18 \\ 0 & 2 \end{vmatrix}$ (b) $\begin{vmatrix} 9 & 27 \\ 4 & 2 \end{vmatrix} = 18 \begin{vmatrix} 1 & 3 \\ 2 & 1 \end{vmatrix}$

4   Which of the following matrices are nonsingular?

(a) $\begin{bmatrix} 5 & 7 & 3 \\ 4 & 8 & 9 \\ 8 & 4 & -15 \end{bmatrix}$ (b) $\begin{bmatrix} 4 & 0 & 1 \\ 19 & 1 & 3 \\ 5 & 4 & 7 \end{bmatrix}$ (c) $\begin{bmatrix} 7 & 0 & 3 \\ 8 & -45 & 2 \\ 4 & 9 & 2 \end{bmatrix}$

5   What can you say about the rank of each matrix in the preceding problem?

6   Do the following three vectors span a 3-space? Why or why not?

$[4 \;\; 6 \;\; 2]$ $[1 \;\; 2 \;\; 0]$ $[3 \;\; 5 \;\; 1]$

7   Let A be an $m \times n$ matrix ($m \leq n$), with rank $r(A) = m$. Show that the matrix AA' must be nonsingular. What can be said about the nonsingularity of the matrix $A'A$?

5.4   Finding the Inverse Matrix

If the matrix A in the linear-equation system $Ax = d$ is nonsingular, then A^{-1} exists, and the solution of the system will be $\bar{x} = A^{-1}d$. We have learned to test the nonsingularity of A by the criterion $|A| \neq 0$. The next question is: How do we find the inverse A^{-1} if A does pass that test?

expansion of a determinant by alien cofactors   Before answering this query, let us discuss another important property of determinants:

PROPERTY VI   The expansion of a determinant by *alien cofactors* (the cofactors of a "wrong" row or column) always yields a value of zero.

Example 1   If we expand the determinant $\begin{vmatrix} 4 & 1 & 2 \\ 5 & 2 & 1 \\ 1 & 0 & 3 \end{vmatrix}$ by using its *first*-row elements but the cofactors of the *second*-row elements

$$|C_{21}| = -\begin{vmatrix} 1 & 2 \\ 0 & 3 \end{vmatrix} = -3 \qquad |C_{22}| = \begin{vmatrix} 4 & 2 \\ 1 & 3 \end{vmatrix} = 10$$

$$|C_{23}| = -\begin{vmatrix} 4 & 1 \\ 1 & 0 \end{vmatrix} = 1$$

we get $a_{11}|C_{21}| + a_{12}|C_{22}| + a_{13}|C_{23}| = 4(-3) + 1(10) + 2(1) = 0$.

More generally, applying the same type of expansion by alien cofactors as described in Example 1 to the determinant $|A| = \begin{vmatrix} a_{11} & a_{12} & a_{13} \\ a_{21} & a_{22} & a_{23} \\ a_{31} & a_{32} & a_{33} \end{vmatrix}$ will yield a zero sum of products as follows:

$$(5.9) \qquad \sum_{j=1}^{3} a_{1j}|C_{2j}| = a_{11}|C_{21}| + a_{12}|C_{22}| + a_{13}|C_{23}|$$

$$= -a_{11}\begin{vmatrix} a_{12} & a_{13} \\ a_{32} & a_{33} \end{vmatrix} + a_{12}\begin{vmatrix} a_{11} & a_{13} \\ a_{31} & a_{33} \end{vmatrix} - a_{13}\begin{vmatrix} a_{11} & a_{12} \\ a_{31} & a_{32} \end{vmatrix}$$

$$= -a_{11}a_{12}a_{33} + a_{11}a_{13}a_{32} + a_{11}a_{12}a_{33} - a_{12}a_{13}a_{31}$$
$$- a_{11}a_{13}a_{32} + a_{12}a_{13}a_{31} = 0$$

The reason for this outcome lies in the fact that the sum of products in (5.9) can be considered as the result of the *regular* expansion by the second row of another determinant $|A^*| \equiv \begin{vmatrix} a_{11} & a_{12} & a_{13} \\ a_{11} & a_{12} & a_{13} \\ a_{31} & a_{32} & a_{33} \end{vmatrix}$, which differs from $|A|$ only in its second row and whose first two rows are identical. As an exercise, the reader should write out the cofactors of the second rows of $|A^*|$ and verify that these are precisely the cofactors which appeared in (5.9)—and with the correct signs. Since $|A^*| = 0$, because of its two identical rows, the expansion by alien cofactors shown in (5.9) will of necessity yield a value of zero also.

Property VI is valid for determinants of all orders and applies when a determinant is expanded by the alien cofactors of any row or any column. Thus we may state, in general, that for a determinant of order n the following holds:

$$(5.10) \quad \sum_{j=1}^{n} a_{ij}|C_{i'j}| = 0 \quad (i \neq i') \quad \text{[expansion by } i\text{th row and}$$

cofactors of i'th row]

$$\sum_{i=1}^{n} a_{ij}|C_{ij'}| = 0 \quad (j \neq j') \quad \text{[expansion by } j\text{th column and}$$

cofactors of j'th column]

The reader should carefully compare (5.10) with (5.8). In the latter (regular Laplace expansion), the subscripts of a_{ij} and of $|C_{ij}|$ must be identical in each product term in the sum. In the expansion by alien cofactors, such as in (5.10), on the other hand, one of the two subscripts (a chosen value of i' or j') is inevitably "out of place."

matrix inversion Property VI, as summarized in (5.10), is of direct help in developing a method of matrix inversion, i.e., of finding the inverse of a matrix.

Assume that an $n \times n$ nonsingular matrix

$$(5.11) \quad \underset{(n \times n)}{A} = \begin{bmatrix} a_{11} & a_{12} & \cdots & a_{1n} \\ a_{21} & a_{22} & \cdots & a_{2n} \\ \cdots\cdots\cdots\cdots\cdots\cdots \\ a_{n1} & a_{n2} & \cdots & a_{nn} \end{bmatrix}$$

is given. Since each element of A has a cofactor $|C_{ij}|$, it is possible to form a matrix of cofactors by replacing each element a_{ij} in (5.11) with its cofactor $|C_{ij}|$. Such a cofactor matrix, denoted by $C = [|C_{ij}|]$, must also be $n \times n$. For our present purposes, however, the transpose of C is of more interest. This transpose C' is referred to as the *adjoint* of A and is symbolized by adj A. Written out, the adjoint takes the form

$$(5.12) \quad \underset{(n \times n)}{C'} \equiv \text{adj } A \equiv \begin{bmatrix} |C_{11}| & |C_{21}| & \cdots & |C_{n1}| \\ |C_{12}| & |C_{22}| & \cdots & |C_{n2}| \\ \cdots\cdots\cdots\cdots\cdots\cdots \\ |C_{1n}| & |C_{2n}| & \cdots & |C_{nn}| \end{bmatrix}$$

The matrices A and C' are conformable for multiplication, and their product AC' is another $n \times n$ matrix in which each element is a sum of products. By utilizing the formula for Laplace expansion as well as Property VI of determinants, the product AC' may be expressed as follows:

$$\underset{(n \times n)}{AC'} = \begin{bmatrix} \sum\limits_{j=1}^{n} a_{1j}|C_{1j}| & \sum\limits_{j=1}^{n} a_{1j}|C_{2j}| & \cdots & \sum\limits_{j=1}^{n} a_{1j}|C_{nj}| \\ \sum\limits_{j=1}^{n} a_{2j}|C_{1j}| & \sum\limits_{j=1}^{n} a_{2j}|C_{2j}| & \cdots & \sum\limits_{j=1}^{n} a_{2j}|C_{nj}| \\ \vdots & \vdots & & \vdots \\ \sum\limits_{j=1}^{n} a_{nj}|C_{1j}| & \sum\limits_{j=1}^{n} a_{nj}|C_{2j}| & \cdots & \sum\limits_{j=1}^{n} a_{nj}|C_{nj}| \end{bmatrix}$$

$$= \begin{bmatrix} |A| & 0 & \cdots & 0 \\ 0 & |A| & \cdots & 0 \\ \vdots & \vdots & & \vdots \\ 0 & 0 & \cdots & |A| \end{bmatrix} \qquad \text{[by (5.8) and (5.10)]}$$

$$= |A| \begin{bmatrix} 1 & 0 & \cdots & 0 \\ 0 & 1 & \cdots & 0 \\ \vdots & \vdots & & \vdots \\ 0 & 0 & \cdots & 1 \end{bmatrix} = |A|I_n \qquad \text{[factoring]}$$

The nonsingularity of matrix A assures us that $|A| \neq 0$. The determinant $|A|$ being a nonzero scalar, it is permissible to divide both sides of the equation $AC' = |A|I$ by $|A|$. The result is

$$\frac{AC'}{|A|} = I \qquad \text{or} \qquad A\frac{C'}{|A|} = I$$

Premultiplying both sides of the last equation by A^{-1}, and using the result that $A^{-1}A = I$, we can get $\dfrac{C'}{|A|} = A^{-1}$, or

$$(5.13) \qquad A^{-1} = \frac{1}{|A|} \operatorname{adj} A \qquad \text{[by (5.12)]}$$

Now, we have found a way to invert the matrix A!

The general procedure for finding the inverse of a square matrix A thus involves the following steps: (1) Find $|A|$. We need to proceed with the subsequent steps if and only if $|A| \neq 0$, for if $|A| = 0$ the inverse in (5.13) will be undefined. (2) Find the cofactors of all the elements of A, and arrange them as a cofactor matrix $C = [|C_{ij}|]$. (3) Take the transpose of C to get adj A. (4) Divide adj A by the determinant $|A|$. The result will be the desired inverse A^{-1}.

Example 2   Find the inverse of $A = \begin{bmatrix} 3 & 2 \\ 1 & 0 \end{bmatrix}$. Since $|A| = -2 \neq 0$, the inverse A^{-1} exists. The cofactor of each element is in this case a 1×1 determinant, which is simply defined as the scalar element of that determinant itself (that is, $|a_{ij}| \equiv a_{ij}$). Thus, we have

$$C = \begin{bmatrix} |C_{11}| & |C_{12}| \\ |C_{21}| & |C_{22}| \end{bmatrix} = \begin{bmatrix} 0 & -1 \\ -2 & 3 \end{bmatrix}$$

where the reader should observe the minus signs attached to 1 and 2, as required for cofactors. Transposing the cofactor matrix yields

$$\operatorname{adj} A = \begin{bmatrix} 0 & -2 \\ -1 & 3 \end{bmatrix}$$

so the inverse A^{-1} can be written as

$$A^{-1} = \frac{1}{|A|} \text{ adj } A = -\frac{1}{2}\begin{bmatrix} 0 & -2 \\ -1 & 3 \end{bmatrix} = \begin{bmatrix} 0 & 1 \\ \frac{1}{2} & -\frac{3}{2} \end{bmatrix}$$

Example 3   Find the inverse of $B = \begin{bmatrix} 4 & 1 & -1 \\ 0 & 3 & 2 \\ 3 & 0 & 7 \end{bmatrix}$. Since $|B| = 99 \neq 0$,

the inverse B^{-1} also exists. The cofactor matrix is

$$\begin{bmatrix} \begin{vmatrix} 3 & 2 \\ 0 & 7 \end{vmatrix} & -\begin{vmatrix} 0 & 2 \\ 3 & 7 \end{vmatrix} & \begin{vmatrix} 0 & 3 \\ 3 & 0 \end{vmatrix} \\ -\begin{vmatrix} 1 & -1 \\ 0 & 7 \end{vmatrix} & \begin{vmatrix} 4 & -1 \\ 3 & 7 \end{vmatrix} & -\begin{vmatrix} 4 & 1 \\ 3 & 0 \end{vmatrix} \\ \begin{vmatrix} 1 & -1 \\ 3 & 2 \end{vmatrix} & -\begin{vmatrix} 4 & -1 \\ 0 & 2 \end{vmatrix} & \begin{vmatrix} 4 & 1 \\ 0 & 3 \end{vmatrix} \end{bmatrix} = \begin{bmatrix} 21 & 6 & -9 \\ -7 & 31 & 3 \\ 5 & -8 & 12 \end{bmatrix}$$

Therefore,

$$\text{adj } B = \begin{bmatrix} 21 & -7 & 5 \\ 6 & 31 & -8 \\ -9 & 3 & 12 \end{bmatrix}$$

and the desired inverse matrix is

$$B^{-1} = \frac{1}{|B|} \text{ adj } B = \frac{1}{99}\begin{bmatrix} 21 & -7 & 5 \\ 6 & 31 & -8 \\ -9 & 3 & 12 \end{bmatrix}$$

The reader can check that the results in the above two examples do satisfy $AA^{-1} = A^{-1}A = I$ and $BB^{-1} = B^{-1}B = I$, respectively.

EXERCISE 5.4

1   Suppose that we expand a fourth-order determinant by its *third column* and the cofactors of the *second-column* elements. How would you write the resulting sum of products in $\sum$ notation? What will be the sum of products in $\sum$ notation if we expand it by the *second row* and the cofactors of the *fourth-row* elements?

2   Find the inverse of each of the following matrices:

(a) $A = \begin{bmatrix} 3 & 8 \\ 0 & 1 \end{bmatrix}$ (c) $C = \begin{bmatrix} 7 & 7 \\ 3 & -1 \end{bmatrix}$

(b) $B = \begin{bmatrix} 1 & 0 \\ 0 & 2 \end{bmatrix}$

3   Find the inverse of each of the following matrices:

(a) $D = \begin{bmatrix} 3 & -1 & 2 \\ 1 & 0 & 3 \\ 4 & 0 & 2 \end{bmatrix}$ (c) $F = \begin{bmatrix} 1 & 0 & 0 \\ 0 & 0 & 1 \\ 0 & 1 & 0 \end{bmatrix}$

(b) $E = \begin{bmatrix} 4 & -2 & 1 \\ 7 & 3 & 3 \\ 2 & 0 & 1 \end{bmatrix}$

5.5   Cramer's Rule

The method of matrix inversion just discussed enables us to derive a convenient, practical way of solving a linear-equation system, which is known as *Cramer's rule*.

derivation of the rule   Given an equation system $Ax = d$, where A is $n \times n$, the solution can be written as

$$\bar{x} = A^{-1}d = \frac{1}{|A|} (\text{adj } A)d \qquad [\text{by (5.13)}]$$

provided that A is nonsingular. According to (5.12), this means that

$$\begin{bmatrix} \bar{x}_1 \\ \bar{x}_2 \\ \vdots \\ \bar{x}_n \end{bmatrix} = \frac{1}{|A|} \begin{bmatrix} |C_{11}| & |C_{21}| & \cdots & |C_{n1}| \\ |C_{12}| & |C_{22}| & \cdots & |C_{n2}| \\ \hdotsfor{4} \\ |C_{1n}| & |C_{2n}| & \cdots & |C_{nn}| \end{bmatrix} \begin{bmatrix} d_1 \\ d_2 \\ \vdots \\ d_n \end{bmatrix}$$

$$= \frac{1}{|A|} \begin{bmatrix} d_1|C_{11}| + d_2|C_{21}| + \cdots + d_n|C_{n1}| \\ d_1|C_{12}| + d_2|C_{22}| + \cdots + d_n|C_{n2}| \\ \hdotsfor{1} \\ d_1|C_{1n}| + d_2|C_{2n}| + \cdots + d_n|C_{nn}| \end{bmatrix}$$

$$= \frac{1}{|A|} \begin{bmatrix} \sum\limits_{i=1}^{n} d_i|C_{i1}| \\ \sum\limits_{i=1}^{n} d_i|C_{i2}| \\ \vdots \\ \sum\limits_{i=1}^{n} d_i|C_{in}| \end{bmatrix}$$

Equating the corresponding elements on the two sides of the equation, we obtain the solution values

$$(5.14) \qquad \bar{x}_1 = \frac{1}{|A|} \sum_{i=1}^{n} d_i|C_{i1}| \qquad \bar{x}_2 = \frac{1}{|A|} \sum_{i=1}^{n} d_i|C_{i2}| \qquad (\text{etc.})$$

The $\sum$ terms in (5.14) look unfamiliar. What do they mean? From (5.8), we see that the Laplace expansion of a determinant $|A|$ by its first column can be expressed in the form $\sum_{i=1}^{n} a_{i1}|C_{i1}|$. If we replace the first column of $|A|$ by the column vector d but keep all the other columns intact, then a new determinant will result, which we can call $|A_1|$—the subscript 1 indicating that the first column has been replaced by d. The expansion of $|A_1|$ by its first column (the d column) will yield the expression $\sum_{i=1}^{n} d_i|C_{i1}|$, because the elements d_i now take the place of the elements a_{i1}. Returning to (5.14), we see therefore that

$$\bar{x}_1 = \frac{1}{|A|} |A_1|$$

Similarly, if we replace the second column of $|A|$ by the column vector d, while retaining all the other columns, the expansion of the new determinant $|A_2|$ by its second column (the d column) will result in the expression $\sum_{i=1}^{n} d_i|C_{i2}|$. When divided by $|A|$, this latter sum will give us the solution value $\bar{x}_2$; and so on.

This procedure can now be generalized: To find the solution value of the jth variable $\bar{x}_j$, we can merely replace the jth column of the determinant $|A|$ by the constant terms $d_1 \cdots d_n$ to get a new determinant $|A_j|$ and then divide $|A_j|$ by the original determinant $|A|$. Thus, the solution of the system $Ax = d$ can be expressed as

$$(5.15) \qquad \bar{x}_j = \frac{|A_j|}{|A|} = \frac{1}{|A|} \begin{vmatrix} a_{11} & a_{12} & \cdots & d_1 & \cdots & a_{1n} \\ a_{21} & a_{22} & \cdots & d_2 & \cdots & a_{2n} \\ \vdots & \vdots & & \vdots & & \vdots \\ a_{n1} & a_{n2} & \cdots & d_n & \cdots & a_{nn} \end{vmatrix}$$

$$\underset{(j\text{th column replaced by } d)}{\uparrow}$$

The result in (5.15) is the statement of Cramer's rule.

Example 1 Find the solution of the equation system

$$5x_1 + 3x_2 = 30$$
$$6x_1 - 2x_2 = 8$$

The coefficients and the constant terms give the following determinants:

$$|A| = \begin{vmatrix} 5 & 3 \\ 6 & -2 \end{vmatrix} = -28 \qquad |A_1| = \begin{vmatrix} 30 & 3 \\ 8 & -2 \end{vmatrix} = -84$$

$$|A_2| = \begin{vmatrix} 5 & 30 \\ 6 & 8 \end{vmatrix} = -140$$

Therefore, by virtue of (5.15), we can immediately write

$$\bar{x}_1 = \frac{|A_1|}{|A|} = \frac{-84}{-28} = 3 \quad \text{and} \quad \bar{x}_2 = \frac{|A_2|}{|A|} = \frac{-140}{-28} = 5$$

Example 2   Find the solution of the equation system

$$
\begin{aligned}
7x_1 - x_2 - x_3 &= 0 \\
10x_1 - 2x_2 + x_3 &= 8 \\
6x_1 + 3x_2 - 2x_3 &= 7
\end{aligned}
$$

The relevant determinants $|A|$ and $|A_j|$ are found to be

$$
|A| = \begin{vmatrix} 7 & -1 & -1 \\ 10 & -2 & 1 \\ 6 & 3 & -2 \end{vmatrix} = -61 \qquad
|A_1| = \begin{vmatrix} 0 & -1 & -1 \\ 8 & -2 & 1 \\ 7 & 3 & -2 \end{vmatrix} = -61
$$

$$
|A_2| = \begin{vmatrix} 7 & 0 & -1 \\ 10 & 8 & 1 \\ 6 & 7 & -2 \end{vmatrix} = -183 \qquad
|A_3| = \begin{vmatrix} 7 & -1 & 0 \\ 10 & -2 & 8 \\ 6 & 3 & 7 \end{vmatrix} = -244
$$

thus the solution values of the variables are

$$\bar{x}_1 = \frac{|A_1|}{|A|} = \frac{-61}{-61} = 1 \qquad \bar{x}_2 = \frac{|A_2|}{|A|} = \frac{-183}{-61} = 3$$

$$\bar{x}_3 = \frac{|A_3|}{|A|} = \frac{-244}{-61} = 4$$

Notice that in each of these examples we find $|A| \neq 0$. This is a necessary condition for the application of Cramer's rule, as it is for the existence of the inverse A^{-1}. Cramer's rule is, after all, based upon the concept of the inverse matrix, even though in practice it bypasses the process of matrix inversion.

note on homogeneous-equation systems   The equation systems $Ax = d$ considered above can have any constants in the vector d. If $d = 0$, that is, if $d_1 = d_2 = \cdots = d_n = 0$, however, the equation system will become

$$Ax = 0$$

where 0 is a zero vector. This special case is referred to as a *homogeneous-equation system*.[1]

If the matrix A is nonsingular, a homogeneous-equation system can yield

---

[1] The word "homogeneous" describes the property that when all the variables $x_1, \ldots, x_n$ are multiplied by the same number, the equation system will remain valid. This is possible only if the constant terms (those unattached to any x_i) are all zero.

    Static (or Equilibrium) Analysis

only a "trivial solution," namely, $\bar{x}_1 = \bar{x}_2 = \cdots = \bar{x}_n = 0$. This follows from the fact that the solution $\bar{x} = A^{-1}d$ will in this case become

$$\underset{(n \times 1)}{\bar{x}} = \underset{(n \times n)}{A^{-1}} \underset{(n \times 1)}{0} = \underset{(n \times 1)}{0}$$

Alternatively, this outcome can be derived from Cramer's rule. The fact that $d = 0$ implies that $|A_j|$, for all j, must contain a whole column of zeros, and thus the solution will turn out to be

$$\bar{x}_j = \frac{|A_j|}{|A|} = \frac{0}{|A|} = 0 \qquad (j = 1, 2, \ldots, n)$$

Curiously enough, the *only* way to get a *nontrivial* solution from a homogeneous-equation system is to have $|A| = 0$, that is, to have a *singular* coefficient matrix A! In that event, we have

$$\bar{x}_j = \frac{|A_j|}{|A|} = \frac{0}{0}$$

where the $0/0$ expression is not equal to zero but is, rather, something undefined. Consequently, Cramer's rule is not applicable. This does not mean that we cannot obtain solutions; it means only that we cannot get a unique solution.

Consider the homogeneous-equation system

$$(5.16) \qquad \begin{array}{l} a_{11}x_1 + a_{12}x_2 = 0 \\ a_{21}x_1 + a_{22}x_2 = 0 \end{array}$$

It is self-evident that $\bar{x}_1 = \bar{x}_2 = 0$ is a solution, but that solution is trivial. Now, assume that the coefficient matrix A is singular, so that $|A| = 0$. This implies that the row vector $[a_{11} \quad a_{12}]$ is a multiple of the row vector $[a_{21} \quad a_{22}]$; consequently, one of the two equations is redundant. By deleting, say, the second equation from (5.16), we end up with one (the first) equation in two variables, the solution of which is $\bar{x}_1 = (-a_{12}/a_{11})\bar{x}_2$. This solution is nontrivial and well defined if $a_{11} \neq 0$, but it really represents an infinite number of solutions because, for every possible value of $\bar{x}_2$, there is a corresponding value $\bar{x}_1$ such that the pair constitutes a solution. Thus no unique nontrivial solution exists for this homogeneous-equation system. This last statement is also generally valid for the n-variable case.

EXERCISE 5.5

1 Use Cramer's rule to solve the following systems of equations:

(a) $\begin{array}{l} 2x_1 + x_2 = 24 \\ 3x_1 - 2x_2 = 8 \end{array}$ 　　　　(b) $\begin{array}{l} 5x_1 - 2x_2 = 15 \\ 4x_1 + x_2 = 12 \end{array}$

2 For each equation system in the preceding problem, find the inverse of the coefficient matrix and obtain the solution by using the equation $\bar{x} = A^{-1}d$. Does the answer check with those obtained by applying Cramer's rule?

3 Use Cramer's rule to solve the following systems of equations:

(*a*)
$$\begin{aligned} 2x_1 - x_2 &= 2 \\ 3x_2 + 2x_3 &= 16 \\ 5x_1 + 3x_3 &= 21 \end{aligned}$$

(*b*)
$$\begin{aligned} -x + y + z &= a \\ x - y + z &= b \\ x + y - z &= c \end{aligned}$$

4 Show that Cramer's rule can be derived directly by the following procedure: Multiply the *i*th equation of the system $Ax = d$ by the cofactor $|C_{ij}|$; add all the (new) equations; then assign the values 1, 2, . . . , n to the index j, successively, to get the solution values $\bar{x}_1, \bar{x}_2, \ldots, \bar{x}_n$ as shown in (5.14). [*Hint:* Apply (5.8) and (5.10).]

5.6 Application to Market and National-Income Models

Simple equilibrium models such as those discussed in Chap. 3 can be solved with ease by Cramer's rule or by matrix inversion.

market model The two-commodity model described in (3.12) can be written (after eliminating the quantity variables) as a system of two linear equations, as in (3.13′):

$$\begin{aligned} c_1 P_1 + c_2 P_2 &= -c_0 \\ \gamma_1 P_1 + \gamma_2 P_2 &= -\gamma_0 \end{aligned}$$

The three determinants needed—$|A|$, $|A_1|$, and $|A_2|$—have the following values:

$$|A| = \begin{vmatrix} c_1 & c_2 \\ \gamma_1 & \gamma_2 \end{vmatrix} = c_1\gamma_2 - c_2\gamma_1$$

$$|A_1| = \begin{vmatrix} -c_0 & c_2 \\ -\gamma_0 & \gamma_2 \end{vmatrix} = -c_0\gamma_2 + c_2\gamma_0$$

$$|A_2| = \begin{vmatrix} c_1 & -c_0 \\ \gamma_1 & -\gamma_0 \end{vmatrix} = -c_1\gamma_0 + c_0\gamma_1$$

Therefore the equilibrium prices must be

$$\bar{P}_1 = \frac{|A_1|}{|A|} = \frac{c_2\gamma_0 - c_0\gamma_2}{c_1\gamma_2 - c_2\gamma_1} \qquad \bar{P}_2 = \frac{|A_2|}{|A|} = \frac{c_0\gamma_1 - c_1\gamma_0}{c_1\gamma_2 - c_2\gamma_1}$$

which are precisely those obtained in (3.14) and (3.15). The equilibrium quantities can then be found, as before, by setting $P_1 = \bar{P}_1$ and $P_2 = \bar{P}_2$ in the demand or supply equations.

national-income model   The simple national-income model cited in (3.23) can also be solved by the use of Cramer's rule. As written in (3.23), the model consists of the following two simultaneous equations:

$$Y = C + I_0 + G_0$$
$$C = a + bY$$

These can be rearranged into the form

$$Y - C = I_0 + G_0$$
$$-bY + C = a$$

so that the endogenous variables Y and C appear only on the left of the equals signs, whereas the exogenous variables and the unattached parameter appear only on the right. The coefficient matrix now takes the form $\begin{bmatrix} 1 & -1 \\ -b & 1 \end{bmatrix}$, and the column vector of constants (data), $\begin{bmatrix} I_0 + G_0 \\ a \end{bmatrix}$. Note that the sum $I_0 + G_0$ is considered as a single entity, i.e., a single element in the constant vector.

Cramer's rule now leads immediately to the following solution:

$$\bar{Y} = \frac{\begin{vmatrix} (I_0 + G_0) & -1 \\ a & 1 \end{vmatrix}}{\begin{vmatrix} 1 & -1 \\ -b & 1 \end{vmatrix}} = \frac{I_0 + G_0 + a}{1 - b}$$

$$\bar{C} = \frac{\begin{vmatrix} 1 & (I_0 + G_0) \\ -b & a \end{vmatrix}}{\begin{vmatrix} 1 & -1 \\ -b & 1 \end{vmatrix}} = \frac{a + b(I_0 + G_0)}{1 - b}$$

The reader should check that the solution values just obtained are identical with those shown in (3.24) and (3.25).

Let us now try to solve this model by inverting the coefficient matrix. Since the coefficient matrix is $A = \begin{bmatrix} 1 & -1 \\ -b & 1 \end{bmatrix}$, its cofactor matrix will be $\begin{bmatrix} 1 & b \\ 1 & 1 \end{bmatrix}$, and we therefore have adj $A = \begin{bmatrix} 1 & 1 \\ b & 1 \end{bmatrix}$. It follows that the inverse matrix is

$$A^{-1} = \frac{1}{|A|} \text{adj } A = \frac{1}{1 - b} \begin{bmatrix} 1 & 1 \\ b & 1 \end{bmatrix}$$

We know that, for the equation system $Ax = d$, the solution is expressible as $\bar{x} = A^{-1}d$. Applied to the present model, this means that

$$\begin{bmatrix} \bar{Y} \\ \bar{C} \end{bmatrix} = \frac{1}{1-b} \begin{bmatrix} 1 & 1 \\ b & 1 \end{bmatrix} \begin{bmatrix} I_0 + G_0 \\ a \end{bmatrix} = \frac{1}{1-b} \begin{bmatrix} I_0 + G_0 + a \\ b(I_0 + G_0) + a \end{bmatrix}$$

It is easy to see that this is again the same solution as obtained before.

matrix algebra versus elimination of variables   The two economic models used for illustration here both involve two equations only, and thus only second-order determinants need be evaluated. For large equation systems, higher-order determinants will appear, and their evaluation may prove to be no simple task. Nor is the inversion of large matrices exactly child's play. From the computational point of view, in fact, matrix inversion and Cramer's rule are not necessarily more efficient than the method of successive elimination of variables.

If so, one may ask, why use the matrix methods at all? As we have seen from the preceding pages, matrix algebra has given us a compact notation for any linear-equation system, and also furnishes a determinantal criterion for testing the existence of a unique solution. These are advantages not otherwise available. In addition to these, it may be mentioned that, unlike the elimination-of-variables method, which affords no means of analytically expressing the solution, the matrix-inversion method and Cramer's rule do provide the handy expressions $\bar{x} = A^{-1}d$ and $\bar{x}_j = |A_j|/|A|$. Such analytical expressions of the solution are useful not only because they are in themselves a summary statement of the actual solution procedure, but also because they make possible the performance of further mathematical operations on the solution as written, if so desired.

Under certain circumstances, matrix methods can even claim a computational advantage, such as when the task is to solve at the same time several equation systems having an identical coefficient matrix A but different constant-term vectors. In such cases, the elimination method would require that the computational procedure be repeated each time a new equation system is considered. With the matrix-inversion method, however, we are required to find the common inverse matrix A^{-1} *only once*; then the same inverse can be used to premultiply all the constant-term vectors pertaining to the various equation systems involved, in order to obtain their respective solutions. This particular computational advantage will take on great practical significance when we consider the solution of the Leontief input-output models in the next section.

5.7   Leontief Input-Output Models

In its "static" version, Professor Leontief's input-output analysis[1] deals with this particular question: What level of output should each of the n industries in an economy produce, in order that it will just be sufficient to satisfy the total demand for that product?

The rationale for the term *input-output analysis* is quite plain to see. The output of any industry (say, the steel industry) is needed as an input in many other industries, or even for that industry itself; therefore the "correct" level of steel output will depend on the input requirements of all the n industries. In turn, the output of many other industries will enter into the steel industry as inputs, and consequently the "correct" levels of the other products will in turn depend partly upon the input requirements of the steel industry. In view of this interindustry dependence, any set of "correct" output levels for the n industries must be one that is consistent with all the input requirements in the economy, so that no bottlenecks will arise anywhere. In this light, it is clear that input-output analysis should be of great use in production planning, such as in planning for the economic development of a country or for a program of national defense.

Strictly speaking, input-output analysis is not a form of the general equilibrium analysis as discussed in Chap. 3. Although the interdependence of the various industries is emphasized, the "correct" output levels envisaged are those which satisfy technical input-output relationships rather than market equilibrium conditions. Nevertheless, the problem posed in input-output analysis also boils down to one of solving a system of simultaneous equations, and matrix algebra can again be of service.

structure of an input-output model   Since an input-output model normally encompasses a large number of industries, its framework is of necessity rather involved. To simplify the problem, the following assumptions are as a rule adopted: (1) Each industry produces only one homogeneous commodity. (Broadly interpreted, this does permit the case of two or more jointly produced commodities, provided they are produced in a fixed proportion to one another.) (2) Each industry uses a fixed input ratio (or factor combination) for the production of its output. (3) Production in every industry is subject to constant returns to scale, so that a k-fold change in every input will result in an exactly k-fold change in the output. These assumptions are, of course, unrealistic. A saving grace is that, if an industry produces two different commodities or uses

[1] Wassily W. Leontief, *The Structure of American Economy 1919–1939*, 2d ed., Oxford University Press, Fair Lawn, N.J., 1951.

two different possible factor combinations, then that industry may—at least conceptually—be broken down into two separate industries.

From these assumptions we see that, in order to produce each unit of the jth commodity, the input need for the ith commodity must be a fixed amount, which we shall denote by a_{ij}. Specifically, the production of each unit of the jth commodity will require a_{1j} (amount) of the first commodity, a_{2j} of the second commodity, . . . , and a_{nj} of the nth commodity. (The order of the subscripts in a_{ij} is easy to remember: the first subscript refers to the input, and the second to the output, so that a_{ij} indicates how much of the ith commodity is used for the production of each unit of the jth commodity.) For our purposes, we may assume prices to be given and, thus, adopt "a dollar's worth" of each commodity as its unit. Then the statement $a_{32} = 0.35$ will mean that 35 cents' worth of the third commodity is required as an input for producing a dollar's worth of the second commodity. The a_{ij} symbol will be referred to as an *input coefficient*.

For an n-industry economy, the input coefficients can be arranged into a matrix $A = [a_{ij}]$, as in Table 5.1, in which each *column* specifies the input requirements for the production of one unit of the output of a particular industry. The second column, for example, states that to produce a unit (a dollar's worth) of commodity II, the inputs needed are: a_{12} units of commodity I, a_{22} units of commodity II, etc. If no industry uses its own product as an input, then the elements in the principal diagonal of matrix A will all be zero.

the open model   If, besides the n industries, the model contains an "open" sector (say, households) which exogenously determines a *final demand* (non-input demand) for the product of each industry and which supplies a *primary input* (say, labor service) not produced by the n industries themselves, then the model is an *open model*.

TABLE 5.1

Input	Output				
	I	II	III	⋯	N
I	a_{11}	a_{12}	a_{13}	⋯	a_{1n}
II	a_{21}	a_{22}	a_{23}	⋯	a_{2n}
III	a_{31}	a_{32}	a_{33}	⋯	a_{3n}
⋮	⋮	⋮	⋮		⋮
N	a_{n1}	a_{n2}	a_{n3}	⋯	a_{nn}

In view of the presence of the open sector, the sum of the elements in each column of the input-coefficient matrix A (or *input matrix A*, for short) must be less than 1. Each column sum represents the *partial* input cost (not including the cost of the primary input) incurred in producing a dollar's worth of some commodity; if this sum is greater than or equal to $1, therefore, production will not be economically justifiable. Symbolically, this fact may be stated thus:

$$\sum_{i=1}^{n} a_{ij} < 1 \qquad (j = 1, 2, \ldots, n)$$

where the summation is over i, that is, over the elements appearing in the various *rows* of a specific column j. Carrying this line of thought a step further, it may also be stated that, since the value of output ($1) must be fully absorbed by the payments to all factors of production, the amount by which the column sum falls short of $1 must represent the payment to the primary input of the open sector. Thus the value of the primary input needed in producing a unit of the jth commodity should be $1 - \sum_{i=1}^{n} a_{ij}$.

If industry I is to produce an output just sufficient to meet the input requirements of the n industries as well as the final demand of the open sector, its output level x_1 must satisfy the following equation:

$$x_1 = a_{11}x_1 + a_{12}x_2 + \cdots + a_{1n}x_n + d_1$$

or $\quad (1 - a_{11})x_1 - a_{12}x_2 - \cdots - a_{1n}x_n = d_1$

where d_1 denotes the final demand for its output and $a_{1j}x_j$ represents the input requirement of the jth industry.[1] Note that, aside from the first coefficient, $(1 - a_{11})$, the remaining coefficients in the last equation are transplanted directly from the first row of Table 5.1, except that they are now prefixed with minus signs. Similarly, the corresponding equation for industry II will have the same coefficients as in the second row of Table 5.1 (again with minus signs added), except that the variable x_2 will have the coefficient $(1 - a_{22})$ instead of $-a_{22}$. For the entire set of n industries, the "correct" output levels can therefore be summarized by the following system of n linear equations:

(5.17)
$$\begin{aligned}
(1 - a_{11})x_1 - \quad & a_{12}x_2 - \cdots - & a_{1n}x_n &= d_1 \\
- a_{21}x_1 + (1 - a_{22})x_2 - \cdots - & a_{2n}x_n &= d_2 \\
\cdots\cdots\cdots\cdots\cdots\cdots\cdots\cdots\cdots & & \\
- a_{n1}x_1 - \quad & a_{n2}x_2 - \cdots + (1 - a_{nn})x_n &= d_n
\end{aligned}$$

[1] The reader is warned not to add up the input coefficients across a row, for such a sum—say, $a_{11} + a_{12} + \cdots + a_{1n}$—is devoid of economic meaning. The sum of the products $a_{11}x_1 + a_{12}x_2 + \cdots + a_{1n}x_n$, on the other hand, does have an economic meaning; it represents the total amount of x_1 needed as input for all the n industries.

Linear Models and Matrix Algebra (continued)

In matrix notation, this may be written as

$$(5.17') \qquad \begin{bmatrix} (1 - a_{11}) & -a_{12} & \cdots & -a_{1n} \\ -a_{21} & (1 - a_{22}) & \cdots & -a_{2n} \\ \vdots & \vdots & & \vdots \\ -a_{n1} & -a_{n2} & \cdots & (1 - a_{nn}) \end{bmatrix} \begin{bmatrix} x_1 \\ x_2 \\ \vdots \\ x_n \end{bmatrix} = \begin{bmatrix} d_1 \\ d_2 \\ \vdots \\ d_n \end{bmatrix}$$

If the 1s in the principal diagonal of the matrix on the left are ignored, the matrix is simply $-A = [-a_{ij}]$. As it is, on the other hand, the matrix is the *sum* of the identity matrix I_n (with 1s in its principal diagonal and with 0s everywhere else) and the matrix $-A$. Thus (5.17') can also be written

$$(5.17'') \qquad (I - A)x = d$$

where x and d are, respectively, the variable vector and the final-demand (constant-term) vector. The matrix $(I - A)$ is called the *technology matrix*. If $(I - A)$ is nonsingular—and there is no a priori reason why it should not be—then the inverse $(I - A)^{-1}$ can be found, and (5.17'') will have the unique solution

$$(5.18) \qquad \bar{x} = (I - A)^{-1}d$$

numerical example   For purposes of illustration, suppose that there are only three industries in the economy and that the input-coefficient matrix is as follows (let us use decimal values this time):

$$(5.19) \qquad A = \begin{bmatrix} a_{11} & a_{12} & a_{13} \\ a_{21} & a_{22} & a_{23} \\ a_{31} & a_{32} & a_{33} \end{bmatrix} = \begin{bmatrix} 0.2 & 0.3 & 0.2 \\ 0.4 & 0.1 & 0.2 \\ 0.1 & 0.3 & 0.2 \end{bmatrix}$$

Note that in A each column sum is less than 1, as it should be. Further, if we denote by a_{0j} the dollar amount of the primary input used in producing a dollar's worth of the jth commodity, then we can write [by subtracting each column sum in (5.19) from 1]:

$$(5.20) \qquad a_{01} = 0.3 \qquad a_{02} = 0.3 \qquad \text{and} \qquad a_{03} = 0.4$$

With the matrix A above, the open input-output system can be expressed in the form $(I - A)x = d$ as follows:

$$(5.21) \qquad \begin{bmatrix} 0.8 & -0.3 & -0.2 \\ -0.4 & 0.9 & -0.2 \\ -0.1 & -0.3 & 0.8 \end{bmatrix} \begin{bmatrix} x_1 \\ x_2 \\ x_3 \end{bmatrix} = \begin{bmatrix} d_1 \\ d_2 \\ d_3 \end{bmatrix}$$

Here we have deliberately not given specific values to the final demands d_1, d_2, and d_3. In this way, by keeping the vector d in parametric form, our solution will appear as a "formula" into which we can feed various specific d vectors and thereby obtain various corresponding specific solutions.

By inverting the 3×3 technology matrix $(I - A)$, the solution of (5.21) can be found, approximately (because of rounding of decimal figures), to be:

$$\begin{bmatrix} \bar{x}_1 \\ \bar{x}_2 \\ \bar{x}_3 \end{bmatrix} = (I - A)^{-1}d = \frac{1}{0.384} \begin{bmatrix} 0.66 & 0.30 & 0.24 \\ 0.34 & 0.62 & 0.24 \\ 0.21 & 0.27 & 0.60 \end{bmatrix} \begin{bmatrix} d_1 \\ d_2 \\ d_3 \end{bmatrix}$$

If the specific final-demand vector (say, the final-output target of a development program) happens to be $d = \begin{bmatrix} 10 \\ 5 \\ 6 \end{bmatrix}$, in billions of dollars, then the following specific solution values will emerge (again in billions of dollars):

$$\bar{x}_1 = \frac{1}{0.384} [0.66(10) + 0.30(5) + 0.24(6)] = \frac{9.54}{0.384} = 24.84$$

and similarly,

$$\bar{x}_2 = \frac{7.94}{0.384} = 20.68 \qquad \text{and} \qquad \bar{x}_3 = \frac{7.05}{0.384} = 18.36$$

An important question now arises. The production of the output mix $\bar{x}_1$, $\bar{x}_2$, and $\bar{x}_3$ must entail a definite required amount of the primary input. Would the amount *required* be consistent with what is *available* in the economy? On the basis of (5.20), the required primary input may be calculated as follows:

$$\sum_{j=1}^{3} a_{0j}\bar{x}_j = 0.3(24.84) + 0.3(20.68) + 0.4(18.36) = \$21.00 \text{ billion}$$

Therefore, the specific final demand $d = \begin{bmatrix} 10 \\ 5 \\ 6 \end{bmatrix}$ will be feasible if and only if the available amount of the primary input is at least \$21 billion. If the amount available falls short, then that particular production target will, of course, have to be revised downward accordingly.

One important feature of the above analysis is that, as long as the input coefficients remain the same, the inverse $(I - A)^{-1}$ will not change; therefore only *one* matrix inversion needs to be performed, even if we are to consider a hundred or a thousand different final-demand vectors—such as a spectrum of alternative development targets. This can mean considerable savings in computational effort as compared with the elimination-of-variables method, especially if large equation systems are involved.[1]

---

[1] If we use Cramer's rule, however, this advantage will be lost. In that case, the solution will be $\bar{x}_j = |(I - A)_j|/|I - A|$, and each time a different final-demand vector d is used, we shall have to reevaluate the determinants $|(I - A)_j|$. This would be much more time-consuming than the multiplication of a known $(I - A)^{-1}$ with a new vector d.

finding the inverse by approximation   For large equation systems, the task of inverting a matrix can be exceedingly lengthy and tedious. Even though electronic computers can aid us, simpler computational schemes would still be desirable. For the input-output models under consideration, there does exist a method of finding an approximation to the inverse $(I - A)^{-1}$ to any desired degree of accuracy; thus it is possible to avoid the process of matrix inversion entirely.

Let us first consider the following matrix multiplication ($m =$ a positive integer):

$$(I - A)(I + A + A^2 + \cdots + A^m)$$
$$= I(I + A + A^2 + \cdots + A^m) - A(I + A + A^2 + \cdots + A^m)$$
$$= (I + A + A^2 + \cdots + A^m) - (A + A^2 + \cdots + A^m + A^{m+1})$$
$$= I - A^{m+1}$$

Had the result of the multiplication been the identity matrix I alone, we could have taken the matrix sum $(I + A + A^2 + \cdots + A^m)$ as the inverse of $(I - A)$. It is the presence of the $-A^{m+1}$ term that spoils things! Fortunately, though, there remains for us a second-best course, for if the matrix A^{m+1} can be made to approach an $n \times n$ null matrix, then $I - A^{m+1}$ will approach I, and accordingly the said sum matrix $(I + A + A^2 + \cdots + A^m)$ will approach the desired inverse $(I - A)^{-1}$. By making A^{m+1} approach a null matrix, therefore, we can obtain an *approximation inverse* by adding the matrices $I, A, A^2, \ldots, A^m$.

But can we make A^{m+1} approach a null matrix? And if so, how? The answer to the first question is yes if—as is true of the input-output models under consideration—the elements in *each* column of matrix A are nonnegative numbers adding up to *less than 1*, such as illustrated in (5.19). For such cases, A^{m+1} can be made to approach a null matrix by making the power m sufficiently large, i.e., by a long-enough process of repeated self-multiplication of matrix A. We shall sketch the proof for this statement presently, but if for now its validity is granted, the procedure of computing the approximation inverse becomes very clear: We can simply calculate the successive matrices $A^2, A^3, \ldots,$ till there emerges a matrix A^{m+1} whose elements are, by a preselected standard, all of a negligible order of magnitude ("approaching zero"). When that happens, we can terminate the multiplication process and add up all the matrices already obtained, to form the approximation inverse $(I + A + A^2 + \cdots + A^m)$.†

---

† The approximation of $(I - A)^{-1}$ by $(I + A + A^2 + \cdots + A^m)$ is reminiscent of the approximation of the infinite series

$$(1 - r)^{-1} = \frac{1}{1 - r} = 1 + r + r^2 + \cdots \qquad (0 < r < 1)$$

by the sum $(1 + r + r^2 + \cdots + r^n)$. Since the subsequent terms in the series become progressively smaller, we can approximate $(1 - r)^{-1}$ to any desired degree of accuracy by an appropriate choice of the number n.

Static (or Equilibrium) Analysis

Note that, when the matrix A is such that A^{m+1} approaches the null matrix as m is increased indefinitely, the approximation inverse $(I + A + A^2 + \cdots + A^m)$ will also have the property that all its elements are nonnegative. The first two terms in the sum, I and A, obviously contain nonnegative elements only. But so do all powers of A, because the self-multiplication of A involves nothing other than the multiplication and addition of the nonnegative elements of A itself. Inasmuch as the final-demand vector d also contains only non-negative elements, it should be clear from (5.18) that the solution output levels must also be nonnegative. This, of course, is precisely what we wanted them to be.

Let us now sketch the proof for the assertion that, given a nonnegative input-coefficient matrix $A = [a_{ij}]$ whose column sums are each less than 1, the matrix A^{m+1} will approach a null matrix as m is increased indefinitely.[1] For this purpose, we shall need the concept of the *norm* of a matrix A, which is defined as the *largest column sum* in A and is denoted by $N(A)$. In the matrix of (5.19), for instance, we have $N(A) = 0.7$; this is the first column sum, which happens also to be equal to the second column sum. It is immediately clear that no element in a matrix can ever exceed the value of the norm; that is,

$$a_{ij} \leq N(A) \qquad \text{(for all } i,j)$$

In the input-output context, we have $N(A) < 1$, and all $a_{ij} < 1$. Actually, the matrix A being nonnegative, we must have

$$0 < N(A) < 1$$

Regarding norms of matrices, there is a theorem stating that, given any two (conformable) matrices A and B, the norm of the product matrix AB can never exceed the product of $N(A)$ and $N(B)$:

$$(5.22) \qquad N(AB) \leq N(A)N(B)$$

In the special case of $A = B$, where the matrix is square, this result means that

$$(5.23) \qquad N(A^2) \leq [N(A)]^2$$

When $B = A^2$, (5.22) and (5.23) together imply that

$$N(A^3) \leq N(A)N(A^2) \leq N(A)[N(A)]^2 = [N(A)]^3$$

The generalized version of the last result is

$$(5.24) \qquad N(A^m) \leq [N(A)]^m$$

It is in this light that the fact $0 < N(A) < 1$ acquires significance, for as m

---

[1] For a more detailed discussion, see Frederick V. Waugh, "Inversion of the Leontief Matrix by Power Series," *Econometrica*, April 1950, pp. 142–154.

becomes infinite, $[N(A)]^m$ must approach zero if $N(A)$ is a positive fraction. By (5.24), this means that $N(A^m)$ must also approach zero, since $N(A^m)$ is at most as large as $[N(A)]^m$. If so, however, then the elements in the matrix A^m must approach zero also when m is increased indefinitely, because no element in the latter matrix can exceed the value of the norm $N(A^m)$. Thus, by making m sufficiently large, the matrix A^{m+1} can be made to approach a null matrix, when the condition $0 < N(A) < 1$ is satisfied.

the closed model   If the exogenous sector of the open input-output model is absorbed into the system as just another *industry*, the model will become a *closed model*. In such a model, final demand and primary input do not appear; in their place will be the input requirements and the output of the newly conceived industry. All goods will now be *intermediate* in nature, because everything that is produced is produced only for the sake of satisfying the input requirements of the $(n + 1)$ industries in the model.

At first glance, the conversion of the open sector into an additional industry would not seem to create any significant change in the analysis. Actually, however, since the new industry is assumed to have a fixed input ratio as does any other industry, the supply of what used to be the primary input must now bear a fixed proportion to what used to be called the final demand. More concretely, this may mean, for example, that households will consume each commodity in a fixed proportion to the labor service they supply. This certainly constitutes a significant change in the analytical framework involved.

Mathematically, the disappearance of the final demands means that we will now have a homogeneous-equation system. Assuming four industries only (including the new one, designated by the subscript 0), the "correct" output levels will, by analogy to (5.17'), be those which satisfy the equation system:

$$
\begin{bmatrix}
(1 - a_{00}) & -a_{01} & -a_{02} & -a_{03} \\
-a_{10} & (1 - a_{11}) & -a_{12} & -a_{13} \\
-a_{20} & -a_{21} & (1 - a_{22}) & -a_{23} \\
-a_{30} & -a_{31} & -a_{32} & (1 - a_{33})
\end{bmatrix}
\begin{bmatrix}
x_0 \\
x_1 \\
x_2 \\
x_3
\end{bmatrix}
=
\begin{bmatrix}
0 \\
0 \\
0 \\
0
\end{bmatrix}
$$

Being homogeneous, this equation system can have a nontrivial solution if and only if the 4×4 technology matrix $(I - A)$ has a vanishing determinant. The latter condition is indeed always fulfilled: In a closed model, there is no more primary input; hence each column sum in the input-coefficient matrix A must now be exactly equal to (rather than less than) 1; that is, $a_{0j} + a_{1j} + a_{2j} + a_{3j} = 1$, or

$$a_{0j} = 1 - a_{1j} - a_{2j} - a_{3j}$$

But this implies that, in every column of the matrix $(I - A)$ above, the top element is always equal to the negative of the sum of the other three elements. Consequently, the four rows are linearly dependent, and we must find $|I - A| = 0$. This guarantees that the system does possess nontrivial solutions; in fact, it has an infinite number of them. This means that in a closed model, with a homogeneous-equation system, no unique "correct" output mix exists. We can determine the output levels $\bar{x}_1, \ldots, \bar{x}_4$ in proportion to one another, but cannot fix their absolute levels unless additional restrictions are imposed on the model.

EXERCISE 5.7

1 Solve the national-income model in Exercise 3.5-1 by Cramer's rule.

2 On the basis of the model in (5.21), if the final demands are $d_1 = 20$, $d_2 = 5$, and $d_3 = 10$ (all in billions of dollars), what will be the solution output levels for the three industries? (Round off final answers to two decimal places.)

3 Using the information in (5.20), calculate the total amount of primary input required to produce the solution output levels of the preceding problem.

4 Given the input-coefficient matrix and the final-demand vector

$$A = \begin{bmatrix} 0.3 & 0.4 & 0.2 \\ 0.2 & 0.0 & 0.5 \\ 0.1 & 0.3 & 0.1 \end{bmatrix} \quad \text{and} \quad d = \begin{bmatrix} 100 \\ 40 \\ 50 \end{bmatrix}$$

find the "correct" output levels for the three industries. (Round off final answers to two decimal places.)

5.8   Limitations of Static Analysis

In the discussion of static equilibrium in the market or in the national income, our primary concern was to find the equilibrium values of the endogenous variables in the model. A fundamental point that was ignored in such an analysis is the actual process of adjustments and readjustments of the variables ultimately leading to the equilibrium state (if it is at all attainable). We asked only about where we shall arrive but did not question when or what may happen along the way.

The static type of analysis fails, therefore, to take into account two problems of importance. One is that, since the adjustment process may take a long time to complete, an equilibrium state as determined within a particular frame of static analysis may have lost its relevance before it is even attained if the exogenous forces in the model have undergone some changes in the meantime. This is the problem of shifts of the equilibrium state. The second is that, even if the adjustment process is allowed to run its course undisturbed, the equilibrium state envisaged in a static analysis may be altogether unattainable. This would be the case of a so-called "unstable equilibrium," which is characterized by the fact that the adjustment process will drive the variables further away from, rather than progressively closer to, that equilibrium state. To disregard the adjustment process, therefore, is to assume away the problem of attainability of equilibrium.

The shifts of the equilibrium state (in response to exogenous changes) pertain to a type of analysis called *comparative statics*, and the question of attainability and stability of equilibrium falls within the realm of *dynamic analysis*. Each of these clearly serves to fill a significant gap in the static analysis, and it is thus imperative to inquire into those areas of analysis also. We shall leave the study of dynamic analysis to Part 5 of the book and shall next turn our attention to the problem of comparative statics.

THREE

COMPARATIVE-STATIC ANALYSIS

6

COMPARATIVE STATICS
AND THE CONCEPT OF DERIVATIVE

The present and the two following chapters will be devoted to the methods of
comparative-static analysis.

6.1   The Nature of Comparative Statics

Comparative statics, as the name suggests, is concerned with the comparison of
different equilibrium states that are associated with different sets of values of
parameters and exogenous variables. For purposes of such a comparison, we
always start by assuming a given initial equilibrium state. In the isolated-market
model, for example, such an initial equilibrium will be represented by a
determinate price $\bar{P}$ and a corresponding quantity $\bar{Q}$. Similarly, in the simple
national-income model of (3.23), the initial equilibrium will be specified by a
determinate $\bar{Y}$ and a corresponding $\bar{C}$. Now if we let a disequilibrating change
occur in the model—in the form of a variation in the value of some parameter
or exogenous variable—the initial equilibrium will, of course, be upset. As a
result, the various endogenous variables must undergo certain adjustments. If it
is assumed that a new equilibrium state relevant to the new values of the data
can be defined and attained, the question posed in the comparative-static
analysis is: How would the new equilibrium compare with the old?

It should be noted that in comparative statics we again disregard the process of adjustment of the variables; we merely compare the initial (*pre*change) equilibrium state with the final (*post*change) equilibrium state. Also, we again preclude the possibility of instability of equilibrium, for we assume the new equilibrium to be attainable, just as we do for the old.

A comparative-static analysis can be either qualitative or quantitative in nature. If we are interested only in the question of, say, whether an increase in investment I_0 will increase or decrease the equilibrium income $\bar{Y}$, then the analysis will be qualitative because the *direction* of change is the only matter considered. But if we are concerned with the *magnitude* of the change in $\bar{Y}$ resulting from a given change in I_0 (that is, the size of the investment multiplier), then the analysis will obviously be quantitative. By obtaining a quantitative answer, however, we can automatically tell the direction of change from its algebraic sign. Hence the quantitative analysis always embraces the qualitative.

It should be clear that the problem under consideration is essentially one of finding a *rate of change*: the rate of change of the equilibrium value of an endogenous variable with respect to the change in a particular parameter or exogenous variable. For this reason, the mathematical concept of *derivative* takes on preponderant significance in comparative statics, because that concept —the most fundamental one in the branch of mathematics known as *differential calculus*—is directly concerned with the notion of rate of change! Later on, moreover, we shall find the concept of derivative to be of extreme importance for optimization problems as well.

6.2 Rate of Change and the Derivative

Even though our present context is concerned only with the rates of change of the equilibrium values of the variables in a model, we may carry on the discussion in a more general manner by considering the rate of change of any variable y in response to a change in another variable x, where the two variables are related to each other by the function

$$y = f(x)$$

Applied in the comparative-static context, the variable y will represent the equilibrium value of an endogenous variable, and x will be some parameter. The reader will note that, for a start, we are restricting ourselves to the simple case where there is only a single parameter or exogenous variable in the model. Once we have mastered this simplified case, however, the extension to the case of more parameters will prove relatively easy.

the difference quotient   Since the notion of "change" figures prominently in the present context, a special symbol is needed to represent it. When the variable x changes from the value x_0 to a new value x_1, the change is measured by the difference $x_1 - x_0$. Hence, using the symbol Δ (the Greek capital delta, for "difference") to denote the change, we write $\Delta x = x_1 - x_0$. Also needed is a way of denoting the value of the function $f(x)$ at various values of x. The standard practice is to use the notation $f(x_i)$ to represent the value of $f(x)$ when $x = x_i$. Thus, for the function $f(x) = 5 + x^2$, we have $f(0) = 5 + 0 = 5$; and similarly, $f(1) = 6$, $f(2) = 9$, etc.

When x changes from an initial value x_0 to $(x_0 + \Delta x)$, the value of the function $y = f(x)$ changes from $f(x_0)$ to $f(x_0 + \Delta x)$. The change in y per unit of change in x can be represented by the *difference quotient*

$$(6.1) \qquad \frac{\Delta y}{\Delta x} = \frac{f(x_0 + \Delta x) - f(x_0)}{\Delta x}$$

This quotient, which measures the average rate of change of y, can be calculated if we know the initial value of x, or x_0, and the magnitude of change in x, or Δx. That is, $\Delta y / \Delta x$ is a function of x_0 and Δx.

Example 1   Given $y = f(x) = 3x^2 - 4$, we can write:

$$f(x_0) = 3(x_0)^2 - 4 \qquad f(x_0 + \Delta x) = 3(x_0 + \Delta x)^2 - 4$$

Therefore, the difference quotient is

$$(6.2) \qquad \frac{\Delta y}{\Delta x} = \frac{3(x_0 + \Delta x)^2 - 4 - (3x_0^2 - 4)}{\Delta x} = \frac{6x_0 \Delta x + 3(\Delta x)^2}{\Delta x}$$

$$= 6x_0 + 3\Delta x$$

which can be evaluated if we are given x_0 and Δx. Let $x_0 = 3$ and $\Delta x = 4$; then the average rate of change of y will be $6(3) + 3(4) = 30$. This means that, on the average, as x changes from 3 to 7, the change in y is 30 units per unit change in x.

the derivative   Frequently, we are interested in the rate of change of y when Δx is very small. In such a case, it is possible to obtain an approximation of $\Delta y / \Delta x$ by dropping all the terms in the difference quotient involving the expression Δx. In (6.2), for instance, if Δx is very small, we may simply take the term $6x_0$ on the right as an approximation of $\Delta y / \Delta x$. The smaller the value of Δx, of course, the closer is the approximation to the true value of $\Delta y / \Delta x$.

As Δx approaches zero (meaning that it gets closer and closer to, but never actually reaches, zero), $(6x_0 + 3\Delta x)$ will approach the value $6x_0$, and by the same token, $\Delta y/\Delta x$ will approach $6x_0$ also. Symbolically, this fact is expressed either by the statement $\Delta y/\Delta x \to 6x_0$ as $\Delta x \to 0$, or by the equation

$$(6.3) \qquad \lim_{\Delta x \to 0} \frac{\Delta y}{\Delta x} = \lim_{\Delta x \to 0} (6x_0 + 3\Delta x) = 6x_0$$

where the symbol $\lim_{\Delta x \to 0}$ is read: The limit of ... as Δx approaches 0. If, as $\Delta x \to 0$, the limit of the difference quotient $\Delta y/\Delta x$ exists, that limit is identified as the derivative of the function $y = f(x)$.

Several points should be noted about the derivative. First, a derivative is a *function*; in fact, in this usage the word *derivative* really means a derived function. The original function $y = f(x)$ is a *primitive function*, and the derivative is another function derived from it. Whereas the difference quotient is a function of x_0 and Δx, the reader should observe—from (6.3), for instance—that the derivative is a function of x_0 only. This is because Δx is already compelled to approach zero, and therefore it should not be regarded as another variable in the function. Let us also add that so far we have used the subscripted symbol x_0 only in order to stress the fact that a change in x must start from some specific value of x. Now that this is understood, we may delete the subscript and simply state that the derivative, like the primitive function, is itself a function of the independent variable x. That is, for each value of x, there is a unique corresponding value for the derivative function.

Second, since the derivative is merely a limit of the difference quotient, which measures a rate of change of y, the derivative must of necessity also be a measure of some rate of change. In view of the fact that the change in x envisaged in the derivative concept is infinitesimal (that is, $\Delta x \to 0$), however, the rate measured by the derivative is in the nature of an *instantaneous* rate of change.

Third, there is the matter of notation. Derivative functions are commonly denoted in two ways. Given a primitive function $y = f(x)$, one way of denoting its derivative (if it exists) is to use the symbol $f'(x)$, or simply f'; this notation is attributed to the mathematician Lagrange. The other common notation is dy/dx, devised by the mathematician Leibniz. [Actually there is a third notation, Dy, or $Df(x)$, but we shall not use it in the following discussion.] The notation $f'(x)$, which resembles the notation for the primitive function $f(x)$, has the advantage of conveying the idea that the derivative is itself a function of x. The reason for expressing it as $f'(x)$—rather than, say, $\phi(x)$—is to emphasize that the function f' is derived from the primitive function f. The alternative notation, dy/dx, serves instead to emphasize that the value of a derivative measures a rate of change. The letter d is the counterpart of the Greek Δ, and dy/dx differs from $\Delta y/\Delta x$ chiefly in that the former is the limit of the latter as Δx approaches zero. In the subsequent discussion, we shall use both of these notations, depending on which seems the more convenient in a particular context.

Using these two notations, we may define the derivative of a given function $y = f(x)$ as follows:

$$\frac{dy}{dx} \equiv f'(x) \equiv \lim_{\Delta x \to 0} \frac{\Delta y}{\Delta x}$$

Example 2   Referring to the function $y = 3x^2 - 4$ again, we have shown its difference quotient to be (6.2), and the limit of that quotient to be (6.3). On the basis of the latter, we may now write (replacing x_0 with x):

$$\frac{dy}{dx} = 6x \qquad \text{or} \qquad f'(x) = 6x$$

Note that different values of x will give the derivative correspondingly different values. For instance, when $x = 3$, we have $f'(x) = 6(3) = 18$; but when $x = 4$, we find that $f'(4) = 6(4) = 24$.

EXERCISE 6.2

1   Given the function $y = 3x^2 + 7$:

    (a)   Find the difference quotient as a function of x and Δx. (Use x in lieu of x_0.)

    (b)   Find the derivative dy/dx.

    (c)   Find $f'(3)$ and $f'(4)$.

2   Given the function $y = 9x^2 - 4x$:

    (a)   Find the difference quotient as a function of x and Δx.

    (b)   Find the derivative dy/dx.

    (c)   Find $f'(2)$ and $f'(3)$.

3   Given the function $y = 5x - 2$:

    (a)   Find the difference quotient $\Delta y/\Delta x$. What type of function is it?

    (b)   Since the expression Δx does not appear in the function $\Delta y/\Delta x$ above, does it make any difference to the value of $\Delta y/\Delta x$ whether Δx is large or small? Consequently, what is the limit of the difference quotient as Δx approaches zero?

6.3   The Derivative and the Slope of a Curve

Elementary economics tells us that, given a total-cost function $C = f(Q)$, where C denotes total cost and Q the output, the marginal cost (MC) is defined as the change in total cost resulting from a unit increase in output; that is, MC =

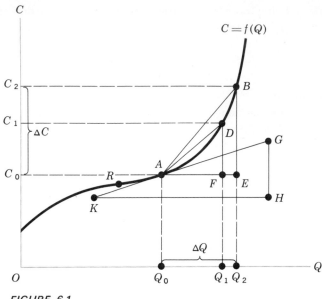

FIGURE 6.1

$\Delta C/\Delta Q$. It is understood that ΔQ is an extremely small change. For the case of a product that has discrete units (integers only), a change of one unit is the smallest change possible; but for the case of a product whose quantity is a continuous variable, ΔQ will refer to an infinitesimal change. In this latter case, it is well known that the marginal cost can be measured by the slope of the total-cost curve. But the slope of the total-cost curve is nothing but the limit of the ratio $\Delta C/\Delta Q$, when ΔQ approaches zero. Thus the concept of the slope of a curve is merely the geometric counterpart of the concept of the derivative. Both have to do with the "marginal" notion so extensively used in economics.

In Fig. 6.1, we have drawn a total-cost curve C, which is the graph of the (primitive) function $C = f(Q)$. Suppose that we consider Q_0 as the initial output level from which an increase in output is measured, then the relevant point on the cost curve will be A. If output is to be raised to $Q_0 + \Delta Q = Q_2$, the total cost will be increased from C_0 to $C_0 + \Delta C = C_2$; thus $\Delta C/\Delta Q = (C_2 - C_0)/(Q_2 - Q_0)$. Geometrically, this is the ratio of two line segments, EB/AE, or the *slope* of the line AB. This particular ratio measures an average rate of change—the *average* marginal cost for the particular ΔQ pictured—and represents a difference quotient. As such, it is a function of the initial value Q_0 and the amount of change ΔQ.

What happens when we vary the magnitude of ΔQ? If a smaller output increment is contemplated (say, from Q_0 to Q_1 only), then the average marginal cost will be measured by the slope of the line AD instead. Moreover, as we reduce the output increment further and further, flatter and flatter lines will result until, in the limit (as $\Delta Q \to 0$), we obtain the line KG (which is the *tangent line* to the cost curve at point A) as the relevant line. The slope of KG $(= HG/KH)$ measures the slope of the total-cost curve at point A and represents the limit of $\Delta C/\Delta Q$, as $\Delta Q \to 0$, when initial output is at $Q = Q_0$. Therefore, in terms of the derivative, the slope of the $C = f(Q)$ curve at point A corresponds to the particular derivative value $f'(Q_0)$.

What if the initial output level is changed from Q_0 to, say, Q_2? In that case, point B on the curve will replace point A as the relevant point, and the slope of the curve at the new point B will give us the derivative value $f'(Q_2)$. Analogous results are obtainable for alternative initial output levels. In general, the derivative $f'(Q)$—a function of Q—will vary as Q changes.

6.4   The Concept of Limit

The derivative dy/dx has been defined as the limit of the difference quotient $\Delta y/\Delta x$ as $\Delta x \to 0$. If we adopt the shorthand symbols $q \equiv \Delta y/\Delta x$ (q for quotient) and $v \equiv \Delta x$ (v for variation), then we have

$$\frac{dy}{dx} = \lim_{\Delta x \to 0} \frac{\Delta y}{\Delta x} = \lim_{v \to 0} q$$

In view of the fact that the derivative concept relies heavily on the notion of limit, it is imperative that we get a clear idea about that notion.

left-side limit and right-side limit   The concept of limit is concerned with the question: What value does one variable (say, q) approach as another variable (say, v) approaches a specific value (say, zero)? In order for this question to make sense, q must of course be a function of v; say, $q = g(v)$. Our immediate interest is in finding the limit of q as $v \to 0$, but we may just as easily explore the more general case of $v \to N$, where N is any finite real number. Then, $\lim_{v \to 0} q$ will be merely a special case of $\lim_{v \to N} q$ where $N = 0$. In the course of the discussion, we shall actually also consider the limit of q as $v \to +\infty$ (plus infinity) or as $v \to -\infty$ (minus infinity).

When we say $v \to N$, the variable v can approach the number N either from values greater than N, or from values less than N. If, as $v \to N$ from the left side (from values less than N), q approaches a finite number L, then we call L the *left-side limit* of q. On the other hand, if L is the number that q tends to as $v \to N$ from the right side (from values greater than N), then we call L the *right-side limit* of q. The left- and right-side limits may or may not be equal.

The left-side limit of q is symbolized by $\lim_{v \to N^-} q$ (minus sign signifies from values less than N), and the right-side limit is written as $\lim_{v \to N^+} q$. When—and only when—the two limits have a common finite value (say, L), we consider the limit of q to exist and write it as $\lim_{v \to N} q = L$. Note that L must be a *finite* number. If we have the situation of $\lim_{v \to N} q = \infty$ (or $-\infty$), we shall consider q to possess *no* limit, because $\lim_{v \to N} q = \infty$ means that $q \to \infty$ as $v \to N$, and if q will assume *ever-increasing* values as v tends to N, it would be contradictory to say that q has a limit. As a convenient way of expressing the fact that $q \to \infty$ as $v \to N$, however, people do write $\lim_{v \to N} q = \infty$ and speak of q as having an "infinite limit."

In certain cases, only the limit of one side needs to be considered. In taking the limit of q as $v \to +\infty$, for instance, only the left-side limit of q is relevant, because v can approach $+\infty$ only from the left. Similarly, for the case of $v \to -\infty$, only the right-side limit is relevant. Whether the limit of q exists in these cases will depend only on whether q approaches a finite value as $v \to +\infty$, or as $v \to -\infty$.

It is important to realize that the symbol ∞ (infinity) is not a number, and therefore it cannot be subjected to the usual algebraic operations. We cannot have $3 + \infty$ or $1/\infty$; nor can we write $q = \infty$, which is not the same as $q \to \infty$. However, it is acceptable to express the *limit* of q as "$=$" (as against $\to$) ∞, for this merely indicates that $q \to \infty$.

graphical illustrations   Let us illustrate, in Fig. 6.2, several possible situations regarding the limit of a function $q = g(v)$.

Diagram *a* shows a smooth curve. As the variable v tends to the value N from *either* side on the horizontal axis, the variable q will tend to the value L. In this case, the left-side limit is identical with the right-side limit; therefore we can write $\lim_{v \to N} q = L$.

The curve drawn in diagram *b* is not smooth; it has a sharp turning point directly above the point N. Nevertheless, as v tends to N from either side, q again tends to an identical value L. The limit of q again exists and is equal to L.

Diagram *c* shows what is known as a *step function*.[1] In this case, as v tends

---

[1] This name is easily explained by the shape of the curve. But step functions can be expressed algebraically, too. The one illustrated in Fig. 6.2c can be expressed by the equation

$$q = \begin{cases} L_1 & \text{(for } 0 \le v < N) \\ L_2 & \text{(for } N \le v) \end{cases}$$

Note that, in each subset of its domain described above, the function appears as a distinct constant function, which constitutes a "step" in the graph.

In economics, step functions can be used, for instance, to show the various prices charged for different quantities purchased (the curve shown in Fig. 6.2c pictures *quantity discount*) or the various tax rates applicable to different income brackets.

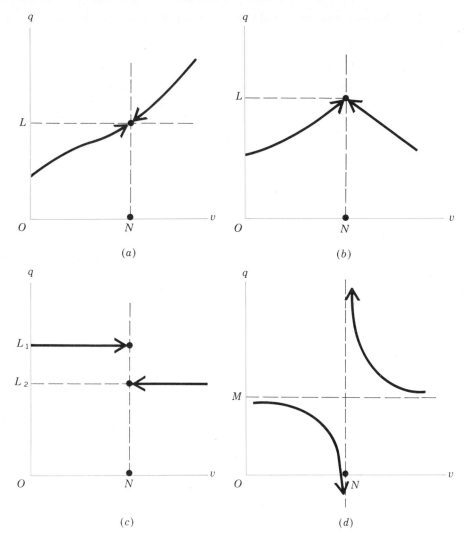

FIGURE 6.2

to N, the left-side limit of q is L_1, but the right-side limit is L_2, a different number. Hence, q does not have a limit as $v \to N$.

Lastly, in diagram d, as v tends to N, the left-side limit of q is $-\infty$, whereas the right-side limit is $+\infty$, because the two parts of the (hyperbolic) curve will fall and rise indefinitely while approaching the broken vertical line as an asymptote. Again, $\lim_{v \to N} q$ does not exist. On the other hand, if we are considering a different sort of limit in diagram d, namely, $\lim_{v \to +\infty} q$, then only the left-side limit has relevance, and we do find that limit to exist: $\lim\limits_{v \to +\infty} q = M$. Analogously, the reader can verify that $\lim\limits_{v \to -\infty} q = M$ as well.

It is also possible to apply the concepts of left-side and right-side limits to the discussion of the marginal cost in Fig. 6.1. In that context, the variables q and v will refer, respectively, to the quotient $\Delta C/\Delta Q$ and to the magnitude of ΔQ, with all changes being measured from point A on the curve. In other words, q will refer to the slope of such lines as AB, AD, and KG, whereas v will refer to the length of such lines as $Q_0 Q_2$ ($=$ line AE) and $Q_0 Q_1$ ($=$ line AF). We have already seen that, as v approaches zero from a positive value, q will approach a value equal to the slope of line KG. Similarly, we can establish that, if ΔQ approaches zero from a negative value (i.e., as the *decrease* in output becomes less and less), the quotient $\Delta C/\Delta Q$, as measured by the slope of such lines as RA (not drawn), will also approach a value equal to the slope of line KG. Indeed, the situation here is very much akin to that illustrated in Fig. 6.2a. Thus the slope of KG in Fig. 6.1 (the counterpart of L in Fig. 6.2) is indeed the limit of the quotient q as v tends to zero, and as such it gives us the marginal cost at the output level $Q = Q_0$.

evaluation of a limit   Let us now illustrate the algebraic evaluation of a limit of a given function $q = g(v)$.

Example 1   Given $q = 2 + v^2$, find $\lim\limits_{v \to 0} q$. To take the left-side limit, we substitute the series of negative values -1, $-\frac{1}{10}$, $-\frac{1}{100}$, . . . (in that order) for v and find that $(2 + v^2)$ will decrease steadily and approach 2 (because v^2 will gradually approach 0). Next, for the right-side limit, we substitute the series of positive values 1, $\frac{1}{10}$, $\frac{1}{100}$, . . . (in that order) for v and find the same limit as before. Inasmuch as the two limits are identical, we consider the limit of q to exist and write $\lim\limits_{v \to 0} q = 2$.

It is tempting to regard the answer just obtained as the outcome of setting $v = 0$ in the equation $q = 2 + v^2$, but this temptation should in general be resisted. In evaluating $\lim\limits_{v \to N} q$, we only let v *tend to* N but, as a rule, do not let $v = N$. Indeed, we can quite legitimately speak of the limit of q as $v \to N$, even if N is *not* in the domain of the function $q = g(v)$. In this latter case, if we try to set $v = N$, q will clearly be undefined.

Example 2   Given $q = (1 - v^2)/(1 - v)$, find $\lim\limits_{v \to 1} q$. Here, $N = 1$ is not in the domain of the function, and we cannot set $v = 1$ because that would involve division by zero. Moreover, even the limit-evaluation procedure of letting

$v \to 1$, as used in Example 1, will cause difficulty, for the denominator $(1 - v)$ will approach zero when $v \to 1$, and we will still have no way of performing the division in the limit.

One way out of this difficulty is to try to transform the given ratio to a form in which v will not appear in the denominator. Since $v \to 1$ implies that $v \neq 1$, so that $(1 - v)$ is nonzero, it is legitimate to divide the expression $(1 - v^2)$ by $(1 - v)$, and write[1]

$$q = \frac{1 - v^2}{1 - v} = 1 + v \qquad (v \neq 1)$$

In this new expression for q, there is no longer a denominator with v in it. Since $(1 + v) \to 2$ as $v \to 1$ from *either* side, we may conclude that $\lim_{v \to 1} q = 2$.

Example 3   Given $q = (2v + 5)/(v + 1)$, find $\lim_{v \to +\infty} q$. The variable v again appears in *both* the numerator and the denominator. If we let $v \to +\infty$ in both, the result will be a ratio between two infinitely large numbers, which does not have a clear meaning. To get out of the difficulty, we try this time to transform the given ratio to a form in which the variable v will not appear in the numerator.[2] This, again, can be accomplished by dividing out the given ratio. Since $(2v + 5)$ is not evenly divisible by $(v + 1)$, however, the result will contain a remainder term as follows:

$$q = \frac{2v + 5}{v + 1} = 2 + \frac{3}{v + 1}$$

But, at any rate, this new expression for q no longer has a numerator with v in it. Noting that the remainder $3/(v + 1) \to 0$ as $v \to +\infty$, we can then conclude that $\lim_{v \to +\infty} q = 2$.

There also exist several useful theorems on the evaluation of limits. These will be discussed in Sec. 6.6.

[1] The division can be performed, as in the case of numbers, in the following manner:

$$
\begin{array}{r}
1 + v \\
1 - v \overline{\smash{\big)}\; 1 \qquad\quad - v^2} \\
\underline{1 - v} \\
v - v^2 \\
\underline{v - v^2}
\end{array}
$$

Alternatively, we may resort to factoring as follows:

$$\frac{1 - v^2}{1 - v} = \frac{(1 + v)(1 - v)}{1 - v} = 1 + v \qquad (v \neq 1)$$

[2] Note that, unlike the $v \to 0$ case, where we want to take v out of the *denominator* in order to avoid division by zero, the $v \to \infty$ case is better served by taking v out of the *numerator*. As $v \to \infty$, an expression containing v in the numerator will become infinite. but an expression with v in the denominator will, more conveniently for us, approach zero and quietly vanish from the scene.

formal view of the limit concept The above discussion should have conveyed some general ideas about the concept of limit. Let us now give it a more precise definition. Since such a definition will make use of the concept of *neighborhood* of a point on a line (in particular, a specific number as a point on the line of real numbers), we shall first explain the latter term.

For a given number L, there can always be found a number $(L - a_1) < L$ and another number $(L + a_2) > L$, where a_1 and a_2 are some arbitrary positive numbers. The set of all numbers falling between $(L - a_1)$ and $(L + a_2)$ is called the *interval* between those two numbers. If the numbers $(L - a_1)$ and $(L + a_2)$ are included in the set, the set is a *closed interval*; if they are excluded, the set is an *open interval*. A closed interval between $(L - a_1)$ and $(L + a_2)$ is denoted by the bracketed expression

$$[L - a_1, L + a_2] \equiv \{q \mid L - a_1 \leq q \leq L + a_2\}$$

and the corresponding *open* interval is denoted with parentheses:

(6.4) $\qquad (L - a_1, L + a_2) \equiv \{q \mid L - a_1 < q < L + a_2\}$

Thus, [ ] relate to the weak inequality sign $\leq$, whereas ( ) relate to the strict inequality sign $<$. But in both types of intervals, the smaller number $(L - a_1)$ is always listed first. Later on, we shall also have occasion to refer to *half-open and half-closed* intervals such as (3,5] and [6,∞), which have the following meanings:

$$(3,5] \equiv \{x \mid 3 < x \leq 5\} \qquad [6,\infty) \equiv \{x \mid 6 \leq x < \infty\}$$

Now we may define a *neighborhood* of L to be an open interval as defined in (6.4), which is an interval "covering" the number L.† Depending on the magnitudes of the arbitrary numbers a_1 and a_2, it is possible to construct various neighborhoods for the given number L. Using the concept of neighborhood, the limit of a function may then be defined as follows:

> As v approaches a number N, the limit of $q = g(v)$ is the number L, if, for every neighborhood of L that can be chosen, *however small*, there can be found a corresponding neighborhood of N (excluding the point $v = N$) in the domain of the function such that, for every value of v in that N-neighborhood, its image q lies in the chosen L-neighborhood.

This statement can be clarified with the help of Fig. 6.3, which resembles Fig. 6.2*a*. From what was learned about the latter figure, we know that $\lim_{v \to N} q = L$ in Fig. 6.3. Let us show that L does indeed fulfill the new definition

† The identification of an open interval as the neighborhood of a point is valid only when we are considering a point on a line (one-dimensional space). In the case of a point in a plane (two-dimensional space), its neighborhood must be thought of as an area, say, a circular area around the point.

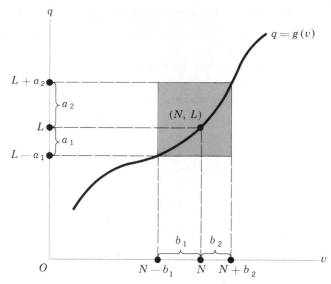

$q = g(v)$

(N, L)

FIGURE 6.3

of a limit. As the first step, select an arbitrary small neighborhood of L, say, $(L - a_1, L + a_2)$. (This should have been made even smaller, but we are keeping it relatively large to facilitate exposition.) Now construct a neighborhood of N, say, $(N - b_1, N + b_2)$, such that the two neighborhoods (when extended into quadrant I) will together define a rectangle (shaded in diagram) with two of its corners lying on the given curve. It can then be verified that, for every value of v in this neighborhood of N (not counting $v = N$), the corresponding value of $q = g(v)$ lies in the chosen neighborhood of L. In fact, no matter how *small* an L-neighborhood we choose, a (correspondingly small) N-neighborhood can be found with the property just cited. Thus L fulfills the definition of a limit, as was to be demonstrated.

We can also apply the above definition to the step function of Fig. 6.2c in order to show that neither L_1 nor L_2 qualifies as $\lim_{v \to N} q$. If we choose a very small neighborhood of L_1—say, just a hair's width on each side of L_1—then, no matter what neighborhood we pick for N, the rectangle associated with the two neighborhoods cannot possibly enclose the lower step of the function. Consequently, for any value of $v > N$, the corresponding value of q (located on the lower step) will not be in the neighborhood of L_1, and thus L_1 fails the test for a limit. By similar reasoning, L_2 must also be dismissed as a candidate for $\lim_{v \to N} q$. In fact, in this case no limit exists for q as $v \to N$.

The fulfillment of the definition can also be checked algebraically rather than by graph. For instance, consider again the function

$$(6.5) \qquad q = \frac{1 - v^2}{1 - v} = 1 + v \qquad (v \neq 1)$$

It has been found in Example 2 that $\lim_{v \to 1} q = 2$; thus, here we have $N = 1$ and $L = 2$. To verify that $L = 2$ is indeed the limit of q, we must demonstrate that, for every chosen neighborhood of L, $(2 - a_1, 2 + a_2)$, there exists a neighborhood of N, $(1 - b_1, 1 + b_2)$, such that, whenever v is in this neighborhood of N, q must be in the chosen neighborhood of L. This means essentially that, for given values of a_1 and a_2, however small, two numbers b_1 and b_2 must be found such that, whenever the inequality

$$(6.6) \qquad 1 - b_1 < v < 1 + b_2 \qquad (v \neq 1)$$

is satisfied, another inequality of the form

$$(6.7) \qquad 2 - a_1 < q < 2 + a_2$$

must also be satisfied. To find such a pair of numbers b_1 and b_2, let us first rewrite (6.7) by substituting (6.5):

$$(6.7') \qquad 2 - a_1 < 1 + v < 2 + a_2$$

This, in turn, can be transformed into the inequality

$$(6.7'') \qquad 1 - a_1 < v < 1 + a_2$$

A comparison of (6.7'')—a variant of (6.7)—with (6.6) suggests that if we choose the two numbers b_1 and b_2 to be $b_1 = a_1$ and $b_2 = a_2$, then the two inequalities (6.6) and (6.7) will always be satisfied simultaneously. Thus the neighborhood of N, $(1 - b_1, 1 + b_2)$, as required in the definition of a limit, can indeed be found for the case of $L = 2$, and this establishes $L = 2$ as the limit.

Let us now utilize the definition of a limit in the opposite way, to show that another value (say, 3) cannot qualify as $\lim_{v \to 1} q$ for the function in (6.5). If 3 were that limit, it would have to be true that, for every chosen neighborhood of 3, $(3 - a_1, 3 + a_2)$, there exists a neighborhood of 1, $(1 - b_1, 1 + b_2)$, such that, whenever v is in the latter neighborhood, q must be in the former neighborhood. That is, whenever the inequality

$$1 - b_1 < v < 1 + b_2$$

is satisfied, another inequality in the form

$$3 - a_1 < 1 + v < 3 + a_2$$

or $\qquad 2 - a_1 < v < 2 + a_2$

must also be satisfied. The *only* way to achieve this result is to choose $b_1 = a_1 - 1$ and $b_2 = a_2 + 1$. This would imply that the neighborhood of 1 is to be the open interval $(2 - a_1, 2 + a_2)$. According to the definition of a limit, however, a_1 and a_2 can be made arbitrarily small, say, $a_1 = a_2 = 0.1$. In that case, the last-mentioned interval will turn out to be (1.9,2.1) which lies entirely to the right of the point $v = 1$ on the horizontal axis and, hence, does not even qualify as a neighborhood of 1. Thus the definition of a limit cannot be fulfilled by the number 3. A similar procedure can be employed to show that *any* number other than 2 will contradict the definition of a limit in the present case.

In general, if one number satisfies the definition of a limit of q as $v \to N$, then no other number can. If a limit exists, it will be unique.

EXERCISE 6.4

1   Given the function $q = (v^2 + v - 56)/(v - 7)$, find the left-side limit and the right-side limit of q as v approaches 7. Can we conclude from these answers that q has a limit as v approaches 7?

2   Given $q = [(v + 2)^2 - 4]/v$, find:

(a) $\lim\limits_{v \to 0} q$ (b) $\lim\limits_{v \to 2} q$ (c) $\lim\limits_{v \to a} q$

3   Given $q = 5 - 1/v$, find:

(a) $\lim\limits_{v \to +\infty} q$ (b) $\lim\limits_{v \to -\infty} q$

4   Use Fig. 6.3 to show that we *cannot* consider the number $(L + a_2)$ as the limit of q as v tends to N.

6.5   Digression on Inequalities and Absolute Values

We have encountered inequality signs many times before. In the discussion of the last section, we also applied mathematical operations to inequalities. In transforming (6.7′) into (6.7″), for example, we subtracted 1 from each side of the inequality. What rules of operations apply to inequalities (as opposed to equations)?

rules of inequalities   To begin with, let us state an important property of inequalities: Inequalities are *transitive*. This means that, if $a > b$ and if $b > c$, then $a > c$. Since equalities (equations) are also transitive, the transitivity property should apply to "weak" inequalities ($\geq$ or $\leq$) as well as to "strict" ones ($>$ or $<$). Thus we have

$$a > b, b > c \;\Rightarrow\; a > c$$
$$a \geq b, b \geq c \;\Rightarrow\; a \geq c$$

This property is what makes possible the writing of a *continued inequality*, such as $3 < a < b < 8$ or $7 \leq x \leq 24$. (In writing a continued inequality, the inequality signs are as a rule arranged in the same direction, usually with the smallest number on the left.)

The most important rules of inequalities are those governing the addition (subtraction) of a number to (from) an inequality, the multiplication or division of an inequality by a number, and the squaring of an inequality. Specifically, these rules are:

RULE I   (*Addition and Subtraction*) $a > b \;\Rightarrow\; a \pm k > b \pm k$
An inequality will continue to hold if an equal quantity is added to or subtracted from each side. This rule may be generalized thus: If $a > b > c$, then $a \pm k > b \pm k > c \pm k$.

RULE II   (*Multiplication and Division*)

$$a > b \;\Rightarrow\; \begin{cases} ka > kb & (k > 0) \\ ka < kb & (k < 0) \end{cases}$$

The multiplication of both sides by a *positive* number preserves the inequality, but a *negative* multiplier will cause the *sense* (or *direction*) of the inequality to be reversed.

Example 1   Since $6 > 5$, multiplication by 3 will yield $3(6) > 3(5)$, or $18 > 15$; but multiplication by -3 will result in $(-3)6 < (-3)5$, or $-18 < -15$.

Division of an inequality by a number n is equivalent to multiplication by the number $1/n$; therefore the rule on division is subsumed under the rule on multiplication.

RULE III   (*Squaring*) $a > b, (b \geq 0) \;\Rightarrow\; a^2 > b^2$
If its two sides are both nonnegative, then the inequality will continue to hold when both sides are squared.

Example 2   Since $4 > 3$ and since both sides are positive, we have $4^2 > 3^2$, or $16 > 9$. Similarly, since $2 > 0$, it follows that $2^2 > 0^2$, or $4 > 0$.

The above three rules have been stated in terms of strict inequalities, but their validity is unaffected if the $>$ signs are replaced by $\geq$ signs.

absolute values and inequalities   When the domain of a variable x is an open interval (a,b), the domain may be denoted by the set $\{x \mid a < x < b\}$ or, more simply, by the inequality $a < x < b$. Similarly, if it is a closed interval $[a,b]$, it may be expressed by the weak inequality $a \leq x \leq b$. In the special case of an interval of the form $(-a,a)$—say, $(-10,10)$—it may be represented either by the inequality $-10 < x < 10$ or, alternatively, by the inequality

$$|x| < 10$$

where the symbol $|x|$ denotes the *absolute value* (or *numerical value*) of x.

For any real number n, the absolute value of n is defined as follows:[1]

$$(6.8) \qquad |n| \equiv \begin{cases} n & \text{(if } n > 0) \\ -n & \text{(if } n < 0) \\ 0 & \text{(if } n = 0) \end{cases}$$

Note that, if $n = 15$, then $|15| = 15$; but if $n = -15$, we find

$$|-15| = -(-15) = 15$$

also. In effect, therefore, the absolute value of any real number is simply its numerical value after the sign is removed. For this reason, we always have $|n| = |-n|$. The absolute value of n is also called the *modulus* of n.

Given the expression $|x| = 10$, we may conclude from (6.8) that x must be either 10 or -10. By the same token, the expression $|x| < 10$ means that (1) if $x > 0$, then $x \equiv |x| < 10$, so that x must be less than 10; but also (2) if $x < 0$, then according to (6.8) we have $-x \equiv |x| < 10$, or $x > -10$, so that x must be greater than -10. Hence, by combining the two parts of this result, we see that x must lie within the open interval $(-10,10)$. In general, we can write

$$(6.9) \qquad |x| < n \quad \Leftrightarrow \quad -n < x < n \qquad (n > 0)$$

which can also be extended to weak inequalities as follows:

$$(6.10) \qquad |x| \leq n \quad \Leftrightarrow \quad -n \leq x \leq n \qquad (n \geq 0)$$

Being themselves numbers, the absolute values of two numbers m and n can be added, subtracted, multiplied, and divided. The following properties characterize absolute values:

$$|m| + |n| \geq |m + n|$$

$$|m| \cdot |n| = |m \cdot n|$$

$$\frac{|m|}{|n|} = \left|\frac{m}{n}\right|$$

[1] The absolute-value notation is similar to that of a first-order determinant, but these two concepts are entirely different. The definition of a first-order determinant is $|a_{ij}| \equiv a_{ij}$, regardless of the sign of a_{ij}. In the definition of the absolute value $|n|$, the sign of n will make a difference. The context of the discussion would normally make it clear whether an absolute value or a first-order determinant is under consideration.

The first of these, interestingly, involves an inequality rather than an equation. The reason for this is easily seen: Whereas the left-hand expression $|m| + |n|$ is definitely a *sum* of two numerical values (both taken as positive), the expression $|m + n|$ is the numerical value of *either* a sum (if m and n are, say, both positive) *or* a difference (if m and n have opposite signs). Thus the left side may exceed the right side.

Example 3   If $m = 5$ and $n = 3$, then $|m| + |n| = |m + n| = 8$. But if $m = 5$ and $n = -3$, then $|m| + |n| = 5 + 3 = 8$, whereas

$$|m + n| = |5 - 3| = 2$$

a smaller number.

In the other two properties, on the other hand, it makes no difference whether m and n have identical or opposite signs, since, in taking the absolute value of the product or quotient on the right-hand side, the sign of the latter term will be removed in any case.

Example 4   If $m = 7$ and $n = 8$, then $|m| \cdot |n| = |m \cdot n| = 7(8) = 56$. But even if $m = -7$ and $n = 8$ (opposite signs), we still get the same result from

$$|m| \cdot |n| = |-7| \cdot |8| = 7(8) = 56$$

and $$|m \cdot n| = |-7(8)| = 7(8) = 56$$

solution of an inequality   Like an equation, an inequality containing a variable (say, x) may have a solution; the solution, if it exists, is a set of values of x for which the inequality holds. Such a solution will itself usually be in the form of an inequality.

Example 5   Find the solution of the inequality

$$3x - 3 > x + 1$$

As in solving an equation, the variable terms should first be collected on one side of the inequality. By adding $(3 - x)$ to both sides, we obtain

$$3x - 3 + 3 - x > x + 1 + 3 - x$$

or $$2x > 4$$

Multiplying both sides by $\frac{1}{2}$ (which does not reverse the sense of the inequality, because $\frac{1}{2} > 0$) will then yield the solution

$$x > 2$$

which is itself an inequality. This solution is not a single number, but a set of numbers. Therefore we may also express the solution as the set $\{x \mid x > 2\}$ or as the open interval $(2, \infty)$.

Example 6   Solve the inequality $|1 - x| \leq 3$. First, let us get rid of the absolute-value notation by utilizing (6.10). The given inequality is equivalent to the statement that

$$-3 \leq 1 - x \leq 3$$

or, after subtracting 1 from each side,

$$-4 \leq -x \leq 2$$

The multiplication of each side by (-1) then yields

$$4 \geq x \geq -2$$

where the sense of inequality has been duly reversed. Writing the smaller number first, we may express the solution in the form of the inequality

$$-2 \leq x \leq 4$$

or in the form of the set $\{x \mid -2 \leq x \leq 4\}$ or the closed interval $[-2,4]$.

Sometimes, a problem may call for the satisfaction of several inequalities in several variables simultaneously; then we must solve a system of simultaneous inequalities. This problem arises, for example, in mathematical programming and game theory, which will be discussed in the final part of the book.

EXERCISE 6.5

1   Solve the following inequalities:

    (a) $3x - 1 < 7x + 2$ (c) $5x + 1 < x + 5$

    (b) $2x + 5 < x - 1$

2   If $9x - 3 < 0$ and $9x > 0$, express these in a continued inequality and find its solution.

3   Solve the following:

    (a) $|x + 1| < 6$ (b) $|1 - 3x| < 2$ (c) $|2x + 3| \leq 5$

6.6   Limit Theorems

Our interest in rates of change led us to the consideration of the concept of derivative, which, being in the nature of the limit of a difference quotient, in turn prompted us to study questions of the existence and evaluation of a limit. The basic process of limit evaluation, as illustrated in Sec. 6.4, involves letting the variable v approach a particular number (say, N) and observing the value which q approaches. When actually evaluating the limit of a function, however, we may draw upon certain established limit theorems, which can materially simplify the task, especially for complicated functions.

theorems involving a single function   When a single function $q = g(v)$ is involved, the following theorems are applicable:

THEOREM I   If $q = av + b$, then $\lim_{v \to N} q = aN + b$ (a and b are constants).

Example 1   Given $q = 5v + 7$, we have $\lim_{v \to 2} q = 5(2) + 7 = 17$. Similarly, $\lim_{v \to 0} q = 5(0) + 7 = 7$.

THEOREM II   If $q = g(v) = b$, then $\lim_{v \to N} q = b$.

This theorem, which says that the limit of a constant function is the constant in that function, is merely a special case of Theorem I, with $a = 0$. (The reader has already encountered an example of this case in Exercise 6.2-3.)

THEOREM III   If $q = v$, then $\lim_{v \to N} q = N$.

$\qquad\qquad$ If $q = v^k$, then $\lim_{v \to N} q = N^k$.

Example 2   Given $q = v^3$, we have $\lim_{v \to 2} q = (2)^3 = 8$.

theorems involving two functions   If we have two functions of the same independent variable v, $q_1 = g(v)$ and $q_2 = h(v)$, and if *both* functions possess limits as follows:

$$\lim_{v \to N} q_1 = L_1 \qquad \lim_{v \to N} q_2 = L_2$$

where L_1 and L_2 are two *finite* numbers, then the following theorems are applicable.

THEOREM IV   (*Sum-Difference Limit Theorem*)

$$\lim_{v \to N} (q_1 \pm q_2) = L_1 \pm L_2$$

The limit of a sum (difference) of two functions is the sum (difference) of their respective limits.

In particular, we note that

$$\lim_{v \to N} 2q_1 = \lim_{v \to N} (q_1 + q_1) = L_1 + L_1 = 2L_1$$

which is in line with Theorem I.

THEOREM V   (Product Limit Theorem)

$$\lim_{v \to N} (q_1 q_2) = L_1 L_2$$

The limit of a product of two functions is the product of their limits.

Applied to the square of a function, this gives

$$\lim_{v \to N} (q_1 q_1) = L_1 L_1 = L_1{}^2$$

which is in line with Theorem III.

THEOREM VI   (Quotient Limit Theorem)

$$\lim_{v \to N} \frac{q_1}{q_2} = \frac{L_1}{L_2} \qquad (L_2 \neq 0)$$

The limit of a quotient of two functions is the quotient of their limits. Naturally, the limit L_2 is restricted to be nonzero; otherwise the quotient is undefined.

Example 3   Find $\lim_{v \to 0} (1 + v)/(2 + v)$. Since we have here $\lim_{v \to 0} (1 + v) = 1$ and $\lim (2 + v) = 2$, the desired limit is $\frac{1}{2}$.

The reader is reminded that L_1 and L_2 represent finite numbers; otherwise these theorems do not apply. In the case of Theorem VI, furthermore, L_2 must be nonzero as well. If these restrictions are not satisfied, then we must fall back on the method of limit evaluation illustrated in Examples 2 and 3 of Sec. 6.4, which relate to the cases, respectively, of L_2 being zero and of L_2 being infinite.

limit of a polynomial function   With the above limit theorems at our disposal, we can easily evaluate the limit of any polynomial function

$$(6.11) \qquad q = g(v) = a_0 + a_1 v + a_2 v^2 + \cdots + a_n v^n$$

as v tends to the number N. Since the limits of the separate terms are, respectively,

$$\lim_{v \to N} a_0 = a_0 \qquad \lim_{v \to N} a_1 v = a_1 N \qquad \lim_{v \to N} a_2 v^2 = a_2 N^2 \qquad \text{(etc.)}$$

the limit of the polynomial function is (by the sum limit theorem)

$$(6.12) \qquad \lim_{v \to N} q = a_0 + a_1 N + a_2 N^2 + \cdots + a_n N^n$$

This limit is also, we note, actually equal to $g(N)$, that is, equal to the value of the function in (6.11) when $v = N$. This particular result will prove important in discussing the concept of *continuity* of the polynomial function.

EXERCISE 6.6

1   Find the limits of the function $q = 3 - 9v + v^2$:

     (a)   As $v \to 0$ (b)   As $v \to 3$ (c)   As $v \to -1$

2   Find the limits of $q = (v + 1)(v - 3)$:

     (a)   As $v \to -1$ (b)   As $v \to 0$ (c)   As $v \to 4$

3   Find the limits of $q = \dfrac{3v + 5}{v + 2}$:

     (a)   As $v \to 0$ (b)   As $v \to 5$ (c)   As $v \to -1$

6.7   Continuity and Differentiability of a Function

The preceding discussion of the concept of limit and its evaluation can now be used to define the continuity and differentiability of a function. These notions bear directly on the derivative of the function, which is what interests us.

continuity of a function   When a function $q = g(v)$ possesses a limit as v tends to the point N in the domain, and when this limit is also equal to $g(N)$— that is, equal to the value of the function at $v = N$—the function is said to be *continuous* at N. As stated above, the term *continuity* involves no less than three requirements: (1) The point N must be in the domain of the function. (2) The function must have a limit as $v \to N$. (3) That limit must be equal in value to $g(N)$.

     It is important to note that while, in discussing the limit of the curve in

Fig. 6.3, the point (N,L) was excluded from consideration, we are no longer excluding it in the present context. Rather, as the third requirement specifically states, the point (N,L) must be on the graph of the function before the function can be considered as continuous at the point N.

Let us check whether the functions shown in Fig. 6.2 are continuous. In diagram a, all three requirements are met at the point N. The point N is in the domain; q has the limit L as $v \to N$; and the limit L happens also to be the value of the function at N. Thus, the function represented by that curve is continuous at N. The same is true of the function depicted in Fig. 6.2b, since L is the limit of the function as v approaches the value N in the domain, and since L is also the value of the function at N. This last graphic example should suffice to establish that the continuity of a function at point N does *not* necessarily imply that the graph of the function is "smooth" at $v = N$, for the point (N,L) in diagram b is actually a "sharp" point and yet the function is continuous at that value of v.

When a function $q = g(v)$ is continuous at all points in the interval (a,b), it is said to be continuous in (or on) that interval. If the function is continuous at all points in a subset S of the domain (where the subset S may be the union of several disjoint intervals), it is said to be continuous in S. And, finally, if the function is continuous at all points in its domain, we say that it is continuous in its domain. Even in this latter case, however, the graph of the function may nevertheless show a discontinuity (a gap) at some value of v, say, at $v = 5$, if that value of v is *not* in its domain.

Again referring to Fig. 6.2, we see that in diagram c the function is *discontinuous* at N because a limit does not exist at that point, in violation of the second requirement of continuity. Nevertheless, the function does fulfill the requirements of continuity in the interval $(0,N)$ of the domain, as well as in the interval $[N,\infty)$. Diagram d obviously is also discontinuous at $v = N$. This time, discontinuity emanates from the fact that N is excluded from the domain, in violation of the first requirement of continuity.

On the basis of the graphs in Fig. 6.2, it appears that sharp points are consistent with continuity, as in diagram b, but that gaps are taboo, as in diagrams c and d. This is indeed the case. Roughly speaking, therefore, a function that is continuous in a particular interval is one whose graph can be drawn for the said interval without lifting the pencil or pen from the paper—a feat which is possible even if there are sharp points, but which is impossible when gaps occur.

polynomial and rational functions   Let us now consider the continuity of certain frequently encountered functions. For any polynomial function, such as $q = g(v)$ in (6.11), we have found from (6.12) that $\lim\limits_{v \to N} q$ exists and is equal to the value of the function at N. Since N is a point (any point) in the domain of the function, we can conclude that any polynomial function is continuous in its domain. This is a very useful piece of information, because polynomial functions will be encountered very often.

What about rational functions? Regarding continuity, there exists an interesting theorem (the continuity theorem) that states: The sum, difference, product, and quotient of any finite number of functions that are continuous in the domain are, respectively, also continuous in the domain. As a result, any rational function (a quotient of two polynomial functions) must also be continuous in its domain.

Example 1   The rational function

$$q = g(v) = \frac{4v^2}{v^2 + 1}$$

is defined for all finite real numbers; thus its domain consists of the interval $(-\infty,\infty)$. For any number N in the domain, the limit of q is (by the quotient limit theorem)

$$\lim_{v \to N} q = \frac{\lim\limits_{v \to N} (4v^2)}{\lim\limits_{v \to N} (v^2 + 1)} = \frac{4N^2}{N^2 + 1}$$

which is equal to $g(N)$. Thus the three requirements of continuity are all met at N. Moreover, we note that N can represent any point in the domain of this function; consequently, this function is continuous in its domain.

Example 2   The rational function

$$q = \frac{v^3 + v^2 - 4v - 4}{v^2 - 4}$$

is not defined at $v = 2$ and at $v = -2$. Since those two values of v are not in the domain, the function is discontinuous at $v = -2$ and $v = 2$, despite the fact that a limit of q exists as $v \to -2$ or 2. Graphically this function will display a gap at each of these two values of v. But for other values of v (those which *are* in the domain), this function is continuous.

differentiability of a function   The previous discussion has provided us with the tools for ascertaining whether any function $q = g(v)$ has a limit as $v \to 0$. If we have a primitive function $y = f(x)$ in mind, and if q represents the difference quotient $\Delta y / \Delta x$, and v, the magnitude of Δx, then the fact that $\lim\limits_{v \to 0} q$ exists (at, say, $x = x_0$) will mean that the derivative dy/dx exists (at $x = x_0$). In such an event, the function $y = f(x)$ is said to be *differentiable* (at $x = x_0$); this is because the process of obtaining the derivative dy/dx is called *differentiation* (or *derivation*).

There is an important general test for differentiability: The function $y = f(x)$ is differentiable at the point $x = x_0$ in the domain *only if* the function is continuous at $x = x_0$. In other words, the continuity of a function is a *necessary* condition for differentiability of that function (though, as we shall see later, this condition is not *sufficient*).

To prove this, we must demonstrate that continuity of $y = f(x)$ follows from differentiability. How do we symbolically express the differentiability and the continuity of $y = f(x)$ at a point $x = x_0$ in the domain? Differentiability means that, for the given *initial value* $x = x_0$, the difference quotient

$$\frac{\Delta y}{\Delta x} = \frac{f(x_0 + \Delta x) - f(x_0)}{\Delta x}$$

has a limit as $\Delta x \to 0$. The notation $(x_0 + \Delta x)$, though ideal for conveying the idea of a change, is cumbersome to use. We can now switch to a simpler way of expressing $\Delta y / \Delta x$ thus: (1) by replacing x_0 with the symbol N as the initial value, and (2) by replacing $(x_0 + \Delta x)$ with the symbol x—this latter is justifiable because the postchange value of x can be any number (depending on the magnitude of change) and, hence, is a variable denotable by x. The equivalence of the two notation systems is demonstrated in Fig. 6.4, where the old notations appear (in brackets) along with the new. Note that, under the new system, the expression $\Delta x \to 0$ will become $x \to N$, which is perfectly analogous to the expression $v \to N$ used before in connection with the function $q = g(v)$. Thus, the above difference quotient can be equivalently expressed as

$$\frac{\Delta y}{\Delta x} = \frac{f(x) - f(N)}{x - N}$$

and the differentiability of $f(x)$ at the point $x = N$ in the domain is therefore to be represented by the statement that the derivative at $x = N$ exists, that is,

$$(6.13) \qquad f'(N) \equiv \lim_{\Delta x \to 0} \frac{\Delta y}{\Delta x} \equiv \lim_{x \to N} \frac{f(x) - f(N)}{x - N}$$

exists.

Continuity, on the other hand, means that: (1) $x = N$ must be in the domain of the function $y = f(x)$, (2) y must have a limit as $x \to N$, and (3) the

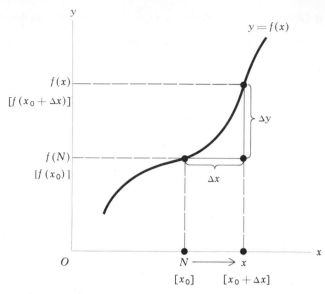

FIGURE 6.4

said limit of y must be equal to $f(N)$. Since we have assumed $x = N$ to be in the domain to begin with, continuity can be symbolically expressed by

$$(6.14) \qquad \lim_{x \to N} f(x) = f(N)$$

What we want to show is, therefore, that the continuity condition (6.14) follows from the differentiability condition (6.13). First, since the notation $x \to N$ implies that $x \neq N$, so that $x - N$ is a nonzero number, it is permissible to write the following identity:

$$(6.15) \qquad f(x) - f(N) \equiv \frac{f(x) - f(N)}{x - N} (x - N)$$

Taking the limit of each side of (6.15) as $x \to N$ yields the following results:

$$\text{Left side} = \lim_{x \to N} f(x) - \lim_{x \to N} f(N) \qquad \text{[difference limit theorem]}$$

$$= \lim_{x \to N} f(x) - f(N) \qquad \text{[}f(N) \text{ is a constant]}$$

$$\text{Right side} = \lim_{x \to N} \frac{f(x) - f(N)}{x - N} \lim_{x \to N} (x - N) \qquad \text{[product limit theorem]}$$

$$= f'(N)(\lim_{x \to N} x - \lim_{x \to N} N) \qquad \text{[by (6.13) and difference limit theorem]}$$

$$= f'(N)(N - N) = 0$$

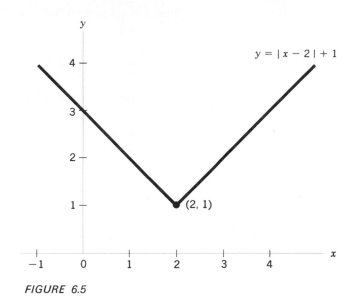

$$y = |x - 2| + 1$$

(2, 1)

FIGURE 6.5

Note that we could not have written these results, if condition (6.13) had not been granted, for if $f'(N)$ did not exist, then the right-side expression (and hence also the left-side expression) in (6.15) would not possess a limit. If $f'(N)$ does exist, however, the two sides will have limits as shown above. Moreover, when the left-side result and the right-side result are equated, we get $\lim_{x \to N} f(x) -$ $f(N) = 0$, which is identical with (6.14). Thus we have proved that continuity, as shown in (6.14), follows from differentiability, as shown in (6.13). In general, if a function is differentiable at every point in its domain, we may conclude that it must be continuous in its domain.

Although differentiability implies continuity, the converse is not true. That is, continuity is a *necessary*, but *not* a *sufficient*, condition for differentiability. To demonstrate this, we merely have to produce a counterexample. Let us consider the function

$$(6.16) \qquad y = f(x) = |x - 2| + 1$$

which is graphed in Fig. 6.5. As can be readily shown, this function is not differentiable, though continuous, when $x = 2$. That the function is continuous at $x = 2$ is easy to establish. First, $x = 2$ is in the domain of the function. Second, the limit of y exists as x tends to 2; to be specific, $\lim_{x \to 2^+} y = \lim_{x \to 2^-} y = 1$. Third, $f(2)$ is also found to be 1. Thus all three requirements of continuity are met. To show that the function f is *not* differentiable at $x = 2$, we must show that the limit of the difference quotient

$$\lim_{x \to 2} \frac{f(x) - f(2)}{x - 2} = \lim_{x \to 2} \frac{|x - 2| + 1 - 1}{x - 2} = \lim_{x \to 2} \frac{|x - 2|}{x - 2}$$

does *not* exist. This involves the demonstration of a disparity between the left-side and the right-side limits. Since, in considering the right-side limit, x must exceed 2, according to the definition of absolute value in (6.8) we have $|x - 2| = x - 2$. Thus the right-side limit is

$$\lim_{x \to 2^+} \frac{|x - 2|}{x - 2} = \lim_{x \to 2^+} \frac{x - 2}{x - 2} = \lim_{x \to 2^+} 1 = 1$$

On the other hand, in considering the left-side limit, x must be less than 2; thus, according to (6.8), $|x - 2| = -(x - 2)$. Consequently, the left-side limit is

$$\lim_{x \to 2^-} \frac{|x - 2|}{x - 2} = \lim_{x \to 2^-} \frac{-(x - 2)}{x - 2} = \lim_{x \to 2^-} (-1) = -1$$

which is different from the right-side limit. This shows that continuity does not guarantee differentiability. As a matter of fact, all differentiable functions are continuous, but not all continuous functions are differentiable.

In Fig. 6.5, the nondifferentiability of the function at $x = 2$ is manifested in the fact that the point (2,1) has no tangent line defined, and hence no definite slope can be assigned to the point. Specifically, to the left of that point, the curve has a slope of -1, but to the right it has a slope of $+1$, and the slopes on the two sides display no tendency to approach a common magnitude at $x = 2$. The point (2,1) is, of course, a special point; it is the only sharp point on the curve. At other points on the curve, the derivative is defined and the function is differentiable. More specifically, the function in (6.16) can be divided into two linear functions as follows:

Left part: $y = -(x - 2) + 1 = 3 - x$ $(x \leq 2)$

Right part: $y = \quad (x - 2) + 1 = x - 1$ $(x > 2)$

The left part is differentiable in the interval $(-\infty, 2)$, and the right part is differentiable in the interval $(2, \infty)$ in the domain.

In general, differentiability is a more restrictive condition than continuity, because it requires something beyond continuity. Continuity at a point only rules out the presence of a gap, whereas differentiability rules out "sharpness" as well. Therefore, differentiability calls for "smoothness" of the function (curve) as well as its continuity. Most of the *specific* functions encountered in economics have the property that they are differentiable everywhere. When *general* functions are used, they are often assumed to be everywhere differentiable, as we shall do in the subsequent discussion.

EXERCISE 6.7

1 A function $y = f(x)$ is discontinuous at $x = x_0$ when *any* of the three requirements for continuity is violated at $x = x_0$. Construct three graphs to illustrate the violation of each of those requirements.

2 Taking the set of all finite real numbers as the domain of the function $q = g(v) = v^2 - 2v - 3$:

(a) Find the limit of q as v tends to N (a finite real number).
(b) Check whether this limit is equal to $g(N)$.
(c) Check whether the function is continuous at N and continuous in its domain.

3 Given the function $q = g(v) = \dfrac{v + 2}{v^2 + 2}$:

(a) Use the limit theorems to find $\lim\limits_{v \to N} q$, N being a finite real number.
(b) Check whether this limit is equal to $g(N)$.
(c) Check the continuity of the function $g(v)$ at N and in its domain $(-\infty, \infty)$.

4 Given $y = f(x) = \dfrac{x^2 - x - 12}{x - 4}$:

(a) Is it possible to apply the quotient limit theorem to find the limit of this function as $x \to 4$?
(b) Is this function continuous at $x = 4$? Why?
(c) Find a function that, for $x \neq 4$, is equivalent to the above function, and obtain from the equivalent function the limit of y as $x \to 4$.

5 In the rational function in Example 2, the numerator is evenly divisible by the denominator, the quotient being $v + 1$. Can we for that reason replace that function outright by $q = v + 1$? Why or why not?

6 On the basis of the graphs of the six functions in Fig. 2.8, would you conclude that each such function is differentiable at every point in its domain? Explain.

RULES OF DIFFERENTIATION AND THEIR USE IN COMPARATIVE STATICS

The central problem of comparative-static analysis, that of finding a rate of change, can be identified with the problem of finding the derivative of some function $y = f(x)$, provided that only a small change in x is being considered. Even though the derivative dy/dx is defined as the limit of the difference quotient $q = g(v)$ as $v \to 0$, it is by no means necessary to undertake the process of limit-taking each time the derivative of a function is sought, for there exist various rules of differentiation (derivation) that will enable us to obtain the desired derivatives directly. Instead of going into comparative-static models immediately, therefore, let us begin by learning some rules of differentiation.

7.1 Rules of Differentiation for a Function of One Variable

First, let us discuss three rules that apply, respectively, to the following types of functions of a single independent variable: $y = k$ (constant function), $y = x^n$, and $y = cx^n$ (power functions). All these have smooth, continuous graphs and are therefore differentiable everywhere.

constant-function rule   The derivative of a constant function $y = f(x) = k$ is zero. Symbolically, this may be expressed variously as

$$\frac{dy}{dx} = 0 \quad \text{or} \quad \frac{dk}{dx} = 0 \quad \text{or} \quad f'(x) = 0$$

In fact, we may also write these in the form

$$\frac{d}{dx} y = \frac{d}{dx} f(x) = \frac{d}{dx} k = 0$$

where the derivative symbol has been separated into two parts, d/dx on the one hand, and y [or $f(x)$ or k] on the other. The first part, d/dx, may be taken as an *operator symbol*, which instructs us to perform a particular mathematical operation. Just as the operator symbol $\sqrt{}$ instructs us to take a square root, the symbol d/dx represents an instruction to take the derivative of, or to differentiate, (some function) with respect to the variable x. The function to be operated on (to be differentiated) is indicated in the second part; here it is $y = f(x) = k$.

The proof of the rule is as follows: Given $f(x) = k$, we have $f(N) = k$ for any value of N. Thus the value of $f'(N)$—the value of the derivative at $x = N$—as defined in (6.13) will be

$$f'(N) = \lim_{x \to N} \frac{f(x) - f(N)}{x - N} = \lim_{x \to N} \frac{k - k}{x - N} = \lim_{x \to N} 0 = 0$$

Moreover, since N represents any value of x at all, the result $f'(N) = 0$ can be immediately generalized to $f'(x) = 0$. This proves the rule.

As discussed before, the derivative of a function has its geometric counterpart in the slope of the curve. The graph of a constant function, say, a fixed-cost function $C_F = f(Q) = \$1200$, is a horizontal straight line with a zero slope throughout. Correspondingly, the derivative must also be zero:

$$\frac{d}{dQ} C_F = \frac{d}{dQ} 1200 = 0 \quad \text{or} \quad f'(Q) = 0$$

power-function rule   The derivative of a power function $y = f(x) = x^n$ is nx^{n-1}. Symbolically, this is expressed as

$$(7.1) \qquad \frac{d}{dx} x^n = nx^{n-1} \quad \text{or} \quad f'(x) = nx^{n-1}$$

Example 1   The derivative of $y = x^3$ is $\dfrac{dy}{dx} = \dfrac{d}{dx} x^3 = 3x^2$.

Example 2   The derivative of $y = x^9$ is $\dfrac{d}{dx} x^9 = 9x^8$.

This rule is valid for any real-valued power of x; that is, the exponent can be any real number. But we shall prove it only for the case of n being some positive integer. In the simplest case, that of $n = 1$, the function is $f(x) = x$, and according to the rule, the derivative is

$$f'(x) = \frac{d}{dx} x = 1(x^0) = 1$$

The proof of this result follows easily from the definition of $f'(N)$ in (6.13): Given $f(x) = x$, the derivative value at any value of x, say, $x = N$, is

$$f'(N) = \lim_{x \to N} \frac{f(x) - f(N)}{x - N} = \lim_{x \to N} \frac{x - N}{x - N} = \lim_{x \to N} 1 = 1$$

Since N represents any value of x, it is permissible to write $f'(x) = 1$. This proves the rule for the case of $n = 1$. As the graphical counterpart of this result, we see that the function $y = f(x) = x$ plots as a $45°$ line, and it has a slope of $+1$ throughout.

For the cases of larger integers, $n = 2, 3, \ldots$, let us first note the following identities:

$$\frac{x^2 - N^2}{x - N} = x + N \qquad \text{[2 terms on the right]}$$

$$\frac{x^3 - N^3}{x - N} = x^2 + Nx + N^2 \qquad \text{[3 terms on the right]}$$

$$\vdots$$

(7.2) $$\frac{x^n - N^n}{x - N} = x^{n-1} + Nx^{n-2} + N^2 x^{n-3} + \cdots + N^{n-1}$$

$$\text{[n terms on the right]}$$

On the basis of (7.2), we can express the derivative of a power function $f(x) = x^n$ at $x = N$ as follows:

(7.3) $$f'(N) = \lim_{x \to N} \frac{f(x) - f(N)}{x - N} = \lim_{x \to N} \frac{x^n - N^n}{x - N}$$

$$= \lim_{x \to N} (x^{n-1} + Nx^{n-2} + \cdots + N^{n-1}) \qquad \text{[by (7.2)]}$$

$$= \lim_{x \to N} x^{n-1} + \lim_{x \to N} Nx^{n-2} + \cdots + \lim_{x \to N} N^{n-1}$$

$$\text{[sum limit theorem]}$$

$$= N^{n-1} + N^{n-1} + \cdots + N^{n-1} \qquad \text{[a total of n terms]}$$

$$= nN^{n-1}$$

Again, N is any value of x; thus this last result can be generalized to

$$f'(x) = nx^{n-1}$$

which proves the rule for n, any positive integer.

As mentioned above, this rule applies even when the exponent n in the power expression x^n is not a positive integer. The following examples serve to illustrate its application to the latter cases.

Example 3   Find the derivative of $y = x^0$. Applying (7.1), we find

$$\frac{d}{dx} x^0 = 0(x^{-1}) = 0$$

Example 4   Find the derivative of $y = 1/x^3$. This involves the reciprocal of a power, but by rewriting the function as $y = x^{-3}$, we can again apply (7.1) to get the derivative:

$$\frac{d}{dx} x^{-3} = -3x^{-4} \qquad \left[= \frac{-3}{x^4} \right]$$

Example 5   Find the derivative of $y = \sqrt{x}$. A square root is involved in this case, but since $\sqrt{x} = x^{1/2}$, the derivative can be found as follows:

$$\frac{d}{dx} x^{1/2} = \frac{1}{2} x^{-1/2} \qquad \left[= \frac{1}{2\sqrt{x}} \right]$$

The reader will observe that derivatives are themselves functions of the independent variable x. In Example 1, for instance, the derivative is $dy/dx = 3x^2$, or $f'(x) = 3x^2$, so that a different value of x will result in a different value of the derivative, such as

$$f'(1) = 3(1)^2 = 3 \qquad f'(2) = 3(2)^2 = 12$$

These specific values of the derivative can be expressed alternatively as

$$\left. \frac{dy}{dx} \right|_{x=1} = 3 \qquad \left. \frac{dy}{dx} \right|_{x=2} = 12$$

but the notations $f'(1)$ and $f'(2)$ are obviously preferable because of their simplicity.

It is of the utmost importance to realize that, to find the derivative values $f'(1)$, $f'(2)$, etc., we must *first* differentiate the function $f(x)$, in order to get the derivative function $f'(x)$, and *then* let x assume specific values in $f'(x)$. To substitute specific values of x into the primitive function $f(x)$ prior to differentiation is definitely not permissible. As an illustration, if we let $x = 1$ in the function of Example 1 before differentiation, the function will degenerate into $y = x = 1$ —a constant function—which will yield a zero derivative rather than the correct answer of $f'(x) = 3x^2$.

power-function rule generalized   When a multiplicative constant c appears in the power function, so that $f(x) = cx^n$, its derivative is

$$\frac{d}{dx}\, cx^n = cnx^{n-1} \qquad \text{or} \qquad f'(x) = cnx^{n-1}$$

This result shows that, in differentiating cx^n, we can simply retain the multiplicative constant c intact and then differentiate the term x^n according to (7.1).

Example 6   Given $y = 2x$, we have $dy/dx = 2x^0 = 2$.

Example 7   Given $f(x) = 4x^3$, the derivative is $f'(x) = 12x^2$.

Example 8   The derivative of $f(x) = 3x^{-2}$ is $f'(x) = -6x^{-3}$.

For a proof of this new rule, consider the fact that for any value of x, say, $x = N$, the value of the derivative of $f(x) = cx^n$ is

$$f'(N) = \lim_{x \to N} \frac{f(x) - f(N)}{x - N} = \lim_{x \to N} \frac{cx^n - cN^n}{x - N} = \lim_{x \to N} c\left(\frac{x^n - N^n}{x - N}\right)$$

$$= \lim_{x \to N} c \lim_{x \to N} \frac{x^n - N^n}{x - N} \qquad \text{[product limit theorem]}$$

$$= c \lim_{x \to N} \frac{x^n - N^n}{x - N} \qquad \text{[limit of a constant]}$$

$$= cnN^{n-1} \qquad \text{[from (7.3)]}$$

In view that N is any value of x, this last result can be generalized immediately to $f'(x) = cnx^{n-1}$, which proves the rule.

EXERCISE 7.1

1   Find the derivative of each of the following functions:

    (a) $y = x^{19}$ (c) $y = 4x^6$ (e) $w = -4u^3$

    (b) $y = 63$ (d) $w = 3u^{-1}$

2   Find the following:

    (a) $\dfrac{d}{dx}(-x^{-4})$ (c) $\dfrac{d}{dw}\, 9w^4$ (e) $\dfrac{d}{du}\, au^b$

    (b) $\dfrac{d}{dx}\, 2x^{1/3}$ (d) $\dfrac{d}{dx}\, cx^2$

3   Find $f'(1)$ and $f'(2)$ from the following functions:

(a) $y = f(x) = 8x$ (c) $f(x) = -3x^{-2}$ (e) $f(w) = \frac{1}{4}w^{1/2}$

(b) $y = f(x) = cx^2$ (d) $f(x) = \frac{2}{3}x^{3/2}$

7.2   Rules of Differentiation Involving Two or More Functions of the Same Variable

The three rules presented in the preceding section are each concerned with a single given function $f(x)$. Now suppose that we have two *differentiable* functions of the same variable x, say, $f(x)$ and $g(x)$, and we want to differentiate the sum, difference, product, or quotient formed with these two functions. In such circumstances, are there appropriate rules that apply? More concretely, given two functions—say, $f(x) = 3x^2$ and $g(x) = 9x^{12}$—how do we get the derivative of, say, $3x^2 + 9x^{12}$, or the derivative of $(3x^2)(9x^{12})$?

sum-difference rule   The derivative of a sum (difference) of two functions is the sum (difference) of the derivatives of the two functions:

$$\frac{d}{dx}[f(x) \pm g(x)] = \frac{d}{dx}f(x) \pm \frac{d}{dx}g(x) = f'(x) \pm g'(x)$$

The proof of this again involves the application of the definition of a derivative and of the various limit theorems. We shall omit the proof and, instead, merely verify its validity and illustrate its application.

Example 1   From the function $y = 14x^3$, we can obtain the derivative $dy/dx = 42x^2$. But $14x^3 = 5x^3 + 9x^3$, so that y may be regarded as the sum of two functions $f(x) = 5x^3$ and $g(x) = 9x^3$. According to the sum rule, we then have

$$\frac{dy}{dx} = \frac{d}{dx}(5x^3 + 9x^3) = \frac{d}{dx}5x^3 + \frac{d}{dx}9x^3 = 15x^2 + 27x^2 = 42x^2$$

which is identical with our earlier result.

This rule, stated above in terms of two functions, can easily be extended to more functions. Thus, it is also valid to write

$$\frac{d}{dx}[f(x) \pm g(x) \pm h(x)] = f'(x) \pm g'(x) \pm h'(x)$$

Example 2   The function cited in Example 1, $y = 14x^3$, can be written as $y = 2x^3 + 13x^3 - x^3$. The derivative of the latter, according to the sum-difference rule, is

$$\frac{dy}{dx} = \frac{d}{dx}(2x^3 + 13x^3 - x^3) = 6x^2 + 39x^2 - 3x^2 = 42x^2$$

which again checks with the previous answer.

This rule is of great practical importance. With it at our disposal, it is now possible to find the derivative of any polynomial function, since the latter is nothing but a sum of power functions.

Example 3 $\dfrac{d}{dx}(ax^2 + bx + c) = 2ax + b$

Example 4

$$\frac{d}{dx}(7x^4 + 2x^3 - 3x + 37) = 28x^3 + 6x^2 - 3 + 0 = 28x^3 + 6x^2 - 3$$

Note that in the last two examples the constants c and 37, do not really produce any effect on the derivative, because the derivative of a constant term is zero. In contrast to the *multiplicative* constant, which is retained during differentiation, the *additive* constant drops out. This fact provides the mathematical explanation of the well-known economic principle that the fixed cost of a firm does not affect its marginal cost. Given a short-run total-cost function

$$C = Q^3 - 4Q^2 + 10Q + 75$$

the marginal-cost function (for very small changes in output) is the limit of the quotient $\Delta C/\Delta Q$, or the derivative of the C function:

$$\frac{dC}{dQ} = 3Q^2 - 8Q + 10$$

whereas the fixed cost is represented by the additive constant 75. Since the latter drops out during the process of deriving dC/dQ, the magnitude of the fixed cost obviously cannot affect the marginal cost.

In general, if a primitive function $y = f(x)$ represents a *total* function, then the derivative function dy/dx is its *marginal* function. Both functions can, of course, be plotted against the variable x graphically; and because of the correspondence between the derivative of a function and the slope of its curve, for each value of x the marginal function should show the slope of the total function at that value of x. In Fig. 7.1a, a linear (constant-slope) total function

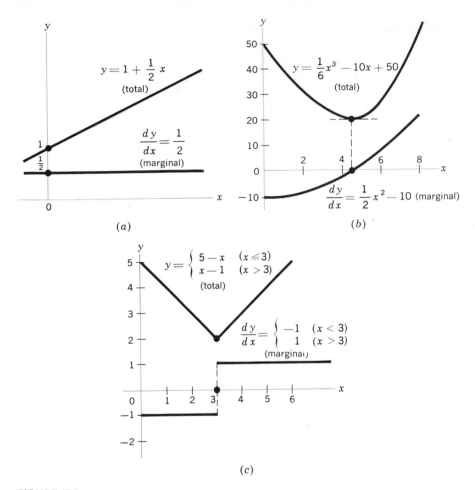

FIGURE 7.1

is seen to have a constant marginal function. On the other hand, the nonlinear (varying-slope) total function in diagram *b* gives rise to a curved marginal function, which lies below (above) the horizontal axis when the total function is negatively (positively) sloped. And, finally, the reader may note from diagram *c* (cf. Fig. 6.5) that "nonsmoothness" of a total function will result in a gap (discontinuity) in the marginal or derivative function. This is in sharp contrast to the everywhere-smooth total function in diagram *b* which gives rise to a continuous marginal function. For this reason, the *smoothness* of a *primitive* function can be linked to the *continuity* of its *derivative* function. In particular, instead of saying that a certain function is smooth (and differentiable), we may alternatively characterize it as a function with a continuous derivative function.

product rule   The derivative of the product of two (differentiable) functions is equal to: the first function times the derivative of the second function, plus the second function times the derivative of the first function:

$$(7.4) \qquad \frac{d}{dx}[f(x)g(x)] = f(x)\frac{d}{dx}g(x) + g(x)\frac{d}{dx}f(x)$$

$$= f(x)g'(x) + g(x)f'(x)$$

Example 5   Find the derivative of $y = (2x + 3)(3x^2)$. Let $f(x) = 2x + 3$ and $g(x) = 3x^2$. Then it follows that $f'(x) = 2$ and $g'(x) = 6x$, and according to (7.4) the desired derivative is

$$\frac{d}{dx}[(2x + 3)(3x^2)] = (2x + 3)(6x) + (3x^2)(2) = 18x^2 + 18x$$

This result can be checked by first multiplying out $f(x)g(x)$ and then taking the derivative of the product polynomial. The product polynomial is in this case $f(x)g(x) = (2x + 3)(3x^2) = 6x^3 + 9x^2$, and direct differentiation does yield the same derivative, $18x^2 + 18x$.

The important point to remember is that the derivative of a product of two functions is *not* the simple product of the two separate derivatives. Since this differs from what intuitive generalization leads one to expect, let us produce a proof for (7.4). According to (6.13), the value of the derivative of $f(x)g(x)$ when $x = N$ should be

$$(7.5) \qquad \frac{d}{dx}[f(x)g(x)]\Big|_{x=N} = \lim_{x \to N} \frac{f(x)g(x) - f(N)g(N)}{x - N}$$

But, by adding *and* subtracting $f(x)g(N)$ in the numerator (thereby leaving the original magnitude unchanged), we can transform the quotient on the right of (7.5) as follows:

$$\frac{f(x)g(x) - f(x)g(N) + f(x)g(N) - f(N)g(N)}{x - N} = f(x)\frac{g(x) - g(N)}{x - N}$$

$$+ g(N)\frac{f(x) - f(N)}{x - N}$$

Substituting this for the quotient on the right of (7.5) and taking its limit, we then get

$$(7.5') \qquad \frac{d}{dx}[f(x)g(x)]\Big|_{x=N} = \lim_{x \to N} f(x) \lim_{x \to N} \frac{g(x) - g(N)}{x - N}$$

$$+ \lim_{x \to N} g(N) \lim_{x \to N} \frac{f(x) - f(N)}{x - N}$$

The four limit expressions in (7.5′) are easily evaluated. The first one is $f(N)$, and the third is $g(N)$ (limit of a constant). The remaining two are, according to (6.13), respectively, $g'(N)$ and $f'(N)$. Thus (7.5′) reduces to

$$(7.5'') \qquad \frac{d}{dx}[f(x)g(x)]\Big|_{x=N} = f(N)g'(N) + g(N)f'(N)$$

And, since N represents any value of x, (7.5″) remains valid if we replace every N symbol by x. This proves the rule.

As an extension of the rule to the case of *three* functions, we have

$$(7.6) \qquad \frac{d}{dx}[f(x)g(x)h(x)] = f'(x)g(x)h(x) + f(x)g'(x)h(x) + f(x)g(x)h'(x)$$

In words, the derivative of the product of three functions is equal to: the product of the second and third functions times the derivative of the first, plus the product of the first and third functions times the derivative of the second, plus the product of the first and second functions times the derivative of the third. This result can be derived by the repeated application of (7.4): First treat the product $g(x)h(x)$ as a single function, say, $\phi(x)$, so that the original product of three functions will become a product of *two* functions, $f(x)\phi(x)$. To this, (7.4) is applicable. After the derivative of $f(x)\phi(x)$ is obtained, we may reapply (7.4) to the product $g(x)h(x) \equiv \phi(x)$ to get $\phi'(x)$. Then (7.6) will follow. The details are left to the reader as an exercise.

The validity of a rule is one thing; its serviceability is something else. Why do we need the product rule when we can resort to the alternative procedure of multiplying out the two functions $f(x)$ and $g(x)$ and then taking the derivative of the product directly? One answer to that question is: The alternative procedure is feasible only for *specific* (numerical or parametric) functions, whereas the product rule is applicable even when the functions are given in the *general* form. Let us illustrate with an economic example.

finding marginal-revenue function from average-revenue function

If we are given an average-revenue (AR) function in specific form,

$$AR = 15 - Q$$

the marginal-revenue (MR) function can be found by first multiplying AR by Q to get the total-revenue (R) function:

$$R \equiv AR \cdot Q = (15 - Q)Q = 15Q - Q^2$$

and then differentiating R:

$$MR \equiv \frac{dR}{dQ} = 15 - 2Q$$

But if the AR function is given in the general form $AR = f(Q)$, then the total-revenue function will also be in a general form:

$$R \equiv AR \cdot Q = f(Q) \cdot Q$$

and therefore the "multiply out" approach will be to no avail. However, R being a product of two functions of Q, namely, $f(Q)$ and Q itself, the product rule may be put to work. Thus, we can differentiate R to get the MR function as follows:

$$(7.7) \qquad MR \equiv \frac{dR}{dQ} = f(Q) \cdot 1 + Q \cdot f'(Q) = f(Q) + Qf'(Q)$$

However, can such a general result tell us anything significant about the MR? Indeed it can. Recalling that $f(Q)$ denotes the AR function, let us rearrange (7.7) and write

$$(7.7') \qquad MR - AR = MR - f(Q) = Qf'(Q)$$

This gives us an important relationship between MR and AR: namely, they will always differ by the amount $Qf'(Q)$.

It remains to examine the expression $Qf'(Q)$. Its first component Q denotes output and is always nonnegative. The other component, $f'(Q)$, represents the slope of the AR curve plotted against Q. Since "average revenue" and "price" are but different names for the same thing:

$$AR \equiv \frac{R}{Q} \equiv \frac{PQ}{Q} \equiv P$$

the AR curve can also be regarded as a curve relating price P to output Q: $P = f(Q)$. Viewed in this light, the AR curve is simply the *inverse* of the demand curve for the product of the firm, i.e., the demand curve plotted after the P and Q axes are reversed. Under pure competition, the AR curve is a horizontal straight line, so that $f'(Q) = 0$ and, from (7.7'), $MR - AR = 0$ for all possible values of Q. Thus the MR curve and the AR curve must coincide. Under imperfect competition, on the other hand, the AR curve is normally downward-sloping, as in Fig. 7.2, so that $f'(Q) < 0$ and, from (7.7'), $MR - AR < 0$ for all positive levels of output. In this case, therefore, the MR curve must lie below the AR curve.

The conclusion just stated is *qualitative* in nature; it concerns only the relative positions of the two curves. But (7.7') also furnishes the *quantitative* information that the MR curve will fall short of the AR curve at any output level Q by precisely the amount $Qf'(Q)$. Let us look at Fig. 7.2 again and consider the particular output level N. For that output, the expression $Qf'(Q)$ specifically becomes $Nf'(N)$; if we can find the magnitude of $Nf'(N)$ in the diagram, we shall know how far below the average-revenue point G the corresponding marginal-revenue point must lie.

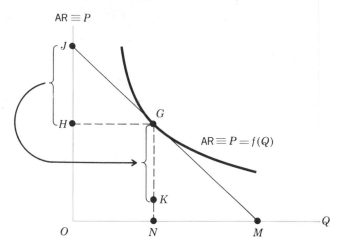

FIGURE 7.2

The magnitude of N is already specified. And $f'(N)$ is simply the slope of the AR curve at the point G (where $Q = N$), that is, the slope of the tangent line JM measured by the ratio of two distances OJ/OM. However, we see that $OJ/OM = HJ/HG$; besides, distance HG is precisely the amount of output under consideration, N. Thus we find

$$Nf'(N) = HG\,\frac{HJ}{HG} = HJ$$

to be the distance by which the marginal revenue must lie below the average revenue at the output N. Accordingly, if we mark a vertical distance $KG = HJ$ directly beneath point G, then the point K must be a point on the MR curve.

The same procedure can be used to locate other points on the MR curve. All we must do, for any chosen point G' on the curve, is first to draw a tangent to the AR curve at G' that will meet the vertical axis at some point J'. Then draw a horizontal line from G' to the vertical axis, and label the intersection with the axis as H'. If we mark a vertical distance $K'G' = H'J'$ directly beneath point G', then the point K' will be a point on the MR curve. This is the graphical way of deriving an MR curve from a given AR curve. Strictly speaking, the accurate drawing of a tangent line requires a knowledge of the value of the derivative at the relevant output, that is, $f'(N)$; hence the graphical method just outlined cannot quite exist by itself. An important exception is the case of a linear AR curve, where the tangent to any point on the curve is simply the given line itself, so that there is in effect no need to draw any tangent at all. Then the above graphical method will apply in a straightforward way.

quotient rule   The derivative of the quotient of two functions, $f(x)/g(x)$, is

$$\frac{d}{dx}\frac{f(x)}{g(x)} = \frac{f'(x)g(x) - f(x)g'(x)}{g^2(x)}$$

In the numerator of the right-hand expression, we find two product terms, each involving the derivative of only one of the two original functions. Note that $f'(x)$ appears in the positive term, and $g'(x)$ in the negative term. The denominator consists of the square of the function $g(x)$; that is, $g^2(x) \equiv [g(x)]^2$.

Example 6 $\dfrac{d}{dx}\left(\dfrac{2x - 3}{x + 1}\right) = \dfrac{2(x + 1) - (2x - 3)(1)}{(x + 1)^2} = \dfrac{5}{(x + 1)^2}$

Example 7 $\dfrac{d}{dx}\left(\dfrac{5x}{x^2 + 1}\right) = \dfrac{5(x^2 + 1) - 5x(2x)}{(x^2 + 1)^2} = \dfrac{5(1 - x^2)}{(x^2 + 1)^2}$

Example 8 $\dfrac{d}{dx}\left(\dfrac{ax^2 + b}{cx}\right) = \dfrac{2ax(cx) - (ax^2 + b)(c)}{(cx)^2} = \dfrac{c(ax^2 - b)}{(cx)^2} = \dfrac{ax^2 - b}{cx^2}$

This rule can be proved as follows. For any value of $x = N$, we have

(7.8) $\dfrac{d}{dx}\dfrac{f(x)}{g(x)}\bigg|_{x=N} = \lim_{x \to N} \dfrac{f(x)/g(x) - f(N)/g(N)}{x - N}$

The quotient expression following the limit sign can be rewritten in the form

$$\frac{f(x)g(N) - f(N)g(x)}{g(x)g(N)} \frac{1}{x - N}$$

By adding *and* subtracting $f(N)g(N)$ in the numerator and rearranging, we can further transform the expression to

$$\frac{1}{g(x)g(N)}\left[\frac{f(x)g(N) - f(N)g(N) + f(N)g(N) - f(N)g(x)}{x - N}\right]$$

$$= \frac{1}{g(x)g(N)}\left[g(N)\frac{f(x) - f(N)}{x - N} - f(N)\frac{g(x) - g(N)}{x - N}\right]$$

Substituting this result into (7.8) and taking the limit, we then have

$$\frac{d}{dx}\frac{f(x)}{g(x)}\bigg|_{x=N} = \lim_{x \to N}\frac{1}{g(x)g(N)}\left[\lim_{x \to N}g(N)\lim_{x \to N}\frac{f(x) - f(N)}{x - N}\right.$$

$$\left. - \lim_{x \to N}f(N)\lim_{x \to N}\frac{g(x) - g(N)}{x - N}\right]$$

$$= \frac{1}{g^2(N)}[g(N)f'(N) - f(N)g'(N)] \qquad \text{[by (6.13)]}$$

which can be generalized by replacing the symbol N with x, because N represents any value of x. This proves the quotient rule.

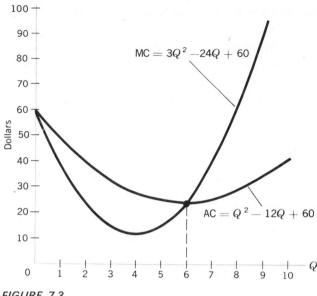

FIGURE 7.3

relationship between marginal-cost and average-cost functions As an
economic application of the quotient rule, let us consider the rate of change
of average cost when output varies.

Given a total-cost function $C = C(Q)$, the average-cost (AC) function will
be a quotient of two functions of Q: $AC \equiv C(Q)/Q$. Therefore, the rate of change
of AC with respect to Q can be found by differentiating AC as follows:

$$(7.9) \qquad \frac{d}{dQ} \frac{C(Q)}{Q} = \frac{[C'(Q) \cdot Q - C(Q) \cdot 1]}{Q^2} = \frac{1}{Q} \left[C'(Q) - \frac{C(Q)}{Q} \right]$$

From this it follows that, for $Q > 0$,

$\frac{1}{Q}[MC - AC]$

$$(7.10) \qquad \frac{d}{dQ} \frac{C(Q)}{Q} \gtreqless 0 \qquad \text{iff} \qquad C'(Q) \gtreqless \frac{C(Q)}{Q}$$

Since the derivative $C'(Q)$ represents the marginal-cost (MC) function, and
$C(Q)/Q$ represents the AC function, the economic meaning of (7.10) is as follows:
The slope of the AC curve will be positive, zero, or negative if and only if the
marginal-cost curve lies above, intersects, or lies below the AC curve. This is
illustrated in Fig. 7.3, where the MC and AC functions plotted are based on the
specific total-cost function

$$C = Q^3 - 12Q^2 + 60Q$$

To the left of $Q = 6$, AC is declining, and thus MC lies below it; to the right, the opposite is true. At $Q = 6$, AC has a slope of zero, and MC and AC have the same value.[1]

The qualitative conclusion in (7.10) is stated explicitly in terms of cost functions. However, its validity remains unaffected if we interpret $C(Q)$ as *any other* differentiable total function, with $C(Q)/Q$ and $C'(Q)$ as its corresponding average and marginal functions. Thus this result gives us a *general* marginal-average relationship. In particular, we may point out, the fact that MR lies below AR when AR is downward-sloping, as discussed in connection with Fig. 7.2, is nothing but a special case of the general result in (7.10).

EXERCISE 7.2

 1   Given the total-cost function $C = Q^3 - 6Q^2 + 14Q + 75$, write out a variable-cost (VC) function. Find the derivative of the VC function, and interpret the economic meaning of that derivative.

2   Differentiate the following by using the product rule:

     (a) $(9x^2 - 2)(3x + 1)$ (d) $(ax + b)(cx^2)$
     (b) $(3x + 11)(6x^2 - x)$ (e) $(2 - 3x)(1 + x)(x + 2)$
     (c) $x^2(4x + 6)$ (f) $(x^2 + 3)x^{-1}$

3   (a)   Given AR $= 60 - 2Q$, plot the average-revenue curve, and then find the MR curve by the method of Fig. 7.2.
     (b)   Find the total-revenue function and the marginal-revenue function mathematically from the given AR function.
     (c)   Does the graphically derived MR curve in (a) check with the mathematically derived MR function in (b)?
     (d)   Comparing the AR and MR functions, what can you conclude about their relative slopes?

4   Provide a mathematical proof for the general result that, given a *linear* average curve, the corresponding marginal curve must have the same vertical intercept but will be twice as steep as the average curve.

5   Prove the result in (7.6) by first treating $g(x)h(x)$ as a single function, $g(x)h(x) \equiv \phi(x)$, and then applying the product rule (7.4).

---

[1] Note that (7.10) does *not* state that, when AC is negatively sloped, MC must also be negatively sloped; it merely says that AC must exceed MC in that circumstance. At $Q = 5$ in Fig. 7.3, for instance, AC is declining but MC is rising, so that their slopes will have opposite signs.

                   Comparative-Static Analysis

6   Find the derivatives of:

(a) $(x^2 + 3)/x$ (Check the result against Exercise 7.2-2f above.)
(b) $(x + 7)/x$ (c) $4x/(x + 5)$ (d) $(ax^2 + b)/(cx + d)$

7   Given the function $f(x) = ax + b$, find the derivatives of:

(a) $f(x)$ (b) $xf(x)$ (c) $1/f(x)$ (d) $f(x)/x$

8   On the basis of the specific AC and MC functions shown in Fig. 7.3, differentiate the AC function, and verify the result in (7.9).

7.3   Rules of Differentiation Involving Functions of Different Variables

In the preceding section, we discussed the rules of differentiation of a sum, difference, product, or quotient of two (or more) differentiable functions of the same variable. Now we shall consider cases where there are two or more differentiable functions, each of which has a *distinct* independent variable.

chain rule   If we have a function $z = f(y)$, where y is in turn a function of another variable x, say, $y = g(x)$, then the derivative of z with respect to x is equal to: the derivative of z with respect to y, times the derivative of y with respect to x. Expressed symbolically,

$$(7.11) \qquad \frac{dz}{dx} = \frac{dz}{dy}\frac{dy}{dx} = f'(y)g'(x)$$

This rule, known as the *chain rule*, appeals easily to intuition. Given a Δx, there must result a corresponding Δy via the function $y = g(x)$, but this Δy will in turn bring about a Δz via the function $z = f(y)$. Thus there is a "chain reaction" as follows:

$$\Delta x \xrightarrow{\text{via } g} \Delta y \xrightarrow{\text{via } f} \Delta z$$

The two links in this chain entail two difference quotients, $\Delta y/\Delta x$ and $\Delta z/\Delta y$, but when they are multiplied, the Δy will cancel itself out, and we end up with

$$\frac{\Delta z}{\Delta y}\frac{\Delta y}{\Delta x} = \frac{\Delta z}{\Delta x}$$

a difference quotient that relates Δz to Δx. If we take the limit of these difference quotients as $\Delta x \to 0$ (which implies $\Delta y \to 0$), each difference quotient will turn into a derivative; i.e., we shall have $(dz/dy)(dy/dx) = dz/dx$. This is precisely the result in (7.11).

In view of the function $y = g(x)$, we can express the function $z = f(y)$ as $z = f[g(x)]$, where the contiguous appearance of the two function signs f and g indicates that this is a *composite function* (function of a function). It is for this reason that the chain rule is also referred to as the *composite-function rule* or *function-of-a-function rule*.

The extension of the chain rule to three or more functions is straightforward. If we have $z = f(y)$, $y = g(x)$, and $x = h(w)$, then

$$\frac{dz}{dw} = \frac{dz}{dy}\frac{dy}{dx}\frac{dx}{dw} = f'(y)g'(x)h'(w)$$

and similarly for cases in which more functions are involved.

Example 1   If $z = 3y^2$, where $y = 2x + 5$, then

$$\frac{dz}{dx} = \frac{dz}{dy}\frac{dy}{dx} = 6y(2) = 12y = 12(2x + 5)$$

Example 2   If $z = y - 3$, where $y = x^3$, then

$$\frac{dz}{dx} = 1(3x^2) = 3x^2$$

Example 3   The usefulness of this rule can best be appreciated when we must differentiate a function such as $z = (x^2 + 3x - 2)^{17}$. Without the chain rule at our disposal, dz/dx can be found only via the laborious route of first multiplying out the 17th-power expression. With the chain rule, however, we can take a shortcut by defining a new, *intermediate* variable $y = x^2 + 3x - 2$, so that we get in effect two functions linked in a chain:

$$z = y^{17} \quad \text{and} \quad y = x^2 + 3x - 2$$

The derivative dz/dx can then be found as follows:

$$\frac{dz}{dx} = \frac{dz}{dy}\frac{dy}{dx} = 17y^{16}(2x + 3) = 17(x^2 + 3x - 2)^{16}(2x + 3)$$

Example 4   Given a total-revenue function of a firm $R = f(Q)$, where output Q is a function of labor input L, or $Q = g(L)$, find dR/dL. By the chain rule, we have

$$\frac{dR}{dL} = \frac{dR}{dQ}\frac{dQ}{dL} = f'(Q)g'(L)$$

Translated into economic terms, dR/dQ is the MR function and dQ/dL is the marginal-physical-product-of-labor (MPP$_L$) function. Similarly, dR/dL has the connotation of the marginal-revenue-product-of-labor (MRP$_L$) function. Thus the result shown above constitutes the mathematical statement of the well-known result in economics that MRP$_L$ = MR $\cdot$ MPP$_L$.

inverse-function rule   If the function $y = f(x)$ represents a one-to-one mapping, i.e., if the function is such that a different value of x will always yield a different value of y, then the function f will have an *inverse function* $x = f^{-1}(y)$ (read: x is an inverse function of y). What the existence of an inverse function essentially means is that, in this case, not only will a given value of x yield a unique value of y [that is, $y = f(x)$], but also a given value of y will yield a unique value of x. (*Warning:* f^{-1} does not mean $1/f$.)

To take a nonnumerical instance, we may exemplify the one-to-one mapping by the mapping from the set of all husbands to the set of all wives in a monogamous society. Each husband has a unique wife, and each wife has a unique husband. In contrast, the mapping from the set of all fathers to the set of all sons is not one-to-one, because a father may have more than one son, albeit each son has a unique father.

When x and y refer specifically to numbers, the property of one-to-one mapping is seen to be unique to the class of functions known as *monotonic functions*. Given a function $f(x)$, if successively larger values of the independent variable x *always* lead to successively larger values of $f(x)$, that is, if

$$x_1 > x_2 \quad \Rightarrow \quad f(x_1) > f(x_2)$$

then the function f is said to be an *increasing* (or *monotonically increasing*) function.[1] If successive increases in x *always* lead to successive decreases in $f(x)$, that is, if

$$x_1 > x_2 \quad \Rightarrow \quad f(x_1) < f(x_2)$$

on the other hand, the function is said to be a *decreasing* (or *monotonically decreasing*) function. In either of these cases, an inverse function f^{-1} exists.

---

[1] Some writers prefer to define an *increasing function* as a function with the property that

$$x_1 > x_2 \quad \Rightarrow \quad f(x_1) \geq f(x_2) \qquad \text{[with a weak inequality]}$$

and then reserve the term *strictly increasing function* for the case where

$$x_1 > x_2 \quad \Rightarrow \quad f(x_1) > f(x_2) \qquad \text{[with a strict inequality]}$$

Under this usage, an ascending step function qualifies as an increasing (though not strictly increasing) function, despite the fact that its graph contains horizontal segments. We shall not follow this usage in the present book. Instead, we shall consider an ascending step function to be, not an increasing function, but a *nondecreasing* one. By the same token, we shall regard a descending step function, not as a decreasing function, but as a *nonincreasing* one.

A practical way of ascertaining the monotonicity of a given function $y = f(x)$ is to check whether the derivative $f'(x)$ always adheres to the same algebraic sign (not zero) for all values of x. Geometrically, this means that its slope is either always upward or always downward. Thus a firm's demand curve $Q = f(P)$ that has a negative slope throughout is monotonic. As such, it has an inverse function $P = f^{-1}(Q)$, which, as mentioned previously, gives the average-revenue curve of the firm, since $P \equiv AR$.

Example 5   The function

$$y = 5x + 25$$

has the derivative $dy/dx = 5$, which is positive regardless of the value of x; thus the function is monotonic. (In this case it is increasing, because the derivative is positive.) It follows that an inverse function exists. In the present case, the inverse function is easily found by solving the given equation $y = 5x + 25$ for x. The result is the function

$$x = \tfrac{1}{5}y - 5$$

It is interesting to note that this inverse function is also monotonic, and increasing, because $dx/dy = \tfrac{1}{5} > 0$ for all values of y.

Generally speaking, if an inverse function exists, then the original and the inverse functions must both be monotonic. Moreover, if f^{-1} is the inverse function of f, then f must be the inverse function of f^{-1}; that is, f and f^{-1} must be inverses of each other.

It is easy to verify that the graph of $y = f(x)$ and that of $x = f^{-1}(y)$ are one and the same, only with the axes reversed. If one lays the x axis of the f^{-1} graph over the x axis of the f graph (and similarly for the y axis), the two curves will coincide. On the other hand, if the x axis of the f^{-1} graph is laid over the y axis of the f graph (and vice versa), then the two curves will become *mirror images* of each other with reference to the $45°$ line drawn through the origin. This mirror-image relationship provides us with an easy way of graphing the inverse function f^{-1}, once the graph of the original function f is given. (The reader should try this with the two functions in Example 5.)

For inverse functions, the rule of differentiation is

$$\frac{dx}{dy} = \frac{1}{dy/dx}$$

This means that the derivative of the inverse function is the reciprocal of the derivative of the original function; as such, dx/dy must take the same sign as dy/dx, so that if f is increasing (decreasing), then so must be f^{-1}.

As a verification of this rule, we can refer back to Example 5, where dy/dx was found to be 5, and dx/dy equal to $\frac{1}{5}$. These two derivatives are indeed reciprocal to each other and have the same sign.

In that simple example, the inverse function is relatively easy to obtain, so that its derivative dx/dy can be found directly from the inverse function. As the next example shows, however, the inverse function is sometimes difficult to express explicitly, and thus direct differentiation may not be practicable. The usefulness of the inverse-function rule then becomes more fully apparent.

Example 6   Given $y = x^5 + x$, find dx/dy. First of all, since

$$\frac{dy}{dx} = 5x^4 + 1 > 0$$

for any value of x, the given function is monotonically increasing, and an inverse function exists. To solve the given equation for x may not be such an easy task, but the derivative of the inverse function can nevertheless be found quickly by use of the inverse-function rule:

$$\frac{dx}{dy} = \frac{1}{dy/dx} = \frac{1}{5x^4 + 1}$$

The inverse-function rule is, strictly speaking, applicable only when the function involved is a one-to-one mapping. In fact, however, we do have some leeway. For instance, when dealing with a U-shaped curve (not monotonic), we may consider the downward- and the upward-sloping segments of the curve as representing two *separate* functions, each with a restricted domain, and each being monotonic in the restricted domain. To each of these, the inverse-function rule can then again be applied.

EXERCISE 7.3

1   Given $y = u^3 + 1$, where $u = 5 - x^2$, find dy/dx by the chain rule.

2   Given $w = ay^2$ and $y = bx^2 + cx$, find dw/dx by the chain rule.

3   Use the chain rule to find dy/dx for the following:

   (a) $y = (3x^2 - 7)^3$ (b) $y = (8x^3 - 5)^6$ (c) $y = (ax + b)^4$

4   Given $y = (16x + 3)^{-2}$, use the chain rule to find dy/dx. Then rewrite the function as $y = 1/(16x + 3)^2$ and find dy/dx by the quotient rule. Are the answers identical?

5   Given $y = 7x + 21$, find its inverse function. Then find dy/dx and dx/dy, and verify the inverse-function rule. Also verify that the graphs of the two functions bear a mirror-image relationship to each other.

6   Are the following functions monotonic?

  (a) $y = -x^6 + 5$ $(x > 0)$ (b) $y = 9x^5 + x^3 + 4x$

  For each monotonic function, find dx/dy by the inverse-function rule.

7.4   Partial Differentiation

Hitherto, we have considered only the derivatives of functions of a single independent variable. In comparative-static analysis, however, we are likely to encounter the situation in which several parameters appear in a model, so that the equilibrium value of each endogenous variable may be a function of more than one parameter. Therefore, as a final preparation for the application of the concept of derivative to comparative statics, we must learn how to find the derivative of a function of more than one variable.

partial derivatives   Let us consider a function

  (7.12) $y = f(x_1, x_2, \ldots, x_n)$

where the variables x_i $(i = 1, 2, \ldots, n)$ are all *independent* of one another, so that each can vary by itself without affecting the others. If the variable x_1 undergoes a change Δx_1 while $x_2, \ldots, x_n$ all remain fixed, there will be a corresponding change in y, namely, Δy. The difference quotient in this case can be expressed as

  (7.13) $\dfrac{\Delta y}{\Delta x_1} = \dfrac{f(x_1 + \Delta x_1, x_2, \ldots, x_n) - f(x_1, x_2, \ldots, x_n)}{\Delta x_1}$

If we take the limit of $\Delta y/\Delta x_1$ as $\Delta x_1 \to 0$, that limit will constitute a derivative. We call it the *partial derivative* of y with respect to x_1, to indicate that all the other independent variables in the function are held constant when taking this particular derivative. Similar partial derivatives can be defined for infinitesimal changes in the other independent variables. The process of taking partial derivatives is called *partial differentiation*.

  Partial derivatives are assigned distinctive symbols. In lieu of the letter d (as in dy/dx), we employ the symbol ∂, which is a variant of the Greek δ (lower case delta). Thus we shall now write $\partial y/\partial x_i$, which is read: the partial derivative of y with respect to x_i. The partial-derivative symbol sometimes is also written as $\dfrac{\partial}{\partial x_i}\, y$; in that case, its $\partial/\partial x_i$ part can be regarded as an operator symbol instructing us to take the partial derivative of (some function) with respect to the variable x_i. Since the function involved here is denoted in (7.12) by f, it is also permissible to write $\partial f/\partial x_i$.

Is there also a partial-derivative counterpart for the symbol $f'(x)$ that we used before? The answer is yes. Instead of f', however, we now use f_1, f_2, etc., where the subscript indicates which independent variable (alone) is being allowed to vary. If the function in (7.12) happens to be written in terms of unsubscripted variables, such as $y = f(u,v,w)$, then the partial derivatives may be denoted by f_u, f_v, and f_w rather than f_1, f_2, and f_3.

In line with these notations, and on the basis of (7.12) and (7.13), we can now define

$$f_1 \equiv \frac{\partial y}{\partial x_1} \equiv \lim_{\Delta x_1 \to 0} \frac{\Delta y}{\Delta x_1}$$

as the first in the set of n partial derivatives of the function f.

techniques of partial differentiation　　Partial differentiation differs from the previously discussed differentiation primarily in that we must hold $(n - 1)$ independent variables *constant* while allowing *one* variable to vary. Inasmuch as we have learned how to handle *constants* in differentiation, the actual differentiation should pose little problem.

Example 1　　Given $y = f(x_1,x_2) = 3x_1{}^2 + x_1x_2 + 4x_2{}^2$, find the partial derivatives. When finding $\partial y/\partial x_1$ (or f_1), we must bear in mind that x_2 is to be treated as a constant during differentiation. As such, x_2 will drop out in the process if it is an *additive* constant (such as the term $4x_2{}^2$) but will be retained if it is a *multiplicative* constant (such as in the term x_1x_2). Thus we have

$$\frac{\partial y}{\partial x_1} \equiv f_1 = 6x_1 + x_2$$

Similarly, by treating x_1 as a constant, we find that

$$\frac{\partial y}{\partial x_2} \equiv f_2 = x_1 + 8x_2$$

Note that, like the primitive function f, both partial derivatives are themselves functions of the variables x_1 and x_2. That is, we may write them as two derived functions

$$f_1 = f_1(x_1,x_2) \quad \text{and} \quad f_2 = f_2(x_1,x_2)$$

For the point $(x_1,x_2) = (1,3)$ in the domain of the function f, for example, the partial derivatives will take the following specific values:

$$f_1(1,3) = 6(1) + 3 = 9 \quad \text{and} \quad f_2(1,3) = 1 + 8(3) = 25$$

Example 2 Given $y = f(u,v) = (u + 4)(3u + 2v)$, the partial derivatives can be found by use of the product rule. By holding v constant, we have

$$f_u = (u + 4)(3) + 1(3u + 2v) = 2(3u + v + 6)$$

Similarly, by holding u constant, we find that

$$f_v = (u + 4)(2) + 0(3u + 2v) = 2(u + 4)$$

When $u = 2$ and $v = 1$, these derivatives will take the following values:

$$f_u(2,1) = 2(13) = 26 \quad \text{and} \quad f_v(2,1) = 2(6) = 12$$

Example 3 Given $y = (3u - 2v)/(u^2 + 3v)$, the partial derivatives can be found by use of the quotient rule:

$$\frac{\partial y}{\partial u} = \frac{3(u^2 + 3v) - 2u(3u - 2v)}{(u^2 + 3v)^2} = \frac{-3u^2 + 4uv + 9v}{(u^2 + 3v)^2}$$

$$\frac{\partial y}{\partial v} = \frac{-2(u^2 + 3v) - 3(3u - 2v)}{(u^2 + 3v)^2} = \frac{-u(2u + 9)}{(u^2 + 3v)^2}$$

geometric interpretation of partial derivatives As a special type of derivative, a partial derivative is a measure of the instantaneous rates of change of some variable, and in that capacity it again has a geometric counterpart in the slope of a particular curve.

Let us consider a production function $Q = Q(K,L)$, where Q, K, and L denote output, capital input, and labor input, respectively. This function is a particular two-variable version of (7.12), with $n = 2$. We can therefore define two partial derivatives $\partial Q/\partial K$ (or Q_K) and $\partial Q/\partial L$ (or Q_L). The partial derivative Q_K relates to the rates of change in output with respect to infinitesimal changes in capital, while labor input is held constant. Thus Q_K symbolizes the marginal-physical-product-of-capital (MPP_K) function. Similarly, the partial derivative Q_L is the mathematical representation of the MPP_L function.

Geometrically, the production function $Q = Q(K,L)$ can be depicted by a *production surface* in a 3-space, such as is shown in Fig. 7.4. The variable Q is plotted vertically, so that for any point (K,L) in the base plane (KL plane) the height of the surface will indicate the output Q. The domain of the function should consist of the entire nonnegative quadrant of the base plane, but for our purposes it is sufficient to consider a subset of it, the rectangle OK_0BL_0. As a

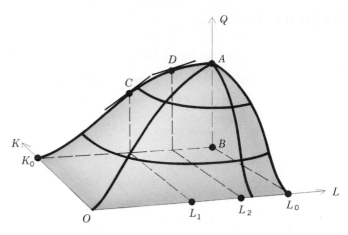

FIGURE 7.4

consequence, only a small portion of the production surface is shown in the figure.

Let us now hold capital fixed at the level K_0 and consider only variations in the input L. By setting $K = K_0$, all points in our (curtailed) domain become irrelevant except those on the line segment K_0B. By the same token, only the curve K_0CDA (a cross section of the production surface) will be germane to the present discussion. This curve represents a total-physical-product-of-labor (TPP$_L$) curve for a fixed amount of capital $K = K_0$; thus we may read from its slope the rate of change of Q with respect to changes in L while K is held constant. It is clear, therefore, that the slope of a curve such as K_0CDA represents the geometric counterpart of the partial derivative Q_L. Once again, we note that the slope of a total (TPP$_L$) curve is its corresponding marginal (MPP$_L \equiv Q_L$) curve.

It was mentioned earlier that a partial derivative is a function of all the independent variables of the primitive function. That Q_L is a function of L is immediately obvious from the K_0CDA curve itself. When $L = L_1$, the value of Q_L is equal to the slope of the curve at point C; but when $L = L_2$, the relevant slope is the one at point D. Why is Q_L also a function of K? The answer is that K can be fixed at various levels, and for each fixed level of K, there will result a different TPP$_L$ curve (a different cross section of the production surface), with inevitable repercussions on the derivative Q_L. Hence Q_L is also a function of K.

An analogous interpretation can be given to the partial derivative Q_K. If the labor input is held constant instead of K (say, at the level of L_0), then the line segment L_0B will be the relevant subset of the domain, and the curve L_0A will indicate the relevant subset of the production surface. The partial derivative Q_K can then be interpreted as the slope of the curve L_0A—bearing in mind that the K axis extends from southeast to northwest in Fig. 7.4. It should be noted that Q_K is again a function of both the variables L and K.

EXERCISE 7.4

1 Find $\partial y/\partial x_1$ and $\partial y/\partial x_2$ for each of the following functions:

(a) $y = 2x_1{}^3 - 11x_1{}^2x_2 + 3x_2{}^2$ (c) $y = (2x_1 + 3)(x_2 - 2)$

(b) $y = 6x_1 + 16x_1x_2{}^2 - 9x_2{}^3$ (d) $y = (2x_1 + 3)/(x_2 - 2)$

2 Find f_x and f_y from the following:

(a) $f(x,y) = x^2 + 5xy - y^3$ (c) $f(x,y) = \dfrac{2x - 3y}{x + y}$

(b) $f(x,y) = (x^2 - 7y)(x - 2)$ (d) $f(x,y) = \dfrac{x^2 - 1}{xy}$

3 From the answers to the preceding problem, find $f_x(1,2)$—the value of the partial derivative f_x when $x = 1$ and $y = 2$—for each function.

4 If the utility function of an individual takes the form

$$U = U(x_1,x_2) = (x_1 + 2)^2(x_2 + 3)^3$$

where U is total utility, and x_1 and x_2 are the quantities of two commodities consumed:

(a) Find the marginal-utility function of each of the two commodities.
(b) Find the value of the marginal utility of the first commodity when 3 units of each commodity are consumed.

7.5   Applications to Comparative-Static Analysis

Equipped with the knowledge of the various rules of differentiation, we can at last tackle the problem posed in comparative-static analysis: namely, how will the equilibrium value of an endogenous variable change when there is a change in any of the exogenous variables or parameters?

market model   First let us consider again the simple one-commodity market model of (3.1). That model, the reader will recall, can be written in the form of two equations:

$$Q = a - bP \qquad (a,b > 0) \qquad \text{[demand]}$$
$$Q = -c + dP \qquad (c,d > 0) \qquad \text{[supply]}$$

with solutions

$$(7.14) \qquad \bar{P} = \frac{a + c}{b + d}$$

$$(7.15) \qquad \bar{Q} = \frac{ad - bc}{b + d}$$

These solutions will be referred to as being in the *reduced form*: the two endogenous variables have been reduced to explicit expressions of the four mutually independent parameters a, b, c, and d.

To find how an infinitesimal change in one of the parameters will affect the value of $\bar{P}$, one has only to differentiate (7.14) partially with respect to each of the parameters. If the *sign* of a partial derivative, say, $\partial\bar{P}/\partial a$, can be determined from the given information about the parameters, we shall know the direction in which $\bar{P}$ will move when the parameter a changes; this constitutes a qualitative conclusion. If the magnitude of $\partial\bar{P}/\partial a$ can be ascertained, it will constitute a quantitative conclusion.

Similarly, we can draw qualitative or quantitative conclusions from the partial derivatives of $\bar{Q}$ with respect to each parameter, such as $\partial\bar{Q}/\partial a$. To avoid misunderstanding, however, a clear distinction should be made between the two derivatives $\partial\bar{Q}/\partial a$ and $\partial Q/\partial a$. The latter derivative is a concept appropriate to the demand function taken alone, and without regard to the supply function. The derivative $\partial\bar{Q}/\partial a$ pertains, on the other hand, to the equilibrium quantity in (7.15) which, being in the nature of a solution of the model, takes into account the interaction of demand and supply together. To emphasize this distinction, we shall refer to the partial derivatives of $\bar{P}$ and $\bar{Q}$ with respect to the parameters as *comparative-static derivatives*.

Concentrating on $\bar{P}$ for the time being, we can get the following four partial derivatives from (7.14):

$$\frac{\partial\bar{P}}{\partial a} = \frac{1}{b + d} \qquad \left[\text{parameter } a \text{ has the coefficient } \frac{1}{b + d}\right]$$

$$\frac{\partial\bar{P}}{\partial b} = \frac{0(b + d) - 1(a + c)}{(b + d)^2} = \frac{-(a + c)}{(b + d)^2} \qquad [\text{quotient rule}]$$

$$\frac{\partial\bar{P}}{\partial c} = \frac{1}{b + d} \left(= \frac{\partial\bar{P}}{\partial a}\right)$$

$$\frac{\partial\bar{P}}{\partial d} = \frac{0(b + d) - 1(a + c)}{(b + d)^2} = \frac{-(a + c)}{(b + d)^2} \left(= \frac{\partial\bar{P}}{\partial b}\right)$$

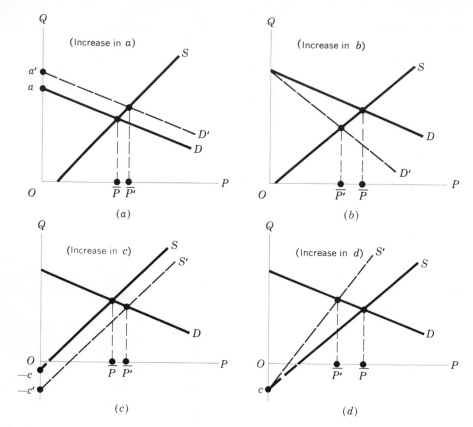

FIGURE 7.5

Since all the parameters are restricted to being positive in the present model, we can conclude that

$$(7.16) \qquad \frac{\partial \bar{P}}{\partial a} = \frac{\partial \bar{P}}{\partial c} > 0 \qquad \text{and} \qquad \frac{\partial \bar{P}}{\partial b} = \frac{\partial \bar{P}}{\partial d} < 0$$

For a fuller appreciation of the results in (7.16), let us look at Fig. 7.5, where each diagram shows a change in *one* of the parameters. As before, we are plotting Q (rather than P) on the vertical axis.

Diagram a pictures an increase in the parameter a (to a'). This means a higher vertical intercept for the demand curve, and inasmuch as the parameter b (the slope parameter) is unchanged, the increase in a results in a parallel upward shift of the demand curve from D to D'. The intersection of D' and the supply curve S determines an equilibrium price $\bar{P}'$, which is greater than the old equilibrium price $\bar{P}$. This corroborates the result that $\partial \bar{P}/\partial a > 0$, although for the sake of exposition we have shown in diagram a a much larger change in the parameter a than what the concept of derivative implies.

Comparative-Static Analysis

The situation in diagram c has a similar interpretation; but since the increase takes place in the parameter c, the result is a parallel shift of the supply curve instead. Note that this shift is downward because the supply curve has a vertical intercept of $-c$; thus an increase in c would mean a change in the intercept, say, from -2 to -4. The graphical comparative-static result, that $\bar{P}'$ exceeds $\bar{P}$, again conforms to what the positive sign of the derivative $\partial \bar{P}/\partial c$ would lead us to expect.

Diagrams b and d illustrate the effects of changes in the slope parameters b and d of the two functions in the model. An increase in b means that the slope of the demand curve will assume a larger numerical (absolute) value; i.e., it will become steeper. In accordance with the result $\partial \bar{P}/\partial b < 0$, we find a decrease in $\bar{P}$ in this diagram. The increase in d that makes the supply curve steeper also results in a decrease in the equilibrium price. This is, of course, again in line with the negative sign of the comparative-static derivative $\partial \bar{P}/\partial d$.

Thus far, all the results in (7.16) seem to have been obtainable graphically. If so, why should we bother to learn differentiation at all? The answer is that the differentiation approach has at least two major advantages. First, the graphical technique is subject to a dimensional restriction, but differentiation is not. Even when the number of endogenous variables and parameters is such that the equilibrium state cannot be shown graphically, we can nevertheless apply the differentiation techniques to the problem. Second, the differentiation method can yield results that are on a higher level of generality. The results in (7.16) will remain valid, regardless of the specific values that the parameters a, b, c, and d take, as long as they satisfy the sign restrictions. So the comparative-static conclusions of this model are, in effect, applicable to an infinite number of combinations of (linear) demand and supply functions. In contrast, the graphical approach deals only with some specific members of the family of demand and supply curves, and the analytical result derived therefrom is applicable, strictly speaking, only to the specific functions depicted.

The above serves to illustrate the application of partial differentiation to comparative-static analysis of the simple market model, but only half of the task has actually been accomplished, for we can also find the comparative-static derivatives pertaining to $\bar{Q}$. This we shall leave to the reader as an exercise.

national-income model   In place of the simple national-income model discussed in Chap. 3, let us study a slightly enlarged model with three endogenous variables, Y (national income), C (consumption), and T (tax collection):

$$\begin{aligned} Y &= C + I_0 + G_0 \\ C &= \alpha + \beta(Y - T) \qquad (\alpha > 0; 0 < \beta < 1) \\ T &= \gamma + \delta Y \qquad (\gamma > 0; 0 < \delta < 1) \end{aligned}$$

(7.17)

The first equation in this system gives the equilibrium condition for national income, while the second and third equations show, respectively, how C and T are determined in the model.

The restrictions on the values of the parameters α, β, γ, and δ can be explained thus: α is positive because consumption is positive even if disposable income $(Y - T)$ is zero; β is a positive fraction because it represents the marginal propensity to consume; γ is positive because even if Y is zero the government will still have a positive tax revenue (from tax bases other than income); and finally, δ is a positive fraction because it represents an income-tax rate, and as such it cannot exceed 100 percent. The exogenous variables I_0 (investment) and G_0 (government expenditure) are, of course, nonnegative. All the parameters and exogenous variables are assumed to be independent of one another, so that any one of them can be assigned a new value without affecting the others.

This model can be solved for $\overline{Y}$ by substituting the third equation of (7.17) into the second and then substituting the resulting equation into the first. The equilibrium income (in reduced form) is

$$(7.18) \qquad \overline{Y} = \frac{\alpha - \beta\gamma + I_0 + G_0}{1 - \beta + \beta\delta}$$

Similar equilibrium values can also be found for the endogenous variables C and T, but we shall concentrate on the equilibrium income.

From (7.18), there can be obtained six comparative-static derivatives. Among these, the following three have special policy significance:

$$(7.19) \qquad \frac{\partial \overline{Y}}{\partial G_0} = \frac{1}{1 - \beta + \beta\delta} > 0$$

$$(7.20) \qquad \frac{\partial \overline{Y}}{\partial \gamma} = \frac{-\beta}{1 - \beta + \beta\delta} < 0$$

$$(7.21) \qquad \frac{\partial \overline{Y}}{\partial \delta} = \frac{-\beta(\alpha - \beta\gamma + I_0 + G_0)}{(1 - \beta + \beta\delta)^2} = \frac{-\beta\overline{Y}}{1 - \beta + \beta\delta} < 0 \quad \text{[by (7.18)]}$$

The partial derivative in (7.19) gives us the *government-expenditure multiplier*. It has a positive sign here because β is less than 1, and $\beta\delta$ is greater than zero. If numerical values are given for the parameters β and δ, we can also find the numerical value of this multiplier from (7.19). The derivative in (7.20) may be called the *nonincome-tax multiplier*, because it shows how a change in γ, the government revenue from nonincome-tax sources, will affect the equilibrium income. This multiplier is negative in the present model because the denominator in (7.20) is positive and the numerator is negative. Lastly, the partial derivative in (7.21) represents an *income-tax-rate multiplier*. For any positive equilibrium income, this multiplier is also negative in the model.

Again, the reader should note the difference between the two derivatives $\partial \bar{Y}/\partial G_0$ and $\partial Y/\partial G_0$. The former is derived from (7.18), the expression for the equilibrium income. The latter, obtainable from the first equation in (7.17), is $\partial Y/\partial G_0 = 1$, which is altogether different in magnitude and in concept.

input-output model   The solution of an open input-output model appears as a matrix equation $\bar{x} = (I - A)^{-1}d$. If we denote the inverse matrix $(I - A)^{-1}$ by $B = [b_{ij}]$, then, for instance, the solution for a three-industry economy can be written as $\bar{x} = Bd$, or

$$(7.22) \qquad \begin{bmatrix} \bar{x}_1 \\ \bar{x}_2 \\ \bar{x}_3 \end{bmatrix} = \begin{bmatrix} b_{11} & b_{12} & b_{13} \\ b_{21} & b_{22} & b_{23} \\ b_{31} & b_{32} & b_{33} \end{bmatrix} \begin{bmatrix} d_1 \\ d_2 \\ d_3 \end{bmatrix}$$

What will be the rates of change of the solution values $\bar{x}_j$ with respect to the exogenous final demands d_1, d_2, and d_3? The general answer is that

$$(7.23) \qquad \frac{\partial \bar{x}_j}{\partial d_k} = b_{jk} \qquad (j,k = 1,2,3)$$

To see this, let us multiply out Bd in (7.22) and express the solution as

$$\begin{bmatrix} \bar{x}_1 \\ \bar{x}_2 \\ \bar{x}_3 \end{bmatrix} = \begin{bmatrix} b_{11}d_1 + b_{12}d_2 + b_{13}d_3 \\ b_{21}d_1 + b_{22}d_2 + b_{23}d_3 \\ b_{31}d_1 + b_{32}d_2 + b_{33}d_3 \end{bmatrix}$$

In this system of three equations, each one gives a particular solution value as a function of the exogenous final demands. Partial differentiation of these will produce a total of nine comparative-static derivatives:

$$(7.23') \qquad \begin{array}{ccc} \dfrac{\partial \bar{x}_1}{\partial d_1} = b_{11} & \dfrac{\partial \bar{x}_1}{\partial d_2} = b_{12} & \dfrac{\partial \bar{x}_1}{\partial d_3} = b_{13} \\[3mm] \dfrac{\partial \bar{x}_2}{\partial d_1} = b_{21} & \dfrac{\partial \bar{x}_2}{\partial d_2} = b_{22} & \dfrac{\partial \bar{x}_2}{\partial d_3} = b_{23} \\[3mm] \dfrac{\partial \bar{x}_3}{\partial d_1} = b_{31} & \dfrac{\partial \bar{x}_3}{\partial d_2} = b_{32} & \dfrac{\partial \bar{x}_3}{\partial d_3} = b_{33} \end{array}$$

This is simply the expanded version of (7.23).

Reading (7.23') as three distinct columns, we may combine the three derivatives in each column into a matrix (vector) derivative:

$$(7.23'') \qquad \frac{\partial \bar{x}}{\partial d_1} \equiv \frac{\partial}{\partial d_1} \begin{bmatrix} \bar{x}_1 \\ \bar{x}_2 \\ \bar{x}_3 \end{bmatrix} = \begin{bmatrix} b_{11} \\ b_{21} \\ b_{31} \end{bmatrix} \qquad \frac{\partial \bar{x}}{\partial d_2} = \begin{bmatrix} b_{12} \\ b_{22} \\ b_{32} \end{bmatrix} \qquad \frac{\partial \bar{x}}{\partial d_3} = \begin{bmatrix} b_{13} \\ b_{23} \\ b_{33} \end{bmatrix}$$

Since the three column vectors in (7.23″) are merely the columns of the matrix B, by further consolidation we can summarize the nine derivatives in a single matrix derivative $\partial \bar{x}/\partial d$. Given $\bar{x} = Bd$, we can simply write

$$\frac{\partial \bar{x}}{\partial d} = \begin{bmatrix} b_{11} & b_{12} & b_{13} \\ b_{21} & b_{22} & b_{23} \\ b_{31} & b_{32} & b_{33} \end{bmatrix} = B$$

This is a compact way of denoting all the comparative-static derivatives of our open input-output model. Obviously, this matrix derivative can easily be extended from the present three-industry model to the general n-industry case.

Comparative-static derivatives of the input-output model are useful as tools of economic planning, for they provide the answer to the question: If the planning targets, as reflected in $(d_1, d_2, \ldots, d_n)$, are revised, and if we wish to take care of all direct and indirect requirements in the economy so as to be completely free of bottlenecks, how must we change the output goals of the n industries?

EXERCISE 7.5

1   Examine the comparative-static properties of the equilibrium quantity in (7.15), and check your results by graphic analysis.

2   On the basis of (7.18), find the partial derivatives $\partial \bar{Y}/\partial I_0$, $\partial \bar{Y}/\partial \alpha$, and $\partial \bar{Y}/\partial \beta$. Interpret their meanings and determine their signs.

3   The numerical input-output model (5.21) was solved in Sec. 5.7.

     (a)   How many comparative-static derivatives can be derived?
     (b)   Write out these derivatives in the form of (7.23′) and (7.23″).

7.6   Note on Jacobian Determinants

The study of partial derivatives above was motivated solely by comparative-static considerations. But partial derivatives also provide a means of testing whether there exists functional (linear *or* nonlinear) dependence among a set of n functions in n variables. This is related to the notion of Jacobian determinants (named after Jacobi).

Consider the two functions

$$(7.24) \qquad \begin{aligned} y_1 &= 2x_1 + 3x_2 \\ y_2 &= 4x_1^2 + 12x_1x_2 + 9x_2^2 \end{aligned}$$

If we get all the four partial derivatives

$$\frac{\partial y_1}{\partial x_1} = 2 \qquad \frac{\partial y_1}{\partial x_2} = 3 \qquad \frac{\partial y_2}{\partial x_1} = 8x_1 + 12x_2 \qquad \frac{\partial y_2}{\partial x_2} = 12x_1 + 18x_2$$

and arrange them into a square matrix in a prescribed order, called a *Jacobian matrix* and denoted by J, and then take its determinant, the result will be what is known as a *Jacobian determinant* (or a *Jacobian*, for short), denoted by $|J|$:

$$(7.25) \qquad |J| \equiv \begin{vmatrix} \dfrac{\partial y_1}{\partial x_1} & \dfrac{\partial y_1}{\partial x_2} \\ \dfrac{\partial y_2}{\partial x_1} & \dfrac{\partial y_2}{\partial x_2} \end{vmatrix} = \begin{vmatrix} 2 & 3 \\ (8x_1 + 12x_2) & (12x_1 + 18x_2) \end{vmatrix}$$

For economy of space, this Jacobian is sometimes also expressed as

$$|J| \equiv \begin{vmatrix} \dfrac{\partial(y_1,y_2)}{\partial(x_1,x_2)} \end{vmatrix}$$

More generally, if we have n differentiable functions in n variables, not necessarily linear,

$$(7.26) \qquad \begin{aligned} y_1 &= f^1(x_1,x_2,\ldots,x_n) \\ y_2 &= f^2(x_1,x_2,\ldots,x_n) \\ &\ \cdots\cdots\cdots\cdots\cdots \\ y_n &= f^n(x_1,x_2,\ldots,x_n) \end{aligned}$$

where the symbol f^n denotes the nth function (and *not* the function raised to the nth power), we can derive a total of n^2 partial derivatives. Together, they will give rise to the Jacobian

$$(7.27) \qquad |J| \equiv \begin{vmatrix} \dfrac{\partial(y_1,y_2,\ldots,y_n)}{\partial(x_1,x_2,\ldots,x_n)} \end{vmatrix} \equiv \begin{vmatrix} \dfrac{\partial y_1}{\partial x_1} & \dfrac{\partial y_1}{\partial x_2} & \cdots & \dfrac{\partial y_1}{\partial x_n} \\ \multicolumn{4}{c}{\cdots\cdots\cdots\cdots\cdots\cdots} \\ \dfrac{\partial y_n}{\partial x_1} & \dfrac{\partial y_n}{\partial x_2} & \cdots & \dfrac{\partial y_n}{\partial x_n} \end{vmatrix}$$

A Jacobian test for the existence of functional dependence among a set of n functions is provided by the following theorem: The Jacobian $|J|$ defined in (7.27) will be identically zero for all values of $x_1, \ldots, x_n$ if and only if the n functions $f^1, \ldots, f^n$ in (7.26) are functionally (linearly or nonlinearly) dependent.

As an example, for the two functions in (7.24) the Jacobian as given in (7.25) has the value

$$|J| = (24x_1 + 36x_2) - (24x_1 + 36x_2) = 0$$

That is, the Jacobian vanishes for all values of x_1 and x_2. Therefore, according to the theorem, the two functions in (7.24) must be dependent. The reader can verify that y_2 is simply y_1 squared; thus they are indeed functionally dependent —here *non*linearly dependent.

Let us now consider the special case of *linear* functions. We have earlier shown that the rows of the coefficient matrix A of a linear-equation system

(7.28)
$$
\begin{aligned}
a_{11}x_1 + a_{12}x_2 + \cdots + a_{1n}x_n &= d_1 \\
a_{21}x_1 + a_{22}x_2 + \cdots + a_{2n}x_n &= d_2 \\
&\cdots \cdots \cdots \cdots \cdots \cdots \cdots \\
a_{n1}x_1 + a_{n2}x_2 + \cdots + a_{nn}x_n &= d_n
\end{aligned}
$$

are linearly dependent if and only if the determinant $|A| = 0$. This result can now be interpreted as a special application of the Jacobian criterion of functional dependence.

Take the left side of each equation in (7.28) as a separate function of the n variables $x_1, \ldots, x_n$, and denote these functions by $y_1, \ldots, y_n$. The partial derivatives of these functions will turn out to be $\partial y_1 / \partial x_1 = a_{11}$, $\partial y_1 / \partial x_2 = a_{12}$, etc., so that we may write, in general, $\partial y_i / \partial x_j = a_{ij}$. In view of this, the elements of the Jacobian of these n functions will be precisely the elements of the coefficient matrix A, already arranged in the correct order. That is, we have $|J| = |A|$, and thus the Jacobian criterion of functional dependence among $y_1, \ldots, y_n$—or, what amounts to the same thing, functional dependence among the rows of the coefficient matrix A—is equivalent to the criterion $|A| = 0$ in the present linear case.

In the above, the Jacobian was discussed in the context of a system of n functions in n variables. It should be pointed out, however, that the Jacobian in (7.27) is defined even if each function in (7.26) contains more than n variables, say, $n + 2$ variables:

$$
y_i = f^i(x_1, \ldots, x_n, x_{n+1}, x_{n+2}) \qquad (i = 1, 2, \ldots, n)
$$

In such a case, by holding x_{n+1} and x_{n+2} constant (or treating them as parameters), we can form a Jacobian by using the partial derivatives of the n functions with respect to the first n variables. Moreover, by holding a different pair of the x variables constant, we can form a different Jacobian. Such a situation will indeed be encountered in the next chapter, in connection with the discussion of the implicit-function theorem.

EXERCISE 7.6

1   Use Jacobian determinants to test the existence of functional dependence between the functions paired below:

(a) $y_1 = x_1^2 + 3x_2^2$
     $y_2 = 2x_1 + 5$
(b) $y_1 = 3x_1^2 + x_2$
     $y_2 = 9x_1^4 + 6x_1^2(x_2 + 4) + x_2(x_2 + 8) + 16$

2   Consider (7.22) as a set of three functions $\bar{x}_i = f^i(d_1,d_2,d_3)$ (with $i = 1,2,3$).

(a)   Write out the 3×3 Jacobian. Does it have some relation to (7.23')? Can we write $|J| = |B|$?

(b)   Since $B \equiv (I - A)^{-1}$, can we conclude that $|B| \neq 0$? What can we infer about the three equations in (7.22)?

COMPARATIVE-STATIC ANALYSIS OF GENERAL-FUNCTION MODELS

The study of partial derivatives has enabled us, in the preceding chapter, to handle the simpler type of comparative-static problems, in which the equilibrium solution of the model can be explicitly stated in the reduced form. In that case, partial differentiation of the solution will directly yield the desired comparative-static information. The reader will recall that the definition of the partial derivative requires the absence of any functional relationship among the independent variables (say, x_i), so that x_1 can vary without affecting the values of $x_2, x_3, \ldots, x_n$. As applied to comparative-static analysis, this means that the parameters and/or exogenous variables which appear in the reduced-form solution must be mutually independent. Since these are indeed defined as predetermined data for purposes of the model, the possibility of their mutually affecting one another is inherently ruled out. The procedure of partial differentiation adopted in the last chapter is therefore fully justifiable.

However, no such expediency should be expected when, owing to the inclusion of general functions in a model, no explicit reduced-form solution can be obtained. In such cases, we will have to find the comparative-static derivatives directly from the originally given equations in the model. Take, for instance, a simple national-income model with two endogenous variables Y and C:

$$Y = C + I_0 + G_0$$
$$C = C(Y, T_0) \qquad [T_0 \text{: exogenous tax collection}]$$

which is reducible to a single equation (an equilibrium condition)

$$Y = C(Y, T_0) + I_0 + G_0$$

to be solved for $\bar{Y}$. Because of the general form of the C function, however, no explicit solution is available. We must, therefore, find the comparative-static derivatives directly from this equation. How might we approach the problem? What special difficulty might we encounter?

Let us suppose that an equilibrium solution $\bar{Y}$ does exist. Then, under certain rather general conditions (to be discussed later), we may take $\bar{Y}$ to be a differentiable function of the exogenous variables I_0, G_0, and T_0. Hence, we may write the equation

$$\bar{Y} = \bar{Y}(I_0, G_0, T_0)$$

even though we are unable to determine explicitly the form which this function takes. Furthermore, in some neighborhood of the equilibrium value $\bar{Y}$, the following identical equality will hold:

$$\bar{Y} \equiv C(\bar{Y}, T_0) + I_0 + G_0$$

This type of identity will be referred to as an *equilibrium identity* because it is nothing but the equilibrium condition with the Y variable replaced by its equilibrium value $\bar{Y}$. Now that $\bar{Y}$ has entered into the picture, it may seem at first blush that simple partial differentiation of this identity will yield any desired comparative-static derivative, say, $\partial \bar{Y} / \partial T_0$. This, unfortunately, is not the case. Since $\bar{Y}$ is a function of T_0, the two arguments of the C function are *not* independent. Specifically, T_0 can in this case affect C not only *directly*, but also *indirectly* via $\bar{Y}$. Consequently, partial differentiation is no longer appropriate for our purposes. How, then, do we tackle this situation?

The answer is that we must resort to *total differentiation* (as against partial differentiation). Based on the notion of *total differentials*, the process of total differentiation can lead us to the related concept of *total derivative*, which measures the rate of change of a function such as $C(\bar{Y}, T_0)$ with respect to the argument T_0, when T_0 also affects the other argument, $\bar{Y}$. Thus, once we become familiar with these concepts, we shall be able to deal with functions whose arguments are not all independent, and that would remove the major stumbling block we have so far encountered in our study of the comparative statics of a general-function model. As a prelude to the discussion of these concepts, however, we should first introduce the notion of *differentials*.

8.1   Differentials

The symbol dy/dx, for the derivative of the function $y = f(x)$, has hitherto been regarded as a single entity. We shall now reinterpret it as a ratio of two quantities, dy and dx.

differentials and derivatives   Given a function $y = f(x)$, a specific Δx will call forth a corresponding Δy, and we can use the difference quotient $\Delta y/\Delta x$ to represent the rate of change of y with respect to x. Since it is true that

$$(8.1) \qquad \Delta y \equiv \left(\frac{\Delta y}{\Delta x}\right) \Delta x$$

the magnitude of Δy can be found, once the rate of change $\Delta y/\Delta x$ and the variation in x are known.

When Δx is infinitesimal, Δy will also be infinitesimal, and the difference quotient $\Delta y/\Delta x$ will turn into the derivative dy/dx. Then, if we denote the infinitesimal changes in x and y, respectively, by dx and dy (in place of Δx and Δy), the identity (8.1) will become

$$(8.2) \qquad dy \equiv \left(\frac{dy}{dx}\right) dx \qquad \text{or} \qquad dy \equiv f'(x)\, dx$$

The symbols dy and dx are called the *differentials* of y and x, respectively.

Dividing the two identities in (8.2) throughout by dx, we have

$$(8.2') \qquad \frac{(dy)}{(dx)} \equiv \left(\frac{dy}{dx}\right) \qquad \text{or} \qquad \frac{(dy)}{(dx)} \equiv f'(x)$$

This result shows that the derivative $(dy/dx) \equiv f'(x)$ may be interpreted as the quotient of two separate differentials dy and dx.

On the basis of (8.2), once we are given the derivative of a function $y = f(x)$, the differential dy can immediately be written.

Example 1   Given $y = 3x^2 + 7x - 5$, find dy. The derivative of the function is $dy/dx = 6x + 7$; thus the desired differential is

$$(8.3) \qquad dy = (6x + 7)\, dx$$

This result can be used to calculate the change in y resulting from a given change in x. It should be remembered, however, that the differentials dy and dx refer to infinitesimal changes only; hence, if we put an x change of substantial magnitude (Δx) into (8.3), the resulting dy can only serve as an approximation to the exact value of the corresponding y change (Δy). Let us calculate dy from (8.3), assuming that x is to change from 5 to 5.01. To do this, we set $x = 5$ and $dx = 0.01$ and substitute these into (8.3). The result is $dy = 37(0.01) = 0.37$. How does this figure compare with the *actual* change in y? When $x = 5$ (before change), we can compute from the given function that $y = 105$, but when $x = 5.01$ (after change), we get $y = 105.3703$. The true change in y is therefore $\Delta y = 0.3703$, for which our answer $dy = 0.37$ constitutes an approximation with an error of 0.0003.

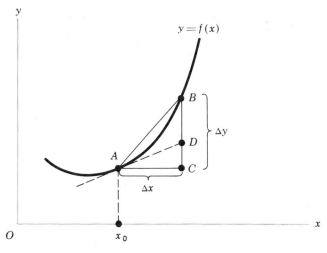

FIGURE 8.1

The source of error in the approximation can be illustrated in general by means of Fig. 8.1. For the given Δx depicted in the figure (distance AC), the true change in y, or Δy, is the distance CB. Had we used the slope of line AB ($= \Delta y/\Delta x = CB/AC$) as the relevant rate of change and applied (8.1) to find Δy, we would have obtained the correct answer:

$$\Delta y = \left(\frac{\Delta y}{\Delta x}\right)\Delta x = \frac{CB}{AC}\,AC = CB$$

But, in using (8.3)—a specific version of (8.2)—we actually employed the derivative dy/dx in lieu of $\Delta y/\Delta x$; that is, we used the slope of the tangent line AD ($= CD/AC$) instead of the slope of line AB in the calculation. Thus we obtained the answer

$$dy = \left(\frac{dy}{dx}\right)\Delta x = \frac{CD}{AC}\,AC = CD$$

which differs from the true change CB by an error of DB. This error can, of course, be expected to become smaller, the smaller is the Δx, that is, the closer the point B moves toward point A.

The process of finding the differential dy is called *differentiation*. The reader will recall that we have been using this term as a synonym for derivation, without having given an adequate explanation. In the light of our interpretation of a derivative as a quotient of two differentials, however, the rationale of the term becomes self-evident. It is still somewhat ambiguous, though, to use the single term differentiation to refer to the process of finding the differential dy as well as to that of finding the derivative dy/dx. To avoid confusion, the usual practice is to qualify the word differentiation with the phrase "with respect to x" when we take the derivative dy/dx. It should be clear from (8.2) that, given a function $y = f(x)$, we can always: (1) transform a known differential dy into the derivative dy/dx by dividing it by dx, and (2) transform a known derivative dy/dx into the differential dy by multiplying it by dx.

differentials and point elasticity   As an illustration of the application of differentials in economics, let us consider the notion of the elasticity of a function. For a demand function $Q = f(P)$, for instance, the elasticity is defined as $(\Delta Q/Q)/(\Delta P/P)$. Now, if the change in P is infinitesimal, the expressions ΔP and ΔQ will reduce to the differentials dP and dQ, and the elasticity measure will then assume the sense of the *point elasticity* of demand, denoted by ε_d (the Greek epsilon, for "elasticity"):[1]

$$(8.4) \qquad \varepsilon_d \equiv \frac{dQ/Q}{dP/P} = \frac{dQ/dP}{Q/P}$$

Observe that in the expression on the extreme right we have rearranged the differentials dQ and dP into a ratio dQ/dP, which can be construed as the derivative, or the *marginal* function, of the demand function $Q = f(P)$. Since we can interpret similarly the ratio Q/P in the denominator as the *average* function of the demand function, the point elasticity of demand ε_d in (8.4) is seen to be the ratio of the marginal function to the average function of the demand function.

Indeed, this last-described relationship is valid not only for the demand function but also for any other function, because for any given *total* function $y = f(x)$ we can write the formula for the point elasticity of y with respect to x as

$$(8.5) \qquad \varepsilon_{yx} = \frac{dy/dx}{y/x} = \frac{\text{marginal function}}{\text{average function}}$$

As a matter of convention, the *absolute* value of the elasticity measure is used in deciding whether the function is elastic at a particular point. In the case of a demand function, for instance, we stipulate:

$$\text{The demand is} \begin{Bmatrix} \text{elastic} \\ \text{of unit elasticity} \\ \text{inelastic} \end{Bmatrix} \text{at a point when } |\varepsilon_d| \gtreqless 1.$$

---

[1] The point-elasticity measure can alternatively be interpreted as the limit of $\dfrac{\Delta Q/Q}{\Delta P/P} = \dfrac{\Delta Q/\Delta P}{Q/P}$ as $\Delta P \to 0$, which gives the same result as (8.4).

Comparative-Static Analysis

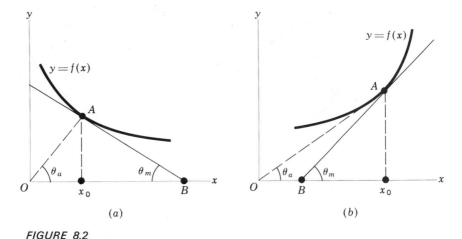

FIGURE 8.2

Example 2　Find ε_d if the demand function is $Q = 100 - 2P$. The marginal function and the average function of the given demand are

$$\frac{dQ}{dP} = -2 \quad \text{and} \quad \frac{Q}{P} = \frac{100 - 2P}{P}$$

so their ratio will give us

$$\varepsilon_d = \frac{-P}{50 - P}$$

As written, the elasticity is shown as a function of P. As soon as a specific price is chosen, however, the point elasticity will be determinate in magnitude. When $P = 25$, for instance, we have $\varepsilon_d = -1$, or $|\varepsilon_d| = 1$, so that the demand elasticity is unitary at that point. When $P = 30$, in contrast, we have $|\varepsilon_d| = 1.5$; hence, demand is elastic at that price. More generally, it may be verified that we have $|\varepsilon_d| > 1$ for $25 < P < 50$ and $|\varepsilon_d| < 1$ for $0 < P < 25$ in the present example. (Can a price $P > 50$ be considered meaningful here?)

At the risk of digressing a trifle, it may also be added here that the interpretation of the ratio of two differentials as a derivative—and the consequent transformation of the elasticity formula of a function into a ratio of its marginal to its average—makes possible a quick way of determining the point elasticity graphically. The two diagrams in Fig. 8.2 illustrate the cases, respectively, of a negatively sloped curve and a positively sloped curve. In each case, the value of the marginal function at point A on the curve, or at $x = x_0$ in the domain, is measured by the slope of the tangent line AB. The value of the average function, on the other hand, is in each case measured by the slope of line OA (the line

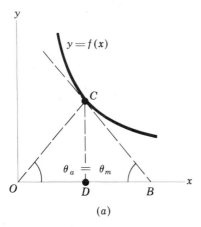

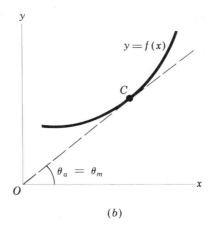

FIGURE 8.3

joining the point of origin with the given point A on the curve, like a radius vector), because at point A we have $y = x_0 A$ and $x = O x_0$, so that the average is $y/x = x_0 A / O x_0 = $ slope of OA. The elasticity at point A can thus be readily ascertained by comparing the *numerical* values of the two slopes involved: If AB is steeper than OA, the function is elastic at point A; in the opposite case, it is inelastic at A. Accordingly, the function pictured in Fig. 8.2a is inelastic at A (or at $x = x_0$), whereas the one in diagram b is elastic at A.

Moreover, the two slopes under comparison are directly dependent on the respective sizes of the two angles θ_m and θ_a (Greek letter theta; the subscripts m and a indicate marginal and average, respectively). Thus we may, alternatively, compare these two angles instead of the two corresponding slopes. Referring to Fig. 8.2 again, the reader can see that $\theta_m < \theta_a$ at point A in diagram a, indicating that the marginal falls short of the average in numerical value; thus the function is inelastic at point A. The exact opposite is true in diagram b.

Sometimes, we are interested in locating a point of unitary elasticity on a given curve. This can now be done easily. If the curve is negatively sloped, as in Fig. 8.3a, we should find a point C such that the line OC and the tangent BC will make the same-sized angle with the x axis, though in the opposite direction. In the case of a positively sloped curve, as in Fig. 8.3b, one has only to find a point C such that the tangent line at C, when properly extended, passes through the point of origin.

We must warn the reader that the graphical method just described is based on the assumption that the function $y = f(x)$ is plotted with the dependent variable y on the vertical axis. In particular, in applying the method to a demand curve, we should make sure that Q is on the vertical axis. (Suppose that Q is actually plotted on the horizontal axis. How should our method of reading the point elasticity be modified?)

EXERCISE 8.1

1   Given $y = 2x^2 - 4x + 9$:

   (a) Find the differential dy.
   (b) When x changes from 2 to 2.05, what is the value of dy?
   (c) Find the true value of Δy, and determine the error involved when dy is used as an approximation to Δy.
   (d) Determine the error of approximation when x undergoes a smaller change, from 2 to 2.01. Is the error smaller than in (c)?

2   Find the differential dy, given:

   (a) $y = -x(x^2 + 3)$ (b) $y = (x - 8)(x + 5)$ (c) $y = \dfrac{x}{x^2 + 1}$

3   Given the import function $M = f(Y)$, where M is imports and Y is national income, show that the income elasticity of imports ε_{MY} is the ratio of the marginal propensity to import to the average propensity to import.

4   Given the consumption function $C = a + bY$ (with $a > 0$; $0 < b < 1$):
   (a) Find its marginal function and its average function.
   (b) Find the income elasticity of consumption ε_{CY}, and determine its sign, assuming $Y > 0$.
   (c) Show that this consumption function is inelastic at all positive income levels.

5   Find the point elasticity of demand, given $Q = k/P^n$, where k and n are constants. Is the value of the elasticity dependent on the price P?

8.2   Total Differentials

The concept of differentials can easily be extended to a function of two or more independent variables. Consider a saving function

   (8.6) $S = S(Y,i)$

where S is savings, Y is national income, and i is interest rate. This function is assumed—as all the functions we shall use here will be assumed—to be continuous and to possess continuous (partial) derivatives, which is another way of saying that it is smooth and differentiable everywhere. We know that the partial derivative $\partial S/\partial Y$ (or S_Y) measures the rate of change of S with respect to an infinitesimal change in Y or, in short, that it signifies the marginal propensity to save. As a result, the change in S due to the small change in Y may be represented by the expression $(\partial S/\partial Y)\,dY$, which is comparable to the right-hand expression in (8.2). By the same token, the change in S resulting from an infinitesimal change in i can be denoted as $(\partial S/\partial i)\,di$. The total change in S will then be equal to

$$dS = \frac{\partial S}{\partial Y}\,dY + \frac{\partial S}{\partial i}\,di$$

or, in an alternative notation,

$$dS = S_Y\,dY + S_i\,di$$

The expression dS, being the *sum* of the changes from both sources, is called the *total differential* of the saving function. And the process of finding such a total differential is called *total differentiation*.

It is possible, of course, that Y may change while i remains constant. In that case, $di = 0$, and the total differential will reduce to a *partial differential*: $dS = (\partial S/\partial Y)\,dY$. Dividing both sides by dY, we get

$$\frac{\partial S}{\partial Y} = \left(\frac{dS}{dY}\right)_{i\ \text{constant}}$$

Thus it is clear that the partial derivative $\partial S/\partial Y$ can also be interpreted as the ratio of two differentials dS and dY, with the proviso that i, the other independent variable in the function, is held constant. In a wholly analogous manner, we can form another partial differential $dS = (\partial S/\partial i)\,di$ when $dY = 0$, and can then interpret the partial derivative $\partial S/\partial i$ as the ratio of the differential dS (with Y held constant) to the differential di. Note that although dS and di can now each stand alone as a differential, the expression $\partial S/\partial i$ remains as a single entity.

The more general case of a function of n independent variables can be exemplified by, say, a utility function in the general form

(8.7) $U = U(x_1, x_2, \ldots, x_n)$

The total differential of this function can be written as

$$dU = \frac{\partial U}{\partial x_1}\,dx_1 + \frac{\partial U}{\partial x_2}\,dx_2 + \cdots + \frac{\partial U}{\partial x_n}\,dx_n$$

or $dU = U_1\,dx_1 + U_2\,dx_2 + \cdots + U_n\,dx_n = \displaystyle\sum_{i=1}^{n} U_i\,dx_i$

in which each term on the right side indicates the amount of change in U resulting from a small change in one of the independent variables. Economically, the first term, $U_1\,dx_1$, means the marginal utility of the first commodity times the increment in consumption of that commodity, and similarly for the other terms. The sum of these thus represents the total change in utility originating from all possible sources of change.

Like any other function, the saving function (8.6) and the utility function (8.7) can both be expected to give rise to elasticity measures similar to that defined in (8.5). But each elasticity measure must in these instances be defined in terms of the change in *one* of the independent variables only; there will thus be *two* such elasticity measures to the saving function, and n of them to the utility function. These are accordingly called *partial elasticities*. For the saving function, the partial elasticities may be written as

$$\varepsilon_{SY} = \frac{\partial S/\partial Y}{S/Y} = \frac{\partial S}{\partial Y}\frac{Y}{S} \quad \text{and} \quad \varepsilon_{Si} = \frac{\partial S/\partial i}{S/i} = \frac{\partial S}{\partial i}\frac{i}{S}$$

For the utility function, the n partial elasticities can be concisely denoted as follows:

$$\varepsilon_{Ux_i} = \frac{\partial U}{\partial x_i}\frac{x_i}{U} \quad (i = 1, 2, \ldots, n)$$

EXERCISE 8.2

1   Find the total differential, given:

(a) $z = 3x^2 + xy - 2y^3$ (b) $U = 2x_1 + 5x_1x_2 + x_2^2$

2   From the answers to the preceding problem:

(a) Find dz (as an approximation to Δz) when x changes from 2 to 2.01 and y changes from 4 to 4.02.
(b) Find dU (as an approximation to ΔU) when x_1 changes from 3 to 3.001 and x_2 changes from 5 to 5.003.

3   Find the total differential, given:

(a) $y = \dfrac{x_1}{x_1 + x_2}$ (b) $y = \dfrac{x_1x_2}{x_1 + x_2}$

4   The supply function of a certain commodity is:

$$Q = a + bP^2 + R^{1/2} \quad (a < 0, b > 0) \quad [R: \text{rainfall}]$$

(a) Find the price elasticity of supply ε_{QP}, and the rainfall elasticity of supply ε_{QR}.
(b) How do these partial elasticities vary with P and R? In a monotonic fashion (for positive P and R)?

8.3   Rules of Differentials

A straightforward way of finding the total differential dy, given a function

$$y = f(x_1, x_2)$$

is to find the partial derivatives f_1 and f_2 and substitute these into the equation

$$dy = f_1\, dx_1 + f_2\, dx_2$$

But sometimes it may be more convenient to apply certain rules of differentials which, in view of their striking resemblance to the derivative formulas studied before, are exceedingly easy to remember.

Let u and v be two functions of the variables x_1 and x_2; then the following rules are valid:[1]

RULE I $d(cu^n) = cnu^{n-1}\, du$ [cf. power-function rule]

RULE II $d(u \pm v) = du \pm dv$ [cf. sum-difference rule]

RULE III $d(uv) = v\, du + u\, dv$ [cf. product rule]

RULE IV $d\left(\dfrac{u}{v}\right) = \dfrac{1}{v^2}(v\, du - u\, dv)$ [cf. quotient rule]

Instead of proving these rules here, we shall merely illustrate their practical application.

Example 1   Find the total differential dy of the function

$$y = 5x_1{}^2 + 3x_2$$

The straightforward method calls for the evaluation of the partial derivatives $f_1 = 10x_1$ and $f_2 = 3$, which will then enable us to write

$$dy = f_1\, dx_1 + f_2\, dx_2 = 10x_1\, dx_1 + 3dx_2$$

We may, however, let $u = 5x_1{}^2$ and $v = 3x_2$ and apply the above-mentioned rules to get the identical answer as follows:

$$dy = d(5x_1{}^2) + d(3x_2) \qquad \text{[by Rule II]}$$
$$= 10x_1\, dx_1 + 3dx_2 \qquad \text{[by Rule I]}$$

---

[1] All the rules of differentials discussed in this section are also applicable when u and v are themselves the independent variables (rather than functions of some other variables x_1 and x_2).

Comparative-Static Analysis

Example 2   Find the total differential of the function

$$y = 3x_1{}^2 + x_1 x_2{}^2$$

Since $f_1 = 6x_1 + x_2{}^2$ and $f_2 = 2x_1 x_2$, the desired differential is

$$dy = (6x_1 + x_2{}^2)\, dx_1 + 2x_1 x_2\, dx_2$$

By applying the given rules, the same result can be arrived at thus:

$$dy = d(3x_1{}^2) + d(x_1 x_2{}^2) \qquad \text{[by Rule II]}$$
$$= 6x_1\, dx_1 + x_2{}^2\, dx_1 + x_1\, d(x_2{}^2) \qquad \text{[by Rules I and III]}$$
$$= (6x_1 + x_2{}^2)\, dx_1 + 2x_1 x_2\, dx_2 \qquad \text{[by Rule I]}$$

Example 3   Find the total differential of the function

$$y = \frac{x_1 + x_2}{2x_1{}^2}$$

In view of the fact that the partial derivatives in this case are

$$f_1 = \frac{-(x_1 + 2x_2)}{2x_1{}^3} \qquad \text{and} \qquad f_2 = \frac{1}{2x_1{}^2}$$

(check these as an exercise), the desired differential is

$$dy = \frac{-(x_1 + 2x_2)}{2x_1{}^3}\, dx_1 + \frac{1}{2x_1{}^2}\, dx_2$$

However, the same result may also be obtained by application of the rules as follows:

$$dy = \frac{1}{4x_1{}^4}\, [2x_1{}^2\, d(x_1 + x_2) - (x_1 + x_2)\, d(2x_1{}^2)] \qquad \text{[by Rule IV]}$$

$$= \frac{1}{4x_1{}^4}\, [2x_1{}^2(dx_1 + dx_2) - (x_1 + x_2)4x_1\, dx_1] \qquad \text{[by Rules II and I]}$$

$$= \frac{1}{4x_1{}^4}\, [-2x_1(x_1 + 2x_2)\, dx_1 + 2x_1{}^2\, dx_2]$$

$$= \frac{-(x_1 + 2x_2)}{2x_1{}^3}\, dx_1 + \frac{1}{2x_1{}^2}\, dx_2$$

These rules can naturally be extended to cases where more than two functions of x_1 and x_2 are involved. In particular, we can add the following two rules to the previous collection:

RULE V $d(u \pm v \pm w) = du \pm dv \pm dw$

RULE VI $d(uvw) = vw\,du + uw\,dv + uv\,dw$

To derive Rule VI, we can employ the familiar trick of first letting $z = vw$, so that

$$d(uvw) = d(uz) = z\,du + u\,dz \qquad \text{[by Rule III]}$$

Then, by applying Rule III again to dz, we get the intermediate result

$$dz = d(vw) = w\,dv + v\,dw$$

which, when substituted into the preceding equation, will yield

$$d(uvw) = vw\,du + u(w\,dv + v\,dw) = vw\,du + uw\,dv + uv\,dw$$

as the desired final result. A similar procedure can be employed to derive Rule V.

EXERCISE 8.3

1   Use the rules of differentials to find (a) dz from $z = 3x^2 + xy - 2y^3$ and (b) dU from $U = 2x_1 + 5x_1x_2 + x_2{}^2$. Check your answers against those obtained for Exercise 8.2-1.

2   Use the rules of differentials to find dy from the following functions:

(a) $y = \dfrac{x_1}{x_1 + x_2}$ \qquad\qquad\qquad (b) $y = \dfrac{x_1x_2}{x_1 + x_2}$

Check your answers against those obtained for Exercise 8.2-3.

3   Given $y = 3x_1(2x_2 - 1)(x_3 + 5)$
   (a) Find dy by Rule VI.
   (b) Find the partial differential of y, if $dx_2 = dx_3 = 0$.
   (c) Derive from the above result the partial derivative $\partial y/\partial x_1$.

4   Prove Rules I, II, III, and IV, assuming u and v to be the independent variables (rather than functions of some other variables). (*Hint:* Apply the definitions of differential and total differential.)

8.4   Total Derivatives

With the notion of differentials at our disposal, we are now equipped to answer the question posed at the beginning of the chapter: How do we find the rate of change of the function $C(\overline{Y}, T_0)$ with respect to T_0, when $\overline{Y}$ and T_0 are related?

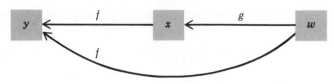

FIGURE 8.4

As previously mentioned, the answer lies in the concept of total derivative. Unlike a *partial* derivative, a *total* derivative does not require the argument $\overline{Y}$ to remain constant as T_0 varies, and can thus allow for the postulated relationship between the two arguments.

finding the total derivative   To carry on the discussion in a more general framework, let us consider any function

(8.8) $y = f(x, w)$ where $x = g(w)$

with the three variables y, x, and w related to one another as in Fig. 8.4. In this figure, which we shall refer to as a *channel map*, it is clearly seen that w—the ultimate source of change in this case—can affect y through two channels: (1) *indirectly*, via the function g and then f (the straight arrows), and (2) *directly*, via the function f (the curved arrow). Whereas the partial derivative f_w is adequate for expressing the direct effect alone, a total derivative is needed to express both effects jointly.

To obtain this total derivative, we first differentiate y totally, to get the total differential $dy = f_x\, dx + f_w\, dw$. When both sides of this equation are divided by the differential dw, the result is

(8.9) $$\frac{dy}{dw} = f_x \frac{dx}{dw} + f_w \frac{dw}{dw}$$

$$= \frac{\partial y}{\partial x} \frac{dx}{dw} + \frac{\partial y}{\partial w} \qquad \left[\frac{dw}{dw} = 1\right]$$

Since the ratio of two differentials may be interpreted as a derivative, the expression dy/dw on the left may be regarded as some measure of the rate of change of y with respect to w. Moreover, if the two terms on the right side of (8.9) can be identified, respectively, as the indirect and the direct effects of w on y, then dy/dw will indeed be the total derivative we are seeking. Now, the second term $(\partial y/\partial w)$ is already known to measure the direct effect, and it thus corresponds to the curved arrow in Fig. 8.4. That the first term $\left(\dfrac{\partial y}{\partial x} \dfrac{dx}{dw}\right)$ measures the indirect effect will also become evident when we analyze it with the help of some arrows as follows:[1]

$$\left(\frac{\partial y}{\partial x} \leftarrow - - - \frac{-dx}{dw}\right)$$

The change in w (namely, dw) is in the first instance transmitted to the variable x, and through the resulting change in x (namely, dx) it is relayed to the variable y. But this is precisely the indirect effect, as depicted by the sequence of straight arrows in Fig. 8.4. Hence, the expression in (8.9) does indeed represent the desired total derivative. The process of finding the total derivative dy/dw is referred to as *total differentiation of y with respect to w*.

Example 1   Find the total derivative dy/dw, given the function

$$y = f(x,\, w) = 3x - w^2 \qquad \text{where} \qquad x = g(w) = 2w^2 + w + 4$$

By virtue of (8.9), the total derivative should be

$$\frac{dy}{dw} = 3(4w + 1) + (-2w) = 10w + 3$$

As a check, we may substitute the function g into the function f, to get

$$y = 3(2w^2 + w + 4) - w^2 = 5w^2 + 3w + 12$$

which is now a function of w alone. The derivative dy/dw is then easily found to be $10w + 3$, the identical answer.

Example 2   If we have a utility function $U = U(c,s)$, where c is the amount of coffee consumed and s is the amount of sugar consumed, and another function $s = g(c)$ indicating the complementarity between these two goods, then we can simply write

$$U = U[c,g(c)]$$

from which it follows that

$$\frac{dU}{dc} = \frac{\partial U}{\partial c} + \frac{\partial U}{\partial g(c)}\, g'(c)$$

---

[1] The expression $\dfrac{\partial y}{\partial x}\dfrac{dx}{dw}$ is reminiscent of the chain rule (composite-function rule) discussed earlier, except that here a partial derivative appears because f happens to be a function of more than one variable.

Comparative-Static Analysis

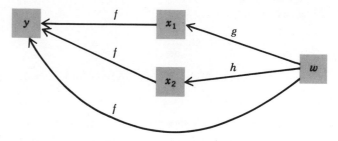

FIGURE 8.5

a variation on the theme   The situation is only slightly more complicated when we have

$$(8.10) \qquad y = f(x_1,x_2,w) \qquad \text{where} \quad \begin{cases} x_1 = g(w) \\ x_2 = h(w) \end{cases}$$

The channel map will now appear as in Fig. 8.5. This time, the variable w can affect y through three channels: (1) indirectly, via the function g and then f, (2) again indirectly, via the function h and then f, and (3) directly via f. From our previous experience, these three effects are expected to be expressible, respectively, as $\dfrac{\partial y}{\partial x_1}\dfrac{dx_1}{dw}$, $\dfrac{\partial y}{\partial x_2}\dfrac{dx_2}{dw}$, and $\dfrac{\partial y}{\partial w}$. This expectation is indeed correct, for when we take the total differential of y, and then divide both sides by dw, we do get

$$(8.11) \qquad \frac{dy}{dw} = f_1 \frac{dx_1}{dw} + f_2 \frac{dx_2}{dw} + f_w \frac{dw}{dw}$$

$$= \frac{\partial y}{\partial x_1}\frac{dx_1}{dw} + \frac{\partial y}{\partial x_2}\frac{dx_2}{dw} + \frac{\partial y}{\partial w}$$

which is comparable to (8.9) above.

Example 3   Suppose that we have a production function

$$Q = Q(K,L) = 25KL - K^2 - 2L^2$$

where the two factors K and L are functions of time t,

$$K = g(t) = 0.3t \qquad L = h(t) = 0.2t$$

The functions g and h convey the information that the amount of capital and labor available will be increasing over time. To find the rate of change of output with respect to time, we can simply apply the total-derivative formula (8.11).

Thus, we have

$$\frac{dQ}{dt} = Q_K \frac{dK}{dt} + Q_L \frac{dL}{dt}$$

$$= (25L - 2K)(0.3) + (25K - 4L)(0.2) = 4.4K + 6.7L = 2.66t$$

another variation on the theme   When the ultimate source of change, w in (8.10), is replaced by two coexisting sources, u and v, the situation becomes the following:

$$(8.12) \qquad y = f(x_1, x_2, u, v) \qquad \text{where} \qquad \begin{cases} x_1 = g(u,v) \\ x_2 = h(u,v) \end{cases}$$

While the channel map will now contain more arrows, the principle of its construction remains the same; we shall, therefore, leave it to the reader to draw. To find the total derivative of y with respect to u (while v is held constant), we may once again resort to taking the total differential of y, and then dividing through by the differential du, with the result:

$$\frac{dy}{du} = \frac{\partial y}{\partial x_1}\frac{dx_1}{du} + \frac{\partial y}{\partial x_2}\frac{dx_2}{du} + \frac{\partial y}{\partial u}\frac{du}{du} + \frac{\partial y}{\partial v}\frac{dv}{du}$$

$$= \frac{\partial y}{\partial x_1}\frac{dx_1}{du} + \frac{\partial y}{\partial x_2}\frac{dx_2}{du} + \frac{\partial y}{\partial u} \qquad \left[\frac{dv}{du} = 0 \text{ since } v \text{ is constant}\right]$$

In view of the fact that we are varying u while holding v constant (as a single derivative cannot handle changes in u and v both), however, the above result must be modified in two ways: (1) The derivatives dx_1/du and dx_2/du on the right should be rewritten with the partial sign as $\partial x_1/\partial u$ and $\partial x_2/\partial u$. This is in line with the functions g and h in (8.12). (2) The ratio dy/du on the left should also be interpreted as a *partial* derivative, even though—being derived through the process of total differentiation of y—it is actually in the nature of a *total* derivative. For this reason, we shall refer to it by the explicit name of *partial total derivative*, and denote it by $\S y/\S u$ (with $\S$ rather than ∂), in order to distinguish it from the simple partial derivative $\partial y/\partial u$ which, as the above result shows, is but one of three component terms that add up to the partial total derivative.[1]

With these modifications, our result becomes

$$(8.13) \qquad \frac{\S y}{\S u} = \frac{\partial y}{\partial x_1}\frac{\partial x_1}{\partial u} + \frac{\partial y}{\partial x_2}\frac{\partial x_2}{\partial u} + \frac{\partial y}{\partial u}$$

which is comparable to (8.11). Note the appearance of the symbol $\partial y/\partial u$ on the

---

[1] An alternative way of denoting this partial total derivative is:

$$\left.\frac{dy}{du}\right|_{v \text{ constant}} \qquad \text{or} \qquad \left.\frac{dy}{du}\right|_{dv=0}$$

Comparative-Static Analysis

right, which necessitates the adoption of the new symbol $\S y/\S u$ on the left to indicate the broader concept of a partial total derivative. In a perfectly analogous manner, we can derive the other partial total derivative, $\S y/\S v$. Inasmuch as the roles of u and v are symmetrical in (8.12), however, a simpler alternative is available to us. All we have to do to obtain $\S y/\S v$ is to replace the symbol u in (8.13) by the symbol v throughout.

The use of the new symbols $\S y/\S u$ and $\S y/\S v$ for the partial total derivatives, if unconventional, serves the good purpose of avoiding confusion with the simple partial derivatives $\partial y/\partial u$ and $\partial y/\partial v$ that can arise from the function f alone in (8.12). However, in the special case where the f function takes the form of $y = f(x_1,x_2)$ without the arguments u and v, the simple partial derivatives $\partial y/\partial u$ and $\partial y/\partial v$ are not defined. Hence, it may not be inappropriate in such a case to use the latter symbols for the partial total derivatives of y with respect to u and v, since no confusion is possible. Even in that event, though, the use of a special symbol is advisable for the sake of greater clarity.

some general remarks   To conclude this section, we offer three general remarks regarding total derivative and total differentiation:

1   In the cases we have discussed, the situation involves without exception a variable that is functionally dependent on a second variable, which is in turn dependent functionally on a third variable. As a consequence, the notion of a *chain* inevitably enters the picture, as evidenced by the appearance of a product (or products) of two derivative expressions as the component(s) of a total derivative. For this reason, the total-derivative formulas in (8.9), (8.11), and (8.13) can also be regarded as expressions of the chain rule, or the composite-function rule—a more sophisticated version of the chain rule introduced in Sec. 7.3.

2   The chain of derivatives does not have to be limited to only two "links" (two derivatives being multiplied); the concept of total derivative should be extendible to cases where there are three or more links in the composite function.

3   In all cases discussed, total derivatives—including those which have been called *partial total derivatives*—measure rates of change with respect to some *ultimate* variables in the chain or, in other words, with respect to certain variables which are in a sense *exogenous* and which are *not* expressed as functions of some other variables. The essence of the total derivative and of the process of total differentiation is to make due allowance for *all* the channels, indirect as well as direct, through which the effects of a change in an *ultimate* variable can possibly be carried to the particular dependent variable under study.

EXERCISE 8.4

1   Find the total derivative dz/dy, given:

    (a) $z = f(x,y) = 2x + xy - y^2$, where $x = g(y) = 3y^2$

    (b) $z = 5x^2 - 3xy + 2y^2$, where $x = 1/y$

    (c) $z = (x + y)(x - 2y)$, where $x = 2 - 7y$

2   Find the total derivative dz/dt, given:

    (a) $z = x^2 - 8xy - y^3$, where $x = 3t$ and $y = 1 - t$

    (b) $z = 3u + vt$, where $u = 2t^2$ and $v = t + 1$

    (c) $z = f(x,y,t)$, where $x = a + bt$ and $y = c + dt$

3   Find the partial total derivatives $\oint W/\oint u$ and $\oint W/\oint v$ if:

    (a) $W = ax^2 + bxy + cu$, where $x = \alpha u + \beta v$ and $y = \gamma u$

    (b) $W = f(x_1,x_2)$, where $x_1 = 5u^2 + 3v$ and $x_2 = u - 4v^3$

4   Draw a channel map appropriate to the case of (8.12).

5   Derive the expression for $\oint y/\oint v$ formally from (8.12) by taking the total differential of y and then dividing by dv.

8.5   Derivatives of Implicit Functions

The concept of total differentials can also enable us to find the derivatives of so-called "implicit functions."

implicit functions   A function given in the form of $y = f(x)$, say,

(8.14) $y = f(x) = 3x^4$

is called an *explicit function*, because the variable y is explicitly expressed as a function of x. If this function is written alternatively in the equivalent form

(8.14') $y - 3x^4 = 0$

however, we no longer have an explicit function. Rather, the function (8.14) is then only *implicitly* defined by the equation (8.14'). When we are (only) given an equation in the form of (8.14'), therefore, the function $y = f(x)$ which it implies, and whose specific form may not even be known to us, is referred to as an *implicit function*.

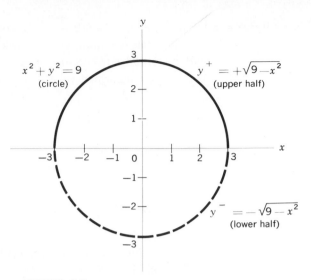

$x^2 + y^2 = 9$
(circle)

$y^+ = +\sqrt{9-x^2}$
(upper half)

$y^- = -\sqrt{9-x^2}$
(lower half)

FIGURE 8.6

An equation in the form of (8.14′) can be denoted in general by $F(y,x) = 0$, because its left side is a function of the two variables y and x. Note that we are using the capital letter F here to distinguish it from the function f; the function F, representing the left-side expression in (8.14′), has two arguments, y and x, whereas the function f, representing the implicit function, has only one argument, x. There may, of course, be more than two arguments in the F function. For instance, we may encounter an equation $F(y, x_1, \ldots, x_m) = 0$. Such an equation *may* also define an implicit function $y = f(x_1, \ldots, x_m)$.

The equivocal word "may" in the last sentence was used advisedly. For, whereas an explicit function, say, $y = f(x)$, can always be transformed into an equation $F(y,x) = 0$ by simply transposing the $f(x)$ expression to the left side of the equals sign, the reverse transformation is not always possible. Indeed, in certain cases, a given equation in the form of $F(y,x) = 0$ may not implicitly define a function $y = f(x)$. For instance, the equation $x^2 + y^2 = 0$ is satisfied only at the point of origin $(0,0)$, and hence yields no meaningful function to speak of. As another example, the equation

(8.15) $F(y,x) = x^2 + y^2 - 9 = 0$

implies not a function, but a relation, because (8.15) plots as a circle, as shown in Fig. 8.6, so that no unique value of y corresponds to each value of x. Note, however, that if we restrict y to nonnegative values, then we will have the upper half of the circle only, and that does constitute a function, namely, $y = +\sqrt{9 - x^2}$. Similarly, the lower half of the circle, with y values nonpositive, constitutes another function, $y = -\sqrt{9 - x^2}$. In contrast, neither the left half nor the right half of the circle can qualify as a function.

In view of this uncertainty, it becomes of interest to ask whether there are known general conditions under which we can be sure that a given equation in the form of

$$(8.16) \qquad F(y, x_1, \ldots, x_m) = 0$$

does indeed define an implicit function

$$(8.17) \qquad y = f(x_1, \ldots, x_m)$$

The answer to this lies in the so-called "implicit-function theorem," which states that:

> Given (8.16), if (a) the function F has continuous partial derivatives $F_y, F_1, \ldots, F_m$, and if (b) at a point $(y_0, x_{10}, \ldots, x_{m0})$ satisfying the equation (8.16), F_y is nonzero, then there exists an m-dimensional neighborhood of $(x_{10}, \ldots, x_{m0})$, N, in which y is an implicitly defined function of the variables $x_1, \ldots, x_m$, in the form of (8.17). This implicit function satisfies $y_0 = f(x_{10}, \ldots, x_{m0})$. It also satisfies the equation (8.16) for *every* m-tuple $(x_1, \ldots, x_m)$ in the neighborhood N—thereby giving (8.16) the status of an *identity* in that neighborhood. Moreover, the implicit function f is continuous, and has continuous partial derivatives $f_1, \ldots, f_m$.

Let us apply this theorem to the equation of the circle, (8.15), which contains only one x variable. First, we can duly verify that $F_y = 2y$ and $F_x = 2x$ are continuous, as required. Then we note that F_y is nonzero except when $y = 0$, that is, except at the left-most point $(-3,0)$ and the right-most point $(3,0)$ on the circle. Thus, around any point on the circle except $(-3,0)$ and $(3,0)$, we can construct a neighborhood in which the equation (8.15) defines an implicit function $y = f(x)$. This is easily verifiable in Fig. 8.6, where it is indeed possible to draw, say, a rectangle around any point on the circle—except $(-3,0)$ and $(3,0)$—such that the portion of the circle enclosed therein will constitute the graph of a function, with a unique y value for each value of x in that rectangle.

Several things should be noted about the implicit-function theorem. First, the conditions cited in the theorem are in the nature of sufficient (but not necessary) conditions. This means that if we find $F_y = 0$ at a point satisfying (8.16), we cannot use the theorem to deny the existence of an implicit function around that point. For such a function may in fact exist (see Exercise 8.5-4).[1]

---

[1] On the other hand, if $F_y = 0$ in an entire neighborhood, then it can be concluded that no implicit function is defined in that neighborhood. By the same token if $F_y = 0$ identically, then no implicit function exists anywhere.

Secondly, even if an implicit function f is assured to exist, the theorem gives no clue as to the specific form the function f takes. Nor, for that matter, does it tell us the exact size of the neighborhood N in which the implicit function is defined. However, despite these limitations, this theorem is one of great importance. For whenever the conditions of the theorem are satisfied, it now becomes meaningful to talk about and make use of a function such as (8.17), even if our model may contain an equation (8.16) which is difficult or impossible to solve explicitly for y in terms of the x variables. Moreover, since the theorem also guarantees the existence of the partial derivatives $f_1, \ldots, f_m$, it is now also meaningful to talk about these derivatives of the implicit function.

derivatives of implicit functions   If the equation $F(y, x_1, \ldots, x_m) = 0$ can be solved for y, then we can explicitly write out the function $y = f(x_1, \ldots, x_m)$, and find its derivatives by the methods learned before. For instance, (8.15) can be solved to yield two separate functions

$$(8.15')\qquad \begin{aligned} y^+ &= +\sqrt{9 - x^2} \qquad \text{[upper half of circle]}\\ y^- &= -\sqrt{9 - x^2} \qquad \text{[lower half of circle]} \end{aligned}$$

and their derivatives can be found as follows:

$$\frac{dy^+}{dx} = \frac{d}{dx}\,(9 - x^2)^{1/2} = \tfrac{1}{2}(9 - x^2)^{-1/2}(-2x)$$

$$= \frac{-x}{\sqrt{9 - x^2}} = \frac{-x}{y^+} \qquad (y^+ \neq 0)$$

(8.18)

$$\frac{dy^-}{dx} = \frac{d}{dx}\,[-(9 - x^2)^{1/2}] = -\tfrac{1}{2}(9 - x^2)^{-1/2}(-2x)$$

$$= \frac{x}{\sqrt{9 - x^2}} = \frac{-x}{y^-} \qquad (y^- \neq 0)$$

But what if the given equation, $F(y, x_1, \ldots, x_m) = 0$, cannot be solved for y explicitly? In this case, if under the terms of the implicit-function theorem an implicit function is known to exist, we can still obtain the desired derivatives without having to solve for y first. To do this, we make use of the so-called "implicit-function rule"—a rule that can give us the derivatives of *every* implicit function defined by the given equation. The development of this rule depends on the following basic facts: (1) If two expressions are *identically* equal, then their respective total differentials must be equal.[1] (2) Differentiation of an expression that involves $y, x_1, \ldots, x_m$ will yield an expression involving the differentials $dy, dx_1, \ldots, dx_m$. (3) If we divide dy by dx_1, and let all the other differentials $(dx_2, \ldots, dx_m)$ be zero, the quotient can be interpreted as the partial derivative $\partial y / \partial x_1$; similar derivatives can be obtained if we divide dy by dx_2, etc. Applying these facts to the equation $F(y, x_1, \ldots, x_m) = 0$—which, we recall, has the status of an *identity* in the neighborhood N in which the implicit function is defined—we can write $dF = d0$, or

$$F_y \, dy + F_1 \, dx_1 + \cdots + F_m \, dx_m = 0$$

Suppose that only y and x_1 are allowed to vary (only dy and dx_1 are *not* set equal to zero). Then the above equation reduces to $F_y \, dy + F_1 \, dx_1 = 0$. Upon dividing through by dx_1, and solving for dy/dx_1, we then get

$$\left. \frac{dy}{dx_1} \right|_{\text{other variables constant}} \equiv \frac{\partial y}{\partial x_1} = -\frac{F_1}{F_y}$$

By similar means, we can derive all the other partial derivatives of the implicit function f. These may conveniently be summarized in a general rule—the *implicit-function rule*—as follows: Given $F(y, x_1, \ldots, x_m) = 0$, if an implicit function $y = f(x_1, \ldots, x_m)$ exists, then the partial derivatives of f are

$$(8.19) \qquad \frac{\partial y}{\partial x_i} = -\frac{F_i}{F_y} \qquad (i = 1, 2, \ldots, m)$$

In the simple case where the given equation is $F(y,x) = 0$, the rule gives

$$(8.19') \qquad \frac{dy}{dx} = -\frac{F_x}{F_y}$$

---

[1] Take, for example, the identity

$$x^2 - y^2 \equiv (x + y)(x - y)$$

This is an identity because the two sides are equal for *any* values of x and y that one may assign. Taking the total differential of each side, we have

$$\begin{aligned} d(\text{left side}) &= 2x \, dx - 2y \, dy \\ d(\text{right side}) &= (x - y) \, d(x + y) + (x + y) \, d(x - y) \\ &= (x - y)(dx + dy) + (x + y)(dx - dy) \\ &= 2x \, dx - 2y \, dy \end{aligned}$$

The two results are indeed equal. If two expressions are *not* identically equal, but are equal only for certain specific values of the variables, however, their total differentials will *not* be equal. The equation

$$x^2 - y^2 = x^2 + y^2 - 2$$

for instance, is valid only for $y = \pm 1$. The total differentials of the two sides are

$$\begin{aligned} d(\text{left side}) &= 2x \, dx - 2y \, dy \\ d(\text{right side}) &= 2x \, dx + 2y \, dy \end{aligned}$$

which are not equal. Note, in particular, that they are not even equal at $y = \pm 1$.

Comparative-Static Analysis

What this rule states is that, even if the specific form of the implicit function is not known to us, we can nevertheless find its derivative(s) by taking the *negative* of the ratio of a pair of partial derivatives of the F function which appears in the given equation that defines the implicit function. Observe that F_y always appears in the denominator of the ratio. This being the case, it is not admissible to have $F_y = 0$. Since the implicit-function theorem specifies that $F_y \neq 0$ at the point around which the implicit function is defined, the problem of a zero denominator is automatically taken care of in the relevant neighborhood of that point.

Example 1   Find dy/dx for the implicit function defined by (8.14'). Since $F(y,x)$ takes the form of $y - 3x^4$, we have, by (8.19'),

$$\frac{dy}{dx} = -\frac{F_x}{F_y} = -\frac{-12x^3}{1} = 12x^3$$

In this particular case, we can easily solve the given equation for y, to get $y = 3x^4$. Thus the correctness of the above derivative is easily verified.

Example 2   Find dy/dx for the implicit functions defined by the equation of the circle (8.15). This time we have $F(y,x) = x^2 + y^2 - 9$; thus $F_y = 2y$ and $F_x = 2x$. By (8.19'), the desired derivative is

$$\frac{dy}{dx} = -\frac{2x}{2y} = -\frac{x}{y} \qquad (y \neq 0)\dagger$$

Earlier, it was asserted that the implicit-function rule gives us the derivative of *every* implicit function defined by a given equation. Let us verify this with the two functions in (8.15') and their derivatives in (8.18). If we substitute y^+ for y in the implicit-function-rule result $dy/dx = -x/y$, we will indeed obtain the derivative dy^+/dx as shown in (8.18); similarly, the substitution of y^- for y will yield the other derivative in (8.18). Thus our earlier assertion is duly verified.

Example 3   Find $\partial y/\partial x$ for any implicit function(s) that may be defined by the equation $F(y,x,w) = y^3x^2 + w^3 + yxw - 3 = 0$. This equation is not easily solved for y. But since F_y, F_x, and F_w are all obviously continuous, and since $F_y = 3y^2x^2 + xw$ is indeed nonzero at a point such as $(1,1,1)$ which satisfies the given equation, an implicit function $y = f(x,w)$ assuredly exists around that point at least. It is thus meaningful to talk about the derivative $\partial y/\partial x$. By

† The restriction $y \neq 0$ is of course perfectly consistent with our earlier discussion of the equation (8.15) that follows the statement of the implicit-function theorem.

(8.19), moreover, we can immediately write

$$\frac{\partial y}{\partial x} = -\frac{F_x}{F_y} = -\frac{2y^3x + yw}{3y^2x^2 + xw}$$

At the point $(1,1,1)$, this derivative has the value $-\frac{3}{4}$.

Example 4   Assume that the equation $F(Q,K,L) = 0$ implicitly defines a production function $Q = f(K,L)$. Let us find a way of expressing the marginal physical products MPP_K and MPP_L in relation to the function F. Since the marginal products are simply the partial derivatives $\partial Q/\partial K$ and $\partial Q/\partial L$, we can apply the implicit-function rule and write

$$\text{MPP}_K \equiv \frac{\partial Q}{\partial K} = -\frac{F_K}{F_Q} \qquad \text{and} \qquad \text{MPP}_L \equiv \frac{\partial Q}{\partial L} = -\frac{F_L}{F_Q}$$

Aside from these, we can obtain yet another partial derivative,

$$\frac{\partial K}{\partial L} = -\frac{F_L}{F_K}$$

from the equation $F(Q,K,L) = 0$. What is the economic meaning of $\partial K/\partial L$? The partial sign implies that the other variable, Q, is being held constant; it follows that the changes in K and L described by this derivative are in the nature of "compensatory" changes designed to keep the output Q constant at a specified level. These are therefore the type of changes pertaining to movements *along* a production *isoquant*. As a matter of fact, the derivative $\partial K/\partial L$ is the measure of the slope of such an isoquant, which is negative in the normal case. The numerical value of $\partial K/\partial L$, on the other hand, is the measure of the *marginal rate of technical substitution* between the two inputs.

extension to the simultaneous-equation case   The implicit-function theorem also comes in a more general and powerful version that deals with the conditions under which a set of simultaneous equations

(8.20)
$$F^1(y_1,\ldots,y_n; x_1,\ldots,x_m) = 0$$
$$F^2(y_1,\ldots,y_n; x_1,\ldots,x_m) = 0$$
$$\cdots\cdots\cdots\cdots\cdots\cdots\cdots$$
$$F^n(y_1,\ldots,y_n; x_1,\ldots,x_m) = 0$$

will assuredly define a set of implicit functions[1]

---

[1] To view it another way, what these conditions serve to do is to assure us that the *n* equations in (8.20) can *in principle* be solved for the *n* y-variables, even if we may not be able to obtain the solution (8.21) in an explicit form.

$$
\begin{aligned}
y_1 &= f^1(x_1, \dots, x_m) \\
y_2 &= f^2(x_1, \dots, x_m) \\
&\quad \cdots\cdots\cdots\cdots\cdots \\
y_n &= f^n(x_1, \dots, x_m)
\end{aligned}
$$

(8.21)

The generalized version of the theorem states that:

Given the equation system (8.20), if (a) the functions $F^1, \dots, F^n$ all have continuous partial derivatives with respect to all the y and x variables, and if (b) at a point $(y_{10}, \dots, y_{n0}; x_{10}, \dots, x_{m0})$ satisfying (8.20), the following Jacobian determinant is nonzero:

$$
|J| \equiv \left| \frac{\partial(F^1, \dots, F^n)}{\partial(y_1, \dots, y_n)} \right| \equiv
\begin{vmatrix}
\dfrac{\partial F^1}{\partial y_1} & \dfrac{\partial F^1}{\partial y_2} & \cdots & \dfrac{\partial F^1}{\partial y_n} \\[2mm]
\dfrac{\partial F^2}{\partial y_1} & \dfrac{\partial F^2}{\partial y_2} & \cdots & \dfrac{\partial F^2}{\partial y_n} \\[1mm]
\cdots\cdots\cdots\cdots\cdots\cdots\cdots \\[1mm]
\dfrac{\partial F^n}{\partial y_1} & \dfrac{\partial F^n}{\partial y_2} & \cdots & \dfrac{\partial F^n}{\partial y_n}
\end{vmatrix}
\neq 0
$$

then there exists an m-dimensional neighborhood of $(x_{10}, \dots, x_{m0})$, N, in which the variables $y_1, \dots, y_n$ are functions of the variables $x_1, \dots, x_m$ in the form of (8.21). These implicit functions satisfy

$$
y_{10} = f^1(x_{10}, \dots, x_{m0})
$$
$$
\cdots\cdots\cdots\cdots\cdots\cdots
$$
$$
y_{n0} = f^n(x_{10}, \dots, x_{m0})
$$

They also satisfy (8.20) for *every* m-tuple $(x_1, \dots, x_m)$ in the neighborhood N—thereby giving (8.20) the status of a set of *identities* as far as this neighborhood is concerned. Moreover, the implicit functions $f^1, \dots, f^n$ are continuous and have continuous partial derivatives with respect to all the x variables.

As in the single-equation case, it is possible to find the partial derivatives of the implicit functions directly from the n equations in (8.20), without having to solve them for the y variables. Taking advantage of the fact that, in the neighborhood N, (8.20) has the status of identities, we can take the total differential of each of these, and write $dF^j = 0$ $(j = 1, 2, \dots, n)$. The result is a set of equations involving the differentials $dy_1, \dots, dy_n$ and $dx_1, \dots, dx_m$. Specifically, after transposing the dx_i terms to the right of the equals signs, we have

$$\frac{\partial F^1}{\partial y_1} dy_1 + \frac{\partial F^1}{\partial y_2} dy_2 + \cdots + \frac{\partial F^1}{\partial y_n} dy_n$$

$$= -\left(\frac{\partial F^1}{\partial x_1} dx_1 + \cdots + \frac{\partial F^1}{\partial x_m} dx_m\right)$$

$$\frac{\partial F^2}{\partial y_1} dy_1 + \frac{\partial F^2}{\partial y_2} dy_2 + \cdots + \frac{\partial F^2}{\partial y_n} dy_n$$

(8.22)

$$= -\left(\frac{\partial F^2}{\partial x_1} dx_1 + \cdots + \frac{\partial F^2}{\partial x_m} dx_m\right)$$

$$\cdots\cdots\cdots\cdots\cdots\cdots\cdots\cdots\cdots\cdots\cdots\cdots\cdots\cdots$$

$$\frac{\partial F^n}{\partial y_1} dy_1 + \frac{\partial F^n}{\partial y_2} dy_2 + \cdots + \frac{\partial F^n}{\partial y_n} dy_n$$

$$= -\left(\frac{\partial F^n}{\partial x_1} dx_1 + \cdots + \frac{\partial F^n}{\partial x_m} dx_m\right)$$

Since all the partial derivatives appearing in (8.22) will take specific (constant) values when evaluated at the point $(y_{10}, \ldots, y_{n0}; x_{10}, \ldots, x_{m0})$—the point around which the implicit functions (8.21) are defined—we have here a system of n *linear* equations, in which the differentials dy_j (considered to be endogenous) are expressed in terms of the differentials dx_i (considered to be exogenous). Now, suppose that we let all the differentials dx_i be zero except dx_1 (that is, only x_1 is allowed to vary); then all the terms involving $dx_2, \ldots, dx_m$ will drop out of the system. Suppose, further, that we divide each remaining term by dx_1; then there will emerge the expressions $dy_1/dx_1, \ldots, dy_n/dx_1$. These, however, should be interpreted as *partial* derivatives of (8.21) because all the x variables have been held constant except x_1. Thus, by taking the steps just described, we are led to the desired partial derivatives of the implicit functions. Note that, in fact, we can obtain in one swoop a total of n of these (here, they are $\partial y_1/\partial x_1, \ldots, \partial y_n/\partial x_1$).

What results from the above-cited steps is the following linear system:

$$\frac{\partial F^1}{\partial y_1}\left(\frac{\partial y_1}{\partial x_1}\right) + \frac{\partial F^1}{\partial y_2}\left(\frac{\partial y_2}{\partial x_1}\right) + \cdots + \frac{\partial F^1}{\partial y_n}\left(\frac{\partial y_n}{\partial x_1}\right) = -\frac{\partial F^1}{\partial x_1}$$

(8.23)

$$\frac{\partial F^2}{\partial y_1}\left(\frac{\partial y_1}{\partial x_1}\right) + \frac{\partial F^2}{\partial y_2}\left(\frac{\partial y_2}{\partial x_1}\right) + \cdots + \frac{\partial F^2}{\partial y_n}\left(\frac{\partial y_n}{\partial x_1}\right) = -\frac{\partial F^2}{\partial x_1}$$

$$\cdots\cdots\cdots\cdots\cdots\cdots\cdots\cdots\cdots\cdots\cdots\cdots\cdots\cdots$$

$$\frac{\partial F^n}{\partial y_1}\left(\frac{\partial y_1}{\partial x_1}\right) + \frac{\partial F^n}{\partial y_2}\left(\frac{\partial y_2}{\partial x_1}\right) + \cdots + \frac{\partial F^n}{\partial y_n}\left(\frac{\partial y_n}{\partial x_1}\right) = -\frac{\partial F^n}{\partial x_1}$$

where, for visual clarity, we have placed parentheses around those derivatives for which we are seeking a solution, to distinguish them from the other derivatives that are now considered to be constants. In matrix notation, this system can be written as

$$(8.23') \quad \begin{bmatrix} \dfrac{\partial F^1}{\partial y_1} & \dfrac{\partial F^1}{\partial y_2} & \cdots & \dfrac{\partial F^1}{\partial y_n} \\[2ex] \dfrac{\partial F^2}{\partial y_1} & \dfrac{\partial F^2}{\partial y_2} & \cdots & \dfrac{\partial F^2}{\partial y_n} \\[2ex] \cdots\cdots\cdots\cdots\cdots \\[1ex] \dfrac{\partial F^n}{\partial y_1} & \dfrac{\partial F^n}{\partial y_2} & \cdots & \dfrac{\partial F^n}{\partial y_n} \end{bmatrix} \begin{bmatrix} \left(\dfrac{\partial y_1}{\partial x_1}\right) \\[2ex] \left(\dfrac{\partial y_2}{\partial x_1}\right) \\[2ex] \vdots \\[1ex] \left(\dfrac{\partial y_n}{\partial x_1}\right) \end{bmatrix} = \begin{bmatrix} -\dfrac{\partial F^1}{\partial x_1} \\[2ex] -\dfrac{\partial F^2}{\partial x_1} \\[2ex] \vdots \\[1ex] -\dfrac{\partial F^n}{\partial x_1} \end{bmatrix}$$

Since the determinant of the coefficient matrix in (8.23') is nothing but the particular Jacobian determinant $|J|$ which is known to be nonzero under conditions of the implicit-function theorem, and since the system must be nonhomogeneous (why?), there should be a unique solution to (8.23'). By Cramer's rule, this solution may be expressed analytically as follows:

$$(8.24) \quad \left(\frac{\partial y_j}{\partial x_1}\right) = \frac{|J_j|}{|J|} \qquad (j = 1, 2, \ldots, n) \qquad [\text{see } (5.15)]$$

By a suitable adaptation of this procedure, the partial derivatives of the implicit functions with respect to the other variables, $x_2, \ldots, x_m$, can also be obtained.

Similarly to the implicit-function rule (8.19) for the single-equation case, the procedure just described calls only for the use of the partial derivatives of the F functions—evaluated at the point $(y_{10}, \ldots, y_{n0}; x_{10}, \ldots, x_{m0})$—in the calculation of the partial derivatives of the implicit functions $f^1, \ldots, f^n$. Thus the matrix equation (8.23') and its analytical solution (8.24) are in effect a statement of the simultaneous-equation version of the implicit-function rule.

Note that the requirement $|J| \neq 0$ rules out a zero denominator in (8.24), just as the requirement $F_y \neq 0$ did in the implicit-function rule (8.19) and (8.19'). Note, also, that the role played by the condition $|J| \neq 0$ in guaranteeing a unique (albeit implicit) solution (8.21) to the general (possibly *nonlinear*) system (8.20), is very similar to the role of the nonsingularity condition $|A| \neq 0$ in a *linear* system $Ax = d$.

Example 5   Let the national-income model (7.17) be rewritten in the form

$$(8.25) \quad \begin{aligned} Y - C - I_0 - G_0 &= 0 \\ C - \alpha - \beta(Y - T) &= 0 \\ T - \gamma - \delta Y &= 0 \end{aligned}$$

If we take the endogenous variables (Y,C,T) to be (y_1,y_2,y_3), and take the exogenous variables and parameters $(I_0,G_0,\alpha,\beta,\gamma,\delta)$ to be $(x_1,x_2,\ldots,x_6)$, then the left-side expression in each equation can be regarded as a specific F function, in the form of $F^j(Y,C,T; I_0,G_0,\alpha,\beta,\gamma,\delta)$. Thus (8.25) is a specific case of (8.20), with $n = 3$ and $m = 6$. Since the functions F^1, F^2, and F^3 do have continuous partial derivatives, and since the relevant Jacobian determinant (the one involving only the endogenous variables),

$$(8.26) \quad |J| = \begin{vmatrix} \dfrac{\partial F^1}{\partial Y} & \dfrac{\partial F^1}{\partial C} & \dfrac{\partial F^1}{\partial T} \\[2mm] \dfrac{\partial F^2}{\partial Y} & \dfrac{\partial F^2}{\partial C} & \dfrac{\partial F^2}{\partial T} \\[2mm] \dfrac{\partial F^3}{\partial Y} & \dfrac{\partial F^3}{\partial C} & \dfrac{\partial F^3}{\partial T} \end{vmatrix} = \begin{vmatrix} 1 & -1 & 0 \\ -\beta & 1 & \beta \\ -\delta & 0 & 1 \end{vmatrix} = 1 - \beta + \beta\delta$$

is always nonzero (both β and δ being restricted to be positive fractions), we can take Y, C and T to be implicit functions of $(I_0,G_0,\alpha,\beta,\gamma,\delta)$ *at* and *around* any point that satisfies (8.25). But a point that satisfies (8.25) would be an equilibrium solution, relating to $\bar{Y}$, $\bar{C}$ and $\bar{T}$. Hence, what the implicit-function theorem tells us is that we are justified in writing

$$\bar{Y} = f^1(I_0,G_0,\alpha,\beta,\gamma,\delta)$$
$$\bar{C} = f^2(I_0,G_0,\alpha,\beta,\gamma,\delta)$$
$$\bar{T} = f^3(I_0,G_0,\alpha,\beta,\gamma,\delta)$$

indicating that the equilibrium values of the endogenous variables are implicit functions of the exogenous variables and the parameters.

The partial derivatives of the implicit functions, such as $\partial\bar{Y}/\partial I_0$ and $\partial\bar{Y}/\partial G_0$, are in the nature of comparative-static derivatives. To find these, we need only the partial derivatives of the F functions, evaluated at the equilibrium state of the model. Moreover, since $n = 3$, three of these can be found in one operation. Suppose we now hold all exogenous variables and parameters fixed except G_0. Then, by adapting the result in (8.23′), we may write the equation

$$\begin{bmatrix} 1 & -1 & 0 \\ -\beta & 1 & \beta \\ -\delta & 0 & 1 \end{bmatrix} \begin{bmatrix} \partial\bar{Y}/\partial G_0 \\ \partial\bar{C}/\partial G_0 \\ \partial\bar{T}/\partial G_0 \end{bmatrix} = \begin{bmatrix} 1 \\ 0 \\ 0 \end{bmatrix}$$

from which three comparative-static derivatives (all with respect to G_0) can be calculated. The first one, representing the government-expenditure multiplier, will for instance come out to be

$$\frac{\partial\bar{Y}}{\partial G_0} = \frac{\begin{vmatrix} 1 & -1 & 0 \\ 0 & 1 & \beta \\ 0 & 0 & 1 \end{vmatrix}}{|J|} = \frac{1}{1 - \beta + \beta\delta} \quad \text{[by (8.26)]}$$

This is of course nothing but the result obtained earlier in (7.19). Note, however, that in the present approach we have worked only with implicit functions, and have completely bypassed the step of solving the system (8.25) explicitly for $\bar{Y}$, $\bar{C}$, and $\bar{T}$. It is this particular feature of the method that will now enable us to tackle the comparative statics of general-function models which, by their very nature, can yield no explicit solution.

EXERCISE 8.5

1. Assuming that the equation $F(U, x_1, x_2, \ldots, x_n) = 0$ implicitly defines a utility function $U = f(x_1, x_2, \ldots, x_n)$:

   (a) Find the expressions for $\partial U/\partial x_2$, $\partial U/\partial x_n$, $\partial x_3/\partial x_2$, and $\partial x_4/\partial x_n$.
   (b) Interpret their respective economic meanings.

2. Given the equation $F(y, x) = 0$ shown below, is an implicit function $y = f(x)$ defined around the point $(y = 3,\ x = 1)$?

   (a) $x^3 - 2x^2 y + 3xy^2 - 22 = 0$
   (b) $2x^2 + 4xy - y^4 + 67 = 0$

   If your answer is affirmative, find dy/dx by the implicit-function rule, and evaluate it at the said point.

3. Given $x^2 + 3xy + 2yz + y^2 + z^2 - 11 = 0$, is an implicit function $z = f(x, y)$ defined around the point $(x = 1,\ y = 2,\ z = 0)$? If so, find $\partial z/\partial x$ and $\partial z/\partial y$ by the implicit-function rule, and evaluate them at that point.

4. By considering the equation $F(y, x) = (x - y)^3 = 0$ in a neighborhood around the point of origin, prove that the conditions cited in the implicit-function theorem are *not* in the nature of *necessary* conditions.

5. If the equation $F(x, y, z) = 0$ implicitly defines each of the three variables as a function of the other two variables, and if all the derivatives in question exist, find the value of $\dfrac{\partial z}{\partial x} \dfrac{\partial x}{\partial y} \dfrac{\partial y}{\partial z}$.

6. Justify the assertion in the text that the equation system (8.23′) must be nonhomogeneous.

7 From the national-income model (8.25), find the nonincome-tax multiplier and the income-tax-rate multiplier by the implicit-function rule. Check your results against (7.20) and (7.21).

8.6 Comparative Statics of General-Function Models

When we first considered the problem of comparative-static analysis, in Chap. 7, we dealt with the case where the equilibrium values of the endogenous variables of the model are expressible explicitly in terms of the exogenous variables and parameters. There, the technique of simple partial differentiation was all we needed. When a model contains functions expressed in the general form, however, that technique becomes inapplicable because of the unavailability of explicit solutions. Instead, a new technique must be employed that makes use of such concepts as total differentials, total derivatives, as well as the implicit-function theorem and the implicit-function rule. We shall illustrate this first with a market model, and then move on to a national-income model.

market model   Consider a single-commodity market, where the quantity demanded Q_d is a function not only of price P but also of an exogenously determined income Y_0. The quantity supplied Q_s, on the other hand, is a function of price alone. If these functions are not given in specific forms, our model may be written generally as follows:

$$
\begin{aligned}
Q_d &= Q_s \\
(8.27) \quad Q_d &= D(P, Y_0) \quad & (\partial D/\partial P < 0;\, \partial D/\partial Y_0 > 0) \\
Q_s &= S(P) \quad & (dS/dP > 0)
\end{aligned}
$$

Both the D and S functions are assumed to possess continuous derivatives or, in other words, to have smooth graphs. Moreover, in order to ensure economic relevance, we have imposed definite restrictions on the signs of these derivatives. By the restriction $dS/dP > 0$, the supply function is stipulated to be monotonically increasing, though it is permitted to be either linear or nonlinear. Similarly, by the restrictions on the two partial derivatives of the demand function, we indicate that it is a decreasing function of price but an increasing function of income. These restrictions serve to confine our analysis to the "normal" case we expect to encounter.

In drawing the usual type of two-dimensional demand curve, the income level is assumed to be held fixed. When income changes, it will upset a given equilibrium by causing a shift of the demand curve. Similarly, in (8.27), Y_0 can cause a disequilibrating change through the demand function. Here, Y_0 is the only exogenous variable or parameter; thus the comparative-static analysis of this model will be concerned exclusively with how a change in Y_0 will affect the equilibrium position of the model.

The equilibrium position of the market is defined by the equilibrium condition $Q_d = Q_s$, which, upon substitution and rearrangement, can be expressed by

$$(8.28) \qquad D(P, Y_0) - S(P) = 0$$

Even though this equation cannot be solved explicitly for the equilibrium price, $\bar{P}$, we shall assume that there does exist a static equilibrium—for otherwise there would be no point in even raising the question of comparative statics. From our experience with specific-function models, we have learned to expect $\bar{P}$ to be a function of the exogenous variable Y_0:

$$(8.29) \qquad \bar{P} = \bar{P}(Y_0)$$

But, now, we can provide a rigorous foundation for this expectation by appealing to the implicit-function theorem. Inasmuch as (8.28) is in the form of $F(P, Y_0) = 0$, the satisfaction of the conditions of the implicit-function theorem will guarantee that every value of Y_0 will yield a unique value of $\bar{P}$ in the neighborhood of a point satisfying (8.28), that is, in the neighborhood of an (initial or "old") equilibrium solution. In that case, we can indeed write the implicit function $\bar{P} = \bar{P}(Y_0)$, and discuss its derivative, $d\bar{P}/dY_0$—the very comparative-static derivative we desire—which is known to exist. Let us, therefore, check those conditions. First, the function $F(P, Y_0)$ indeed possesses continuous derivatives; this is because, by assumption, its two additive components $D(P, Y_0)$ and $S(P)$ have continuous derivatives. Secondly, the partial derivative of F with respect to P, namely, $F_P = \partial D/\partial P - dS/dP$, is negative, and hence nonzero, no matter where it is evaluated. Thus, the implicit-function theorem applies, and (8.29) is indeed legitimate.

According to the same theorem, the equilibrium condition (8.28) can now be taken to be an identity in some neighborhood of the equilibrium solution. Consequently, we may write the equilibrium identity

$$(8.30) \qquad D(\bar{P}, Y_0) - S(\bar{P}) \equiv 0$$

It then requires only a straight application of the implicit-function rule to produce the comparative-static derivative, $d\bar{P}/dY_0$, which, for visual clarity, we shall from here on enclose in parentheses to distinguish it from the regular derivative expressions that merely constitute part of the model specification.

The result is

$$(8.31) \qquad \left(\frac{d\bar{P}}{dY_0}\right) = -\frac{\partial F/\partial Y_0}{\partial F/\partial \bar{P}} = -\frac{\partial D/\partial Y_0}{\partial D/\partial \bar{P} - dS/d\bar{P}} > 0$$

In this result, the expression $\partial D/\partial \bar{P}$ refers to the derivative $\partial D/\partial P$ evaluated at the initial equilibrium, i.e., at $P = \bar{P}$; a similar interpretation attaches to $dS/d\bar{P}$. In fact, $\partial D/\partial Y_0$ must be evaluated at the equilibrium point as well. By virtue of the sign specifications in (8.27), $(d\bar{P}/dY_0)$ is invariably positive. Thus our *qualitative* conclusion is that a small increase (decrease) in the income level will always result in an increase (decrease) in the equilibrium price. If the values which the derivatives of the demand and supply functions take at the initial equilibrium are known, then (8.31) will of course yield a *quantitative* conclusion also.

The above discussion is concerned with the effect of a change in Y_0 on $\bar{P}$. Is it possible also to find out the effect on the equilibrium quantity $\bar{Q}\,(= \bar{Q}_d = \bar{Q}_s)$? The answer is yes. Since, in the equilibrium state, we have $\bar{Q} = S(\bar{P})$, and since $\bar{P} = \bar{P}(Y_0)$, we may apply the chain rule to get the derivative

$$(8.32) \qquad \left(\frac{d\bar{Q}}{dY_0}\right) = \frac{dS}{d\bar{P}}\left(\frac{d\bar{P}}{dY_0}\right) > 0 \qquad \left[\text{since } \frac{dS}{d\bar{P}} > 0\right]$$

Thus the equilibrium quantity is also positively related to Y_0 in this model. Again, (8.32) can supply a quantitative conclusion if the values which the various derivatives take at the equilibrium are known.

The results in (8.31) and (8.32), which exhaust the comparative-static contents of the model (since the latter contains only one exogenous and two endogenous variables), are not surprising. In fact, they convey no more than the proposition that an upward shift of the demand curve will result in a higher equilibrium price as well as a higher equilibrium quantity. This same proposition, it may seem, could have been arrived at in a flash from a simple graphic analysis! This sounds plausible, but one should not lose sight of the far, far more general character of the analytical procedure we have used here. The graphic analysis, let us reiterate, is by its very nature limited to a specific set of curves (the geometric counterpart of a specific set of functions); its conclusions are therefore, strictly speaking, relevant and applicable to only that set of curves. In sharp contrast, the formulation in (8.27), simplified as it is, covers the entire set of possible combinations of negatively sloped demand curves and positively sloped supply curves. Thus it is vastly more general. Also, the analytical procedure used here can handle many problems of greater complexity that would prove to be beyond the capabilities of the graphic approach.

simultaneous-equation approach   The above analysis of model (8.27) was carried out on the basis of a single equation, namely, (8.30). Since only one endogenous variable can fruitfully be incorporated into one equation, the inclusion of $\bar{P}$ means the exclusion of $\bar{Q}$. As a result, we were compelled to find $(d\bar{P}/dY_0)$ first and then to infer $(d\bar{Q}/dY_0)$ in a subsequent step. Now we shall show how $\bar{P}$ and $\bar{Q}$ can be studied simultaneously. There being two endogenous variables, we shall accordingly set up a two-equation system. First, letting $Q = Q_d = Q_s$ in (8.27) and rearranging, we can express our market model as

$$(8.33) \qquad \begin{aligned} F^1(P,Q;\ Y_0) &= D(P,Y_0) - Q = 0 \\ F^2(P,Q;\ Y_0) &= S(P) - Q = 0 \end{aligned}$$

which is in the form of (8.20), with $n = 2$ and $m = 1$. It becomes of interest, once again, to check the conditions of the implicit-function theorem. First, since the demand and supply functions are both assumed to possess continuous derivatives, so must the functions F^1 and F^2. Secondly, the endogenous-variable Jacobian (the one involving P and Q) indeed turns out to be nonzero, regardless of where it is evaluated, because

$$(8.34) \qquad |J| = \begin{vmatrix} \dfrac{\partial F^1}{\partial P} & \dfrac{\partial F^1}{\partial Q} \\[2mm] \dfrac{\partial F^2}{\partial P} & \dfrac{\partial F^2}{\partial Q} \end{vmatrix} = \begin{vmatrix} \dfrac{\partial D}{\partial P} & -1 \\[2mm] \dfrac{dS}{dP} & -1 \end{vmatrix} = \dfrac{dS}{dP} - \dfrac{\partial D}{\partial P} > 0$$

Hence, if an equilibrium solution $(\bar{P},\bar{Q})$ exists (as we must assume in order to make it meaningful to talk about comparative statics), the implicit-function theorem tells us that we can write the implicit functions

$$(8.35) \qquad \bar{P} = \bar{P}(Y_0) \qquad \text{and} \qquad \bar{Q} = \bar{Q}(Y_0)$$

even though we cannot solve for $\bar{P}$ and $\bar{Q}$ explicitly. These functions are known to have continuous derivatives. Moreover, (8.33) will have the status of a pair of identities in some neighborhood of the equilibrium state, so that we may also write

$$(8.36) \qquad \begin{aligned} D(\bar{P},Y_0) - \bar{Q} &\equiv 0 \\ S(\bar{P}) - \bar{Q} &\equiv 0 \end{aligned}$$

From these, $(d\bar{P}/dY_0)$ and $(d\bar{Q}/dY_0)$ can be found simultaneously.

Taking the total differential of each identity in turn, and rearranging, we can get a linear system in $d\bar{P}$ and $d\bar{Q}$:

$$\frac{\partial D}{\partial \bar{P}}\, d\bar{P} - d\bar{Q} = -\frac{\partial D}{\partial Y_0}\, dY_0$$

$$\frac{dS}{d\bar{P}}\, d\bar{P} - d\bar{Q} = 0$$

This system is *linear* because all the derivatives appearing therein are constants when evaluated at the initial equilibrium, and because dY_0 (an arbitrary disequilibrating change in the exogenous variable) is also a constant. Upon dividing through by dY_0, and interpreting the quotient of two differentials as a derivative, we have the matrix equation[1]

$$\begin{bmatrix} \dfrac{\partial D}{\partial \bar{P}} & -1 \\[2ex] \dfrac{dS}{d\bar{P}} & -1 \end{bmatrix} \begin{bmatrix} \left(\dfrac{d\bar{P}}{dY_0}\right) \\[2ex] \left(\dfrac{d\bar{Q}}{dY_0}\right) \end{bmatrix} = \begin{bmatrix} -\dfrac{\partial D}{\partial Y_0} \\[2ex] 0 \end{bmatrix}$$

By Cramer's rule, and using (8.34), we then find the solution to be

(8.37)

$$\left(\dfrac{d\bar{P}}{dY_0}\right) = \dfrac{\begin{vmatrix} -\dfrac{\partial D}{\partial Y_0} & -1 \\[2ex] 0 & -1 \end{vmatrix}}{|J|} = \dfrac{\dfrac{\partial D}{\partial Y_0}}{|J|}$$

$$\left(\dfrac{d\bar{Q}}{dY_0}\right) = \dfrac{\begin{vmatrix} \dfrac{\partial D}{\partial \bar{P}} & -\dfrac{\partial D}{\partial Y_0} \\[2ex] \dfrac{dS}{d\bar{P}} & 0 \end{vmatrix}}{|J|} = \dfrac{\dfrac{dS}{d\bar{P}}\dfrac{\partial D}{\partial Y_0}}{|J|}$$

where all the derivatives of the demand and supply functions (including those appearing in the Jacobian) are to be evaluated at the initial equilibrium. The reader can check that the results just obtained are identical with those obtained earlier in (8.31) and (8.32), by means of the single-equation approach.

use of total derivatives   Both the single-equation and the simultaneous-equation approaches illustrated above have one feature in common: we take the *total differentials* of both sides of an equilibrium identity and then equate the two results. Instead of taking the total differentials, however, it is possible to take, and equate, the *total derivatives* of the two sides of the equilibrium identity with respect to a particular exogenous variable or parameter.

In the single-equation approach, for instance, the equilibrium identity is

$$D(\bar{P}, Y_0) - S(\bar{P}) \equiv 0 \qquad \text{[from (8.30)]}$$

where $\bar{P} = \bar{P}(Y_0)$ [from (8.29)]

Taking the total derivative of the equilibrium identity with respect to Y_0—which

---

[1] Without going through the steps of total differentiation and division by dY_0, the same matrix equation can be obtained from an adaptation of the implicit-function rule (8.23').

Comparative-Static Analysis

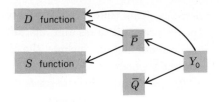

FIGURE 8.7

takes into account the indirect as well as the direct effects of a change in Y_0—will therefore give us the equation

$$\frac{\partial D}{\partial \bar{P}}\left(\frac{d\bar{P}}{dY_0}\right) + \frac{\partial D}{\partial Y_0} - \frac{dS}{d\bar{P}}\left(\frac{d\bar{P}}{dY_0}\right) = 0$$

$$\underset{\substack{\text{(indirect effect} \\ \text{of } Y_0 \text{ on } D)}}{} \quad \underset{\substack{\text{(direct effect} \\ \text{of } Y_0 \text{ on } D)}}{} \quad \underset{\substack{\text{(indirect effect} \\ \text{of } Y_0 \text{ on } S\;)}}{}$$

When this is solved for $(d\bar{P}/dY_0)$, the result is identical with the one in (8.31).

In the simultaneous-equation approach, on the other hand, there is a pair of equilibrium identities:

$$D(\bar{P}, Y_0) - \bar{Q} \equiv 0$$
$$S(\bar{P}) - \bar{Q} \equiv 0 \qquad \text{[from (8.36)]}$$

where $\qquad \bar{P} = \bar{P}(Y_0) \qquad \bar{Q} = \bar{Q}(Y_0) \qquad$ [from (8.35)]

The various effects of Y_0 are now harder to keep track of, but with the help of the channel map in Fig. 8.7, the pattern should become very clear. This channel map tells us, for instance, that when differentiating the D function with respect to Y_0, we must allow for the indirect effect of Y_0 upon D through $\bar{P}$, as well as the direct effect of Y_0 (curved arrow). In differentiating the S function with respect to Y_0, on the other hand, there is only the indirect effect (through $\bar{P}$) to be taken into account. Thus, the result of totally differentiating the two identities with respect to Y_0 is, upon rearrangement, the following pair of equations:

$$\frac{\partial D}{\partial \bar{P}}\left(\frac{d\bar{P}}{dY_0}\right) - \left(\frac{d\bar{Q}}{dY_0}\right) = -\frac{\partial D}{\partial Y_0}$$

$$\frac{dS}{d\bar{P}}\left(\frac{d\bar{P}}{dY_0}\right) - \left(\frac{d\bar{Q}}{dY_0}\right) = 0$$

These are, of course, identical with the equations obtained by the total-differential method, and they lead again to the comparative-static derivatives in (8.37).

national-income model   The procedure just illustrated will now be applied to a national-income model, also to be formulated in terms of general functions. This time, for the sake of variety, let us abstract from government expenditures and taxes and, instead, add foreign trade relations into the model. Furthermore, let us include the money market, à la Hicks,[1] along with the market for goods.

More specifically, the *goods market* will be assumed to be characterized by the following four functions:

1   Investment expenditure I is a decreasing function of interest rate i:

$$I = I(i) \qquad (I' < 0)$$

where $I' \equiv dI/di$ is the derivative of the investment function.

2   Savings S is an increasing function of national income Y as well as interest rate i, with the marginal propensity to save being a positive fraction:

$$S = S(Y,i) \qquad (0 < S_Y < 1; S_i > 0)$$

where $S_Y \equiv \partial S/\partial Y$ (marginal propensity to save) and $S_i \equiv \partial S/\partial i$ are the partial derivatives.

3   The expenditure on imports M is a function of national income, with the marginal propensity to import being another positive fraction:

$$M = M(Y) \qquad (0 < M' < 1)$$

4   The amount of exports X is exogenously determined:

$$X = X_0$$

In the *money market*, we have two more functions as follows:

5   The quantity demanded of money M_d is an increasing function of national income (*transactions demand*) but a decreasing function of interest rate (*speculative demand*):

$$M_d = L(Y,i) \qquad (L_Y > 0; L_i < 0)$$

The function symbol L is employed here because the money demand function is customarily referred to as the *liquidity function*. The symbol M_d, representing money demand, should be carefully distinguished from the symbol M, for imports.

6   The money supply is exogenously determined, as a matter of *monetary policy*:

$$M_s = M_{s0}$$

All the derivatives cited above are assumed to be continuous.

---

[1] J. R. Hicks, "Mr. Keynes and the 'Classics': A Suggested Interpretation," *Econometrica*, April, 1937, pp. 147–159.

The attainment of equilibrium in this model requires the simultaneous satisfaction of the equilibrium condition of the goods market—injections = leakages, or $I + X = S + M$—as well as that of the money market—demand for money = supply of money, or $M_d = M_s$. On the basis of the general functions cited above, the equilibrium state may be described by the following pair of conditions:

$$(8.38) \qquad \begin{aligned} I(i) + X_0 &= S(Y,i) + M(Y) \\ L(Y,i) &= M_{s0} \end{aligned}$$

Since the symbols I, S, M, and L are merely function symbols, we have in effect only two endogenous variables, income Y and interest rate i, plus two exogenous variables, exports X_0 (based on foreign decisions) and M_{s0} (determined by the monetary authorities). Thus, (8.38) can be expressed in the form of (8.20), with $n = m = 2$:

$$(8.38') \qquad \begin{aligned} F^1(Y,i; X_0, M_{s0}) &= I(i) + X_0 - S(Y,i) - M(Y) = 0 \\ F^2(Y,i; X_0, M_{s0}) &= L(Y,i) - M_{s0} = 0 \end{aligned}$$

This system satisfies the conditions of the implicit-function theorem, because (a) F^1 and F^2 have continuous derivatives as a consequence of the assumed continuity of the derivatives of all functions appearing in our model, and (b) the endogenous-variable Jacobian is nonzero when evaluated at the initial equilibrium (which we assume to exist) as well as elsewhere:

$$(8.39) \qquad |J| = \begin{vmatrix} \partial F^1/\partial Y & \partial F^1/\partial i \\ \partial F^2/\partial Y & \partial F^2/\partial i \end{vmatrix} = \begin{vmatrix} -S_Y - M' & I' - S_i \\ L_Y & L_i \end{vmatrix}$$

$$= -L_i(S_Y + M') - L_Y(I' - S_i) > 0$$

Hence, the implicit functions

$$(8.40) \qquad \bar{Y} = \bar{Y}(X_0, M_{s0}) \qquad \text{and} \qquad \bar{i} = \bar{i}(X_0, M_{s0})$$

can be written, even though we are unable to solve for $\bar{Y}$ and $\bar{i}$ explicitly. Furthermore, we may take (8.38') to be a pair of identities in some neighborhood of the equilibrium, so that we may also write

$$(8.41) \qquad \begin{aligned} I(\bar{i}) + X_0 - S(\bar{Y},\bar{i}) - M(\bar{Y}) &\equiv 0 \\ L(\bar{Y},\bar{i}) - M_{s0} &\equiv 0 \end{aligned}$$

From these equilibrium identities, a total of four comparative-static derivatives will emerge, two relating to X_0 and the other two relating to M_{s0}. But we shall derive here only the former two, leaving the other two to be derived by the reader as an exercise.

Accordingly, after taking the total differential of each identity in (8.41), we set dM_{s0} to zero, so that dX_0 will remain as the sole disequilibrating factor.

Next, dividing through by dX_0, and interpreting each quotient of two differentials as a partial derivative (partial, because the other exogenous variable M_{s0} is being held constant), we arrive at the matrix equation

$$(8.42) \quad \begin{bmatrix} -S_Y - M' & I' - S_i \\ L_Y & L_i \end{bmatrix} \begin{bmatrix} (\partial \bar{Y}/\partial X_0) \\ (\partial \bar{\imath}/\partial X_0) \end{bmatrix} = \begin{bmatrix} -1 \\ 0 \end{bmatrix}$$

The solution is, by Cramer's rule and using (8.39),

$$(8.43) \quad \left(\frac{\partial \bar{Y}}{\partial X_0} \right) = \frac{\begin{vmatrix} -1 & I' - S_i \\ 0 & L_i \end{vmatrix}}{|J|} = \frac{-L_i}{|J|} > 0$$

$$\left(\frac{\partial \bar{\imath}}{\partial X_0} \right) = \frac{\begin{vmatrix} -S_Y - M' & -1 \\ L_Y & 0 \end{vmatrix}}{|J|} = \frac{L_Y}{|J|} > 0$$

where all the derivatives on the right side of the equals sign (including those appearing in the Jacobian) are to be evaluated at the initial equilibrium, that is, at $Y = \bar{Y}$ and $i = \bar{\imath}$. When the specific values of these derivatives are known, (8.43) yields quantitative conclusions regarding the effect of a change in exports. Without the knowledge of those values, however, we must settle for the qualitative conclusions that both $\bar{Y}$ and $\bar{\imath}$ will increase with exports in the present model.

As in the market model, instead of using total differentials, the option is open to us to take the *total derivatives* of the equilibrium identities in (8.41) with respect to the particular exogenous variable under study, X_0. In so doing, we must of course bear in mind the implicit solutions (8.40). The various ways in which X_0 can affect the different components of the model—as given in (8.41) and (8.40)—are summarized in the channel map in Fig. 8.8. It should be noted, in particular, that in differentiating the saving function or the liquidity function with respect to X_0, we must allow for *two* indirect effects—one through $\bar{\imath}$ and the other through $\bar{Y}$. With the help of this channel map, we can differentiate the equilibrium identities totally with respect to X_0, to get the following pair of equations:

$$I' \left(\frac{\partial \bar{\imath}}{\partial X_0} \right) + 1 - S_Y \left(\frac{\partial \bar{Y}}{\partial X_0} \right) - S_i \left(\frac{\partial \bar{\imath}}{\partial X_0} \right) - M' \left(\frac{\partial \bar{Y}}{\partial X_0} \right) = 0$$

$$L_Y \left(\frac{\partial \bar{Y}}{\partial X_0} \right) + L_i \left(\frac{\partial \bar{\imath}}{\partial X_0} \right) = 0$$

Since the other exogenous variable, M_{s0}, is being held constant, the left side of each of these equations represents the *partial total* derivative of the left-side expression in the corresponding equilibrium identity. However, the comparative-static derivatives $(\partial \bar{Y}/\partial X_0)$ and $(\partial \bar{\imath}/\partial X_0)$, being derivatives of the implicit

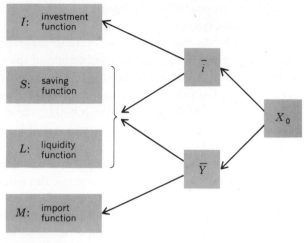

FIGURE 8.8

functions (8.40), are plain *partial* derivatives. When properly condensed, these two equations reduce exactly to (8.42). So the total-differential method and the total-derivative method yield identical results.

The reader will observe that $(\partial \bar{Y}/\partial X_0)$ is in the nature of an export multiplier. Since the export-induced increase in the equilibrium income will, by virtue of the import function $M = M(Y)$, cause the imports to rise as well, we can again apply the chain rule to find the (auxiliary) comparative-static derivative:

$$\left(\frac{\partial \bar{M}}{\partial X_0}\right) = M'\left(\frac{\partial \bar{Y}}{\partial X_0}\right) = \frac{-M'L_i}{|J|}$$

The sign of this derivative is positive because $M' > 0$. By a perfectly analogous procedure, we can also find the other auxiliary comparative-static derivatives, such as $(\partial \bar{I}/\partial X_0)$ and $(\partial \bar{S}/\partial X_0)$.

summary of the procedure   In the analysis of the general-function market model and national-income model, we relied chiefly on the implicit-function theorem to enable us to write the implicit solutions such as

$$\bar{P} = \bar{P}(Y_0) \qquad \text{and} \qquad \bar{\imath} = \bar{\imath}(X_0, M_{s0})$$

Our subsequent search for the comparative-static derivatives such as $(d\bar{P}/dY_0)$ and $(\partial \bar{\imath}/\partial X_0)$ then rests for its meaningfulness upon the known fact—thanks again to the implicit-function theorem—that the $\bar{P}$ and $\bar{i}$ functions do possess continuous derivatives.

To facilitate the application of that theorem, we make it a standard practice to write the equilibrium condition(s) of the model in the form of (8.16) or (8.20). We then check whether (a) the F function(s) have continuous derivatives, and (b) the value of F_y or the endogenous-variable Jacobian determinant (as the case may be) is nonzero at the initial equilibrium of the model. However, as long as the individual functions in the model have continuous derivatives— an assumption which is often adopted as a matter of course in general-function models—the first condition above is automatically satisfied. As a practical matter, therefore, it is needed only to check the value of F_y or the endogenous-variable Jacobian. And if it is nonzero at the equilibrium, we may proceed at once to the task of finding the comparative-static derivatives.

To that end, the implicit-function rule is of help. For the single-equation case, simply set the endogenous variable equal to its equilibrium value (e.g., set $P = \bar{P}$) in the equilibrium condition, and then apply the rule as stated in (8.19) to the resulting equilibrium identity. For the simultaneous-equation case, we must also first set all endogenous variables equal to their respective equilibrium values in the equilibrium conditions. Then we can either apply the implicit-function rule as stated in (8.24) to the resulting equilibrium identities, or carry out the several steps outlined below: (1) Take the total differential of each equilibrium identity in turn. (2) Select one, and only one, exogenous variable (say, X_0) as the sole disequilibrating factor, and set the differentials of all other exogenous variables equal to zero. Then divide all remaining terms in each identity by dX_0, and interpret each quotient of two differentials as a comparative-static derivative—a partial one if the model contains two or more exogenous variables.[1] (3) Solve the resulting equation system for the comparative-static derivatives appearing therein, and interpret their economic meanings. In this step, if Cramer's rule is used, we can take advantage of the fact that, earlier, in checking the condition $|J| \neq 0$, we have in fact already calculated the determinant of the coefficient matrix of the equation system now being solved. (4) For the analysis of another disequilibrating factor (another exogenous variable) if any, repeat steps (2) and (3). Although a different group of comparative-static derivatives will emerge in the new equation system, the coefficient matrix will be the same as before, and thus the known value of $|J|$ can again be put to use. Given a model with m exogenous variables, it will take exactly m applications of the above-described procedure to catch all the comparative-static derivatives there are.

---

[1] Instead of taking steps (1) and (2), we may equivalently resort to the total-derivative method by differentiating (both sides of) each equilibrium identity totally with respect to the selected exogenous variable. In so doing, a channel map will prove to be of help.

EXERCISE 8.6

1   In the very short run, the supply of a commodity is fixed; thus we may write $Q_s = S_0$. Assume that the demand function for this commodity takes the form

$$Q_d = D(P,t_0) \qquad (\partial D/\partial P < 0; \partial D/\partial t_0 > 0)$$

where t_0 represents given consumer taste for the commodity, and where both partial derivatives are continuous.

    (a)   Is the implicit-function theorem applicable?
    (b)   How would you write the equilibrium solution for P and Q?
    (c)   How would $\bar{P}$ and $\bar{Q}$ vary with a change in consumer taste?

2   Analyze the comparative-static properties of the following market model, in which r represents rainfall and the other symbols have their usual meanings:

$$Q_d = Q_s$$
$$Q_d = D(P,Y_0) \qquad (\partial D/\partial P < 0; \partial D/\partial Y_0 > 0)$$
$$Q_s = S(P,r_0) \qquad (\partial S/\partial P > 0)$$

Assume that all partial derivatives are continuous and that $\partial S/\partial r_0$ has no definite sign.

3   From the national-income model in (8.38), find $(\partial \bar{Y}/\partial M_{s0})$ and $(\partial \bar{\imath}/\partial M_{s0})$, and interpret their economic meanings. Use *both* the total-differential method and the total-derivative method, and verify that the end results are the same.

4   Consider the following national-income model, in which we have ignored taxes:

$$Y - C(Y) - I(i) - G_0 = 0 \qquad (0 < C' < 1; I' < 0)$$
$$kY + L(i) - M_{s0} = 0 \qquad (k = \text{positive constant}; L' < 0)$$

    (a)   Is the first equation in the nature of an equilibrium condition?
    (b)   What is the total quantity demanded for money in this model?
    (c)   Analyze the comparative statics of the model when money supply changes (monetary policy) and when government expenditure changes (fiscal policy).

8.7   Limitations of Comparative Statics

Comparative statics is a useful area of study, because in economics we are often interested in finding out how a disequilibrating change in a parameter will affect the equilibrium state of a model. It is important to realize, however, that by its very nature comparative statics ignores the process of adjustment from the old equilibrium to the new and also neglects the time element involved in that adjustment process. As a consequence, it must of necessity also disregard the possibility that, because of the inherent instability of the model, the new equilibrium may not be attainable ever. The study of the process of adjustment per se belongs to the field of *economic dynamics*. When we come to that, particular attention will be directed toward the manner in which a variable will change over time, and explicit consideration will be given to the question of stability of equilibrium.

The important topic of dynamics, however, must wait its turn. Meanwhile, in the next part of the book, we shall undertake to study the problem of *optimization*, an exceedingly important special variety of equilibrium analysis with attendant comparative-static implications (and complications) of its own.

FOUR

OPTIMIZATION PROBLEMS

OPTIMIZATION: A SPECIAL VARIETY
OF EQUILIBRIUM ANALYSIS

When we first introduced the term equilibrium in Chap. 3, we made a broad distinction between goal and nongoal equilibrium. In the latter type, exemplified by our study of market and national-income models, the interplay of certain opposing forces in the model—e.g., the forces of demand and supply in the market models and the forces of leakages and injections in the income models—dictates an equilibrium state, if any, in which these opposing forces are just balanced against each other, thus obviating any further tendency to change. The attainment of this type of equilibrium is the outcome of the impersonal balancing of these forces and does not require the conscious effort on the part of anyone to accomplish a specified goal. True, the consuming households behind the forces of demand and the firms behind the forces of supply are each striving for an optimal position under the given circumstances, but as far as the market itself is concerned, no one is aiming at any particular equilibrium price or equilibrium quantity (unless, of course, the government happens to be trying to peg the price). Similarly, in national-income determination, the impersonal balancing of leakages and injections is what brings about an equilibrium state, and no conscious effort at reaching any particular goal (such as an attempt to alter an undesirable income level by means of monetary or fiscal policies) needs to be involved at all.

In the present part of the book, however, our attention will be turned to the study of *goal equilibrium*, in which the equilibrium state is defined as the optimum position for a given economic unit (a household, a business firm, or even an entire economy) and in which the said economic unit will be deliberately striving for attainment of that equilibrium. As a result, in this context—but only in this context—our earlier warning that equilibrium does not imply desirability will become irrelevant and immaterial. In this part of the book, only the classical techniques for locating optimum positions—those using differential calculus—will be introduced. More modern developments, known as mathematical programming, will be discussed in Part 6.

9.1 Optimum Values and Extreme Values

Economics is by and large a science of choice. When any kind of an economic project is to be carried out, such as the production of a specified level of output, there are usually a number of alternative ways of accomplishing it. One (or more) of these alternatives will, however, be more desirable than others from the standpoint of some criterion, and it is the essence of the optimization problem to choose, on the basis of that specified criterion, the best alternative available.

The most common criterion of choice among alternatives in economics is the goal of *maximizing* something (such as maximizing a firm's profit, a consumer's utility, or the rate of growth of a firm or of a country's economy) or of *minimizing* something (such as minimizing the cost of producing a given output). Economically, we may categorize such maximization and minimization processes under the general heading of *optimization*, meaning "the quest for the best." From a purely mathematical point of view, however, the terms maximum and minimum do not carry with them any connotation of optimality. Therefore, the collective term for maximum and minimum, as mathematical concepts, is the more matter-of-fact designation *extremum*, meaning an extreme value.

In working out an optimization problem, the first order of business is to delineate an *objective function* in which the dependent variable represents the object of maximization or minimization and in which the set of independent variables indicates the objects whose magnitudes the economic unit in question can pick and choose, with a view to optimizing. We shall therefore refer to the independent variables as *choice variables*.[1] The essence of the optimization process is simply to find the set of values of the choice variables that will yield the desired extremum of the objective function.

For example, a business firm may seek to maximize profit π, that is, to maximize the difference between total revenue R and total cost C. Since, within the framework of a given state of technology and a given market demand for the firm's product, R and C are both functions of the output level Q, it follows that π is also expressible as a function of Q:

$$\pi(Q) = R(Q) - C(Q)$$

[1] They can also be called *decision variables*, or *policy variables*.

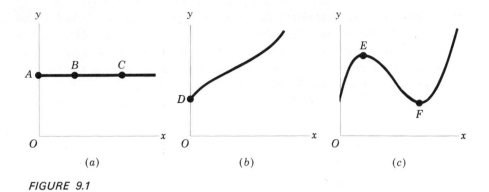

(a)   (b)   (c)

FIGURE 9.1

This equation constitutes the relevant objective function, with π as the object of maximization and Q as the (only) choice variable. The optimization problem is then that of choosing the level of Q such that π will be a maximum. Note that the *optimal* level of π is by definition its *maximal* level, but the optimal level of the choice variable Q is itself not required to be either a maximum or a minimum.

To cast the problem into a more general mold for further discussion (though still confining ourselves to objective functions of one variable only), let us consider the general function

$$y = f(x)$$

and attempt to develop a procedure for finding the level of x that will maximize or minimize the value of y. It will be assumed in this discussion that the function f is continuous and possesses a continuous derivative.

9.2   Relative Maximum and Minimum: First-Derivative Test

Since the objective function $y = f(x)$ is stated in the general form, there is no restriction as to whether it is linear or nonlinear, or whether it is monotonic or contains both increasing and decreasing parts. From among the many possible types of functions compatible with the above objective-function form, we have selected three specific cases to be depicted in Fig. 9.1. Simple as they may be, the graphs in Fig. 9.1 should give us valuable insight into the problem of locating the maximum or minimum value of the function $y = f(x)$.

relative versus absolute extremum   If the objective function is a constant function, as in Fig. 9.1a, all values of the choice variable x will result in the same value of y, and the height of each point on the graph of the function (such as A or B or C) may be considered a maximum or, for that matter, a minimum—or, indeed, neither. In this case, there is in effect no significant choice to be made regarding the value of x, and the economic content of the function is therefore nil so far as optimization is concerned.

In diagram b, the function is monotonically increasing, and there is no finite maximum if the set of nonnegative real numbers is taken to be its domain. However, we may consider the end point D on the left (the y intercept) as representing a minimum; in fact, it is in this case the *absolute* (or *global*) minimum in the range of the function.

The points E and F in diagram c, on the other hand, are examples of a *relative* (or *local*) extremum, in the sense that each of these points represents an extremum in the immediate neighborhood of the point only. The fact that point F is a relative minimum is, of course, no guarantee that it is also the global minimum of the function, although this may happen to be the case. Similarly, a relative maximum point such as E may or may not be a global maximum. Note also that a function can very well have several relative extrema, some of which may be maxima while others are minima.

In most economic problems that we shall be dealing with, our primary, if not exclusive, concern will be with extreme values other than end-point values, for with most such problems the domain of the objective function is restricted to be the set of nonnegative numbers, and thus an end point (on the left) will represent the zero level of the choice variable, which is of no practical interest. Actually, the type of function most frequently encountered in economic analysis is that shown in diagram c, or some variant thereof which contains only a single bend in the curve. We shall therefore continue our discussion mainly with reference to the search for *relative* extrema such as points E and F. This will, however, by no means foreclose the knowledge of an absolute maximum if we want it, because an absolute maximum must be either a relative maximum or one of the end points of the function, so that if we know all the relative maxima it is necessary only to select the largest of these and compare it with the end points in order to determine the absolute maximum. The absolute minimum of a function can be found analogously. Hereafter, the extreme values considered will be *relative* or *local* ones, unless indicated otherwise.

first-derivative test   As a matter of terminology, from now on we shall refer to the derivative of a function alternatively as its *first* derivative (short for *first-order* derivative). The reason for this will become apparent shortly.

Given a function $y = f(x)$, the first derivative $f'(x)$ plays a major role in our search for its extreme values. This is due to the fact that, if a relative

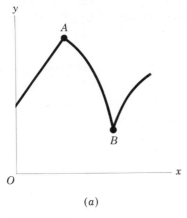

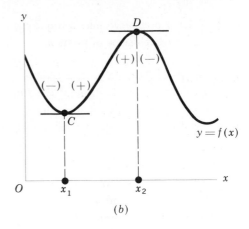

(a)   (b)

FIGURE 9.2

extremum of the function occurs at $x = x_0$, then either (1) we have $f'(x_0) = 0$, or (2) $f'(x_0)$ does not exist. The second eventuality is illustrated in Fig. 9.2a, where both points A and B depict relative extreme values of y, and yet no derivative is defined at either of these sharp points. Since in the present discussion we are assuming that $y = f(x)$ is continuous and possesses a continuous derivative, however, we are in effect ruling out sharp points. For smooth functions, relative extreme values can occur only where the first derivative has a zero value. This is illustrated by points C and D in Fig. 9.2b, both of which represent extreme values, and both of which are characterized by a zero slope—$f'(x_1) = 0$ and $f'(x_2) = 0$. It is also easy to see that when the slope is nonzero we cannot possibly have either a minimum (the bottom of a valley) or a maximum (the peak of a hill).

We must add, however, that a zero slope, while *necessary*, is *not sufficient* to establish a relative extremum. An example of the case where a zero derivative is not associated with an extremum will be presented shortly. By appending a certain proviso to the zero-derivative condition, however, we can obtain a decisive test for a relative extremum. This may be stated as follows:

FIRST-DERIVATIVE TEST FOR RELATIVE EXTREMUM   If the first derivative of a function $f(x)$ at a point $x = x_0$ is $f'(x_0) = 0$, then the value of the function at this point, $f(x_0)$, will be

a   A relative *maximum* if the derivative $f'(x)$ changes its sign from positive to negative from the left of the point x_0 to its right

b   A relative *minimum* if $f'(x)$ turns from negative to positive from the left of x_0 to its right *c*   Neither a relative maximum nor a relative minimum if $f'(x)$ has the same sign on both sides of point x_0

Let us call the value x_0 a *critical value* of x if $f'(x_0) = 0$, and refer to $f(x_0)$ as a *stationary value* of y (or of the function f). The point with coordinates x_0 and $f(x_0)$ can, accordingly, be called a *stationary point*. (The rationale for the word "stationary" should be self-evident—wherever the slope is zero, the point in question is never situated on an upward or downward incline, but is rather at a standstill position.) Then, graphically, the first possibility listed in this test will establish the stationary point as the peak of a hill, such as point D in Fig. 9.2*b*, whereas the second possibility will establish the stationary point as the bottom of a valley, such as point C in the same diagram. Note, however, that in view of the existence of a third possibility, yet to be discussed, we are unable to regard the equation $f'(x_0) = 0$ as a *sufficient condition* for a relative extremum. But we now see that, *if* the necessary condition $f'(x_0) = 0$ is satisfied, *then* the change-of-derivative-sign proviso will serve as a *sufficient condition* for a relative maximum or minimum, depending on the direction of the sign change.

Let us now explain the third possibility. In Fig. 9.3*a*, the function f is shown to attain a zero slope at point J (when $x = j$). Even though $f'(j)$ is zero —which makes $f(j)$ a stationary value—the derivative does not change its sign from one side of $x = j$ to the other; therefore, according to the test above, point J gives neither a maximum nor a minimum, as is duly confirmed by the graph of the function. Rather, it exemplifies what is known as an *inflection point*.

The characteristic feature of an inflection point is that, at that point, the derivative (as against the primitive) function reaches an extreme value. Since this can be either a maximum or a minimum, we have two types of inflection points. In Fig. 9.3*a'*, where we have plotted the derivative $f'(x)$, we see that its value is zero when $x = j$ (see point J') but is positive on both sides of point J'; this makes J' a *minimum* point of the derivative function $f'(x)$.

The other type of inflection point is portrayed in Fig. 9.3*b*, where the slope of the function $g(x)$ increases till the point K is reached and decreases thereafter. Consequently, the graph of the derivative function $g'(x)$ will assume the shape shown in diagram *b'*, where point K' gives a *maximum* value of the derivative function $g'(x)$.†

To sum up: A relative extremum must be a stationary value, but a stationary value may be associated with either a relative extremum or an inflection point. To find the relative maximum or minimum of a given function, therefore, the procedure should be first to find the stationary values of the function where $f'(x) = 0$ and then to apply the first-derivative test to determine

† Note that a zero derivative value, while a necessary condition for a relative extremum, is *not* required for an inflection point; for the derivative $g'(x)$ has a positive value at $x = k$, and yet point K is an inflection point.

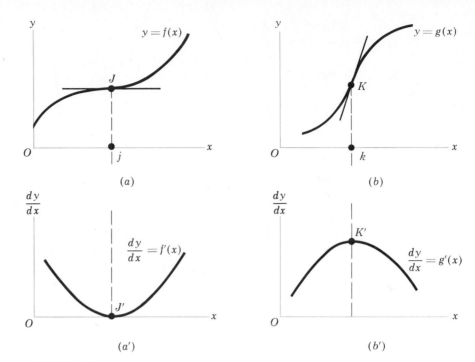

FIGURE 9.3

whether each of the stationary values is a relative maximum, a relative minimum, or neither.

Example 1   Find the relative extrema of the function

$$y = f(x) = x^3 - 12x^2 + 36x + 8$$

First, we find the derivative function to be

$$f'(x) = 3x^2 - 24x + 36$$

To get the critical values, i.e., the values of x where $f'(x) = 0$, we set the quadratic derivative function equal to zero and get a quadratic equation:

$$3x^2 - 24x + 36 = 0$$

By factoring the polynomial or by applying the quadratic formula, we can obtain the following pair of roots (solutions):

$$\bar{x}_1 = 2 \quad \text{[at which we have } f'(2) = 0 \text{ and } f(2) = 40]$$
$$\bar{x}_2 = 6 \quad \text{[at which we have } f'(6) = 0 \text{ and } f(6) = 8]$$

Since $f'(2) = f'(6) = 0$, these two values of x are the critical values we desire.

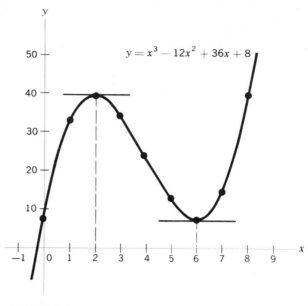

FIGURE 9.4

It is easy to verify that $f'(x) > 0$ for $x < 2$ and that $f'(x) < 0$ for $x > 2$ in the immediate neighborhood of $x = 2$; thus, the corresponding value of the function $f(2) = 40$ is established as a relative maximum. Similarly, since $f'(x) < 0$ for $x < 6$ and $f'(x) > 0$ for $x > 6$ in the immediate neighborhood of $x = 6$, the value of the function $f(6) = 8$ must be a relative minimum.

The graph of the function of this example is shown in Fig. 9.4. Such a graph may be used to verify the location of extreme values obtained through use of the first-derivative test. But, in reality, in most cases "helpfulness" flows in the opposite direction—the mathematically derived extreme values will help in plotting the graph. The accurate plotting of a graph ideally requires knowledge of the value of the function at every point in the domain; but as a matter of actual practice, only a few points in the domain are selected for purposes of plotting, and the rest of the points typically are filled in by interpolation. The pitfall of this practice is that, unless we hit upon the stationary point(s) by coincidence, we shall miss the exact location of the turning point(s) in the curve. Now, with the first-derivative test at our disposal, it becomes possible to determine these turning points precisely.

Example 2   Find the relative extremum of the average-cost function

$$AC = f(Q) = Q^2 - 5Q + 8$$

We know that the derivative here is $f'(Q) = 2Q - 5$, a linear function. Setting

$f'(Q)$ equal to zero, we get the linear equation $2Q - 5 = 0$, which has the single root $\bar{Q} = 2.5$. This is the only critical value in this case. To apply the first-derivative test, let us find the values of the derivative at, say, $Q = 2.4$ and $Q = 2.6$, respectively. Since $f'(2.4) = -0.2 < 0$ whereas $f'(2.6) = 0.2 > 0$, we can conclude that the stationary value $AC = f(2.5) = 1.75$ represents a relative minimum. The graph of the function of this example is actually a U-shaped curve, so that the relative minimum we have found will also be the absolute minimum. Our knowledge of the exact location of this point should be of great help in plotting the AC curve.

EXERCISE 9.2

1   Find the stationary values of the following (check whether maxima or minima or inflection points), assuming the domain to be the set of all real numbers:

(a) $y = -x^2 + 4x + 7$ (c) $y = x^2 + 3$
(b) $y = 2x^2 + x$ (d) $y = 3x^2 - x + 1$

2   Find the stationary values of the following (check whether maxima or minima or inflection points), assuming the domain to be the interval $[0, \infty)$:

(a) $y = x^3 - 3x + 5$
(b) $y = \frac{1}{3}x^3 - 2x^2 + 4x + 10$
(c) $y = -x^3 + 4.5x^2 - 6x + 6$

3   Show that the function $y = x + 1/x$ (with $x \neq 0$) has two relative extrema, one being a maximum and the other a minimum. Is the "minimum" larger or smaller than the "maximum"? How is this paradoxical result possible? (*Hint:* Plot the function—the graph will help to explain.)

4   Let $T = \phi(x)$ be a *total* function (total product, total cost, etc.):

(a)   Write out the expressions for the *marginal* function M and the *average* function A.
(b)   Show that, when A reaches a relative extremum, M and A must have the same value.
(c)   What general principle does this suggest in connection with the drawing of a marginal curve and an average curve in the same diagram?
(d)   What can you conclude about the elasticity of the total function T at the point where A reaches an extreme value?

9.3 Second and Higher Derivatives

Hitherto we have considered only the first derivative $f'(x)$ of a function $y = f(x)$; now let us introduce the concept of *second derivative* (short for *second-order derivative*), and derivatives of even higher orders. These will enable us to develop alternative criteria for locating the relative extrema of a function.

derivative of a derivative   Since it is a function of x, the first derivative $f'(x)$ should itself be differentiable with respect to x, provided that it is continuous and smooth. The result of this differentiation, known as the second derivative of the function f, is denoted by

$f''(x)$ where the double prime indicates that $f(x)$ has been differentiated twice, and where the expression (x) following the double prime suggests that the second derivative is again a function of x

or

$\dfrac{d^2y}{dx^2}$ where the notation stems from the consideration that the second derivative means, in fact, $\dfrac{d}{dx}\left(\dfrac{dy}{dx}\right)$; hence the d^2 in the numerator and dx^2 in the denominator of this symbol.

As a function of x, the second derivative can be differentiated with respect to x again to produce a *third* derivative, which in turn can be the source of a *fourth* derivative, and so on ad infinitum, as long as the differentiability condition is met. These higher-order derivatives are symbolized along the same line as the second derivative:

$$f'''(x), f^{(4)}(x), \ldots, f^{(n)}(x) \qquad \text{[with superscripts in ( )]}$$

or $\dfrac{d^3y}{dx^3}, \dfrac{d^4y}{dx^4}, \ldots, \dfrac{d^ny}{dx^n}$

Example 1   Find the first through the fifth derivatives of the function

$$y = f(x) = 4x^4 - x^3 + 17x^2 + 3x - 1$$

The desired derivatives are as follows:

$$f'(x) = 16x^3 - 3x^2 + 34x + 3$$
$$f''(x) = 48x^2 - 6x + 34$$
$$f'''(x) = 96x - 6$$
$$f^{(4)}(x) = 96$$
$$f^{(5)}(x) = 0$$

In this particular (polynomial-function) example, each successive derivative emerges as a simpler expression than the one before, until we reach a fifth derivative, which is identically zero. This is not generally true, however, of all types of functions, as the next example will show. Something else which should be pointed out is that the statement "the fifth derivative is zero" must not be confused with the statement "the fifth derivative does not exist," which describes an altogether different situation. Note, also, that $f^{(5)}(x) = 0$ (zero at all values of x) is not the same as $f^{(5)}(x_0) = 0$ (zero at x_0 only).

Example 2   Find the first four derivatives of the rational function

$$y = g(x) = \frac{x}{1 + x} \qquad (x \neq -1)$$

These derivatives can be found either by use of the quotient rule or, after rewriting the function as $y = x(1 + x)^{-1}$, by the product rule:

$$\left. \begin{array}{l} g'(x) = (1 + x)^{-2} \\ g''(x) = -2(1 + x)^{-3} \\ g'''(x) = 6(1 + x)^{-4} \\ g^{(4)}(x) = -24(1 + x)^{-5} \end{array} \right\} \qquad (x \neq -1)$$

In this case, repeated derivation evidently does not tend to simplify the derivative expression.

Note that, like the primitive function $g(x)$, all the successive derivatives obtained are themselves functions of x. Given specific values of x, these derivative functions will then take specific values. When $x = 2$, for instance, the second derivative in Example 2 can be evaluated as

$$g''(2) = -2(3)^{-3} = \frac{-2}{27}$$

and similarly for other values of x. It is of the utmost importance to realize that to evaluate this second derivative $g''(x)$ at $x = 2$, as we did, we must first obtain $g''(x)$ from $g'(x)$ and then substitute $x = 2$ into the equation for $g''(x)$. It is *incorrect* to substitute $x = 2$ into $g(x)$ or $g'(x)$ *prior to* the differentiation process leading to $g''(x)$.

interpretation of the second derivative   The derivative function $f'(x)$ measures the rate of change of the function f. By the same token, the second-derivative function f'' is the measure of the rate of change of the first derivative f'; in other words, the second derivative measures the *rate of change* of the *rate of change* of the original function f. To put it differently, with a given infinitesimal

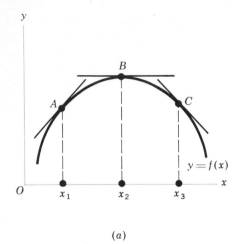

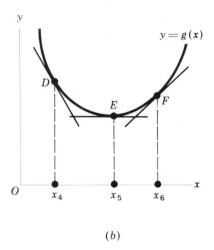

FIGURE 9.5

(a)

(b)

increase in the independent variable x from a point $x = x_0$,

$$\left.\begin{matrix} f'(x_0) > 0 \\ f'(x_0) < 0 \end{matrix}\right\} \text{ means that the } \textit{value of the function} \text{ tends to } \left\{\begin{matrix} \text{increase} \\ \text{decrease} \end{matrix}\right.$$

whereas, with regard to the second derivative,

$$\left.\begin{matrix} f''(x_0) > 0 \\ f''(x_0) < 0 \end{matrix}\right\} \text{ means that the } \textit{slope of the curve} \text{ tends to } \left\{\begin{matrix} \text{increase} \\ \text{decrease} \end{matrix}\right.$$

Thus, a positive first derivative coupled with a positive second derivative at $x = x_0$ will imply that the slope of the curve at that point is *positive and increasing*—the value of the function is increasing at an increasing rate. Likewise, a positive first derivative with a negative second derivative indicates that the slope of the curve is *positive but decreasing*—the value of the function is increasing at a decreasing rate. The case of a negative first derivative can be interpreted analogously, but a warning should accompany this case: When $f'(x_0) < 0$ and $f''(x_0) > 0$, the slope of the curve is *negative and increasing*, but this does *not* mean that the slope is changing, say, from (-10) to (-11); on the contrary, the change should be from (-11), a smaller number, to (-10), a larger number. In other words, the negative slope must tend to be *less* steep as x increases. Lastly, when $f'(x_0) < 0$ and $f''(x_0) < 0$, the slope of the curve must be *negative and decreasing*. This refers to a negative slope that tends to become *steeper* as x increases.

Since we have been talking about slopes, it may be useful to continue the discussion with a graphical illustration. In Fig. 9.5 we have marked out six points (A, B, C, D, E, and F) on the two parabolas shown; each of these points illustrates a different combination of first- and second-derivative signs, as follows:

If at	the derivative signs are		we can illustrate it by
$x = x_1$	$f'(x_1) > 0$	$f''(x_1) < 0$	point A
$x = x_2$	$f'(x_2) = 0$	$f''(x_2) < 0$	point B
$x = x_3$	$f'(x_3) < 0$	$f''(x_3) < 0$	point C
$x = x_4$	$g'(x_4) < 0$	$g''(x_4) > 0$	point D
$x = x_5$	$g'(x_5) = 0$	$g''(x_5) > 0$	point E
$x = x_6$	$g'(x_6) > 0$	$g''(x_6) > 0$	point F

From this, we see that a *negative* second derivative (the first three cases) is consistently reflected in an inverse U-shaped curve, or a portion thereof, because the curve in question is required to have a smaller and smaller slope as x increases. In contrast, a *positive* second derivative (the last three cases) consistently leads to a U-shaped curve, or a portion thereof, since the curve in question must display a larger and larger slope as x increases. Viewing the two curves in Fig. 9.5 from the standpoint of the horizontal axis, we find the one in diagram a to be concave throughout, whereas the one in diagram b is convex throughout. Since concavity and convexity are descriptions of how the curve "bends," we may now expect the second derivative of a function to inform us about the *curvature* of its graph, just as the first derivative tells us about its *slope*.

Although the words "concave" and "convex" are sufficient to convey the differing curvature of the two curves in Fig. 9.5, most writers today will label them as *strictly concave* and *strictly convex*, respectively. In line with this terminology, a function whose graph is strictly concave (strictly convex) is called a *strictly concave (strictly convex) function*. The precise geometric characterization of a strictly concave function is as follows: If we pick any pair of points M and N on its curve, and join them by a straight line, the line segment MN must lie entirely *below* the curve, except at points M and N. The characterization of a strictly convex function can be obtained by substituting the word *above* for the word *below* in the last statement. The reader should try this out in Fig. 9.5. If the characterizing condition is relaxed somewhat, so that the line segment MN is allowed *either* to lie below the curve, *or* to lie along (coincide with) the curve, then we will be describing instead a *concave function*, without the adverb "strictly." Similarly, if the line segment MN *either* lies above, *or* lies along the curve, then the function is *convex*, again without the adverb "strictly." Note that, since the line segment MN may coincide with a (nonstrictly) concave or convex curve, the latter may very well contain a linear segment. In contrast, a *strictly* concave or convex curve can never contain a linear segment anywhere. It follows that while a strictly concave (convex) function is automatically a concave (convex) function, the converse is not true.[1]

From our earlier discussion of the second derivative, we may now infer that if the second derivative $f''(x)$ is negative for all x, then the primitive function $f(x)$ must be a strictly concave function. Similarly, $f(x)$ must be strictly convex, if $f''(x)$ is positive for all x. Despite this, it is *not* valid to reverse the above inference and say that, if $f(x)$ is strictly concave (strictly convex), then $f''(x)$ must be negative (positive) for all x. This is because, in certain exceptional cases, the second derivative may have a *zero* value at a stationary point on such a curve. An example of this can be found in the function $y = f(x) = x^4$, which plots as a strictly convex curve, but whose derivatives

$$f'(x) = 4x^3 \qquad f''(x) = 12x^2$$

indicate that, at the stationary point where $x = 0$, the value of the second derivative is $f''(0) = 0$. Note, however, that at any other point, with $x \neq 0$, the second derivative of this function does have the (expected) positive sign. Aside from the possibility of a zero value at a stationary point, therefore, the second derivative of a strictly concave or convex function may be expected in general to adhere to a single algebraic sign.

For other types of functions, the second derivative may take both positive and negative values, depending on the value of x. In Fig. 9.3a and b, for instance, both $f(x)$ and $g(x)$ undergo a sign change in the second derivative at their respective inflection points J and K. According to Fig. 9.3a', the slope of $f'(x)$— that is, the value of $f''(x)$—changes from negative to positive at $x = j$; the exact opposite occurs with the slope of $g'(x)$—that is, the value of $g''(x)$—on the basis of Fig. 9.3b'. Translated into curvature terms, this means that the graph of $f(x)$ switches from concave to convex at point J, whereas the graph of $g(x)$ has the reverse change at point K. Consequently, instead of characterizing an inflection point as a point where the first derivative reaches an extreme value, we may now characterize it alternatively as a point where the function undergoes a change in curvature or a change in the sign of its second derivative.

an application   The two curves in Fig. 9.5 exemplify the graphs of quadratic functions, which may be expressed generally in the form

$$y = ax^2 + bx + c \qquad (a \neq 0)$$

From our discussion of the second derivative, we can now derive a convenient

---

[1] We shall discuss these concepts further in Sec. 11.4 below.

way of determining whether a given quadratic function will have a strictly convex (U-shaped) or a strictly concave (inverse U-shaped) graph.

Since the second derivative of the quadratic function cited is $d^2y/dx^2 = 2a$, we see that this derivative will always have the same algebraic sign as the coefficient a. Recalling that a positive second derivative implies a strictly convex curve, we can infer that a positive coefficient a in the above quadratic function gives rise to a U-shaped graph. In contrast, a negative coefficient a leads to a strictly concave curve, shaped like an inverted U.

As intimated at the end of Sec. 9.2, the relative extremum of this function will also prove to be its absolute extremum, because in a quadratic function there can be found only a single valley or peak, evident in a U or inverted U, respectively.

EXERCISE 9.3

1 Find the second derivatives of the following functions:

(a) $ax^2 + bx + c$

(c) $\dfrac{2x}{1-x}$ $(x \neq 1)$

(b) $4x^4 - 3x - 18$

(d) $\dfrac{1+x}{1-x}$ $(x \neq 1)$

2 Find the third derivatives of the functions in the preceding problem.

3 Which of the following quadratic functions are strictly convex?

(a) $y = 5x^2 - 4x + 13$

(c) $u = 9 - x^2$

(b) $w = -3x^2 + 39$

(d) $v = 2 - 5x + x^2$

4 Draw (a) a concave curve which is *not* strictly concave, and (b) a curve which qualifies as a concave curve as well as a convex curve.

5 Given the function $y = a - \dfrac{b}{c+x}$ ($a,b,c > 0$; $x \geq 0$), determine the general shape of its graph by examining (a) its first and second derivatives, (b) its vertical intercept, and (c) the limit of y as x tends to infinity. If this function is to be used as a consumption function, how should the parameters be restricted in order to make it economically sensible?

9.4   Second-Derivative Test

Returning to the pair of extreme points B and E in Fig. 9.5 and remembering the newly established relationship between the second derivative and the curvature of a curve, we should be able to see the validity of the following criterion for a relative extremum:

SECOND-DERIVATIVE TEST FOR RELATIVE EXTREMUM   If the first derivative of a function f at the point $x = x_0$ is $f'(x_0) = 0$, then the value of the function at that point, or $f(x_0)$, will be

a   A relative *maximum* if the second derivative is $f''(x_0) < 0$
b   A relative *minimum* if the second derivative is $f''(x_0) > 0$

As was the case with the first-derivative test, the condition $f'(x_0) = 0$ is a *necessary* condition here. If this condition is satisfied, then the negative (positive) sign of the second derivative becomes a *sufficient* condition for a relative maximum (minimum). These two conditions are often referred to, respectively, as the *first-order condition* and the *second-order condition* for a relative extremum, on account of the particular order of derivative involved in each.

The second-derivative test is, in general, more convenient to use than the first-derivative test. However, unlike the latter, the second-derivative test has the drawback of being "incomplete," in the sense that one possible outcome, $f''(x_0) = 0$, is left undiscussed. When a zero second derivative is encountered, this test fails, and we must then either revert to the first-derivative test or else resort to another test, to be developed below, involving the third or even higher derivatives.

At this juncture, we shall simply point out that, in the case of $f''(x_0) = 0$, the point x_0 may in some circumstances yield an inflection point. This possibility may be seen from Fig. 9.3a and a'. When $x = j$, $f'(x)$ reaches a minimum value; thus $f''(j)$ must be zero. The corresponding point on the function, J, is an inflection point. In still other circumstances, however, a relative extremum may exist at $x = x_0$ when $f''(x_0) = 0$. This may be seen from the function $y = x^4$, for which the critical value is $x = 0$, since $f'(x) = 4x^3$ and $f'(0) = 0$. At this value of x, the second derivative $f''(x) = 12x^2$ assumes the value of zero also, and yet the value of the function $f(0) = 0$ is a minimum, for any nonzero value of x will yield a value of y greater than zero. Hence the case of $f''(x_0) = 0$ must be considered indeterminate.

Example 1   Find the relative extremum of the function

$$y = f(x) = 4x^2 - x$$

The first and second derivatives are

$$f'(x) = 8x - 1 \quad \text{and} \quad f''(x) = 8$$

Setting $f'(x)$ equal to zero and solving the resulting equation, we find the (only) critical value to be $\bar{x} = \frac{1}{8}$, which yields the (only) stationary value $f(\frac{1}{8}) = -\frac{1}{16}$. Because the second derivative is positive (in this case it is indeed positive for any value of x), the extremum is established as a minimum.

Example 2   Find the relative extrema of the function

$$y = g(x) = x^3 - 3x^2 + 2$$

The first two derivatives of this function are

$$g'(x) = 3x^2 - 6x \quad \text{and} \quad g''(x) = 6x - 6$$

Setting $g'(x)$ equal to zero and solving the resulting quadratic equation

$$3x^2 - 6x = 0$$

we obtain the critical values

$$\bar{x}_1 = 0 \quad \text{and} \quad \bar{x}_2 = 2$$

which in turn yield the two stationary values:

$$g(0) = 2 \qquad \text{[a maximum because } g''(0) = -6 < 0]$$
$$g(2) = -2 \qquad \text{[a minimum because } g''(2) = 6 > 0]$$

conditions for profit maximization   We shall now present some economic examples of extreme-value problems, i.e., problems of optimization.

One of the first things that a student of economics learns is that, in order to maximize profit, a firm must choose the output level such that $MC = MR$. Let us show the mathematical derivation of this condition. To keep the analysis on a general level, we shall work with a total-revenue function $R = R(Q)$ and a total-cost function $C = C(Q)$, both of which are functions of a single variable Q. From these it follows that a profit function (the objective function) may also be formulated in terms of Q (the choice variable):

$$(9.1) \qquad \pi = \pi(Q) = R(Q) - C(Q)$$

To find the profit-maximizing output level, we must fulfill the necessary condition for a maximum: $d\pi/dQ = 0$. Accordingly, let us differentiate (9.1) with respect to Q and set the resulting derivative $d\pi/dQ$ equal to zero:

(9.2) $\quad\dfrac{d\pi}{dQ} \equiv \pi'(Q) = R'(Q) - C'(Q)$

$\qquad\qquad = 0 \qquad \text{iff } R'(Q) = C'(Q)$

Thus the *optimum* output (*equilibrium* output) $\bar{Q}$ must satisfy the equation $R'(\bar{Q}) = C'(\bar{Q})$, or MR $=$ MC. This condition constitutes the first-order condition for profit maximization.

However, the fulfillment of the first-order condition may yield a minimum rather than a maximum; thus we must check the second-order condition next. We can obtain the second derivative by differentiating the first derivative in (9.2) with respect to Q:

$$\dfrac{d^2\pi}{dQ^2} \equiv \pi''(Q) = R''(Q) - C''(Q)$$

$\qquad < 0 \qquad \text{iff } R''(Q) < C''(Q)$

For an output level $\bar{Q}$ that fulfills $R'(\bar{Q}) = C'(\bar{Q})$, the satisfaction of the second-order condition $R''(\bar{Q}) < C''(\bar{Q})$ will be sufficient to establish it as a profit-maximizing output. Economically, this would mean that, if the rate of change of MR is less than the rate of change of MC at the output where MC $=$ MR, then that output will maximize profit.

These conditions are illustrated in Fig. 9.6. In diagram *a* we have drawn a total-revenue and a total-cost curve, which are seen to intersect twice, at output levels of Q_2 and Q_4. In the open interval (Q_2,Q_4), total revenue R exceeds total cost C, and thus π is positive. But in the intervals $[0,Q_2)$ and $(Q_4,Q_5]$, where Q_5 represents the upper limit of the firm's productive capacity, π is negative. This fact is reflected in diagram *b*, where the profit curve—obtained by plotting the vertical distance between the R and C curves for each level of output—lies above the horizontal axis only in the interval (Q_2,Q_4).

When we set $d\pi/dQ = 0$, in fulfillment of the first-order condition, it is our intention to locate the peak point K on the profit curve, at output Q_3, where the slope of the curve is zero. However, the relative-minimum point M (output Q_1) will also offer itself as a candidate, because it too meets the zero-slope requirement. Thus we shall later resort to the second-order condition to sift out the "wrong" kind of extremum.

The first-order condition $d\pi/dQ = 0$ is equivalent to the condition $R'(Q) = C'(Q)$. In diagram *a*, the output level Q_3 satisfies this equation, because the R and C curves do have the same slope at Q_3 (the tangent lines drawn to the two curves at H and J are parallel to each other). The same is true for output Q_1. Since the equality of the slopes of R and C means the equality of MR and MC, outputs Q_3 and Q_1 must obviously be where the MR and MC curves intersect, as illustrated in diagram *c*.

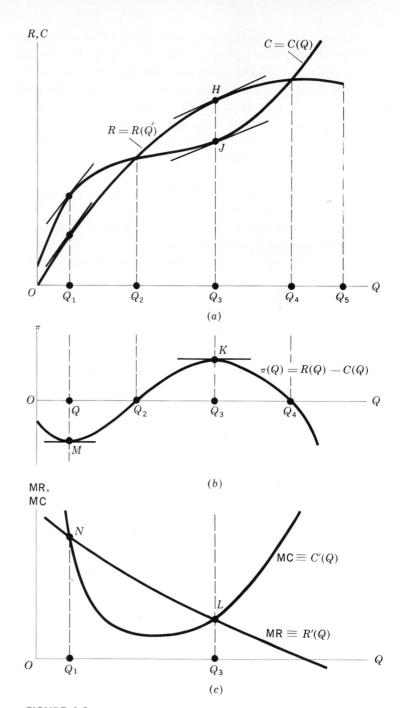

FIGURE 9.6

How does the second-order condition enter into the picture? Let us first look at diagram b. At point K, the second derivative of the π function will (barring the exceptional zero-value case) have a negative value, $\pi''(Q_3) < 0$, because the curve is inverse U-shaped around K; this means that Q_3 will maximize profit. At point M, on the other hand, we would expect that $\pi''(Q_1) > 0$; thus Q_1 provides a relative minimum for π instead. The second-order condition for maximum can, of course, be stated alternatively as $R''(Q) < C''(Q)$, that is, that the slope of the MR curve be less than the slope of the MC curve. From diagram c, it is immediately apparent that output Q_3 fulfills this condition, since the slope of MR is negative while that of MC is positive at point L. But output Q_1 violates this condition because both MC and MR have negative slopes, and that of MR is *numerically smaller* than that of MC at point N, which implies that $R''(Q)$ is *larger* than $C''(Q)$ at the latter point.

For a more concrete illustration of the profit-maximization problem, let us assume that

$$R(Q) = 1000Q - 2Q^2$$
$$C(Q) = Q^3 - 59Q^2 + 1315Q + 2000$$

Therefore,

$$\pi = R - C = -Q^3 + 57Q^2 - 315Q - 2000$$

where R, C, and π are all in dollar units, while Q is in units of (say) tons per week. This profit function has two critical values, because

$$\frac{d\pi}{dQ} = -3Q^2 + 114Q - 315 = 0 \qquad \text{when } Q = \begin{cases} 3 \\ 35 \end{cases}$$

But since the second derivative is

$$\frac{d^2\pi}{dQ^2} = -6Q + 114 \qquad \begin{cases} >0 \text{ when } Q = 3 \\ <0 \text{ when } Q = 35 \end{cases}$$

the output of 35 (tons per week) is the only profit-maximizing one.

The substitution of the solution value $\bar{Q} = 35$ into the profit function will reveal that the maximum profit is \$13,925 per week in the present case.

maximizing excise-tax revenue   A monopolist firm is known to have the following types of total-revenue and total-cost functions:

$$R = -\alpha Q^2 + \beta Q \qquad (\alpha, \beta > 0)$$
$$C = aQ^2 + bQ + c \qquad (a, b, c > 0)$$

Suppose that the government plans to levy an excise tax on the product of this

       Optimization Problems

firm and wishes to maximize the tax revenue T from this source. What tax rate t (dollars per unit of output) should the government choose?

For this problem, the objective function is the tax-revenue function

$$(9.3) \qquad T = t\bar{Q}$$

where $\bar{Q}$ stands for the monopolist's equilibrium output *after* the imposition of the excise tax. Since the cost and revenue functions of the monopolist are known, it is easy to find out what $\bar{Q}$ will be. We must remember, however, that the tax levy will alter the cost picture of the firm, so that we should write a new (postlevy) total-cost function

$$\begin{aligned} C* &= C + tQ \\ &= aQ^2 + (b + t)Q + c \end{aligned}$$

to be used in calculating the equilibrium output $\bar{Q}$.

In order to find $\bar{Q}$, we can either formulate a profit function

$$\pi = R - C*$$

and proceed as we did for (9.1), or proceed as follows: First derive the MR and MC* functions and then equate these in fulfillment of the first-order profit-maximization condition for the monopolist. Let us follow the latter procedure.

From the new total-cost function $C*$, we can derive the marginal-cost function by straight derivation:

$$\text{MC*} \equiv \frac{dC*}{dQ} = 2aQ + b + t$$

Similarly, the derivative of the total-revenue function R (which is unaffected by the tax levy) will give us

$$\text{MR} \equiv \frac{dR}{dQ} = -2\alpha Q + \beta$$

Equating MC* and MR and solving for Q, we find the monopolist's equilibrium output to be

$$\bar{Q} = \frac{\beta - b - t}{2(a + \alpha)}$$

Substituting this expression into the objective function of the government, (9.3), we get the more specific and more informative tax-revenue function

$$T = \frac{t(\beta - b - t)}{2(a + \alpha)}$$

which shows T as a function of the only choice variable t (a, b, α, and β are parametric constants).

For the maximization of T, we must satisfy the first-order condition; i.e., we must set the first derivative

$$\frac{dT}{dt} = \frac{\beta - b - 2t}{2(a + \alpha)}$$

equal to zero. Since the quotient will be zero only if its numerator is zero, we can simply set $\beta - b - 2t = 0$ and find the revenue-maximizing tax rate to be

$$t = \frac{\beta - b}{2}$$

But does this tax rate indeed maximize, rather than minimize, the tax revenue? Let us check the second-order condition. The second derivative is

$$\frac{d^2T}{dt^2} = \frac{-2}{2(a + \alpha)} = \frac{-1}{a + \alpha}$$

which is a negative quantity; therefore the second-order condition for maximum is met, and the solution $\bar{t}$ does constitute the answer we have been seeking.

coefficients of a cubic total-cost function　　The search for a maximum or minimum may be an end in itself, but it may also be a preliminary step to some other analytical objective.

Suppose that we want to represent a short-run total-cost function by a cubic function as follows:

$$(9.4) \qquad C = aQ^3 + bQ^2 + cQ + d$$

To make economic sense, the coefficients a, b, c, and d must obviously be restricted in certain ways. What kind of restrictions would economic common sense dictate?

First of all, since the coefficient d represents the fixed cost, it should in the short-run context be positive: $d > 0$. This takes care of one restriction. Second, since we may expect marginal cost to be positive at all levels of output, the C function must be made monotonically increasing. It was mentioned earlier that, in general, the graph of a cubic function will contain two wiggles, as illustrated in Fig. 9.4; in the present case, we want the curve to wiggle without bending down, so that the slope of the curve is kept consistently upward, as in Fig. 9.6a. This requirement will entail definite restrictions on the coefficients a, b, and c.

First let us note that we can be sure of the positivity of marginal cost at all levels of output if the *absolute minimum* of the MC function is *positive*, i.e., if the said minimum occurs (in the first quadrant) above the horizontal axis, as in Fig. 9.6c. The MC function in the present case is the quadratic function

$$\mathrm{MC} = C'(Q) = 3aQ^2 + 2bQ + c$$

For this to possess a positive absolute minimum in the first quadrant, it is necessary (though not sufficient) that its graph be U-shaped. (With an inverse-U in the first quadrant, in contrast, the absolute minimum will be MC $= 0$ instead.) Consequently, we should impose the restriction $a > 0$ in order to make the coefficient of the Q^2 term positive. If so, then the absolute minimum of MC— identical with its sole relative minimum—will be found at the bottom of the U. It now remains to find the conditions under which this minimum will be positive.

According to our knowledge of relative extremum, the minimum of MC will occur where

$$\frac{d}{dQ} \, MC = 6aQ + 2b = 0$$

The output level that satisfies this condition, namely,

$$Q^* = \frac{-2b}{6a} = \frac{-b}{3a}$$

minimizes (rather than maximizes) MC because the second derivative $d^2(MC)/dQ^2 = 6a$ is assuredly positive in view of the restriction $a > 0$. The knowledge of Q^* enables us to calculate the minimum level of MC, but we may first infer the sign of coefficient b from it: Inasmuch as negative output levels are ruled out, we see that b can never be positive (given $a > 0$). Moreover, if the law of diminishing returns is assumed to set in at a positive output level (that is, if MC is assumed to have an initial declining segment), then Q^* should be positive (rather than zero). In that event, b should be restricted to being negative.

Next, let us substitute the MC-minimizing output Q^* into the MC function in order to find the minimum level of MC. That level turns out to be

$$MC_{min} = 3a \left(\frac{-b}{3a} \right)^2 + 2b \, \frac{-b}{3a} + c = \frac{3ac - b^2}{3a}$$

Thus, to guarantee the positivity of MC_{min}, we must impose the restriction[1] that $b^2 < 3ac$. This last restriction, it may be noted, in effect also implies the restriction that $c > 0$. (Why?)

In sum, therefore, the coefficients of the total-cost function in (9.4) should be restricted as follows:

$$(9.5) \qquad a,c,d > 0 \qquad b < 0 \qquad b^2 < 3ac$$

---

[1] This restriction may also be obtained by the method of *completing the square*. The MC function can be successively transformed as follows:

$$MC = 3aQ^2 + 2bQ + c$$
$$= \left(3aQ^2 + 2bQ + \frac{b^2}{3a} \right) - \frac{b^2}{3a} + c$$
$$= \left(\sqrt{3a} \, Q + \sqrt{\frac{b^2}{3a}} \right)^2 + \frac{-b^2 + 3ac}{3a}$$

Since the squared expression can possibly be zero, the positivity of MC will be assured—on the knowledge that $a > 0$—only if $b^2 < 3ac$.

EXERCISE 9.4

1 Use the second-derivative test to find the relative maxima and minima in the following:

(a) $y = -x^2 + 4x + 91$

(c) $y = \frac{1}{3}x^3 - 3x^2 + 5x + 3$

(b) $y = 2x^3 + x^2 + 1$

(d) $y = \dfrac{2x}{1 - x}$ $(x \neq 1)$

2 Mr. Greenthumb wishes to mark out a rectangular flower bed along the side wall of his house. The other three sides are to be marked by wire netting, of which he has only 20 ft available. What are the length L and width W of the rectangle that would give him the largest possible planting area? How do you make sure that your answer gives the largest, not the smallest, area? (*Hint:* First write an area function A in terms of *one* variable, either L or W alone.)

3 A firm has the following total-cost and demand functions:

$$C = \tfrac{1}{3}Q^3 - 7Q^2 + 111Q + 50$$
$$Q = 100 - P$$

(a) Does the total-cost function satisfy the coefficient restrictions of (9.5)?
(b) Write out the total-revenue function R in terms of Q.
(c) Formulate the total-profit function π in terms of Q.
(d) Find the profit-maximizing level of output $\bar{Q}$.
(e) What is the maximum profit?

4 From the information of the preceding problem, obtain the MR function and the MC function. Then find the profit-maximizing level of output by equating the MR and MC functions. Do you get the same answer?

5 Given the total-cost function in (9.4), and assuming that the coefficients satisfy the restrictions of (9.5), find the relative minimum of average variable cost. Is this also an absolute minimum? Is this a positive or negative number?

6 In the second-derivative test, strict inequalities <0 and >0 are applied to $f''(x_0)$ to yield *sufficient* conditions for relative maximum and minimum. Suppose that we use weak inequalities instead. Can we consider $f''(x_0) \leq 0$ as a *necessary* condition for a relative maximum, and $f''(x_0) \geq 0$ a *necessary* condition for a relative minimum? Explain.

Optimization Problems

9.5   Digression on Maclaurin and Taylor Series   *ignore*

The time has now come for us to develop a test for relative extrema that can apply even when the second derivative turns out to have a zero value at the stationary point. Before we can do that, however, it will first be necessary to discuss the so-called "expansion" of a function $y = f(x)$ into what are known, respectively, as a *Maclaurin series* (expansion around the point $x = 0$) and a *Taylor series* (expansion around any point $x = x_0$).

To *expand* a function $y = f(x)$ around a point x_0 means, in the present context, to transform that function into a polynomial form in which the coefficients of the various terms are expressed in terms of the derivative values $f'(x_0)$, $f''(x_0)$, etc.—all evaluated at the point of expansion x_0. In the Maclaurin series, these will be evaluated at $x = 0$; thus we have $f'(0)$, $f''(0)$, etc., in the coefficients. The result of expansion may be referred to as a *power series* because, being a polynomial, it consists of a sum of power functions.

Maclaurin series of a polynomial function   Let us consider first the expansion of a *polynomial* function of the nth degree,

$$(9.6) \qquad f(x) = a_0 + a_1 x + a_2 x^2 + a_3 x^3 + \cdots + a_n x^n$$

Since this involves the transformation of one polynomial into another, it may seem a sterile and purposeless exercise, but actually it will serve to shed much light on the whole idea of expansion.

Since the power series after expansion will involve the derivatives of various orders of the function f, let us find these first. By successive differentiation of (9.6), we can get the derivatives as follows:

$$f'(x) = a_1 + 2a_2 x + 3a_3 x^2 + \cdots + na_n x^{n-1}$$
$$f''(x) = 2a_2 + 6a_3 x + 12a_4 x^2 + \cdots + n(n-1)a_n x^{n-2}$$
$$f'''(x) = 6a_3 + 24a_4 x + 60a_5 x^2 + \cdots + n(n-1)(n-2)a_n x^{n-3}$$
$$\vdots$$
$$f^{(n)}(x) = n(n-1)(n-2)\cdots(3)(2)(1)a_n$$

Note that each successive differentiation reduces the number of terms by one—the additive constant in front drops out—till, in the nth derivative, we are left with a single constant term (a product term). These derivatives can be evaluated at various points of x; here we shall evaluate them at $x = 0$, with the result that all terms involving x will drop out. We are then left with the following exceptionally neat derivative values:

$$(9.7) \qquad f'(0) = a_1 \qquad f''(0) = 2a_2 \qquad f'''(0) = 6a_3 \qquad \cdots$$
$$f^{(n)}(0) = n(n-1)(n-2)\cdots(3)(2)(1)a_n$$

If we now adopt a shorthand symbol $n!$ (read: n factorial), defined as

$$n! \equiv n(n-1)(n-2)\cdots(3)(2)(1)$$

so that, for example, $2! = 2 \times 1 = 2$ and $3! = 3 \times 2 \times 1 = 6$, etc. (with $0!$ defined as equal to 1), then the result in (9.7) can be rewritten as

$$a_1 = \frac{f'(0)}{1!} \qquad a_2 = \frac{f''(0)}{2!} \qquad a_3 = \frac{f'''(0)}{3!} \qquad \cdots \qquad a_n = \frac{f^{(n)}(0)}{n!}$$

Substituting these into (9.6), and utilizing the obvious fact that $f(0) = a_0$, we can now express the given function $f(x)$ as a new polynomial in which the coefficients are expressed in terms of derivatives evaluated at $x = 0$:†

$$(9.8) \qquad f(x) = \frac{f(0)}{0!} + \frac{f'(0)}{1!}x + \frac{f''(0)}{2!}x^2 + \frac{f'''(0)}{3!}x^3 + \cdots + \frac{f^{(n)}(0)}{n!}x^n$$

This new polynomial, the Maclaurin series of the polynomial function $f(x)$, represents the expansion of the function $f(x)$ around zero ($x = 0$).

Example 1   Find the Maclaurin series for the function

$$(9.9) \qquad f(x) = 2 + 4x + 3x^2$$

This function has the derivatives

$$\begin{aligned} f'(x) &= 4 + 6x \\ f''(x) &= 6 \end{aligned} \qquad \text{so that} \qquad \begin{cases} f'(0) = 4 \\ f''(0) = 6 \end{cases}$$

Thus the Maclaurin series is

$$f(x) = f(0) + f'(0)x + \frac{f''(0)}{2}x^2$$
$$= 2 + 4x + 3x^2$$

This verifies that the Maclaurin series does indeed correctly represent the given function.

Taylor series of a polynomial function   More generally, the polynomial function in (9.6) can be expanded around any point x_0, not necessarily zero. In the interest of simplicity, we shall explain this by means of the specific quadratic function in (9.9) and generalize the result later.

For the purpose of expansion around a specific point x_0, we may first interpret any given value of x as a *deviation* from x_0. More specifically, we shall

---

† Since $0! = 1$ and $1! = 1$, the first two terms on the right of the equals sign in (9.8) can be written more simply as $f(0)$, and $f'(0)x$, respectively. We have included the denominators $0!$ and $1!$ here to call attention to the symmetry among the various terms in the expansion.

           Optimization Problems

let $x = x_0 + \delta$, where δ represents the deviation from the value x_0. Upon such interpretation, the given function (9.9) and its derivatives will now become

$$
\begin{aligned}
f(x) &= 2 + 4(x_0 + \delta) + 3(x_0 + \delta)^2 \\
(9.10) \qquad f'(x) &= 4 + 6(x_0 + \delta) \\
f''(x) &= 6
\end{aligned}
$$

We know that the expression $(x_0 + \delta) = x$ is a variable in the function, but since x_0 in the present context is a *fixed* number, only δ can be properly regarded as a variable in (9.10). Consequently, $f(x)$ is in fact a function of δ, say, $g(\delta)$:

$$
g(\delta) = 2 + 4(x_0 + \delta) + 3(x_0 + \delta)^2 \qquad [\equiv f(x)]
$$

with derivatives

$$
\begin{aligned}
g'(\delta) &= 4 + 6(x_0 + \delta) \qquad [\equiv f'(x)] \\
g''(\delta) &= 6 \qquad\qquad\qquad\ [\equiv f''(x)]
\end{aligned}
$$

We already know how to expand $g(\delta)$ around zero ($\delta = 0$). According to (9.8), such an expansion will yield the following Maclaurin series:

$$
(9.11) \qquad g(\delta) = \frac{g(0)}{0!} + \frac{g'(0)}{1!}\delta + \frac{g''(0)}{2!}\delta^2
$$

But since we have let $x = x_0 + \delta$, the fact that $\delta = 0$ will imply that $x = x_0$; hence, on the basis of the identity $g(\delta) \equiv f(x)$, we can write for the case of $\delta = 0$:

$$
g(0) = f(x_0) \qquad g'(0) = f'(x_0) \qquad g''(0) = f''(x_0)
$$

Upon substituting these into (9.11), we find the result to represent the expansion of $f(x)$ around the point x_0, because the coefficients involve the derivatives $f'(x_0), f''(x_0)$, etc., all evaluated at $x = x_0$:

$$
(9.12) \qquad f(x)\,[= g(\delta)] = \frac{f(x_0)}{0!} + \frac{f'(x_0)}{1!}(x - x_0) + \frac{f''(x_0)}{2!}(x - x_0)^2
$$

The reader should compare this result—a Taylor series of $f(x)$—with the Maclaurin series of $g(\delta)$ in (9.11).

Since for the specific function under consideration, namely, (9.9), we have

$$
f(x_0) = 2 + 4x_0 + 3x_0{}^2 \qquad f'(x_0) = 4 + 6x_0 \qquad f''(x_0) = 6
$$

the Taylor-series formula (9.12) will yield

$$
\begin{aligned}
f(x) &= 2 + 4x_0 + 3x_0{}^2 + (4 + 6x_0)(x - x_0) + \tfrac{6}{2}(x - x_0)^2 \\
&= 2 + 4x + 3x^2
\end{aligned}
$$

This verifies that the Taylor series does correctly represent the given function.

The expansion formula in (9.12) can be generalized to apply to the nth-degree polynomial of (9.6). The generalized Taylor-series formula is

$$(9.13) \qquad f(x) = \frac{f(x_0)}{0!} + \frac{f'(x_0)}{1!} (x - x_0) + \frac{f''(x_0)}{2!} (x - x_0)^2 + \cdots$$

$$+ \frac{f^{(n)}(x_0)}{n!} (x - x_0)^n$$

This differs from the Maclaurin series of (9.8) only in the replacement of zero by x_0 as the point of expansion and in the replacement of x by the expression $(x - x_0)$. What (9.13) tells us is that, given an nth-degree polynomial $f(x)$, if we let $x = 7$ (say) in the terms on the right of (9.13), select an arbitrary number x_0, then evaluate and add these terms, we will end up exactly with $f(7)$—the value of $f(x)$ at $x = 7$.

expansion of an arbitrary function   Heretofore, we have shown how an nth-degree polynomial function can be expressed in another nth-degree polynomial form. As it turns out, it is also possible to express any *arbitrary* function $\phi(x)$—one that is not even necessarily a polynomial—in a polynomial form similar to (9.13), provided that $\phi(x)$ has finite, continuous derivatives up to the desired degree at the expansion point x_0.

According to a mathematical proposition known as *Taylor's theorem*, given an arbitrary function $\phi(x)$, if we know the value of the function at $x = x_0$ [that is, $\phi(x_0)$] and the values of its derivatives at x_0 [that is, $\phi'(x_0)$, $\phi''(x_0)$, etc.], then this function can be expanded around the point x_0 as follows ($n =$ a fixed positive integer arbitrarily chosen):

$$(9.14) \qquad \phi(x) = \left[\frac{\phi(x_0)}{0!} + \frac{\phi'(x_0)}{1!} (x - x_0) \right.$$

$$\left. + \frac{\phi''(x_0)}{2!} (x - x_0)^2 + \cdots + \frac{\phi^{(n)}(x_0)}{n!} (x - x_0)^n \right] + R_n$$

$$\equiv P_n + R_n$$

where P_n represents the (bracketed) nth-degree polynomial [the first $(n + 1)$ terms on the right], and R_n denotes a *remainder*, to be explained below. The presence of R_n distinguishes (9.14) from (9.13), and for this reason (9.14) is called the *Taylor series with remainder*. The form of the polynomial P_n and the size of the remainder R_n will depend on the value of n we choose. The larger the n, the more terms there will be in P_n; accordingly, R_n will in general assume a different value for each different n. This fact explains the need for the subscript n in these two symbols. As a memory aid, we can identify n as the order of the highest derivative in P_n. (In the special case of $n = 0$, no derivative will appear in P_n at all.)

The appearance of R_n in (9.14) is due to the fact that we are here dealing with an arbitrary function ϕ which cannot always be transformed *exactly* into the polynomial form shown in (9.13). Therefore, a remainder term is included as a supplement to the P_n part, in order to represent the difference between $\phi(x)$ and the polynomial P_n. Looked at differently, P_n may be considered a polynomial approximation to $\phi(x)$, with the term R_n as a measure of the error of approximation. If we choose $n = 1$, for example, we have

$$\phi(x) = [\phi(x_0) + \phi'(x_0)(x - x_0)] + R_1 = P_1 + R_1$$

where P_1 consists of $n + 1 = 2$ terms and constitutes a *linear* approximation to $\phi(x)$. If we choose $n = 2$, a second-power term will appear, so that

$$\phi(x) = \left[\phi(x_0) + \phi'(x_0)(x - x_0) + \frac{\phi''(x_0)}{2!}(x - x_0)^2 \right] + R_2 = P_2 + R_2$$

where P_2, consisting of $n + 1 = 3$ terms, will be a *quadratic* approximation to $\phi(x)$. And so forth.

We should mention, in passing, that the arbitrary function $\phi(x)$ would obviously encompass the nth-degree polynomial of (9.6) as a special case. For this case, if the expansion is into another nth-degree polynomial, the result of (9.13) will exactly apply; or in other words, we can use the result in (9.14), with $R_n = 0$. However, if the given nth-degree polynomial $f(x)$ is expanded into a polynomial of *lesser* degree, then the latter can only be considered an approximation to $f(x)$, and a remainder will appear; accordingly, the result in (9.14) can be applied with a nonzero remainder. Thus the Taylor series in the form of (9.14) is perfectly general.

Example 2   Expand the function

$$\phi(x) = \frac{1}{1 + x}$$

around the point $x_0 = 1$, with $n = 4$. We shall need the first four derivatives of $\phi(x)$, which are

$$\phi'(x) = -(1 + x)^{-2} \qquad \text{so that} \qquad \phi'(1) = -(2)^{-2} = \frac{-1}{4}$$

$$\phi''(x) = 2(1 + x)^{-3} \qquad\qquad\qquad \phi''(1) = 2(2)^{-3} = \frac{1}{4}$$

$$\phi'''(x) = -6(1 + x)^{-4} \qquad\qquad\qquad \phi'''(1) = -6(2)^{-4} = \frac{-3}{8}$$

$$\phi^{(4)}(x) = 24(1 + x)^{-5} \qquad\qquad\qquad \phi^{(4)}(1) = 24(2)^{-5} = \frac{3}{4}$$

Also, we see that $\phi(1) = \frac{1}{2}$. Thus, setting $x_0 = 1$ in (9.14) and utilizing the information derived above, we obtain the following Taylor series with remainder:

$$\phi(x) = \frac{1}{2} - \frac{1}{4}(x-1) + \frac{1}{8}(x-1)^2 - \frac{1}{16}(x-1)^3 + \frac{1}{32}(x-1)^4 + R_4$$

$$= \frac{31}{32} - \frac{13}{16}x + \frac{1}{2}x^2 - \frac{3}{16}x^3 + \frac{1}{32}x^4 + R_4$$

It is possible, of course, to choose $x_0 = 0$ as the point of expansion here, too. In that case, with x_0 set equal to zero in (9.14), the expansion will result in a *Maclaurin series with remainder*.

Example 3   Expand the function in Example 2 around $x_0 = 0$, with $n = 4$. Evaluating the four derivatives at the new point of expansion, we find that

$$\phi'(0) = -1 \qquad \phi''(0) = 2 \qquad \phi'''(0) = -6 \qquad \phi^{(4)}(0) = 24$$

Setting $x_0 = 0$ in (9.14) and utilizing these derivative values, we obtain the following Maclaurin series with remainder:

$$\phi(x) = \phi(0) + \phi'(0)x + \frac{\phi''(0)}{2!}x^2 + \frac{\phi'''(0)}{3!}x^3 + \frac{\phi^{(4)}(0)}{4!}x^4 + R_4$$

$$= 1 + (-1)x + \frac{2}{2}x^2 + \frac{-6}{6}x^3 + \frac{24}{24}x^4 + R_4$$

$$= 1 - x + x^2 - x^3 + x^4 + R_4$$

The reader may find it of interest that, if the expression $1/(1+x)$ is divided out, we get precisely the result just derived.

Lagrange form of the remainder   Now we must comment further on the remainder term. According to what is called the *Lagrange form of the remainder*, we can express R_n as

(9.15) $$R_n = \frac{\phi^{(n+1)}(p)}{(n+1)!}(x - x_0)^{n+1}$$

where p is some number between x (the point where we wish to evaluate the arbitrary function ϕ) and x_0 (the point where we expand the function ϕ). Note that this expression closely resembles the term which should logically follow the last term in P_n in (9.14), except that the derivative involved is here to be evaluated at a point p instead of x_0. Since the point p is not otherwise specified, this formula does not really enable us to calculate R_n; nevertheless, it does have great analytical significance. Let us therefore illustrate its meaning graphically, although we shall do it only for the simple case of $n = 0$.

Optimization Problems

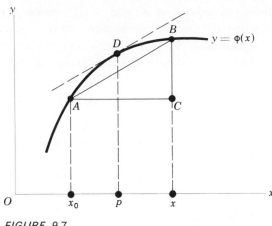

FIGURE 9.7

When $n = 0$, no derivatives whatever will appear in the polynomial part P_0; therefore (9.14) reduces to

$$\phi(x) = P_0 + R_0 = \phi(x_0) + \phi'(p)(x - x_0)$$

or $\quad \phi(x) - \phi(x_0) = \phi'(p)(x - x_0)$

This result, a simple version of the *mean-value theorem*, states that the difference between the value of the function ϕ at x_0 and at any other x value can be expressed as the product of the difference $(x - x_0)$ and the derivative ϕ' evaluated at p (with p being some point between x and x_0). Let us look at Fig. 9.7, where the function $\phi(x)$ is shown as a continuous curve with derivative values defined at all points. Let x_0 be the chosen point of expansion, and let x be *any* point on the horizontal axis. If we try to approximate $\phi(x)$, or distance xB, by $\phi(x_0)$, or distance x_0A, it will involve an error equal to $\phi(x) - \phi(x_0)$, or the distance CB. What the mean-value theorem says is that the error CB—which constitutes the remainder term R_0 in the expansion—can be expressed as $\phi'(p)(x - x_0)$, where p is some point between x and x_0. First we locate, on the curve between points A and B, a point D such that the tangent line at D is parallel to line AB; such a point D must exist, since the curve passes from A to B in a continuous and smooth manner. Then, the remainder will be

$$R_0 = CB = \frac{CB}{AC} AC = (\text{slope of } AB) \cdot AC$$

$$= (\text{slope of tangent at } D) \cdot AC$$

$$= (\text{slope of curve at } x = p) \cdot AC = \phi'(p)(x - x_0)$$

where the point p is between x and x_0, as required. This demonstrates the rationale of the Lagrange form of the remainder for the case $n = 0$. We can always express R_0 as $\phi'(p)(x - x_0)$ because, even though p cannot be specified in a definite way, we can be sure that such a point exists.

Equation (9.15) provides a way of expressing the remainder term R_n, but it does not eliminate R_n as a source of discrepancy between $\phi(x)$ and the polynomial P_n. However, if it happens that

$$R_n \to 0 \text{ as } n \to \infty \qquad \text{so that} \qquad P_n \to \phi(x) \text{ as } n \to \infty$$

then it will be possible to make P_n as accurate an approximation to $\phi(x)$ as we desire by choosing a large enough value for n, that is, by including a great enough number of terms in the polynomial P_n.† In this (convenient) event, the Taylor series is said to be *convergent* to $\phi(x)$ at the point of expansion. An example of this will be discussed in Sec. 10.2 below.

EXERCISE 9.5

1   Find the value of the following factorial expressions:

(a) $5!$ (b) $7!$ (c) $\dfrac{4!}{3!}$ (d) $\dfrac{6!}{3!}$ (e) $\dfrac{(n + 2)!}{n!}$

2   Find the first five terms of the Maclaurin series (i.e., choose $n = 4$ and let $x_0 = 0$) for:

(a) $\phi(x) = \dfrac{1}{1 - x}$ (b) $\phi(x) = \dfrac{1 - x}{1 + x}$

3   Find the Taylor series, with $n = 4$ and $x_0 = -2$, for the two functions in the preceding problem.

4   On the basis of the Taylor series with the Lagrange form of the remainder [see (9.14) and (9.15)], show that at the point of expansion $(x = x_0)$ the Taylor series will always give *exactly* the value of the function at that point, $\phi(x_0)$, not merely an approximation.

9.6   nth-Derivative Test for Relative Extremum of a Function of One Variable

The expansion of a function into a Taylor (or Maclaurin) series is useful as an approximation device in the circumstance that $R_n \to 0$ as $n \to \infty$, but our present concern is with its application in the development of a general test for a relative extremum.

† This should be reminiscent of the method of finding the inverse matrix by approximation, as discussed in Sec. 5.7.

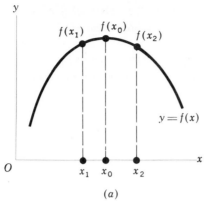 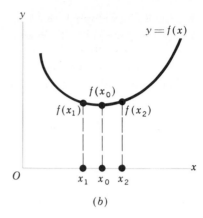

$$(a) \qquad\qquad\qquad (b)$$

FIGURE 9.8

Taylor expansion and relative extremum

As a preparatory step for that task, let us redefine a relative extremum as follows:

> A function $f(x)$ attains a relative maximum (minimum) value at x_0 if $f(x) - f(x_0)$ is negative (positive) for values of x in the immediate neighborhood of x_0, both to its left and to its right.

This can be made clear by reference to Fig. 9.8, where x_1 is a value of x to the left of x_0, and x_2 is a value of x to the right of x_0. In diagram a, $f(x_0)$ is a relative maximum; thus $f(x_0)$ exceeds both $f(x_1)$ and $f(x_2)$. In short, $f(x) - f(x_0)$ is negative for any value of x in the immediate neighborhood of x_0. The opposite is true of diagram b, where $f(x_0)$ is a relative minimum, and thus $f(x) - f(x_0) > 0$.

Assuming $f(x)$ to have finite, continuous derivatives up to the desired order at the point $x = x_0$, the function $f(x)$—not necessarily polynomial—can be expanded around the point x_0 as a Taylor series. On the basis of (9.14) (after duly changing ϕ to f), and using the Lagrange form of the remainder, we can write

$$(9.16) \qquad f(x) - f(x_0) = f'(x_0)(x - x_0) + \frac{f''(x_0)}{2!}(x - x_0)^2 + \cdots$$

$$+ \frac{f^{(n)}(x_0)}{n!}(x - x_0)^n + \frac{f^{(n+1)}(p)}{(n+1)!}(x - x_0)^{n+1}$$

If we can determine the sign of the expression $f(x) - f(x_0)$, we can immediately come to a conclusion as to whether $f(x_0)$ is an extremum, and if so, whether it is a maximum or a minimum. For this, it is necessary to examine the right-hand sum of (9.16). Altogether, there are $(n + 1)$ terms in this sum—n terms from P_n, plus the remainder—and thus the actual number of terms is indefinite, being dependent upon the value of n we choose. However, by properly choosing n, we can always make sure that there will exist only a single term on the right, thereby drastically simplifying the task of evaluating the sign of $f(x) - f(x_0)$ and determining whether $f(x_0)$ is an extremum, and if so, which kind.

some specific cases   This will become clearer through some specific illustrations:

CASE 1 $f'(x_0) \neq 0$

If the first derivative at x_0 is nonzero, let us choose $n = 0$; then there will be only $n + 1 = 1$ term on the right side, implying that only the remainder R_0 will be there. That is, we have

$$f(x) - f(x_0) = \frac{f'(p)}{1!} (x - x_0) = f'(p)(x - x_0)$$

where p is some number between x_0 and a value of x in the immediate neighborhood of x_0. Note that p must accordingly be very, very close to x_0.

What is the sign of the expression on the right? Because of the continuity of the derivative, $f'(p)$ will have the same sign as $f'(x_0)$ since, as mentioned above, p is very, very close to x_0. In the present case, $f'(p)$ must be nonzero; in fact, it must be a specific positive or negative number. But what about the $(x - x_0)$ part? When we go from the left of x_0 to its right, x shifts from a magnitude $x_1 < x_0$ to a magnitude $x_2 > x_0$ (see Fig. 9.8). Consequently, the expression $(x - x_0)$ must turn from negative to positive as we move, and $f(x) - f(x_0) = f'(p)(x - x_0)$ must also change sign from the left of x_0 to its right. However, this violates our new definition of a relative extremum; accordingly, there cannot exist a relative extremum at $f(x_0)$ when $f'(x_0) \neq 0$—a fact that is already well known to us.

CASE 2 $f'(x_0) = 0; f''(x_0) \neq 0$

In this case, choose $n = 1$, so that initially there will be $n + 1 = 2$ terms on the right. But one of these terms will vanish because $f'(x_0) = 0$, and we shall again be left with only one term to evaluate:

$$f(x) - f(x_0) = f'(x_0)(x - x_0) + \frac{f''(p)}{2!} (x - x_0)^2$$

$$= \tfrac{1}{2} f''(p)(x - x_0)^2 \qquad [\text{because } f'(x_0) = 0]$$

As before, $f''(p)$ will have the same sign as $f''(x_0)$, which is specified and unvarying; whereas the $(x - x_0)^2$ part, being a square, is invariably positive. Thus the expression $f(x) - f(x_0)$ must take the same sign as $f''(x_0)$ and, according to the above definition of relative extremum, will specify

A relative maximum of $f(x)$ if $f''(x_0) < 0$

A relative minimum of $f(x)$ if $f''(x_0) > 0$ [with $f'(x_0) = 0$]

The reader will recognize this as the second-derivative test introduced earlier.

CASE 3 $\quad f'(x_0) = f''(x_0) = 0$, but $f'''(x_0) \neq 0$

Here we are encountering a situation that the second-derivative test is incapable of handling, for $f''(x_0)$ is now zero. With the help of the Taylor series, however, a conclusive result can be established without difficulty.

Let us choose $n = 2$; then three terms will initially appear on the right. But two of these will drop out because $f'(x_0) = f''(x_0) = 0$, so that we again have only one term to evaluate:

$$f(x) - f(x_0) = f'(x_0)(x - x_0) + \frac{1}{2} f''(x_0)(x - x_0)^2 + \frac{1}{3!} f'''(p)(x - x_0)^3$$

$$= \frac{1}{6} f'''(p)(x - x_0)^3$$

As previously, the sign of $f'''(p)$ is identical with that of $f'''(x_0)$ because of the continuity of the derivative and because p is very close to x_0. But the $(x - x_0)^3$ part has a varying sign. Specifically, since $(x - x_0)$ is negative to the left of x_0, so also will be $(x - x_0)^3$; yet, to the right of x_0, the $(x - x_0)^3$ part will be positive. Again there is a change in the sign of $f(x) - f(x_0)$ as we pass through x_0, which violates the definition of a relative extremum. However, we know that x_0 is a critical value [$f'(x_0) = 0$], and thus it must give an inflection point, inasmuch as it does not give a relative extremum.

CASE 4 $\quad f'(x_0) = f''(x_0) = \cdots = f^{(n-1)}(x_0) = 0$, but $f^{(n)}(x_0) \neq 0$

This is a very general case, and we can therefore derive a general result from it. Note that here all the derivative values are zero until we arrive at the nth one.

Analogously to the preceding three cases, the Taylor series for Case 4 will reduce to

$$f(x) - f(x_0) = \frac{1}{n!} f^{(n)}(p)(x - x_0)^n$$

Again, $f^{(n)}(p)$ takes the same sign as $f^{(n)}(x_0)$, which is unvarying. The sign of the $(x - x_0)^n$ part, on the other hand, will *vary* if n is *odd* (cf. Cases 1 and 3) and will *remain unchanged* (positive) if n is *even* (cf. Case 2). When n is odd, accordingly, $f(x) - f(x_0)$ will change sign as we pass through the point x_0, thereby violating the definition of a relative extremum (which means that x_0 must give us an inflection point). But when n is even, $f(x) - f(x_0)$ will not change sign from the left of x_0 to its right, and this will establish the stationary value $f(x_0)$ as a relative maximum or minimum, depending on whether $f^{(n)}(x_0)$ is negative or positive.

nth-derivative test   At last, then, we may state the following general test:

nth-DERIVATIVE TEST FOR RELATIVE EXTREMUM OF A FUNCTION OF ONE VARIABLE   If the first derivative of a function $f(x)$ at x_0 is $f'(x_0) = 0$ and if the first *nonzero* derivative value at x_0 encountered in successive derivation is that of the nth derivative, $f^{(n)}(x_0)$, then the stationary point with value $f(x_0)$ will be

a   A relative *maximum* if n is an even number and $f^{(n)}(x_0) < 0$
b   A relative *minimum* if n is an even number but $f^{(n)}(x_0) > 0$
c   An *inflection point* if n is odd

This test is "complete" in the sense that it covers all the possible contingencies which may occur. With the exception of a constant function (which requires no test for extremum anyway), a function must sooner or later yield some *nonzero* derivative value at a given point x_0, where $f'(x_0) = 0$. And when that nonzero derivative value is found, the above test will specify the nature of the value $f(x_0)$ as either a relative maximum, a relative minimum, or an inflection point.

Example 1   Examine the function $y = (7 - x)^4$ for its relative extremum. Since $f'(x) = -4(7 - x)^3$ is zero when $x = 7$, we take $x = 7$ as the critical value for testing, with $y = 0$ as the stationary value of the function. By successive derivation (continued until we encounter a nonzero derivative value at the point $x = 7$), we get

$$f''(x) = 12(7 - x)^2 \quad \text{so that} \quad f''(7) = 0$$
$$f'''(x) = -24(7 - x) \qquad\qquad\qquad f'''(7) = 0$$
$$f^{(4)}(x) = 24 \qquad\qquad\qquad\qquad f^{(4)}(7) = 24$$

Since 4 is an even number and since $f^{(4)}(7)$ is positive, we conclude that the point $(7,0)$ represents a relative minimum.

EXERCISE 9.6

1 Find the stationary values of:

(a) $y = x^3$ (b) $y = -x^4$ (c) $y = x^6$

Determine by the nth-derivative test whether they represent relative maxima, relative minima, or inflection points.

2 Find the stationary values of the following functions:

(a) $y = (x - 1)^3$ (b) $y = (x - 2)^4$

Use the nth-derivative test to determine the exact nature of these stationary values.

10
EXPONENTIAL AND LOGARITHMIC FUNCTIONS

The nth-derivative test developed in the preceding chapter equips us for the task of locating the extreme values of any objective function, as long as it involves only one choice variable and possesses derivatives to the desired order. In the examples cited in Chap. 9, however, we made use only of polynomial and rational functions, for which we know how to obtain the necessary derivatives. Suppose that our objective function happened to be an *exponential* one, such as

$$y = 8^{x-\sqrt{x}}$$

Then we are still helpless in applying the derivative criterion, because we have yet to learn how to differentiate such a function. This is what we shall do in the present chapter.

Exponential functions, as well as the closely related logarithmic functions, have important applications in economics, especially in connection with growth problems, and in economic dynamics in general. The particular application relevant to the present part of the book, however, involves a class of optimization problems in which the choice variable is *time*. For example, a wine dealer may have a stock of wine, the market value of which, owing to improved vintage, is known to increase with time in some prescribed fashion. His problem is to determine the best time to sell that stock on the basis of the wine-value function, after taking into account the interest cost involved in having the money capital tied up in his stock. Exponential functions may enter into such a problem in two ways. In the first place, the value of the wine may increase with time according to some *exponential law of growth*. In that event, we would have an exponential wine-value function. This is only a possibility, of course, and not a certainty.

When we give consideration to the interest cost, however, a *sure* entry is provided for an exponential function because of the fact of interest compounding, which will be explained presently. Thus we must study the nature of exponential functions before we can discuss this type of optimization problem.

Since our primary purpose is to deal with time as a choice variable, let us now switch to the symbol t—in lieu of x—to indicate the independent variable in the subsequent discussion. (However, this same symbol t can very well represent variables other than time also.)

10.1   The Nature of Exponential Functions

As introduced in connection with polynomial functions, the term *exponent* means an indicator of the power to which a variable is to be raised. In power expressions such as x^3 or x^5, the exponents are *constants*; but there is no reason why we cannot also have a *variable* exponent, such as in 3^x or 3^t, where the number 3 is to be raised to varying powers (various values of x). A function whose *independent* variable appears in the role of an exponent is called an *exponential function*.

simple exponential function   In its simple version, the exponential function may be represented in the form

$$(10.1) \qquad y = f(t) = b^t \qquad (b > 1)$$

where y and t are the dependent and independent variables, respectively, and b denotes a fixed *base* of the exponent. The domain of such a function is the set of all real numbers. Thus, unlike the exponents in a polynomial function, the variable exponent t in (10.1) is not limited to positive integers—unless we wish to impose such a restriction.

But why the restriction of $b > 1$? The explanation is as follows. In view of the fact that the domain of the function in (10.1) consists of the set of all real numbers, it is possible for t to take a value such as $\frac{1}{2}$. If b is allowed to be negative, the half power of b will involve taking the square root of a negative number. This is not an impossible task, but it necessitates the concept of an *imaginary* number ($i \equiv \sqrt{-1}$), which we intend to introduce somewhat later. For now, therefore, let us take the easy way out by restricting b to be positive. Once we adopt the restriction $b > 0$, however, we might as well go all the way to the restriction $b > 1$: The restriction $b > 1$ differs from $b > 0$ only in the further exclusion of the cases of (1) $0 < b < 1$ and (2) $b = 1$; but as will be shown, the first case can be subsumed under the restriction $b > 1$, whereas the

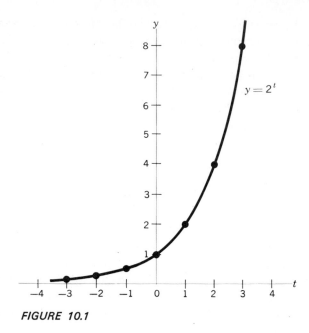

$y = 2^t$

FIGURE 10.1

second case can be dismissed outright. Consider the first case. If $b = \frac{1}{5}$, then we have

$$y = \left(\frac{1}{5}\right)^t = \frac{1}{5^t} = 5^{-t}$$

This shows that a function with a fractional base can easily be rewritten into one with a base greater than 1. As for the second case, the fact that $b = 1$ will give us the function $y = 1^t = 1$, so that the exponential function actually degenerates into a constant function; it may therefore be disqualified as a member of the exponential family.

graphical form   The graph of the exponential function in (10.1) takes the general shape of the curve in Fig. 10.1. The curve drawn is based on the value $b = 2$; but even for other values of b, the same general configuration will prevail.

Several salient features of this type of exponential curve may be noted. First, it is continuous and smooth everywhere; thus the function should be everywhere differentiable. Second, it is monotonically increasing, and in fact y increases at an increasing rate throughout. Consequently, both the first and second derivatives of the function $y = b^t$ should be positive—a fact we should be able to confirm after we have developed the relevant differentiation formulas. Third, we note that, even though the domain of the function contains negative as well as positive numbers, the range of the function is limited to the open interval $(0,\infty)$. That is, the dependent variable y is invariably *positive*, regardless of the sign of the independent variable t.

The monotonicity of the exponential function entails at least two interesting and significant implications. First, we may infer that the exponential function must have an inverse function, which is itself monotonic. This inverse function, we shall find, turns out to be a *logarithmic* function. Second, since monotonicity means that there is a unique value of t for a given value of y and since the range of the exponential function is the interval $(0,\infty)$, it follows that we should be able to express *any positive number* as a unique power of a base $b > 1$. This can be seen from Fig. 10.1, where the curve of $y = 2^t$ covers all the positive values of y in its range; therefore any positive value of y must be expressible as some unique power of the number 2. Actually, even if the base is changed to some other real number greater than 1, the same range holds, so that it is possible to express any positive number y as a power of any base $b > 1$.

generalized exponential function   This last point deserves closer scrutiny. If a positive y can indeed be expressed as powers of various alternative bases, then there must exist a general procedure of *base conversion*. In the case of the function $y = 9^t$, for instance, we can readily transform it into $y = (3^2)^t = 3^{2t}$, thereby converting the base from 9 to 3, provided that the exponent is duly altered from t to $2t$. This change in exponent, necessitated by the base conversion, does not create any new type of function, for, if we let $w = 2t$, then $y = 3^{2t} = 3^w$ is still in the form of (10.1). From the point of view of the base 3, however, the exponent is now $2t$ rather than t. What is the effect of adding a numerical coefficient (here, 2) to the exponent t?

The answer is to be found in Fig. 10.2a, where two curves are drawn—one for the function $y = f(t) = b^t$ and one for another function $y = g(t) = b^{2t}$. Since the exponent in the latter is exactly twice that of the former, and since the identical base is adopted for the two functions, the assignment of an arbitrary value $t = t_0$ in the function g and $t = 2t_0$ in the function f must yield the same value:

$$f(2t_0) = g(t_0) = b^{2t_0} = y_0$$

Thus the distance y_0J will be half of y_0K. By similar reasoning, for any value of y, the function g should be exactly halfway between the function f and the vertical axis. It may be concluded, therefore, that the *doubling* of the exponent has the effect of compressing the exponential curve *halfway* toward the y axis, whereas *halving* the exponent will extend the curve away from the y axis to *twice* the horizontal distance.

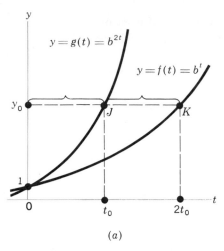

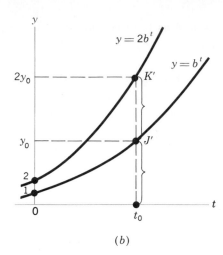

FIGURE 10.2

It is of interest that both functions share the same vertical intercept

$$f(0) = g(0) = b^0 = 1$$

The change of the exponent t to $2t$, or to any other multiple of t, will leave the vertical intercept unaffected. In terms of *compressing*, this is because compressing a zero horizontal distance will still yield a zero distance.

The change of exponent is one way of modifying—and generalizing—the exponential function of (10.1); another is to attach a coefficient to b^t, such as $2b^t$. [Warning: $2b^t \neq (2b)^t$.] The effect of such a coefficient is also to compress or extend the curve, except that this time the direction is vertical. In Fig. 10.2b, the higher curve represents $y = 2b^t$, and the lower one is $y = b^t$. For every value of t, the former must obviously be twice as high, because it has a y value twice as large as the latter. Thus we have $t_0 J' = J'K'$. Note that the vertical intercept, too, is changed in the present case. We may conclude that *doubling* the coefficient (here, from 1 to 2) serves to extend the curve away from the horizontal axis to *twice* the vertical distance, whereas *halving* the coefficient will compress the curve *halfway* toward the t axis.

With the knowledge of the two modifications discussed above, the exponential function $y = b^t$ can now be generalized to the form

$$(10.2) \qquad y = ab^{ct}$$

where a and c are "compressing" or "extending" agents. When assigned various values, they will alter the position of the exponential curve, thus generating a whole family of exponential curves (functions). If a and c are positive, the general configuration shown in Fig. 10.2 will prevail; if a or c or both are *negative*, however, then fundamental modifications will occur in the configuration of the curve. (See Exercise 10.1-5 below.)

a preferred base   What prompted the discussion of the change of exponent from t to ct was the question of base conversion. But, granting the feasibility of base conversion, why would one want to do it anyhow? One answer is that some bases are more convenient than others as far as mathematical manipulations are concerned.

Curiously enough, in calculus, the preferred base happens to be a certain irrational number denoted by the symbol e:

$$e = 2.71828 \ldots$$

When this base e is used in an exponential function, it is referred to as a *natural exponential function*, examples of which are

$$y = e^t \qquad y = e^{3t} \qquad y = Ae^{rt}$$

These illustrative functions can also be expressed by the alternative notations

$$y = \exp{(t)} \qquad y = \exp{(3t)} \qquad y = A \exp{(rt)}$$

where the abbreviation exp (for exponential) indicates that e is to have the expression in parentheses as its exponent.

The choice of such an outlandish number as $e = 2.71828 \ldots$ as the preferred base will no doubt seem bewildering. But there is an excellent reason for this choice, for the function e^t possesses the remarkable property of being its own derivative! That is,

$$\frac{d}{dt} e^t = e^t$$

a fact which will reduce the work of differentiation to practically no work at all. Moreover, armed with this differentiation rule—to be proved later in this chapter —it will also be easy to find the derivative of a more complicated natural exponential function such as $y = Ae^{rt}$. To do this, first let $w = rt$, so that the function becomes

$$y = Ae^w \qquad \text{where } w = rt, \text{ and } A, r \text{ are constants}$$

Then, by the chain rule, we can write

$$\frac{dy}{dt} = \frac{dy}{dw}\frac{dw}{dt} = Ae^w(r) = rAe^{rt}$$

That is,

$$(10.3) \qquad \frac{d}{dt} Ae^{rt} = rAe^{rt}$$

The mathematical convenience of the base e should thus be clear.

EXERCISE 10.1

1   Plot in a single diagram the graphs of the exponential functions $y = 3^t$ and $y = 3^{2t}$.

   (a) Do the two graphs display the same general positional relationship as shown in Fig. 10.2a?
   (b) Do these two curves share the same y intercept? Why?
   (c) Sketch the graph of the function $y = 3^{3t}$ in the same diagram.

2   Plot in a single diagram the graphs of the exponential functions $y = 4^t$ and $y = 3(4^t)$.

   (a) Do the two graphs display the general positional relationship suggested in Fig. 10.2b?
   (b) Do the two curves have the same y intercept? Why?
   (c) Sketch the graph of the function $y = \frac{3}{2}(4^t)$ in the same diagram.

3   Taking for granted that e^t is its own derivative, use the chain rule to find dy/dt for the following:

   (a) $y = e^{5t}$ (b) $y = 7e^{3t}$ (c) $y = 3e^{2t}$

4   In view of our discussion about (10.1), do you expect the function $y = e^t$ to be monotonically increasing at an increasing rate? Verify your answer by determining the signs of the first and second derivatives of this function. In doing so, remember that the domain of this function is the set of all real numbers, i.e., the interval $(-\infty,\infty)$.

5   In (10.2), if negative values are assigned to a and c, the general shape of the curves in Fig. 10.2 will no longer prevail. Examine the change in curve configuration by contrasting (a) the case of $a = -1$ against the case of $a = 1$, and (b) the case of $c = -1$ against the case of $c = 1$.

Optimization Problems

10.2   Natural Exponential Functions and the Problem of Growth

The pertinent questions still unanswered are: How is the number e defined? Does it have any economic meaning in addition to its mathematical significance as a convenient base? And, in what ways do natural exponential functions apply to economic analysis?

the number e   Let us consider the following function:

$$(10.4) \qquad f(m) = \left(1 + \frac{1}{m}\right)^m$$

If larger and larger values are assigned to m, then $f(m)$ will also assume larger values; specifically, we find that

$$f(1) = (1 + \tfrac{1}{1})^1 = 2$$
$$f(2) = (1 + \tfrac{1}{2})^2 = 2.25$$
$$f(3) = (1 + \tfrac{1}{3})^3 = 2.37037 \ldots$$
$$f(4) = (1 + \tfrac{1}{4})^4 = 2.44141 \ldots$$
$$\vdots$$

Moreover, if m is increased indefinitely, then $f(m)$ will converge to the number $2.71828 \ldots \equiv e$; thus e may be defined as the limit of (10.4) as $m \to \infty$:

$$(10.5) \qquad e \equiv \lim_{m \to \infty} f(m) = \lim_{m \to \infty} \left(1 + \frac{1}{m}\right)^m$$

That the approximate value of e is 2.71828 can be verified by finding the Maclaurin series of the function $\phi(x) = e^x$—with x used here to facilitate the application of the expansion formula (9.14). Such a series will give us a polynomial approximation to e^x, and thus the value of e ($=e^1$) may be approximated by setting $x = 1$ in that polynomial. If the remainder term R_n approaches zero as the number of terms in the series is increased indefinitely, i.e., if the series is convergent to $\phi(x)$, then we can indeed approximate the value of e to any desired degree of accuracy by making the number of included terms sufficiently large.

To this end, we need to have derivatives of various orders for the function. Accepting the fact that the first derivative of e^x is e^x itself, we can see that the derivative of $\phi(x)$ is simply e^x and, similarly, that the second, third, or any higher-order derivatives must be e^x as well. Hence, when we evaluate all the derivatives at the expansion point ($x_0 = 0$), we have the gratifyingly neat result

$$\phi'(0) = \phi''(0) = \cdots = \phi^{(n)}(0) = e^0 = 1$$

Consequently, by setting $x_0 = 0$ in (9.14), the Maclaurin series of e^x is

$$e^x = \phi(x) = \phi(0) + \phi'(0)x + \frac{\phi''(0)}{2!} x^2 + \frac{\phi'''(0)}{3!} x^3 + \cdots$$

$$+ \frac{\phi^{(n)}(0)}{n!} x^n + R_n$$

$$= 1 + x + \frac{1}{2!} x^2 + \frac{1}{3!} x^3 + \cdots + \frac{1}{n!} x^n + R_n$$

The remainder term R_n, according to (9.15), can be written as

$$R_n = \frac{\phi^{(n+1)}(p)}{(n+1)!} x^{n+1} = \frac{e^p}{(n+1)!} x^{n+1}$$

$$[\phi^{(n+1)}(x) = e^x; \therefore \phi^{(n+1)}(p) = e^p]$$

Inasmuch as the factorial expression $(n + 1)!$ will increase in value more rapidly than the power expression x^{n+1} (for a finite x) as n increases, it follows that $R_n \to 0$ as $n \to \infty$. Thus the Maclaurin series converges, and the value of e^x may, as a result, be expressed as an *infinite series*—an expression involving an infinite number $(n \to \infty)$ of additive terms which follow a consistent, recognizable pattern of formation, and in which the remainder term R_n disappears $(R_n \to 0)$:

$$(10.6) \qquad e^x = 1 + x + \frac{1}{2!} x^2 + \frac{1}{3!} x^3 + \frac{1}{4!} x^4 + \frac{1}{5!} x^5 + \cdots$$

As a special case, for $x = 1$ (carrying calculations to five decimal places), we find that

$$e = 1 + 1 + \frac{1}{2!} + \frac{1}{3!} + \frac{1}{4!} + \frac{1}{5!} + \cdots$$

$$= 2 + 0.5 + 0.16667 + 0.04167 + 0.00833 + 0.00139$$

$$+ 0.00020 + 0.00002 + 0.00000 + \cdots = 2.71828$$

which is accurate to five decimal places. Note that we need not worry about the subsequent terms in the infinite series, because they will be of negligible magnitude if we are concerned only with five decimal places.

an economic interpretation of e   Mathematically, the number e is the limit expression in (10.5). But does it also possess some economic meaning? The answer is that it can be interpreted as the result of a special process of interest compounding.

Suppose that, starting out with a principal (or capital) of $1, we find a hypothetical banker to offer us the unusual interest rate of 100 percent per annum ($1 interest per year). If interest is to be compounded once a year, the

Optimization Problems

value of our asset at the end of the year will become \$2; we shall denote this value by $V(1)$, where the number in parentheses indicates the frequency of compounding within 1 year:

$$V(1) = \text{initial principal } (1 + \text{interest rate})$$
$$= 1(1 + 100\%) = (1 + \tfrac{1}{1})^1 = 2$$

If interest is compounded semiannually, however, an interest amounting to 50 percent (half of 100 percent) of principal will accrue at the end of 6 months. We shall therefore have \$1.50 as the new principal during the second 6-month period, in which interest will be calculated at 50 percent of \$1.50. Thus our year-end asset value will be $1.50(1 + 50\%)$; that is,

$$V(2) = (1 + 50\%)(1 + 50\%) = (1 + \tfrac{1}{2})^2$$

By analogous reasoning, we can write $V(3) = (1 + \tfrac{1}{3})^3$, $V(4) = (1 + \tfrac{1}{4})^4$, etc.; or, in general,

$$(10.7) \qquad V(m) = \left(1 + \frac{1}{m}\right)^m$$

where m represents the frequency of compounding in 1 year.

In the limiting case, when interest is compounded *continuously* during the year, i.e., when m becomes infinite, the value of the asset will grow in a "snowballing" fashion, becoming at the end of 1 year

$$\lim_{m \to \infty} V(m) = \lim_{m \to \infty} \left(1 + \frac{1}{m}\right)^m = e \text{ (dollars)} \qquad [\text{by } (10.5)]$$

Thus, the number $e = 2.71828$ can be interpreted as the year-end value to which a principal of \$1 will grow if interest at the rate of 100 percent per annum is compounded continuously.

The reader will note that the interest rate of 100 percent is only a *nominal interest rate*, for if \$1 becomes $\$e = \$2.718$ after 1 year, the *effective interest rate* is in this case approximately 172 percent per annum.

interest compounding and the function Ae^{rt}   The continuous interest-compounding process just discussed can be generalized in three directions, to allow for: (1) more years of compounding, (2) a principal other than \$1, and (3) a nominal interest rate other than 100 percent.

If a principal of \$1 becomes $\$e$ after 1 year of continuous compounding and if we let $\$e$ be the new principal in the second year (during which every dollar will again grow into $\$e$), our asset value at the end of 2 years will obviously become $\$e(e) = \$e^2$. By the same token, it will become $\$e^3$ at the end of 3 years or, more generally, will become $\$e^t$ after t years.

Next, let us change the principal from \$1 to an unspecified amount, \$$A$. This change is easily taken care of: if \$1 will grow into \$$e^t$ after t years of continuous compounding at the nominal rate of 100 percent per annum, it stands to reason that \$$A$ will grow into \$$Ae^t$.

How about a nominal interest rate of other than 100 percent, for instance, $r = 0.05 \ (= 5 \text{ percent})$? The effect of this rate change is to alter the expression Ae^t to Ae^{rt}, as can be verified from the following. With an initial principal of \$$A$, to be invested for t years at a nominal interest rate r, the compound-interest formula (10.7) must be modified to the form

$$(10.8) \qquad V(m) = A\left(1 + \frac{r}{m}\right)^{mt}$$

The insertion of the coefficient A reflects the change of principal from the previous level of \$1. The quotient expression r/m means that, in each of the m compounding periods in a year, only $1/m$ of the nominal rate r will actually be applicable. Finally, the exponent mt tells us that, since interest is to be compounded m times a year, there should be a total of mt compoundings in t years.

The formula (10.8) can be transformed into an alternative form

$$(10.8') \qquad V(m) = A\left[\left(1 + \frac{r}{m}\right)^{m/r}\right]^{rt}$$

$$= A\left[\left(1 + \frac{1}{w}\right)^{w}\right]^{rt} \qquad \text{where } w \equiv \frac{m}{r}$$

As the frequency of compounding m is increased, the newly created variable w must increase pari passu; thus, as $m \to \infty$, we have $w \to \infty$, and the bracketed expression in (10.8'), by virtue of (10.5), tends to the number e. Consequently, we find the asset value in the generalized continuous-compounding process to be

$$(10.8'') \qquad V \equiv \lim_{m \to \infty} V(m) = Ae^{rt}$$

as anticipated above.

Note that, in (10.8), t is a *discrete* (as against a *continuous*) variable: it can only take values that are integral multiples of $1/m$. For example, if $m = 4$ (compounding on a quarterly basis), then t can only take the values of $\frac{1}{4}$, $\frac{1}{2}$, $\frac{3}{4}$, 1, etc., indicating that $V(m)$ will assume a new value only at the end of each new quarter. When $m \to \infty$, as in (10.8''), however, $1/m$ will become infinitesimal, and accordingly the variable t will become continuous. In that case, it becomes legitimate to speak of fractions of a year and to let t be, say, 1.2 or 2.35.

The upshot is that the expressions e, e^t, Ae^t, and Ae^{rt} can all be interpreted economically in connection with continuous interest compounding, as summarized in Table 10.1.

Optimization Problems

instantaneous rate of growth   It should be pointed out, however, that interest compounding is an illustrative, not an exclusive, interpretation of the natural exponential function Ae^{rt}. Interest compounding merely exemplifies the general process of *exponential growth* (here, the growth of a sum of money capital over time), and we can apply the function equally well to the growth of population, wealth, or real capital.

Applied to some context other than interest compounding, the coefficient r in Ae^{rt} no longer denotes the nominal interest rate. What economic meaning does it then take? The answer is that r can be reinterpreted as the *instantaneous rate of growth* of the function Ae^{rt}. (In fact, this is why we have adopted the symbol r, for rate of growth, in the first place.) Given the function $V = Ae^{rt}$, which gives the value of V at each point of time t, the rate of change of V is to be found in the derivative

$$\frac{dV}{dt} = rAe^{rt} = rV \qquad \text{[see (10.3)]}$$

But the *rate of growth* of V is simply the *rate of change* in V expressed in relative (percentage) terms, i.e., expressed as a ratio to the value of V itself. Thus, for any given point of time, we have

$$(10.9) \qquad \text{Rate of growth of } V \equiv \frac{dV/dt}{V} = \frac{rV}{V} = r$$

as was stated above.

Several observations should be made about this rate of growth. But, first, let us clarify a fundamental point regarding the concept of time, namely, the distinction between a *point* of time and a *period* of time. The variable V (denoting a sum of money, or the size of population, etc.) is a *stock* concept, which is concerned with the question: How much of it *exists* at a given moment? As such, V is related to the *point* concept of time; at each point of time, V takes a unique

TABLE 10.1

Principal ($)	Nominal interest rate	Years of continuous compounding	Asset value, at the end of compounding process ($)
1	100% (=1)	1	e
1	100%	t	e^t
A	100%	t	Ae^t
A	r	t	Ae^{rt}

value. The change in V, on the other hand, represents a *flow*, which involves the question: How much of it *takes place* during a given time span? Hence a change in V and, by the same token, the rate of change of V must have reference to some specified period of time, say, per year.

With this understanding, let us return to (10.9) for some comments: (1) The rate of growth defined in (10.9) is an *instantaneous* rate of growth. Since the derivative $dV/dt = rAe^{rt}$ takes a different value at a different point of t, as will $V = Ae^{rt}$, their ratio must also have reference to a specific point (or *instant*) of t. In this sense, the rate of growth is instantaneous. (2) In the present case, however, the instantaneous rate of growth happens to be a constant r, with the rate of growth thus remaining uniform at all points of time. This may not, of course, be true of all growth situations actually encountered. (3) Even though the rate of growth r is measured instantaneously, as of a particular point of time, its magnitude nevertheless has the connotation of so many percent *per unit of time*, say, per year (if t is measured in year units). Growth, by its very nature, can occur only over a time interval. This is why a single still picture (recording the situation at one instant) could never portray, say, the growth of a child, whereas two still pictures taken at different times—say, a year apart—can accomplish this. To say that V has a rate of growth of r at the instant $t = t_0$, therefore, really means that, if the rate r prevailing at $t = t_0$ is allowed to continue undisturbed for one whole unit of time (1 year), then V will have grown by the amount rV at the end of the year. (4) For the exponential function $V = Ae^{rt}$, the *percentage rate* of growth is constant at all points of t, but the *absolute amount* of increment of V increases as time goes on, because the percentage rate will be calculated on larger and larger bases.

Upon interpreting r as the instantaneous rate of growth, it is clear that little effort will henceforth be required to find the rate of growth of a natural exponential function of the form $y = Ae^{rt}$, provided that r is a constant. Given a function $y = 75e^{0.02t}$, for instance, we can immediately read off the rate of growth of y as 0.02, or 2 percent per period.

continuous versus discrete growth   The above discussion, though analytically interesting, is still open to question insofar as economic relevance is concerned, because in actuality growth does not always take place on a *continuous* basis—not even in interest compounding. Fortunately, however, even for cases of *discrete* growth, where changes occur only once per period rather than from instant to instant, the continuous exponential growth function can be justifiably used.

For one thing, in cases where the frequency of compounding is relatively high, though not infinite, the continuous pattern of growth may be regarded as an approximation to the true growth pattern. But, more importantly, we can show that a problem of discrete or discontinuous growth can always be transformed into an equivalent continuous version.

Suppose that we have a geometric pattern of growth (say, the *discrete* compounding of interest) as shown by the following sequence:

$$A, A(1 + i), A(1 + i)^2, A(1 + i)^3, \cdots$$

where the effective interest rate per period is denoted by i and where the exponent of the expression $(1 + i)$ denotes the number of periods covered in the compounding. If we consider $(1 + i)$ to be the base b in an exponential expression, then the above sequence may be summarized by the exponential function Ab^t —except that, because of the discrete nature of the problem, t is restricted to integer values only. Moreover, $b = 1 + i$ is a positive number (positive even if i is a *negative* interest rate, say, -0.04), so that it can always be expressed as a power of any real number greater than 1, including e. This means that there must exist a number r such that[1]

$$1 + i = b = e^r$$

Thus we can transform Ab^t into a natural exponential function:

$$A(1 + i)^t = Ab^t = Ae^{rt}$$

For any given value of t—in this context, integer values of t—the function Ae^{rt} will, of course, yield exactly the same value as $A(1 + i)^t$, such as $A(1 + i) = Ae^r$ and $A(1 + i)^2 = Ae^{2r}$. Consequently, even though a *discrete* case $A(1 + i)^t$ is being considered, we may still work with the *continuous* natural exponential function Ae^{rt}. This explains why natural exponential functions are extensively applied in economic analysis despite the fact that not all growth patterns may actually be continuous.

discounting and negative growth   Let us now turn briefly from interest compounding to the closely related concept of *discounting*. In a compound-interest problem, we seek to compute the *future value* V (principal plus interest) from a given *present value* A (initial principal). The problem of *discounting* is the opposite one, that of finding the present value A of a given sum V which is to be available t years from now.

Let us take the discrete case first. If the amount of principal A will grow into the future value of $A(1 + i)^t$ after t years of annual compounding at the interest rate i per annum, i.e., if

$$V = A(1 + i)^t$$

[1] The method of finding the number r, given a specific value of b, will be discussed in Sec. 10.4.

then, by dividing both sides of the equation by the nonzero expression $(1 + i)^t$, we can get the discounting formula:

$$(10.10) \qquad A = \frac{V}{(1 + i)^t} = V(1 + i)^{-t}$$

which involves a negative exponent. It should be realized that in this formula the roles of V and A have been reversed: V is now a given, whereas A is the unknown, to be computed from i (rate of discount) and t (number of years), as well as V.

Similarly, for the continuous case, if the principal A will grow into Ae^{rt} after t years of continuous compounding at the rate r in accordance with the formula

$$V = Ae^{rt}$$

then we can derive the corresponding continuous-discounting formula simply by dividing both sides of the last equation by e^{rt}:

$$(10.11) \qquad A = \frac{V}{e^{rt}} = Ve^{-rt}$$

Here again, we have A (rather than V) as the unknown, to be computed from a given future value V, a nominal rate of discount r, and the number of years t.

Taking (10.11) as an exponential growth function, we can immediately read $-r$ as the instantaneous rate of growth of A. Being negative, this rate is sometimes referred to as a *rate of decay*. Just as interest compounding exemplifies the process of growth, discounting illustrates *negative* growth.

EXERCISE 10.2

1 Use the infinite-series form of e^x in (10.6) to find the approximate value of:

(a) e^2 (b) $\sqrt{e}\,(=e^{1/2})$

(Round off your calculation of each term to 3 decimal places, and continue with the series till you get a term 0.000.)

2 Given the function $\phi(x) = e^{2x}$:

(a) Write the polynomial part P_n of its Maclaurin series. [*Hint:* First find the successive derivatives of $\phi(x)$.]

(b) Write the Lagrange form of the remainder R_n. Determine whether $R_n \to 0$ as $n \to \infty$, that is, whether the series is convergent to $\phi(x)$.

(c)   If convergent, so that $\phi(x)$ may be expressed as an infinite series, write out this series.

3   Write an exponential expression for the value:

(a)   \$10, compounded continuously at the interest rate of 5% for 3 years
(b)   \$700, compounded continuously at the interest rate of 4% for 2 years
(These interest rates are nominal rates per annum.)

4   What is the instantaneous rate of growth of y in each of the following?

(a) $y = e^{0.07t}$

(b) $y = 3e^{0.07t}$

(c) $y = Ae^{0.2t}$

(d) $y = 0.03e^{t}$

5   Show that the two functions $y_1 = Ae^{rt}$ (interest compounding) and $y_2 = Ae^{-rt}$ (discounting) are mirror images of each other with reference to the y axis. [Cf. Exercise 10.1-5, part (b).]

10.3   Logarithms

Exponential functions are closely related to *logarithmic functions (log functions*, for short). Before we can discuss log functions, we must first understand the meaning of the term *logarithm*.

the meaning of logarithm   When we have two numbers such as 4 and 16, which can be related to each other by the equation $4^2 = 16$, we define the *exponent* 2 to be the *logarithm* of 16 to the base of 4, and write

$$\log_4 16 = 2$$

It should be clear from this example that the logarithm is nothing but the *power* to which a base (4) must be raised to attain a particular number (16). In general, we may state that

(10.12) $y = b^t \quad \Leftrightarrow \quad t = \log_b y$

which indicates that the log of y to the base b (denoted by $\log_b y$) is the power to which the base b must be raised in order to attain the value y. For this reason, it is correct, even though tautological, to write

$$b^{\log_b y} = y$$

In the discussion of exponential functions, we emphasized that the function

$y = b^t$ (with $b > 1$) is monotonically increasing. This means that, for any positive value of y, there is a *unique* exponent t (not necessarily positive) such that $y = b^t$; moreover, the larger the value of y, the larger must be t, as can be seen from Fig. 10.2. Translated into logarithms, the monotonicity of the exponential function implies that any positive number y must possess a *unique* logarithm t to a base $b > 1$ such that the larger the y, the larger its logarithm. As Figs. 10.1 and 10.2 show, y is necessarily positive in the exponential function $y = b^t$; consequently, a negative number or zero cannot possess a logarithm.

common log and natural log   The base of the logarithm, $b > 1$, does not have to be restricted to any particular number, but in actual log applications two numbers are commonly chosen as bases—the number 10 and the number e. When 10 is the base, the logarithm is known as *common logarithm*, symbolized by $\log_{10}$ (or if the context is clear, simply by log). With e as the base, on the other hand, the logarithm is referred to as *natural logarithm* and is denoted either by $\log_e$ or by ln (for natural log). We may also use the symbol log (without subscript e) if it is not ambiguous in the particular context.

Common logarithms, used frequently in *computational* work, are exemplified by the following:

$$\log_{10} 1000 = 3 \quad [\text{because } 10^3 = 1000]$$
$$\log_{10} 100 = 2 \quad [\text{because } 10^2 = 100]$$
$$\log_{10} 10 = 1 \quad [\text{because } 10^1 = 10]$$
$$\log_{10} 1 = 0 \quad [\text{because } 10^0 = 1]$$
$$\log_{10} 0.1 = -1 \quad [\text{because } 10^{-1} = 0.1]$$
$$\log_{10} 0.01 = -2 \quad [\text{because } 10^{-2} = 0.01]$$

The reader should observe the close relation between the set of numbers immediately to the left of the equals signs and the set of numbers immediately to the right. From these, it should be apparent that the common logarithm of a number between 10 and 100 must be between 1 and 2 and that the common logarithm of a number between 1 and 10 must be a positive fraction, etc. The exact logarithms can easily be obtained from a table of common logarithms.[1]

In *analytical* work, however, natural logarithms prove vastly more convenient to use than common logarithms. Since, by the definition of logarithm, we have the relationship

$$(10.13) \qquad y = e^t \qquad \Leftrightarrow \qquad t = \log_e y \ (\text{or } t = \ln y)$$

---

[1] More fundamentally, the value of a logarithm, like the value of e, can be calculated (or approximated) by resorting to a Maclaurin-series expansion of a log function, in a manner similar to that outlined in (10.6). However, we shall not venture into this matter here.

it is easy to see that the analytical convenience of e in exponential functions will automatically extend into the realm of logarithms with e as the base.

The following examples will serve to illustrate natural logarithms:

$$\ln e^3 = \log_e e^3 = 3$$
$$\ln e^2 = \log_e e^2 = 2$$
$$\ln e^1 = \log_e e^1 = 1$$
$$\ln 1 = \log_e e^0 = 0$$
$$\ln \frac{1}{e} = \log_e e^{-1} = -1$$

The general principle emerging from these examples is that, given an expression e^n, where n is any real number, we can automatically read the exponent n as the natural log of e^n. In general, therefore, we have the result that $\ln e^n = n$.†

Common log and natural log are convertible into each other; i.e., the base of a logarithm can be changed, just as the base of an exponential expression can. A pair of conversion formulas will be developed after we have studied the basic rules of logarithms.

rules of logarithms   Logarithms are in the nature of exponents; therefore, they obey certain rules closely related to the rules of exponents introduced in Sec. 2.5. These can be of great help in simplifying mathematical operations. The first three rules are stated only in terms of natural log, but they are also valid when the symbol ln is replaced by $\log_b$.

RULE I   (*Log of a Product*) $\ln (uv) = \ln u + \ln v$ $(u,v > 0)$

Example 1 $\ln (e^6 e^4) = \ln e^6 + \ln e^4 = 6 + 4 = 10$

Example 2 $\ln (Ae^7) = \ln A + \ln e^7 = \ln A + 7$

Proof   By definition, $\ln u$ is the power to which e must be raised to attain the value of u; thus $e^{\ln u} = u$.‡ Similarly, we have $e^{\ln v} = v$ and $e^{\ln (uv)} = uv$. The latter is an exponential expression for uv. However, another expression of uv is obtainable by direct multiplication of u and v:

$$uv = e^{\ln u} e^{\ln v} = e^{\ln u + \ln v}$$

† As a mnemonic device, observe that when the symbol ln (or $\log_e$) is placed at the left of the expression e^n, the symbol ln seems to cancel out the symbol e, leaving n as the answer.
‡ Note that when e is raised to the power ln u, the symbol e and the symbol ln again seem to cancel out, leaving u as the answer.

Thus, by equating the two expressions for uv, we find that

$$e^{\ln (uv)} = e^{\ln u + \ln v} \qquad \text{or} \qquad \ln (uv) = \ln u + \ln v$$

RULE II   (*Log of a Quotient*) $\ln (u/v) = \ln u - \ln v$ $(u,v > 0)$

Example 3 $\ln (e^2/c) = \ln e^2 - \ln c = 2 - \ln c$

Example 4 $\ln (e^2/e^5) = \ln e^2 - \ln e^5 = 2 - 5 = -3$

The proof of this rule is very similar to that of Rule I and is therefore left to the reader as an exercise.

RULE III   (*Log of a Power*) $\ln u^a = a \ln u$ $(u > 0)$

Example 5 $\ln e^{15} = 15 \ln e = 15$

Example 6 $\ln A^3 = 3 \ln A$

Proof   By definition, $e^{\ln u} = u$; and similarly, $e^{\ln u^a} = u^a$. However, another expression for u^a can be formed as follows:

$$u^a = (e^{\ln u})^a = e^{a \ln u}$$

By equating the exponents in the two expressions for u^a, we obtain the desired result, $\ln u^a = a \ln u$.

These three rules are useful devices for simplifying the mathematical operations in certain types of problems. Rule I serves to convert, via logarithms, a multiplicative operation (uv) into an additive one $(\ln u + \ln v)$; Rule II turns a division (u/v) into a subtraction $(\ln u - \ln v)$; and Rule III enables us to reduce a power to a multiplicative constant. Moreover, these rules can be used in combination.

Example 7 $\ln (uv^a) = \ln u + \ln v^a = \ln u + a \ln v$

The reader is warned, however, that when we have *additive* expressions to begin with, logarithms may be of no help at all. In particular, it should be remembered that

$$\ln (u \pm v) \neq \ln u \pm \ln v$$

Let us now introduce two additional rules concerned with changes in the base of a logarithm.

RULE IV   (*Conversion of Log Base*) $\log_b u = (\log_b e)(\log_e u)$ $(u > 0)$

This rule, which resembles the chain rule in spirit (witness the "chain" $b \nearrow^e \searrow_e \nearrow^u$), enables us to derive a logarithm $\log_e u$ (to base e) from the logarithm $\log_b u$ (to base b), or vice versa.

Proof   Let $u = e^p$, so that $p = \log_e u$. Then it follows that

$$\log_b u = \log_b e^p = p \log_b e = (\log_e u)(\log_b e)$$

Rule IV can readily be generalized to

$$\log_b u = (\log_b c)(\log_c u)$$

where c is some base other than b.

RULE V   (*Inversion of Log Base*) $\log_b e = \dfrac{1}{\log_e b}$

This rule, which resembles the inverse-function rule of differentiation, enables us to obtain the log of b to the base e immediately upon being given the log of e to the base b, and vice versa. (This rule can also be generalized to the form $\log_b c = 1/\log_c b$.)

Proof   As an application of Rule IV, let $u = b$; then we have

$$\log_b b = (\log_b e)(\log_e b)$$

But the left-side expression is $\log_b b = 1$; therefore $\log_b e$ and $\log_e b$ must be reciprocal to each other, as Rule V asserts.

From the last two rules, it is easy to derive the following pair of conversion formulas between common log and natural log:

$$(10.14) \qquad \begin{aligned} \log_{10} N &= (\log_{10} e)(\log_e N) = 0.4343 \log_e N \\ \log_e N &= (\log_e 10)(\log_{10} N) = 2.3026 \log_{10} N \end{aligned}$$

for N a positive real number. The first equals sign in each formula is easily justified by Rule IV. In the first formula, the value 0.4343 (the common log of 2.71828) is found from a table of common logarithms; in the second, the value 2.3026 (the natural log of 10) is merely the reciprocal of 0.4343, so calculated because of Rule V.

Example 8 $\log_e 100 = 2.3026 (\log_{10} 100) = 2.3026(2) = 4.6052$. Conversely, we have $\log_{10} 100 = 0.4343(\log_e 100) = 0.4343(4.6052) = 2$.

an application   The above rules of logarithms enable us to solve with ease certain simple *exponential equations* (exponential *functions* set equal to zero). For instance, if we seek to find the value of x that satisfies the equation

$$ab^x - c = 0 \qquad (a,b,c > 0)$$

we can first try to transform this exponential equation, by the use of logarithms, into a *linear* equation and then solve it as such. For this purpose, the c term should first be transposed to the right side:

$$ab^x = c$$

Whereas we do not have a simple log expression for the sum $(ab^x - c)$, we do have convenient log expressions for ab^x and for c individually. Thus, after the transposition of c and upon taking the log (say, to base 10) of both sides, we have

$$\log a + x \log b = \log c$$

which is a linear equation in the variable x, with the solution

$$x = \frac{\log c - \log a}{\log b}$$

EXERCISE 10.3

1   What are the values of the following logarithms?

(a) $\log_{10} 10{,}000$ (c) $\log_{10} 1{,}000{,}000$ (e) $\log_3 81$
(b) $\log_{10} 0.0001$ (d) $\log_2 8$ (f) $\log_5 3125$

2   What are the values of the following logarithms?

(a) $\log_e e^{-4}$ (c) $\log_e \left(\dfrac{1}{e}\right)$ (e) $\ln \dfrac{1}{e^3}$

(b) $\log_e e^5$ (d) $\ln e^6$ (f) $\ln e^2$

3   Evaluate the following by application of the rules of logarithms:

(a) $\log_{10} (100)^{14}$ (d) $\ln Ae^2$ (g) $1/(\log_{16} 2)$
(b) $\log_{10} \frac{1}{100}$ (e) $\ln ABe^{-4}$ (h) $\log_{32} 2$
(c) $\ln (3/B)$ (f) $(\log_4 e)(\log_e 64)$

4   Which of the following are valid?

(a) $\ln u - 2 = \ln \dfrac{u}{e^2}$ (c) $\ln u + \ln v - \ln w = \ln \dfrac{uv}{w}$

(b) $3 + \ln v = \ln \dfrac{e^3}{v}$ (d) $\ln 3 + \ln 5 = \ln 8$

5   Prove that $\ln (u/v) = \ln u - \ln v$.

Optimization Problems

10.4 Logarithmic Functions

When a variable is expressed as a function of the logarithm of another variable, the function is referred to as a *logarithmic function*. We have already seen two versions of this type of function in (10.12) and (10.13), namely,

$$t = \log_b y \quad \text{and} \quad t = \log_e y \ (= \ln y)$$

which differ from each other only in regard to the base of the logarithm.

log functions and exponential functions   As we stated earlier, log functions are inverse functions of certain exponential functions. An examination of the above two log functions will confirm that they are indeed the respective inverse functions of the exponential functions

$$y = b^t \quad \text{and} \quad y = e^t$$

because the log functions cited are the results of reversing the roles of the dependent and independent variables of the corresponding exponential functions. The reader should realize, of course, that the symbol t is being used here as a general symbol, and it does not necessarily stand for *time*. Even when it does, its appearance as a *dependent* variable does not mean that time is *determined* by some variable y; it means only that a given value of y is associated with a unique point of time.

As inverse functions of monotonically increasing (exponential) functions, logarithmic functions must also be monotonically increasing, which is in line with our earlier statement that the larger a number, the larger is its logarithm to any given base. This property may be expressed symbolically in terms of the following two propositions: For two positive values of y (y_1 and y_2),

$$(10.15) \qquad \begin{aligned} \ln y_1 &= \ln y_2 \quad \Leftrightarrow \quad y_1 = y_2 \\ \ln y_1 &> \ln y_2 \quad \Leftrightarrow \quad y_1 > y_2 \end{aligned}$$

These propositions are also valid, of course, if we replace ln by $\log_b$.

the graphical form   The monotonicity and other general properties of logarithmic functions can be clearly observed from their graphs. Given the graph of the exponential function $y = e^t$, we can obtain the graph of the corresponding log function by replotting the original graph with the two axes transposed. The result of such replotting is illustrated in Fig. 10.3. The reader will note that if diagram *b* were laid over diagram *a*, with y axis on y axis and t axis on t axis, the two curves should coincide exactly. As they actually appear in Fig. 10.3— with interchanged axes—on the other hand, the two curves are seen to be mirror

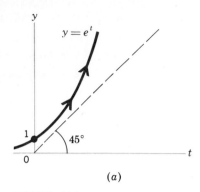
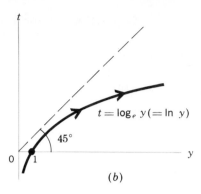

FIGURE 10.3

images of each other (as the graphs of any pair of inverse functions must be) with reference to the 45° line drawn through the origin.

This mirror-image relationship has several noteworthy implications. For one, although both are monotonically increasing, the log curve increases at a *decreasing rate* (second derivative negative), in contradistinction to the exponential curve, which increases at an increasing rate. Another interesting contrast is that, while the exponential function has a positive *range*, the log function has a positive *domain* instead. (This latter restriction on the domain of the log function is, of course, merely another way of stating that only positive numbers possess logarithms.) A third consequence of the mirror-image relationship is that, just as $y = e^t$ has a vertical intercept at 1, the log function $t = \log_e y$ must cross the horizontal axis at $y = 1$, indicating that $\log_e 1 = 0$. Inasmuch as this horizontal intercept is unaffected by the base of the logarithm—for instance, $\log_{10} 1 = 0$ also—we may infer from the general shape of the log curve in Fig. 10.3b that, for *any* base,

$$(10.16) \qquad \left. \begin{array}{c} 0 < y < 1 \\ y = 1 \\ y > 1 \end{array} \right\} \Leftrightarrow \left\{ \begin{array}{c} \log y < 0 \\ \log y = 0 \\ \log y > 0 \end{array} \right.$$

For verification, the reader may check the two sets of examples of common and natural logarithms given in Sec. 10.3. Furthermore, we may note that

$$(10.16') \qquad \log y \to \left\{ \begin{array}{c} \infty \\ -\infty \end{array} \right\} \text{ as } y \to \left\{ \begin{array}{c} \infty \\ 0^+ \end{array} \right.$$

The graphical comparison of the logarithmic function and the exponential function in Fig. 10.3 is based on the simple functions $y = e^t$ and $t = \ln y$. The same general result will prevail if we compare the generalized exponential function $y = Ae^{rt}$ with its corresponding log function. With the (positive) constants A and r to *compress* or *extend* the exponential curve, it will nevertheless resemble the general shape of Fig. 10.3a, except that its vertical intercept will be at $y = A$ rather than at $y = 1$ (when $t = 0$, we have $y = Ae^0 = A$). Its inverse function, accordingly, must have a *horizontal* intercept at $y = A$. In general, with reference to the 45° line, the corresponding log curve will be a mirror image of the exponential curve.

If the specific algebraic expression of the inverse of $y = Ae^{rt}$ is desired, it can be obtained by taking the natural log of both sides of this exponential function [which, according to the first proposition in (10.15), will leave the equation undisturbed] and then solving for t:

$$\ln y = \ln (Ae^{rt}) = \ln A + rt \ln e = \ln A + rt$$

hence

$$(10.17) \qquad t = \frac{\ln y - \ln A}{r} \qquad (r \neq 0)$$

This result, a log function, constitutes the inverse of the exponential function $y = Ae^{rt}$. As claimed earlier, the function in (10.17) has a horizontal intercept at $y = A$, because when $y = A$, we have $\ln y = \ln A$, and therefore $t = 0$.

base conversion   In Sec. 10.2, it was stated that the exponential function $y = Ab^t$ can always be converted into a *natural* exponential function $y = Ae^{rt}$. We are now ready to derive a conversion formula. Instead of Ab^t, however, let us consider the conversion of the more general expression Ab^{ct} into Ae^{rt}. Since the essence of the problem is to find an r from given values of b and c such that

$$e^r = b^c$$

all that is necessary is to express r as a function of b and c. Such a task is easily accomplished by taking the natural log of both sides of the last equation:

$$\ln e^r = \ln b^c$$

The left side can immediately be read as equal to r, so that the desired function (conversion formula) emerges as

$$(10.18) \qquad r = \ln b^c = c \ln b$$

This indicates that the function $y = Ab^{ct}$ can always be rewritten in the natural-base form, $y = Ae^{(c \ln b)t}$.

Example 1   Convert $y = 2^t$ to a natural exponential function. Here, we have $A = 1, b = 2$, and $c = 1$. Hence, $r = c \ln b = \ln 2$, and the desired exponential function is

$$y = Ae^{rt} = e^{(\ln 2)t}$$

If we like, we can also calculate the numerical value of $(\ln 2)$ by use of (10.14) and a table of common logarithms as follows:

$$(10.19) \qquad \ln 2 = 2.3026 \log_{10} 2 = 2.3026(0.3010) = 0.6931$$

Then we may express the earlier result alternatively as $y = e^{0.6931t}$.

Example 2   Convert $y = 3(5)^{2t}$ to a natural exponential function. In this example, $A = 3, b = 5$, and $c = 2$, and formula (10.18) gives us $r = 2 \ln 5$. Therefore the desired function is

$$y = Ae^{rt} = 3e^{(2 \ln 5)t}$$

Again, if we like, we can calculate that

$$2 \ln 5 = \ln 25 = 2.3026 \log_{10} 25 = 2.3026(1.3979) = 3.2188$$

so the earlier result can be alternatively expressed as $y = 3e^{3.2188t}$.

It is also possible, of course, to convert log functions of the form $t = \log_b y$ into equivalent natural log functions. To that end, it is sufficient to apply Rule IV of logarithms, which may be expressed as

$$\log_b y = (\log_b e)(\log_e y)$$

The direct substitution of this result into the given log function will immediately give us the desired natural log function:

$$
\begin{aligned}
t = \log_b y &= (\log_b e)(\log_e y) \\
&= \frac{1}{\log_e b} \log_e y \qquad \text{[by Rule V of logarithms]} \\
&= \frac{\ln y}{\ln b}
\end{aligned}
$$

By the same procedure, we can transform the more general log function $t = a \log_b (cy)$ into the equivalent form

$$t = a(\log_b e)(\log_e cy) = \frac{a}{\log_e b} \log_e (cy) = \frac{a}{\ln b} \ln (cy)$$

Example 3   Convert the function $t = \log_2 y$ into the natural log form. Since in this example we have $b = 2$ and $a = c = 1$, the desired function is

$$t = \frac{1}{\ln 2} \ln y$$

By (10.19), however, we may also express it as $t = (1/0.6931) \ln y$.

Example 4   Convert the function $t = 7 \log_{10} 2y$ into a natural logarithmic function. The values of the constants are in this case $a = 7$, $b = 10$, and $c = 2$; consequently, the desired function is

$$t = \frac{7}{\ln 10} \ln 2y$$

But since $\ln 10 = 2.3026$, as (10.14) indicates, the above function can be rewritten as $t = (7/2.3026) \ln 2y = 3.0400 \ln 2y$.

In the above discussion, we have followed the practice of expressing t as a function of y when the function is logarithmic. The only reason for doing so is our desire to stress the inverse-function relationship between the exponential and logarithmic functions. When a log function is studied *by itself*, we shall write $y = \ln t$ (rather than $t = \ln y$), as is customary. Naturally, nothing in the analytical aspect of the discussion will be affected by such an interchange of symbols.

EXERCISE 10.4

1   The form of the inverse function of $y = Ae^{rt}$ in (10.17) requires r to be nonzero. What is the meaning of this requirement when viewed in reference to the original exponential function $y = Ae^{rt}$?

2   (*a*)   Sketch a graph of the exponential function $y = Ae^{rt}$; indicate the value of the vertical intercept.

    (*b*)   Then sketch the graph of the log function $t = \dfrac{\ln y - \ln A}{r}$, and indicate the value of the horizontal intercept.

3   Find the inverse function of $y = ab^{ct}$. (*Hint:* Take log to the base b.)

4   Transform the following functions to their natural exponential forms:

    (*a*) $y = 8^{3t}$ (*c*) $y = 5(5)^t$

    (*b*) $y = 2(7)^{2t}$ (*d*) $y = 2(15)^{4t}$

5 Transform the following functions to their natural logarithmic forms:

(a) $t = \log_7 y$

(b) $t = \log_8 3y$

(c) $t = 3 \log_{15} 9y$

(d) $t = 2 \log_{10} y$

6 Find the continuous-compounding nominal interest rate per annum (r) that is equivalent to a discrete-compounding interest rate (i) of

(a) 5 percent per annum, compounded annually

(b) 5 percent per annum, compounded semiannually

(c) 6 percent per annum, compounded semiannually

(d) 6 percent per annum, compounded quarterly

10.5 Derivatives of Exponential and Logarithmic Functions

Earlier it was claimed that the function e^t is its own derivative. As it turns out, the natural log function, $\ln t$, possesses a rather convenient derivative also, namely, $d(\ln t)/dt = 1/t$. This fact reinforces our preference for the base e. Let us now prove the validity of these two derivative formulas, and then we shall deduce the derivative formulas for certain variants of the exponential and log expressions e^t and $\ln t$.

log-function rule   The derivative of the log function $y = \ln t$ is

$$\frac{dy}{dt} = \frac{d}{dt} \ln t = \frac{1}{t}$$

To prove this, we recall that, by definition, the derivative of $y = f(t) = \ln t$ has the following value at $t = N$:

$$f'(N) = \lim_{t \to N} \frac{f(t) - f(N)}{t - N} = \lim_{t \to N} \frac{\ln t - \ln N}{t - N} = \lim_{t \to N} \frac{\ln (t/N)}{t - N}$$

$$\text{[by Rule II of logarithms]}$$

Now let us introduce a shorthand symbol $m \equiv \dfrac{N}{t - N}$. Then we can write

$\dfrac{1}{t - N} = \dfrac{m}{N}$, and also $\dfrac{t}{N} = 1 + \dfrac{t - N}{N} = 1 + \dfrac{1}{m}$. Thus the expression to the right of the limit sign above can be converted to the form

$$\frac{1}{t - N} \ln \frac{t}{N} = \frac{m}{N} \ln \left(1 + \frac{1}{m} \right) = \frac{1}{N} \ln \left(1 + \frac{1}{m} \right)^m$$

$$\text{[by Rule III of logarithms]}$$

The reader will note that, when t tends to N, m will tend to infinity. Thus, to find the desired derivative value, we may take the limit of the last expression above as $m \to \infty$:

$$f'(N) = \lim_{m \to \infty} \frac{1}{N} \ln \left(1 + \frac{1}{m}\right)^m = \frac{1}{N} \ln e = \frac{1}{N} \qquad \text{[by (10.5)]}$$

Since N can be any number for which a logarithm is defined, however, we can generalize this result, and write $f'(t) = d(\ln t)/dt = 1/t$. This proves the log-function rule.

exponential-function rule The derivative of the function $y = e^t$ is

$$\frac{dy}{dt} = \frac{d}{dt} e^t = e^t$$

This result follows easily from the log-function rule. We know that the inverse function of the function $y = e^t$ is $t = \ln y$, with derivative $dt/dy = 1/y$. Thus, by the inverse-function rule, we may write immediately

$$\frac{dy}{dt} = \frac{1}{dt/dy} = \frac{1}{1/y} = y = e^t$$

the rules generalized The above two rules can be extended to cases where the variable t in the expression e^t and $\ln t$ is replaced by some *function* of t, say, $f(t)$. For this purpose, we may resort to the chain rule for help.

Given a function $y = e^{f(t)}$, we can first let $u = f(t)$, so that $y = e^u$. Then, by the chain rule, the derivative emerges as

$$\frac{d}{dt} e^{f(t)} = \frac{d}{dt} e^u = \frac{d}{du} e^u \frac{du}{dt} = e^u \frac{du}{dt} = e^{f(t)} f'(t)$$

Similarly, given a function $y = \ln f(t)$, we can first let $v = f(t)$, so as to form a chain: $y = \ln v$, where $v = f(t)$. Then, by the chain rule, we have

$$\frac{d}{dt} \ln f(t) = \frac{d}{dt} \ln v = \frac{d}{dv} \ln v \frac{dv}{dt} = \frac{1}{v} \frac{dv}{dt} = \frac{1}{f(t)} f'(t)$$

In sum, the generalized versions of the two rules are

$$(10.20) \quad \begin{aligned} \frac{d}{dt} e^{f(t)} &= f'(t) e^{f(t)} \\ \frac{d}{dt} \ln f(t) &= \frac{f'(t)}{f(t)} \end{aligned} \qquad \begin{aligned} \text{or } \frac{d}{dt} e^u &= e^u \frac{du}{dt} \\ \text{or } \frac{d}{dt} \ln v &= \frac{1}{v} \frac{dv}{dt} \end{aligned}$$

The reader will note that the only real modification introduced in (10.20) beyond the simpler rules $de^t/dt = e^t$ and $d(\ln t)/dt = 1/t$ is the multiplicative factor $f'(t)$.

Example 1   Find the derivative of the function $y = e^{rt}$. Here, the exponent is $rt = f(t)$, with $f'(t) = r$; thus

$$\frac{dy}{dt} = \frac{d}{dt} e^{rt} = re^{rt}$$

Example 2   Find dy/dt from the function $y = e^{-t}$. In this case, $f(t) = -t$, so that $f'(t) = -1$. As a result,

$$\frac{dy}{dt} = \frac{d}{dt} e^{-t} = -e^{-t}$$

Example 3   Find dy/dt from the function $y = \ln at$. Since in this case $f(t) = at$, with $f'(t) = a$, the derivative is

$$\frac{d}{dt} \ln at = \frac{a}{at} = \frac{1}{t}$$

which is, interestingly enough, identical with the derivative of $y = \ln t$.

This example illustrates the fact that a multiplicative constant of t *within* a log expression drops out in the process of derivation. But note that, for a constant k, we have

$$\frac{d}{dt} k \ln t = k \frac{d}{dt} \ln t = \frac{k}{t}$$

thus a multiplicative constant *without* the log expression is still retained in derivation.

Example 4   Find the derivative of the function $y = \ln t^c$. With $f(t) = t^c$ and $f'(t) = ct^{c-1}$, the formula in (10.20) yields

$$\frac{d}{dt} \ln t^c = \frac{ct^{c-1}}{t^c} = \frac{c}{t}$$

Example 5   Find dy/dt from $y = t^3 \ln t^2$. This function being a product of two terms t^3 and $\ln t^2$, the product rule should be used:

$$\frac{dy}{dt} = t^3 \frac{d}{dt} \ln t^2 + \ln t^2 \frac{d}{dt} t^3$$

$$= t^3 \left(\frac{2t}{t^2}\right) + (\ln t^2)(3t^2)$$

$$= 2t^2 + 3t^2(2 \ln t) \qquad \text{[Rule III of logarithms]}$$

$$= 2t^2(1 + 3 \ln t)$$

the case of base b   For exponential and log functions with base b, the derivatives are

(10.21)
$$\frac{d}{dt} b^t = b^t \ln b \qquad \left[\text{Warning:} \frac{d}{dt} b^t \neq tb^{t-1}\right]$$

$$\frac{d}{dt} \log_b t = \frac{1}{t \ln b}$$

Note that in the special case of base e (when $b = e$), we have $\ln b = \ln e = 1$, so that these two derivatives will reduce to $(d/dt)e^t = e^t$ and $(d/dt) \ln t = 1/t$, respectively.

The proofs for (10.21) are not difficult. For the case of b^t, the proof is based on the identity $b \equiv e^{\ln b}$, which enables us to write

$$b^t = e^{(\ln b)t} = e^{t \ln b}$$

(We write $t \ln b$, instead of $\ln b\, t$, in order to emphasize that t is not a part of the log expression.) Hence,

$$\frac{d}{dt} b^t = \frac{d}{dt} e^{t \ln b} = (\ln b)(e^{t \ln b}) \qquad \text{[by (10.20)]}$$

$$= (\ln b)(b^t) = b^t \ln b$$

To prove the second part of (10.21), on the other hand, we rely on the basic log property that

$$\log_b t = (\log_b e)(\log_e t) = \frac{1}{\ln b} \ln t$$

which leads us to the derivative

$$\frac{d}{dt} \log_b t = \frac{d}{dt}\left(\frac{1}{\ln b} \ln t\right) = \frac{1}{\ln b} \frac{d}{dt} \ln t = \frac{1}{\ln b}\left(\frac{1}{t}\right)$$

The more general versions of these two formulas are

(10.21′)
$$\frac{d}{dt} b^{f(t)} = f'(t)\, b^{f(t)} \ln b$$

$$\frac{d}{dt} \log_b f(t) = \frac{f'(t)}{f(t)} \frac{1}{\ln b}$$

Again, it is seen that if $b = e$, then $\ln b = 1$, and these formulas will reduce to (10.20).

Example 6   Find the derivative of the function $y = 12^{1-t}$. Here, $b = 12$, $f(t) = 1 - t$, and $f'(t) = -1$; thus

$$\frac{dy}{dt} = -(12)^{1-t} \ln 12$$

Exponential and Logarithmic Functions   **309**

Example 7   Find dy/dt from $y = t \log_5 [t^2/(1 + t)]$. Obviously, we must use the product rule here. If we refer to the log expression in this function as L, then $y = tL$ and

$$(10.22) \qquad \frac{dy}{dt} = t\frac{dL}{dt} + L\frac{dt}{dt} = t\frac{dL}{dt} + L$$

We need to know what dL/dt is. Since $L = \log_5 [t^2/(1 + t)]$, it follows that

$$\frac{d}{dt}L = \frac{d}{dt}[\log_5 t^2 - \log_5 (1 + t)] \qquad \text{[by Rule II of logarithms]}$$

$$= \frac{2t}{t^2 \ln 5} - \frac{1}{(1 + t) \ln 5} \qquad \text{[by (10.21$'$)]}$$

$$= \frac{2(1 + t) - t}{t(1 + t) \ln 5} = \frac{2 + t}{t(1 + t) \ln 5}$$

Upon substituting this result into (10.22), the desired derivative is found to be

$$\frac{dy}{dt} = \frac{2 + t}{(1 + t) \ln 5} + \log_5 \left(\frac{t^2}{1 + t}\right)$$

higher derivatives   Higher derivatives of exponential and log functions, like those of other types of functions, are merely the results of repeated differentiation.

Example 8   Find the *second* derivative of $y = b^t$ (with $b > 1$). The first derivative, by (10.21), is $y'(t) = b^t \ln b$ (where $\ln b$ is, of course, a constant); thus, by differentiating once more with respect to t, we have

$$y''(t) = \frac{d}{dt}y'(t) = \left(\frac{d}{dt}b^t\right)\ln b = (b^t \ln b)\ln b = b^t(\ln b)^2$$

Note that $y = b^t$ is always positive and $\ln b$ (for $b > 1$) is also positive [by (10.16)]; thus $y'(t) = b^t \ln b$ must be positive. And $y''(t)$, being a product of b^t and a squared number, is also positive. These facts confirm our previous statement that the exponential function $y = b^t$ increases monotonically at an increasing rate.

Example 9   Find the *second* derivative of $y = \ln t$. The first derivative is $y' = 1/t = t^{-1}$; hence, the second derivative is

$$y'' = -t^{-2} = \frac{-1}{t^2}$$

Inasmuch as the domain of this function consists of the open interval $(0,\infty)$,

$y' = 1/t$ must be a positive number. On the other hand, y'' is always negative. Together, these conclusions serve to confirm our earlier allegation that the log function $y = \ln t$ increases monotonically at a decreasing rate.

an application   One of the prime virtues of the logarithm is its ability to convert a multiplication into an addition, and a division into a subtraction. This property can be exploited when we are differentiating a complicated product or quotient of any type of functions (not necessarily exponential or logarithmic).

Example 10   Find dy/dx from

$$y = \frac{x^2}{(x + 3)(2x + 1)}$$

Instead of applying the product and quotient rules, we may first take the natural log of both sides of the equation to reduce the function to the form

$$\ln y = \ln x^2 - \ln (x + 3) - \ln (2x + 1)$$

According to (10.20), the derivative of the left side with respect to x can be expressed as

$$\frac{d}{dx}(\text{left side}) = \frac{1}{y}\frac{dy}{dx}$$

whereas the right side will yield

$$\frac{d}{dx}(\text{right side}) = \frac{2x}{x^2} - \frac{1}{x + 3} - \frac{2}{2x + 1} = \frac{7x + 6}{x(x + 3)(2x + 1)}$$

When the two results are equated and both sides are multiplied by y, we get the desired derivative as follows:

$$\frac{dy}{dx} = \frac{7x + 6}{x(x + 3)(2x + 1)}\, y$$

$$= \frac{7x + 6}{x(x + 3)(2x + 1)}\, \frac{x^2}{(x + 3)(2x + 1)} = \frac{x(7x + 6)}{(x + 3)^2(2x + 1)^2}$$

Example 11   Find dy/dx from $y = x^a e^{kx - c}$. Taking the natural log of both sides, we have

$$\ln y = a \ln x + \ln e^{kx - c} = a \ln x + kx - c$$

Thus
$$\frac{1}{y}\frac{dy}{dx} = \frac{a}{x} + k$$

and
$$\frac{dy}{dx} = \left(\frac{a}{x} + k\right) x^a e^{kx - c}$$

EXERCISE 10.5

1   Find the derivatives of:

(a) $y = e^{2t+3}$

(b) $y = e^{1-5t}$

(c) $y = e^{t^2+1}$

(d) $y = 3e^{2-t^2}$

(e) $y = e^{ax^2+bx+c}$

(f) $y = xe^x$

(g) $y = x^2e^{2x}$

(h) $y = axe^{bx+c}$

2   (a) Verify the derivative in Example 3 by utilizing the equation $\ln at = \ln a + \ln t$.

(b) Verify the result in Example 4 by utilizing the equation $\ln t^c = c \ln t$.

3   Find the derivatives of:

(a) $y = \ln 3t^5$

(b) $y = \ln at^c$

(c) $y = \ln (t + 2)$

(d) $y = 5 \ln (t + 1)^2$

(e) $y = \ln x - \ln (1 + x)$

(f) $y = \ln [x(1 - x)^8]$

(g) $y = \ln \left(\dfrac{3x}{1 + x} \right)$

(h) $y = 3x^4 \ln x^2$

4   Find the derivatives of:

(a) $y = 5^t$

(b) $y = \log_2 (t + 1)$

(c) $y = 11^{2t+3}$

(d) $y = \log_7 5x^2$

(e) $y = \log_2 (8x^2 + 3)$

(f) $y = x^2 \log_3 x$

5   Prove the two formulas in (10.21′). [*Hint:* Use (10.21), and apply the chain rule.]

6   Show that the function $V = Ae^{rt}$ (with $A, r > 0$) and the function $A = Ve^{-rt}$ (with $V, r > 0$) are both monotonic, but in opposite directions, and that they are both strictly convex in shape. (Cf. Exercise 10.2-5.)

7   Find the derivatives of the following by first taking the natural log of both sides:

(a) $y = \dfrac{3x}{(x + 2)(x + 4)}$

(b) $y = (x^2 + 3)e^{x^2+1}$

10.6   Optimal Timing

What we have learned about exponential and log functions can now be applied to some simple problems of optimal timing.

a problem of wine storage   Suppose that a wine dealer is in possession of a particular quantity (say, a case) of wine, which he can either sell at the present time ($t = 0$) for a sum of $\$K$ or else store for a variable length of time and then sell at a higher value. The growing value (V) of the wine is known to be the following function of time:

$$(10.23) \qquad V = Ke^{\sqrt{t}} \qquad [= K \exp{(t^{1/2})}]$$

so that if $t = 0$ (sell now), then $V = K$. The problem is: When should he sell it in order to maximize profit, assuming the storage cost to be nil?[1]

Since the cost of wine is a "sunk" cost—the wine is already paid for by the dealer—and since storage cost is assumed to be nonexistent, to maximize profit is the same as maximizing the sales revenue, or the value of V. There is one catch, however: Each value of V corresponding to a specific point of t represents a dollar sum receivable at a different date and, because of the interest element involved, is not directly comparable with the V value of another date. The way out of this difficulty is to *discount* each V figure to its *present-value* equivalent (the value at time $t = 0$), for then all the V values will be on a comparable footing.

Let us assume that the interest rate on the continuous-compounding basis is at the level of r. Then, according to (10.11), the present value of V can be expressed as

$$(10.23') \qquad A(t) = Ve^{-rt} = Ke^{\sqrt{t}}\, e^{-rt} = Ke^{\sqrt{t}-rt}$$

where A, denoting the present value of V, is itself a function of t. Therefore our problem amounts to finding the value of t that maximizes A.

maximization conditions   The first-order condition for maximizing A is to have $dA/dt = 0$. To find this derivative, we can first take the natural log of both sides of (10.23') as follows:

$$\ln A(t) = \ln K + \ln e^{\sqrt{t}-rt} = \ln K + (t^{1/2} - rt)$$

Upon differentiating both sides with respect to t, we get

$$\frac{1}{A}\frac{dA}{dt} = \frac{1}{2}t^{-1/2} - r$$

or

$$\frac{dA}{dt} = A\left(\frac{1}{2}t^{-1/2} - r\right)$$

[1] The consideration of storage cost will entail a difficulty we are not yet equipped to handle. Later, in Chap. 13, we shall return to this problem.

Since $A \neq 0$, the necessary condition $dA/dt = 0$ can be fulfilled if and only if

$$\frac{1}{2} t^{-1/2} = r \quad \text{or} \quad \frac{1}{2\sqrt{t}} = r \quad \text{or} \quad \frac{1}{2r} = \sqrt{t}$$

This implies that the optimum length of storage time is

$$\bar{t} = \left(\frac{1}{2r}\right)^2 = \frac{1}{4r^2}$$

If $r = 0.10$, for instance, then $\bar{t} = 25$, and the dealer should store the case of wine for 25 years. Note that the higher the rate of interest (rate of discount) is, the shorter the optimum storage period will be.

The first-order condition, $1/(2\sqrt{t}) = r$, admits of an easy economic interpretation. The left-hand expression merely represents the rate of growth of wine value V, because from (10.23)

$$\frac{dV}{dt} = \frac{d}{dt} K \exp(t^{1/2}) = K \frac{d}{dt} \exp(t^{1/2}) \qquad [K \text{ constant}]$$

$$= K \left(\frac{1}{2} t^{-1/2}\right) \exp(t^{1/2}) \qquad [\text{by (10.20)}]$$

$$= \left(\frac{1}{2} t^{-1/2}\right) V \qquad [\text{by (10.23)}]$$

so that the rate of growth of V is indeed the left-hand expression in the first-order condition:

$$r_V \equiv \frac{dV/dt}{V} = \frac{1}{2} t^{-1/2} = \frac{1}{2\sqrt{t}}$$

The right-hand expression r is, in contrast, the rate of interest or the rate of compound-interest growth of the cash fund receivable *if* the wine is sold right away—an *opportunity-cost* aspect of storing the wine. Thus, the equating of the two instantaneous rates, as illustrated in Fig. 10.4, is an attempt to hold onto the wine until the advantage of storage is completely wiped out, i.e., to wait till the moment when the (declining) rate of growth of wine value is just matched by the (constant) interest rate on cash sales receipts.

The next order of business is to check whether the value of $\bar{t}$ satisfies the second-order condition for maximization of A. The second derivative of A is

$$\frac{d^2 A}{dt^2} = \frac{d}{dt} A \left(\frac{1}{2} t^{-1/2} - r\right) = A \frac{d}{dt} \left(\frac{1}{2} t^{-1/2} - r\right) + \left(\frac{1}{2} t^{-1/2} - r\right) \frac{dA}{dt}$$

But, since the final term drops out when we evaluate it at the equilibrium

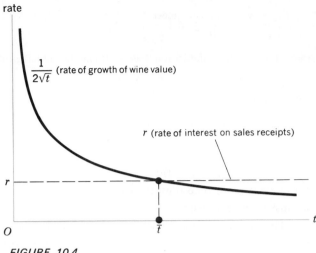

rate

$\dfrac{1}{2\sqrt{t}}$ (rate of growth of wine value)

r (rate of interest on sales receipts)

r

O

$\bar{t}$

t

FIGURE 10.4

(optimum) point, where $dA/dt = 0$, we are left with

$$\frac{d^2A}{dt^2} = A \frac{d}{dt}\left(\frac{1}{2}t^{-1/2} - r\right) = A\left(-\frac{1}{4}t^{-3/2}\right) = \frac{-A}{4\sqrt{t^3}}$$

In view that $A > 0$ and $t > 0$, this second derivative is negative, thereby assuring that the solution value $\bar{t}$ is indeed profit-maximizing.

a problem of timber cutting

A similar problem, which involves a choice of the best time to take action, is that of timber cutting.

Suppose the value of timber (already planted on some given land) is the following increasing function of time:

$$V = 2^{\sqrt{t}}$$

expressed in units of \$1000. Assuming a discount rate of r (on the continuous basis) and also assuming zero upkeep cost during the period of timber growth, what is the optimal time to cut the timber for sale?

As in the wine problem, we should first convert V into its present value:

$$A(t) = Ve^{-rt} = 2^{\sqrt{t}}e^{-rt}$$

thus $\ln A = \ln 2^{\sqrt{t}} + \ln e^{-rt} = \sqrt{t}\ln 2 - rt = t^{1/2}\ln 2 - rt$

To maximize A, we must set $dA/dt = 0$. The first derivative is obtainable by differentiating $\ln A$ with respect to t and then multiplying by A:

$$\frac{1}{A}\frac{dA}{dt} = \frac{1}{2}t^{-1/2}\ln 2 - r$$

thus
$$\frac{dA}{dt} = A\left(\frac{\ln 2}{2\sqrt{t}} - r\right)$$

Since $A \neq 0$, the condition $dA/dt = 0$ can be met if and only if

$$\frac{\ln 2}{2\sqrt{t}} = r \qquad \text{or} \qquad \sqrt{t} = \frac{\ln 2}{2r}$$

Consequently, the optimum number of years of growth is

$$\bar{t} = \left(\frac{\ln 2}{2r}\right)^2$$

It is evident from this solution that, the higher the rate of discount, the earlier the timber should be cut.

To make sure that $\bar{t}$ is a maximizing (instead of minimizing) solution, the second-order condition should be checked. But this will be left to the reader as an exercise.

In this example, we have abstracted from planting cost by assuming that the trees are already planted, in which case the (sunk) planting cost is legitimately excludable from consideration in the optimization decision. If the decision is not one of when to harvest but one of whether or not to plant at all, then the planting cost (incurred at the *present*) must be duly compared with the *present* value of the timber output, computed with t set at the optimum value $\bar{t}$. For instance, if $r = 0.05$, then we have

$$\bar{t} = \left(\frac{0.6931}{0.10}\right)^2 = (6.931)^2 = 48.0 \text{ years}$$

and $\quad \bar{A} = 2^{6.931}e^{-0.05(48.0)} = (121.9)e^{-2.40}$
$$= 121.9(0.9072) = \$110.59 \text{ (in thousands)}$$

So only a planting cost lower than $\bar{A}$ will make the venture worthwhile—again, provided that upkeep cost is nil.

EXERCISE 10.6

1   If the value of wine grows according to the function $V = Ke^{2\sqrt{t}}$, instead of as in (10.23), how long should the dealer store the wine?

2   Check the second-order condition for the timber-cutting problem.

3   As a generalization of the optimization problem illustrated in the present section, show that:

(a) With any value function $V = f(t)$ and a given continuous rate of discount r, the first-order condition for the present value A of V to reach a maximum is that the rate of growth of V be equal to r.

(b) The second-order condition for maximum really amounts to the requirement that the rate of growth of V be decreasing with time.

10.7 Further Applications of Exponential and Logarithmic Derivatives

Aside from their use in optimization problems, the derivative formulas of Sec. 10.5 have further useful economic applications.

finding the rate of growth   When a variable y is a function of time, $y = f(t)$, its instantaneous rate of growth is defined as

$$(10.24) \qquad r_y \equiv \frac{dy/dt}{y} = \frac{f'(t)}{f(t)} = \frac{\text{marginal function}}{\text{total function}}$$

But, from (10.20), we see that this ratio is precisely the derivative of $\ln f(t) = \ln y$. Thus, to find the instantaneous rate of growth of a function of time $f(t)$, we can —instead of differentiating it with respect to t, and then dividing by $f(t)$—simply take its natural log and then differentiate $\ln f(t)$ with respect to time.[1] This alternative method may often (though not always) turn out to be the simpler approach, especially if $f(t)$ is a multiplicative or divisional expression which, upon logarithm-taking, will reduce to a sum or difference of additive terms.

Example 1   Find the rate of growth of $V = Ae^{rt}$, where t denotes time. It is already known to us that the rate of growth of V is r, but let us check it by finding the derivative of $\ln V$:

$$\ln V = \ln A + rt \ln e = \ln A + rt \qquad [A \text{ constant}]$$

Therefore,

$$r_V = \frac{d}{dt} \ln V = 0 + \frac{d}{dt} rt = r$$

as was to be demonstrated.

---

[1] If we plot the natural log of a function $f(t)$ against t in a two-dimensional diagram, the slope of the curve, accordingly, will tell us the rate of growth of $f(t)$. This provides the rationale for the so-called "semilog scale" charts.

Example 2   Find the rate of growth of $y = 4^t$. In this case, we have

$$\ln y = \ln 4^t = t \ln 4$$

Hence $r_y = \dfrac{d}{dt} \ln y = \ln 4$

This is as it should be, because $e^{\ln 4} \equiv 4$, and consequently, $y = 4^t$ can be rewritten as $y = e^{(\ln 4)t}$, which would immediately enable us to read $(\ln 4)$ as the rate of growth of y.

rate of growth of a combination of functions   To carry this discussion a step further, let us examine the instantaneous rate of growth of a *product* of two functions of time:

$$y = uv \qquad \text{where} \quad \begin{cases} u = f(t) \\ v = g(t) \end{cases}$$

Taking the natural log of y, we obtain

$$\ln y = \ln u + \ln v$$

Thus, the desired rate of growth is

$$r_y = \frac{d}{dt} \ln y = \frac{d}{dt} \ln u + \frac{d}{dt} \ln v$$

But the two terms on the right side are the rates of growth of u and v, respectively. Thus, we have

$$r_{(uv)} \, (= r_y) = r_u + r_v$$

Expressed in words, the instantaneous rate of growth of a *product* is the *sum* of the instantaneous rates of growth of the components.

By a similar procedure, the rate of growth of a *quotient* can be shown to be the *difference* between the rates of growth of the components (see Exercise 10.7-2).

Example 3   If consumption C is growing at the rate α, and if population H (for "heads") is growing at the rate β, what is the rate of growth of per-capita consumption? Since per-capita consumption is equal to C/H, its rate of growth should be

$$r_{(C/H)} = r_C - r_H = \alpha - \beta$$

Now consider the instantaneous rate of growth of a *sum* of two functions of time:

$$z = u + v \qquad \text{where} \quad \begin{cases} u = f(t) \\ v = g(t) \end{cases}$$

This time, the natural log will be

$$\ln z = \ln (u + v) \qquad [\neq \ln u + \ln v]$$

Thus
$$r_z = \frac{d}{dt} \ln z = \frac{d}{dt} \ln (u + v)$$

$$= \frac{1}{u + v} \frac{d}{dt} (u + v) \qquad [\text{by } (10.20)]$$

$$= \frac{1}{u + v} [f'(t) + g'(t)]$$

But from (10.24) we have $r_u = f'(t)/f(t)$, so that $f'(t) = f(t)r_u = ur_u$. Similarly, we have $g'(t) = vr_v$. As a result, we can write

$$r_{(u+v)} \ (= r_z) = \frac{u}{u + v} r_u + \frac{v}{u + v} r_v$$

which is a formula showing that the rate of growth of a *sum* is a *weighted average* of the rates of growth of the components.

By the same token, we can find (see Exercise 10.7-3)

$$r_{(u-v)} = \frac{u}{u - v} r_u - \frac{v}{u - v} r_v$$

Example 4   The exports of goods of a country, $G = G(t)$, has a growth rate of $t/3$, and its exports of services, $S = S(t)$, has a growth rate of $t/5$. What is the growth rate of its total exports? Since total exports is $X(t) = G(t) + S(t)$, a sum, its rate of growth should be

$$r_X = \frac{G}{X} r_G + \frac{S}{X} r_S$$

$$= \frac{G}{X}\left(\frac{t}{3}\right) + \frac{S}{X}\left(\frac{t}{5}\right) = \frac{5G + 3S}{15X} t$$

At any given point of t, the growth rate r_X will have a specific value, because G, S, and X will all take specific values once t is specified.

finding the point elasticity   We have seen that, given $y = f(t)$, the derivative of $\ln y$ measures the instantaneous rate of growth of y. If t is not a time variable, this derivative can be reinterpreted to mean the instantaneous *rate of proportional change* of the function, which is a more general concept than that of the rate of growth. Now let us see what happens when, given a function $y = f(x)$, we differentiate $(\ln y)$ with respect to $(\ln x)$ rather than to x.

To begin with, let us define $u \equiv \ln y$ and $v \equiv \ln x$. Then we can observe a chain of relationship linking u to y, and thence to x and v as follows:

$$u \equiv \ln y \qquad y = f(x) \qquad x \equiv e^{\ln x} \equiv e^v$$

Accordingly, the derivative of $(\ln y)$ with respect to $(\ln x)$ is

$$\frac{d(\ln y)}{d(\ln x)} = \frac{du}{dv} = \frac{du}{dy}\frac{dy}{dx}\frac{dx}{dv}$$

$$= \left(\frac{d}{dy}\ln y\right)\left(\frac{dy}{dx}\right)\left(\frac{d}{dv}e^v\right) = \frac{1}{y}\frac{dy}{dx}e^v = \frac{1}{y}\frac{dy}{dx}x = \frac{dy}{dx}\frac{x}{y}$$

But this expression is precisely that of the point elasticity of the function. Hence we have established the general principle that, for a function $y = f(x)$, the point elasticity of y with respect to x is

$$(10.25) \qquad \varepsilon_{yx} \equiv \frac{dy}{dx}\frac{x}{y} = \frac{d(\ln y)}{d(\ln x)}$$

It should be noted that the subscript yx in this symbol is an indicator that y and x are the two variables involved and does not imply the multiplication of y and x. This is unlike the case of $r_{(uv)}$, where the subscript *does* denote a product. Again, we now have an alternative way of finding the point elasticity of a function by use of logarithms, which may often turn out to be an easier approach, especially if the given function comes in the form of a multiplicative or divisional expression.

Example 5   Find the point elasticity of demand, given that $Q = k/P$, where k is a positive constant. This is the equation of a rectangular hyperbola (see Fig. 2.8d); and, as is well known, a demand function of this form has a unitary point elasticity at all points. To show this, we shall apply (10.25). Since the natural log of the demand function is

$$\ln Q = \ln k - \ln P$$

the elasticity of demand (Q with respect to P) is indeed

$$\varepsilon_d = \frac{d(\ln Q)}{d(\ln P)} = -1 \qquad \text{or} \qquad |\varepsilon_d| = 1$$

The result in (10.25) was derived by use of the chain rule of derivatives. It is of interest that a similar chain rule holds for elasticities; i.e., given a function $y = g(w)$, where $w = h(x)$, we have

$$\varepsilon_{yx} = \varepsilon_{yw}\varepsilon_{wx}$$

The proof is as follows:

$$\varepsilon_{yw}\varepsilon_{wx} = \left(\frac{dy}{dw}\frac{w}{y}\right)\left(\frac{dw}{dx}\frac{x}{w}\right) = \frac{dy}{dw}\frac{dw}{dx}\frac{w}{y}\frac{x}{w} = \frac{dy}{dx}\frac{x}{y} = \varepsilon_{yx}$$

EXERCISE 10.7

1   Find the instantaneous rate of growth:

(a) $y = 3t^2$ (c) $y = ab^t$ (e) $y = t/3^t$
(b) $y = at^c$ (d) $y = 2^t(t^2)$

2   Prove that if $y = u/v$, where $u = f(t)$ and $v = g(t)$, then the rate of growth of y will be $r_y = r_u - r_v$.

3   Prove the rate-of-growth formula for $r_{(u-v)}$.

4   (a) Given $y = wz$, where $w = g(x)$ and $z = h(x)$, establish that

$$\varepsilon_{yx} = \varepsilon_{wx} + \varepsilon_{zx}$$

(b) Given $y = u/v$, where $u = G(x)$ and $v = H(x)$, establish that

$$\varepsilon_{yx} = \varepsilon_{ux} - \varepsilon_{vx}$$

(*Hint:* Take natural log.)

5   Given $y = f(x)$, show that $d(\log_b y)/d(\log_b x)$—log to base b rather than e— also measures the point elasticity ε_{yx}.

6   (a) Show that, if the demand for money M_d is a function of the national income $Y = Y(t)$ and the interest rate $i = i(t)$, then the rate of growth of M_d can be expressed as

$$r_{M_d} = \varepsilon_{M_d Y}\, r_Y + \varepsilon_{M_d i}\, r_i$$

(b) Suppose that the rate of growth of money supply is r_{M_s}. How do we express the rate of growth of E, the excess demand for money, in terms of r_Y, r_i, and r_{M_s}?

7   Given the production function $Q = F(K,L)$, find a general expression for the rate of growth of Q in terms of the rates of growth of K and L.

11

THE CASE OF MORE
THAN ONE CHOICE VARIABLE

The problem of optimization was discussed in Chap. 9 within the framework of an objective function with a single choice variable. In the last chapter, the discussion was extended to exponential objective functions, but we still dealt with one choice variable only. Now we must develop a way of finding the extreme values of an objective function that involves two or more choice variables. Only then will we be able to tackle the type of problem confronting, say, a multi-product firm, where the profit-maximizing decision consists of the choice of optimal output levels for several commodities and the optimal combination of several different inputs.

We shall discuss first the case of an objective function of two choice variables, $z = f(x,y)$, in order to take advantage of its graphability. Later the analytical results can be generalized to the nongraphable n-variable case. Regardless of the number of variables, however, we shall assume throughout that, when written in a general form, our objective function possesses finite, continuous partial derivatives to any desired order. This will assure the smoothness and differentiability of the objective function as well as its partial derivatives.

For functions of several variables, extreme values are again of two kinds, absolute (global) or relative (local); as before, we shall confine our attention mainly to the search for relative extrema. For this reason, we shall again drop the adjective *relative*, with the understanding that any reference to extreme values will, unless otherwise specified, be to relative ones.

11.1 Second-Order Partial Derivatives and Total Differentials

In finding the extrema of functions of one variable, the criterion used hinges primarily on the signs of the first and second derivatives. When a larger number of choice variables is present, the algebraic signs of derivatives will again play a dominant role in the locating of extreme values. But the nature of the context will now dictate that we use *partial* derivatives instead. As we saw in Chap. 7, partial derivatives are measures of rates of change. Being themselves functions of the independent variables of the primitive function, they are capable of yielding, through repeated differentiation, partial derivatives of various higher orders. The second-order (or second) partial derivatives will prove of special importance in the subsequent discussion.

second-order partial derivatives   The function $z = f(x,y)$ can give rise to *two* first-order partial derivatives,

$$f_x \equiv \frac{\partial z}{\partial x} \quad \text{and} \quad f_y \equiv \frac{\partial z}{\partial y}$$

Since f_x is itself a function of x (as well as of y), we can measure the rate of change of f_x with respect to x, while y remains fixed, by a particular second partial derivative denoted either by f_{xx} or by $\partial^2 z/\partial x^2$:

$$f_{xx} \equiv \frac{\partial}{\partial x}(f_x) \quad \text{or} \quad \frac{\partial^2 z}{\partial x^2} \equiv \frac{\partial}{\partial x}\left(\frac{\partial z}{\partial x}\right)$$

The notation f_{xx} has a double subscript signifying that the primitive function f has been differentiated partially with respect to x twice, whereas the notation $\partial^2 z/\partial x^2$ resembles that of $d^2 z/dx^2$ except for the use of the partial symbol. In a perfectly analogous manner, we can use the second partial derivative

$$f_{yy} \equiv \frac{\partial}{\partial y}(f_y) \quad \text{or} \quad \frac{\partial^2 z}{\partial y^2} = \frac{\partial}{\partial y}\left(\frac{\partial z}{\partial y}\right)$$

to denote the rate of change of f_y with respect to y, while x is held constant.

Recall, however, that f_x is also a function of y and that f_y is also a function of x. Hence, there can be written two more second partial derivatives:

$$f_{xy} \equiv \frac{\partial^2 z}{\partial x\, \partial y} \equiv \frac{\partial}{\partial x}\left(\frac{\partial z}{\partial y}\right) \quad \text{and} \quad f_{yx} \equiv \frac{\partial^2 z}{\partial y\, \partial x} \equiv \frac{\partial}{\partial y}\left(\frac{\partial z}{\partial x}\right)$$

These are called *cross* (or *mixed*) *partial derivatives* because each measures the rate of change of one first-order partial derivative with respect to the "other" variable.

It bears repeating that the second-order partial derivatives of $z = f(x,y)$, like z and the first derivatives f_x and f_y, are also functions of the variables x and y. When that fact requires emphasis, we can write f_{xx} as $f_{xx}(x,y)$, and f_{xy} as $f_{xy}(x,y)$, etc. And, along the same line, we can use the notation $f_{yx}(1,2)$ to denote the value of f_{yx} evaluated at $x = 1$ and $y = 2$, etc.

Even though f_{xy} and f_{yx} have been separately defined, they will—according to a proposition known as *Young's theorem*—be identical with each other as long as the two cross partial derivatives are both continuous. In that case, the sequential order in which partial differentiation is undertaken becomes immaterial, because $f_{xy} = f_{yx}$. For the ordinary types of *specific* functions with which we work, this continuity condition is usually met; for *general* functions, as mentioned earlier, we always assume the continuity condition to hold. Hence, we may in general expect to find identical cross partial derivatives. In fact, the theorem applies also to functions of three or more variables. Given $z = g(u,v,w)$, for instance, the mixed partial derivatives will be characterized by $g_{uv} = g_{vu}$, $g_{vw} = g_{wv}$, etc., provided that the continuity condition is fulfilled.

Example 1   Find the four second-order partial derivatives of

$$z = x^3 + 5xy - y^2$$

The first partial derivatives of this function are

$$f_x = 3x^2 + 5y \qquad \text{and} \qquad f_y = 5x - 2y$$

Therefore, upon further differentiation, we get

$$f_{xx} = 6x \qquad f_{yx} = 5 \qquad f_{xy} = 5 \qquad f_{yy} = -2$$

As expected, f_{yx} and f_{xy} are identical.

Example 2   Find all the second partial derivatives of $z = x^2 e^{-y}$. In this case, the first partial derivatives are

$$f_x = 2xe^{-y} \qquad \text{and} \qquad f_y = -x^2 e^{-y}$$

Thus we have

$$f_{xx} = 2e^{-y} \qquad f_{yx} = -2xe^{-y} \qquad f_{xy} = -2xe^{-y} \qquad f_{yy} = x^2 e^{-y}$$

Again, we see that $f_{yx} = f_{xy}$.

Note that the second partial derivatives are all functions of the original variables x and y. This fact is clear enough in Example 2, but it is true even for Example 1, although some second partial derivatives happen to be *constant* functions in that case.

second-order total differential   The concept of partial derivatives enables us to write the total differential of a function. In Sec. 8.2, we learned that, for a function $z = f(x,y)$, the total differential can be written as

(11.1) $$dz \text{ (or } df) = f_x \, dx + f_y \, dy$$

This equation, constructed from first-order partial derivatives, gives us the value of dz (change in z) for given values of dx and dy, which are changes measured from some specific point (x_0,y_0) in the domain.

Now, with the second-order partial derivatives at our command, we can also give expression to a *second-order total differential*, $d^2z \equiv d(dz)$, as a measure of the change in dz itself. The symbol $d(dz)$ makes it clear that dz itself is to undergo differentiation. But before that can be done, we must first know the following: Of what variables is dz a function? To answer this question, we first recall that, in the equation $dz = f_x \, dx + f_y \, dy$, the symbols dx and dy represent *given* or *arbitrary* variations of the variables x and y, and they must, therefore, be treated as *constants* during differentiation. It follows then that dz varies with f_x and f_y, and, since f_x and f_y are functions of x and y, we must consider dz to be a function of x and y, just as z is.

With this in mind, we can apply the definition of differential—as illustrated in (11.1)—directly to dz, in order to get d^2z (or d^2f) as follows:

(11.2) $$d^2z \equiv d(dz) = \frac{\partial(dz)}{\partial x} \, dx + \frac{\partial(dz)}{\partial y} \, dy \qquad [\text{cf. (11.1)}]$$

$$= \frac{\partial}{\partial x} (f_x \, dx + f_y \, dy) \, dx + \frac{\partial}{\partial y} (f_x \, dx + f_y \, dy) \, dy$$

$$= (f_{xx} \, dx + f_{xy} \, dy) \, dx + (f_{yx} \, dx + f_{yy} \, dy) \, dy$$

$$- f_{xx} \, dx^2 + f_{xy} \, dy \, dx + f_{yx} \, dx \, dy + f_{yy} \, dy^2$$

$$= f_{xx} \, dx^2 + 2f_{xy} \, dx \, dy + f_{yy} \, dy^2 \qquad [f_{xy} = f_{yx}]$$

Note that the exponent 2 appears in (11.2) in two different ways. In the symbol d^2z, the exponent (to d) indicates the *second-order* total differential of z; but in the symbol $dx^2 \equiv (dx)^2$, the exponent denotes the *squaring* of the first-order differential dx.

The result in (11.2) shows the magnitude of d^2z (the change in dz) in terms of given values of dx and dy, measured from some point (x_0,y_0) in the domain. In order to calculate d^2z, however, we also need to know the second-order partial derivatives f_{xx}, f_{xy}, and f_{yy}, all evaluated at (x_0,y_0)—just as we need the first-order partial derivatives to calculate dz from (11.1).

Example 3   Given $z = x^3 + 5xy - y^2$, find dz and d^2z. This function is the same one which appeared in Example 1, so that, substituting the various derivatives already obtained there into (11.1) and (11.2), we find

$$dz = (3x^2 + 5y) \, dx + (5x - 2y) \, dy$$

and $\quad d^2z = 6x \, dx^2 + 10dx \, dy - 2dy^2$

An alternative way of reaching these results is by direct differentiation of the function:

$$\begin{aligned} dz &= d(x^3) + d(5xy) - d(y^2) \\ &= 3x^2 \, dx + 5y \, dx + 5x \, dy - 2y \, dy \end{aligned}$$

Further differentiation of dz (bearing in mind that dx and dy are constants) will then yield

$$\begin{aligned} d^2z &= d(3x^2) \, dx + d(5y) \, dx + d(5x) \, dy - d(2y) \, dy \\ &= (6x \, dx) \, dx + (5dy) \, dx + (5dx) \, dy - (2dy) \, dy \\ &= 6x \, dx^2 + 10dx \, dy - 2dy^2 \end{aligned}$$

At the point $x = 1$ and $y = 2$, for instance, we have

$$dz = 13dx + dy \quad \text{and} \quad d^2z = 6dx^2 + 10dx \, dy - 2dy^2$$

And for given dx and dy from the point $x = 1$ and $y = 2$ in the domain, the sign of dz tells the direction of change of z, whereas the sign of d^2z reveals whether dz is increasing ($d^2z > 0$) or decreasing ($d^2z < 0$).

EXERCISE 11.1

1   Find the four second-order partial derivatives of each of the following:

(a) $f(x,y) = x^3 + y^3 - 3xy$ (c) $f(x,y) = 2^x e^y$
(b) $f(x,y) = x^2 y + xy^2$ (d) $f(x,y) = 7x \ln (1 + y)$

2   Find the first-order and second-order total differentials, df and d^2f, of the four functions in the preceding problem.

3   Given the production function $Q = f(K,L) = K^\alpha L^\beta$, where α and β are positive fractions, find the four second-order partial derivatives, determine their signs, and interpret the results economically.

4   On the basis of a production function $Q = f(K,L)$, write out an expression for dQ and for d^2Q. For given values of input changes, dK and dL, what will determine the change in output, dQ? What will determine the change in dQ itself?

Optimization Problems

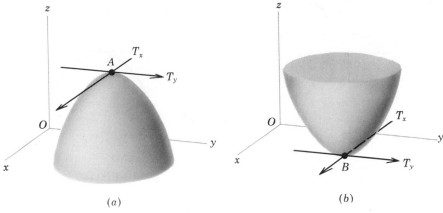

(a)   (b)

FIGURE 11.1

11.2   Extreme Values of a Function of Two Variables

In the case of a function of one independent variable, an extreme value is represented graphically by the peak of a hill or the bottom of a valley in a two-dimensional graph. With *two* independent variables, the graph of the function—$z = f(x,y)$—becomes a surface in a 3-space, and even though the extreme values are still to be associated with peaks and bottoms, these "hills" and "valleys" themselves now take on a three-dimensional character. The two diagrams in Fig. 11.1 will serve to illustrate. Point A in diagram a, for instance, constitutes a maximum, because the value of z at this point is larger than at any other point in its immediate neighborhood. Similarly, point B in diagram b represents a minimum, because everywhere in its immediate neighborhood the value of the function exceeds that at point B.

first-order condition   Being the peak of a hill and the bottom of a valley, respectively, points A and B are characterized by the fact that a tangent line T_x drawn through such a point parallel to the xz plane and a tangent line T_y drawn parallel to the yz plane will both have zero slopes. In other words, T_x will be parallel to the x axis, and T_y parallel to the y axis. This may be seen from two cross-section views of the hill of Fig. 11.1a, as illustrated in Fig. 11.2. The curve in Fig. 11.2a shows the subset of the surface resulting when the hill is cut from point A by a plane parallel to the xz plane, whereas diagram b is what results from cutting the hill at point A by a plane parallel to the yz plane. The tangent lines T_x and T_y are perfectly flat. A cross-section examination of the valley in Fig. 11.1b will yield similar results, of course, but with U-shaped cross-section curves.

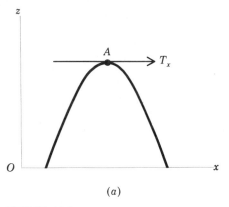

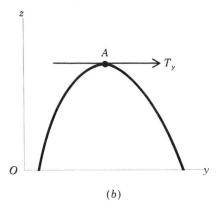

(a)   (b)

FIGURE 11.2

The fact that T_x is drawn parallel to the xz plane implies that we are holding fixed the value of y, and the fact that T_x has zero slope means that $\partial z/\partial x = 0$ at the point in question. Similarly, the zero slope of T_y implies $\partial z/\partial y = 0$. Hence, in terms of partial derivatives, we have at points A and B:

$$f_x = f_y = 0 \qquad \left[\text{or } \frac{\partial z}{\partial x} = \frac{\partial z}{\partial y} = 0\right]$$

Intuitively, it is quite evident that, unless both f_x and f_y are equal to zero simultaneously at a given point on the surface, that point cannot qualify as a peak or a bottom point. Consequently, $f_x = f_y = 0$ constitutes the *necessary condition* for an extremum in the value of z.

From the viewpoint of total differentials, we can state that, for z to attain an extreme value at a point on the surface, it is necessary that momentarily z be neither rising nor falling at that point. That is to say, in the instantaneous sense, z must be in a stationary position, so that $dz = 0$. Since

$$dz = f_x\, dx + f_y\, dy$$

and since dx and dy (representing arbitrary variations in x and y) are not necessarily both zero, the only way to assure a zero dz under *all* circumstances is to have f_x and f_y equal to zero simultaneously. It is clear, therefore, that $dz = 0$ and $f_x = f_y = 0$ are equivalent conditions.[1]

The condition just stated is referred to as the *first-order condition* for extremum, because only the first-order differential or the first-order partial

---

[1] The reader should note that, even though not explicitly brought into the discussion of the optimization of a function of a single variable $y = f(x)$, the zero-differential condition is also applicable in that case. However, in the single-variable context, only one derivative will be involved: To have the differential $dy = f'(x)\, dx$ vanish for any arbitrary variation dx, it is necessary that $f'(x) = 0$.

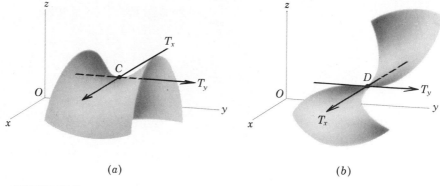

(a)   (b)

FIGURE 11.3

derivatives are involved. As before, the first-order condition is *necessary* but *not sufficient*. That it is not sufficient to establish an extremum can be seen from the two diagrams in Fig. 11.3. At point C in diagram a, both T_x and T_y have zero slopes, but this point does not qualify as an extremum: Whereas it is a *minimum* when viewed against the background of the yz plane, it turns out to be a *maximum* when looked at against the xz plane! A point with such a "dual personality" is referred to, for graphical reasons, as a *saddle point*. Similarly, point D in Fig. 11.3b, while characterized by flat T_x and T_y, is no extremum either; its location on the twisted surface makes it an *inflection point*, whether viewed against the xz or the yz plane. These counterexamples decidedly rule out the first-order condition as a sufficient condition for an extremum.

To develop a sufficient condition, we must look to second-order partial derivatives or to the second-order total differential.

second-order condition   In the case of a function of one variable $y = \phi(x)$, if we have a stationary value $\phi(x_0)$—which satisfies the *necessary* condition $\phi'(x_0) = 0$—the second-order condition $\phi''(x_0) < 0$ will be *sufficient* to establish that value as a maximum. Similarly, the condition $\phi''(x_0) > 0$ will be sufficient to establish a minimum. One might be tempted to generalize from this that, given $z = f(x,y)$, the corresponding sufficient condition to establish a stationary value $f(x_0,y_0)$ as an extremum is for the second partial derivative values $f_{xx}(x_0,y_0)$ and $f_{yy}(x_0,y_0)$ to be negative (for a maximum) and positive (for a minimum). In fact, the two diagrams in Fig. 11.1 seemingly would bear out this generalization. But the generalization happens to be invalid.

The second partial derivatives f_{xx} and f_{yy} are concerned only with the shape of the surface in the two basic directions relating to T_x (north-south) and T_y (east-west). If f_{xx} and f_{yy} are negative at point A, for instance, then the two

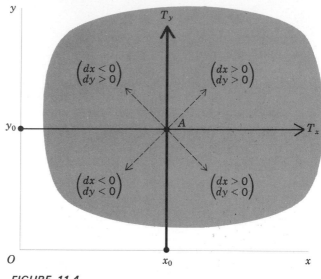

FIGURE 11.4

particular cross sections shown in Fig. 11.2 will be inverse U-shaped. By no means, however, is the possibility ruled out that another cross section of the surface at A, say, in the northeast-southwest direction, may be U-shaped, so that the surface "curls up" from point A in the said direction. This would obviously disqualify A as a maximum point. To eliminate this sort of "misbehavior" in the *other* directions, we must take into account the cross partial derivative f_{xy} alongside f_{xx} and f_{yy}.

To see how f_{xy} will actually enter into the picture, let us first discuss the second-order condition in terms of the second-order total differential d^2z and then translate the result into terms of second partial derivatives. In Fig. 11.4, we depict a bird's-eye view of some surface. The point A on the surface, which lies directly above the point (x_0, y_0) in the domain, is assumed to satisfy the condition $f_x(x_0, y_0) = f_y(x_0, y_0) = 0$, so that, at point A, we have

$$(11.3) \qquad dz(x_0, y_0) = f_x(x_0, y_0)\, dx + f_y(x_0, y_0)\, dy = 0$$

Therefore, point A is a prospective candidate for an extremum. Whether or not it really qualifies will depend on the surface configuration in the neighborhood of point A. Two special cases are of interest to us. The first is the situation wherein a movement on the surface from point A in *any* direction—not necessarily those of the tangents T_x and T_y—invariably results in a decrease in z. This condition will establish the surface to be a hill such as in Fig. 11.1a and will establish A as its peak. However, to have a decrease in z in every direction from A is tantamount to having $dz < 0$ for any values of dx and dy, not both zero.

Since it was earlier established that, at A, we have $dz(x_0, y_0) = 0$, the requirement of a negative dz away from A means that dz must be decreasing from an initial level of zero. In other words, the requirement entails that $d(dz) \equiv d^2z < 0$. Thus, when the first-order condition $dz = 0$ is satisfied at point A, the condition $d^2z < 0$ at A for any values of dx and dy (not both zero), is sufficient to establish the point as a peak and $f(x_0, y_0)$ as a maximum value of the function $z = f(x, y)$.

The second case is the opposite one of having a positive d^2z for *any* values of dx and dy, not both zero. Since $dz = 0$ at point A, the condition $d^2z > 0$ means that the surface will curl up from A in every possible direction towards you, as you look at Fig. 11.4, thereby establishing A as the bottom of a valley, as illustrated in Fig. 11.1b. When the necessary condition $dz = 0$ is already satisfied, therefore, the condition that $d^2z > 0$ for any values of dx and dy (not both zero) is a sufficient condition for a minimum of z.

Referring back to (11.2), we see that, for given values of dx and dy, the sign of d^2z hinges on f_{xx}, f_{yy}, and f_{xy}. So the sufficient condition regarding d^2z should be translatable into a condition regarding the signs of the second-order partial derivatives of the function. The actual translation will require a knowledge of quadratic forms, which will be discussed in the next section, but the result may be stated here first: For any values of dx and dy, not both zero,

$$d^2z \begin{cases} < 0 & \text{iff } f_{xx} < 0;\, f_{yy} < 0;\, \text{and } f_{xx}f_{yy} > f_{xy}^{\,2} \\ > 0 & \text{iff } f_{xx} > 0;\, f_{yy} > 0;\, \text{and } f_{xx}f_{yy} > f_{xy}^{\,2} \end{cases}$$

The reader will note that f_{xy} does enter explicitly into this condition. On the basis of this result, we can state the conditions for extremum in terms of second partial derivatives as in Table 11.1. It should be understood that all the second partial derivatives are to be evaluated at the stationary point where $f_x = f_y = 0$. It should also be stressed that the second-order condition, although *sufficient*, is *not necessary* for an extremum. In particular, if a stationary value is characterized by $f_{xx}f_{yy} = f_{xy}^{\,2}$ in violation of the second-order condition, that value may nevertheless turn out to be an extremum. But this is something that

TABLE 11.1

Conditions for extremum: z = f(x,y)

Condition	Maximum	Minimum
First-order	$f_x = f_y = 0$	$f_x = f_y = 0$
Second-order	$f_{xx}, f_{yy} < 0$ and $f_{xx}f_{yy} > f_{xy}^{\,2}$	$f_{xx}, f_{yy} > 0$ and $f_{xx}f_{yy} > f_{xy}^{\,2}$

requires further investigation, and we shall not attempt to pursue this matter here, because of its extreme complexity. On the other hand, if, as another type of violation, a stationary value is characterized by $f_{xx}f_{yy} < f_{xy}^2$, then we may conclusively identify it as a saddle point, because the sign of d^2z will be indefinite in that case. In view of this uncertainty, this test is only an incomplete test.

Example 1   Find the extreme value(s) of $z = 8x^3 + 2xy - 3x^2 + y^2 + 1$. First let us find all the first and second partial derivatives:

$$f_x = 24x^2 + 2y - 6x \qquad f_y = 2x + 2y$$
$$f_{xx} = 48x - 6 \qquad f_{yy} = 2 \qquad f_{xy} = 2$$

The first-order condition calls for satisfaction of the simultaneous equations $f_x = 0$ and $f_y = 0$; that is,

$$24x^2 + 2y - 6x = 0$$
$$2y + 2x = 0$$

The second equation implies that $y = -x$, and when this information is substituted into the first equation, we get $24x^2 - 8x = 0$, which yields the pair of solutions

$$\bar{x}_1 = 0 \qquad [\text{implying } \bar{y}_1 = -\bar{x}_1 = 0]$$
$$\bar{x}_2 = \tfrac{1}{3} \qquad [\text{implying } \bar{y}_2 = -\tfrac{1}{3}]$$

To apply the second-order condition, we note that, when

$$\bar{x}_1 = \bar{y}_1 = 0$$

f_{xx} turns out to be -6, while f_{yy} is 2, so that $f_{xx}f_{yy}$ is negative and is necessarily less than a squared value f_{xy}^2. This fails the second-order condition. The fact that f_{xx} and f_{yy} have opposite signs suggests, of course, that the surface in question will curl upward in one direction but downward in another, thereby giving rise to a saddle point.

What about the other solution? When evaluated at $\bar{x}_2 = \tfrac{1}{3}$, we find that $f_{xx} = 10$, which, together with the fact that $f_{yy} = f_{xy} = 2$, meets all three parts of the second-order condition for a minimum. Therefore, by setting $x = \tfrac{1}{3}$ and $y = -\tfrac{1}{3}$ in the given function, we can obtain as a minimum of z the value $\bar{z} = \tfrac{23}{27}$. In the present example, there thus exists only one relative extremum (a minimum), which can be represented by the ordered triple

$$(\bar{x}, \bar{y}, \bar{z}) = \left(\frac{1}{3}, \frac{-1}{3}, \frac{23}{27} \right)$$

Example 2   Find the extreme value(s) of $z = x + 2ey - e^x - e^{2y}$. The relevant derivatives of this function are

$$f_x = 1 - e^x \qquad f_y = 2e - 2e^{2y}$$
$$f_{xx} = -e^x \qquad f_{yy} = -4e^{2y} \qquad f_{xy} = 0$$

To satisfy the necessary condition, we must have

$$1 - e^x = 0$$
$$2e - 2e^{2y} = 0$$

which has only one solution, namely, $\bar{x} = 0$ and $\bar{y} = \frac{1}{2}$. To ascertain the status of the value of z corresponding to this solution (the stationary value), we evaluate the second-order derivatives at $x = 0$ and $y = \frac{1}{2}$, and find that $f_{xx} = -1$, $f_{yy} = -4e$, and $f_{xy} = 0$. Since f_{xx} and f_{yy} are both negative and since, in addition, $(-1)(-4e) > 0$, we may conclude that the z value in question, namely,

$$\bar{z} = 0 + e - e^0 - e^1 = -1$$

is a maximum value of the function. This maximum point on the given surface can be denoted by the ordered triple $(\bar{x}, \bar{y}, \bar{z}) = (0, \frac{1}{2}, -1)$.

Again, the reader should note that, to evaluate the second partial derivatives at $\bar{x}$ and $\bar{y}$, differentiation must be undertaken first, and then the specific values of $\bar{x}$ and $\bar{y}$ are to be substituted into the derivatives as the final step.

EXERCISE 11.2

Find the extreme value(s) of each of the following functions, and determine whether they are maxima or minima:

1    $z = x^2 + xy + 2y^2 + 3$

2    $z = -x^2 + xy - y^2 + 2x + y$

3    $z = ax^2 + by^2 + c$; consider each of the three subcases:

    (a) $a > 0, b > 0$ (c) a and b opposite in sign
    (b) $a < 0, b < 0$

4    $z = e^{2x} - 2x + 2y^2 + 3$

11.3   Quadratic Forms—An Excursion

The expression for d^2z on the last line of (11.2) exemplifies what are known as *quadratic forms*, for which there exist established criteria for determining whether their signs are always positive or negative. Since the second-order condition for extremum bears directly on the question of whether d^2z is always positive or negative, those criteria are of direct interest.

To begin with, we define a *form* as a polynomial expression in which each component term has a uniform degree. Our earlier encounter with polynomials was confined to the case of a single variable: $a_0 + a_1x + \cdots + a_nx^n$. When more variables are involved, each term of a polynomial may contain either one variable or several variables, each raised to a nonnegative integer power, such as $3x + 4x^2y^3 - 2yz$. In the special case where each term has a uniform degree— i.e., where the sum of exponents in each term is uniform—the polynomial is called a *form*. For example, $4x - 9y + z$ is a *linear form* in three variables, because each of its terms is of the first degree. On the other hand, the polynomial $4x^2 - xy + 3y^2$, in which each term is of the second degree (sum of integer exponents $= 2$), constitutes a *quadratic form* in two variables. We may also encounter quadratic forms in three variables, such as $x^2 + 2xy - yw + 7w^2$, or indeed in n variables.

second-order total differential as a quadratic form   If we consider the differentials dx and dy in (11.2) as variables and the partial derivatives as coefficients, i.e., if we let

$$(11.4) \quad \begin{array}{ll} u \equiv dx & v \equiv dy \\ a \equiv f_{xx} & b \equiv f_{yy} \quad h \equiv f_{xy}\,[\,=f_{yx}] \end{array}$$

then the second-order total differential of (11.2), namely,

$$d^2z = f_{xx}\,dx^2 + 2f_{xy}\,dx\,dy + f_{yy}\,dy^2$$

can easily be identified as a quadratic form q in the two variables u and v:

$$(11.2') \quad q = au^2 + 2huv + bv^2$$

Note that, in this quadratic form, $dx \equiv u$ and $dy \equiv v$ are cast in the role of variables, whereas the second partial derivatives are treated as constants—the exact opposite of the situation when we were differentiating dz to get d^2z. The reason for this reversal lies in the changed nature of the problem we are now dealing with. The second-order condition for extremum requires d^2z to be definitely positive (for a minimum) and definitely negative (for a maximum), regardless of the values that dx and dy actually take (so long as they are not both zero) and regardless of whether dx and dy represent increases or decreases. It is obvious, therefore, that in the present context dx and dy must be considered as *variables*. The second partial derivatives, on the other hand, will assume specific values at the points we are examining as possible extremum points, and thus may be regarded as *constants*.

The major question becomes, then: What restrictions must be placed upon a, b, and h in (11.2'), when u and v are allowed to take any values, in order to assure a *positive q* or a *negative q*?

positive and negative definiteness   As a matter of terminology, let us remark that a quadratic form q is said to be

$$\left.\begin{array}{l} \textit{positive definite} \\ \textit{positive semidefinite} \\ \textit{negative semidefinite} \\ \textit{negative definite} \end{array}\right\} \text{if } q \text{ is invariably} \left\{\begin{array}{ll} \text{positive} & (> 0) \\ \text{nonnegative} & (\geq 0) \\ \text{nonpositive} & (\leq 0) \\ \text{negative} & (< 0) \end{array}\right.$$

regardless of the values of the variables in the quadratic form, not all zero. If q changes signs when the variables assume different values, on the other hand, q is said to be *indefinite*. What interests us here primarily is the conditions that will make the quadratic form $q = d^2z$ positive definite (for the minimum-value problem) and negative definite (for the maximum-value problem).

For the two-variable case of (11.2'), these conditions are relatively easy to derive. In the first place, we see that the signs of the first and third terms in (11.2') are independent of the values of the variables u and v, because these variables appear in squares. Thus it is easy to specify the condition for the positive or negative definiteness of these terms alone, by restricting the signs of a and b. The trouble spot lies in the middle term. But if we can convert the entire polynomial into an expression such that the variables u and v appear only in some squares, then the definiteness of the sign of q will again become tractable.

The device that will do the trick is that of completing the square. By adding h^2v^2/a to, and subtracting the same quantity from, the right side of (11.2'), we can rewrite the quadratic form as follows:

$$q = au^2 + 2huv + \frac{h^2}{a}v^2 + bv^2 - \frac{h^2}{a}v^2$$

$$= a\left(u^2 + \frac{2h}{a}uv + \frac{h^2}{a^2}v^2\right) + \left(b - \frac{h^2}{a}\right)v^2$$

$$= a\left(u + \frac{h}{a}v\right)^2 + \frac{ab - h^2}{a}(v^2)$$

Now that the variables u and v appear only in squares, we can predicate the sign of q entirely on the values of the coefficients a, b, and h as follows:

(11.5) q is $\begin{Bmatrix}\text{positive definite} \\ \text{negative definite}\end{Bmatrix}$ iff $\begin{Bmatrix}a > 0 \\ a < 0\end{Bmatrix}$ and $ab - h^2 > 0$

Note two things: First, $ab - h^2$ should be *positive* in both cases. Second, as a prerequisite for the positivity of $ab - h^2$, the product ab must be positive (since it must exceed the squared term h^2); hence, the above condition automatically implies that a and b must take the identical algebraic sign.

The condition just derived may be stated more succinctly by the use of determinants. We observe first that the quadratic form in (11.2′) can be rearranged into the following square, symmetric format:

$$q = \quad a(u^2) + h(uv)$$
$$+ \, h(vu) + b(v^2)$$

with the squared terms placed on the diagonal and with the $2huv$ term split into two equal parts and placed off the diagonal. The coefficients will now form a symmetric matrix, with a and b on the principal diagonal and h off the diagonal. Viewed in this light, the quadratic form is also easily seen to be the 1×1 matrix (a scalar) resulting from the following matrix multiplication:

$$q = \begin{bmatrix} u & v \end{bmatrix} \begin{bmatrix} a & h \\ h & b \end{bmatrix} \begin{bmatrix} u \\ v \end{bmatrix}$$

The determinant of the 2×2 coefficient matrix, $\begin{vmatrix} a & h \\ h & b \end{vmatrix}$—which is referred to as the *discriminant* of the quadratic form q, and which we shall therefore denote by $|D|$—supplies the clue to the criterion in (11.5), for the latter can be alternatively expressed as:

(11.5′) q is $\begin{Bmatrix}\text{positive definite} \\ \text{negative definite}\end{Bmatrix}$ iff $\begin{Bmatrix}|a| > 0 \\ |a| < 0\end{Bmatrix}$ and $\begin{vmatrix} a & h \\ h & b \end{vmatrix} > 0$

The determinant $|a| = a$ is a subdeterminant of $|D|$ that consists of the *first* element on the principal diagonal; thus it is called the *first principal minor* of $|D|$. The determinant $\begin{vmatrix} a & h \\ h & b \end{vmatrix}$ can also be considered a subdeterminant of $|D|$; since it involves the *first and second* elements on the principal diagonal, it is called the *second principal minor* of $|D|$. In the present case, there are only two principal minors available, and their signs will serve to determine the positive or negative definiteness of q.

When (11.5′) is translated, via (11.4), into terms of the second-order total differential d^2z, we have

$$d^2z \text{ is } \begin{Bmatrix} \text{positive definite} \\ \text{negative definite} \end{Bmatrix} \text{ iff } \begin{Bmatrix} f_{xx} > 0 \\ f_{xx} < 0 \end{Bmatrix} \text{ and } \begin{vmatrix} f_{xx} & f_{xy} \\ f_{xy} & f_{yy} \end{vmatrix} = f_{xx}f_{yy} - f_{xy}{}^2 > 0$$

Recalling that the last inequality above implies that f_{xx} and f_{yy} are required to take the *same* sign, we see that this is precisely the second-order condition presented in Table 11.1.

In general, the discriminant of a quadratic form

$$q = au^2 + 2huv + bv^2$$

is the symmetric determinant $\begin{vmatrix} a & h \\ h & b \end{vmatrix}$. In the particular case of the quadratic form

$$d^2z = f_{xx}\,dx^2 + 2f_{xy}\,dx\,dy + f_{yy}\,dy^2$$

the discriminant is a determinant with the second-order partial derivatives as its elements. Such a determinant is called a *Hessian determinant* (or simply a *Hessian*). In the two-variable case, the Hessian is

$$|H| = \begin{vmatrix} f_{xx} & f_{xy} \\ f_{yx} & f_{yy} \end{vmatrix}$$

which, in view of Young's theorem ($f_{xy} = f_{yx}$), is symmetric—as a discriminant should be. The reader should carefully distinguish the Hessian determinant from the Jacobian determinant discussed in Sec. 7.6.

Example 1   Is $q = 5u^2 + 3uv + 2v^2$ either positive or negative definite ? The discriminant of q is $\begin{vmatrix} 5 & 1.5 \\ 1.5 & 2 \end{vmatrix}$, with principal minors

$$5 > 0 \qquad \text{and} \qquad \begin{vmatrix} 5 & 1.5 \\ 1.5 & 2 \end{vmatrix} = 7.75 > 0$$

Therefore q is positive definite.

Example 2   Given $f_{xx} = -2$, $f_{xy} = 1$, and $f_{yy} = -1$ at a certain point on a function $z = f(x,y)$, does d^2z have a definite sign at that point regardless of the values of dx and dy ? The discriminant of the quadratic form d^2z is in this case $\begin{vmatrix} -2 & 1 \\ 1 & -1 \end{vmatrix}$, with principal minors

$$-2 < 0 \qquad \text{and} \qquad \begin{vmatrix} -2 & 1 \\ 1 & -1 \end{vmatrix} = 1 > 0$$

Thus d^2z is negative definite.

three-variable quadratic forms   Can similar conditions be obtained for a quadratic form in *three* variables?

A quadratic form with three variables u_1, u_2, and u_3 may be generally represented as

$$
(11.6) \qquad
\begin{aligned}
q(u_1,u_2,u_3) = \; & d_{11}(u_1{}^2) \; + d_{12}(u_1 u_2) + d_{13}(u_1 u_3) \\
+ \; & d_{21}(u_2 u_1) + d_{22}(u_2{}^2) \; + d_{23}(u_2 u_3) \\
+ \; & d_{31}(u_3 u_1) + d_{32}(u_3 u_2) + d_{33}(u_3{}^2) \\
= \; & \sum_{i=1}^{3} \sum_{j=1}^{3} d_{ij} u_i u_j
\end{aligned}
$$

where the double-$\sum$ (double-sum) notation means that both the index i and the index j are allowed to take the values 1, 2, and 3; and thus the double-sum expression is equivalent to the 3×3 array shown above. Such a square array of the quadratic form is, incidentally, always to be considered a symmetric one, even though we have written the pair of coefficients (d_{12}, d_{21}) or (d_{23}, d_{32}) as if the two members of each pair were different. For if the term in the quadratic form involving the variables u_1 and u_2 happens to be, say, $12 u_1 u_2$, we can always let $d_{12} = d_{21} = 6$, so that $d_{12} u_1 u_2 = d_{21} u_2 u_1$, and a similar procedure may be applied to make the other off-diagonal elements symmetrical.

Actually, this three-variable quadratic form is again expressible as a product of three matrices:

$$
(11.6') \qquad
q(u_1,u_2,u_3) =
\begin{bmatrix} u_1 & u_2 & u_3 \end{bmatrix}
\begin{bmatrix}
d_{11} & d_{12} & d_{13} \\
d_{21} & d_{22} & d_{23} \\
d_{31} & d_{32} & d_{33}
\end{bmatrix}
\begin{bmatrix} u_1 \\ u_2 \\ u_3 \end{bmatrix}
\equiv u'Du
$$

As in the two-variable case, the first matrix (a row vector) and the third matrix (a column vector) merely list the variables, and the middle one (D) is a symmetric coefficient matrix from the square-array version of the quadratic form in (11.6). This time, however, a total of *three* principal minors can be formed from its discriminant, namely,

$$
|D_1| \equiv d_{11} \qquad
|D_2| \equiv \begin{vmatrix} d_{11} & d_{12} \\ d_{21} & d_{22} \end{vmatrix} \qquad
|D_3| \equiv \begin{vmatrix} d_{11} & d_{12} & d_{13} \\ d_{21} & d_{22} & d_{23} \\ d_{31} & d_{32} & d_{33} \end{vmatrix}
$$

where $|D_i|$ denotes the ith principal minor of the discriminant $|D|$.† It turns out that the conditions for positive or negative definiteness can again be stated in terms of certain sign restrictions on these principal minors.

By the now-familiar device of completing the square, the quadratic form in (11.6) can be converted into an expression in which the three variables appear

---

† We have so far viewed the *i*th principal minor $|D_i|$ as a subdeterminant formed by retaining the first *i* principal-diagonal elements of $|D|$. Since the notion of a *minor* implies the *deletion* of something from the original determinant, however, the reader may prefer to view the *i*th principal minor alternatively as a subdeterminant formed by deleting the last $(n - i)$ rows and columns of $|D|$.

only as components of some squares. Specifically, recalling that $a_{12} = a_{21}$, etc., we have

$$q = d_{11}\left(u_1 + \frac{d_{12}}{d_{11}}u_2 + \frac{d_{13}}{d_{11}}u_3\right)^2$$

$$+ \frac{d_{11}d_{22} - d_{12}^2}{d_{11}}\left(u_2 + \frac{d_{11}d_{23} - d_{12}d_{13}}{d_{11}d_{22} - d_{12}^2}u_3\right)^2$$

$$+ \frac{d_{11}d_{22}d_{33} - d_{11}d_{23}^2 - d_{22}d_{13}^2 - d_{33}d_{12}^2 + 2d_{12}d_{13}d_{23}}{d_{11}d_{22} - d_{12}^2}(u_3)^2$$

This sum of squares will be positive (negative) for any values of u_1, u_2, and u_3, not all zero, if and only if the coefficients of the three squared expressions are all positive (negative). But the three coefficients (in the order given) can be expressed in terms of the three principal minors as follows:

$$|D_1| \qquad \frac{|D_2|}{|D_1|} \qquad \frac{|D_3|}{|D_2|}$$

Hence, for *positive definiteness*, the necessary-and-sufficient condition is threefold:

$$|D_1| > 0$$
$$|D_2| > 0 \qquad \text{[given that } |D_1| > 0 \text{ already]}$$
$$|D_3| > 0 \qquad \text{[given that } |D_2| > 0 \text{ already]}$$

In other words, the three principal minors must all be positive. For *negative definiteness*, on the other hand, the necessary-and-sufficient condition becomes:

$$|D_1| < 0$$
$$|D_2| > 0 \qquad \text{[given that } |D_1| < 0 \text{ already]}$$
$$|D_3| < 0 \qquad \text{[given that } |D_2| > 0 \text{ already]}$$

That is, the three principal minors must alternate in sign in the specified manner.

Example 3   Determine whether $q = u_1^2 + 6u_2^2 + 3u_3^2 - 2u_1u_2 - 4u_2u_3$ is either positive or negative definite. The discriminant of q is

$$\begin{vmatrix} 1 & -1 & 0 \\ -1 & 6 & -2 \\ 0 & -2 & 3 \end{vmatrix}$$

with principal minors as follows:

$$1 > 0 \qquad \begin{vmatrix} 1 & -1 \\ -1 & 6 \end{vmatrix} = 5 > 0 \qquad \text{and} \qquad \begin{vmatrix} 1 & -1 & 0 \\ -1 & 6 & -2 \\ 0 & -2 & 3 \end{vmatrix} = 11 > 0$$

Therefore, the quadratic form is positive definite.

Example 4   Determine whether $q = 2u^2 + 3v^2 - w^2 + 6uv - 8uw - 2vw$ is either positive or negative definite. The discriminant may be written as

$$\begin{vmatrix} 2 & 3 & -4 \\ 3 & 3 & -1 \\ -4 & -1 & -1 \end{vmatrix},$$ and we find its first principal minor to be $2 > 0$, but the second

principal minor is $\begin{vmatrix} 2 & 3 \\ 3 & 3 \end{vmatrix} = -3 < 0$. This violates the condition for both positive

and negative definiteness; thus q is neither positive nor negative definite.

n-variable quadratic forms   As an extension of the above result to the n-variable case, we shall state without proof that, for the quadratic form

$$q(u_1, u_2, \ldots, u_n) = \sum_{i=1}^{n} \sum_{j=1}^{n} d_{ij} u_i u_j \qquad \text{[where } d_{ij} = d_{ji}]$$
$$= \underset{(1 \times n)}{u'} \underset{(n \times n)}{D} \underset{(n \times 1)}{u} \qquad \text{[cf. (11.6$'$)]}$$

the necessary-and-sufficient condition for *positive definiteness* is that the principal minors of $|D|$, namely,

$$|D_1| \equiv d_{11} \qquad |D_2| \equiv \begin{vmatrix} d_{11} & d_{12} \\ d_{21} & d_{22} \end{vmatrix} \qquad \cdots \qquad |D_n| \equiv \begin{vmatrix} d_{11} & d_{12} & \cdots & d_{1n} \\ d_{21} & d_{22} & \cdots & d_{2n} \\ \multicolumn{4}{c}{\cdots\cdots\cdots\cdots\cdots} \\ d_{n1} & d_{n2} & \cdots & d_{nn} \end{vmatrix}$$

all be positive. The corresponding necessary-and-sufficient condition for *negative definiteness* is that the principal minors alternate in sign as follows:

$$|D_1| < 0 \qquad |D_2| > 0 \qquad |D_3| < 0 \qquad \text{(etc.)}$$

so that all the *odd*-numbered principal minors are negative and all *even*-numbered ones are positive. The nth principal minor, $|D_n| = |D|$, should be positive if n is even, but negative if n is odd.

checking sign-definiteness by characteristic roots   Aside from the above determinantal test for the sign-definiteness of a quadratic form $u'Du$, there is an alternative test that utilizes the concept of the so-called "characteristic roots" of the matrix D.

   This concept arises in a problem of the following nature: Given an $n \times n$ matrix D, can we find a scalar r, and an $n \times 1$ vector $x \neq 0$, such that the matrix equation

(11.7) $Dx = rx$

is satisfied? If so, then the scalar r is referred to as a *characteristic root* of matrix D, and x a *characteristic vector* of that matrix.[1] The equation $Dx = rx$ can be rewritten as $Dx - rIx = 0$, or

(11.7') $\quad (D - rI)x = 0 \qquad$ where 0 is $n \times 1$

This, of course, represents a system of n homogeneous linear equations. Since we want a nontrivial solution for x, the coefficient matrix $(D - rI)$—called the *characteristic matrix* of D—is required to be singular. In other words, its determinant must be made to vanish:

(11.8) $\quad |D - rI| = \begin{vmatrix} d_{11} - r & d_{12} & \cdots & d_{1n} \\ d_{21} & d_{22} - r & \cdots & d_{2n} \\ \hdotsfor{4} \\ d_{n1} & d_{n2} & \cdots & d_{nn} - r \end{vmatrix} = 0$

Equation (11.8) is called the *characteristic equation* of matrix D. Since the determinant $|D - rI|$ will yield, upon Laplace expansion, an nth-degree polynomial in the variable r, (11.8) is in fact an nth-degree polynomial equation. There will thus be a total of n roots, $(r_1, \ldots, r_n)$, each of which qualifies as a characteristic root. If D is symmetric, as is the case in the quadratic-form context, the characteristic roots will always turn out to be real numbers, but they can take either algebraic sign, or be zero. Inasmuch as these values of r will all make the determinant $|D - rI|$ vanish, the substitution of any of these (say, r_i) into the equation system (11.7') will produce a corresponding vector $x|_{r=r_i}$. More accurately, the system being homogeneous, it will yield an infinite number of vectors corresponding to the root r_i. We shall, however, apply a process of *normalization* (to be explained below) and select a particular member of that infinite set as *the* characteristic vector corresponding to r_i; this vector will be denoted by v_i. With a total of n characteristic roots, there should be a total of n such corresponding characteristic vectors.

Example 5 $\quad$ Find the characteristic roots and vectors of the matrix $\begin{bmatrix} 2 & 2 \\ 2 & -1 \end{bmatrix}$.

By substituting the given matrix for D in (11.8), we can get the equation

$\begin{vmatrix} 2 - r & 2 \\ 2 & -1 - r \end{vmatrix} = r^2 - r - 6 = 0$

with roots $r_1 = 3$ and $r_2 = -2$. When the first root is used, the matrix equation (11.7') will take the form of

$\begin{bmatrix} 2 - 3 & 2 \\ 2 & -1 - 3 \end{bmatrix} \begin{bmatrix} x_1 \\ x_2 \end{bmatrix} = \begin{bmatrix} -1 & 2 \\ 2 & -4 \end{bmatrix} \begin{bmatrix} x_1 \\ x_2 \end{bmatrix} = \begin{bmatrix} 0 \\ 0 \end{bmatrix}$

The two rows of the coefficient matrix being linearly dependent, as we would expect in view of (11.8), there is an infinite number of solutions, which can be

---

[1] Characteristic roots are also known by the alternative names of *latent roots*, or *eigenvalues*. Characteristic vectors are also called *eigenvectors*.

expressed by the equation $x_1 = 2x_2$. To force out a unique solution, we *normalize* the solution by imposing the restriction $x_1^2 + x_2^2 = 1$.† Then, since

$$x_1^2 + x_2^2 = (2x_2)^2 + x_2^2 = 5x_2^2 = 1$$

we can obtain (by taking the positive square root) $x_2 = 1/\sqrt{5}$, and also $x_1 = 2x_2 = 2/\sqrt{5}$. Thus the first characteristic vector is

$$v_1 = \begin{bmatrix} 2/\sqrt{5} \\ 1/\sqrt{5} \end{bmatrix}$$

Similarly, by using the second root $r_2 = -2$ in (11.7′), we get the equation

$$\begin{bmatrix} 2 - (-2) & 2 \\ 2 & -1 - (-2) \end{bmatrix} \begin{bmatrix} x_1 \\ x_2 \end{bmatrix} = \begin{bmatrix} 4 & 2 \\ 2 & 1 \end{bmatrix} \begin{bmatrix} x_1 \\ x_2 \end{bmatrix} = \begin{bmatrix} 0 \\ 0 \end{bmatrix}$$

which has the solution $x_1 = -\frac{1}{2}x_2$. Upon normalization, we find

$$x_1^2 + x_2^2 = (-\tfrac{1}{2}x_2)^2 + x_2^2 = \tfrac{5}{4}x_2^2 = 1$$

which yields $x_2 = 2/\sqrt{5}$ and $x_1 = -1/\sqrt{5}$. Thus the second characteristic vector is

$$v_2 = \begin{bmatrix} -1/\sqrt{5} \\ 2/\sqrt{5} \end{bmatrix}$$

The set of characteristic vectors obtained in this manner possesses two important properties: First, the scalar product $v_i'v_i$ $(i = 1,2, \ldots, n)$ must be equal to unity, since

$$v_i'v_i = [x_1 \quad x_2 \quad \cdots \quad x_n] \begin{bmatrix} x_1 \\ x_2 \\ \vdots \\ x_n \end{bmatrix} = \sum_{i=1}^{n} x_i^2 = 1 \qquad \text{[by normalization]}$$

Secondly, the scalar product $v_i'v_j$ (where $i \neq j$) can always be taken to be zero.[1] In sum, therefore, we may write that

---

† More generally, for the *n*-variable case, we require that $\sum\limits_{i=1}^{n} x_i^2 = 1$.

[1] To demonstrate this, we note that, by (11.7), we may write $Dv_j = r_jv_j$, and $Dv_i = r_iv_i$. By premultiplying both sides of each of these equations by an appropriate row vector, we have

$$v_i'Dv_j = v_i'r_jv_j = r_jv_i'v_j \qquad \text{[since } r_j \text{ is a scalar]}$$
$$v_j'Dv_i = v_j'r_iv_i = r_iv_j'v_i = r_iv_i'v_j \qquad \text{[since } v_i'v_j = v_j'v_i]$$

Since $v_i'Dv_j$ and $v_j'Dv_i$ are both 1×1, and since they are transposes of each other (recall that $D' = D$ because D is symmetric), they must represent the same scalar. It follows that the extreme-right expressions in these two equations are equal; hence, by subtracting, we have

$$(r_j - r_i)v_i'v_j = 0$$

Now if $r_j \neq r_i$ (distinct roots), then $v_i'v_j$ has to be zero in order for the equation to hold, and this establishes our claim. If $r_j = r_i$ (repeated roots), moreover, it will always be possible, as it turns out, to find two linearly independent normalized vectors satisfying $v_i'v_j = 0$. Thus, we may state in general that $v_i'v_j = 0$, whenever $i \neq j$.

(11.9) $v_i'v_i = 1$ and $v_i'v_j = 0$ $(i \neq j)$

These properties will prove useful below. As a matter of terminology, when two vectors yield a zero-valued scalar product, the vectors are said to be *orthogonal* (perpendicular) to each other.[1] Hence, each pair of characteristic vectors of matrix D must be orthogonal. The other property, $v_i'v_i = 1$, is indicative of normalization. Together, these two properties account for the fact that the characteristic vectors $(v_1, \ldots, v_n)$ are said to be a set of *orthonormal* vectors. The reader should try to verify the orthonormality of the two characteristic vectors found in Example 5.

Now we are ready to explain how the characteristic roots and characteristic vectors of matrix D can be of service in determining the sign-definiteness of the quadratic form $u'Du$. In essence, the idea is again to transform $u'Du$ (which involves not only squared terms $u_1{}^2, \ldots, u_n{}^2$, but also cross-product terms such as u_1u_2 and u_2u_3) into a form that contains only squared terms. Thus, the approach is similar in intent to the completing-the-square process used in deriving the determinantal test above. However, in the present case, the transformation will have the additional feature that each squared term has as its coefficient one of the characteristic roots, so that the signs of the n roots will provide sufficient information for determining the sign-definiteness of the quadratic form.

The transformation that will do the trick is as follows: Let the characteristic vectors $v_1, \ldots, v_n$ constitute the columns of a matrix T:

$$\underset{(n \times n)}{T} = [v_1 \quad v_2 \quad \cdots \quad v_n]$$

and then apply the transformation $\underset{(n \times 1)}{u} = \underset{(n \times n)}{T} \underset{(n \times 1)}{y}$ to the quadratic form $u'Du$:

$$u'Du = (Ty)'D(Ty) = y'T'DTy \quad \text{[by (4.11)]}$$
$$= y'Ry \quad \text{where} \quad R \equiv T'DT$$

As a result, the original quadratic form in the variables u_i is now turned into another quadratic form in the variables y_i. Since the u_i variables and the y_i variables take the same range of values, the transformation does not affect the sign-definiteness of the quadratic form. Thus we may now just as well consider the sign of the quadratic form $y'Ry$ instead. What makes this latter quadratic form intriguing is that the matrix R will turn out to be a diagonal one, with the roots $r_1, \ldots, r_n$ of matrix D displayed along its diagonal, and with zeros everywhere else, so that we have in fact

---

[1] As a simple illustration of this, think of the two unit vectors of a 2-space, $e_1 = \begin{bmatrix} 1 \\ 0 \end{bmatrix}$ and $e_2 = \begin{bmatrix} 0 \\ 1 \end{bmatrix}$. These vectors lie, respectively, on the two axes, and are thus perpendicular. At the same time, we do find that $e_1'e_2 = e_2'e_1 = 0$.

$$(11.10) \qquad u'Du = y'Ry = [y_1 \ \ y_2 \ \ \cdots \ \ y_n] \begin{bmatrix} r_1 & 0 & \cdots & 0 \\ 0 & r_2 & \cdots & 0 \\ \multicolumn{4}{c}{\dotfill} \\ 0 & 0 & \cdots & r_n \end{bmatrix} \begin{bmatrix} y_1 \\ y_2 \\ \vdots \\ y_n \end{bmatrix}$$

$$= r_1 y_1^2 + r_2 y_2^2 + \cdots + r_n y_n^2$$

which is an expression involving squared terms only. The transformation $R \equiv T'DT$ provides us, therefore, with a procedure for *diagonalizing* the symmetric matrix D into the special diagonal matrix R.

Example 6   Verify that the matrix $\begin{bmatrix} 2 & 2 \\ 2 & -1 \end{bmatrix}$ given in Example 5 can be diagonalized into the matrix $\begin{bmatrix} r_1 & 0 \\ 0 & r_2 \end{bmatrix} = \begin{bmatrix} 3 & 0 \\ 0 & -2 \end{bmatrix}$. On the basis of the characteristic vectors found in Example 5, the transformation matrix T should be

$$T = [v_1 \ \ v_2] = \begin{bmatrix} 2/\sqrt{5} & -1/\sqrt{5} \\ 1/\sqrt{5} & 2/\sqrt{5} \end{bmatrix}$$

Thus we may write

$$R \equiv T'DT = \begin{bmatrix} \dfrac{2}{\sqrt{5}} & \dfrac{1}{\sqrt{5}} \\ -\dfrac{1}{\sqrt{5}} & \dfrac{2}{\sqrt{5}} \end{bmatrix} \begin{bmatrix} 2 & 2 \\ 2 & -1 \end{bmatrix} \begin{bmatrix} \dfrac{2}{\sqrt{5}} & -\dfrac{1}{\sqrt{5}} \\ \dfrac{1}{\sqrt{5}} & \dfrac{2}{\sqrt{5}} \end{bmatrix} = \begin{bmatrix} 3 & 0 \\ 0 & -2 \end{bmatrix}$$

which duly verifies the diagonalization process.

To prove the diagonalization result in (11.10), let us (partially) write out the matrix R as follows:

$$R \equiv T'DT = \begin{bmatrix} v_1' \\ v_2' \\ \vdots \\ v_n' \end{bmatrix} D [v_1 \ \ v_2 \ \ \cdots \ \ v_n]$$

The reader may easily verify that $D[v_1 \ \ v_2 \ \ \cdots \ \ v_n]$ can be rewritten as $[Dv_1 \ \ Dv_2 \ \ \cdots \ \ Dv_n]$. Besides, by (11.7), we can further rewrite this as $[r_1 v_1 \ \ r_2 v_2 \ \ \cdots \ \ r_n v_n]$. Hence, we see that

$$R = \begin{bmatrix} v_1' \\ v_2' \\ \vdots \\ v_n' \end{bmatrix} [r_1 v_1 \ \ r_2 v_2 \ \ \cdots \ \ r_n v_n] = \begin{bmatrix} r_1 v_1' v_1 & r_2 v_1' v_2 & \cdots & r_n v_1' v_n \\ r_1 v_2' v_1 & r_2 v_2' v_2 & \cdots & r_n v_2' v_n \\ \multicolumn{4}{c}{\dotfill} \\ r_1 v_n' v_1 & r_2 v_n' v_2 & \cdots & r_n v_n' v_n \end{bmatrix}$$

$$= \begin{bmatrix} r_1 & 0 & \cdots & 0 \\ 0 & r_2 & \cdots & 0 \\ \vdots & \vdots & & \vdots \\ 0 & 0 & \cdots & r_n \end{bmatrix} \qquad \text{[by (11.9)]}$$

which is precisely what we intended to show.

In view of the result in (11.10), we may formally state the following test for the sign-definiteness of a quadratic form:

a $q = u'Du$ is positive (negative) definite, if and only if *every* characteristic root of D is positive (negative)

b $q = u'Du$ is positive (negative) semidefinite, if and only if *all* characteristic roots of D are nonnegative (nonpositive), and *at least one* root is zero

c $q = u'Du$ is indefinite, if and only if some of the characteristic roots of D are positive and some are negative

Note that, in applying this test, all we need are the characteristic roots; the characteristic vectors are not required unless we wish to find the transformation matrix T. Note, too, that this test is a complete one—it covers all possible cases that may arise. Unfortunately, however, it also has a serious drawback, namely, when the matrix D is of a high dimension, it may not be easy to solve the polynomial equation (11.8) to find the characteristic roots needed for the test. In such cases, the determinantal test may yet prove to be more serviceable, even though it is not a complete test.

EXERCISE 11.3

1   By direct matrix multiplication, express each matrix product below as a quadratic form:

(a) $\begin{bmatrix} u & v \end{bmatrix} \begin{bmatrix} 4 & 2 \\ 2 & 3 \end{bmatrix} \begin{bmatrix} u \\ v \end{bmatrix}$

(c) $\begin{bmatrix} x & y \end{bmatrix} \begin{bmatrix} 5 & 2 \\ 4 & 0 \end{bmatrix} \begin{bmatrix} x \\ y \end{bmatrix}$

(b) $\begin{bmatrix} u & v \end{bmatrix} \begin{bmatrix} -2 & 3 \\ 1 & -4 \end{bmatrix} \begin{bmatrix} u \\ v \end{bmatrix}$

(d) $\begin{bmatrix} dx & dy \end{bmatrix} \begin{bmatrix} f_{xx} & f_{xy} \\ f_{yx} & f_{yy} \end{bmatrix} \begin{bmatrix} dx \\ dy \end{bmatrix}$

2   In the preceding problem, in (b) and (c), the coefficient matrices are not symmetric with respect to the principal diagonal. Verify that by averaging the off-diagonal elements and thus converting them, respectively, into $\begin{bmatrix} -2 & 2 \\ 2 & -4 \end{bmatrix}$ and $\begin{bmatrix} 5 & 3 \\ 3 & 0 \end{bmatrix}$ we will get the same quadratic forms as before.

3   On the basis of their coefficient matrices (the *symmetric* versions), determine by the determinantal test whether the quadratic forms in Exercise 11.3-1a, b, and c are either positive definite or negative definite.

4   Express each quadratic form below as a matrix product involving a *symmetric* coefficient matrix:

(a) $q = 3u^2 - 4uv + 7v^2$

(b) $q = u^2 + 5uv + 2v^2$

(c) $q = 10uv - u^2 - 31v^2$

(d) $q = 6xy - 2x^2 - 5y^2$

(e) $q = 3u_1{}^2 - 2u_1u_2 + 4u_1u_3 + 5u_2{}^2 + 4u_3{}^2 - 2u_2u_3$

(f) $q = -u^2 + 2uv - 4uw - 4v^2 - 7w^2$

5   From the discriminants obtained from the symmetric coefficient matrices of the preceding problem, ascertain by the determinantal test which of the quadratic forms are positive definite and which are negative definite.

6   Find the characteristic roots of each of the following matrices:

(a) $D = \begin{bmatrix} 4 & 2 \\ 2 & 3 \end{bmatrix}$ (b) $E = \begin{bmatrix} -2 & 2 \\ 2 & -4 \end{bmatrix}$ (c) $F = \begin{bmatrix} 5 & 3 \\ 3 & 0 \end{bmatrix}$

What can you conclude about the signs of the quadratic forms $u'Du$, $u'Eu$ and $u'Fu$? (Check your results against Exercise 11.3-3.)

7   Find the characteristic vectors of the matrix $\begin{bmatrix} 4 & 2 \\ 2 & 1 \end{bmatrix}$.

8   Given a quadratic form $u'Du$, where D is 2×2, the characteristic equation of D can be written as

$$\begin{vmatrix} d_{11} - r & d_{12} \\ d_{21} & d_{22} - r \end{vmatrix} = 0 \qquad (d_{12} = d_{21})$$

Expand the determinant; express the roots of this equation by use of the quadratic formula; and deduce the following:

(a)   No imaginary number (a number involving $\sqrt{-1}$) can occur in r_1 and r_2.

(b)   To have repeated roots, matrix D must be in the form of $\begin{bmatrix} c & 0 \\ 0 & c \end{bmatrix}$.

(c)   To have either positive or negative semidefiniteness, the discriminant of the quadratic form must vanish, that is, $|D| = 0$.

11.4   Objective Functions with More Than Two Variables

When there appear in an objective function $n > 2$ choice variables, it is no longer possible to graph the function, although we can still speak of a *hypersurface* in an $(n + 1)$-dimensional space. On such a (nongraphable) hypersurface, there again may exist $(n + 1)$-dimensional analogs of peaks of hills and bottoms of valleys. How do we identify them?

In the two-variable case, the availability of the visual aid of Fig. 11.1 prompted us to approach the problem of extremum identification first from the point of view of partial derivatives, then by a consideration of the same problem in terms of total differentials. Now that we are familiar with total differentials, we can attack our problem directly by means of the latter concept.

first-order condition for extremum   Let us explicitly consider a function of three choice variables,

$$z = f(x_1, x_2, x_3)$$

with first partial derivatives f_1, f_2, and f_3 and second partial derivatives f_{ij} ($\equiv \partial^2 z / \partial x_i \, \partial x_j$), with $i, j = 1, 2, 3$. By virtue of Young's theorem, we have $f_{ij} = f_{ji}$.

Our understanding of the nature of extreme values indicates that, to have a maximum or a minimum in z, it is necessary that z be instantaneously in a stationary position; that is, $dz = 0$. Since the value of dz is simply the following sum:

(11.11) $$dz = f_1 \, dx_1 + f_2 \, dx_2 + f_3 \, dx_3$$

and since dx_1, dx_2, and dx_3 are arbitrary (infinitesimal) variations in the independent variables x_1, x_2, and x_3, not necessarily zero, the only way to guarantee a zero dz is to have $f_1 = f_2 = f_3 = 0$. Thus, again, the necessary condition for extremum is that all the first-order partial derivatives be zero, the same as for the two-variable case.

As a special case, note that if we happen to be working with a function $z = f(x_1, x_2, x_3)$ implicitly defined by an equation $F(z, x_1, x_2, x_3) = 0$, where

$$f_i \equiv \frac{\partial z}{\partial x_i} = \frac{-\partial F / \partial x_i}{\partial F / \partial z} \qquad (i = 1, 2, 3)$$

then the first-order condition $f_1 = f_2 = f_3 = 0$ will amount to the condition

$$\frac{\partial F}{\partial x_1} = \frac{\partial F}{\partial x_2} = \frac{\partial F}{\partial x_3} = 0$$

since the value of the denominator $\partial F / \partial z \neq 0$ makes no difference.

second-order condition   The satisfaction of the first-order condition will earmark certain values of z as the stationary values of the objective function. If at a stationary value of z we find that $d^2 z$ is positive definite (for any variations dx_i, not all zero), this will suffice to establish that value of z as a minimum.

Analogously, the negative definiteness of d^2z is a sufficient condition for the stationary value to be a maximum. This raises the questions of how to express d^2z when there are three variables in the function and how to determine its positive or negative definiteness.

The expression for d^2z can be obtained by differentiating dz in (11.11). In such a process, as in (11.2), we should treat the derivatives f_i as variables and the differentials dx_i as constants. Thus, we have

$$(11.12) \qquad d^2z = d(dz) = \frac{\partial(dz)}{\partial x_1} dx_1 + \frac{\partial(dz)}{\partial x_2} dx_2 + \frac{\partial(dz)}{\partial x_3} dx_3$$

$$= \frac{\partial}{\partial x_1}(f_1\,dx_1 + f_2\,dx_2 + f_3\,dx_3)\,dx_1$$

$$+ \frac{\partial}{\partial x_2}(f_1\,dx_1 + f_2\,dx_2 + f_3\,dx_3)\,dx_2$$

$$+ \frac{\partial}{\partial x_3}(f_1\,dx_1 + f_2\,dx_2 + f_3\,dx_3)\,dx_3$$

$$= \begin{array}{l} f_{11}\,dx_1{}^2 \quad + f_{12}\,dx_1\,dx_2 + f_{13}\,dx_1\,dx_3 \\ + f_{21}\,dx_2\,dx_1 + f_{22}\,dx_2{}^2 \quad + f_{23}\,dx_2\,dx_3 \\ + f_{31}\,dx_3\,dx_1 + f_{32}\,dx_3\,dx_2 + f_{33}\,dx_3{}^2 \end{array}$$

which is a quadratic form similar to (11.6). Consequently, the criteria for positive and negative definiteness we learned earlier are directly applicable here.

In determining the positive or negative definiteness of d^2z, we must again, as we did in (11.2'), regard dx_i as variables that can take any values (though not all zero), while considering the derivatives f_{ij} as coefficients upon which to impose certain restrictions. The coefficients in (11.12) give rise to the symmetric Hessian determinant

$$|H| = \begin{vmatrix} f_{11} & f_{12} & f_{13} \\ f_{21} & f_{22} & f_{23} \\ f_{31} & f_{32} & f_{33} \end{vmatrix}$$

whose principal minors may be denoted as

$$|H_1| = f_{11} \qquad |H_2| = \begin{vmatrix} f_{11} & f_{12} \\ f_{21} & f_{22} \end{vmatrix} \qquad |H_3| = |H|$$

Thus, on the basis of the determinantal criteria for positive and negative definiteness, we may state the second-order condition for an extremum of z as follows:

$$(11.13) \qquad d^2z \text{ is } \begin{cases} \text{positive definite } (z \text{ minimum}) \\ \text{negative definite } (z \text{ maximum}) \end{cases} \text{ if}$$

$$\begin{cases} |H_1| > 0; \ |H_2| > 0; \ |H_3| > 0 \\ |H_1| < 0; \ |H_2| > 0; \ |H_3| < 0 \end{cases}$$

When the necessary condition $f_1 = f_2 = f_3 = 0$ is already fulfilled, the second-order condition as stated here will constitute the sufficient condition for minimum and maximum of z, respectively.

We may, of course, also apply the characteristic-root test, and associate the positive definiteness (negative definiteness) of d^2z with the positivity (negativity) of all the characteristic roots of the *Hessian matrix* $\begin{bmatrix} f_{11} & f_{12} & f_{13} \\ f_{21} & f_{22} & f_{23} \\ f_{31} & f_{32} & f_{33} \end{bmatrix}$. When computational (as against theoretical) work is involved, as in numerical examples and problems, however, primary reliance is best to be placed on the determinantal test, because of the difficulties that may be encountered in solving for the characteristic roots of 3×3 or higher-dimensional matrices.

Example 1   Find the extreme value(s) of

$$z = 2x_1^2 + x_1 x_2 + 4x_2^2 + x_1 x_3 + x_3^2 + 2$$

The necessary condition for extremum involves the simultaneous satisfaction of the following three equations:

$$
\begin{aligned}
(f_1 =)\quad & 4x_1 + x_2 + x_3 = 0 \\
(f_2 =)\quad & x_1 + 8x_2 = 0 \\
(f_3 =)\quad & x_1 + 2x_3 = 0
\end{aligned}
$$

Being a homogeneous linear-equation system, in which all the three equations are independent (the determinant of the coefficient matrix does not vanish), the system has only the single solution $\bar{x}_1 = \bar{x}_2 = \bar{x}_3 = 0$. This means that there is only one stationary value, $\bar{z} = 2$.

The Hessian determinant of this function is

$$|H| = \begin{vmatrix} f_{11} & f_{12} & f_{13} \\ f_{21} & f_{22} & f_{23} \\ f_{31} & f_{32} & f_{33} \end{vmatrix} = \begin{vmatrix} 4 & 1 & 1 \\ 1 & 8 & 0 \\ 1 & 0 & 2 \end{vmatrix}$$

the principal minors of which are all positive:

$$|H_1| = 4 \qquad |H_2| = 31 \qquad |H_3| = 54$$

Thus we can conclude, by (11.13), that $\bar{z} = 2$ is a minimum.

Example 2   Find the extreme value(s) of

$$z = -x_1^3 + 3x_1 x_3 + 2x_2 - x_2^2 - 3x_3^2$$

The first partial derivatives are found to be

$$f_1 = -3x_1^2 + 3x_3 \qquad f_2 = 2 - 2x_2 \qquad f_3 = 3x_1 - 6x_3$$

By setting all f_i equal to zero, in fulfillment of the necessary condition, we get three simultaneous equations, one nonlinear and two linear:

$$
\begin{aligned}
-3x_1{}^2 \quad\quad + 3x_3 &= 0 \\
-2x_2 \quad\quad &= -2 \\
3x_1 \quad\quad - 6x_3 &= 0
\end{aligned}
$$

Since the second equation gives $\bar{x}_2 = 1$ and the third equation implies $\bar{x}_1 = 2\bar{x}_3$, substitution of these into the first equation yields two solutions:

$$
(\bar{x}_1,\bar{x}_2,\bar{x}_3) = \begin{cases} (0,1,0), \text{ implying } \bar{z} = 1 \\ (\tfrac{1}{2},1,\tfrac{1}{4}), \text{ implying } \bar{z} = \tfrac{17}{16} \end{cases}
$$

The second-order partial derivatives, properly arranged, give us the Hessian

$$
|H| = \begin{vmatrix} -6x_1 & 0 & 3 \\ 0 & -2 & 0 \\ 3 & 0 & -6 \end{vmatrix}
$$

in which the first element $(-6x_1)$ reduces to 0 under the first solution (with $\bar{x}_1 = 0$) and to -3 under the second (with $\bar{x}_1 = \tfrac{1}{2}$). It is immediately obvious that the first solution does not fulfill the second-order condition, since $|H_1| = 0$. Under the second solution, however, we find that

$$
|H_1| = -3 \quad |H_2| = 6 \quad \text{and} \quad |H_3| = -18
$$

which duly alternate in sign. Consequently, according to (11.13), the solution $\bar{z} = \tfrac{17}{16}$ is a maximum.

n-variable case   When there are n choice variables, the objective function may be expressed as

$$
z = f(x_1,x_2, \ldots, x_n)
$$

The total differential will then be

$$
dz = f_1 \, dx_1 + f_2 \, dx_2 + \cdots + f_n \, dx_n
$$

so that the necessary condition for extremum ($dz = 0$) is that all the n first-order partial derivatives be zero.

The second-order differential d^2z will again be a quadratic form, derivable analogously to (11.12) and expressible by an $n \times n$ array. The coefficients of that array, properly arranged, will now give the (symmetric) Hessian

$$
|H| = \begin{vmatrix} f_{11} & f_{12} & \cdots & f_{1n} \\ f_{21} & f_{22} & \cdots & f_{2n} \\ \cdots & \cdots & \cdots & \cdots \\ f_{n1} & f_{n2} & \cdots & f_{nn} \end{vmatrix}
$$

with principal minors $|H_1|$, $|H_2|$, ..., $|H_n|$, as defined before. The second-order condition for extremum is, as before, that all the n principal minors be positive (for a minimum in z) and that they duly alternate in sign (for a maximum in z), the first one being negative.

In summary, then—if we concentrate on the determinantal test—we have the criteria as listed in Table 11.2, which is valid for an objective function of any number of choice variables. As special cases, we can have $n = 1$ or $n = 2$. When $n = 1$, the objective function is $z = f(x)$, and the conditions for maximization, $f_1 = 0$ and $|H_1| < 0$, will reduce to $f'(x) = 0$ and $f''(x) < 0$, exactly as we learned in Sec. 9.4. Similarly, when $n = 2$, the objective function is $z = f(x_1, x_2)$, so that the first-order condition for maximum will be $f_1 = f_2 = 0$, whereas the second-order condition will be

$$f_{11} < 0 \qquad \text{and} \qquad \begin{vmatrix} f_{11} & f_{12} \\ f_{21} & f_{22} \end{vmatrix} = f_{11}f_{22} - f_{12}{}^2 > 0$$

which is merely a restatement of the information presented in Table 11.1.

second-order condition in relation to strict concavity and convexity

The second-order condition—be it stated in terms of the principal minors of the Hessian determinant, or the characteristic roots of the Hessian matrix—is always concerned with the question of whether a stationary point is the peak of a hill, or the bottom of a valley. In other words, it has to do with how a curve, or surface, or hypersurface (as the case may be), bends itself around the stationary

TABLE 11.2

Conditions for extremum: $z = f(x_1, x_2, ..., x_n)$

Condition	Maximum	Minimum
First-order	$f_1 = f_2 = \cdots = f_n = 0$ (or $dz = 0$ for arbitrary dx_i)	$f_1 = f_2 = \cdots = f_n = 0$ (or $dz = 0$ for arbitrary dx_i)
Second-order	$|H_1| < 0;\ |H_2| > 0;$ $|H_3| < 0; \ldots$ (or d^2z negative definite)*	$|H_1|, |H_2|, \ldots, |H_n| > 0$ (or d^2z positive definite)*

* Instead of stating the d^2z is negative (positive) definite, some writers prefer to state that the *Hessian matrix H* (to be distinguished from the Hessian determinant $|H|$) is negative (positive) definite. In this usage, observe that the sign-definiteness of a matrix refers to the sign of the *quadratic form* with which that matrix is associated, but implies nothing at all about the signs of the *elements* of that matrix.

point. In the single-choice-variable case, $y = f(x)$, strict concavity and strict convexity have been found to be of interest, because they are associated, respectively, with inverse U-shaped and U-shaped curves, as illustrated in Fig. 9.5. Such functions are again of interest when the objective function contains two or more choice variables. This is because a function such as $z = f(x_1, \ldots, x_n)$ —assumed here to be twice-differentiable so that second-order partial derivatives, and hence d^2z, are defined—qualifies as a strictly concave (strictly convex) function if and only if d^2z is negative (positive) definite at every point on the function.[1] It follows that a stationary point of a strictly concave (strictly convex) function must be a relative maximum (minimum) by the criteria in Table 11.2. In fact, in such a case, the relative extremum must also be an absolute (or global) extremum, and a unique one at that.[2] We shall later illustrate this by an example. But, first, we must extend the definition of strict concavity and strict convexity from the one-variable case (Sec. 9.3) to a more general context.

For the two-variable case, $z = f(x,y)$, we can give *strict concavity* (*strict convexity*) a geometric characterization as follows: When we pick *any pair* of distinct points M and N on the surface of the f function, and join them into a line segment MN, the latter must lie entirely below (above) the surface, except at points M and N. The case of a strictly concave function is illustrated in Fig. 11.5, where M and N, two arbitrary points, are joined together by a (broken) line segment as well as a (solid) arc, the latter consisting of points on the surface that lie directly above line segment MN. Since strict concavity requires arc MN to lie above line segment MN (except at M and N) for *any* pair of points M and N, the surface must typically be dome-shaped. Analogously, the surface of a strictly convex function must typically be bowl-shaped.[3] The reader will note that the definition, as stated, does not require the dome or the bowl to be everywhere smooth; if, for example, the peak of the dome in Fig. 11.5 is a sharp point, the definition for strict concavity can still be met. In our present context, however, smoothness must be assumed because we need to work with the various derivatives of the function.

To facilitate generalization to the nongraphable n-dimensional case, it is necessary to translate the geometric definition into an equivalent algebraic version. Returning to Fig. 11.5, let $u = (x_1, y_1)$ and $v = (x_2, y_2)$ be any two distinct ordered pairs (2-vectors) in the domain of $z = f(x,y)$. Then the z values (height of surface) corresponding to these will be $f(u) = f(x_1, y_1)$, and $f(v) =$

---

[1] Similarly, a function is concave (convex) if and only if d^2z is *either* negative (positive) definite, *or* negative (positive) semidefinite at every point on the function. Note that *semi*definiteness of d^2z can be associated with concavity or convexity, but *not* with *strict* concavity or convexity.

[2] A relative extremum of a concave or convex function must actually also be an absolute extremum. However, such an absolute extremum may not be unique, i.e., there may exist two or more stationary points with the identical absolute extreme value—unless the function happens to be *strictly* concave or convex.

[3] For a nonstrictly concave (convex) function, line segment *MN* is allowed *either* to lie below (above) the surface, *or* to lie on the surface itself. Graphically, this means that a portion of the surface, or even the entire surface, may be flat rather than curved.

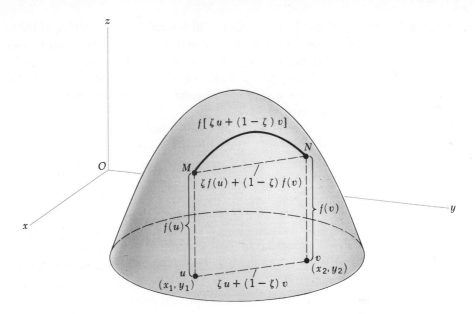

$f[\zeta u + (1 - \zeta)v]$

$\zeta f(u) + (1 - \zeta)f(v)$

N

M

$f(v)$

$f(u)$

v
(x_2, y_2)

u
(x_1, y_1)

$\zeta u + (1 - \zeta)v$

FIGURE 11.5

$f(x_2, y_2)$, respectively. It will be assumed that if u and v are in the domain, then all the points on the line segment uv are also in the domain. Now since each point on the said line segment is in the nature of a "weighted average" of u and v, we can denote this line segment by the expression $\zeta u + (1 - \zeta)v$, where ζ (the Greek letter zeta)—unlike u and v—is a scalar with the range of values $0 \leq \zeta \leq 1$.† By the same token, line segment MN, which can be taken as the set of all weighted averages of $f(u)$ and $f(v)$, can be expressed by $\zeta f(u) + (1 - \zeta)f(v)$, with ζ again varying from 0 to 1. What about the arc MN along the surface? Since that arc shows the values of the function evaluated at the various points on line segment uv, it can be written simply as $f[\zeta u + (1 - \zeta)v]$. Using these expressions, we may state the following algebraic definition: For any pair of distinct points u and v in the domain of the function f, and for all values of ζ in the open interval $(0,1)$,

$$(11.14) \qquad \text{The function } f \text{ is strictly} \begin{Bmatrix} \text{concave} \\ \text{convex} \end{Bmatrix}$$

$$\text{iff} \qquad \underbrace{\zeta f(u) + (1 - \zeta)f(v)}_{\text{height of line segment}} \begin{Bmatrix} < \\ > \end{Bmatrix} \underbrace{f[\zeta u + (1 - \zeta)v]}_{\text{height of arc}}$$

† The weighted-average expression $\zeta u + (1 - \zeta)v$, for any specific value of ζ between 0 and 1, is technically known as a *convex combination* of the (vectors) u and v. Leaving a detailed explanation of this concept to Sec. 18.3, we shall merely note here that, when $\zeta = 0$, the given expression reduces to the vector v and, similarly, when $\zeta = 1$, the expression reduces to the vector u. An intermediate value of ζ, on the other hand, gives us a sort of "average" of the two vectors u and v.

A simple modification of (11.14) can also yield the algebraic definition of (non-strictly) concave or convex functions; but we shall leave this to the reader as an exercise. Note that, in (11.14), we let ζ take the values in the open interval $(0,1)$, thereby excluding $\zeta = 0$ and $\zeta = 1$ from consideration. This is only to be expected, since we want to compare line segment MN with arc MN exclusive of points M and N themselves.

The algebraic definition (11.14) is applicable generally to a function of any number of variables, say, $z = f(x_1, \ldots, x_n)$. Indeed, we can use (11.14) verbatim, as long as we take care to reinterpret u and v as a pair of n-vectors instead of 2-vectors.

Example 3   Let us consider the function $z = f(x,y) = x^2 + y^2$, for which second-order partial derivatives are obviously defined. We shall first show that this function satisfies the definition of strict convexity, and then verify that d^2z is indeed positive definite at every point on the function, as was earlier claimed to be necessarily the case. Lastly, we shall check that the relative minimum of the function is actually also the unique absolute minimum.

Let $u = (x_1, y_1)$ and $v = (x_2, y_2)$ be any two distinct points in the domain. Then the left-side expression in the inequality of (11.14) can be written as

(11.15) $\zeta f(x_1, y_1) + (1 - \zeta)f(x_2, y_2)$
$$= \zeta(x_1^2 + y_1^2) + (1 - \zeta)(x_2^2 + y_2^2)$$
$$= \zeta x_1^2 + (1 - \zeta)x_2^2 + \zeta y_1^2 + (1 - \zeta)y_2^2$$

whereas the right-side expression will appear as

(11.16) $f[\zeta(x_1, y_1) + (1 - \zeta)(x_2, y_2)]$
$$= f[\underbrace{\zeta x_1 + (1 - \zeta)x_2}_{\text{value of } x}, \underbrace{\zeta y_1 + (1 - \zeta)y_2}_{\text{value of } y}]$$
$$= [\zeta x_1 + (1 - \zeta)x_2]^2 + [\zeta y_1 + (1 - \zeta)y_2]^2$$

Subtracting (11.16) from (11.15), and rearranging terms, we find the difference to be

(11.17) $\zeta(1 - \zeta)[(x_1 - x_2)^2 + (y_1 - y_2)^2]$

Since ζ is restricted to be a positive fraction, $\zeta(1 - \zeta)$ must be positive. Moreover, since (x_1, y_1) and (x_2, y_2) are distinct points, we must have either $x_1 \neq x_2$, or $y_1 \neq y_2$, or both, so that the bracketed expression in (11.17) must be positive as well. In other words, (11.17) must be positive, and hence (11.15) must be greater than (11.16). According to (11.14), this establishes the given function to be strictly convex.

Let us now check d^2z, or the second-order condition. The first partial derivatives of the function being $f_x = 2x$ and $f_y = 2y$, the second-order ones are readily found to be $f_{xx} = 2$, $f_{xy} = f_{yx} = 0$, and $f_{yy} = 2$. Thus the Hessian determinant is $\begin{vmatrix} 2 & 0 \\ 0 & 2 \end{vmatrix}$, with $|H_1| = 2$, and $|H_2| = 4$, implying that d^2z is positive definite and that the sufficient condition for minimum is satisfied. Besides, since the positivity of $|H_1|$ and $|H_2|$ is independent of the choice of the x and y values (f_{xx}, f_{xy}, and f_{yy} are all constant functions here), d^2z is positive definite at every point on the function.

Lastly, we note that there exists in this example only one stationary point, namely, $(\bar{x},\bar{y},\bar{z}) = (0,0,0)$. An inspection of the function should also make it clear that $\bar{z} = 0$ is not only a relative minimum, but also the unique absolute minimum, because *any* point in the domain other than $(0,0)$ will make $z = x^2 + y^2$ positive, or greater than $\bar{z}$. As an alternative way of viewing this property, the reader may observe that $z = x^2 + y^2$ happens to be a positive-definite quadratic form, which, by definition, takes positive values only, so long as x and y are not both zero. Consequently, the zero $\bar{z}$ value corresponding to $x = y = 0$ must be a unique absolute (global) minimum.

Because of the above-illustrated relationship between the strict concavity (strict convexity) of a smooth objective function $z = f(x_1, \ldots, x_n)$ and the negative (positive) definiteness of d^2z, any prior knowledge that the function f is strictly concave or convex will make it unnecessary to check the second-order condition. It is to take advantage of this fact that, in general-function optimization models, the objective function is sometimes assumed from the outset to be strictly concave or convex, as the case may call for.[1] Such an assumption will not only obviate the need for checking the second-order condition, but also guarantee the globality and uniqueness of the extremum found. Note, however, that if the context of the problem does not require the globality and uniqueness features—e.g., when we are only interested in knowing whether d^2z has a particular definite sign at a particular stationary point—then the function f only needs to be strictly concave or convex in a neighborhood of the stationary point in question, but not necessarily so over the entire domain of the function.

EXERCISE 11.4

1   Express the quadratic-form expression for d^2z in (11.12) as a product of three matrices.

2   What values of x, y, and w will satisfy the first-order condition for the extremum of a function $z = (x,y,w)$ implicitly defined by the equation $xy - y + 3yw - x^2 - 2y^2 + z^2 - w^2 = 0$?

---

[1] If the objective function is given in a *specific* instead of general form, then its strict concavity or convexity will no longer be something that we may assume, but rather a matter to be checked, either by means of (11.14) or by an equivalent geometric consideration.

3   Find the extreme values, if any, of the following functions (indicate whether maximum or minimum):

(a) $z = x_1{}^2 - 3x_1x_2 + 3x_2{}^2 + 4x_2x_3 + 6x_3{}^2$
(b) $z = 5 - (x_1{}^2 + x_2{}^2 + x_3{}^2)$
(c) $z = x_1{}^2 + x_1x_3 - x_2 + x_2{}^2 + x_2x_3 + 3x_3{}^2$

4   Find the extreme values, if any, of the following functions (indicate whether maximum or minimum):

(a) $z = e^{2x} - e^y + e^{w^2} - 2(x + e^w) + y$
(b) $z = e^{2x} + e^{-y} + e^{w^2} - (2x + 2e^w - y)$

5   Give an algebraic definition of nonstrictly concave and convex functions.

6   Show that if a function $f(x_1, \ldots, x_n)$ is convex, then the function $-f(x_1, \ldots, x_n)$ must be concave. Is it also true that if f is strictly convex, then the function $-f$ must be strictly concave?

7   Check by (11.14) that the following are strictly convex functions:

(a) $z = x^2$ (b) $z = x^2 + 2y^2$ (c) $z = 2x^2 - xy + y^2$

11.5   Economic Examples

At the beginning of this chapter, the case of a multiproduct firm was cited as an illustration of the general problem of optimization with more than one choice variable. We should now be equipped to handle that problem and others of a similar nature.

problem of a multiproduct firm

Example 1   Let us first postulate a two-product firm under circumstances of pure competition. Since with pure competition the prices of both commodities must be taken as exogenous, these will be denoted by P_{10} and P_{20}, respectively. Accordingly, the firm's revenue function will be

$$R = P_{10}Q_1 + P_{20}Q_2$$

where Q_i represents the output level of the ith product per unit of time. The firm's cost function will be assumed to be

$$C = 2Q_1{}^2 + Q_1Q_2 + 2Q_2{}^2$$

Note that $\partial C/\partial Q_1 = 4Q_1 + Q_2$ (the marginal cost of the first product) is a function not only of Q_1 but also of Q_2. Similarly, the marginal cost of the second product will also depend, in part, on the output level of the first product. Thus, according to the assumed cost function, the two commodities are seen to be technically related in production.

The profit function of this hypothetical firm can now be written readily as

$$\pi = R - C = P_{10}Q_1 + P_{20}Q_2 - 2Q_1{}^2 - Q_1Q_2 - 2Q_2{}^2$$

a function of two choice variables (Q_1 and Q_2) and two price parameters. It is our task to find the levels of Q_1 and Q_2 that, in combination, will maximize π. For this purpose, we first find the first-order partial derivatives of the profit function:

(11.18)

$$\pi_1 \left(\equiv \frac{\partial \pi}{\partial Q_1} \right) = P_{10} - 4Q_1 - Q_2$$

$$\pi_2 \left(\equiv \frac{\partial \pi}{\partial Q_2} \right) = P_{20} - Q_1 - 4Q_2$$

Setting these both equal to zero, to satisfy the necessary condition for maximum, we get the two simultaneous equations

$$4Q_1 + Q_2 = P_{10}$$
$$Q_1 + 4Q_2 = P_{20}$$

which yield the solution

$$\bar{Q}_1 = \frac{4P_{10} - P_{20}}{15} \qquad \text{and} \qquad \bar{Q}_2 = \frac{4P_{20} - P_{10}}{15}$$

Thus, if $P_{10} = 12$ and $P_{20} = 18$, for example, we have $\bar{Q}_1 = 2$ and $\bar{Q}_2 = 4$, implying an optimal profit $\bar{\pi} = 48$ per unit of time.

To be sure that this does represent a maximum profit, let us check the second-order condition. The second partial derivatives, obtainable by partial differentiation of (11.18), give us the following Hessian:

$$|H| = \begin{vmatrix} \pi_{11} & \pi_{12} \\ \pi_{21} & \pi_{22} \end{vmatrix} = \begin{vmatrix} -4 & -1 \\ -1 & -4 \end{vmatrix}$$

Since $|H_1| = -4 < 0$ and $|H_2| = 15 > 0$, the above solution does maximize the profit.

Example 2   Let us now transplant the problem of Example 1 into the setting of a monopolistic market. By virtue of this new market-structure assumption, the revenue function must be modified to reflect the fact that the prices of the two products will now vary with their output levels (which are assumed to be identical with their sales levels, no inventory accumulation being contemplated in the model). The exact manner in which prices will vary with output levels is, of course, to be found in the demand functions for the firm's two products.

Suppose that the demands facing the monopolist firm are as follows:

$$(11.19) \qquad \begin{aligned} Q_1 &= 40 - 2P_1 + P_2 \\ Q_2 &= 15 + P_1 - P_2 \end{aligned}$$

These equations reveal that the two commodities are related in *consumption*; specifically, they are substitute goods, because an increase in the price of one will raise the demand for the other. As given, (11.19) expresses the quantities demanded Q_1 and Q_2 as functions of prices, but for our present purposes it will be more convenient to have prices P_1 and P_2 expressed in terms of the sales volumes Q_1 and Q_2, that is, to have average-revenue functions for the two products. The latter can easily be obtained by transforming (11.19). Since (11.19) can be rewritten as

$$\begin{aligned} -2P_1 + P_2 &= Q_1 - 40 \\ P_1 - P_2 &= Q_2 - 15 \end{aligned}$$

we may (considering Q_1 and Q_2 as parameters) apply Cramer's rule to solve for P_1 and P_2 as follows:

$$(11.19') \qquad \begin{aligned} P_1 &= 55 - Q_1 - Q_2 \\ P_2 &= 70 - Q_1 - 2Q_2 \end{aligned}$$

These constitute the desired average-revenue functions, since $P_1 \equiv AR_1$ and $P_2 \equiv AR_2$.

Consequently, the firm's total-revenue function can be written as

$$\begin{aligned} R &= P_1 Q_1 + P_2 Q_2 \\ &= (55 - Q_1 - Q_2)Q_1 + (70 - Q_1 - 2Q_2)Q_2 \qquad \text{[by (11.19')]} \\ &= 55Q_1 + 70Q_2 - 2Q_1 Q_2 - Q_1{}^2 - 2Q_2{}^2 \end{aligned}$$

If we again assume the total-cost function to be

$$C = Q_1{}^2 + Q_1 Q_2 + Q_2{}^2$$

then it follows that the profit function will be

$$(11.20) \qquad \pi = R - C = 55Q_1 + 70Q_2 - 3Q_1 Q_2 - 2Q_1{}^2 - 3Q_2{}^2$$

which is an objective function in two choice variables. Once the profit-maximizing output levels $\bar{Q}_1$ and $\bar{Q}_2$ are found, however, the optimal prices $\bar{P}_1$ and $\bar{P}_2$ are easy enough to find from (11.19').

The objective function yields the following first and second partial derivatives:

$$\begin{aligned} \pi_1 &= 55 - 3Q_2 - 4Q_1 & \pi_2 &= 70 - 3Q_1 - 6Q_2 \\ \pi_{11} &= -4 & \pi_{12} = \pi_{21} &= -3 & \pi_{22} &= -6 \end{aligned}$$

To satisfy the first-order condition for a maximum of π, we must have $\pi_1 = \pi_2 = 0$; that is,

$$4Q_1 + 3Q_2 = 55$$
$$3Q_1 + 6Q_2 = 70$$

Thus the solution output levels (per unit of time) are

$$(\bar{Q}_1, \bar{Q}_2) = (8, 7\tfrac{2}{3})$$

Upon substitution of this result into (11.19') and (11.20), respectively, we find that

$$\bar{P}_1 = 39\tfrac{1}{3} \qquad \bar{P}_2 = 46\tfrac{2}{3} \qquad \text{and} \qquad \bar{\pi} = 488\tfrac{1}{3} \qquad \text{(per unit of time)}$$

Inasmuch as the Hessian is $\begin{vmatrix} -4 & -3 \\ -3 & -6 \end{vmatrix}$, we have

$$|H_1| = -4 < 0 \qquad \text{and} \qquad |H_2| = 15 > 0$$

so that the value of $\bar{\pi}$ does represent the maximum profit.

price discrimination   Even in a single-product firm, there can arise an optimization problem involving two or more choice variables. Such would be the case, for instance, when a monopolistic firm sells a single product in two or more separate markets (e.g., domestic and foreign) and therefore must decide upon the quantities (Q_1, Q_2, etc.) to be supplied to the respective markets in order to maximize profit. The several markets will, in general, have different demand conditions, and if demand elasticities differ in the various markets, profit maximization will entail the practice of price discrimination. Let us derive this familiar conclusion mathematically.

Example 3   For a change of pace, this time let us use three choice variables, i.e., assume three separate markets. Also, let us work with general rather than numerical functions. Accordingly, our monopolistic firm will simply be assumed to have total-revenue and total-cost functions as follows:

$$R = R_1(Q_1) + R_2(Q_2) + R_3(Q_3)$$
$$C = C(Q) \qquad \text{where } Q = Q_1 + Q_2 + Q_3$$

The symbol R_i, be it noted, represents here the revenue function of the ith market, rather than a derivative in the sense of f_i. Each such revenue function naturally implies a particular demand structure, which will generally be different from those prevailing in the other two markets. On the cost side, on the other hand, only one cost function is postulated, since a single firm is producing for all three markets. In view of the fact that $Q = Q_1 + Q_2 + Q_3$, total cost C is also basically a function of Q_1, Q_2, and Q_3, which constitute the choice variables of the model. We can, of course, rewrite $C(Q)$ as $C(Q_1 + Q_2 + Q_3)$. It should be noted, however, that even though the latter version contains three independent variables, the function should nevertheless be considered as having a single argument only, because the sum of Q_i is really a single entity. In contrast, if the function appears in the form $C(Q_1,Q_2,Q_3)$, then there can be counted as many arguments as independent variables.

Now the profit function is

$$\pi = R_1(Q_1) + R_2(Q_2) + R_3(Q_3) - C(Q)$$

with first partial derivatives $\pi_i \equiv \partial\pi/\partial Q_i$ (for $i = 1,2,3$) as follows:

$$\pi_1 = R_1'(Q_1) - C'(Q)\frac{\partial Q}{\partial Q_1} = R_1'(Q_1) - C'(Q) \quad \left[\text{since } \frac{\partial Q}{\partial Q_1} = 1\right]$$

(11.21) $$\pi_2 = R_2'(Q_2) - C'(Q)\frac{\partial Q}{\partial Q_2} = R_2'(Q_2) - C'(Q) \quad \left[\text{since } \frac{\partial Q}{\partial Q_2} = 1\right]$$

$$\pi_3 = R_3'(Q_3) - C'(Q)\frac{\partial Q}{\partial Q_3} = R_3'(Q_3) - C'(Q) \quad \left[\text{since } \frac{\partial Q}{\partial Q_3} = 1\right]$$

Setting these equal to zero simultaneously will give us

$$C'(Q) = R_1'(Q_1) = R_2'(Q_2) = R_3'(Q_3)$$

That is,

$$\text{MC} = \text{MR}_1 = \text{MR}_2 = \text{MR}_3$$

Thus, the levels of Q_1, Q_2, and Q_3 should be chosen such that the marginal revenue in each market is equated to the marginal cost of the total output Q.

To see the implications of this condition with regard to price discrimination, let us first find out how the MR in any market is specifically related to the price in that market. Since the revenue in each market is $R_i = P_iQ_i$, it follows that the marginal revenue must be

$$\text{MR}_i \equiv \frac{dR_i}{dQ_i} = P_i\frac{dQ_i}{dQ_i} + Q_i\frac{dP_i}{dQ_i}$$

$$= P_i\left(1 + \frac{dP_i}{dQ_i}\frac{Q_i}{P_i}\right) = P_i\left(1 + \frac{1}{\varepsilon_{di}}\right) \quad [\text{by (8.4)}]$$

where ε_{di}, the point elasticity of demand in the ith market, is normally negative. Consequently, the relationship between MR_i and P_i can be expressed alternatively by the equation

(11.22) $$\text{MR}_i = P_i\left(1 - \frac{1}{|\varepsilon_{di}|}\right)$$

The reader will recall that $|\varepsilon_{di}|$ is, in general, a function of P_i, so that when $\bar{Q}_i$ is chosen, and $\bar{P}_i$ thus specified, $|\varepsilon_{di}|$ will also assume a specific value, which can be either greater than, or less than, or equal to one. But if $|\varepsilon_{di}| < 1$ (demand being inelastic at a point), then its reciprocal will exceed one, and the parenthesized expression in (11.22) will be negative, thereby implying a negative value for MR_i. Similarly, if $|\varepsilon_{di}| = 1$ (unitary elasticity), then MR_i will take a zero value. Inasmuch as a firm's MC is positive, the first-order condition $MC = MR_i$ requires the firm to operate at a positive level of MR_i. Hence the firm's chosen sales levels Q_i must be such that the corresponding point elasticity of demand in each market is greater than one.

The first-order condition $MR_1 = MR_2 = MR_3$ can now be translated, via (11.22), into the following:

$$P_1\left(1 - \frac{1}{|\varepsilon_{d1}|}\right) = P_2\left(1 - \frac{1}{|\varepsilon_{d2}|}\right) = P_3\left(1 - \frac{1}{|\varepsilon_{d3}|}\right)$$

From this it can readily be inferred that the *smaller* the value of $|\varepsilon_d|$ (at the chosen level of output) in a particular market, the *higher* the price charged in that market must be—hence, price discrimination—if profit is to be maximized.

The maximization of profit also requires us to check the second-order condition. From (11.21), the second partial derivatives are found to be

$$\pi_{11} = R_1''(Q_1) - C''(Q)\,\frac{\partial Q}{\partial Q_1} = R_1''(Q_1) - C''(Q)$$

$$\pi_{22} = R_2''(Q_2) - C''(Q)\,\frac{\partial Q}{\partial Q_2} = R_2''(Q_2) - C''(Q)$$

$$\pi_{33} = R_3''(Q_3) - C''(Q)\,\frac{\partial Q}{\partial Q_3} = R_3''(Q_3) - C''(Q)$$

and $\quad \pi_{12} = \pi_{21} = \pi_{13} = \pi_{31} = \pi_{23} = \pi_{32} = -C''(Q)\quad \left[\text{since } \dfrac{\partial Q}{\partial Q_i} = 1\right]$

so that we have (after shortening the second-derivative notation)

$$|H| = \begin{vmatrix} R_1'' - C'' & -C'' & -C'' \\ -C'' & R_2'' - C'' & -C'' \\ -C'' & -C'' & R_3'' - C'' \end{vmatrix}$$

The second-order condition is therefore translatable into the following threefold requirement:

1 $|H_1| = R_1'' - C'' < 0$; that is, the slope of MR_1 must be less than the slope of MC of the entire output [cf. the situation of point L in Fig. 9.6c], but since any of the three markets can be taken as the "first" market, this in effect also implies $R_2'' - C'' < 0$ and $R_3'' - C'' < 0$.

2    $|H_2| = (R_1'' - C'')(R_2'' - C'') - (C'')^2 > 0$; or, $R_1''R_2'' - (R_1'' + R_2'')C'' > 0$.

3    $|H_3| = R_1''R_2''R_3'' - (R_1''R_2'' + R_1''R_3'' + R_2''R_3'')C'' < 0$.

The satisfaction of this tripartite requirement will be sufficient to assure the maximization of profit when the first-order condition is met.

Example 4   To make the above example more concrete, let us now give a numerical version. Suppose that our monopolistic firm has the average-revenue functions

$$\begin{array}{lll}
P_1 = 63 - 4Q_1 & \text{so that} & R_1 = P_1Q_1 = 63Q_1 - 4Q_1{}^2 \\
P_2 = 105 - 5Q_2 & & R_2 = P_2Q_2 = 105Q_2 - 5Q_2{}^2 \\
P_3 = 75 - 6Q_3 & & R_3 = P_3Q_3 = 75Q_3 - 6Q_3{}^2
\end{array}$$

and that the total-cost function is

$$C = 20 + 15Q$$

Then the marginal functions will be

$$R_1' = 63 - 8Q_1 \qquad R_2' = 105 - 10Q_2 \qquad R_3' = 75 - 12Q_3 \qquad C' = 15$$

When each marginal revenue R_i' is set equal to the marginal cost C' of the total output, the equilibrium quantities are found to be

$$\bar{Q}_1 = 6 \qquad \bar{Q}_2 = 9 \qquad \text{and} \qquad \bar{Q}_3 = 5$$

Thus, $\bar{Q} = \sum_{i=1}^{3} \bar{Q}_i = 20$

Substituting these solutions into the revenue and cost equations, we get $\bar{\pi} = 679$ as the total profit from the triple-market business operation.

     That this profit is maximal can be seen from the fact that the second derivatives are

$$R_1'' = -8 \qquad R_2'' = -10 \qquad R_3'' = -12 \qquad C'' = 0$$

so that all three parts of the second-order condition are duly satisfied.

     It is easy to see from the average-revenue functions that the firm should charge the discriminatory prices $\bar{P}_1 = 39$, $\bar{P}_2 = 60$, and $\bar{P}_3 = 45$ in the three markets. As the reader can readily verify, the point elasticity of demand is lowest in the second market, in which the highest price is charged.

input decisions of a firm   Instead of output levels Q_i, the choice variables of a firm may also appear in the guise of input levels.

Example 5   Let us assume the following circumstances: (1) Two inputs a and b are used in the production of a single product Q of a hypothetical firm. (2) The prices of both inputs, P_a and P_b, are beyond the control of the firm, as is the output price P; hence we shall denote them by P_{a0}, P_{b0}, and P_0, respectively. (3) The production process takes t_0 years (t_0 being some positive fraction) to complete; thus the revenue from sales should be duly discounted before it can be properly compared with the cost of production, which is incurred at the present time. The rate of discount, on a continuous basis, is assumed to be given at r_0.

Upon assumption 1, we can write a general production function $Q = Q(a,b)$, with marginal physical products Q_a and Q_b. Assumption 2 enables us to express the total cost as

$$C = aP_{a0} + bP_{b0}$$

and the total revenue as

$$R = P_0 Q(a,b)$$

To write the profit function, however, we must first discount the revenue by multiplying it by the constant $e^{-r_0 t_0}$—which, to avoid complicated superscripts with subscripts, we shall write as e^{-rt}. Thus, the profit function will be

$$\pi = P_0 Q(a,b)e^{-rt} - aP_{a0} - bP_{b0}$$

in which a and b are the only choice variables.

To maximize profit, it is necessary that the first partial derivatives

$$(11.23)$$
$$\pi_a \left(\equiv \frac{\partial \pi}{\partial a} \right) = P_0 Q_a e^{-rt} - P_{a0}$$

$$\pi_b \left(\equiv \frac{\partial \pi}{\partial b} \right) = P_0 Q_b e^{-rt} - P_{b0}$$

both be zero. This means that

$$(11.24) \qquad P_0 Q_a e^{-rt} = P_{a0} \qquad \text{and} \qquad P_0 Q_b e^{-rt} = P_{b0}$$

Since $P_0 Q_a$ (the price of the product times the marginal product of input a) represents the *value of marginal product of input a* (VMP$_a$), the first equation merely says that the present value of VMP$_a$ should be equated to the given price of input a. The second equation is the same prerequisite applied to input b.

Note that, to fulfill the condition (11.24), the marginal physical products Q_a and Q_b must both be positive, because P_0, P_{a0}, P_{b0}, and e^{-rt} all have positive values. This has an important interpretation in terms of an *isoquant*, which is defined as the locus of input combinations that yield the same output level. When plotted in the ab plane, isoquants will generally appear like those drawn

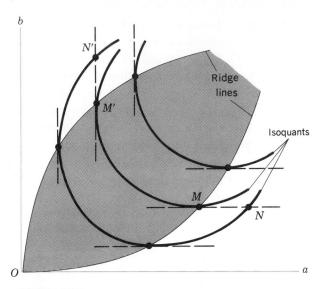

FIGURE 11.6

in Fig. 11.6. Inasmuch as each of them pertains to a fixed output level, along any isoquant we must have

$$dQ = Q_a \, da + Q_b \, db = 0$$

which implies that the slope of an isoquant is expressible as

$$(11.25) \qquad \frac{db}{da} = -\frac{Q_a}{Q_b} \qquad \left(= -\frac{\text{MPP}_a}{\text{MPP}_b} \right)$$

Thus, to have Q_a and Q_b both positive is to confine the firm's input choice to the negatively sloped segments of the isoquants only. In Fig. 11.6, the relevant region of operation is accordingly restricted to the shaded area defined by the two so-called "ridge lines." Outside the shaded area, where the isoquants are characterized by positive slopes, the marginal product of one input must be negative. The movement from the input combination at M to the one at N, for instance, indicates that with input b held constant the *increase* in input a leads us to a *lower* isoquant (a smaller output); thus, Q_a must be negative. Similarly, a movement from M' to N' illustrates the negativity of Q_b. Note that when we confine our attention to the shaded area, each isoquant can be taken as a function of the form $b = \phi(a)$, because for every admissible value of a, the isoquant determines a unique value of b.

The second-order condition revolves around the second partial derivatives of π, obtainable from (11.23). Bearing in mind that Q_a and Q_b, being derivatives, are themselves functions of the variables a and b, we can find π_{aa}, $\pi_{ab} = \pi_{ba}$, and

Optimization Problems

π_{bb}, and arrange them into a Hessian:

$$(11.26) \qquad |H| = \begin{vmatrix} \pi_{aa} & \pi_{ab} \\ \pi_{ab} & \pi_{bb} \end{vmatrix} = \begin{vmatrix} P_0 Q_{aa} e^{-rt} & P_0 Q_{ab} e^{-rt} \\ P_0 Q_{ab} e^{-rt} & P_0 Q_{bb} e^{-rt} \end{vmatrix}$$

For a stationary value of π to be a maximum, it is sufficient that

$$|H_1| < 0 \qquad \text{[that is, } \pi_{aa} < 0 \text{, which can obtain iff } Q_{aa} < 0 \text{]}$$
$$|H_2| = |H| > 0 \quad \text{[that is, } \pi_{aa}\pi_{bb} > \pi_{ab}{}^2 \text{, which can obtain iff } Q_{aa}Q_{bb} > Q_{ab}{}^2 \text{]}$$

Thus, we note, the second-order condition can be tested either with the π_{ij} derivatives or the Q_{ij} derivatives, whichever are more convenient.

The symbol Q_{aa} denotes the rate of change of Q_a ($\equiv$ MPP$_a$) as input a changes while input b is fixed; similarly, Q_{bb} denotes the rate of change of Q_b ($\equiv$ MPP$_b$) as input b changes alone. So the second-order condition stipulates, in part, that the MPP of both inputs be *diminishing* at the chosen input levels $\bar{a}$ and $\bar{b}$. Observe, however, that diminishing MPP$_a$ and MPP$_b$ do *not* guarantee the satisfaction of the second-order condition, because the latter condition also involves the magnitude of $Q_{ab} = Q_{ba}$, which measures the rate of change of MPP of one input as the amount of the other input varies.

Upon further examination it emerges that, just as the first-order condition specifies the isoquant to be negatively sloped at the chosen input combination (as shown in the shaded area of Fig. 11.6), the second-order condition really amounts to specifying that same isoquant to be strictly convex at the chosen input combination. The curvature of the isoquant is associated with the sign of the second derivative d^2b/da^2. To obtain the latter, (11.25) must be differentiated totally with respect to a, bearing in mind that Q_a and Q_b are both derivative functions of a and b and yet that, on an isoquant, b is itself a function of a; that is,

$$Q_a = Q_a(a,b) \qquad Q_b = Q_b(a,b) \qquad \text{and} \qquad b = \phi(a)$$

The total differentiation thus proceeds as follows:

$$(11.27) \qquad \frac{d^2b}{da^2} = \frac{d}{da}\left(-\frac{Q_a}{Q_b}\right) = -\frac{1}{Q_b{}^2}\left[Q_b \frac{dQ_a}{da} - Q_a \frac{dQ_b}{da}\right]$$

Since b is a function of a on the isoquant, the total-derivative formula (8.9) gives us

$$(11.28) \qquad \begin{aligned} \frac{dQ_a}{da} &= \frac{\partial Q_a}{\partial b}\frac{db}{da} + \frac{\partial Q_a}{\partial a} = Q_{ba}\frac{db}{da} + Q_{aa} \\[2mm] \frac{dQ_b}{da} &= \frac{\partial Q_b}{\partial b}\frac{db}{da} + \frac{\partial Q_b}{\partial a} = Q_{bb}\frac{db}{da} + Q_{ab} \end{aligned}$$

The Case of More Than One Choice Variable

After substituting (11.25) into (11.28) and then substituting the latter into (11.27), we can rewrite the second derivative as

$$(11.29) \qquad \frac{d^2b}{da^2} = -\frac{1}{Q_b{}^2}\left[Q_{aa}Q_b - Q_{ba}Q_a - Q_{ab}Q_a + Q_{bb}Q_a{}^2\left(\frac{1}{Q_b}\right)\right]$$

$$= -\frac{1}{Q_b{}^3}\left[Q_{aa}(Q_b)^2 - 2Q_{ab}(Q_a)(Q_b) + Q_{bb}(Q_a)^2\right]$$

It is to be noted that the expression in brackets (last line) is a quadratic form in two variables Q_a and Q_b. If the second-order condition is fulfilled, so that

$$Q_{aa} < 0 \qquad \text{and} \qquad \begin{vmatrix} Q_{aa} & -Q_{ab} \\ -Q_{ab} & Q_{bb} \end{vmatrix} > 0$$

then, by virtue of (11.5′), the said quadratic form must be negative definite. This will in turn make d^2b/da^2 positive, because Q_b has been constrained to be positive by the first-order condition. Thus the fulfillment of the second-order condition means that the relevant (negatively-sloped) isoquant is strictly convex at the chosen input combination, as was asserted.

The concept of strict convexity, as applied to an isoquant $b = \phi(a)$, which is drawn in the two-dimensional ab plane, should be carefully distinguished from the same concept as applied to the production function $Q(a,b)$ itself, which is drawn in the three-dimensional abQ space. Note, in particular, that if we are to apply the concept of strict concavity or convexity to the production function in the present context, then, in order to produce the desired results $Q_{aa} < 0$ and $Q_{aa}Q_{bb} > Q_{ab}{}^2$, the appropriate stipulation is that $Q(a,b)$ be strictly *concave* (dome-shaped), which is in sharp contradistinction to the stipulation that the relevant isoquant be strictly *convex* (U-shaped, or shaped like a part of a U).

Example 6   Next, suppose that interest is compounded *quarterly* instead, at a given interest rate of i_0 per quarter. Also suppose that the production process takes exactly a quarter of a year. The profit function of the last example will then become

$$\pi = P_0Q(a,b)(1 + i_0)^{-1} - aP_{a0} - bP_{b0}$$

The first-order condition is now found to be

$$P_0Q_a(1 + i_0)^{-1} - P_{a0} = 0$$
$$P_0Q_b(1 + i_0)^{-1} - P_{b0} = 0$$

with an analytical interpretation entirely the same as in Example 5, except for the different manner of discounting.

The reader can readily see that the same sufficient condition derived in the preceding example must apply here as well.

EXERCISE 11.5

1   If the competitive firm of Example 1 has the cost function $C = 2Q_1{}^2 + 2Q_2{}^2$ instead, then:

   (a)   Will the production of the two goods still be technically related?
   (b)   What will be the optimal levels of Q_1 and Q_2?
   (c)   What is the value of π_{12}? What does this imply economically?

2   If the demand functions in Example 2 are

$$Q_1 = 40 - 2P_1 - P_2$$
$$Q_2 = 35 - P_1 - P_2$$

   will the two commodities still be related in consumption? If so, in what way?

3   A two-product firm has the demand functions given in the preceding problem, and the cost function $C = Q_1{}^2 + 2Q_2{}^2 + 10$.

   (a)   Find the output levels which will satisfy the necessary condition for maximum profit.
   (b)   Check the satisfaction of the second-order condition.
   (c)   What is the maximal profit?

4   On the basis of the equilibrium price and quantity in Example 4, calculate the point elasticity of demand $|\varepsilon_{di}|$ (for $i = 1,2,3$). Which market has the highest and the lowest demand elasticities?

5   If the cost function of Example 4 is changed to $C = 20 + 15Q + Q^2$:

   (a)   Find the new marginal-cost function.
   (b)   Find the new equilibrium quantities $\bar{Q}_1$, $\bar{Q}_2$, and $\bar{Q}_3$ (using fractions).
   (c)   Find the new equilibrium prices.
   (d)   Verify that the second-order condition is met by the above solution.

6   In Example 6, how will you rewrite the profit function if the following conditions hold?

   (a)   Interest is compounded semiannually at an interest rate of i_0 per annum, and the production process takes 1 year.
   (b)   Interest is compounded quarterly at an interest rate of i_0 per annum, and the production process takes 9 months.

11.6   Comparative-Static Aspects of Optimization

Optimization, being a special variety of static equilibrium analysis, is naturally also subject to investigations of the comparative-static sort. The idea, again, is to find out how a change in any parameter will affect the equilibrium position of the model, which in the present context refers to the optimal values of the choice variables (and the optimal value of the objective function). Since no new technique is involved beyond those discussed in Part 3, we may proceed directly with some illustrations, based on the examples introduced in the preceding section.

reduced-form solutions   Example 1 of Sec. 11.5 contains two parameters (or exogenous variables), P_{10} and P_{20}; it is not surprising, therefore, that the optimal output levels of this two-product firm are expressed strictly in terms of these parameters:

$$\bar{Q}_1 = \frac{4P_{10} - P_{20}}{15} \quad \text{and} \quad \bar{Q}_2 = \frac{4P_{20} - P_{10}}{15}$$

These are reduced-form solutions, and simple partial differentiation alone is sufficient to tell us all the comparative-static properties of the model, namely,

$$\frac{\partial \bar{Q}_1}{\partial P_{10}} = \frac{4}{15} \qquad \frac{\partial \bar{Q}_1}{\partial P_{20}} = -\frac{1}{15} \qquad \frac{\partial \bar{Q}_2}{\partial P_{10}} = -\frac{1}{15} \qquad \frac{\partial \bar{Q}_2}{\partial P_{20}} = \frac{4}{15}$$

For maximum profit, each product of the firm should be produced in a larger quantity if its market price rises or if the market price of the other product falls.

Of course, these conclusions follow only from the particular assumptions of the model in question. We may point out, in particular, that the effects of a change in P_{10} on $\bar{Q}_2$ and of P_{20} on $\bar{Q}_1$, are consequences of the assumed technical relation on the production side of these two commodities, and that in the absence of such a relation we shall have

$$\frac{\partial \bar{Q}_1}{\partial P_{20}} = \frac{\partial \bar{Q}_2}{\partial P_{10}} = 0$$

Moving on to Example 2, we note that the optimal output levels are there stated, numerically, as $\bar{Q}_1 = 8$ and $\bar{Q}_2 = 7\frac{2}{3}$—no parameters appear. In fact, all the constants in the equations of the model are numerical rather than parametric, so that by the time we reach the solution stage those constants have all lost their respective identities through the process of arithmetic manipulation. What this serves to underscore is the fundamental lack of generality in the use of numerical constants and the consequent lack of comparative-static content in the equilibrium solution.

On the other hand, the *non*use of numerical constants is no guarantee that a problem will automatically become amenable to comparative-static analysis. The price-discrimination problem (Example 3), for instance, was primarily set up for the study of the equilibrium (profit-maximization) condition, and no parameter was introduced at all. Accordingly, even though stated in terms of general functions, a reformulation will be necessary if a comparative-static study is contemplated.

general-function models   The input-decision problem of Example 5 illustrates the case where a general-function formulation does embrace several parameters—in fact, no less than five (P_0, P_{a0}, P_{b0}, r, and t), where we have, as before, omitted the 0 subscripts from the exogenous variables r_0 and t_0. How do we derive the comparative-static properties of this model?

The answer lies again in the application of the implicit-function theorem. But, unlike the cases of nongoal-equilibrium models of the market or of national-income determination, where we worked with the equilibrium conditions of the model, the present context of goal equilibrium dictates that we work with the first-order conditions of optimization. For Example 5, these conditions are stated in (11.24). Collecting all terms in (11.24) to the left of the equals signs, and making explicit that Q_a and Q_b are both functions of the endogenous (choice) variables a and b, we can rewrite the first-order conditions in the format of (8.20) as follows:

(11.30)
$$F^1(a,b;P_0,P_{a0},P_{b0},r,t) = P_0 Q_a(a,b)e^{-rt} - P_{a0} = 0$$
$$F^2(a,b;P_0,P_{a0},P_{b0},r,t) = P_0 Q_b(a,b)e^{-rt} - P_{b0} = 0$$

The functions F^1 and F^2 are assumed to possess continuous derivatives. Thus it would be possible to apply the implicit-function theorem, provided that the Jacobian of this system with respect to the endogenous variables a and b does not vanish at the initial equilibrium. The said Jacobian turns out to be nothing but the Hessian determinant of the π function of Example 5:

(11.31)
$$|J| = \begin{vmatrix} \dfrac{\partial F^1}{\partial a} & \dfrac{\partial F^1}{\partial b} \\[2ex] \dfrac{\partial F^2}{\partial a} & \dfrac{\partial F^2}{\partial b} \end{vmatrix} = \begin{vmatrix} P_0 Q_{aa}e^{-rt} & P_0 Q_{ab}e^{-rt} \\[1ex] P_0 Q_{ab}e^{-rt} & P_0 Q_{bb}e^{-rt} \end{vmatrix} = |H|$$

[by (11.26)]

Hence, if we assume that the second-order condition for profit-maximization is satisfied, then $|H|$ must be positive, and so must be $|J|$, at the initial equilibrium or optimum. In that event, the implicit-function theorem will enable us to write the pair of implicit functions

$$(11.32) \quad \begin{aligned} \bar{a} &= \bar{a}(P_0, P_{a0}, P_{b0}, r, t) \\ \bar{b} &= \bar{b}(P_0, P_{a0}, P_{b0}, r, t) \end{aligned}$$

as well as the pair of identities

$$(11.33) \quad \begin{aligned} P_0 Q_a(\bar{a}, \bar{b}) e^{-rt} - P_{a0} &\equiv 0 \\ P_0 Q_b(\bar{a}, \bar{b}) e^{-rt} - P_{b0} &\equiv 0 \end{aligned}$$

To study the comparative statics of the model, first take the total differential of each identity in (11.33). For the time being, we shall permit all the exogenous variables to vary, so that the result of total differentiation will involve $d\bar{a}$, $d\bar{b}$, as well as dP_0, dP_{a0}, dP_{b0}, dr, and dt. If we place on the left side of the equals sign only those terms involving $d\bar{a}$ and $d\bar{b}$, the result will be

$$(11.34) \quad \begin{aligned} P_0 Q_{aa} e^{-rt}\, d\bar{a} + P_0 Q_{ab} e^{-rt}\, d\bar{b} \\ = -Q_a e^{-rt}\, dP_0 + dP_{a0} + P_0 Q_a t e^{-rt}\, dr + P_0 Q_a r e^{-rt}\, dt \\ P_0 Q_{ab} e^{-rt}\, d\bar{a} + P_0 Q_{bb} e^{-rt}\, d\bar{b} \\ = -Q_b e^{-rt}\, dP_0 + dP_{b0} + P_0 Q_b t e^{-rt}\, dr + P_0 Q_b r e^{-rt}\, dt \end{aligned}$$

where, be it noted, the first and second derivatives of Q are all to be evaluated at the equilibrium, i.e., at $\bar{a}$ and $\bar{b}$. The reader will also note that the coefficients of $d\bar{a}$ and $d\bar{b}$ on the left are precisely the elements of the Jacobian in (11.31).

To derive the specific comparative-static derivatives—of which there are a total of ten (why?)—we now shall allow only a single exogenous variable to vary at a time. Suppose we let P_0 vary, alone. Then $dP_0 \neq 0$, but $dP_{a0} = dP_{b0} = dr = dt = 0$, so that only the first term will remain on the right side of each equation in (11.34). Dividing through by dP_0, and interpreting the ratio $d\bar{a}/dP_0$ to be the comparative-static derivative $(\partial\bar{a}/\partial P_0)$, and similarly for the ratio $d\bar{b}/dP_0$, we can write the matrix equation

$$\begin{bmatrix} P_0 Q_{aa} e^{-rt} & P_0 Q_{ab} e^{-rt} \\ P_0 Q_{ab} e^{-rt} & P_0 Q_{bb} e^{-rt} \end{bmatrix} \begin{bmatrix} (\partial\bar{a}/\partial P_0) \\ (\partial\bar{b}/\partial P_0) \end{bmatrix} = \begin{bmatrix} -Q_a e^{-rt} \\ -Q_b e^{-rt} \end{bmatrix}$$

The solution, by Cramer's rule, is found to be

$$(11.35) \quad \begin{aligned} \left(\frac{\partial\bar{a}}{\partial P_0}\right) &= \frac{(Q_b Q_{ab} - Q_a Q_{bb}) P_0 e^{-2rt}}{|J|} \\ \left(\frac{\partial\bar{b}}{\partial P_0}\right) &= \frac{(Q_a Q_{ab} - Q_b Q_{aa}) P_0 e^{-2rt}}{|J|} \end{aligned}$$

If the reader prefers, it may be added here, there is available an alternative method for obtaining these results: One may simply differentiate the two identities in (11.33) *totally* with respect to P_0 (while holding the other four exogenous variables fixed), bearing in mind that P_0 can affect $\bar{a}$ and $\bar{b}$ via (11.32).

Let us now analyze the signs of the comparative-static derivatives in (11.35). On the assumption that the second-order condition is satisfied, the Jacobian in the denominator must be positive. The second-order condition also implies that Q_{aa} and Q_{bb} are negative, just as the first-order condition implies that Q_a and Q_b are positive. Moreover, the expression $P_0 e^{-2rt}$ is certainly positive. Thus, if $Q_{ab} > 0$ (if increasing one input will raise the MPP of the other input), we can conclude that both $(\partial\bar{a}/\partial P_0)$ and $(\partial\bar{b}/\partial P_0)$ will be positive, implying that an increase in the product price will result in increased employment of both inputs in equilibrium. If $Q_{ab} < 0$, on the other hand, the sign of each derivative in (11.35) will depend on the relative strength of the negative force and the positive force in the parenthetical expression on the right.

Next, let the exogenous variable r vary, alone. Then all the terms on the right of (11.34) will vanish except those involving dr. Dividing through by $dr \neq 0$, we now obtain the following matrix equation

$$\begin{bmatrix} P_0 Q_{aa} e^{-rt} & P_0 Q_{ab} e^{-rt} \\ P_0 Q_{ab} e^{-rt} & P_0 Q_{bb} e^{-rt} \end{bmatrix} \begin{bmatrix} (\partial\bar{a}/\partial r) \\ (\partial\bar{b}/\partial r) \end{bmatrix} = \begin{bmatrix} P_0 Q_a t e^{-rt} \\ P_0 Q_b t e^{-rt} \end{bmatrix}$$

with the solution

$$(11.36) \qquad \left(\frac{\partial\bar{a}}{\partial r}\right) = \frac{t(Q_a Q_{bb} - Q_b Q_{ab})(P_0 e^{-rt})^2}{|J|}$$

$$\left(\frac{\partial\bar{b}}{\partial r}\right) = \frac{t(Q_b Q_{aa} - Q_a Q_{ab})(P_0 e^{-rt})^2}{|J|}$$

Both of these comparative-static derivatives will be negative if Q_{ab} is positive, but indeterminate in sign if Q_{ab} is negative.

By a similar procedure, we may find the effects of variations in the remaining parameters. Actually, in view of the symmetry between r and t in (11.33) it is immediately obvious that both $(\partial\bar{a}/\partial t)$ and $(\partial\bar{b}/\partial t)$ will be similar in appearance to (11.36).

The effects of changes in P_{a0} and P_{b0} are left to the reader to analyze. As the reader will find, the sign restriction of the second-order condition will again be useful in evaluating the comparative-static derivatives, because it can tell us the signs of Q_{aa} and Q_{bb} as well as the Jacobian $|J|$ at the initial equilibrium (optimum). This goes to show that, aside from distinguishing between maximum and minimum, the second-order condition also has a vital role to play in the study of shifts in equilibrium positions as well.

EXERCISE 11.6

For the following exercises, assume that $Q_{ab} > 0$.

1   On the basis of the model described in (11.30) through (11.33), find the comparative-static derivatives $(\partial \bar{a}/\partial P_{a0})$ and $(\partial \bar{b}/\partial P_{a0})$. Interpret the economic meaning of the result. Then analyze the effects on $\bar{a}$ and $\bar{b}$ of a change in P_{b0}.

2   For the problem of Example 6 in Sec. 11.5:

    (*a*)   How many parameters are there? Enumerate them.

    (*b*)   Following the procedure described in (11.30) through (11.35), and assuming that the second-order condition is satisfied, find the comparative-static derivatives $(\partial \bar{a}/\partial P_0)$ and $(\partial \bar{b}/\partial P_0)$. Evaluate their signs and interpret their economic meanings.

    (*c*)   Find $(\partial \bar{a}/\partial i_0)$ and $(\partial \bar{b}/\partial i_0)$, evaluate their signs, and interpret their economic meanings.

3   Show that the results in (11.35) can be obtained alternatively by differentiating the two identities in (11.33) *totally* with respect to P_0, while holding the other exogenous variables fixed. Bear in mind that P_0 can affect $\bar{a}$ and $\bar{b}$ by virtue of (11.32).

12

CONSTRAINED OPTIMIZATION

The last chapter presented a general method for finding the (relative) extrema of an objective function of two or more choice variables. One important feature of that discussion is that all the choice variables are *independent* of one another, in the sense that the decision made regarding one variable does not impinge upon the choices of the remaining variables. For instance, a two-product firm can choose any value for Q_1 and any value for Q_2 it wishes, without the two choices limiting each other.

If the said firm is somehow required to observe a restriction (such as a production quota) in the form of $Q_1 + Q_2 = 950$, however, the independence between the choice variables will be lost. In that event, the firm's profit-maximizing output levels $\bar{Q}_1$ and $\bar{Q}_2$ not only will be simultaneous but also will be dependent, because the higher $\bar{Q}_1$ is, the lower $\bar{Q}_2$ must correspondingly be, in order to stay within the combined quota of 950. The new optimum satisfying the production quota will constitute a *constrained optimum*, which, in general, may be expected to differ from the *free optimum* discussed in the preceding chapter.

A restriction, such as the production quota mentioned above, establishes a relationship between the two variables in their roles as choice variables, but this should be distinguished from other types of relationships that may link the variables together. For instance, in Example 2 of Sec. 11.5, the two products of the firm are related in consumption (substitutes) as well as in production (as is reflected in the cost function), but that fact does not qualify the problem as one of constrained optimization, since the two output variables are still *independent as choice variables*. Only the dependence of the variables qua choice variables gives rise to a constrained optimum.

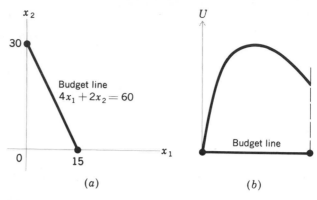

FIGURE 12.1

12.1 Effects of a Constraint

The primary purpose of imposing a constraint is to give due cognizance to certain limiting factors present in the optimization problem under discussion.

We have already seen the limitation on output choices that result from a production quota. For further illustration, let us consider a consumer with the simple utility (index) function

$$(12.1) \qquad U = x_1 x_2 + 2x_1$$

Since the marginal utilities—the partial derivatives $U_1 \equiv \partial U/\partial x_1$ and $U_2 \equiv \partial U/\partial x_2$—are positive for all positive levels of x_1 and x_2 here, to have U maximized without any constraint, the consumer should purchase an *infinite* amount of both goods, a solution that obviously has little practical relevance. To render the optimization problem meaningful, the purchasing power of the consumer must also be taken into account; i.e., a *budget constraint* should be incorporated into the problem. If the consumer intends to spend a given sum, say, $60, on the two goods and if the current prices are $P_{10} = 4$ and $P_{20} = 2$, then the budget constraint can be expressed by the linear equation

$$(12.2) \qquad 4x_1 + 2x_2 = 60$$

Such a constraint, like the production quota referred to earlier, will render the choices of $\bar{x}_1$ and $\bar{x}_2$ mutually dependent.

The problem now is to maximize (12.1), subject to the constraint stated in (12.2). Mathematically, what the constraint (variously called *restraint, side relation,* or *subsidiary condition*) does is to narrow the domain, and hence the range, of the objective function. The domain of (12.1) would normally be the set $\{(x_1,x_2) \mid x_1 \geq 0, \ x_2 \geq 0\}$. Graphically, the domain is represented by the nonnegative quadrant of the x_1x_2 plane in Fig. 12.1a. After the budget constraint

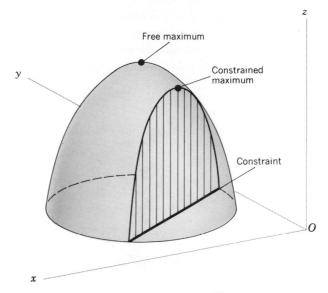

FIGURE 12.2

(12.2) is added, however, we can admit only those values of the variables which satisfy this latter equation, so that the domain is immediately reduced to the set of points lying on the budget line. This will automatically affect the range of the objective function, too; only that subset of the utility surface lying directly above the budget-constraint line will now be relevant. The said subset (a cross section of the surface) may look like the curve in Fig. 12.1*b*, where *U* is plotted on the vertical axis, with the budget line of diagram *a* placed on the horizontal axis. Our interest, then, is only in the location of the maximum on the curve in diagram *b*.

In general, for a function $z = f(x,y)$, the difference between a constrained extremum and a free extremum may be illustrated in the three-dimensional graph of Fig. 12.2. The free extremum in this particular graph is the peak point of the entire dome, but the constrained extremum is at the peak of the inverse U-shaped curve situated on top of (i.e., lying directly above) the constraint line. In general, a constrained maximum can be expected to have a lower value than the free maximum, although, by coincidence, the two maxima may happen to have the same value. But the constrained maximum can never exceed the free maximum.

It is interesting to note that, had we added another constraint intersecting the first constraint in the *xy* plane, the two constraints together would have restricted the domain to a single point (their intersection). Since that would automatically narrow the range of the objective function to a single point on the

z surface, the locating of the extremum would become a trivial matter. In the usual problem, the number and the nature of the constraints are likely to be such as to restrict, but not eliminate, the possibility of choice. Specifically, the number of constraints should be less than the number of choice variables.

12.2   Finding the Stationary Values

Even without any new technique of solution, the constrained maximum in the simple example defined by (12.1) and (12.2) can easily be found. Since the constraint (12.2) implies

$$(12.2') \qquad x_2 = \frac{60 - 4x_1}{2} = 30 - 2x_1$$

we can combine the constraint with the objective function by substituting (12.2′) into (12.1). The result will be an objective function in one variable only:

$$U = x_1(30 - 2x_1) + 2x_1 = 32x_1 - 2x_1{}^2$$

which can be handled with the method already learned. By setting $dU/dx_1 = 32 - 4x_1$ equal to zero, we get the solution $\bar{x}_1 = 8$, which by virtue of (12.2′) immediately leads to $\bar{x}_2 = 30 - 2(8) = 14$. From (12.1), we can then find the stationary value $\overline{U} = 128$; and since the second derivative is $d^2U/dx_1{}^2 = -4 < 0$, that stationary value constitutes a (constrained) maximum of U.†

When the constraint is itself a complicated function, or when there are several constraints to consider, however, the technique of substitution and elimination of variables could become a burdensome task. More importantly, when the constraint comes in a form such that we cannot solve it to express one variable (x_2) as an explicit function of the other (x_1), the elimination method would in fact be of no avail—even if x_2 were known to be an implicit function of x_1, that is, even if the conditions of the implicit-function theorem were satisfied. In such cases, we may resort to a method known as the *method of Lagrange (undetermined) multiplier*, which, as we shall see, has distinct analytical advantages.

Lagrange-multiplier method   The essence of the Lagrange-multiplier method is to convert a constrained-extremum problem into a form such that the first-order condition of the free-extremum problem can still be applied.

† The reader may recall that for the flower-bed problem of Exercise 9.4-2 the same technique of substitution was applied to find the maximum area, using a constraint (the available quantity of wire netting) to eliminate one of the two variables (the length or the width of the flower bed).

Given the problem of maximizing $U = x_1 x_2 + 2x_1$, subject to the constraint $4x_1 + 2x_2 = 60$ [from (12.1) and (12.2)], let us write what is referred to as the *Lagrangean function*, which is a modified version of the objective function that incorporates the constraint as follows:

(12.3) $\qquad Z = x_1 x_2 + 2x_1 + \lambda(60 - 4x_1 - 2x_2)$

The symbol λ (the Greek letter lambda), representing some as yet undetermined number, is called a *Lagrange (undetermined) multiplier*. If we can somehow be assured that $4x_1 + 2x_2 = 60$, so that the constraint will be satisfied, then the last term in (12.3) will vanish regardless of the value of λ. In that event, Z will be identical with U. Moreover, with the constraint out of the way, we only have to seek the *free* maximum of Z, in lieu of the *constrained* maximum of U. The question is: How can we make the parenthetical expression in (12.3) vanish?

The tactic that will accomplish this is simply to treat λ as an additional variable in (12.3), i.e., to let $Z = Z(\lambda, x_1, x_2)$. For then the first-order condition for free extremum will consist of the set of simultaneous equations

$$\begin{aligned}
Z_\lambda \ (\equiv \partial Z/\partial \lambda) &= 60 - 4x_1 - 2x_2 = 0 \\
\text{(12.4)} \qquad Z_1 \ (\equiv \partial Z/\partial x_1) &= x_2 + 2 - 4\lambda = 0 \\
Z_2 \ (\equiv \partial Z/\partial x_2) &= x_1 - 2\lambda = 0
\end{aligned}$$

and the first equation will automatically guarantee the satisfaction of the constraint. Thus, by incorporating the constraint into the Lagrangean function Z and by treating the Lagrange multiplier as an extra variable, we can obtain the constrained extremum $\bar{U}$ simply by screening the stationary values of Z, taken as a *free* function.

Solving (12.4) for the critical values of the variables, we find $\bar{x}_1 = 8$, $\bar{x}_2 = 14$ (and $\bar{\lambda} = 4$). As expected, the values of $\bar{x}_1$ and $\bar{x}_2$ check with the answers already obtained by the substitution method. Furthermore, it is clear from (12.3) that $\bar{Z} = 128$; this is identical with the value of $\bar{U}$ found earlier, as it should be.

In general, given an objective function

(12.5) $\qquad z = f(x,y)$

subject to the constraint

(12.6) $\qquad g(x,y) = c$

where c is a constant,[1] we can write the Lagrangean function as

(12.7) $\qquad Z = f(x,y) + \lambda[c - g(x,y)]$

---

[1] It is also possible to subsume the constant c under the constraint function so that (12.6) appears as $G(x, y) = 0$, where $G(x, y) \equiv c - g(x, y)$. In that case, (12.7) should be changed to $Z = f(x, y) + \lambda G(x, y)$.

Constrained Optimization

For stationary values of Z, regarded as a function of the three variables λ, x, and y, the necessary condition is

$$
\begin{aligned}
Z_\lambda &= c - g(x,y) = 0 \\
(12.8) \qquad Z_x &= f_x - \lambda g_x = 0 \\
Z_y &= f_y - \lambda g_y = 0
\end{aligned}
$$

Since the first equation in (12.8) is nothing but a restatement of (12.6), the stationary values of the Lagrangean function Z will automatically fulfill the constraint of the original function z. And since the expression $\lambda[c - g(x,y)]$ is now assuredly zero, the stationary values of Z in (12.7) must be identical with those of (12.5), subject to (12.6).

Let us illustrate the method with two more examples.

Example 1   Find the extremum of

$$z = xy \qquad \text{subject to} \qquad x + y = 6$$

The first step is to write the Lagrangean function

$$Z = xy + \lambda(6 - x - y)$$

For a stationary value of Z, it is necessary that

$$
\left.
\begin{aligned}
Z_\lambda &= 6 - x - y = 0 \\
Z_x &= y - \lambda = 0 \\
Z_y &= x - \lambda = 0
\end{aligned}
\right\}
\quad \text{or} \quad
\left\{
\begin{aligned}
x + y &= 6 \\
-\lambda \quad + y &= 0 \\
-\lambda + x \quad &= 0
\end{aligned}
\right.
$$

Thus, by Cramer's rule or some other method, we can find

$$\bar{\lambda} = 3 \qquad \bar{x} = 3 \qquad \bar{y} = 3$$

The stationary value is $\bar{Z} = \bar{z} = 9$, which must be tested against a second-order condition before we can tell whether it is a maximum or minimum (or neither). That will be taken up later.

Example 2   Find the extremum of

$$z = x_1^2 + x_2^2 \qquad \text{subject to} \qquad x_1 + 4x_2 = 2$$

The Lagrangean function is

$$Z = x_1^2 + x_2^2 + \lambda(2 - x_1 - 4x_2)$$

for which the necessary condition for a stationary value is

$$
\left.
\begin{aligned}
Z_\lambda &= 2 - x_1 - 4x_2 = 0 \\
Z_1 &= 2x_1 - \lambda = 0 \\
Z_2 &= 2x_2 - 4\lambda = 0
\end{aligned}
\right\}
\quad \text{or} \quad
\left\{
\begin{aligned}
x_1 + 4x_2 &= 2 \\
-\lambda + 2x_1 \quad &= 0 \\
-4\lambda \quad + 2x_2 &= 0
\end{aligned}
\right.
$$

The stationary value of Z, defined by the solution

$$\bar{\lambda} = \tfrac{4}{17} \qquad \bar{x}_1 = \tfrac{2}{17} \qquad \bar{x}_2 = \tfrac{8}{17}$$

is therefore $\bar{Z} = \bar{z} = \tfrac{4}{17}$. Again, a second-order condition must be consulted before we can tell whether $\bar{z}$ is a maximum or a minimum.

total-differential approach   In the discussion of the free extremum of $z = f(x,y)$, it was learned that the necessary condition may be stated in terms of the total differential dz as follows:

$$(12.9) \qquad dz = f_x\, dx + f_y\, dy = 0$$

This statement remains valid after a constraint $g(x,y) = c$ is added. However, with the constraint in the picture, we can no longer take dx and dy both as "arbitrary" variations as before. For if $g(x,y) = c$, then dg must be equal to dc, which is zero since c is a constant. Hence,

$$(12.10) \qquad (dg =)\; g_x\, dx + g_y\, dy = 0$$

and this relation makes dx and dy dependent on each other. The necessary condition therefore becomes $dz = 0$ [(12.9)], subject to $g = c$, and hence also subject to $dg = 0$ [(12.10)]. By visual inspection of (12.9) and (12.10), it should be clear that, in order to satisfy this necessary condition, we must have

$$(12.11) \qquad \frac{f_x}{g_x} = \frac{f_y}{g_y}$$

This result can be verified by solving (12.10) for dy and substituting the result into (12.9). The condition (12.11), together with the constraint $g(x,y) = c$, will provide two equations from which to find the critical values of x and y.†

Does the total-differential approach yield the same first-order condition as the Lagrange-multiplier method? Let us compare (12.8) with the result just obtained. The first equation in (12.8) merely repeats the constraint; the new result requires its satisfaction also. The last two equations in (12.8) can be rewritten, respectively, as

$$(12.11') \qquad \frac{f_x}{g_x} = \lambda \qquad \text{and} \qquad \frac{f_y}{g_y} = \lambda$$

and these convey precisely the same information as (12.11). Note, however, that whereas the total-differential approach yields only the values of $\bar{x}$ and $\bar{y}$, the

---

† Note that the constraint $g = c$ is still to be considered along with (12.11), even though we have utilized the equation $dg = 0$—that is, (12.10)—in deriving (12.11). While $g = c$ necessarily implies $dg = 0$, the converse is not true: $dg = 0$ merely implies $g = $ a constant (not necessarily c). Unless the constraint is explicitly considered, therefore, some information will be unwittingly left out of the problem.

Lagrange-multiplier method also gives the value of $\bar{\lambda}$ as a direct by-product. As it turns out, $\bar{\lambda}$ provides a measure of the sensitivity of $\bar{Z}$ (and $\bar{z}$) to a shift of the constraint, as we shall presently demonstrate. Therefore, the Lagrange-multiplier method offers the advantage of containing certain built-in comparative-static information in the solution.

an interpretation of the Lagrange multiplier   To show that $\bar{\lambda}$ indeed measures the sensitivity of $\bar{Z}$ to changes in the constraint, let us perform a comparative-static analysis on the first-order conditions (12.8). Since λ, x, and y are endogenous, the only available exogenous variable is the constraint parameter c. A change in c would cause a shift of the constraint curve in the xy plane, and thereby alter the optimal solution. In particular, the effect of an *increase* in c (a larger budget, or a larger production quota) would indicate how the optimal solution is affected by a *relaxation* of the constraint.

To do the comparative-static analysis, we again resort to the implicit-function theorem. Taking the three equations in (12.8) to be in the form of $F^j(\lambda,x,y;c) = 0$ (with $j = 1$, 2, 3), and assuming them to have continuous partial derivatives, we must first check that the following endogenous-variable Jacobian (where $f_{xy} = f_{yx}$, and $g_{xy} = g_{yx}$)

$$
(12.12) \quad |J| = \begin{vmatrix} \dfrac{\partial F^1}{\partial \lambda} & \dfrac{\partial F^1}{\partial x} & \dfrac{\partial F^1}{\partial y} \\[2mm] \dfrac{\partial F^2}{\partial \lambda} & \dfrac{\partial F^2}{\partial x} & \dfrac{\partial F^2}{\partial y} \\[2mm] \dfrac{\partial F^3}{\partial \lambda} & \dfrac{\partial F^3}{\partial x} & \dfrac{\partial F^3}{\partial y} \end{vmatrix} = \begin{vmatrix} 0 & -g_x & -g_y \\[2mm] -g_x & f_{xx} - \lambda g_{xx} & f_{xy} - \lambda g_{xy} \\[2mm] -g_y & f_{xy} - \lambda g_{xy} & f_{yy} - \lambda g_{yy} \end{vmatrix}
$$

does not vanish in the optimal state. At this moment, there is certainly no inkling that this would be the case. But our previous experience with the comparative statics of optimization problems [see the discussion of (11.31)] would suggest that this Jacobian is closely related to the second-order sufficient condition, and that if the sufficient condition is satisfied, then the Jacobian will be nonzero at the equilibrium (optimum). Leaving the full demonstration of this fact to the following section, let us proceed on the assumption that $|J| \neq 0$. If so, then we can express $\bar{\lambda}$, $\bar{x}$, and $\bar{y}$ all as implicit functions of the parameter c:

$$(12.13) \qquad \bar{\lambda} = \bar{\lambda}(c) \qquad \bar{x} = \bar{x}(c) \qquad \text{and} \qquad \bar{y} = \bar{y}(c)$$

all of which will have continuous derivatives. Also, we have the identities

$$
(12.14) \quad \begin{aligned} c - g(\bar{x},\bar{y}) &\equiv 0 \\ f_x(\bar{x},\bar{y}) - \bar{\lambda} g_x(\bar{x},\bar{y}) &\equiv 0 \\ f_y(\bar{x},\bar{y}) - \bar{\lambda} g_y(\bar{x},\bar{y}) &\equiv 0 \end{aligned}
$$

Now since the optimal value of Z depends on $\bar{\lambda}$, $\bar{x}$, and $\bar{y}$, that is,

(12.15) $\bar{Z} = f(\bar{x},\bar{y}) + \bar{\lambda}[c - g(\bar{x},\bar{y})]$

we may, in view of (12.13), consider $\bar{Z}$ to be a function of c alone. Differentiating $\bar{Z}$ totally with respect to c, we find

$$\frac{d\bar{Z}}{dc} = f_x \frac{d\bar{x}}{dc} + f_y \frac{d\bar{y}}{dc} + [c - g(\bar{x},\bar{y})] \frac{d\bar{\lambda}}{dc} + \bar{\lambda}\left(1 - g_x \frac{d\bar{x}}{dc} - g_y \frac{d\bar{y}}{dc}\right)$$

$$= (f_x - \bar{\lambda}g_x)\frac{d\bar{x}}{dc} + (f_y - \bar{\lambda}g_y)\frac{d\bar{y}}{dc} + [c - g(\bar{x},\bar{y})]\frac{d\bar{\lambda}}{dc} + \bar{\lambda}$$

where f_x, f_y, g_x, and g_y are all to be evaluated at the optimum. By (12.14), however, the first three terms on the right side will all drop out. Thus we are left with the simple result

(12.16) $\dfrac{d\bar{Z}}{dc} = \bar{\lambda}$

which validates our claim that the solution value of the Lagrange multiplier constitutes a measure of the effect of a change in the constraint via the parameter c on the optimal value of the objective function.

n-variable and multiconstraint cases   The generalization of the Lagrange-multiplier method to n variables can be easily carried out if we write the choice variables in subscript notation. The objective function will then be in the form

$z = f(x_1, x_2, \ldots, x_n)$

subject to the constraint

$g(x_1, x_2, \ldots, x_n) = c$

It follows that the Lagrangean function will be

$Z = f(x_1, x_2, \ldots, x_n) + \lambda[c - g(x_1, x_2, \ldots, x_n)]$

for which the first-order condition will consist of the following $(n + 1)$ simultaneous equations:

$Z_\lambda = c - g(x_1, x_2, \ldots, x_n) = 0$
$Z_1 = f_1 - \lambda g_1 = 0$
$Z_2 = f_2 - \lambda g_2 = 0$
$\cdots\cdots\cdots\cdots\cdots$
$Z_n = f_n - \lambda g_n = 0$

Again, the first of these equations will assure that the constraint is met, even though we are to focus our attention on the *free* Lagrangean function.

When there is more than one constraint, the Lagrange-multiplier method is again applicable, provided that we introduce as many such multipliers as there are constraints in the Lagrangean function.

Let an n-variable function be subject simultaneously to the two constraints

$$g(x_1, x_2, \ldots, x_n) = c \quad \text{and} \quad h(x_1, x_2, \ldots, x_n) = d$$

Then, adopting λ and μ (the Greek letter mu) as the two undetermined multipliers, we may construct a Lagrangean function as follows:

$$Z = f(x_1, x_2, \ldots, x_n) + \lambda[c - g(x_1, x_2, \ldots, x_n)] + \mu[d - h(x_1, x_2, \ldots, x_n)]$$

This function will have the same value as the original objective function f if both constraints are fulfilled, i.e., if the last two terms in the Lagrangean function both vanish. Considering λ and μ as variables, we now count $(n + 2)$ variables altogether; thus the first-order condition will in this case consist of the following $(n + 2)$ simultaneous equations:

$$Z_\lambda = c - g(x_1, x_2, \ldots, x_n) = 0$$
$$Z_\mu = d - h(x_1, x_2, \ldots, x_n) = 0$$
$$Z_i = f_i - \lambda g_i - \mu h_i = 0 \qquad (i = 1, 2, \ldots, n)$$

These will normally enable us to solve for all the x_i as well as λ and μ. As before, the first two equations of the necessary condition represent essentially a mere restatement of the two constraints.

EXERCISE 12.2

1 Use the Lagrange-multiplier method to find the stationary value of z:

(a) $z = xy$, subject to $x + 2y = 2$
(b) $z = x(y + 2)$, subject to $x + y = 1$
(c) $z = x - 3y - xy$, subject to $x + y = 6$

2 In the above problem, find whether a slight relaxation of the constraint will increase or decrease the optimal value of z. At what rate?

3 Write the Lagrangean function and the first-order condition for stationary values (without solving the equations) for each of the following:

(a) $z = x + 2y + 3w + xy - yw$, subject to $x + y + 2w = 10$
(b) $z = x^2 + 2xy + yw^2$, subject to $2x + y + w^2 = 24$ and $x + w = 8$

4 If, instead of $g(x,y) = c$, the constraint is written in the form of $G(x,y) = 0$, how should the Lagrangean function and the first-order condition be modified as a consequence?

5 In discussing the total-differential approach, it was pointed out that, given the constraint $g(x,y) = c$, we may deduce that $dg = 0$. By the same token, we can further deduce that $d^2g = d(dg) = d(0) = 0$. Yet, in our earlier discussion of the unconstrained extremum of a function $z = f(x,y)$, we had a situation where $dz = 0$ is accompanied by either a positive definite or a negative definite d^2z, rather than $d^2z = 0$. How do you account for this disparity of treatment in the two cases?

12.3 Second-Order Condition

The introduction of a Lagrange multiplier as an additional variable makes it possible to apply to the constrained-extremum problem the same first-order condition used in the free-extremum problem. It is tempting to go a step further and borrow the second-order condition as well. This, however, should not be done. For even though $\bar{Z}$ is indeed a standard type of extremum with respect to the choice variables, it is *not* so with respect to the Lagrange multiplier. Specifically, we can see from (12.15) that, unlike $\bar{x}$ and $\bar{y}$, if $\bar{\lambda}$ is replaced by any other value of λ, no effect will be produced on $\bar{Z}$, since $[c - g(\bar{x},\bar{y})]$ is identically zero. Thus the role played by λ in the optimal solution differs basically from that of x and y.† While it is harmless to treat λ as just another choice variable in the discussion of the first-order condition, we must be careful not to apply blindly the second-order condition developed for the free-extremum problem to the present constrained case. Rather, we must derive a new second-order condition. As we shall see, such a condition can again be stated in terms of the second-order total differential d^2z. However, the presence of the constraint will entail certain significant modifications of the criterion.

second-order total differential It has been mentioned that, inasmuch as the constraint $g(x,y) = c$ means $dg = g_x\,dx + g_y\,dy = 0$, as in (12.10), dx and dy no longer are both arbitrary. We may, of course, still take (say) dx as an

† In a more general framework of constrained optimization known as "nonlinear programming," to be discussed in Chap. 20, it will be shown that, with inequality constraints, if $\bar{Z}$ is a maximum (minimum) with respect to x and y, then it will be a minimum (maximum) with respect to λ. In other words, the point $(\bar{\lambda}, \bar{x}, \bar{y})$ is a saddle point. The present case—where $\bar{Z}$ is a genuine extremum with respect to x and y, but is invariant with respect to λ—may be considered as a degenerate case of saddle point. The saddle-point nature of the solution $(\bar{\lambda}, \bar{x}, \bar{y})$ also leads to the important concept of "duality." But this subject is best to be pursued later.

arbitrary variation, but then dy must be regarded as dependent on dx, always to be chosen so as to satisfy (12.10), i.e., to satisfy $dy = -(g_x/g_y)\,dx$. Viewed differently, once the value of dx is specified, dy will depend on g_x and g_y, but since the latter derivatives in turn depend on the variables x and y, dy will also depend on x and y. Obviously, then, the earlier formula for d^2z in (11.2), being based on the arbitrariness of both dx and dy, can no longer apply.

To find an appropriate new expression for d^2z, we must treat dy as a variable dependent on x and y during differentiation (if dx is to be considered a constant). Thus,

$$d^2z = d(dz) = \frac{\partial(dz)}{\partial x}\,dx + \frac{\partial(dz)}{\partial y}\,dy$$

$$= \frac{\partial}{\partial x}(f_x\,dx + f_y\,dy)\,dx + \frac{\partial}{\partial y}(f_x\,dx + f_y\,dy)\,dy$$

$$= \left[f_{xx}\,dx + \left(f_{xy}\,dy + f_y\,\frac{\partial dy}{\partial x}\right)\right]dx$$

$$\qquad\qquad + \left[f_{yx}\,dx + \left(f_{yy}\,dy + f_y\,\frac{\partial dy}{\partial y}\right)\right]dy$$

$$= f_{xx}\,dx^2 + f_{xy}\,dy\,dx + f_y\,\frac{\partial(dy)}{\partial x}\,dx$$

$$\qquad\qquad + f_{yx}\,dx\,dy + f_{yy}\,dy^2 + f_y\,\frac{\partial(dy)}{\partial y}\,dy$$

Since the third and the sixth terms can be reduced to

$$f_y\left[\frac{\partial(dy)}{\partial x}\,dx + \frac{\partial(dy)}{\partial y}\,dy\right] = f_y\,d(dy) = f_y\,d^2y$$

the desired expression for d^2z is

(12.17) $\qquad d^2z = f_{xx}\,dx^2 + 2f_{xy}\,dx\,dy + f_{yy}\,dy^2 + f_y\,d^2y$

which differs from (11.2) only by the last term, $f_y\,d^2y$.

It should be noted that this last term is in the *first* degree [d^2y is *not* the same as $(dy)^2$]; thus its presence in (12.17) disqualifies d^2z as a quadratic form. However, d^2z can be transformed into a quadratic form by virtue of the constraint $g(x,y) = c$. Since the constraint implies $dg = 0$ and also $d^2g = d(dg) = 0$, so by the procedure used in obtaining (12.17) we can get

$$(d^2g =) g_{xx}\,dx^2 + 2g_{xy}\,dx\,dy + g_{yy}\,dy^2 + g_y\,d^2y = 0$$

Solving this last equation for d^2y and substituting the result in (12.17), we are able to eliminate the first-degree expression d^2y and write d^2z as the following

384

quadratic form:

$$d^2z = \left(f_{xx} - \frac{f_y}{g_y}g_{xx}\right)dx^2 + 2\left(f_{xy} - \frac{f_y}{g_y}g_{xy}\right)dx\,dy + \left(f_{yy} - \frac{f_y}{g_y}g_{yy}\right)dy^2$$

Because of (12.11'), the first parenthetical coefficient is reducible to $(f_{xx} - \lambda g_{xx})$, and similarly for the other terms. However, by partially differentiating the derivatives in (12.8), the reader will find that the following second derivatives

$$(12.18) \quad \begin{aligned} Z_{xx} &= f_{xx} - \lambda g_{xx} \\ Z_{xy} &= f_{xy} - \lambda g_{xy} = Z_{yx} \\ Z_{yy} &= f_{yy} - \lambda g_{yy} \end{aligned}$$

are precisely equal to these parenthetical coefficients. Hence, if we make use of the Lagrangean function, we can finally express d^2z more neatly as follows:

$$(12.17') \quad \begin{aligned} d^2z = &\quad Z_{xx}\,dx^2 \quad + Z_{xy}\,dx\,dy \\ &+ Z_{yx}\,dy\,dx + Z_{yy}\,dy^2 \end{aligned}$$

The coefficients of (12.17') are simply the second partial derivatives of Z with respect to the choice variables x and y; together, therefore, they can give rise to a Hessian determinant.

For an extreme value of $z = f(x,y)$, subject to $g(x,y) = c$, the second-order condition can be couched in terms of the positive- or negative-definiteness of d^2z. The "catch" in the present context is that we are concerned with the sign-definiteness of d^2z not for all possible values of dx and dy, but only for those satisfying the (linear) equation $dg = 0$ in (12.10). Thus the second-order condition for extremum should be stated as follows:

For minimum z: d^2z positive definite, subject to $dg = 0$.

For maximum z: d^2z negative definite, subject to $dg = 0$.

the bordered Hessian   As in the case of free extremum, it is possible to express the second-order condition in determinantal form. In place of the Hessian determinant $|H|$, however, in the constrained-extremum case we shall encounter what is known as a *bordered Hessian*.

In preparation for the development of this idea, let us first analyze the conditions for the sign-definiteness of a two-variable quadratic form, subject to a linear constraint, say,

$$q = au^2 + 2huv + bv^2 \quad \text{subject to} \quad \alpha u + \beta v = 0$$

Since the constraint implies $v = -(\alpha/\beta)u$, we can rewrite q as a function of one variable only:

$$q = au^2 - 2h\frac{\alpha}{\beta}u^2 + b\frac{\alpha^2}{\beta^2}u^2 = (a\beta^2 - 2h\alpha\beta + b\alpha^2)\frac{u^2}{\beta^2}$$

It is obvious that q will be positive (negative) definite if and only if the expression in parentheses is positive (negative). Now, it so happens that the following symmetric determinant

$$\begin{vmatrix} 0 & \alpha & \beta \\ \alpha & a & h \\ \beta & h & b \end{vmatrix} = 2h\alpha\beta - a\beta^2 - b\alpha^2$$

is exactly the *negative* of the said parenthetical expression. Consequently, for values of u and v, not both zero, that satisfy the equation $\alpha u + \beta v = 0$, we can state alternatively that, subject to the given constraint,

$$q \text{ is } \begin{Bmatrix} \text{positive definite} \\ \text{negative definite} \end{Bmatrix} \quad \text{iff} \quad \begin{vmatrix} 0 & \alpha & \beta \\ \alpha & a & h \\ \beta & h & b \end{vmatrix} \begin{Bmatrix} < 0 \\ > 0 \end{Bmatrix}$$

It is noteworthy that the determinant used in this criterion is nothing but the discriminant of the original quadratic form $\begin{vmatrix} a & h \\ h & b \end{vmatrix}$, with a border placed on top and a similar border on the left. Furthermore, the border is merely composed of the two coefficients α and β from the constraint, plus a zero in the principal diagonal. This bordered discriminant is symmetric.

Example 1   Determine whether $q = 4u^2 + 4uv + 3v^2$, subject to $u - 2v = 0$, is either positive or negative definite. We first form the bordered discriminant $\begin{vmatrix} 0 & 1 & -2 \\ 1 & 4 & 2 \\ -2 & 2 & 3 \end{vmatrix}$, which is made symmetric by splitting the coefficient of uv into two equal parts for insertion into the determinant. Inasmuch as the determinant has a negative value (-27), q must be positive definite.

When applied to the quadratic form d^2z in (12.17'), the variables u and v become dx and dy, respectively, and the (plain) discriminant consists of the Hessian $\begin{vmatrix} Z_{xx} & Z_{xy} \\ Z_{yx} & Z_{yy} \end{vmatrix}$. Moreover, the constraint to the quadratic form being $g_x\,dx + g_y\,dy = 0$, we have $\alpha = g_x$ and $\beta = g_y$. Thus, for values of dx and dy, not both zero, that satisfy the said constraint, we now have the following determinantal criterion for the second-order condition:

$$d^2z \text{ is } \begin{Bmatrix} \text{positive definite} \\ \text{negative definite} \end{Bmatrix} \quad \text{iff} \quad \begin{vmatrix} 0 & g_x & g_y \\ g_x & Z_{xx} & Z_{xy} \\ g_y & Z_{yx} & Z_{yy} \end{vmatrix} \begin{Bmatrix} < 0 \\ > 0 \end{Bmatrix}$$

The determinant to the right, often referred to as a bordered Hessian, shall be denoted by $|\bar{H}|$, where the bar on top symbolizes the border. On the basis of this, we may conclude that, given a stationary value of $z = f(x,y)$ or of $Z = f(x,y) + \lambda[c - g(x,y)]$, a positive $|\bar{H}|$ is sufficient to establish it as a relative maximum of z; similarly, a negative $|\bar{H}|$ is sufficient to establish it as a minimum—all the derivatives involved in $|\bar{H}|$ being evaluated at the critical values of x and y.

Now that we have derived the second-order condition, it is an easy matter to verify that, as earlier claimed, the satisfaction of this sufficient condition will guarantee that the endogenous-variable Jacobian (12.12) does not vanish in the optimal state. Substituting (12.18) into (12.12), and multiplying both the first column and the first row of the Jacobian by -1 (which will leave the value of the determinant unaltered), we see that

$$(12.19) \qquad |J| = \begin{vmatrix} 0 & g_x & g_y \\ g_x & Z_{xx} & Z_{xy} \\ g_y & Z_{yx} & Z_{yy} \end{vmatrix} = |\bar{H}|$$

That is, the endogenous-variable Jacobian is identical with the bordered Hessian —a result similar to (11.31) where it was shown that, in the free-extremum context, the endogenous-variable Jacobian is identical with the plain Hessian. If, in fulfillment of the sufficient condition, we have $|\bar{H}| \neq 0$ at the optimum, then $|J|$ must also be nonzero. Consequently, in applying the implicit-function theorem to the present context, it would not be amiss to substitute the condition $|\bar{H}| \neq 0$ for the usual condition $|J| \neq 0$. This practice will be followed when we analyze the comparative statics of constrained-optimization problems below.

Example 2   Let us now return to Example 1 of Sec. 12.2 and ascertain whether the stationary value found there gives a maximum or a minimum. Since $Z_x = y - \lambda$ and $Z_y = x - \lambda$, the second-order partial derivatives are $Z_{xx} = 0$, $Z_{xy} = Z_{yx} = 1$, and $Z_{yy} = 0$. The border elements we need are $g_x = 1$ and $g_y = 1$. Thus we find that

$$|\bar{H}| = \begin{vmatrix} 0 & 1 & 1 \\ 1 & 0 & 1 \\ 1 & 1 & 0 \end{vmatrix} = 2 > 0$$

which establishes the value $\bar{z} = 9$ as a maximum.

Example 3   Continuing on to Example 2 of Sec. 12.2, we see that $Z_1 = 2x_1 - \lambda$ and $Z_2 = 2x_2 - 4\lambda$. These yield $Z_{11} = 2$, $Z_{12} = Z_{21} = 0$, and $Z_{22} = 2$. From the constraint $x_1 + 4x_2 = 2$, we obtain $g_1 = 1$ and $g_2 = 4$. It follows that the bordered Hessian is

$$|\bar{H}| = \begin{vmatrix} 0 & 1 & 4 \\ 1 & 2 & 0 \\ 4 & 0 & 2 \end{vmatrix} = -34 < 0$$

so that the value $\bar{z} = \frac{4}{17}$ is a minimum.

n-variable case   When the objective function takes the form

$$z = f(x_1, x_2, \ldots, x_n) \qquad \text{subject to} \qquad g(x_1, x_2, \ldots, x_n) = c$$

the second-order condition still hinges on the sign of d^2z. Since the latter will be a constrained quadratic form in the variables $dx_1, dx_2, \ldots, dx_n$, subject to the relation

$$(dg =)\, g_1\, dx_1 + g_2\, dx_2 + \cdots + g_n\, dx_n = 0$$

the conditions for the positive- or negative-definiteness of d^2z will again involve a bordered Hessian. But this time these conditions must be expressed in terms of the bordered principal minors of the Hessian.

Given a bordered Hessian

$$|\bar{H}| = \begin{vmatrix} 0 & g_1 & g_2 & \cdots & g_n \\ g_1 & Z_{11} & Z_{12} & \cdots & Z_{1n} \\ g_2 & Z_{21} & Z_{22} & \cdots & Z_{2n} \\ \cdots\cdots\cdots\cdots\cdots\cdots \\ g_n & Z_{n1} & Z_{n2} & \cdots & Z_{nn} \end{vmatrix}$$

its bordered principal minors can be defined as

$$|\bar{H}_2| \equiv \begin{vmatrix} 0 & g_1 & g_2 \\ g_1 & Z_{11} & Z_{12} \\ g_2 & Z_{21} & Z_{22} \end{vmatrix} \qquad |\bar{H}_3| \equiv \begin{vmatrix} 0 & g_1 & g_2 & g_3 \\ g_1 & Z_{11} & Z_{12} & Z_{13} \\ g_2 & Z_{21} & Z_{22} & Z_{23} \\ g_3 & Z_{31} & Z_{32} & Z_{33} \end{vmatrix} \qquad \text{(etc.)}$$

with the last one being $|\bar{H}_n| = |\bar{H}|$. In the newly introduced symbols, the horizontal bar above H again means bordered, and the subscript indicates the order of the principal minor being bordered. For instance, $|\bar{H}_2|$ involves the second principal minor of the (plain) Hessian, bordered with 0, g_1, and g_2; and similarly for the others. The conditions for positive- and negative-definiteness of d^2z will then be

$$d^2z \text{ is } \begin{cases} \text{positive definite} \\ \text{negative definite} \end{cases} \qquad \text{iff} \qquad \begin{cases} |\bar{H}_2|, |\bar{H}_3|, \ldots, |\bar{H}_n| < 0 \\ |\bar{H}_2| > 0;\ |\bar{H}_3| < 0;\ |\bar{H}_4| > 0; \ldots \end{cases}$$

In the former, all the bordered principal minors, starting with $|\bar{H}_2|$, must be negative; in the latter, they must alternate in sign. As previously, a positive-definite d^2z is sufficient to establish a stationary value of z as its minimum, whereas a negative-definite d^2z is sufficient to establish it as a maximum.

Drawing the threads of the discussion together, we may summarize the conditions for constrained extremum in Table 12.1. The reader will recognize, however, that the criterion stated in the table is not complete. The second-order condition being *not* necessary, failure to satisfy the criteria stated does not preclude the possibility that the stationary value is nonetheless a maximum or a minimum as the case may be; such an eventuality is not covered in the table. In the usual economic applications, however, the second-order sufficient condition is either satisfied, or assumed to be satisfied, so that the information in the table is adequate. The reader is urged to compare the results contained in Table 12.1 with those in Table 11.2 for the free-extremum case.

multiconstraint case   When more than one constraint appears in the problem, the second-order condition will involve a Hessian with more than one border. Suppose that there are n choice variables and m constraints $(m < n)$ of the form $g^j(x_1, \ldots, x_n) = c_j$. Then the Lagrangean function will be

$$Z = f(x_1, \ldots, x_n) + \sum_{j=1}^{m} \lambda_j[c_j - g^j(x_1, \ldots, x_n)]$$

and the bordered Hessian will appear as

$$|\bar{H}| \equiv \begin{vmatrix} 0 & 0 & \cdots & 0 & g_1^1 & g_2^1 & \cdots & g_n^1 \\ 0 & 0 & \cdots & 0 & g_1^2 & g_2^2 & \cdots & g_n^2 \\ & & & & & & & \\ 0 & 0 & \cdots & 0 & g_1^m & g_2^m & \cdots & g_n^m \\ g_1^1 & g_1^2 & \cdots & g_1^m & Z_{11} & Z_{12} & \cdots & Z_{1n} \\ g_2^1 & g_2^2 & \cdots & g_2^m & Z_{21} & Z_{22} & \cdots & Z_{2n} \\ & & & & & & & \\ g_n^1 & g_n^2 & \cdots & g_n^m & Z_{n1} & Z_{n2} & \cdots & Z_{nn} \end{vmatrix}$$

where $g_i^j \equiv \partial g^j/\partial x_i$ are the partial derivatives of the constraint functions, and the double-subscripted Z symbols denote, as before, the second-order partial

TABLE 12.1

Conditions for constrained extremum: $z = f(x_1, x_2, \ldots, x_n)$, **subject to** $g(x_1, x_2, \ldots, x_n) = c$; **with** $Z = f(x_1, x_2, \ldots, x_n) + \lambda[c - g(x_1, x_2, \ldots, x_n)]$

Condition	Maximum	Minimum
First-order	$Z_\lambda = Z_1 = Z_2 = \cdots = Z_n = 0$ (or $dz = 0$, subject to $g = c$)	$Z_\lambda = Z_1 = Z_2 = \cdots = Z_n = 0$ (or $dz = 0$, subject to $g = c$)
Second-order	$|\bar{H}_2| > 0; |\bar{H}_3| < 0;$ $|\bar{H}_4| > 0; \ldots$ (or d^2z negative definite, subject to $dg = 0$)	$|\bar{H}_2|, |\bar{H}_3|, \ldots, |\bar{H}_n| < 0$ (or d^2z positive definite, subject to $dg = 0$)

derivatives of the Lagrangean function. Note that we have partitioned the bordered Hessian into four *areas* for visual clarity. The upper-left area consists of zeros only, and the lower-right area is simply the plain Hessian. The other two areas, containing the g_i^j derivatives, bear a mirror-image relationship to each other with reference to the principal diagonal, thereby resulting in a symmetric array of elements in the entire bordered Hessian.

Various bordered principal minors can be formed from $|\bar{H}|$. The one that contains Z_{22} as the last element of its principal diagonal may be denoted by $|\bar{H}_2|$, as before. By including one more row and one more column, so that Z_{33} enters into the scene, we will have $|\bar{H}_3|$, and so forth. With this symbolism, we can state the second-order sufficient condition in terms of the signs of the following $(n - m)$ bordered principal minors:

$$|\bar{H}_{m+1}|, |\bar{H}_{m+2}|, \ldots, |\bar{H}_n|(= |\bar{H}|)$$

For a maximum of z, a sufficient condition is that these bordered principal minors alternate in sign, the sign of $|\bar{H}_{m+1}|$ being that of $(-1)^{m+1}$. For a minimum of z, a sufficient condition is that these bordered principal minors all take the same sign, namely, that of $(-1)^m$.

Note that it makes an important difference whether we have an odd or even number of constraints, because (-1) raised to an odd power will yield the opposite sign to the case of an even power. Note, also, that when $m = 1$, the condition just stated reduces to that presented in Table 12.1.

EXERCISE 12.3

1   Use the bordered Hessian to determine whether the stationary value of z obtained in each part of Exercise 12.2-1 is a maximum or a minimum.

2   In stating the second-order conditions for constrained maximum and minimum, we specified the algebraic signs of $|\bar{H}_2|$, $|\bar{H}_3|$, $|\bar{H}_4|$, etc., but not of $|\bar{H}_1|$. Write out an appropriate expression for $|\bar{H}_1|$, and verify that it will invariably take the negative sign.

3   Recalling Property II of determinants (Sec. 5.3), show that:

(a)   By appropriately interchanging two rows and/or two columns of $|\bar{H}_2|$ and duly altering the sign of the determinant after each interchange, it can be transformed into

$$\begin{vmatrix} Z_{11} & Z_{12} & g_1 \\ Z_{21} & Z_{22} & g_2 \\ g_1 & g_2 & 0 \end{vmatrix}$$

(b) By a similar procedure, $|\bar{H}_3|$ can be transformed into

$$\begin{vmatrix} Z_{11} & Z_{12} & Z_{13} & g_1 \\ Z_{21} & Z_{22} & Z_{23} & g_2 \\ Z_{31} & Z_{32} & Z_{33} & g_3 \\ g_1 & g_2 & g_3 & 0 \end{vmatrix}$$

What alternative way of "bordering" the principal minors of the Hessian do these results suggest?

4 Write out the bordered Hessian for a constrained-optimization problem with four choice variables and two constraints. Then state specifically the second-order sufficient condition for a maximum and for a minimum of z, respectively.

12.4   Utility Maximization and Consumer Demand

The maximization of a numerical utility function was cited earlier as an example of constrained optimization. Let us now reexamine this problem in more detail. For simplicity, we shall still allow our hypothetical consumer the choice of only two goods, both of which have continuous, positive marginal-utility functions. The prices of both goods are market-determined, hence exogenous, though we shall in this section omit the zero subscript from the price symbols. If the purchasing power of the consumer is a given amount B (for budget), the problem posed will be that of maximizing the utility (index) function

$$U = U(x,y) \qquad (U_x, U_y > 0)$$

subject to

$$xP_x + yP_y = B$$

first-order condition   The Lagrangean function of this optimization model is

$$Z = U(x,y) + \lambda(B - xP_x - yP_y)$$

As the first-order condition, we have the following set of simultaneous equations:

$$\begin{align} Z_\lambda &= B - xP_x - yP_y = 0 \\ (12.20) \qquad Z_x &= U_x - \lambda P_x = 0 \\ Z_y &= U_y - \lambda P_y = 0 \end{align}$$

Since the last two equations are equivalent to

$$(12.20') \qquad \frac{U_x}{P_x} = \frac{U_y}{P_y} = \lambda$$

the first-order condition in effect calls for the satisfaction of (12.20′), subject to the budget constraint—the first equation in (12.20). What (12.20′) states is merely the familiar proposition in classical consumer theory that, in order to maximize utility, the consumer must allocate his budget so as to equalize the ratio of marginal utility to price for every commodity. Specifically, in the equilibrium or optimum, these ratios should have the common value λ. As we learned earlier, λ measures the comparative-static effect of the constraint constant on the optimal value of the objective function. Hence, we have in the present context $\lambda = (\partial \bar{U}/\partial B)$; that is, the optimal value of the Lagrange multiplier can be interpreted to mean the *marginal utility of money* (budget money) when the consumer's utility is maximized.

If we restate the condition in (12.20′) in the form

$$(12.20'') \qquad \frac{U_x}{U_y} = \frac{P_x}{P_y}$$

the first-order condition can be given an alternative interpretation, in terms of indifference curves.

An *indifference curve* is defined as the locus of the combinations of x and y that will yield a constant level of U. This means that on an indifference curve we must find

$$dU = U_x \, dx + U_y \, dy = 0$$

with the implication that $dy/dx = -U_x/U_y$. Accordingly, if we plot an indifference curve in the xy plane, as in Fig. 12.3, its slope, dy/dx, must be equal to the negative of the marginal-utility ratio U_x/U_y. (Since we assume $U_x, U_y > 0$, the slope of the indifference curve must be negative.) Conversely, since U_x/U_y is the negative of the indifference-curve slope, it must represent the *marginal rate of substitution* between the two goods.

What about the meaning of P_x/P_y? As we shall presently see, this ratio represents the negative of the slope of the graph of the budget constraint. The budget constraint, $xP_x + yP_y = B$, can be written alternatively as

$$y = \frac{B}{P_y} - \frac{P_x}{P_y} x$$

so that, when plotted in the xy plane as in Fig. 12.3, it will obviously emerge as a straight line with slope $-P_x/P_y$ (and vertical intercept B/P_y).

In this light, the new version of the first-order condition—(12.20″) plus the

Optimization Problems

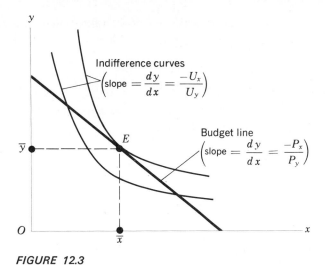

FIGURE 12.3

budget constraint—discloses that, to maximize utility, the consumer must allocate his budget so that the slope of his budget line is equal to the slope of some indifference curve, while nonetheless remaining on the budget line. This condition is met at point E, a point of tangency between the budget line and one of the indifference curves in Fig. 12.3.

second-order condition   If the bordered Hessian in the present problem is positive, i.e., if

$$(12.21) \qquad |\bar{H}| = \begin{vmatrix} 0 & P_x & P_y \\ P_x & U_{xx} & U_{xy} \\ P_y & U_{yx} & U_{yy} \end{vmatrix} = 2P_x P_y U_{xy} - P_y^2 U_{xx} - P_x^2 U_{yy} > 0$$

(with all the derivatives evaluated at the critical values $\bar{x}$ and $\bar{y}$), then the stationary value of U will assuredly be a maximum. The presence of the derivatives U_{xx}, U_{yy}, and U_{xy} in (12.21) clearly suggests that fulfillment of the condition would entail certain restrictions on the utility function and, hence, on the shape of the indifference curves. What are these restrictions?

Considering first the shape of the indifference curves, we can show that a positive $|\bar{H}|$ means essentially the strict convexity of the (downward-sloping) indifference curve at the point of tangency E. Just as the downward slope of an indifference curve is indicated by a negative $dy/dx \ (= -U_x/U_y)$, its strict convexity hinges on a positive d^2y/dx^2. To get d^2y/dx^2, we can differentiate $-U_x/U_y$ with respect to x; but in doing so, we should bear in mind not only that both U_x and U_y (being derivatives) are functions of x and y but also that, along

Constrained Optimization

a given indifference curve, y is itself a function of x. Accordingly, U_x and U_y can both be considered functions of x alone; therefore, we can get a total derivative

$$(12.22) \qquad \frac{d^2y}{dx^2} = \frac{d}{dx}\left(-\frac{U_x}{U_y}\right) = -\frac{1}{U_y{}^2}\left(U_y\frac{dU_x}{dx} - U_x\frac{dU_y}{dx}\right)$$

Since x can affect U_x and U_y not only directly but also indirectly, via the intermediary of y, we have

$$(12.23) \qquad \frac{dU_x}{dx} = U_{xx} + U_{yx}\frac{dy}{dx} \qquad \frac{dU_y}{dx} = U_{xy} + U_{yy}\frac{dy}{dx}$$

where dy/dx refers to the slope of the indifference curve. Now, at the point of tangency E—the only point relevant to the discussion of the second-order condition—this slope is identical with that of the budget constraint; that is, $dy/dx = -P_x/P_y$. Thus we can rewrite (12.23) as

$$(12.23') \qquad \frac{dU_x}{dx} = U_{xx} - U_{yx}\frac{P_x}{P_y} \qquad \frac{dU_y}{dx} = U_{xy} - U_{yy}\frac{P_x}{P_y}$$

Substituting (12.23′) into (12.22) and utilizing the information that

$$U_x = \frac{U_y P_x}{P_y} \qquad \text{[from (12.20″)]}$$

and then factoring out $U_y/P_y{}^2$, we can finally transform (12.22) into

$$(12.22') \qquad \frac{d^2y}{dx^2} = \frac{2P_x P_y U_{xy} - P_y{}^2 U_{xx} - P_x{}^2 U_{yy}}{U_y P_y{}^2} = \frac{|\bar{H}|}{U_y P_y{}^2}$$

It is clear that when the second-order condition for maximum in (12.21) is fulfilled, the second derivative in (12.22′) is positive, so that the indifference curve must be strictly convex. We recall, however, that the derivatives in $|\bar{H}|$ are evaluated at the critical values $\bar{x}$ and $\bar{y}$ only, and thus the convexity condition pertains only to that point of tangency. Naturally, if all the indifference curves happen to be strictly convex everywhere, then the point of tangency with a budget line will always produce a utility-maximizing combination of x and y wherever that point may be.

strictly concave and strictly quasiconcave utility functions   Our next question is: What types of utility function will produce strictly convex indifference curves as shown in Fig. 12.3 and thus satisfy the second-order condition (12.21)? Two functions that qualify are illustrated in Fig. 12.4. Diagram a depicts a smooth, strictly concave function similar to the one in Fig. 11.1a except that, because of the assumption of positive U_x and U_y, we have only

Optimization Problems

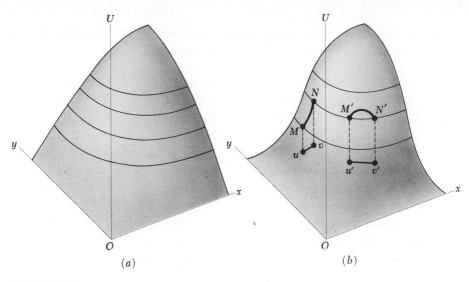

FIGURE 12.4

drawn the ascending portion of a dome-shaped surface. When this surface is cut with a plane parallel to the xy plane, we obtain for each of such cuts a curve which, when projected onto the xy plane, will become a strictly convex downward-sloping indifference curve as drawn in Fig. 12.3. Strict concavity in a smooth utility function is, therefore, sufficient to fulfill the second-order condition. By examining Fig. 12.4b, however, it should be evident that strict concavity is not necessary, for the desired indifference curves can also be obtained from diagram b, even though the utility surface shown therein is not strictly concave —in fact, not even concave.

Generally shaped like a bell, though shown here only as the ascending portion of a bell, the type of surface in Fig. 12.4b exemplifies the so-called *strictly quasiconcave function*. Its defining geometric property is that, for any pair of distinct points u and v in its domain, if the line segment uv (which is assumed to lie entirely in the domain) gives rise to the arc MN on the surface, and if M is lower than or equal in height to N, then all the points on arc MN other than M and N must be higher than M. Algebraically, a function f is said to be strictly quasiconcave if, for any two distinct points u and v in the domain, and for all values of ζ, $0 < \zeta < 1$, we have

$$(12.24) \qquad f(u) \le f(v) \qquad \Rightarrow \qquad f[\zeta u + (1 - \zeta)v] > f(u)$$

or, equivalently,

$$(12.24') \qquad f[\zeta u + (1 - \zeta)v] > \min \{f(u), f(v)\}$$

Constrained Optimization

where the right-side expression in the last inequality is read: the minimum of the set of values $f(u)$ and $f(v)$. That this definition is satisfied by the function in Fig. 12.4b can be verified by examining such arcs as MN (M lower than N) and $M'N'$ (M' and N' of equal height). Note that, in the case of arc $M'N'$, it is the heavy arch, not the light curve that passes through M' and N' as part of an indifference curve, that lies directly above the line segment $u'v'$. The interesting thing is, however, that the definition (12.24) is actually also satisfied by the strictly concave function in Fig. 12.4a. What this suggests is that a strictly concave function is always strictly quasiconcave, although, as we have seen, the converse is not true.

From the above, it may be concluded that, in order to generate strictly convex downward-sloping indifference curves as shown in Fig. 12.3, all we need is to specify a smooth, increasing, strictly quasiconcave utility function. Such a function may contain convex as well as concave portions, as shown in Fig. 12.4b, so that marginal utilities U_x and U_y may be either increasing or diminishing. It follows that strict convexity of indifference curves does not imply diminishing marginal utilities, a fact that can also be verified in (12.21), where the positivity of $|\bar{H}|$ by no means requires the negativity of U_{xx} and U_{yy}. Viewed the other way around, (12.21) also indicates that diminishing marginal utilities may not mean strictly convex indifference curves, since to have $U_{xx} < 0$ and $U_{yy} < 0$, without anything said about the cross partial derivatives $U_{xy} = U_{yx}$, certainly does not guarantee a positive $|\bar{H}|$. However, if we adopt the stronger assumption of a strictly concave utility function, then we will have the features of diminishing marginal utilities and strictly convex indifference curves simultaneously.

In our model, U_x and U_y are assumed to have continuous derivatives. As a result, the utility surface must be drawn as a smooth one. But the definition (12.24) does not in itself require smoothness in the function. To give an illustration in the one-variable framework, the curve in Fig. 12.5a contains a sharp point M, yet it qualifies nonetheless as a strictly quasiconcave curve. The same diagram also illustrates that a strictly quasiconcave curve (or surface) does not have to be sloped in a single direction throughout, although it can.

Now that we have defined strict quasiconcavity of a function, it is easy to explain the related concepts of strict quasiconvexity and (nonstrict) quasiconcavity and quasiconvexity. The algebraic definition of a *strictly quasiconvex* function is given by

$$(12.25) \qquad f(u) \leq f(v) \qquad \Rightarrow \qquad f[\zeta u + (1 - \zeta)v] < f(v) \qquad (0 < \zeta < 1)$$

or, equivalently,

$$(12.25') \qquad f[\zeta u + (1 - \zeta)v] < \max \{f(u), f(v)\}$$

where the right-side expression is read: the maximum of the set of values $f(u)$

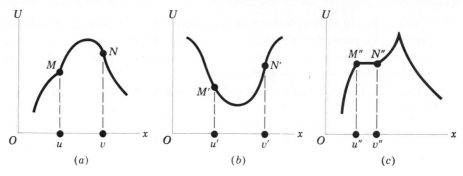

FIGURE 12.5

and $f(v)$. Geometrically, this type of function has the shape of an inverted bell, as illustrated in Fig. 12.5b. Note that arc $M'N'$ in diagram b satisfies (12.25) but fails (12.24), whereas the exact opposite is true of arc MN in diagram a.

To define (nonstrict) *quasiconcavity*, it is only necessary to change the strict inequality sign $>$ in (12.24) and (12.24$'$) to the weak inequality sign $\geq$. Geometrically, this will allow the surface to contain a flat portion, or, in the one-variable case, a horizontal line segment. The latter is illustrated in Fig. 12.5c, where every point on arc $M''N''$ is of uniform height, and that arc satisfies (12.24$'$) as an equality rather than inequality. To define (nonstrict) *quasiconvexity*, we only need to replace the $<$ sign in (12.25) and (12.25$'$) by the $\leq$ sign. The reader will observe that if a function f is quasiconcave, then the function $-f$ must be quasiconvex, and vice versa.

comparative-static analysis   In our consumer model, the prices P_x and P_y are exogenous, as is the amount of the budget, B. If we assume the satisfaction of the second-order condition, then we can analyze the comparative-static properties of the model on the basis of the first-order condition (12.20), viewed as a set of equations $F^j = 0$ (with $j = 1, 2, 3$), where each F^j function has continuous partial derivatives. As pointed out in (12.19), the endogenous-variable Jacobian of this set of equations must have the same value as the bordered Hessian; that is, $|J| = |\bar{H}|$. Thus, when the second-order condition (12.21) is met, $|J|$ must be positive and it does not vanish at the initial optimum. Consequently, the implicit-function theorem is applicable, and we may express the optimal values of the endogenous variables as implicit functions of the exogenous variables:

$$
\begin{aligned}
\bar{\lambda} &= \bar{\lambda}(P_x, P_y, B) \\
(12.26) \quad \bar{x} &= \bar{x}(P_x, P_y, B) \\
\bar{y} &= \bar{y}(P_x, P_y, B)
\end{aligned}
$$

These are known to possess continuous derivatives that give comparative-static information. In particular, the derivatives of the last two functions $\bar{x}$ and $\bar{y}$, which are descriptive of the consumer's demand behavior, can tell us how the consumer will react to changes in prices and in his budget. To find these derivatives, however, we must first convert (12.20) into a set of equilibrium identities as follows:

$$
\begin{array}{ll}
& B - \bar{x}P_x - \bar{y}P_y \equiv 0 \\
(12.27) \quad & U_x(\bar{x},\bar{y}) - \lambda P_x \equiv 0 \\
& U_y(\bar{x},\bar{y}) - \lambda P_y \equiv 0
\end{array}
$$

By taking the total differential of each identity in turn (allowing every variable to change), and noting that $U_{xy} = U_{yx}$, we then arrive at the linear system

$$
\begin{array}{ll}
& - P_x \; d\bar{x} - P_y \; d\bar{y} = \bar{x} \; dP_x + \bar{y} \; dP_y - dB \\
(12.28) \quad & -P_x \; d\lambda + U_{xx} \; d\bar{x} + U_{xy} \; d\bar{y} = \lambda \; dP_x \\
& -P_y \; d\lambda + U_{yx} \; d\bar{x} + U_{yy} \; d\bar{y} = \qquad \lambda \; dP_y
\end{array}
$$

To study the effect of a change in the budget size (also referred to as the *income* of the consumer), let $dP_x = dP_y = 0$, but keep $dB \neq 0$. Then, after dividing (12.28) through by dB, and interpreting each ratio of differentials as a partial derivative, we can write the matrix equation[1]

$$
(12.29) \quad
\begin{bmatrix}
0 & -P_x & -P_y \\
-P_x & U_{xx} & U_{xy} \\
-P_y & U_{yx} & U_{yy}
\end{bmatrix}
\begin{bmatrix}
(\partial\lambda/\partial B) \\
(\partial\bar{x}/\partial B) \\
(\partial\bar{y}/\partial B)
\end{bmatrix}
=
\begin{bmatrix}
-1 \\
0 \\
0
\end{bmatrix}
$$

As the reader can verify, the array of elements in the coefficient matrix is exactly the same as what would appear in the Jacobian $|J|$, which has the same value as the bordered Hessian $|\bar{H}|$ although the latter has P_x and P_y (rather than $-P_x$ and $-P_y$) in the first row and the first column. By Cramer's rule, we can solve for all three comparative-static derivatives, but we shall confine our attention to the following two:

$$
(12.30) \quad
\left(\frac{\partial\bar{x}}{\partial B}\right) = \frac{1}{|J|}
\begin{vmatrix}
0 & -1 & -P_y \\
-P_x & 0 & U_{xy} \\
-P_y & 0 & U_{yy}
\end{vmatrix}
= \frac{1}{|J|}
\begin{vmatrix}
-P_x & U_{xy} \\
-P_y & U_{yy}
\end{vmatrix}
$$

$$
(12.31) \quad
\left(\frac{\partial\bar{y}}{\partial B}\right) = \frac{1}{|J|}
\begin{vmatrix}
0 & -P_x & -1 \\
-P_x & U_{xx} & 0 \\
-P_y & U_{yx} & 0
\end{vmatrix}
= \frac{-1}{|J|}
\begin{vmatrix}
-P_x & U_{xx} \\
-P_y & U_{yx}
\end{vmatrix}
$$

By the second-order condition, $|J| = |\bar{H}|$ is positive, as are P_x and P_y. Unfortunately, in the absence of additional information about the relative magnitudes

---

[1] The matrix equation (12.29) can also be obtained by totally differentiating (12.27) with respect to B, while bearing in mind the implicit solutions in (12.26).

of P_x, P_y, and the U_{ij}, we are still unable to ascertain the signs of these two comparative-static derivatives. This means that, as the consumer's budget (or income) increases, his optimal purchases $\bar{x}$ and $\bar{y}$ may *either* increase *or* decrease. In case, say, $\bar{x}$ decreases as B increases, product x is referred to as an *inferior good* as against a *normal good*.

Next, we may analyze the effect of a change in P_x. Letting $dP_y = dB = 0$ this time, but keeping $dP_x \neq 0$, and then dividing (12.28) through by dP_x, we obtain another matrix equation

$$(12.32) \qquad \begin{bmatrix} 0 & -P_x & -P_y \\ -P_x & U_{xx} & U_{xy} \\ -P_y & U_{yx} & U_{yy} \end{bmatrix} \begin{bmatrix} (\partial\bar{\lambda}/\partial P_x) \\ (\partial\bar{x}/\partial P_x) \\ (\partial\bar{y}/\partial P_x) \end{bmatrix} = \begin{bmatrix} \bar{x} \\ \bar{\lambda} \\ 0 \end{bmatrix}$$

From this, the following comparative-static derivatives emerge:

$$(12.33) \qquad \left(\frac{\partial\bar{x}}{\partial P_x}\right) = \frac{1}{|J|} \begin{vmatrix} 0 & \bar{x} & -P_y \\ -P_x & \bar{\lambda} & U_{xy} \\ -P_y & 0 & U_{yy} \end{vmatrix}$$

$$= \frac{-\bar{x}}{|J|} \begin{vmatrix} -P_x & U_{xy} \\ -P_y & U_{yy} \end{vmatrix} + \frac{\bar{\lambda}}{|J|} \begin{vmatrix} 0 & -P_y \\ -P_y & U_{yy} \end{vmatrix}$$

$$\equiv T_1 + T_2 \qquad [T_i \text{ means the } i\text{th term}]$$

$$(12.34) \qquad \left(\frac{\partial\bar{y}}{\partial P_x}\right) = \frac{1}{|J|} \begin{vmatrix} 0 & -P_x & \bar{x} \\ -P_x & U_{xx} & \bar{\lambda} \\ -P_y & U_{yx} & 0 \end{vmatrix}$$

$$= \frac{\bar{x}}{|J|} \begin{vmatrix} -P_x & U_{xx} \\ -P_y & U_{yx} \end{vmatrix} - \frac{\bar{\lambda}}{|J|} \begin{vmatrix} 0 & -P_x \\ -P_y & U_{yx} \end{vmatrix}$$

$$\equiv T_3 + T_4$$

How do we interpret these two results? The first one, $(\partial\bar{x}/\partial P_x)$, tells how a change in P_x affects the optimal purchase of x; it thus provides the basis for the study of our consumer's demand function for x. There are two component terms in this effect. The first term, T_1, can be rewritten, by using (12.30), as $-(\partial\bar{x}/\partial B)\bar{x}$. In this light, T_1 seems to be a measure of the effect of a change in B (budget, or income) upon the optimal purchase $\bar{x}$, with $\bar{x}$ itself serving as a weighting factor. However, since this derivative obviously is concerned with a price change, T_1 must be interpreted as the *income effect* of a *price change*. As P_x rises, the decline in the consumer's real income will produce an effect on $\bar{x}$ similar to that of an actual decrease in B; hence the use of the term $-(\partial\bar{x}/\partial B)$. Understandably, the more prominent the place of commodity x in the total budget, the greater this income effect will be—and hence the appearance of the weighting factor $\bar{x}$ in T_1. This interpretation can be demonstrated more rigorously by expressing the consumer's effectual income loss by the differential $dB = -\bar{x}\, dP_x$. Then we have

$$(12.35) \qquad \bar{x} = -\frac{dB}{dP_x}$$

and $\qquad T_1 = -\left(\frac{\partial \bar{x}}{\partial B}\right)\bar{x} = \left(\frac{\partial \bar{x}}{\partial B}\right)\frac{dB}{dP_x}$

which shows T_1 to be the measure of the effect of dP_x on $\bar{x}$ via B, that is, the income effect.

If we now compensate the consumer for his effectual income loss by giving him an income increment numerically equal to dB, then, because of the neutralization of the income effect, the remaining component in the comparative-static derivative $(\partial \bar{x}/\partial P_x)$, namely, T_2, will measure the variation in $\bar{x}$ due entirely to price-induced substitution of one commodity for another, i.e., the *substitution effect* of the change in P_x. To see this more clearly, let us return to (12.28), and see how the income compensation will modify the situation. When studying the effect of dP_x only (with $dP_y = dB = 0$), the first equation in (12.28) can be written as $-P_x\,d\bar{x} - P_y\,d\bar{y} = \bar{x}\,dP_x$. Since the indication of the effectual income loss of the consumer lies in the expression $\bar{x}\,dP_x$ (which, incidentally, appears only in the first equation), to compensate the consumer means to set this term equal to zero. If so, the vector of constants in (12.32) must be changed from $\begin{bmatrix} \bar{x} \\ \lambda \\ 0 \end{bmatrix}$ to $\begin{bmatrix} 0 \\ \lambda \\ 0 \end{bmatrix}$, and the income-compensated version of the derivative $(\partial \bar{x}/\partial P_x)$ will be

$$\left(\frac{\partial \bar{x}}{\partial P_x}\right)_{\text{compensated}} = \frac{1}{|J|}\begin{vmatrix} 0 & 0 & -P_y \\ -P_x & \lambda & U_{xy} \\ -P_y & 0 & U_{yy} \end{vmatrix} = \frac{\lambda}{|J|}\begin{vmatrix} 0 & -P_y \\ -P_y & U_{yy} \end{vmatrix} = T_2$$

Hence, we may express (12.33) in the form

$$(12.33') \qquad \left(\frac{\partial \bar{x}}{\partial P_x}\right) = T_1 + T_2 = \underbrace{-\left(\frac{\partial \bar{x}}{\partial B}\right)\bar{x}}_{\text{income effect}} + \underbrace{\left(\frac{\partial \bar{x}}{\partial P_x}\right)_{\text{compensated}}}_{\text{substitution effect}}$$

This result, which decomposes the comparative-static derivative $(\partial \bar{x}/\partial P_x)$ into two components, an income effect and a substitution effect, is known as the *Slutsky equation.*

What can we say about the sign of $(\partial \bar{x}/\partial P_x)$? The substitution effect T_2 is clearly negative, because $|J| > 0$ and $\lambda > 0$ [see (12.20')]. The income effect T_1, on the other hand, is indeterminate in sign according to (12.30). Should it be negative, it would reinforce T_2; in that event, an increase in P_x must decrease the purchase of x, and the demand curve of the utility-maximizing consumer will be negatively sloped. Should it be positive, but relatively small in magnitude, it would dilute the substitution effect, though the overall result would still be a downward-sloping demand curve. But in case T_1 is positive and dominates T_2 (such as when $\bar{x}$ is a significant item in the consumer budget, thus providing an overwhelming weighting factor), then a rise in P_x will actually lead to a *larger* purchase of x, a special demand situation characteristic of what are called *Giffen goods*. Normally, of course, we would expect $(\partial \bar{x}/\partial P_x)$ to be negative.

Finally, let us examine the comparative-static derivative in (12.34), $(\partial \bar{y}/\partial P_x) = T_3 + T_4$, which has to do with the *cross effect* of a change in the price of x on the optimal purchase of y. The term T_3 bears a striking resemblance to term T_1 and again has the interpretation of an income effect.[1] Note that the weighting factor here is again $\bar{x}$ (rather than $\bar{y}$); this is because we are studying the effect of a change in P_x on effectual income, which depends for its magnitude upon the relative importance of $\bar{x}$ (not $\bar{y}$) in the consumer budget. Naturally, the remaining term, T_4, is again a measure of the substitution effect.

The sign of T_3 is, according to (12.31), dependent on such factors as U_{xx}, U_{yx}, etc., and is indeterminate without further restrictions on the model. However, the substitution effect T_4 will surely be positive in our model, since $\bar{\lambda}$, P_x, P_y and $|J|$ are all positive. This means that, unless more than offset by a negative income effect, an increase in the price of x will always increase the purchase of y in our two-commodity model. In other words, when the consumer can only choose between two goods, these goods must bear a relationship to each other as substitutes.

Even though the above analysis relates to the effects of a change in P_x, our results are readily adaptable to the case of a change in P_y. Our model happens to be such that the positions occupied by the variables x and y are perfectly symmetrical. Thus, to infer the effects of a change in P_y, all that it takes is to interchange the roles of x and y in the results already obtained above.

proportionate changes in prices and income It is also of interest to ask how $\bar{x}$ and $\bar{y}$ will be affected when all three parameters P_x, P_y, and B are changed in the same proportion. Such a question still lies within the realm of comparative statics, but unlike the preceding analysis, the present inquiry now involves the simultaneous variation of all the parameters.

When both prices are raised, along with income, by the same multiple k, every term in the budget constraint will increase k-fold, to become

$$kB - kxP_x - kyP_y = 0$$

---

[1] The reader who needs a stronger dose of assurance that T_3 represents the income effect can use (12.31) and (12.35) to write

$$T_3 = -\left(\frac{\partial \bar{y}}{\partial B}\right)\bar{x} = \left(\frac{\partial \bar{y}}{\partial B}\right)\frac{dB}{dP_x}$$

Thus T_3 is the effect of a change in P_x on $\bar{y}$ via the income factor B.

Inasmuch as the common factor k can be canceled out, however, this new constraint is in fact identical with the old. The utility function, moreover, is independent of these parameters. Consequently, the old equilibrium levels of x and y will continue to prevail; that is, the consumer equilibrium position in our model is invariant to *equal* proportionate changes in all the prices and in his income. Thus, in the present model, the consumer is seen to be free from any "money illusion."

Symbolically, this situation can be described by the equations

$$\bar{x}(P_x,P_y,B) = \bar{x}(kP_x,kP_y,kB)$$
$$\bar{y}(P_x,P_y,B) = \bar{y}(kP_x,kP_y,kB)$$

The functions $\bar{x}$ and $\bar{y}$, with the *invariance* property just cited, are no ordinary functions; they are examples of a special class of function known as *homogeneous functions*, which have interesting economic applications. We shall therefore examine these briefly in the next section.

EXERCISE 12.4

1   Given $U = (x + 2)(y + 1)$ and $P_x = 2$, $P_y = 5$, and $B = 51$:

    (a)   Write the Lagrangean function.
    (b)   Find the optimal levels of purchase $\bar{x}$ and $\bar{y}$.
    (c)   Is the second-order condition for maximum fulfilled?
    (d)   Does the set of solutions in (b) give any comparative-static information?

2   Assume that $U = (x + 2)(y + 1)$, but this time assign no specific numerical values to the price and income parameters.

    (a)   Write the Lagrangean function.
    (b)   Find $\bar{x}$, $\bar{y}$, and $\bar{\lambda}$ in terms of the parameters P_x, P_y, and B.
    (c)   Check whether the second-order condition for maximum is fulfilled.
    (d)   By setting $P_x = 2$, $P_y = 5$, and $B = 51$, check the validity of your answer to the preceding problem.

3   Can your set of solutions ($\bar{x}$ and $\bar{y}$) in Exercise 12.4-2 yield any comparative-static information? Find all the comparative-static derivatives you can, evaluate their signs, and interpret their economic meanings.

4   From the utility function $U = (x + 2)(y + 1)$ and the constraint $xP_x + yP_y = B$ of Exercise 12.4-2, we have already found the U_{ij} and $|\bar{H}|$, as well as $\bar{x}$ and $\bar{\lambda}$. Moreover, we recall that $|J| = |\bar{H}|$.

(a) Substitute these into (12.30) and (12.31) to find $(\partial\bar{x}/\partial B)$ and $(\partial\bar{y}/\partial B)$.

(b) Substitute into (12.33) and (12.34) to find $(\partial\bar{x}/\partial P_x)$ and $(\partial\bar{y}/\partial P_x)$.

Do these results check with those obtained in Exercise 12.4-3?

5   In your solutions $\bar{x}$ and $\bar{y}$ in Exercise 12.4-2, will the levels of optimal purchase change if the income and the two prices are all doubled?

6   When studying the effect of dP_x alone, the first equation in (12.28) reduces to $-P_x\,d\bar{x} - P_y\,d\bar{y} = \bar{x}\,dP_x$, and when we compensate the consumer's effectual income loss by dropping the term $\bar{x}\,dP_x$, the equation becomes $-P_x\,d\bar{x} - P_y\,d\bar{y} = 0$. Show that this result can be obtained alternatively from a compensation procedure whereby we try to keep the consumer's optimal utility level $\bar{U}$ (rather than effectual income) unchanged, so that the term T_2 can alternatively be interpreted as $(\partial\bar{x}/\partial P_x)_{\bar{U}=\text{constant}}$. [*Hint:* Make use of (12.20'').]

7   Draw a strictly quasiconcave curve $y = f(x)$ which is

(a) also quasiconvex   (d) not concave

(b) not quasiconvex   (e) neither concave nor convex

(c) not convex   (f) both concave and convex

8   Are the following functions quasiconcave? Strictly quasiconcave? First check graphically; then check by the algebraic definition. Assume that $x \geq 0$.

(a) $f(x) = a$ (c) $f(x) = a + cx^2$ $(c < 0)$

(b) $f(x) = a + bx$ $(b > 0)$

9   Show that the utility function $U(x,y) = ax + by$, $(a,b > 0)$, is quasiconcave, but not strictly so, for nonnegative values of x and y. Deduce from the given function the general shape of the indifference curves, and show that they are (as expected) not strictly convex curves.

12.5   Note on Homogeneous Functions

A function is said to be homogeneous of degree r, if multiplication of each of its independent variables by a constant k will alter the value of the function by the proportion k^r, that is, if

$$f(kx_1, \ldots, kx_n) = k^r f(x_1, \ldots, x_n)$$

In general, k can take any value. However, in order for the above equation to make sense, $(kx_1, \ldots, kx_n)$ must not lie outside the domain of the function f. For this reason, in economic applications the constant k is usually taken to be positive, because most economic variables do not admit negative values.

Example 1   Given the function $f(x,y,w) = x/y + 2w/3x$, if we multiply each variable by k, we get

$$f(kx,ky,kw) = \frac{(kx)}{(ky)} + \frac{2(kw)}{3(kx)} = \frac{x}{y} + \frac{2w}{3x} = f(x,y,w) = k^0 f(x,y,w)$$

In this particular example, the value of the function will *not* be affected at all by equal proportionate variations in all the independent variables; or, one might say, the value of the function is changed by a multiple of k^0 ($= 1$). This makes the function f a homogeneous function of degree zero.

The reader will observe that the functions $\bar{x}$ and $\bar{y}$ cited at the end of the preceding section are both homogeneous of degree zero.

Example 2   When we multiply each variable in the function

$$g(x,y,w) = \frac{x^2}{y} + \frac{2w^2}{x}$$

by k, we get

$$g(kx,ky,kw) = \frac{(kx)^2}{(ky)} + \frac{2(kw)^2}{(kx)} = k\left(\frac{x^2}{y} + \frac{2w^2}{x}\right) = kg(x,y,w)$$

The function g is homogeneous of degree one (or, of the first degree); multiplication of each variable by k will alter the value of the function exactly k-fold as well.

Example 3   Now, consider the function $h(x,y,w) = 2x^2 + 3yw - w^2$. A similar multiplication this time will give us

$$h(kx,ky,kw) = 2(kx)^2 + 3(ky)(kw) - (kw)^2 = k^2 h(x,y,w)$$

Thus the function h is homogeneous of degree two; in this case, a doubling of all variables, for example, will quadruple the value of the function.

linear homogeneity   In the discussion of production functions, wide use is made of homogeneous functions of the first degree. These are often referred to as *linearly homogeneous* functions, the adverb "linearly" modifying the adjective "homogeneous." Some writers, however, seem to prefer the somewhat misleading terminology *linear* homogeneous functions, or even *linear and* homogeneous functions, which tends to convey, wrongly, the impression that the functions themselves are linear. On the basis of the function g in Example 2 above, we know that a function which is homogeneous of the first degree is *not necessarily* linear in itself. Hence the reader is advised to avoid using the terms "linear homogeneous functions" and "linear and homogeneous functions" unless, of course, the functions in question are indeed linear. Note, however, that it is not incorrect to speak of "linear homogeneity," meaning homogeneity of degree one, because to modify a noun (homogeneity) does call for the use of an adjective (linear).

Since the primary field of application of linearly homogeneous functions is in the theory of production, let us adopt as the framework of our discussion a production function in the form, say,

$$(12.36) \qquad Q = f(K,L)$$

Whether applied at the *micro* or the *macro* level, the mathematical assumption of linear homogeneity would amount to the economic assumption of constant returns to scale, because linear homogeneity means that raising all inputs (independent variables) k-fold will always raise the output (value of the function) exactly k-fold also.

What unique properties characterize a linearly homogeneous production function?

PROPERTY I   The average physical product of labor (APP_L) and of capital (APP_K) can be expressed as functions of the capital-labor ratio, $K^* \equiv K/L$, alone.

To prove this, we multiply each independent variable in (12.36) by a factor $k = 1/L$. By virtue of linear homogeneity, this will change output Q to $kQ = Q/L$. The right side of (12.36) will correspondingly become

$$f\left(\frac{K}{L}, \frac{L}{L}\right) = f\left(\frac{K}{L}, 1\right) = f(K^*,1)$$

Since the variables K and L in the original function are to be replaced (whenever they appear) by K^* and 1, respectively, the right side in effect becomes a function of the capital-labor ratio K^* alone, say, $\phi(K^*)$, which is a function with a single argument, K^*, even though two independent variables K and L are actually involved in that argument. Equating the two sides, we have

$$(12.37) \qquad APP_L \equiv \frac{Q}{L} = \phi(K^*)$$

The expression for APP_K is then found to be

$$(12.38) \qquad APP_K \equiv \frac{Q}{K} = \frac{Q}{L}\frac{L}{K} = \frac{\phi(K^*)}{K^*}$$

Both average products being functions of K^* alone, linear homogeneity implies that, as long as the K/L ratio is kept constant (whatever the absolute levels of K and L), the average products will be constant, too. Therefore, while the production function is homogeneous of degree one, both APP_L and APP_K are homogeneous of degree *zero* in the variables K and L, since equal proportionate changes in K and L (a constant K^*) will not alter the magnitudes of the average products.

PROPERTY II   The marginal physical products MPP_L and MPP_K can likewise be expressed as functions of K^* alone.

To find the marginal products, we first write the total product as

(12.36′) $Q = L\phi(K^*)$ [by (12.37)]

and then differentiate Q with respect to K and L. For this purpose, we shall find the following two preliminary results to be of service:

(12.39) $\dfrac{\partial K^*}{\partial K} = \dfrac{\partial}{\partial K}\left(\dfrac{K}{L}\right) = \dfrac{1}{L}$ $\dfrac{\partial K^*}{\partial L} = \dfrac{\partial}{\partial L}\left(\dfrac{K}{L}\right) = \dfrac{-K}{L^2}$

The results of differentiation are

(12.40) $MPP_K \equiv \dfrac{\partial Q}{\partial K} = \dfrac{\partial}{\partial K}[L\phi(K^*)]$

$= L\dfrac{\partial \phi(K^*)}{\partial K} = L\dfrac{d\phi(K^*)}{dK^*}\dfrac{\partial K^*}{\partial K}$ [chain rule]

$= L\phi'(K^*)\left(\dfrac{1}{L}\right) = \phi'(K^*)$ [by (12.39)]

(12.41) $MPP_L = \dfrac{\partial Q}{\partial L} = \dfrac{\partial}{\partial L}\left[L\phi(K^*)\right]$

$= \phi(K^*) + L\dfrac{\partial \phi(K^*)}{\partial L}$ [product rule]

$= \phi(K^*) + L\phi'(K^*)\dfrac{\partial K^*}{\partial L}$ [chain rule]

$= \phi(K^*) + L\phi'(K^*)\dfrac{-K}{L^2}$ [by (12.39)]

$= \phi(K^*) - K^*\phi'(K^*)$

which indeed show that MPP_K and MPP_L are functions of K^* alone.

Like average products, the marginal products will remain the same as long as the capital-labor ratio is held constant; they are homogeneous of degree zero in the variables K and L.

PROPERTY III   (*Euler's Theorem*) $K\dfrac{\partial Q}{\partial K} + L\dfrac{\partial Q}{\partial L} \equiv Q$

Proof $K\dfrac{\partial Q}{\partial K} + L\dfrac{\partial Q}{\partial L} = K\phi'(K^*) + L[\phi(K^*) - K^*\phi'(K^*)]$

$$\text{[by (12.40), (12.41)]}$$

$$= K\phi'(K^*) + L\phi(K^*) - K\phi'(K^*) \qquad [K^* \equiv K/L]$$

$$= L\phi(K^*) = Q \qquad\qquad\qquad \text{[by (12.36')]}$$

Since the proof is valid for *any* values of K and L, the property can be written as an identical equality. What this property says is that the value of a linearly homogeneous function can always be expressed as a sum of terms, each of which being the product of one of the independent variables and the first-order partial derivative with respect to that variable. The reader should take care to distinguish clearly between the identity $K\dfrac{\partial Q}{\partial K} + L\dfrac{\partial Q}{\partial L} \equiv Q$ [Euler's theorem, which applies only to the constant-returns-to-scale case of $Q = f(K,L)$] and the equation $dQ = \dfrac{\partial Q}{\partial K}\,dK + \dfrac{\partial Q}{\partial L}\,dL$ [total differential of Q, for *any* function $Q = f(K,L)$].

Economically, this property means that under conditions of constant returns to scale, if each input factor is paid the amount of its marginal product, the total product will be exactly exhausted by the distributive shares for all the input factors, or, equivalently, the pure economic profit will be zero. Since this situation is descriptive of the long-run equilibrium under pure competition, it was once thought that only linearly homogeneous production functions would make sense in economics. This, of course, is not the case. For one thing, the zero economic profit in the long-run equilibrium can be brought about by the forces of competition, including the entry and exit of firms, regardless of the specific nature of the production functions actually prevailing. Moreover, when imperfect competition exists in the factor markets, the payment to the factors may not be equal to the marginal products, and, consequently, Euler's theorem becomes irrelevant to the distribution picture. While linearly homogeneous production functions are often convenient to work with because of the various mathematical properties they are known to possess, there are other meaningful production functions too.

Cobb-Douglas production function   One specific production function widely used in economic analysis is the *Cobb-Douglas production function*:

(12.42) $Q = AK^\alpha L^{1-\alpha}$

where A is a positive constant, and α is a positive fraction. What we shall consider here first is a generalized version of this function, namely,

(12.43) $\qquad Q = AK^\alpha L^\beta$

where β is another positive fraction which may or may not be equal to $1 - \alpha$. Some of the major features of this function are: (1) It is homogeneous of degree $(\alpha + \beta)$. (2) In the special case of $\alpha + \beta = 1$, it is linearly homogeneous. (3) Its isoquants are negatively sloped throughout and strictly convex for positive values of K and L.

Its homogeneity is easily seen from the fact that, by changing K and L to kK and kL, respectively, the output will be changed to

$$A(kK)^\alpha(kL)^\beta = k^{\alpha+\beta}(AK^\alpha L^\beta) = k^{\alpha+\beta}Q$$

That is, the function is homogeneous of degree $(\alpha + \beta)$. In case $\alpha + \beta = 1$, there will be constant returns to scale, because the function will be linearly homogeneous. That its isoquants have negative slopes and strict convexity can be verified from the signs of the derivatives dK/dL and d^2K/dL^2 (or the signs of dL/dK and d^2L/dK^2). For any given output Q_0, (12.43) can be written as

$$AK^\alpha L^\beta = Q_0$$

Taking the natural log of both sides and transposing, we find that

$$\ln A + \alpha \ln K + \beta \ln L - \ln Q_0 = 0$$

which implicitly defines K as a function of L.† By the implicit-function rule and the log rule, therefore, we have

$$\frac{dK}{dL} = -\frac{\partial F/\partial L}{\partial F/\partial K} = -\frac{(\beta/L)}{(\alpha/K)} = -\frac{\beta K}{\alpha L} < 0$$

Then it follows that

$$\frac{d^2K}{dL^2} = \frac{d}{dL}\left(-\frac{\beta K}{\alpha L}\right) = -\frac{\beta}{\alpha}\frac{d}{dL}\left(\frac{K}{L}\right) = -\frac{\beta}{\alpha}\frac{1}{L^2}\left(L\frac{dK}{dL} - K\right) > 0$$

The signs of these derivatives establish the isoquant (any isoquant) to be downward-sloping throughout and strictly convex in the KL plane for positive values of K and L.

Let us now examine the $\alpha + \beta = 1$ case (the Cobb-Douglas function proper), to verify the three properties of linear homogeneity cited earlier. First

---

† The conditions of the implicit-function theorem are satisfied, because F (the left-side expression) has continuous partial derivatives, and because $\partial F/\partial K = \alpha/K \neq 0$ for positive values of K.

Optimization Problems

of all, the total product in this special case is expressible as

$$(12.42') \qquad Q = AK^\alpha L^{1-\alpha} = A \left(\frac{K}{L}\right)^\alpha L = LA(K^*)^\alpha$$

where the expression $A(K^*)^\alpha$ is a specific version of the general expression $\phi(K^*)$ used before. Therefore, the average products are

$$(12.44) \qquad \text{APP}_L = \frac{Q}{L} = A(K^*)^\alpha \qquad \text{APP}_K = \frac{Q}{K} = \frac{Q}{L}\frac{L}{K} = \frac{A(K^*)^\alpha}{K^*}$$
$$= A(K^*)^{\alpha-1}$$

both of which are now functions of K^* alone.

Second, differentiation of $Q = AK^\alpha L^{1-\alpha}$ yields the marginal products:

$$(12.45)$$
$$\frac{\partial Q}{\partial K} = A\alpha K^{\alpha-1} L^{-(\alpha-1)} = A\alpha \left(\frac{K}{L}\right)^{\alpha-1} = A\alpha(K^*)^{\alpha-1}$$

$$\frac{\partial Q}{\partial L} = AK^\alpha(1-\alpha)L^{-\alpha} = A(1-\alpha)\left(\frac{K}{L}\right)^\alpha = A(1-\alpha)(K^*)^\alpha$$

and these are also functions of K^* alone.

Lastly, we can verify Euler's theorem by using (12.45) as follows:

$$K\frac{\partial Q}{\partial K} + L\frac{\partial Q}{\partial L} = KA\alpha(K^*)^{\alpha-1} + LA(1-\alpha)(K^*)^\alpha$$
$$= LA(K^*)^\alpha \left[\frac{K\alpha}{LK^*} + 1 - \alpha\right]$$
$$= LA(K^*)^\alpha[\alpha + 1 - \alpha] = LA(K^*)^\alpha = Q \qquad \text{[by (12.42')]}$$

Interesting economic meanings can be assigned to the exponents α and $(1-\alpha)$ in the linearly homogeneous Cobb-Douglas production function. If each input is assumed to be paid by the amount of its marginal product, then the relative share of total product accruing to capital will be

$$\frac{K(\partial Q/\partial K)}{Q} = \frac{KA\alpha(K^*)^{\alpha-1}}{LA(K^*)^\alpha} = \alpha$$

Similarly, labor's relative share will be

$$\frac{L(\partial Q/\partial L)}{Q} = \frac{LA(1-\alpha)(K^*)^\alpha}{LA(K^*)^\alpha} = 1 - \alpha$$

Thus the exponent of each input variable indicates the relative share of that input in the total product. Looking at it another way, we can also interpret the exponent of each input variable as the partial elasticity of output with respect to that input. This is because the capital-share expression given above is equivalent to the expression $\dfrac{\partial Q/\partial K}{Q/K} \equiv \varepsilon_{QK}$ and, similarly, the labor-share expression above is precisely that of ε_{QL}.

What about the meaning of the constant A? For given values of K and L, the magnitude of A will proportionately affect the level of Q. Hence A may be considered as an *efficiency parameter*, i.e., as an indicator of the state of technology.

extensions of the results   We have discussed linear homogeneity in the specific context of production functions, but the properties cited are equally valid in other contexts, provided that the variables K, L, and Q are properly reinterpreted.

Furthermore, it is possible to extend our results to the case of more than two variables. With a linearly homogeneous function

$$y = f(x_1, x_2, \ldots, x_n)$$

we can again divide each variable by x_1 (that is, multiply by $1/x_1$) and get the result

$$y = x_1 \phi \left(\frac{x_2}{x_1}, \frac{x_3}{x_1}, \ldots, \frac{x_n}{x_1} \right)$$

which is comparable to (12.36′). Moreover, Euler's theorem is easily extended to the form

$$\sum_{i=1}^{n} x_i f_i = y$$

where the partial derivatives of the original function f (namely, f_i) are again homogeneous of degree zero in the variables x_i, as in the two-variable case.

The above extensions can, in fact, also be generalized with relative ease to a homogeneous function of degree r. In the first place, by definition of homogeneity, we can in the present case write

$$y = x_1{}^r \phi \left(\frac{x_2}{x_1}, \frac{x_3}{x_1}, \ldots, \frac{x_n}{x_1} \right)$$

The modified version of Euler's theorem will now appear in the form

$$\sum_{i=1}^{n} x_i f_i = ry$$

where a multiplicative constant r has been attached to the dependent variable y on the right. And, finally, the partial derivatives of the original function f, the f_i, will all be homogeneous of degree $(r - 1)$ in the variables x_i. The reader can thus see that the linear-homogeneity case is merely a special case thereof, in which $r = 1$.

EXERCISE 12.5

1   Determine whether the following functions are homogeneous. If so, of what degree?

(a) $f(x,y) = \sqrt{xy}$

(b) $f(x,y) = (x^2 - y^2)^{1/2}$

(c) $f(x,y) = x^3 - xy + y^3$

(d) $f(x,y) = 2x + y + 3\sqrt{xy}$

(e) $f(x,y,w) = \dfrac{xy^2}{w} + 2xw$

(f) $f(x,y,w) = x^4 - 5yw^3$

2   Show that the function (12.36) can be expressed alternatively as $Q = K\psi\left(\dfrac{L}{K}\right)$ instead of $Q = L\phi(K^*)$.

3   Deduce from Euler's theorem that, with constant returns to scale:

(a) When $\text{MPP}_K = 0$, APP_L will be equal to MPP_L.
(b) When $\text{MPP}_L = 0$, APP_K will be equal to MPP_K

4   On the basis of (12.37) through (12.41), deduce that the following will hold under conditions of constant returns to scale:

(a) An APP_L curve can be plotted against $K^*\ (=\ K/L)$ as the independent variable (on the horizontal axis).
(b) MPP_K is measured by the slope of that APP_L curve.
(c) APP_K is measured by the slope of the radius vector to the APP_L curve.
(d) $\text{MPP}_L = \text{APP}_L - K^*(\text{MPP}_K) = \text{APP}_L - K^*(\text{slope of } \text{APP}_L)$.

5   Use (12.44) and (12.45) to verify that the relations described in Exercise 12.5-4b, c, and d are obeyed by the Cobb-Douglas production function.

6   Given the production function $Q = AK^\alpha L^\beta$, show that:

(a) $\alpha + \beta > 1$ implies increasing returns to scale.
(b) $\alpha + \beta < 1$ implies decreasing returns to scale.
(c) α and β are, respectively, the partial elasticities of output with respect to capital and labor inputs.

12.6 Least-Cost Combination of Inputs

As another example of constrained optimization, let us discuss the problem of finding the least-cost input combination for the production of a specified level of output Q_0 representing, say, a customer's special order. Here we shall work with a general production function; later on, however, reference will be made to homogeneous production functions.

first-order condition   Assuming a production function with two variable inputs, $Q = Q(a,b)$, where $Q_a, Q_b > 0$ in the relevant subset of the domain [see Fig. 11.6], and assuming both input prices to be exogenous (though again omitting the zero subscript), we may formulate the problem as one of minimizing the cost

$$C = aP_a + bP_b$$

subject to the output constraint

$$Q(a,b) = Q_0$$

Hence, the Lagrangean function is

$$Z = aP_a + bP_b + \mu[Q_0 - Q(a,b)]$$

To satisfy the first-order condition for a minimum C, the input levels (the choice variables) must satisfy the following simultaneous equations:

$$Z_\mu = Q_0 - Q(a,b) = 0$$
$$Z_a = P_a - \mu Q_a = 0$$
$$Z_b = P_b - \mu Q_b = 0$$

The first equation in this set is merely the constraint restated, and the last two imply the condition

$$(12.46) \qquad \frac{P_a}{Q_a} = \frac{P_b}{Q_b} = \mu$$

At the point of optimal input combination, the input-price–marginal-product ratio must be the same for each input. Since this ratio measures the amount of outlay per unit of marginal product of the input in question, the Lagrange multiplier μ can be given the interpretation of the marginal cost of production in the optimum state. This interpretation is, of course, entirely consistent with our earlier discovery in (12.16) that the optimal value of the Lagrange multiplier measures the comparative-static effect which the constant in the constraint equation produces on the optimal value of the objective function, that is, $\bar{\mu} = (\partial \bar{C}/\partial Q_0)$.

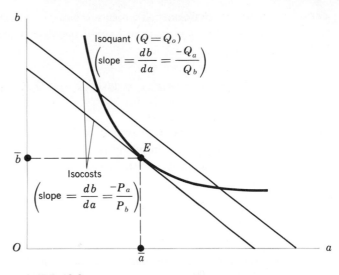

FIGURE 12.6

Equation (12.46) can be alternatively written in the form

$$(12.46') \qquad \frac{P_a}{P_b} = \frac{Q_a}{Q_b}$$

which the reader should compare with (12.20″). Presented in this form, the first-order condition can be explained in terms of isoquants and isocosts. As we learned in (11.25), the Q_a/Q_b ratio is the negative of the slope of an isoquant; that is, it is a measure of the *marginal rate of technical substitution of a for b* (MRTS$_{ab}$). In the present model, the output level is specified at Q_0; thus only one isoquant is involved, as shown in Fig. 12.6.

The P_a/P_b ratio, on the other hand, represents the negative of the slope of *isocosts* (a notion comparable with the budget line in consumer theory). An isocost, defined as the locus of the input combinations that entail the same total cost, is expressible by the linear equation

$$C_0 = aP_a + bP_b \qquad \text{or} \qquad b = \frac{C_0}{P_b} - \frac{P_a}{P_b}a$$

where C_0 stands for a (parametric) cost figure. When plotted in the ab plane, as in Fig. 12.6, therefore, it yields a family of straight lines with slope $-P_a/P_b$ (and vertical intercept C_0/P_b). The equality of the two ratios therefore amounts to the equality of the slopes of the isoquant and a selected isocost. Since we are compelled to stay on the given isoquant, this condition leads us to the point of tangency E and the input combination $(\bar{a},\bar{b})$.

second-order condition   To assure a *minimum* cost, it is sufficient (after the first-order condition is met) to have a negative bordered Hessian, i.e., to have

$$|\bar{H}| = \begin{vmatrix} 0 & Q_a & Q_b \\ Q_a & -\mu Q_{aa} & -\mu Q_{ab} \\ Q_b & -\mu Q_{ba} & -\mu Q_{bb} \end{vmatrix} = \mu(Q_{aa}Q_b{}^2 - 2Q_{ab}Q_aQ_b + Q_{bb}Q_a{}^2) < 0$$

Since the optimal value of μ (marginal cost) is positive, this reduces to the condition that the expression in parentheses be negative.

From (11.29), we recall that the curvature of an isoquant is represented by the second derivative

$$\frac{d^2b}{da^2} = \frac{-1}{Q_b{}^3}(Q_{aa}Q_b{}^2 - 2Q_{ab}Q_aQ_b + Q_{bb}Q_a{}^2)$$

When the isoquant is strictly convex at the point of tangency, we have the inequality $d^2b/da^2 > 0$, which implies—since Q_b (marginal product of b) is positive—that the expression in parentheses is negative. Thus the strict convexity of the isoquant of Fig. 12.6 at the point of its tangency with an isocost will guarantee the satisfaction of the second-order condition stated above. Conversely, if the second-order condition is satisfied, then the isoquant must be strictly convex at the point of tangency.

In Sec. 12.4, in connection with the model of consumer utility-maximization, it was shown that an increasing, strictly quasiconcave utility function $U = U(x,y)$ gives rise to strictly convex, downward-sloping indifference curves. Since isoquants and indifference curves are very similar in nature, we can reason by analogy that an increasing, strictly quasiconcave production function $Q = Q(a,b)$ will give rise to strictly convex, downward-sloping isoquants. We have already assumed that $Q = Q(a,b)$ is an increasing function, that is, Q_a and Q_b are both positive. Had we specified in addition that the production function is strictly quasiconcave, the second-order condition would have been satisfied automatically.

the expansion path   Let us now turn to one of the comparative-static aspects of this model. Assuming *fixed* input prices, let us postulate successive increases of Q_0 (ascent to higher and higher isoquants) and trace the effect on the least-cost combination $\bar{b}/\bar{a}$. Each shift of the isoquant, of course, will result in a new point of tangency, with a higher isocost. The locus of such points of tangency, known as the *expansion path* of the firm, serves to describe the least-cost combinations required to produce varying levels of Q_0. Two possible shapes of the expansion path are shown in Fig. 12.7.

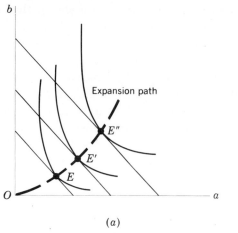

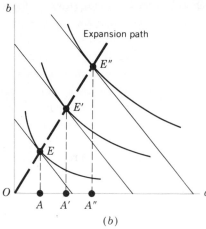

(a)

(b)

FIGURE 12.7

If we assume the strict convexity of the isoquants (hence, satisfaction of the second-order condition), the expansion path will be derivable directly from the first-order condition (12.46′). Let us illustrate this for the generalized version of the Cobb-Douglas production function.

The condition (12.46′) requires the equality of the input-price ratio and the marginal-product ratio. For the function $Q = Aa^\alpha b^\beta$, this means that each point on the expansion path must satisfy

$$\frac{P_a}{P_b} = \frac{Q_a}{Q_b} = \frac{A\alpha a^{\alpha-1}b^\beta}{Aa^\alpha \beta b^{\beta-1}} = \frac{\alpha b}{\beta a}$$

implying that the optimal input ratio should be

(12.47) $$\frac{\bar{b}}{\bar{a}} = \frac{\beta P_a}{\alpha P_b} = \text{a constant}$$

since α, β, and the input prices are all constant. As a result, all points on the expansion path must show the same *fixed* input ratio; i.e., the expansion path must be a straight line emanating from the point of origin. This is illustrated in Fig. 12.7b, where the input ratios at the various points of tangency (AE/OA, $A'E'/OA'$ and $A''E''/OA''$) are all equal.

The straight-line expansion path is characteristic of the generalized Cobb-Douglas function whether or not $\alpha + \beta = 1$, because the derivation of the result in (12.47) does not rely on the equation $\alpha + \beta = 1$. As a matter of fact, any homogeneous production function (not necessarily the Cobb-Douglas) will give rise to a straight-line expansion path, because of the following reason: If it is homogeneous of (say) degree r, then the marginal-product functions Q_a and Q_b

Constrained Optimization

should both be homogeneous of degree $(r - 1)$ in the inputs a and b; thus a k-fold increase in both inputs will produce a k^{r-1}-fold change in the values of *both* Q_a and Q_b, which will leave the Q_a/Q_b ratio intact. Therefore, if the first-order condition $P_a/P_b = Q_a/Q_b$ is fulfilled at given input prices by a particular input combination (a_0, b_0), it must also be fulfilled by a combination (ka_0, kb_0)— precisely as is depicted by the straight-line expansion path in Fig. 12.7b.

Although *any* homogeneous production function can give rise to a straight-line expansion path, the specific degree of homogeneity does make a significant difference in the interpretation of the expansion path. In Fig. 12.7b, we have drawn the distance OE equal to that of EE', so that point E' involves a doubling of the scale of point E. Now if the production function is homogeneous of degree *one*, the output at E' must be twice $(2^1 = 2)$ that of E. But if the degree of homogeneity is *two*, the output at E' will be four times $(2^2 = 4)$ that of E. Thus, the spacing of the isoquants for $Q = 1$, $Q = 2$, . . . , will be widely different for different degrees of homogeneity.

elasticity of substitution   Another aspect of comparative statics has to do with the effect of a change in the P_a/P_b ratio upon the least-cost input combination $\bar{b}/\bar{a}$ for producing the same given output Q_0 (that is, while we stay on the same isoquant).

When the (exogenous) input-price ratio P_a/P_b rises, we can normally expect the optimal input ratio $\bar{b}/\bar{a}$ also to rise, because input b (now relatively cheaper) will tend to be substituted for input a. The *direction* of substitution is clear, but what about its *extent*? The extent of input substitution can be measured by the following point-elasticity expression, called the *elasticity of substitution* and denoted by σ (lower-case Greek letter sigma, for "substitution"):

$$(12.48) \qquad \sigma \equiv \frac{\text{relative change in } (\bar{b}/\bar{a})}{\text{relative change in } (P_a/P_b)}$$

$$= \frac{\dfrac{d(\bar{b}/\bar{a})}{\bar{b}/\bar{a}}}{\dfrac{d(P_a/P_b)}{P_a/P_b}} = \frac{\dfrac{d(\bar{b}/\bar{a})}{d(P_a/P_b)}}{\dfrac{\bar{b}/\bar{a}}{P_a/P_b}}$$

The value of σ can be anywhere between 0 and ∞; the larger the σ, the greater the substitutability between the two inputs. The limiting case of $\sigma = 0$ is where the two inputs must be used in a fixed proportion as complements to each other. The other limiting case, with σ infinite, is where the two inputs are perfect substitutes for each other. Note that, if $(\bar{b}/\bar{a})$ is considered as a function of

(P_a/P_b), then the elasticity σ will again be the ratio of a *marginal* function to an *average* function.[1]

For illustration, let us calculate the elasticity of substitution for the generalized Cobb-Douglas production function. We learned earlier that, for this case, the least-cost input combination is specified by

$$\left(\frac{\bar{b}}{\bar{a}}\right) = \frac{\beta}{\alpha}\left(\frac{P_a}{P_b}\right) \qquad \text{[from (12.47)]}$$

This equation is in the form $y = kx$, for which dy/dx (the marginal) and y/x (the average) are both equal to the constant k. That is,

$$\frac{d(\bar{b}/\bar{a})}{d(P_a/P_b)} = \frac{\beta}{\alpha} \qquad \text{and} \qquad \frac{\bar{b}/\bar{a}}{P_a/P_b} = \frac{\beta}{\alpha}$$

Substituting these values into (12.48), we immediately find that $\sigma = 1$; that is, the generalized Cobb-Douglas production function is characterized by a *constant, unitary* elasticity of substitution. Note that the derivation of this result in no way relies upon the assumption that $\alpha + \beta = 1$. Thus the elasticity of substitution of the production function $Q = Aa^{\alpha}b^{\beta}$ will be unitary even if $\alpha + \beta \neq 1$.

CES production function   More recently, there has come into common use another form of production function which, while still characterized by a constant elasticity of substitution (CES), can yield a σ with a (constant) value other than 1.[†] The equation of this function, known as the *CES production function*, is

$$(12.49) \qquad Q = A[\delta K^{-\rho} + (1 - \delta)L^{-\rho}]^{-1/\rho}$$
$$(A > 0; 0 < \delta < 1; \rho > -1)$$

where K and L represent two factors of production, and A, δ, and ρ (lower-case Greek letter rho) are three parameters. The parameter A (the *efficiency parameter*)

---

[1] There is an alternative way of expressing σ. Since, at the point of tangency, we always have

$$\frac{P_a}{P_b} = \frac{Q_a}{Q_b} = \text{MRTS}_{ab}$$

the elasticity of substitution can be defined equivalently as

$$(12.48') \qquad \sigma = \frac{\text{relative change in } (\bar{b}/\bar{a})}{\text{relative change in MRTS}_{ab}} = \frac{\dfrac{d(\bar{b}/\bar{a})}{\bar{b}/\bar{a}}}{\dfrac{d(Q_a/Q_b)}{Q_a/Q_b}} = \frac{\dfrac{d(\bar{b}/\bar{a})}{d(Q_a/Q_b)}}{\dfrac{\bar{b}/\bar{a}}{Q_a/Q_b}}$$

[†] K. J. Arrow, H. B. Chenery, B. S. Minhas, and R. M. Solow, "Capital-Labor Substitution and Economic Efficiency," *Review of Economics and Statistics*, August, 1961, pp. 225–250.

plays the same role as the coefficient A in the Cobb-Douglas function; it serves as an indicator of the state of technology. The parameter δ (the *distribution parameter*), like the α in the Cobb-Douglas function, has to do with the relative factor shares in the product. And the parameter ρ (the *substitution parameter*)—which has no counterpart in the Cobb-Douglas function—is what determines the value of the (constant) elasticity of substitution, as will be shown later.

First, however, let us observe that this function is homogeneous of degree one. If we replace K and L by kK and kL, respectively, the output will change from Q to

$$A[\delta(kK)^{-\rho} + (1 - \delta)(kL)^{-\rho}]^{-1/\rho} = A\{k^{-\rho}[\delta K^{-\rho} + (1 - \delta)L^{-\rho}]\}^{-1/\rho}$$
$$= (k^{-\rho})^{-1/\rho}Q = kQ$$

Consequently, the CES function, like all linearly homogeneous production functions, displays constant returns to scale, qualifies for the application of Euler's theorem, and possesses average products and marginal products that are homogeneous of degree zero in the variables K and L.

We may also note that the isoquants generated by the CES production function are always negatively sloped and strictly convex for positive values of K and L. To show this, let us first find the expressions for the marginal products Q_L and Q_K. Using the notation $[\cdots]$ as a shorthand for $[\delta K^{-\rho} + (1 - \delta)L^{-\rho}]$, we have

(12.50) $$Q_L \equiv \frac{\partial Q}{\partial L} = A\left(-\frac{1}{\rho}\right)[\cdots]^{-(1/\rho)-1}(1 - \delta)(-\rho)L^{-\rho-1}$$

$$= (1 - \delta)A[\cdots]^{-(1+\rho)/\rho}L^{-(1+\rho)}$$

$$= (1 - \delta)\frac{A^{1+\rho}}{A^\rho}[\cdots]^{-(1+\rho)/\rho}L^{-(1+\rho)}$$

$$= \frac{(1 - \delta)}{A^\rho}\left(\frac{Q}{L}\right)^{1+\rho} > 0 \qquad [\text{by (12.49)}]$$

and similarly,

(12.51) $$Q_K \equiv \frac{\partial Q}{\partial K} = \frac{\delta}{A^\rho}\left(\frac{Q}{K}\right)^{1+\rho} > 0$$

Thus the slope of an isoquant (with K plotted vertically and L horizontally) is

(12.52) $$\frac{dK}{dL} = -\frac{Q_L}{Q_K} = -\frac{(1 - \delta)}{\delta}\left(\frac{K}{L}\right)^{1+\rho} < 0 \qquad [\text{see (11.25)}]$$

It can then be easily checked that $d^2K/dL^2 > 0$ (which we leave to the reader as an exercise), implying that the isoquant is strictly convex.

With the marginal products already found, we are ready to discuss the elasticity of substitution of the CES production function. In order to fulfill the least-cost combination condition $Q_L/Q_K = P_L/P_K$, we must have

$$\frac{1-\delta}{\delta}\left(\frac{K}{L}\right)^{1+\rho} = \frac{P_L}{P_K} \qquad \text{[see (12.52)]}$$

Thus the optimal factor ratio is (introducing a shorthand symbol c)

$$(12.53) \qquad \left(\frac{\bar{K}}{\bar{L}}\right) = \left(\frac{\delta}{1-\delta}\right)^{1/(1+\rho)}\left(\frac{P_L}{P_K}\right)^{1/(1+\rho)} \equiv c\left(\frac{P_L}{P_K}\right)^{1/(1+\rho)}$$

Taking $(\bar{K}/\bar{L})$ to be a function of (P_L/P_K), we find the associated marginal and average functions to be as follows:

$$\text{Marginal function} = \frac{d(\bar{K}/\bar{L})}{d(P_L/P_K)} = \frac{c}{1+\rho}\left(\frac{P_L}{P_K}\right)^{1/(1+\rho)-1}$$

$$\text{Average function} = \frac{\bar{K}/\bar{L}}{P_L/P_K} = c\left(\frac{P_L}{P_K}\right)^{1/(1+\rho)-1}$$

Therefore the elasticity of substitution equals[1]

$$(12.54) \qquad \frac{\text{Marginal function}}{\text{Average function}} = \frac{1}{1+\rho}$$

What this shows is that σ is a constant whose magnitude depends on the value of the parameter ρ as follows:

$$\left.\begin{array}{c} -1 < \rho < 0 \\ \rho = 0 \\ 0 < \rho < \infty \end{array}\right\} \Rightarrow \left\{\begin{array}{c} \sigma > 1 \\ \sigma = 1 \\ \sigma < 1 \end{array}\right.$$

Cobb-Douglas function as a special case of the CES function   In this last result, the middle case of $\rho = 0$ leads to a unitary elasticity of substitution which, as we know, is characteristic of the Cobb-Douglas function. This suggests that the (linearly homogeneous) Cobb-Douglas function is a special case of the (linearly homogeneous) CES function. Note that the CES function, as given in (12.49), is undefined when $\rho = 0$, because division by zero is not possible. Nevertheless, we shall demonstrate that, as $\rho \to 0$, the CES function will approach the Cobb-Douglas function.

[1] Of course, we could also have obtained the same result by first taking the logarithms of both sides of (12.53):

$$\ln\left(\frac{\bar{K}}{\bar{L}}\right) = \ln c + \frac{1}{1+\rho}\ln\left(\frac{P_L}{P_K}\right)$$

and then applying the formula for elasticity in (10.25), to get

$$\sigma = \frac{d(\ln \bar{K}/\bar{L})}{d(\ln P_L/P_K)} = \frac{1}{1+\rho}$$

For this demonstration, we shall rely on a technique known as *L'Hôpital's rule*. This rule has to do with the evaluation of the limit of a function $f(x) = \dfrac{m(x)}{n(x)}$ as $x \to a$ (where a can be either finite or infinite), when it happens that the numerator $m(x)$ and the denominator $n(x)$ either (a) both tend to zero as $x \to a$, thus resulting in an expression of the 0/0 form, or (b) both tend to $\pm\infty$ as $x \to a$, thus resulting in an expression in the form of ∞/∞ (or $\infty/-\infty$, or $-\infty/\infty$, or $-\infty/-\infty$). Even though the limit of $f(x)$ cannot be evaluated as the expression stands under these two circumstances, its value can nevertheless be found by using the formula

$$(12.55) \qquad \lim_{x \to a} \frac{m(x)}{n(x)} = \lim_{x \to a} \frac{m'(x)}{n'(x)} \qquad \text{[L'Hôpital's rule]}$$

Example 1 Find the limit of $(1 - x^2)/(1 - x)$ as $x \to 1$. Here, both $m(x)$ and $n(x)$ approach zero as x approaches unity, thus exemplifying circumstance (a). Since $m'(x) = -2x$ and $n'(x) = -1$, we have

$$\lim_{x \to 1} \frac{1 - x^2}{1 - x} = \lim_{x \to 1} \frac{-2x}{-1} = \lim_{x \to 1} 2x = 2$$

This answer is identical with that obtained by another method in Example 2 of Sec. 6.4.

Example 2 Find the limit of $(2x + 5)/(x + 1)$ as $x \to \infty$. When x becomes infinite, both $m(x)$ and $n(x)$ become infinite in the present case, thus we have here an example of circumstance (b). Since $m'(x) = 2$ and $n'(x) = 1$, we can write

$$\lim_{x \to \infty} \frac{2x + 5}{x + 1} = \lim_{x \to \infty} \frac{2}{1} = 2$$

Again, this answer is identical with that obtained by another method in Example 3 of Sec. 6.4.

It may turn out that the right-side expression in (12.55) again falls into the 0/0 or the ∞/∞ format, same as the left-side expression. In such an event, we may reapply L'Hôpital's rule, i.e., we may look for the limit of $m''(x)/n''(x)$ as $x \to a$, and take that limit as our answer. It may also turn out that even though the given function $f(x)$, whose limit we wish to evaluate, is originally not in the form of $m(x)/n(x)$ that falls into the 0/0 or the ∞/∞ format upon limit-taking, a suitable transformation will make $f(x)$ amenable to the application of the rule in (12.55). This latter possibility can be illustrated by the problem of finding the limit of the CES function (12.49)—now viewed as a function $Q(\rho)$—as $\rho \to 0$.

As given, $Q(\rho)$ is not in the form of $m(\rho)/n(\rho)$. Dividing both sides of (12.49) by A, and taking the natural log, however, we do get an expression in that form, namely,

$$(12.56) \qquad \ln \frac{Q}{A} = \frac{-\ln [\delta K^{-\rho} + (1 - \delta)L^{-\rho}]}{\rho} \equiv \frac{m(\rho)}{n(\rho)}$$

Moreover, as $\rho \to 0$, we find that $m(\rho) \to -\ln [\delta + 1 - \delta] = -\ln 1 = 0$, and $n(\rho) \to 0$. Thus L'Hôpital's rule can be used to find the limit of $\ln (Q/A)$. Once that is done, the limit of Q can also be found: Since $Q/A = e^{\ln (Q/A)}$, so that $Q = Ae^{\ln (Q/A)}$, it follows that

$$(12.57) \qquad \lim Q = \lim Ae^{\ln (Q/A)} = Ae^{\lim \ln (Q/A)}$$

From (12.56), let us first find $m'(\rho)$ and $n'(\rho)$, as required by L'Hôpital's rule. The latter is simply $n'(\rho) = 1$. The former is

$$m'(\rho) = \frac{-1}{[\delta K^{-\rho} + (1 - \delta)L^{-\rho}]} \frac{d}{d\rho} [\delta K^{-\rho} + (1 - \delta)L^{-\rho}] \qquad \text{[chain rule]}$$

$$= \frac{-[-\delta K^{-\rho} \ln K - (1 - \delta)L^{-\rho} \ln L]}{[\delta K^{-\rho} + (1 - \delta)L^{-\rho}]} \qquad \text{[by (10.21')]}$$

By (12.55), therefore, we have

$$\lim_{\rho \to 0} \ln \frac{Q}{A} = \lim_{\rho \to 0} \frac{m'(\rho)}{n'(\rho)} = \frac{\delta \ln K + (1 - \delta) \ln L}{1} = \ln (K^{\delta}L^{1-\delta})$$

In view of this result, when e is raised to the power of $\lim_{\rho \to 0} \ln (Q/A)$, the outcome is simply $K^{\delta}L^{1-\delta}$. Hence, by (12.57), we finally arrive at the result

$$\lim_{\rho \to 0} Q = AK^{\delta}L^{1-\delta}$$

showing that, as $\rho \to 0$, the CES function indeed tends to the Cobb-Douglas function.

EXERCISE 12.6

1 Supply a proof for the assertion in Fig. 12.6 that the slope of the isoquant is equal to $-Q_a/Q_b$. Then discuss the conditions under which the isoquant will be negatively sloped.

2   In Fig. 12.7, the isocosts are drawn as parallel lines. What does the parallelism imply?

3   Suppose that the isoquants in Fig. 12.7b are derived from a particular homogeneous production function $Q = Q(a,b)$. Noting that $OE = EE' = E'E''$, what must be the ratios between the output levels represented by the three isoquants if the function Q is homogeneous

(a) of degree one?   (b) of degree two?

4   For the generalized Cobb-Douglas case, if we plot the ratio $\bar{b}/\bar{a}$ against the ratio P_a/P_b, what type of curve will result? Does this result depend on the assumption that $\alpha + \beta = 1$? How do you read the elasticity of substitution graphically from this curve? (*Hint:* Review Figs. 8.2 and 8.3.)

5   By differentiating (12.50) with respect to L and (12.51) with respect to K, establish that the CES production function is characterized by diminishing returns to each input for all positive levels of input.

6   Show that, on an isoquant of the CES function, $d^2K/dL^2 > 0$. (*Note:* This involves total rather than partial derivation.)

7   For the CES function, if each factor of production is paid according to its marginal product, what will be the ratio of labor's share of product to capital's share of product? Would a larger value of δ mean a larger relative share for capital?

8   Show that by writing the CES function as $Q = A[\delta K^{-\rho} + (1 - \delta)L^{-\rho}]^{-r/\rho}$, where $r > 0$ is a new parameter, we can introduce increasing returns to scale and decreasing returns to scale.

9   Evaluate the following:

(a) $\lim\limits_{x \to 4} \dfrac{x^2 - x - 12}{x - 4}$ (c) $\lim\limits_{x \to 0} \dfrac{5^x - e^x}{x}$

(b) $\lim\limits_{x \to 0} \dfrac{e^x - 1}{x}$ (d) $\lim\limits_{x \to \infty} \dfrac{\ln x}{x}$

10 By use of L'Hôpital's rule, show that

(a) $\lim\limits_{x \to \infty} \dfrac{x^n}{e^x} = 0$ (b) $\lim\limits_{x \to 0^+} x \ln x = 0$ (c) $\lim\limits_{x \to 0^+} x^x = 1$

12.7   Some Concluding Remarks

We have now come to the end of this discussion of (classical) optimization analysis. Our somewhat arduous journey has taken us (1) from the case of a single choice variable to the more general n-variable case, (2) from the polynomial objective function to the exponential and logarithmic, and (3) from the free extremum to the constrained extremum. With this background, the reader can go a long way in dealing with problems of optimization.

It would be well to point out, however, that the classical techniques presented above are limited in several ways. First of all, the extremum identified by the use of differential calculus is of necessity a relative rather than an absolute one. In other words, a maximum so identified is maximal only in relation to its neighboring points (somewhat like a winner of a local beauty contest). Thus, in a sense, the criterion of maximality or minimality is myopic.

Second, as the reader is well aware, the statement of the necessary and sufficient conditions for maximum and minimum in terms of the first and second derivatives implies that differentiability is a sine qua non for application of the methods we discussed. Discontinuity and kinks in the function are taboo.

Third, we are only equipped to cope with equations. Even though inequalities often do appear in our models as part of the model specifications (such as $U_x > 0$), the relevant mathematical operation is performed only on equations. In the utility-maximization model, for instance, the budget constraint is stated in the form that the total expenditure be *equal to* (and not "less than *or* equal to") a given sum. Thus the consumer is denied the option of saving part of his funds. It may be argued, of course, that this objection will dissolve if we envisage the act of saving as a purchase of a savings deposit—an additional commodity to be incorporated into the consumer's utility function. But the fact remains that the method of calculus is limited by its inability to handle inequalities. It is precisely for this reason, of course, that we never explicitly specify in a classical optimization problem that the values of the choice variables must be nonnegative, as economic common sense may often require. Instead, we just hope that, with a properly constructed model, the solution values will indeed come out with the economically sensible sign.

Lest the reader gather the impression that all our work has been in vain, we should hasten to add that some of these limitations are not as damaging as they may appear. For example, with the knowledge of all the possible relative maxima and the end-point values of the objective function (which should not be difficult to calculate), it is usually possible to determine the *absolute* maximum. In many cases, moreover, the nature of the economic model is such that there exists only one relative extremum which at the same time is also the absolute extremum.

However, the required assumptions of smooth continuity (e.g., the smoothly continuous substitution of one input for another) and equational constraint do not, indeed, always smack of realism. In a subsequent part of the book, on the subject of mathematical programming, we shall remedy this deficiency by developing a different approach to optimization problems that permits consideration of constraints in the form of inequalities. Moreover, in that context we shall, in a certain sense, relax the prerequisite of smoothness.

That topic, however, shall be reserved for discussion in Part 6. Meanwhile, in order for the reader to gain a proper appreciation of the full sweep of the major categories of economic analysis—from statics to comparative statics, and thence to dynamics—we shall first venture, in Part 5, into the as yet unexplored territory of dynamic analysis. Since the mathematical techniques used in dynamic analysis are intimately related to the methods of differential calculus we have just learned, there is also a pedagogical advantage in discussing dynamics first. Nevertheless, a reader anxious to familiarize himself with mathematical programming may skip Part 5 and proceed directly to Part 6, without any methodological difficulty.

FIVE

DYNAMIC ANALYSIS

13

ECONOMIC DYNAMICS
AND INTEGRAL CALCULUS

The term *dynamics*, as applied to economic analysis, has different meanings for different economists. Professor Baumol, in his *Economic Dynamics*,[1] has discussed several types of dynamic analysis, each with a different connotation for the term. And, in an interesting article on semantics,[2] Professor Machlup has enumerated a whole list of varying senses in which the term has been used, including one that is mercilessly revealing of human nature: "Typically, 'Statics' was what those benighted opponents have been writing; 'Dynamics' was one's own, vastly superior theory."

In recent years, however, the term dynamics has acquired an almost exclusive usage; it now refers to the type of analysis in which the object is either to trace and study the specific time paths of the variables or to determine whether, given sufficient time, these variables will tend to converge to certain (equilibrium) values. This type of information is important because it fills a serious gap that marred our study of statics and comparative statics. In the latter, we always make the arbitrary assumption that the process of economic adjustment must inevitably lead to equilibrium. In a dynamic analysis, the question of "attainability" can be squarely faced, rather than assumed away.

One salient feature of dynamic analysis is the *dating* of the variables, which introduces a consideration of *time* into the picture. This can be done in two ways, however: time can be considered either as a *continuous* variable or as a *discrete* variable. In the former case, something is happening to the variable at each

---

[1] William J. Baumol, *Economic Dynamics*, 3d ed., The Macmillan Company, New York, 1970.
[2] Fritz Machlup, "Statics and Dynamics: Kaleidoscopic Words," *Southern Economic Journal*, October, 1959, pp. 91–110; reprinted in Machlup, *Essays on Economic Semantics*, Prentice-Hall, Inc., Englewood Cliffs, N.J., 1963, pp. 9–42.

point of time (such as in continuous interest compounding); whereas in the latter, the variable undergoes a change only once within a *period* of time (e.g., interest is added only at the end of every 6 months). One of these time concepts may be more appropriate than the other in certain contexts, but as we have seen, the continuous case can usually be regarded as the limit for the discrete case when the discrete time periods become very, very short.

We shall discuss first the continuous-time case, to which the mathematical techniques of *integral calculus* and *differential equations* are pertinent. Later, in Chaps. 16 and 17, we shall turn to the discrete-time case, which utilizes the methods of *difference equations*.

13.1   Dynamics and Integration

In a static model, generally speaking, the problem is to find the values of the endogenous variables that will satisfy some specified equilibrium condition(s). Applied to the context of optimization models, the task becomes one of finding the values of the choice variables that will maximize (or minimize) a specific objective function—with the first-order condition serving as the equilibrium condition, provided that the second-order condition poses no problem. In a dynamic model, by contrast, the problem usually involves the delineation of the time path of some variable, on the basis of a known pattern of change (say, a given instantaneous rate of change).

An example should make this clear. Suppose that population size H is known to change over time at the rate

$$(13.1) \qquad \frac{dH}{dt} = t^{-1/2}$$

We then ask the question: What is the time path of population, $H = H(t)$, that corresponds to (13.1)? That is, what specific form of the function $H(t)$ will relate the population size H to time t so as to conform to the rate of change specified in (13.1)?

The reader will recognize that, if we know the function $H = H(t)$ to begin with, then the derivative dH/dt can be found by differentiation. But in the problem now confronting us, the shoe is on the other foot: we are called upon to uncover the *primitive* function from a given *derived* function, rather than the reverse. Mathematically, we shall need the exact opposite of the method of differentiation, or of differential calculus.

The relevant method, known as *integration*, or *integral calculus*, will be studied below. For the time being, let us be content with the observation that the function $H(t) = 2t^{1/2}$ does indeed have a derivative of the form in (13.1), thus apparently qualifying as a solution to our problem. The trouble is that there also exist similar functions, such as $H(t) = 2t^{1/2} + 15$ or $H(t) = 2t^{1/2} + 99$ or, more generally,

$$(13.2) \qquad H(t) = 2t^{1/2} + c \qquad (c = \text{an arbitrary constant})$$

which all possess exactly the same derivative (13.1). No unique time path can be determined, therefore, unless the value of the constant c can somehow be made definite. To accomplish this, additional information must be built into the model, usually in the form of what is known as an *initial condition* or *boundary condition*.

If we have knowledge of the initial population $H(0)$—that is, the value of H at $t = 0$, let us say, $H(0) = 100$—then the value of the constant c can be made determinate. Setting $t = 0$ in (13.2), we get

$$H(0) = 2(0)^{1/2} + c = c$$

But if $H(0) = 100$, then $c = 100$, and (13.2) becomes

$$(13.2') \qquad H(t) = 2t^{1/2} + 100$$

where the constant is no longer arbitrary. More generally, for any given initial population $H(0)$, the time path will be

$$(13.2'') \qquad H(t) = 2t^{1/2} + H(0)$$

so that the population size H at any point of time will, in the present example, consist of the sum of the initial population $H(0)$ and another term involving the time variable t. Such a time path indeed charts the complete itinerary of the variable H over time, and thus it truly constitutes the solution to our dynamic model. [Equation (13.1) is also a function of t. Why can't it be considered a solution as well?]

Simple as it is, this population example illustrates the quintessence of the problems of economic dynamics. Given the pattern of behavior of a variable over time, we seek to find a function that will describe the time path of the variable. In the process, we shall encounter one or more arbitrary constants, but if we possess sufficient additional information in the form of *initial conditions*, it will always be possible to definitize these arbitrary constants.

In the simpler types of problems, such as the one cited above, the solution can be found by the method of integral calculus, which deals with the process of tracing a given derivative function back to its primitive function. In more complicated cases, we can also resort to the known techniques of the closely related branch of mathematics known as *differential equations*. Since a differential equation is defined as any equation containing differential or derivative expressions, (13.1) surely qualifies as one; consequently, by finding its solution, we have in fact already solved a differential equation, albeit an exceedingly simple one.

Let us now proceed to the study of the basic concepts of integral calculus. Since we discussed differential calculus with x (rather than t) as the independent variable, for the sake of symmetry we shall use x here, too. For convenience, however, in the present discussion we shall denote the primitive and derived functions by $F(x)$ and $f(x)$, respectively, rather than distinguish them by the use of a prime.

13.2 Indefinite Integrals

the nature of integrals   It has been mentioned that integration is the reverse of differentiation. If the differentiation of a given primitive function $F(x)$ yields the derivative $f(x)$, then we can "integrate" $f(x)$ to find $F(x)$, provided that appropriate information is available to us to definitize the arbitrary constant which will come up in the process of integration. The function $F(x)$ is referred to as an *integral* (or *antiderivative*) of the function $f(x)$. These two types of processes may thus be likened to two ways of studying a family tree: *Integration* involves the tracing of the parentage of the function $f(x)$, whereas *differentiation* seeks out the progeny of the function $F(x)$. But note this difference: While the (differentiable) primitive function $F(x)$ invariably produces a lone offspring, namely, a unique derivative $f(x)$, the derived function $f(x)$ is traceable to an infinite number of possible parents through integration, because if $F(x)$ is an integral of $f(x)$, then so also must be $F(x)$ plus any constant, as we saw in (13.2).

We need a special notation to denote the required integration of $f(x)$ with respect to x. The standard one is

$$\int f(x)\, dx$$

The symbol on the left—an elongated S (with the connotation of sum, to be explained later)—is called the *integral sign*, whereas the $f(x)$ part is known as the *integrand* (the function to be integrated), and the dx part—similar to the dx in the differentiation operator d/dx—reminds us that the operation is to be performed with respect to the variable x. However, the reader may also take $f(x)\, dx$ as a single entity and interpret it as the differential of the primitive function $F(x)$ [that is, $dF(x) = f(x)\, dx$]. Then, the integral sign in front can be viewed as an instruction to reverse the differentiation process that gave rise to the differential. With this new symbolism, we can write that

$$(13.3) \qquad \frac{d}{dx} F(x) = f(x) \quad \Rightarrow \quad \int f(x)\, dx = F(x) + c$$

where the presence of c, an arbitrary *constant of integration*, serves to indicate the multiple parentage of the integrand.

The integral $\int f(x)\,dx$ is, more specifically, known as the *indefinite integral* of $f(x)$ (as against the *definite integral* to be discussed in the next section), because it has no definite numerical value. Being equal to $F(x) + c$, its value will in general vary with the value of x (even if c is definitized). Thus, like a derivative, an indefinite integral is itself a function of the variable x.

basic rules of integration   Just as there are rules of derivation, we can also develop certain rules of integration. As may be expected, the latter are heavily dependent on the rules of derivation with which we are already familiar. From the following derivative formula for a power function,

$$\frac{d}{dx}\left(\frac{x^{n+1}}{n+1}\right) = x^n \quad (n \neq -1)$$

for instance, we see that the expression $x^{n+1}/(n+1)$ is the primitive function for the derivative function x^n; thus, by substituting these for $F(x)$ and $f(x)$ in (13.3), we may state the result as a rule of integration.

RULE I   (*The Power Rule*) $\displaystyle\int x^n\,dx = \frac{1}{n+1}\,x^{n+1} + c \quad (n \neq -1)$

Example 1   Find $\int x^3\,dx$. Here, we have $n = 3$, and therefore

$$\int x^3\,dx = \frac{1}{4}\,x^4 + c$$

Example 2   Find $\int x\,dx$. Since $n = 1$, we have

$$\int x\,dx = \frac{1}{2}\,x^2 + c$$

Example 3   What is $\int 1\,dx$? To find this integral, we recall that $x^0 = 1$, so that we can let $n = 0$ in the power rule and get

$$\int 1\,dx = x + c$$

[$\int 1\,dx$ is sometimes written simply as $\int dx$, since $1\,dx = dx$.]

Example 4   Find $\int \sqrt{x^3}\,dx$. Since $\sqrt{x^3} = x^{3/2}$, we have $n = \frac{3}{2}$; therefore,

$$\int \sqrt{x^3}\,dx = \frac{x^{5/2}}{\frac{5}{2}} + c = \frac{2}{5}\,\sqrt{x^5} + c$$

Example 5   Find $\int \dfrac{1}{x^4} \, dx$. Since $1/x^4 = x^{-4}$, we have $n = -4$. Thus the integral is

$$\int \frac{1}{x^4} \, dx = \frac{x^{-4+1}}{-4+1} + c = -\frac{1}{3x^3} + c$$

The reader will note that the correctness of the results of integration can always be checked by differentiation; if the integration is correct, the derivative of the integral must be equal to the integrand.

The derivative formulas for simple exponential and logarithmic functions have been shown to be

$$\frac{d}{dx} e^x = e^x \qquad \text{and} \qquad \frac{d}{dx} \ln x = \frac{1}{x} \qquad (x > 0)$$

From these, two other basic rules of integration emerge.

RULE II   *(The Exponential Rule)* $\displaystyle\int e^x \, dx = e^x + c$

RULE III   *(The Logarithmic Rule)* $\displaystyle\int \frac{1}{x} \, dx = \ln x + c \qquad (x > 0)$

It is of interest that the integrand involved in Rule III is $1/x = x^{-1}$, which is a special form of the power function x^n with $n = -1$. This particular integrand is inadmissible under the power rule, but now is duly taken care of by the logarithmic rule.

As stated, the logarithmic rule is placed under the restriction $x > 0$, because logarithms do not exist for nonpositive values of x. A more general formulation of the rule, which can take care of negative values of x, is

$$\int \frac{1}{x} \, dx = \ln |x| + c \qquad (x \neq 0)$$

which also implies that $(d/dx) \ln |x| = 1/x$, just as $(d/dx) \ln x = 1/x$. The reader should convince himself that the replacement of x (with the restriction $x > 0$) by $|x|$ (with the restriction $x \neq 0$) does not vitiate the formula in any way.

Also, as a matter of notation, it should be pointed out that the integral $\int \dfrac{1}{x} \, dx$ is sometimes also written as $\int \dfrac{dx}{x}$.

rules of operation   The three rules given above amply illustrate the spirit underlying all such rules of integration. Each rule always corresponds to a certain derivative formula. Also, a constant is always appended at the end (even though it may later be eliminated by use of a given initial condition) to indicate that a whole family of primitive functions can give rise to the given form of the integrand.

To be able to deal with more complicated integrands, however, we shall also find the following two rules of operation with regard to integrals helpful.

RULE IV   (*The Integral of a Sum*)   The integral of the sum of a finite number of functions is the sum of the integrals of those functions. For the two-function case, this means that

$$\int [f(x) + g(x)]\, dx = \int f(x)\, dx + \int g(x)\, dx$$

This rule is a natural consequence of the fact that

$$\underbrace{\frac{d}{dx}\,[F(x) + G(x)]}_{A} = \underbrace{\frac{d}{dx}\,F(x) + \frac{d}{dx}\,G(x)}_{B} = \underbrace{f(x) + g(x)}_{C}$$

Inasmuch as $A = C$, on the basis of (13.3) we can write

(13.4) $$\int [f(x) + g(x)]\, dx = F(x) + G(x) + c$$

But, from the fact that $B = C$, it follows that

$$\int f(x)\, dx = F(x) + c_1 \quad \text{and} \quad \int g(x)\, dx = G(x) + c_2$$

Thus we can obtain (by addition)

(13.5) $$\int f(x)\, dx + \int g(x)\, dx = F(x) + G(x) + c_1 + c_2$$

The constants c, c_1, and c_2 being arbitrary in value, we can let $c = c_1 + c_2$. Then the right sides of (13.4) and (13.5) will become equal, and as a consequence, their left sides must be equal also. This proves Rule IV.

Example 6   Find $\int (x^3 + x + 1)\, dx$. By Rule IV, this integral can be expressed as a sum of three integrals: $\int x^3\, dx + \int x\, dx + \int 1\, dx$. Since the values of these three integrals have previously been found in Examples 1, 2, and 3, we can simply combine those results to get

$$\int (x^3 + x + 1)\, dx = \left(\frac{x^4}{4} + c_1\right) + \left(\frac{x^2}{2} + c_2\right) + (x + c_3)$$

$$= \frac{x^4}{4} + \frac{x^2}{2} + x + c$$

In the final answer, we have lumped together the three subscripted constants into a single constant c.

As a general practice, all the additive arbitrary constants of integration that come up during the process can always be combined into a single arbitrary constant in the final answer.

Example 7   Find $\int \left(e^x + \dfrac{1}{x} \right) dx$. By Rule IV, this can be written as a sum of two integrals whose values are given in Rules II and III:

$$\int \left(e^x + \frac{1}{x} \right) dx = \int e^x \, dx + \int \frac{1}{x} \, dx = e^x + \ln |x| + c$$

Note that we have directly written c in this example, instead of first writing out c_1 and c_2 and then combining them into c.

RULE V   (*The Integral of a Multiple*)   The integral of k times an integrand (k being a constant) is k times the integral of that integrand. In symbols,

$$\int kf(x) \, dx = k \int f(x) \, dx$$

What this rule amounts to, operationally, is that a multiplicative constant can be "factored out" of the integral sign. (Warning: A *variable* term *cannot* be factored out in this fashion!) To prove this rule, we recall that k times $f(x)$ merely means adding $f(x)$ k times; therefore, by Rule IV,

$$\int kf(x) \, dx = \int \underbrace{[f(x) + f(x) + \cdots + f(x)]}_{k \text{ terms}} \, dx$$

$$= \underbrace{\int f(x) \, dx + \int f(x) \, dx + \cdots + \int f(x) \, dx}_{k \text{ terms}} = k \int f(x) \, dx$$

Example 8   Find $\int -f(x) \, dx$. Here $k = -1$, and thus

$$\int -f(x) \, dx = - \int f(x) \, dx$$

That is, the integral of the negative of a function is the negative of the integral of that function.

Example 9   Find $\int 2x^2\,dx$. Factoring out the 2 and applying Rule I, we have

$$\int 2x^2\,dx = 2\int x^2\,dx = 2\left(\frac{x^3}{3} + c_1\right) = \frac{2}{3}x^3 + c$$

Example 10   Find $\int 3x^2\,dx$. In this case, factoring out the multiplicative constant yields

$$\int 3x^2\,dx = 3\int x^2\,dx = 3\left(\frac{x^3}{3} + c_1\right) = x^3 + c$$

Note that, in contrast to the preceding example, the term x^3 in the final answer does not have any fractional expression attached to it. This neat result is due to the fact that 3 (the multiplicative constant of the integrand) happens to be precisely equal to 2 (the power of the function) plus 1. Referring to the power rule (Rule I), we see that the multiplicative constant $(n + 1)$ will in such a case cancel out the fraction $1/(n + 1)$, thereby yielding $(x^{n+1} + c)$ as the answer.

In general, whenever we have an expression $(n + 1)x^n$ as the integrand, there is really no need to factor out the constant $(n + 1)$ and then integrate x^n; instead, we may write $x^{n+1} + c$ as the answer right away.

Example 11   Find $\int \left(5e^x - x^{-2} + \dfrac{3}{x}\right) dx$. This example illustrates both Rules IV and V; actually, it illustrates the first three rules as well:

$$\int \left(5e^x - \frac{1}{x^2} + \frac{3}{x}\right) dx = 5\int e^x\,dx - \int x^{-2}\,dx + 3\int \frac{1}{x}\,dx$$

$$\text{[by Rules IV and V]}$$

$$= (5e^x + c_1) - \left(\frac{x^{-1}}{-1} + c_2\right) + (3\ln|x| + c_3)$$

$$= 5e^x + \frac{1}{x} + 3\ln|x| + c$$

The correctness of the result can again be verified by differentiation, of course.

rules involving substitution   Now we shall introduce two more rules of integration which seek to simplify the process of integration, when the circumstances are appropriate, by a substitution of the original variable of integration. Whenever the newly introduced variable of integration makes the integration process easier than under the old, these rules will become of service.

RULE VI (*The Substitution Rule*) The integral of $f(u)(du/dx)$ with respect to the variable x is the integral of $f(u)$ with respect to the variable u:

$$\int f(u) \frac{du}{dx} \, dx = \int f(u) \, du = F(u) + c$$

where the operation $\int du$ has been substituted for the operation $\int dx$.

This rule, which is the integral-calculus counterpart of the chain rule, may indeed be proved by means of the chain rule itself. Given a function $F(u)$, where $u = u(x)$, the chain rule states that

$$\frac{d}{dx} F(u) = \frac{d}{du} F(u) \frac{du}{dx} = F'(u) \frac{du}{dx} = f(u) \frac{du}{dx}$$

Since $f(u)(du/dx)$ is the derivative of $F(u)$, it follows from (13.3) that the integral (antiderivative) of the former must be

$$\int f(u) \frac{du}{dx} \, dx = F(u) + c$$

The reader may note that this result, in fact, follows also from the *canceling* of the two dx expressions on the left.

Example 12 Find $\int 2x(x^2 + 1) \, dx$. The answer to this can be obtained by first multiplying out the integrand:

$$\int 2x(x^2 + 1) \, dx = \int (2x^3 + 2x) \, dx = \frac{x^4}{2} + x^2 + c$$

but let us now do it by the substitution rule. Let $u = x^2 + 1$; then $du/dx = 2x$, or $dx = du/2x$. Substitution of $du/2x$ for dx will yield

$$\int 2x(x^2 + 1) \, dx = \int 2xu \frac{du}{2x} = \int u \, du = \frac{u^2}{2} + c_1$$

$$= \frac{1}{2} (x^4 + 2x^2 + 1) + c_1 = \frac{1}{2} x^4 + x^2 + c$$

where $c = \frac{1}{2} + c_1$. The same answer can also be obtained by substituting du/dx for $2x$ (instead of $du/2x$ for dx).

Example 13 Find $\int 6x^2(x^3 + 2)^9 \, dx$. The integrand of this example is not easily multiplied out, and thus the substitution rule now has a better opportunity to display its effectiveness. Let $u = x^3 + 2$; then $du/dx = 3x^2$, so that

$$\int 6x^2(x^3 + 2)^9 \, dx = \int \left(2 \frac{du}{dx} \right) u^9 \, dx = \int 2u^9 \, du$$

$$= \frac{2}{10} u^{10} + c = \frac{1}{5} (x^3 + 2)^{10} + c$$

Example 14   Find $\int 8e^{2x+3}\,dx$. Let $u = 2x + 3$; then $du/dx = 2$, or $dx = du/2$. Hence,

$$\int 8e^{2x+3}\,dx = \int 8e^u\,\frac{du}{2} = 4\int e^u\,du = 4e^u + c = 4e^{2x+3} + c$$

Example 15   Find $\int \dfrac{2x^3 + 1}{x^4 + 2x}\,dx$. Let $u = x^4 + 2x$; then

$$\frac{du}{dx} = 4x^3 + 2$$

Thus we have

$$\int \frac{2x^3 + 1}{x^4 + 2x}\,dx = \int \frac{\frac{1}{2}(du/dx)}{u}\,dx = \frac{1}{2}\int \frac{du}{u} = \frac{1}{2}\ln|u| + c$$

$$= \frac{1}{2}\ln|x^4 + 2x| + c$$

As these examples show, this rule is of help whenever we can—by the judicious choice of a function $u = u(x)$—express the integrand (a function of x) as the product of $f(u)$ (a function of u) and du/dx (the derivative of the u function which we have chosen). However, as illustrated by the last three examples, this rule can be used also when the original integrand is transformable into a constant multiple of $f(u)(du/dx)$. This would not affect the applicability because the constant multiplier can be factored out of the integral sign, which would then leave an integrand of the form $f(u)(du/dx)$, as required in the substitution rule. When the substitution of variables results in a *variable* multiple of $f(u)(du/dx)$, say, x times the latter, however, factoring is not permissible, and this rule will be of no help. In fact, there exists no general formula giving the integral of a product of two functions in terms of the separate integrals of those functions; nor do we have a general formula giving the integral of a quotient of two functions in terms of their separate integrals. Herein lies the reason why integration, on the whole, is more difficult than differentiation and why, with complicated integrands, it is more convenient to look up the answer in prepared tables of integration formulas rather than to undertake the integration by oneself.

RULE VII   (*Integration by Parts*)   The integral of v with respect to u is equal to uv less the integral of u with respect to v:

$$\int v\,du = uv - \int u\,dv$$

The essence of this rule is to replace the operation $\int du$ by the operation $\int dv$.

The rationale behind this result is relatively simple. First, the product rule of differentials gives us

$$d(uv) = v\,du + u\,dv$$

If we integrate both sides of the equation (i.e., integrate each differential), we get a new equation

$$\int d(uv) = \int v\,du + \int u\,dv$$

or $uv = \int v\,du + \int u\,dv$ [no constant is needed on the left (why?)]

Then, by subtracting $\int u\,dv$ from both sides, the result stated above emerges.

Example 16   Find $\int x(x+1)^{1/2}\,dx$. Unlike Examples 12 and 13, the present example is not amenable to the type of substitution used in Rule VI. (Why?) However, we may consider the given integral to be in the form of $\int v\,du$, and apply Rule VII. To this end, we shall let $v = x$, implying $dv = dx$, and also let $u = \frac{2}{3}(x+1)^{3/2}$, so that $du = (x+1)^{1/2}\,dx$. Then we can find the integral to be

$$\int x(x+1)^{1/2}\,dx = \int v\,du = uv - \int u\,dv$$

$$= \frac{2}{3}(x+1)^{3/2}x - \int \frac{2}{3}(x+1)^{3/2}\,dx = \frac{2}{3}(x+1)^{3/2}x - \frac{4}{15}(x+1)^{5/2} + c$$

Example 17   Find $\int \ln x\,dx$. We cannot apply the logarithmic rule here, because that rule deals with the integrand $1/x$, not $\ln x$. Nor can we use Rule VI. But if we let $v = \ln x$, implying $dv = (1/x)\,dx$, and also let $u = x$, so that $du = dx$, then the integration can be performed as follows:

$$\int \ln x\,dx = \int v\,du = uv - \int u\,dv$$

$$= x\ln x - \int dx = x\ln x - x + c = x(\ln x - 1) + c$$

Example 18   Find $\int xe^x\,dx$. In this case, we shall simply let $v = x$, and $u = e^x$, so that $dv = dx$ and $du = e^x\,dx$. Applying Rule VII, we then have

$$\int xe^x\,dx = \int v\,du = uv - \int u\,dv$$

$$= e^x x - \int e^x\,dx = e^x x - e^x + c = e^x(x-1) + c$$

The validity of this result, like those of the preceding examples, can of course be readily checked by differentiation.

EXERCISE 13.2

1   Find the following:

(a) $\displaystyle\int 16x^{-3}\,dx \qquad (x \neq 0)$

(d) $\displaystyle\int (2x^5 - 3x^2 + 2)\,dx$

(b) $\displaystyle\int 16x^{15}\,dx$

(e) $\displaystyle\int (ax^2 + bx)\,dx$

(c) $\displaystyle\int (x^5 - 3x)\,dx$

(f) $\displaystyle\int (2ax + b)(ax^2 + bx)^7\,dx$

2   Find:

(a) $\displaystyle\int 13e^x\,dx$

(d) $\displaystyle\int 3e^{-(2x+7)}\,dx$

(b) $\displaystyle\int \left(e^x + \frac{4}{x}\right)dx \qquad (x \neq 0)$

(e) $\displaystyle\int 4xe^{x^2+3}\,dx$

(c) $\displaystyle\int \left(5e^x + \frac{3}{x^2}\right)dx \qquad (x \neq 0)$

(f) $\displaystyle\int xe^{x^2+9}\,dx$

3   Find:

(a) $\displaystyle\int \frac{3dx}{x} \qquad (x \neq 0)$

(c) $\displaystyle\int \frac{2x}{x^2 + 3}\,dx$

(b) $\displaystyle\int \frac{dx}{x + 3} \qquad (x \neq -3)$

(d) $\displaystyle\int \frac{x}{3x^2 + 5}\,dx$

4   Given n constants k_i (with $i = 1, 2, \ldots, n$) and n functions $f_i(x)$, deduce from Rules IV and V that

$$\int \sum_{i=1}^{n} k_i f_i(x)\,dx = \sum_{i=1}^{n} k_i \int f_i(x)\,dx$$

5   Find:

(a) $\displaystyle\int (x + 3)(x + 1)^{1/2}\,dx$

(b) $\displaystyle\int \ln 2x\,dx$

(c) $\displaystyle\int x \ln x\,dx$

13.3   Definite Integrals

meaning of definite integrals   All the integrals cited in the preceding section are of the *indefinite* variety: each is a function of a variable and, hence, possesses no definite numerical value. Now, for a given indefinite integral of a continuous function $f(x)$,

$$\int f(x)\, dx = F(x) + c$$

if we choose two values of x in the domain, say, a and b $(a < b)$, substitute them successively into the right side of the equation, and form the difference

$$[F(b) + c] - [F(a) + c] = F(b) - F(a)$$

we get a numerical value that is independent of the arbitrary constant c. This value is called the *definite integral* of $f(x)$ from a to b. We refer to a as the *lower limit of integration* and to b as the *upper limit of integration*.

In order to indicate the limits of integration, we now modify the integral sign to the form $\int_a^b$. The evaluation of the definite integral is then symbolized in the following steps:

$$(13.6) \qquad \int_a^b f(x)\, dx = F(x) \Big]_a^b = F(b) - F(a)$$

where the symbol $\Big]_a^b$ $\left(\text{also written } \Big|_a^b \text{ or } \Big[\ \cdots\ \Big]_a^b\right)$ is an instruction to substitute b and a, successively, for x in the result of integration to get $F(b)$ and $F(a)$, and then take their difference, as indicated on the right of (13.6). As the first step, however, we must find the indefinite integral, though we may omit the constant c, since the latter will drop out in the process of difference-taking anyway.

The result in (13.6) constitutes a part of what is known as the *fundamental theorem of calculus*: If a function $f(x)$ is continuous in an interval, then the function has integrals (antiderivatives) in that interval; furthermore, if $F(x)$ is any integral of $f(x)$, then for any two points a and b in the interval we have

$$\int_a^b f(x)\, dx = F(b) - F(a).$$

Example 1   Evaluate $\int_1^5 3x^2\, dx$. Since the indefinite integral is $x^3 + c$, this definite integral has the value

$$\int_1^5 3x^2\, dx = x^3 \Big]_1^5 = (5)^3 - (1)^3 = 125 - 1 = 124$$

Example 2   Evaluate $\int_a^b ke^x\, dx$. Here, the limits of integration are given in symbols; consequently, the result of integration is also in terms of those symbols:

$$\int_a^b ke^x\, dx = ke^x \bigg]_a^b = k(e^b - e^a)$$

Example 3   Evaluate $\int_0^4 \left(\dfrac{1}{1+x} + 2x\right) dx$. The indefinite integral is $\ln|1+x| + x^2 + c$; thus the answer is

$$\int_0^4 \left(\frac{1}{1+x} + 2x\right) dx = \left[\ln|1+x| + x^2\right]_0^4$$

$$= (\ln 5 + 16) - (\ln 1 + 0)$$
$$= \ln 5 + 16 \qquad [\text{since } \ln 1 = 0]$$

It is important to realize that the limits of integration a and b both refer to values of the variable x. Were we to use the substitution-of-variables technique (Rules VI and VII) during integration and introduce a variable, u, care should be taken *not* to consider a and b as the limits of u. The next example will illustrate this point.

Example 4   Evaluate $\int_1^2 (2x^3 - 1)^2(6x^2)\, dx$. Let $u = 2x^3 - 1$; then $du/dx = 6x^2$, or $du = 6x^2\, dx$. Now notice that, when $x = 1$, u will be 1 but that, when $x = 2$, u will be 15; in other words, the limits of integration in terms of the variable u should be 1 (lower) and 15 (upper). Rewriting the given integral in u will therefore give us not $\int_1^2 u^2\, du$ but

$$\int_1^{15} u^2\, du = \frac{1}{3} u^3 \bigg]_1^{15} = \frac{1}{3}(15^3 - 1^3) = 1124\tfrac{2}{3}$$

Alternatively, we may first convert u back to x and then use the original limits of 1 and 2 to get the identical answer:

$$\left[\frac{1}{3} u^3\right]_{u=1}^{u=15} = \left[\frac{1}{3}(2x^3 - 1)^3\right]_{x=1}^{x=2} = \frac{1}{3}(15^3 - 1^3) = 1124\tfrac{2}{3}$$

a definite integral as an area under a curve   Every definite integral has a definite value. That value may be interpreted geometrically to be a particular area under a given curve.

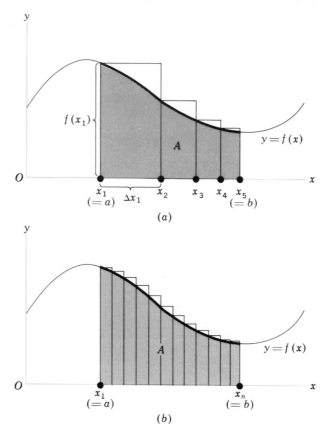

$f(x_1)$

A

$y = f(x)$

x_1 $\quad$ x_2 $\quad$ x_3 $\quad$ x_4 $\quad$ x_5
$(=a)$ $\quad \Delta x_1$ $\qquad\qquad\qquad (=b)$

(a)

A

$y = f(x)$

x_1 $\qquad\qquad\qquad x_n$
$(=a)$ $\qquad\qquad\qquad (=b)$

(b)

FIGURE 13.1

In Fig. 13.1 is drawn the graph of a continuous function $y = f(x)$. If we seek to measure the (shaded) area A enclosed by the curve and the x axis between the two points a and b in the domain, we may proceed in the following manner. First, we divide the interval $[a,b]$ into n subintervals (not necessarily equal in length). Four of these are drawn in diagram a—that is, $n = 4$—the first being $[x_1,x_2]$ and the last being $[x_4,x_5]$. Since each of these represents a change in x, we may refer to them as $\Delta x_1, \ldots, \Delta x_4$, respectively. Now, on the subintervals let us construct four rectangular blocks such that the height of each block is equal to the highest value of the function attained in that block (which happens to occur at the left-side boundary of each rectangle here). The first block thus has a height $f(x_1)$ and a width Δx_1, and the ith block, in general, will have a height $f(x_i)$ and a width Δx_i. The total area A^* of this set of blocks is the sum

$$A^* = \sum_{i=1}^{n} f(x_i)\,\Delta x_i \qquad (n = 4 \text{ in Fig. 13.1a})$$

This, though, is obviously *not* the area under the curve we seek, but only a very rough approximation thereof.

What makes A^* deviate from the true value of A is the unshaded portion of the rectangular blocks; these make A^* an *overestimate* of A. If the unshaded portion can be shrunk in size and be made to approach zero, however, the approximation value A^* will correspondingly approach the true value A. This result will materialize when we try a finer and finer segmentation of the interval $[a,b]$, so that n is increased and Δx_i is shortened indefinitely. Then the blocks will become more slender (if more numerous), and the protrusion beyond the curve will diminish, as can be seen in diagram b. Carried to the limit, this "slenderizing" operation will yield

$$(13.7) \qquad \lim_{n \to \infty} \sum_{i=1}^{n} f(x_i)\, \Delta x_i = \lim_{n \to \infty} A^* = \text{area } A$$

provided that this limit exists. (It does in the present case.) This equation, indeed, constitutes the formal definition of an area under a curve.

The summation expression in (13.7), $\sum_{i=1}^{n} f(x_i)\, \Delta x_i$, bears a certain resemblance to the definite integral expression

$$\int_{a}^{b} f(x)\, dx$$

and we may indeed interpret these to have essentially the same connotation.

When the change Δx_i is infinitesimal, we may replace it with the symbol dx_i. Moreover, the subscript i may be dropped because each of these infinitesimal changes can be equally well represented by the symbol dx. Thus we may rewrite $f(x_i)\, \Delta x_i$ into $f(x)\, dx$. What about the summation sign? The $\sum_{i=1}^{n}$ notation represents the sum of a *finite* number of terms. When $n \to \infty$, so that an *infinite* number of *infinitesimal* blocks are added, the $\sum_{i=1}^{n}$ notation is no longer appropriate and is replaced by $\int_{a}^{b}$, where the elongated S symbol again indicates a sum, and where a and b (just as $i = 1$ and n) serve to specify the lower and upper limits of this sum.[1] In this light, we may regard the definite integral as a shorthand for the limit-of-a-sum expression in (13.7). That is,

$$\int_{a}^{b} f(x)\, dx \equiv \lim_{n \to \infty} \sum_{i=1}^{n} f(x_i)\, \Delta x_i = \text{area } A$$

---

[1] If n becomes *countably* infinite, we may still use the summation sign in the form of $\sum_{i=1}^{\infty}$, with $i = 1, 2, \ldots$. In the present context, however, n is becoming *noncountably* infinite. Accordingly, we should use $\int_{a}^{b}$.

Thus the said definite integral (referred to as a *Riemann integral*) now has an *area* connotation as well as a *sum* connotation, because $\int_a^b$ is the continuous counterpart of the discrete concept of $\sum_{i=1}^n$.

In Fig. 13.1, we attempted to approximate area A by systematically reducing an *overestimate* $A*$ by finer segmentation of the interval $[a,b]$. The resulting limit of the sum of block areas is called the *upper integral*—an approximation from above. We could also have approximated area A from below by forming rectangular blocks inscribed by the curve rather than protruding beyond it (see Exercise 13.3-3). The total area $A**$ of this new set of blocks will *under-*estimate A, but as segmentation of $[a,b]$ becomes finer and finer, we shall again find $\lim_{n \to \infty} A** = A$. The last-cited limit of the sum of block areas is called the *lower integral*. If, and only if, the upper integral and lower integral are equal in value, then the Riemann integral $\int_a^b f(x) \, dx$ is defined, and the function $f(x)$ is said to be *Riemann integrable*. There exist theorems specifying the conditions under which a function $f(x)$ is integrable. According to the fundamental theorem of calculus, a function is integrable in $[a,b]$ if it is continuous in that interval. As long as we are working with continuous functions, therefore, we should have no worries in this regard.

Another point may be noted. Although the area A in Fig. 13.1 happens to lie entirely under a decreasing portion of the curve $y = f(x)$, the conceptual equating of a definite integral with an area is valid also for upward-sloping portions of the curve. In fact, both types of slopes may even be involved simultaneously; e.g., we can calculate $\int_0^b f(x) \, dx$ as the area under the curve in Fig. 13.1 above the line Ob.

Note that, if we calculate the area B in Fig. 13.2 by the definite integral $\int_a^b f(x) \, dx$, however, the answer will come out negative because the height of each rectangular block involved in this area is negative. This gives rise to the notion of a *negative area*, an area that lies *below* the x axis and *above* a given curve. In case we are interested in the numerical rather than the algebraic value of such an area, therefore, we should take the absolute value of the relevant definite integral. The area $C = \int_c^d f(x) \, dx$, on the other hand, has a positive sign even though it lies in the negative region of the x axis; this is because each rectangular block has a positive height as well as a positive width when we are moving from c to d. From this, the implication is clear that interchange of the two limits of integration would, by reversing the direction of movement, alter the sign of Δx_i

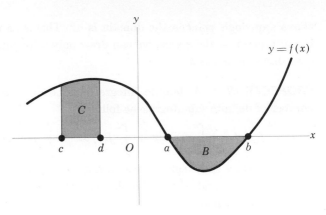

FIGURE 13.2

and of the definite integral. Applied to area B, we see that the definite integral $\int_b^a f(x)\, dx$ (from b to a) will give the negative of the area B; this will measure the numerical value of this area.

some properties of definite integrals   The discussion in the preceding paragraph leads us to the following property of definite integrals.

PROPERTY I   The interchange of the limits of integration changes the sign of the definite integral:

$$\int_b^a f(x)\, dx = -\int_a^b f(x)\, dx$$

This can be proved as follows:

$$\int_b^a f(x)\, dx = F(a) - F(b) = -[F(b) - F(a)] = -\int_a^b f(x)\, dx$$

Definite integrals also possess some other general properties.

PROPERTY II   A definite integral has a value of zero when the two limits of integration are identical:

$$\int_a^a f(x)\, dx = F(a) - F(a) = 0$$

Under the "area" interpretation, this means that the area (under a curve) above any single *point* in the domain is nil. This is as it should be, because on top of a point on the x axis, we can draw only a (one-dimensional) *line*, never a (two-dimensional) *area*.

PROPERTY III   A definite integral can be expressed as a sum of a finite number of definite subintegrals as follows:

$$\int_a^d f(x)\ dx = \int_a^b f(x)\ dx + \int_b^c f(x)\ dx + \int_c^d f(x)\ dx \qquad (a < b < c < d)$$

Only three subintegrals are shown in this equation, but the extension to the case of n subintegrals should be obvious. This property is sometimes described as the *additivity property*.

In terms of area, this means that the area (under the curve) lying above the interval $[a,d]$ on the x axis can be obtained by summing the areas lying above the subintervals in the set $\{[a,b], [b,c], [c,d]\}$. Note that, since we are dealing with closed intervals, the border points b and c have each been included in *two* areas. Is this not double counting? It indeed is. But fortunately no damage is done, because by Property II the area above a single point is zero, so that the double counting produces no effect on the calculation. But, needless to say, the double counting of any *interval* is never permitted.

Earlier, it was mentioned that all continuous functions are Riemann integrable. Now, by Property III, we can also find the definite integrals (areas) of certain discontinuous functions. Consider the step function in Fig. 13.3a. In spite of the discontinuity at point b in the interval $[a,c]$, we can find the shaded area from the sum

$$\int_a^b f(x)\ dx + \int_b^c f(x)\ dx$$

The same also applies to the curve in diagram b.

PROPERTY IV $\displaystyle\int_a^b - f(x)\ dx = -\int_a^b f(x)\ dx$

PROPERTY V $\displaystyle\int_a^b kf(x)\ dx = k\int_a^b f(x)\ dx$

PROPERTY VI $\displaystyle\int_a^b [f(x) + g(x)]\ dx = \int_a^b f(x)\ dx + \int_a^b g(x)\ dx$

PROPERTY VII   Given $u(x)$ and $v(x)$, $\displaystyle\int_{x=a}^{x=b} v\ du = uv\ \Big|_{x=a}^{x=b} - \int_{x=a}^{x=b} u\ dv$

These last four properties, all borrowed from the rules of indefinite integration, should require no further explanation.

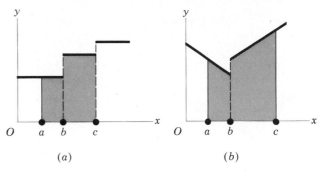

FIGURE 13.3

another look at the indefinite integral   We introduced the definite integral by way of attaching two limits of integration to an indefinite integral. Now that we know the meaning of the definite integral, let us see how we can revert from the latter to the indefinite integral.

Suppose that, instead of fixing the upper limit of integration at b, we allow it to be a variable, designated simply as x. Then the integral will take the form

$$\int_a^x f(x)\, dx = F(x) - F(a)$$

which, being a function of x, denotes a *variable* area under the curve of $f(x)$. But since the last term on the right is a constant, this integral must be a member of the family of primitive functions of $f(x)$, which we denoted earlier as $F(x) + c$. If we set $c = -F(a)$, then the above integral becomes exactly the indefinite integral $\int f(x)\, dx$.

From this point of view, therefore, we may consider the $\int$ symbol to mean the same as $\int_a^x$, provided that it is understood that in the latter version of the symbol the lower limit of integration is related to the constant of integration by the equation $c = -F(a)$.

EXERCISE 13.3

1   Evaluate the following:

(a) $\displaystyle\int_1^3 \frac{1}{2} x^2\, dx$

(b) $\displaystyle\int_2^4 (x^3 - 3x^2)\, dx$

(c) $\displaystyle\int_0^1 x(x^2 + 6)\, dx$

(e) $\displaystyle\int_{-1}^1 (ax^2 + bx + c)\, dx$

(d) $\displaystyle\int_1^4 \sqrt{x}\, dx$

(f) $\displaystyle\int_4^2 x^2\left(\frac{1}{3}x^3 + 1\right) dx$

2   Evaluate the following:

(a) $\displaystyle\int_1^2 e^{-2x}\, dx$

(c) $\displaystyle\int_2^3 (e^{2x} + e^x)\, dx$

(b) $\displaystyle\int_{-1}^{e-2} \frac{dx}{x + 2}$

(d) $\displaystyle\int_e^6 \left(\frac{1}{x} + \frac{1}{1 + x}\right) dx$

3   In Fig. 13.1a, take the lowest value of the function attained in each sub-interval as the height of the rectangular block, i.e., take $f(x_2)$ instead of $f(x_1)$ as the height of the first block, though still retaining Δx_1 as its width, and do likewise for the other blocks.

(a)   Write a summation expression for the total area A^{**} of the new rectangles.

(b)   Does A^{**} overestimate or underestimate the desired area A?

(c)   Would A^{**} tend to approach or to deviate further from A if a finer segmentation of $[a,b]$ were introduced? (*Hint:* Try a diagram.)

(d)   In the limit, when the number n of subintervals approaches ∞, would the approximation value A^{**} approach the true value A, just as the approximation value A^* did?

(e)   What can you conclude from the above about the Riemann integrability of the function $f(x)$ in the figure?

4   The definite integral $\displaystyle\int_a^b f(x)\, dx$ is said to represent an area under a curve.

Does this curve refer to the graph of the integrand $f(x)$, or of the primitive function $F(x)$? If we plot the graph of the $F(x)$ function, how can we show the above definite integral on it—by an area, a line segment, or a point?

13.4   Improper Integrals

Certain integrals are said to be "improper." We may briefly discuss two varieties thereof.

infinite limits of integration   When we have definite integrals of the form

$$\int_a^\infty f(x)\, dx \quad\text{and}\quad \int_{-\infty}^b f(x)\, dx$$

with one limit of integration being infinite, we refer to them as *improper integrals*. In these cases, it is not possible to evaluate the integrals as, respectively,

$$F(\infty) - F(a) \quad\text{and}\quad F(b) - F(-\infty)$$

because ∞ is not a number, and therefore it cannot be substituted for x in the function $F(x)$. Instead, we must resort once more to the concept of limits.

The first improper integral cited above can be defined to be the limit of another (proper) integral as the latter's upper limit of integration tends to ∞; that is,

$$(13.8) \qquad \int_a^\infty f(x)\, dx \equiv \lim_{b\to\infty} \int_a^b f(x)\, dx$$

If this limit exists, the improper integral is said to be convergent (or to converge), and the limiting process will yield the value of the integral. If the limit does not exist, the improper integral is said to be divergent, and is in fact meaningless. By the same token, we can define

$$(13.8') \qquad \int_{-\infty}^b f(x)\, dx \equiv \lim_{a\to-\infty} \int_a^b f(x)\, dx$$

with the same criterion of convergence and divergence.

Example 1   Evaluate $\displaystyle\int_1^\infty \frac{dx}{x^2}$. First we note that

$$\int_1^b \frac{dx}{x^2} = \frac{-1}{x}\bigg]_1^b = \frac{-1}{b} + 1$$

Hence, in line with (13.8), the desired integral is

$$\int_1^\infty \frac{dx}{x^2} = \lim_{b\to\infty} \int_1^b \frac{dx}{x^2} = \lim_{b\to\infty} \left(\frac{-1}{b} + 1\right) = 1$$

This improper integral does converge, and it has a value of 1.

Since the limit expression is cumbersome to write, some people prefer to omit the "lim" notation and write simply

$$\int_1^\infty \frac{dx}{x^2} = \frac{-1}{x}\bigg]_1^\infty = 0 + 1 = 1$$

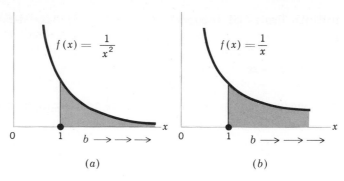

FIGURE 13.4

Even when written in this form, however, the improper integral should never-theless be interpreted with the limit concept in mind.

Graphically speaking, this improper integral still has the connotation of an area. But since the upper limit of integration is allowed to take on increasingly larger values in this case, the right-side boundary must be extended eastward indefinitely, as shown in Fig. 13.4*a*. Despite this, we are able to consider the area to have the definite (limit) value of 1.

Example 2   Evaluate $\displaystyle\int_{1}^{\infty} \frac{dx}{x}$. As before, we first find

$$\int_{1}^{b} \frac{dx}{x} = \ln |x| \Big]_{1}^{b} = \ln |b| - \ln 1 = \ln b \qquad [\text{since } b > 1 > 0]$$

When we let $b \to \infty$, by (10.16′) we have $\ln b \to \infty$. Thus the given improper integral is divergent.

Figure 13.4*b* shows the graph of the function $1/x$, as well as the area corresponding to the given integral. The indefinite eastward extension of the right-side boundary will result this time in an infinite area, even though the shape of the graph displays a superficial similarity to that of diagram *a*.

What if both limits of integration are infinite? A direct extension of (13.8) and (13.8′) would suggest the definition

$$(13.8'') \qquad \int_{-\infty}^{\infty} f(x)\, dx = \lim_{\substack{b \to +\infty \\ a \to -\infty}} \int_{a}^{b} f(x)\, dx$$

Again, this improper integral is said to converge if and only if the limit in question exists.

infinite integrand   Even with finite limits of integration, an integral can yet be improper if the integrand becomes infinite somewhere in the interval of integration $[a,b]$. To evaluate such an integral, we must again rely upon the concept of a limit.

Example 3   Evaluate $\int_0^1 \frac{1}{x}\, dx$. This integral is improper because, as Fig. 13.4*b* shows, the integrand is infinite at the lower limit of integration ($1/x \to \infty$ as $x \to 0^+$). Therefore we should first find the integral

$$\int_a^1 \frac{1}{x}\, dx = \ln |x| \Big]_a^1 = \ln 1 - \ln |a| = -\ln a \qquad [\text{for } a > 0]$$

and then evaluate its limit as $a \to 0^+$:

$$\int_0^1 \frac{1}{x}\, dx \equiv \lim_{a \to 0^+} \int_a^1 \frac{1}{x}\, dx = \lim_{a \to 0^+} (-\ln a)$$

Since this limit does not exist (as $a \to 0^+$, $\ln a \to -\infty$), the given integral is divergent.

Example 4   Evaluate $\int_0^9 x^{-1/2}\, dx$. When $x \to 0^+$, the integrand $1/\sqrt{x}$ becomes infinite; the integral is improper. Again, we can first find

$$\int_a^9 x^{-1/2}\, dx = 2x^{1/2} \Big]_a^9 = 6 - 2\sqrt{a}$$

The limit of this expression as $a \to 0^+$ is $6 - 0 = 6$. Thus the given integral is convergent (to 6).

The situation where the integrand becomes infinite at the *upper* limit of integration is perfectly similar. It is an altogether different proposition, however, when an infinite value of the integrand occurs in the open interval (a,b) rather than at a or b. In this eventuality, it is necessary to take advantage of the additivity of definite integrals and first decompose the given integral into subintegrals. Assume that $f(x) \to \infty$ as $x \to p$, with p being a point in the interval (a,b); then, by the additivity property, we have

$$\int_a^b f(x)\, dx = \int_a^p f(x)\, dx + \int_p^b f(x)\, dx$$

The given integral on the left can be considered as convergent if and only if each subintegral has a limit.

Example 5   Evaluate $\int_{-1}^{1} \dfrac{1}{x^3} \, dx$. The integrand tends to be infinite when x approaches zero; thus we must write the given integral as the sum

$$\int_{-1}^{1} x^{-3} \, dx = \int_{-1}^{0} x^{-3} \, dx + \int_{0}^{1} x^{-3} \, dx \qquad (\text{say}, \equiv I_1 + I_2)$$

The integral I_1 is divergent, because

$$\lim_{b \to 0^-} \int_{-1}^{b} x^{-3} \, dx = \lim_{b \to 0^-} \left[\frac{-1}{2} x^{-2} \right]_{-1}^{b} = \lim_{b \to 0^-} \left(-\frac{1}{2b^2} + \frac{1}{2} \right) = -\infty$$

Thus, we can conclude immediately, without having to evaluate I_2, that the given integral is divergent.

EXERCISE 13.4

1 Check the definite integrals given in Exercises 13.3-1 and 13.3-2 to determine whether any of them is improper. If this is true for any, indicate which variety of improper integral each one is.

2 Which of the following integrals are improper, and why ?

(a) $\displaystyle\int_{0}^{\infty} e^{-rt} \, dt$ (c) $\displaystyle\int_{0}^{1} x^{-2/3} \, dx$ (e) $\displaystyle\int_{1}^{5} \frac{dx}{x - 2}$

(b) $\displaystyle\int_{2}^{3} x^4 \, dx$ (d) $\displaystyle\int_{-\infty}^{0} e^{rt} \, dt$ (f) $\displaystyle\int_{-3}^{4} 6 \, dx$

3 Evaluate all the *improper* integrals in the preceding problem.

4 Evaluate the integral I_2 of Example 5, and show that it is also divergent.

13.5   Some Economic Applications of Integrals

Integrals are used in economic analysis in various ways. We shall illustrate a few simple applications in the present section and then show the application to the celebrated Domar growth model in the next.

from a marginal function to a total function   Given a total function (e.g., a total-cost function), the process of differentiation can yield the marginal function (e.g., the marginal-cost function). Being the opposite of differentiation, the process of integration should enable us, conversely, to infer the total function from a given marginal function.

Example 1   If the marginal cost (MC) of a firm is the following function of output, $C'(Q) = 2e^{0.2Q}$, and if the fixed cost is $C_F = 90$, find the total-cost function $C(Q)$. By integrating $C'(Q)$ with respect to Q, we find that

$$(13.9) \qquad \int 2e^{0.2Q} \, dQ = 2\frac{1}{0.2} e^{0.2Q} + c = 10e^{0.2Q} + c$$

This result may be taken as the desired $C(Q)$ function except that, in view of the arbitrary constant c, the answer appears indeterminate. Fortunately, the information that $C_F = 90$ can be used as an initial condition to definitize the constant: When $Q = 0$, total cost C will consist solely of C_F. Setting $Q = 0$ in the result of (13.9), therefore, we should get a value of 90; that is, $10e^0 + c = 90$. But this would imply that $c = 90 - 10 = 80$. Hence, the total-cost function is

$$C(Q) = 10e^{0.2Q} + 80$$

Note that, unlike the case of (13.2) where the arbitrary constant c has the same value as the initial value of the variable $H(0)$, in the present example we have $c = 80$ but $C(0) \equiv C_F = 90$, so that the two take different values. In general, it should *not* be assumed that the arbitrary constant c will always be equal to the initial value of the total function.

Example 2   If the marginal propensity to save (MPS) is the following function of income, $S'(Y) = 0.3 - 0.1Y^{-1/2}$, and if the aggregate savings S is nil when income Y is 81, find the saving function $S(Y)$. As the MPS is the derivative of the S function, the problem now calls for the integration of $S'(Y)$:

$$S(Y) = \int (0.3 - 0.1Y^{-1/2}) \, dY = 0.3Y - 0.2Y^{1/2} + c$$

The specific value of the constant c can be found from the fact that $S = 0$ when $Y = 81$. Even though, strictly speaking, this is not an *initial* condition (not relating to $Y = 0$), substitution of this information into the above integral will nevertheless serve to definitize c. Since

$$0 = 0.3(81) - 0.2(9) + c \quad \Rightarrow \quad c = -22.5$$

the desired saving function is

$$S(Y) = 0.3Y - 0.2Y^{1/2} - 22.5$$

The technique illustrated in the above two examples can be extended directly to other problems involving the search for total functions (such as total revenue, total consumption) from given marginal functions. It may also be reiterated that in problems of this type the validity of the answer (an integral) can always be checked by differentiation.

investment and capital formation   Capital formation is the process of adding to a given stock of capital. Regarding this process as continuous over time, we may express capital stock as a function of time, $K(t)$, and use the derivative dK/dt to denote the rate of capital formation.[1] But the rate of capital formation at time t is identical with the rate of *net-investment* flow at time t, denoted by $I(t)$. Thus, capital stock K and net investment I are related by the following two equations:

$$\frac{dK}{dt} \equiv I(t)$$

and $$K(t) = \int I(t)\, dt = \int \frac{dK}{dt}\, dt = \int dK$$

The first equation above is an identity; it shows the synonymity between net investment and the increment of capital. Since $I(t)$ is the derivative of $K(t)$, it stands to reason that $K(t)$ will be the integral or antiderivative of $I(t)$, as shown in the second equation. The transformation of the integrand in the latter equation is also easy to comprehend: The switch from I to dK/dt is by definition, and the next transformation is by cancellation of two identical differentials, i.e., by the substitution rule.

Example 3   Suppose that the investment flow is described by the equation $I(t) = 3t^{1/2}$ and that the initial capital stock, at time $t = 0$, is $K(0)$. What is the time path of capital K? By integrating $I(t)$ with respect to t, we obtain

$$K(t) = \int I(t)\, dt = \int 3t^{1/2}\, dt = 2t^{3/2} + c$$

Next, letting $t = 0$ in the leftmost and rightmost expressions, we find $K(0) = c$. Therefore, the time path of K is

(13.10) $$K(t) = 2t^{3/2} + K(0)$$

The reader should observe the basic similarity between the results in (13.10) and in (13.2″).

---

[1] As a matter of notation, the derivative of a variable with respect to *time* often is also denoted by a dot placed over the variable, such as $\dot{K} \equiv dK/dt$. In dynamic analysis, where derivatives with respect to *time* occur in abundance, this more concise symbol can contribute substantially to notational simplicity. However, a dot, being such a tiny mark, is easily lost sight of or misplaced; thus, great care is required in using this symbol.

The concept of the definite integral will enter into the picture when one desires to find the amount of capital formation during some interval of time (rather than the time path of K). Since $\int I(t)\, dt = K(t)$, we may write the definite integral

$$\int_a^b I(t)\, dt = K(t) \Big]_a^b = K(b) - K(a)$$

to indicate the total capital accumulation during the time interval $[a,b]$. Of course, it also represents an area under the $I(t)$ curve. Be it noted, however, that in the graph of the $K(t)$ function, this definite integral would appear instead as a vertical distance—more specifically, as the difference between the two vertical distances $K(b)$ and $K(a)$. (cf. Exercise 13.3-4.)

To appreciate this distinction between $K(t)$ and $I(t)$ more fully, let us emphasize that capital K is a *stock* concept, whereas investment I is a *flow* concept. Accordingly, while $K(t)$ tells us the *amount* of K existing at each point of time, $I(t)$ gives us the information about the *rate* of (net) investment per year (or per period of time) which is prevailing at each point of time. Thus, in order to calculate the *amount* of net investment undertaken (capital accumulation), we must first specify the length of the interval involved. This fact can also be seen when we rewrite the identity $dK/dt \equiv I(t)$ as $dK \equiv I(t)\, dt$, which states that dK, the increment in K, is based not only on $I(t)$, the rate of flow, but also on dt, the time elapsed. It is this need to specify the time interval in the expression $I(t)\, dt$ that brings the definite integral into the picture, and gives rise to the *area* representation under the $I(t)$—as against the $K(t)$—curve.

Example 4   If net investment is a constant flow at $I(t) = 1000$ (dollars per year), what will be the total net investment (capital formation) during a year, from $t = 0$ to $t = 1$? Obviously, the answer is $1000; this can be obtained formally as follows:

$$\int_0^1 I(t)\, dt = \int_0^1 1000\, dt = 1000t \Big]_0^1 = 1000$$

The reader can verify that the same answer will emerge if, instead, the year involved is from $t = 1$ to $t = 2$.

Example 5   If $I(t) = 3t^{1/2}$ (thousands of dollars per year)—a nonconstant flow—what will be the capital formation during the time interval $[1,4]$, that is, during the second, third, and fourth years? The answer lies in the definite integral

$$\int_1^4 3t^{1/2}\, dt = 2t^{3/2} \Big]_1^4 = 16 - 2 = 14$$

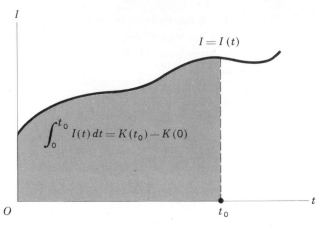

$$\int_0^{t_0} I(t)\,dt = K(t_0) - K(0)$$

$I = I(t)$

O t_0

FIGURE 13.5

On the basis of the preceding examples, we may express the amount of capital accumulation during the time interval $[0,t]$, for any investment rate $I(t)$, by the definite integral

$$\int_0^t I(t)\,dt = K(t)\Big]_0^t = K(t) - K(0)$$

Figure 13.5 illustrates the case of the time interval $[0,t_0]$. Viewed differently, the above equation yields the following expression for the time path $K(t)$:

$$K(t) = K(0) + \int_0^t I(t)\,dt$$

The amount of K at any time t is the initial capital plus the total capital accumulation that has occurred since.

present value of a cash flow   Our earlier discussion of discounting and present value, limited to the case of a *single* future value V, led us to the discounting formulas

$$A = V(1 + i)^{-t} \qquad [discrete \text{ case}]$$

and $\quad A = Ve^{-rt} \qquad\qquad [continuous \text{ case}]$

Now suppose that we have a stream or flow of future values—a series of revenues receivable at various times or of cost outlays payable at various times. How do we compute the present value of the entire "cash stream," or cash flow? In the *discrete* case, if we assume three future revenue figures $R_t\ (t = 1,2,3)$

available at the end of the tth year and also assume an interest rate of i per annum, the present values of R_t will be, respectively,

$$R_1(1 + i)^{-1} \qquad R_2(1 + i)^{-2} \qquad R_3(1 + i)^{-3}$$

It follows that the total present value is the sum

$$(13.11) \qquad \Pi = \sum_{t=1}^{3} R_t(1 + i)^{-t}$$

(Π is the upper-case Greek letter pi, signifying *present*.) This differs from the single-value formula only in the replacement of V by R_t and in the insertion of the $\sum$ sign.

The idea of the sum readily carries over to the case of a continuous cash flow, but in the latter context the $\sum$ symbol must give way, of course, to the definite integral sign. Consider a continuous revenue stream at the rate of $R(t)$ dollars per year. This means that at $t = t_1$ the rate of flow is $R(t_1)$ dollars per year, but at another point of time $t = t_2$ the rate will be $R(t_2)$ dollars per year— with t taken as a continuous variable. If, at any point of time t we allow an infinitesimal time interval dt to pass, then the amount of revenue during the interval $[t, t + dt]$ can be written as $R(t) \, dt$ [cf. the previous discussion of $dK \equiv I(t) \, dt$]. When discounted at the nominal rate of r per year, its present value should be $R(t)e^{-rt} \, dt$. If we let our problem be that of finding the total present value of a three-year stream, then our answer is to be found in the following definite integral:

$$(13.11') \qquad \Pi = \int_0^3 R(t)e^{-rt} \, dt$$

This expression, the continuous version of the sum in (13.11), differs from the single-value formula only in the replacement of V by $R(t)$ and in the appending of the definite integral symbol.[1]

Example 6   What is the present value of a continuous revenue flow lasting for y years at the constant rate of D dollars per year and discounted at the nominal rate of r per year? According to (13.11'), we have

$$(13.12) \qquad \Pi = \int_0^y De^{-rt} \, dt = D \int_0^y e^{-rt} \, dt = D \left[\frac{-1}{r} e^{-rt} \right]_0^y$$

$$= \frac{-D}{r} e^{-rt} \bigg]_{t=0}^{t=y} = \frac{-D}{r} (e^{-ry} - 1) = \frac{D}{r} (1 - e^{-ry})$$

[1] It may be noted that, whereas the upper summation index and the upper limit of integration are identical at 3, the lower summation index 1 differs from the lower limit of integration 0. This is because the first revenue in the discrete stream, by assumption, will not be forthcoming until $t = 1$ (end of first year), but the revenue flow in the continuous case is assumed to commence immediately after $t = 0$.

Thus, Π depends on D, r, and y. If $D = \$3000$, $r = 0.06$, and $y = 2$, for instance, we have

$$\Pi = \frac{3000}{0.06}(1 - e^{-0.12}) = 50{,}000(1 - 0.8869) = \$5655 \qquad \text{[approximately]}$$

The value of Π naturally is always positive; this follows from the positivity of D and r, as well as $(1 - e^{-ry})$. (The number e raised to any negative power will always give a positive fractional value, as can be seen from the second quadrant of Fig. 10.3a.)

Example 7   In the wine-storage problem of Sec. 10.6, we assumed zero storage cost. That simplifying assumption was necessitated by our ignorance of a way to compute the present value of a cost flow. With this ignorance behind us, we are now ready to permit the wine dealer to incur storage costs.

Let the purchase cost of the case of wine be an amount C, incurred at the present time. Its (future) sale value, which varies with time, may be generally denoted as $V(t)$—its present value being $V(t)e^{-rt}$. Whereas the sale value represents a single future value (because there can be only one sale transaction on this case of wine), the storage cost is a stream. Assuming this cost to be a constant stream at the rate of s dollars per year, the total present value of the storage cost incurred in a total of t years will amount to

$$\int_0^t se^{-rt}\, dt = \frac{s}{r}(1 - e^{-rt}) \qquad \text{[cf. (13.12)]}$$

Thus the *net* present value—what the dealer would seek to maximize—can be expressed as

$$N(t) = V(t)e^{-rt} - \frac{s}{r}(1 - e^{-rt}) - C = \left[V(t) + \frac{s}{r}\right]e^{-rt} - \frac{s}{r} - C$$

which is an objective function in a single choice variable t.

To maximize $N(t)$, the value of t must be chosen such that $N'(t) = 0$, assuming due fulfillment of the second-order condition. This first derivative is

$$N'(t) = V'(t)e^{-rt} - r\left[V(t) + \frac{s}{r}\right]e^{-rt} \qquad \text{[product rule]}$$

$$= [V'(t) - rV(t) - s]e^{-rt}$$

which will be zero if and only if

$$V'(t) = rV(t) + s$$

Thus, this last equation may be taken as the optimization condition for the choice of the time of sale $\bar{t}$.

The economic interpretation of this condition appeals easily to intuitive reasoning: $V'(t)$ represents the rate of change of the sale value, or the increment in V, if sale is postponed for a year, while the two terms on the right side indicate, respectively, the increments in the interest cost and the storage cost entailed by such a postponement of sale (revenue and cost both being reckoned at time $\bar{t}$). So, the idea of the equating of the two sides is to us just some "old wine in a new bottle," for it is nothing but the same MC = MR condition in another guise!

present value of a perpetual flow   If a cash flow were to persist forever—a situation exemplified by the interest from a perpetual bond or the revenue from an indestructible capital asset such as land—the present value of the flow would be

$$\Pi = \int_0^\infty R(t)e^{-rt}\, dt$$

which is an improper integral.

Example 8   Find the present value of a perpetual income stream flowing at the uniform rate of D dollars per year, if the continuous rate of discount is r. Since, in evaluating an improper integral, we simply take the limit of a proper integral, the result in (13.12) can still be of help. Specifically, we can write

$$\Pi = \int_0^\infty De^{-rt}\, dt = \lim_{y\to\infty} \int_0^y De^{-rt}\, dt = \lim_{y\to\infty} \frac{D}{r}(1 - e^{-ry}) = \frac{D}{r}$$

Note that the y parameter (number of years) has disappeared from the final answer. This is as it should be, for here we are dealing with a *perpetual* flow. The reader may also observe that our result (present value = rate of revenue ÷ rate of discount) corresponds precisely to the familiar formula for the so-called "capitalization" of an asset with a perpetual yield.

EXERCISE 13.5

1   Given the following marginal-revenue functions:

   (a) $R'(Q) = 75 - 1.6Q$ (b) $R'(Q) = 10(1 + Q)^{-2}$

   find in each case the total-revenue function $R(Q)$. What initial condition can you introduce to definitize the constant of integration?

2 (a) Given the marginal propensity to import $M'(Y) = 0.1$ and the information that $M = 20$ when $Y = 0$, find the import function $M(Y)$.

(b) Given the marginal propensity to consume $C'(Y) = 0.7 + 0.1Y^{-1/2}$ and the information that $C = Y$ when $Y = 121$, find the consumption function $C(Y)$.

3 Assume that the rate of investment is described by the function $I(t) = 12t^{1/3}$ and that $K(0) = 25$:

(a) Find the time path of capital stock K.

(b) Find the amount of capital accumulation during the time intervals $[0,1]$ and $[1,3]$, respectively.

4 If net investment has been occurring since the beginning of history at the rate of $I(t) = 100e^{0.2t}$ per year:

(a) Find the total capital accumulation undertaken up to the present time $(t = 0)$.

(b) Determine the present capital stock $K(0)$.

5 Given a continuous income stream at the constant rate of \$1000 per year:

(a) What will be the present value Π if the income stream lasts for 2 years and the continuous discount rate is 0.05 per year?

(b) What will be the present value Π if the income stream terminates after exactly 3 years and the discount rate is 0.04?

6 What is the present value of a perpetual cash flow of:

(a) \$1000 per year, discounted at $r = 5\%$?

(b) \$2460 per year, discounted at $r = 6\%$?

7 In the present-value formula (13.12), find whether Π is directly or inversely related to the parameters D, y, and r. [*Hint:* The sign of $\partial\Pi/\partial r$ depends, after factoring out e^{-ry}, on the sign of $(ry - e^{ry} + 1)$. One way of evaluating the sign of this parenthetical expression—call it p—is to note that $p = 0$ when $ry = 0$; therefore the derivative $dp/d(ry)$ should tell us about the sign of p when ry is positive rather than zero.]

13.6 Domar Growth Model

In the population-growth problem of (13.1) and (13.2) and the capital-formation problem of (13.10), the common objective is to delineate a time path on the basis of some given pattern of change of a variable. In the well-known growth model of Professor Domar,[1] on the other hand, the idea is to stipulate the type of time path required to prevail if a certain equilibrium condition of the economy is to be satisfied.

the framework   The basic premises of the Domar model are as follows:

1   Any change in the rate of investment flow per year $I(t)$ will produce a dual effect: it will affect the aggregate demand as well as the productive capacity of the economy.

2   The demand effect of a change in $I(t)$ operates through the multiplier process, so that an increase in $I(t)$ will raise the rate of income flow per year $Y(t)$ by a multiple of the increment in $I(t)$. The multiplier is $k = 1/s$, where s stands for the given (constant) marginal propensity to save. On the assumption that $I(t)$ is the only (parametric) expenditure flow that influences the rate of income flow, we can then state that

$$(13.13) \qquad \frac{dY}{dt} = \frac{dI}{dt} \frac{1}{s}$$

3   The capacity effect of investment is to be measured by the change in the rate of *potential* output the economy is capable of producing. Assuming a constant capacity-capital ratio, we can write

$$\frac{\kappa}{K} \equiv \rho \qquad (= \text{a constant})$$

where κ (the Greek letter kappa) stands for capacity or potential output flow per year, and ρ (the Greek letter rho) denotes the given capacity-capital ratio. This implies, of course, that with a capital stock $K(t)$ the economy is potentially capable of producing an annual product, or income, amounting to $\kappa \equiv \rho K$ dollars. Note that, from $\kappa \equiv \rho K$ (the production function), it follows that $d\kappa = \rho \, dK$, and

$$(13.14) \qquad \frac{d\kappa}{dt} = \rho \frac{dK}{dt} = \rho I$$

In Domar's model, equilibrium is defined to be a situation in which productive capacity is fully utilized. To have equilibrium is, therefore, to require the aggregate demand to be exactly equal to the potential output producible in a year; that is, $Y = \kappa$. If we start initially from an equilibrium situation, however, the requirement will reduce to the balancing of the respective *changes*

[1] Evsey D. Domar, "Capital Expansion, Rate of Growth, and Employment," *Econometrica*, April, 1946, pp. 137–147; reprinted in Domar, *Essays in the Theory of Economic Growth*, Oxford University Press, Fair Lawn, N.J., 1957, pp. 70–82.

in capacity and in aggregate demand; that is,

$$(13.15) \qquad \frac{dY}{dt} = \frac{d\kappa}{dt}$$

What kind of time path of investment $I(t)$ can satisfy this equilibrium condition at all times?

finding the solution   To answer this question, we first substitute (13.13) and (13.14) into the equilibrium condition (13.15). The result is the following differential equation:

$$(13.16) \qquad \frac{dI}{dt}\frac{1}{s} = \rho I \qquad \text{or} \qquad \frac{1}{I}\frac{dI}{dt} = \rho s$$

Since (13.16) specifies a definite pattern of change for I, we should be able to find the equilibrium (or required) investment path from it.

In this simple case, the solution is obtainable by directly integrating both sides of the second equation in (13.16) with respect to t. The fact that the two sides are identical in equilibrium assures the equality of their integrals. Thus,

$$\int \frac{1}{I}\frac{dI}{dt}\,dt = \int \rho s\,dt$$

By the substitution rule and the log rule, the left side gives us

$$\int \frac{dI}{I} = \ln |I| + c_1$$

whereas the right side yields (ρs being a constant)

$$\int \rho s\,dt = \rho s t + c_2$$

Equating the two results and combining the two constants, we have

$$\ln |I| = \rho s t + c$$

Letting each side of this last equation serve as the exponent of e, we can write

$$e^{\ln |I|} = e^{(\rho s t + c)}$$

or $|I| = e^{\rho s t}e^{c} = Ae^{\rho s t}$ where $A \equiv e^{c}$

If we take investment to be positive, then $|I| = I$, so that the above result becomes $I(t) = Ae^{\rho s t}$, where A is arbitrary. To get rid of this arbitrary constant, we set $t = 0$ in the equation $I(t) = Ae^{\rho s t}$, to get $I(0) = Ae^{0} = A$. This definitizes

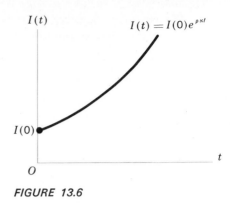

$$I(t) = I(0)e^{\rho st}$$

FIGURE 13.6

the constant A, and enables us to express the solution—the required investment path—as

(13.17) $I(t) = I(0)e^{\rho st}$

where $I(0)$ denotes the initial rate of investment.[1]

This result has a somewhat disquieting economic meaning: In order to maintain the balance between capacity and demand over time, the rate of investment flow must grow precisely at the exponential rate of ρs, along a path such as illustrated in Fig. 13.6. Obviously, the larger will be the required rate of growth of investment, the larger the capacity-capital ratio and the marginal propensity to save happen to be. But at any rate, once the values of ρ and s are known, the required growth path of investment becomes very rigidly set.

the razor's edge   It now becomes relevant to ask: What will happen if the *actual* rate of growth of investment—call that rate r—differs from the *required* rate ρs?

Domar's approach is to define a *coefficient of utilization*

$$u = \lim_{t \to \infty} \frac{Y(t)}{\kappa(t)} \qquad [u = 1 \text{ means full utilization of capacity}]$$

and show that $u = r/\rho s$, so that $u \gtreqqless 1$ as $r \gtreqqless \rho s$. In other words, if there is a discrepancy between the actual and the required rates ($r \neq \rho s$), then we will find in the end (as $t \to \infty$) either a shortage of capacity ($u > 1$) or a surplus of capacity ($u < 1$), depending on whether r is greater or less than ρs.

---

[1] The solution (13.17) will remain valid even if we let investment be negative in the result $|I| = Ae^{\rho st}$. See Exercise 13.6-2.

We can show, however, that the conclusion about capacity shortage and surplus really applies at any time t, not only as $t \to \infty$. For a growth rate of r implies that

$$I(t) = I(0)e^{rt} \qquad \text{and} \qquad \frac{dI}{dt} = rI(0)e^{rt}$$

Therefore, by (13.13) and (13.14), we have

$$\frac{dY}{dt} = \frac{1}{s}\frac{dI}{dt} = \frac{r}{s}I(0)e^{rt}$$

$$\frac{d\kappa}{dt} = \rho I(t) = \rho I(0)e^{rt}$$

The ratio between these two derivatives,

$$\frac{dY/dt}{d\kappa/dt} = \frac{r}{\rho s}$$

should tell us the relative magnitudes of the demand-creating effect and the capacity-generating effect of investment at any time t, under the actual growth rate of r. If r (the actual rate) exceeds ρs (the required rate), then $dY/dt > d\kappa/dt$, and the demand effect will outstrip the capacity effect, causing a shortage of capacity. Conversely, if $r < \rho s$, then there will be a deficiency in aggregate demand and, hence, a surplus of capacity.

The curious thing about this conclusion is that if investment actually grows at a *faster* rate than required ($r > \rho s$), the end result will be a *shortage* rather than surplus of capacity. It is equally curious that if the actual growth of investment lags behind the required rate ($r < \rho s$), we will encounter a capacity *surplus* rather than shortage. Indeed, because of such paradoxical results, if we now allow the entrepreneurs to adjust the actual growth rate r (hitherto taken to be a constant) according to the prevailing capacity situation, they will most certainly make the "wrong" kind of adjustment. In the case of $r > \rho s$, for instance, the emergent capacity shortage will motivate an even faster rate of investment. But this would mean an increase in r, instead of the reduction called for under the circumstances. Consequently, the discrepancy between the two rates of growth would be intensified rather than reduced.

The upshot is that, given the parametric constants ρ and s, the only way to avoid both shortage and surplus of productive capacity is to guide the investment flow ever so carefully along the equilibrium path with a growth rate $\bar{r} = \rho s$. And, as we have shown, any deviation from such a "razor's edge" time path will bring about a persistent failure to satisfy the norm of full utilization which Domar envisaged in this model. This is perhaps not too joyful a prospect to contemplate. Fortunately, more flexible results become possible when certain assumptions of the Domar model are modified, as we shall see from the growth model of Professor Solow, to be discussed in the next chapter.

EXERCISE 13.6

1   How many factors of production are explicitly considered in the Domar model? What does this fact imply with regard to the capital-labor ratio in production?

2   Show that even if we let investment be negative in the equation $|I| = Ae^{\rho st}$, upon definitizing the arbitrary constant A we will still end up with the solution (13.17).

3   Show that the result in (13.17) can be obtained alternatively by finding— and equating—the *definite* integrals of both sides of (13.16),

$$\frac{1}{I}\frac{dI}{dt} = \rho s$$

with respect to the variable t, with limits of integration $t = 0$ and $t = t$. Remember that when we change the variable of integration from t to I, the limits of integration will change from $t = 0$ and $t = t$, respectively, to $I = I(0)$ and $I = I(t)$. [*Hint:* $\ln u - \ln v = \ln (u/v)$.]

14

CONTINUOUS TIME: FIRST-ORDER DIFFERENTIAL EQUATIONS

In the Domar growth model, we have solved a simple differential equation by direct integration. For more complicated differential equations, there are various established methods of solution. Even in the latter cases, however, the fundamental idea underlying the methods of solution is still the techniques of integral calculus. For this reason, the solution to a differential equation is often referred to as the *integral* of that equation.

Only *first-order* differential equations will be discussed in the present chapter. In this context, the word *order* refers to the highest order of the derivatives (or differentials) appearing in the differential equation; thus a first-order differential equation can contain only the first derivative, say, dy/dt.

14.1 First-Order Linear Differential Equations with Constant Coefficient and Constant Term

The first derivative dy/dt is the only one that can appear in a first-order differential equation, but it may enter in various powers: dy/dt, $(dy/dt)^2$, or $(dy/dt)^3$. The highest power attained by the derivative in the equation is referred to as the *degree* of the differential equation. In case the derivative dy/dt appears only in the first degree, and likewise the dependent variable y, and furthermore, no product of the form $y(dy/dt)$ occurs, then the equation is said to be *linear*. Thus a first-order linear differential equation will generally take the form[1]

---

[1] The reader will note that the derivative term *dy/dt* in (14.1) has a unit coefficient. This is not to imply that it can never actually have a nonunit coefficient, but when such a coefficient appears, we can always "normalize" the equation by dividing each term by the said coefficient. For this reason, the form given in (14.1) may nonetheless be regarded as a *general* representation.

(14.1) $$\frac{dy}{dt} + u(t)y = w(t)$$

where u and w are two functions of t, as is y. In contrast to dy/dt and y, however, no restriction whatsoever is placed on the independent variable t. Thus the function u and w may very well represent such expressions as t^2 and e^t or some more complicated functions of t; on the other hand, u and w may also be constants.

This last point leads us to a further classification. When the function u (the coefficient of the dependent variable y) is a constant, and when the function w is a constant additive term, then (14.1) reduces to the special case of a first-order linear differential equation with *constant coefficient and constant term*. In this section, we shall deal only with this simple variety of differential equations.

the homogeneous case   If u and w are constant functions and if w happens to be identically zero, then (14.1) will become

(14.2) $$\frac{dy}{dt} + ay = 0$$

where a is some constant. This differential equation is said to be *homogeneous*, on account of the zero constant term (compare with homogeneous-equation systems). More accurately, this equation is homogeneous because every term therein is uniformly in the first degree in terms of y and dy/dt; in particular, the constant 0—unlike any other constant—can be regarded as in the first degree in terms of y because $0y = 0$.

Equation (14.2) can be written alternatively as

(14.2′) $$\frac{1}{y}\frac{dy}{dt} = -a$$

But the reader will recognize that the differential equation (13.16) we met in the Domar model is precisely of this form. Therefore, by analogy, we should be able to write the solution of (14.2) or (14.2′) immediately as follows:

(14.3) $$y(t) = Ae^{-at}$$ [*general* solution]

or

(14.3′) $$y(t) = y(0)e^{-at}$$ [*definite* solution]

In (14.3), there appears an arbitrary constant A; therefore it is a *general solution*. When any particular value is substituted for A, the solution becomes a *particular solution* of (14.2); there is an infinite number of particular solutions, one for each possible value of A, including the value $y(0)$. This latter value, however, has a special significance: $y(0)$ is the only value that can make the solution satisfy the initial condition. Since this represents the result of definitizing the arbitrary constant, we shall refer to (14.3′) as the *definite solution* of the differential equation (14.2) or (14.2′).

The reader should observe two things about the solution of a differential equation: First, the solution is not a number or some value, but rather a function $y(t)$. Second, the solution $y(t)$ is free of any derivative or differential expressions, so that as soon as a specific value of t is substituted into it, a corresponding value of y can directly be calculated.

the nonhomogeneous case   When a nonzero constant takes the place of the zero in (14.2), we have a *nonhomogeneous* differential equation

$$(14.4) \qquad \frac{dy}{dt} + ay = b$$

The solution of this equation will consist of the sum of two terms, one of which is called the *complementary function* (denoted by y_c), and the other known as the *particular integral* (denoted by y_p). As will be shown, each of these has a significant economic interpretation in the context of economic dynamics. Here, we shall present only the method of solution; its rationale will become clear later.

Even though our objective is to solve the *non*homogeneous equation (14.4), frequently we shall have to refer to its homogeneous version, as shown in (14.2). For convenient reference, let us call the latter the *reduced equation* of (14.4). The nonhomogeneous equation (14.4) itself can accordingly be referred to as the *complete equation*. It turns out that the complementary function y_c is nothing but the general solution of the reduced equation, whereas the particular integral y_p is simply *any* particular solution of the complete equation.

Our discussion of the homogeneous case has already given us the general solution of the reduced equation, and we may therefore write

$$y_c = Ae^{-at} \qquad \text{[by (14.3)]}$$

What about the particular integral? Since the particular integral is *any* particular solution of the complete equation, let us first try the simplest possible type of solution, namely, y being some constant $(y = k)$. If y is a constant, then it follows that $dy/dt = 0$, and (14.4) will become $ay = b$, with the solution $y = b/a$. Therefore, the constant solution will work as long as $a \neq 0$. In that case, we have

$$y_p = \frac{b}{a} \qquad (a \neq 0)$$

The sum of the complementary function and the particular integral then constitutes the general solution of the complete equation (14.4):

$$(14.5) \qquad y(t) = y_c + y_p = Ae^{-at} + \frac{b}{a} \qquad \text{[general solution, case of } a \neq 0\text{]}$$

What makes this a general solution is the presence of the arbitrary constant A. We may, of course, definitize this constant by means of an initial condition. Let us say that y takes the value $y(0)$ when $t = 0$. Then, by setting $t = 0$ in (14.5), we find that

$$y(0) = A + \frac{b}{a} \qquad \text{and} \qquad A = y(0) - \frac{b}{a}$$

thus we can rewrite (14.5) into

$$(14.5') \qquad y(t) = \left[y(0) - \frac{b}{a} \right] e^{-at} + \frac{b}{a} \qquad \text{[definite solution, case of } a \neq 0\text{]}$$

It should be noted that the use of the initial condition to definitize the arbitrary constant is—and should be—undertaken as the *final* step, after we have found the general solution to the complete equation. Since the values of both y_c and y_p are related to the value of $y(0)$, both of these must be taken into account in definitizing the constant A.

Example 1　　Solve the equation $dy/dt + 2y = 6$, with the initial condition $y(0) = 10$. Here, we have $a = 2$ and $b = 6$; thus, by (14.5'), the solution is

$$y(t) = [10 - 3]e^{-2t} + 3 = 7e^{-2t} + 3$$

Example 2　　Solve the equation $dy/dt + 4y = 0$, with the initial condition $y(0) = 1$. Since $a = 4$ and $b = 0$, we have

$$y(t) = [1 - 0]e^{-4t} + 0 = e^{-4t}$$

The same answer could have been obtained from (14.3'), the formula for the homogeneous case.

The homogeneous equation (14.2) is merely a special case of the non-homogeneous equation (14.4) when $b = 0$. Consequently, the formula (14.3') is also a special case of formula (14.5') under the circumstance that $b = 0$.

What if $a = 0$, so that the solution in (14.5') is undefined? In that case, the differential equation is of the extremely simple form

$$(14.6) \qquad \frac{dy}{dt} = b$$

By straight integration, its general solution can be readily found to be

(14.7) $y(t) = bt + c$

Where c is an arbitrary constant. The two component terms in (14.7) can, in fact, again be identified as the complementary function and the particular integral of the given differential equation, respectively. Since $a = 0$, the complementary function can be expressed simply as

$$y_c = Ae^{-at} = Ae^0 = A \qquad (A = \text{an arbitrary constant})$$

As to the particular integral, the fact that the constant solution $y = k$ fails to work in the present case of $a = 0$ suggests that we should try instead a *non-constant* solution. Let us consider the simplest possible type of the latter, namely, $y = kt$. If $y = kt$, then $dy/dt = k$, and the complete equation (14.6) will reduce to $k = b$, so that we may write

$$y_p = bt \qquad (a = 0)$$

Our new trial solution indeed works! The general solution of (14.6) is therefore

(14.7′) $y(t) = y_c + y_p = A + bt$ [general solution, case of $a = 0$]

which is identical with the result in (14.7), because c and A are but alternative notations for an arbitrary constant. Note, however, that in the present case, y_c is a constant whereas y_p is a function of time—the exact opposite of the situation in (14.5).

By definitizing the arbitrary constant, we find the definite solution to be

(14.7″) $y(t) = y(0) + bt$ [definite solution, case of $a = 0$]

Example 3   Solve the equation $dy/dt = 2$, with the initial condition $y(0) = 5$. The solution is, by (14.7″),

$$y(t) = 5 + 2t$$

verification of the solution   It is a characteristic common to all solutions of differential equations that their validity can always be checked by differentiation.

If we try that on the solution (14.5′), we can obtain the derivative

$$\frac{dy}{dt} = -a\left[y(0) - \frac{b}{a}\right]e^{-at}$$

When this expression for dy/dt and the expression for $y(t)$ as shown in (14.5′) are substituted into the left side of the differential equation (14.4), that side should reduce exactly to the value of the constant term b on the right side of (14.4) if the solution is correct. Performing this substitution, we indeed find that

$$-a\left[y(0) - \frac{b}{a}\right]e^{-at} + a\left\{\left[y(0) - \frac{b}{a}\right]e^{-at} + \frac{b}{a}\right\} = b$$

Thus our solution is correct, provided that it also fulfills the initial condition. To check the latter, let us set $t = 0$ in the solution (14.5'). Since the result

$$y(0) = \left[y(0) - \frac{b}{a}\right] + \frac{b}{a} = y(0)$$

is an identity, the solution evidently also fulfills the initial condition.

It is recommended that, as a final step in the process of solving a differential equation, the reader should make it a habit to check the validity of his answer by making sure (1) that the derivative of the time path $y(t)$ is consistent with the given differential equation and (2) that the definite solution satisfies the initial condition.

EXERCISE 14.1

1   Find y_c, y_p, the general solution, and the definite solution of each differential equation:

(a) $\dfrac{dy}{dt} + 4y = 8$ $\qquad y(0) = 2$ $\qquad$ (c) $\dfrac{dy}{dt} + 10y = 15$ $\qquad y(0) = 0$

(b) $\dfrac{dy}{dt} - 2y = 0$ $\qquad y(0) = 3$ $\qquad$ (d) $2\dfrac{dy}{dt} + 4y = 6$ $\qquad y(0) = 1$

(Hint: Normalize.)

2   Check the validity of your answers to the preceding problem.

3   Find the solution of each of the following by using an appropriate formula developed in the text:

(a) $\dfrac{dy}{dt} + y = 4$ $\qquad y(0) = 0$ $\qquad$ (d) $\dfrac{dy}{dt} + 4y = 2$ $\qquad y(0) = 1$

(b) $\dfrac{dy}{dt} = 15$ $\qquad y(0) = 1$ $\qquad$ (e) $\dfrac{dy}{dt} - 7y = 7$ $\qquad y(0) = 7$

(c) $\dfrac{dy}{dt} - y = 0$ $\qquad y(0) = 10$ $\qquad$ (f) $3\dfrac{dy}{dt} + 6y = 5$ $\qquad y(0) = 0$

4   Check the validity of your answers to the preceding problem.

14.2 Dynamics of Market Price

In the (macro) Domar growth model, we found an application of the *homogeneous* case of linear differential equations of the first order. To illustrate the *non-homogeneous* case, let us present a (micro) dynamic model of the market.

the framework Suppose that, for a particular commodity, the demand and supply functions are as follows:

$$(14.8) \qquad \begin{aligned} Q_d &= a - bP && (a,b > 0) \\ Q_s &= -c + dP && (c,d > 0) \end{aligned}$$

Then, according to (3.4), the equilibrium price should be

$$(14.9) \qquad \bar{P} = \frac{a + c}{b + d} \qquad (= \text{some positive constant})$$

If it happens that the initial price $P(0)$ is precisely at the level of $\bar{P}$, the market will clearly be in equilibrium instantly, and no dynamic analysis at all will be needed. In the more likely case of $P(0) \neq \bar{P}$, however, $\bar{P}$ is attainable (if ever) only after a due process of adjustment, during which not only will price change over time but Q_d and Q_s, being functions of P, must change over time as well. It is in this light that the price and quantity variables can *all* be taken as *functions of time*.

Our dynamic question is this: Given sufficient time for the adjustment process to work itself out, does it tend to bring price to the equilibrium level $\bar{P}$? That is, does the time path $P(t)$ tend to converge to $\bar{P}$, as $t \to \infty$?

the time path To answer this question, we must first find the time path $P(t)$. But that, in turn, requires a specific pattern of price change to be prescribed first. In general, price changes are governed by the relative strength of the demand and supply forces in the market. Let us assume, for the sake of simplicity, that the rate of price change (with respect to time) at any moment is always directly proportional to the *excess demand* $(Q_d - Q_s)$ prevailing at that moment. Such a pattern of change can be expressed symbolically as

$$(14.10) \qquad \frac{dP}{dt} = \alpha(Q_d - Q_s) \qquad (\alpha > 0)$$

where α represents a (constant) *adjustment coefficient*. With this pattern of change, we can have $dP/dt = 0$ if and only if $Q_d = Q_s$. In this connection, it may be instructive to note two senses of the term *equilibrium price*: the intertemporal sense (P being constant over time) and the market-clearing sense (the equilibrium price being one that equates Q_d and Q_s). In the present model, the two senses happen to coincide with each other, but this may not be true of all models.

By virtue of the demand and supply functions in (14.8), we can express (14.10) specifically in the form

$$\frac{dP}{dt} = \alpha(a - bP + c - dP) = \alpha(a + c) - \alpha(b + d)P$$

or

$$(14.10') \qquad \frac{dP}{dt} + \alpha(b + d)P = \alpha(a + c)$$

Since this is precisely in the form of the differential equation (14.4), and since the coefficient of P is nonzero, we can apply the solution formula (14.5') and write the solution—the time path of price—as

$$(14.11) \qquad P(t) = \left[P(0) - \frac{a + c}{b + d}\right]e^{-\alpha(b+d)t} + \frac{a + c}{b + d}$$

$$= [P(0) - \bar{P}]e^{-kt} + \bar{P} \qquad \text{where } k \equiv \alpha(b + d)$$
$$\text{[by (14.9)]}$$

the dynamic stability of equilibrium   In the end, the question originally posed, namely, whether $P(t) \to \bar{P}$ as $t \to \infty$, amounts to the question of whether the first term on the right of (14.11) will tend to zero as $t \to \infty$. Since $P(0)$ and $\bar{P}$ are both constant, the key factor will be the exponential expression e^{-kt}. In view of the fact that $k > 0$, that expression does tend to zero as $t \to \infty$. Consequently, with the assumptions of our model, the time path will indeed lead the price toward the equilibrium position. In a situation of this sort, where the time path of the relevant variable $P(t)$ *converges* to the level $\bar{P}$—interpreted here in its role as the intertemporal (rather than market-clearing) equilibrium—the equilibrium is said to be *dynamically stable*.

The concept of dynamic stability is an important one. Let us examine it further by a more detailed analysis of (14.11). Depending on the relative magnitudes of $P(0)$ and $\bar{P}$, the solution (14.11) really encompasses three possible cases. The first is $P(0) = \bar{P}$, which implies $P(t) = \bar{P}$. In that event, the time path of price can be drawn as the horizontal straight line in Fig. 14.1. As mentioned earlier, the attainment of equilibrium is in this case immediate. Second, we may have $P(0) > \bar{P}$. In this case, the first term on the right of (14.11) is positive, but it will decrease as the increase in t lowers the value of e^{-kt}. Thus the time path will approach the equilibrium level $\bar{P}$ from above, as illustrated by the top curve in Fig. 14.1. Third, in the opposite case of $P(0) < \bar{P}$, the equilibrium level $\bar{P}$ will be approached from below, as illustrated by the bottom curve in the same figure.

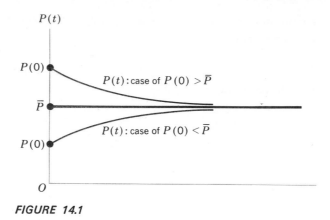

FIGURE 14.1

In general, to have dynamic stability, the *deviation* of the time path from equilibrium must either be identically zero (as in case 1) or steadily decrease with time (as in cases 2 and 3).

A comparison of (14.11) with (14.5') tells us that the $\bar{P}$ term, the counterpart of b/a, is nothing but the particular integral y_p, whereas the exponential term is the (definitized) complementary function y_c. Thus, we now have an economic interpretation for y_c and y_p; y_p represents the *intertemporal equilibrium level* of the relevant variable, and y_c is the *deviation from equilibrium*. Dynamic stability amounts, therefore, to the asymptotic vanishing of the complementary function as t becomes infinite.

In this model, the particular integral is a constant, so we have a *stationary equilibrium* in the intertemporal sense, represented by $\bar{P}$. If the particular integral is nonconstant, as in (14.7'), on the other hand, we may interpret it as a *moving equilibrium*.

an alternative use of the model   What we have done above is to analyze the dynamic stability of equilibrium (the convergence of the time path), given certain sign specifications for the parameters. An alternative type of inquiry is: In order to achieve dynamic stability, what specific restrictions must be imposed upon the parameters?

The answer to that is contained in the solution (14.11). If we take the general case of $P(0) \neq \bar{P}$, we see that the first (y_c) term in (14.11) will tend to zero as $t \to \infty$ if and only if $k > 0$—that is, if and only if

$$\alpha(b + d) > 0$$

Thus, we can take this last inequality as the required restriction on the parameters α (the adjustment coefficient of price), b (the negative of the slope of the

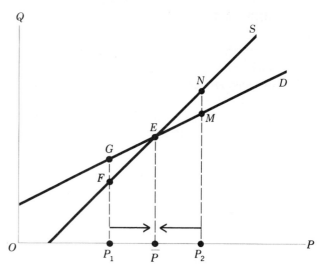

FIGURE 14.2

demand curve, plotted with Q on the *vertical* axis), and d (the slope of the supply curve, plotted similarly).

In case the price adjustment is of the "normal" type, i.e., in case $\alpha > 0$, so that excess demand drives price up rather than down, then this restriction becomes merely $(b + d) > 0$ or, equivalently,

$$d > -b$$

To have dynamic stability in that event, the slope of the supply must exceed the slope of the demand. When both demand and supply are normally sloped $(-b < 0, d > 0)$, this requirement is obviously met, but even if one of the curves is sloped "perversely," the condition may still be fulfilled, such as when $d = 1$ and $-b = {}^1\!/_2$ (positively sloped demand). The latter situation is illustrated in Fig. 14.2, where the equilibrium price $\bar{P}$ is, as usual, determined by the point of intersection of the two curves. If the initial price happens to be at P_1, then Q_d (distance P_1G) will exceed Q_s (distance P_1F), and the excess demand (FG) will drive price up. On the other hand, if price is initially at P_2, then there will be a *negative* excess demand MN, which will drive the price down. As the two arrows in the figure show, therefore, the price adjustment in this case will be *toward* the equilibrium, no matter which side of $\bar{P}$ we start from. We should emphasize, however, that while these arrows can display the direction, they are incapable of indicating the magnitude of change. Thus Fig. 14.2 is basically static, not dynamic, in nature, and can serve only to illustrate, not to replace, the dynamic analysis presented above.

EXERCISE 14.2

1　If both the demand and supply in Fig. 14.2 are negatively sloped instead, which curve should be steeper in order to have dynamic stability? Does your answer conform to the criterion $d > -b$?

2　Show that (14.10') can be rewritten as $dP/dt + k(P - \bar{P}) = 0$. If we let $P - \bar{P} \equiv \delta$ (signifying deviation), so that $d\delta/dt = dP/dt$, the differential equation can be further rewritten as

$$\frac{d\delta}{dt} + k\delta = 0$$

Find the time path $\delta(t)$, and discuss its economic implications.

14.3　Variable Coefficient and Variable Term

In the more general case of a first-order linear differential equation

(14.12)　　$\dfrac{dy}{dt} + uy = w$

u and w represent, respectively, a variable coefficient and a variable term, both being functions of t, as is y. How do we find the time path $y(t)$ in this case?

the homogeneous case　　For the homogeneous case, where $w = 0$, the solution is still easy to obtain. Since the differential equation is in the form

(14.13)　　$\dfrac{dy}{dt} + uy = 0$　　or　　$\dfrac{1}{y}\dfrac{dy}{dt} = -u$

we may get, by integrating both sides in turn with respect to t,

$$\text{Left side} = \int \frac{1}{y}\frac{dy}{dt}\,dt = \int \frac{dy}{y} = \ln y + c \qquad (\text{assuming } y > 0)$$

$$\text{Right side} = \int -u\,dt = -\int u\,dt$$

Thus, by equating the above, we have

$$\ln y = -c - \int u\,dt$$

and

(14.14)　　$y(t) = e^{\ln y} = e^{-c}e^{-\int u\,dt} = Ae^{-\int u\,dt}$　　where $A \equiv e^{-c}$

This is the general solution of the differential equation (14.13). As compared with the general solution (14.3) of the constant-coefficient case, the only difference is that the expression e^{-at} is now replaced by the more complicated expression $e^{-\int u\,dt}$. This distinction can be better appreciated if we interpret the exponent at as the integral $\int a\,dt = at$ (plus a constant which can be subsumed under the A term, since e raised to a constant power is a constant). Then the difference in fact turns into a similarity, because in both cases we are integrating the coefficient of the y term—a in one case, and u in the other—with respect to t, and taking the negative of the resulting integral as the exponent of e.

Once the general solution is obtained, it is a relatively simple matter to get the definite solution with the help of an appropriate initial condition.

Example 1   Find the general solution of the equation $\dfrac{dy}{dt} + 3t^2y = 0$. Here we have $u = 3t^2$, and $\int u\,dt = \int 3t^2\,dt = t^3 + k$. Therefore, by (14.14), we may write the solution as

$$y(t) = Ae^{-(t^3+k)} = Ae^{-t^3}e^{-k} = Be^{-t^3} \qquad \text{where } B \equiv Ae^{-k}$$

The reader will observe that, had we omitted the constant of integration k from consideration, we would have lost no information, because then we would have obtained $y(t) = Ae^{-t^3}$, which is really the identical solution since A and B both represent arbitrary constants. In other words, the expression e^{-k}, where the constant k makes its only appearance, can always be subsumed under the other constant A.

the nonhomogeneous case   For the nonhomogeneous case, where $w \neq 0$, the solution is not as easy to obtain. We shall try to find that solution via the concept of exact differential equations, to be discussed in the next section. It does no harm, however, to state the result here first: Given the differential equation (14.12), the general solution is

$$(14.15) \qquad y(t) = e^{-\int u\,dt}\left(A + \int we^{\int u\,dt}\,dt\right)$$

where A is an arbitrary constant that can be definitized if we have an appropriate initial condition.

It is of interest that this general solution, like the solution in the constant-coefficient constant-term case, again consists of two additive components. Furthermore, one of these two, $Ae^{-\int u\,dt}$, is nothing but the general solution of the reduced (homogeneous) equation, derived earlier in (14.14), and is therefore in the nature of a complementary function.

Example 2 Find the general solution of the equation $\dfrac{dy}{dt} + 2ty = t$. Here we have

$$u = 2t \qquad w = t \qquad \text{and} \qquad \int u\, dt = t^2 + k$$

Thus, by (14.15), we have

$$y(t) = e^{-(t^2+k)}\left(A + \int te^{t^2+k}\, dt\right)$$

$$= e^{-t^2}e^{-k}\left(A + e^k \int te^{t^2}\, dt\right)$$

$$= Ae^{-k}e^{-t^2} + e^{-t^2}\left(\frac{1}{2}e^{t^2} + c\right) \qquad [e^{-k}e^k = 1]$$

$$= (Ae^{-k} + c)e^{-t^2} + \frac{1}{2}$$

$$= Be^{-t^2} + \frac{1}{2} \qquad \text{where } B \equiv Ae^{-k} + c \text{ is arbitrary}$$

The validity of this solution can again be checked by differentiation.

It is interesting to note that, as in Example 1 above, we could again have omitted the constant of integration k, as well as the constant of integration c, without affecting the final outcome. This is because both k and c may be subsumed under the arbitrary constant B in the final solution. The reader is urged to try out the simpler process of applying (14.15) without using the constants k and c, and verify that the same solution will obtain.

Example 3 Solve the equation $\dfrac{dy}{dt} + 4ty = 4t$. This time we shall omit the constants of integration. Since

$$u = 4t \qquad w = 4t \qquad \text{and} \qquad \int u\, dt = 2t^2 \qquad \text{[constant omitted]}$$

the general solution is, by (14.15),

$$y(t) = e^{-2t^2}\left(A + \int 4te^{2t^2}\, dt\right) = e^{-2t^2}(A + e^{2t^2}) \qquad \text{[constant omitted]}$$

$$= Ae^{-2t^2} + 1$$

As may be expected, the omission of the constants of integration serves to simplify the procedure substantially.

The differential equation $\dfrac{dy}{dt} + uy = w$ in (14.12) is more general than the

equation $\dfrac{dy}{dt} + ay = b$ in (14.4), since u and w are not necessarily constant, as

are a and b. Accordingly, solution formula (14.15) is also more general than solution formula (14.5). In fact, when we set $u = a$ and $w = b$, (14.15) should reduce to (14.5). This is indeed the case. For when we have

$$u = a \qquad w = b \qquad \text{and} \qquad \int u \, dt = at \qquad \text{[constant omitted]}$$

then (14.15) becomes

$$y(t) = e^{-at}\left(A + \int be^{at}\, dt\right) = e^{-at}\left(A + \frac{b}{a}e^{at}\right) \qquad \text{[constant omitted]}$$

$$= Ae^{-at} + \frac{b}{a}$$

which is identical with (14.5).

EXERCISE 14.3

Solve the following first-order linear differential equations; if an initial condition is given, definitize the arbitrary constant:

1    $\dfrac{dy}{dt} + 5y = 10$

2    $\dfrac{dy}{dt} + ty = 0$

3    $\dfrac{dy}{dt} + 2ty = t \qquad y(0) = \dfrac{3}{2}$

4    $\dfrac{dy}{dt} + t^2 y = 3t^2 \qquad y(0) = 4$

5    $2\dfrac{dy}{dt} + 12y + 2e^t = 0 \qquad y(0) = \dfrac{6}{7}$

6    $dy + (3t^2 y - e^{-t^3})\, dt = 0 \qquad$ (*Hint:* Transform.)

7    $\dfrac{dy}{dt} + y = t \qquad$ (*Hint:* Review integration by parts, Sec. 13.2.)

14.4   Exact Differential Equations

We shall now introduce the concept of exact differential equations, and use the solution method pertaining thereto to obtain the solution formula (14.15) cited above for the differential equation (14.12). Even though our immediate purpose is to use it to solve a *linear* differential equation, an exact differential equation can be either linear or nonlinear by itself.

exact differential equations   Given a function of two variables $F(y,t)$, its total differential is

$$dF(y,t) = \frac{\partial F}{\partial y}\,dy + \frac{\partial F}{\partial t}\,dt$$

When this differential is set equal to zero, the resulting equation

$$\frac{\partial F}{\partial y}\,dy + \frac{\partial F}{\partial t}\,dt = 0$$

is known as an *exact differential equation*, because its left side is exactly the differential of the function $F(y,t)$. For instance, given

$$F(y,t) = y^2 t + k \qquad [k \text{ a constant}]$$

the total differential is

$$dF = 2yt\,dy + y^2\,dt$$

thus the differential equation

$$(14.16) \qquad 2yt\,dy + y^2\,dt = 0 \qquad \text{or} \qquad \frac{dy}{dt} + \frac{y^2}{2yt} = 0$$

is exact.

In general, a differential equation

$$(14.17) \qquad M\,dy + N\,dt = 0$$

is exact if and only if $M = \partial F/\partial y$ and $N = \partial F/\partial t$ for some function $F(y,t)$. By Young's theorem, which states that $\partial^2 F/\partial t\,\partial y = \partial^2 F/\partial y\,\partial t$, however, we can also state that (14.17) is exact if and only if

$$(14.18) \qquad \frac{\partial M}{\partial t} = \frac{\partial N}{\partial y}$$

This last equation gives us a simple test for the exactness of a differential equation. Applied to (14.16), where $M = 2yt$ and $N = y^2$, this test yields $\partial M/\partial t = 2y = \partial N/\partial y$; thus the exactness of the said differential equation is duly verified.

Note that no restrictions have been placed on the terms M and N with regard to the manner in which the variable y occurs. Thus an exact differential equation may very well be *nonlinear* (in y). Nevertheless, it will always be of the first order and the first degree.

Being exact, the differential equation merely says

$$dF(y,t) = 0$$

Thus its general solution should clearly be in the form

$$F(y,t) = c$$

To solve an exact differential equation is basically, therefore, to search for the (primitive) function $F(y,t)$. Let us outline a method of finding this for the equation $M\ dy + N\ dt = 0$.

method of solution   As a first step, since $M = \partial F/\partial y$, the function F must contain the integral of M with respect to the variable y; hence we can write out a preliminary result—in a yet indeterminate form—as follows:

$$(14.19) \qquad F(y,t) = \int M\ dy + \psi(t)$$

Here M, a *partial* derivative, is to be integrated with respect to y only; that is, t is to be treated as a constant in the integration process, just as it was treated as a constant in the partial differentiation of $F(y,t)$ that resulted in $M = \partial F/\partial y$.† Since, in differentiating $F(y,t)$ partially with respect to y, any additive term containing only the variable t and/or some constants (but with no y) would drop out, we must now take care to reinstate such terms in the integration process. This explains why we have introduced in (14.19) a general term $\psi(t)$, which, though not exactly the same as a constant of integration, has a precisely identical role to play as the latter. It is relatively easy to get $\int M\ dy$; but how do we pin down the exact form of this $\psi(t)$ term?

The trick is to utilize the fact that $N = \partial F/\partial t$. But the procedure is best explained with the help of specific examples.

Example 1   Solve the exact differential equation

$$2yt\ dy + y^2\ dt = 0 \qquad \text{[reproduced from (14.16)]}$$

In this equation, we have

$$M = 2yt \qquad \text{and} \qquad N = y^2$$

† Some writers employ the operator symbol $\int (\cdots)\ \partial y$ to emphasize that the integration is with respect to y only. We shall still use the symbol $\int (\cdots)\ dy$ here, since there is little possibility of confusion.

Step i: By (14.19), we can first write the preliminary result

$$F(y,t) = \int 2yt \, dy + \psi(t) = y^2 t + \psi(t)$$

Note that we have omitted the constant of integration, because it can automatically be merged into the expression $\psi(t)$.

Step ii: If we differentiate the above result partially with respect to t, we can obtain

$$\frac{\partial F}{\partial t} = y^2 + \psi'(t)$$

But since $N = \partial F/\partial t$, we can equate $N = y^2$ and $\partial F/\partial t = y^2 + \psi'(t)$, to get

$$\psi'(t) = 0$$

Step iii: Integration of the last result gives us

$$\psi(t) = \int \psi'(t) \, dt = \int 0 \, dt = k$$

and now we have a specific form of $\psi(t)$. It happens in the present case that $\psi(t)$ is simply a constant; more generally, it is a function of t.

Step iv: The results of steps *i* and *iii* can be combined to yield

$$F(y,t) = y^2 t + k$$

The solution of the exact differential equation should then be $F(y,t) = c$. But since the constant k can be merged into c, we may write the solution simply as

$$y^2 t = c \qquad \text{or} \qquad y(t) = ct^{-1/2}$$

where c is arbitrary.

Example 2   Solve the equation $(t + 2y) \, dy + (y + 3t^2) \, dt = 0$. First let us check whether this is an exact differential equation. Setting $M = t + 2y$ and $N = y + 3t^2$, we find that $\partial M/\partial t = 1 = \partial N/\partial y$. Thus the equation passes the exactness test. To find its solution, we again follow the procedure outlined in Example 1.

Step i: Apply (14.19) and write

$$F(y,t) = \int (t + 2y) \, dy + \psi(t) = yt + y^2 + \psi(t)$$

$$[\text{constant merged into } \psi(t)]$$

Step ii: Differentiate this result with respect to t, to get

$$\frac{\partial F}{\partial t} = y + \psi'(t)$$

Then, equating this to $N = y + 3t^2$, we find that

$$\psi'(t) = 3t^2$$

Step iii: Integrate this last result to get

$$\psi(t) = \int 3t^2 \, dt = t^3 \qquad \text{[constant may be omitted]}$$

Step iv: Combine the results of steps *i* and *iii* to get the complete form of the function $F(y,t)$:

$$F(y,t) = yt + y^2 + t^3$$

which implies that the solution of the given differential equation is

$$yt + y^2 + t^3 = c$$

The reader should verify that setting the total differential of this equation equal to zero will indeed produce the given differential equation.

This four-step procedure can be used to solve any exact differential equation. Interestingly, it may even be applicable when the given equation is *not* exact. To see this, however, we must first introduce the concept of integrating factor.

integrating factor   Sometimes an inexact differential equation can be made exact by multiplying every term of the equation by a particular common factor. Such a factor is called an *integrating factor*.

Example 3   The differential equation

$$2t \, dy + y \, dt = 0$$

is not exact, because it does not satisfy (14.18):

$$\frac{\partial M}{\partial t} = \frac{\partial}{\partial t} \, (2t) = 2 \neq \frac{\partial N}{\partial y} = \frac{\partial}{\partial y} \, (y) = 1$$

However, if we multiply each term by y, the given equation will turn into (14.16), which has been established to be exact. Thus y is an integrating factor for the differential equation in the present example.

When an integrating factor can be found for an inexact differential equation, it is always possible to render it exact, and then the four-step solution procedure can be readily put to use.

solution of first-order linear differential equations   The general first-order linear differential equation

$$\frac{dy}{dt} + uy = w$$

which, in the format of (14.17), can be expressed as

(14.20) $dy + (uy - w)\,dt = 0$

has a known integrating factor, namely,

$$e^{\int u\,dt} \equiv \exp\left(\int u\,dt\right)$$

Let us verify this claim by an example.

Example 4   Transform $dy + (2ty - t)\,dt = 0$ into an exact differential equation. As can easily be checked, the equation is inexact in the form given. But since it is in the general format of (14.20), with $u = 2t$ and $\int u\,dt = t^2 + c$, we are supposed to find

$$e^{t^2+c} = e^c e^{t^2} = A e^{t^2}   \text{(with } A \text{ arbitrary)}$$

to be an integrating factor.

Multiplying each term of the given differential equation by this expression, we get the equivalent equation

$$A e^{t^2}\,dy + A e^{t^2}(2ty - t)\,dt = 0$$

From this, however, we may cancel the common multiplicative constant A without affecting its exactness. In retrospect, then, we see that the constant of integration in the integrating factor $\exp\left(\int u\,dt\right)$, which gave rise to A, could have been safely omitted.

Now, taking $M = e^{t^2}$ and $N = e^{t^2}(2ty - t)$, we find that

$$\frac{\partial M}{\partial t} = 2te^{t^2} = \frac{\partial N}{\partial y}$$

Thus the original differential equation has indeed been made exact by use of the above-indicated integrating factor.

The general first-order linear differential equation (14.20) can be made exact by the same type of integrating factor. When every term of (14.20) is multiplied by $\exp\left(\int u\,dt\right)$, we obtain

(14.20′) $\underbrace{\exp\left(\int u\,dt\right)dy}_{M} + \underbrace{\exp\left(\int u\,dt\right)(uy - w)\,dt}_{N} = 0$

This is now an *exact* differential equation, because by letting

$$z \equiv \int u \, dt \qquad \left[\text{so that } M = e^z, \ N = e^z(uy - w), \text{ and } \frac{dz}{dt} = u \right]$$

and by applying the chain rule, we can find that

$$\frac{\partial M}{\partial t} = \frac{\partial}{\partial t} e^z = \frac{\partial e^z}{\partial z} \frac{dz}{dt} = e^z \frac{dz}{dt} = e^z u$$

and $\qquad \dfrac{\partial N}{\partial y} = \dfrac{\partial}{\partial y} e^z(uy - w) = e^z u \left(= \dfrac{\partial M}{\partial t} \right)$

Consequently, we can find its solution by the four-step procedure.

Step i: First, we apply (14.19) to get

$$F(y,t) = \int e^z \, dy + \psi(t) = ye^z + \psi(t)$$

The integral $\int e^z \, dy$ comes out to be ye^z because $z \equiv \int u \, dt$ is a function of t only, as is u.

Step ii: Next, we differentiate the above result with respect to t:

$$\frac{\partial F}{\partial t} = \frac{\partial}{\partial t} ye^z + \psi'(t) = ye^z \frac{dz}{dt} + \psi'(t) = ye^z u + \psi'(t)$$

Since this can be equated to $N = e^z(uy - w) = e^z uy - e^z w$, we may infer that

$$\psi'(t) = -we^z$$

Step iii: Straight integration now yields

$$\psi(t) = \int -we^z \, dt = -\int we^z \, dt$$

In the absence of specific information about w and u (and hence z), nothing further can be done with this integral, and we must be contented with this rather general expression for $\psi(t)$.

Step iv: Substituting this $\psi(t)$ expression into step i, we find

$$F(y,t) = ye^z - \int we^z \, dt = ye^{\int u \, dt} - \int we^{\int u \, dt} \, dt$$

so the general solution of the exact differential equation (14.20')—and hence the solution of the equivalent, though inexact, first-order linear differential equation

(14.20)—is

$$ye^{\int u\,dt} - \int we^{\int u\,dt}\,dt = A \qquad [A \text{ is arbitrary}]$$

or

(14.21) $\qquad y(t) = e^{-\int u\,dt}\left(A + \int we^{\int u\,dt}\,dt\right)$

which is exactly the result given earlier in (14.15).

a variant of the Domar model　As an economic application of the solution formula (14.21), let us consider a variant of the Domar model in which the propensity to save is allowed to vary over time. In that case, the demand effect of investment should be expressed by the equation

$$\frac{dY}{dt} = \frac{dI}{dt}\frac{1}{s(t)} \qquad [\text{cf. (13.13)}]$$

although the capacity effect would remain as before:

$$\frac{d\kappa}{dt} = \rho I \qquad [\text{from (13.14)}]$$

When these two effects are equated, we get the basic differential equation

$$\frac{dI}{dt}\frac{1}{s(t)} = \rho I$$

or $\qquad dI - \rho s(t)I\,dt = 0$

which is in the form of (14.20), with $u = -\rho s(t)$ and $w = 0$. Its general solution is therefore obtainable from (14.21):

(14.22) $\qquad I(t) = e^{-\int -\rho s(t)\,dt}\left(A + \int 0\,dt\right) = Ae^{\int \rho s(t)\,dt}$

$$\left[\int 0\,dt = \text{constant; hence, it has been merged into } A\right]$$

Next, we shall definitize the constant A by using the initial condition that the rate of investment flow at $t = 0$ is $I(0)$. To facilitate the process, however, let us first introduce a notation for the primitive function of $\rho s(t)$, namely,

$$\int \rho s(t)\,dt = F(t) + c$$

The general solution (14.22) can then be rewritten as

(14.22') $\qquad I(t) = Ae^{F(t)+c} = Ae^c e^{F(t)}$

When $t = 0$, this equation gives $I(0) = Ae^c e^{F(0)}$, which implies that

$$Ae^c = I(0)e^{-F(0)}$$

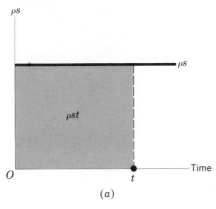

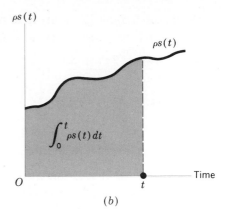

(a)   (b)

FIGURE 14.3

Substituting this into (14.22'), we then get

(14.22") $\quad I(t) = I(0)e^{-F(0)}e^{F(t)} = I(0)e^{F(t)-F(0)}$

$$= I(0) \exp [F(t) - F(0)] = I(0) \exp \left(\int_0^t \rho s(t) \, dt \right)$$

[by (13.6)]

and this constitutes the definite solution of the model.

  The required investment path shown in (14.22") differs from the solution (13.17) of the previous version of the Domar model only in the substitution of the definite integral $\int_0^t \rho s(t) \, dt$ for the product ρst as the exponent of e. The rationale of this substitution is easily clarified with the help of Fig. 14.3. In diagram a, depicting the case where ρ and s are both constant, the product ρst has the geometric meaning of a rectangular area under the ρs curve or line, extending in time from zero to some point t. When s becomes a nonconstant function of time, the $\rho s(t)$ curve will in general no longer be a horizontal straight line. In that case, the area under the curve must be measured by the definite integral indicated in diagram b. Hence, the change of the exponent. The reader will note that the definite integral version is perfectly general; even if s is a constant, the definite integral can still be used, because then we will have $\int_0^t \rho s \, dt = \rho st$, plus a constant that can be subsumed elsewhere.

EXERCISE 14.4

1 Verify that each of the following differential equations is exact, and solve by the four-step procedure:

  (a) $2yt^3 \, dy + 3y^2t^2 \, dt = 0$

(b) $3y^2t \, dy + (y^3 + 2t) \, dt = 0$

(c) $t(1 + 2y) \, dy + y(1 + y) \, dt = 0$

(d) $\dfrac{dy}{dt} + \dfrac{2y^4t + 3t^2}{4y^3t^2} = 0$

[*Hint:* First convert to the form of (14.17).]

2   Test whether the following differential equations are exact; if not, determine whether we can use t, y, or y^2 as an integrating factor:

(a) $2(t^3 + 1) \, dy + 3yt^2 \, dt = 0$

(b) $4y^3t \, dy + (2y^4 + 3t) \, dt = 0$

3   By applying the four-step procedure to the general exact differential equation $M \, dy + N \, dt = 0$, derive the following formula for the general solution of an exact differential equation:

$$\int M \, dy + \int N \, dt - \int \left(\frac{\partial}{\partial t} \int M \, dy \right) dt = c$$

14.5   Nonlinear Differential Equations of the First Order and First Degree

In a *linear* differential equation, we restrict to the *first degree* not only the derivative dy/dt but also the dependent variable y, and we do not allow the product $y(dy/dt)$ to appear. When y appears in a power higher than one, the equation becomes *nonlinear* even if it only contains the derivative dy/dt in the first degree. In general, an equation in the form

(14.23) $f(y,t) \, dy + g(y,t) \, dt = 0$

or

(14.23') $\dfrac{dy}{dt} = h(y,t)$

where there is no restriction on the powers of y and t, constitutes a first-order first-degree nonlinear differential equation. Certain varieties of such equations can be solved with relative ease by more or less routine procedures. We shall briefly discuss three cases.

exact differential equations   The first is the now-familiar case of exact differential equations. As was pointed out earlier, the y variable can appear in an exact equation in a high power, as in (14.16)—$2yt\, dy + y^2\, dt = 0$—which the reader should compare with (14.23). True, the cancellation of the common factor y from both terms on the left will reduce the equation to a linear form, but the exactness property will be lost in that event. As an *exact* differential equation, therefore, it must be regarded as nonlinear.

Since the solution method for exact differential equations has already been discussed, no further comment is necessary here.

separable variables   The differential equation in (14.23)

$$f(y,t)\, dy + g(y,t)\, dt = 0$$

may happen to possess the convenient property that the function f is in the variable y alone, while the function g involves only the variable t, so that the equation reduces to the special form

(14.24) $f(y)\, dy + g(t)\, dt = 0$

In such an event, the variables are said to be *separable*, because the terms involving y—consolidated into $f(y)$—can be mathematically separated from the terms involving t, which are collected under $g(t)$. To solve this special type of equation, only simple integration techniques are required.

Example 1   Solve the equation $3y^2\, dy - t\, dt = 0$. First let us rewrite the equation as

$$3y^2\, dy = t\, dt$$

Integrating the two sides (each of which is a differential) and equating the results, we get

$$\int 3y^2\, dy = \int t\, dt$$

That is,

$$y^3 + c_1 = \frac{1}{2} t^2 + c_2$$

Thus the general solution can be written as

$$y^3 = \frac{1}{2} t^2 + c \qquad \text{or} \qquad y(t) = \left(\frac{1}{2} t^2 + c \right)^{1/3}$$

The notable point here is that the integration of each term is performed with respect to a different variable; it is this which makes the separable-variable equation comparatively easy to handle.

Example 2   Solve the equation $2t\,dy + y\,dt = 0$. At first glance, this differential equation does not seem to belong in this spot, because it fails to conform to the general form of (14.24). To be specific, the coefficients of dy and dt are seen to involve the "wrong" variables. However, a simple transformation —dividing through by $2yt$ ($\neq 0$)—will reduce the equation to the separable-variable form

$$\frac{1}{y}\,dy + \frac{1}{2t}\,dt = 0$$

From our experience with Example 1, we can work toward the solution (without first transposing a term) as follows:[1]

$$\int \frac{1}{y}\,dy + \int \frac{1}{2t}\,dt = c$$

so $\ln y + \dfrac{1}{2}\ln t = c$ or $\ln (yt^{1/2}) = c$

Thus the solution is

$$yt^{1/2} = e^c = k \qquad \text{or} \qquad y(t) = kt^{-1/2}$$

where k is an arbitrary constant, just as the symbols c and A employed elsewhere.

The reader should note that, instead of solving the equation in Example 2 as we did, we could also have transformed it first into an exact differential equation (by the integrating factor y) and then solved it as such. The solution, already given in Example 1 of Sec. 14.4, must of course be identical with the one just obtained by separation of variables. The point is that a given differential equation can often be solvable in more than one way, and therefore one may have a choice of the method to be used. In other cases, a differential equation that is not amenable to a particular method may nonetheless become so after an appropriate transformation.

equations reducible to the linear form   If the differential equation $dy/dt = h(y,t)$ happens to take the specific nonlinear form

(14.25) $$\frac{dy}{dt} + Ry = Ty^n$$

where R and T are two functions of t, and n is any number other than 0 and 1

---

[1] In the integration process, we should, strictly speaking, have written $\ln |y|$ and $\frac{1}{2}\ln |t|$. If y and t can be assumed to be positive, as is appropriate in the majority of economic contexts, then the result given in the text will obtain.

(what if $n = 0$ or $n = 1$?), then the equation—referred to as a *Bernoulli equation* —can always be reduced to a linear differential equation and solved as such.

The reduction procedure is relatively simple: First, we can divide (14.25) by y^n, to get

$$y^{-n} \frac{dy}{dt} + Ry^{1-n} = T$$

If we adopt a shorthand variable z as follows:

$$z = y^{1-n} \qquad \left[\text{so that } \frac{dz}{dt} = \frac{dz}{dy} \frac{dy}{dt} = (1 - n)y^{-n} \frac{dy}{dt} \right]$$

then the preceding equation can be written as

$$\frac{1}{1 - n} \frac{dz}{dt} + Rz = T$$

Moreover, after multiplying through by $(1 - n) \, dt$ and rearranging, we can transform the equation into

$$(14.25') \qquad dz + [(1 - n)Rz - (1 - n)T] \, dt = 0$$

This is seen to be a first-order linear differential equation of the form (14.20), in which the variable z has taken the place of y.

Clearly, we can apply formula (14.21) to find its solution $z(t)$. Then, as a final step, we can translate z back to y by reverse substitution.

Example 3 Solve the equation $dy/dt + ty = 3ty^2$. This is a Bernoulli equation, with $n = 2$ (giving us $z = y^{1-n} = y^{-1}$), $R = t$, and $T = 3t$. Thus, by (14.25'), we can write the linearized differential equation as

$$dz + (-tz + 3t) \, dt = 0$$

By applying formula (14.21), the solution can be found to be

$$z(t) = c \exp\left(\tfrac{1}{2}t^2\right) + 3$$

(As an exercise, trace out the steps leading to this solution.)

Since our primary interest lies in the solution $y(t)$ rather than $z(t)$, we must perform a reverse transformation using the equation $z = y^{-1}$, or $y = z^{-1}$. By taking the reciprocal of $z(t)$, therefore, we get

$$y(t) = \frac{1}{c \exp\left(\tfrac{1}{2}t^2\right) + 3}$$

as the desired solution. This is a general solution, because an arbitrary constant c is present.

Example 4 Solve the equation $dy/dt + (1/t)y = y^3$. Here, we have $n = 3$ (thus $z = y^{-2}$), $R = 1/t$, and $T = 1$; thus the equation can be linearized into the form

$$dz + \left(\frac{-2}{t}z + 2\right)dt = 0$$

As the reader can verify, by the use of formula (14.21), the solution of this differential equation is

$$z(t) = ct^2 + 2t$$

It then follows, by the reverse transformation $y = z^{-1/2}$, that the general solution, in the original variable, is to be written as

$$y(t) = (ct^2 + 2t)^{-1/2}$$

As an exercise, the reader should check the validity of the solutions of these last two examples by differentiation.

EXERCISE 14.5

1 Determine, for each of the following, (1) whether the variables are separable and (2) whether the equation is linear or else can be linearized:

(a) $2t\, dy + 2y\, dt = 0$

(c) $\dfrac{dy}{dt} = -\dfrac{t}{y}$

(b) $\dfrac{y}{y+t}\, dy + \dfrac{2t}{y+t}\, dt = 0$

(d) $\dfrac{dy}{dt} = 3y^2 t$

2 Solve (a) and (b) in Exercise 14.5-1 by separation of variables, taking y and t to be positive. Check your answers by differentiation.

3 Solve (c) in Exercise 14.5-1 as a separable-variable equation and, also, as a Bernoulli equation.

4 Solve (d) in Exercise 14.5-1 as a separable-variable equation and, also, as a Bernoulli equation.

5 Verify the correctness of the intermediate solution $z(t) = ct^2 + 2t$ in Example 4 by showing that its derivative dz/dt is consistent with the linearized differential equation.

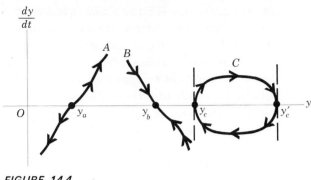

FIGURE 14.4

14.6　The Qualitative-Graphic Approach

The several cases of nonlinear differential equations previously discussed (exact differential equations, separable-variable equations, and Bernoulli equations) have all been solved *quantitatively*. That is, we have in every case sought and found a time-path equation which, for each value of t, tells the specific corresponding value of y.

At times, we may not be able to find a quantitative solution from a given differential equation. Yet, in such cases, it may nonetheless be possible to ascertain the *qualitative* properties of the time path—primarily, whether $y(t)$ converges—by directly observing the differential equation itself or by analyzing its graph. Even if quantitative solutions are available, moreover, we may still employ the techniques of qualitative analysis if the qualitative aspect of the time path is our principal or exclusive concern.

the phase diagram　Given a first-order differential equation in the general form

$$\frac{dy}{dt} = f(y)$$

either linear or nonlinear in the variable y, we can plot dy/dt against y as in Fig. 14.4. Such a geometric representation, feasible whenever dy/dt is a function of y alone, is called a *phase diagram*, and the graph representing the function f is a *phase line*. Once a phase line is known, its configuration will impart significant qualitative information regarding the time path $y(t)$. The clue to this lies in the following two general remarks:

1   Anywhere *above* the horizontal axis (where $dy/dt > 0$), y must be increasing over time and thus, as far as the y axis is concerned, must be moving from left to right. By analogous reasoning, any point *below* the horizontal axis must be associated with a leftward movement in the variable y, because the negativity of dy/dt means that y decreases over time. These directional tendencies explain why the arrowheads on the illustrative phase lines in Fig. 14.4 are drawn as they are. Above the horizontal axis, the arrows are uniformly pointed toward the right—toward the northeast or southeast or due east, as the case may be. The opposite is true below the y axis. Moreover, these results are independent of the algebraic sign of y; even if phase line A (or any other) is transplanted to the left of the vertical axis, the direction of the arrows will not be affected in the slightest.

2   An equilibrium level of y—in the intertemporal sense of the term—if it exists, can occur only on the horizontal axis, where $dy/dt = 0$ (y stationary over time). To find an equilibrium, therefore, it is necessary only to consider the intersection of the phase line with the y axis.[1] To test the dynamic stability of equilibrium, on the other hand, we should also check whether, regardless of the initial position of y, the phase line will always guide it toward the equilibrium position at the said intersection.

types of time path   On the basis of the above general remarks, we may observe three different types of time paths from the illustrative phase lines in Fig. 14.4.

Phase line A has an equilibrium at point y_a; but *above* as well as *below* that point, the arrowheads consistently lead away from equilibrium. Thus, although equilibrium will be attained if it happens that $y(0) = y_a$, the more usual case of $y(0) \neq y_a$ will result in y being ever-increasing [if $y(0) > y_a$] or ever-decreasing [if $y(0) < y_a$]. Besides, in this case the deviation of y from y_a tends to grow at an increasing pace because, as we follow the arrowheads on the phase line, we deviate farther from the y axis, thereby encountering ever-increasing numerical values of dy/dt as well. The time path $y(t)$ implied by phase line A can therefore be represented by the curves shown in Fig. 14.5a, where y is plotted against t (rather than dy/dt against y). The equilibrium y_a is dynamically unstable.

In contrast, phase line B implies a stable equilibrium at y_b. If $y(0) = y_b$, equilibrium will prevail at once. But the important feature of phase line B is that, even if $y(0) \neq y_b$, the movement along the phase line will guide y toward the level of y_b. The time path $y(t)$ corresponding to this type of phase line will

---

[1] However, not all intersections represent equilibrium positions. We shall see this when we discuss phase line *C* in Fig. 14.4.

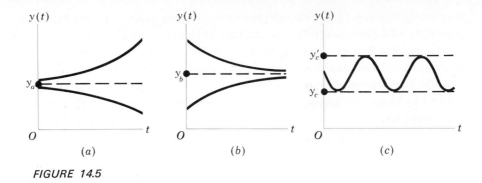

FIGURE 14.5

therefore be of the form shown in Fig. 14.5*b*, which is reminiscent of the dynamic market model.

The above discussion suggests that, in general, it is the slope of the phase line at its intersection point which holds the key to the dynamic stability of equilibrium or the convergence of the time path. A (finite) *positive* slope, such as at point y_a, makes for dynamic *instability*; whereas a (finite) *negative* slope, such as at y_b, implies dynamic *stability*.

This generalization can help us to draw qualitative inferences about given differential equations without even having to draw phase lines. Take the linear differential equation in (14.4), for instance:

$$\frac{dy}{dt} + ay = b \qquad \text{or} \qquad \frac{dy}{dt} = -ay + b$$

Since the phase line will obviously have the (constant) slope $-a$, here assumed nonzero, we may immediately infer (without drawing the line) that

$$a \gtrless 0 \quad \Leftrightarrow \quad y(t) \begin{Bmatrix} \text{converges to} \\ \text{diverges from} \end{Bmatrix} \text{equilibrium}$$

As we may expect, this result coincides perfectly with what the quantitative solution of this equation tells us:

$$y(t) = \left[y(0) - \frac{b}{a} \right] e^{-at} + \frac{b}{a} \qquad \text{[from (14.5')]}$$

We have learned that the convergence of $y(t)$ hinges on the prospect that $e^{-at} \to 0$ as $t \to \infty$. This can happen if and only if $a > 0$; if $a < 0$, then $e^{-at} \to \infty$ as $t \to \infty$, and $y(t)$ cannot converge. Thus, our conclusion is one and the same, whether it is arrived at quantitatively or qualitatively.

It remains to discuss phase line C, which, being a closed loop sitting across the horizontal axis, does not qualify as a *function* but shows instead a *relation* between dy/dt and y.† The interesting new element that emerges in this case is the possibility of a periodically fluctuating time path. The way that phase line C is drawn, we shall find y fluctuating between the two values y_c and y'_c in a perpetual motion. In order to generate the periodic fluctuation, the loop must, of course, straddle the horizontal axis in such a manner that dy/dt can alternately be positive and negative. Besides, at the two intersection points y_c and y'_c, the phase line should have an infinite slope; otherwise the intersection will resemble either y_a or y_b, neither of which permits a continual flow of arrowheads. The type of time path $y(t)$ corresponding to this looped phase line is illustrated in Fig. 14.5c. Note that, whenever $y(t)$ hits the upper bound y'_c or the lower bound y_c, we have $dy/dt = 0$ (local extrema); but these values certainly do not represent equilibrium values of y. In terms of Fig. 14.4, this means that not all intersections between a phase line and the y axis are equilibrium positions.

In sum, for the study of the dynamic stability of equilibrium (or the convergence of the time path), one has the alternative either of finding the time path itself or else of simply drawing the inference from its phase line. We shall illustrate the application of the latter approach with the Solow growth model.

EXERCISE 14.6

1   Plot the phase line for each of the following, and discuss its qualitative implications:

(a) $\dfrac{dy}{dt} = y - 2$ (c) $\dfrac{dy}{dt} = 4 - \dfrac{y}{2}$

(b) $\dfrac{dy}{dt} = 1 - y$ (d) $\dfrac{dy}{dt} = 3y - 2$

2   Plot the phase line for each of the following and interpret:

(a) $\dfrac{dy}{dt} = (y + 1)^2 - 12$ $(y > 0)$

(b) $\dfrac{dy}{dt} = \dfrac{1}{2}y - y^2$ $(y > 0)$

3   Given $dy/dt = (y - 3)(y - 5) = y^2 - 8y + 15$:

(a) Deduce that there are two possible equilibrium levels of y, one at $y = 3$ and the other at $y = 5$.

† This can arise from a second-degree differential equation $(dy/dt)^2 = f(y)$.

(b)   Find the sign of $\dfrac{d}{dy}\left(\dfrac{dy}{dt}\right)$ at $y = 3$ and $y = 5$, respectively. Can you infer from these whether the equilibrium points are dynamically stable or unstable?

14.7   Solow Growth Model

The growth model of Professor Solow[1] is purported to show, among other things, that the razor's-edge growth path of the Domar model is primarily a result of the particular production-function assumption adopted therein and that, under alternative circumstances, the need of delicate balancing may not arise.

the framework   In the Domar model, output is explicitly stated as a function of capital alone: $\kappa = \rho K$ (the productive capacity, or potential output, is a constant multiple of the stock of capital). The absence of a labor input in the production function carries the implication that labor is always combined with capital in a *fixed* proportion, so that it is necessary to consider explicitly only one of these factors of production. Solow, in contrast, seeks to analyze the case where capital and labor can be combined in *varying* proportions. Thus his production function appears in the form

$$Q = f(K,L) \qquad (K,L > 0)$$

where Q is output (net of depreciation), K is capital, and L is labor force—all being used in the *macro* sense. It is assumed that f_K and f_L are positive (positive marginal products), and f_{KK} and f_{LL} are negative (diminishing returns to each input). Furthermore, the production function f is taken to be linearly homogeneous (constant returns to scale). Consequently, it is possible to write

$$(14.26) \qquad Q = Lf\left(\frac{K}{L}, 1\right) = L\phi(K^*) \qquad \text{where } K^* \equiv \frac{K}{L}$$

In view of the assumed signs of f_K and f_{KK}, the newly introduced ϕ function (which, be it noted, has only a single argument, K^*) must be characterized by a positive first derivative and a negative second derivative. To verify this claim, we first recall from (12.40) that

$$f_K \equiv \text{MPP}_K = \phi'(K^*)$$

---

[1] Robert M. Solow, "A Contribution to the Theory of Economic Growth," *Quarterly Journal of Economics*, February, 1956, pp. 65–94.

hence $f_K > 0$ automatically means $\phi'(K^*) > 0$. Then, since

$$f_{KK} = \frac{\partial}{\partial K}\, \phi'(K^*) = \frac{d\phi'(K^*)}{dK^*}\frac{\partial K^*}{\partial K} = \phi''(K^*)\frac{1}{L} \qquad \text{[see (12.39)]}$$

the assumption $f_{KK} < 0$ leads directly to the result $\phi''(K^*) < 0$. Thus the ϕ function—which, according to (12.37), gives the APP_L for every capital-labor ratio—is one that increases with K^* at a decreasing rate.

Given that Q depends on K and L, it is necessary now to stipulate how the latter two variables themselves are determined. Solow's assumptions are:

$$(14.27) \qquad \dot{K}\left(\equiv \frac{dK}{dt}\right) = sQ \qquad \text{[constant proportion of Q is invested]}$$

$$(14.28) \qquad L = L_0 e^{\lambda t} \qquad (\lambda > 0) \qquad \text{[labor force grows exponentially]}$$

The symbol s represents a (constant) marginal propensity to save, and L_0 and λ are, respectively, the initial labor force and the rate of growth of labor.

If we make a point of keeping labor fully employed at all times, the two L's in (14.26) and (14.28) should be equated to each other. Then, the three equations of the model can be condensed, through substitution, into a single equation:

$$(14.29) \qquad \dot{K} = sL_0 e^{\lambda t}\phi(K^*)$$

This is a differential equation, but whereas the function ϕ is in terms of the variable K^*, the derivative on the left is in terms of the variable K. In order to unify the variable, we must first establish a relationship between $\dot{K}$ and $\dot{K}^*$ ($\equiv dK^*/dt$), so that we can transform $\dot{K}$ into $\dot{K}^*$. Now, since $K^* \equiv K/L$, it follows that

$$K = K^*L = K^*L_0 e^{\lambda t}$$

and thus, by the product rule,

$$(14.30) \qquad \dot{K} = L_0 e^{\lambda t}\frac{d}{dt}K^* + K^*\frac{d}{dt}L_0 e^{\lambda t}$$

$$= L_0 e^{\lambda t}\dot{K}^* + K^*\lambda L_0 e^{\lambda t}$$

Upon substituting (14.30) into (14.29) and dividing through by $L_0 e^{\lambda t}$, we can finally have the differential equation expressed in a single variable K^*, as desired:

$$(14.31) \qquad \dot{K}^* = s\phi(K^*) - \lambda K^*$$

This differential equation, with two parameters s and λ, is the fundamental equation of the Solow model.

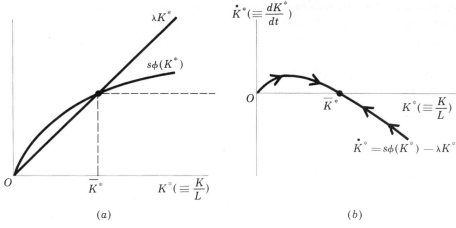

FIGURE 14.6

a qualitative-graphic analysis   Equation (14.31) being in a general-function form, no specific quantitative solution is available. Nevertheless, we can analyze it qualitatively. To this end, we should plot a phase line, with $\dot{K}^*$ on the vertical axis and K^* on the horizontal.

Since (14.31) contains two terms on the right, however, let us first plot these as two separate curves. The λK^* term, a linear function of K^*, will obviously show up in Fig. 14.6a as a straight line, with a zero vertical intercept and a slope equal to λ. The $s\phi(K^*)$ term, on the other hand, will plot as a curve that increases at a decreasing rate, like $\phi(K^*)$, since $s\phi(K^*)$ is merely a constant fraction of the $\phi(K^*)$ curve. If we consider K to be an indispensable factor of production, we must start the $s\phi(K^*)$ curve from the point of origin; this is because if $K = 0$ and thus $K^* = 0$, Q must also be zero, as will be $\phi(K^*)$ and $s\phi(K^*)$. The way the curve is actually drawn also reflects the implicit assumption that there exists a set of K^* values for which $s\phi(K^*)$ exceeds λK^*, so that the two curves intersect at some positive value of K^*, namely, $\bar{K}^*$.

Based upon these two curves, the value of $\dot{K}^*$ for each value of K^* can be measured by the vertical distance between the two curves. Plotting the values of $\dot{K}^*$ against K^*, as in Fig. 14.6b, will then yield the phase line we need. Note that, since the two curves in diagram a intersect when the capital-labor ratio is $\bar{K}^*$, the phase line in diagram b must cross the horizontal axis at $\bar{K}^*$. This marks $\bar{K}^*$ as the (intertemporal) equilibrium capital-labor ratio.

Inasmuch as the phase line has a negative slope at $\bar{K}^*$, the equilibrium is readily identified as a stable one; given any (positive) initial value of K^*, the dynamic movement of the model must lead us convergently to the level of $\bar{K}^*$. The significant point is that once this equilibrium is attained—and thus the capital-labor ratio is (by definition) unvarying over time—capital must thereafter grow apace with labor, at the identical rate λ. This will imply, in turn, that net investment must grow at the rate λ (see Exercise 14.7-2). Note, however, that "must" is used here not in the sense of requirement, but with the implication of automaticity. Thus, what the Solow model serves to show is that, given a rate of growth of labor λ, the economy by itself, and without the delicate balancing à la Domar, can eventually reach a state of steady growth in which investment will grow at the rate λ, the same as K and L. Moreover, in order to satisfy (14.26), Q must grow at the same rate as well because $\phi(K^*)$ is a constant when the capital-labor ratio remains unvarying at the level of $\bar{K}^*$. Such a situation, in which the relevant variables all grow at an identical rate, is called a *steady state* —a generalization of the concept of *stationary state*, in which the relevant variables all remain constant, or in other words all grow at the zero rate.

Note that, in the above analysis, the production function is assumed for convenience to be invariant over time. If the state of technology is allowed to improve, on the other hand, the production function will have to be duly modified. For instance, it may be written instead in the form

$$ Q = T(t)f(K,L) \qquad \left(\frac{dT}{dt} > 0 \right) $$

where T, some measure of technology, is an increasing function of time. Because of the increasing multiplicative term $T(t)$, a fixed amount of K and L will turn out a larger output at a future date than at present. In this event, the $s\phi(K^*)$ curve in Fig. 14.6 will be subject to a secular upward shift, resulting in successively higher intersections with the λK^* ray and also in larger values of $\bar{K}^*$. With technological improvement, therefore, it will become possible, in a succession of steady states, to have a larger and larger amount of capital equipment available to each representative worker in the economy, with a concomitant rise in productivity.

a quantitative illustration   The above analysis had to be qualitative, owing to the presence of a general function $\phi(K^*)$ in the model. But if we specify the production function to be a linearly homogeneous Cobb-Douglas function, for instance, then a quantitative solution can be found as well.

Let us write the production function as

$$ Q = K^\alpha L^{1-\alpha} = L \left(\frac{K}{L} \right)^\alpha = LK^{*\alpha} $$

so that $\phi(K^*) = K^{*\alpha}$. Then (14.31) becomes

$$ \dot{K}^* = sK^{*\alpha} - \lambda K^* \qquad \text{or} \qquad \dot{K}^* + \lambda K^* = sK^{*\alpha} $$

which is a Bernoulli equation in the variable K^* [see (14.25)], with $R = \lambda$, $T = s$, and $n = \alpha$. Letting $z = (K^*)^{1-\alpha}$, we obtain its linearized version

$$dz + [(1 - \alpha)\lambda z - (1 - \alpha)s]\,dt = 0$$

or
$$\frac{dz}{dt} + \underbrace{(1 - \alpha)\lambda}_{a} z = \underbrace{(1 - \alpha)s}_{b}$$

This is a linear differential equation with a constant coefficient a and a constant term b. Thus, by formula (14.5′), we have

$$z(t) = \left[z(0) - \frac{s}{\lambda} \right] e^{-(1-\alpha)\lambda t} + \frac{s}{\lambda}$$

The substitution of $z = (K^*)^{1-\alpha}$ will then yield the final solution

$$(K^*)^{1-\alpha} = \left[(K_0^*)^{1-\alpha} - \frac{s}{\lambda} \right] e^{-(1-\alpha)\lambda t} + \frac{s}{\lambda}$$

where K_0^* is the initial value of the capital-labor ratio K^*.

This solution is what determines the time path of K^*. Recalling that $(1 - \alpha)$ and λ are both positive, we see that as $t \to \infty$ the exponential expression will approach zero; consequently,

$$(K^*)^{1-\alpha} \to \frac{s}{\lambda} \qquad \text{or} \qquad K^* \to \left(\frac{s}{\lambda} \right)^{1/(1-\alpha)}$$

Therefore, the capital-labor ratio will approach the latter constant as its equilibrium value. This equilibrium or steady-state value, $\bar{K}^*$, varies directly with the magnitude of the propensity to consume s, and inversely with the growth rate of labor force λ.

EXERCISE 14.7

1 Divide (14.31) through by K^*, and interpret the resulting equation in terms of the growth rates of K^*, K, and L. [*Hint:* Utilize (14.26) and (14.27); also see Exercise 10.7-2.]

2 Show that, if capital is growing at the rate λ (that is, $K = Ae^{\lambda t}$), net investment I must also be growing at the rate λ.

3 If the production function in the Solow model is $Q = T(t)f(K,L)$, with the function f being linearly homogeneous, $T(t)$ growing at the rate ρ, and L growing at the rate λ, what must be the rate of growth of Q in the steady state?

15

HIGHER-ORDER DIFFERENTIAL EQUATIONS

In the last chapter, we discussed the methods of solving a *first-order* differential equation, one in which there appears no derivative (or differential) of orders higher than 1. At times, however, the specification of a model may involve the second derivative or a derivative of an even higher order. We may, for instance, be given a function describing "the rate of change of the rate of change" of the income variable Y, say,

$$\frac{d^2 Y}{dt^2} = kY$$

from which we are supposed to find the time path of Y. In this event, the given function constitutes a *second-order* differential equation, and the task of finding the time path $Y(t)$ is that of *solving* the second-order differential equation. The present chapter is concerned with the methods of solution and the economic applications of such higher-order differential equations, but we shall confine our discussion to the *linear* case only.

A simple variety of linear differential equations of order n is of the following form:

$$(15.1) \qquad \frac{d^n y}{dt^n} + a_1 \frac{d^{n-1} y}{dt^{n-1}} + \cdots + a_{n-1} \frac{dy}{dt} + a_n y = b$$

or, in an alternative notation,

$$(15.1') \qquad y^{(n)}(t) + a_1 y^{(n-1)}(t) + \cdots + a_{n-1} y'(t) + a_n y = b$$

This equation is of *order n*, because the nth derivative (the first term on the left) is the highest derivative present. It is *linear,* since all the derivatives, as well as the dependent variable y, appear only in the first degree, and moreover, no product term occurs in which y and any of its derivatives are multiplied together. The reader will note, in addition, that this differential equation is characterized by *constant coefficients* (the a's) and a *constant term* (b). The constancy of the coefficients is an assumption we shall retain throughout this chapter. The constant term b, on the other hand, is adopted here as a first approach; later, in Sec. 15.6, we shall drop it in favor of a variable term.

15.1 Second-Order Linear Differential Equations with Constant Coefficients and Constant Term

For pedagogical reasons, let us discuss the method of solution first for the *second-order* case ($n = 2$). The relevant differential equation is then the simple one

$$(15.2) \qquad y''(t) + a_1 y'(t) + a_2 y = b$$

where a_1, a_2, and b are all constants. If the term b is identically zero, we have a *homogeneous* equation, but if b is a nonzero constant, the equation is *nonhomogeneous.* Our discussion will proceed on the assumption that (15.2) is nonhomogeneous; in solving the nonhomogeneous version of (15.2), the solution of the homogeneous version will emerge automatically as a by-product.

In this connection, we recall a proposition introduced in Sec. 14.1 which is equally applicable here: If y_c is the *complementary function,* i.e., the general solution (with arbitrary constants) of the reduced equation of (15.2) and if y_p is the *particular integral,* i.e., any particular solution (with no arbitrary constants) of the complete equation (15.2), then $y(t) = y_c + y_p$ will be the general solution of the complete equation. As was explained previously, the y_p component provides us with the equilibrium value of the variable y in the intertemporal sense of the term, whereas the y_c component reveals, for each point of time, the deviation of the time path $y(t)$ from the equilibrium.

the particular integral   For the case of constant coefficients and constant term, the particular integral is relatively easy to find. Since the particular integral can be *any* solution of (15.2), i.e., any value of y that satisfies this nonhomogeneous equation, we should always try the simplest possible type: namely, $y = $ a constant. If $y = $ a constant, it follows that

$$y'(t) = y''(t) = 0$$

so that (15.2) will in effect become $a_2 y = b$, with the solution $y = b/a_2$. Thus, the desired particular integral is

$$(15.3) \qquad y_p = \frac{b}{a_2} \qquad (a_2 \neq 0)$$

Since the process of finding the value of y_p involves the condition $y'(t) = 0$, the rationale for considering that value as an intertemporal equilibrium becomes self-evident.

Example 1 Find the particular integral of the equation

$$y''(t) + y'(t) - 2y = -10$$

The relevant coefficients here are $a_2 = -2$ and $b = -10$. Therefore, the particular integral is $y_p = -10/(-2) = 5$.

What if $a_2 = 0$—so that the expression b/a_2 is not defined? In such a situation, since the constant solution for y_p fails to work, we must try some *nonconstant* form of solution. Taking the simplest possibility, we may try $y = kt$. Since $a_2 = 0$, the differential equation is now

$$y''(t) + a_1 y'(t) = b$$

but if $y = kt$, which implies $y'(t) = k$ and $y''(t) = 0$, this equation will reduce to $a_1 k = b$. This determines the value of k as b/a_1, thereby giving us the particular integral

$$(15.3') \qquad y_p = \frac{b}{a_1} t \qquad (a_2 = 0; a_1 \neq 0)$$

Inasmuch as y_p is in this case a nonconstant function of time, we shall regard it as a moving equilibrium.

Example 2 Find the y_p of the equation $y''(t) + y'(t) = -10$. Here, we have $a_2 = 0$, $a_1 = 1$, and $b = -10$. Thus, by (15.3'), we can write

$$y_p = -10t$$

If it happens that a_1 is also zero, then the solution form of $y = kt$ will also break down, because the expression bt/a_1 will now be undefined. We ought, then, to try a solution of the form $y = kt^2$. With $a_1 = a_2 = 0$, the differential equation now reduces to the extremely simple form

$$y''(t) = b$$

and if $y = kt^2$, which implies $y'(t) = 2kt$ and $y''(t) = 2k$, the differential equation can be written as $2k = b$. Thus, we find $k = b/2$, and the particular integral will be

$$(15.3'') \qquad y_p = \frac{b}{2}t^2 \qquad (a_1 = a_2 = 0)$$

The equilibrium represented by this particular integral is again a moving equilibrium.

Example 3   Find the y_p of the equation $y''(t) = -10$. Since the coefficients are $a_1 = a_2 = 0$ and $b = -10$, formula $(15.3'')$ is applicable. The desired answer is $y_p = -5t^2$.

the complementary function   The complementary function of (15.2) is defined to be the general solution of its reduced (homogeneous) equation

$$(15.4) \qquad y''(t) + a_1 y'(t) + a_2 y = 0$$

This is why we stated that the solution of a homogeneous equation will always be a *by-product* in the process of solving a complete equation.

Even though we have never tackled such an equation before, our experience with the complementary function of the first-order differential equations can supply us with a useful hint. From the solutions (14.3), (14.3′), (14.5), and (14.5′), it is clear that exponential expressions of the form Ae^{rt} figure very prominently in the complementary functions of first-order differential equations with constant coefficients. Then why not try a solution of the form $y = Ae^{rt}$ in the second-order equation, too?

In using the trial solution $y = Ae^{rt}$, we make the general assumption that $Ae^{rt} \neq 0$, for otherwise the time path of y will simply be a horizontal straight line lying on the t axis, and nothing further really needs to be said or done. With $Ae^{rt} \neq 0$, however, we now face the task of finding the particular values of A and r that will make the trial solution work. Since the solution $y = Ae^{rt}$ implies

$$y'(t) = rAe^{rt} \qquad \text{and} \qquad y''(t) = r^2 Ae^{rt}$$

the differential equation (15.4) can, on the basis of the postulated solution and the above two derivatives, be transformed into

$$(15.4') \qquad Ae^{rt}(r^2 + a_1 r + a_2) = 0$$

As long as we choose only those values of A and r that satisfy $(15.4')$, the trial solution $y = Ae^{rt}$ should work. However, since $Ae^{rt} \neq 0$, $(15.4')$ can be simplified to

$$(15.4'') \qquad r^2 + a_1 r + a_2 = 0$$

Higher-Order Differential Equations   **505**

In fact, then, the solution $y = Ae^{rt}$ will work as long as we pick only the r values that satisfy (15.4″), regardless of the value of the other constant A. Equation (15.4″) is known as the *characteristic equation* (or *auxiliary equation*) of the homogeneous equation (15.4)—or of the complete equation (15.2).

Since (15.4″) is a quadratic equation in r, we can find two roots (solutions), referred to in the present context as *characteristic roots*, as follows:[1]

$$(15.5) \qquad r_1, r_2 = \frac{-a_1 \pm \sqrt{a_1^2 - 4a_2}}{2}$$

These two roots bear a simple but interesting relationship to each other, which can serve as a means of checking our calculation: The *sum* of the two roots is always equal to $-a_1$, and their *product* is always equal to a_2. The proof of this statement is straightforward:

$$r_1 + r_2 = \frac{-a_1 + \sqrt{a_1^2 - 4a_2}}{2}$$

$$(15.6) \qquad\qquad\qquad\qquad + \frac{-a_1 - \sqrt{a_1^2 - 4a_2}}{2} = \frac{-2a_1}{2} = -a_1$$

$$r_1 r_2 = \frac{(-a_1)^2 - (a_1^2 - 4a_2)}{4} = \frac{4a_2}{4} = a_2$$

The values of these two roots are the only values we may assign to r in the solution $y = Ae^{rt}$. But this means that, in effect, there are *two* solutions which will work, namely,

$$y_1 = A_1 e^{r_1 t} \qquad \text{and} \qquad y_2 = A_2 e^{r_2 t}$$

where A_1 and A_2 are two arbitrary constants, and r_1 and r_2 are the characteristic roots found from (15.5). Since we want only *one* general solution, however, there seems to be one too many. Two alternatives are now open to us: (1) pick either y_1 or y_2 at random, or (2) combine them in some fashion.

The first alternative, though simpler, is unacceptable. There is only one arbitrary constant in y_1 or y_2, but to qualify as a general solution of a *second-order* differential equation, the expression must contain *two* arbitrary constants. This requirement stems from the fact that, in proceeding from a function $y(t)$ to its second derivative $y''(t)$, we "lose" two constants during the two rounds of differentiation; therefore, to revert from a second-order differential equation to the primitive function $y(t)$, two constants should be reinstated. That leaves us only the alternative of combining y_1 and y_2, so as to include both constants A_1

---

[1] Note that the quadratic equation (15.4″) is in the normalized form; the coefficient of the r^2 term is 1. In applying formula (15.5) to find the characteristic roots of a differential equation, we must first make sure that the characteristic equation is indeed in the normalized form.

and A_2. As it turns out, we can simply take their *sum*, $y_1 + y_2$, as the general solution of (15.4). Let us demonstrate that, if y_1 and y_2, respectively, satisfy (15.4), then the sum $(y_1 + y_2)$ will also do so. If y_1 and y_2 are indeed solutions of (15.4), then by substituting each of these into (15.4), we must find that the following two equations hold:

$$y_1''(t) + a_1 y_1'(t) + a_2 y_1 = 0$$

$$y_2''(t) + a_1 y_2'(t) + a_2 y_2 = 0$$

By adding these equations, however, we find that

$$\underbrace{[y_1''(t) + y_2''(t)]}_{=\ \frac{d^2}{dt^2}\ (y_1+y_2)} + a_1 \underbrace{[y_1'(t) + y_2'(t)]}_{=\ \frac{d}{dt}\ (y_1+y_2)} + a_2(y_1 + y_2) = 0$$

Thus, like y_1 or y_2, the sum $(y_1 + y_2)$ satisfies the equation (15.4) as well. Accordingly, the general solution of the homogeneous equation (15.4) or the complementary function of the complete equation (15.2) can, in general, be written as $y_c = y_1 + y_2$.

A more careful examination of the characteristic-root formula (15.5) indicates, however, that as far as the values of r_1 and r_2 are concerned, three possible cases can arise, some of which may necessitate a modification of our result that $y_c = y_1 + y_2$.

CASE 1   (*Distinct Real Roots*)   When $a_1^2 > 4a_2$, the square root in (15.5) is a real number, and the two roots r_1 and r_2 will take *distinct* real values, because the square root is added to $-a_1$ for r_1, and subtracted from $-a_1$ for r_2. In this case, we can indeed write

$$(15.7) \qquad y_c = y_1 + y_2 = A_1 e^{r_1 t} + A_2 e^{r_2 t} \qquad (r_1 \neq r_2)$$

The two roots being distinct, the two exponential expressions must be linearly independent (neither is a multiple of the other); consequently, A_1 and A_2 will always remain as separate entities and provide us with two constants, as required.

Example 4   Solve the differential equation

$$y''(t) + y'(t) - 2y = -10$$

The particular integral of this equation has already been found to be $y_p = 5$, in Example 1. Let us find the complementary function. Since the coefficients of the equation are $a_1 = 1$ and $a_2 = -2$, the characteristic roots are, by (15.5),

$$r_1, r_2 = \frac{-1 \pm \sqrt{1 + 8}}{2} = \frac{-1 \pm 3}{2} = 1, -2$$

(Check: $r_1 + r_2 = -1 = -a_1$; $r_1r_2 = -2 = a_2$.) Since the roots are distinct real numbers, the complementary function is $y_c = A_1e^t + A_2e^{-2t}$. Therefore, the general solution can be written as

(15.8) $y(t) = y_c + y_p = A_1e^t + A_2e^{-2t} + 5$

In order to definitize the constants A_1 and A_2, there is need now for *two* initial conditions. Let these conditions be $y(0) = 12$ and $y'(0) = -2$. That is, when $t = 0$, $y(t)$ and $y'(t)$ are, respectively, 12 and -2. Setting $t = 0$ in (15.8), we find that

$$y(0) = A_1 + A_2 + 5$$

Differentiating (15.8) with respect to t and then setting $t = 0$ in the derivative, we find that

$$y'(t) = A_1e^t - 2A_2e^{-2t} \qquad \text{and} \qquad y'(0) = A_1 - 2A_2$$

To fulfill the two initial conditions, therefore, we must set $y(0) = 12$ and $y'(0) = -2$, which results in the following pair of simultaneous equations:

$$A_1 + A_2 = 7$$
$$A_1 - 2A_2 = -2$$

with solutions $A_1 = 4$ and $A_2 = 3$. Thus the definite solution of the differential equation is

(15.8') $y(t) = 4e^t + 3e^{-2t} + 5$

As before, we can check the validity of this solution by differentiation. The first and second derivatives of (15.8') are

$$y'(t) = 4e^t - 6e^{-2t} \qquad \text{and} \qquad y''(t) = 4e^t + 12e^{-2t}$$

When these are substituted into the given differential equation along with (15.8'), the result is an identity $-10 = -10$. Thus the solution is correct. As the reader can easily verify, (15.8') also satisfies both of the initial conditions.

CASE 2   (*Repeated Real Roots*)   When the coefficients in the differential equation are such that $a_1{}^2 = 4a_2$, the square root in (15.5) will vanish, and the two characteristic roots will take an identical value:

$$r (= r_1 = r_2) = -\frac{a_1}{2}$$

Such roots are known as *repeated roots*, or *multiple* (here, *double*) *roots*.

If we attempt to write the complementary function as $y_c = y_1 + y_2$, the sum will in this case collapse into a single expression

$$y_c = A_1e^{rt} + A_2e^{rt} = (A_1 + A_2)e^{rt} = A_3e^{rt}$$

leaving us with only one constant. This is not sufficient to lead us from a second-order differential equation back to its primitive function. The only way out is to find another eligible component term for the sum—a term which satisfies (15.4) and yet which is linearly independent of the term $A_3 e^{rt}$, so as to preclude such "collapsing."

An expression that will satisfy these requirements is $A_4 t e^{rt}$. Since the variable t has entered into it multiplicatively, this component term is obviously linearly independent of the $A_3 e^{rt}$ term; thus it will enable us to introduce another constant, A_4. But does $A_4 t e^{rt}$ qualify as a solution of (15.4)? If we try $y = A_4 t e^{rt}$, then, by the product rule, we can find its first and second derivatives to be

$$y'(t) = (rt + 1)A_4 e^{rt} \quad \text{and} \quad y''(t) = (r^2 t + 2r)A_4 e^{rt}$$

Substituting these expressions of y, y', and y'' into the left side of (15.4), we get the expression

$$[(r^2 t + 2r) + a_1(rt + 1) + a_2 t]A_4 e^{rt}$$

Inasmuch as, in the present context, we have $a_1^2 = 4a_2$ and $r = -a_1/2$, this last expression vanishes identically and thus is always equal to the right side of (15.4); this shows that $A_4 t e^{rt}$ does indeed qualify as a solution.

Hence, the complementary function of the double-root case can be written as

(15.9) $\qquad y_c = A_3 e^{rt} + A_4 t e^{rt}$

Example 5 $\qquad$ Solve the differential equation

$$y''(t) + 6y'(t) + 9y = 27$$

Here, the coefficients are $a_1 = 6$ and $a_2 = 9$; since $a_1^2 = 4a_2$, the roots will be repeated. According to formula (15.5), we have $r = -a_1/2 = -3$. Thus, in line with the result in (15.9), the complementary function may be written as

$$y_c = A_3 e^{-3t} + A_4 t e^{-3t}$$

The general solution of the given differential equation is now also readily obtainable. Trying a constant solution for the particular integral, we get $y_p = 3$. It follows that the general solution of the complete equation is

$$y(t) = y_c + y_p = A_3 e^{-3t} + A_4 t e^{-3t} + 3$$

The two arbitrary constants can again be definitized with two initial conditions. Suppose that the initial conditions are $y(0) = 5$ and $y'(0) = -5$. By setting $t = 0$ in the above general solution, we should find $y(0) = 5$; that is,

$$y(0) = A_3 + 3 = 5$$

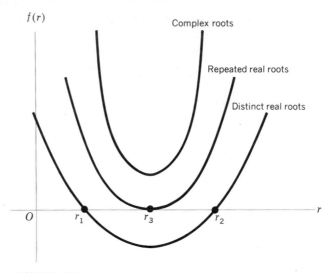

$f(r)$

Complex roots

Repeated real roots

Distinct real roots

O r_1 r_3 r_2 r

FIGURE 15.1

This yields $A_3 = 2$. Next, by differentiating the general solution and then setting $t = 0$ and also $A_3 = 2$, we must have $y'(0) = -5$. That is,

$$y'(t) = -3A_3e^{-3t} - 3A_4te^{-3t} + A_4e^{-3t}$$

and $y'(0) = -6 + A_4 = -5$

This yields $A_4 = 1$. Thus we can finally write the definite solution of the given equation as

$$y(t) = 2e^{-3t} + te^{-3t} + 3$$

CASE 3   (*Complex Roots*)   There remains a third possibility regarding the relative magnitude of the coefficients a_1 and a_2, namely, $a_1{}^2 < 4a_2$. When this eventuality occurs, formula (15.5) will involve the square root of a *negative* number, which cannot be handled before we are properly introduced to the concepts of *imaginary* and *complex* numbers. For the time being, therefore, we shall be content with the mere cataloging of this case and shall leave the full discussion of it to a later section.

The three cases cited above can be illustrated by the three curves in Fig. 15.1, each of which represents a different version of the quadratic function $f(r) = r^2 + a_1r + a_2$. As we learned earlier, when such a function is set equal to zero, the result is a quadratic *equation* $f(r) = 0$, and to solve the latter equation is merely to "find the zeros of the quadratic *function*." Graphically, this means

Dynamic Analysis

that the roots of the equation are to be found on the horizontal axis, where $f(r) = 0$.

In the case of the lowest curve in Fig. 15.1, its position is such that it intersects the horizontal axis twice; thus we can find two distinct roots r_1 and r_2, both of which satisfy the quadratic equation $f(r) = 0$ and both of which, of course, are real-valued. Thus the lowest curve illustrates Case 1. Turning to the middle curve, we note that it meets the horizontal axis only once, at r_3. This latter is the only value of r that can satisfy the equation $f(r) = 0$. Therefore, the middle curve illustrates Case 2. Lastly, we note that the top curve does not meet the horizontal axis at all, and there is thus no real-valued root to the equation $f(r) = 0$. As we shall see in a later section, even though no real roots exist in such a case (Case 3), we can still find two complex numbers that satisfy the equation.

Meanwhile, let us first examine an economic model involving only real roots.

EXERCISE 15.1

1   Find the particular integral of each equation:

(a) $y''(t) - 2y'(t) + 3y = 2$ (d) $y''(t) + 2y'(t) - y = -5$
(b) $y''(t) + y'(t) = 4$ (e) $y''(t) = 8$
(c) $y''(t) + 3y = 9$

2   Find the complementary function of each equation:

(a) $y''(t) + 3y'(t) - 4y = 12$ (c) $y''(t) - 2y'(t) + y = 3$
(b) $y''(t) + 5y'(t) + 4y = 1$ (d) $y''(t) + 8y'(t) + 16y = 8$

3   Find the general solution of each differential equation in the preceding problem, and then definitize the solution with the initial conditions $y(0) = 4$ and $y'(0) = 2$.

4   Verify that the definite solution in Example 5: (a) fulfills the two initial conditions and (b) has first and second derivatives which conform to the given differential equation.

15.2   Domar Burden-of-Debt Model

When the government incurs a larger and larger debt through continual net borrowing, the interest charges on the public debt naturally must grow, provided that the interest rate is not falling. Assuming that the entire amount of the interest charges is to be paid for with tax revenue, then the absolute amount of tax collection must also rise continually as a result, thus imposing a "burden" on the public. According to Domar,[1] however, the burden of the public debt should be measured not by the absolute amount of interest charges (or the tax it necessitates), but by the proportion the additional tax bears to the national income. It is argued that, if income happens to be increasing, then an absolute increase in tax collection may not really inflict any hardship on the public. Domar seeks to analyze the burden of public debt under several alternative situations of income growth, of which we shall consider two.

In this discussion, the following assumptions are made. First, the rate of net borrowing is always proportional to the rate of national-income flow; i.e., a constant fraction of national income always gets to become new public debt. Then, denoting the total public debt outstanding by $D(t)$, we may write

$$(15.10) \qquad D'(t) = \alpha Y(t) \qquad (0 < \alpha < 1)$$

Second, the interest rate is taken to be a constant i, so that the interest-induced tax $T(t)$ is always proportional to the total outstanding debt:

$$T(t) = iD(t)$$

CASE 1   (*Income Grows at Constant Relative Rate*)   If income grows at a constant relative rate β, then the following equation holds:

$$(15.11) \qquad Y'(t) = \beta Y(t) \qquad (0 < \beta < 1)$$

Our objective is to find the debt burden

$$B(t) \equiv \frac{T(t)}{Y(t)} = \frac{iD(t)}{Y(t)}$$

on the basis of the postulated income-growth pattern. To this end, we must first find the time paths $D(t)$ and $Y(t)$.

One possible approach is to integrate (15.11) in order to get $Y(t)$ and then to substitute this into (15.10) and solve the resulting first-order differential equation for $D(t)$. As an illustration for the present chapter, however, let us treat the problem as one of solving a second-order differential equation. By differentiating (15.10) with respect to t and utilizing (15.11) and (15.10) successively, we obtain the equation

$$D''(t) = \alpha Y'(t) = \alpha\beta Y(t) = \beta D'(t)$$

[1] Evsey D. Domar, "The 'Burden of the Debt' and the National Income," *American Economic Review*, December, 1944, pp. 798–827; reprinted in Domar, *Essays in the Theory of Economic Growth*, Oxford University Press, Fair Lawn, N.J., 1957, pp. 35–69.

That is,

(15.12) $D''(t) - \beta D'(t) = 0$

This is a second-order differential equation in the form of (15.2), with coefficients $a_1 = -\beta$ and $a_2 = b = 0$. Thus, by using the various formulas developed earlier, we can readily find that

$$y_p = 0 \qquad \text{[by (15.3')]}$$

$$r_1, r_2 = \frac{1}{2} (\beta \pm \sqrt{\beta^2}) = \beta, 0 \qquad \text{[by (15.5)]} \qquad \text{[distinct roots]}$$

and $$y_c = A_1 e^{\beta t} + A_2 \qquad \text{[by (15.7)]}$$

The general solution of (15.12) is therefore

$$D(t) = A_1 e^{\beta t} + A_2$$

In order to definitize this, let us denote the initial values of D and Y as $D(0) = D_0$ and $Y(0) = Y_0$. Setting $t = 0$ in the general solution, we find that

(15.13) $D(0) = A_1 + A_2 = D_0$

Next, by setting $t = 0$ in the derivative of the general solution, we can get the equation $D'(0) = \beta A_1$; but since (15.10) implies $D'(0) = \alpha Y(0) = \alpha Y_0$, it follows that

(15.14) $\beta A_1 = \alpha Y_0$

Solved simultaneously, (15.13) and (15.14) yield the values

$$A_1 = \frac{\alpha}{\beta} Y_0 \qquad \text{and} \qquad A_2 = D_0 - \frac{\alpha}{\beta} Y_0$$

so that the definite solution of (15.12) is in the form

$$D(t) = \frac{\alpha}{\beta} Y_0 e^{\beta t} + D_0 - \frac{\alpha}{\beta} Y_0$$

This depicts the time path of the public debt.

The other time path, $Y(t)$, is easier to find. In fact, we can see immediately from (15.11) that $Y(t) = A e^{\beta t}$, or

$$Y(t) = Y_0 e^{\beta t}$$

after the initial condition is taken into consideration. Consequently, it is now possible to write the burden function as follows:

$$B(t) = \frac{iD(t)}{Y(t)} = \frac{i(\alpha/\beta) Y_0 e^{\beta t} + iD_0 - i(\alpha/\beta) Y_0}{Y_0 e^{\beta t}}$$

The relevant dynamic question is: What will happen to $B(t)$ if new government borrowing is to continue indefinitely at the indicated rate? This is tantamount to asking: What is the limit of $B(t)$ as t becomes infinite? Since both the numerator and the denominator become infinite as $t \to \infty$, we shall apply L'Hôpital's rule (12.55) to evaluate this limit.[1] Differentiating both members of the fraction with respect to t, we can write

$$\lim_{t \to \infty} B(t) = \lim_{t \to \infty} \frac{\beta i(\alpha/\beta) Y_0 e^{\beta t}}{\beta Y_0 e^{\beta t}} = \lim_{t \to \infty} \frac{i\alpha}{\beta} = \frac{i\alpha}{\beta}$$

Thus, if income grows at a constant relative rate, the debt burden will not increase without bounds but will approach a finite limit whose magnitude depends on the values of the parameters α, β, and i.

CASE 2 (*Income Grows by Constant Absolute Increments*) If income grows instead by a constant amount per unit of time, then (15.11) must be replaced by the equation

$$(15.15) \qquad Y'(t) = \gamma \qquad (\gamma > 0)$$

In that case, by differentiating (15.10) and substituting (15.15) into the result, we obtain the second-order differential equation

$$(15.16) \qquad D''(t) = \alpha\gamma$$

This is a special case of (15.2), with coefficients $a_1 = a_2 = 0$ and $b = \alpha\gamma$. It follows that

$$y_p = \frac{1}{2}\alpha\gamma t^2 \qquad \text{[by (15.3'')]}$$

$$r_1 = r_2 = 0 \qquad \text{[by (15.5)]} \qquad \text{[repeated roots]}$$

$$\text{and} \qquad y_c = A_3 + A_4 t \qquad \text{[by (15.9)]}$$

Thus, the general solution of (15.16) is

$$D(t) = A_3 + A_4 t + \frac{1}{2}\alpha\gamma t^2$$

To definitize this solution, we again denote the initial values of D and Y by D_0 and Y_0, respectively. By setting $t = 0$ in the solution, it is found that $A_3 = D_0$. Next, by differentiating $D(t)$ and setting $t = 0$, it is found that

---

[1] An alternative way is to multiply both the numerator and the denominator by $e^{-\beta t}$, thereby producing an expression with an exponential term in the numerator only.

$D'(0) = A_4$. But since (15.10) implies that $D'(0) = \alpha Y_0$, we may equate the two expressions for $D'(0)$, to get $A_4 = \alpha Y_0$. The substitution of these values into the general solution then yields the following definite solution:

$$D(t) = D_0 + \alpha Y_0 t + \frac{1}{2}\alpha\gamma t^2$$

We next seek the time path of Y. In view of the fact that the derivative of $Y(t)$ is a constant γ, we can immediately infer that $Y(t) = \gamma t + c$ or, after taking into account the initial value of Y, that

$$Y(t) = Y_0 + \gamma t$$

This information enables us to express the burden function as

$$B(t) = \frac{iD(t)}{Y(t)} = \frac{iD_0 + i\alpha Y_0 t + \frac{1}{2}i\alpha\gamma t^2}{Y_0 + \gamma t}$$

Once again, we wish to evaluate the limit of $B(t)$ as t becomes infinite, and once again, L'Hôpital's rule can be of help. Upon differentiating the numerator and the denominator of $B(t)$, respectively, with respect to t, we find this time

$$\lim_{t \to \infty} B(t) = \lim_{t \to \infty} \frac{i\alpha Y_0 + i\alpha\gamma t}{\gamma} = \infty$$

Unlike the situation in Case 1, therefore, the debt burden in the present case does grow indefinitely, as government borrowing is continued at the rate indicated. It appears, therefore, that the question of whether the debt burden can stay at a tolerable level will depend on the pattern of income growth.

EXERCISE 15.2

1   If income remains constant over time, the burden-of-debt model will consist of the equations

$$D'(t) = \alpha Y(t) \qquad \text{and} \qquad Y'(t) = 0$$

(a)   What second-order differential equation is implied by this version of the model?
(b)   Find the definite solution, $D(t)$.
(c)   Analyze the burden function $B(t)$ for this case.

2   How would you evaluate the limit of $B(t)$, as $t \to \infty$, in the second (repeated-root) case of the burden-of-debt model without using L'Hôpital's rule?

15.3   Complex Numbers and Circular Functions

The two cases of the burden-of-debt model illustrate, respectively, the cases of distinct real characteristic roots and of repeated real roots, which we are well equipped to handle. In the present section, we shall study the concepts of complex numbers (and circular functions), so that we shall be prepared to handle the case of complex roots as well.

imaginary and complex numbers   The square of a real number—whether positive or negative—is always positive. Thus, only a positive number can have a real-valued square root. Conceptually, however, we can define a number $i \equiv \sqrt{-1}$, which when squared will equal -1. Being the square root of a negative number, i is obviously not real-valued; it is therefore referred to as an *imaginary number*. With it at our disposal, we may also write a host of other imaginary numbers, such as $\sqrt{-9} = \sqrt{9}\sqrt{-1} = 3i$ and $\sqrt{-2} = \sqrt{2}\,i$.

Extending its application a step further, we may construct yet another type of number—one that contains a *real* part as well as an *imaginary* part, such as $(8 + i)$ and $(3 + 5i)$. Known as *complex numbers*, these can be represented generally in the form $(h + vi)$, where h and v are two real numbers.[1] Of course, in case $v = 0$, the complex number will reduce to a real number, whereas if $h = 0$, it will become an imaginary number. Thus the *set of all real numbers* (call it **R**) constitutes a subset of the *set of all complex numbers* (call it **C**). Similarly, the *set of all imaginary numbers* (call it **I**) also constitutes a subset of **C**. That is, $R \subset C$, and $I \subset C$. Furthermore, since the terms *real* and *imaginary* are mutually exclusive, the sets **R** and **I** must be disjoint; that is $R \cap I = \varnothing$.

A complex number $(h + vi)$ can be represented graphically in what is called an *Argand diagram*, as illustrated in Fig. 15.2. By plotting h horizontally on the *real axis* and v vertically on the *imaginary axis*, the number $(h + vi)$ can be specified by the point (h,v), which we have alternatively labeled C. The values of h and v are algebraically signed, of course, so that if $h < 0$, the point C will be to the left of the point of origin; similarly, a negative v will mean a location below the horizontal axis.

Given the values of h and v, we can also calculate the length of the line OC by applying Pythagoras' theorem, which states that the square of the hypotenuse of a right-angled triangle is the sum of the squares of the other two sides. Denoting the length of OC by R (for radius vector), we have

$$(15.17) \qquad R^2 = h^2 + v^2 \qquad \text{and} \qquad R = \sqrt{h^2 + v^2}$$

---

[1] We employ the symbols h (for horizontal) and v (for vertical) in the general complex-number notation, because we shall presently plot the values of h and v, respectively, on the horizontal and vertical axes of a two-dimensional diagram.

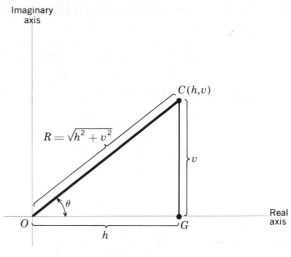

FIGURE 15.2

where the square root is always taken to be positive. The value of R is sometimes called the *absolute value*, or *modulus*, of the complex number $(h + vi)$. (Note that changing the signs of h and v will produce no effect on the absolute value of the complex number, R.) Like h and v, then, R is real-valued, but unlike these other values, R is always positive. We shall find the number R to be of great importance in the ensuing discussion.

complex roots   Meanwhile, let us return to formula (15.5) and examine the case of complex characteristic roots. When the coefficients of a second-order differential equation are such that $a_1{}^2 < 4a_2$, the square-root expression in (15.5) can be written as

$$\sqrt{a_1{}^2 - 4a_2} = \sqrt{4a_2 - a_1{}^2}\sqrt{-1} = \sqrt{4a_2 - a_1{}^2}\,i$$

Hence, if we adopt the shorthand

$$h = \frac{-a_1}{2} \quad \text{and} \quad v = \frac{\sqrt{4a_2 - a_1{}^2}}{2}$$

the two roots can be denoted by a pair of *conjugate complex numbers*:

$$r_1, r_2 = h \pm vi$$

These two complex roots are said to be "conjugate" because they always appear together, one being the *sum* of h and vi, and the other being the *difference* between h and vi. Note that they share the same absolute value R.

Example 1   Find the roots of the characteristic equation $r^2 + r + 4 = 0$. Applying the familiar formula, we have

$$r_1, r_2 = \frac{-1 \pm \sqrt{-15}}{2} = \frac{-1 \pm \sqrt{15}\sqrt{-1}}{2} = \frac{-1}{2} \pm \frac{\sqrt{15}}{2}i$$

which constitute a pair of conjugate complex numbers.

As before, we can use (15.6) to check our calculations. If correct, we should have $r_1 + r_2 = -a_1 (= -1)$ and $r_1 r_2 = a_2 (= 4)$. Since we do find

$$r_1 + r_2 = \left(\frac{-1}{2} + \frac{\sqrt{15}\,i}{2}\right) + \left(\frac{-1}{2} - \frac{\sqrt{15}\,i}{2}\right)$$

$$= \frac{-1}{2} + \frac{-1}{2} = -1$$

and $$r_1 r_2 = \left(\frac{-1}{2} + \frac{\sqrt{15}\,i}{2}\right)\left(\frac{-1}{2} - \frac{\sqrt{15}\,i}{2}\right)$$

$$= \left(\frac{-1}{2}\right)^2 - \left(\frac{\sqrt{15}\,i}{2}\right)^2 = \frac{1}{4} - \frac{-15}{4} = 4$$

our calculation is indeed validated.

Even in the complex-root case (Case 3), we may express the complementary function of a differential equation according to (15.7); that is,

$$(15.18) \qquad y_c = A_5 e^{(h+vi)t} + A_6 e^{(h-vi)t} = e^{ht}(A_5 e^{vit} + A_6 e^{-vit})$$

But a new feature has been introduced: the number i now appears in the exponents of the two expressions in parentheses. How do we interpret such imaginary exponential functions?

To facilitate their interpretation, it will prove helpful first to transform these expressions into equivalent *circular-function* forms. As we shall presently see, the latter functions characteristically involve periodic fluctuations of a variable. Consequently, the complementary function (15.18), being translatable into circular-function forms, can also be expected to generate a cyclical type of time path.

circular functions   Consider a circle with its center at the point of origin and with a radius of length R, as shown in Fig. 15.3. Let the radius, like the hand of a clock, rotate in the counterclockwise direction. Starting from the position OA, it will gradually move into the position OP, followed successively by such positions as OB, OC, and OD; and at the end of a cycle, it will return to OA. Thereafter, the cycle will simply repeat itself.

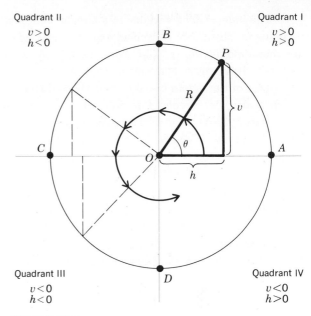

FIGURE 15.3

When in a specific position—say, OP—the clock hand will make a definite angle θ with line OA, and the tip of the hand (P) will determine a vertical distance v and a horizontal distance h. As the angle θ changes during the process of rotation, v and h will vary, although R will not. Thus the ratios v/R and h/R must change with θ; that is, these two ratios are both functions of the angle θ. Specifically, v/R and h/R are called, respectively, the *sine* (function) of θ and the *cosine* (function) of θ:

$$(15.19) \qquad \sin \theta \equiv \frac{v}{R}$$

$$(15.19') \qquad \cos \theta \equiv \frac{h}{R}$$

In view of their connection with a circle, these functions are referred to as *circular functions*. Since they are also associated with a triangle, however, they are alternatively called *trigonometric functions*. Another (and fancier) name for them is *sinusoidal functions*. The sine and cosine functions are not the only circular functions; another frequently encountered one is the *tangent* function, defined as

$$\tan \theta = \frac{\sin \theta}{\cos \theta} = \frac{v}{h} \qquad (h \neq 0)$$

Our major concern here, however, will be with the sine and cosine functions.

The independent variable in a circular function is the angle θ, so that the mapping involved here is from an *angle* to a *ratio of two distances*. Usually, angles are measured in *degrees* (for example, 30, 45, and 90°); in analytical work, however, it is more convenient to measure angles in *radians* instead. The advantage of the radian measure stems from the fact that, when θ is so measured, the derivatives of circular functions will come out in neater expressions—much as the base e gives us neater derivatives for exponential and logarithmic functions. But just how much is a radian? To explain this, let us return to Fig. 15.3, where we have drawn the point P so that the length of the *arc AP* is exactly equal to the radius R. A *radian* (abbreviated as *rad*) can then be defined as the size of the angle θ (in Fig. 15.3) formed by such an R-length arc. Since the circumference of the circle has a total length of $2\pi R$ (where $\pi = 3.14159\ldots$), a complete circle must involve an angle of 2π rad altogether. In terms of degrees, however, a complete circle makes an angle of $360°$; thus, by equating $360°$ to 2π rad, we can arrive at the following conversion table:

Degrees	360	270	180	90	45	0
Radians	2π	$\dfrac{3\pi}{2}$	π	$\dfrac{\pi}{2}$	$\dfrac{\pi}{4}$	0

properties of the sine and cosine functions   Given the length of R, the value of $\sin\theta$ hinges upon the way the value of v changes in response to changes in the angle θ. In the starting position OA, we have $v = 0$. As the clock hand moves counterclockwise, v starts to assume an increasing positive value, culminating in the maximum value of $v = R$ when the hand coincides with OB, that is, when $\theta = \pi/2$ rad $(= 90°)$. Further movement will gradually shorten v, until its value becomes zero when the hand is in the position OC—when $\theta = \pi$ rad $(= 180°)$. As the hand enters the third quadrant, v begins to assume negative values; in the position OD, we have $v = -R$. In the fourth quadrant, v is still negative, but it will increase from the value of $-R$ toward the value of $v = 0$, which is attained when the hand returns to OA—that is, when $\theta = 2\pi$ rad $(= 360°)$. The cycle then repeats itself.

When these illustrative values of v are substituted into (15.19), we can obtain the results shown in the "$\sin\theta$" row of Table 15.1. For a more complete

TABLE 15.1

θ	0	$\dfrac{1}{2}\pi$	π	$\dfrac{3}{2}\pi$	2π
$\sin\theta$	0	1	0	-1	0
$\cos\theta$	1	0	-1	0	1

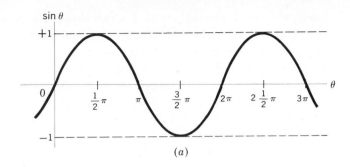

(a)

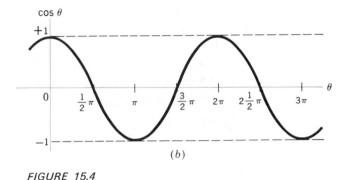

(b)

FIGURE 15.4

description of the sine function, however, the reader is referred to the graph in Fig. 15.4a, where the values of sin θ are plotted against those of θ (expressed in radians).

The value of cos θ, in contrast, depends instead upon the way that h changes in response to changes in θ. In the starting position OA, we have $h = R$. Then h gradually shrinks, till $h = 0$ when $\theta = \pi/2$ (position OB). In the second quadrant, h turns negative, and when $\theta = \pi$ (position OC), $h = -R$. The value of h gradually increases from $-R$ to zero in the third quadrant, and when $\theta = 3\pi/2$ (position OD), we find that $h = 0$. In the fourth quadrant, h turns positive again, and when the hand returns to position OA ($\theta = 2\pi$), we again have $h = R$. The cycle then repeats itself.

The substitution of these illustrative values of h into (15.19′) yields the results in the bottom row of Table 15.1, but Fig. 15.4b gives a more complete depiction of the cosine function.

The sin θ and cos θ functions share the same domain, namely, the set of all real numbers (radian measures of θ). In this connection, it may be pointed out that a *negative* angle simply refers to the reverse rotation of the clock hand; for instance, a clockwise movement from OA to OD in Fig. 15.3 generates an angle of $-\pi/2$ rad ($= -90°$). There is also a common range for the two functions, namely, the closed interval $[-1,1]$. For this reason, the graphs of $\sin \theta$ and $\cos \theta$ are, in Fig. 15.4, confined to a definite horizontal band.

A major distinguishing property of the sine and cosine functions is that both are *periodic*; their values will repeat themselves for every 2π rad (a complete circle) the angle θ travels through. Each function is therefore said to have a *period* of 2π. In view of this periodicity feature, the following equations hold (for n any integer):

$$\sin (\theta + 2n\pi) = \sin \theta \qquad \cos (\theta + 2n\pi) = \cos \theta$$

That is, adding (or subtracting) any integer multiple of 2π to any angle θ will affect neither the value of $\sin \theta$ nor that of $\cos \theta$.

The graphs of the sine and cosine functions indicate a constant range of fluctuation in each period, namely, ± 1. This is sometimes alternately described by saying that the *amplitude* of fluctuation is 1. By virtue of the identical period and the identical amplitude, we see that the $\cos \theta$ curve, if shifted rightward by $\pi/2$, will be exactly coincident with the $\sin \theta$ curve. These two curves are therefore said to differ only in *phase*, i.e., to differ only in the location of the peak in each period. Symbolically, this fact may be stated by the equation

$$\cos \theta = \sin \left(\theta + \frac{\pi}{2} \right)$$

The sine and cosine functions obey certain identities. Among these, the more frequently used are

(15.20)
$$\sin (-\theta) \equiv -\sin \theta$$
$$\cos (-\theta) \equiv \cos \theta$$

(15.21)
$$\sin^2 \theta + \cos^2 \theta \equiv 1 \qquad [\text{where } \sin^2 \theta \equiv (\sin \theta)^2, \text{ etc.}]$$

(15.22)
$$\sin (\theta_1 \pm \theta_2) \equiv \sin \theta_1 \cos \theta_2 \pm \cos \theta_1 \sin \theta_2$$
$$\cos (\theta_1 \pm \theta_2) \equiv \cos \theta_1 \cos \theta_2 \mp \sin \theta_1 \sin \theta_2$$

The pair of identities (15.20) serves to underscore the fact that the cosine function is symmetrical with respect to the vertical axis (that is, θ and $-\theta$ always yield the same cosine value), while the sine function is not. Shown in (15.21) is the fact that, for any magnitude of θ, the sum of the squares of its sine and cosine is always unity. And the set of identities in (15.22) gives the sine and cosine of the sum and difference of two angles θ_1 and θ_2. These identities will prove useful in the subsequent discussion.

Finally, a word about derivatives. Being continuous and smooth, both $\sin \theta$ and $\cos \theta$ are differentiable. The derivatives, $d(\sin \theta)/d\theta$ and $d(\cos \theta)/d\theta$, are obtainable by taking the limits, respectively, of the difference quotients $\Delta(\sin \theta)/\Delta \theta$ and $\Delta(\cos \theta)/\Delta \theta$ as $\Delta \theta \to 0$. The results, stated here without proof, are

$$(15.23) \qquad \frac{d}{d\theta} \sin \theta = \cos \theta$$

$$(15.23') \qquad \frac{d}{d\theta} \cos \theta = -\sin \theta$$

It should be emphasized, however, that these derivative formulas are valid only when θ is measured in radians; if measured in degrees, for instance, (15.23) will become $d(\sin \theta)/d\theta = (\pi/180) \cos \theta$ instead. It is for the sake of getting rid of the factor $(\pi/180)$ that radian measures are preferred to degree measures in analytical work.

Example 2   Find the slope of the sin θ curve at $\theta = \pi/2$. The slope of the sine curve is given by its derivative ($= \cos \theta$). Thus, at $\theta = \pi/2$, the slope should be $\cos (\pi/2) = 0$. The reader may refer to Fig. 15.4 for verification of this result.

Example 3   Find the second derivative of sin θ. From (15.23), we know that the first derivative of sin θ is cos θ, therefore the desired second derivative is

$$\frac{d^2}{d\theta^2} \sin \theta = \frac{d}{d\theta} \cos \theta = -\sin \theta$$

Euler relations   In Sec. 9.5, it was shown that any function which has finite, continuous derivatives up to the desired order can be expanded into a polynomial function. Moreover, if the remainder term R_n in the resulting Taylor series (expansion at any point x_0) or Maclaurin series (expansion at $x_0 = 0$) happens to approach zero as the number of terms n becomes infinite, the polynomial may be written as an infinite series. We shall now expand the sine and cosine functions and then attempt to show how the imaginary exponential expressions encountered in (15.18) can be transformed into circular functions having equivalent expansions.

For the sine function, write $\phi(\theta) = \sin \theta$; it then follows that $\phi(0) = \sin 0 = 0$. By successive derivation, we can get

$$\left. \begin{aligned} \phi'(\theta) &= \cos \theta \\ \phi''(\theta) &= -\sin \theta \\ \phi'''(\theta) &= -\cos \theta \\ \phi^{(4)}(\theta) &= \sin \theta \\ \phi^{(5)}(\theta) &= \cos \theta \\ &\vdots \end{aligned} \right\} \Rightarrow \left\{ \begin{aligned} \phi'(0) &= \cos 0 = 1 \\ \phi''(0) &= -\sin 0 = 0 \\ \phi'''(0) &= -\cos 0 = -1 \\ \phi^{(4)}(0) &= \sin 0 = 0 \\ \phi^{(5)}(0) &= \cos 0 = 1 \\ &\vdots \end{aligned} \right.$$

When substituted into (9.14), where θ now replaces x, these will give us the following Maclaurin series with remainder:

$$\sin \theta = 0 + \theta + 0 - \frac{\theta^3}{3!} + 0 + \frac{\theta^5}{5!} + \cdots + \frac{\phi^{(n+1)}(p)}{(n+1)!} \theta^{n+1}$$

Now, the expression $\phi^{(n+1)}(p)$ in the last (remainder) term, which represents the $(n+1)$st derivative evaluated at $\theta = p$, can only take the form of $\pm \cos p$ or $\pm \sin p$ and, as such, can only take a value in the interval $[-1,1]$, regardless of how large n is. On the other hand, $(n+1)!$ will grow rapidly as $n \to \infty$—in fact, much more rapidly than θ^{n+1} as n increases. Hence, the remainder term will approach zero as $n \to \infty$, and we can therefore express the Maclaurin series as an infinite series:

$$(15.24) \qquad \sin \theta = \theta - \frac{\theta^3}{3!} + \frac{\theta^5}{5!} - \frac{\theta^7}{7!} + \cdots$$

Similarly, if we write $\psi(\theta) = \cos \theta$, then $\psi(0) = \cos 0 = 1$, and the successive derivatives will be

$$\left. \begin{aligned} \psi'(\theta) &= -\sin \theta \\ \psi''(\theta) &= -\cos \theta \\ \psi'''(\theta) &= \sin \theta \\ \psi^{(4)}(\theta) &= \cos \theta \\ \psi^{(5)}(\theta) &= -\sin \theta \\ &\vdots \end{aligned} \right\} \Rightarrow \left(\begin{aligned} \psi'(0) &= -\sin 0 = 0 \\ \psi''(0) &= -\cos 0 = -1 \\ \psi'''(0) &= \sin 0 = 0 \\ \psi^{(4)}(0) &= \cos 0 = 1 \\ \psi^{(5)}(0) &= -\sin 0 = 0 \\ &\vdots \end{aligned} \right.$$

On the basis of these derivatives, we can expand $\cos \theta$ as follows:

$$\cos \theta = 1 + 0 - \frac{\theta^2}{2!} + 0 + \frac{\theta^4}{4!} + \cdots + \frac{\psi^{(n+1)}(p)}{(n+1)!} \theta^{n+1}$$

Since the remainder term will again tend toward zero as $n \to \infty$, the cosine function is also expressible as an infinite series, as follows:

$$(15.25) \qquad \cos \theta = 1 - \frac{\theta^2}{2!} + \frac{\theta^4}{4!} - \frac{\theta^6}{6!} + \cdots$$

The reader must have noticed that, with (15.24) and (15.25) at hand, we are now capable of constructing a table of sine and cosine values for all possible values of θ (in radians). However, our immediate interest lies in finding the relationship between imaginary exponential expressions and circular functions. To this end, let us now expand the two exponential expressions $e^{i\theta}$ and $e^{-i\theta}$. The reader will recognize that these are but special cases of the expression e^x, which has previously been shown, in (10.6), to have the expansion

$$e^x = 1 + x + \frac{1}{2!} x^2 + \frac{1}{3!} x^3 + \frac{1}{4!} x^4 + \cdots$$

Letting $x = i\theta$, therefore, we can immediately obtain

$$e^{i\theta} = 1 + i\theta + \frac{(i\theta)^2}{2!} + \frac{(i\theta)^3}{3!} + \frac{(i\theta)^4}{4!} + \frac{(i\theta)^5}{5!} + \cdots$$

$$= 1 + i\theta - \frac{\theta^2}{2!} - \frac{i\theta^3}{3!} + \frac{\theta^4}{4!} + \frac{i\theta^5}{5!} - \cdots$$

$$= \left(1 - \frac{\theta^2}{2!} + \frac{\theta^4}{4!} - \cdots\right) + i\left(\theta - \frac{\theta^3}{3!} + \frac{\theta^5}{5!} - \cdots\right)$$

Similarly, by setting $x = -i\theta$, the following result will emerge:

$$e^{-i\theta} = 1 - i\theta + \frac{(-i\theta)^2}{2!} + \frac{(-i\theta)^3}{3!} + \frac{(-i\theta)^4}{4!} + \frac{(-i\theta)^5}{5!} + \cdots$$

$$= 1 - i\theta - \frac{\theta^2}{2!} + \frac{i\theta^3}{3!} + \frac{\theta^4}{4!} - \frac{i\theta^5}{5!} - \cdots$$

$$= \left(1 - \frac{\theta^2}{2!} + \frac{\theta^4}{4!} - \cdots\right) - i\left(\theta - \frac{\theta^3}{3!} + \frac{\theta^5}{5!} - \cdots\right)$$

By substituting (15.24) and (15.25) into the above two results, the following pair of identities—known as the *Euler relations*—can readily be established:

(15.26) $e^{i\theta} \equiv \cos\theta + i\sin\theta$

(15.26′) $e^{-i\theta} \equiv \cos\theta - i\sin\theta$

These will enable us to translate any imaginary exponential function into an equivalent linear combination of sine and cosine functions, and vice versa.

Example 4   Find the value of $e^{i\pi}$. First let us convert this expression into a trigonometric expression. By setting $\theta = \pi$ in (15.26), it is found that $e^{i\pi} = \cos\pi + i\sin\pi$. Since $\cos\pi = -1$ and $\sin\pi = 0$, it follows that $e^{i\pi} = -1$.

Example 5   Show that $e^{-i\pi/2} = -i$. Setting $\theta = \pi/2$ in (15.26′), we have

$$e^{-i\pi/2} = \cos\frac{\pi}{2} - i\sin\frac{\pi}{2} = 0 - i(1) = -i$$

alternative representations of complex numbers   So far, we have represented a pair of conjugate complex numbers in the general form $(h \pm vi)$. Since h and v refer to the abscissa and ordinate in the cartesian coordinate system of an Argand diagram, the expression $(h \pm vi)$ represents the *cartesian form* of a pair of conjugate complex numbers. As a by-product of the discussion of circular functions and Euler relations, we can now express $(h \pm vi)$ in two other ways.

Referring to Fig. 15.2, we see that as soon as h and v are specified, the angle θ and the value of R will also be determinate. Since a given θ and a given R can together identify a unique point in the Argand diagram, we may employ θ and R to specify the particular pair of complex numbers. By rewriting the definitions of the sine and cosine functions in (15.19) and (15.19') as

$$(15.27) \qquad v = R \sin \theta \qquad \text{and} \qquad h = R \cos \theta$$

the conjugate complex numbers $(h \pm vi)$ can be transformed as follows:

$$h \pm vi = R \cos \theta \pm Ri \sin \theta = R(\cos \theta \pm i \sin \theta)$$

By doing so, we have in effect switched from the cartesian coordinates of the complex numbers (h and v) to what are called their *polar coordinates* (R and θ). The right-hand expression in the above equation, accordingly, exemplifies the *polar form* of a pair of conjugate complex numbers.

Furthermore, in view of the Euler relations, the polar form may also be rewritten into the *exponential form* as follows: $R(\cos \theta \pm i \sin \theta) = Re^{\pm i\theta}$. Hence, we have a total of three alternative representations of the conjugate complex numbers:

$$(15.28) \qquad h \pm vi = R(\cos \theta \pm i \sin \theta) = Re^{\pm i\theta}$$

If we are given the values of R and θ, the transformation to h and v is straightforward: we use the two equations in (15.27). What about the reverse transformation? With given values of h and v, no difficulty arises in finding the corresponding value of R, which is equal to $\sqrt{h^2 + v^2}$. But a slight complication arises in regard to θ: the desired value of θ (in radians) is that which satisfies the two conditions $\cos \theta = h/R$ and $\sin \theta = v/R$; but for given values of h and v, θ is not unique! (Why?) Fortunately, the problem is not serious, for by confining our attention to the interval $[0,2\pi)$ in the domain, the indeterminacy is quickly resolved.

Example 6   Find the cartesian form of the complex number $5e^{3i\pi/2}$. Here we have $R = 5$ and $\theta = 3\pi/2$; hence, by (15.27) and Table 15.1,

$$h = 5 \cos \frac{3\pi}{2} = 0 \qquad \text{and} \qquad v = 5 \sin \frac{3\pi}{2} = -5$$

The cartesian form is thus simply $h + vi = -5i$.

Example 7   Find the polar and exponential forms of $(1 + \sqrt{3}\,i)$. In this case, we have $h = 1$ and $v = \sqrt{3}$; thus $R = \sqrt{1 + 3} = 2$. Table 15.1 is of no use in locating the value of θ this time, but Table 15.2, which lists some additional

Dynamic Analysis

selected values of $\sin \theta$ and $\cos \theta$, will help. Specifically, we are seeking the value of θ such that $\cos \theta = h/R = \frac{1}{2}$ and $\sin \theta = v/R = \sqrt{3}/2$. The value $\theta = \pi/3$ meets the requirements. Thus, according to (15.28), the desired transformation is

$$1 + \sqrt{3}\,i = 2\left(\cos \frac{\pi}{3} + i \sin \frac{\pi}{3}\right) = 2e^{i\pi/3}$$

Before leaving this topic, let us note an important extension of the result in (15.28). Supposing that we have the nth power of a complex number—say, $(h + vi)^n$—how do we write its polar and exponential forms? The exponential form is the easier to derive. Since $h + vi = Re^{i\theta}$, it follows that

$$(h + vi)^n = (Re^{i\theta})^n = R^n e^{in\theta}$$

Similarly, we can write

$$(h - vi)^n = (Re^{-i\theta})^n = R^n e^{-in\theta}$$

The reader should observe that the power n has brought about two changes: (1) R now becomes R^n, and (2) θ now becomes $n\theta$. When these two changes are inserted into the polar form in (15.28), we find that

$$(15.28') \qquad (h \pm vi)^n = R^n(\cos n\theta \pm i \sin n\theta)$$

That is,

$$[R(\cos \theta \pm i \sin \theta)]^n = R^n(\cos n\theta \pm i \sin n\theta)$$

Known as *De Moivre's theorem*, this result indicates that, to raise a complex number to the nth power, one must simply modify its polar coordinates by raising R to the nth power and multiplying θ by n.

TABLE 15.2

θ	$\dfrac{\pi}{6}$	$\dfrac{\pi}{4}$		$\dfrac{\pi}{3}$	$\dfrac{3\pi}{4}$
$\sin \theta$	$\dfrac{1}{2}$	$\dfrac{1}{\sqrt{2}}$	$\left(= \dfrac{\sqrt{2}}{2}\right)$	$\dfrac{\sqrt{3}}{2}$	$\dfrac{1}{\sqrt{2}}$ $\left(= \dfrac{\sqrt{2}}{2}\right)$
$\cos \theta$	$\dfrac{\sqrt{3}}{2}$	$\dfrac{1}{\sqrt{2}}$	$\left(= \dfrac{\sqrt{2}}{2}\right)$	$\dfrac{1}{2}$	$\dfrac{-1}{\sqrt{2}}$ $\left(= \dfrac{-\sqrt{2}}{2}\right)$

EXERCISE 15.3

1   Find the roots of the following quadratic equations:

(a) $r^2 - 3r + 9 = 0$ (c) $2x^2 + x + 8 = 0$

(b) $r^2 + 4r + 13 = 0$

2   (a)   How many degrees are there in a radian?

(b)   How many radians are there in a degree?

3   With reference to Fig. 15.3, and by using Pythagoras' theorem, prove that

(a) $\sin^2 \theta + \cos^2 \theta \equiv 1$ (b) $\sin \dfrac{\pi}{4} = \cos \dfrac{\pi}{4} = \dfrac{1}{\sqrt{2}}$

(*Hint*: When $\theta = \pi/4$, the line OP makes a 45° line.)

4   By means of the identities (15.20), (15.21), and (15.22), show that:

(a) $\sin 2\theta \equiv 2 \sin \theta \cos \theta$

(b) $\cos 2\theta \equiv 1 - 2 \sin^2 \theta$

(c) $\sin (\theta_1 + \theta_2) + \sin (\theta_1 - \theta_2) \equiv 2 \sin \theta_1 \cos \theta_2$

(d) $1 + \tan^2 \theta \equiv \dfrac{1}{\cos^2 \theta}$

(e) $\sin \left(\dfrac{\pi}{2} - \theta \right) \equiv \cos \theta$

(f) $\cos \left(\dfrac{\pi}{2} - \theta \right) \equiv \sin \theta$

5   By applying the chain rule:

(a)   Write out the derivative formulas for $\dfrac{d}{d\theta} \sin f(\theta)$ and $\dfrac{d}{d\theta} \cos f(\theta)$, where $f(\theta)$ is a function of θ.

(b)   Find the derivatives of $\cos (\theta^3)$, $\sin (\theta^2 + 3\theta)$, $\cos (e^\theta)$, and $\sin \left(\dfrac{1}{\theta} \right)$.

6   From the Euler relations, deduce that:

(a) $e^{-i\pi} = -1$ (c) $e^{i\pi/4} = \dfrac{1}{\sqrt{2}} (1 + i)$

(b) $e^{i\pi/3} = \dfrac{1}{2} (1 + \sqrt{3}\, i)$ (d) $e^{-3i\pi/4} = \dfrac{-1}{\sqrt{2}} (1 + i)$

Dynamic Analysis

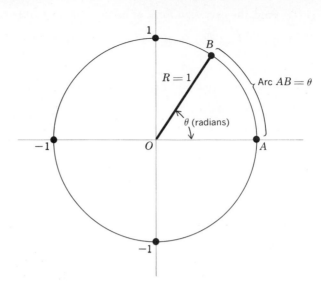

FIGURE 15.5

Furthermore, if we employ the shorthand symbols

$$\alpha \equiv A_5 + A_6 \qquad \text{and} \qquad \beta \equiv (A_5 - A_6)i$$

it is possible to simplify (15.29) into[1]

$$(15.29') \qquad y_c = e^{ht}(\alpha \cos vt + \beta \sin vt)$$

where the new arbitrary constants α and β are later to be definitized.

The meticulous reader may feel somewhat uneasy about the substitution of θ by vt in the foregoing procedure. The variable θ measures an angle, but vt is a magnitude in units of t (in our context, time). Therefore, how can we make the substitution $\theta = vt$? The answer to this question can best be explained with reference to the *unit circle* (a circle with radius $R = 1$) in Fig. 15.5. True, we have been using θ to designate an angle; but since the angle is measured in radian units, the value of θ is always the ratio of the length of arc AB to the radius R. When $R = 1$, we have specifically

$$\theta \equiv \frac{\text{arc } AB}{R} \equiv \frac{\text{arc } AB}{1} \equiv \text{arc } AB$$

---

[1] The fact that, in defining β, we include in it the imaginary number i is by no means an attempt to "sweep the dirt under the rug." We are justified in doing so because β, being an *arbitrary* constant, can take an imaginary as well as a real value. Nor is it necessarily true that, as defined, β will turn out to be imaginary. Actually, if A_5 and A_6 are a pair of conjugate complex numbers (say, $A_5, A_6 = m \pm ni$), then α and β will both be real—$\alpha = A_5 + A_6 = 2m$ and $\beta = (A_5 - A_6)i = (2ni)i = -2n$—even though the number i appears in the definition of β.

Dynamic Analysis

7 Find the cartesian form of each complex number:

(a) $2\left(\cos\dfrac{\pi}{6} + i\sin\dfrac{\pi}{6}\right)$ (b) $4e^{i\pi/3}$ (c) $\sqrt{2}\,e^{-i\pi/4}$

8 Find the polar and exponential forms of the following complex numbers:

(a) $\dfrac{3}{2} + \dfrac{3\sqrt{3}}{2}\,i$ (b) $4(\sqrt{3} + i)$

15.4 Analysis of the Complex-Root Case

With the concepts of complex numbers and circular functions at our disposal, we are now prepared to approach the complex-root case (Case 3), referred to in Sec. 15.1. The reader will recall that the classification of the three cases, according to the nature of the characteristic roots, is concerned only with the complementary function of a differential equation. Thus, we can continue to focus our attention on the reduced equation

$$y''(t) + a_1 y'(t) + a_2 y = 0 \qquad \text{[reproduced from (15.4)]}$$

the complementary function When the values of the coefficients a_1 and a_2 are such that $a_1{}^2 < 4a_2$, the characteristic roots will be the pair of conjugate complex numbers

$$r_1, r_2 = h \pm vi$$

where $\qquad h = -\dfrac{1}{2}a_1 \qquad$ and $\qquad v = \dfrac{1}{2}\sqrt{4a_2 - a_1{}^2}$

The complementary function, as was already previewed, will thus be in the form

$$y_c = e^{ht}(A_5 e^{vit} + A_6 e^{-vit}) \qquad \text{[reproduced from (15.18)]}$$

Let us first transform the imaginary exponential expressions in the parentheses into equivalent trigonometric expressions, so that we may interpret the complementary function as a circular function. This may be accomplished by using the Euler relations. Letting $\theta = vt$ in (15.26) and (15.26'), we find that

$$e^{vit} = \cos vt + i\sin vt \qquad \text{and} \qquad e^{-vit} = \cos vt - i\sin vt$$

From these, it follows that the complementary function in (15.18) can be rewritten as

$$(15.29) \qquad y_c = e^{ht}[A_5(\cos vt + i\sin vt) + A_6(\cos vt - i\sin vt)]$$
$$= e^{ht}[(A_5 + A_6)\cos vt + (A_5 - A_6)i\sin vt]$$

Higher-Order Differential Equations **529**

In other words, θ is not only the radian measure of the angle but also the length of the arc AB, which is a number rather than an angle. If the passing of time is charted on the circumference of the unit circle (counterclockwise), rather than on a straight line as we do in plotting a time series, then it really makes no difference whatsoever whether we consider the lapse of time as an increase in the radian measure of the angle θ or as a lengthening of the arc AB. Even if $R \neq 1$, moreover, the same line of reasoning can apply, except that in that case θ will be equal to (arc $AB)/R$ instead; i.e., the angle θ and the arc AB will bear a fixed proportion to each other, instead of being equal. Thus, the substitution $\theta = vt$ is indeed legitimate.

an example of solution   Let us find the solution of the differential equation

$$y''(t) + 2y'(t) + 17y = 34$$

with the initial conditions $y(0) = 3$ and $y'(0) = 11$.

Since $a_1 = 2$, $a_2 = 17$, and $b = 34$, we can immediately find the particular integral to be

$$y_p = \frac{b}{a_2} = \frac{34}{17} = 2 \qquad \text{[by (15.3)]}$$

Moreover, since $a_1{}^2 = 4 < 4a_2 = 68$, the characteristic roots will be the pair of conjugate complex numbers $(h \pm vi)$, where

$$h = -\frac{1}{2}a_1 = -1 \qquad \text{and} \qquad v = \frac{1}{2}\sqrt{4a_2 - a_1{}^2} = \frac{1}{2}\sqrt{64} = 4$$

Hence, by (15.29'), the complementary function is

$$y_c = e^{-t}(\alpha \cos 4t + \beta \sin 4t)$$

Combining y_c and y_p, the general solution can be expressed as

$$y(t) = e^{-t}(\alpha \cos 4t + \beta \sin 4t) + 2$$

To definitize the constants α and β, we utilize the two initial conditions. First, by setting $t = 0$ in the general solution, we find that

$$y(0) = e^0(\alpha \cos 0 + \beta \sin 0) + 2$$
$$= (\alpha + 0) + 2 = \alpha + 2 \qquad \text{[$\cos 0 = 1$; $\sin 0 = 0$]}$$

By the initial condition $y(0) = 3$, we can thus specify $\alpha = 1$. Next, let us differentiate the general solution with respect to t—using the product rule and the derivative formulas (15.23) and (15.23') while bearing in mind the chain rule [Exercise 15.3-5]—to find $y'(t)$ and then $y'(0)$:

$$y'(t) = -e^{-t}(\alpha \cos 4t + \beta \sin 4t) + e^{-t}[\alpha(-4 \sin 4t) + 4\beta \cos 4t]$$

so that

$$y'(0) = -(\alpha \cos 0 + \beta \sin 0) + (-4\alpha \sin 0 + 4\beta \cos 0)$$
$$= -(\alpha + 0) + (0 + 4\beta) = 4\beta - \alpha$$

By the second initial condition $y'(0) = 11$, and in view that $\alpha = 1$, it then becomes clear that $\beta = 3$.† The definite solution is, therefore,

$$(15.30) \qquad y(t) = e^{-t}(\cos 4t + 3 \sin 4t) + 2$$

As before, the y_p component $(= 2)$ can be interpreted as the intertemporal equilibrium level of y, whereas the y_c component represents the deviation from equilibrium. Owing to the presence of circular functions in y_c, the time path (15.30) may be expected to exhibit a fluctuating pattern. But what specific pattern will it involve?

the time path   We are familiar with the paths of a simple sine or cosine function, as shown in Fig. 15.4. Now we must study the paths of certain variants and combinations of sine and cosine functions so that we can interpret, in general, the complementary function (15.29′)

$$y_c = e^{ht}(\alpha \cos vt + \beta \sin vt)$$

and, in particular, the y_c component of (15.30).

Let us first examine the term $(\alpha \cos vt)$. By itself, the expression $(\cos vt)$ is a circular function of (vt), with period 2π $(= 6.2832)$ and amplitude 1. The period of 2π means that the graph will repeat its configuration every time that (vt) increases by 2π. When t alone is taken as the independent variable, however, repetition will occur every time t increases by $2\pi/v$, so that with reference to t— as is appropriate in dynamic economic analysis—we shall consider the period of $(\cos vt)$ to be $2\pi/v$. (The amplitude, however, remains at 1.) Now, when a multiplicative constant α is attached to $(\cos vt)$, it will cause the range of fluctuation to change from ± 1 to $\pm \alpha$. Thus the amplitude now becomes α, though the period is unaffected by this constant. In short, $(\alpha \cos vt)$ is a cosine function of t, with period $2\pi/v$ and amplitude α. By the same token, $(\beta \sin vt)$ is a sine function of t, with period $2\pi/v$ and amplitude β.

There being a common period, the sum $(\alpha \cos vt + \beta \sin vt)$ will also display a repeating cycle every time t increases by $2\pi/v$. To show this more rigorously, let us note that for given values of α and β we can always find two constants A

† Note that, here, β indeed turns out to be a real number, even though we have included the imaginary number i in its definition.

and ε, such that

$$\alpha = A \cos \varepsilon \qquad \text{and} \qquad \beta = -A \sin \varepsilon$$

Thus we may express the said sum as

$$\begin{aligned}
\alpha \cos vt + \beta \sin vt &= A \cos \varepsilon \cos vt - A \sin \varepsilon \sin vt \\
&= A(\cos vt \cos \varepsilon - \sin vt \sin \varepsilon) \\
&= A \cos (vt + \varepsilon) \qquad [\text{by } (15.22)]
\end{aligned}$$

This is a modified cosine function of t, with amplitude A and period $2\pi/v$, because every time that t increases by $2\pi/v$, $(vt + \varepsilon)$ will increase by 2π, which will complete a cycle on the cosine curve.

Had y_c consisted only of the expression $(\alpha \cos vt + \beta \sin vt)$, the implication would have been that the time path of y would be a never-ending, constant-amplitude fluctuation around the equilibrium value of y, as represented by y_p. But there is, in fact, also the multiplicative term e^{ht} to consider. This latter term is of major importance, for, as we shall see, it holds the key to the question of whether the time path will converge.

If $h > 0$, the value of e^{ht} will increase continually as t increases. This will produce a magnifying effect on the amplitude of $(\alpha \cos vt + \beta \sin vt)$ and cause ever-greater deviations from the equilibrium in each successive cycle. As illustrated in Fig. 15.6a, the time path will in this case be characterized by *explosive fluctuation*. If $h = 0$, on the other hand, then $e^{ht} = 1$, and the complementary function will simply be $(\alpha \cos vt + \beta \sin vt)$, which has been shown to have a constant amplitude. In this second case, each cycle will display a uniform pattern of deviation from the equilibrium as illustrated by the time path in Fig. 15.6b. This is a time path with *uniform fluctuation*. Lastly, if $h < 0$, the term e^{ht} will continually decrease as t increases, and each successive cycle will have a smaller amplitude than the preceding one, much as the way a ripple dies down. This, the stable-equilibrium case, is illustrated in Fig. 15.6c, where the time path is characterized by *damped fluctuation*. The solution in (15.30), with $h = -1$, exemplifies this last case. It should be clear that only the case of damped fluctuation can produce a *convergent* time path; in the other two cases, the time path is *nonconvergent* or *divergent*.[1]

In all three diagrams of Fig. 15.6, the intertemporal equilibrium is assumed to be stationary. If it is a moving one, the three types of time path depicted will still fluctuate around it, but since a moving equilibrium generally plots as a curve rather than a horizontal straight line, the fluctuation will take on the nature of, say, a series of business cycles around a secular trend.

---

[1] We shall use the two words *nonconvergent* and *divergent* interchangeably, although the latter is more strictly applicable to the explosive than to the uniform variety of nonconvergence.

Higher-Order Differential Equations

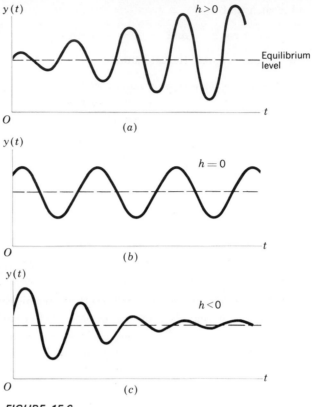

y(t)

h > 0

Equilibrium level

t

O

(a)

y(t)

h = 0

t

O

(b)

y(t)

h < 0

t

O

(c)

FIGURE 15.6

EXERCISE 15.4

Find the y_p and the y_c, the general solution, and the definite solution of each of the following:

1     $y''(t) - 4y'(t) + 8y = 0$ $y(0) = 3; y'(0) = 7$

2     $y''(t) + 4y'(t) + 8y = 2$ $y(0) = \frac{5}{4}; y'(0) = 2$

3     $y''(t) + 3y'(t) + 4y = 12$ $y(0) = 2; y'(0) = 2$

4     $y''(t) - 2y'(t) + 5y = 5$ $y(0) = 6; y'(0) = 3$

5     $y''(t) + 9y = 3$ $y(0) = 1; y'(0) = 3$

6     $2y''(t) - 12y'(t) + 20y = 40$ $y(0) = 4; y'(0) = 5$

7 Which of the above six differential equations yield time paths with (a) damped fluctuation; (b) uniform fluctuation; (c) explosive fluctuation?

15.5 A Market Model with Price Expectations

In the earlier formulation of the dynamic market model, both Q_d and Q_s are taken to be functions of the current price P alone. More realistically, however, buyers and sellers may base their market behavior not only on the current price but also on the price *trend* prevailing at the time. For the price trend is likely to lead them to certain *expectations* regarding the price level in the future, and these expectations will, in turn, influence their demand and supply decisions.

price trend and price expectations In the continuous-time context, the price-trend information is to be found primarily in the two derivatives dP/dt (whether price is rising) and d^2P/dt^2 (whether increasing at an increasing rate). To take the price trend into account, therefore, we should include these derivatives as additional variables in the demand and supply functions:

$$Q_d = D[P(t),P'(t),P''(t)]$$
$$Q_s = S[P(t),P'(t),P''(t)]$$

If we confine ourselves to the linear version of these functions and simplify the notation for the independent variables to P, P', and P'', we can write

$$
\begin{aligned}
&\text{(15.31)} &&Q_d = j_1 + k_1P + m_1P' + n_1P'' &&(j_1 > 0;\, k_1 < 0)\\
& &&Q_s = j_2 + k_2P + m_2P' + n_2P'' &&(j_2 < 0;\, k_2 > 0)
\end{aligned}
$$

where the sign restrictions on the parameters j_i and k_i are merely carryovers from the previous market models, but the parameters m_i and n_i are new.

The latter parameters, upon which we have not placed any restrictions, play a significant role in the model, for it is in these parameters that buyers' and sellers' price expectations are embodied. If $m_1 > 0$, for instance, then a rising price will cause Q_d to increase. This would suggest that buyers expect the rising price to *continue* to rise and hence they prefer to increase their purchases now, while price is still relatively low. The opposite sign, on the other hand, would signify the expectation of a prompt reversal of the price trend; hence they prefer to cut purchases now and wait for price to go down again. In either case, of course, there is an element of speculation in the buyers' behavior. The other parameters—m_2, n_1, and n_2—can be similarly interpreted.

the time path of price   Before we can find the time path of price P, we must first postulate, or otherwise determine, the pattern of change which P will follow. In the market model of Sec. 14.2, it was the assumed process of price adjustment, $dP/dt = \alpha(Q_d - Q_s)$, that supplied this information. And, as was pointed out there, that particular assumption carries the implication that the intertemporal sense and the market-clearing sense of equilibrium price are coincident. In the present model, however, we shall seek to illustrate a different type of market adjustment, namely that the market price is to be set at a level so as to clear the market at every point of time. If so, then every price reached in the market is a market-clearing equilibrium price, even though it may not qualify as an intertemporal equilibrium price. Here, therefore, the two senses of equilibrium are no longer identical with each other.

What kind of pattern of change will now emerge? If $Q_d = Q_s$ at all times, then the two functions in (15.31) can be combined into a single equation

$$(n_1 - n_2)P'' + (m_1 - m_2)P' + (k_1 - k_2)P = -(j_1 - j_2)$$

Moreover, by using the following shorthand,

(15.32) $n \equiv n_1 - n_2$ $m \equiv m_1 - m_2$ $k \equiv k_1 - k_2$ $j \equiv j_1 - j_2$

we may rewrite it (after normalizing) as

(15.33) $P'' + \left(\dfrac{m}{n}\right)P' + \left(\dfrac{k}{n}\right)P = \left(-\dfrac{j}{n}\right)$ $(n \neq 0)$

The reader will recognize this to be a differential equation of the form (15.2), with the following substitutions:

$$y = P \qquad a_1 = \frac{m}{n} \qquad a_2 = \frac{k}{n} \qquad b = -\frac{j}{n}$$

And it is (15.33) that embodies the needed information about the pattern of change of P.

The intertemporal equilibrium price implied in (15.33) is to be found from the particular integral P_p (formerly y_p), which has the value

$$P_p = \frac{b}{a_2} = -\frac{j/n}{k/n} = -\frac{j}{k} \qquad (k \neq 0)$$

By the sign restrictions on j_i and k_i, we know that $-j = j_2 - j_1 < 0$ and $k = k_1 - k_2 < 0$; it follows that $P_p = -j/k$ will be positive, as we would expect the equilibrium price to be. Moreover, j and k being (parametric) constants, the equilibrium price will represent a stationary rather than a moving equilibrium.

It remains to find the complementary function P_c (formerly y_c). Unlike the debt-burden model, the present model admits of complex as well as real characteristic roots; thus three possible cases may arise.

CASE 1   *(Distinct Real Roots)* $\left(\dfrac{m}{n}\right)^2 > 4\left(\dfrac{k}{n}\right)$

The complementary function of this case is, by (15.7),

$$P_c = A_1 e^{r_1 t} + A_2 e^{r_2 t}$$

where

$$r_1, r_2 = \frac{1}{2}\left[-\frac{m}{n} \pm \sqrt{\left(\frac{m}{n}\right)^2 - 4\left(\frac{k}{n}\right)}\right]$$

Accordingly, the general solution will be

(15.34) $P(t) = P_c + P_p = A_1 e^{r_1 t} + A_2 e^{r_2 t} - \dfrac{j}{k}$

CASE 2   *(Double Real Roots)* $\left(\dfrac{m}{n}\right)^2 = 4\left(\dfrac{k}{n}\right)$

In this case, the characteristic roots take the single value

$$r = -\frac{m}{2n}$$

thus, by (15.9), the general solution may be written as

(15.34') $P(t) = A_3 e^{-mt/2n} + A_4 t e^{-mt/2n} - \dfrac{j}{k}$

CASE 3   *(Complex Roots)* $\left(\dfrac{m}{n}\right)^2 < 4\left(\dfrac{k}{n}\right)$

In this third and last case, the characteristic roots are the pair of conjugate complex numbers

$$r_1, r_2 = h \pm vi$$

where $h = -m/2n$ and $v = \frac{1}{2}\sqrt{4(k/n) - (m/n)^2}$.
Therefore, by (15.29'), we have the general solution

(15.34'') $P(t) = e^{ht}(\alpha \cos vt + \beta \sin vt) - \dfrac{j}{k}$

Example 1   Find $P(t)$, given demand and supply functions

$$Q_d = 10 - P - 4P' + P''$$
$$Q_s = -2 + 2P + 5P' + 10P''$$

with initial conditions $P(0) = 5$ and $P'(0) = \frac{1}{2}$. The coefficients in the two equations give us

$$j = 10 - (-2) = 12 \qquad k = -1 - 2 = -3$$
$$m = -4 - 5 = -9 \qquad n = 1 - 10 = -9$$

Hence we have $(m/n)^2 = 1 < 4(k/n) = \frac{4}{3}$, which marks this as an illustration of Case 3. The specific values of h and v in the complex roots are

$$h = -\frac{1}{2} \qquad \text{and} \qquad v = \frac{1}{2}\sqrt{\frac{1}{3}} = \frac{1}{2\sqrt{3}} = \frac{\sqrt{3}}{6}$$

Substituting these into (15.34″) yields the general solution

$$P(t) = e^{-t/2}\left(\alpha \cos \frac{\sqrt{3}}{6} t + \beta \sin \frac{\sqrt{3}}{6} t\right) + 4$$

Setting $t = 0$ in this solution, we find that

$$P(0) = e^0(\alpha \cos 0 + \beta \sin 0) + 4 = \alpha + 4 \qquad [\cos 0 = 1; \sin 0 = 0]$$

Since $P(0)$ should be 5, we conclude that $\alpha = 1$. Further, by differentiating $P(t)$ and setting $t = 0$, we have

$$P'(t) = -\frac{1}{2}e^{-t/2}\left(\alpha \cos \frac{\sqrt{3}}{6} t + \beta \sin \frac{\sqrt{3}}{6} t\right)$$

$$+ e^{-t/2}\left(-\alpha \sin \frac{\sqrt{3}}{6} t + \beta \cos \frac{\sqrt{3}}{6} t\right)\frac{\sqrt{3}}{6} \qquad [\text{chain rule}]$$

$$\text{and} \qquad P'(0) = -\frac{1}{2}(\alpha + 0) + (0 + \beta)\frac{\sqrt{3}}{6} = -\frac{1}{2} + \frac{\sqrt{3}}{6}\beta \qquad [\alpha = 1]$$

Since $P'(0)$ should be $\frac{1}{2}$, we determine that $\beta = 6/\sqrt{3} = 2\sqrt{3}$. Consequently, the definite solution should be written as

$$P(t) = e^{-t/2}\left(\cos \frac{\sqrt{3}}{6} t + 2\sqrt{3} \sin \frac{\sqrt{3}}{6} t\right) + 4$$

This time path is obviously one with periodic fluctuation, the period being $2\pi/v = 2\pi \div (\sqrt{3}/6) = 21.77$. That is, there will be a cycle every time that t increases by 21.77. In view of the multiplicative term $e^{-t/2}$, moreover, the fluctuation must be damped. The time path—starting at the given initial price $P(0) = 5$—will converge, after a series of fluctuations, to the stationary intertemporal equilibrium price $\bar{P} = 4$.

dynamic stability of equilibrium To conclude this section, let us consider in general terms the question of dynamic stability for the three cases outlined above. The crucial factor, as we may expect, is to be found in the characteristic roots of the differential equation.

Take the solution (15.34) under Case 1. In order to have convergence, it is the necessary-and-sufficient condition that r_1 and r_2 both be negative, for then, and only then, will both exponential terms tend to zero as $t \to \infty$, so that $P(t) \to -j/k$. Note that, as stated, this condition does not even permit *one* of the roots to be positive or zero. If $r_1 = 2$ and $r_2 = -5$, for example, it may appear at first glance that the second root, with a higher absolute value, can outweigh the first. In actuality, however, it is the *positive* root that will dominate, because as t increases, e^{2t} will get increasingly larger, whereas e^{-5t} will dwindle away.

For Case 2, the important factors are the exponential expressions e^{rt} and te^{rt}. To have e^{rt} decrease with t, we must again require $r < 0$. But what about te^{rt}? As it turns out, the expression te^{rt} (or more generally, $t^k e^{rt}$) possesses the same general type of path as e^{rt} (for $r \neq 0$). Thus, the necessary-and-sufficient condition for convergence is, again, that the double roots r be negative. (See Exercise 15.5-5.)

In the complex-root case (Case 3), there are two parts of the conjugate roots to consider: h and v. The presence of v being confined to the trigonometric expressions in the solution (15.34''), it can affect only the period, but not the amplitude, of the path. The real part (h) of the roots, on the other hand, does enter into the convergence-determining exponential term in front. Thus, the condition for dynamic stability of equilibrium is simply $h < 0$, as we had occasion to explain.

Accordingly, we may sum up the foregoing discussion in a single statement: In all three cases analyzed, the time path will converge to the intertemporal equilibrium if and only if the *real parts* of the characteristic roots are *negative*. This criterion, in fact, enables us to ascertain the convergence of the solution of a second-order differential equation by inspecting its characteristic roots alone, without the necessity of finding the exact time path itself.

EXERCISE 15.5

1   Assume the following demand and supply in the model of this section

$$Q_d = 10 - 2P + 3P' - P''$$
$$Q_s = -5 + 3P - 7P' + 4P''$$

and initial conditions $P(0) = 5$ and $P'(0) = 3$.

(a)   Find the time path $P(t)$.

(b) What is the intertemporal equilibrium price?

(c) Does the time path converge to equilibrium? With or without periodic fluctuation?

2 Assume the demand and supply to be

$$Q_d = 9 - P + P' + 3P''$$
$$Q_s = -1 + 4P - P' + 5P''$$

and assume $P(0) = 4$ and $P'(0) = 4$.

(a) Find the time path $P(t)$.

(b) What is the intertemporal equilibrium price?

(c) Does the time path converge to equilibrium? With or without periodic fluctuation?

3 Show that, when $(m/n)^2 < 4(k/n)$, the dynamic stability of equilibrium requires that m and n be of the same algebraic sign.

4 For each of the following, find the characteristic roots, and infer the convergence or divergence of the time path without actually finding the time path:

(a) $P'' + 3P' + 2P = 4$ (d) $P'' + 2P' + 5P = 3$

(b) $P'' - 2P' - 3P = -8$ (e) $P'' - 3P' + 10P = 7$

(c) $P'' - 4P' + 4P = 9$ (f) $P'' + 5P' + 8P = 10$

5 Prove that, as $t \to \infty$, the limit of te^{rt} is zero if $r < 0$, but is infinite if $r > 0$. (*Hint:* Apply L'Hôpital's rule.)

15.6 Differential Equations with a Variable Term

In the differential equations considered above,

$$y''(t) + a_1 y'(t) + a_2 y = b$$

the right-hand term b is a constant. What if, instead of b, we have on the right a *variable term*: i.e., some function of t such as bt^2, e^{bt}, or $b \sin t$? The answer is that we must then modify our particular integral y_p. Fortunately, the complementary function is not affected by the existence of a variable term, because y_c deals only with the reduced equation, whose right side is always zero.

method of undetermined coefficients   We shall explain a method of finding y_p, known as the *method of undetermined coefficients*, which is applicable to constant-coefficient variable-term differential equations, as long as the variable term can yield, upon successive differentiation, only a *finite* number of distinct types of expression (apart from multiplicative constants). The explanation of this method can best be carried out with a concrete illustration.

Example 1   Find the particular integral of

$$(15.35) \qquad y''(t) + 5y'(t) + 3y = 6t^2 - t - 1$$

By definition, the particular integral is a value of y satisfying the given equation, i.e., a value of y that will make the left side identically equal to the right side regardless of the value of t. Since the left side contains the function $y(t)$ and the derivatives $y'(t)$ and $y''(t)$—whereas the right side contains multiples of the expressions t^2, t, and a constant—we ask: What general function form of $y(t)$, along with its first and second derivatives, will give us the three types of expression t^2, t, and a constant? The obvious answer is a function of the form $B_1t^2 + B_2t + B_3$ (where B_i are coefficients yet to be determined), for if we write the particular integral as

$$y(t) = B_1t^2 + B_2t + B_3$$

we can derive

$$(15.36) \qquad y'(t) = 2B_1t + B_2 \qquad \text{and} \qquad y''(t) = 2B_1$$

and these three equations are indeed composed of the said types of expressions. Substituting these into (15.35) and collecting terms, we get

$$\text{Left side} = (3B_1)t^2 + (10B_1 + 3B_2)t + (2B_1 + 5B_2 + 3B_3)$$

And when this is equated term-by-term to the right side, we can determine the coefficients B_i as follows:

$$\left.\begin{matrix} 3B_1 = 6 \\ 10B_1 + 3B_2 = -1 \\ 2B_1 + 5B_2 + 3B_3 = -1 \end{matrix}\right\} \Rightarrow \begin{cases} B_1 = 2 \\ B_2 = -7 \\ B_3 = 10 \end{cases}$$

Thus the desired particular integral can be written as

$$y_p = 2t^2 - 7t + 10$$

This method can work only when the number of expression types is finite. (See Exercise 15.6-1.) In general, when this prerequisite is met, the particular integral may be taken as being in the form of a linear combination of all the distinct expression types contained in the given variable term, as well as in all its derivatives.

Example 2   As a further illustration, let us find the general form for the particular integral suitable for the variable term $(b \sin t)$. Repeated differentiation yields, in this case, the successive derivatives $(b \cos t)$, $(-b \sin t)$, $(-b \cos t)$, $(b \sin t)$, etc., which involve only two distinct types of expression. We may therefore try a particular integral of the form $(B_1 \sin t + B_2 \cos t)$.

a modification   In certain cases, a complication arises in applying the method. When the coefficient of the y term in the given differential equation is zero, such as in

$$y''(t) + 5y'(t) = 6t^2 - t - 1$$

the previously used trial form for the y_p, namely, $B_1 t^2 + B_2 t + B_3$, will fail to work. The cause of this failure is that, since the $y(t)$ term is out of the picture and since only derivatives $y'(t)$ and $y''(t)$ as shown in (15.36) will be substituted into the left side, no $B_1 t^2$ term will ever appear on the left to be equated to the $6t^2$ term on the right. The way out of this kind of difficulty is to use the trial solution $t(B_1 t^2 + B_2 t + B_3)$ instead; or if this too fails, to use $t^2(B_1 t^2 + B_2 t + B_3)$, etc.

Indeed, the same trick may be employed in yet another difficult circumstance, as is illustrated in the next example.

Example 3   Find the particular integral of

$$(15.37) \qquad y''(t) + 3y'(t) - 4y = 2e^{-4t}$$

Here, the variable term is in the form of e^{-4t}, but all of its successive derivatives (namely, $-8e^{-4t}$, $32e^{-4t}$, $-128e^{-4t}$, etc.) take the same form as well. If we try the solution

$$y(t) = Be^{-4t} \qquad [\text{with } y'(t) = -4Be^{-4t} \text{ and } y''(t) = 16Be^{-4t}]$$

and substitute these into (15.37), we obtain the inauspicious result that

$$(15.38) \qquad \text{Left side} = (16 - 12 - 4)Be^{-4t} = 0$$

which obviously cannot be equated to the right-hand term $2e^{-4t}$.

What causes this to happen is the fact that the exponential coefficient in the variable term (-4) happens to be equal to one of the roots of the characteristic equation of (15.37):

$$r^2 + 3r - 4 = 0 \qquad (\text{roots } r_1, r_2 = 1, -4)$$

The characteristic equation, it will be recalled, is obtained through a process of differentiation;[1] but the expression $(16 - 12 - 4)$ in (15.38) is derived through the same process. Not surprisingly, therefore, $(16 - 12 - 4)$ is merely a specific version of $(r^2 + 3r - 4)$ with r set equal to -4. Since -4 happens to be a characteristic root, the quadratic expression

$$r^2 + 3r - 4 = 16 - 12 - 4$$

must of necessity be identically zero.

To cope with this situation, let us try instead the solution

$$y(t) = Bte^{-4t}$$

with derivatives

$$y'(t) = (1 - 4t)Be^{-4t} \quad \text{and} \quad y''(t) = (-8 + 16t)Be^{-4t}$$

Substituting these into (15.37) will now yield: left side $= -5Be^{-4t}$. When this is equated to the right side, we determine the coefficient to be $B = -2/5$. Consequently, the desired particular integral of (15.37) can be written as

$$y_p = \frac{-2}{5} te^{-4t}$$

EXERCISE 15.6

1   Show that the method of undetermined coefficients is inapplicable to the differential equation $y''(t) + ay'(t) + by = t^{-1}$.

2   Find the particular integral of each of the following equations by the method of undetermined coefficients:

   (a) $y''(t) + 2y'(t) + y = t$
   (b) $y''(t) + 4y'(t) + y = 2t^2$
   (c) $y''(t) + y'(t) + 2y = e^t$
   (d) $y''(t) + y'(t) + 3y = \sin t$

15.7   Higher-Order Linear Differential Equations

The methods of solution introduced above are readily extended to an nth-order linear differential equation. With constant coefficients and a constant term, such an equation can be written generally as

$$(15.39) \qquad y^{(n)}(t) + a_1 y^{(n-1)}(t) + \cdots + a_{n-1}y'(t) + a_n y = b$$

[1] See the text discussion leading to (15.4").

finding the solution   In this case of constant coefficients and constant term, the presence of the higher derivatives does not materially affect the method of finding the particular integral discussed earlier.

If we try the simplest possible type of solution, $y = k$, we can see that all the derivatives from $y'(t)$ to $y^{(n)}(t)$ will be zero; hence (15.39) will reduce to $a_n k = b$, and we can write

$$y_p = k = \frac{b}{a_n} \quad (a_n \neq 0) \quad \text{[cf. (15.3)]}$$

In case $a_n = 0$, however, we must try a solution of the form $y = kt$. Then, since $y'(t) = k$, but all the higher derivatives will vanish, (15.39) can be reduced to $a_{n-1}k = b$, thereby yielding the particular integral

$$y_p = kt = \frac{b}{a_{n-1}} t \quad (a_n = 0; a_{n-1} \neq 0) \quad \text{[cf. (15.3')]}$$

If it happens that $a_n = a_{n-1} = 0$, then this last solution will fail, too; instead, a solution of the form $y = kt^2$ must be tried. Further adaptations of this procedure should be obvious.

As for the complementary function, inclusion of the higher-order derivatives in the differential equation has the effect of raising the degree of the characteristic equation. The complementary function is defined as the general solution of the reduced equation

$$(15.40) \qquad y^{(n)}(t) + a_1 y^{(n-1)}(t) + \cdots + a_{n-1} y'(t) + a_n y = 0$$

Trying $y = Ae^{rt} (\neq 0)$ as a solution and utilizing the knowledge that this implies $y'(t) = rAe^{rt}, y''(t) = r^2 Ae^{rt}, \ldots, y^{(n)}(t) = r^n Ae^{rt}$, we can rewrite (15.40) as

$$Ae^{rt}(r^n + a_1 r^{n-1} + \cdots + a_{n-1}r + a_n) = 0$$

This equation is satisfied by any value of r which satisfies the following (nth-degree polynomial) characteristic equation

$$(15.40') \qquad r^n + a_1 r^{n-1} + \cdots + a_{n-1}r + a_n = 0$$

There will, of course, be n roots to this polynomial, and each of these should be included in the general solution of (15.40). Thus our complementary function should in general be in the form

$$y_c = A_1 e^{r_1 t} + A_2 e^{r_2 t} + \cdots + A_n e^{r_n t} \qquad \left(= \sum_{i=1}^{n} A_i e^{r_i t} \right)$$

As before, however, some modifications must be made in case the n roots are not all real and distinct. First, suppose that there are repeated roots, say, $r_1 = r_2 = r_3$. Then, to avoid "collapsing," we must write the first three terms of the solution as $A_1 e^{r_1 t} + A_2 t e^{r_1 t} + A_3 t^2 e^{r_1 t}$ [cf. (15.9)]. In case we have $r_4 = r_1$ as well, then the fourth term must be altered to $A_4 t^3 e^{r_1 t}$, etc.

Second, suppose that two of the roots are complex, say,

$$r_5, r_6 = h \pm vi$$

then the fifth and sixth terms in the above solution should be combined into the following expression:

$$e^{ht}(\alpha \cos vt + \beta \sin vt) \qquad \text{[cf. (15.29')]}$$

By the same token, if two *distinct* pairs of complex roots are found, there must be two such trigonometric expressions (with a different set of values of h, v, α, and β for each).[1] As a further possibility, if there happen to be two pairs of *repeated* complex roots, then we should use e^{ht} as the multiplicative term for one but use $t e^{ht}$ for the other. Also, even though h and v have identical values in the repeated complex roots, a different pair of arbitrary constants must now be assigned to each.

Once y_p and y_c are found, the general solution of the complete equation (15.39) follows easily. As before, it is simply the sum of the complementary function and the particular integral: $y(t) = y_c + y_p$. In this general solution, we can count a total of n arbitrary constants—an A_i for each real root, and a different pair of constants, such as (α, β), for each pair of complex roots. Thus, to definitize the solution, as many as n initial conditions will be required.

Example 1 Find the general solution of

$$y^{(4)}(t) + 6y'''(t) + 14y''(t) + 16y'(t) + 8y = 24$$

The particular integral of this fourth-order equation is simply

$$y_p = \frac{24}{8} = 3$$

Its characteristic equation is, by (15.40'),

$$r^4 + 6r^3 + 14r^2 + 16r + 8 = 0$$

which can be factored into the form

$$(r + 2)(r + 2)(r^2 + 2r + 2) = 0$$

From the first two parenthetical expressions, we can obtain the double roots $r_1 = r_2 = -2$, but the last (quadratic) expression yields the pair of complex

---

[1] It is of interest to note that, inasmuch as complex roots always come in conjugate pairs, we can be sure of having *at least one* real root when the differential equation is of an *odd* order, i.e., when *n* is an odd number.

roots r_3, $r_4 = -1 \pm i$, with $h = -1$ and $v = 1$. Consequently, the complementary function is

$$y_c = A_1 e^{-2t} + A_2 t e^{-2t} + e^{-t}(\alpha \cos t + \beta \sin t)$$

and the general solution is

$$y(t) = A_1 e^{-2t} + A_2 t e^{-2t} + e^{-t}(\alpha \cos t + \beta \sin t) + 3$$

The four constants A_1, A_2, α, and β can be definitized, of course, if we are given four initial conditions.

Note that all the characteristic roots in this example either are real and negative or are complex and with a negative real part. The time path must therefore be convergent, and the equilibrium is dynamically stable.

convergence and the Routh theorem   The solution of a high-degree characteristic equation is not always an easy task. For this reason, it should be of tremendous help if we can find a way of ascertaining the convergence or divergence of a time path without having to solve for the characteristic roots. Fortunately, there does exist such a method, which can provide a qualitative (though nongraphic) analysis of a differential equation.

This method is to be found in the *Routh theorem*,[1] which states that:

The real parts of all of the roots of the nth-degree polynomial equation

$$a_0 r^n + a_1 r^{n-1} + \cdots + a_{n-1} r + a_n = 0$$

are negative if and only if the first n of the following sequence of determinants

$$|a_1|; \quad \begin{vmatrix} a_1 & a_3 \\ a_0 & a_2 \end{vmatrix}; \quad \begin{vmatrix} a_1 & a_3 & a_5 \\ a_0 & a_2 & a_4 \\ 0 & a_1 & a_3 \end{vmatrix}; \quad \begin{vmatrix} a_1 & a_3 & a_5 & a_7 \\ a_0 & a_2 & a_4 & a_6 \\ 0 & a_1 & a_3 & a_5 \\ 0 & a_0 & a_2 & a_4 \end{vmatrix}; \cdots$$

are all positive.

In applying this theorem, it should be remembered that $|a_1| \equiv a_1$. Further, it is to be understood that we should take $a_m = 0$ for all $m > n$. For example, given a third-degree polynomial equation ($n = 3$), we need to examine the signs of the first *three* determinants above; for that purpose, we should set $a_4 = a_5 = 0$.

The relevance of this theorem to the convergence problem should become self-evident once we recall that, in order for the time path $y(t)$ to converge, all

---

[1] For a discussion of this theorem, and a sketch of its proof, see Paul A. Samuelson, *Foundations of Economic Analysis*, Harvard University Press, 1947, pp. 429–435, and the references there cited.

the characteristic roots of the differential equation must have negative real parts. Since the characteristic equation (15.40′) is an nth-degree polynomial equation, with $a_0 = 1$, the Routh theorem can be of direct help in the testing of convergence. In fact, we note that the coefficients of the characteristic equation (15.40′) are wholly identical with those of the given differential equation (15.40), so that it is perfectly acceptable to substitute the coefficients of (15.40) directly into the sequence of determinants shown above for testing, provided that we always take $a_0 = 1$. Inasmuch as the condition cited in the theorem is given on the "if and only if" basis, it obviously constitutes a necessary-and-sufficient condition.

Example 2   Test by the Routh theorem whether the differential equation of Example 1 above has a convergent time path. This equation is of the fourth order, so that $n = 4$. The coefficients are $a_0 = 1$, $a_1 = 6$, $a_2 = 14$, $a_3 = 16$, $a_4 = 8$, and $a_5 = a_6 = a_7 = 0$. Substituting these into the first four determinants, we find their values to be 6, 68, 800, and 6400, respectively. Because they are all positive, we can conclude that the time path is convergent.

EXERCISE 15.7

1   Find the particular integral of each of the following:

(a) $y'''(t) + 2y''(t) + y'(t) + 2y = 8$
(b) $y'''(t) + y''(t) + 3y'(t) = 1$
(c) $3y'''(t) + 9y''(t) = 1$

(d) $\dfrac{d^4y}{dt^4} + \dfrac{d^2y}{dt^2} = 4$

2   Find the y_p and the y_c (and hence the general solution) of:

(a) $y'''(t) - 2y''(t) - y'(t) + 2y = 4$
     $[Hint: r^3 - 2r^2 - r + 2 = (r - 1)(r + 1)(r - 2)]$
(b) $y'''(t) + 7y''(t) + 15y'(t) + 9y = 0$
     $[Hint: r^3 + 7r^2 + 15r + 9 = (r + 1)(r^2 + 6r + 9)]$
(c) $y'''(t) + 6y''(t) + 10y'(t) + 8y = 8$
     $[Hint: r^3 + 6r^2 + 10r + 8 = (r + 4)(r^2 + 2r + 2)]$

3   On the basis of the signs of the characteristic roots obtained in the preceding problem, analyze the dynamic stability of equilibrium. Then check your answer by the Routh theorem.

4   Without finding their characteristic roots, determine whether the following
     differential equations will give rise to convergent time paths:

(a) $y'''(t) - 10y''(t) + 27y'(t) - 18y = 3$
(b) $y'''(t) + 11y''(t) + 34y'(t) + 24y = 5$
(c) $y'''(t) + 4y''(t) + 5y'(t) - 2y = -2$

16

DISCRETE TIME: FIRST-ORDER DIFFERENCE EQUATIONS

In the continuous-time context, the pattern of change of a variable y is embodied in the derivatives $y'(t)$, $y''(t)$, etc. The time change involved in these is infinitesimal in magnitude. When time is, instead, taken to be a *discrete* variable, so that the variable t is allowed to take only integer values, the concept of the derivative obviously will no longer be appropriate. Then, as we shall see, the pattern of change of the variable y must be described by so-called "differences," rather than by derivatives or differentials, of $y(t)$. Accordingly, the techniques of differential equations will give way to those of *difference equations*.

When we are dealing with discrete time, the variable y will change its value only when the variable t changes from one integer value to the next, such as from $t = 1$ to $t = 2$. Meanwhile, nothing is supposed to happen to y. In this light, it becomes more convenient to interpret the values of t as referring to *periods*—rather than *points*—of time, with $t = 1$ denoting period 1 and $t = 2$ denoting period 2, and so forth. Then we may simply regard y as having one unique value in each time period. In view of this interpretation, the discrete-time version of economic dynamics is often referred to as *period analysis*. It should be emphasized, however, that "period" is being used here not in the calendar sense but in the analytical sense. Hence, a period may involve one extent of calendar time in a particular economic model, but an altogether different one in another. Even in the same model, moreover, each successive period should not necessarily be construed as meaning equal calendar time. In the analytical sense, a period is merely a length of time that elapses before the variable y undergoes a change.

As the reader will recall, however, discrete time and continuous time really have much in common. In particular, if the time period in the discrete-time case is very, very short, it will closely approach the continuous-time case in essence.

16.1   Discrete Time, Differences, and Difference Equations

The change from continuous time to discrete time produces no effect on the fundamental nature of dynamic analysis, although the formulation of the problem must be altered. Basically, our dynamic problem is still to find a time path from some given pattern of change of a variable y over time. But the pattern of change should now be represented by the difference quotient $\Delta y/\Delta t$, which is the discrete-time counterpart of the derivative dy/dt. Recall, however, that t can only take integer values; thus, when we are comparing the values of y in two consecutive periods, we must have $\Delta t = 1$. For this reason, the difference quotient $\Delta y/\Delta t$ can be simplified to the expression Δy; this is called the *first difference* of y. The symbol Δ, meaning difference, can accordingly be interpreted as a directive to take the first difference of (y). As such, it constitutes the discrete-time counterpart of the operator symbol d/dt.

The expression Δy can take various values, of course, depending on which two consecutive time periods are involved in the difference-taking (or "differencing"). To avoid ambiguity, let us add a time subscript to y and define the first difference more specifically, as follows:

(16.1) $\Delta y_t \equiv y_{t+1} - y_t$

where y_t means the value of y in the tth period, and y_{t+1} is its value in the period immediately following the tth period. With this symbolism, we may describe the pattern of change of y by an equation such as

(16.2) $\Delta y_t = 2$

or

(16.3) $\Delta y_t = -0.1y_t$

Equations of this type are called *difference equations*. The reader should note the striking resemblance between the last two equations, on the one hand, and the differential equations $dy/dt = 2$ and $dy/dt = -0.1y$ on the other.

Even though difference equations derive their name from difference expressions such as Δy_t, there are alternate equivalent forms of such equations which are completely free of Δ expressions and which are more convenient to use. By virtue of (16.1), we can rewrite (16.2) as

(16.2') $y_{t+1} - y_t = 2$

or

(16.2") $\qquad y_{t+1} = y_t + 2$

For (16.3), the corresponding alternate equivalent forms are

(16.3') $\qquad y_{t+1} - 0.9y_t = 0$

or

(16.3") $\qquad y_{t+1} = 0.9y_t$

The double-prime-numbered versions will prove convenient when we are calculating a y value from a known y value of the preceding period. In later discussions, however, we shall employ mostly the single-prime-numbered versions, i.e., those of (16.2') and (16.3').

It is important to note that the choice of time subscripts in a difference equation is somewhat arbitrary. For instance, without any change in meaning, (16.2') can be rewritten as $y_t - y_{t-1} = 2$, where $(t-1)$ refers to the period immediately preceding the tth. Or, we may express it equivalently as $y_{t+2} - y_{t+1} = 2$.

Also, it may be pointed out that, although we have consistently used subscripted y symbols, it is also acceptable to use $y(t)$, $y(t+1)$, and $y(t-1)$ in their stead. In order to avoid using the notation $y(t)$ for both continuous-time and discrete-time cases, however, in the discussion of period analysis we shall adhere to the subscript device.

Analogous to differential equations, difference equations can be either linear or nonlinear, homogeneous or nonhomogeneous, and of the first or second (or higher) orders. Take (16.2') for instance. It can be classified as: (1) linear, for no y term (of any period) is raised to the second (or higher) power; (2) nonhomogeneous, since the right-hand side (where there is no y term) is nonzero; and (3) of the first order, because there exists only a *first difference* Δy_t, involving a one-period time lag only. (In contrast, a second-order difference equation, to be discussed in the ensuing chapter, involves a two-period lag and thus entails three y terms: y_{t+2}, y_{t+1}, as well as y_t.)

Actually, (16.2') can also be characterized as having constant coefficients and a constant term $(=2)$. Since the constant-coefficient case is the only one we shall consider, this characterization will henceforth be implicitly assumed. Throughout the present chapter, the constant-term feature will also be retained, though a method of dealing with the variable-term case will be discussed in the next chapter.

The reader should check that the equation (16.3') is also linear and of the first order; but unlike (16.2'), it is homogeneous.

16.2 Solving a First-Order Difference Equation

In solving a differential equation, our objective was to find a time path $y(t)$. As we know, such a time path is a function of time which is totally free from any derivative (or differential) expressions and which is perfectly consistent with the given differential equation as well as with its initial conditions. The time path we seek from a difference equation is similar in nature. Again, it should be a function of t—a formula defining the values of y in every time period—which is consistent with the given difference equation as well as with its initial conditions. Besides, it must not contain any difference expressions such as Δy_t (or expressions like $y_{t+1} - y_t$).

Solving differential equations is, in the final analysis, a matter of integration. How do we solve a difference equation?

iterative method   Before developing a general method of attack, let us first explain a relatively pedestrian method, the *iterative method*—which, though crude, will prove immensely revealing of the essential nature of a so-called "solution."

In this chapter we are concerned only with the first-order case; thus the difference equation describes the pattern of change of y between *two* consecutive periods only. Once such a pattern is specified, such as by (16.2″), and once we are given an initial value y_0, it is no problem to find y_1 from the equation. Similarly, once y_1 is found, y_2 will be immediately obtainable, and so forth, by repeated application (iteration) of the pattern of change specified in the difference equation. The results of iteration will then permit us to infer a time path.

Example 1   Find the solution of the difference equation (16.2), assuming an initial value of $y_0 = 15$. To carry out the iterative process, it is more convenient to use the alternative form of the difference equation (16.2″), namely, $y_{t+1} = y_t + 2$, with $y_0 = 15$. From this equation, we can deduce step-by-step that

$$y_1 = y_0 + 2$$
$$y_2 = y_1 + 2 = (y_0 + 2) + 2 = y_0 + 2(2)$$
$$y_3 = y_2 + 2 = [y_0 + 2(2)] + 2 = y_0 + 3(2)$$
$$\vdots \qquad \vdots \qquad\qquad \vdots \qquad\qquad \vdots$$

and, in general, for any period t,

$$(16.4) \qquad y_t = y_0 + t(2) = 15 + 2t$$

This last equation indicates the y value of any time period (including the initial period $t = 0$); it therefore constitutes the solution of (16.2).

The process of iteration is crude—it corresponds roughly to solving simple differential equations by straight integration—but it serves to point out clearly the manner in which a time path is generated. In general, the value of y_t will depend in a specified way on the value of y in the immediately preceding period (y_{t-1}); thus a given initial value y_0 will successively lead to $y_1, y_2, \ldots$, via the prescribed pattern of change.

Example 2   Solve the difference equation (16.3); this time, let the initial value be unspecified and denoted simply by y_0. Again it is more convenient to work with the alternative version in (16.3''), namely, $y_{t+1} = 0.9y_t$. By iteration, we have

$$y_1 = 0.9y_0$$
$$y_2 = 0.9y_1 = 0.9(0.9y_0) = (0.9)^2 y_0$$
$$y_3 = 0.9y_2 = 0.9(0.9)^2 y_0 = (0.9)^3 y_0$$
$$\vdots \qquad \vdots \qquad \quad \vdots \qquad \qquad \vdots$$

In general, we can summarize these into the solution

$$(16.5) \qquad y_t = (0.9)^t y_0$$

To heighten interest, we can lend some economic content to this example. In the simple multiplier analysis, a single investment expenditure in period 0 will call forth successive rounds of spending, which in turn will bring about varying amounts of income increment in succeeding time periods. Using y to denote *income increment*, we have y_0 = the amount of investment in period 0; but the subsequent income increments will depend on the marginal propensity to consume (MPC). If MPC = 0.9 and if the income of each period is consumed only in the next period, then 90 percent of y_0 will be consumed in period 1, resulting in an income increment in period 1 of $y_1 = 0.9y_0$. By similar reasoning, we can find $y_2 = 0.9y_1$, etc. These, we see, are precisely the results of the iterative process cited above. In other words, the multiplier process of income generation can be described by a difference equation such as (16.3''), and a solution like (16.5) will tell us what the magnitude of income increment is to be in any time period t.

Example 3   Solve the homogeneous difference equation

$$my_{t+1} - ny_t = 0$$

Upon normalizing and transposing, this may be written as

$$y_{t+1} = \left(\frac{n}{m}\right) y_t$$

which is the same as (16.3") in Example 2 except for the replacement of 0.9 by n/m. Hence, by analogy, the solution should be

$$y_t = \left(\frac{n}{m}\right)^t y_0$$

The reader is requested to watch the term $\left(\frac{n}{m}\right)^t$. It is through this term that various values of t will lead to their corresponding values of y. It therefore corresponds to the expression e^{rt} in the solutions to differential equations. If we write it more generally as b^t (b for base) and attach the more general multiplicative constant A (instead of y_0), then we see that the solution of the general homogeneous difference equation of Example 3 will be in the form

$$y_t = Ab^t$$

We shall find that this expression Ab^t will play the same important role in difference equations as the expression Ae^{rt} did in differential equations.[1] However, even though both are exponential expressions, the former is to the base b, whereas the latter is to the base e. It stands to reason that, just as the type of the continuous-time path $y(t)$ depends heavily on the value of r, the discrete-time path y_t will hinge principally upon the value of b.

general method   By this time, the reader must have become quite impressed with the various similarities between differential and difference equations. As might be conjectured, the general method of solution presently to be explained will again parallel that for differential equations.

Suppose that we are seeking the solution to the first-order difference equation

(16.6) $y_{t+1} + ay_t = c$

where a and c are two constants. The general solution will consist of the sum of two components: a *particular integral* y_p,† which is *any* solution of the complete nonhomogeneous equation (16.6), and a *complementary function* y_c, which is the general solution of the reduced equation of (16.6):

(16.7) $y_{t+1} + ay_t = 0$

The y_p component will again represent the intertemporal equilibrium level of y, and the y_c component signifies the deviations of the time path from that

---

[1] The observant reader may object to this statement by pointing out that the solution (16.4) in Example 1 does not contain a term in the form of Ab^t. This latter fact, however, arises only because in Example 1 we have $b = n/m = 1/1 = 1$, so that the term Ab^t reduces to a constant.
† We are borrowing this term from differential equations, even though no "integral" is involved here. Some writers call it a *particular solution*.

equilibrium. The sum of y_c and y_p will constitute a *general* solution, because of the presence of an arbitrary constant. As before, in order to definitize the solution, an initial condition will be needed.

Let us first deal with the complementary function. Our experience with Example 3 suggests that we may try a solution of the form $y_t = Ab^t$ (with $Ab^t \neq 0$, for otherwise y_t will turn out simply to be a horizontal straight line lying on the t axis); in that case, we also have $y_{t+1} = Ab^{t+1}$. If these values of y_t and y_{t+1} hold, the homogeneous equation (16.7) will become

$$Ab^{t+1} + aAb^t = 0$$

which, upon canceling the nonzero common factor Ab^t, yields

$$b + a = 0 \quad \text{or} \quad b = -a$$

This means that, for the trial solution to work, we must set $b = -a$; thus the complementary function should be written as

$$y_c \ (= Ab^t) = A(-a)^t$$

Now let us search for the particular integral which has to do with the complete equation (16.6). In this regard, Example 3 is of no help at all, because that example relates only to a homogeneous equation. However, we note that for y_p we can choose *any* solution of (16.6), so that, if a trial solution of the simplest form $y_t = k$ (a constant) can work out, no real difficulty will be encountered. Now, if $y_t = k$, then y will maintain the same constant value over time, and we must have $y_{t+1} = k$ also. Substitution of these values into (16.6) yields

$$k + ak = c \quad \text{and} \quad k = \frac{c}{1 + a}$$

Since this particular k value satisfies the equation, the particular integral can be written as

$$y_p \ (= k) = \frac{c}{1 + a} \quad (a \neq -1)$$

This being a constant, a stationary equilibrium is indicated in this case.

If it happens that $a = -1$, as in Example 1, however, the particular integral $c/(1 + a)$ is not defined, and some other solution of the nonhomogeneous equation (16.6) must be sought. In this event, we employ the now-familiar trick of trying a solution of the form $y_t = kt$. This implies, of course, that $y_{t+1} = k(t + 1)$. Substituting these into (16.6), we find

$$k(t + 1) + akt = c \quad \text{and} \quad k = \frac{c}{t + 1 + at} = c$$

$$[\text{because } a = -1]$$

thus $\quad y_p \ (= kt) = ct$

This form of the particular integral is a nonconstant function of t; it therefore represents a moving equilibrium.

Adding y_c and y_p together, we may now write the general solution in one of the two following forms:

$$(16.8) \qquad y_t = A(-a)^t + \frac{c}{1+a} \qquad \text{[general solution, case of } a \neq -1]$$

$$(16.9) \qquad y_t = A(-a)^t + ct = A + ct \quad \text{[general solution, case of } a = -1]$$

Neither of these is completely determinate, in view of the arbitrary constant A. To eliminate this arbitrary constant, we resort to the initial condition that $y_t = y_0$ when $t = 0$. Letting $t = 0$ in (16.8), we have

$$y_0 = A + \frac{c}{1+a} \qquad \text{and} \qquad A = y_0 - \frac{c}{1+a}$$

Consequently, the definite version of (16.8) is

$$(16.8') \qquad y_t = \left(y_0 - \frac{c}{1+a}\right)(-a)^t + \frac{c}{1+a}$$

$$\text{[definite solution, case of } a \neq -1]$$

Letting $t = 0$ in (16.9), on the other hand, we find $y_0 = A$, so that the definite version of (16.9) is

$$(16.9') \qquad y_t = y_0 + ct \qquad \text{[definite solution, case of } a = -1]$$

If this last result is applied to Example 1 above, the solution that emerges will be exactly the same as the iterative solution (16.4).

The reader should check the validity of each of these solutions by the following two steps: First, by letting $t = 0$ in (16.8'), see that the latter equation reduces to the identity $y_0 = y_0$, signifying the satisfaction of the initial condition. Second, by substituting the y_t formula (16.8') and a similar y_{t+1} formula—obtained by replacing t with $(t + 1)$ in (16.8')—into (16.6), see that the latter reduces to the identity $c = c$, signifying that the time path is consistent with the given difference equation. The check on the validity of solution (16.9') is analogous.

Example 4   Solve the first-order difference equation

$$y_{t+1} - 5y_t = 1 \qquad (y_0 = \tfrac{7}{4})$$

Following the procedure used in deriving (16.8'), we can find y_c by trying a solution $y_t = Ab^t$ (which implies $y_{t+1} = Ab^{t+1}$). Substituting these values into the homogeneous version $y_{t+1} - 5y_t = 0$ and canceling the common factor Ab^t, we get $b = 5$. Thus,

$$y_c = A(5)^t$$

To find y_p, try the solution $y_t = k$, which implies $y_{t+1} = k$. Substituting these into the complete difference equation, we find $k = -\frac{1}{4}$. Hence

$$y_p = -\frac{1}{4}$$

It follows that the general solution is

$$y_t = y_c + y_p = A(5)^t - \frac{1}{4}$$

Letting $t = 0$ here and utilizing the initial condition $y_0 = \frac{7}{4}$, we obtain $A = 2$. Thus the definite solution may finally be written as

$$y_t = 2(5)^t - \frac{1}{4}$$

Since the given difference equation of this example is a special case of (16.6), with $a = -5$, $c = 1$, and $y_0 = \frac{7}{4}$, and since (16.8′) is the solution "formula" for this type of difference equation, we could have found our solution by inserting the specific parameter values into (16.8′), with the result that

$$y_t = \left(\frac{7}{4} - \frac{1}{1-5} \right) (5)^t + \frac{1}{1-5} = 2(5)^t - \frac{1}{4}$$

which checks perfectly with the earlier answer.

Note that the y_{t+1} term in (16.6) has a unit coefficient. If a given difference equation has a nonunit coefficient for this term, it must be normalized before using the solution formula (16.8′).

EXERCISE 16.2

1 Convert the following difference equations into the form of (16.2″):

    (a) $\Delta y_t = 7$ (b) $\Delta y_t = 0.2y_t$ (c) $\Delta y_t = 2y_t - 9$

2 Solve the following difference equations by iteration:

    (a) $y_{t+1} = y_t + 1$ $(y_0 = 10)$
    (b) $y_{t+1} = \alpha y_t$ $(y_0 = \beta)$
    (c) $y_{t+1} = \alpha y_t - \beta$ $(y_t = y_0$ when $t = 0)$

3 Rewrite the equations in the preceding problem in the form of (16.6), and solve by applying formula (16.8′) or (16.9′), whichever is appropriate. Do your answers check with those obtained by the iterative method?

4   For each of the following difference equations, use the procedure illustrated in the derivation of (16.8') and (16.9') to find y_c, y_p, and the definite solution:

(a) $y_{t+1} + 3y_t = 4$ $(y_0 = 4)$
(b) $2y_{t+1} - y_t = 2$ $(y_0 = 7)$
(c) $y_{t+1} = 0.2y_t + 8$ $(y_0 = 1)$

16.3   Dynamic Stability of Equilibrium

In the continuous-time case, the dynamic stability of equilibrium depends on the Ae^{rt} term in the complementary function. In period analysis, the corresponding role is played by the Ab^t term in the complementary function. Since its interpretation is somewhat more complicated than Ae^{rt}, let us try to clarify it before proceeding further.

significance of b   Whether the equilibrium is dynamically stable is a question of whether or not the complementary function will tend to zero as $t \to \infty$. Basically, we must analyze the path of the term Ab^t as t is increased indefinitely. Obviously, the value of b (the base of this exponential term) is of the utmost importance in this regard. Let us first consider its significance alone, by disregarding the coefficient A (or by assuming $A = 1$).

For analytical purposes, we can divide the range of possible values of b, namely, $(-\infty, +\infty)$, into seven distinct regions, as set forth in the first two columns of Table 16.1, arranged in descending order of magnitude of b. These regions are also marked off in Fig. 16.1 on a vertical b scale, with the points $+1$,

TABLE 16.1

Value of b^t

Region	Value of b		b^t	$t = 0$	$t = 1$	$t = 2$	$t = 3$	$t = 4 \cdots$
I	$b > 1$	$(\|b\| > 1)$	e.g., $(2)^t$	1	2	4	8	16
II	$b = 1$	$(\|b\| = 1)$	$(1)^t$	1	1	1	1	1
III	$0 < b < 1$	$(\|b\| < 1)$	e.g., $(\frac{1}{2})^t$	1	$\frac{1}{2}$	$\frac{1}{4}$	$\frac{1}{8}$	$\frac{1}{16}$
IV	$b = 0$	$(\|b\| = 0)$	$(0)^t$	0	0	0	0	0
V	$-1 < b < 0$	$(\|b\| < 1)$	e.g., $(-\frac{1}{2})^t$	1	$-\frac{1}{2}$	$\frac{1}{4}$	$-\frac{1}{8}$	$\frac{1}{16}$
VI	$b = -1$	$(\|b\| = 1)$	$(-1)^t$	1	-1	1	-1	1
VII	$b < -1$	$(\|b\| > 1)$	e.g., $(-2)^t$	1	-2	4	-8	16

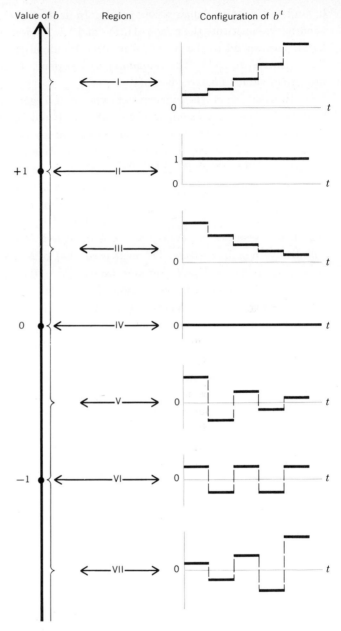

FIGURE 16.1

0, and -1 as the demarcation points. In fact, these latter three points in themselves constitute the regions II, IV, and VI. Regions III and V, on the other hand, correspond to the set of all positive fractions and the set of all negative fractions, respectively. The remaining two regions, I and VII, are where the numerical value of b exceeds unity.

In each region, the exponential expression b^t generates a different type of time path. These are exemplified in Table 16.1 and illustrated in Fig. 16.1. In region I (where $b > 1$), b^t must increase with t at an increasing pace. The general configuration of the time path will therefore assume the shape of the top graph in Fig. 16.1. Note that this graph is shown as a step function rather than as a smooth curve; this is because we are dealing with period analysis. In region II ($b = 1$), b^t will remain at unity for all values of t. Its graph will thus be a horizontal straight line. Next, in region III, b^t represents a positive fraction raised to integer powers. As the power is increased, b^t must decrease, though it will always remain positive. The next case, that of $b = 0$ in region IV, is quite similar to the case of $b = 1$; but here we have $b^t = 0$ rather than $b^t = 1$, so that its graph will coincide with the horizontal axis. However, this case is of peripheral interest only, since we have earlier adopted the assumption that $Ab^t \neq 0$, which implies $b \neq 0$.

When we move into the negative regions, an interesting new phenomenon occurs: The value of b^t will *alternate* between positive and negative values from period to period! This fact is clearly brought out in the last three rows of Table 16.1 and in the last three graphs of Fig. 16.1. In region V, where b is a negative fraction, the alternating time path tends to get closer and closer to the horizontal axis (cf. the positive-fraction region, III). In contrast, when $b = -1$ (region VI), a perpetual alternation between $+1$ and -1 results. And finally, when $b < -1$ (region VII), the alternating time path will deviate farther and farther from the horizontal axis.

What is striking is that, whereas the phenomenon of a fluctuating time path cannot possibly arise from a single Ae^{rt} term (the complex-root case of the second-order differential equation requires a *pair* of complex roots), fluctuation can be generated by a single b^t (or Ab^t) term. Note, however, that the character of the fluctuation is somewhat different; unlike the circular-function pattern, the fluctuation depicted in Fig. 16.1 is nonsmooth. For this reason, we shall employ the word *oscillation* to denote the new, nonsmooth type of fluctuation, even though many writers do use the terms fluctuation and oscillation interchangeably.

The essence of the above discussion can be conveyed in the following general statement: The time path of b^t ($b \neq 0$) will be

$$\left.\begin{matrix} \text{Nonoscillatory} \\ \text{Oscillatory} \end{matrix}\right\} \quad \text{if} \quad \begin{cases} b > 0 \\ b < 0 \end{cases}$$

$$
\left.\begin{array}{l} \text{Explosive} \\ \text{Damped} \end{array}\right\} \quad \text{if} \quad \left\{\begin{array}{l} |b| > 1 \\ |b| < 1 \end{array}\right.
$$

It is important to note that, whereas the convergence of the expression e^{rt} depends on the *sign* of r, the convergence of the b^t expression hinges, instead, on the *absolute value* of b.

the role of A   So far we have deliberately left out the multiplicative constant A. But its effects—of which there are two—are relatively easy to take into account. First, the *magnitude* of A can serve to "blow up" (if, say, $A = 3$) or "pare down" (if, say, $A = \frac{1}{5}$) the values of b^t. That is, it can produce a *scale effect* without changing the basic configuration of the time path. The *sign* of A, on the other hand, does materially affect the shape of the path because, if b^t is multiplied by $A = -1$, then each time path shown in Fig. 16.1 will be replaced by its own mirror image with reference to the horizontal axis. Thus, a negative A can produce a *mirror effect* as well as a scale effect.

convergence to equilibrium   The above discussion presents the interpretation of the Ab^t term in the complementary function, which, as we recall, represents the deviations from some intertemporal equilibrium level. If a term (say) $y_p = 5$ is added to the Ab^t term, the time path must be shifted up vertically by a constant value of 5. This will in no way affect the convergence or divergence of the time path, but it will alter the level with reference to which convergence or divergence is gauged. What Fig. 16.1 pictures is the convergence (or lack of it) of the Ab^t expression to zero. When the y_p is included, then it becomes a question of the convergence of the time path $y_t = y_c + y_p$ to the equilibrium level y_p.

In this connection, let us add a word of explanation for the special case of $b = 1$ (region II). A time path such as

$$
y_t = A(1)^t + y_p = A + y_p
$$

gives the impression that it converges, because the multiplicative term $(1)^t = 1$ produces no explosive effect. Observe, however, that y_t will now take the value $(A + y_p)$ rather than the equilibrium value y_p; in fact, it can never reach y_p (unless $A = 0$). As an illustration of this type of situation, we can cite the time path in (16.9), in which a moving equilibrium $y_p = ct$ is involved. This time path is to be considered divergent, not because of the appearance of t in the particular integral but because, with a nonzero A, there will be a constant deviation from the moving equilibrium. Thus, in stipulating the condition for convergence of time path y_t to the equilibrium y_p, we must rule out the case of $b = 1$.

In sum, the solution

$$y_t = Ab^t + y_p$$

is convergent if and only if $|b| < 1$.

Example 1   What kind of time path is represented by $y_t = 2(-\frac{4}{5})^t + 9$? Since $b = -\frac{4}{5} < 0$, the time path is oscillatory. But since $|b| = \frac{4}{5} < 1$, the oscillation is damped, and the time path converges to the equilibrium level of 9.

The reader should take care not to confuse $2(-\frac{4}{5})^t$ with $-2(\frac{4}{5})^t$, which represent entirely different time-path configurations.

Example 2   How do you characterize the time path $y_t = 3(2)^t + 4$? Since $b = 2 > 0$, no oscillation will occur. But since $|b| = 2 > 1$, the time path will explode and will diverge from the equilibrium level of 4.

EXERCISE 16.3

1   Discuss the nature of the following time paths:

(a) $y_t = 3^t + 1$ (c) $y_t = 5(-\frac{1}{10})^t + 3$
(b) $y_t = 2(\frac{1}{3})^t$ (d) $y_t = -3(\frac{1}{4})^t + 2$

2   What is the nature of the time path obtained from each of the difference equations in Exercise 16.2-4?

3   Find the solutions of the following, and determine whether the time paths are oscillatory and convergent:

(a) $y_{t+1} - \frac{1}{3}y_t = 6$ $(y_0 = 1)$
(b) $y_{t+1} + 2y_t = 1$ $(y_0 = 1)$
(c) $y_{t+1} + \frac{1}{4}y_t = 5$ $(y_0 = 2)$
(d) $y_{t+1} - y_t = 3$ $(y_0 = 2)$

16.4   The Cobweb Model

To illustrate the use of first-order difference equations in economic analysis, we shall cite two variants of the market model for a single commodity. The first variant, known as the *cobweb model*, differs from our earlier market models in that it treats Q_s as a function not of current price but of the price of the preceding time period.

the model   Consider a situation in which the producer's output decision must be made one period in advance of the actual sale—such as in agricultural production, where planting must precede by an appreciable length of time the harvesting and sale of the output. Let us assume that the output decision in period t is based on the then-prevailing price P_t. Since this output will not be available for sale until period $(t + 1)$, however, P_t will determine not Q_{st}, but $Q_{s,t+1}$. Thus we now have a "lagged" supply function[1]

$$Q_{s,t+1} = S(P_t)$$

or, equivalently,

$$Q_{st} = S(P_{t-1})$$

When such a supply function interacts with a demand function of the form

$$Q_{dt} = D(P_t)$$

interesting dynamic price patterns will result.

Taking the linear versions of these (lagged) supply and (unlagged) demand functions, and assuming that in each time period the market price is always set at a level which clears the market, we have a market model with the following three equations:

$$\begin{aligned}
&Q_{dt} = Q_{st}\\
(16.10) \quad &Q_{dt} = \alpha - \beta P_t & (\alpha,\beta > 0)\\
&Q_{st} = -\gamma + \delta P_{t-1} & (\gamma,\delta > 0)
\end{aligned}$$

By substituting the last two equations into the first, however, the model can be reduced to a single first-order difference equation as follows:

$$\beta P_t + \delta P_{t-1} = \alpha + \gamma$$

In order to solve this equation, it is desirable first to normalize it and shift the time subscripts ahead by one period [alter t to $(t + 1)$, etc.]. The result,

$$(16.11) \quad P_{t+1} + \frac{\delta}{\beta} P_t = \frac{\alpha + \gamma}{\beta}$$

will then be a replica of (16.6), with the substitutions

$$y = P \qquad a = \frac{\delta}{\beta} \qquad \text{and} \qquad c = \frac{\alpha + \gamma}{\beta}$$

Inasmuch as δ and β are both positive, it follows that $a \neq -1$. Consequently,

---

[1] We are making the implicit assumption here that the entire output of a period will be placed on the market, with no part of it held in storage. Such an assumption is appropriate when the commodity in question is perishable or when no inventory is ever kept. A model with inventory will be considered in the next section.

we can apply formula (16.8'), to get the time path

$$(16.12) \qquad P_t = \left(P_0 - \frac{\alpha + \gamma}{\beta + \delta}\right)\left(-\frac{\delta}{\beta}\right)^t + \frac{\alpha + \gamma}{\beta + \delta}$$

where P_0 represents the initial price.

the cobwebs Three points may be observed in regard to this time path. In the first place, the expression $(\alpha + \gamma)/(\beta + \delta)$, which constitutes the particular integral of the difference equation, can be taken as the intertemporal equilibrium price of the model:[1]

$$\bar{P} = \frac{\alpha + \gamma}{\beta + \delta}$$

Being a constant, this is a stationary equilibrium. Substituting $\bar{P}$ into our solution, we can express the time path P_t alternatively in the form

$$(16.12') \qquad P_t = (P_0 - \bar{P})\left(-\frac{\delta}{\beta}\right)^t + \bar{P}$$

This leads us to the second point, namely, the significance of the expression $(P_0 - \bar{P})$. Since this corresponds to the constant A in the Ab^t term, its sign will bear on the question of whether the time path will commence above or below the equilibrium (mirror effect), whereas its magnitude will decide how far above or below (scale effect). Lastly, there is the expression $(-\delta/\beta)$, which corresponds to the b component of Ab^t. Since our model specification has it that $\beta, \delta > 0$, we must have an oscillatory time path. It is this fact which gives rise to the cobweb phenomenon, as we shall presently see. There can, of course, arise *three* possible varieties of oscillation patterns in the model. According to Table 16.1 or Fig. 16.1, the oscillation will be

$$\left.\begin{array}{l} \text{Explosive} \\ \text{Uniform} \\ \text{Damped} \end{array}\right\} \quad \text{if} \quad \delta \gtreqless \beta$$

In order to visualize the cobwebs, let us depict the model (16.10) in Fig. 16.2. The second equation of (16.10) plots as a downward-sloping linear demand curve, with its slope numerically equal to β. Similarly, a linear supply curve with a slope equal to δ can be drawn from the third equation, if we let the Q axis represent in this instance a *lagged* quantity supplied. The case of $\delta > \beta$ (S steeper than D) and the case of $\delta < \beta$ (S flatter than D) are illustrated in

---

[1] As far as the market-clearing sense of equilibrium is concerned, the price reached in each period is an equilibrium price, because we have assumed that $Q_{dt} = Q_{st}$ for every t.

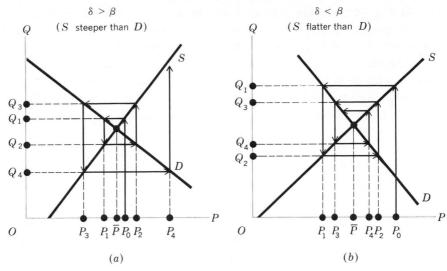

FIGURE 16.2

diagrams a and b, respectively. In either case, however, the intersection of D and S will yield the intertemporal equilibrium price $\bar{P}$.

When $\delta > \beta$, as in diagram a, the interaction of demand and supply will produce an explosive price path as follows. Given an initial price P_0 (here assumed above $\bar{P}$), we can follow the arrowhead and read off on the S curve that the quantity supplied in the next period (period 1) will be Q_1. In order to clear the market, the quantity demanded in period 1 must also be Q_1, which is possible if and only if price is set at the level of P_1 (see downward arrow). Now, via the S curve, the price P_1 will lead to Q_2 as the quantity supplied in period 2, and to clear the market in the latter period, price must be set at the level of P_2 according to the demand curve. Repeating this reasoning, we can trace out the prices and quantities in subsequent periods by simply following the arrowheads in the diagram, thereby spinning a "cobweb" around the demand and supply curves. By comparing the price levels, $P_0, P_1, P_2, \ldots$, we observe in this case not only an oscillatory pattern of change but also a tendency for price to widen its deviation from $\bar{P}$ as time goes by. With the cobweb being spun from inside out, the time path is divergent and the oscillation explosive.

By way of contrast, in the case of diagram b, where $\delta < \beta$, a similar spinning process will create a cobweb which is center-oriented. From P_0, if we follow the arrowheads, we shall be led ever closer to the intersection of the demand and supply curves, where $\bar{P}$ is. While still oscillatory, this price path is convergent.

In Fig. 16.2 we have not shown a third possibility, namely, that of $\delta = \beta$. The procedure of graphical analysis involved, however, is perfectly analogous to the other two cases. It is therefore left to the reader as an exercise.

The above discussion has dealt only with the time path of P (that is, P_t); after P_t is found, however, it takes but a short step to get to the time path of Q. The second equation of (16.10) relates Q_{dt} to P_t, so that if (16.12) or (16.12') is substituted into the demand equation, the time path of Q_{dt} can be obtained immediately. Moreover, since Q_{dt} must be equal to Q_{st} in each time period (clearance of market), we can simply refer to the time path as Q_t rather than Q_{dt}. On the basis of Fig. 16.2, the rationale of this substitution is easily seen. Each point on the D curve relates a P_i to a Q_i pertaining to the same time period; therefore the demand function can serve to map the time path of price into the time path of quantity.

The reader will note that the graphical technique of Fig. 16.2 is applicable even when the D and S curves are nonlinear.

EXERCISE 16.4

1   On the basis of (16.10), find the time path of Q, and analyze the condition for its convergence.

2   Draw a diagram similar to those of Fig. 16.2 to show that, for the case of $\delta = \beta$, the price will oscillate uniformly with neither damping nor explosion.

3   Given demand and supply for the cobweb model as follows, find the intertemporal equilibrium price, and determine whether the equilibrium is stable:

(a) $Q_{dt} = 18 - 3P_t$ $Q_{st} = -3 + 4P_{t-1}$
(b) $Q_{dt} = 22 - 3P_t$ $Q_{st} = -2 + P_{t-1}$
(c) $Q_{dt} = 19 - 6P_t$ $Q_{st} = 6P_{t-1} - 5$

4   In model (16.10), let the $Q_{dt} = Q_{st}$ condition and the demand function remain as they are, but change the supply function to

$$Q_{st} = -\gamma + \delta P_t^*$$

where P_t^* denotes the *expected price* of period t. Furthermore, suppose that sellers have the "adaptive" type of price expectation:[1]

[1] See Marc Nerlove, "Adaptive Expectations and Cobweb Phenomena," *Quarterly Journal of Economics*, May, 1958, pp. 227–240.

$$P_t^* = P_{t-1}^* + \eta(P_{t-1} - P_{t-1}^*) \qquad (0 < \eta \leq 1)$$

where η (the Greek letter eta) is the expectation-adjustment coefficient.

(a) Give an economic interpretation to the adaptive expectation equation. What happens if η takes its maximum value? Can we consider the cobweb model as a special case of the present model?

(b) Show that the new model can be represented by the first-order difference equation

$$P_{t+1} - \left(1 - \eta - \frac{\eta \delta}{\beta}\right) P_t = \frac{\eta(\alpha + \gamma)}{\beta}$$

(*Hint:* Solve the supply function for P_t^*, and use the information that $Q_{st} = Q_{dt} = \alpha - \beta P_t$.)

(c) Find the time path of price. Is this path necessarily oscillatory? Can it be oscillatory? Under what circumstances?

(d) Show that the time path P_t, if oscillatory, will converge only if $1 - 2/\eta < -\delta/\beta$. As compared with the cobweb solution (16.12) or (16.12′), does the new model have a wider or narrower range for the stability-inducing values of $-\delta/\beta$?

16.5 A Market Model with Inventory

In the preceding model, price is assumed to be set in such a way as to clear the current output of every time period. The implication of that assumption is either that the commodity is a perishable which cannot be stocked or that, though it is stockable, no inventory is ever kept. Now we shall construct a model in which sellers do keep an inventory of the commodity.

the model   Let us assume the following: (1) Both the quantity demanded, Q_{dt}, and the quantity currently produced, Q_{st}, are unlagged linear functions of price P_t. (2) The adjustment of price is effected not through market clearance in every period, but through a process of price-setting by the sellers: At the beginning of each period, the sellers set a price for that period after taking into consideration the inventory situation. If, as a result of the preceding-period price, inventory accumulated, the current-period price is set at a lower level than before; but if inventory decumulated instead, then the current price is set higher than before. (3) The price adjustment made from period to period is inversely proportional to the observed change in inventory (stock).

With these assumptions, we can write the following equations in the model:

$$(16.13) \qquad \begin{array}{ll} Q_{dt} = \alpha - \beta P_t & (\alpha, \beta > 0) \\ Q_{st} = -\gamma + \delta P_t & (\gamma, \delta > 0) \\ P_{t+1} = P_t - \sigma(Q_{st} - Q_{dt}) & (\sigma > 0) \end{array}$$

where σ denotes the *stock-induced-price-adjustment* coefficient. The reader will note that (16.13) is really nothing but the discrete-time counterpart of the market model of Sec. 14.2, although we have now couched the price-adjustment process in terms of *inventory* $(Q_{st} - Q_{dt})$ rather than *excess demand* $(Q_{dt} - Q_{st})$. Nevertheless, the analytical results will turn out to be much different; for one thing, with discrete time, we may encounter the phenomenon of oscillations. Let us derive and analyze the time path P_t.

time path By substituting the first two equations into the third, the model can be condensed into a single difference equation:

$$(16.14) \qquad P_{t+1} - [1 - \sigma(\beta + \delta)]P_t = \sigma(\alpha + \gamma)$$

and its solution is given by (16.8′):

$$(16.15) \qquad P_t = \left(P_0 - \frac{\alpha + \gamma}{\beta + \delta}\right)[1 - \sigma(\beta + \delta)]^t + \frac{\alpha + \gamma}{\beta + \delta}$$

$$= (P_0 - \bar{P})[1 - \sigma(\beta + \delta)]^t + \bar{P}$$

Obviously, therefore, the dynamic stability of the model will hinge on the expression $1 - \sigma(\beta + \delta)$; for convenience, let us refer to this expression as b.

With reference to Table 16.1, we see that, in analyzing the exponential expression b^t, seven distinct regions of b values may be defined. However, since our model specifications $(\sigma, \beta, \delta > 0)$ have effectually ruled out the first two regions, there remain only five possible cases, as listed in Table 16.2. For each of these regions, the b specification of the second column can be translated into an equivalent σ specification, as shown in the third column. For instance, for region III, the b specification is $0 < b < 1$; therefore we can write

$$0 < 1 - \sigma(\beta + \delta) < 1$$

$$-1 < -\sigma(\beta + \delta) < 0 \qquad \text{[subtracting 1 from all three parts]}$$

and $\qquad \dfrac{1}{\beta + \delta} > \sigma > 0 \qquad \text{[dividing through by } -(\beta + \delta)]$

This last gives us the desired equivalent σ specification for region III. The translation for the other regions may be carried out analogously. Since the type of time path pertaining to each region is already known from Fig. 16.1, the σ

specification will enable us to tell from given values of σ, β, and δ the general nature of the time path P_t, as outlined in the last column of Table 16.2.

Example 1   If the sellers in our model always increase (decrease) the price by 10 percent of the amount of the decrease (increase) in inventory, and if the demand curve has a slope of -1 and the supply curve a slope of 15 (both slopes with respect to the price axis), what type of time path P_t shall we find?

Here, we have $\sigma = 0.1$, $\beta = 1$, and $\delta = 15$. Since $1/(\beta + \delta) = \frac{1}{16}$ and $2/(\beta + \delta) = \frac{1}{8}$, the value of $\sigma(=\frac{1}{10})$ lies between the former two values; it is thus a case of region V. The time path P_t will be characterized by damped oscillation.

graphical summary of the results   The substance of Table 16.2, which contains as many as five different possible cases of σ specification, can be made much easier to grasp if the results are presented graphically. Inasmuch as the σ specification involves essentially a comparison of the relative magnitudes of the parameters σ and $(\beta + \delta)$, let us plot σ against $(\beta + \delta)$, as in Fig. 16.3. Note that we need only concern ourselves with the positive quadrant because, by model specification, σ and $(\beta + \delta)$ are both positive. From Table 16.2, it is clear that regions IV and VI are specified by the equations $\sigma = 1/(\beta + \delta)$ and

TABLE 16.2

Region	Value of $b \equiv 1 - \sigma(\beta + \delta)$	Value of σ	Nature of time path P_t
III	$0 < b < 1$	$0 < \sigma < \dfrac{1}{\beta + \delta}$	Nonoscillatory and convergent
IV	$b = 0$	$\sigma = \dfrac{1}{\beta + \delta}$	Remaining in equilibrium[1]
V	$-1 < b < 0$	$\dfrac{1}{\beta + \delta} < \sigma < \dfrac{2}{\beta + \delta}$	With damped oscillation
VI	$b = -1$	$\sigma = \dfrac{2}{\beta + \delta}$	With uniform oscillation
VII	$b < -1$	$\sigma > \dfrac{2}{\beta + \delta}$	With explosive oscillation

[1] The fact that price will be remaining in equilibrium in this case can also be seen directly from (16.14). With $\sigma = 1/(\beta + \delta)$, the coefficient of P_t will vanish, and (16.14) will reduce to $P_{t+1} = \sigma(\alpha + \gamma) = (\alpha + \gamma)/(\beta + \delta) = \bar{P}$.

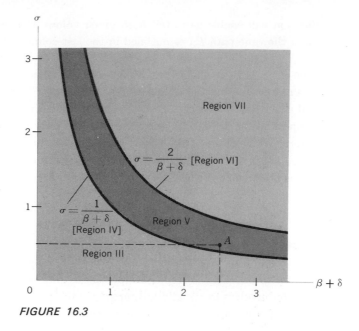

FIGURE 16.3

$\sigma = 2/(\beta + \delta)$, respectively. Since each of these plots as a rectangular hyperbola, the two regions are graphically represented by the two hyperbolic curves in Fig. 16.3. Once we have the two hyperbolas, moreover, the other three regions will immediately fall into place. Region III, for instance, is merely the set of points lying below the lower hyperbola, where we have σ less than $1/(\beta + \delta)$. Similarly, region V is represented by the set of points falling between the two hyperbolas, whereas all the points located above the higher hyperbola pertain to region VII.

Example 2   If $\sigma = \frac{1}{2}$, $\beta = 1$, and $\delta = \frac{3}{2}$, will our model (16.13) yield a convergent time path P_t? The given parametric values correspond to point A in Fig. 16.3. Since it falls within region V, the time path is convergent, though oscillatory.

The reader will note that, in the two models just presented, our analytical results are in each instance stated as a set of alternative possible cases—three types of oscillatory paths for the cobwebs, and five types of time paths in the inventory model. This richness of analytical results stems, of course, from the parametric formulation of the models. As the reader well knows, the fact that our result cannot be stated in a single unequivocal answer is a merit rather than a weakness.

EXERCISE 16.5

1 In solving (16.14), why should formula (16.8') be used instead of (16.9')?

2 On the basis of Table 16.2, check the validity of the translation from the b specification to the σ specification for regions IV through VII.

3 If model (16.13) has the following numerical form:

$$Q_{dt} = 21 - 2P_t$$
$$Q_{st} = -3 + 6P_t$$
$$P_{t+1} = P_t - 0.3(Q_{st} - Q_{dt})$$

find the time path P_t and determine whether it is convergent.

4 Suppose that, in model (16.13), the supply in each period is a fixed quantity, say, $Q_{st} = k$, instead of a function of price. Analyze the behavior of price over time. What restriction should be imposed on k to make the solution economically meaningful?

16.6 Nonlinear Difference Equations— the Qualitative-Graphic Approach

Thus far we have only utilized *linear* difference equations in our models; but the facts of economic life may not always acquiesce to the convenience of linearity. Fortunately, when nonlinearity occurs in the case of first-order difference-equation models, there exists an easy method of analysis that is applicable under fairly general conditions. This method, graphic in nature, closely resembles that of the qualitative analysis of first-order differential equations presented in Sec. 14.6.

phase diagram Nonlinear difference equations in which only the variables y_{t+1} and y_t appear, such as

$$y_{t+1} + y_t{}^3 = 5 \quad \text{or} \quad y_{t+1} + \sin y_t - \ln y_t = 3$$

can be categorically represented by the equation

$$y_{t+1} = f(y_t)$$

where f can be a function of any degree of complexity, as long as it is a function of y_t alone. When the two variables y_{t+1} and y_t are plotted against each other in a cartesian coordinate plane, the resulting diagram constitutes a *phase diagram*, and the curve corresponding to f is a *phase line*. From these, it is possible to analyze the time path of the variable by the process of iteration.

The terms phase diagram and phase line are used here in analogy to the differential-equation case; but note one dissimilarity in the construction of the diagram. In the differential-equation case, we plotted dy/dt against y as in Fig. 14.4, so that, in order to be perfectly analogous in the present case, we should have Δy_t on the vertical axis and y_t on the horizontal. This is not impossible to do, but it is much more convenient to place y_{t+1} on the vertical axis instead, as we have done in Fig. 16.4. The reader will also note the presence of a 45° line in each diagram of Fig. 16.4; this line will prove to be of great service in carrying out our graphic analysis.

Let us illustrate the procedure involved by means of Fig. 16.4a, where we have drawn a phase line (labeled f_1) representing a specific difference equation $y_{t+1} = f_1(y_t)$. If we are given an initial value y_0 (plotted on the horizontal axis), by iteration we can trace out all the subsequent values of y as follows. First, since the phase line f_1 maps the initial value y_0 into y_1 according to the equation

$$y_1 = f_1(y_0)$$

we can go straight up from y_0 to the phase line, hit point A, and read its height on the vertical axis as the value of y_1. Next, we seek to map y_1 into y_2 according to the equation

$$y_2 = f_1(y_1)$$

For this purpose, we must first plot y_1 on the horizontal axis—similarly to y_0 during the first mapping. This required transplotting of y_1 from the vertical axis to the horizontal is most easily accomplished by the use of the 45° line, which, having a slope of $+1$, is the locus of points with identical abscissa and ordinate, such as (2,2) and (5,5). Thus, to transplot y_1 from the vertical axis, we can simply go across to the 45° line, hit point B, and then turn straight down to the horizontal axis to locate the point y_1. By repeating this process, we can map y_1 to y_2 via point C on the phase line, and then use the 45° line for transplotting y_2, etc.

Now that the nature of the iteration is clear, however, we may observe that the desired iteration can be achieved simply by following the arrowheads from y_0 to A (on the phase line), to B (on the 45° line), to C (on the phase line), etc. —always alternating between the two lines—without it ever being necessary to resort to the axes again.

types of time path The graphic iterations just outlined are, of course, equally applicable to the other three diagrams in Fig. 16.4. Actually, these four

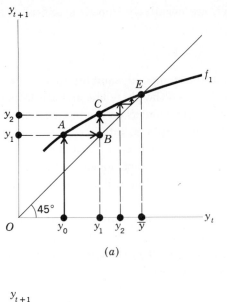

(a)

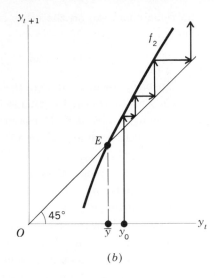

(b)

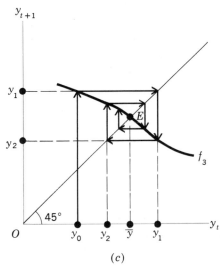

(c)

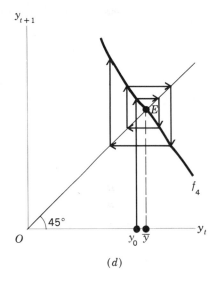

(d)

FIGURE 16.4

diagrams serve to illustrate four major varieties of phase lines, each implying a different type of time path. The first two phase lines, f_1 and f_2, are characterized by positive slopes, with one being less than unity and the other one greater than unity:

$$0 < f_1'(y_t) < 1 \qquad \text{and} \qquad f_2'(y_t) > 1$$

The remaining two, on the other hand, are negatively sloped; specifically, we have

$$-1 < f_3'(y_t) < 0 \qquad \text{and} \qquad f_4'(y_t) < -1$$

In each diagram of Fig. 16.4, the intertemporal equilibrium value of y (namely $\bar{y}$) is located at the intersection between the phase line and the 45° line, which we have labeled E. This is so because the point E on the phase line, being simultaneously a point on the 45° line, will map a y_t into a y_{t+1} of identical value; and when $y_{t+1} = y_t$, by definition y must be in equilibrium intertemporally. Our principal task is to determine whether, given an initial value $y_0 \neq \bar{y}$, the pattern of change implied by the phase line will lead us consistently toward $\bar{y}$ (convergent) or away from it (divergent).

For the phase line f_1, the iterative process leads from y_0 to $\bar{y}$ in a steady path, without oscillation. The reader can verify that, if y_0 is placed to the right of $\bar{y}$, there will also be a steady movement toward $\bar{y}$, though it will be in the leftward direction. These time paths are convergent to equilibrium, and their general configurations would be of the same type as shown in region III of Fig. 16.1.

Given the phase line f_2, whose slope exceeds unity, however, a divergent time path will emerge. From an initial value y_0 greater than $\bar{y}$, the arrowheads will lead steadily away from the equilibrium to higher and higher y values. As the reader can verify, an initial value lower than $\bar{y}$ will cause a similar steady divergent movement, though in the opposite direction.

When the phase line is negatively inclined, as in f_3 and f_4, the steady movement gives way to oscillation, and there will now be the phenomenon of *overshooting* the equilibrium mark. In diagram c, y_0 leads to y_1, which exceeds $\bar{y}$, only to be followed by y_2, which falls short of $\bar{y}$, etc. The convergence of the time path will, in such cases, depend on the slope of the phase line being less than 1 in its absolute value. This is the case of the phase line f_3, where the extent of overshooting tends to diminish in successive periods. For the phase line f_4, whose slope exceeds 1 numerically, on the other hand, the opposite tendency prevails, thereby giving rise to a divergent time path.

The oscillatory time paths generated by phase lines f_3 and f_4 are reminiscent of the cobwebs in Fig. 16.2. In Fig. 16.4c or d, however, the cobweb is spun around a phase line (which contains a lag) and the 45° line, instead of around a demand curve and a (lagged) supply curve. Here, a 45° line is used as a mechanical aid for transplotting a value of y, whereas in Fig. 16.2, the D curve (which plays a role similar to that of the 45° line in Fig. 16.4) is an integral part of the model itself. Specifically, once Q_{st} is determined on the supply curve, we let the arrowheads hit the D curve for the explicit purpose of finding a price that will "clear the market," as was the rule of the game in the cobweb model. Consequently, there is a basic difference in the labeling of the axes: in Fig. 16.2 there are two entirely different variables, P and Q, but in Fig. 16.4 the axes represent the values of the same variable y in two consecutive periods. The reader should note, however, that if we analyze the graph of the difference equation (16.11) which summarizes the cobweb model, rather than the separate demand and supply functions in (16.10), then the resulting diagram will be a phase line such as shown in Fig. 16.4. In other words, there really exist two alternative ways of graphically analyzing the cobweb model, which will yield the identical result.

The basic rule emerging from the above consideration of the phase line is that the *algebraic sign* of its slope determines whether there will be *oscillation*, and the *absolute value* of its slope governs the question of *convergence*. If the phase line happens to contain both positively and negatively sloped segments, and if the absolute value of its slope is at some points greater (and elsewhere less) than 1, the time path will naturally become more complicated. However, even in such cases, the graphic-iterative analysis can be employed with equal ease. Of course, an initial value must be given to us before the iteration can be duly started. Indeed, in these more complicated cases, a different initial value can lead to a time path of an altogether different breed (see Exercises 16.6-2 and 16.6-3 below).

an economic example   We shall now cite an economic example of a non-linear difference equation. In Fig. 16.4, the four nonlinear phase lines all happen to be of the smooth variety; in the present example, we shall show a nonsmooth phase line.

As a point of departure, let us take the *linear* difference equation (16.11) of the cobweb model and rewrite it as

$$(16.16) \qquad P_{t+1} = \frac{\alpha + \gamma}{\beta} - \frac{\delta}{\beta} P_t \qquad \left(\frac{\delta}{\beta} > 0 \right)$$

This is in the format of $P_{t+1} = f(P_t)$, with $f'(P_t) = -\delta/\beta < 0$. We have plotted this linear phase line in Fig. 16.5 on the assumption that the slope is greater than 1 in absolute value, implying *explosive* oscillation.

Now let there be imposed a legal price ceiling $\hat{P}$ (read: P caret or, less formally, P hat). This can be shown in Fig. 16.5 as a horizontal straight line because, irrespective of the level of P_t, P_{t+1} is now forbidden to exceed the level of $\hat{P}$. What this does is to invalidate that part of the phase line lying above $\hat{P}$ or, to view it differently, to bend down the upper part of the phase line to the level of $\hat{P}$, thus resulting in a kinked phase line.[1] In view of the kink, the new

---

[1] Strictly speaking, we should also "bend" that part of the phase line lying to the right of the point $\hat{P}$ on the horizontal axis. But it does no harm to leave it as it is, so long as the other end has already been bent, because the transplotting of P_{t+1} to the horizontal axis will carry the upper limit of $\hat{P}$ over to the P_t axis automatically.

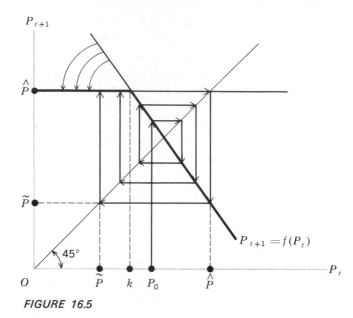

FIGURE 16.5

(heavy) phase line is not only nonlinear but nonsmooth as well. Like a step function, this kinked line will require more than one equation to express it algebraically:

$$(16.16') \qquad P_{t+1} = \begin{cases} \hat{P} & \text{(for } P_t \le k) \\ \dfrac{\alpha + \gamma}{\beta} - \dfrac{\delta}{\beta} P_t & \text{(for } P_t > k) \end{cases}$$

where k denotes the value of P_t corresponding to the kink.

Assuming an initial price P_0, let us trace out the time path of price iteratively. During the first stage of iteration, when the downward-sloping segment of the phase line is in effect, the explosive oscillatory tendency will clearly manifest itself. After a few periods, however, the arrowheads will begin to hit the ceiling price, and thereafter the time path will develop into a perpetual cyclical movement between $\hat{P}$ and an effectual *price floor* $\tilde{P}$ (read: P tilde or, less formally, P wiggle). Thus, by virtue of the price ceiling, the intrinsic explosive tendency of the model is effectively contained, and the ever-widening oscillation is now tamed into a uniform oscillation.

What is significant about this result is that, whereas in the case of a linear phase line a uniformly oscillatory path can be produced (as the reader can verify) if and only if the slope of the phase line is -1, now after the introduction of nonlinearity the same analytical result can arise when the phase line has a slope other than -1. The economic implication of this fact is of considerable import. If one observes a more or less uniform oscillation in the actual time path of a variable and attempts to explain it by means of a *linear* model, he will be forced to rely on the rather special—and implausible—model specification that the phase-line slope is exactly -1. But if nonlinearity is introduced, in either the smooth or the nonsmooth variety, then a host of more reasonable assumptions can be used, each of which can equally account for the observed feature of uniform oscillation.

EXERCISE 16.6

1   In difference-equation models, the variable t can only take integer values. Does this imply that in the phase diagrams of Fig. 16.4 the variables y_t and y_{t+1} must be considered as discrete variables?

2   As a phase line, use the left half of an inverse U-shaped curve, and let it intersect the 45° line at two points L (left) and R (right).

   (a)   Is this a case of multiple equilibria?
   (b)   If the initial value y_0 lies to the left of L, what kind of time path will be obtained?
   (c)   What if the initial value lies between L and R?
   (d)   What if the initial value lies to the right of R?
   (e)   What can you conclude about the dynamic stability of equilibrium at L and at R, respectively?

3   As a phase line, use an inverse U-shaped curve. Let its upward-sloping segment intersect the 45° line at point L, and let its downward-sloping segment intersect the 45° line at point R. Answer the same five questions raised in the preceding problem. (*Note:* Your answer will depend on the particular way the phase line is drawn; explore various possibilities.)

4   In Fig. 16.5, rescind the legal price ceiling and impose a minimum price P_m instead.

   (a)   How will the phase line change?
   (b)   Will it be kinked? Nonlinear?
   (c)   Will there also develop a uniformly oscillatory movement in price?

5   With reference to (16.16′) and Fig. 16.5, show that the constant k can be expressed as

$$k = \frac{\alpha + \gamma}{\delta} - \frac{\beta}{\delta} \bar{P}$$

17

HIGHER-ORDER DIFFERENCE EQUATIONS AND SIMULTANEOUS-EQUATION DYNAMIC MODELS

The economic models in the preceding chapter involve difference equations that relate P_t and P_{t-1} to each other. As the P value in one period can uniquely determine the P value in the next, the time path of P becomes fully determinate once an initial value P_0 is specified. It may happen, however, that the value of an economic variable in period t (say, y_t) depends not only on y_{t-1} but also on y_{t-2}. Such a situation will give rise to a difference equation of the second order.

Strictly speaking, a *second-order difference equation* is one that involves an expression $\Delta^2 y_t$, called the *second difference* of y_t, but contains no differences of order higher than 2. The symbol Δ^2, the discrete-time counterpart of the symbol d^2/dt^2, is an instruction to "take the second difference" as follows:

$$
\begin{aligned}
\Delta^2 y_t &= \Delta(\Delta y_t) = \Delta(y_{t+1} - y_t) && \text{[by (16.1)]} \\
&= (y_{t+2} - y_{t+1}) - (y_{t+1} - y_t) && \text{[again by (16.1)]}\dagger \\
&= y_{t+2} - 2y_{t+1} + y_t
\end{aligned}
$$

Thus a second difference of y_t is transformable into a sum of terms involving a two-period time lag. Since expressions like $\Delta^2 y_t$ and Δy_t are quite cumbersome to work with, we shall simply redefine a second-order difference equation as one involving a two-period time lag in the variable. Similarly, a third-order difference equation will involve a three-period time lag, etc.

---

† That is, we first move the subscripts in the $(y_{t+1} - y_t)$ expression forward by one period, to get a new expression $(y_{t+2} - y_{t+1})$, and then we subtract from the latter the original expression. Note that, since the resulting difference may be written as $\Delta y_{t+1} - \Delta y_t$, we may infer the following rule of operation:

$$\Delta(y_{t+1} - y_t) = \Delta y_{t+1} - \Delta y_t$$

This is reminiscent of the rule applicable to the derivative of a sum or difference.

Let us first concentrate on the method of solving a second-order difference equation, leaving the generalization to higher-order equations for a later section. To keep the scope of discussion manageable, we shall only deal with linear difference equations with constant coefficients in the present chapter. However, both the constant-term and variable-term varieties will be examined below.

17.1 Second-Order Linear Difference Equations with Constant Coefficients and Constant Term

A simple variety of second-order difference equation takes the form

$$(17.1) \qquad y_{t+2} + a_1 y_{t+1} + a_2 y_t = c$$

The reader will recognize this equation to be linear, nonhomogeneous, and with constant coefficients (a_1, a_2) and constant term c.

particular integral As before, the solution of (17.1) may be expected to have two components: a particular integral y_p representing the intertemporal equilibrium level of y, and a complementary function y_c specifying, for every time period, the deviation from the equilibrium. The particular integral, defined as any solution of the complete equation, can sometimes be found simply by trying a solution of the form $y_t = k$. Substituting this constant value of y into (17.1), we obtain

$$k + a_1 k + a_2 k = c \qquad \text{and} \qquad k = \frac{c}{1 + a_1 + a_2}$$

Thus, as long as $(1 + a_1 + a_2) \neq 0$, the particular integral is

$$(17.2) \qquad y_p \, (= k) = \frac{c}{1 + a_1 + a_2} \qquad \text{(case of } a_1 + a_2 \neq -1\text{)}$$

Example 1 Find the particular integral of $y_{t+2} - 3y_{t+1} + 4y_t = 6$. Here we have $a_1 = -3$, $a_2 = 4$, and $c = 6$. Since $a_1 + a_2 \neq -1$, the particular integral can be obtained from (17.2) as follows:

$$y_p = \frac{6}{1 - 3 + 4} = 3$$

In case $a_1 + a_2 = -1$, then the trial solution $y_t = k$ breaks down, and we must try $y_t = kt$ instead. Substituting the latter into (17.1) and bearing in mind that we now have $y_{t+1} = k(t + 1)$ and $y_{t+2} = k(t + 2)$, we find that

$$k(t + 2) + a_1 k(t + 1) + a_2 kt = c$$

and $\quad k = \dfrac{c}{(1 + a_1 + a_2)t + a_1 + 2} = \dfrac{c}{a_1 + 2}$

[since $a_1 + a_2 = -1$]

Thus we can write the particular integral as

$$(17.2') \qquad y_p\,(= kt) = \frac{c}{a_1 + 2}\, t \qquad \text{(case of } a_1 + a_2 = -1; a_1 \neq -2)$$

Example 2   Find the particular integral of $y_{t+2} + y_{t+1} - 2y_t = 12$. Here, $a_1 = 1$, $a_2 = -2$, and $c = 12$. Obviously, formula (17.2) is not applicable, but (17.2') is. Thus,

$$y_p = \frac{12}{1 + 2}\, t = 4t$$

This particular integral represents a moving equilibrium.

If $a_1 + a_2 = -1$, but at the same time $a_1 = -2$ (that is, if $a_1 = -2$ and $a_2 = 1$), then we can adopt a trial solution of the form $y_t = kt^2$, which implies $y_{t+1} = k(t + 1)^2$, etc. The reader may verify that, in this case, the particular integral will turn out to be

$$(17.2'') \qquad y_p = kt^2 = \frac{c}{2}\, t^2 \qquad \text{(case of } a_1 = -2; a_2 = 1)$$

However, since this formula applies only to the unique case of the difference equation $y_{t+2} - 2y_{t+1} + y_t = c$, its usefulness is rather limited.

complementary function   To find the complementary function, we must concentrate on the reduced equation

$$(17.3) \qquad y_{t+2} + a_1 y_{t+1} + a_2 y_t = 0$$

Our experience with first-order difference equations has taught us that the expression Ab^t plays a prominent role in the general solution of such an equation. Let us therefore try a solution of the form $y_t = Ab^t$, which will naturally imply that $y_{t+1} = Ab^{t+1}$, and so on. It is our task now to determine the values of A and b.

Upon substitution of the trial solution into (17.3), the equation becomes

$$Ab^{t+2} + a_1 Ab^{t+1} + a_2 Ab^t = 0$$

or, after canceling the (nonzero) common factor of Ab^t,

(17.3′) $b^2 + a_1 b + a_2 = 0$

This quadratic equation—the *characteristic equation* of (17.3) or of (17.1)—which is comparable to (15.4″), possesses the two *characteristic roots*

(17.4) $b_1, b_2 = \dfrac{-a_1 \pm \sqrt{a_1{}^2 - 4a_2}}{2}$

each of which is acceptable in the solution Ab^t. In fact, *both b_1 and b_2 should appear in the general solution of the homogeneous difference equation (17.3) because, just as in the case of differential equations, this general solution must consist of two *linearly independent* parts, each with its own multiplicative arbitrary constant.

Three possible situations may be encountered in regard to the characteristic roots, depending on the square-root expression in (17.4). These, the reader will find, parallel very closely the analysis of second-order differential equations in Sec. 15.1.

CASE I   (*Distinct Real Roots*)   When $a_1{}^2 > 4a_2$, the square root in (17.4) is a real number, and b_1 and b_2 will be real and distinct. In that event, $b_1{}^t$ and $b_2{}^t$ are linearly independent, and the complementary function can simply be written as a linear combination of these expressions; that is,

(17.5) $y_c = A_1 b_1{}^t + A_2 b_2{}^t$

The reader should compare this with (15.7).

Example 3   Find the solution of $y_{t+2} + y_{t+1} - 2y_t = 12$. This equation has the coefficients $a_1 = 1$ and $a_2 = -2$; from (17.4), the characteristic roots can be found to be $b_1, b_2 = 1, -2$. Thus, the complementary function is

$$y_c = A_1(1)^t + A_2(-2)^t = A_1 + A_2(-2)^t$$

Since, in Example 2, the particular integral of the given difference equation has already been found to be $y_p = 4t$, we can write the general solution as

$$y_t = y_c + y_p = A_1 + A_2(-2)^t + 4t$$

There are still two arbitrary constants A_1 and A_2 to be definitized; to accomplish this, *two* initial conditions are necessary. Suppose that we are given $y_0 = 4$ and $y_1 = 5$. Then, since by letting $t = 0$ and $t = 1$ successively in the general solution we find

$$y_0 = A_1 + A_2 \qquad (= 4 \text{ by the first initial condition})$$
$$y_1 = A_1 - 2A_2 + 4 \qquad (= 5 \text{ by the second initial condition})$$

the arbitrary constants can be definitized to $A_1 = 3$ and $A_2 = 1$. The definite solution then can finally be written as

$$y_t = 3 + (-2)^t + 4t$$

CASE 2 *(Repeated Real Roots)* When $a_1{}^2 = 4a_2$, the square root in (17.4) vanishes, and the characteristic roots will be repeated:

$$b\ (= b_1 = b_2) = -\frac{a_1}{2}$$

Now, if we express the complementary function in the form of (17.5), the two components will collapse into a single term:

$$A_1 b_1{}^t + A_2 b_2{}^t = (A_1 + A_2)b^t \equiv A_3 b^t$$

This will not do, because we are now short of one constant.

To supply the missing component—which, we recall, should be linearly independent of the term $A_3 b^t$—the old trick of multiplying b^t by the variable t will again work. The new component term is therefore to take the form $A_4 t b^t$. That this is linearly independent of $A_3 b^t$ should be obvious, for we can never obtain the expression $A_4 t b^t$ by attaching a constant coefficient to $A_3 b^t$. That $A_4 t b^t$ does indeed qualify as a solution of the homogeneous equation (17.3), just as $A_3 b^t$ does, can easily be verified by substituting $y_t = A_4 t b^t$ [and $y_{t+1} = A_4(t + 1)b^{t+1}$, etc.] into (17.3)† and seeing that the latter will reduce to an identity $0 = 0$.

The complementary function for the repeated-root case is therefore

(17.6) $$y_c = A_3 b^t + A_4 t b^t$$

which the reader should compare with (15.9).

Example 4 Find the complementary function of $y_{t+2} + 6y_{t+1} + 9y_t = 4$. The coefficients being $a_1 = 6$ and $a_2 = 9$, the characteristic roots are found to be $b_1 = b_2 = -3$. We therefore have

$$y_c = A_3(-3)^t + A_4 t(-3)^t$$

If we proceed a step further, we can easily find $y_p = \frac{1}{4}$, so that the general solution of the given difference equation is

$$y_t = A_3(-3)^t + A_4 t(-3)^t + \frac{1}{4}$$

Given two initial conditions, A_3 and A_4 can again be assigned definite values.

---

† In this substitution it should be kept in mind that we have in the present case $a_1{}^2 = 4a_2$ and $b = -a_1/2$.

CASE 3 *(Complex Roots)* Under the remaining possibility of $a_1{}^2 < 4a_2$, the characteristic roots will be conjugate complex. Specifically, they will be in the form

$$b_1, b_2 = h \pm vi$$

where

(17.7) $\qquad h = -\dfrac{a_1}{2} \qquad$ and $\qquad v = \dfrac{\sqrt{4a_2 - a_1{}^2}}{2}$

The complementary function itself will thus become

$$y_c = A_5 b_1{}^t + A_6 b_2{}^t = A_5(h + vi)^t + A_6(h - vi)^t$$

As it stands, y_c is not easily interpreted. But fortunately, thanks to De Moivre's theorem, given in (15.28′), this complementary function can easily be transformed into trigonometric terms, which we have learned to interpret.

According to the said theorem, we can write

$$(h \pm vi)^t = R^t(\cos \theta t \pm i \sin \theta t)$$

where the value of R (always taken to be positive) is, by (15.17),

(17.8) $\qquad R = \sqrt{h^2 + v^2} = \sqrt{\dfrac{a_1{}^2 + 4a_2 - a_1{}^2}{4}} = \sqrt{a_2}$

and θ is the radian measure of the angle in the interval $[0, 2\pi)$, which fulfills the conditions

(17.9) $\qquad \cos \theta = \dfrac{h}{R} = \dfrac{h}{\sqrt{a_2}} \qquad$ and $\qquad \sin \theta = \dfrac{v}{R} = \dfrac{v}{\sqrt{a_2}}$

Therefore, the complementary function can be transformed as follows:

$$(17.10) \qquad y_c = A_5 R^t(\cos \theta t + i \sin \theta t) + A_6 R^t(\cos \theta t - i \sin \theta t)$$

$$= R^t[(A_5 + A_6) \cos \theta t + (A_5 - A_6)i \sin \theta t]$$

$$= R^t(A_7 \cos \theta t + A_8 \sin \theta t)$$

Here, we have adopted the shorthand symbols

$$A_7 \equiv A_5 + A_6 \qquad \text{and} \qquad A_8 \equiv (A_5 - A_6)i$$

in lieu of the α and β used in (15.29′) for the differential-equation case. A far more important difference is that, in (17.10), we have the expressions $\cos \theta t$ and $\sin \theta t$, in contrast to the expressions $\cos vt$ and $\sin vt$ found in (15.29′). Note, also, that the multiplicative factor R^t has replaced the differential-equation counterpart of e^{ht}.

To give specific content to this complementary function, we need to know R, θ, A_7, and A_8. The values of R and θ, defined in (17.8) and (17.9), are obtainable as soon as we find the real part h and the imaginary part v of the complex characteristic roots from (17.7), while the arbitrary constants A_7 and A_8 can be definitized later, given two initial conditions.

Example 5   Find the general solution of $y_{t+2} + \frac{1}{4}y_t = 5$. With coefficients $a_1 = 0$ and $a_2 = \frac{1}{4}$, this constitutes an illustration of the complex-root case of $a_1^2 < 4a_2$. By (17.7), the real and imaginary parts of the roots are $h = 0$ and $v = \frac{1}{2}$. We can also find, by (17.8), that $R = \frac{1}{2}$. Since the value of θ is that which can satisfy the two equations

$$\cos \theta = \frac{h}{R} = 0 \quad \text{and} \quad \sin \theta = \frac{v}{R} = 1$$

it may be concluded, from Table 15.1, that

$$\theta = \frac{\pi}{2}$$

Consequently, the complementary function is

$$y_c = \left(\frac{1}{2}\right)^t \left(A_7 \cos \frac{\pi}{2} t + A_8 \sin \frac{\pi}{2} t\right)$$

To find y_p, let us try a constant solution $y_t = k$ in the complete equation. This yields $k = 4$; thus, $y_p = 4$, and the general solution can be written as

$$(17.11) \qquad y_t = \left(\frac{1}{2}\right)^t \left(A_7 \cos \frac{\pi}{2} t + A_8 \sin \frac{\pi}{2} t\right) + 4$$

Example 6   Find the general solution of $y_{t+2} - 4y_{t+1} + 16y_t = 0$. In the first place, the particular integral is easily found to be $y_p = 0$. This means that the general solution $y_t (= y_c + y_p)$ will be identical with y_c. To find the latter, we see that the coefficients $a_1 = -4$ and $a_2 = 16$ generate two complex roots $h \pm vi$, with

$$h = \frac{4}{2} = 2 \quad \text{and} \quad v = \frac{\sqrt{64 - 16}}{2} = 2\sqrt{3}$$

whereas (17.8) gives us $R = \sqrt{16} = 4$. This means that θ must satisfy the two conditions

$$\cos \theta = \frac{h}{R} = \frac{1}{2} \quad \text{and} \quad \sin \theta = \frac{v}{R} = \frac{\sqrt{3}}{2}$$

Therefore, from Table 15.2, we find that

$$\theta = \frac{\pi}{3}$$

It follows then that the complementary function—which also serves as the general solution here—is

$$(17.12) \qquad y_c \, (= y_t) = 4^t \left(A_7 \cos \frac{\pi}{3} t + A_8 \sin \frac{\pi}{3} t \right)$$

convergence of the time path   As in the case of first-order difference equations, the convergence of the time path y_t hinges solely on whether y_c tends toward zero at $t \to \infty$. What we learned about the various configurations of the expression b^t, in Fig. 16.1, is therefore still applicable, although in the present context we shall have to consider *two* characteristic roots rather than one.

Consider first the case of distinct real roots: $b_1 \neq b_2$. If $|b_1| > 1$ and $|b_2| > 1$, then both component terms in the complementary function (17.5)— $A_1 b_1{}^t$ and $A_2 b_2{}^t$—will be explosive, and thus y_c must be divergent. In the opposite case of $|b_1| < 1$ and $|b_2| < 1$, both terms in y_c will converge toward zero as t is indefinitely increased, as will y_c also. What if $|b_1| > 1$ but $|b_2| < 1$? In this intermediate case, it is evident that the $A_2 b_2{}^t$ term tends to "die down," while the other term tends to deviate farther from zero. It follows that the $A_1 b_1{}^t$ term must eventually dominate the scene and render the path divergent.

Let us call the root with the higher *absolute* value the *dominant root*. Then it appears that it is the dominant root b_1 which really sets the tone of the time path, at least with regard to its ultimate convergence or divergence. Such is indeed the case. We may state, thus, that *a time path will be convergent if and only if the dominant root is less than 1 in absolute value.* The reader can verify that this statement is valid for the cases where both roots are greater than or less than 1 in absolute value (which was discussed above), and where one root has an absolute value of 1 exactly (which was *not* discussed above). Note, however, that even though the eventual convergence depends on the dominant root alone, the *non*dominant root will exert a definite influence on the time path, too, at least in the beginning periods. Therefore, the exact configuration of y_t is still dependent on both roots.

Turning to the repeated-root case, we find the complementary function to consist of the terms $A_3 b^t$ and $A_4 t b^t$, as shown in (17.6). The former is already familiar to us, but a word of explanation is still needed for the latter, which involves a multiplicative t. If $|b| > 1$, the b^t term will be explosive, and the multiplicative t will simply serve to intensify the explosiveness as t increases. If $|b| < 1$, on the other hand, the b^t part (which diminishes as t increases) and the

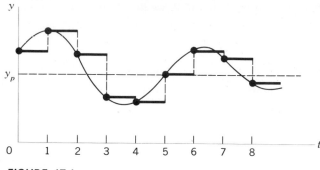

FIGURE 17.1

t part will run counter to each other; i.e., the value of t will offset rather than reinforce b^t. Which force will prove the stronger? The answer is that the damping force of b^t will always win over the exploding force of t. For this reason, the basic requirement for convergence in the repeated-root case is still that the root be less than 1 in absolute value.

Example 7   Analyze the convergence of the solutions in Examples 3 and 4 above. For Example 3, the solution is

$$y_t = 3 + (-2)^t + 4t$$

where the roots are 1 and -2, respectively $[3(1)^t = 3]$, and where there is a moving equilibrium $4t$. The dominant root being -2, the time path will be divergent.

For Example 4, where the solution is

$$y_t = A_3(-3)^t + A_4 t(-3)^t + \frac{1}{4}$$

and where $|b| = 3$, we also have divergence.

Let us now consider the complex-root case. From the general form of the complementary function in (17.10),

$$y_c = R^t(A_7 \cos \theta t + A_8 \sin \theta t)$$

it is clear that the parenthetical expression, like the one in (15.29′), will produce a fluctuating pattern of a periodic nature. However, since the variable t can only take integer values 0, 1, 2, . . . in the present context, we shall catch and utilize only a subset of the points on the graph of a circular function. The y value at each such point will always prevail for a whole period, till the next relevant point is reached. As illustrated in Fig. 17.1, the resulting path is neither the usual oscillatory type (not alternating between values above and below y_p in consecutive

Dynamic Analysis

periods), nor the usual fluctuating type (not smooth); rather, it displays a *stepped* fluctuation. As far as convergence is concerned, though, the decisive factor is really the R^t term, which, like the e^{ht} term in (15.29″), will dictate whether the stepped fluctuation is to be intensified or mitigated as t increases. In the present case, the fluctuation can be gradually narrowed down if and only if $R < 1$. Since R is by definition the absolute value of the conjugate complex roots $(h \pm vi)$, the condition for convergence is again that the characteristic roots be less than unity in absolute value.

To summarize: For all three possible cases of characteristic roots, the time path will converge to a (stationary or moving) intertemporal equilibrium if and only if the absolute value of every root is less than 1.

Example 8   Are the time paths (17.11) and (17.12) convergent? In (17.11) we have $R = \frac{1}{2}$; therefore the time path will converge to the stationary equilibrium $(=4)$. In (17.12), on the other hand, we have $R = 4$, so that the time path will not converge to the equilibrium $(=0)$.

EXERCISE 17.1

1   Write out the characteristic equation for each of the following, and find the characteristic roots:

(a) $y_{t+2} - y_{t+1} + \dfrac{1}{2} y_t = 2$ (c) $y_{t+2} - 4y_{t+1} + 4y_t = 7$

(b) $y_{t+2} + \dfrac{1}{2} y_{t+1} - \dfrac{1}{2} y_t = 5$ (d) $y_{t+2} - 2y_{t+1} + 3y_t = 4$

2   For each of the difference equations in the preceding problem, state on the basis of its characteristic roots whether the time path involves oscillation or stepped fluctuation, and whether it is explosive.

3   Find the particular integrals of the equations in Exercise 17.1-1 above. Do these represent stationary or moving equilibria?

4   Solve the following difference equations:

(a) $y_{t+2} + 3y_{t+1} - \dfrac{7}{4} y_t = 9$ $(y_0 = 6;\ y_1 = 3)$

(b) $y_{t+2} - 2y_{t+1} + 2y_t = 1$ $(y_0 = 3;\ y_1 = 4)$

(c) $y_{t+2} - y_{t+1} + \dfrac{1}{4} y_t = 2$ $(y_0 = 4; y_1 = 7)$

5   Analyze the time paths obtained in the preceding problem.

17.2   Samuelson Multiplier-Accelerator Interaction Model

As an illustration of the use of second-order difference equations in economics, let us cite Professor Samuelson's well-known *interaction* model, which seeks to explore the dynamic process of income determination when the acceleration principle is in operation along with the Keynesian multiplier.[1] Among other things, that model serves to demonstrate that the mere interaction of the multiplier and the accelerator is capable of generating cyclical fluctuations endogenously.

the framework   Suppose that national income Y_t is made up of three component expenditure streams: consumption, C_t; investment, I_t; and government expenditure, G_t. Consumption is envisaged as a function not of current income but of the income of the prior period, Y_{t-1}; for simplicity, it shall be assumed that C_t is strictly proportional to Y_{t-1}. Investment, which is of the "induced" variety, is a function of the prevailing trend of consumer spending. It is through this induced investment, of course, that the acceleration principle enters into the model. Specifically, we shall assume I_t to be in a fixed ratio to the consumption increment $\Delta C_{t-1} \equiv C_t - C_{t-1}$. The third component, G_t, on the other hand, is taken to be exogenous; in fact, we shall assume it to be a constant and simply denote it by G_0.

These assumptions can be translated into the following set of equations:

(17.13)
$$Y_t = C_t + I_t + G_0$$
$$C_t = \gamma Y_{t-1} \qquad (0 < \gamma < 1)$$
$$I_t = \alpha(C_t - C_{t-1}) \qquad (\alpha > 0)$$

where γ (the third letter in the Greek alphabet, and thus a sort of counterpart for c) represents the marginal propensity to consume, and α stands for accelerator (short for *acceleration coefficient*). Note that, if induced investment is expunged from the model, we are left with a first-order difference equation that is descriptive of the dynamic multiplier process (cf. Example 2 of Sec. 16.2). With induced

[1] Paul A. Samuelson, "Interactions between the Multiplier Analysis and the Principles of Acceleration," *Review of Economic Statistics*, May, 1939, pp. 75–78; reprinted in American Economic Association, *Readings in Business Cycle Theory*, Richard D. Irwin, Inc., Homewood, Ill., 1944, pp. 261–269.

investment included, however, we have a second-order difference equation that depicts the interaction of the multiplier and the accelerator.

By virtue of the second equation, we can express I_t in terms of income as follows:

$$I_t = \alpha(\gamma Y_{t-1} - \gamma Y_{t-2}) = \alpha\gamma(Y_{t-1} - Y_{t-2})$$

Upon substituting this and the C_t equation into the first equation in (17.13) and rearranging, the model can be condensed into the single equation

$$Y_t - \gamma(1 + \alpha)Y_{t-1} + \alpha\gamma Y_{t-2} = G_0$$

or, equivalently (after shifting the subscripts forward by two periods),

$$(17.14) \qquad Y_{t+2} - \gamma(1 + \alpha)Y_{t+1} + \alpha\gamma Y_t = G_0$$

As a second-order linear difference equation with constant coefficients and constant term, this can be solved by the method just learned.

the solution   As the particular integral, we have, by (17.2),

$$Y_p = \frac{G_0}{1 - \gamma(1 + \alpha) + \alpha\gamma} = \frac{G_0}{1 - \gamma}$$

It may be noted that the expression $1/(1 - \gamma)$ is merely the multiplier that would prevail in the absence of induced investment. Thus $G_0/(1 - \gamma)$—the exogeneous expenditure item times the multiplier—should give us the equilibrium income in the sense that this income level satisfies the equilibrium condition "national income = total expenditure." [Cf. (3.24).] Being the particular integral of the model, however, it also gives us the intertemporal equilibrium income.

With regard to the complementary function, there are three possible cases. Case 1 ($a_1{}^2 > 4a_2$), in the present context, is characterized by

$$\gamma^2(1 + \alpha)^2 > 4\alpha\gamma \qquad \text{or} \qquad \gamma(1 + \alpha)^2 > 4\alpha$$

$$\text{or} \qquad \gamma > \frac{4\alpha}{(1 + \alpha)^2}$$

Similarly, to characterize Cases 2 and 3, we only need to change the $>$ sign in the last inequality to $=$ and $<$, respectively.

While indicative of the general nature of the characteristic roots, this tripartite classification tells nothing about the convergence of the time path of Y. For the latter purpose, we need to distinguish, under each case, between the *damped* and the *explosive* subcases. We could, of course, simply illustrate these subcases by citing some specific examples; but let us attempt the more rewarding, if more difficult, task of finding the general conditions under which convergence and divergence will prevail.

dynamic stability of equilibrium The difference equation (17.14) has the following characteristic equation:

$$b^2 - \gamma(1 + \alpha)b + \alpha\gamma = 0$$

which can be solved for two roots b_1 and b_2. Since convergence and divergence depend on the values of b_1 and b_2 and since b_1 and b_2, in turn, depend on the values of the parameters α and γ, the conditions for convergence and divergence should be expressible in terms of the values of α and γ. To do this, we can make use of the fact that—by (15.6)—the two characteristic roots are always related to each other by the following two equations:

(17.15) $\qquad b_1 + b_2 = \gamma(1 + \alpha)$

(17.15′) $\qquad b_1 b_2 = \alpha\gamma$

For Case 1, the roots are real and distinct. Since α and γ are both positive, (17.15′) tells us that b_1 and b_2 must possess the same algebraic sign. Furthermore, since $\gamma(1 + \alpha) > 0$, (17.15) indicates that both b_1 and b_2 must be positive. Hence, the time path Y_t cannot have oscillations in Case 1. Even though the signs of b_1 and b_2 are now known, there actually exist as many as five possible combinations of their values, each with its own implication regarding the corresponding values for α and γ:

$$
\begin{array}{llll}
(i) & 0 < b_2 < b_1 < 1 & \Rightarrow & \gamma < 1; \alpha\gamma < 1 \\
(ii) & 0 < b_2 < b_1 = 1 & \Rightarrow & \gamma = 1 \\
(iii) & 0 < b_2 < 1 < b_1 & \Rightarrow & \gamma > 1 \\
(iv) & 1 = b_2 < b_1 & \Rightarrow & \gamma = 1 \\
(v) & 1 < b_2 < b_1 & \Rightarrow & \gamma < 1; \alpha\gamma > 1
\end{array}
$$

Under *Possibility i*, where both b_1 and b_2 take (positive) fractional values, the product $(1 - b_1)(1 - b_2)$ must be positive. When we multiply this expression out, and use (17.15) and (17.15′), we can rewrite it as

$$1 - b_1 - b_2 + b_1 b_2 = 1 - \gamma(1 + \alpha) + \alpha\gamma = 1 - \gamma$$

Hence, the positivity of this implies that $\gamma < 1$, which is of course consistent with the model specification. In contrast, the next three possibilities all violate the model specification since they involve $\gamma \geq 1$; hence, they must be ruled out.[1] But *Possibility v* is again admissible. In this latter situation, b_1 and b_2 are both greater than one, thus the product $(1 - b_1)(1 - b_2) = 1 - \gamma$, being a product

---

[1] To see that *Possibility ii* implies $\gamma = 1$, we reason as follows: Since $b_2 < b_1 = 1$, we may write $b_1 b_2 = b_2$. But $b_1 b_2 = \alpha\gamma$ by (17.15′). Thus $b_2 = \alpha\gamma$. Now, by (17.15), $b_1 + b_2 = \gamma + \alpha\gamma = \gamma + b_2$. Therefore, by subtracting b_2 from both sides, we obtain $\gamma = b_1 = 1$, as claimed.

As to *Possibility iii*, since $0 < b_2 < 1 < b_1$, the product $(1 - b_1)(1 - b_2)$ must be negative because the two component terms are opposite in sign. As earlier shown in the text, this product reduces to $1 - \gamma$, so its negativity means that $\gamma > 1$, as claimed.

Possibility iv can be analyzed similarly, but will be left to the reader as an exercise. (See Exercise 17.2-3.)

of two negative terms, is again positive, implying $\gamma < 1$. Thus we are finally left with only two admissible subcases under Case 1. The first—*Possibility i*—involves fractional roots b_1 and b_2, and therefore yields a convergent time path of Y. The other subcase—*Possibility v*—features roots greater than one, and thus produces a divergent time path. As far as the values of α and γ are concerned, however, the question of convergence and divergence hinges on whether $\alpha\gamma < 1$ or $\alpha\gamma > 1$. This is because $\alpha\gamma = b_1 b_2$ must fall short of (exceed) unity when b_1 and b_2 both are positive fractions (greater than one). These results are summarized in the top part of Table 17.1, where the convergent subcase is labelled 1C, and the divergent subcase 1D.

The analysis of Case 2, with repeated roots, is similar in nature. The roots will now be $b = \gamma(1 + \alpha)/2$, with a positive sign because α and γ are positive. Thus, there is again no oscillation. This time we may classify the value of b into three possibilities only:

$$(vi) \qquad 0 < b < 1 \quad \Rightarrow \quad \gamma < 1; \alpha\gamma < 1$$
$$(vii) \qquad b = 1 \qquad\;\; \Rightarrow \quad \gamma = 1$$
$$(viii) \qquad b > 1 \qquad\;\; \Rightarrow \quad \gamma < 1; \alpha\gamma > 1$$

Under *Possibility vi*, b is a positive fraction, so we can expect the expression

$$(1 - b)^2 = 1 - 2b + b^2 = 1 - \gamma(1 + \alpha) + \alpha\gamma = 1 - \gamma$$

to be positive, which implies that $\gamma < 1$. The same inference can also be made for *Possibility viii*, where $(1 - b)^2$ is again positive. When $b = 1$, as in *Possibility vii*, on the other hand, we have $(1 - b)^2 = 0$ so that $\gamma = 1$, which is in violation of the model specification. Thus we are again left with only two admissible

TABLE 17.1

Case	Subcase	Values of α and γ	Time path Y_t
1 Distinct real roots $\gamma > \dfrac{4\alpha}{(1 + \alpha)^2}$	1C: $0 < b_2 < b_1 < 1$ 1D: $1 < b_2 < b_1$	$\alpha\gamma < 1$ $\alpha\gamma > 1$	Nonoscillatory and nonfluctuating
2 Repeated real roots $\gamma = \dfrac{4\alpha}{(1 + \alpha)^2}$	2C: $0 < b < 1$ 2D: $b > 1$	$\alpha\gamma < 1$ $\alpha\gamma > 1$	Nonoscillatory and nonfluctuating
3 Complex roots $\gamma < \dfrac{4\alpha}{(1 + \alpha)^2}$	3C: $R < 1$ 3D: $R \geq 1$	$\alpha\gamma < 1$ $\alpha\gamma \geq 1$	With stepped fluctuation

subcases. The first—*Possibility vi*—yields a convergent time path, whereas the other—*Possibility viii*—gives a divergent one. In terms of α and γ, the fact that $\alpha\gamma = b_1 b_2 = b^2$ clearly indicates that the convergent and divergent subcases are associated, respectively, with $\alpha\gamma < 1$ and $\alpha\gamma > 1$. These results are listed in the middle part of Table 17.1, where the two subcases are labelled 2C (convergent) and 2D (divergent).

Finally, in Case 3, with complex roots, we will have stepped fluctuation which represents endogenous business cycles. In this case, we should look to the absolute value $R = \sqrt{a_2}$ [see (17.8)] for the clue to convergence and divergence, where a_2 is the coefficient of the y_t term in the difference equation (17.1). In the present model, we have $R = \sqrt{\alpha\gamma}$, which gives rise to the following three possibilities:

$$
\begin{array}{lll}
(ix) & R < 1 & \Rightarrow \quad \alpha\gamma < 1 \\
(x) & R = 1 & \Rightarrow \quad \alpha\gamma = 1 \\
(xi) & R > 1 & \Rightarrow \quad \alpha\gamma > 1
\end{array}
$$

Even though all of these happen to be admissible (see Exercise 17.2-4), only the $R < 1$ possibility entails a convergent time path and qualifies as Subcase 3C in Table 17.1. The other two are thus collectively labelled as Subcase 3D.

In sum, we may conclude from Table 17.1 that a convergent time path can obtain if and only if $\alpha\gamma < 1$.

graphical summary of the results   The above analysis is somewhat involved. A graphical representation should help to put things in a better perspective. In Fig. 17.2, the set of all admissible combinations of α and γ (ordered pairs) is confined by our model specifications to the variously shaded area. Since the values of $\gamma = 0$ and $\gamma = 1$ are excluded, as is the value $\alpha = 0$, the shaded area is a sort of rectangle without sides. The curve corresponding to the equation $\gamma = 4\alpha/(1 + \alpha)^2$ serves to mark off the three major cases of Table 17.1: The points on that curve pertain to Case 2; the points lying to the north of the curve (representing higher γ values) belong to Case 1; those lying to the south (with lower γ values) are of Case 3.

To distinguish between the convergent and divergent subcases, on the other hand, we have to check whether $\alpha\gamma \lesseqgtr 1$. This means that we can draw the graph of $\alpha\gamma = 1$ (a rectangular hyperbola) as another demarcation line. The points lying to the north of this rectangular hyperbola satisfy the inequality $\alpha\gamma > 1$, whereas those located below it correspond to $\alpha\gamma < 1$. It is then possible to mark off the subcases easily. Under Case 1, the broken-line shaded region, being below the hyperbola, corresponds to Subcase 1C, but the solid-line shaded region is associated with Subcase 1D. Under Case 2, which relates to the points

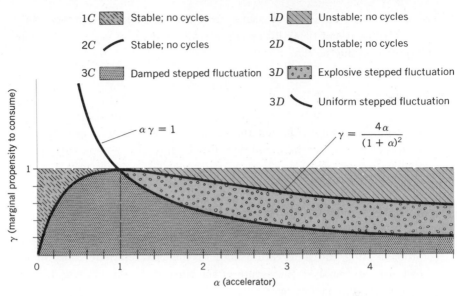

Legend:

1C — Stable; no cycles
2C — Stable; no cycles
3C — Damped stepped fluctuation
1D — Unstable; no cycles
2D — Unstable; no cycles
3D — Explosive stepped fluctuation
3D — Uniform stepped fluctuation

$\alpha \gamma = 1$

$\gamma = \dfrac{4\alpha}{(1 + \alpha)^2}$

γ (marginal propensity to consume)

α (accelerator)

FIGURE 17.2

lying on the curve $\gamma = 4\alpha/(1 + \alpha)^2$, Subcase 2C covers the upward-sloping portion of that curve, and Subcase 2D, the downward-sloping portion. Finally, for Case 3, the rectangular hyperbola serves to separate the dot-shaded region (Subcase 3C) from the pebble-shaded region (Subcase 3D). The latter, the reader should note, also includes the points located *on* the rectangular hyperbola itself, because of the *weak inequality* in the specification $\alpha\gamma \geq 1$.

Since Fig. 17.2 is the repository of all the qualitative information contained in the model, given any ordered pair (α,γ), we can always find the correct subcase graphically by plotting the ordered pair in the diagram.

Example 1   If the accelerator is 0.8 and the marginal propensity to consume is 0.7, what kind of interaction time path will result? The ordered pair (0.8,0.7) is located in the dot-shaded region, Subcase 3C; thus the time path will be characterized by damped stepped fluctuation.

Example 2   What kind of interaction is implied by $\alpha = 2$ and $\gamma = 0.5$? The ordered pair (2,0.5) lies exactly on the rectangular hyperbola, under Subcase 3D. The time path of Y will again display stepped fluctuation, but it will be neither explosive nor damped. By analogy to the cases of uniform oscillation and uniform fluctuation, we may term this situation as "uniform stepped fluctuation." However, the uniformity feature in this latter case cannot in general be expected to be a perfect one, because, similarly to what was done in Fig. 17.1, we can only accept those points on a sine or cosine curve that correspond to integer values of t, but these values of t may hit an entirely different set of points on the curve in each period of fluctuation.

EXERCISE 17.2

1   By consulting Fig. 17.2, find the subcases to which the following sets of values of α and γ pertain, and describe the interaction time path qualitatively.

(a) $\alpha = 3.5; \gamma = 0.8$ (c) $\alpha = 0.2; \gamma = 0.9$

(b) $\alpha = 2; \gamma = 0.7$ (d) $\alpha = 1.5; \gamma = 0.6$

2   From the values of α and γ given in parts (a) and (c) of the preceding problem, find the numerical values of the characteristic roots in each instance, and analyze the nature of the time path. Do your results check with those obtained earlier?

3   Show that *Possibility iv* $(1 = b_2 < b_1)$ implies $\gamma = 1$.

4   Show that, in Case 3, we can never have $\gamma \geq 1$.

17.3   Generalizations to Variable-Term and Higher-Order Equations

We are now ready to extend our methods in two directions, to the variable-term case, and to difference equations of higher orders.

variable term in the form of cm^t   When the constant term c in (17.1) is replaced by a variable term—some function of t—the only effect will be upon the particular integral. (Why?) To find the new particular integral, we can again apply the method of undetermined coefficients. In the differential-equation context (Sec. 15.6), that method requires that the successive derivatives of the variable term take only a finite number of distinct types of expression, apart from multiplicative constants. Applied to difference equations, the requirement should be amended to read: the successive *differences* of the variable term must take only a finite number of distinct expression types, apart from multiplicative constants. Let us illustrate this method by concrete examples, first taking a variable term in the form of cm^t, with c and m being constants.

Example 1　Find the particular integral of

$$y_{t+2} + y_{t+1} - 3y_t = 7^t$$

Here, we have the case of $c = 1$ and $m = 7$. First, let us ascertain whether the variable term 7^t yields a finite number of expression types upon successive differencing. According to the rule of differencing ($\Delta y_t = y_{t+1} - y_t$), the *first* difference of the term is

$$\Delta 7^t = 7^{t+1} - 7^t = (7 - 1)7^t = 6(7)^t$$

Similarly, the *second* difference, $\Delta^2(7^t)$, can be expressed as

$$\Delta(\Delta 7^t) = \Delta 6(7^t) = 6(7)^{t+1} - 6(7)^t = 6(7 - 1)7^t = 36(7)^t$$

Moreover, as can be verified, all successive differences will, like the first and second, be some multiple of 7^t. Since there is only a single expression type, we can try a solution $y_t = B(7)^t$ for the particular integral, where B is an undetermined coefficient.

Substituting the trial solution and its corresponding versions for periods $(t + 1)$ and $(t + 2)$ into the given difference equation, we obtain

$$B(7)^{t+2} + B(7)^{t+1} - 3B(7)^t = 7^t \qquad \text{or} \qquad B(7^2 + 7 - 3)(7)^t = 7^t$$

Thus,

$$B = \frac{1}{49 + 7 - 3} = \frac{1}{53}$$

and we can write the particular integral as

$$y_p = B(7)^t = \frac{1}{53}(7)^t$$

This, of course, represents a moving equilibrium. The reader can verify the correctness of the solution by substituting it into the difference equation and seeing to it that there will result an identity, $7^t = 7^t$.

The result reached in Example 1 can be easily generalized from the variable term 7^t to that of cm^t. From our experience, we expect all the successive differences of cm^t to take the same form of expression: namely, Bm^t, where B is some multiplicative constant. Hence we can try a solution $y_t = Bm^t$ for the particular integral, when given the difference equation

$$(17.16) \qquad y_{t+2} + a_1 y_{t+1} + a_2 y_t = cm^t$$

Using the trial solution $y_t = Bm^t$, which implies $y_{t+1} = Bm^{t+1}$, etc., we can rewrite equation (17.16) as

$$Bm^{t+2} + a_1 Bm^{t+1} + a_2 Bm^t = cm^t$$

or $$B(m^2 + a_1 m + a_2)m^t = cm^t$$

Hence the coefficient B in the trial solution should be

$$B = \frac{c}{m^2 + a_1 m + a_2}$$

and the desired particular integral of (17.16) can be written as

$$(17.17) \qquad y_p = Bm^t = \frac{c}{m^2 + a_1 m + a_2} m^t \qquad (m^2 + a_1 m + a_2 \neq 0)$$

Note that the denominator of B is not allowed to be zero. If it happens to be,[1] we must then use the trial solution $y_t = Btm^t$ instead; or, if that too fails, $y_t = Bt^2 m^t$.

variable term in the form of ct^n   Let us now consider variable terms in the form ct^n, where c and n are constants.

Example 2   Find the particular integral of

$$y_{t+2} + 5y_{t+1} + 2y_t = t^2$$

The first three differences of t^2 (a special case of ct^n with $c = 1$ and $n = 2$) are found as follows:[2]

$$\Delta t^2 = (t + 1)^2 - t^2 = 2t + 1$$
$$\Delta^2 t^2 = \Delta(\Delta t^2) = \Delta(2t + 1) = \Delta 2t + \Delta 1$$
$$\qquad = 2(t + 1) - 2t + 0 = 2 \qquad [\Delta \text{ constant} = 0]$$
$$\Delta^3 t^2 = \Delta(\Delta^2 t^2) = \Delta 2 = 0$$

Since further differencing will only yield zero, there are altogether three distinct types of expression: t^2 (from the variable term itself), t, and a constant (from the successive differences).

Let us therefore try the solution

$$y_t = B_0 + B_1 t + B_2 t^2$$

---

[1] Analogous to the situation in Example 3 of Sec. 15.6, this eventuality will materialize when the constant m happens to be equal to a characteristic root of the difference equation. The characteristic roots of the difference equation above are the values of b that satisfy the equation $b^2 + a_1 b + a_2 = 0$. If one root happens to have the value m, then it must follow that $m^2 + a_1 m + a_2 = 0$.

[2] These results should be compared with the first three derivatives of t^2:

$$\frac{d}{dt} t^2 = 2t \qquad \frac{d^2}{dt^2} t^2 = 2 \qquad \text{and} \qquad \frac{d^3}{dt^3} t^2 = 0$$

for the particular integral, with undetermined coefficients B_0, B_1, and B_2. Note that this solution implies

$$
\begin{aligned}
y_{t+1} &= B_0 + B_1(t+1) + B_2(t+1)^2 \\
&= (B_0 + B_1 + B_2) + (B_1 + 2B_2)t + B_2t^2 \\
y_{t+2} &= B_0 + B_1(t+2) + B_2(t+2)^2 \\
&= (B_0 + 2B_1 + 4B_2) + (B_1 + 4B_2)t + B_2t^2
\end{aligned}
$$

When these are substituted into the difference equation, we obtain

$$
(8B_0 + 7B_1 + 9B_2) + (8B_1 + 14B_2)t + 8B_2t^2 = t^2
$$

Equating the two sides term by term, we see that the undetermined coefficients are required to satisfy the following simultaneous equations:

$$
\begin{aligned}
8B_0 + 7B_1 + 9B_2 &= 0 \\
8B_1 + 14B_2 &= 0 \\
8B_2 &= 1
\end{aligned}
$$

Thus, their values must be $B_0 = {}^{13}/_{256}$, $B_1 = -{}^{7}/_{32}$, and $B_2 = {}^{1}/_{8}$, giving us the particular integral

$$
y_p = \frac{13}{256} - \frac{7}{32}t + \frac{1}{8}t^2
$$

Our experience with the variable term t^2 should enable us to generalize the method to the case of ct^n. In the new trial solution, there should obviously be a term B_nt^n, to correspond to the given variable term. Furthermore, since successive differencing of the term yields the distinct expressions t^{n-1}, t^{n-2}, . . . , t, and B_0 (constant), the new trial solution for the case of the variable term ct^n should be written as

$$
y_t = B_0 + B_1t + B_2t^2 + \cdots + B_nt^n
$$

But the rest of the procedure is entirely the same.

It must be added that such a trial solution may also fail to work. In that event, the trick—already employed on countless other occasions—is again to multiply the original trial solution by a sufficiently high power of t. That is, we can instead try $y_t = t(B_0 + B_1t + B_2t^2)$, etc.

higher-order linear difference equations   The *order* of a difference equation indicates the highest-order difference present in the equation; but it also indicates the maximum number of periods of time lag involved. An nth-order linear difference equation (with constant coefficients and constant term) may thus be written in general as

$$(17.18) \qquad y_{t+n} + a_1 y_{t+n-1} + \cdots + a_{n-1} y_{t+1} + a_n y_t = c$$

The method of finding the particular integral of this does not differ in any substantive way. As a starter, we can still try $y_t = k$ (the case of stationary intertemporal equilibrium). Should this fail, we then try $y_t = kt$ or $y_t = kt^2$, etc., in that order.

In the search for the complementary function, however, we shall now be confronted with a characteristic equation which is an nth-degree polynomial equation:

$$(17.19) \qquad b^n + a_1 b^{n-1} + \cdots + a_{n-1} b + a_n = 0$$

There will now be n characteristic roots b_i (with $i = 1, 2, \ldots, n$), all of which should enter into the complementary function thus:

$$(17.20) \qquad y_c = \sum_{i=1}^{n} A_i b_i^t$$

provided, of course, that the roots are all real and distinct. In case there are repeated real roots (say $b_1 = b_2 = b_3$), then the first three terms in the sum of (17.20) must be modified to

$$A_1 b_1^t + A_2 t b_1^t + A_3 t^2 b_1^t \qquad \text{[cf. (17.6)]}$$

Moreover, if there is a pair of conjugate complex roots—say, b_{n-1}, b_n—then the last two terms in the sum of (17.20) are to be combined into the expression

$$R^t (A_{n-1} \cos \theta t + A_n \sin \theta t)$$

A similar expression can also be assigned to any other pair of complex roots. In case of two *repeated* pairs, however, one of the two must be given a multiplicative factor of tR^t instead of R^t.

After y_p and y_c are both found, the general solution of the complete difference equation (17.18) is again obtained by summing; that is,

$$y_t = y_p + y_c$$

But since there will be a total of n arbitrary constants in this solution, no less than n initial conditions will be required to definitize it.

Example 3   Find the general solution of the third-order difference equation

$$y_{t+3} - \tfrac{7}{8} y_{t+2} + \tfrac{1}{8} y_{t+1} + \tfrac{1}{32} y_t = 9$$

By trying the solution $y_t = k$, the particular integral is easily found to be $y_p = 32$. As for the complementary function, since the cubic characteristic equation

$$b^3 - \tfrac{7}{8} b^2 + \tfrac{1}{8} b + \tfrac{1}{32} = 0$$

can be factored into the form

$$(b - \tfrac{1}{2})(b - \tfrac{1}{2})(b + \tfrac{1}{8}) = 0$$

the roots are $b_1 = b_2 = \tfrac{1}{2}$ and $b_3 = -\tfrac{1}{8}$. This enables us to write

$$y_c = A_1(\tfrac{1}{2})^t + A_2 t(\tfrac{1}{2})^t + A_3(-\tfrac{1}{8})^t$$

Note that the second term contains a multiplicative t; this is due to the presence of repeated roots. The general solution of the given difference equation is then simply the sum of y_c and y_p.

In this example, all three characteristic roots happen to be less than 1 in their absolute values. We can therefore conclude that the solution obtained represents a time path which converges to the stationary equilibrium level of 32.

convergence and the Schur theorem When we have a high-order difference equation that is not easily solved, we can nonetheless determine the convergence of the relevant time path qualitatively without having to struggle with its actual quantitative solution. The reader will recall that the time path can converge if and only if every root of the characteristic equation is less than 1 in absolute value. In view of this, the following theorem—known as the *Schur theorem*[1]—becomes directly applicable:

The roots of the nth-degree polynomial equation

$$a_0 b^n + a_1 b^{n-1} + \cdots + a_{n-1} b + a_n = 0$$

will all be less than unity in absolute value if and only if the following n determinants

$$\Delta_1 = \begin{vmatrix} a_0 & a_n \\ a_n & a_0 \end{vmatrix} \qquad \Delta_2 = \begin{vmatrix} a_0 & 0 & a_n & a_{n-1} \\ a_1 & a_0 & 0 & a_n \\ a_n & 0 & a_0 & a_1 \\ a_{n-1} & a_n & 0 & a_0 \end{vmatrix} \qquad \cdots$$

$$\Delta_n = \begin{vmatrix} a_0 & 0 & \cdots & 0 & a_n & a_{n-1} & \cdots & a_1 \\ a_1 & a_0 & \cdots & 0 & 0 & a_n & \cdots & a_2 \\ \cdots & \cdots & \cdots & \cdots & \cdots & \cdots & \cdots & \cdots \\ a_{n-1} & a_{n-2} & \cdots & a_0 & 0 & 0 & \cdots & a_n \\ a_n & 0 & \cdots & 0 & a_0 & a_1 & \cdots & a_{n-1} \\ a_{n-1} & a_n & \cdots & 0 & 0 & a_0 & \cdots & a_{n-2} \\ \cdots & \cdots & \cdots & \cdots & \cdots & \cdots & \cdots & \cdots \\ a_1 & a_2 & \cdots & a_n & 0 & 0 & \cdots & a_0 \end{vmatrix}$$

are all positive.

---

[1] For a discussion of this theorem and its history, see John S. Chipman, *The Theory of Inter-Sectoral Money Flows and Income Formation*, The Johns Hopkins Press, Baltimore, 1951, pp. 119–120.

Note that, since the condition in the theorem is given on the "if and only if" basis, it is a necessary-and-sufficient condition. Thus the Schur theorem is a perfect difference-equation counterpart of the Routh theorem introduced earlier in the differential-equation framework.

The construction of these determinants is based on a simple procedure. This is best explained with the aid of the dashed lines which partition each determinant into four *areas*. Each area of the kth determinant, Δ_k, always consists of a $k \times k$ subdeterminant. The *upper-left* area has a_0 alone in the diagonal, zeros above the diagonal, and progressively larger subscripts for the successive coefficients in each column below the diagonal elements. When we transpose the elements of the upper-left area, we obtain the *lower-right* area. Turning to the *upper-right* area, we now place the a_n coefficient alone in the diagonal, with zeros below the diagonal, and progressively smaller subscripts for the successive coefficients as we go up each column from the diagonal. When the elements of this area are transposed, we get the *lower-left* area.

The application of this theorem is straightforward. Since the coefficients of the characteristic equation are the same as those appearing on the left side of the original difference equation, we can introduce them directly into the determinants cited. Note that, in our context, we always have $a_0 = 1$.

Example 4   Does the time path of the equation $y_{t+2} + 3y_{t+1} + 2y_t = 12$ converge? Here we have $n = 2$, and the coefficients are $a_0 = 1$, $a_1 = 3$, and $a_2 = 2$. Thus we get

$$\Delta_1 = \begin{vmatrix} a_0 & a_2 \\ a_2 & a_0 \end{vmatrix} = \begin{vmatrix} 1 & 2 \\ 2 & 1 \end{vmatrix} = -3 < 0$$

Since this already violates the convergence condition, there is no need to proceed to Δ_2.

Actually, the characteristic roots of the given difference equation are easily found to be $b_1, b_2 = -1, -2$, which indeed imply a divergent time path.

Example 5   Test the convergence of the path of $y_{t+2} + \frac{1}{6}y_{t+1} - \frac{1}{6}y_t = 2$ by the Schur theorem. Here the coefficients are $a_0 = 1$, $a_1 = \frac{1}{6}$, $a_2 = -\frac{1}{6}$ (with $n = 2$). Thus we have

$$\Delta_1 = \begin{vmatrix} a_0 & a_2 \\ a_2 & a_0 \end{vmatrix} = \begin{vmatrix} 1 & -\frac{1}{6} \\ -\frac{1}{6} & 1 \end{vmatrix} = \frac{35}{36} > 0$$

$$\Delta_2 = \begin{vmatrix} a_0 & 0 & a_2 & a_1 \\ a_1 & a_0 & 0 & a_2 \\ a_2 & 0 & a_0 & a_1 \\ a_1 & a_2 & 0 & a_0 \end{vmatrix} = \begin{vmatrix} 1 & 0 & -\frac{1}{6} & \frac{1}{6} \\ \frac{1}{6} & 1 & 0 & -\frac{1}{6} \\ -\frac{1}{6} & 0 & 1 & \frac{1}{6} \\ \frac{1}{6} & -\frac{1}{6} & 0 & 1 \end{vmatrix} = \frac{1176}{1296} > 0$$

These do fulfill the necessary-and-sufficient condition for convergence.

EXERCISE 17.3

1   Apply the definition of the "differencing" symbol Δ, to find:

    (a) Δt (b) $\Delta^2 t$ (c) Δt^3

Compare the results of differencing with those of differentiation.

2   Find the particular integral of each of the following:

    (a) $y_{t+2} + 2y_{t+1} + y_t = 3^t$
    (b) $y_{t+2} - 5y_{t+1} - 6y_t = 2(6)^t$
    (c) $3y_{t+2} + 9y_t = 3(4)^t$ (*Hint:* Normalize.)

3   Find the particular integrals of:

    (a) $y_{t+2} - 2y_{t+1} + 5y_t = t$
    (b) $y_{t+2} - 2y_{t+1} + 5y_t = 4 + 2t$
    (c) $y_{t+2} + 5y_{t+1} + 2y_t = 18 + 6t + 8t^2$

4   Would you expect that, when the variable term takes the form $m^t + t^n$, the trial solution should be $B(m)^t + (B_0 + B_1 t + \cdots + B_n t^n)$? Why?

5   Find the characteristic roots and the complementary function of:

    (a) $y_{t+3} - \frac{1}{2}y_{t+2} - y_{t+1} + \frac{1}{2}y_t = 0$
    (b) $y_{t+3} - 2y_{t+2} + \frac{5}{4}y_{t+1} - \frac{1}{4}y_t = 1$

[*Hint:* Try factoring out $(b - \frac{1}{2})$ in both characteristic equations.]

6   Test the convergence of the solutions of the following difference equations by the Schur theorem:

    (a) $y_{t+2} + \frac{1}{2}y_{t+1} - \frac{1}{2}y_t = 3$
    (b) $y_{t+2} - \frac{1}{9}y_t = 1$

7   In the case of a third-order difference equation

$$y_{t+3} + a_1 y_{t+2} + a_2 y_{t+1} + a_3 y_t = c$$

what are the exact forms of the determinants involved in the Schur theorem?

17.4 Simultaneous Linear Difference Equations and Differential Equations

Heretofore, our discussion of economic dynamics has been limited to models that are reducible to a single difference (or differential) equation. In certain contexts, however—notably in general-equilibrium and input-output models—the dynamic aspect of the analysis requires the *simultaneous* determination of the time paths of several variables. This would entail simultaneous difference equations or simultaneous differential equations. We shall briefly outline the method of solving such equations in the present section, but we shall confine the discussion to the case of *linear* difference and differential equations with constant coefficients only.

Linear equations may be either first order or higher order. Interestingly, however, when given an nth-order difference (differential) equation, we can always transform it into a mathematically equivalent system of n simultaneous first-order difference (differential) equations. Because of this, we need only consider simultaneous equations of the first order, for when higher-order equations do appear, they can first be duly transformed in a manner to be explained presently, thereby reducing the system to a first-order one.

To illustrate the transformation procedure, let us consider the single difference equation

(17.21) $\qquad y_{t+2} + a_1 y_{t+1} + a_2 y_t = c$

If we concoct an artificial new variable x_t, defined as

$\qquad x_t \equiv y_{t+1} \qquad$ (implying $x_{t+1} \equiv y_{t+2}$)

we can express the original second-order equation by means of *two* first-order (one-period lag) simultaneous equations as follows:

(17.21′) $\qquad \begin{aligned} x_{t+1} & & + a_1 x_t + a_2 y_t & = c \\ y_{t+1} & - & x_t \qquad\quad & = 0 \end{aligned}$

It is easily seen that, as long as the second equation (which defines the variable x_t) is satisfied, the first is identical with the original given equation. By a similar procedure, and using more artificial variables, we can even transform a higher-order single equation into an equivalent system of simultaneous first-order equations. The reader can verify, for instance, that the third-order equation

(17.22) $\qquad y_{t+3} + y_{t+2} - 3y_{t+1} + 2y_t = 0$

can be expressed as

(17.22′) $\qquad \begin{aligned} w_{t+1} & & & + w_t - 3x_t + 2y_t & = 0 \\ & x_{t+1} & & - w_t \qquad\qquad\quad & = 0 \\ & & y_{t+1} & \quad - x_t \qquad & = 0 \end{aligned}$

where $x_t \equiv y_{t+1}$ (so that $x_{t+1} \equiv y_{t+2}$) and $w_t \equiv x_{t+1}$ (so that $w_{t+1} \equiv x_{t+2} \equiv y_{t+3}$). By a perfectly similar procedure, we can also transform an nth-order *differential* equation into a system of n first-order equations. For instance, the second-order differential equation

$$(17.23) \qquad y''(t) + a_1 y'(t) + a_2 y(t) = 0$$

can be transformed, by introducing a new variable $x(t) \equiv y'(t)$, into the following system of two first-order equations:

$$(17.23') \qquad \begin{aligned} x'(t) &+ a_1 x(t) + a_2 y(t) = 0 \\ y'(t) - & x(t) = 0 \end{aligned}$$

In view of the above, there appears to be a double reason for our interest in the method of solving a simultaneous-equation dynamic system: by virtue of its direct applicability to a given *system* of simultaneous difference or differential equations, and also because of its possible use in solving a *single* given higher-order equation which may nevertheless be expressed equivalently as a simultaneous-equation system.

simultaneous difference equations   Suppose that we are given the following system of linear difference equations:

$$(17.24) \qquad \begin{aligned} x_{t+1} &+ 6x_t + 9y_t = 4 \\ y_{t+1} - & x_t = 0 \end{aligned}$$

How do we find the time paths of x and y such that both equations in this system will be satisfied? Essentially, our task is again to seek the particular integrals and complementary functions, and sum these to obtain the desired time paths of the two variables.

Since particular integrals represent intertemporal equilibrium values, let us denote them here by $\bar{x}$ and $\bar{y}$. As before, it is advisable first to try constant solutions, namely, $x_{t+1} = x_t = \bar{x}$ and $y_{t+1} = y_t = \bar{y}$. This will indeed work in the present case, for upon substituting these trial solutions into (17.24) we get

$$(17.25) \qquad \left. \begin{aligned} 7\bar{x} + 9\bar{y} &= 4 \\ -\bar{x} + \bar{y} &= 0 \end{aligned} \right\} \quad \Rightarrow \quad \bar{x} = \bar{y} = \frac{1}{4}$$

(In case this fails to work, however, we must then try solutions of the form $x_t = k_1 t$, $y_t = k_2 t$, etc.)

Drawing upon our previous experience, we should adopt, for the complementary functions, trial solutions of the form

$$(17.26) \qquad x_t = mb^t \qquad \text{and} \qquad y_t = nb^t$$

which will, of course, imply

(17.27) $x_{t+1} = mb^{t+1}$ and $y_{t+1} - nb^{t+1}$

Note that, to simplify matters, we are employing the same base $b \neq 0$ for both variables, although their coefficients are allowed to differ. It is our purpose to find the values of b, m, and n that can make the trial solutions (17.26) satisfy the *reduced* (homogeneous) version of (17.24).

Upon substituting the trial solutions into the reduced version of (17.24) and canceling the common factor $b^t \neq 0$, we obtain the two equations

(17.28) $\begin{aligned} (b + 6)m + 9n &= 0 \\ -m + bn &= 0 \end{aligned}$

This can be considered as a linear homogeneous-equation system in the two variables m and n—if we are willing to consider b as a parameter for the time being. In order to avoid the trivial solution $m = n = 0$ [which, according to (17.26), would result in trivial complementary functions $x_t = y_t = 0$ as well], the determinant of the coefficient matrix in (17.28) is required to vanish (see Sec. 5.5). That is, we must have

(17.29) $\begin{vmatrix} b + 6 & 9 \\ -1 & b \end{vmatrix} = b^2 + 6b + 9 = 0$

From this quadratic equation, we find $b\ (=b_1 = b_2) = -3$ to be the only value which can prevent m and n from both being zero in (17.28). We shall therefore only use this value of b. Equation (17.29) is called the *characteristic equation*, and its roots the *characteristic roots*, of the given simultaneous difference-equation system.

Once we have a specific value of b, (17.28) gives us the corresponding solution values of m and n. The system being homogeneous, however, there will actually emerge an infinite number of solutions for (m,n), expressible in the form of an equation $m = kn$, where k is a constant. In fact, for each root b_i, there will in general be a distinct solution equation $m_i = k_i n_i$. But in the present case of repeated roots, $b = -3$, we only obtain a single equation, $m = -3n$.

If we now let $n = A_3$ (A_3 being an arbitrary constant), so that $m = -3A_3$, then—recalling that $b = -3$—the trial solutions (17.26) will take the specific forms

$x_t = -3A_3(-3)^t$ and $y_t = A_3(-3)^t$

and the complementary functions should be written as

(17.30) $\begin{aligned} x_c &= -3A_3(-3)^t - 3A_4 t(-3)^t \\ y_c &= A_3(-3)^t + A_4 t(-3)^t \end{aligned}$ [by (17.6)]

where A_4 is another arbitrary constant. Moreover, the general solution follows

Dynamic Analysis

easily by combining the particular integrals in (17.25) with the complementary functions just found. All that remains, then, is to definitize the two arbitrary constants A_3 and A_4 with the help of appropriate initial or boundary conditions.

One interesting feature of the above solution is that, since both time paths have identical b^t expressions in them, they must either both converge or both diverge. In the present case, with repeated roots $b = -3$, the time paths of x and y will both display explosive oscillation.

matrix notation In order to bring out the basic parallelism between the methods of solving a single equation and an equation system, the above exposition was carried out without the benefit of matrix notation. Let us now see how the latter can be utilized here. Even though it may seem pointless to apply matrix notation to (17.24), a simple system of two equations only, the possibility of extending that notation to the n-equation case should make it a worthwhile exercise.

First of all, the given system (17.24) may be expressed as

$$(17.24') \qquad \begin{bmatrix} 1 & 0 \\ 0 & 1 \end{bmatrix}\begin{bmatrix} x_{t+1} \\ y_{t+1} \end{bmatrix} + \begin{bmatrix} 6 & 9 \\ -1 & 0 \end{bmatrix}\begin{bmatrix} x_t \\ y_t \end{bmatrix} = \begin{bmatrix} 4 \\ 0 \end{bmatrix}$$

or, more succinctly, as

$$(17.24'') \qquad Iu + Kv = d$$

where I is the 2×2 identity matrix; K is the 2×2 matrix of the coefficients of the x_t and y_t terms; and u, v, and d are column vectors defined as follows:

$$u = \begin{bmatrix} x_{t+1} \\ y_{t+1} \end{bmatrix} \qquad v = \begin{bmatrix} x_t \\ y_t \end{bmatrix} \qquad d = \begin{bmatrix} 4 \\ 0 \end{bmatrix}$$

The reader may find one feature puzzling: Since we know $Iu = u$, why not drop the I? The answer is that, even though it seems redundant now, the identity matrix will be needed in subsequent operations, and therefore we shall retain it as in (17.24").

When we try constant solutions $x_{t+1} = x_t = \bar{x}$ and $y_{t+1} = y_t = \bar{y}$ for the particular integrals, we are in effect setting $u = v = \begin{bmatrix} \bar{x} \\ \bar{y} \end{bmatrix}$; this will reduce (17.24") to

$$(I + K)\begin{bmatrix} \bar{x} \\ \bar{y} \end{bmatrix} = d$$

If the inverse $(I + K)^{-1}$ exists, we can express the particular integrals as

$$(17.25') \qquad \begin{bmatrix} \bar{x} \\ \bar{y} \end{bmatrix} = (I + K)^{-1}d$$

This is of course a general formula, for it is valid for any matrix K and vector d as long as $(I + K)^{-1}$ exists. Applied to our numerical example, we have

$$(I + K)^{-1}d = \begin{bmatrix} 7 & 9 \\ -1 & 1 \end{bmatrix}^{-1}\begin{bmatrix} 4 \\ 0 \end{bmatrix} = \begin{bmatrix} \frac{1}{16} & -\frac{9}{16} \\ \frac{1}{16} & \frac{7}{16} \end{bmatrix}\begin{bmatrix} 4 \\ 0 \end{bmatrix} = \begin{bmatrix} \frac{1}{4} \\ \frac{1}{4} \end{bmatrix}$$

Therefore, $\bar{x} = \bar{y} = \frac{1}{4}$, which checks with (17.25).

Turning to the complementary functions, we see that the trial solutions (17.26) and (17.27) will give the u and v vectors the specific forms

$$u = \begin{bmatrix} mb^{t+1} \\ nb^{t+1} \end{bmatrix} = \begin{bmatrix} m \\ n \end{bmatrix} b^{t+1} \qquad \text{and} \qquad v = \begin{bmatrix} mb^{t} \\ nb^{t} \end{bmatrix} = \begin{bmatrix} m \\ n \end{bmatrix} b^{t}$$

When substituted into the reduced equation of (17.24'')—$Iu + Kv = 0$—these trial solutions will transform the latter into

$$I\begin{bmatrix} m \\ n \end{bmatrix} b^{t+1} + K\begin{bmatrix} m \\ n \end{bmatrix} b^{t} = 0$$

or, after multiplying through by b^{-t} (a scalar) and factoring,

$$(17.28') \qquad (bI + K)\begin{bmatrix} m \\ n \end{bmatrix} = 0$$

where 0 is a zero vector. It is from this that we are to find the appropriate values of b, m, and n to be used in the trial solutions in order to make the latter determinate.

To avoid trivial solutions for m and n, it is necessary that

$$(17.29') \qquad |bI + K| = 0$$

And this is the characteristic equation which will give us the characteristic roots b_i. The reader can verify that if we substitute

$$bI = \begin{bmatrix} b & 0 \\ 0 & b \end{bmatrix} \qquad \text{and} \qquad K = \begin{bmatrix} 6 & 9 \\ -1 & 0 \end{bmatrix}$$

into this equation, the result will precisely be (17.29), yielding the repeated roots $b = -3$.

In general, each root b_i will elicit from (17.28') a particular set of infinite number of solution values of m and n which are tied to each other by the equation $m_i = k_i n_i$. It is therefore possible to write, for each value of b_i,

$$n_i = A_i \qquad \text{and} \qquad m_i = k_i A_i$$

where A_i are arbitrary constants to be definitized later. When substituted into the trial solutions, these expressions for n_i and m_i along with the values b_i will lead to specific forms of complementary functions. If all roots are distinct real

Dynamic Analysis

numbers, we may apply (17.5) and write

$$\begin{bmatrix} x_c \\ y_c \end{bmatrix} = \begin{bmatrix} \Sigma m_i b_i{}^t \\ \Sigma n_i b_i{}^t \end{bmatrix} = \begin{bmatrix} \Sigma k_i A_i b_i{}^t \\ \Sigma A_i b_i{}^t \end{bmatrix}$$

With repeated roots, however, we must apply (17.6) instead and, as a result, the complementary functions will contain terms such as $A_3 b^t$ and $A_4 t b^t$, as in the result (17.30) for our present numerical example. Finally, in the complex-root case, the complementary functions should be written with (17.10) as their prototype.

Finally, to get the general solution, we can simply form the sum

$$\begin{bmatrix} x_t \\ y_t \end{bmatrix} = \begin{bmatrix} x_c \\ y_c \end{bmatrix} + \begin{bmatrix} \bar{x} \\ \bar{y} \end{bmatrix}$$

Then it remains only to definitize the arbitrary constants A_i.

The extension of this procedure to the n-equation system should be self-evident. When n is large, however, the characteristic equation—an nth-degree polynomial equation—may not be easy to solve quantitatively. In that event, we may again find the Schur theorem to be of help in yielding certain qualitative conclusions about the time paths of the variables in the system. All these variables, we recall, are assigned the same base b in the trial solutions, so they must end up with the same $b_i{}^t$ expressions in the complementary functions and share the same convergence properties. Thus a single application of the Schur theorem will enable us to determine the convergence or divergence of the time path of every variable in the system.

simultaneous differential equations   The method of solution just described can also be applied to a first-order linear *differential*-equation system. About the only major modification needed is to change the trial solutions to

(17.31) $x(t) = me^{rt}$ and $y(t) = ne^{rt}$

which will imply that

(17.32) $x'(t) = rme^{rt}$ and $y'(t) = rne^{rt}$

Of course, the characteristic roots are now denoted by r instead of b.

Suppose that we are given the following equation system:

$$(17.33) \qquad \begin{aligned} x'(t) + 2y'(t) + 2x(t) + 5y(t) &= 77 \\ y'(t) + x(t) + 4y(t) &= 61 \end{aligned}$$

First, we can rewrite it in matrix notation as

(17.33') $Ju + Mv = g$

where the matrices are

$$J = \begin{bmatrix} 1 & 2 \\ 0 & 1 \end{bmatrix} \qquad u = \begin{bmatrix} x'(t) \\ y'(t) \end{bmatrix} \qquad M = \begin{bmatrix} 2 & 5 \\ 1 & 4 \end{bmatrix} \qquad v = \begin{bmatrix} x(t) \\ y(t) \end{bmatrix} \qquad g = \begin{bmatrix} 77 \\ 61 \end{bmatrix}$$

Note, that, in view of the appearance of the $2y'(t)$ term in the first equation of (17.33), we have to use the matrix J in place of the identity matrix I, as in (17.24″). Of course, if J is nonsingular (so that J^{-1} exists), then we can in a sense *normalize* (17.33′) by premultiplying every term therein by J^{-1}, to get

(17.33″) $\qquad J^{-1}Ju + J^{-1}Mv = J^{-1}g \qquad$ or $\qquad Iu + Kv = d$

$$(K \equiv J^{-1}M; \, d \equiv J^{-1}g)$$

This new format is an exact duplicate of (17.24″), although it must be remembered that the vectors u and v have altogether different meanings in the two different contexts. In the ensuing development, we shall adhere to the $Ju + Mv = g$ formulation given in (17.33′).

To find the particular integrals, let us try constant solutions $x(t) = \bar{x}$ and $y(t) = \bar{y}$—which imply that $x'(t) = y'(t) = 0$. If these solutions hold, the vectors v and u will become $v = \begin{bmatrix} \bar{x} \\ \bar{y} \end{bmatrix}$ and $u = \begin{bmatrix} 0 \\ 0 \end{bmatrix}$, and (17.33′) will reduce to $Mv = g$. Thus the solution for $\bar{x}$ and $\bar{y}$ can be written as

(17.34) $\qquad \begin{bmatrix} \bar{x} \\ \bar{y} \end{bmatrix} = v = M^{-1}g$

which the reader should contrast with (17.25′). In numerical terms, our present problem yields the following particular integrals:

$$\begin{bmatrix} \bar{x} \\ \bar{y} \end{bmatrix} = \begin{bmatrix} 2 & 5 \\ 1 & 4 \end{bmatrix}^{-1} \begin{bmatrix} 77 \\ 61 \end{bmatrix} = \begin{bmatrix} \frac{4}{3} & -\frac{5}{3} \\ -\frac{1}{3} & \frac{2}{3} \end{bmatrix} \begin{bmatrix} 77 \\ 61 \end{bmatrix} = \begin{bmatrix} 1 \\ 15 \end{bmatrix}$$

Now let us look for the complementary functions. Using the trial solutions suggested in (17.31) and (17.32), the vectors u and v will become

$$u = \begin{bmatrix} m \\ n \end{bmatrix} re^{rt} \qquad \text{and} \qquad v = \begin{bmatrix} m \\ n \end{bmatrix} e^{rt}$$

The substitution of these into the *homogeneous* version of (17.33′)

$$Ju + Mv = 0$$

results in the equation

$$J \begin{bmatrix} m \\ n \end{bmatrix} re^{rt} + M \begin{bmatrix} m \\ n \end{bmatrix} e^{rt} = 0$$

or, after multiplying through by the scalar e^{-rt} and factoring,

(17.35) $\qquad (rJ + M) \begin{bmatrix} m \\ n \end{bmatrix} = 0$

This, the reader should compare with (17.28′). Since our objective is to find *nontrivial* solutions of m and n (so that our trial solutions will also be nontrivial), it is necessary that

(17.36) $$|rJ + M| = 0$$

The analog of (17.29′), this last equation—the characteristic equation of the given equation system—will yield the roots r_i that we need. Then, we can find the corresponding (nontrivial) values of m_i and n_i.

In our present example, the characteristic equation is

(17.36′) $$|rJ + M| = \begin{vmatrix} r + 2 & 2r + 5 \\ 1 & r + 4 \end{vmatrix} = r^2 + 4r + 3 = 0$$

with roots $r_1 = -1$, $r_2 = -3$. Substituting these into (17.35), we get

$$\begin{bmatrix} 1 & 3 \\ 1 & 3 \end{bmatrix} \begin{bmatrix} m_1 \\ n_1 \end{bmatrix} = 0 \qquad \text{(for } r_1 = -1\text{)}$$

$$\begin{bmatrix} -1 & -1 \\ 1 & 1 \end{bmatrix} \begin{bmatrix} m_2 \\ n_2 \end{bmatrix} = 0 \qquad \text{(for } r_2 = -3\text{)}$$

It follows that $m_1 = -3n_1$ and $m_2 = -n_2$, which we may also express as

$$\begin{aligned} m_1 &= 3A_1 \\ n_1 &= -A_1 \end{aligned} \qquad \text{and} \qquad \begin{aligned} m_2 &= A_2 \\ n_2 &= -A_2 \end{aligned}$$

Now that r_i, m_i, and n_i have all been found, the complementary functions can be written as the following linear combinations of exponential expressions:

$$\begin{bmatrix} x_c \\ y_c \end{bmatrix} = \begin{bmatrix} \Sigma m_i e^{r_i t} \\ \Sigma n_i e^{r_i t} \end{bmatrix} \qquad \text{[distinct real roots]}$$

And the general solution will emerge in the form

$$\begin{bmatrix} x(t) \\ y(t) \end{bmatrix} = \begin{bmatrix} x_c \\ y_c \end{bmatrix} + \begin{bmatrix} \bar{x} \\ \bar{y} \end{bmatrix}$$

In our present example, the solution is

$$\begin{bmatrix} x(t) \\ y(t) \end{bmatrix} = \begin{bmatrix} 3A_1 e^{-t} + A_2 e^{-3t} + 1 \\ -A_1 e^{-t} - A_2 e^{-3t} + 15 \end{bmatrix}$$

Moreover, if we are given the initial conditions $x(0) = 6$ and $y(0) = 12$, the arbitrary constants can be found to be $A_1 = 1$ and $A_2 = 2$. These will serve to definitize the above solution.

Once more we may observe that, since the $e^{r_i t}$ expressions are shared by both time paths $x(t)$ and $y(t)$, the latter must either both converge or both diverge. The roots being -1 and -3 in the present case, both time paths will converge to their respective equilibria, namely, $\bar{x} = 1$ and $\bar{y} = 15$.

Even though our example consists of a two-equation system only, the method certainly extends to the general n-equation system. When n is large, quantitative solutions may again be difficult, but once the characteristic equation is found, a qualitative analysis will always be possible by resorting to the Routh theorem.

further comments on the characteristic equation   The term "characteristic equation" has now been encountered in *three* separate contexts: In Sec. 11.3, we spoke of the characteristic equation of a matrix; in Sec. 15.1 and Sec. 17.1, the term was applied to a single linear differential equation and difference equation; now, in this section, we have just introduced the characteristic equation of a system of linear difference or differential equations. Is there a connection between the three?

There indeed is a connection, and a close one. In the first place, given a single equation and an equivalent equation system—as exemplified by the equation (17.21) and the system (17.21'), or the equation (17.23) and the system (17.23')—their characteristic equations must be identical. For illustration, consider the difference equation (17.21), $y_{t+2} + a_1 y_{t+1} + a_2 y_t = c$. We have earlier learned to write its characteristic equation by directly transplanting its constant coefficients into a quadratic equation:

$$b^2 + a_1 b + a_2 = 0$$

What about the equivalent system (17.21')? Taking that system to be in the form of $Iu + Kv = d$, as in (17.24''), we would have the matrix $K = \begin{bmatrix} a_1 & a_2 \\ -1 & 0 \end{bmatrix}$. So the characteristic equation is

$$(17.37) \qquad |bI + K| = \begin{vmatrix} b + a_1 & a_2 \\ -1 & b \end{vmatrix} = b^2 + a_1 b + a_2 = 0$$

$$[\text{by } (17.29')]$$

which is precisely the same as the one obtained from the single equation as was asserted. Naturally, the same type of result holds also for the differential-equation framework, the only difference being that we would, in accordance with our convention, replace the symbol b by the symbol r in the latter framework.

It is also possible to link the characteristic equation of a difference- (or differential-) equation system to that of a particular square matrix, which we shall call D. Referring to the definition in (11.8), but using the symbol b (instead of r) for the difference-equation framework, we can write the characteristic equation of matrix D as follows:

$$(17.38) \qquad |D - bI| = 0$$

In general, if we multiply every element of the determinant $|D - bI|$ by -1, the value of the determinant will be unchanged if matrix D contains an *even* number of rows (or columns), or will change its sign if D contains an *odd* number of rows. In the present case, however, since $|D - bI|$ is to be set equal to zero, multiplying every element by -1 will not matter, regardless of the dimension of matrix D. But to multiply every element of the determinant $|D - bI|$ by -1 is tantamount to multiplying the matrix $(D - bI)$ by -1 (see Example 6 of Sec. 5.3) before taking its determinant. Thus, (17.38) can be rewritten as

$$(17.38') \qquad |bI - D| = 0$$

When this is equated to (17.37), it becomes clear that if we pick the matrix $D = -K$, then its characteristic equation will be identical with that of the system (17.21'). This matrix, $-K$, has a special meaning: If we take the *reduced* version of the system, $Iu + Kv = 0$, and express it in the form of $Iu = -Kv$, or simply $u = -Kv$, we see that $-K$ is the matrix that can transform the vector $v = \begin{bmatrix} x_t \\ y_t \end{bmatrix}$ into the vector $u = \begin{bmatrix} x_{t+1} \\ y_{t+1} \end{bmatrix}$ in that particular equation.

Again, the same reasoning can be adapted to the differential-equation system (17.23'). However, the reader is warned that in the case of a system such as (17.33'), $Ju + Mv = g$, where—unlike in the system (17.23')—the first term is Ju rather than Iu, we should not take $D = -M$. Rather, it is necessary first to normalize the equation $Ju + Mv = g$ into the form of (17.33''), and then take $D = -K = -J^{-1}M$.

In sum, given (1) a single difference or differential equation, and (2) an equivalent equation system, from which we can also obtain (3) an appropriate matrix D, if we try to find the characteristic equations of all three of these, the results must be one and the same.

EXERCISE 17.4

Solve the following two difference-equation systems:

1. $\begin{aligned} x_{t+1} & + x_t + 2y_t = 24 \\ y_{t+1} & + 2x_t - 2y_t = 9 \end{aligned}$ (with $x_0 = 10$ and $y_0 = 9$)

2. $\begin{aligned} x_{t+1} & - x_t - \tfrac{1}{3}y_t = -1 \\ x_{t+1} + y_{t+1} & - \tfrac{1}{6}y_t = 8\tfrac{1}{2} \end{aligned}$ (with $x_0 = 5$ and $y_0 = 4$)

Solve the following two differential-equation systems:

3. $\begin{aligned} x'(t) & - x(t) - 12y(t) = -60 \\ y'(t) & + x(t) + 6y(t) = 36 \end{aligned}$ [with $x(0) = 13$ and $y(0) = 4$]

4      $x'(t)$ $-\ 2x(t) + 3y(t) = 10$

            $y'(t) -\ \ x(t) + 2y(t) = \ 9$ [with $x(0) = 8$ and $y(0) = 5$]

5   Verify that the difference-equation system (17.24) is equivalent to the single equation $y_{t+2} + 6y_{t+1} + 9y_t = 4$, which was earlier solved as Example 4 of Sec. 17.1. How do the solutions obtained by the two different methods compare?

6   Verify that the characteristic equation of the difference equation (17.22) is identical with that of the equivalent system (17.22').

7   On the basis of the differential-equation system (17.33), find the matrix D whose characteristic equation is identical with that of the system. Check that the characteristic equations of the two are indeed the same.

17.5   Dynamic Input-Output Models

Our first confrontation with input-output analysis was concerned with the question: How much should be produced in each industry so that the input requirements of all industries, as well as the final demand (open system), will be exactly satisfied? The context was static, and the problem was to solve a simultaneous-equation system for the *equilibrium* output levels of all industries. When certain additional economic considerations are incorporated into the model, the input-output system can take on a dynamic character, and there will then result a difference- or differential-equation system of the type discussed in the preceding section.

     Three such dynamizing considerations will be considered here. To keep the exposition simple, however, we shall illustrate with two-industry open systems only. Nevertheless, since we shall employ matrix notation, the generalization to the n-industry case should not prove difficult, for it can be accomplished simply by duly changing the dimensions of the matrices involved. For purposes of such generalization, it will prove advisable to denote the variables not by x_t and y_t but by $x_{1,t}$ and $x_{2,t}$, so that we can extend the symbolism to $x_{n,t}$ when needed. The reader will recall that, in the input-output context, x_i represents the output (measured in dollars) of the ith industry; the new subscript t will now add a time dimension to it. The input-coefficient symbol a_{ij} will still mean the dollar worth of the ith commodity required in the production of a dollar's worth of the jth commodity, and d_i will again indicate the final demand for the ith commodity.

time lag in production   In a static two-industry open system, the output of industry I should be set at the level of demand as follows:

$$x_1 = a_{11}x_1 + a_{12}x_2 + d_1$$

Now assume that there is a one-period lag in production, so that the amount demanded in period t will determine not the current output but the output of period $(t + 1)$. To depict this new situation, we must modify the above equation to the form

$$(17.39) \qquad x_{1,t+1} = a_{11}x_{1,t} + a_{12}x_{2,t} + d_{1,t}$$

Similarly, we can write for industry II:

$$(17.39') \qquad x_{2,t+1} = a_{21}x_{1,t} + a_{22}x_{2,t} + d_{2,t}$$

Thus, we now have a system of simultaneous difference equations; this constitutes a dynamic version of the input-output model.

In matrix notation, the system consists of the equation

$$(17.40) \qquad x_{t+1} - Ax_t = d_t$$

$$\text{where} \qquad x_{t+1} = \begin{bmatrix} x_{1,t+1} \\ x_{2,t+1} \end{bmatrix} \quad x_t = \begin{bmatrix} x_{1,t} \\ x_{2,t} \end{bmatrix} \quad A = \begin{bmatrix} a_{11} & a_{12} \\ a_{21} & a_{22} \end{bmatrix} \quad d_t = \begin{bmatrix} d_{1,t} \\ d_{2,t} \end{bmatrix}$$

The reader can see that (17.40) is in the form of (17.24″), with only two exceptions. First, unlike vector u, vector x_{t+1} does not have an identity matrix I as its "coefficient." However, as explained earlier, this really makes no analytical difference. The second, and more substantive, point is that the vector d_t, with a time subscript, implies that the final-demand vector is being viewed as a function of time. If this function is nonconstant, a modification will be required in the method of finding the particular integrals, although the complementary functions will remain unaffected. The following example will illustrate the modified procedure.

Example 1   Given the exponential final-demand vector

$$d_t = \begin{bmatrix} \delta^t \\ \delta^t \end{bmatrix} = \begin{bmatrix} 1 \\ 1 \end{bmatrix} \delta^t \qquad (\delta = \text{a positive scalar})$$

find the particular integrals of the dynamic input-output model (17.40). In line with the method of undetermined coefficients introduced in Sec. 17.3, we should try solutions of the form $x_{1,t} = \beta_1 \delta^t$ and $x_{2,t} = \beta_2 \delta^t$, where β_1 and β_2 are the undetermined coefficients. That is, we should try

$$(17.41) \qquad x_t = \begin{bmatrix} \beta_1 \delta^t \\ \beta_2 \delta^t \end{bmatrix} = \begin{bmatrix} \beta_1 \\ \beta_2 \end{bmatrix} \delta^t$$

which implies[1]

$$x_{t+1} = \begin{bmatrix} \beta_1 \delta^{t+1} \\ \beta_2 \delta^{t+1} \end{bmatrix} = \begin{bmatrix} \beta_1 \delta \\ \beta_2 \delta \end{bmatrix} \delta^t = \begin{bmatrix} \delta & 0 \\ 0 & \delta \end{bmatrix} \begin{bmatrix} \beta_1 \\ \beta_2 \end{bmatrix} \delta^t$$

If the indicated trial solutions hold, then the system (17.40) will become

$$\begin{bmatrix} \delta & 0 \\ 0 & \delta \end{bmatrix} \begin{bmatrix} \beta_1 \\ \beta_2 \end{bmatrix} \delta^t - \begin{bmatrix} a_{11} & a_{12} \\ a_{21} & a_{22} \end{bmatrix} \begin{bmatrix} \beta_1 \\ \beta_2 \end{bmatrix} \delta^t = \begin{bmatrix} 1 \\ 1 \end{bmatrix} \delta^t$$

or, upon canceling the common scalar multiplier $\delta^t \neq 0$,

$$(17.42) \qquad \begin{bmatrix} \delta - a_{11} & -a_{12} \\ -a_{21} & \delta - a_{22} \end{bmatrix} \begin{bmatrix} \beta_1 \\ \beta_2 \end{bmatrix} = \begin{bmatrix} 1 \\ 1 \end{bmatrix}$$

Assuming the coefficient matrix on the extreme left to be nonsingular, we can readily find β_1 and β_2 (by Cramer's rule) to be

$$(17.42') \qquad \beta_1 = \frac{\delta - a_{22} + a_{12}}{\Delta} \qquad \text{and} \qquad \beta_2 = \frac{\delta - a_{11} + a_{21}}{\Delta}$$

where $\Delta \equiv (\delta - a_{11})(\delta - a_{22}) - a_{12}a_{21}$. Since β_1 and β_2 are now expressed entirely in the known values of the parameters, we only need to insert them into the trial solution (17.41) to get the definite expressions for the particular integrals.

A more general version of the type of final-demand vector discussed here is given in Exercise 17.5-1.

The procedure for finding the complementary functions of (17.40) is no different from that presented in the preceding section. Since the homogeneous version of the equation system is $x_{t+1} - Ax_t = 0$, the characteristic equation should be

$$|bI - A| = \begin{vmatrix} b - a_{11} & -a_{12} \\ -a_{21} & b - a_{22} \end{vmatrix} = 0 \qquad [\text{cf. } (17.29')]$$

From this we can find the characteristic roots b_1 and b_2 and thence proceed to the remaining steps of the solution process.

excess demand and output adjustment   The model formulation in (17.40) can also arise from a different economic assumption. Consider the situation

---

[1] The reader will note that the vector $\begin{bmatrix} \beta_1 \delta \\ \beta_2 \delta \end{bmatrix}$ can be rewritten in several equivalent forms:

$$\begin{bmatrix} \beta_1 \\ \beta_2 \end{bmatrix} \delta \qquad \text{or} \qquad \delta \begin{bmatrix} \beta_1 \\ \beta_2 \end{bmatrix} \qquad \text{or} \qquad \delta \begin{bmatrix} 1 & 0 \\ 0 & 1 \end{bmatrix} \begin{bmatrix} \beta_1 \\ \beta_2 \end{bmatrix} = \begin{bmatrix} \delta & 0 \\ 0 & \delta \end{bmatrix} \begin{bmatrix} \beta_1 \\ \beta_2 \end{bmatrix}$$

We choose the third alternative here because in a subsequent step we shall want to add $\begin{bmatrix} \delta & 0 \\ 0 & \delta \end{bmatrix}$ to another 2 × 2 matrix. The first two alternative forms will entail problems of dimension conformability.

in which the excess demand for each product always tends to induce an output increment equal to the excess demand. Since the excess demand for the first product in period t amounts to

$$\underbrace{a_{11}x_{1,t} + a_{12}x_{2,t} + d_{1,t} -}_{\text{(demanded)}} \underbrace{x_{1,t}}_{\text{(supplied)}}$$

the output adjustment (increment) $\Delta x_{1,t}$ is to be set exactly equal to that level:

$$\Delta x_{1,t} \; (\equiv x_{1,t+1} - x_{1,t}) = a_{11}x_{1,t} + a_{12}x_{2,t} + d_{1,t} - x_{1,t}$$

However, if we add $x_{1,t}$ to both sides of this equation, the result will become identical with (17.39). Similarly, our output-adjustment assumption will give an equation the same as (17.39′) for the second industry. In short, the same mathematical model can result from altogether different economic assumptions.

So far, the input-output system has been viewed only in the discrete-time framework. For comparison purposes, let us now cast the output-adjustment process in the continuous-time mold.

In the main, this would call for use of the symbol $x_i(t)$ in lieu of $x_{i,t}$, and of the derivative $x_i'(t)$ in lieu of the difference $\Delta x_{i,t}$. With these changes, our output-adjustment assumption will manifest itself in the following pair of differential equations:

$$x_1'(t) = a_{11}x_1(t) + a_{12}x_2(t) + d_1(t) - x_1(t)$$
$$x_2'(t) = a_{21}x_1(t) + a_{22}x_2(t) + d_2(t) - x_2(t)$$

At any instant of time $t = t_0$, the symbol $x_i(t_0)$ tells us the rate of output flow per unit of time (say, per month) that prevails at the said instant, and $d_i(t_0)$ indicates the final demand per month prevailing at that instant. Hence the right-hand sum in each equation indicates the rate of excess demand per month, measured at $t = t_0$. The derivative $x_i'(t_0)$ at the left, on the other hand, represents the rate of output adjustment per month called forth by the excess demand at $t = t_0$. This adjustment will eradicate the excess demand (and bring about equilibrium) in a month's time, but only if the excess demand and the output adjustment both stay unchanged at the current rates. In actuality, the excess demand will vary with time, as will the induced output adjustment, thus resulting in a cat-and-mouse game of chase. The solution of the system, consisting of the time paths of the output x_i, is therefore merely a chronicle of this chase. If the solution is convergent, the cat (output adjustment) will eventually be able to catch the mouse (excess demand), asymptotically (as $t \to \infty$).

After proper rearrangement, this system of differential equations can be written in the format of (17.33′) as follows:

(17.43) $$Ix' + (I - A)x = d$$

where $$x' = \begin{bmatrix} x_1'(t) \\ x_2'(t) \end{bmatrix} \quad x = \begin{bmatrix} x_1(t) \\ x_2(t) \end{bmatrix} \quad A = \begin{bmatrix} a_{11} & a_{12} \\ a_{21} & a_{22} \end{bmatrix} \quad d = \begin{bmatrix} d_1(t) \\ d_2(t) \end{bmatrix}$$

(the prime denoting derivative, not transpose). The complementary functions can be found by the method discussed earlier. In particular, the characteristic roots are to be found from the equation

$$|rI + (I - A)| = \begin{vmatrix} r + 1 - a_{11} & -a_{12} \\ -a_{21} & r + 1 - a_{22} \end{vmatrix} = 0 \qquad \text{[cf. (17.36)]}$$

As for the particular integrals, if the final-demand vector contains non-constant functions of time $d_1(t)$ and $d_2(t)$ as its elements, a modification will be needed in the method of solution. Let us illustrate with a simple example.

Example 2   Given the final-demand vector

$$d = \begin{bmatrix} \lambda_1 e^{\rho t} \\ \lambda_2 e^{\rho t} \end{bmatrix} = \begin{bmatrix} \lambda_1 \\ \lambda_2 \end{bmatrix} e^{\rho t}$$

where λ_i and ρ are constants, find the particular integrals of the dynamic model (17.43). Using the method of undetermined coefficients, we can try solutions of the form $x_i(t) = \beta_i e^{\rho t}$, which imply, of course, that $x_i'(t) = \rho \beta_i e^{\rho t}$. In matrix notation, these can be written as

$$(17.44) \qquad x = \begin{bmatrix} \beta_1 \\ \beta_2 \end{bmatrix} e^{\rho t}$$

and $\qquad x' = \rho \begin{bmatrix} \beta_1 \\ \beta_2 \end{bmatrix} e^{\rho t} = \begin{bmatrix} \rho & 0 \\ 0 & \rho \end{bmatrix} \begin{bmatrix} \beta_1 \\ \beta_2 \end{bmatrix} e^{\rho t}$ [cf. footnote on page 614]

Upon substituting into (17.43) and canceling the common (nonzero) scalar multiplier $e^{\rho t}$, we obtain

$$\begin{bmatrix} \rho & 0 \\ 0 & \rho \end{bmatrix} \begin{bmatrix} \beta_1 \\ \beta_2 \end{bmatrix} + \begin{bmatrix} 1 - a_{11} & -a_{12} \\ -a_{21} & 1 - a_{22} \end{bmatrix} \begin{bmatrix} \beta_1 \\ \beta_2 \end{bmatrix} = \begin{bmatrix} \lambda_1 \\ \lambda_2 \end{bmatrix}$$

or

$$(17.45) \qquad \begin{bmatrix} \rho + 1 - a_{11} & -a_{12} \\ -a_{21} & \rho + 1 - a_{22} \end{bmatrix} \begin{bmatrix} \beta_1 \\ \beta_2 \end{bmatrix} = \begin{bmatrix} \lambda_1 \\ \lambda_2 \end{bmatrix}$$

If the leftmost matrix is nonsingular, we can apply Cramer's rule and determine the values of the coefficients β_i to be

$$\beta_1 = \frac{\lambda_1(\rho + 1 - a_{22}) + \lambda_2 a_{12}}{\Delta}$$

$(17.45')$

$$\beta_2 = \frac{\lambda_2(\rho + 1 - a_{11}) + \lambda_1 a_{21}}{\Delta}$$

where $\Delta \equiv (\rho + 1 - a_{11})(\rho + 1 - a_{22}) - a_{12} a_{21}$. The *undetermined coefficients* having thus been determined, we can introduce these values into the trial solution (17.44) in order to obtain the desired particular integrals.

capital formation   Another economic consideration that can give rise to a dynamic input-output system is the possibility of capital formation, including the accumulation of inventory.

In the static discussion, we only considered the output level of each product needed to satisfy current demand. The needs for inventory accumulation or capital formation either were ignored or were subsumed under the final-demand vector. To bring capital formation into the open, let us now consider—along with an input-coefficient matrix $A = [a_{ij}]$—a capital-coefficient matrix

$$C = [c_{ij}] = \begin{bmatrix} c_{11} & c_{12} \\ c_{21} & c_{22} \end{bmatrix}$$

where c_{ij} denotes the dollar worth of the ith commodity needed by the jth industry as new capital (either equipment or inventory, depending on the nature of the ith commodity) as a result of an output increment of \$1 in the jth industry. For example, if an increase of \$1 in the output of the soft-drink (jth) industry induces it to add \$2 worth of bottling equipment (ith commodity), then $c_{ij} = 2$. Such a capital coefficient thus reveals a marginal capital-output ratio of sorts, the ratio being limited to one type of capital (the ith commodity) only. Like the input coefficients a_{ij}, the capital coefficients are assumed to be fixed. The idea is for the economy to produce each commodity in such quantity as to satisfy not only the input-requirement demand plus the final demand, but also the capital-requirement demand for it.

If time is *continuous*, output increment is indicated by the derivatives $x_i'(t)$; thus the output of each industry should be set at

$$x_1(t) = \underbrace{a_{11}x_1(t) + a_{12}x_2(t)}_{} + \underbrace{c_{11}x_1'(t) + c_{12}x_2'(t)}_{} + \underbrace{d_1(t)}_{}$$
$$x_2(t) = \underbrace{a_{21}x_1(t) + a_{22}x_2(t)}_{\text{input requirement}} + \underbrace{c_{21}x_1'(t) + c_{22}x_2'(t)}_{\text{capital requirement}} + \underbrace{d_2(t)}_{\substack{\text{final} \\ \text{demand}}}$$

In matrix notation, this is expressible by the equation

$$Ix = Ax + Cx' + d$$

or

(17.46) $$Cx' + (A - I)x = -d$$

If time is *discrete*, the capital requirement in period t will be based on the output increment $x_{i,t} - x_{i,t-1}$ ($\equiv \Delta x_{i,t-1}$); thus the output levels should be set at

$$\begin{bmatrix} x_{1,t} \\ x_{2,t} \end{bmatrix} = \underbrace{\begin{bmatrix} a_{11} & a_{12} \\ a_{21} & a_{22} \end{bmatrix}\begin{bmatrix} x_{1,t} \\ x_{2,t} \end{bmatrix}}_{\text{input requirement}} + \underbrace{\begin{bmatrix} c_{11} & c_{12} \\ c_{21} & c_{22} \end{bmatrix}\begin{bmatrix} x_{1,t} - x_{1,t-1} \\ x_{2,t} - x_{2,t-1} \end{bmatrix}}_{\text{capital requirement}} + \underbrace{\begin{bmatrix} d_{1,t} \\ d_{2,t} \end{bmatrix}}_{\substack{\text{final} \\ \text{demand}}}$$

or $$Ix_t = Ax_t + C(x_t - x_{t-1}) + d_t$$

Moving the time subscript forward by one period, and collecting terms, however, we can write the equation in the form

(17.47) $\quad (I - A - C)x_{t+1} + Cx_t = d_{t+1}$

The differential-equation system (17.46) and the difference-equation system (17.47) can again be solved, of course, by the method of the preceding section. It also goes without saying that these two matrix equations are both extendible to the n-industry case simply by an appropriate redefinition of the matrices and a corresponding change in the dimensions thereof.

In the above, we have discussed how a dynamic input-output model can arise from such considerations as time lags and adjustment mechanisms. When similar considerations are applied to general-equilibrium market models, the latter will tend to become dynamic in much the same way. But, since the formulation of such models is analogous in spirit to input-output models, we shall dispense with a formal discussion thereof and merely refer the reader to the illustrative cases in Exercises 17.5-7 and 17.5-8.

EXERCISE 17.5

1   In Example 1, if the final-demand vector is changed to $d_t = \begin{bmatrix} \lambda_1 \delta^t \\ \lambda_2 \delta^t \end{bmatrix}$, what will the particular integrals be? After finding your answers show that the answers in Example 1 are merely a special case of these, with $\lambda_1 = \lambda_2 = 1$.

2   (a) Show that (17.42) can be written more concisely as

$(\delta I - A)\beta = u$

(b) Of the five symbols used, which are scalars? Vectors? Matrices?
(c) Write the solution for β in matrix form, assuming $(\delta I - A)$ to be nonsingular.

3   (a) Show that (17.45) can be written more concisely as

$(\rho I + I - A)\beta = \lambda$

(b) Which of the five symbols represent scalars, vectors, and matrices, respectively?
(c) Write the solution for β in matrix form, assuming $(\rho I + I - A)$ to be nonsingular.

4   In the capital-formation model, write the characteristic equation for (a) the continuous-time case (17.46); (b) the discrete-time case (17.47).

5   Given $A = \begin{bmatrix} \frac{3}{10} & \frac{4}{10} \\ \frac{3}{10} & \frac{2}{10} \end{bmatrix}$ and $d_t = \begin{bmatrix} (\frac{12}{10})^t \\ (\frac{12}{10})^t \end{bmatrix}$ for the discrete-time production-lag input-output model described in (17.40), find (a) the particular integrals; (b) the complementary functions; and (c) the definite time paths, assuming initial outputs $x_{1,0} = \frac{187}{39}$ and $x_{2,0} = \frac{72}{13}$. (*Note:* Use fractions, not decimals, in all calculations.)

6   Given $A = \begin{bmatrix} \frac{3}{10} & \frac{4}{10} \\ \frac{3}{10} & \frac{2}{10} \end{bmatrix}$ and $d = \begin{bmatrix} e^{t/10} \\ 2e^{t/10} \end{bmatrix}$ for the continuous-time output-adjustment input-output model described in (17.43), find (a) the particular integrals; (b) the complementary functions; and (c) the definite time paths, assuming initial conditions $x_1(0) = \frac{53}{6}$ and $x_2(0) = \frac{25}{6}$. (Again, use fractions, not decimals, in all calculations.)

7   In an n-commodity market, all Q_{di} and Q_{si} (with $i = 1, 2, \ldots, n$) will be functions of the n prices $P_1, \ldots, P_n$, as will also be the excess demand for each commodity $E_i \equiv Q_{di} - Q_{si}$. Assuming linearity, we can write

$$E_1 = a_{10} + a_{11}P_1 + a_{12}P_2 + \cdots + a_{1n}P_n$$
$$E_2 = a_{20} + a_{21}P_1 + a_{22}P_2 + \cdots + a_{2n}P_n$$
$$\cdots\cdots\cdots\cdots\cdots\cdots\cdots\cdots\cdots\cdots\cdots\cdots\cdots$$
$$E_n = a_{n0} + a_{n1}P_1 + a_{n2}P_2 + \cdots + a_{nn}P_n$$

or, in matrix notation,

$$E = a + AP$$

(a)   What do these last four symbols stand for—scalars, vectors, or matrices? What are their respective dimensions?

(b)   Now consider all prices to be functions of time, and assume that $dP_i/dt = \alpha_i E_i$ (with $i = 1, 2, \ldots, n$). What is the economic interpretation of this last set of equations?

(c)   Write out the differential equations showing each dP_i/dt to be a linear function of the n prices.

(d)   Show that, if we let P' denote the $n \times 1$ column vector of the derivatives dP_i/dt, and if we let α denote an $n \times n$ diagonal matrix, with $\alpha_1, \alpha_2, \ldots, \alpha_n$ (in that order) in the principal diagonal and zeros elsewhere, we can write the above differential-equation system in matrix notation as $P' - \alpha AP = \alpha a$.

8   For the n-commodity market of the preceding problem, the discrete-time version will consist of a set of difference equations $\Delta P_{i,t} = \alpha_i E_{i,t}$ (with $i = 1, 2, \ldots, n$), where $E_{i,t} = a_{i0} + a_{i1}P_{1,t} + a_{i2}P_{2,t} + \cdots + a_{in}P_{n,t}$.

(a) Write out the excess-demand equation system, and show that it can be expressed in matrix notation as $E_t = a + AP_t$.

(b) Show that the price adjustment equations can be written as $P_{t+1} - P_t = \alpha E_t$, where α is the $n \times n$ diagonal matrix defined in the preceding problem.

(c) Show that the difference-equation system of the present discrete-time model can be expressed in the form $P_{t+1} - (I + \alpha A)P_t = \alpha a$.

17.6 Limitations of Dynamic Analysis

The static analysis presented in Part 2 of this volume dealt only with the question of what the equilibrium position will be under certain given conditions of a model. The major query was: What values of the variables, *if attained*, will tend to perpetuate themselves? But the *attainability* of the equilibrium position is taken for granted. When we proceeded to the realm of comparative statics, in Part 3, the central question shifted to the more interesting problem: How will the equilibrium position shift in response to a certain change in a parameter? But the attainability aspect was again brushed aside. It was not until we reached the dynamic analysis in Part 5 that we looked the question of attainability squarely in the eye. Here we specifically ask: If initially we are away from an equilibrium position—say, because of a recent disequilibrating parameter change—will the various forces in the model tend to send us toward the new equilibrium position? Furthermore, in a dynamic analysis, we also learn the particular character of the path (whether steady, fluctuating, or oscillatory) the variable will follow on its way to the equilibrium (if at all). The significance of dynamic analysis should therefore be self-evident.

However, in concluding its discussion, we should also take cognizance of the limitations of dynamic analysis. For one thing, to make the analysis manageable, dynamic models are often formulated in terms of linear equations. While simplicity may thereby be gained, the assumption of linearity will in many cases entail a considerable sacrifice of realism. Since a time path which is germane to a linear model may not always approximate that of a nonlinear counterpart, as we have seen in the price-ceiling example of Sec. 16.6, care must be exercised in the interpretation and application of the results of linear dynamic models. In this connection, however, the qualitative-graphic approach may perform an extremely valuable service, because under quite general conditions it can enable us to incorporate nonlinearity into a model without adding undue complexity to the analysis, as the Solow growth model admirably illustrates.

Another shortcoming usually found in dynamic economic models is the use of constant coefficients in differential or difference equations. Inasmuch as the primary role of the coefficients is to specify the parameters of the model, the constancy of coefficients—again assumed for the sake of mathematical manageability—essentially serves to "freeze" the economic environment of the problem under investigation. In other words, it means that the endogenous adjustment of the model is being studied in a sort of economic vacuum, such that no exogenous factors are allowed to intrude. In certain cases, of course, this problem may not be too serious, because many economic parameters do tend to stay relatively constant over long periods of time. And in some other cases, we may be able to undertake a comparative-dynamic type of analysis, to see how the time path of a variable will be affected by a change in certain parameters. Nevertheless, when we are interpreting a time path that extends into the distant future, we should always be careful not to be overconfident about the validity of the path in its more remote stretches, if simplifying assumptions of constancy have been made.

The reader realizes, of course, that to point out its limitations as has been done here is by no means intended to disparage dynamic analysis as such. Indeed, it will be recalled that each type of analysis hitherto presented has been shown to have its own brand of limitations. As long as it is duly interpreted and properly applied, therefore, dynamic analysis—like any other type of analysis—can play an important part in the study of economic phenomena.

SIX

MATHEMATICAL PROGRAMMING
AND GAME THEORY

18

LINEAR PROGRAMMING

Now that we have covered the entire analytical spectrum of *statics* (including *optimization*), *comparative statics*, and *dynamics*, let us return to the problem of optimization and present some relatively recent developments in that area of analysis. These consist of *mathematical programming* (a general term covering *linear programming* as well as *nonlinear programming*) and *game theory*.

Mathematical programming differs from classical optimization in that it seeks to tackle problems in which the optimizer faces *inequality* constraints— constraints in the form of, say, $g(x,y) \leq c$ rather than $g(x,y) = c$. As a specific illustration, instead of requiring a consumer to spend the exact amount of \$250, the mathematical-programming framework will allow him the freedom of spending either \$250, or less if he chooses. By thus liberalizing the constraint requirement, this new framework of optimization makes the problem at once more interesting and more realistic. But it also calls for the development of new methods of solution, since inequality constraints cannot be handled by the classical techniques of calculus.

Game theory, the other development, departs from our earlier framework of optimization in a still more radical way. Instead of seeking a maximum or minimum value of a variable, the optimizer will be assumed to be looking for a so-called "minimax" or "maximin" value. Thus, there is even to be a new optimization criterion. However, as we shall see, even though it was developed independently of mathematical programming, game theory nevertheless bears a close relationship to the latter.

We shall first discuss the simpler variety of mathematical programming, known as linear programming, in which the objective function as well as the constraint inequalities are all linear.

18.1   Simple Examples of Linear Programming

The essence of linear programming can best be conveyed by means of concrete examples. We shall present two, with one illustrating minimization and the other illustrating maximization.

a problem of diet   To maintain his health, a person must fulfill certain minimum daily requirements for several kinds of nutrients. Assume, for the sake of simplicity, that only three kinds of nutrients need to be considered: calcium, protein, and calories. Also assume that the person's diet is to consist of only two food items, I and II, whose price and nutrient contents are as shown in Table 18.1, where we have also listed the minimum daily requirement for each nutrient. Problem: What combination of the two food items will satisfy the daily requirements and entail the least cost?

If we denote the quantities of the two food items to be purchased each day by x_1 and x_2 (regarded as continuous variables), the problem can be stated mathematically as follows:

$$\begin{aligned}
\text{Minimize} \quad & C = 0.6x_1 + x_2 \\
\text{subject to} \quad & 10x_1 + 4x_2 \geq 20 \\
& 5x_1 + 5x_2 \geq 20 \\
& 2x_1 + 6x_2 \geq 12 \\
\text{and} \quad & x_1, x_2 \geq 0
\end{aligned}$$

(18.1)

The first equation in (18.1), which is a cost function based on the price information in Table 18.1, constitutes the *objective function* of the linear program; here the function is to be minimized. The three inequalities that follow are the *constraints* necessitated by the daily requirements; these are readily translated from the last

TABLE 18.1

	Food I (per lb)	Food II (per lb)	Minimum daily requirement
Price ($)	0.60	1.00	
Calcium (unit*)	10	4	20
Protein (unit*)	5	5	20
Calories (unit*)	2	6	12

* Hypothetical units are employed to allow the use of convenient round numbers in the example.

three rows of the table. The reader will note that, although it is forbidden to fall below the daily requirements, the optimizer *is* (in view of the use of the weak inequality signs $\geq$) allowed to exceed the minimum amounts indicated; it is this feature that mainly distinguishes linear programming from the optimization problems discussed earlier. Lastly, by means of the two additional inequalities, x_1, $x_2 \geq 0$, referred to as *nonnegativity restrictions*, we bring into the open a requirement which, on account of the limitations of the calculus, has to be left implicit in the classical optimization framework, namely, negative purchases are not permissible. It is also worth noting that our problem actually contains more constraints than choice variables. This is something that can never occur in classical optimization problems, but is now made feasible because the constraints have been weakened from equalities to inequalities, and are thus much easier to satisfy.

In short, then, there are three essential ingredients in a linear program: an objective function, a set of constraints, and a set of nonnegativity restrictions. The reader will note that linearity prevails throughout, because no variable is raised to a power other than 1, or is multiplied by any other variable. It is this fact, of course, that gives rise to the name linear programming.

the graphical solution   Since our problem involves only two choice variables, it is amenable to graphical analysis. In Fig. 18.1, let us plot x_1 and x_2 on the two axes. Because of the nonnegativity restrictions, we need only to consider the nonnegative quadrant.

To see what the constraints will entail graphically, let us first pretend that the three constraints are given as equations and plot them as three straight lines as seen in Fig. 18.1a. Each of these lines—labeled as *calcium border*, *protein border*, and *calorie border*, respectively—divides the quadrant into two nonoverlapping regions. Since each constraint is of the $\geq$ type, only the points (ordered pairs) lying in the northeast region or on the border line itself will satisfy the particular constraint involved. To satisfy all three constraints simultaneously, we can thus accept only those ordered pairs (x_1,x_2) which do not lie to the southeast of *any* border line we have constructed. The point (1,2), for instance, does satisfy the calorie constraint, but it fails the other two; it is therefore unfeasible in our linear program. On the other hand, all the points located in the shaded area in diagram *b* do satisfy all three constraints simultaneously. For this reason, the shaded area is called the *feasible region*, and each point (ordered pair) in that region is known as a *feasible solution*. It should be understood that the feasible region includes the points on its (heavy) kinked *boundary*. In particular, the set of points on the horizontal axis $\{(x_1,x_2) \mid x_1 \geq 6,\ x_2 = 0\}$, as well as the set of points on the vertical axis $\{(x_1,x_2) \mid x_1 = 0,\ x_2 \geq 5\}$, are also members of the

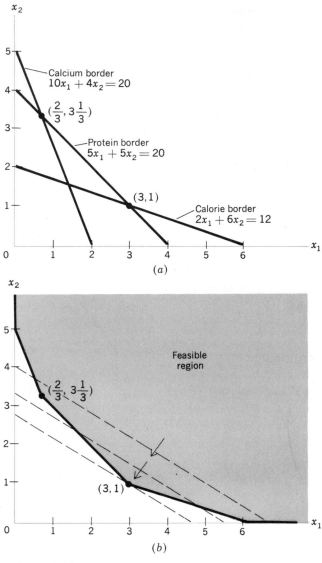

FIGURE 18.1

feasible region. Therefore, the feasible region can be considered as a *closed set* (of ordered pairs), a concept which, akin to that of a closed interval, means a set that includes all its boundary points.

The reader will note that the kinked boundary of the feasible region is composed of selected segments of the three constraint borders and of the axes. Note also that, in our present (two-dimensional) case, the corner points on the

Mathematical Programming and Game Theory

boundary—to be referred to as *extreme points*—occur either at the intersection of two borderlines [e.g., (3,1) and $(\frac{2}{3},3\frac{1}{3})$] or at the intersection of one borderline and one axis [e.g., (0,5) and (6,0)]. These extreme points will prove of great significance in our solution.

The points in the feasible region represent the set of all food combinations that satisfy all the constraints as well as the nonnegativity restrictions, but some of these would entail a lower purchase cost than others. To minimize cost C, it is necessary also to take the objective function into account. Writing the cost function in the form

$$x_2 = C - 0.6x_1$$

and taking C to be a parameter, we can plot this equation as a family of parallel straight lines with the common slope of -0.6. Among these, three possible ones are shown—as dashed lines—in Fig. 18.1*b*. Inasmuch as each of these corresponds to a definite value of C, what have been drawn are in effect three *isocosts*. To minimize cost, then, we must select the lowest possible isocost while still staying in the feasible region. In Fig. 18.1*b*, such a selection leads us to the extreme point (3,1). Thus, the *optimal feasible solution* (or *optimal solution*, for short) of our linear program is $(\bar{x}_1,\bar{x}_2) = (3,1)$. It follows that the minimized cost of diet, calculated at the food prices given, will amount to $\bar{C} = \$2.80$ per day. With this steady daily diet of 3 lb of food I and 1 lb of food II, our hypothetical optimizer may very well get tired of eating, but as far as the cost of living is concerned, the optimal combination certainly cannot be topped.

As described, the diet problem is nothing but a modified version of the least-cost-combination problem. The isocost idea is entirely the same as before, but the smooth isoquant encountered before is now replaced by a feasible region with a kinked boundary. As a result of this, the idea of *point of tangency* in differential calculus must be given up in favor of what may be termed the *point of contact*. In Fig. 18.1*b*, the point of contact is an extreme point on the boundary. This fact, let us point out, is no mere coincidence. As we shall show below, the optimal solutions of all linear programs are always to be found at extreme points. Since an extreme point always represents the intersection of two constraint borders (or of one border and one axis), we can, after pinpointing the optimal corner, find the optimal solution $(\bar{x}_1,\bar{x}_2)$ by simultaneously solving the equations of the two relevant intersecting lines. In our present example, the optimal corner is at the intersection of the protein and calorie borders. Thus, by solving the following two equations

$$5x_1 + 5x_2 = 20$$
$$2x_1 + 6x_2 = 12$$

we can find $(\bar{x}_1,\bar{x}_2) = (3,1)$.

The reader should note that while this solution *exactly* fulfills the requirements for protein and calorie, it *overfulfills* the calcium requirement. This is a situation that cannot possibly arise if all the constraints are strict equations.

effect of price changes   Let us now pose a comparative-static question: What will happen to the optimal solution if food prices P_1 and P_2 are changed? Since the slope of the isocosts is measured by the ratio $-P_1/P_2$ (in our example, $-0.60/1.00 = -0.6$), the immediate effect of price changes will be upon the isocosts. But several possibilities may arise.

First, if the two prices change in exactly the same proportion, then the slope of the isocosts will remain unchanged. In that event, the original optimal solution $(\bar{x}_1, \bar{x}_2)$ must continue to prevail, although the cost figure $\bar{C}$ will, naturally, rise or fall *pari passu* with P_1 and P_2.

Second, the two prices may change by different proportions, but the difference may be relatively minor. In such a case, the slope of the isocosts will undergo a small change, say, from -0.6 to -0.4 or to -0.8. As the reader can verify—by drawing a family of isocosts with slope -0.8 in Fig. 18.1*b*—a slope change of this magnitude will still leave the original optimal solution unaffected. Thus, unlike the point of tangency in differential calculus, the point of contact (the optimal corner) is insensitive to small changes in the price parameters.

As yet another possibility, suppose that both prices now become equal, say, at $P_1 = P_2 = 1$. Then the isocosts, now having a slope of -1, will be parallel to the protein border. The lowest possible new isocost will then contact the feasible region not at a single point but along an entire edge of its boundary, with the result that each point on the line segment extending from $(3,1)$ to $(\frac{2}{3}, 3\frac{1}{3})$ is equally optimal. As far as the optimizing individual is concerned, the multiple-optimum phenomenon poses no problem; on the contrary, it may be counted as a blessing because it can now make possible some variation in his menu. But, for us, this phenomenon seems to call for a retraction of our earlier statement that optimal solutions are always to be found at extreme points. A moment's reflection will indicate, however, that we are still on safe ground, for even in this multiple-optimum case, an optimal solution has occurred at a corner—nay, at *two* corners! In fact, if we confine our attention to extreme points only, we run no risk of missing any better solution. We shall find that it is this line of thinking which underlies the so-called "simplex method" of solution to be introduced below.

a production problem   Let us turn next to another simple example, this time in the realm of production.

The assumptions are as follows: A business firm produces two lines of product, I and II, with a plant that consists of three production departments: cutting, mixing, and packaging. The equipment in each department can be used for 8 hr a day; thus we shall regard 8 hr as the daily capacity in each department. The process of production can be summarized as follows: (1) Product I is first cut, then packaged. Each ton of this product uses up $\frac{1}{2}$ hr of the cutting capacity and $\frac{1}{3}$ hr of the packaging capacity. (2) Product II is first mixed, then packaged. Each ton of this product uses up 1 hr of the mixing capacity and $\frac{2}{3}$ hr of the packaging capacity. Finally, products I and II can be sold at prices of $80 and $60 per ton, respectively, but after deducting the variable costs incurred, they yield on a net basis $40 and $30 per ton. These latter amounts may be considered either as net-revenue figures (net of variable costs) or as gross-profit figures (gross of fixed costs). For simplicity, we shall refer to them here as "profits per ton." Problem: What output combination should the firm choose in order to maximize the total (gross) profit?

To answer this, we may first arrange the given information in tabular form, as in Table 18.2, and then translate the problem into the following linear program in the two continuous choice variables x_1 and x_2:

$$\text{Maximize} \quad \pi = 40x_1 + 30x_2$$

(18.2)

$$\begin{aligned}
\text{subject to} \quad & x_1 && \leq 16 && [\textit{cutting} \text{ constraint}] \\
& x_2 \leq 8 && && [\textit{mixing} \text{ constraint}] \\
& x_1 + 2x_2 \leq 24 && && [\textit{packaging} \text{ constraint}]
\end{aligned}$$

$$\text{and} \quad x_1, x_2 \geq 0$$

Note that, although the cutting constraint should, according to Table 18.2, be $\frac{1}{2}x_1 \leq 8$, we have multiplied both sides by 2 to get rid of the fractional expression.

TABLE 18.2

	Hours of processing needed per ton of		Daily capacity (hours)
	Product I	Product II	
Cutting	$\frac{1}{2}$	0	8
Mixing	0	1	8
Packaging	$\frac{1}{3}$	$\frac{2}{3}$	8
Profit per ton	$40	$30	

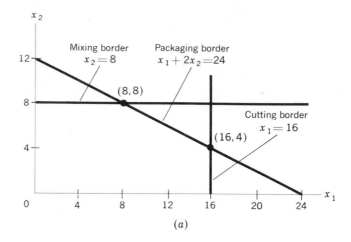

(a)

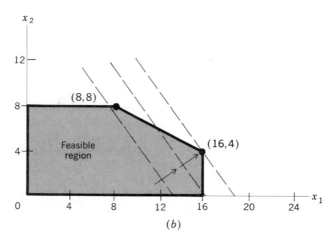

(b)

FIGURE 18.2

Similarly, we have modified the packaging constraint by a multiplier of 3. The problem encountered is now one of maximization. Also, the constraints are now of the $\leq$ type, for even though we can never exceed the capacity, we are nevertheless free to leave part of it idle. However, the nonnegativity restrictions still appear in the same form as in the minimization problem.

the graphical solution   The linear program in (18.2) can again be solved graphically, as is shown in Fig. 18.2. By virtue of the nonnegativity restrictions, the problem is again confined to the nonnegative quadrant, in which we can draw three constraint borders. The cutting border ($x_1 = 16$) and the mixing border

$(x_2 = 8)$ plot, respectively, as a vertical line and a horizontal line in Fig. 18.2a, whereas the packaging border appears as a slanting line that intersects the other two borders at the points (16,4) and (8,8).

Our constraints being of the $\leq$ type, the feasible region will this time consist of the set of points which meet the following three locational specifications simultaneously: (1) on or below the mixing border, (2) on or to the left of the cutting border, and (3) on or below the packaging border. The set of all qualified points is graphically represented by the shaded area in Fig. 18.2b. Since the boundary points on all sides of this area are feasible as well as the interior points, the feasible region is a closed set. In the present case, the set is also said to be *strictly bounded*, which means, roughly speaking, that the shaded area is capable of being "packed" into a box of a definite size. (In contrast, the feasible region in Fig. 18.1b is only *bounded from below*.)

Finally, let us consider the objective function. Rewriting the latter as

$$x_2 = \frac{\pi}{30} - \frac{4}{3} x_1$$

and taking π to be a parameter, we may plot this equation as a family of straight lines with the common slope of $-\frac{4}{3}$, three of which are shown (as dashed lines) in diagram b. Since each of these is associated with a specific value of the profit parameter π, we may call them *isoprofits*. Our objective, of course, is to attain the highest possible isoprofit while still remaining in the feasible region. Thus we must select the extreme point (16,4) as representing the best output combination. That is, the optimal solution is $\bar{x}_1 = 16$ tons per day, and $\bar{x}_2 = 4$ tons per day. Substituting these values into the objective function, we can then find the maximized profit to be $\bar{\pi} = \$760$ per day.

The reader will note that, while the cutting and packaging constraints are exactly fulfilled by the solution (16,4), the mixing constraint is not; to maximize profit, part of the mixing capacity is to be left unused. Such a result will be inconceivable if the constraints are all in the form of strict equations.

Speaking of the form of constraints, we should mention that, although the constraints in the above two examples are either all of the $\leq$ type (maximization problem) or all of the $\geq$ type (minimization problem), they need not always be so. It may be desired, for example, to restrict the calorie intake in the diet problem by the dual constraint of "no less than 2000" (for health) and "no more than 3500" (for weight control), in which case both types of inequalities will appear. But this will not affect our method of solution, for in (18.2) we have already seen the $\geq$ type of nonnegativity restrictions capable of coexisting with the $\leq$ type of capacity constraints. When both types of constraints are present, however, there does arise the possibility of inconsistent constraints; if, in the case of Fig. 18.3a, the problem requires us to be above border I and yet also to be

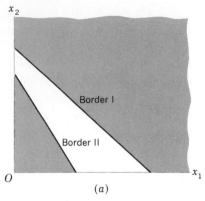

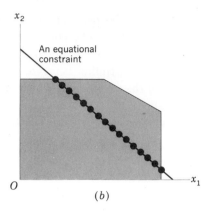

FIGURE 18.3

below border II, the feasible region will be a null set, and the problem cannot be solved.

A linear program may in fact also include one or more *equational* constraints. Figure 18.3b shows a (shaded) feasible region similar to the one in Fig. 18.2b, but if an equational constraint is added, the set of feasible solutions will shrink from the shaded area to the dotted line segment—the intersection of the shaded area and the new constraint line. Nevertheless, the same method of solution will apply.

EXERCISE 18.1

1   Solve the following problems graphically:

(a)   Maximize $\pi = 2x_1 + 5x_2$
  subject to

$$x_1 \leq 4$$
$$x_2 \leq 3$$
$$x_1 + 2x_2 \leq 8$$

and

$$x_1, x_2 \geq 0$$

(b)   Minimize $C = 12x_1 + 42x_2$
  subject to

$$x_1 + 2x_2 \geq 3$$
$$x_1 + 4x_2 \geq 4$$
$$3x_1 + x_2 \geq 3$$

and

$$x_1, x_2 \geq 0$$

2   What special features distinguish the graphical solutions of the following problems? What cause these features to arise?

(a) Minimize $\quad C = 6x_1 + 24x_2$
    subject to $\quad\quad x_1 + 2x_2 \geq 3$
    $$x_1 + 4x_2 \geq 4$$
    and $\quad\quad\quad\quad x_1, x_2 \geq 0$

(b) Minimize $\quad C = 6x_1 + 30x_2$
    subject to the same constraints as in (a)

3　A boy has been dating two girls, Mary and Nancy. From experience, he knows that: (1) Mary, the sophisticate, likes to go to more exclusive places where a date (3 hr) will cost \$12. Nancy, on the other hand, likes more popular entertainment so that a date (3 hr) will cost \$8. (2) His budget allows \$48 per month for dates. His class work leaves at most 18 hr and 4000 calories of his energy per month for social activities. (3) Each date with Mary consumes 500 calories of energy, but being more vivacious, Nancy takes twice that much. If he expects 6 units of pleasure from a date with Mary and 5 units of pleasure from a date with Nancy, how must he plan his social life in order to maximize pleasure? (Assume that the number of dates is a continuous variable, so that it is possible to have a whole date as well as a fractional date, or mini-date.)

4　In the preceding problem, if the time constraint is removed, how will the answer be affected?

5　A homeowner wants to paint his house. It has to be a one-coat job; to satisfy this requirement, the paint must have a viscosity of at least 200 centipoises. Another requirement is that, for a desired level of brilliance, there must be at least 14 g of a chemical ingredient Y in each gallon of the paint. In addition, for a desired degree of durability, at least 30 g of another chemical Z must be present in each gallon of the paint.

　　There are two kinds of paint (I and II) available to him. Type I costs \$6, and II costs \$4 per gal. Their specifications include the following:

	Paint I (per gal)	Paint II (per gal)
Viscosity (centipoises)	400	100
Y (grams)	20	10
Z (grams)	20	60

The homeowner decides to blend I and II, in order to meet the three requirements at a minimum cost. How much of I and II (call these x_1 and

x_2) should be used in *each gallon* of the blend? What is the minimized cost of the blended paint? (*Hint:* Aside from the usual constraints, there should be an equational constraint $x_1 + x_2 = 1$. Why?)

6   In the preceding problem, if the prices of paints I and II are reversed, how will the blend be affected? What will be the minimized cost per gallon of the new blend?

18.2   General Formulation of Linear Programs

The two examples of the preceding section illustrated the case of two choice variables and three constraints. When there are n choice variables and m constraints instead, the linear program will still take the same general form—with a linear objective function, a set of linear-inequality constraints, and a set of nonnegativity restrictions as its major ingredients. The generalized n-variable linear program can be stated in three alternative ways: in longhand, in Σ notation, or in matrix notation.

longhand   When completely written out, a maximization program in n variables and subject to m constraints will appear as follows:

$$
\begin{aligned}
\text{Maximize} \quad & \pi = c_1 x_1 + c_2 x_2 + \cdots + c_n x_n \\
\text{subject to} \quad & a_{11} x_1 + a_{12} x_2 + \cdots + a_{1n} x_n \leq r_1 \\
& a_{21} x_1 + a_{22} x_2 + \cdots + a_{2n} x_n \leq r_2 \\
& \qquad \vdots \qquad\qquad \vdots \qquad\qquad\qquad \vdots \qquad \vdots \\
& a_{m1} x_1 + a_{m2} x_2 + \cdots + a_{mn} x_n \leq r_m \\
\text{and} \quad & x_j \geq 0 \quad (j = 1, 2, \ldots, n)
\end{aligned}
$$

(18.3)

In (18.3), we have borrowed the π symbol from the production example to serve as a general symbol for the *maximand* (the object to be maximized), even though in many contexts the objective function may be something other than a profit function. The choice variables are denoted by x_j (with $j = 1, 2, \ldots, n$), and their coefficients in the objective function are symbolized by c_j (with $j = 1, 2, \ldots, n$), which are a set of given constants. The r_i symbols ($i = 1, 2, \ldots, m$)—another set of constants—represent, on the other hand, the "restrictions" imposed in the program. For the sake of uniformity, we have written all the m constraints as $\leq$ inequalities, but no loss of generality is thereby entailed. In particular, it may be noted that, in case a $\geq$ constraint appears, we can always convert it into the $\leq$ form simply by multiplying both sides by -1. Lastly, the reader will note that the coefficients of the choice variables in the constraints are denoted by a_{ij}, where the double subscripts can serve to pinpoint the specific location of each coefficient. Since there are altogether m constraints in n variables (where m can be greater than, equal to, or less than n), the coefficients a_{ij} will form a rectangular matrix of dimension $m \times n$.

Analogously, a minimization program may be written in longhand as follows:

$$
\begin{aligned}
\text{Minimize} \quad & C = c_1 x_1 + c_2 x_2 + \cdots + c_n x_n \\
\text{subject to} \quad & a_{11} x_1 + a_{12} x_2 + \cdots + a_{1n} x_n \geq r_1 \\
& a_{21} x_1 + a_{22} x_2 + \cdots + a_{2n} x_n \geq r_2 \\
& \quad \vdots \qquad \vdots \qquad\qquad \vdots \qquad \vdots \\
& a_{m1} x_1 + a_{m2} x_2 + \cdots + a_{mn} x_n \geq r_m \\
\text{and} \quad & x_j \geq 0 \quad (j = 1, 2, \ldots, n)
\end{aligned}
$$

(18.4)

Again, we have borrowed the C symbol from the diet problem to serve as a general symbol for the *minimand* (the object to be minimized), even though the objective function in many contexts may not be a cost function. The c_j in the objective function still represent a set of given constant coefficients, as are r_i in the constraints, but the symbol r in the present context will signify *requirements* rather than *restrictions*. The symbolism for the choice variables and the coefficients in the constraints has been retained intact. The constraints, however, now appear as $\geq$ inequalities.

Σ notation   A substantial saving in space can be achieved by expressing the linear programs (18.3) and (18.4) in Σ notation:

$$
\begin{aligned}
\text{Maximize} \quad & \pi = \sum_{j=1}^{n} c_j x_j \\[2mm]
\text{subject to} \quad & \sum_{j=1}^{n} a_{ij} x_j \leq r_i \quad (i = 1, 2, \ldots, m) \\[2mm]
\text{and} \quad & x_j \geq 0 \quad\qquad (j = 1, 2, \ldots, n)
\end{aligned}
$$

and similarly,

$$
\begin{aligned}
\text{Minimize} \quad & C = \sum_{j=1}^{n} c_j x_j \\[2mm]
\text{subject to} \quad & \sum_{j=1}^{n} a_{ij} x_j \geq r_i \quad (i = 1, 2, \ldots, m) \\[2mm]
\text{and} \quad & x_j \geq 0 \quad\qquad (j = 1, 2, \ldots, n)
\end{aligned}
$$

Though concise, statements written in Σ notation are inconvenient to operate upon mathematically; therefore, we shall not make use of them below.

matrix notation   To see how matrix notation can be applied, let us first define the following four matrices:

$$(18.5) \qquad c \equiv \begin{bmatrix} c_1 \\ c_2 \\ \vdots \\ c_n \end{bmatrix} \qquad x \equiv \begin{bmatrix} x_1 \\ x_2 \\ \vdots \\ x_n \end{bmatrix} \qquad A \equiv \begin{bmatrix} a_{11} & a_{12} & \cdots & a_{1n} \\ a_{21} & a_{22} & \cdots & a_{2n} \\ \vdots & \vdots & & \vdots \\ a_{m1} & a_{m2} & \cdots & a_{mn} \end{bmatrix} \qquad r \equiv \begin{bmatrix} r_1 \\ r_2 \\ \vdots \\ r_m \end{bmatrix}$$

Three of these are column vectors—c and x being of dimension $n \times 1$, but r being $m \times 1$. Matrix A is an $m \times n$ array.

Upon these definitions, the objective function in (18.3) can be expressed by the equation

$$\pi = \underset{(1 \times n)\,(n \times 1)}{c' \quad x}$$

where, it will be recalled, the vector product $c'x$ is 1×1 and, therefore, represents a scalar. It is in regard to the m constraints, however, that the advantage of matrix notation manifests itself distinctly, for the entire set of constraints in (18.3) can be summarized in a single inequality as follows:

$$\underset{(m \times n)\,(n \times 1)}{A \quad x} \leq \underset{(m \times 1)}{r}$$

Here, the inequality sign is to be interpreted to mean element-by-element inequality, that is, the ith row of matrix Ax is to be less than or equal to the ith row of matrix r, for every i.† Similarly, we can express the n nonnegativity restrictions by the single inequality

$$\underset{(n \times 1)}{x} \geq \underset{(n \times 1)}{0}$$

In short, the linear program in (18.3) is expressible concisely in the form

$$\begin{array}{lll} & \text{Maximize} & \pi = c'x \\ (18.3') & \text{subject to} & Ax \leq r \\ & \text{and} & x \geq 0 \end{array}$$

By the same token, it is possible to state the minimization program in (18.4) in the following simple form:

$$\begin{array}{lll} & \text{Minimize} & C = c'x \\ (18.4') & \text{subject to} & Ax \geq r \\ & \text{and} & x \geq 0 \end{array}$$

toward a method of solution   In the two-variable case ($n = 2$), the graphical method of solution can lead us to an optimal solution without difficulty. This is true regardless of the number of constraints present in the linear program,

---

† The inequality sign $\leq$, when applied to numbers, is often used interchangeably with the sign $\leqq$. When applied to vectors, however, the two signs may be assigned different meanings. For a discussion, see Kelvin Lancaster, *Mathematical Economics*, The Macmillan Company, New York, 1968, p. 250.

because additional constraints can increase only the number of extreme points, but not the dimension of the diagram. When there are three choice variables, however, the method becomes unwieldy, for a three-dimensional graph will be required. And, for the general n-variable case, the method completely breaks down! We must therefore search for a *nongraphical* method of solution that can apply to any number of variables.

First, let us see how the procedure of solution of the two-variable case should normally extend to the n-variable context. For the case of $n = 2$, our field of operation is a 2-space (a plane). By virtue of the nonnegativity restrictions and the constraints, however, we are able to narrow the field down and simply focus our attention on the feasible region, a subset of the 2-space. Then, via the objective function, we finally locate a particular point $(\bar{x}_1, \bar{x}_2)$ in that subset as the optimal solution. For the general n-variable case, we must work instead with an n-space, in which each point represents an ordered n-tuple—$(x_1, x_2, \ldots, x_n)$ —or an n-vector. The nonnegativity restrictions will now confine us to the *nonnegative orthant* (the n-dimensional analog of the nonnegative quadrant), and the constraints will together delineate a subset of the nonnegative orthant as the feasible region. Then, finally, by means of the objective function, we can locate a particular point in the feasible region—$(\bar{x}_1, \bar{x}_2, \ldots, \bar{x}_n)$—as the optimal solution.

As was intimated earlier, however, the optimal solution is always to be found at one of the extreme points of the feasible region; as will be explained below, this happens to be true even for the n-variable case. Consequently, instead of finding the entire feasible region, all we need is a method of determining the set of all extreme points, from among which we can then select the optimal solution.

This convenient result is based on the fact that, regardless of the number of choice variables, the feasible region in a linear program is always what is referred to as a *closed convex set*. Since the theory of convex sets plays a significant part in mathematical programming (and in game theory), it is advisable to get acquainted with it before proceeding to the development of a method of solution for the general n-variable linear program.

EXERCISE 18.2

1   Can the m constraints in (18.3) be written as follows?

$$
\begin{bmatrix} a_{11} \\ a_{21} \\ \vdots \\ a_{m1} \end{bmatrix} x_1 + \begin{bmatrix} a_{12} \\ a_{22} \\ \vdots \\ a_{m2} \end{bmatrix} x_2 + \cdots + \begin{bmatrix} a_{1n} \\ a_{2n} \\ \vdots \\ a_{mn} \end{bmatrix} x_n \leq \begin{bmatrix} r_1 \\ r_2 \\ \vdots \\ r_m \end{bmatrix}
$$

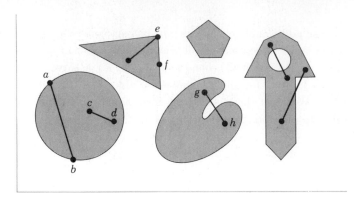

FIGURE 18.4

2   Can the objective function in (18.3) be written as an inner product?

3   Suppose that the first constraint in (18.4) happens to be an equation, $a_{11}x_1 + a_{12}x_2 + \cdots + a_{1n}x_n = r_1$. Show that, by replacing this equation with two appropriately chosen inequalities, we can still adhere to the format of using the $\geq$ sign throughout the constraint section.

18.3   Convex Sets

Generally speaking, a set can be a collection of any kind of objects, but in the present context our concern is only with sets of *points* in an n-space, which includes, as special cases, points on a line (1-space) and points in a plane (2-space). Since a point in an n-space may also be considered an n-tuple or an n-vector, point sets are also sets of n-tuples or of n-vectors. Convex sets represent a special genre of point sets.

the geometric definition   In a 2-space or 3-space, a *convex set* can be defined geometrically as a set with the property that, for any two points in the set, the line segment connecting these two points is also in the set.

It should be obvious that a *straight line* fulfills this definition and constitutes a convex set. By convention, a single *point* is also considered a convex set, and so is a null set (no point). For additional examples, let us look at Fig. 18.4. The disk—i.e., the "solid" circle, or a circle plus all the points within it—is a convex set, because a line joining any two points in the disk lies also in the latter. This is exemplified by line ab, which links two *boundary points*, and line cd, which joins two *interior points*. Note, however, that a (hollow) circle is *not* in itself a convex set. Similarly, a triangle (or a pentagon) is not in itself a convex set, but its solid version is.

Reference has already been made to boundary points as against interior points. In particular, a boundary point which does not lie on a line segment between any other two points in the convex set, such as point *e*, is called an *extreme point*. An extreme point must be a boundary point, but the converse is not true. For instance, point *f* is a boundary point, but since it lies on a line segment in the set, it does not qualify as an extreme point. The set of all extreme points must therefore be a subset of the set of all boundary points. It is interesting to note that, in the special case of a disk, all the boundary points happen to be extreme points as well.

The remaining two solid figures in Fig. 18.4 are not convex sets. The palette-shaped figure is reentrant, and thus a line segment such as *gh* does not lie entirely in the set. In the key-shaped figure, moreover, we find not only the feature of reentrance but also the presence of a hole, which is yet another cause of nonconvexity. Generally speaking, to qualify as a convex set, the set of points must contain no holes, and its boundary must not be indented anywhere.

The geometric definition of convexity also applies readily to point sets in a 3-space. For instance, a solid cube is a convex set, whereas a hollow cylinder is not. When a 4-space or a space of higher dimension is involved, however, the geometric interpretation becomes less obvious. Let us therefore turn to the algebraic definition of convex sets.

the algebraic definition   To this end, it is essential to introduce the concept of *convex combination* of vectors (points), which is a special type of linear combination.

A linear combination of two vectors *u* and *v* can be written as

$$k_1 u + k_2 v$$

where k_1 and k_2 are two scalars. When these two scalars are such that they both lie in the closed interval [0,1] and add up to unity, the linear combination is a convex combination, which can thus be defined as the combination

(18.6) $\zeta u + (1 - \zeta)v$ $(0 \leq \zeta \leq 1)$

As an illustration, the combination $\dfrac{1}{3}\begin{bmatrix} 2 \\ 0 \end{bmatrix} + \dfrac{2}{3}\begin{bmatrix} 4 \\ 9 \end{bmatrix}$ is a convex combination. In view of the fact that these two scalar multipliers are positive fractions adding up to 1, such a convex combination may be interpreted as a *weighted average* of the two vectors.[1]

---

[1] The reader will recall that this interpretation has been made use of earlier, in the discussion of concave and convex functions in Sec. 11.4.

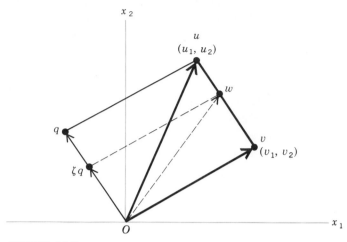

FIGURE 18.5

The unique characteristic of the combination in (18.6) is that, for every acceptable value of ζ, the resulting sum vector always lies on the line segment connecting the points u and v. This can be demonstrated by means of Fig. 18.5, where we have plotted two vectors $u = \begin{bmatrix} u_1 \\ u_2 \end{bmatrix}$ and $v = \begin{bmatrix} v_1 \\ v_2 \end{bmatrix}$ as two points with coordinates (u_1, u_2) and (v_1, v_2), respectively. If we plot another vector q such that $Oquv$ forms a parallelogram, then we have (by virtue of the discussion in Fig. 4.3)

$$u = q + v \qquad \text{or} \qquad q = u - v$$

It follows that a convex combination of vectors u and v (let us call it w) can be expressed in terms of vector q, because

$$w = \zeta u + (1 - \zeta)v = \zeta u + v - \zeta v = \zeta(u - v) + v = \zeta q + v$$

Hence, to plot the vector w, we can simply add ζq and v by the familiar parallelogram method. If the scalar ζ is a positive fraction, the vector ζq will merely be an abridged version of vector q; thus ζq must lie on the line segment Oq. Adding ζq and v, therefore, we must find vector w lying on the line segment uv, for the new, smaller parallelogram is nothing but the original parallelogram with the qu side shifted downward. The exact location of vector w will, of course, vary according to the value of the scalar ζ; by varying ζ from zero to unity, the location of w will shift from v to u. Thus the set of all points on the line segment uv, including u and v themselves, corresponds to the set of all convex combinations of vectors u and v.

In view of the above, a convex set may be defined as follows: A set S is

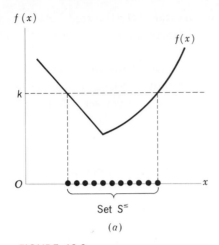
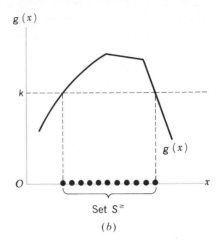

FIGURE 18.6

convex if and only if, for any two points $u \in S$ and $v \in S$, and for every scalar $0 \leq \zeta \leq 1$, it is true that $w = \zeta u + (1 - \zeta)v \in S$. This definition is applicable regardless of the dimension of the space in which the vectors u and v are located.

convex set versus convex function   Even though the identical word *convex* appears in both the term *convex set* and the term *convex function*, it has a widely different connotation in each context. In describing a *set*, the word convex is concerned with whether the set has any holes in it, whereas, in describing a *function*, the word has to do with how a curve or surface bends. What, then, is the rationale for using the same adjective? The answer will become clear if we compare the definition of convex set (given in the preceding paragraph) with that of convex function [see (11.14) and the ensuing sentence]. As the reader will note, both definitions depend on the concept of convex combinations (weighted averages) of vectors (points), and this makes the word convex an appropriate adjective in both contexts.

Aside from the similarity of their names, the concepts of convex set and convex function are related in the sense that the former can be generated by the latter in a certain manner. Specifically, given a convex *function*, $f(x)$, and some constant, k, we can always identify an associated convex *set*, $S^\leq$, defined as follows:

$$(18.7) \quad S^\leq \equiv \{x \mid f(x) \leq k\} \quad [f(x) \text{ convex}]$$

As illustrated in Fig. 18.6a, the set $S^\leq$ consists of all the x values corresponding to the segment of the $f(x)$ curve lying on or below the broken horizontal line. Hence it is the line segment on the horizontal axis marked by the heavy dots, which constitutes a convex set. Note that if the value of the constant k is changed, the definition (18.7) will yield a different line segment, but in any case the result will be a convex set.

Going a step further, we may observe that, even if we are given a *concave* function instead, say, $g(x)$, along with some constant, k, we can still generate an associated convex set, $S^{\geq}$. But the definition of this convex set will differ from (18.7):

$$(18.8) \qquad S^{\geq} \equiv \{x \mid g(x) \geq k\} \qquad [g(x) \text{ concave}]$$

in which the $\geq$ sign appears instead of $\leq$. Geometrically, as shown in Fig. 18.6b, the set $S^{\geq}$ contains all the x values corresponding to the segment of the $g(x)$ curve lying on or above the broken horizontal line. Thus it is again a line segment on the horizontal axis—a convex set.

In the above discussion, we have for simplicity stated the definitions of sets $S^{\leq}$ and $S^{\geq}$ in terms of functions of a single variable, $f(x)$ and $g(x)$. However, the underlying idea can be extended in a straightforward manner to functions of several variables. (See Exercise 18.3-8.)

convex sets in linear programming   The major ingredients of a linear program are the objective function and its m constraints and n nonnegativity restrictions. It turns out that each of these gives rise to a convex set. Moreover, the feasible region is also a convex set.

The objective function always comes in a linear form. For any given value of π (or C), it takes these general forms:

$$
\begin{array}{lll}
\text{2-space:} & \pi_0 = c_1 x_1 + c_2 x_2 & [\text{giving a } \textit{line}] \\
\text{3-space:} & \pi_0 = c_1 x_1 + c_2 x_2 + c_3 x_3 & [\text{giving a } \textit{plane}] \\
(18.9) \quad \text{n-space:} & \pi_0 = c_1 x_1 + c_2 x_2 + \cdots + c_n x_n & \\
& & [\text{giving a } \textit{hyperplane}]
\end{array}
$$

Lines and planes—special cases of hyperplanes—are easily seen to be convex sets. Let us now demonstrate that a hyperplane in an n-space is also a convex set.

Let the set of points that satisfy (18.9) be called the set H; then each point in H will be on the hyperplane defined by the said equation.[1] If we select any two points u and v in the set H, with coordinates $(u_1, u_2, \ldots, u_n)$ and $(v_1, v_2, \ldots, v_n)$, respectively, then, since these coordinates satisfy the equation

---

[1] While a formal definition of the set H calls for the expression

$$H = \{(x_1, x_2, \ldots, x_n) \mid \pi_0 = c_1 x_1 + \cdots + c_n x_n\}$$

or, in vector notation,

$$H = \{x \mid \pi_0 = c'x\} \qquad [\text{by (18.5)}]$$

the set H (the hyperplane) can be more simply specified by (18.9) or by its vector version, $\pi_0 = c'x$.

(18.9), we must—by substituting u_i for x_i and doing the same for v_i—find the following to be true:

$$(18.10) \quad \begin{aligned} \pi_0 &= c_1 u_1 + c_2 u_2 + \cdots + c_n u_n \\ \pi_0 &= c_1 v_1 + c_2 v_2 + \cdots + c_n v_n \end{aligned}$$

In the more succinct vector notation, these can be written as

$$(18.10') \quad \pi_0 = c'u \quad \text{and} \quad \pi_0 = c'v$$

To prove the set H to be convex, it is necessary to show that any convex combination of u and v (call it w) will be in the set H also. That is, w must satisfy (18.9), so that we may validly write $\pi_0 = c'w$. The required demonstration is relatively simple. Since

$$\begin{aligned} c'w &= c'[\zeta u + (1 - \zeta)v] = c'\zeta u + c'(1 - \zeta)v \quad &\text{[distributive law]} \\ &= \zeta c'u + (1 - \zeta)c'v \quad &\text{[scalar multiplication is commutative]} \\ &= \zeta \pi_0 + (1 - \zeta)\pi_0 \quad &\text{[by (18.10$'$)]} \\ &= \pi_0 \end{aligned}$$

the convex combination w *is* in the set H, for any value of ζ in the closed interval $[0,1]$. Consequently, the set H is indeed convex. In fact, H is a closed convex set, since every point on the hyperplane is a boundary point, and the set H does contain all its boundary points.

Considered in relation to the n-space in which it is located, a hyperplane always serves to divide the n-space into two *halfspaces*. In the 2-space case, for example, a straight line will divide the coordinate plane into 2 two-dimensional halfspaces, one to each side of the line—as we have seen from the borders constructed in Figs. 18.1 and 18.2. An n-space can be similarly divided into two n-dimensional halfspaces, but it takes a hyperplane to do it. Depending on whether or not the dividing hyperplane is considered as part of the halfspace in question, we may have either an *open* or a *closed* halfspace. For instance, if we write the two inequalities

$$c'x < 9 \quad \text{and} \quad c'x \geq 9$$

the former will define an *open* halfspace lying to one side of the hyperplane $c'x = 9$, whereas the latter will define a *closed* halfspace containing the points lying to the other side of the said hyperplane as well as the points on the hyperplane itself.

In view of the above, every constraint in (18.3) and (18.4) is seen to define a closed halfspace. Furthermore, so does every nonnegativity restriction, for the inequality (say) $x_1 \geq 0$ is but a special case of the constraint

$$(18.11) \quad a_{11}x_1 + a_{12}x_2 + \cdots + a_{1n}x_n \geq r_1$$

with $a_{11} = 1$ and all the other coefficients (including r_1) set equal to zero. It happens that each of these closed halfspaces is again a convex set.

The validity of this last statement is fairly obvious in the 2-space case. In Fig. 18.1, the set of points lying on or to the right of any constraint border is a convex set, because the line segment joining any two points therein must be in the set, too. Let us now demonstrate that a closed halfspace in an n-space is also convex. Consider the closed halfspace defined by the inequality (18.11), which is alternatively expressible in vector notation as

$$(18.11') \qquad a'x \geq r_1 \qquad (\text{where } a' \equiv [a_{11} \ \ a_{12} \ \ \cdots \ \ a_{1n}])$$

Let u and v be any two points in that halfspace. Then, since u and v both satisfy (18.11'), it follows that

$$a'u \geq r_1 \qquad \text{and} \qquad a'v \geq r_1 \qquad [\text{cf. (18.10')}]$$

For any scalar $0 \leq \zeta \leq 1$, moreover, we may deduce that

$$(18.12) \qquad \zeta a'u \geq \zeta r_1 \qquad \text{and} \qquad (1 - \zeta)a'v \geq (1 - \zeta)r_1$$

Now let $w = \zeta u + (1 - \zeta)v$ be a convex combination of u and v. If w can be shown to satisfy (18.11') also, then the halfspace in question must be convex. For this purpose, we need to form the vector product $a'w$:

$$a'w = a'[\zeta u + (1 - \zeta)v] = \zeta a'u + (1 - \zeta)a'v$$

But, by virtue of (18.12), it is clear that

$$a'w \geq \zeta r_1 + (1 - \zeta)r_1 \qquad \text{or} \qquad a'w \geq r_1$$

Thus the convex combination w, like u and v, also satisfies (18.11'). This proves that a closed halfspace in an n-space is a (closed) convex set.

Pursuing this line of reasoning a bit further, we can also establish the feasible region of a general n-variable linear program to be a closed convex set. As a preliminary, the reader will note that the feasible region always represents the intersection of a total of $m + n$ closed convex sets. In general, any point in the feasible region must by definition simultaneously satisfy a system of $m + n$ linear (weak) inequalities—the m constraints plus the n nonnegativity restrictions. Thus it must simultaneously be a member of $m + n$ closed halfspaces, i.e., must be a point in the *intersection* of those $m + n$ closed convex sets. This being the case, the following theorem will establish the feasible region as a closed convex set: The intersection of a finite number of convex sets is a convex set, and if each of the sets is closed, the intersection will also be closed.

The essence of this theorem can be grasped from Fig. 18.7, where the set S (a solid square) and the set T (a solid triangle) are both convex. Their intersection $S \cap T$, represented by the heavy-shaded area, evidently is also convex. Moreover,

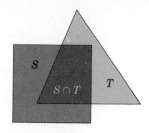

FIGURE 18.7

if S and T are both closed, then $S \cap T$ will also be closed, because the boundary points of the intersection set, which are merely a subset of the boundary points of S and of T, do belong to the intersection set.[1]

For a formal proof of this theorem, let u and v be any two points[2] in the intersection of two convex sets S and T. This means that

$$u, v \in S \qquad \text{and concurrently} \qquad u, v \in T$$

If w is any convex combination of u and v, then, since S is convex by assumption, we must find $w \in S$. Similarly, since T is also assumed convex, it is true that $w \in T$. But the concurrent membership in S and T implies that $w \in (S \cap T)$; that is, any convex combination of u and v will, like u and v themselves, be in the intersection set. This proves that the intersection is convex. By repeating the process, it can then be proved that the intersection of any finite number of convex sets must be a convex set.

extreme points and optimal solution   Two major results that emerge from the foregoing are: (1) For any given value of π (or C), the objective function of an n-variable linear program always defines a hyperplane, which is a closed convex set. (2) The feasible region, being the intersection of $m + n$ closed halfspaces, is also a closed convex set—call it set F. These two results may now be related to each other.

In attempting to optimize, it is always our purpose to "push" the objective hyperplane—by varying the value of π or C—either to the highest possible position (to attain $\bar{\pi}$), or to the lowest possible position (to attain $\bar{C}$), while still staying in the set F. When the optimal position is reached, the optimal hyperplane $\bar{H}$ can contain no interior points of the set F, for if it does we can always "push"

---

[1] Observe that the *union* of two convex sets is not necessarily convex. In Fig. 18.7, the union set $S \cup T$ consists of the entire shaded area, which is reentrant.
[2] The special cases of $S \cap T$ being a null set or a set with only one point are trivial, because such sets are considered to be convex by convention.

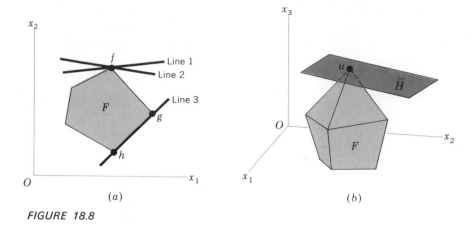

FIGURE 18.8

it farther, to attain a better position. Thus only the boundary points of the set F can appear in the intersection set $\bar{H} \cap F$. This leads us to the concept of supporting hyperplanes.

A *supporting hyperplane* (say, $\bar{H}$) is a hyperplane which has one or more points in common with a convex set (F) but which is so situated that the set F lies on one side of $\bar{H}$ exclusively. Figure 18.8 illustrates this concept for the 2-space and 3-space cases. In diagram a, lines 1, 2, and 3 are examples of supporting hyperplanes (here, lines). Line 1 (or line 2) has only one point in common with the solid polygon F, but line 3 has several. In either case, however, the set F lies exclusively on one side of the supporting line; consequently, only *boundary points* of F can appear on each of these lines. Note that each supporting line contains at least one extreme point of the set F, such as f, g, and h. The 3-space illustration in diagram b is similar, except that the supporting *line* is now replaced by a supporting *plane*. Again, the intersection of $\bar{H}$ and F (this time a solid polyhedron) can consist only of the boundary points of F; as illustrated, only one point (u) is involved, and that point is an extreme point of the set F.

For the general n-space case, the essence of the discussion concerning Fig. 18.8 finds embodiment in the following two theorems:

THEOREM I   Given u, a boundary point of a closed convex set, there is at least one supporting hyperplane at u.

THEOREM II   For a closed convex set bounded from below, there is at least one extreme point in every supporting hyperplane.

The relevance of these to linear programming is obvious. When we attain an optimal solution, the objective hyperplane—representing the optimal isoprofit or isocost—will be a supporting hyperplane. According to Theorem I, every boundary point of the feasible region is a possible candidate for the optimal solution. But Theorem II narrows down the problem by enabling us to confine our attention to *extreme points* only. For even though there may be *non*extreme boundary points present in the same supporting hyperplane, they are associated with the same π (or C) value and, accordingly, are no better than the extreme points and can be disregarded without any loss.

This simple but important fact is used to good advantage in the *simplex method* of solving an n-variable linear program, originally developed by George B. Dantzig,[1] which we shall explain in the next section. A *simplex* is a sort of n-dimensional analog of a triangle, with corners that represent extreme points, and the simplex method provides a systematic procedure whereby we can move from one extreme point of the feasible region to another, till the optimal one is reached. The fact that we may narrow down the field of choice to the extreme points only is one of the special features that distinguish linear programming from classical optimization problems.

local versus global optimum   Another important feature of linear programming which distinguishes it from classical optimization problems is that any solution obtained will give us not only a local (relative) optimum, but also a global (absolute) optimum. The reason for this particular feature is to be found in the following theorem (the globality theorem), which gives sufficient—though not necessary—conditions under which a local optimum will also qualify as a global optimum:

> If the feasible set F is a closed convex set, and if the objective function is a continuous concave (convex) function over the feasible set, then (*a*) any local maximum (minimum) will be a global maximum (minimum), and (*b*) the points in F at which the objective function is optimized will constitute a convex set. If the objective function happens to be *strictly* concave (convex) over the feasible set, then the global maximum (minimum) will be unique.

While these sufficient conditions are not necessarily satisfied in the classical optimization framework, they invariably are in linear programming. As we have seen, the feasible region in linear programming is always a closed convex set. Besides, the objective function being continuous and linear in the choice variables, it can be considered as either a concave or a convex function, depending on whether the problem is one of maximization or minimization. Thus the sufficient conditions stated in the theorem are indeed satisfied, and any optimum found will be global in nature in line with part (*a*) of the theorem.

[1] George B. Dantzig, "Maximization of a Linear Function of Variables Subject to Linear Inequalities," in Tjalling C. Koopmans (ed.), *Activity Analysis of Production and Allocation*, John Wiley & Sons, Inc., New York, 1951, pp. 339–347.

To understand part (b) of the theorem, let us take another look at Fig. 18.8. If the optimal solution of a linear program occurs at a single extreme point, such as point f in diagram a or point u in diagram b, then, by convention, that point constitutes a convex set in itself, and the assertion of the theorem is duly verified. But what if there are multiple optima? Multiple optima occur when the supporting hyperplane touches the feasible set at more than one point, such as when line 3 (diagram a) is the supporting line, or when the supporting plane $\bar{H}$ (diagram b) coincides with one of the faces (flat sides) of the solid polyhedron F. In these instances, the set of all optimal points will find embodiment either in the line segment hg, or some face of the polyhedron F, as the case may be. Thus the set is again a convex set, as the theorem asserts. In view of this, we can be sure that, if there exist a pair of optimal solutions to a linear program (two solutions being equally optimal), then any convex combination or weighted average of the two must also be an optimal solution.

EXERCISE 18.3

1   Do the following constitute convex sets in a 3-space?

(a)   a doughnut   (c)   a bowling pin

(b)   a perfect marble   (d)   a vase

2   The equation $x_1^2 + x_2^2 = 4$ represents a circle with center at (0,0) and with a radius of 2.

(a)   What does the set $\{(x_1,x_2) \mid x_1^2 + x_2^2 \leq 4\}$ represent geometrically?

(b)   Sketch a graph of the set.

(c)   Is this set convex?

3   Sketch a graph for each of the following sets, and indicate whether the set is convex:

(a) $\{(x_1,x_2) \mid x_2 = e^{x_1}\}$

(b) $\{(x_1,x_2) \mid x_2 \geq e^{x_1}\}$

(c) $\{(x_1,x_2) \mid x_2 \leq 3 - x_1^2\}$

(d) $\{(x_1,x_2) \mid x_1 x_2 \geq 1; x_1 > 0; x_2 > 0\}$

4   Plot the vectors $u = \begin{bmatrix} 15 \\ 30 \end{bmatrix}$ and $v = \begin{bmatrix} 30 \\ 20 \end{bmatrix}$.

(a)   Mark the points $\frac{1}{2}u$ and $\frac{1}{2}v$ in the diagram, and verify by parallelogram construction that the convex combination $\frac{1}{2}u + \frac{1}{2}v$ lies on the line segment uv.

(b)   Do the same for the convex combination $\frac{1}{3}u + \frac{2}{3}v$.

5   (a)   Show that, if two points $u = \begin{bmatrix} u_1 \\ u_2 \end{bmatrix}$ and $v = \begin{bmatrix} v_1 \\ v_2 \end{bmatrix}$ satisfy the inequality

$3x_1 + 5x_2 \leq 10$ (that is, $3u_1 + 5u_2 \leq 10$, etc.), then a convex combination $w = \zeta u + (1 - \zeta)v$ will also satisfy this inequality.

(b)   What does this imply regarding the set of points $\{(x_1, x_2) \mid 3x_1 + 5x_2 \leq 10\}$?

6   Given $u = \begin{bmatrix} 10 \\ 6 \end{bmatrix}$ and $v = \begin{bmatrix} 4 \\ 8 \end{bmatrix}$, which of the following are *convex* combinations of u and v?

(a) $\begin{bmatrix} 7 \\ 7 \end{bmatrix}$ (b) $\begin{bmatrix} 5.2 \\ 7.6 \end{bmatrix}$ (c) $\begin{bmatrix} 6.2 \\ 8.2 \end{bmatrix}$

[*Hint:* Does there exist a scalar ζ such that $\zeta u + (1 - \zeta)v = \begin{bmatrix} 7 \\ 7 \end{bmatrix}$?]

7   Given two vectors u and v in the 2-space, find and sketch:

(a)   The set of all linear combinations of u and v

(b)   The set of all nonnegative linear combinations of u and v

(c)   The set of all convex combinations of u and v

8   (a)   Generalize the definitions of the sets $S^{\leq}$ and $S^{\geq}$ in (18.7) and (18.8) to the cases where f and g are functions of n variables.

(b)   Assume that $n = 2$ and that the function f is shaped like an ice cream cone, whereas the function g is shaped like a pyramid. Describe the sets $S^{\leq}$ and $S^{\geq}$.

9   On the basis of Fig. 12.5, do you think that, given a quasiconvex or quasiconcave function and some constant k, it is still possible to delineate a convex set $S^{\leq}$ or $S^{\geq}$ as defined in (18.7) and (18.8)?

18.4   Simplex Method: Finding the Extreme Points

The optimal solution of a linear program is to be found among the extreme points. Given a graphable feasible region F, it is a simple task to find its extreme points, but how do we do it for the nongraphable n-variable case? Let us reexamine the extreme points of the 2-variable case for possible clues.

slacks and surpluses   The extreme points in Figs. 18.1 and 18.2 fall into three major types. These can be adequately illustrated in Fig. 18.9, which reproduces the feasible region of Fig. 18.2b.

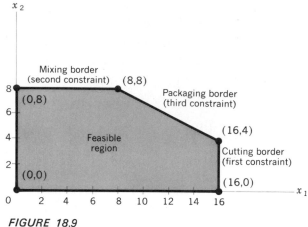

FIGURE 18.9

The first type consists of those which occur at the intersection of two constraint borders; examples of these are found in the points (8,8) and (16,4). While such points do fulfill two of the constraints *exactly*, the remaining constraint is inexactly fulfilled. The point (16,4), for instance, exactly fulfills the cutting and packaging constraints but not the mixing constraint, because the point lies below the mixing border. With the *inexact* fulfillment of some constraint, there must be an underutilization of capacity (or, in the diet problem, an overintake of some nutrient beyond the minimum requirement). That is, a *slack* in capacity utilization (or a *surplus* in nutrient intake) will develop.

Extreme points of the second type, exemplified by (0,8) and (16,0), occur where a constraint border intersects an axis. Being located on one constraint border only, such points can fulfill only one constraint exactly. Viewed differently, there will now develop slacks in *two* constraints.

Lastly, as the third type of extreme point, we have the point of origin (0,0), which fulfills none of the constraints exactly. The (0,0) extreme point, however, is only found in a maximization program, for the feasible region of a minimization program normally excludes the point of origin, as the reader can see from Fig. 18.1b.

The upshot is that in the present example—where the number of constraints (3) exceeds the number of choice variables (2)—each and every extreme point will involve a slack in at least one of the constraints. Furthermore, as should be evident from Fig. 18.9, the specific magnitude of the slacks entailed by each extreme point is easily calculable. When settling on a particular extreme point as the optimal solution, therefore, we are in effect deciding not only the values of $\bar{x}_1$ and $\bar{x}_2$ but also the optimal values of the slacks. Let us try to consider the slacks explicitly, denoting the slack in the ith constraint by the symbol s_i. The

Mathematical Programming and Game Theory

s_i represent *slack variables*, although in the minimization context they will become *surplus variables* instead. These are collectively referred to as *dummy variables*.

Explicit consideration of slacks or surpluses will enable us to transform each constraint inequality into a strict equation. More importantly, it will lead us to an algebraic method of finding the extreme points of the feasible region.

linear program transformed   Let us return to the production problem in (18.2), whose feasible region is already depicted in Fig. 18.9. By adding a slack variable to each constraint and appropriately modifying the objective function and the nonnegativity restrictions, we can rewrite that linear program into the form

$$\text{Maximize} \quad \pi = 40x_1 + 30x_2 + 0s_1 + 0s_2 + 0s_3$$

(18.13)

$$\text{subject to} \quad \begin{aligned} x_1 \quad\quad\quad + s_1 \quad\quad\quad\quad &= 16 \quad \text{[cutting]} \\ x_2 \quad\quad + s_2 \quad\quad &= 8 \quad \text{[mixing]} \\ x_1 + 2x_2 \quad\quad\quad\quad + s_3 &= 24 \quad \text{[packaging]} \end{aligned}$$

and

$$x_1, x_2, s_1, s_2, s_3 \geq 0$$

The reader will note that the three transformed constraints in (18.13) can also be expressed by the following matrix equation:

(18.14)

$$\begin{bmatrix} 1 & 0 & 1 & 0 & 0 \\ 0 & 1 & 0 & 1 & 0 \\ 1 & 2 & 0 & 0 & 1 \end{bmatrix} \begin{bmatrix} x_1 \\ x_2 \\ s_1 \\ s_2 \\ s_3 \end{bmatrix} = \begin{bmatrix} 16 \\ 8 \\ 24 \end{bmatrix}$$

There are now *five* variables in all. The slack variables s_i are, like x_1 and x_2, restricted to be nonnegative. When $s_i > 0$, a slack exists in the ith constraint; when $s_i = 0$, the ith constraint is exactly fulfilled. But s_i can never be negative. In the objective function, the s_i variables are given zero coefficients because slacks do not contribute to profit. Actually, they may be omitted from the objective function altogether. Note that, in a minimization problem, the (nonnegative) dummy variables must appear in the constraints as $-s_i$ instead.

It is an easy matter to find the values of the slacks implied by each extreme point. For the point (0,0), for instance, we can substitute $x_1 = 0$ and $x_2 = 0$ into the three transformed constraints and find that $s_1 = 16$, $s_2 = 8$, and $s_3 = 24$. Thus the point $(x_1, x_2) = (0,0)$ in the two-dimensional *output space* of Fig. 18.9 can be mapped into the point

$$(x_1, x_2, s_1, s_2, s_3) = (0, 0, 16, 8, 24)$$

in a five-dimensional *solution space*, as shown in the first row of Table 18.3. By the same procedure, the reader can verify the mapping of the remaining four extreme points listed there.

What is remarkable about the results of Table 18.3 is the fact that all these five points in the solution space, which represent extreme points, share the common property that exactly *three* of the five variables assume nonzero values. Of course, this is no mere coincidence; besides, three is not just any number, but is the precise number of constraints in our linear program.

To understand this result, let us recall the earlier discussion about counting the number of equations and the number of variables. Normally, assuming consistency and independence, we can expect a system of m equations to yield a determinate solution only when there are exactly m variables in it. In our present case, there are three constraints being considered in (18.14), so that $m = 3$; consequently no more than three of the five variables can be included in the determinate solution with a nonzero value.[1] This will perhaps become clearer when we consider the following vector-equation version of the constraints:

$$(18.14') \quad \begin{bmatrix} 1 \\ 0 \\ 1 \end{bmatrix} x_1 + \begin{bmatrix} 0 \\ 1 \\ 2 \end{bmatrix} x_2 + \begin{bmatrix} 1 \\ 0 \\ 0 \end{bmatrix} s_1 + \begin{bmatrix} 0 \\ 1 \\ 0 \end{bmatrix} s_2 + \begin{bmatrix} 0 \\ 0 \\ 1 \end{bmatrix} s_3 = \begin{bmatrix} 16 \\ 8 \\ 24 \end{bmatrix}$$

If we set any two of the five variables equal to zero, thereby in effect deleting two terms from the left of (18.14'), there will result a system of three equations in three variables. A unique solution can then be obtained, provided that the (retained) coefficient vectors on the left are linearly independent. When the solution values of these three variables are combined with the arbitrarily assigned zero values of the other two variables, the result will be an ordered quintuple such as shown in Table 18.3.

basic feasible solutions and extreme points

However, from the process just described, there can arise two possible situations. First, a negative

---

[1] It may happen, however, that *less* than m variables actually take nonzero values in the solution space. This is known as the case of *degeneracy*, which will be discussed briefly in Sec. 18.6.

TABLE 18.3

Output space (x_1, x_2)	Solution space $\rightarrow (x_1, x_2, s_1, s_2, s_3)$
(0,0)	(0,0,16,8,24)
(16,0)	(16,0, 0,8, 8)
(16,4)	(16,4, 0,4, 0)
(8,8)	(8,8, 8,0, 0)
(0,8)	(0,8,16,0, 8)

solution value may appear; for instance, if we set $x_1 = s_3 = 0$, then (18.14′) will yield $x_2 = 12$, $s_1 = 16$, and $s_2 = -4$. Being in violation of the nonnegativity restrictions, such a solution is obviously *unfeasible* and must be rejected. Graphically, this particular unfeasible solution represents the intersection of the packaging border with the vertical axis, which clearly lies beyond the feasible region—in the complement set $\widetilde{F}$.

Second, all the solution values may turn out to be nonnegative. In this eventuality, the solution will correspond to one of the extreme points of the feasible region, and the solution will constitute a *basic feasible solution* (BFS) of the linear program. It is *feasible* because the solution is in the feasible region: it satisfies the constraints as well as the nonnegativity restrictions. It is *basic* because the availability of this solution is contingent upon the presence of three linearly independent coefficient vectors, which together form a *basis* for a 3-space. (This latter 3-space, referred to as the *requirement space*, has to do with the constraints; its dimension is, of course, determined by the number of constraints we have.) In view of the correspondence noted above, the search for the extreme points now amounts to the search for the basic feasible solutions of the transformed constraint equations.

As an illustration, let us set $x_1 = x_2 = 0$ in (18.14′). Then we have

$$(18.15) \qquad \begin{bmatrix} 1 \\ 0 \\ 0 \end{bmatrix} s_1 + \begin{bmatrix} 0 \\ 1 \\ 0 \end{bmatrix} s_2 + \begin{bmatrix} 0 \\ 0 \\ 1 \end{bmatrix} s_3 = \begin{bmatrix} 16 \\ 8 \\ 24 \end{bmatrix}$$

or equivalently,

$$(18.15′) \qquad \begin{bmatrix} 1 & 0 & 0 \\ 0 & 1 & 0 \\ 0 & 0 & 1 \end{bmatrix} \begin{bmatrix} s_1 \\ s_2 \\ s_3 \end{bmatrix} = \begin{bmatrix} 16 \\ 8 \\ 24 \end{bmatrix}$$

Since the leftmost matrix is an identity matrix that can be dropped without affecting the equation, the solution can be read off directly: $s_1 = 16$, $s_2 = 8$, $s_3 = 24$. The existence of this unique solution is guaranteed by the linear independence of the three coefficient (column) vectors, which, the reader will note, are the unit vectors spanning a 3-space (the requirement space). Inasmuch as the solution is nonnegative, it is a BFS. And, since the solution values give rise to the point (0,0,16,8,24) in the solution space, or the point (0,0) in Fig. 18.9, the BFS does indeed correspond to an extreme point.

Setting another pair of variables in (18.14′) equal to zero will clearly result in an entirely new equation system. If the coefficient vectors are again linearly independent, we shall have a new basis for the requirement space, and a new BFS—provided that the solution is nonnegative—which can locate for us another extreme point. Thus, to move to a different extreme point in the feasible region means essentially to switch to a new basis for the three-dimensional requirement space. This is a fundamental fact that will be utilized in the ensuing discussion.

The significant thing about the BFS concept is that the method of its determination is algebraic instead of geometric, so that it permits a ready extension to the general linear program with m constraints and n choice variables. In the latter case, the requirement space will be m-dimensional, and the solution space of dimension $m + n$. To find a BFS, we now have to let n of the $m + n$ variables be zero in the transformed constraint equations; but the procedure is otherwise no different from the simpler case illustrated in (18.15).

EXERCISE 18.4

1   Transform the following linear programs into the format of (18.13):

    (a)   Maximize $\pi = 3x_1 + 2x_2 + 5x_3$
             subject to

$$3x_1 + x_2 \leq 10$$
$$x_2 + 2x_3 \leq 6$$
$$2x_1 + x_2 + x_3 \leq 8$$

             and

$$x_1, x_2, x_3 \geq 0$$

    (b)   Minimize $C = x_1 + 6x_2 + 2x_3$
             subject to

$$x_1 + 2x_2 \geq 2$$
$$x_1 + x_2 + 3x_3 \geq 12$$

             and

$$x_1, x_2, x_3 \geq 0$$

2   Transform the linear programs in Exercise 18.1-1 by the use of dummy variables.

3   The linear programs of the preceding problem have the following sets of extreme points, respectively:

    (a)   (0,0), (0,3), (2,3), (4,2), (4,0)
    (b)   (4,0), $(2,\frac{1}{2})$, $(\frac{3}{5},\frac{6}{5})$, (0,3)

By substituting these (x_1,x_2) values into the appropriate transformed constraints, find the values of s_i corresponding to each extreme point. Then express the latter as points in the five-dimensional solution space, as in Table 18.3.

4   When the extreme points in the preceding problem are expressed as ordered quintuples, how many nonzero elements do you find in each? Is this result coincidental?

5   What will be the respective dimensions of the requirement space and the solution space if a linear program contains:

(a)   5 choice variables and 3 constraints?
(b)   3 choice variables and 4 constraints?
(c) n choice variables and m constraints?

18.5   Simplex Method: Finding the Optimal Extreme Point

To locate an extreme point is to find a basic feasible solution. But how do we find the *optimal* extreme point and BFS? In a low-dimension program, we can of course find *all* the BFS's, calculate the corresponding values of the maximand (or minimand), and then select the optimal one therefrom. When many variables and constraints are involved, this procedure can entail a great deal of computation. The idea of the simplex method is to start with some initial extreme point, compute the value of the objective function, and then see whether the latter can be improved upon by moving to an adjacent extreme point. If so, we can make the move and then seek to determine whether further improvement is possible by a subsequent move. When finally an extreme point is attained that does not admit of further improvement, it will constitute the optimal solution. This iterative procedure of moving from one corner of the feasible region to another can contribute to computational economy, because only a subset of the set of all extreme points will need to enter in the process.

We shall illustrate the technique involved by continuing our discussion of the transformed linear program in (18.13), which is a maximization problem.

simplex tableau   From (18.15) and (18.15'), we have already found an initial BFS by setting $x_1 = x_2 = 0$. That gives rise to the following quintuple in the solution space, S_1, and a corresponding profit figure, π_1:

$$(18.16) \quad \begin{aligned} S_1 &= (0,0,16,8,24) \\ \pi_1 &= 40(0) + 30(0) = 0 \end{aligned}$$

This same answer can also be obtained schematically by the use of what is called a *simplex tableau*, as shown in Table 18.4.†

In such a tableau, we reserve a column for each choice variable and slack variable; in addition, we have a π column and a constant column. The inclusion of a π column is to enable us to embody in the tableau the information contained

† What is described hereinafter is the *revised simplex method*, which differs from the simplex method by inclusion of the objective function in the tableau.

in the objective function (row 0) as well as the data for the three transformed constraints (rows 1, 2, and 3). All the numbers appearing beneath each variable are merely the coefficients of that variable in the relevant equations, whereas the numbers in the constant column are those unattached to any variable. The vertical line to the left of the constant column is where the equals sign should be in the various equations. Thus, row 0 can be read as $\pi - 40x_1 - 30x_2 = 0$, which is simply a transposed version of our objective function. Similarly, row 1 states that $x_1 + s_1 = 16$ (the first constraint), etc. It may help the reader to note that, if row 0 and the π column are disregarded, the remaining entries in the tableau are exactly those of (18.14) duly transplanted.

According to our previous discussion, to find a BFS is to find a particular *basis* for the three-dimensional requirement space. This means that, disregarding row 0 for the time being, we must pick out from the last three rows three linearly independent column vectors. An obvious choice is the asterisked columns, which together form a 3×3 identity matrix. Consequently, we can take s_1, s_2, and s_3 into the basis—and accordingly set $x_1 = x_2 = 0$. When the x_1 and x_2 columns are (mentally) deleted from the tableau, the three bottom rows will reduce exactly to the form of (18.15'), giving us $(s_1, s_2, s_3) = (16, 8, 24)$, which is non-negative and, hence, a BFS.

Inasmuch as no output is being produced, the profit will be zero, and this BFS is obviously not optimal. Nevertheless, in maximization problems, it is desirable always to adopt as the initial BFS one that includes slack variables only. The slack variables always have linearly independent unit vectors as their coefficient vectors; thus they will invariably supply a ready-made basis.

Actually, the profit information can also be read directly from the tableau. For if row 0 is considered along with the three bottom rows—while still disregarding the x_1 and x_2 columns—the tableau translates into the equation system

$$(18.17) \qquad \begin{bmatrix} 1 & 0 & 0 & 0 \\ 0 & 1 & 0 & 0 \\ 0 & 0 & 1 & 0 \\ 0 & 0 & 0 & 1 \end{bmatrix} \begin{bmatrix} \pi \\ s_1 \\ s_2 \\ s_3 \end{bmatrix} = \begin{bmatrix} 0 \\ 16 \\ 8 \\ 24 \end{bmatrix}$$

TABLE 18.4

Tableau I	π	x_1	x_2	s_1	s_2	s_3	Constant
Row 0	1	-40	-30	0	0	0	$\boxed{0}$
Row 1	0	$\boxed{1}$	0	1	0	0	16
Row 2	0	0	1	0	1	0	8
Row 3	0	1	2	0	0	1	24
				*	*	*	

which reveals not only the slack values but also the additional information that $\pi_1 = 0$ (the subscript 1 here refers to the initial BFS). As a general rule, when a 4×4 identity matrix is present in a tableau, as in Table 18.4, so that a BFS is specified, the value of the objective function associated with that BFS can always be read off the tableau, along with the values of the variables forming the basis of the requirement space. A comparison of (18.17) with Table 18.4 indicates, moreover, that the top element in the constant column of the tableau (boxed for emphasis) is what tells the profit figure, whereas the remaining entries in the constant column show the values of the variables in the basis. In order to avail ourselves of the profit information, henceforth let us always consider the 4×4 rather than the 3×3 identity matrix—or, more generally, the $(m + 1) \times (m + 1)$ rather than the $m \times m$ one.

a pivot step   Now let us endeavor to improve upon the profit by switching to a new BFS, by forming a new basis. The main idea of the basis-changing process, known as *pivoting*, is to replace a column vector currently in the basis by another column vector that is currently excluded. Or, what amounts to the same thing, we must expel a currently included variable (s_1, s_2, or s_3) in favor of a currently excluded one (x_1 or x_2). What criterion can we employ in the selection of the *outgoing* and *incoming* vectors (or variables)?

Since our purpose is to improve upon the profit, it is natural to turn to the objective function for a clue. As written in (18.13), the objective function indicates that the marginal profit rate of x_1 is \$40 and that of x_2 is \$30. It stands to reason that the selection of x_1 as the incoming variable is more promising as a profit booster. In terms of the tableau, the criterion is that we should select that variable which has the *negative entry with the largest absolute value* in row 0. Here, the appropriate entry is -40, and the incoming variable is to be x_1; let us call the x_1 column the *pivot column*.

The pivot column is destined to replace one of the s_i columns, but this raises two problems. First, we must decide which of the latter columns is to go. Second, we must see to it that, as the new member of the basis, the pivot column is linearly independent of the old vectors that are retained. It happens that both problems can be resolved in one sweep, by transforming the pivot column into a unit vector, with 1 in either of the three bottom rows, and 0s elsewhere. Leaving aside the mechanics of this transformation, let us first examine its implication. If the transformed pivot column has its unit element in row 1, so that it looks exactly like the s_1 column, we can certainly let s_1 be the outgoing variable, for this replacement will preserve the linear independence in the basis. Similarly, if the unit element is in row 2, we can let the transformed pivot column replace the s_2 column. In this way, the twin problems of the choice of the outgoing variable and the preservation of linear independence can always be disposed of at once.

It remains to decide on the exact placement of the unit element in the pivot column. For convenience, the pivot-column element to be set equal to 1 will be referred to as the *pivot element*. The overriding consideration in the choice of the pivot element is that we must stay within the capacity limitations of all three production departments. If we let the element in row 3 be the pivot element, for instance, the x_1 column will—after transformation into a unit vector—be identical with the present s_3 column. This means that the variable x_1 will displace the s_3 variable in the second BFS, and as we can see from (18.17), the solution value of x_1 will be $x_1 = 24$ (replacing $s_3 = 24$). However, according to (18.13), this output will violate the cutting constraint and, therefore, is unfeasible. Another way of looking at it is that, if x_1 replaces s_3, the new tableau will have a negative element in the constant column for row 1 (cutting constraint). The resulting solution is then unfeasible, and must be ruled out. On the other hand, if we pick the element in row 1 (encircled) as the pivot element, then the x_1 variable will displace the s_1 variable, and the solution value of x_1 will be $x_1 = 16$ (replacing $s_1 = 16$). Since this (smaller) output does not violate any constraint in (18.13), we can safely accept the encircled element (1) as the pivot element. In this latter case, all the constants in the constant column will remain non-negative in the new tableau. Note that we do not have to worry about the element 0 in row 2 in this connection; the zero coefficient indicates that the x_1 variable is unrelated to the second constraint, so that the introduction of the x_1 variable into the new basis will in no way meet any obstacle from that particular constraint.

The constraint consideration just outlined can be fully taken care of if the pivot element is chosen thus: (1) Pick out those elements in the pivot column— in all rows except row 0—that are *positive*. (2) Divide each of these positive elements into its counterpart in the constant column. (3) Compare the resulting quotients, which we shall refer to as *displacement quotients*, and take the row with the *smallest* quotient as the *pivot row*. (4) Select the element at the intersection of the pivot column and the pivot row as the pivot element.

By selecting the smallest displacement quotient, we can make sure that the output added (x_1) will be small enough to stay within the bounds of all the constraints and that none of the variables will violate the nonnegativity restrictions. In our present example, there are only two such quotients to be compared: $\frac{16}{1}$ and $\frac{24}{1}$. Since the former is the smallest quotient, row 1 should be the pivot row, with the encircled element (1) as the pivot element.

Our next task is to transform the pivot column into a unit vector by setting the pivot element equal to 1, and the other elements therein to 0s. In the present case, the pivot element is already equal to 1, so that nothing has to be done. In general, however, if the pivot element is a number k, we can transform it to 1 by dividing all the elements in the pivot row by k, including the constant-column entry. (This amounts to dividing all the terms in a constraint equation by the same constant.) The row-2 element, already zero, requires no operation either. To transform the element -40 in row 0 to a zero, we add 40 times the pivot row (row 1) to row 0. (This amounts to adding a constant multiple of an equation to another equation, which in no way disturbs the equality.) Similarly, to transform the element 1 in row 3 to a zero, we can subtract the pivot row (row 1) from row 3. The results are given in Table 18.5, where we have a new simplex tableau (Tableau II).

If the reader mentally deletes the x_2 and s_1 columns, Tableau II is seen to represent the following system of equations:

$$(18.18) \quad \begin{bmatrix} 1 & 0 & 0 & 0 \\ 0 & 1 & 0 & 0 \\ 0 & 0 & 1 & 0 \\ 0 & 0 & 0 & 1 \end{bmatrix} \begin{bmatrix} \pi \\ x_1 \\ s_2 \\ s_3 \end{bmatrix} = \begin{bmatrix} 640 \\ 16 \\ 8 \\ 8 \end{bmatrix}$$

from which the solution values of the four variables can be read off readily, since the identity matrix on the left can be dropped. The appearance of the identity matrix is of course not coincidental, for the transformation procedure which led to the solution in (18.18) is intrinsically that of solving an equation system by matrix inversion. But instead of determining the inverse matrix, this time we have gone directly to the identity matrix $AA^{-1} = I$.

Actually, it is possible to read off the solution directly from the constant column of Tableau II without writing out (18.18). In the π column, the *unit element* of this unit vector is in row 0; thus we can read the constant in row 0 as the solution value of π, and similarly for the variables x_1, s_2, and s_3 in the new basis. The x_2 and s_1 columns, which do not contain unit vectors, on the other hand, are excluded from the basis, and their solution values are automatically read to be zero. Consequently, the second basic feasible solution inplies that

$$(18.19) \quad \begin{aligned} S_2 &= (16,0,0,8,8) \\ \pi_2 &= 640 \end{aligned}$$

TABLE 18.5

Tableau II	π	x_1	x_2	s_1	s_2	s_3	Constant
Row 0	1	0	-30	40	0	0	640
Row 1	0	1	0	1	0	0	16
Row 2	0	0	1	0	1	0	8
Row 3	0	0	②	-1	0	1	8

As compared with S_1, we now have a substantially larger profit (640 against 0). In terms of Table 18.3, we have—in undertaking this pivoting step—moved from the first extreme point to the second extreme point.

another pivot step   In row 0 of Tableau II, there is an entry -30 associated with the variable x_2. Since a *negative* entry in row 0 indicates a *positive* marginal profit rate, further profit improvement is possible by letting x_2 replace a zero-profit-rate or a negative-profit-rate variable in the basis. Therefore, we adopt the x_2 column as the next pivot column. As for the pivot row, since the smallest displacement quotient is

$$\min \left\{ \tfrac{8}{1}, \tfrac{8}{2} \right\} = \min \{8,4\} = 4$$

row 3 should be chosen. Hence the pivot element is 2, which we have encircled to call attention.

In order to transform the elements in the x_2 column into 0, 0, 0, and 1 (in that order), we must: (1) add 15 times row 3 (the pivot row) to row 0; (2) leave row 1 intact; (3) subtract $1/2$ times row 3 from row 2; and (4) divide row 3 by 2. The reader is urged to carry out these operations and check the results against Tableau III in Table 18.6.

In Tableau III, the columns with unit vectors pertain to the variables π, x_1, x_2, and s_2, whose solution values can be read off as follows: $\pi = 760$, $x_1 = 16$, $x_2 = 4$ (from row 3), and $s_2 = 4$ (from row 2). Consequently, we can write

$$(18.20) \quad \begin{aligned} S_3 &= (16,4,0,4,0) \\ \pi_3 &= 760 \end{aligned}$$

Two products are now being produced, and the profit has been raised to 760. Again, we can see from Table 18.3 that the second pivot step has taken us to a new extreme point of the feasible region.

We are ready for another pivot step, but since row 0 of Tableau III contains no more negative entries, no further pivoting will prove profitable. To appreciate

TABLE 18.6

Tableau III	π	x_1	x_2	s_1	s_2	s_3	Constant
Row 0	1	0	0	25	0	15	760
Row 1	0	1	0	1	0	0	16
Row 2	0	0	0	$\tfrac{1}{2}$	1	$-\tfrac{1}{2}$	4
Row 3	0	0	1	$-\tfrac{1}{2}$	0	$\tfrac{1}{2}$	4

this fact, let us convert row 0 into the equation

$$\pi = 760 - 25s_1 - 15s_3$$

To maximize π in this equation, we must set $s_1 = s_3 = 0$; but the solution S_3 does just that. Hence S_3 must be optimal! As expected, this optimal solution is identical with the results obtained graphically in Sec. 18.1.

In terms of Fig. 18.9, the simplex method has led us systematically from the point of origin—the initial extreme point—to the next extreme point (16,0), followed by a move to the optimal extreme point (16,4). Note that we have arrived at the optimal solution without having to compare *all* five extreme points. Also note that, by choosing x_1 as the pivot column in Tableau I (in accordance with the marginal-profit-rate criterion), we have traveled to the optimum via a shorter route; had we chosen x_2 as the pivot column, we would have moved to the point (0,8) in Fig. 18.9 first, and that would have required three pivot steps to reach the point (16,4).

EXERCISE 18.5

Add appropriate dummy variables and solve the following linear programs by the simplex method:

1   Maximize $\pi = 4x_1 + 3x_2$

     subject to $\begin{bmatrix} 1 & 1 \\ 2 & 1 \end{bmatrix} \begin{bmatrix} x_1 \\ x_2 \end{bmatrix} \le \begin{bmatrix} 4 \\ 6 \end{bmatrix}$

     and $x_1, x_2 \ge 0$

2   Maximize $\pi = 4x_1 + 3x_2$

     subject to $\begin{bmatrix} 1 & 1 \\ 3 & 2 \end{bmatrix} \begin{bmatrix} x_1 \\ x_2 \end{bmatrix} \le \begin{bmatrix} 5 \\ 12 \end{bmatrix}$

     and $x_1, x_2 \ge 0$

3   Maximize $\pi = 6x_1 + 2x_2 + 5x_3$

     subject to $\begin{bmatrix} 2 & 3 & 1 \\ 1 & 0 & 2 \\ 1 & 2 & 5 \end{bmatrix} \begin{bmatrix} x_1 \\ x_2 \\ x_3 \end{bmatrix} \le \begin{bmatrix} 10 \\ 8 \\ 19 \end{bmatrix}$

     and $x_1, x_2, x_3 \ge 0$

4   Maximize $\pi = 3x_1 + 2x_2 + 6x_3$
     subject to the same constraints as in the preceding problem.

18.6   Further Notes on the Simplex Method

minimization programs and artificial variables   In the maximization problem discussed above, there is no need to search for an initial BFS, because a ready-made one is always available at the point of origin. For minimization problems, however, this is not true, because in those problems the point of origin lies outside the feasible region.

To illustrate, let us transform the diet problem of Sec. 18.1 into the form

$$\text{Minimize} \qquad C = 0.6x_1 + x_2$$

(18.21)   subject to
$$\begin{bmatrix} 10 & 4 & -1 & 0 & 0 \\ 5 & 5 & 0 & -1 & 0 \\ 2 & 6 & 0 & 0 & -1 \end{bmatrix} \begin{bmatrix} x_1 \\ x_2 \\ s_1 \\ s_2 \\ s_3 \end{bmatrix} = \begin{bmatrix} 20 \\ 20 \\ 12 \end{bmatrix}$$

and $x_1, x_2, s_1, s_2, s_3 \geq 0$

Note that the (nonnegative) s_i variables, representing *surpluses* (rather than slacks), are to be *subtracted* from the left sides of the constraints. Hence the last three columns in the coefficient matrix in (18.21) appear as the *negative* of an identity matrix. If we try to set $x_1 = x_2 = 0$, the three constraints will yield the solution $(s_1, s_2, s_3) = (-20, -20, -12)$, which is clearly unfeasible. Therefore we must actively search for some suitable initial BFS.

One method that will obviate this search is to *augment* the program by adding a nonnegative *artificial variable* to every constraint. For reasons to be explained below, the artificial variables, denoted by v_i, should be assigned some *large* coefficients in the objective function—large in relation to the coefficients of the choice variables. If we let these be 100, then the program in (18.21) can be written as follows:[1]

$$\text{Minimize} \qquad C = 0.6x_1 + x_2 + 100(v_1 + v_2 + v_3)$$

(18.21')   subject to
$$\begin{bmatrix} 10 & 4 & -1 & 0 & 0 & 1 & 0 & 0 \\ 5 & 5 & 0 & -1 & 0 & 0 & 1 & 0 \\ 2 & 6 & 0 & 0 & -1 & 0 & 0 & 1 \end{bmatrix} \begin{bmatrix} x_1 \\ x_2 \\ s_1 \\ s_2 \\ s_3 \\ v_1 \\ v_2 \\ v_3 \end{bmatrix} = \begin{bmatrix} 20 \\ 20 \\ 12 \end{bmatrix}$$

and $x_1, x_2, s_1, s_2, s_3, v_1, v_2, v_3 \geq 0$

[1] We have inserted two broken lines in the 3 × 8 coefficient matrix to clarify the association between the three groups of column vectors and the three groups of variables (choice, surplus, and artificial).

Since the artificial variables are associated with three linearly independent unit vectors (which form an identity matrix), similar to the s_i variables in Table 18.4, we may now accept the v_i variables into the initial basis without conducting any real search.

While acceptable in an initial BFS to get us started, these v_i variables—being mere mathematical artifice—must somehow be prevented from entering into our optimal solution. In this regard, we need not worry if the v_i variables are given large coefficients in the objective function, for these coefficients (in our example, 100) represent the *prices* of some artificially created food items, just as 0.6 is the price of food I, so the assignment of inordinately large values to these will automatically make the artificial food items too expensive to be included in the optimal diet. This will then assure $v_1 = v_2 = v_3 = 0$ in the optimal solution and render the augmented linear program (18.21') optimally equivalent to the original version in (18.21).

The simplex method can now be applied in substantially the same way, except for a few simple modifications. First, upon arranging the program in (18.21') into Tableau I in Table 18.7, we see that the v_i columns are not yet in the form of 4-element unit vectors. We first add $100 \times$ (row 1 + row 2 + row 3) to row 0, in order to convert Tableau I to Tableau II. Since the latter does contain a 4×4 identity matrix, we are now able to read off the solution $(C, v_1, v_2, v_3) = (5200, 20, 20, 12)$.

Another modification in the method concerns the criterion for the choice of the pivot column. For minimization programs, we should look for the column —not counting the C column and the constant column—with the *largest positive element* in row 0. The rationale of this new criterion can easily be seen when we convert row 0 of Tableau II into the equation

$$C = 5200 - \tfrac{8497}{5}x_1 - 1499x_2 + 100(s_1 + s_2 + s_3)$$

If we are to choose one of the five variables as the incoming variable to replace an artificial variable in the initial basis, x_1 can obviously contribute most to cost minimization because it has the negative coefficient with the highest absolute value. In terms of Tableau II, however, x_1 is the variable with the largest *positive* coefficient in row 0—hence the above criterion. Accordingly, the x_1 column should be picked as the pivot column.

The choice of the pivot row strictly follows the former procedure. Here, since the smallest displacement quotient is

$$\min \left\{ \tfrac{20}{10}, \tfrac{20}{5}, \tfrac{12}{2} \right\} = \min \{2,4,6\} = 2$$

row 1 is the pivot row, and the (encircled) element 10 is the pivot element. By transforming the pivot column into a unit vector, we end up with Tableau III, which gives us the solution $(C, x_1, v_2, v_3) = (\tfrac{9006}{5}, 2, 10, 8)$. Now that x_1 has replaced

TABLE 18.7

Tableau	Row	C	Choice variables		Surplus variables			Artificial variables			Con-stant
			x_1	x_2	s_1	s_2	s_3	v_1	v_2	v_3	
I	0	1	$-\frac{6}{10}$	-1	0	0	0	-100	-100	-100	0
	1	0	10	4	-1	0	0	1	0	0	20
	2	0	5	5	0	-1	0	0	1	0	20
	3	0	2	6	0	0	-1	0	0	1	12
II	0	1	$\frac{8497}{5}$	1499	-100	-100	-100	0	0	0	$\boxed{5200}$
	1	0	$\boxed{10}$	4	-1	0	0	1	0	0	20
	2	0	5	5	0	-1	0	0	1	0	20
	3	0	2	6	0	0	-1	0	0	1	12
III	0	1	0	$\frac{20{,}481}{25}$	$\frac{3497}{50}$	-100	-100	$-\frac{8497}{50}$	0	0	$\boxed{\frac{9006}{5}}$
	1	0	1	$\frac{2}{5}$	$-\frac{1}{10}$	0	0	$\frac{1}{10}$	0	0	2
	2	0	0	3	$\frac{1}{2}$	-1	0	$-\frac{1}{2}$	1	0	10
	3	0	0	$\boxed{\frac{26}{5}}$	$\frac{1}{5}$	0	-1	$-\frac{1}{5}$	0	1	8
IV	0	1	0	0	$\frac{2498}{65}$	-100	$\frac{7481}{130}$	$-\frac{8998}{65}$	0	$-\frac{20{,}481}{130}$	$\boxed{\frac{35{,}154}{65}}$
	1	0	1	0	$-\frac{3}{26}$	0	$\frac{1}{13}$	$\frac{3}{26}$	0	$-\frac{1}{13}$	$\frac{18}{13}$
	2	0	0	0	$\frac{5}{13}$	-1	$\boxed{\frac{15}{26}}$	$-\frac{5}{13}$	1	$-\frac{15}{26}$	$\frac{70}{13}$
	3	0	0	1	$\frac{1}{26}$	0	$-\frac{5}{26}$	$-\frac{1}{26}$	0	$\frac{5}{26}$	$\frac{20}{13}$
V	0	1	0	0	$\frac{1}{15}$	$-\frac{19}{75}$	0	$-\frac{1501}{15}$	$-\frac{7481}{75}$	-100	$\boxed{\frac{56}{15}}$
	1	0	1	0	$-\frac{1}{6}$	$\frac{2}{15}$	0	$\frac{1}{6}$	$-\frac{2}{15}$	0	$\frac{2}{3}$
	2	0	0	0	$\boxed{\frac{2}{3}}$	$-\frac{26}{15}$	1	$-\frac{2}{3}$	$\frac{26}{15}$	-1	$\frac{28}{3}$
	3	0	0	1	$\frac{1}{6}$	$-\frac{1}{3}$	0	$-\frac{1}{6}$	$\frac{1}{3}$	0	$\frac{10}{3}$
VI	0	1	0	0	0	$-\frac{2}{25}$	$-\frac{1}{10}$	-100	$-\frac{2498}{25}$	$-\frac{999}{10}$	$\boxed{\frac{14}{5}}$
	1	0	1	0	0	$-\frac{3}{10}$	$\frac{1}{4}$	0	$\frac{3}{10}$	$-\frac{1}{4}$	3
	2	0	0	0	1	$-\frac{13}{5}$	$\frac{3}{2}$	-1	$\frac{13}{5}$	$-\frac{3}{2}$	14
	3	0	0	1	0	$\frac{1}{10}$	$-\frac{1}{4}$	0	$-\frac{1}{10}$	$\frac{1}{4}$	1

v_1 in the basis, the cost of diet is substantially reduced: from $5200 to only slightly over $1800.

The subsequent steps are nothing but the same process repeated. But note that it will take two more pivot steps to drive out the remaining two artificial variables. Inasmuch as the introduction of the v_i variables inevitably lengthens the computation process, we should try whenever possible to reduce the number of such variables added. This can be done, for instance, if the first column of the coefficient matrix happens to contain the elements 0, 1, and 0 (rather than 10, 5, 2), for then we may omit v_2 and let x_1 take its place in the initial basis. Similarly, if the elements of that column are 0, 0, and 1, we can instead omit v_3.

From Tableau II on, each successive tableau in Table 18.7 shows a reduction in cost. When the cost is reduced to $\frac{14}{5} = 2.80$ in Tableau VI, we can tell from row 0 that no further reduction is possible because no more *positive* entries are present in the x_j, s_i and v_i columns. Our optimal solution is therefore

$$(\bar{x}_1, \bar{x}_2, \bar{s}_1, \bar{s}_2, \bar{s}_3) = (3,1,14,0,0)$$
$$\bar{C} = \$2.80$$

which is identical with the graphical solution obtained in Sec. 18.1.

another application of artificial variables   The use of artificial variables is not exclusive to minimization problems. In some maximization programs, artificial variables can be used to good advantage, too.

When, in the *maximization* context, one of the constraints (say, the third) happens to be a strict equation, there will be no need for an s_3 variable. In that event, we are "cheated" out of a unit vector in the simplex tableau, and the so-called "ready-made initial BFS" will no longer be available. To remedy the situation, we can let an artificial variable v_3 (for the *third* constraint) fill the void left by the absence of the s_3 variable, for it too can give rise to a unit vector of the correct type.

Of course, to assure that v_3 will be duly barred from the optimal solution, we must in this case assign to it a large *negative* coefficient (negative marginal-profit rate) in the objective function. But otherwise, the application of the simplex method will be the same as before.

degeneracy   The linear programs discussed above have the common property that the vector of constants in the m constraint equations is *not* expressible as a linear combination of *less* than m coefficient vectors. In (18.14′), e.g., the vector on the right side cannot be expressed as a linear combination of less than three of the left-side vectors. As a result, each of the m variables in a basis must take a nonzero value; this is why each point in the solution space of Table 18.3 has exactly three nonzero elements. When this property does not hold, the linear program is said to be *degenerate*.

Insofar as the simplex method is concerned, the only manifestation of degeneracy lies in the appearance of "tied" displacement quotients. That is, two or more quotients will share the distinction of being the smallest, so that two or more rows will be equally strong candidates for the pivot row. Since it is not possible to displace more than one variable at a time, some criterion must be found to break the tie.

One practical, if arbitrary, method is simply to pick the pivot row in such a way that, among the tied variables, the one with the leftmost location in the simplex tableau will actually get to be displaced. With this tie-breaking criterion, it then becomes possible to proceed with the remaining pivot steps in a systematic fashion.

In degeneracy cases, a pivot step may fail to improve profit or reduce cost at all. It may indeed take several pivot steps of the zero-improvement type before the iterative process succeeds in breaking out of the deadlock. Aside from the tie, and the possibility of zero improvement, however, the application of the simplex method to degeneracy cases is again the same as before.

This concludes our introduction to the simplex method, or simplex *algorithm*.[1] The process involved is by itself not difficult, but in linear programs of substantial dimensions the computation task will inevitably be lengthy and tedious. Fortunately, the modern computer is well adapted to precisely the type of repetitive calculations that a linear program entails. By properly giving the computer a set of detailed instructions (i.e., by proper *computer programming*), we can rely on the machine to carry out the successive steps of the simplex algorithm faithfully, untiringly, and at a superhuman speed. High dimensionality then poses little problem.

EXERCISE 18.6

1 Carry out the calculations leading from Tableau II to each succeeding tableau in Table 18.7.

Solve the following by the simplex method:

---

[1] Algorithm is a fancy word meaning a routinized computational procedure.

2   Minimize $C = x_1 + 4x_2$

subject to $\begin{bmatrix} 1 & 2 \\ 3 & 2 \end{bmatrix} \begin{bmatrix} x_1 \\ x_2 \end{bmatrix} \geq \begin{bmatrix} 8 \\ 12 \end{bmatrix}$

and $x_1, x_2 \geq 0$

3   Minimize $C = 2x_1 + 7x_2$

subject to $\begin{bmatrix} 1 & 2 \\ 0 & 1 \end{bmatrix} \begin{bmatrix} x_1 \\ x_2 \end{bmatrix} \geq \begin{bmatrix} 8 \\ 3 \end{bmatrix}$

and $x_1, x_2 \geq 0$

(*Hint:* Only one artificial variable is needed.)

4   Minimize $C = 12x_1 + 42x_2$

subject to $\begin{bmatrix} 1 & 2 \\ 1 & 4 \\ 3 & 1 \end{bmatrix} \begin{bmatrix} x_1 \\ x_2 \end{bmatrix} \geq \begin{bmatrix} 3 \\ 4 \\ 3 \end{bmatrix}$

and $x_1, x_2 \geq 0$

19

LINEAR PROGRAMMING (continued)

19.1   Duality

Hitherto, we have discussed maximization and minimization linear programs as two separate types of problems. But, actually, corresponding to every *minimization* program (to minimize C), there always exists a counterpart *maximization* program (to maximize a new variable, C^*), with the property that $\bar{C}^* = \bar{C}$. Similarly, for every π-maximization program, there always exists a counterpart π^*-minimization program such that $\bar{\pi}^* = \bar{\pi}$. The original linear program is usually referred to as the *primal program* (or simply the *primal*), and its counterpart is known as the *dual program* (or *dual*, for short). In view of this, minimization and maximization programs are really not so disjunct as they were implied to be. In fact, since the optimal values of the objective functions in the primal and in the dual are always identical, we now have the option of picking the easier of the two programs to work with; as we shall see, it is always possible also to translate the solution values of the dual-program variables into those of the primal-program variables, and vice versa.

the dual program   For a clear distinction, let us denote the choice variables of the primal by x_j (as we did), and the choice variables of the dual by y_i. The structures of the primal and the dual are then related to each other as shown in the following two examples.

Example 1

	Primal		*Dual*

Maximize $\pi = 3x_1 + 4x_2 + 3x_3$ Minimize $\pi^* = 12y_1 + 42y_2$

subject to
$$\begin{bmatrix} 1 & 1 & 3 \\ 2 & 4 & 1 \end{bmatrix} \begin{bmatrix} x_1 \\ x_2 \\ x_3 \end{bmatrix} \le \begin{bmatrix} 12 \\ 42 \end{bmatrix}$$
subject to
$$\begin{bmatrix} 1 & 2 \\ 1 & 4 \\ 3 & 1 \end{bmatrix} \begin{bmatrix} y_1 \\ y_2 \end{bmatrix} \ge \begin{bmatrix} 3 \\ 4 \\ 3 \end{bmatrix}$$

and $x_1, x_2, x_3 \ge 0$ and $y_1, y_2 \ge 0$

Example 2

	Primal		*Dual*

Minimize $C = 4x_1 + 3x_2 + 8x_3$ Maximize $C^* = 2y_1 + 5y_2$

subject to
$$\begin{bmatrix} 1 & 0 & 1 \\ 0 & 1 & 2 \end{bmatrix} \begin{bmatrix} x_1 \\ x_2 \\ x_3 \end{bmatrix} \ge \begin{bmatrix} 2 \\ 5 \end{bmatrix}$$
subject to
$$\begin{bmatrix} 1 & 0 \\ 0 & 1 \\ 1 & 2 \end{bmatrix} \begin{bmatrix} y_1 \\ y_2 \end{bmatrix} \le \begin{bmatrix} 4 \\ 3 \\ 8 \end{bmatrix}$$

and $x_1, x_2, x_3 \ge 0$ and $y_1, y_2 \ge 0$

Briefly, the rules of transformation are these: (1) Change "maximize" to "minimize," and vice versa. (Attach an asterisk to the maximand or minimand of the primal to make it a dual minimand or maximand.) (2) The inequality signs in the primal constraints must be reversed in the dual constraints, although the $\ge$ signs in the nonnegativity restrictions are never altered. (3) As the coefficient matrix for the dual constraints, take the transpose of the coefficient matrix of the primal constraints. (4) The row vector of coefficients in the primal objective function is, after it is transposed, taken to be the column vector of constants in the dual constraints. Similarly, the column vector of constants in the primal constraints, after it is transposed, becomes the row vector of coefficients in the dual objective function.

From these rules of transformation, the reader should be able to deduce that the dual of a dual program is the primal itself, provided that we now convert y to x instead and delete (rather than attach) the asterisk in the objective function.

To generalize from the two examples cited above, we may relate the primal and dual programs in matrix notation as follows:

	Primal			*Dual*	
Maximize	$\pi = c'x$		Minimize	$\pi^* = r'y$	
subject to	$Ax \le r$	$\rightarrow$	subject to	$A'y \ge c$	
and	$x \ge 0$		and	$y \ge 0$	

or

Minimize	$C = c'x$		Maximize	$C^* = r'y$	
subject to	$Ax \ge r$	$\rightarrow$	subject to	$A'y \le c$	
and	$x \ge 0$		and	$y \ge 0$	

Note that if the primal has m constraints and n choice variables, so that the matrix A is $m \times n$, then the dual will have n constraints and m choice variables because the matrix A', being the transpose of A, is $n \times m$. The dimensions of the other matrices appearing in the primal program are as follows: c' is $1 \times n$; x is $n \times 1$; and r is $m \times 1$, as shown in (18.5). The vector y in the dual is $m \times 1$.

The fact that the primal and the dual may contain different numbers of constraints and choice variables is why there may be different degrees of ease in their solution. In the two examples above, the primals (with three variables) are not easily solved graphically; but since there are only two variables in the duals, these lend themselves easily to graphical solution. Moreover, even when both the primal and the dual are nongraphable, so that the simplex algorithm must be resorted to anyway, we may still wish to select whichever program has less constraints, because the fewer the constraints, the smaller the dimension of the basis will be and the fewer the dummy variables we must add. And, finally, even when the primal and the dual have an equal (or nearly equal) number of constraints, we may find it easier to take the maximization program, because the latter would normally contain a ready-made initial BFS, so that there is no need to bother with artificial variables.

duality theorems   Although it affords a degree of freedom, this option to choose also raises a problem: If we decide to work with the dual, the solution will consist of the values of $\bar{y}_i$ (and, say, $\bar{C}^*$); but if our real concern is with the primal solution values $\bar{x}_j$ (and $\bar{C}$), how can we infer the primal solution from the dual solution and vice versa? The answer to this lies in the following two theorems.

DUALITY THEOREM I   The optimal values of the primal and the dual objective functions are always identical, provided that optimal feasible solutions do exist; that is, $\bar{C} = \bar{C}^*$ and $\bar{\pi} = \bar{\pi}^*$.

DUALITY THEOREM II   (a) If a certain *choice* variable in a linear program is optimally *nonzero*, then the corresponding *dummy* variable in the counterpart program must be optimally *zero*. That is (using s_i to denote the ith primal dummy variable, and t_j to denote the jth dual dummy variable),

$$\bar{y}_i > 0 \quad \Rightarrow \quad \bar{s}_i = 0 \qquad \text{and} \qquad \bar{x}_j > 0 \quad \Rightarrow \quad \bar{t}_j = 0$$

(b) If a certain *dummy* variable in a linear program is optimally *nonzero*, then the corresponding *choice* variable in the counterpart program must be optimally *zero*. That is,

$$\bar{s}_i > 0 \quad \Rightarrow \quad \bar{y}_i = 0 \quad \text{and} \quad \bar{t}_j > 0 \quad \Rightarrow \quad \bar{x}_j = 0\dagger$$

According to the first theorem, the choice between the primal and the dual is immaterial as far as the optimal value of the objective function is concerned. And by virtue of the second theorem, which states the so-called *complementary slackness* relationship between the choice variables of one program and the dummy variables of the other, the optimal solution obtained for a given linear program will provide sufficient information for us to work out the optimal solution of the counterpart program.

solving the primal via the dual   Let us now illustrate the application of the duality theorems by using Example 1 above. Since the dual program in that example, with only two choice variables, can be solved graphically, let us first find the dual optimal solution by graph and then determine the primal optimal solution by means of the duality theorems.

As the reader can verify, the graphical analysis of the dual yields the following information:

$$(\bar{y}_1, \bar{y}_2) = (2, \tfrac{1}{2})$$

so, from the objective function, we can readily calculate that

$$\bar{\pi}^* = 12(2) + 42(\tfrac{1}{2}) = 45$$

Furthermore, when the $\bar{y}_i$ values are substituted into the dual constraints, the first two constraints are seen to reduce to two equations, whereas the third constraint reduces to a strict inequality. Thus, $\bar{t}_1 = \bar{t}_2 = 0$, whereas $\bar{t}_3 > 0$. On

---

† A feel for the rationale behind the duality theorems can be obtained from the following considerations. The constraint of the primal (the maximization version) can be expressed as

$$Ax + s = r \qquad (s \geq 0)$$

Premultiplying by y', we have

$$y'Ax + y's = y'r \, (= r'y = \pi^*)$$

Similarly, the dual constraint can be written as $A'y - t = c \, (t \geq 0)$. Premultiplying by x', and taking the transpose of every term, we have

$$y'Ax - t'x = c'x \, (= \pi)$$

When we subtract π from π^*, we find

$$\pi^* - \pi = y's + t'x \geq 0 \qquad \text{[by nonnegativity]}$$

Thus π can never exceed π^*. But when π^* is minimized and π is maximized, the two values should be equal; this underlies the result $\bar{\pi} = \bar{\pi}^*$ of Theorem I. Next, since $\bar{\pi} = \bar{\pi}^*$, we must find in a pair of optimal solutions that $\bar{y}'\bar{s} + \bar{t}'\bar{x} = 0$, or

$$(\bar{y}_1 \bar{s}_1 + \cdots + \bar{y}_m \bar{s}_m) + (\bar{t}_1 \bar{x}_1 + \cdots + \bar{t}_n \bar{x}_n) = 0$$

In view of the nonnegativity restrictions, the only way to satisfy this equation is to have each of the $m + n$ terms individually equal to zero. This leads to the result in Theorem II. (The reasoning would be analogous if we started with the minimization version of the primal instead.)

the basis of this information about the dual, we should be able to find the optimal solution of the primal.

Since $\bar{y}_1$ and $\bar{y}_2$ are both nonzero, we must have $\bar{s}_1 = \bar{s}_2 = 0$ by the complementary-slackness relationship given in Duality Theorem II, so that the first two (the only two) primal constraints must optimally be strict equalities. Moreover, since $\bar{t}_3 > 0$, it follows that $\bar{x}_3 = 0$. Thus the constraint section of the primal program in Example 1 will appear in the optimal solution as follows:

$$(19.1) \qquad \begin{bmatrix} 1 & 1 & 3 \\ 2 & 4 & 1 \end{bmatrix} \begin{bmatrix} x_1 \\ x_2 \\ 0 \end{bmatrix} = \begin{bmatrix} 12 \\ 42 \end{bmatrix} \quad \text{or} \quad \begin{bmatrix} 1 & 1 \\ 2 & 4 \end{bmatrix} \begin{bmatrix} x_1 \\ x_2 \end{bmatrix} = \begin{bmatrix} 12 \\ 42 \end{bmatrix}$$

whence we have $\bar{x}_1 = 3$ and $\bar{x}_2 = 9$. We may therefore express the solution values of the primal choice variables by the equation

$$(19.2) \qquad (\bar{x}_1, \bar{x}_2, \bar{x}_3) = (3, 9, 0)$$

This completes the translation from $\bar{y}_i$ to $\bar{x}_j$.

The value of $\bar{\pi}$, according to Duality Theorem I, should be 45. If we substituted the $\bar{x}_j$ values into the primal objective function, the answer will indeed check: $\bar{\pi} = 3(3) + 4(9) + 0 = 45$.

A particularly remarkable and useful fact concerning the duality of linear programs is that, if the dual is solved by the simplex algorithm (rather than by graph), we can in fact directly read from its optimal (final) tableau the *primal* optimal solution as well as that of the dual! This being so, the translation from $\bar{y}_i$ to $\bar{x}_j$ now indeed becomes automatic.

Let us illustrate with the optimal tableau for the dual program of Example 1, which is shown in Table 19.1. From the four unit vectors in this tableau, the dual optimal solution can easily be read off as

$$(\bar{\pi}^*, \bar{y}_1, \bar{y}_2, \bar{t}_3) = (45, 2, \tfrac{1}{2}, \tfrac{7}{2})$$

where t_3 denotes the third dual dummy variable.

TABLE 19.1

Row	π^*	y_1	y_2	t_1	t_2	t_3	v_1	v_2	v_3	Constant
0	1	0	0	-3	-9	0	Not relevant,			45
1	0	0	0	$-\tfrac{11}{2}$	$\tfrac{5}{2}$	1	therefore			$\tfrac{7}{2}$
2	0	0	1	$\tfrac{1}{2}$	$-\tfrac{1}{2}$	0	omitted.			$\tfrac{1}{2}$
3	0	0	1	0	-2	1	0			2

Those four figures are, of course, all taken from the constant column. However, if we look instead in row 0 under the dummy-variable columns and take the *absolute values* of the three entries in the broken rectangle, we get the numbers 3, 9, and 0, which are precisely the values of $\bar{x}_1$, $\bar{x}_2$, and $\bar{x}_3$ in (19.2), arranged in the proper order.[1] As a general rule, we can always associate the t_j columns of a dual optimal tableau with the x_j variables and can read the absolute values of the top elements thereof as the optimal values of the primal choice variables.[2] Furthermore, we can also associate the y_i columns with the primal dummy variables and can read the absolute values of the top elements in those columns as the values of $\bar{s}_i$. In Table 19.1, the two zeros in the broken ellipse in row 0 indicate that $\bar{s}_1 = \bar{s}_2 = 0$, which we already know to be true. Since, in addition, the boxed element in the constant column also tells the value of $\bar{\pi}$ by virtue of Duality Theorem I, all the relevant information concerning the *primal* optimal solution can be gathered by reading row 0 of the *dual* optimal tableau! And by analogy, it is also possible to read the *dual* optimal solution from row 0 of a given *primal* optimal tableau.

This extremely convenient result conforms perfectly in its essence to Duality Theorem II. Any dual variable that takes a nonzero value in the optimal solution—here, y_1, y_2, and t_3—must be characterized by a unit column vector in the optimal tableau. Since the π^* column has preempted the e_1 type of unit vector (with the unit element on top), the unit vectors in the y_1, y_2, and t_3 columns must have a zero top element. According to the method just expounded, we may therefore deduce that $\bar{s}_1 = \bar{s}_2 = \bar{x}_3 = 0$. But this conclusion is precisely what Duality Theorem II is purported to show. Similarly, by converse application of the method, the fact that $\bar{x}_1$ and $\bar{x}_2$ are nonzero (in the primal optimal tableau) will imply that $\bar{t}_1$ and $\bar{t}_2$ must be zero; this will prevent the t_1 and t_2 columns in Table 19.1 from being unit vectors.

EXERCISE 19.1

Given the following primals, formulate their duals:

1   Maximize $\pi = 13x_1 + x_2$

    subject to $2x_1 + x_2 \leq 6$
                      $4x_1 + 3x_2 \leq 14$
    and $x_1, x_2 \geq 0$

---

[1] Taking the absolute values is a necessary step because $\bar{x}_j$ must be nonnegative.
[2] Since the number of dual dummy variables is by construction identical with the number of primal choice variables, no dimensional problem ever arises in this procedure.

2 Minimize $C = x_1 + 3x_2$

subject to $\begin{bmatrix} 1 & 2 \\ 0 & 1 \\ 2 & 3 \end{bmatrix} \begin{bmatrix} x_1 \\ x_2 \end{bmatrix} \geq \begin{bmatrix} 5 \\ 4 \\ 9 \end{bmatrix}$

and $x_1, x_2 \geq 0$

3 Maximize $\pi = c_1 x_1 + c_2 x_2 + c_3 x_3$

subject to $\begin{bmatrix} a_{11} & a_{12} & a_{13} \\ a_{21} & a_{22} & a_{23} \\ a_{31} & a_{32} & a_{33} \end{bmatrix} \begin{bmatrix} x_1 \\ x_2 \\ x_3 \end{bmatrix} \leq \begin{bmatrix} r_1 \\ r_2 \\ r_3 \end{bmatrix}$

and $x_j \geq 0 \qquad (j = 1,2,3)$

4 For the dual of Example 2 in the text, the optimal tableau appears as follows:

Row	C^*	y_1	y_2	t_1	t_2	t_3	Constant
0	1	0	0	0	1	2	19
1	0	0	0	1	2	−1	2
2	0	0	1	0	1	0	3
3	0	1	0	0	−2	1	2

(a) Write out the optimal solution of the dual and of the primal.
(b) Substitute the $\bar{y}_i$ and $\bar{x}_j$, respectively, into the dual and primal objective functions to verify that $\bar{C}^* = \bar{C}$.

5 After a number of pivot steps, the tableau of a given linear program assumes the following form:

Row	π	x_1	x_2	s_1	s_2	Constant
0	1	0	0	2	1	14
1	0	0	1	2	−1	2
2	0	1	0	−1	1	2

(a) Is this an optimal tableau? Why?
(b) What are the values of $\bar{x}_1$, $\bar{x}_2$, and $\bar{\pi}$?
(c) How many choice variables would its dual program contain? Why?

(d) What are the optimal values of the dual choice variables and the dual objective function?

6   Given the information that, for the following linear program,

Minimize $C = x_1 + 4x_2$

subject to $\begin{bmatrix} 1 & 2 \\ 3 & 2 \end{bmatrix} \begin{bmatrix} x_1 \\ x_2 \end{bmatrix} \geq \begin{bmatrix} 8 \\ 12 \end{bmatrix}$

and $x_1, x_2 \geq 0$

the optimal solution involves $\bar{x}_1 = 8$ and $\bar{x}_2 = 0$:

(a) Find $\bar{s}_1$, $\bar{s}_2$, and $\bar{C}$.
(b) Write out the dual program.
(c) On the basis of your answer to (a) above, what must be the value of $\bar{y}_2$? On the basis of the given optimal solution, which dual constraint must be a strict equality?
(d) Use your answer to (c) to solve for $\bar{y}_1$.
(e) Substitute $\bar{y}_1$ and $\bar{y}_2$ into the C^* function and check whether $\bar{C}^* = \bar{C}$.

19.2   Economic Interpretation of a Dual

That the dual of a linear program can serve as a computational stand-in for the primal is now clear. In most cases, however, a dual program may also possess a distinct and significant economic meaning of its own.

dual of the production program   Let us first interpret the dual program of the production problem. In the simple two-product two-constraint case, the primal is in the form

Maximize $\pi = c_1 x_1 + c_2 x_2$

subject to $\begin{bmatrix} a_{11} & a_{12} \\ a_{21} & a_{22} \end{bmatrix} \begin{bmatrix} x_1 \\ x_2 \end{bmatrix} \leq \begin{bmatrix} r_1 \\ r_2 \end{bmatrix}$

and $x_1, x_2 \geq 0$

Accordingly, the dual can be written as

Minimize $\pi^* = r_1 y_1 + r_2 y_2$

(19.3)   subject to $\begin{bmatrix} a_{11} & a_{21} \\ a_{12} & a_{22} \end{bmatrix} \begin{bmatrix} y_1 \\ y_2 \end{bmatrix} \geq \begin{bmatrix} c_1 \\ c_2 \end{bmatrix}$

and $y_1, y_2 \geq 0$

Before we can properly interpret the dual, we must first clarify the general nature of the dual variables, including their unit of measure. In the primal, π denotes total gross profit in dollars.[1] In view of the fact that $\bar{\pi}^* = \bar{\pi}$, the symbol π^* in the dual should also be in dollars, as must be the expression $r_1 y_1 + r_2 y_2$ as well. Since the symbol r_i refers to the total quantity of the ith resource in the firm's fixed plant (labeled in an earlier example as the *capacity* of the ith production department), the symbol y_i must obviously be expressed in units of dollars per unit of the ith resource, for only then will each term $r_i y_i$ come out in dollar units. That is to say, y_i must signify some kind of *valuation* of the resource in question.

However, this value is obviously not a market price; rather, it is a value to be *imputed* to the resource. For this reason, the value of y_i is referred to in the literature as an *accounting price*, or *shadow price*, for the ith resource. We shall find it expedient to regard y_i alternatively as representing the *opportunity cost* of using the ith resource.

Let us examine the three ingredient parts of the dual program in this light. First, what the *nonnegativity restrictions* $y_i \geq 0$ mean is that we are forbidden to impute to any resource a value (opportunity cost) of less than zero. This is certainly an economically sensible requirement. In fact, we should always impute a *positive* value to a resource, unless the latter happens not to be fully utilized, so that a nil opportunity cost is incurred in putting it to productive use. This means that a positive opportunity cost for a resource ($\bar{y}_i > 0$) is always to be associated with the full utilization of the resource in the optimal solution ($\bar{s}_i = 0$). The reader will note that, by this line of interpretation, we are once again led back to the second duality theorem, which—heretofore only mathematically interpreted—has now acquired an economic connotation.

Turning next to the *constraints* in the dual, let us specifically examine the first constraint in (19.3):

(19.4) $a_{11} y_1 + a_{21} y_2 \geq c_1$

Since the coefficient a_{ij} denotes the amount of the ith resource used in producing a unit of the jth product, the left side of (19.4) represents the total opportunity cost of production of a unit of the first product ($j = 1$). The right-hand term c_1 denotes the per-unit gross profit of the first product. Thus, what this constraint requires is that the opportunity cost of production be imputed at a level at least as large as the gross profit from the product.

Now, a moment's reflection will indicate that if the opportunity cost of production is actually to exceed the profit, then the resource allocation must certainly be nonoptimal because, simply by dropping the first product, resources

---

[1] As explained in Sec. 18.1, the total gross profit means here the total sales receipts less the variable costs, but before deducting any fixed costs.

will be released therefrom that can immediately be utilized to better advantage elsewhere. Mathematically, if the $>$ part of the $\geq$ sign in (19.4) holds in the optimal solution, then the first product should not be produced ($\bar{x}_1 = 0$). On the contrary, if the first product is actually produced, i.e., if $\bar{x}_1 \neq 0$, then the opportunity cost of production must be exactly equal to the gross profit, and the $=$ part of the $\geq$ sign in (19.4) must hold in the optimal solution. In short, $\bar{t}_1 > 0 \Rightarrow \bar{x}_1 = 0$, and $\bar{x}_1 > 0 \Rightarrow \bar{t}_1 = 0$. This, however, is again merely a restatement of Duality Theorem II. The second constraint in (19.3) can, of course, be given an analogous interpretation.

Lastly, let us look at the *dual objective function*. Recalling that r_1 and r_2 are the total quantities of available resources in the firm's fixed plant, the expression

$$\pi^* = r_1 y_1 + r_2 y_2$$

evidently denotes the total value to be imputed to those resources. It is the idea of the dual program to minimize this total while fulfilling the constraints as interpreted above. Thus, the correspondence between the primal and dual suggests that to maximize profit by finding the optimal output levels (the primal program) is tantamount to minimizing the total imputed value or opportunity cost of the resources in the plant, with the proviso that the opportunity cost of production of each product must be no less than the gross profit from that product. And the fact that $\bar{\pi} = \bar{\pi}^*$ means that, in the optimal solution, the total gross profit must be imputed or allocated in its entirety to the resources in the plant via the shadow prices. This completes the economic interpretation of the dual.

For simplicity, we have cast the production problem in the simple two-product two-resource mold. But since the reasoning employed in the foregoing discussion does not depend on the assumption that $m = n = 2$, the opportunity-cost interpretation of the dual can readily be generalized to the m-resource n-product framework as well.

dual of the diet problem   By analogous reasoning, the choice variables in the dual of the diet problem can also be given an imputed-value interpretation.

The general diet program is, in matrix notation,

Minimize $C = c'x$
subject to $Ax \geq r$
and $x \geq 0$

where C is the total cost of the diet, c' is the row vector of food prices, x is the column vector of food quantities, A is the matrix of coefficients a_{ij} (the amount of the ith nutrient contained in the jth food), and r is the column vector of minimum nutrient requirements. Accordingly, its dual can be written as

Maximize $\qquad C^* = r'y$

subject to $\qquad A'y \leq c$

and $\qquad\qquad y \geq 0$

where y is the column vector of dual choice variables.

Inasmuch as C is in dollar units, its dual counterpart C^* must also be in dollars. But the elements of vector r' are in physical units of the respective nutrients, so that the elements of vector y should be in units of dollars per unit of the respective nutrients. In other words, the dual choice variables are again in the nature of some kind of valuation; this time they denote the imputed values of the various nutrients. As such, they are never allowed to be negative.

In this light, each dual constraint may be construed to mean that the total value imputed to the nutrients contained in one unit of every food should be no greater than the price of that food. Actually, common sense will forbid us to buy the jth food if its price exceeds the imputed value of its nutrient content, because we would not be getting our money's worth. Therefore, in the optimal solution, we shall buy only those foods for which the imputed values of their respective nutrient contents are exactly equal to their respective prices. The astute reader will observe that this is again a case of Duality Theorem II at work.

As the objective of this dual program, we seek to maximize the total imputed value of the minimum nutrient requirements, subject to the above-cited constraints. When this maximum is attained, we shall have in effect succeeded also in minimizing the cost of our diet while satisfying all the minimum nutrient requirements.

dual choice variables and Lagrange multipliers   The dual choice variables, y_i, have been shown to represent shadow prices, or imputed values. We can also demonstrate that, in the optimal solution, they play the same role in linear programming as Lagrange multipliers do in classical optimization problems, namely, they serve to measure the sensitivity of the optimal value of the primal objective function to changes in the primal constraint constants.

For this demonstration, let us again consider the production problem, and its dual as shown in (19.3). In the optimal solution, the y_i variables take the values $\bar{y}_i$, and the dual objective function becomes $\bar{\pi}^* = r_1\bar{y}_1 + r_2\bar{y}_2$. Since $\bar{\pi} = \bar{\pi}^*$, however, we can also write

$$\bar{\pi} = r_1\bar{y}_1 + r_2\bar{y}_2$$

Hence, by differentiating $\bar{\pi}$ with respect to r_1 and r_2, we can write

$$\bar{y}_1 = \frac{\partial \bar{\pi}}{\partial r_1} \quad \text{and} \quad \bar{y}_2 = \frac{\partial \bar{\pi}}{\partial r_2}$$

which indicate that $\bar{y}_i$ (the optimal value of the ith dual choice variable) is a measure of the sensitivity of $\bar{\pi}$ (the optimized value of the primal objective function) to infinitesimal changes in r_i (the parametric constant in the ith primal constraint). Specifically, $\bar{y}_i$ tells us how a slight relaxation of the ith capacity constraint (increase in the amount of the ith resource) will change the total gross profit in the optimal solution. Since, in the classical problem of maximizing $z = f(x,y)$ subject to $g(x,y) = c$, which gives rise to the Lagrangean function $Z = f(x,y) + \lambda[c - g(x,y)]$, the optimal value of the Lagrange multiplier has the meaning of

$$\bar{\lambda} = \frac{d\bar{Z}}{dc} \quad \text{[see (12.16)]}$$

it is clear that dual choice variables and Lagrange multipliers play the identical role, even though the frameworks in which they do so are different.

The Lagrange-multiplier interpretation of $\bar{y}_i$ is, of course, perfectly consistent with our earlier interpretation of y_i as the imputed value of the ith resource. When the ith constraint is relaxed, the ith resource is made available in greater quantity, and the effect of this on the total profit (the Lagrange-multiplier interpretation) will hinge directly on the magnitude of the imputed value of the ith resource (the earlier interpretation), since, in the optimal solution, the total profit and the total imputed value of the firm's resources must be equated to each other.

EXERCISE 19.2

1   Formulate the dual of the dating problem presented in Exercise 18.1-3, and give it an economic interpretation.

2   In the context of the diet problem, give a Lagrange-multiplier interpretation to the optimal values of the dual choice variables, $\bar{y}_i$, and explain specifically what they serve to measure. Is this interpretation consistent with the imputed-value interpretation of y_i?

19.3 Activity Analysis: Micro Level

Hitherto in our discussion, the constraints section of a linear program is by and large read *horizontally*; i.e., each constraint inequality is viewed as an entity that gives rise to a borderline (or hyperplane), which in turn gives rise to two halfspaces. At one juncture, in connection with the discussion of basic feasible solutions, however, we deviated from the above practice, and read the coefficients in the constraints *vertically* as column vectors, in (18.14′) and (18.15). Such a vertical view provides an alternative way of looking at a linear program.

the concept of activity   Imagine a firm that uses two resources (K and L) to produce two goods (x_1, x_2). If the available resources are limited to K_0 and L_0, the firm's constraints can be written in a single vector equation as follows:

$$(19.5) \qquad \begin{bmatrix} a_{11} \\ a_{21} \end{bmatrix} x_1 + \begin{bmatrix} a_{12} \\ a_{22} \end{bmatrix} x_2 + \begin{bmatrix} 1 \\ 0 \end{bmatrix} s_1 + \begin{bmatrix} 0 \\ 1 \end{bmatrix} s_2 = \begin{bmatrix} K_0 \\ L_0 \end{bmatrix}$$

Reading (19.5) vertically, i.e., taking every variable (with its own coefficient vector) by itself, we can consider each of these as representing a distinct *activity* of the firm. The first activity, for instance, consists of the production of the first product, so that the problem of determining the solution value $\bar{x}_1$ is really that of finding the optimal *level* of the first activity. Similarly, the production of the second product constitutes the firm's second activity. We may even consider each *slack* variable as being associated with a separate activity—that of "leaving some resource idle"—although this is by its very nature more of an *inactivity* than an activity.

The pursuit of each activity will entail definite repercussions upon the resources of the firm. As specified by the first vector in (19.5), each unit of the first activity will consume a_{11} units of capital and a_{21} units of labor. Analogously, the second vector reveals that each unit of the second activity will use up a_{12} units of capital and a_{22} units of labor. These vectors, which we shall call *activity vectors*, are therefore the indicators of the input requirements for a unit increase in the level of the activity in question. Note that, since the slack variables are each exclusively associated with one particular resource, their activity vectors are, respectively, the unit vectors $e_1 \equiv \begin{bmatrix} 1 \\ 0 \end{bmatrix}$ and $e_2 \equiv \begin{bmatrix} 0 \\ 1 \end{bmatrix}$.

If we denote the first two activity vectors by A_1 and A_2 and write the resource vector on the right of (19.5) as r, the vector equation (19.5) can be written more simply as

$$(19.5') \qquad A_1 x_1 + A_2 x_2 + e_1 s_1 + e_2 s_2 = r$$

This equation, which states that the production activities and the slack activities of the firm must together exactly exhaust the total resources available, is to be the constraint in the production linear program of the firm. The idea of the program is then to select nonnegative levels of these four activities such that a certain objective function will be maximized, subject to the resource-exhaustion constraint (19.5′). When viewed in such a light, the problem becomes one of *activity analysis.*

As defined above, an activity vector shows only the *input* requirements of the activity in question. But it is possible to include in the vector the *output* picture as well. Instead of the vector $\begin{bmatrix} a_{11} \\ a_{21} \end{bmatrix}$, for instance, we may—using a plus sign to denote output and a minus sign to indicate input—describe the first activity by the expanded vector $\begin{bmatrix} 1 \\ -a_{11} \\ -a_{21} \end{bmatrix}$, where the top element indicates a unit level of output, and the remaining elements are the inputs required. For our purposes here, however, it is more convenient just to adhere to the input-requirement version of such a vector.

constant returns to scale and fixed input ratios   Viewing the production program in the framework of activity analysis serves to bring to the fore two assumptions regarding the production function that are implicit in the linear program. One is the assumption of constant returns to scale (CRTS), and the other is that of fixed input ratios.

The CRTS assumption is reflected in the fact that the elements in the activity vectors A_1 and A_2 are all constants. Because of this constancy, if $\begin{bmatrix} a_{11} \\ a_{21} \end{bmatrix}$ units of $\begin{bmatrix} K \\ L \end{bmatrix}$ are required to produce one unit of x_1, then to produce k units of x_1 will call for exactly k times as much of each resource. The same is true of the second product; in fact, the CRTS assumption applies also to the slack activities.

The assumption of fixed input ratios can be seen from the fact that each product is producible only by a single activity, for which the capital-labor ratio is rigidly specified by the given activity vector, as shown in (19.5). What this means is that substitution between labor and capital is completely ruled out in our example. But, of course, linear programming is not really that inflexible. In case labor and capital can indeed be combined in (say) three different ratios for the production of x_1, we can easily account for this in the program by listing for the said product three separate activities instead of one, as follows:

$$(19.6) \qquad (A_1 x_1 + A_1^* x_1^* + A_1^{**} x_1^{**}) + A_2 x_2 + e_1 s_1 + e_2 s_2 = r$$

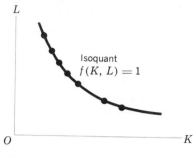

L

Isoquant
$f(K, L) = 1$

O　　　　　　　　　　　　　　　　*K*

FIGURE 19.1

where $A_1 \neq A_1^* \neq A_1^{**}$ are three distinct activity vectors, each describing a different capital-labor ratio under a different productive process, and x_1, x_1^*, and x_1^{**} represent the quantities of the first product to be produced, respectively, under the three processes. In this manner, we can relax the assumption of fixed input ratios. The CRTS assumption, however, is always retained.

Exactly *three* processes are listed in (19.6) for the first product; but since these processes can be used simultaneously in combination, the first product can in reality be produced in *more than three* ways. For instance, if the firm wishes to turn out a total of 12 units of that product, it either can let $x_1 = 3$, $x_1^* = 5$, and $x_1^{**} = 4$ or, alternatively, can select the combination (2,9,1) or (6,0,6) or (3.5,4.5,4), etc. Since each of these possible combinations entails a different overall capital-labor ratio for the production of the total output and can, in fact, be regarded as a distinct way of production, it seems that once we admit multiprocess production into the linear program, the constriction of fixed input ratios will virtually disappear.

But does this mean that the production function implicit in the linear programming framework will be the same as that envisaged in the classical production theory? The answer is, not quite.

production functions: classical analysis versus linear programming
Let us examine the production function of a firm that uses two resources, K and L, to produce a single commodity. To facilitate relating this to the earlier discussions of production functions, let us revert to the symbol Q for output.

In the classical analysis, the production function

$$Q = f(K,L)$$

is assumed to be everywhere continuous and differentiable. For a specific level of output, say, $Q = 1$, the function f will give rise to an isoquant equation

$$1 = f(K,L)$$

which plots as a smooth curve, as in Fig. 19.1. This isoquant indicates continuous

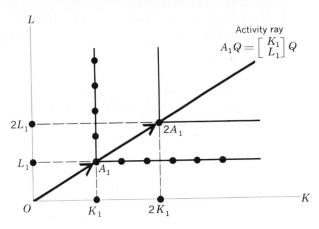

FIGURE 19.2

substitutability between labor and capital. As we persist in substituting, more-over, the rate of substitution will vary continuously. The same is true of the isoquants pertaining to all other conceivable levels of output. But the classical production function *may* or *may not* be characterized by CRTS.

In the linear-programming or activity-analysis framework, the isoquants take on a different appearance. First, let us consider the single-process case, assuming a constant activity vector $A_1 \equiv \begin{bmatrix} K_1 \\ L_1 \end{bmatrix}$ for the first product, which is here considered as the *only* product. Since the output of $Q = 1$ can only be produced with K_1 units of capital and L_1 units of labor, the isoquant equation for this output is

$$1 = g(K_1, L_1)$$

This will plot as a *single* point A_1 in the KL plane in Fig. 19.2, because K_1 and L_1 are two constants, so that $g(K_1, L_1)$ refers only to the value of the production function at a specific point in the domain. The point A_1 is, of course, nothing but the graphical representation of the activity vector defined above. Owing to the CRTS assumption in linear programming, it is easy to deduce that the isoquant for $Q = 2$, again a single point, will be at $2A_1 \equiv 2 \begin{bmatrix} K_1 \\ L_1 \end{bmatrix}$. Furthermore, since all such isoquant points are nonnegative multiples of the activity vector A_1, they must all lie on the straight-line *activity ray* shown in Fig. 19.2.

To use the word *isoquant*—a term normally associated with a curve—to refer to a single point may seem somewhat strange. Actually, it *is* possible to reinterpret the isoquant points in Fig. 19.2 as curves. By virtue of fixed input ratios, we know that, if capital is held at K_1 while labor is increased beyond L_1, the output will remain at $Q = 1$, because the excess labor is sterile in the absence of an accompanying increment in capital. And a similar result holds true for excess capital. This fact, which can be expressed by the equations

$$1 = g(K_1, L_1 + \delta) \qquad \text{and} \qquad 1 = g(K_1 + \delta, L_1) \qquad (\delta \geq 0)$$

means graphically that any point lying due north or due east of A_1 must also yield an output of $Q = 1$. As a result, we may draw the isoquant for $Q = 1$ alternatively as an L-shaped curve with a kink at A_1. By the same token, the isoquant for $Q = 2$ can be depicted as another L-shaped curve with a kink at the point $2A_1$ on the ray. It should be obvious, however, that a kink point—requiring *less* of one resource and *no more* of the other resource than any other fellow point—must be the most efficient input combination on an isoquant. Thus all the other points, said to be *dominated* by the kink point, can be dismissed from consideration.

For this reason, a single-process firm must operate on the activity ray

$$A_1 Q = \begin{bmatrix} K_1 \\ L_1 \end{bmatrix} Q \qquad (Q \geq 0)$$

where Q, the output level, can alternatively be interpreted as the level at which the given activity is to be operated. When we consider the multiprocess production of the same product, however, there will arise a number of activity rays. With (say) four activity vectors,

$$(19.7) \qquad A_1 \equiv \begin{bmatrix} K_1 \\ L_1 \end{bmatrix} \qquad A_2 \equiv \begin{bmatrix} K_2 \\ L_2 \end{bmatrix} \qquad A_3 \equiv \begin{bmatrix} K_3 \\ L_3 \end{bmatrix} \qquad A_4 \equiv \begin{bmatrix} K_4 \\ L_4 \end{bmatrix}$$

each showing a distinct input ratio capable of yielding a unit output, we can draw four activity rays as in Fig. 19.3.† These rays are labeled $A_j Q_j$ ($j = 1, \ldots, 4$), where Q_j represents the amount of the product to be produced under the jth process.

How do we find the isoquant for $Q\ (\equiv \sum_j Q_j) = 1$ in this multiprocess case? In the first place, the four points $A_1, \ldots, A_4$—each signifying the exclusive use of a "pure" process at the unit level—should by definition be included in the said isoquant. But assuming the product to be divisible, it is also possible to operate the processes in various combinations, such as

$$\tfrac{1}{2}A_1 + \tfrac{1}{2}A_2 \qquad \tfrac{1}{3}A_2 + \tfrac{2}{3}A_3 \qquad \tfrac{1}{5}A_3 + \tfrac{4}{5}A_4$$

for as long as the numerical coefficients Q_j in the combination add up to 1, we can obtain the output of $Q = 1$. Mathematically, this means that, to produce a unit output, we must use only *convex combinations* of the pure activity vectors;

---

† Note that, the way we have drawn the activity vectors $A_1, \ldots, A_4$, none of them is "dominated" by the other three in the sense that it requires more K as well as more L for the production of one unit of output, and, being obviously inefficient, will never be put to use.

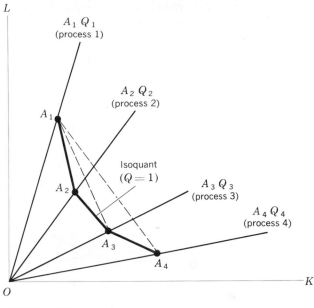

FIGURE 19.3

graphically, this means that the input ratios pertaining to the *combined* processes must lie on the line segments connecting the activity vectors $A_1, \ldots, A_4$.

In this connection, we should note that, while any pair of activity vectors in Fig. 19.3 can theoretically be convex-combined, we need only consider the convex combinations of *adjacent* vectors (such as A_1A_2 and A_2A_3), because the combinations of *nonadjacent* vectors can all be dismissed as being inefficient. Take the (dashed) line segment A_1A_3, for instance. Being located to the northeast of A_1A_2 as well as A_2A_3, all the points on A_1A_3—except the end points A_1 and A_3 themselves—involve larger input requirements for *both* capital and labor than the points on A_1A_2 or A_2A_3; yet the output obtainable is identical at $Q = 1$. The convex combination of A_1 and A_4 (the pair remotest from each other) fares even worse, for the dashed line segment A_1A_4 is seen to lie even farther out, thus entailing even more inputs. In this light, the line segments A_1A_3, A_1A_4, and A_2A_4 (not drawn) are clearly all dominated by A_1A_2, A_2A_3, and A_3A_4, and as such can simply be ignored. The points on the three retained line segments, on the other hand, do not dominate one another; when we switch from one input ratio to another, the *increment* in one resource is accompanied by a *decrement* in the other. Consequently, we may take the kinked line $A_1A_2A_3A_4$ as the isoquant for $Q = 1$.

This isoquant certainly differs from the classical smooth isoquant shown in

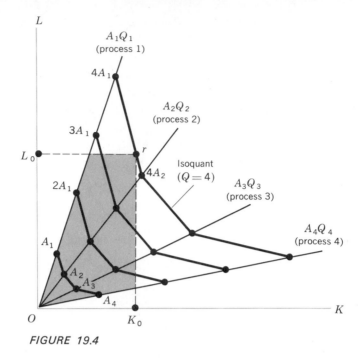

FIGURE 19.4

Fig. 19.1. Though a lot closer to the classical version than the single-process case of Fig. 19.2, the isoquant $A_1A_2A_3A_4$ is not smooth. The rate of substitution tends to stay constant in a certain range, but then it takes a sudden jump. Besides, this feature will remain as long as the firm has at its disposal only a *finite* number of pure processes, for any finite increase in the number of processes will only increase the number of line segments on the isoquant but cannot iron out the sharp points thereon. In this light, therefore, the smooth isoquant of the classical theory must evidently be based on the assumption that an *infinite* number of production processes is available to the firm.

The isoquants for other output levels can be constructed in an analogous manner. For $Q = 2$, for example, we can simply extend each vector A_j to $2A_j$ (by doubling both the abscissa and ordinate of the point) and then join the resulting new vector points by adjacent pairs. By virtue of the CRTS assumption in linear programming, all the points on this new kinked isoquant will be associated with an output $Q = 2$. Four such isoquants have been drawn in Fig. 19.4. But herein lies another difference from the classical approach. For although the CRTS feature can be built into the classical isoquants (by even spacing), it does not have to be; in contrast, CRTS is invariably assumed in linear programming.

Note that, while it is again permissible to add the points lying due north of A_1 and due east of A_4 to the first isoquant $(Q = 1)$, and similarly for the other isoquants, we have refrained from doing so, for the simple reason that such points would be dominated. As a consequence, all the isoquants will lie within the cone-shaped area bounded by the two outermost activity rays, A_1Q_1 and A_4Q_4. Such an area, which constitutes a convex set of points and which is therefore called a *convex cone*, represents the set of all nonnegative linear combinations of two vectors (here A_1 and A_4). That is, if we take all possible nonnegative multiples of the two vectors, and form all possible sums by the parallelogram method, the sum vectors will fill out the conic area.

optimization   Let us now formulate a simple linear program in the light of the activity interpretation of the constraints. Assume that the multiprocess single-product firm depicted in Fig. 19.4 seeks to maximize output Q within the limits of its given resources K_0 and L_0. Then the relevant linear program will be

$$\begin{aligned} \text{Maximize} \quad & Q = Q_1 + Q_2 + Q_3 + Q_4 \\ (19.8) \quad \text{subject to} \quad & A_1Q_1 + A_2Q_2 + A_3Q_3 + A_4Q_4 \leq r \\ \text{and} \quad & Q_j \geq 0 \quad (j = 1, \ldots, 4) \end{aligned}$$

where all the Q symbols are scalars, the A_j symbols denote the activity vectors defined in (19.7), and $r \equiv \begin{bmatrix} K_0 \\ L_0 \end{bmatrix}$ indicates the available resources. For our present purposes, we shall neglect slack activities.

We are able to solve this program graphically despite the fact that there are as many as four choice variables. Since we are reading the constraints *vertically* and since each activity vector is a 2-vector, we can plot each term A_jQ_j in the constraints as an activity ray in the KL coordinate plane (the input space) of Fig. 19.4. By placing the resources rather than the choice variables on the axes, therefore, a four-dimensional problem is reduced to a two-dimensional one.

Inasmuch as the isoquants—which encompass the economically efficient input combinations—are all confined to the convex cone defined by the two outermost activity rays, the firm does not have to look beyond the cone for its optimal solution. But the resource limitation actually will further narrow down its field of choice. If we plot K_0 and L_0 in the diagram, the rectangular area OK_0rL_0 will define the set of all feasible input combinations open to the firm. Deleting from this rectangle what lies beyond the convex cone, we finally find the shaded area (the intersection of the rectangle and the cone) to be the ultimate field of choice.

To maximize output Q means to climb to the highest possible isoquant. Subject to the resource constraint, we see that the maximum output attainable in Fig. 19.4 is $Q = 4$, which requires full utilization of the available resources

K_0 and L_0 at point r. Since point r lies on the line segment joining $4A_1$ and $4A_2$, it is obvious that only the first two processes will be adopted in the optimal solution; i.e., we must set $\bar{Q}_3 = \bar{Q}_4 = 0$. This fact, plus the fact that both K_0 and L_0 are to be fully utilized, implies that $A_1Q_1 + A_2Q_2 = r$, or

$$(19.9) \qquad \begin{bmatrix} K_1 \\ L_1 \end{bmatrix} Q_1 + \begin{bmatrix} K_2 \\ L_2 \end{bmatrix} Q_2 = \begin{bmatrix} K_0 \\ L_0 \end{bmatrix}$$

From this linear system of two equations, we can easily find that

$$\bar{Q}_1 = \frac{K_0 L_2 - K_2 L_0}{K_1 L_2 - K_2 L_1} \qquad \text{and} \qquad \bar{Q}_2 = \frac{K_1 L_0 - K_0 L_1}{K_1 L_2 - K_2 L_1}$$

Or, to approach the problem another way, since r is a convex combination of $4A_1$ and $4A_2$, there must exist a unique scalar ζ in the interval $[0,1]$ such that $\zeta(4A_1) + (1 - \zeta)(4A_2) = r$, that is,

$$(19.10) \qquad 4\zeta \begin{bmatrix} K_1 \\ L_1 \end{bmatrix} + 4(1 - \zeta) \begin{bmatrix} K_2 \\ L_2 \end{bmatrix} = \begin{bmatrix} K_0 \\ L_0 \end{bmatrix}$$

From this, it follows that

$$\zeta = \frac{K_0 - 4K_2}{4(K_1 - K_2)} \qquad \left[\text{also} = \frac{L_0 - 4L_2}{4(L_1 - L_2)} \right]$$

Then, by equating (19.9) and (19.10), we may express the solution values alternatively as

$$\bar{Q}_1 = 4\bar{\zeta} = \frac{K_0 - 4K_2}{K_1 - K_2} \qquad \text{and} \qquad \bar{Q}_2 = 4(1 - \bar{\zeta}) = 4 - \frac{K_0 - 4K_2}{K_1 - K_2}$$

The above problem can, of course, also be solved by the regular simplex method; or the reader may first formulate a dual for the linear program, solve that, and then obtain the solution of the primal. The optimal solution will in either case come out the same. In particular, since there are two constraints, we know that no more than two of the choice variables Q_j need to be nonzero in the optimal solution. This is precisely the result we have just obtained from the activity-analysis version of the problem.

EXERCISE 19.3

1   Assume that a unit of output can be produced by either of the following three combinations of $\begin{bmatrix} K \\ L \end{bmatrix}$:

$$A_1 = \begin{bmatrix} 2 \\ 5 \end{bmatrix} \qquad A_2 = \begin{bmatrix} 3 \\ 2 \end{bmatrix} \qquad A_3 = \begin{bmatrix} 5 \\ 1 \end{bmatrix}$$

(a) Plot the vectors A_1, A_2, and A_3.

(b) Construct an isoquant for output $Q = 1$. How many kinks does the isoquant contain?

(c) Draw the activity rays A_1Q_1, A_2Q_2, and A_3Q_3.

(d) Recalling the assumption of CRTS, construct an isoquant for $Q = 2$.

2   In the preceding problem, if a fourth activity $\begin{bmatrix} 3 \\ 4 \end{bmatrix}$ were also known to be capable of producing a unit output, would you include it on your isoquant for $Q = 1$? Why, or why not?

3   In Exercise 19.3-1, does the isoquant for $Q = 1$ include the following three points?

(a) $(\frac{5}{2}, \frac{7}{2})$ (b) $(\frac{8}{3}, 3)$ (c) $(\frac{7}{2}, \frac{7}{4})$

4   Suppose that a firm has four activities which utilize three resources in the production of its output.

(a) Will its activity rays be located in a 3-space or a 4-space?

(b) Can these rays still define a convex cone?

(c) Is the cone more likely to resemble an ice cream cone or an off-position pyramid? Why?

5   In the problem of Fig. 19.4, if the resource limits were changed to:

(a) $\begin{bmatrix} K_0 \\ L_0 \end{bmatrix} = \begin{bmatrix} 3K_4 \\ 3L_4 \end{bmatrix}$ (b) $\begin{bmatrix} K_0 \\ L_0 \end{bmatrix} = \begin{bmatrix} K_2 + 3K_3 \\ L_2 + 3L_3 \end{bmatrix}$

how would the solution change?

6   In the problem of Fig. 19.4, if point r were moved to a location due north of point $4A_1$, what would be the new optimal solution? How would this differ fundamentally from the type of solution shown in Fig. 19.4?

7   Show that the production function of a firm which uses a single process, with CRTS and fixed input ratios as illustrated in Fig. 19.2, can be represented by the equation $Q = \min \left\{ \dfrac{K}{K_1}, \dfrac{L}{L_1} \right\}$.

19.4 Activity Analysis: Macro Level

Much of what has been said in the preceding section can also be applied at the macro level of analysis. On the firm level, each activity is associated with a separate process of production. On the national level, we may instead consider each activity as representing an industry. Accordingly, the level at which an activity is operated will now specify the output level of the (single) product of an entire industry. If every industry is assumed to be characterized by constant returns to scale and by fixed input ratios, moreover, the input-output relationship of each industry can be summarized by a unique activity ray, on which a point twice as far from the point of origin as another will always mean twice as much output.

Since CRTS and fixed input ratios are the standard assumptions in input-output models, it seems that we should now be able to interpret input-output analysis in terms of activity analysis or linear programming. This is indeed the case.

input-output analysis and linear programming   The inputs required in the operation of each activity (industry) are of two varieties: a *primary* input, which is not the output of any industry; and *intermediate* inputs, which are themselves the outputs of other industries. If we assume a total of n industries, each producing a distinct commodity and if we adopt the same symbols for the input coefficients as in Sec. 5.7, we may find the following three types of vectors to be of interest:

$$(19.11) \qquad \begin{bmatrix} 1 \\ -a_{0j} \\ -a_{1j} \\ -a_{2j} \\ \vdots \\ -a_{nj} \end{bmatrix} \quad \begin{bmatrix} a_{0j} \\ a_{1j} \\ a_{2j} \\ \vdots \\ a_{nj} \end{bmatrix} \quad \begin{bmatrix} a_{1j} \\ a_{2j} \\ \vdots \\ a_{nj} \end{bmatrix}$$

The first of these gives a complete description of the input-output relationship of the jth activity (industry): the first element thereof (1) indicates a unit output of the jth commodity; the second element shows the primary-input requirement for it; and the rest of the elements depict the intermediate-input requirement. The second vector, in which the unit element has been deleted and the signs of all a_{ij} reversed, concentrates on the description of the input side of the industry alone. And the third vector narrows down the perspective even further by listing only the intermediate inputs. The term *activity vector* is often given to the first version in (19.11). But, as we did in the preceding section, we shall reserve this name for a modified version of it to be introduced later.

For the time being, let us consider the third vector in (19.11). There being n industries in the economy, we can write n such vectors. When lumped together, they will form the familiar $n \times n$ matrix:

$$A = \begin{bmatrix} a_{11} & a_{12} & \cdots & a_{1n} \\ a_{21} & a_{22} & & a_{2n} \\ \cdots & \cdots & \cdots & \cdots \\ a_{n1} & a_{n2} & \cdots & a_{nn} \end{bmatrix}$$

Given this matrix, and also an output vector and a final-demand vector as follows:

$$x = \begin{bmatrix} x_1 \\ x_2 \\ \vdots \\ x_n \end{bmatrix} \qquad d = \begin{bmatrix} d_1 \\ d_2 \\ \vdots \\ d_n \end{bmatrix}$$

our task is, in line with the earlier discussion of the open input-output model, to find a vector x such that

$$(19.12) \qquad (I - A)x = d$$

The solution, assuming $(I - A)$ to be nonsingular, is simply

$$(19.13) \qquad \bar{x} = (I - A)^{-1}d$$

No hint of the linear-programming type of optimization is evident in such a formulation of the problem because there is no objective function to optimize and because the equation (19.12), though in the nature of *constraints* on the output level of each industry (each industry should produce enough output to satisfy the total demand), contains no inequalities at all.

However, the same input-output problem can be looked at from a different angle. First of all, it is easy to see that, to ensure the satisfaction of the total demand, it is only necessary for the output of each industry to be *no less than* (rather than *equal to*) the total demand for it. Consequently, it is not unreasonable to change (19.12) to an inequality

$$(I - A)x \geq d$$

However, in order to guard against unwarranted excesses—i.e., to prevent the $>$ part of the $\geq$ sign from going "wild"—we should also append some sort of minimization requirement to this inequality. Assuming labor to be the only primary input, for example, we can seek to minimize the total labor input required for producing the output indicated above. That is, we can endeavor to minimize:

$$L = \sum_{j=1}^{n} a_{0j}x_j = \begin{bmatrix} a_{01} & a_{02} & \cdots & a_{0n} \end{bmatrix} \begin{bmatrix} x_1 \\ x_2 \\ \vdots \\ x_n \end{bmatrix} = A_0'x$$

where L denotes total required labor, and A'_0 denotes the row vector of labor-input coefficients. In addition, since the output levels x_j can never be negative, it is also legitimate to impose the restriction $x \geq 0$. In this light, the input-output model (19.12) can be reformulated in the mathematically equivalent form

$$
\begin{array}{lll}
& \text{Minimize} & L = A'_0 x \\
(19.14) & \text{subject to} & (I - A)x \geq d \\
& \text{and} & x \geq 0
\end{array}
$$

which, the reader will recognize, is merely a standard linear program.

the solution   The linear program (19.14) can be solved by either of two approaches. One is to read the n constraints *horizontally*, and the other is to read them *vertically*.

When read horizontally, the n constraints give rise to n closed halfspaces which, together with the nonnegativity restrictions, will define a feasible region (a convex set) in the nonnegative orthant. The objective function, on the other hand, will generate a family of isolabor hyperplanes. To find the optimal solution is to select a point in the feasible region that is on the isolabor hyperplane with the minimum value of L. That point ($\bar{x}$), however, will of necessity turn out to be the one given in (19.13), for if labor is an indispensable input for every commodity produced, then the output vector with the least labor requirement must necessarily be that which contains no excess output over total demand. That is, the optimal output vector is necessarily $\bar{x} = (I - A)^{-1}d$, the solution of the regular input-output model.[1]

Now, let us read the constraints vertically. Since the matrix $(I - A)$ consists of the following n vectors:

$$
\begin{bmatrix} 1 - a_{11} \\ -a_{21} \\ \vdots \\ -a_{n1} \end{bmatrix}
\quad
\begin{bmatrix} -a_{12} \\ 1 - a_{22} \\ \vdots \\ -a_{n2} \end{bmatrix}
\quad \cdots \quad
\begin{bmatrix} -a_{1n} \\ -a_{2n} \\ \vdots \\ 1 - a_{nn} \end{bmatrix}
$$

we may plot these as activity vectors in an n-space. Specifically, we should plot them in the final-demand space (with the jth axis indicating the final demand for x_j)—just as the activity vectors in (19.5) should be plotted in the input space (KL space). These vectors are then to be linearly combined via a set of nonnegative coefficients $x_1, \ldots, x_n$, and the set of all such nonnegative combinations will take the form of a *convex polyhedral cone*—the n-dimensional analog of the convex cone encountered in Fig. 19.4. An illustrative pictorial view of such a cone is given in Fig. 19.5 for the case of $n = 3$. If the three arrows

---

[1] Note that, in this case, all of the constraints will be fulfilled exactly. This result comes about because the number of constraints is identical with the number of choice variables in the present problem.

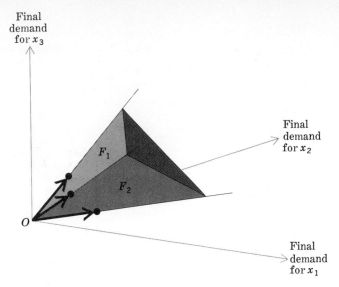

Final
demand
for x_3

Final
demand
for x_2

F_1

F_2

O

Final
demand
for x_1

FIGURE 19.5

locate three vectors, then the set of all *nonnegative combinations* of two of these vectors (by parallelogram) will consist of a triangular flat surface such as F_1 and F_2, which are two-dimensional convex cones similar to the one in Fig. 19.4. If, further, we form all the possible nonnegative combinations of the points on F_1 and F_2, however, we shall also fill out the space bounded by the surfaces F_1, F_2, and F_3 (which lurks behind). Thus the totality of the nonnegative combinations of the three given vectors will be the set of points located either on the boundary or in the interior of the pyramidlike solid in Fig. 19.5. This solid, a closed convex set, is called a convex polyhedral cone, and the surfaces F_1, F_2, and F_3 are called the *faces*, or *facets*, of the cone.

Whereas the illustrative convex polyhedral cone in Fig. 19.5 is drawn entirely in the nonnegative orthant, this will not be the case in an input-output linear program. In the three-industry model, the constraints will take the form

$$(19.15) \qquad \begin{bmatrix} 1 - a_{11} \\ -a_{21} \\ -a_{31} \end{bmatrix} x_1 + \begin{bmatrix} -a_{12} \\ 1 - a_{22} \\ -a_{32} \end{bmatrix} x_2 + \begin{bmatrix} -a_{13} \\ -a_{23} \\ 1 - a_{33} \end{bmatrix} x_3 \geq \begin{bmatrix} d_1 \\ d_2 \\ d_3 \end{bmatrix}$$

and inasmuch as all the a_{ij} coefficients are either positive fractions or zeros, the elements in the three activity vectors will be signed thus (in the nonzero case):

Vector 1   Vector 2   Vector 3

$$\begin{bmatrix} + \\ - \\ - \end{bmatrix} \qquad \begin{bmatrix} - \\ + \\ - \end{bmatrix} \qquad \begin{bmatrix} - \\ - \\ + \end{bmatrix}$$

Consequent to the presence of the negative elements in the vectors, the activity rays must lie outside the nonnegative orthant. In Fig. 19.6a, which presents a

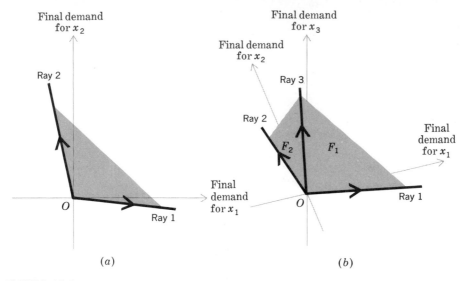

Final demand
for x_2

Ray 2

Ray 1

O

(a)

Final demand
for x_3

Final demand
for x_2

Ray 3

Ray 2

F_2 F_1

Final
demand
for x_1

O

Ray 1

Final
demand
for x_1

(b)

FIGURE 19.6

bird's-eye view of our 3-space, ray 1 is seen, for example, to be positive in the x_1 direction but negative in the x_2 direction; actually, it is also negative in the x_3 direction—i.e., it extends *away* from our viewpoint. Ray 2 is to be similarly interpreted. When pictured in the 3-space in Fig. 19.6b, such rays must therefore give rise to a convex polyhedral cone that "wraps" the nonnegative orthant. Interestingly, the nonnegative orthant is now a subset of the convex polyhedral cone, which is the exact opposite of the situation in Fig. 19.5.

We have now interpreted the nonnegative combinations of the three vectors on the left of (19.15) as corresponding to points in a convex polyhedral cone. How do we interpret the remaining expression $\geq d$? The vector point d, with coordinates (d_1,d_2,d_3), is located directly above the point $(d_1,d_2,0)$ in the base plane of Fig. 19.7. What the expression $\geq d$ does is to define a subset of the final-demand space, satisfying the condition that the demand met for the jth commodity is no less than the specific amount d_j ($j = 1,2,3$). If we take point d as a new point of origin and draw three new axes parallel to the three original ones (see arrows), then the said subset will, in terms of relative position, be to the point d as the nonnegative orthant is to the point of origin. Since it looks like an upper room of a house, let us refer to it as the d *loft*.

When (19.15) is read in its entirety, therefore, the instruction is for us to confine our attention to those points in the convex polyhedral cone that are in the d loft. But since the d loft is a subset of the nonnegative orthant, and hence a subset of the cone, all that this indicates is that the d loft alone need be taken into consideration.

The objective of the linear program is then to minimize L while still remaining in the d loft, i.e., to pick from among a family of isolabor planes—

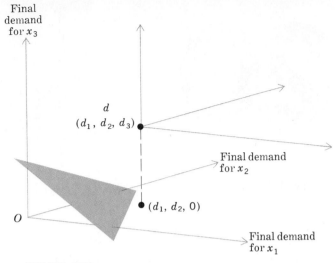

FIGURE 19.7

or, more accurately, plane segments—the lowest one having a point in common with the d loft. Since such plane segments, all parallel, are typically shaped like the shaded triangle in Fig. 19.7 (see Exercise 19.4-4), the optimal one will be the one that touches the d loft at point d itself. Consequently, the constraint (19.15) must optimally be a strict equality. This, then, will again lead us back to the formulation (19.12) and to the same solution arrived at earlier in (19.13).

EXERCISE 19.4

1   In the input-output model discussed in the text, there is no limitation imposed on labor availability. If there were only a limited amount L_0 available, what additional constraint must be added to the model? Write it in both summation notation and vector notation.

2   The point of origin is an element of any cone (referred to as the *vertex* of the cone). Explain from the activity-analysis viewpoint why this should be the case.

3   Given the three vectors $\begin{bmatrix} 1 \\ 1 \end{bmatrix}$, $\begin{bmatrix} 2 \\ -1 \end{bmatrix}$, and $\begin{bmatrix} 3 \\ 1 \end{bmatrix}$, draw the cone that will be generated by nonnegative combinations of these vectors.

4   (*a*)   Supply an explanation for the triangular shape of the isolabor plane segment illustrated in Fig. 19.7. (*Hint:* Review the discussion of isoquant construction for Fig. 19.3)

    (*b*)   Why are the isolabor plane segments all parallel?

NONLINEAR PROGRAMMING

Linear programming, as discussed in the last two chapters, is in a very real sense an improvement over the classical optimization framework, since constraints may now enter into the problem as inequalities, and, accordingly, we can also explicitly introduce nonnegativity restrictions into the problem. However, the necessity of confining the objective function and the constraints to the linear mold can sometimes be a significant drawback. As a further improvement, therefore, we would welcome an optimization framework that can handle nonlinear objective functions as well as nonlinear inequality constraints. Such a framework is found in *nonlinear programming*.

20.1   The Nature of Nonlinear Programming

The maximization problem of nonlinear programming has the following general format:

$$
\begin{aligned}
\text{Maximize} \quad & \pi = f(x_1, x_2, \ldots, x_n) \\
\text{subject to} \quad & g^1(x_1, x_2, \ldots, x_n) \leq r_1 \\
& g^2(x_1, x_2, \ldots, x_n) \leq r_2 \\
& \quad\quad \ldots\ldots\ldots\ldots\ldots\ldots \\
& g^m(x_1, x_2, \ldots, x_n) \leq r_m \\
\text{and} \quad & x_j \geq 0 \quad (j = 1, 2, \ldots, n)
\end{aligned}
$$

(20.1)

Denoting the n-tuple of choice variables by the unsubscripted symbol x, we can write (20.1) more succinctly as

$$
\begin{array}{lll}
\text{Maximize} & \pi = f(x) & \\
(20.1') \quad \text{subject to} & g^i(x) \le r_i & (i = 1, 2, \ldots, m) \\
\text{and} & x \ge 0 &
\end{array}
$$

Similarly, the minimization problem can be written in the form of

$$
\begin{array}{ll}
\text{Minimize} & C = f(x_1, x_2, \ldots, x_n) \\
\text{subject to} & g^1(x_1, x_2, \ldots, x_n) \ge r_1 \\
& g^2(x_1, x_2, \ldots, x_n) \ge r_2 \\
(20.2) & \qquad \cdots\cdots\cdots\cdots\cdots \\
& g^m(x_1, x_2, \ldots, x_n) \ge r_m \\
\text{and} & x_j \ge 0 \qquad (j = 1, 2, \ldots, n)
\end{array}
$$

or, more succinctly,

$$
\begin{array}{lll}
\text{Minimize} & C = f(x) & \\
(20.2') \quad \text{subject to} & g^i(x) \ge r_i & (i = 1, 2, \ldots, m) \\
\text{and} & x \ge 0 &
\end{array}
$$

From the above, it is clear that a nonlinear program, like a linear one, also consists of three ingredients—an objective function, a set of m constraints, and a set of nonnegativity restrictions on the n choice variables. As in linear programming, m can be either greater than, equal to, or less than n. All the functions in the problem, $f(x)$ and $g^i(x)$, are assumed to be differentiable. Note, also, that in order to be consistent with our earlier discussion of linear programming, we are again adopting only the $\le$ type of constraints in the maximization problem and the $\ge$ type in the minimization problem. In case the reverse type of inequality occurs, it can readily be converted by multiplying through by -1.

The formulations in (20.1) and (20.2) are manifestly the most general optimization problems encountered so far in this volume. As such, they encompass all the previously discussed optimization problems as special cases. Linear programs are obviously special cases. If we take the objective function by itself, we have the free-extremum problem. And, finally, adding to the objective function the constraint section in its strict-equality version and with $m < n$, we obtain the classical problem of constrained optimization.[1]

nonlinearities in economics　　Nonlinearities can arise in various ways. In the production problem in linear programming, the per-unit gross profit of each

---

[1] Actually, the connection between nonlinear programming and classical optimization is even closer than has been indicated. For it is possible, if desired, to transform a nonlinear-programming problem into a classical one by taking the following two steps: (1) Introduce m dummy variables to convert the inequality constraints into equational ones. (2) Regard each of the n choice variables and each of the m dummy variables as the square of a new, artificial variable, to ensure nonnegativity. (See Exercise 20.1-6.)

product was assumed to be a constant. But it can very well be a decreasing function of the output level, either because a larger output tends to depress the market price (average revenue), or because increased production tends to raise the average variable cost of the product. If so, the linear objective function $\pi = c_1 x_1 + \cdots + c_n x_n$ must be replaced by a nonlinear version, such as $\pi = c_1(x_1)x_1 + \cdots + c_n(x_n)x_n$, where $c_j(x_j)$ denotes a decreasing function of the variable x_j.

Similarly, in the constraint section, it may happen that the input requirement for resource i in the production of product j decreases with the output level of product j. For instance, the later units of production may conceivably be processable at greater speed than the earlier ones, so that less machine time will be used up by each successive unit of output. This will, of course, undermine the constancy of the coefficient a_{ij}, as assumed in linear programming. It may also happen that the coefficient a_{ij} depends on the output level, not only of product j, but also of another product k. Then there will arise in the constraint section a term which involves the product of the two variables x_j and x_k, and linearity will again be lost.

Whenever the economic circumstances illustrated above are descriptive of the problem at hand, a nonlinear formulation will be more appropriate than a linear one. Unfortunately, many of the convenient features of linear programming will then become unavailable. This fact can be illustrated by some simple nonlinear programs that can be solved graphically.

graphical solution   We shall present here three specific examples, each of which will serve to spotlight certain features that distinguish nonlinear programming from linear programming.

Example 1   Minimize $C = (x_1 - 4)^2 + (x_2 - 4)^2$
subject to
$$2x_1 + 3x_2 \geq 6$$
$$-3x_1 - 2x_2 \geq -12$$
and $x_1, x_2 \geq 0$

The constraints of this problem being linear, the shape of the feasible region does not differ fundamentally from that of a linear program. Shown as the shaded area in Fig. 20.1a, the feasible region derives its southwestern border from the first constraint, and its northeastern border from the second. Since the objective function is nonlinear, it does not generate a family of parallel, straight isovalue lines. Instead, we get a family of concentric circles, with center at (4,4) and with each successively smaller circle being associated with a lower value of C. In a free-extremum problem, we would of course choose the point $(x_1, x_2) = (4, 4)$, which yields the minimum value $C = 0$. Being confined to the shaded region, however, the best we can do is to pick the point $(\bar{x}_1, \bar{x}_2) = (2\frac{2}{13}, 2\frac{10}{13})$, where the

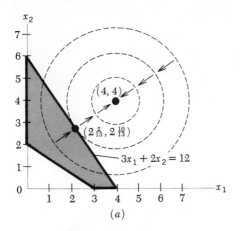

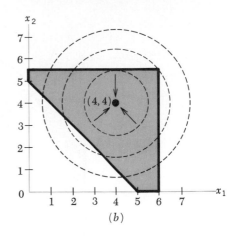

FIGURE 20.1

northeastern border is tangent to one of the circles.[1] The minimized value of C is then $\bar{C} = (2\frac{2}{13} - 4)^2 + (2\frac{10}{13} - 4)^2 = 4\frac{12}{13}$.

The reader will note that, here, the optimal solution is *not* located at an extreme point of the feasible region, as we would expect in linear programming. Consequently, only *one* constraint is seen to be exactly fulfilled, instead of two. Note, also, that whereas to go northeastward towards the point (4,4) will at first decrease C, to stay on the same course beyond that point will lead to higher values of C instead. Thus we are no longer justified, as under linear programming, in pushing the isovalue curve as far as possible in one single specific direction.

Example 2   Minimize $C = (x_1 - 4)^2 + (x_2 - 4)^2$

subject to $\begin{aligned} x_1 + x_2 &\geq 5 \\ -x_1 &\geq -6 \\ -2x_2 &\geq -11 \end{aligned}$

and $x_1, x_2 \geq 0$

---

[1] While the exact values of $\bar{x}_1$ and $\bar{x}_2$ are hardly ascertainable graphically, they can be found algebraically once we have the geometric information in Fig. 20.1a. First, since the optimal point lies on the northeastern border, it must satisfy the equation

$3x_1 + 2x_2 = 12$ [from the second constraint]

Next, the circle which is tangent to that border at that point must have the same slope as that border, namely, $-3/2$. Since the slope of the circle is [using the implicit-function rule on the equation $F(x_1, x_2) = (x_1 - 4)^2 + (x_2 - 4)^2 - C = 0$]:

$$\frac{dx_2}{dx_1} = -\frac{\partial F/\partial x_1}{\partial F/\partial x_2} = -\frac{2(x_1 - 4)}{2(x_2 - 4)} = -\frac{x_1 - 4}{x_2 - 4}$$

it follows that, by setting this equal to $-3/2$, we can obtain another equation

$2x_1 - 3x_2 = -4$

Solved simultaneously, these two equations yield the exact values of $\bar{x}_1$ and $\bar{x}_2$.

Nonlinear Programming   701

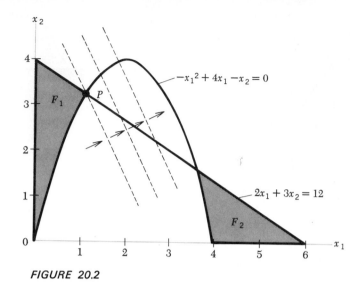

FIGURE 20.2

The present problem differs from the preceding one only in its constraint section. In view of the linearity in the constraints, the feasible region is again a solid polygon, but its new geographic location in relation to the isovalue circles yields a totally new type of outcome. As Fig. 20.1b shows, the free-minimum solution point (4,4) is now contained in the interior of the feasible set, so the constrained optimal solution is also found in that point, with $\bar{C} = 0$. In this example, therefore, the optimal solution does not even lie on the boundary of the feasible region, and, consequently, *none* of the constraints is exactly fulfilled at the optimal solution. In contrast to linear programming, it is now no longer possible to narrow down our field of choice to the set of extreme points of the feasible region.

Example 3   Maximize $\pi = 2x_1 + x_2$
             subject to $-x_1^2 + 4x_1 - x_2 \leq 0$
                                  $2x_1 + 3x_2 \leq 12$
             and $x_1, x_2 \geq 0$

In this example, nonlinearity enters through the first constraint. Rewriting the latter in the form of $x_2 \geq -x_1^2 + 4x_1$, where the right-side expression is a quadratic function of x_1, we see that this constraint requires us to pick only the points lying on or above the parabola shown in Fig. 20.2. The second constraint, on the other hand, instructs us to stay on or below a negatively sloped straight line. All told, therefore, the feasible region consists of two disjoint parts, F_1 and F_2. Hence, in this case, the feasible region is not even a convex set!

From the linear objective function, we get a family of linear isovalue curves. As far as F_1 is concerned, point P yields the highest π value, but since F_2 is also feasible, point P qualifies only as a local optimum, not a global one. In fact, any point in F_2 is a better choice than point P. This serves to illustrate that, when the feasible set is not convex, the sufficient conditions of the globality theorem (Sec. 18.3) fail to be satisfied, and a local optimum is therefore not necessarily a global one as well.

To sum up: Nonlinear programming differs from linear programming in at least the following five respects, some of which are closely related to each other: (1) The field of choice extends over the entire feasible region, not merely the set of its extreme points. (2) The number of exactly fulfilled constraints (and non-negativity restrictions) may not be equal to the number of choice variables. (3) Adherence to a uniform direction of movement may not lead to continually increasing (or decreasing) values of the objective function. (4) The feasible region may not be a convex set. (5) A local optimum may not be a global optimum. As a result of these differences, solution methods appropriate for linear programming become largely inapplicable in the nonlinear framework, and new methods become necessary. In this chapter, however, our attention will primarily be focused, not on solution algorithms (which tend to be involved and specialized), but on certain analytical results (necessary conditions and sufficient conditions) that provide the *qualitative* characterizations of an optimal solution, rather than the *quantitative* solution itself.

EXERCISE 20.1

Solve the following three nonlinear programs graphically; in each case, give the specific values of $\bar{x}_1$ and $\bar{x}_2$:

1   Minimize $C = x_1{}^2 + x_2{}^2$
    subject to $x_1 x_2 \geq 25$
    and $x_1, x_2 \geq 0$

2   Maximize $\pi = x_1{}^2 + (x_2 - 2)^2$
    subject to $5x_1 + 3x_2 \leq 15$
    and $x_1, x_2 \geq 0$

3   Minimize $C = x_1 + x_2$
    subject to $x_1{}^2 + x_2 \geq 9$
                $-x_1 x_2 \geq -8$
    and $x_1, x_2 \geq 0$

4 A firm has the linear demand function $x_1 = a - bP_1$ for its first product and $x_2 = c - dP_2$ for the second product. If the average variable costs for the two products are, respectively, $V_1 = m + x_1$ and $V_2 = n + x_2{}^2$, find its total-gross-profit objective function.

5 The objective function $C = (x_1 - 4)^2 + (x_2 - 4)^2$ in Examples 1 and 2 in the text generates a family of isovalue concentric circles in the $x_1 x_2$ plane. If we introduce a third dimension, C, perpendicular to the $x_1 x_2$ plane, what kind of surface will the objective function yield?

6 Transform the nonlinear program in Exercise 20.1-1 into an equivalent classical constrained-optimization problem by (1) using a dummy variable s, and (2) expressing x_1, x_2, and s as the squares of three other variables, u, v, and w, respectively. Solve this problem in the classical manner, and compare your solution with the graphical solution obtained earlier.

20.2   Kuhn-Tucker Conditions

In the classical optimization problem, with no explicit restrictions on the signs of the choice variables, and with no inequalities in the constraints, the first-order condition for a relative or local extremum is simply that the first partial derivatives of the objective function with respect to all the choice variables and the Lagrange multipliers be zero. In nonlinear programming, there exists a similar type of first-order condition, known as the *Kuhn-Tucker conditions*.[1] As we shall see, however, while the classical first-order condition is always necessary, the Kuhn-Tucker conditions cannot be accorded the status of necessary conditions unless a certain proviso is satisfied. On the other hand, under certain specific circumstances, the Kuhn-Tucker conditions turn out to be *sufficient conditions*, or even *necessary-and-sufficient* conditions as well.

Since the Kuhn-Tucker conditions are the single most important analytical result in nonlinear programming, it is essential to have a proper understanding of those conditions as well as their implications. For the sake of expository convenience, we shall develop these conditions in two steps.

effect of nonnegativity restrictions   As the first step, consider a problem with nonnegativity restrictions, but with no other constraints. Taking the

---

[1] H. W. Kuhn and A. W. Tucker, "Nonlinear Programming," in J. Neyman (ed.), *Proceedings of the Second Berkeley Symposium on Mathematical Statistics and Probability*, University of California Press, Berkeley, California, 1951, pp. 481–492.

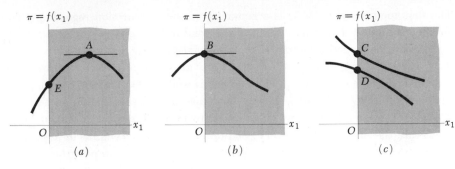

FIGURE 20.3

single-variable case, in particular, we have:

$$(20.3) \quad \begin{array}{ll} \text{Maximize} & \pi = f(x_1) \\ \text{subject to} & x_1 \geq 0 \end{array}$$

where the function f is assumed to be differentiable. In view of the restriction $x_1 \geq 0$, three possible situations may arise. First, if a local maximum of π occurs in the interior of the shaded feasible region in Fig. 20.3, such as at point A in diagram a, then we have an *interior solution*. The first-order condition in this case is $d\pi/dx_1 = f'(x_1) = 0$, same as in the classical problem. Secondly, as illustrated by point B in diagram b, a local maximum can also occur on the vertical axis, where $x_1 = 0$. Even in this second case, where we have a *boundary solution*, the first-order condition $f'(x_1) = 0$ nevertheless remains valid. However, as a third possibility, a local maximum may in the present context take the position of point C or point D in diagram c, because to qualify as a local maximum in the problem (20.3), the candidate point merely has to be higher than the neighboring points *within* the feasible region. In view of this last possibility, the maximum point in a problem like (20.3) can be characterized, not only by the equation $f'(x_1) = 0$, but also by the inequality $f'(x_1) < 0$. Note, on the other hand, that the opposite inequality, $f'(x_1) > 0$, can safely be ruled out, for at a point where the curve is upward-sloping, we can never have a maximum, even if that point is located on the vertical axis, such as point E in diagram a.

The upshot of the above discussion is that, in order for a value of x_1 to give a local maximum of π in the problem (20.3), it must satisfy one of the following three conditions:

$$(20.4) \quad f'(x_1) = 0 \quad \text{and} \quad x_1 > 0 \quad \text{[point } A\text{]}$$
$$(20.5) \quad f'(x_1) = 0 \quad \text{and} \quad x_1 = 0 \quad \text{[point } B\text{]}$$
$$(20.6) \quad f'(x_1) < 0 \quad \text{and} \quad x_1 = 0 \quad \text{[points } C \text{ and } D\text{]}$$

Actually, these three conditions can be consolidated into a single statement:

$$(20.7) \quad f'(x_1) \leq 0 \quad x_1 \geq 0 \quad \text{and} \quad x_1 f'(x_1) = 0$$

The first inequality in (20.7) is a summary of the information regarding $f'(x_1)$ enumerated in (20.4) through (20.6). The second inequality is a similar summary for x_1; in fact, it merely reiterates the nonnegativity restriction of the problem. And, as the third part of (20.7), we have an equation which expresses an important feature common to (20.4), (20.5), as well as (20.6), namely that, of the two quantities x_1 and $f'(x_1)$, *at least one* must take a zero value, so that the product of the two must be zero. Taken together, the three parts of (20.7) constitute the first-order necessary condition for a local maximum in a problem where the choice variable must be nonnegative. But going a step further, we can also take them to be necessary for a *global* maximum. This is because a global maximum must also be a local maximum (e.g., Miss America must also be a title winner at the state level) and, as such, must also satisfy the necessary condition for a local maximum.

When the problem contains n choice variables:

$$(20.8) \quad \begin{aligned} &\text{Maximize} & \pi &= f(x_1, x_2, \ldots, x_n) \\ &\text{subject to} & x_j &\geq 0 \quad (j = 1, 2, \ldots, n) \end{aligned}$$

the classical first-order condition $f_1 = f_2 = \cdots = f_n = 0$ must be similarly modified. To do this, we can apply the same type of reasoning underlying (20.7) to each choice variable, x_j, taken by itself. Graphically, this amounts to viewing the horizontal axis in Fig. 20.3 as representing each x_j in turn. The required modification of the first-order condition then readily suggests itself:

$$(20.9) \quad f_j \leq 0 \qquad x_j \geq 0 \quad \text{and} \quad x_j f_j = 0 \qquad (j = 1, 2, \ldots, n)$$

where f_j is the partial derivative $\partial \pi / \partial x_j$.

effect of inequality constraints   With this background, we now proceed to the second step, and try to include inequality constraints as well. For simplicity, let us first deal with a problem with three variables ($n = 3$) and two constraints ($m = 2$):

$$(20.10) \quad \begin{aligned} &\text{Maximize} & \pi &= f(x_1, x_2, x_3) \\ &\text{subject to} & g^1(x_1, x_2, x_3) &\leq r_1 \\ & & g^2(x_1, x_2, x_3) &\leq r_2 \\ &\text{and} & x_1, x_2, x_3 &\geq 0 \end{aligned}$$

which, with the help of two dummy variables s_1 and s_2, can be transformed into the equivalent form

$$(20.10') \quad \begin{aligned} &\text{Maximize} & \pi &= f(x_1, x_2, x_3) \\ &\text{subject to} & g^1(x_1, x_2, x_3) + s_1 &= r_1 \\ & & g^2(x_1, x_2, x_3) + s_2 &= r_2 \\ &\text{and} & x_1, x_2, x_3, s_1, s_2 &\geq 0 \end{aligned}$$

If the nonnegativity restrictions are absent, we may, in line with the classical approach, form the Lagrangean function (denoting the Lagrange multiplier here by y rather than λ):

$$(20.11) \qquad Z^* = f(x_1, x_2, x_3) + y_1[r_1 - g^1(x_1, x_2, x_3) - s_1] \\ + y_2[r_2 - g^2(x_1, x_2, x_3) - s_2]$$

and write the first-order condition as

$$\frac{\partial Z^*}{\partial x_1} = \frac{\partial Z^*}{\partial x_2} = \frac{\partial Z^*}{\partial x_3} = \frac{\partial Z^*}{\partial s_1} = \frac{\partial Z^*}{\partial s_2} = \frac{\partial Z^*}{\partial y_1} = \frac{\partial Z^*}{\partial y_2} = 0$$

But since the x_j and s_i variables do have to be nonnegative, the first-order condition on those variables should be modified in accordance with (20.9). Consequently, we obtain the following set of conditions instead:

$$(20.12) \qquad \begin{array}{lll} \dfrac{\partial Z^*}{\partial x_j} \leq 0 & x_j \geq 0 \quad \text{and} & x_j \dfrac{\partial Z^*}{\partial x_j} = 0 \\[2mm] \dfrac{\partial Z^*}{\partial s_i} \leq 0 & s_i \geq 0 \quad \text{and} & s_i \dfrac{\partial Z^*}{\partial s_i} = 0 \\[2mm] \dfrac{\partial Z^*}{\partial y_i} = 0 & & \left(\begin{array}{l} i = 1, 2 \\ j = 1, 2, 3 \end{array} \right) \end{array}$$

The reader may note that the derivatives $\partial Z^*/\partial y_i$ are still to be set strictly equal to zero. (Why?)

Each line of (20.12) relates to a different type of variable. But we can consolidate the last two lines and, in the process, eliminate the dummy variables s_i from the first-order condition. Inasmuch as $\partial Z^*/\partial s_i = -y_i$, the second line tells us that we must have $-y_i \leq 0$, $s_i \geq 0$ and, $-s_i y_i = 0$, or, equivalently,

$$(20.13) \qquad s_i \geq 0 \qquad y_i \geq 0 \qquad \text{and} \qquad y_i s_i = 0$$

But the third line—a restatement of the constraints in (20.10′)—means that $s_i = r_i - g^i(x_1, x_2, x_3)$. By substituting the latter into (20.13), therefore, we can combine the second and third lines of (20.12) into a single statement:

$$r_i - g^i(x_1, x_2, x_3) \geq 0 \qquad y_i \geq 0 \qquad \text{and} \qquad y_i[r_i - g^i(x_1, x_2, x_3)] = 0$$

This enables us to express the first-order condition (20.12) in an equivalent form *without* the dummy variables. Using the symbol g_j^i to denote $\partial g^i/\partial x_j$, we now write

$$(20.14) \qquad \begin{array}{l} \dfrac{\partial Z^*}{\partial x_j} = f_j - (y_1 g_j^1 + y_2 g_j^2) \leq 0 \quad x_j \geq 0 \quad \text{and} \quad x_j \dfrac{\partial Z^*}{\partial x_j} = 0 \\[2mm] r_i - g^i(x_1, x_2, x_3) \geq 0 \ y_i \geq 0 \ \text{and} \ y_i[r_i - g^i(x_1, x_2, x_3)] = 0 \end{array}$$

These, then, are the Kuhn-Tucker conditions for the problem (20.10), or, more accurately, one version of the Kuhn-Tucker conditions, expressed in terms of the Lagrangean function Z^* in (20.11).

Now that we know the results, though, it is possible to obtain the same set of conditions more directly by using a different Lagrangean function. Given the problem (20.10), let us ignore the nonnegativity restrictions as well as the inequality signs in the constraints and write the purely classical type of Lagrangean function, Z:

$$(20.15) \qquad Z = f(x_1, x_2, x_3) + y_1[r_1 - g^1(x_1, x_2, x_3)] + y_2[r_2 - g^2(x_1, x_2, x_3)]$$

Then let us (1) set the partial derivatives $\partial Z/\partial x_j \leq 0$, but $\partial Z/\partial y_i \geq 0$, (2) impose nonnegativity restrictions on x_j and y_i, and (3) require complementary slackness to prevail between each variable and the partial derivative of Z with respect to that variable, that is, require their product to vanish. Since the results of these steps, namely,

$$(20.16) \qquad \begin{aligned} \frac{\partial Z}{\partial x_j} &= f_j - (y_1 g_j^1 + y_2 g_j^2) \leq 0 & x_j \geq 0 & \quad\text{and}\quad & x_j \frac{\partial Z}{\partial x_j} = 0 \\ \frac{\partial Z}{\partial y_i} &= r_i - g^i(x_1, x_2, x_3) \geq 0 & y_i \geq 0 & \quad\text{and}\quad & y_i \frac{\partial Z}{\partial y_i} = 0 \end{aligned}$$

are identical with (20.14), the Kuhn-Tucker conditions are expressible also in terms of the Lagrangean function Z (as against Z^*). Note that, by switching from Z^* to Z, we can not only arrive at the Kuhn-Tucker conditions more directly, but also identify the expression $r_i - g^i(x_1, x_2, x_3)$—which was left nameless in (20.14)—as the partial derivative $\partial Z/\partial y_i$. In the subsequent discussion, therefore, we shall only use the (20.16) version of the Kuhn-Tucker conditions, based on the Lagrangean function Z.

interpretation of the Kuhn-Tucker conditions   Parts of the Kuhn-Tucker conditions (20.16) are merely a restatement of certain aspects of the given problem. Thus the conditions $x_j \geq 0$ merely repeat the nonnegativity restrictions, and the conditions $\partial Z/\partial y_i \geq 0$ merely reiterate the constraints. To include these in (20.16), however, has the important advantage of revealing more clearly the remarkable symmetry between the two types of variables, x_j (choice variables) and y_i (Lagrange multipliers). To each variable in each category, there corresponds a marginal condition—$\partial Z/\partial x_j \leq 0$ or $\partial Z/\partial y_i \geq 0$—to be satisfied by the optimal solution. Each of the variables must be nonnegative as well. And, finally, each variable is characterized by complementary slackness in relation to a particular partial derivative of the Lagrangean function Z. This means that, for each x_j, we must find in the optimal solution that *either* the marginal condition holds as an equality, as in the classical context, *or* the choice variable in question must take a zero value, *or* both. Analogously, for each y_i, we must find in the optimal solution that *either* the marginal condition holds as an equality—meaning that the ith constraint is exactly fulfilled—or the Lagrange multiplier vanishes, *or* both.

An even more explicit interpretation is possible, when we look at the expanded expressions for $\partial Z/\partial x_j$ and $\partial Z/\partial y_i$ in (20.16). Assume the problem to be the familiar production problem. Then we have

$$f_j \equiv \text{the marginal gross profit of the } j\text{th product}$$
$$y_i \equiv \text{the shadow price of the } i\text{th resource}$$
$$g_j^i \equiv \text{the amount of the } i\text{th resource used up in producing the marginal}$$
$$\text{unit of the } j\text{th product}$$
$$y_i g_j^i \equiv \text{the marginal imputed cost of the } i\text{th resource incurred in}$$
$$\text{producing a unit of the } j\text{th product}$$
$$\sum_i y_i g_j^i \equiv \text{the aggregate marginal imputed cost of the } j\text{th product}$$

Thus the marginal condition

$$\frac{\partial Z}{\partial x_j} = f_j - \sum_i y_i g_j^i \leq 0$$

requires that the marginal gross profit of the jth product be no greater than its aggregate marginal imputed cost. The complementary-slackness condition then means that, if the optimal solution calls for the active production of the jth product ($\bar{x}_j > 0$), the marginal gross profit must be exactly equal to the aggregate marginal imputed cost ($\partial Z/\partial \bar{x}_j = 0$), as would be the situation in the classical optimization problem. If, on the other hand, the marginal gross profit optimally falls short of the aggregate imputed cost ($\partial Z/\partial \bar{x}_j < 0$), that product must not be produced ($\bar{x}_j = 0$).† This latter situation is something that can never occur in the classical context, for if the marginal gross profit is less than the marginal imputed cost, then the output should in that framework be reduced all the way to the level where the marginal condition is satisfied as an equality. What causes the situation of $\partial Z/\partial \bar{x}_j < 0$ to qualify as an optimal one here, is the explicit specification of nonnegativity in the present framework. For then the most we can do in the way of output reduction is to lower production to the level $\bar{x}_j = 0$, and if we still find $\partial Z/\partial \bar{x}_j < 0$ at the zero output, we stop there anyway.

As for the remaining conditions, which relate to the variables y_i, their meanings are even easier to perceive. First of all, the marginal condition $\partial Z/\partial y_i \geq 0$ merely requires the firm to stay within the capacity limitation of every resource in the plant. The complementary-slackness condition then

---

† Note that, given the equation $ab = 0$, where a and b are real numbers, we can legitimately infer that $a \neq 0$ implies $b = 0$, but it is not true that $a = 0$ implies $b \neq 0$, since $b = 0$ is also consistent with $a = 0$.

stipulates that, if the ith resource is not fully used in the optimal solution ($\partial Z/\partial \bar{y}_i > 0$), the shadow price of that resource—which is never allowed to be negative—must be set equal to zero ($\bar{y}_i = 0$). On the other hand, if a resource has a positive shadow price in the optimal solution ($\bar{y}_i > 0$), then it is perforce a fully utilized resource ($\partial Z/\partial \bar{y}_i = 0$).

It is also possible, of course, to take the Lagrange-multiplier value $\bar{y}_i$ to be a measure of how the optimal value of the objective function reacts to a slight relaxation of the ith constraint (see Sec. 12.2). In that light, complementary slackness would mean that, if the ith constraint is optimally not binding ($\partial Z/\partial \bar{y}_i > 0$), then relaxing that particular constraint will not affect the optimal value of the gross profit ($\bar{y}_i = 0$)—just as loosening a belt which is not constricting one's waist to begin with will not produce any greater comfort. If, on the other hand, a slight relaxation of the ith constraint (increasing the endowment of the ith resource) does increase the gross profit ($\bar{y}_i > 0$), then that resource constraint must in fact be binding in the optimal solution ($\partial Z/\partial \bar{y}_i = 0$).

the n-variable m-constraint case   The above discussion can be generalized in a straightforward manner to the maximization problem given in (20.1) or (20.1′). Since there are now n choice variables and m constraints, the Lagrangean function Z will appear in the more general form

$$(20.17) \qquad Z = f(x_1, x_2, \ldots, x_n) + \sum_{i=1}^{m} y_i[r_i - g^i(x_1, x_2, \ldots, x_n)]$$

And the Kuhn-Tucker conditions will simply be

$$(20.18) \qquad \frac{\partial Z}{\partial x_j} \leq 0 \qquad x_j \geq 0 \qquad \text{and} \qquad x_j \frac{\partial Z}{\partial x_j} = 0$$
$$\frac{\partial Z}{\partial y_i} \geq 0 \qquad y_i \geq 0 \qquad \text{and} \qquad y_i \frac{\partial Z}{\partial y_i} = 0 \qquad \text{[maximization]}$$
$$\begin{pmatrix} i = 1, 2, \ldots, m \\ j = 1, 2, \ldots, n \end{pmatrix}$$

Here, in order to avoid a cluttered appearance, we have not written out the expanded expressions for the partial derivatives $\partial Z/\partial x_j$ and $\partial Z/\partial y_i$. But the reader is urged to write them out for a more detailed view of the Kuhn-Tucker conditions, similar to what was given in (20.16). Note that, aside from the change in the dimension of the problem, the Kuhn-Tucker conditions remain entirely the same as in the three-variable, two-constraint case discussed before. The interpretation of these conditions should naturally also remain the same.

What if the problem is one of *minimization*, as in (20.2) or (20.2′)? One way of handling it is to convert the problem into a maximization problem and then apply (20.18). To minimize C is equivalent to *maximizing* $-C$, so such a conversion is always feasible. But we must, of course, also reverse the constraint inequalities by multiplying every constraint through by -1. Instead of going through the conversion process, however, we may—again using the Lagrangean function Z as defined in (20.17)—directly apply the minimization version of the Kuhn-Tucker conditions as follows:

$$(20.19) \quad \begin{array}{ccccc} \dfrac{\partial Z}{\partial x_j} \geq 0 & x_j \geq 0 & \text{and} & x_j \dfrac{\partial Z}{\partial x_j} = 0 & \\[2ex] \dfrac{\partial Z}{\partial y_i} \leq 0 & y_i \geq 0 & \text{and} & y_i \dfrac{\partial Z}{\partial y_i} = 0 & \end{array} \quad \text{[minimization]}$$

$$\begin{pmatrix} i = 1, 2, \ldots, m \\ j = 1, 2, \ldots, n \end{pmatrix}$$

This the reader should compare with (20.18).

Reading (20.18) and (20.19) horizontally (*row*wise), we see that the Kuhn-Tucker conditions for both maximization and minimization problems consist of a set of conditions relating to the choice variables x_j (first row), and another set relating to the Lagrange multipliers y_i (second row). Reading them vertically (*column*wise), on the other hand, we note that, for each x_j and y_i, there is a marginal condition (first column), a nonnegativity restriction (second column), and a complementary-slackness condition (third column). In any given problem, the marginal conditions pertaining to the choice variables always differ, as a group, from the marginal conditions for the Lagrange multipliers in the sense of inequality they take. Also, the marginal conditions for a maximization problem always differ, as a group, from those of a minimization problem in the sense of inequality they take.

Subject to a proviso to be explained in the next section, the Kuhn-Tucker maximum conditions (20.18) and minimum conditions (20.19) are necessary conditions for a local maximum and a local minimum, respectively. But since a global maximum (minimum) must also be a local maximum (minimum), the Kuhn-Tucker conditions can also be taken as necessary conditions for a global maximum (minimum), subject to the same proviso.

an example   Let us check whether the Kuhn-Tucker conditions are satisfied by the solution in Example 1 of Sec. 20.1, as illustrated in Fig. 20.1a. The Lagrangean function for this problem is

$$Z = (x_1 - 4)^2 + (x_2 - 4)^2 + y_1(6 - 2x_1 - 3x_2) + y_2(-12 + 3x_1 + 2x_2)$$

Since the problem is one of minimization, the appropriate conditions are (20.19), which include the four marginal conditions

$$\frac{\partial Z}{\partial x_1} = 2(x_1 - 4) - 2y_1 + 3y_2 \geq 0$$

$$\frac{\partial Z}{\partial x_2} = 2(x_2 - 4) - 3y_1 + 2y_2 \geq 0$$

$$\frac{\partial Z}{\partial y_1} = 6 - 2x_1 - 3x_2 \leq 0$$

$$\frac{\partial Z}{\partial y_2} = -12 + 3x_1 + 2x_2 \leq 0$$

plus the nonnegativity and complementary-slackness conditions. The question is: Can we find nonnegative values $\bar{y}_1$ and $\bar{y}_2$ which, together with the optimal values $\bar{x}_1 = 2\frac{2}{13} = \frac{28}{13}$ and $\bar{x}_2 = 2\frac{10}{13} = \frac{36}{13}$, will satisfy all those conditions?

Given that $\bar{x}_1$ and $\bar{x}_2$ are both nonzero, complementary slackness dictates that $\partial Z/\partial x_1 = 0$ and $\partial Z/\partial x_2 = 0$. Thus, after substituting the $\bar{x}_1$ and $\bar{x}_2$ values into the first two marginal conditions, the latter become two equations

$$-2y_1 + 3y_2 = \tfrac{48}{13}$$
$$-3y_1 + 2y_2 = \tfrac{32}{13}$$

with solution $\bar{y}_1 = 0$, and $\bar{y}_2 = \frac{16}{13} = 1\frac{3}{13}$, which are nonnegative, as required. Since these values, together with $\bar{x}_1$ and $\bar{x}_2$, imply that $\partial Z/\partial \bar{x}_1 = 0$, $\partial Z/\partial \bar{x}_2 = 0$, $\partial Z/\partial \bar{y}_1 < 0$, and $\partial Z/\partial \bar{y}_2 = 0$, which satisfy the marginal inequalities as well as the complementary-slackness conditions, all the Kuhn-Tucker minimum conditions are satisfied.

EXERCISE 20.2

1   Draw a set of diagrams similar to Fig. 20.3 for the minimization case, and deduce a set of necessary conditions for a local minimum corresponding to (20.4) through (20.6). Then condense these conditions into a single statement similar to (20.7).

2   (a) Show that, in (20.18), instead of writing

$$y_i \frac{\partial Z}{\partial y_i} = 0 \qquad (i = 1, \ldots, m)$$

as a set of m separate conditions, it is sufficient to write a single equation in the form of

$$\sum_{i=1}^{m} y_i \frac{\partial Z}{\partial y_i} = 0$$

(b) Can we do the same for the set of conditions

$$x_j \frac{\partial Z}{\partial x_j} = 0 \qquad (j = 1, \ldots, n)$$

3 Using the reasoning of the preceding problem, which set (or sets) of conditions in (20.19) can be condensed into a single equation?

4 Given the minimization problem (20.2), and using the Lagrangean function (20.17), take the derivatives $\partial Z/\partial x_j$ and $\partial Z/\partial y_i$ and write out the expanded version of the Kuhn-Tucker minimum conditions (20.19).

5 Convert the minimization problem (20.2) into a maximization problem, formulate the Lagrangean function, take the derivatives with respect to x_j and y_i, and apply the Kuhn-Tucker maximum conditions (20.18). Are the results consistent with those obtained in the preceding problem?

6 Check the applicability of the Kuhn-Tucker conditions to Example 2 of Sec. 20.1 as follows:
(a) Write the Lagrangean function and the Kuhn-Tucker conditions.
(b) From the solution given in Fig. 20.1b, find the optimal values of $\partial Z/\partial y_i$ ($i = 1, 2, 3$). What can we then conclude about $\bar{y}_i$?
(c) Now find the optimal values of $\partial Z/\partial x_1$ and $\partial Z/\partial x_2$.
(d) Are all the Kuhn-Tucker conditions satisfied?

20.3 The Constraint Qualification

In the last section, it was pointed out that the Kuhn-Tucker conditions are necessary conditions *only if* a particular proviso is satisfied. That proviso, called the *constraint qualification*, imposes a certain restriction on the constraint functions of a nonlinear program, for the specific purpose of ruling out certain irregularities on the boundary of the feasible set, that would invalidate the Kuhn-Tucker conditions should the optimal solution occur there.

irregularities at boundary points   Let us first illustrate the nature of such irregularities by means of some concrete examples.

Example 1   Maximize $\pi = x_1$
            subject to $x_2 - (1 - x_1)^3 \le 0$
            and $x_1, x_2 \ge 0$

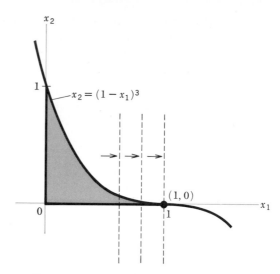

FIGURE 20.4

As shown in Fig. 20.4, the feasible region is the set of points that lie in the first quadrant on or below the curve $x_2 = (1 - x_1)^3$. Since the objective function directs us to maximize x_1, the optimal solution is the point $(1,0)$. But this solution fails to satisfy the Kuhn-Tucker maximum conditions. To check this, we first write the Lagrangean function

$$Z = x_1 + y_1[-x_2 + (1 - x_1)^3]$$

As the first marginal condition, we should then have

$$\frac{\partial Z}{\partial x_1} = 1 - 3y_1(1 - x_1)^2 \leq 0$$

In fact, since $\bar{x}_1 = 1$ is positive, complementary slackness requires that this derivative vanish when evaluated at the point $(1,0)$. However, the actual value we get happens to be $\partial Z/\partial \bar{x}_1 = 1$, thus violating the above marginal condition.

The reason for this anomaly is that the optimal solution, $(1,0)$, occurs in this example at an outward-pointing *cusp*, which constitutes one type of irregularity that can invalidate the Kuhn-Tucker conditions at a boundary optimal solution. A cusp is a sharp point formed when a curve takes a sudden reversal in direction, such that the slope of the curve on one side of the point is the same as the slope of the curve on the other side of the point. Here, the boundary of the feasible region at first follows the constraint curve, but when the point $(1,0)$ is reached, it takes an abrupt turn westward and follows the trail of the horizontal axis thereafter. Since the slopes of both the curved side and the horizontal side of the boundary are zero at the point $(1,0)$, that point is a cusp.

Mathematical Programming and Game Theory

Cusps are the most frequently cited culprit for the failure of the Kuhn-Tucker conditions, but the truth is that the presence of a cusp is neither necessary nor sufficient to cause those conditions to fail at an optimal solution. The following two examples will confirm this.

Example 2   To the problem of the preceding example, let us add a new constraint

$$2x_1 + x_2 \leq 2$$

whose border, $x_2 = 2 - 2x_1$, plots as a straight line with slope -2 which passes through the optimal point in Fig. 20.4. Clearly, the feasible region remains the same as before, and so does the optimal solution at the cusp. But if we write the new Lagrangean function

$$Z = x_1 + y_1[-x_2 + (1 - x_1)^3] + y_2[2 - 2x_1 - x_2]$$

and the marginal conditions

$$\frac{\partial Z}{\partial x_1} = 1 - 3y_1(1 - x_1)^2 - 2y_2 \leq 0$$

$$\frac{\partial Z}{\partial x_2} = -y_1 - y_2 \leq 0$$

$$\frac{\partial Z}{\partial y_1} = -x_2 + (1 - x_1)^3 \geq 0$$

$$\frac{\partial Z}{\partial y_2} = 2 - 2x_1 - x_2 \geq 0$$

it turns out that the values $\bar{x}_1 = 1$, $\bar{x}_2 = 0$, $\bar{y}_1 = 1$, and $\bar{y}_2 = \frac{1}{2}$ do satisfy the above four inequalities, as well as the nonnegativity and complementary-slackness conditions. As a matter of fact, $\bar{y}_1$ can be assigned any nonnegative value (not just 1), and all the conditions can still be satisfied—which goes to show that the optimal value of a Lagrange multiplier is not necessarily unique. More importantly, however, this example shows that the Kuhn-Tucker conditions can remain valid despite the cusp.

Example 3   The feasible region of the problem

Maximize	$\pi = x_2 - x_1^2$
subject to	$-(10 - x_1^2 - x_2)^3 \leq 0$
	$-x_1 \leq -2$
and	$x_1, x_2 \geq 0$

as shown in Fig. 20.5, contains no cusp anywhere. Yet, at the optimal solution, (2,6), the Kuhn-Tucker conditions nonetheless fail to hold. For, with the

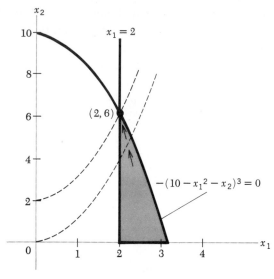

FIGURE 20.5

Lagrangean function

$$Z = x_2 - x_1^2 + y_1(10 - x_1^2 - x_2)^3 + y_2(-2 + x_1)$$

the second marginal condition would require that

$$\frac{\partial Z}{\partial x_2} = 1 - 3y_1(10 - x_1^2 - x_2)^2 \le 0$$

Indeed, since $\bar{x}_2$ is positive, this derivative should vanish when evaluated at the point (2,6). But actually we get $\partial Z/\partial \bar{x}_2 = 1$, regardless of the value assigned to y_1. Thus the Kuhn-Tucker conditions can fail even in the absence of a cusp—nay, even when the feasible region is a convex set as in Fig. 20.5. The fundamental reason why cusps are neither necessary nor sufficient for the failure of the Kuhn-Tucker conditions is that the irregularities referred to above relate, not to the shape of the feasible region per se, but to the forms of the constraint functions themselves.

the constraint qualification   Boundary irregularities—cusp or no cusp—will not occur if a certain constraint qualification is satisfied.

To explain this, let $\bar{x} \equiv (\bar{x}_1, \bar{x}_2, \ldots, \bar{x}_n)$ be a (solution) point at the boundary of the feasible region and let $dx \equiv (dx_1, dx_2, \ldots, dx_n)$ represent a particular direction of movement from the said boundary point. The direction-of-movement interpretation of the vector dx is perfectly in line with our earlier interpretation of a vector as a directed line segment (an arrow), but here, the point of departure is the point $\bar{x}$ instead of the point of origin, and so the vector dx is *not* in the nature of a radius vector. We shall now impose two requirements on the vector dx. First, if the jth choice variable has a zero value at the point $\bar{x}$, then we shall only permit a nonnegative change on the x_j axis, that is,

$$(20.20) \qquad dx_j \geq 0 \quad \text{if} \quad \bar{x}_j = 0$$

Secondly, if the ith constraint is exactly fulfilled at the point $\bar{x}$, then we shall only allow values of $dx_1, \ldots, dx_n$ such that the value of the constraint function $g^i(\bar{x})$ will not increase (for a maximization problem) or will not decrease (for a minimization problem), that is,

$$(20.21) \qquad dg^i(\bar{x}) = g_1^i \, dx_1 + g_2^i \, dx_2 + \cdots + g_n^i \, dx_n \quad \begin{cases} \leq 0 \text{ (maximization)} \\ \geq 0 \text{ (minimization)} \end{cases}$$

$$\text{if} \qquad g^i(\bar{x}) = r_i$$

where all the partial derivatives g_j^i are to be evaluated at $\bar{x}$. If a vector dx satisfies (20.20) and (20.21), we shall call it a *test vector*. Finally, if there exists a differentiable arc that (1) emanates from the point $\bar{x}$, (2) is contained entirely in the feasible region, and (3) is tangent to a given test vector, we shall call it a *qualifying arc* for that test vector. With this background, the constraint qualification can be stated simply as follows:

> The constraint qualification is satisfied if, for any point $\bar{x}$ on the boundary of the feasible region, there exists a qualifying arc for every test vector dx.

Example 4   We shall show that the optimal point (1,0) of Example 1 in Fig. 20.4, which fails the Kuhn-Tucker conditions, also fails the constraint qualification. At that point, $\bar{x}_2 = 0$, thus the test vectors must satisfy

$$dx_2 \geq 0 \qquad \text{[by (20.20)]}$$

Moreover, since the (only) constraint, $g^1 = x_2 - (1 - x_1)^3 \leq 0$, is exactly fulfilled at (1,0), we must let

$$g_1^1 \, dx_1 + g_2^1 \, dx_2 = 3(1 - \bar{x}_1)^2 \, dx_1 + dx_2 = dx_2 \leq 0 \qquad \text{[by (20.21)]}$$

These two requirements imply that we must let $dx_2 = 0$. On the other hand, we are free to choose dx_1. Thus the vector $(dx_1, dx_2) = (2,0)$ is an acceptable test vector. But this vector would appear as an arrow that starts from (1,0) and points in the due-east direction in Fig. 20.4 (not drawn), for which there exists no qualifying arc. Hence the optimal solution point violates the constraint qualification.

Example 5   Referring to Example 2 above, let us now illustrate that, after an additional constraint $2x_1 + x_2 \leq 2$ is added to Fig. 20.4, the point $(1,0)$ will satisfy the constraint qualification, thereby revalidating the Kuhn-Tucker conditions.

As in Example 4, we have to require $dx_2 \geq 0$ (because $\bar{x}_2 = 0$) and $dx_2 \leq 0$ (because the first constraint is exactly fulfilled); thus, $dx_2 = 0$. But the second constraint is also exactly fulfilled, thereby requiring

$$g_1^2 \, dx_1 + g_2^2 \, dx_2 = 2 \, dx_1 + dx_2 = 2 \, dx_1 \leq 0 \qquad \text{[by (20.21)]}$$

With nonpositive dx_1 and zero dx_2, the only admissible test vectors—aside from the null vector itself—are those pointing in the due-west direction in Fig. 20.4 from $(1,0)$. All of these would lie along the horizontal axis in the feasible region, and there can certainly be found a qualifying arc for each test vector. Hence, this time the constraint qualification indeed is satisfied.

linear constraints   Earlier, in Example 3, it was demonstrated that convexity of the feasible set does not guarantee the validity of the Kuhn-Tucker conditions as necessary conditions. However, if the feasible region is a convex set formed by *linear* constraints only, then the constraint qualification will invariably be met, and the Kuhn-Tucker conditions will always hold at an optimal solution. This being the case, we need never worry about boundary irregularities when dealing with a nonlinear program with linear constraints, or, as a special case, a linear program per se.

Example 6   Let us illustrate the linear-constraint result in the two-variable two-constraint framework. For a maximization problem, the linear constraints can be written as

$$a_{11}x_1 + a_{12}x_2 \leq r_1$$
$$a_{21}x_1 + a_{22}x_2 \leq r_2$$

where we shall take all the parameters to be positive. Then, as indicated in Fig. 20.6, the first constraint border will have a slope of $-a_{11}/a_{12} < 0$, and the second, a slope of $-a_{21}/a_{22} < 0$. The boundary points of the shaded feasible region fall into the following five types: (1) the point of origin, where the two axes intersect, (2) points that lie on one axis segment, such as J and S, (3) points at the intersection of one axis and one constraint border, namely, K and R, (4) points lying on a single constraint border, such as L and N, and (5) the point of intersection of the two constraints, M. We may briefly examine each type in turn with reference to the satisfaction of the constraint qualification.

(1) At the origin, no constraint is exactly fulfilled, so we may ignore (20.21). But since $x_1 = x_2 = 0$, we must choose test vectors with $dx_1 \geq 0$ and

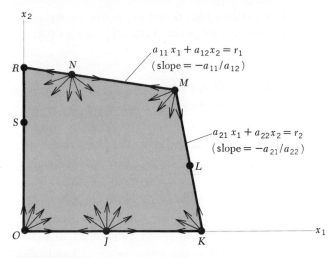

FIGURE 20.6

$dx_2 \geq 0$, by (20.20). Hence all test vectors from the origin must point in the due-east, due-north, or northeast directions, as depicted in Fig. 20.6. These vectors all happen to fall within the feasible set, and a qualifying arc clearly can be found for each.

(2) At a point like J, we can again ignore (20.21). The fact that $x_2 = 0$ means that we must choose $dx_2 \geq 0$, but our choice of dx_1 is free. Hence all vectors would be acceptable except those pointing southward ($dx_2 < 0$). Again all such vectors fall within the feasible region, and there exists a qualifying arc for each. The analysis of point S is similar.

(3) At points K and R, both (20.20) and (20.21) must be considered. Specifically, at K, we have to choose $dx_2 \geq 0$ since $x_2 = 0$, so that we must rule out all southward arrows. The second constraint being exactly fulfilled, moreover, the test vectors for point K must satisfy

$$(20.22) \qquad g_1^2 \, dx_1 + g_2^2 \, dx_2 = a_{21} \, dx_1 + a_{22} \, dx_2 \leq 0$$

Since at K we also have $a_{21}x_1 + a_{22}x_2 = r_2$ (second constraint border), however, we may add this equality to (20.22) and modify the restriction on the test vectors to the form

$$(20.22') \qquad a_{21}(x_1 + dx_1) + a_{22}(x_2 + dx_2) \leq r_2$$

Interpreting $(x_j + dx_j)$ to be the new value of x_j attained at the arrowhead of a test vector, we may construe (20.22') to mean that all test vectors must have their arrowheads located on or below the second constraint border. Consequently, all these vectors must again fall within the feasible region, so that a qualifying arc can be found for each. The analysis of point R is analogous.

(4) At points like L and N, neither variable is zero and (20.20) can be ignored. However, for point N, (20.21) dictates that

$$(20.23) \qquad g_1^1 \, dx_1 + g_2^1 \, dx_2 = a_{11} \, dx_1 + a_{12} \, dx_2 \leq 0$$

Since point N satisfies $a_{11}x_1 + a_{12}x_2 = r_1$ (first constraint border), we may add this equality to (20.23) and write

$$(20.23') \qquad a_{11}(x_1 + dx_1) + a_{12}(x_2 + dx_2) \leq r_1$$

This would require the test vectors to have arrowheads located on or below the first constraint border in Fig. 20.6. Thus we obtain essentially the same kind of result encountered in the other cases. The analysis of point L is analogous.

(5) At point M, we may again disregard (20.20), but this time (20.21) requires all test vectors to satisfy both (20.22) and (20.23). Since we may modify the latter conditions to the forms in (20.22') and (20.23'), all test vectors must now have their arrowheads located on or below the first as well as the second constraint borders. The result thus again duplicates those of the previous cases.

In this example, it so happens that, for every type of boundary point considered, the test vectors all lie within the feasible region. While this locational feature makes the qualifying arcs easy to find, it is by no means a prerequisite for their existence. In a problem with a nonlinear constraint border, in particular, the constraint border itself may serve as a qualifying arc for some test vector that lies outside of the feasible region. An example of this can be found in one of the problems in Exercise 20.3.

EXERCISE 20.3

1   Check whether the solution point $(\bar{x}_1, \bar{x}_2) = (2,6)$ in Example 3 satisfies the constraint qualification.

2   Maximize $\pi = x_1$
    subject to $x_1^2 + x_2^2 \leq 1$
    and $x_1, x_2 \geq 0$

Solve graphically and check whether the optimal-solution point satisfies (a) the constraint qualification, and (b) the Kuhn-Tucker maximum conditions.

3   Minimize $C = x_1$
    subject to $x_1^2 - x_2 \geq 0$
    and $x_1, x_2 \geq 0$

Solve graphically. Does the optimal solution occur at a cusp? Check whether the optimal solution satisfies (a) the constraint qualification, and (b) the Kuhn-Tucker minimum conditions.

4   Minimize $C = 2x_1 + x_2$
     subject to $x_1{}^2 - 4x_1 + x_2 \geq 0$
                   $-2x_1 - 3x_2 \geq -12$
     and $x_1, x_2 \geq 0$

Solve graphically for the global minimum, and check whether the optimal solution satisfies (a) the constraint qualification, and (b) the Kuhn-Tucker conditions. (*Hint:* The feasible region is identical with that depicted in Fig. 20.2.)

5   Minimize $C = x_1$
     subject to $-x_2 - (1 - x_1)^3 \geq 0$
     and $x_1, x_2 \geq 0$

Show that (a) the optimal solution $(\bar{x}_1, \bar{x}_2) = (1,0)$ does not satisfy the Kuhn-Tucker conditions, but (b) by introducing a new multiplier $y_0 \geq 0$, and modifying the Lagrangean function (20.17) to the form

$$Z_0 = y_0 f(x_1, x_2, \ldots, x_n) + \sum_{i=1}^{m} y_i[r_i - g^i(x_1, x_2, \ldots, x_n)]$$

the Kuhn-Tucker conditions can be satisfied at (1,0). (*Note:* The Kuhn-Tucker conditions on the multipliers extend only to $y_1, \ldots, y_m$, but not to y_0.)

20.4   Kuhn-Tucker Sufficiency Theorem: Concave Programming

Our discussion hitherto has been concerned with *necessary* conditions for a maximum or minimum in nonlinear programming. Necessary conditions are useful as a screening device to reject unqualified candidates for optimal solution. In nonlinear programming, for instance, any interior point in the feasible region that fails the Kuhn-Tucker conditions cannot possibly be an optimal solution. Similarly, a boundary point that satisfies the constraint qualification but fails the Kuhn-Tucker conditions can safely be ruled out as an optimal solution. If a point x^0 does meet the necessary conditions, however, we should not then conclude that x^0 constitutes an optimal solution, because certain unqualified candidates may very well pass the screening test, the way an inflection point can satisfy the first-order condition $dy/dx = 0$ in the simplest optimization problem. In other

words, with the necessary conditions as a fishing net, we may catch genuine optimal solutions as well as spurious ones.

To have a *sufficient* condition is a different story, for if a point $\bar{x}$ satisfies a sufficient condition for a maximum, then that point must maximize the objective function. In this sense, sufficient conditions provide a more definitive type of test. But they also happen to have their own shortcoming, namely, a sufficient condition as such may not be necessary, so that a genuine optimal solution may nonetheless fail to satisfy the sufficient condition. In other words, with a sufficient condition as a fishing net, we may fail to catch a true optimal solution.

The most gratifying situation is of course one where we possess a necessary-and-sufficient condition. All optimal solutions can be caught by means of such a condition, and yet we do not run the risk of admitting any unqualified candidates.

In this section, we shall show that, under certain circumstances, the Kuhn-Tucker conditions can be regarded as *sufficient* conditions for an extremum, or they may even emerge as *necessary-and-sufficient* conditions.

the Kuhn-Tucker sufficiency theorem   In classical optimization problems, the statement of the sufficient condition for an extremum involves the concept of second derivatives, which, in general, have to do with the concavity and convexity of the objective function. Here, in nonlinear programming, the statement of sufficient conditions will again involve the notions of concavity and convexity, except that these notions will now be applied not only to the objective function $f(x)$, but also to the constraint functions $g^i(x)$.

For the *maximization* problem, Kuhn and Tucker offer the following statement of sufficient conditions (sufficiency theorem):

> Given the nonlinear program
>
> Maximize $\pi = f(x)$
> subject to $g^i(x) \leq r_i$ $(i = 1, 2, \ldots, m)$
> and $x \geq 0$
>
> if the following conditions are satisfied:
>
> (a)   the objective function $f(x)$ is differentiable and *concave* in the non-negative orthant
> (b)   each constraint function $g^i(x)$ is differentiable and *convex* in the nonnegative orthant
> (c)   the point $\bar{x}$ satisfies the Kuhn-Tucker maximum conditions
>
> then $\bar{x}$ gives a global maximum of $\pi = f(x)$.

Note that, in this theorem, the constraint qualification is nowhere mentioned. This is because we have already assumed, in condition (c), that the Kuhn-

Tucker conditions are satisfied at $\bar{x}$ and, consequently, the question of the constraint qualification is no longer an issue.

As it stands, the above theorem indicates that conditions (a), (b), and (c) are sufficient to establish $\bar{x}$ to be an optimal solution. Looking at it differently, however, we may also interpret it to mean that, given (a) and (b), then the Kuhn-Tucker maximum conditions are sufficient for a maximum. In the preceding section, we learned that the Kuhn-Tucker conditions, though not necessary per se, become necessary when the constraint qualification is satisfied. Combining this information with the sufficiency theorem, we may now state that, if the constraint qualification is satisfied and if conditions (a) and (b) are realized, then the Kuhn-Tucker maximum conditions will be *necessary and sufficient* for a maximum. This would be the case, for instance, when all the constraints are linear inequalities, which is sufficient for satisfying the constraint qualification. Later, we shall introduce another set of circumstances that will guarantee the satisfaction of the constraint qualification, even if the $g^i(x)$ functions are not all linear.

The maximization problem dealt with in the sufficiency theorem above is often referred to as *concave programming*. This name arises because Kuhn and Tucker adopt the $\geq$ inequality instead of the $\leq$ inequality in every constraint, so that condition (b) would require the $g^i(x)$ functions to be *all concave*, like the $f(x)$ function. But we have modified the formulation in order to achieve consistency with our earlier discussion of linear programming. Though different in form, the two formulations are of course equivalent in substance.

As stated above, the sufficiency theorem deals only with maximization problems. But adaptation to *minimization* problems is by no means difficult. Aside from the appropriate changes in the theorem to reflect the reversal of the problem itself, all we have to do is to interchange the two words *concave* and *convex* in conditions (a) and (b) and to use the Kuhn-Tucker *minimum* conditions in condition (c). (See Exercise 20.4-1.)

Since the Kuhn-Tucker sufficiency theorem is relatively easy to prove, we shall reproduce the proof below. To facilitate that, however, we shall first make some preliminary remarks about concave and convex functions.

remarks on concave and convex functions   The first remark has to do with the definition of a concave function. In Chap. 11 (Fig. 11.5), the definition of concavity was based on a comparison of the height of a line segment and the height of an arc. When the function in question is differentiable, however, we may alternatively base the definition of concavity on the first derivative(s) of the function. In the one-variable case, a function $f(w)$ is concave if, for a given point $\bar{w}$, and for any other point w in the domain, we have

$$(20.24) \qquad f(w) \leq f(\bar{w}) + f'(\bar{w})(w - \bar{w})$$

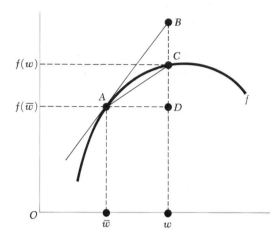

FIGURE 20.7

In Fig. 20.7, let A be a given point on a concave curve f, with height equal to $f(\overline{w})$ and with tangent line AB. As we move rightward on the horizontal axis from $\overline{w}$ to some point $w > \overline{w}$, the concave curve (if *strictly* concave, as drawn) would curl progressively away from the tangent line AB, so that the point C, with a height equal to $f(w)$, will lie below point B. In that case, the slope of line AC will be less than that of AB. On the other hand, if the curve is *nonstrictly* concave, then it may contain a straight line segment, so that, say, the curve segment AC may happen to be linear and coincident with AB. If so, the slope of AC is equal to that of AB. Taken together, these two situations imply that

$$\left(\text{Slope of } AC = \frac{DC}{AD} = \right)\frac{f(w) - f(\overline{w})}{w - \overline{w}} \le (\text{slope of } AB =)f'(\overline{w})$$

which leads directly to (20.24). Since (20.24) stipulates that, for any point A on the curve, slope of $AC \le$ slope of tangent AB, what it does is essentially to require the graph of the concave function $f(w)$ to lie everywhere on or below each of its tangent lines.

A similar definition can be stated for a differentiable concave function of several variables, $f(x) = f(x_1, x_2, \ldots, x_n)$. Such a function is concave if, for a given point $\overline{x}$ and for any other point x in the domain, we have

$$(20.25) \qquad f(x) \le f(\overline{x}) + \sum_{j=1}^{n} f_j(\overline{x})(x_j - \overline{x}_j)$$

where $f_j(\overline{x})$ means the partial derivative f_j evaluated at the point $\overline{x}$.† This

---

† To define a *convex* function, the inequality in (20.25) should be reversed.

Mathematical Programming and Game Theory

statement requires the graph of the concave function $f(x)$ to lie everywhere on or below each of its tangent planes or hyperplanes.

The second remark to be made here is simply that the sum of concave functions is also a concave function. This assertion is as easy to prove as it is intuitively appealing. All that one has to do is to apply (20.25) to a second concave function $g(x)$ to get a similar inequality, and then add the latter to (20.25). The result will indicate that the sum $f(x) + g(x)$ also satisfies the definition of a concave function. (See Exercise 20.4-3.) It follows naturally that the sum of convex functions is also a convex function.

Example 1   Is the function $f(x_1, x_2) = (x_1 - a)^2 + (x_2 - b)^2$ convex? Let us first expand the expression and write

$$f(x_1, x_2) = x_1^2 - 2ax_1 + a^2 + x_2^2 - 2bx_2 + b^2$$

The first term x_1^2 (a U-shaped curve when plotted against x_1) is convex in x_1, but independent of x_2. The latter means that x_1^2 is a constant function of x_2, and hence a linear function of x_2; as such, it can be taken as a convex function of x_2 as well. In short, x_1^2 is convex in the two variables x_1 and x_2. By the same argument, the term x_2^2 is also convex in x_1 and x_2. Turning to the remaining terms, we note that they are all linear and thus convex in x_1 and x_2. The consequence is that $f(x_1, x_2)$ is just a sum of convex functions, and must itself be a convex function of the two variables x_1 and x_2.

If this particular function happens to be the objective function of a *minimization* problem, it will satisfy condition (*a*) of the Kuhn-Tucker sufficiency theorem. In a *maximization* problem, in contrast, this objective function violates condition (*a*). What if this function is viewed as a constraint function $g(x_1, x_2)$? In that case, it would be acceptable under condition (*b*) of the sufficiency theorem for a *maximization* problem, but not for a *minimization* problem.

Example 2   Is the function $g(x_1, x_2) = \ln x_1 - \exp(-x_2)$ concave? The log function is concave in x_1, and therefore also concave in the two variables x_1 and x_2. The exponential function $\exp(-x_2)$, showing exponential decay, is convex in x_2. Thus its negative is concave in x_2, and therefore also concave in the two variables x_1 and x_2. The function $g(x_1, x_2)$, being the sum of two concave functions, must also be concave in x_1 and x_2.

proof of the sufficiency theorem   For the maximization problem, the Lagrangean function can be expressed as

$$(20.26) \qquad Z = f(x) + \sum_{i=1}^{m} \bar{y}_i[r_i - g^i(x)] \qquad [\text{cf. (20.17)}]$$

Nonlinear Programming 725

where we have assigned the specific values $\bar{y}_i$ to the Lagrange multipliers, thereby making Z a function of the x_j variables alone. In line with conditions (a) and (b) of the sufficiency theorem, let us postulate $f(x)$ to be concave and each $g^i(x)$ to be convex, which makes each $-g^i(x)$ concave. Then Z, being a sum of concave functions, must also be concave in x. Applying (20.25) to it, therefore, we get

$$(20.27) \qquad Z(x) \leq Z(\bar{x}) + \sum_{j=1}^{n} \frac{\partial Z}{\partial \bar{x}_j} (x_j - \bar{x}_j)$$

where $\bar{x}$ is some specific point in the domain, and $\partial Z / \partial \bar{x}_j$ is the partial derivative $\partial Z / \partial x_j$ evaluated at $\bar{x}$. In particular, let us select as $\bar{x}$ and $\bar{y}$ those values of choice variables and Lagrange multipliers that satisfy the Kuhn-Tucker maximum conditions, in line with condition (c) of the sufficiency theorem. Then the $\sum$ expression in (20.27) can be shown to be nonpositive, so that its deletion will not upset the inequality, thereby enabling us to infer that $Z(x) \leq Z(\bar{x})$.

To see this, decompose the $\sum$ expression into two terms:

$$T_1 = \sum_{j=1}^{n} \frac{\partial Z}{\partial \bar{x}_j} x_j \qquad \text{and} \qquad T_2 = -\sum_{j=1}^{n} \frac{\partial Z}{\partial \bar{x}_j} \bar{x}_j$$

By virtue of complementary slackness at point $\bar{x}$, T_2 must vanish. As to T_1, which involves x_j rather than $\bar{x}_j$, so that complementary slackness does not apply, we can only be sure that $\partial Z / \partial \bar{x}_j \leq 0$ (marginal condition) and $x_j \geq 0$ (model specification) for every j. Thus T_1 is nonpositive. Adding up the two terms, we find the $\sum$ expression in (20.27) nonpositive, and therefore we can conclude that

$$(20.28) \qquad Z(x) \leq Z(\bar{x})$$

or, by reference to (20.26),

$$(20.28') \qquad f(x) + \sum_{i=1}^{m} \bar{y}_i[r_i - g^i(x)] \leq f(\bar{x}) + \sum_{i=1}^{m} \bar{y}_i[r_i - g^i(\bar{x})]$$

If we can show that the two $\sum$ expressions in (20.28') can be deleted without upsetting the inequality, then we can conclude that $f(x) \leq f(\bar{x})$, which will establish the claim that $\bar{x}$ maximizes the objective function $f(x)$. This indeed can be done. The $\sum$ expression on the left is necessarily nonnegative because, for each i, we have $\bar{y}_i \geq 0$ (nonnegativity) and $r_i - g^i(x) \geq 0$ (constraint specification). In contrast, the $\sum$ expression on the right must vanish, because $[r_i - g^i(\bar{x})]$ is nothing but $\partial Z / \partial \bar{y}_i$, so that complementary slackness applies. Consequently, $f(x) \leq f(\bar{x})$, and $\bar{x}$ is indeed the optimal solution.

The maximum value $\bar{\pi} = f(\bar{x})$ is a *global* maximum. One way of showing this is that the validity of the inequality $f(x) \leq f(\bar{x})$ does not hinge on x being located in any restricted neighborhood of $\bar{x}$. More formally, however, we may have recourse to the globality theorem introduced in Sec. 18.3. Our objective function is assumed to be differentiable and concave. As to the constraints, since each $g^i(x)$ is convex, the result in (18.7)—when properly generalized to the n-dimensional case—would indicate that the set

$$S_i^{\leq} \equiv \{x \mid g^i(x) \leq r_i\}$$

must be a convex set, in fact a closed convex set. Moreover, the feasible region is simply the intersection of the closed convex sets $S_i^{\leq}$, $i = 1, 2, \ldots, m$, so the feasible set is also a closed convex set. Consequently, the globality theorem is applicable, and any local maximum must be a global maximum. Note that, if the objective function $f(x)$ is *strictly* concave, then the global maximum will be unique.

In the above, by starting from the postulated conditions that (*a*) the $f(x)$ function is differentiable and concave, (*b*) each $g^i(x)$ function is differentiable and convex, and (*c*) point $\bar{x}$ satisfies the Kuhn-Tucker maximum conditions, we deduced that $\bar{x}$ does maximize π. The sufficiency theorem is therefore validated.

saddle point   The result in (20.28)—derived on the basis of a specifically chosen $\bar{y}$—means that, given $\bar{y}$, $\bar{x}$ *maximizes* the Lagrangean function Z among all admissible x. As it turns out, it is also true that, given $\bar{x}$, $\bar{y}$ *minimizes* Z among all admissible y. That is, we have in fact

(20.29) $Z(x, \bar{y}) \leq Z(\bar{x}, \bar{y}) \leq Z(\bar{x}, y)$

Since this situation is akin to the one depicted in Fig. 11.3*a*, the point $(\bar{x}, \bar{y})$ is called a *saddle point*, and $Z(\bar{x}, \bar{y})$ a *saddle value* of the Lagrangean function.

It may be recalled that the first inequality in (20.29), which is merely a restatement of (20.28) with the explicit mention that $\bar{y}$ is given, follows from the fact that Z is *concave* in the variables x, given $\bar{y}$. We can also show that the second inequality in (20.29) is tied to the fact that Z is *convex* in the variables y, given $\bar{x}$. Setting $x = \bar{x}$ in the Lagrangean function, we have

$$Z = f(\bar{x}) + \sum_{i=1}^{m} y_i[r_i - g^i(\bar{x})]$$

Since r_i and $g^i(\bar{x})$ represent constants, Z is clearly linear in the variables y_i, and thus convex in y_i. In the light of the footnote to the definition (20.25), we may then write

(20.30) $Z(y) \geq Z(\bar{y}) + \sum_{i=1}^{m} \dfrac{\partial Z}{\partial \bar{y}_i}(y_i - \bar{y}_i)$ [cf. (20.27)]

where we may take $\bar{y}$ to be the y value satisfying the Kuhn-Tucker maximum conditions. Then, by the same type of analysis of (20.27), we can show that the $\sum$ expression in (20.30) must be nonnegative, so that its deletion does not affect the validity of the inequality. Hence, we get $Z(\bar{y}) \leq Z(y)$ or, more completely,

$Z(\bar{x},\bar{y}) \leq Z(\bar{x},y)$. In view of this discussion, we may characterize a saddle point $(\bar{x},\bar{y})$ as a point where the given function $Z(x,y)$ is concave with respect to one set of independent variables (here, x), but convex with respect to another (here, y).

When applied to linear programming, the saddle-point notion is especially interesting, because it leads directly to the concept of duality. In general, a pair of primal and dual linear programs may be written in vector notation as follows:

Maximize	$\pi = c'x$		Minimize	$\pi^* = r'y$
subject to	$Ax \leq r$		subject to	$A'y \geq c$
and	$x \geq 0$		and	$y \geq 0$

The Lagrangean function (20.17) for each of these emerges in the form

$$Z = c'x + y'(r - Ax) = c'x + y'r - y'Ax \qquad \text{[primal]}$$
$$\text{and} \qquad Z' = r'y + x'(c - A'y) = r'y + x'c - x'A'y \qquad \text{[dual]}$$

Note that Z and Z' are transposes of each other. Since Z and Z' are both 1×1, they obviously represent an identical scalar. Thus we are actually maximizing the identical Lagrangean function with respect to the x_j variables (primal program), while minimizing it with respect to the y_i variables (dual program). When the optimal solutions $\bar{x}$ and $\bar{y}$ are attained in these two programs, they must accordingly satisfy the inequality (20.29). This goes to show that the concept of duality and the notion of saddle point amount to the same thing.

By complementary slackness, the $y'(r - Ax)$ component of Z above must vanish in the optimal solution [cf. (20.14), the last equation]. Similarly, the $x'(c - A'y)$ component of Z' must vanish. These facts give us the essence of Duality Theorem II of Sec. 19.1. Going a step further, by subtracting these vanishing components from Z and Z', respectively, we find in the optimal solution that $\bar{Z} = c'\bar{x} = \bar{\pi}$ and $\bar{Z}' = r'\bar{y} = \bar{\pi}^*$. The fact that $\bar{Z} = \bar{Z}'$ then implies $\bar{\pi} = \bar{\pi}^*$, which is the essence of Duality Theorem I. It thus appears that the duality feature of linear programming reveals itself most clearly when the problem is viewed in the context of nonlinear programming.

EXERCISE 20.4

1 Given: Minimize $C = F(x)$

subject to $G^i(x) \geq r_i \qquad (i = 1, 2, \ldots, m)$

and $x \geq 0$

(a) Convert it into a maximization problem.

(b) What in the present problem are the equivalents of the f and g^i functions in the Kuhn-Tucker sufficiency theorem?

(c) Hence, what concavity-convexity conditions should be placed on the F and G^i functions to make the sufficient conditions for a maximum applicable here?

(d) On the basis of the above, how would you state the Kuhn-Tucker sufficient conditions for a *minimum*?

2 Demonstrate that, when the sufficient conditions for a minimum are satisfied by the minimization program given in the preceding problem, the globality theorem will again be applicable, so that the minimum attained will be global.

3 Prove that if $f(x)$ and $g(x)$ are both concave in x, then $f(x) + g(x)$ is also concave in x.

4 In (20.29), does $Z(\bar{x},\bar{y})$ constitute a unique saddle value? How would you modify (20.29) to describe a unique saddle value?

5 Is the Kuhn-Tucker sufficiency theorem applicable to:

(a) Maximize $\quad \pi = x_1$

subject to $\quad x_1{}^2 + x_2{}^2 \leq 1$

and $\quad x_1, x_2 \geq 0$

(b) Minimize $\quad C = (x_1 - 3)^2 + (x_2 - 4)^2$

subject to $\quad x_1 + x_2 \geq 4$

and $\quad x_1, x_2 \geq 0$

(c) Minimize $\quad C = 2x_1 + x_2$

subject to $\quad x_1{}^2 - 4x_1 + x_2 \geq 0$

and $\quad x_1, x_2 \geq 0$

20.5 Arrow-Enthoven Sufficiency Theorem: Quasiconcave Programming

To apply the Kuhn-Tucker sufficiency theorem, certain concavity-convexity specifications must be met. These constitute quite stringent requirements. In a more recently introduced sufficiency theorem—the Arrow-Enthoven sufficiency theorem[1]—these specifications have been relaxed to the extent of requiring only *quasiconcavity* and *quasiconvexity* in the objective and constraint functions. With

---

[1] Kenneth J. Arrow and Alain C. Enthoven, "Quasi-concave Programming," *Econometrica*, October, 1961, pp. 779–800.

the requirements thus weakened, the scope of applicability of the sufficient conditions is correspondingly widened.

In the original formulation of the Arrow-Enthoven paper, with a maximization problem and with constraints in the $\geq$ form, the $f(x)$ and $g^i(x)$ functions must uniformly be quasiconcave in order for their theorem to be applicable. This gives rise to the name *quasiconcave programming*. In our discussion here, however, we shall again use the $\leq$ inequality in the constraints of a maximization problem and the $\geq$ inequality in the minimization problem.

the Arrow-Enthoven sufficiency theorem   The theorem is as follows:

Given the nonlinear program

Maximize $\pi = f(x)$

subject to $g^i(x) \leq r_i$ $(i = 1, 2, \ldots, m)$

and $x \geq 0$

if the following conditions are satisfied:

(a)   the objective function $f(x)$ is differentiable and *quasiconcave* in the nonnegative orthant

(b)   each constraint function $g^i(x)$ is differentiable and *quasiconvex* in the nonnegative orthant

(c)   the point $\bar{x}$ satisfies the Kuhn-Tucker maximum conditions

(d)   any *one* of the following is satisfied:

(d-i) $f_j(\bar{x}) < 0$ for at least one variable x_j

(d-ii) $f_j(\bar{x}) > 0$ for some variable x_j that can take on a positive value without violating the constraints

(d-iii)   the n derivatives $f_j(\bar{x})$ are not all zero, and the function $f(x)$ is twice differentiable in the neighborhood of $\bar{x}$ [i.e., all the second-order partial derivatives of $f(x)$ exist at $\bar{x}$]

(d-iv)   the function $f(x)$ is concave

then $\bar{x}$ gives a global maximum of $\pi = f(x)$.

Since the proof of this theorem is somewhat involved, we shall omit it here. However, we do want to call the reader's attention to a few important features of this theorem. For one thing, while Arrow and Enthoven have succeeded in weakening the concavity-convexity specifications to their quasiconcavity-quasiconvexity counterparts, they find it necessary to append a new requirement, (d). Note, though, that only *one* of the four alternatives listed under (d) is required to form a complete set of sufficient conditions. In effect, therefore, the above theorem contains as many as *four* different sets of sufficient conditions for a maximum. In the case of (*d-iv*), with $f(x)$ concave, it would appear that the Arrow-Enthoven sufficiency theorem becomes identical with the Kuhn-Tucker sufficiency theorem. But this is not true. Inasmuch as Arrow and Enthoven only require the constraint functions $g^i(x)$ to be *quasi*convex, their sufficient conditions are still weaker.

As stated, the theorem lumps together the conditions (*a*) through (*d*) as a set of sufficient conditions. But it is also possible to interpret it to mean that, when (*a*), (*b*), and (*d*) are satisfied, then the Kuhn-Tucker maximum conditions become sufficient conditions for a maximum. Furthermore, if the constraint qualification is also satisfied, then the Kuhn-Tucker conditions will become necessary and sufficient for a maximum.

Like the Kuhn-Tucker theorem, the Arrow-Enthoven theorem can be adapted to the *minimization* framework with ease. Aside from the obvious changes that are needed to reverse the direction of optimization, we simply have to interchange the words *quasiconcave* and *quasiconvex* in conditions (*a*) and (*b*), replace the Kuhn-Tucker maximum conditions by the minimum conditions, reverse the inequalities in (*d-i*) and (*d-ii*), and change the word *concave* to *convex* in (*d-iv*).

a constraint-qualification test   It was earlier mentioned that if all constraint functions are linear, then the constraint qualification is satisfied. In case the $g^i(x)$ functions are nonlinear, the following test offered by Arrow and Enthoven may prove useful in determining whether the constraint qualification is satisfied:

For a maximization problem, if

(*a*)   every constraint function $g^i(x)$ is differentiable and quasiconvex

(*b*)   there exists a point x^0 in the nonnegative orthant such that all the constraints are satisfied as strict inequalities at x^0

(*c*)   *one* of the following is true:

(*c-i*)   every $g^i(x)$ function is convex

(*c-ii*)   the partial derivatives of every $g^i(x)$ are not all zero when evaluated at every point x in the feasible region

then the constraint qualification is satisfied.

Again, this test can be adapted to the minimization problem with ease. To do so, just change the word *quasiconvex* to *quasiconcave* in condition (*a*), and change the word *convex* to *concave* in (*c-i*). The application of this test will be illustrated later.

checking quasiconcavity and quasiconvexity   Whether working with a maximization or a minimization problem, we must, in order to apply the Arrow-Enthoven theorem and their constraint-qualification test, first check the $f(x)$ and $g^i(x)$ functions against the quasiconcavity-quasiconvexity specifications. For such a check, we may use the definitions introduced in Sec. 12.4, to wit, for any real number ζ $(0 < \zeta < 1)$, a function

(20.31) f is $\begin{cases} \text{quasiconcave} \\ \text{quasiconvex} \end{cases}$ if

$$f(u) \leq f(v) \quad \Rightarrow \quad f[\zeta u + (1 - \zeta)v] \begin{cases} \geq f(u) \\ \leq f(v) \end{cases}$$

But we may find it convenient sometimes to use the alternative definitions that, for any real number k,

(20.31′) f is $\begin{cases} \text{quasiconcave} \\ \text{quasiconvex} \end{cases}$ if

the set $\begin{cases} S^{\geq} \equiv \{u \mid f(u) \geq k\} \\ S^{\leq} \equiv \{v \mid f(v) \leq k\} \end{cases}$ is a convex set

As the reader may recall, these characterizations of quasiconcave and quasiconvex functions have been briefly previewed in Exercise 18.3-9. But a few examples may further clarify the idea.

Example 1   Any monotonic function of a single variable is quasiconcave as well as quasiconvex. If we draw the graph of a monotonic function $f(w)$, pick any value w_0, and let $k = f(w_0)$, then the set $S^{\geq}$ (which lie on the w axis) will include all the points located on *one* side of w_0. Thus $S^{\geq}$ is a convex set, and $f(w)$ is quasiconcave. By the same token, the set $S^{\leq}$ will consist of all the points on the w axis that lie on the *other* side of w_0. Since this latter set is also convex, $f(w)$ is quasiconvex as well.

Example 2   Any concave (convex) function is quasiconcave (quasiconvex). The reason for this should be clear from our earlier discussion of Fig. 18.6, and no further explanation is needed. We do want to emphasize here, however, that the converse statement is not true, i.e., a quasiconcave (quasiconvex) function is not necessarily concave (convex). This is because the convexity criterion of the sets $S^{\geq}$ and $S^{\leq}$, while sufficient for the quasiconcavity and quasiconvexity of a function, are only necessary (but *not* sufficient) for the concavity and convexity of that function.

Example 3   The function $z = f(x_1, x_2) = x_1 x_2$ is quasiconcave for nonnegative values of x_1 and x_2. To check by (20.31′), we first set $x_1 x_2 = k$ to get the equation for the isovalue curves. Like x_1 and x_2, k must be a nonnegative number. In case $k > 0$, the isovalue curve is a rectangular hyperbola in the x_1x_2 plane. The set $S^{\geq} = \{(x_1, x_2) \mid f(x_1, x_2) = x_1x_2 \geq k\}$, consisting of all the points on or above the rectangular hyperbola, is a convex set. In the other possibility, with $k = 0$, the isovalue curve as defined by $x_1x_2 = 0$ will be L-shaped, with the L coincident with the nonnegative segments of the two axes. The set $S^{\geq}$, consisting this time of the entire nonnegative quadrant, is again a convex set. Thus, by (20.31′), the function $z = x_1x_2$ is indeed quasiconcave for $x_1, x_2 \geq 0$. As such, it could qualify, for instance, as the objective function of a maximization problem, or as one of the constraint functions of a minimization problem, to which the Arrow-Enthoven sufficiency theorem is applicable.

The reader is cautioned not to confuse the shape of the isovalue curves $x_1x_2 = k$ (which are defined in the x_1x_2 plane) with the shape of the surface $z = x_1x_2$ (which is defined in the x_1x_2z space). The characteristics of the z surface is what we are attempting to determine; the shape of the isovalue curves is of interest to us here only as a means to delineate the sets $S^{\geq}$, which then enable us to check the definitions in (20.31′).

Example 4   The function $f(x_1, x_2) = (x_1 - a)^2 + (x_2 - b)^2$ is quasiconvex. Let us check this by (20.31′). Setting $(x_1 - a)^2 + (x_2 - b)^2 = k$, we see that k must be nonnegative. For each k, the isovalue curve is a circle in the x_1x_2 plane with center at (a,b) and with radius $\sqrt{k}$. Since $S^{\leq} = \{(x_1, x_2) \mid f(x_1, x_2) \leq k\}$ is the set of all points on or inside the circle, it constitutes a convex set. This is true even when $k = 0$, that is, when the circle degenerates into the single point (a,b). Thus the given function is quasiconvex, and it could qualify as the objective function of a minimization problem, or one of the constraint functions of a maximization problem, to which the Arrow-Enthoven sufficiency theorem is applicable.

The reader may recall that, in Example 1 of Sec. 20.4, this function was already established to be a convex function. Thus it is possible to conclude from this immediately that it is quasiconvex. In our earlier demonstration of the convexity of this function, we made use of the fact that the sum of concave (convex) functions is a concave (convex) function. It should be pointed out that no similar rule exists for quasiconcave and quasiconvex functions. That is, the sum of quasiconcave (quasiconvex) functions is *not necessarily* a quasiconcave (quasiconvex) function. (See Exercise 20.5-3.)

EXERCISE 20.5

1   Justify the changes suggested in the text for the Arrow-Enthoven sufficiency theorem and the constraint-qualification test when these are applied to a minimization problem.

2   Is the constraint-qualification test in the nature of a set of necessary conditions, or sufficient conditions?

3   Let $f(w)$ plot as a negatively sloped curve shaped like the right half of a bell in the first quadrant, passing through the points (0,5), (2,4), (3,2), and (5,1). Let $g(w)$ plot as a positively sloped 45° line. Are these two functions quasiconcave? Now plot the sum $f(w) + g(w)$. Is this sum a quasiconcave function?

4   Are the following functions quasiconcave, quasiconvex, neither, or both?

(a) $C(Q) = 4Q^3 - 3Q^2 + Q + 15, \quad Q \geq 0$ (*Hint:* Review the discussion of the cubic total-cost function, Sec. 9.4.)

(b) $f(w) = w^3 - 2w$

(c) $f(x_1, x_2) = 6x_1 - 9x_2$

(d) $f(x_1, x_2) = x_2 - \ln x_1$

(e) $Q(K,L) = K^\alpha L^\beta \quad (K, L \geq 0; \alpha, \beta > 0)$

5   Which functions in the preceding problem are mathematically acceptable as the objective function of a *maximization* problem to which the Arrow-Enthoven sufficiency theorem is applicable?

6   Is the constraint qualification satisfied, given that the constraints of a *maximization* problem are:

(a) $x_1^2 + (x_2 - 5)^2 \leq 4$ and $5x_1 + x_2 \leq 10$

(b) $x_1 + x_2 \leq 8$ and $-x_1 x_2 \leq -8$ (*Note:* $-x_1 x_2$ is not convex.)

20.6   Economic Applications

We are now ready to show some simple economic applications of the two sufficiency theorems.

utility maximization revisited   In our previous encounter with consumer theory in Sec. 12.4, the problem was stated in the form of: Maximize $U = U(x_1, x_2)$, subject to $P_1 x_1 + P_2 x_2 = B$. The constraint appears as an equation, and the choice variables are not specifically restricted to be nonnegative. It is now possible to restate the problem in a more realistic format.

Taking the n-variable case, we can write it as a nonlinear program

$$\begin{array}{lll} & \text{Maximize} & U = U(x_1, \ldots, x_n) \\ (20.32) & \text{subject to} & P_1 x_1 + \cdots + P_n x_n \leq B \\ & \text{and} & x_1, \ldots, x_n \geq 0 \end{array}$$

where all the prices are taken to be exogenous.

Since the (only) constraint function $g^1(x) = P_1 x_1 + \cdots + P_n x_n$ is linear, the constraint qualification is satisfied, and the Kuhn-Tucker maximum conditions are necessary and sufficient if the other conditions cited in either of the two sufficiency theorems are met. To apply the Kuhn-Tucker theorem, we would want $U(x)$ to be differentiable and concave, and $g^1(x)$ to be differentiable and convex. The latter is automatically satisfied since $g^1(x)$ is linear, but the former has to be taken care of by explicit model specification. In checking the Arrow-Enthoven theorem, however, we note that it is only needed to specify $U(x)$ to be differentiable and quasiconcave—a considerably less stringent requirement—provided, of course, that condition (d) can be duly satisfied. If, for instance, there exists some commodity j that lies within the reach of the consumer's budget and yields a positive marginal utility always (nonsatiation), then we will automatically have $U_j(\bar{x}) > 0$ and condition (d-ii) will be fulfilled. But there are of course other ways to satisfy condition (d) so as to make the Kuhn-Tucker maximum conditions necessary and sufficient.

The quasiconcavity specification is perfectly in line with our earlier discussion of the classical consumer theory in Sec. 12.4. Recall, however, that there—in a two-commodity model with an equality constraint—the $U(x)$ function was specified to be *strictly* quasiconcave. The purpose of the strictness assumption was to rule out any horizontal platforms on the bell-shaped utility surface in the $x_1 x_2 U$ space, so that each isovalue set (here, indifference set) will emerge as a thin curve rather than a wide zone. For only then would it make sense to speak of a point-of-tangency optimal solution in the classical tradition. Things are different when the budget constraint is an inequality instead. Since what we are seeking is no longer a point of tangency, but an optimal point within a feasible region, it is now acceptable to have horizontal platforms on the utility surface, and there is thus no need to specify *strict* quasiconcavity.

In Sec. 12.4, the $U(x)$ function was also assumed to be an *increasing* function of x_1 and x_2. Economically, this implies nonsatiation in both commodities. Graphically, this restricts the utility surface to the ascending portion of a bell only, so that the indifference curves will be the usual downward-sloping, convex type rather than the round or oval loops illustrated in Fig. 20.8. The rationale for this assumption is again to be found in the tangency-solution feature of the classical framework. For although a tangency point like H would indeed represent the best choice under the circumstances (because ascent to the

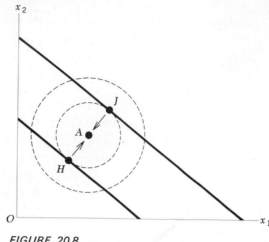

FIGURE 20.8

peak of the utility surface, via a movement towards point A in the base plane, is precluded by the budget), tangency points on the far side of the peak, such as J, would clearly be nonoptimal and should categorically be excluded. Turning to the nonlinear-programming framework, we see that the assumption of nonsatiation can also be of service—to satisfy condition (d-ii). However, since condition (d) in the Arrow-Enthoven sufficiency theorem can be taken care of in other ways, it is not absolutely necessary to assume that $U(x)$ is increasing.

The Kuhn-Tucker conditions for this problem are easy to write and interpret. These will therefore be left to the reader.

least-cost combination revisited

Let the production function of a firm be of the Cobb-Douglas type: $Q = K^\alpha L^\beta$, where α, $\beta > 0$. Also let the input prices $P_K > 0$ and $P_L > 0$ be exogenously determined. Then the least-cost combination problem can be stated as the nonlinear program

$$
\begin{aligned}
&\text{Minimize} && C = P_K K + P_L L \\
(20.33)\quad &\text{subject to} && K^\alpha L^\beta \geq Q_0 \quad (Q_0 > 0) \\
&\text{and} && K, L \geq 0
\end{aligned}
$$

The objective function being linear, it is automatically convex as well as quasiconvex. The (only) constraint function, $K^\alpha L^\beta$, is quasiconcave regardless of whether $\alpha + \beta \lesseqgtr 1$, that is, regardless of whether returns to scale are increasing, constant, or decreasing [see Exercise 20.5-4(e)]. However, this function is *not* concave if $\alpha + \beta > 1$ (increasing returns to scale). In the latter case, each successive unit increment in output will require less than proportionate increase in the two inputs. Geometrically, the successive isoquants for unit increments in output will become more and more tightly spaced as we move away from the point of origin on any given ray in the KL plane. Accordingly, the projection of such a ray onto the production surface will produce a curve showing increasingly more rapid ascent, so that the surface cannot be concave.

In view of this, the Kuhn-Tucker sufficiency theorem becomes inapplicable when there are increasing returns to scale. In contrast, the Arrow-Enthoven theorem is applicable even then. For a minimization problem, the latter theorem specifies a quasiconvex objective function and quasiconcave constraint function(s). These specifications are indeed met in the present problem. In addition, condition (d-i) is satisfied, because for a minimization problem we are supposed to have $f_j(\bar{x}) > 0$ for some choice variable x_j, and we do have here $\partial C/\partial K = P_K > 0$ and $\partial C/\partial L = P_L > 0$ for all values of K and L, including $\bar{K}$ and $\bar{L}$.

Going a step further, we may also ascertain that the constraint function $g^1 = K^\alpha L^\beta$ passes the constraint-qualification test. First, g^1 is a quasiconcave function. Secondly, there certainly exists a nonnegative ordered pair (K,L) that satisfies the constraint as a strict inequality. Thirdly, since every point in the feasible region is characterized by $K > 0$ and $L > 0$ (otherwise Q_0 cannot be positive), the partial derivatives $\partial g^1/\partial K = \alpha K^{\alpha-1}L^\beta$ and $\partial g^1/\partial L = \beta K^\alpha L^{\beta-1}$ are both positive everywhere in the feasible region, thus satisfying condition (c-ii) of the test. Consequently, with the constraint qualification satisfied, the Kuhn-Tucker minimum conditions can be taken as necessary-and-sufficient.

the sales-maximizing firm   In the standard analysis of a firm, the objective of profit maximization is usually assumed. However, when the firm in question is a corporation in which ownership and management are separate, it may very well be rational for the management to pursue the alternative goal of maximizing the sales (revenue).[1] The total revenue is often taken as an important indicator of the competitive position of the firm within the industry. Moreover, increases in sales revenue are often taken to be a sign of managerial success. It is even conceivable that the remuneration of the management depends directly on this particular performance index. Thus sales maximization appears to be a plausible alternative objective in the corporate setup, provided that, to avoid possible stockholder discontent, the management always sees to it that the profit level never falls below a certain prescribed minimum.

If so, the problem of the management is to maximize $R = R(Q)$, subject

---

[1] William J. Baumol, "On the Theory of Oligopoly," *Economica*, August, 1958, pp. 187–198. See also Baumol's *Business Behavior, Value and Growth*, revised edition, Harcourt, Brace, & World, Inc., New York, 1967.

to $\pi = R(Q) - C(Q) \geq \pi_0$, or

Maximize $R = R(Q)$

subject to $C(Q) - R(Q) \leq -\pi_0$ $(\pi_0 > 0)$

and $Q \geq 0$

As long as $R(Q)$ is differentiable and concave and $C(Q)$ is differentiable and convex—which would imply that the constraint function $C(Q) - R(Q)$ is also differentiable and convex—the Kuhn-Tucker sufficiency theorem can be applied. Furthermore, the constraint-qualification test can also be satisfied under those assumptions. Thus the Kuhn-Tucker maximum conditions become necessary and sufficient in this problem.

It is interesting to note that we cannot hope to attain greater generality in this case by relaxing the concavity-convexity assumptions to a quasiconcave $R(Q)$ and a quasiconvex $C(Q)$. Under these weaker assumptions, the constraint function $C(Q) - R(Q)$ is the sum of two quasiconvex functions, which gives no guarantee that it is also quasiconvex. Hence the Arrow-Enthoven sufficiency theorem does not automatically become applicable, unless, of course, the constraint function is rendered quasiconvex via a direct, new assumption.

For this problem, with the Lagrangean function

$$Z = R(Q) + y[-\pi_0 - C(Q) + R(Q)]$$

the Kuhn-Tucker conditions consist of the marginal conditions

(20.34)
$$\frac{\partial Z}{\partial Q} = R'(Q) - yC'(Q) + yR'(Q) \leq 0$$

$$\frac{\partial Z}{\partial y} = -\pi_0 - C(Q) + R(Q) \geq 0$$

plus the nonnegativity and complementary-slackness conditions. Ordinarily, we would expect $R(0) = 0$ and $C(0) > 0$. Thus a zero output would yield $\partial Z/\partial y = -\pi_0 - C(0) < 0$, which violates the second marginal condition. We must therefore take $Q > 0$ instead. By complementary slackness, this implies that $\partial Z/\partial Q = 0$. Solving this latter equation, we obtain the sales-maximizing output rule

$$R'(Q) = \frac{y}{1 + y} C'(Q)$$

In this result, the value of y is either zero or positive. If $y = 0$, the rule reduces to $R'(Q) = 0$, and the firm will push its output all the way to the level where the marginal revenue vanishes. This would be sales maximization in its purest form, because the firm would in that case proceed to the very peak of the total-revenue curve. But such extreme behavior becomes unfeasible when a sufficiently high minimum profit, π_0, is prescribed. In this new situation, we must have

$y > 0$, which implies that $\partial Z / \partial y = 0$ (the constraint is exactly fulfilled at the optimum). Observe that, even then, the rule would imply that

$$R'(Q) < C'(Q) \qquad \left[\text{since } \frac{y}{1 + y} < 1 \right]$$

and this would generally yield a higher output level than the profit-maximizing rule $R'(Q) = C'(Q)$. This will be illustrated in a numerical example below.

solving a nonlinear program via the Kuhn-Tucker conditions   Our discussion of the Kuhn-Tucker conditions has thus far been concentrated on their *analytical* roles (in necessary conditions and sufficient conditions), but these conditions can also play a *computational* role if they happen to be necessary and sufficient,[1] and if the number of choice variables is reasonably small. We shall illustrate the procedure involved with a numerical example of a sales-maximizing firm.

Let the firm have revenue and cost functions

$$R = 32Q - Q^2 \quad \text{[concave]} \qquad \text{and} \qquad C = Q^2 + 8Q + 4 \quad \text{[convex]}$$

and let the minimum profit be $\pi_0 = 18$. Under these circumstances, the Kuhn-Tucker conditions indeed are necessary and sufficient. On the basis of (20.34), the two marginal conditions will now take the specific form of

$$\frac{\partial Z}{\partial Q} = 32 - 2Q - y(4Q - 24) \leq 0$$

$$\frac{\partial Z}{\partial y} = -2Q^2 + 24Q - 22 \geq 0$$

The value of Q must be either positive or zero. Trying $Q = 0$ first, we immediately encounter a contradiction in the second marginal condition. Thus we must let $Q > 0$ instead. If so, we may infer from complementary slackness that $\partial Z / \partial Q = 0$, which gives us an equation in two variables. The value of y in that equation must be either positive or zero. Trying $y = 0$ and solving for Q, we get $Q = 16$. Although acceptable in itself, this value of Q would imply $\partial Z / \partial y = -150$, in violation of the second marginal condition (the profit constraint). Thus we must let $y > 0$ instead. But then it follows that $\partial Z / \partial y = 0$ by complementary slackness. Solving this new equation, we obtain the two roots $Q_1 = 11$ and $Q_2 = 1$. But since only the first root is consistent with the condition $\partial Z / \partial Q = 0$, the sales-maximizing output is $\bar{Q} = 11$. In contrast, the $R'(Q) = C'(Q)$ rule would lead to a lower figure, $Q = 6$, as the profit-maximizing output.

---

[1] If they are only sufficient, but not necessary, then an optimal solution may fail the Kuhn-Tucker conditions, so the latter will become ineffective as a fishing net to catch such a solution.

From the above, it should be clear that the computational procedure involved is essentially one of trial and error. The basic idea is first to try a zero value for each choice variable. Setting a variable equal to zero always simplifies the marginal conditions by causing certain terms to drop out. If appropriate nonnegative values of Lagrange multipliers can then be found that satisfy all the marginal inequalities, the zero solution will be optimal. If, on the other hand, the zero solution violates some of the inequalities, then we must let one or more choice variables be positive. For every positive choice variable, we may, by complementary slackness, convert an inequality marginal condition into a strict equation. Properly solved, such equations will lead us either to a solution, or to a contradiction that would then compel us to try something else. If a solution exists, such trials will eventually enable us to uncover it.

Note that, in a two-variable problem, we must try out no less than four (2^2) possible combinations of choice-variable signs: (0,0), (0,+), (+,0), and (+,+). A three-variable problem will present as many as eight (2^3) possibilities to check, and the complexity will grow rapidly as the number of choice variables increases. This method is therefore unsuitable for high-dimensional nonlinear programs.

EXERCISE 20.6

1   Write out the Kuhn-Tucker conditions for the problem (20.32).

2   Write out the Kuhn-Tucker conditions for the problem (20.33).

3   Let the total revenue R of a sales-maximizing firm depend on output Q and advertising expenditure A, and let its total cost consist of production cost C and advertising cost A.

(a)   Reformulate the nonlinear program given in the text.
(b)   What restrictions must be placed on the R and C functions to make the Kuhn-Tucker sufficiency theorem applicable?
(c)   What restrictions are needed to make the Arrow-Enthoven sufficiency theorem applicable?

4   Minimize $C = x_1^2 + x_2^2$
     subject to $x_1 + x_2 \geq 2$
     and $x_1, x_2 \geq 0$

(a)   Is the Kuhn-Tucker sufficiency theorem applicable to this problem? Are the Kuhn-Tucker minimum conditions necessary and sufficient?

(b) Write out the Kuhn-Tucker conditions and use these to seek out the optimal solution by trial and error. What are the values of $\bar{x}_1$ and $\bar{x}_2$?

5   (a) Formulate a nonlinear program that answers the question: What is the shortest distance (d) from the point of origin (0,0) to any point lying on or above the straight line passing through the points (0,2) and (2,0). (*Hint:* Use Pythagoras' theorem.)

(b) How does the present program differ from the one given in the preceding problem? Would it be possible to take the solution ($\bar{x}_1$, $\bar{x}_2$) of the latter as the solution of the present problem? Why?

(c) What is the shortest distance, $\bar{d}$?

21

GAME THEORY

The discussion of mathematical programming has modified the framework of optimization problems by the inclusion of constraints in the form of inequalities, but the nature of the optimizing process remains that either of *maximizing* or of *minimizing*, never any mixture of the two. In the context of game theory, however, the very framework of optimization is changed to that of finding either the maximum among a set of minima (*maximin*) or the minimum among a set of maxima (*minimax*).

21.1   Basic Concepts of Game Theory

A *game* is a situation in which two or more participants, the *players*, confront one another in pursuit of certain conflicting objectives. Being in conflict, it is obvious that not all players' objectives can be simultaneously realized. Thus some players may win and receive a *positive payoff*, whereas others may lose and get a *negative payoff*.

There are basically two major categories of games: *games of chance* and *games of strategy*. The former is exemplified by the game in which each of n players is dealt a card, and the player with the highest card wins a dollar from each of the other players. No skill is involved in such a game. In games of strategy, on the other hand, the outcome depends primarily on the deliberate choice of a course of action—the *strategy*—by each participant. Skill does enter in and, with it, there also enters the problem of optimization. Obviously, this category of games is the only one of interest to us.

Games of strategy can naturally be found in abundance in the realm of gambling; but examples are also to be found in the battle of the sexes (how to maneuver the husband to buy her that fur coat), in international politics (how to get the upper hand in a peace negotiation), in economics (how to enlarge our share of the market relative to our competitors), and so forth. In each of these examples, a player is seeking a strategy that will result in the attainment of a particular objective, but the opposing player(s) will try to optimize from their standpoint, too. The final outcome of the game will thus depend *jointly* on the strategies chosen by *all* participants in the game.

two-person constant-sum games   Under the category of games of strategy, we can make a further classification on the basis of several criteria. Depending on the number of players, we may have *two-person, three-person,* or *n-person* games. "Person" really means "participating party" in this context. In a game of wage negotiation, for instance, there are *two* parties confronting each other across the bargaining table, namely, labor and management. Despite the fact that many individuals sit at each side of the table, this must be considered as essentially a *two*-person game. Similarly, an international disarmament conference is an *n*-person game, where *n* denotes the number of conferring nations, regardless of the number of individuals in each country's delegation. As may be expected, the theory of two-person games is more fully developed than that of the more complicated *n*-person games.

Depending on the payoff situation, a game can be classified as either *constant-sum* or *nonconstant-sum*. In the former type, the payoffs of all players at the end of the game will always add up to a fixed constant, whatever the strategies chosen by the various players. Suppose that two gas stations are in a contest for higher sales (measured in dollars) through price warfare. Also suppose that the total demand for gasoline facing these stations has a unitary elasticity throughout, so that the customers' total expenditure will be $100 per day regardless of the price charged. Then one outcome of this game—the result of a particular combination of price strategies—might be a sales distribution described by the ordered pair ($30, $70), while another outcome—the result of a different combination of price strategies—might be ($60, $40). But the sum of the two sales figures will stay invariably at the $100 level. This is therefore a constant-sum game. Such a game therefore can only *redistribute*, but never *create*, the object of payoff (in this case, sales). In contrast, the game would become a nonconstant-sum one if price-cutting tends to induce customers to raise their total expenditure on gasoline. Note that, had the object of payoff been changed to *profit* instead of sales, then the above price-war game would also have been nonconstant-sum, because the profit figures would be affected by the *cost* picture, which in turn depends on the varying numbers of gallons sold at various price levels pertaining to different combinations of price strategies.

payoff matrix   We shall hereafter confine our discussion to two-person constant-sum games. In such games, if there is a finite number of strategies at the disposal of each player, the total number of possible outcomes of the game will also be finite. The game can then be completely described by means of a *payoff matrix*, such as is shown in Table 21.1.

In this table, we have assumed that player 1 has only two strategies available, but player 2 has three. The total number of possible outcomes is therefore $2 \times 3 = 6$. For each possible outcome, there is a corresponding payoff to each player; what Table 21.1 shows are only the payoffs to player 1. Thus, the entry 30 represents what player 1 will get if both players adopt their respective first strategies. To facilitate reference, let us consider that entry as the a_{11} element of the payoff matrix $A = [a_{ij}]$. Then we may write

$$(21.1) \qquad A = \begin{bmatrix} a_{11} & a_{12} & a_{13} \\ a_{21} & a_{22} & a_{23} \end{bmatrix} = \begin{bmatrix} 30 & 60 & 50 \\ 50 & 40 & 70 \end{bmatrix}$$

Here, the first subscript of a_{ij} always refers to the strategy adopted by player 1, and the second subscript, to the strategy of player 2. This convention requires the listing of strategies in the particular format illustrated in Table 21.1: those of player 1 in a vertical sequence, and those of player 2 horizontally. Inasmuch as the payoff matrix A must be a rectangular array of numbers, the game under discussion is often referred to as a *rectangular game*.

Naturally, the payoff situation for player 2 can also be depicted by a rectangular array, say, a matrix B. Since, in a constant-sum game, the payoff to player 2 under any given outcome of the game is necessarily equal to that specific constant minus the payoff to player 1, matrix B is readily calculable

TABLE 21.1

	Strategies of player 2		
Strategies of player 1	1	2	3
1	30	60	50
2	50	40	70

from matrix A. If the constant sum is 100, then the matrix in (21.1) must imply

$$(21.2) \quad B = \begin{bmatrix} (100-30) & (100-60) & (100-50) \\ (100-50) & (100-40) & (100-70) \end{bmatrix} = \begin{bmatrix} 70 & 40 & 50 \\ 50 & 60 & 30 \end{bmatrix}$$

In view of the fact that a known matrix A always has a unique matrix B as its counterpart, it is sufficient to consider matrix A (the payoffs to player 1) alone.

zero-sum games   In a constant-sum game, the *constant* can be any number; in the special case where it is zero, the game becomes a *zero-sum game*. If there are only two players in a zero-sum game, one player's payoff must be the *negative* of the payoff to the other; because a player can only win what his opponent loses.

As an economic example of this, consider two firms in a duopolistic market that are striving to lure away each other's established customers. Since such a contest involves existing customers only, the number of customers won over by one firm must be identical with the number of customers lost to the other. The game is thus zero-sum.

It is possible to reformulate a nonzero-constant-sum game as a zero-sum one. Let us take the gasoline-station example again, and assume that the two stations, respectively, have the payoff matrices A and B in (21.1) and (21.2). As they stand, the elements in A and B represent *sales*. Given an original sales distribution—say, ($50, $50)—however, we can express the payoffs in terms of *gains in sales* instead. In that case, we can, by subtracting the original sales (50) from every element, obtain two new payoff matrices A^* and B^*:

$$(21.3) \quad A^* = \begin{bmatrix} -20 & 10 & 0 \\ 0 & -10 & 20 \end{bmatrix} \quad B^* = \begin{bmatrix} 20 & -10 & 0 \\ 0 & 10 & -20 \end{bmatrix}$$

Since we now have

$$a_{ij}^* + b_{ij}^* = 0 \quad \text{(for all } i \text{ and } j)$$

A^* and B^* will add up to a 2×3 zero matrix. Thus the modified version of the game is zero-sum. As the reader can verify, even if the original sales distribution is unequal, say, ($40, $60)—in which case, we ought to subtract 40 from every element of A and 60 from every element of B—the modified payoff matrices will still imply a zero-sum game.

The type of transformation just outlined alters the numbers in the payoff matrices, but it does not affect the fundamental structure of the game. If a particular strategy can maximize a firm's absolute sales level, it should of necessity be the strategy that can maximize the *gain* in sales from whatever initial level there was. Similarly, the worst strategy will remain the worst under either criterion. Mathematically, the transformation only shifts the origin of measurement.

In fact, there exists a theorem to the effect that optimal strategies are *invariant* with respect to the following payoff-matrix transformation:

$$(21.4) \quad A = \begin{bmatrix} a_{11} & a_{12} \\ a_{21} & a_{22} \end{bmatrix} \quad \rightarrow \quad A^* = \begin{bmatrix} ka_{11} + c & ka_{12} + c \\ ka_{21} + c & ka_{22} + c \end{bmatrix}$$

where k and c are two constants. This transformation theorem not only justifies the previous translation of a constant-sum game to a zero-sum game in (21.3), but also makes it possible—for computational convenience—to tidy up any payoff matrix containing fractions or negative numbers.

Example 1 Given the payoff matrix $A = \begin{bmatrix} -8 & 4 \\ 3 & -2 \end{bmatrix}$, we can add 8 to every element to get $A^* = \begin{bmatrix} 0 & 12 \\ 11 & 6 \end{bmatrix}$, where no negative element now appears. As mentioned before, the choice of optimal strategies will be unaffected by the transformation performed. Note, however, that the final payoff should still be read from the *original* matrix A instead of A^*. In case we wish to read the final payoff from A^*, then care must be taken to subtract 8 from it first.

Example 2 Given the payoff matrix $A = \begin{bmatrix} \frac{1}{2} & -\frac{1}{3} \\ 2 & 4 \end{bmatrix}$, we can multiply each element by 6, then add 2 to it to obtain $A^* = \begin{bmatrix} 5 & 0 \\ 14 & 26 \end{bmatrix}$ as the adjusted payoff matrix. We repeat that, when the final outcome of the game has been determined, the actual payoff should be read from the *original* matrix A. If read from A^*, the figure should first be duly adjusted back, by subtracting 2 and then dividing by 6.

EXERCISE 21.1

1 Given the following sets of payoff matrices A and B (for players 1 and 2, respectively), indicate whether each of these two-person games is constant-sum. If the latter is true, also indicate whether it is zero-sum.

(a) $A = \begin{bmatrix} 2 & 6 & 3 \\ 4 & 0 & 5 \end{bmatrix}$ $B = \begin{bmatrix} 7 & 3 & 6 \\ 5 & 9 & 1 \end{bmatrix}$

(b) $A = \begin{bmatrix} 4 & 9 \\ 6 & 0 \end{bmatrix}$ $B = \begin{bmatrix} 1 & -4 \\ -1 & 5 \end{bmatrix}$

$$(c) \quad A = \begin{bmatrix} 6 & 8 & 3 \\ 3 & 2 & -2 \\ -1 & 0 & -3 \end{bmatrix} \quad B = \begin{bmatrix} -6 & -8 & -3 \\ -3 & -2 & 2 \\ 1 & 0 & 3 \end{bmatrix}$$

2 If the total payoff for the two players in a constant-sum game is \$500, write out the matrix B, given a matrix A as follows:

$$(a) \quad A = \begin{bmatrix} 250 & 124 \\ 361 & 316 \end{bmatrix} \qquad (b) \quad A = \begin{bmatrix} 167 & 203 & 352 \\ 480 & 317 & 216 \end{bmatrix}$$

3 If player 1 has 32 possible strategies and if player 2 has 24, how many possible outcomes of the game will there be?

4 In the gasoline-station example, translate the *sales* payoff matrices A and B in (21.1) and (21.2) into *gains in sales* payoff matrices A^* and B^*, assuming the original sales distribution to be:

(a)   (\$40, \$60)   (b)   (\$30, \$70)

Do the results show the transformed game to be zero-sum?

21.2   Saddle-Point Solutions of Rectangular Games

While the structure of a two-person, constant-sum game is completely summarized in a single payoff matrix A, this matrix alone does not enable us to tell the final outcome of the game. For the latter, it is necessary first to postulate the behavioral patterns of the two players, i.e., to specify the manner in which each participant will play the game. A player can be aggressive, and even reckless; in that case he may aim at the highest possible payoff, realizing that if his opponent is more shrewd, he himself may end up with a substantial loss. Or a player can be the cautious type, trying to avoid the riskier course of action but realizing that, if his possible loss will not be spectacular, nor might be his prospective gain. In the established theory of games, both players are assumed to be of the latter type.

conservative gamesmanship   Given the knowledge of player 1's payoff matrix as follows:

$$(21.5) \quad A = \begin{bmatrix} 7 & 8 & 4 \\ 4 & 7 & 2 \end{bmatrix}$$

how are our cautious, risk-averting players supposed to behave?

First of all, we must assume that although each player has knowledge of (or is able to make an educated guess about) the payoff matrix A, he is ignorant about the exact strategy the opponent plans to adopt; otherwise the game would be reduced to mere child's play. For illustration, if player 1 knows for sure that the opponent is adopting strategy 2, then only the second column of matrix A will be relevant, and player 1 can simply adopt strategy 1 (first row) in order to maximize his payoff at 8. Thus the possession of information about the opponent will greatly simplify one's problem. It is, of course, this kind of advantage which explains the popularity of military or industrial espionage activities!

If ignorant of the opponent's plan, however, a conservative player 1 may instead proceed thus: (1) determine the least payoff he can receive under each of his own strategies (the minimum in each row of A), and (2) choose the strategy (row) that has the largest minimum. This way, he can be sure that whatever the opponent does, he will not end up with the worst of all worlds, because he has specifically (in the second step above) avoided some less-favorable outcomes (the lower row minima). By the same token, he can never attain the best possible outcome, because he has deliberately (in the first step above) shut his eyes to some more favorable outcomes. Herein lies the inherent conservatism of this approach.

Applying this procedure to the payoff matrix in (21.5), player 1 will find the minima of the two rows to be 4 and 2, respectively, as shown in Table 21.2. The maximum among these, called the *maximin* (the maximum among a set of row minima), is 4, which occurs in the first row. Hence the (conservatively) optimal strategy for player 1 is his strategy 1.

What about player 2? In order to pursue the same type of conservative gamesmanship, player 2 must seek his own maximin. More specifically, he should find the maximum among the set of *column* (not row) minima in his own payoff matrix B. If we assume the present game to be 10-sum, then matrix B and player 2's maximin will be as in Table 21.3, which leads him to adopt his strategy 3 (third column) as the (conservatively) optimal strategy. However, in view of the constant-sum nature of the game, the choice of the maximum among the column minima in matrix B must yield the same strategy that gives the minimum among

TABLE 21.2

Payoff matrix	Row minima	Maximin
$A = \begin{bmatrix} 7 & 8 & 4 \\ 4 & 7 & 2 \end{bmatrix}$	$(4) \rightarrow$ 2	4

the column maxima in matrix A. Therefore we can work with matrix A instead. As Table 21.4 shows, if player 2 tries to find the *minimax* (the minimum among a set of column maxima) in matrix A, he will settle on the same optimal strategy, namely, strategy 3. Besides, the minimax payoff being 4 (to player 1), the corresponding payoff to player 2 must be $10 - 4 = 6$, which checks with the answer obtained from matrix B.

In sum, the conservative gamesmanship postulated above essentially amounts to the search for a maximin or a minimax. While one may question the empirical relevance of the assumption of conservative players, one can hardly deny that it does open up a fresh and interesting framework of optimization.

saddle-point solution   Returning to our game, we observe that player 1 will pick strategy 1 (Table 21.2) so that he can get a payoff of *at least* $a_{13} = 4$, whereas player 2 will pick strategy 3 (Table 21.4) so that player 1 will get a payoff of *at most* $a_{13} = 4$. With this particular pairing of strategies, the final payoff will indeed be a_{13}, because the two conservative antagonists seem to have agreed upon a "solution" to the game.

This result comes about because the element $a_{13} = 4$ is in the present case at once the maximin and the minimax of matrix A. More formally, it is because matrix A satisfies the equation

$$(21.6) \qquad \max_{i} \min_{j} (a_{ij}) = \min_{j} \max_{i} (a_{ij})$$

TABLE 21.3

Payoff matrix	$B = \begin{bmatrix} 3 & 2 & 6 \\ 6 & 3 & 8 \end{bmatrix}$
Column minima	3 2 ⑥
	↓
Maximin	6

TABLE 21.4

Payoff matrix	$A = \begin{bmatrix} 7 & 8 & 4 \\ 4 & 7 & 2 \end{bmatrix}$
Column maxima	7 8 ④
	↓
Minimax	4

If somewhat formidable in appearance, the symbols in this equation are not difficult to interpret, provided we bear in mind that the subscript i refers to rows and that j refers to columns. The symbol $\min_j$ is simply a directive to minimize columnwise among the j's. For example, in the matrix A of Table 21.2 we find

	$j = 1$	$j = 2$	$j = 3$
$i = 1$	7	8	4
$i = 2$	4	7	2

Thus, for $i = 1$ (row 1), we have

$$\min_j (a_{1j}) = 4$$

and for $i = 2$ (row 2), we have

$$\min_j (a_{2j}) = 2$$

Consequently, if these results are exhibited in a vector, we can write

$$\min_j (a_{ij}) = \begin{bmatrix} 4 \\ 2 \end{bmatrix}$$

which is just a listing of the row minima. When the above expression is preceded by the expression $\max_i$—which means to maximize rowwise among the i's—we obtain

$$\max_i \min_j (a_{ij}) = \max_i \begin{bmatrix} 4 \\ 2 \end{bmatrix} = 4$$

In short, then, the left-hand expression in (21.6) is just a concise description of the procedure for determining the maximin, as outlined in Table 21.2. Analogously, the right side of (21.6) is the mathematical expression of the minimax procedure outlined in Table 21.4. When the payoff matrix A satisfies (21.6), the element that is the maximin will be the minimax as well, which in the present case is $a_{13} = 4$.

When an element serves both as a maximin and as a minimax, it is called a *saddle point*—a maximum from one point of view, but a minimum from the other. In case a saddle point is present in a payoff matrix, we can always take it as a solution of the game. This has already been illustrated in Tables 21.2 and 21.4, where $a_{13} = 4$ is a saddle point. As another illustration, let us examine Table 21.5. Here the maximin and minimax are again equal, both being the element $a_{22} = 5$. Clearly, this latter element—a saddle point—yields the solution of the game. From the subscripts of a_{22}, we can deduce that each player will choose his respective strategy 2 as optimal. Moreover, the element 5 indicates that player 1 will receive a payoff of 5, whereas—assuming the game to be zero-sum—player 2 will have a payoff of -5. In such a case, 5 is said to be the *value of the game*. Thus the game is completely solved.

The existence of a saddle point in the payoff matrix makes the solution of the game determinate. Unfortunately, it also makes it monotonous, because in repeated plays of the same game, the identical solution will invariably emerge. It is rather in games wherein no saddle point exists that more varied plays will appear; these we shall discuss in the following section.

dominated strategies   Before we examine that problem, however, a word may be said about a special phenomenon which characterizes some of the payoff matrices introduced above. If an element-by-element comparison is made of the first two rows in the matrix of Table 21.5, row 1 will reveal an inferior payoff to player 1, whichever strategy player 2 happens to adopt. There is no earthly reason, therefore, for player 1 ever to consider adopting strategy 1 (first row) when strategy 2 is available to him. Strategy 1 is thus said to be *dominated* by strategy 2 and can be removed forthright from the payoff matrix.

Actually, a dominated strategy does not even have to be inferior in every element, for so long as a strategy is *no better anywhere* than another strategy, it may be considered as dominated by the latter. Accordingly, a strategy involving payoffs (4, 8, 12) is regarded as dominated by another one with payoffs (5, 8, 12). However, when a strategy has *some* payoffs *larger* but *some* payoffs *less* than the corresponding elements in another strategy, *neither* of them dominates the other. For example, row 2 and row 3 in Table 21.5 do not dominate each other.

TABLE 21.5

	row min
$A = \begin{bmatrix} 4 & 3 & 6 \\ 6 & 5 & 8 \\ 7 & 1 & 5 \end{bmatrix}$	3 ⑤ → maximin 1
column max 7 ⑤ 8	
↓	
minimax	

Domination can also, of course, occur among the columns. In Table 21.5, column 2 dominates column 3 from the standpoint of player 2, because the former involves a lower payoff to his opponent (player 1) in every row. Thus, player 2 will never adopt strategy 3 when strategy 2 is available to him. For this reason, column 3 may also be removed from the payoff matrix.

After these dominated strategies (from both players' points of view) are expunged, the payoff matrix will reduce to

$$A = \begin{bmatrix} - & - & - \\ 6 & 5 & - \\ 7 & 1 & - \end{bmatrix}$$

Note that the solution point $a_{22} = 5$ is still retained in the reduced matrix. Furthermore, in the latter, the element $a_{22} = 5$ still constitutes a saddle point. The removal of dominated strategies, while simplifying the payoff matrix, will produce no effect on the final outcome of the game. As the reader can verify, the above matrix can actually be further reduced. But the solution point will stay.

EXERCISE 21.2

1 Given payoff matrix $A = \begin{bmatrix} 1 & 4 & 2 \\ 8 & 9 & 2 \\ 7 & 6 & 5 \end{bmatrix}$,

(a) List the row minima, and find the maximin.
(b) List the column maxima, and find the minimax.
(c) Is there a saddle point ? If so, which element is it ?
(d) What are the optimal strategies for the two players ?
(e) What is the payoff to player 1 ?
(f) Can you tell the payoff to player 2 without additional information ?

2 If the payoff matrix of the preceding problem is changed to

$$A = \begin{bmatrix} 10 & 4 & 7 & 8 \\ 3 & 3 & 6 & 0 \\ 6 & -1 & 5 & 3 \end{bmatrix}$$

how will you answer the same six questions ?

3 (a) In the payoff matrix of the preceding problem, seek out the dominated rows and columns. Also indicate the *dominating* rows and columns.
(b) If we remove all the dominated rows and columns, will the saddle point also be taken away ?

4   Find the saddle point, if any, in each of the following:

(a) $A = \begin{bmatrix} 4 & 0 & 1 \\ 5 & 3 & 8 \end{bmatrix}$
(b) $A = \begin{bmatrix} 6 & 0 & 7 \\ 3 & 1 & 6 \\ 5 & 4 & 2 \end{bmatrix}$

5   On the basis of the matrix $A = \begin{bmatrix} 6 & 2 & -3 \\ 5 & 0 & -1 \\ 3 & 4 & 7 \end{bmatrix}$, find:

(a) $\min_{j} (a_{1j})$ (d) $\max_{i} (a_{i1})$ (g) $\max_{i} \min_{j} (a_{ij})$

(b) $\min_{j} (a_{2j})$ (e) $\max_{i} (a_{i2})$ (h) $\min_{j} \max_{i} (a_{ij})$

(c) $\min_{j} (a_{3j})$ (f) $\max_{i} (a_{i3})$

6   Does the matrix in the preceding problem satisfy (21.6)? Hence, is there a saddle point?

21.3   Mixed Strategy: The Case of No Saddle Point

Let us now explore the case where the payoff matrix contains no saddle point. Consider a simple rectangular game with the following payoff matrix:

(21.7) $A = \begin{bmatrix} 4 & 1 \\ 2 & 3 \end{bmatrix}$

As the reader can readily verify, player 1's maximin is $a_{21} = 2$, whereas player 2's minimax is $a_{22} = 3$. Thus no saddle point exists. Optimally, both players should adopt their respective strategy 2; but if so, the actual outcome will be a payoff of $a_{22} = 3$ to player 1, even though he only expected the maximin ($= 2$). Pleasantly surprised, he tries to stick to the same strategy in repeated plays, but his opponent will soon learn to switch to strategy 1 (column 1), thereby reducing player 1's payoff to $a_{21} = 2$. Noticing player 2's consistent adoption of strategy 1, player 1 will also switch to his own strategy 1, which—in combination with player 2's strategy 1—can improve the payoff to $a_{11} = 4$. This will cause his opponent to revise his strategy again, and so on. As a result, varied plays will now occur in the game; this makes the game more interesting but also causes it to be apparently indeterminate in its outcome.

mixed strategy and expected payoff   A major feature of the above game is that each player should avoid the use of the same strategy in repeated plays, because adherence to the same strategy, like revealing a country's military plans to the enemy, will place oneself at a definite disadvantage. In other words, a *mixed strategy* should be adopted in lieu of the *pure strategy* appropriate in the saddle-point case. However, while the purpose of a mixed strategy is to keep the opponent in the dark by being unpredictable, by no means does it imply a totally random pattern of play. To the contrary, the conservative gamesmanship posited here would call for the careful selection of a particular *mixture* of pure strategies that can yield the optimal total payoff in the long run.

   First, let us see how a mixed strategy works. Suppose that player 1 decides arbitrarily to use strategy 1 (row 1) 20 times out of 30 and strategy 2 (row 2) 10 times out of 30; then the *relative frequencies* of the two strategies (2:1) are determinate. But the exact sequence in which the two strategies are used in successive plays of the game must be deliberately left indefinite, in order to achieve the desired unpredictability. For this purpose, he may use, for instance, a "random device" as follows: Place two red balls and one white ball of the same size into a bag; draw a ball from the bag before each individual play; adopt strategy 1 if the ball is red, but strategy 2 if it is white. In the long run—but only in the long run—the relative frequencies of the appearance of the red and white balls will tend to be in the ratio of 2:1, as intended.

   Let us denote the intended relative frequency of the ith strategy by the symbol x_i. Then the particular mixture specified above is

(21.8) $(x_1, x_2) = (\frac{2}{3}, \frac{1}{3})$

Needless to say, each x_i is by definition a number between 0 and 1. Furthermore, the sum of the x_i must be unity. Symbolically, the relative frequencies x_i will always have the properties that[1]

(21.9) $x_i \geq 0$ and $\sum_i x_i = 1$

   Given the mixture in (21.8), what payoff can player 1 expect to receive in repeated plays of the game with payoff matrix (21.7)? First, let us assume the opponent to use strategy 1 purely—which makes the first column $\begin{bmatrix} 4 \\ 2 \end{bmatrix}$ relevant. In view of the choice of the mixture (21.8), player 1 should, in the long run, get a payoff 4 in two-thirds of all plays and a payoff 2 in one-third of all plays. The *expected payoff per play* (E) should therefore, in the probability sense, be

---

[1] Strictly speaking, we should write $0 \leq x_i \leq 1$ instead of $x_i \geq 0$; but by virtue of the second property, namely $\Sigma x_i = 1$, the ≤ 1 part of the statement will prove redundant and thus may be omitted.

the weighted average

$$E_1 = \tfrac{2}{3}(4) + \tfrac{1}{3}(2) = \tfrac{10}{3}$$

where the subscript in E_1 serves notice that player 2 is assumed to use his strategy 1 purely. This equation can be written alternatively as

$$E_1 = [\tfrac{2}{3} \ \tfrac{1}{3}] \begin{bmatrix} 4 \\ 2 \end{bmatrix}$$

where the row vector specifies the mixed strategy involved, and the column vector the relevant column from the payoff matrix. Similarly, if player 2 is assumed to use his strategy 2 purely, so that the second column of (21.7) becomes applicable, we can calculate another expected payoff

$$E_2 = [\tfrac{2}{3} \ \tfrac{1}{3}] \begin{bmatrix} 1 \\ 3 \end{bmatrix} = \tfrac{2}{3} + \tfrac{3}{3} = \tfrac{5}{3}$$

But if player 2 also mixes his strategies, player 1's expected payoff will fall somewhere in between the above two weighted averages. The important point is that the *minimum expected payoff* which player 1 can count on with the mixed strategy described in (21.8) is $E_2 = \tfrac{5}{3}$.

The mixture shown in (21.8) was only *arbitrarily* chosen. Suppose, now, that we select another arbitrary mixture

$$(21.8') \qquad (x_1', x_2') = (\tfrac{1}{10}, \tfrac{9}{10})$$

The expected payoffs will then become

$$E_1' = [\tfrac{1}{10} \ \tfrac{9}{10}] \begin{bmatrix} 4 \\ 2 \end{bmatrix} = \tfrac{11}{5}$$

$$E_2' = [\tfrac{1}{10} \ \tfrac{9}{10}] \begin{bmatrix} 1 \\ 3 \end{bmatrix} = \tfrac{14}{5}$$

provided that player 2 uses his strategies purely. If player 2 also tries to mix his strategies, then the expected payoff to player 1 will again lie between the last two figures. Therefore, the minimum expected payoff to player 1 under this new mixture will be $E_1' = \tfrac{11}{5}$. Even though this is an appreciable improvement over the $\tfrac{5}{3}$ figure for the first mixture, there is no assurance that the mixture in (21.8') is the *best* available. The *maximin* principle—now to be applied to the expected payoff E, rather than to the original entries in the payoff matrix —obliges player 1 to search for that particular mixture which will yield *the largest possible minimum expected payoff per play*, i.e., will yield the *maximin E*.

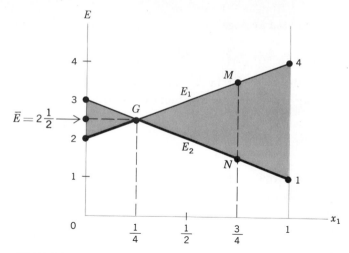

FIGURE 21.1

the graphical solution   When there are only *two rows* in the payoff matrix, a remarkably simple graphical method can be employed to find the maximin mixed strategy for player 1.

Our task is to find the optimal values of the two variables x_1 and x_2. Since $x_1 + x_2 = 1$, however, it is sufficient merely to find the value of $\bar{x}_1$; once that is found, we immediately have $\bar{x}_2 = 1 - \bar{x}_1$. With this understanding, we can plot the variable E (expected payoff) against the single independent variable x_1 as in Fig. 21.1. Note that, inasmuch as x_1 cannot fall below zero or exceed unity, only the interval $[0, 1]$ needs to be plotted on the horizontal axis.

Now, on the basis of the payoff matrix $A = \begin{bmatrix} 4 & 1 \\ 2 & 3 \end{bmatrix}$ in (21.7), we can write the expected payoffs E_1 and E_2 in terms of the yet-to-be-determined relative frequencies x_1 and $(1 - x_1)$ as follows:

(21.10)
$$E_1 = \begin{bmatrix} x_1 & 1 - x_1 \end{bmatrix} \begin{bmatrix} 4 \\ 2 \end{bmatrix} = 2x_1 + 2$$

$$E_2 = \begin{bmatrix} x_1 & 1 - x_1 \end{bmatrix} \begin{bmatrix} 1 \\ 3 \end{bmatrix} = 3 - 2x_1$$

Each of these expresses the expected payoff E as a linear function of x_1 and plots as a straight line. For any chosen value of x_1, say, $x_1 = \frac{3}{4}$, the height of the point M on line E_1 indicates the expected payoff to player 1 when the opponent adopts his pure strategy 1, whereas the height of point N on line E_2 shows the value of E when player 2 uses strategy 2. It follows that the intermediate points on the line segment MN are associated with the expected payoffs corresponding to various mixtures—convex combinations—of player 2's strategies. The shaded area, which consists of two separate triangles in this case, thus shows the set of all possible expected payoffs. What the *maximin* principle dictates is that player 1 should delineate the set of all minimum expected payoffs and then find the value of x_1 which maximizes from among that set of minima. In Fig. 21.1, the minima set is simply the set of points on the lower boundary of the shaded area (the heavy kinked line). The maximum in this set is, of course, point G.

Since G is at the intersection of lines E_1 and E_2, the solution value of x_1 can be obtained by equating E_1 and E_2 in (21.10). Thus, we have

$$2x_1 + 2 = 3 - 2x_1$$

and $\qquad \bar{x}_1 = \tfrac{1}{4}$

It can then be deduced that the optimal values of x_2 and E are, respectively,

$$\bar{x}_2 = 1 - \tfrac{1}{4} = \tfrac{3}{4}$$

and

(21.11) $\qquad \bar{E}(= \bar{E}_1) = 2\bar{x}_1 + 2 = \tfrac{5}{2}$

These results can also be confirmed graphically in Fig. 21.1. With this optimal mixed strategy, $(\bar{x}_1, \bar{x}_2) = (\tfrac{1}{4}, \tfrac{3}{4})$—which, incidentally, requires him to place one red ball and three white balls in his bag—player 1 can expect a payoff of at least $\tfrac{5}{2}$ per play in repeated plays of the game, regardless of what player 2 does.

Inasmuch as there are also only *two columns* in the payoff matrix (21.7), the same method can be adapted to the problem of finding the optimal mixed strategy of player 2. Applying the *minimax* principle, he should find a pair of relative frequencies for his strategies, (y_1, y_2), with the properties

$$y_j \geq 0 \qquad \text{and} \qquad \sum_j y_j = 1 \qquad [\text{cf. (21.9)}]$$

that will minimize the maximal expected payoffs to player 1 under various circumstances.

If player 1 uses strategy 1 (row 1), the row vector [4 1] in (21.7) will determine the payoff, and thus player 2's mixture (y_1, y_2) or $(y_1, 1 - y_1)$ will in general yield

(21.12) $\qquad E_{(1)} = [4 \quad 1] \begin{bmatrix} y_1 \\ 1 - y_1 \end{bmatrix} = 3y_1 + 1$

where the parenthesized subscript indicates the particular strategy assumed for player 1. Analogously, in case player 1 uses strategy 2, so that the row

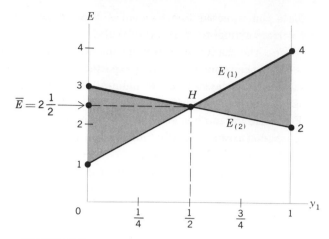

FIGURE 21.2

vector [2 3] becomes relevant, we have

$$(21.13) \qquad E_{(2)} = \begin{bmatrix} 2 & 3 \end{bmatrix} \begin{bmatrix} y_1 \\ 1 - y_1 \end{bmatrix} = 3 - y_1$$

These two equations are represented graphically by the two straight lines in Fig. 21.2, where E is plotted against the independent variable y_1.

In accordance with the minimax principle, player 2 must first delineate the set of maximal expected payoffs to player 1 corresponding to all the possible values of y_1 in the interval $[0, 1]$. The upper boundary of the shaded area comprises this desired set. Since the minimum of that set occurs at point H—at the intersection of lines $E_{(1)}$ and $E_{(2)}$—we can equate (21.12) and (21.13) to find the value of $\bar{y}_1$:

$$3y_1 + 1 = 3 - y_1$$

whence $\qquad \bar{y}_1 = \tfrac{1}{2}$

From this, it follows that

$$\bar{y}_2 = 1 - \tfrac{1}{2} = \tfrac{1}{2}$$

and

$$(21.14) \qquad \bar{E}(= \bar{E}_{(1)}) = 3\bar{y}_1 + 1 = \tfrac{5}{2}$$

These solutions are also duly confirmed in Fig. 21.2. Therefore, if player 2 adopts this optimal mixed strategy $(\bar{y}_1, \bar{y}_2) = (\tfrac{1}{2}, \tfrac{1}{2})$, he can keep the expected payoff of his opponent to at most $\tfrac{5}{2}$ per play in repeated plays of the game, regardless of what player 1 does. The reader will observe that the *minimax*

Mathematical Programming and Game Theory

value of the expected payoff to player 1 in (21.14) and the *maximin* value found in (21.11) are precisely the same.

To sum up: From what seemed at first glance to be an indeterminate game, we have demonstrated by the above example that there can nevertheless be found determinate optimal *mixed strategies* for both players which lead to an *optimal expected payoff* of a definite magnitude. Moreover, the value of $\bar{E}$ is at once the *maximin* for player 1 and the *minimax* for player 2; as such, it provides a solution to the game, even though no saddle point exists in the payoff matrix. When duly generalized, these observations lead to the so-called *minimax theorem*, or *fundamental theorem of game theory*: For *any* two-person constant-sum game, there always exist a maximin expected payoff and a minimax expected payoff that are equal to each other.

further comments on the graphical solution   The observant reader must have noticed that the phrase "in repeated plays of the game" has appeared several times in the above discussion. It bears reiterating that the concept of optimal relative frequencies $(\bar{x}_1, \bar{x}_2)$ and $(\bar{y}_1, \bar{y}_2)$ is strictly relevant only in the long pull, when the same game is played over and over again. In every individual play, a player can only use one (pure) strategy, since the balls in the bag can, in each drawing, only come out either red or white, but never pink. It is only in the long run that the intended mixture of strategies can be translated into reality, such as using strategy 1 in 25 times out of 100 individual plays. By the same token, the optimal expected payoff per game ($\bar{E}$) is also a long-run—and probabilistic—concept; insofar as each single play is concerned, the player will indeed realize a payoff other than $\bar{E}$. This should become clear when we recall that the actual payoff in each play can only be one of the four entries of the payoff matrix in (21.7), namely, 4, 1, 2, or 3, whereas the value of $\bar{E}$ is according to Fig. 21.1 equal to $\frac{5}{2}$, which differs from every payoff entry. In this connection, it is of interest to note that since the pure-strategy optimal payoffs are

$$a_{21} = 2 \quad \text{[player 1's maximin]}$$
$$a_{22} = 3 \quad \text{[player 2's minimax]}$$

the mixed-strategy optimal payoff, $\bar{E} = \frac{5}{2}$, represents an improvement for *both* players. Instead of the pure-strategy maximin of 2, player 1 can now expect $\frac{5}{2}$; yet player 2 also finds this to his taste because $\frac{5}{2}$ is less than the pure-strategy minimax of 3.

The above-described graphical method of solution is applicable whenever a player has no more than two pure strategies available to him. For then he can just plot E against x_1 alone, knowing that once $\bar{x}_1$ is found, then it follows that $\bar{x}_2 = 1 - \bar{x}_1$. Note, however, that the applicability of the method depends in

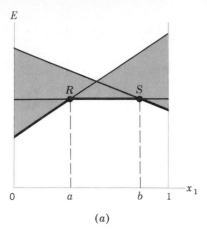

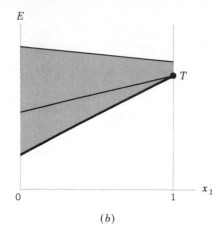

FIGURE 21.3

no way upon the number of pure strategies available to the *opponent*. This latter number will determine the number of straight lines which would together define the shaded area, but it cannot affect the dimension of the graph. In each diagram of Fig. 21.3, for instance, the opponent (player 2) is assumed to have a total of *three* pure strategies open to him; thus there are drawn three lines E_1, E_2, and E_3 (not labeled). While the shaded area is now shaped differently, its lower boundary is not any harder to delineate. Nor is it any more difficult to locate the maximum on that boundary.

Figure 21.3 also serves to illustrate two varieties of outcome that differ basically from the one in Fig. 21.1. In diagram *a*, all the points on the line segment RS on the lower boundary of the shaded area are equally optimal, because RS happens to be parallel to the horizontal axis. This is then a case of multiple solution, in which the optimal value of x_1 consists of the closed interval $[a, b]$ or, more formally,

$$\bar{x}_1 = \{x_1 \mid a \leq x_1 \leq b\}$$

Note that point R is the intersection of a pair of straight lines. Thus, by setting the two equations corresponding to those lines equal to each other, we can always find the exact value of a algebraically. The value of b can also be found similarly, since point S is another intersection of two lines.

In diagram *b*, the highest point on the lower boundary is point T, which corresponds to $x_1 = 1$. This time the solution is unique, but since the optimal mixture is $(\bar{x}_1, \bar{x}_2) = (1, 0)$, player 1 is told to adopt his strategy 1 exclusively. The "mixture" is not a mixture at all! It seems, therefore, that although the graphical method was discussed primarily in the context of mixed-strategy situations, it is equally applicable to games with pure-strategy solutions.

EXERCISE 21.3

For each of the following games, find the maximin mixed strategy $(\bar{x}_1, \bar{x}_2)$ for player 1, and calculate the optimal expected payoff per game $\bar{E}$:

1 $\quad A = \begin{bmatrix} 7 & 5 \\ 2 & 9 \end{bmatrix}$

4 $\quad A = \begin{bmatrix} 6 & -2 & 3 \\ 0 & 3 & 3 \end{bmatrix}$

2 $\quad A = \begin{bmatrix} 8 & 5 \\ 2 & 0 \end{bmatrix}$

5 $\quad A = \begin{bmatrix} 6 & 0 & 3 \\ 0 & 10 & 3 \end{bmatrix}$

3 $\quad A = \begin{bmatrix} 5 & 7 & 2 \\ 0 & -1 & 8 \end{bmatrix}$

6 $\quad A = \begin{bmatrix} 10 & -1 & 3 & 7 \\ 2 & 4 & 1 & 0 \end{bmatrix}$

21.4   The Rectangular Game as a Linear Program

The graphical method expounded above is easy to use, but it is appropriate only when the payoff matrix is either $2 \times n$ or $m \times 2$ in dimension. To generalize our discussion to the case of an $m \times n$ payoff matrix, it is necessary to emancipate ourselves from graphs entirely. Fortunately, it can be demonstrated that the solving of a rectangular game is mathematically equivalent to solving a linear program. Since we know how to solve linear programs of any dimension, all we need is a procedure for converting a rectangular game into a linear program.

process of conversion   The clue to this is to be found in Fig. 21.4, which reproduces the two expected-payoff lines of Fig. 21.1, based on the payoff matrix (21.7). Instead of the shading in Fig. 21.1, let us now shade the area below the heavy kinked line. The new shading, unlike the old, delineates a *convex set* of points which is closed and bounded from above. Mathematically, this convex set is the intersection of four closed halfspaces defined by the following four inequalities:

$$(21.15) \qquad E \leq 2x_1 + 2 \qquad E \leq -2x_1 + 3 \qquad x_1 \geq 0 \qquad x_1 \leq 1$$

Viewed in this light, the search for the maximin point G becomes a matter of finding the highest possible horizontal supporting line to our convex set (see arrows). Moreover, if we regard the desired supporting line as a member of a family of horizontal lines generated by a linear *objective function*, we may express

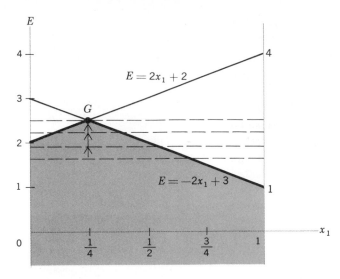

FIGURE 21.4

the problem as follows:

$$\text{Maximize} \quad E$$

(21.16)
$$\text{subject to} \quad E \leq \quad 2x_1 + 2$$
$$E \leq -2x_1 + 3$$

$$\text{and} \quad 0 \leq \quad x_1 \leq 1$$

This is not quite in the customary form of a linear program, but a few simple transformations will reduce (21.16) to the familiar format. First, of course, the last line in (21.16) may be replaced by the following [see (21.9)]:

(21.16′)
$$x_1 + x_2 = 1 \quad \text{[an additional constraint]}$$
$$x_1, x_2 \geq 0 \quad \text{[nonnegativity restrictions]}$$

But since this introduces x_2 into the picture, the other two constraints in (21.16) must be modified accordingly.

From (21.10) we see that, if the expression $(1 - x_1)$ in the row vector is changed to x_2, the right-hand expressions $(2x_1 + 2)$ and $(3 - 2x_1)$ in the two equations will become $(4x_1 + 2x_2)$ and $(x_1 + 3x_2)$, respectively. Substituting these into (21.16) and rearranging terms, we can express the two constraints as

(21.16″)
$$E \leq 4x_1 + 2x_2 \quad \text{or} \quad -4x_1 - 2x_2 + E \leq 0$$
$$E \leq \quad x_1 + 3x_2 \quad \text{or} \quad - x_1 - 3x_2 + E \leq 0$$

where we are now apparently treating E as a third choice variable.

Mathematical Programming and Game Theory

To qualify E as a third variable, however, we are compelled to subject it to the traditional nonnegativity restriction, $E \geq 0$. Are we justified in doing so? The sign of E, we recall, hinges entirely on the payoff matrix. If all entries in the matrix are nonnegative, as in (21.7), then it is necessarily true that $E \geq 0$. But if the payoff matrix contains one or more negative elements, then the legitimacy of the latter restriction will become problematic. Fortunately, the transformation theorem introduced earlier in connection with (21.4) assures us that the optimal strategy of a game is invariant with respect to the addition of a constant c to every element in the matrix. Hence, given a payoff matrix such as $A = \begin{bmatrix} -3 & -1 \\ -2 & -5 \end{bmatrix}$, we can—by adding 5—first transform it to $A^* = \begin{bmatrix} 2 & 4 \\ 3 & 0 \end{bmatrix}$. Then we can write $E^* \geq 0$, where $E^* = E + 5$, and formulate the program in terms of E^* instead. The optimal strategies will still come out to be the same; the only adjustment needed in interpreting the solution of the transformed program is to subtract 5 from $\bar{E}^*$ to get $\bar{E}$.

Lastly, the objective function in (21.16) may also be rewritten into the customary form:

$$(21.16''') \qquad \pi = 0x_1 + 0x_2 + E$$

Thus, by combining (21.16'), (21.16''), and (21.16'''), the linear program in (21.16) will now assume the form

$$\begin{aligned}
\text{Maximize} \quad & \pi = & 0x_1 + 0x_2 + E \\
\text{subject to} \quad & & -4x_1 - 2x_2 + E \leq 0 \\
(21.17) \quad & & -x_1 - 3x_2 + E \leq 0 \\
& & x_1 + x_2 \quad\quad\; = 1 \\
\text{and} \quad & & x_1, x_2, E \quad\;\; \geq 0
\end{aligned}$$

which differs from the standard maximization program only in the presence of a *strict equality*, $x_1 + x_2 = 1$. The simplex method is now fully applicable, although the fact that no slack variable is needed for the third constraint will necessitate the introduction of an artificial variable, in order to "manufacture" a ready-made initial basic feasible solution.

However, if we wish, we may take the liberty of simply writing $x_1 + x_2 \leq 1$, instead of $x_1 + x_2 = 1$, in the third constraint. This seemingly arbitrary step may be intuitively justified as follows: Should the expected payoff $\bar{E}$ be positive, then the player certainly would not miss any opportunity of playing the game; i.e., he would play 100 percent of the time. In that event, we will find $\bar{x}_1 + \bar{x}_2 = 1$ rather than $\bar{x}_1 + \bar{x}_2 < 1$ anyway. Should $\bar{E}$ be zero, on the other hand, the player would be indifferent about whether to play or not to play, so that he might play only 80 percent of the time, with the result that $\bar{x}_1 + \bar{x}_2 < 1$. But even in this latter event, we can (by not counting the other 20 percent of the plays) scale up the $\bar{x}_1$ and $\bar{x}_2$ so that they will add up to 1. In short, as long as $\bar{E} > 0$, the liberty we took makes no difference, whereas in case $\bar{E} = 0$, a scaling adjustment will easily take care of the complication and guarantee a solution that satisfies the condition $\bar{x}_1 + \bar{x}_2 = 1$.

By incorporating this last modification into the linear program, then, we finally arrive at the completely standardized format:

$$\text{Maximize} \quad \pi = 0x_1 + 0x_2 + E$$

(21.18)   subject to
$$\begin{bmatrix} -4 & -2 & 1 \\ -1 & -3 & 1 \\ 1 & 1 & 0 \end{bmatrix} \begin{bmatrix} x_1 \\ x_2 \\ E \end{bmatrix} \leq \begin{bmatrix} 0 \\ 0 \\ 1 \end{bmatrix}$$

and $$x_1, x_2, E \geq 0$$

The reader should note that in the 3×3 coefficient matrix, the third row and the third column (each of which contains a series of 1s followed by a 0) serve to *border* a 2×2 matrix that represents $-A'$, i.e., the payoff matrix $A = \begin{bmatrix} 4 & 1 \\ 2 & 3 \end{bmatrix}$ in (21.7) duly transposed and multiplied by -1. This suggests an easy rule for deriving the coefficient matrix of the constraints once the payoff matrix A is given:

$$\begin{bmatrix} -4 & -2 & 1 \\ -1 & -3 & 1 \\ 1 & 1 & 0 \end{bmatrix} = \begin{bmatrix} -A' & 1 \\ & 1 \\ \hline 1 & 1 & 0 \end{bmatrix}$$

Note also that the column vector of constants on the right of the constraints consists merely of a series of 0s followed by a unit element.

To sum up, the conversion process involves the following steps:

1   Check whether the payoff matrix is nonnegative. If so, proceed to the ensuing steps. If not, add an appropriate constant to each element to make the matrix nonnegative.

2   Write a linear objective function in which the relative-frequency variables x_i are assigned zero coefficients, whereas the expected-payoff variable E— taken to be the last variable—is given a unit coefficient. Since we are taking player 1's viewpoint, this objective function is to be maximized.

3   In the constraints, the coefficient matrix on the left is the matrix $-A'$ bordered with unit elements *on the right* and *at the bottom*, and having a zero as the last element in the principal diagonal. The column vector to the right of the $\leq$ sign, on the other hand, is a series of 0s followed by a single unit element.

4   All the variables x_i and E are restricted to be nonnegative.

5   In interpreting the solution, make sure to reverse the adjustment of the payoff matrix cited in the first step above.

The conversion process just outlined can naturally be applied also to the general rectangular game with an $m \times n$ payoff matrix

$$
A = \begin{bmatrix}
a_{11} & a_{12} & \cdots & a_{1n} \\
a_{21} & a_{22} & \cdots & a_{2n} \\
\multicolumn{4}{c}{\dotfill} \\
a_{m1} & a_{m2} & \cdots & a_{mn}
\end{bmatrix}
$$

Since player 1 now possesses m pure strategies in all, there will be a total of $(m + 1)$ variables in the linear program, namely, the x_i (with $i = 1, \ldots, m$) plus the variable E. Assuming the matrix A to be nonnegative, we can immediately construct the corresponding linear program as follows:

$$\text{Maximize} \qquad \pi = 0x_1 + \cdots + 0x_m + E$$

(21.19)   subject to
$$
\left[
\begin{array}{ccc|c}
 & & & 1 \\
 & -A' & & \vdots \\
 & & & 1 \\
\hline
1 & \cdots & 1 & 0
\end{array}
\right]
\begin{bmatrix} x_1 \\ \vdots \\ x_m \\ E \end{bmatrix}
\leq
\begin{bmatrix} 0 \\ \vdots \\ 0 \\ 1 \end{bmatrix}
$$

and $x_1, \ldots, x_m, E \geq 0$

the simplex solution   According to the graphical approach in Fig. 21.1, the game described by the linear program (21.18) has the maximin solution

$$(\bar{x}_1, \bar{x}_2) = (\tfrac{1}{4}, \tfrac{3}{4})$$

It is only to be expected that the identical solution will emerge from the simplex method, as illustrated in Table 21.6

Tableau I is constructed from (21.18), after the addition of three slack variables s_1, s_2, and s_3. A ready-made initial solution is easily spotted; it includes in it the variable π and the three slack variables. Checking over row 0, it is obvious that column E should be chosen as the pivot column, since it has the largest (in this case, the only) negative entry. In selecting the pivot row, however, we find a tie between row 1 and row 2 for the minimum displacement quotient. In this, we are now witnessing an actual example of degeneracy. According to the proposed tie-breaking practice, we decide to take row 1 as the pivot row, so that s_1 rather than s_2 will be displaced from the basis. Then, by duly converting the E column into a unit vector (with elements 0, 1, 0, 0), we are led to Tableau II.

From there on, the straight application of the method suffices; but note that the maximand does not rise above the zero level until Tableau IV, the optimal tableau, is reached. The result

$$(\bar{\pi}, \bar{x}_1, \bar{x}_2, \bar{E}) = (\tfrac{5}{2}, \tfrac{1}{4}, \tfrac{3}{4}, \tfrac{5}{2})$$

checks, of course, with the previously obtained solution. Note that we have here $\bar{\pi} = \tfrac{5}{2}$, which is identical with the value of $\bar{E}$. This should not surprise us, because in our objective function we have deliberately defined π to be identical with E.

EXERCISE 21.4

1   Convert the six games in Exercise 21.3 into corresponding linear programs. (*Note:* Watch out for payoff matrices with negative elements.)

2   Solve the first and second linear programs in Exercise 21.4-1 by the simplex method, and check your answers against Exercises 21.3-1 and 21.3-2.

TABLE 21.6

Tableau	Row	π	x_1	x_2	E	s_1	s_2	s_3	Constant
	0	1	0	0	-1	0	0	0	$\boxed{0}$
I	1	0	-4	-2	$\textcircled{1}$	1	0	0	0
	2	0	-1	-3	1	0	1	0	0
	3	0	1	1	0	0	0	1	1
	0	1	-4	-2	0	1	0	0	$\boxed{0}$
II	1	0	-4	-2	1	1	0	0	0
	2	0	$\textcircled{3}$	-1	0	-1	1	0	0
	3	0	1	1	0	0	0	1	1
	0	1	0	$-\tfrac{10}{3}$	0	$-\tfrac{1}{3}$	$\tfrac{4}{3}$	0	$\boxed{0}$
III	1	0	0	$-\tfrac{10}{3}$	1	$-\tfrac{1}{3}$	$\tfrac{4}{3}$	0	0
	2	0	1	$-\tfrac{1}{3}$	0	$-\tfrac{1}{3}$	$\tfrac{1}{3}$	0	0
	3	0	0	$\textcircled{\tfrac{4}{3}}$	0	$\tfrac{1}{3}$	$-\tfrac{1}{3}$	1	1
	0	1	0	0	0	$\tfrac{1}{2}$	$\tfrac{1}{2}$	$\tfrac{5}{2}$	$\boxed{\tfrac{5}{2}}$
IV	1	0	0	0	1	$\tfrac{1}{4}$	$\tfrac{1}{4}$	$\tfrac{5}{2}$	$\tfrac{5}{2}$
	2	0	1	0	0	$-\tfrac{1}{4}$	$\tfrac{1}{4}$	$\tfrac{1}{4}$	$\tfrac{1}{4}$
	3	0	0	1	0	$\tfrac{1}{4}$	$-\tfrac{1}{4}$	$\tfrac{3}{4}$	$\tfrac{3}{4}$

3   Solve the third linear program in Exercise 21.4-1, and check your answer against Exercise 21.3-3.

4   In (21.19), what are the dimensions of the coefficient matrix, the variable vector, and the constant vector in the constraint section?

21.5   Duality Once Again

After having solved a game as if it were a linear program, it is only natural to ask: Is there any economic meaning to the dual of that program? The answer is yes indeed. Whereas the primal yields the maximin expected payoff, the dual will give its minimax counterpart. Furthermore, just as player 1 can find his optimal mixed strategy $(\bar{x}_1, \ldots, \bar{x}_m)$ from the primal, player 2 can likewise find his best mixture $(\bar{y}_1, \ldots, \bar{y}_n)$ from the dual.

the dual program   Let us first formulate the dual of the program (21.18). Since there are three constraints, the dual must have three choice variables, which we designate as y_1, y_2, and F. Then we may immediately write

$$\text{Minimize} \qquad \pi^* = 0y_1 + 0y_2 + F$$

$$(21.20) \qquad \text{subject to} \qquad \begin{bmatrix} -4 & -1 & 1 \\ -2 & -3 & 1 \\ 1 & 1 & 0 \end{bmatrix} \begin{bmatrix} y_1 \\ y_2 \\ F \end{bmatrix} \geq \begin{bmatrix} 0 \\ 0 \\ 1 \end{bmatrix}$$

$$\text{and} \qquad y_1, y_2, F \geq 0$$

It may be noticed that the coefficient matrix in the constraints is again a bordered matrix, but the $-A'$ part is now replaced by $-A$.

It remains to be demonstrated that the solution to the dual will yield the optimal solution for player 2. Before attempting such a demonstration, however, let us first check whether the solution of this dual will indeed conform to player 2's minimax solution obtained in Fig. 21.2, namely,

$$(\bar{y}_1, \bar{y}_2) = (\tfrac{1}{2}, \tfrac{1}{2}) \qquad (\text{minimax payoff} = \tfrac{5}{2})$$

To this end, the reader will recall that, when two linear programs are dual to each other, the optimal simplex tableau of either program will always contain the solution of the other. Thus, from the last tableau in Table 21.6, we can immediately read from row 0 that

$$(\bar{y}_1, \bar{y}_2, \bar{F}) = (\tfrac{1}{2}, \tfrac{1}{2}, \tfrac{5}{2})$$

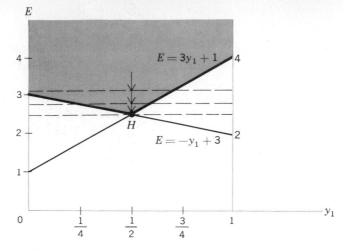

FIGURE 21.5

This result checks with that of Fig. 21.2, provided that we interpret $\bar{F}(=\bar{\pi}^*)$ as the minimax expected payoff.

player 2's linear program   To rationalize our economic interpretation of the dual, however, we should formulate independently a linear program describing the game as player 2 sees it, and then show that it is identical with the dual derived in (21.20). Since the process of formulation closely parallels that which led to (21.18), a brief sketch should be sufficient.

First, let us reproduce in Fig. 21.5 the two expected-payoff lines of Fig. 21.2, but again shade the diagram differently—this time above the heavy kinked line. The new shaded area, a closed convex set bounded from below, is the intersection of four closed halfspaces defined by the following inequalities:

$$E \geq 3y_1 + 1 \qquad E \geq -y_1 + 3 \qquad y_1 \geq 0 \qquad y_1 \leq 1 \qquad \text{[cf. (21.15)]}$$

In this light, the locating of the minimax point H becomes the problem of finding the lowest horizontal supporting line to the said convex set (see arrows). Therefore, we may conceive of the problem as one of minimizing a linear objective function, subject to the inequalities just enumerated.

By applying the same type of transformation to the above inequalities as we did to (21.15)—this time utilizing (21.12) and (21.13) instead of (21.10) for the explicit introduction of the y_2 variable—we obtain

$$-4y_1 - y_2 + E \geq 0$$
$$-2y_1 - 3y_2 + E \geq 0$$
$$y_1 + y_2 = 1$$
$$y_1, y_2, E \geq 0$$

Next, if we now change $y_1 + y_2 = 1$ to $y_1 + y_2 \geq 1$† and introduce an appropriate objective function, the following linear program for player 2 will emerge:

Minimize $\quad \pi^* = 0y_1 + 0y_2 + E$

subject to $\quad \begin{bmatrix} -4 & -1 & 1 \\ -2 & -3 & 1 \\ 1 & 1 & 0 \end{bmatrix} \begin{bmatrix} y_1 \\ y_2 \\ E \end{bmatrix} \geq \begin{bmatrix} 0 \\ 0 \\ 1 \end{bmatrix}$

and $\quad y_1, y_2, E \geq 0$

While formulated independently, this program is obviously the same as the dual program in (21.20), except for the minor detail that in the dual the variable F is used in place of E. The only reason a new variable F was introduced in the dual is that we could not presume then that the meaning of the third dual variable would be identical with E. Now that we know $F \equiv E$, we may simply drop the symbol F altogether and use E in both the primal and the dual.

Even though the above illustration is limited to the simple case of a 2×2 payoff matrix, what we said about the application of duality to game theory applies also to larger rectangular games. Accordingly, the dual of the general program in (21.19) should again represent the same game looked at from the opponent's point of view.

EXERCISE 21.5

1   Solve the dual program (21.20) by the simplex method.

2   Given a 3×5 payoff matrix, how many choice variables will there be—besides E—in the primal program and in the dual program?

3   Given the following payoff matrices, formulate the linear programs from the viewpoint of player 2:

$(a) \quad A = \begin{bmatrix} 4 & 2 \\ 0 & 9 \end{bmatrix}$ $\qquad (c) \quad A = \begin{bmatrix} -1 & 4 & -3 \\ 0 & -2 & 8 \end{bmatrix}$

$(b) \quad A = \begin{bmatrix} 8 & 9 & 5 \\ 7 & 6 & 0 \end{bmatrix}$

4   Write the dual of (21.19).

† Since E (payoff to player 1) is nonnegative, player 2 would naturally prefer not to play the game whenever possible. This is why we must impose the restriction in the form $\Sigma y_j \geq 1$ (instead of ≤ 1).

5   From the final tableaus obtained in Exercise 21.4-2, read the values of $\bar{y}_1$, $\bar{y}_2$, and $\bar{E}$.

6   From the final tableau obtained in Exercise 21.4-3:

    (a)   Read the values of $\bar{y}_1$, $\bar{y}_2$, and $\bar{y}_3$.

    (b)   Read the value of $\bar{E}$. (*Warning:* We want $\bar{E}$ pertaining to the original payoff matrix, not $\bar{E}^*$.)

21.6   Limitations of Mathematical Programming and Game Theory

Mathematical programming and game theory have served to broaden the framework of our discussion of optimization to the cases of inequality constraints and of maximin and minimax objectives. Actually, even though these two relatively recent developments in mathematical economics evolved from independent sources, they have been shown as having much in common.

The applications of mathematical programming and game theory are quite broad. The former is capable of handling many problems that involve cost minimization subject to certain constraints regarding the minimum quality of the product, or output (or profit) maximization subject to certain limitations of capacity. Apart from its use in practical industrial management, mathematical programming also enables us to view the theory of production and resource allocation in a new light. As for game theory, its application to the analysis of duopoly situations should be obvious. Also, even if a firm has more than one competitor, as under oligopoly, a two-person game may nonetheless be relevant if we are willing to lump all the competitors together and designate them jointly as player 2. It should be pointed out, too, that there also exist theories of many-person and nonconstant-sum games, which, for reasons of space limitations, we have omitted from the discussion.

However, mathematical programming and game theory are not without limitations of their own. In game theory, for instance, without regard to the personality and psyche of the players involved, an arbitrary guiding principle —that of conservative gamesmanship—has been forced upon them. By this device, we are assured of a solution, but when a game is played, it is the participants—not the game theorist—who must define what is to be considered as the desired objective, and it is just possible that the attainment of a maximin or a minimax may not be their cup of tea! Second, granted that the player is a conservative gamesman, he will still need a complete knowledge of the payoff matrix before he can determine his optimal strategy. But the real-life player (say the gasoline station owner who was introduced at the beginning of this chapter) may not always possess full information as to what the payoff will be for each and every possible combination of strategies available to him and his opponent. Thus the determinacy of the solution may be illusory.

What about mathematical programming? For one thing, in the above discussion we have always assumed the choice variables to be continuous. In actuality, though, one or more of the variables may admit of integer values only—an optimal output of 3.75 airplanes, e.g., would not quite make practical sense. This complication fortunately is well taken care of by an offshoot of mathematical-programming techniques, known as *integer programming*, which yields only integer solution values. A more serious limitation—and this is a limitation not only of mathematical programming, but of all the optimization frameworks considered in this volume—lies in the *static* nature of the solution. In writing an optimal solution, say, $(\bar{x}_1, \ldots, \bar{x}_n)$, we are expressing the best choice that can be made of each variable x_j under a set of given circumstances, but since each $\bar{x}_j$ represents a single numerical value, it can only pertain either to a single point of time, or to a period of time during which all the circumstances postulated in the problem experience no changes. In either case, the problem and its solution are static. A *dynamic* optimization problem, in contrast, would ask for the complete *optimal time path* of each choice variable in a given period, not just a single optimal value. To solve such a problem, however, we must first acquire a knowledge of the mathematical methods of *calculus of variations*, *optimal control theory*, and *dynamic programming*. Since these topics can hardly be explained with a proper degree of thoroughness and clarity within a limited number of pages, they are best to be relegated to a separate volume.

Thus, we have now brought another part of the book to a close by pointing out the limitations of the techniques and analyses involved. The purpose of this is not, of course, to discredit the mathematical methods that have just been painstakingly expounded; rather it is to caution the reader not to attribute to them a degree of omnipotence they do not possess. Indeed, it is an essential part of learning always to have a clear awareness of the limitations of the analytical methods one studies, because without it one is apt to become a slave to the techniques, rather than be their master!

THE GREEK ALPHABET

Α	α	alpha
Β	β	beta
Γ	γ	gamma
Δ	δ	delta
Ε	ε	epsilon
Ζ	ζ	zeta
Η	η	eta
Θ	θ	theta
Ι	ι	iota
Κ	κ	kappa
Λ	λ	lambda
Μ	μ	mu
Ν	ν	nu
Ξ	ξ	xi
Ο	o	omicron
Π	π	pi
Ρ	ρ	rho
Σ	σ	sigma
Τ	τ	tau
Υ	υ	upsilon
Φ	ϕ (or φ)	phi
Χ	χ	chi
Ψ	ψ	psi
Ω	ω	omega

A SHORT READING LIST

The interested reader may find the following books of help:

ABADIE, J. (ed.): *Nonlinear Programming*, North-Holland Publishing Company, Amsterdam, 1967. (A collection of papers on certain theoretical and computational aspects of nonlinear programming; Chapter 2, by Abadie, deals with the Kuhn-Tucker theorem in relation to the constraint qualification.)

ALLEN, R. G. D.: *Macro-Economic Theory: A Mathematical Treatment*, St Martin's Press, Inc., New York, 1967. (A comprehensive mathematical treatment of macroeconomic topics, including growth models and cycle models.)

————: *Mathematical Analysis for Economists*, Macmillan & Co., Ltd., London, 1938. (A clear exposition of differential and integral calculus; determinants are discussed, but not matrices; no set theory, and no mathematical programming.)

————: *Mathematical Economics*, 2d ed., St Martin's Press, Inc., New York, 1959. (Discusses a legion of mathematical economic models; explains linear differential and difference equations and matrix algebra.)

ALMON, C.: *Matrix Methods in Economics*, Addison-Wesley Publishing Company, Inc., Reading, Mass., 1967. (Matrix methods are discussed in relation to linear-equation systems, input-output models, linear programming, and nonlinear programming. Characteristic roots and characteristic vectors are also covered.)

BAUMOL, W. J.: *Economic Dynamics: An Introduction*, 3d ed., The Macmillan Company, New York, 1970. (Part IV gives a lucid explanation of simple difference equations; Part V treats simultaneous difference equations; differential equations are only briefly discussed.)

BURMEISTER, E., AND A. R. DOBELL: *Mathematical Theories of Economic Growth*, The Macmillan Company, New York, 1970. (A thorough and systematic exposition of growth models of varying degrees of complexity.)

BUSHAW, D. W., AND R. W. CLOWER: *Introduction to Mathematical Economics*, Richard D. Irwin, Inc., Homewood, Ill., 1957. (The first half of the book is a mathematical treatment of price theory; the second half, a survey of mathematical methods.)

CODDINGTON, E. A., AND N. LEVINSON: *Theory of Ordinary Differential Equations*, McGraw-Hill Book Company, New York, 1955. (A mathematical text on differential equations.)

COURANT, R.: *Differential and Integral Calculus* (trans. E. J. McShane), Interscience Publishers, Inc., New York, vol. I, 2d ed., 1937, vol. II, 1936. (A classic treatise on calculus.)

————, AND F. JOHN: *Introduction to Calculus and Analysis*, Interscience Publishers, Inc., New York, 1965. (An updated version of the preceding title.)

DOMAR, E. D.: *Essays in the Theory of Economic Growth*, Oxford University Press, Fair Lawn, N.J., 1957. (Applications of differential equations to various economic models.)

DORFMAN, R., P. A. SAMUELSON, AND R. M. SOLOW: *Linear Programming and Economic Analysis*, McGraw-Hill Book Company, New York, 1958. (A detailed treatment of linear programming, game theory, and input-output analysis.)

FRISCH, R.: *Maxima and Minima: Theory and Economic Applications* (in collaboration with A. Nataf), Rand McNally & Company, Chicago, Ill., 1966. (A thorough treatment of extremum problems, done primarily in the classical tradition.)

GOLDBERG, S.: *Introduction to Difference Equations*, John Wiley & Sons, Inc., New York, 1958. (With economic applications.)

HADLEY, G.: *Linear Algebra*, Addison-Wesley Publishing Company, Inc., Reading, Mass., 1961. (Covers matrices, determinants, convex sets, etc.)

————: *Linear Programming*, Addison-Wesley Publishing Company, Inc., Reading, Mass., 1962. (A clearly written, mathematically oriented exposition.)

————: *Nonlinear and Dynamic Programming*, Addison-Wesley Publishing Company, Inc., Reading, Mass., 1964. (Covers nonlinear programming, stochastic programming, integer programming, and dynamic programming; computational aspects are emphasized.)

HALMOS, P. R.: *Naive Set Theory*, D. Van Nostrand Company, Inc., Princeton, N.J., 1960. (An informal and, hence, readable introduction to the basics of set theory.)

HENDERSON, J. M., AND R. E. QUANDT: *Microeconomic Theory: A Mathematical Approach*, 2d ed., McGraw-Hill Book Company, New York, 1971. (A comprehensive mathematical treatment of microeconomic topics.)

INTRILIGATOR, M. D.: *Mathematical Optimization and Economic Theory*, Prentice-Hall, Inc., Englewood Cliffs, N.J., 1971. (A thorough discussion of optimization methods, including the classical techniques, linear and nonlinear programming, and dynamic optimization; also applications to the theories of the consumer and the firm, general equilibrium and welfare economics, and theories of growth.)

KEMENY, J. G., J. L. SNELL, AND G. L. THOMPSON: *Introduction to Finite Mathematics*, 2d ed., Prentice-Hall, Inc., Englewood Cliffs, N.J., 1966. (Covers such topics as sets, matrices, probability, and linear programming.)

KOOPMANS, T. C. (ed.): *Activity Analysis of Production and Allocation*, John Wiley & Sons, Inc., New York, 1951. (Contains a number of important papers on linear programming and activity analysis.)

————: *Three Essays on the State of Economic Science*, McGraw-Hill Book Company, New York, 1957. (The first essay contains a good exposition of convex sets; the third essay discusses the interaction of *tools* and *problems* in economics.)

LANCASTER, K.: *Mathematical Economics*, The Macmillan Company, New York, 1968. (A standard reference work on mathematical economics, more up-to-date than R. G. D. Allen's 1959 book. The first three-fifths of the volume deals with economic topics, including optimization, static, and dynamic models; the remainder of the volume presents reviews of mathematical techniques, written rather concisely.)

LEONTIEF, W. W.: *The Structure of American Economy, 1919–1939*, 2d ed., Oxford University Press, Fair Lawn, N.J., 1951. (The pioneering work in input-output analysis.)

———— (ed.): *Studies in the Structure of the American Economy*, Oxford University Press, Fair Lawn, N.J., 1953. (A series of papers on input-output analysis.)

McKINSEY, J. C. C.: *Introduction to the Theory of Games*, McGraw-Hill Book Company, New York, 1952. (An extensive treatment of game theory.)

QUIRK, J., AND R. SAPOSNIK: *Introduction to General Equilibrium Theory and Welfare Economics*, McGraw-Hill Book Company, New York, 1968. (A survey of the subject, using many of the mathematical techniques covered in the present book.)

SAMUELSON, P. A.: *Foundations of Economic Analysis*, Harvard University Press, Cambridge, Mass., 1947. (A classic in mathematical economics, but the reading is very difficult.)

THOMAS, G. B.: *Calculus and Analytic Geometry*, 4th ed., Addison-Wesley Publishing Company, Inc., Reading, Mass., 1968. (A clearly written introduction to calculus.)

VANCE, E. P.: *Modern Algebra and Trigonometry*, 2d ed., Addison-Wesley Publishing Company, Inc., Reading, Mass., 1968. (Covers such topics as real and complex numbers, inequalities, absolute values, and various types of functions.)

VON NEUMANN, J., AND O. MORGENSTERN: *Theory of Games and Economic Behavior*, 3d ed., Princeton University Press, Princeton, N.J., 1953. (The pioneering work in game theory; difficult reading.)

WILLIAMS, J. D.: *The Compleat Strategyst*, rev. ed., McGraw-Hill Book Company, New York, 1965. (A fascinating introduction to game theory.)

YAMANE, T.: *Mathematics for Economists: An Elementary Survey*, 2d ed., Prentice-Hall, Inc., Englewood Cliffs, N.J., 1968. (Comprehensive, yet rather concise, coverage of mathematical topics; very few economic illustrations are given.)

INDEX

Extremum:
    constrained versus free, 373
    global versus local, 246, 649

Facet, 695
Factorial, 268
Factoring:
    of determinant and matrix, 107
    of integrand, 434
    of polynomial, 48
Feasible region, 627
Feasible solution, 627
Final demand, 124
First-derivative test, 247–248
First-order condition, 258, 331, 351, 389, 704
Flow concept, 292, 455
Fluctuation, 533
    (*See also* Time path)
Form, 334
Fraction, 11
Friedman, M., 7
Function, 23–24
    algebraic versus nonalgebraic, 29
    concave versus convex, 255–256
    continuous versus discontinuous, 156–157
    decreasing versus increasing, 181
    explicit versus implicit, 216
    general versus specific, 34–35
    graphical form of, 28, 521
    quasiconcave versus quasiconvex,
      395–397, 732–733
Function-of-function rule, 180

Game, 742
    classification of, 742–746
    and duality, 767–769
    in relation to linear programming, 761–765
    value of, 751
Game theory, fundamental theorem of, 759
Giffen good, 401
Globality theorem, 649
Goldsmith, R., 7
Growth, 291
    continuous versus discrete, 292–293
    negative, 294
    rate of, 291, 317–319

Halfspace, 645
Hessian determinant, 337, 350
    bordered, 385–387
Hessian matrix, 349, 351
Hicks, J. R., 234
Homogeneous-equation system, 118–119, 130
Homogeneous function, 403
    linearly, 404–407
Hyperplane, 644
    supporting, 648
Hypersurface, 34, 346

i, the number, 516
Idempotent matrix, 86, 88, 94
Identity, 10
Identity matrix, 85

Image, 24
    mirror (*see* Mirror image)
Imaginary number, 516
Implicit function, 216
Implicit-function rule, 219–220, 225
Implicit-function theorem, 218, 222–223
    applied to market model, 229, 231
    applied to national-income models,
      225–227, 235
    applied to optimization models, 369–370,
      380–381, 397–398
Income effect, 399
Independence (*see* Dependence)
Indifference curve, 392
    curvature and slope of, 392–394
    and second-order condition, 394
    and shape of utility surface, 394–395
Inequality, 149–150
    solution of, 152–153
Inferior good, 399
Infinite series, 288
Inflection point, 248, 256, 329
Initial condition, 429
Inner product, 66
Input coefficient, 124
Input matrix, 125
Input-output model:
    closed, 130–131
    comparative statics of, 193–194
    dynamic, 612–618
    open, 124–126
    in relation to linear programming, 692–694
    static, 123–127
Integers, 11
Integral, 430, 466
    definite, 440–447
    improper, 448–452
    indefinite, 430–438, 447
    lower versus upper, 444
    particular (*see* Particular integral)
Integral calculus, 428
Integrand, 430
Integrating factor, 483, 484
Integration, 430
    constant of, 430
    limits of, 440
    by parts, 437–438
    rules of, 431–438, 445–446
Intercept:
    horizontal, 302
    vertical, 27
Interest rate, 289
Interior point, 640
Interior solution, 705
Intersection set, 15
Interval, closed versus open, 146
Inventory, 567
Inverse function, 181–182
Inverse-function rule, 182
Inverse matrix, 90–92
    approximation, 128
    finding the, 113–114
    and solution of linear-equation system, 93
Investment, 234
    and capital formation, 454–456
    induced, 588
Irrational number, 11–12

Money:
    demand for, 234
    illusion, 402
    marginal utility of, 392
Monotonic function, 181–182
Multiplier:
    export, 237
    government-expenditure, 192
    income-tax-rate, 192
    interaction of, with accelerator, 588–594
    Lagrange (*see* Lagrange multiplier)
    nonincome-tax, 192

n-space, 74
n-vector, 74
National-income models, 56–58, 121–122, 233–235
    comparative statics of, 191–193, 225–227, 233–237
    dynamic, 588–594
Necessary condition, 96, 721–722
Necessary-and-sufficient condition, 96–97, 722
Negative definiteness, 335
    conditions for, 339, 340, 345
Negative semidefiniteness, 335
    condition for, 345
Neighborhood, 146
Nerlove, M., 566*n*.
Neyman, J., 704*n*.
Nonlinear programming, 698
    in relation to linear programming, 703, 728
Nonnegative combination, 694–695
Nonnegative restriction, 627, 699
Nonsingularity, 90
    conditions for, 97, 109–110
Norm, 129
Normalization of characteristic vector, 342
*n*th-derivative test, 278
Null matrix, 86
Null set, 14
Null vector, 75

Objective function, 244, 626, 699
One-to-one correspondence, 21, 73, 181
Optimal feasible solution, 629
Optimal timing, 312–316
Optimization, 244
    constrained (*see* Constrained optimum)
Ordered *n*-tuple, 63
Ordered pair, 20
Ordinate, 45
Orthant, 639
Orthogonal vectors, 343
Orthonormal vectors, 343
Oscillation, 560
    (*See also* Time path)

Parabola, 27
Parameter, 9
Partial derivative, 184–187
    cross (mixed), 323
    second-order, 323
Partial total derivative, 214–215, 236

Particular integral, 468, 554
    of first-order difference equation, 554–555
    of first-order differential equation, 468, 470
    and intertemporal equilibrium, 474, 504
    of second-order difference equation, 579–580
    of second-order differential equation, 503–505
    of variable-term difference equation, 594–597
    of variable-term differential equation, 540–543
Payoff, 742
    expected, 754
Payoff matrix, 744
    transformation of, 746
Period, 522
Period analysis, 549
Phase, 522
Phase diagram, 493–496, 571–575
Pivoting, 659–663
Polar coordinates, 526
Polynomial function, 26
    continuity of, 157–158
    limit of, 155–156
Positive definiteness, 335
    conditions for, 339, 340, 345
Positive semidefiniteness, 335
    condition for, 345
Power-function rule, 165, 168
Power series, 267
Present value, 293–294
    of cash flow, 456–458
    of perpetual flow, 459
Price discrimination, 359–362
Price expectations, 535
    adaptive, 566–567
Primal program, 670
    in relation to dual program, 671
Primary input, 124
Primitive function, 138
Principal diagonal, 68
Principal minor, 336, 338, 340
    bordered, 388
Product rule, 172–173
Production function, 186
    CES, 417–419
    Cobb-Douglas, 407–410, 415, 419–421
    in linear programming, 684–689
    linearly homogeneous, 404–407
    and returns to scale, 405, 411, 683
Profit, maximization of, 259–262
Pythagoras' theorem, 79, 516

Quadratic equation, 45
Quadratic form, 334, 338, 340
    constrained, 385–386
    sign-definiteness of, 345
Quadratic formula, 46
Quadratic function, 26–27, 34
    versus quadratic equation, 45
Qualifying arc, 717
Quasiconcave function, 395–397, 414, 732–733
Quasiconcave programming, 730
Quasiconvex function, 396–397, 732–733
Quotient rule, 176

Value:
   of function, 24
   of game, 751
   of marginal product, 363
Variable, 9
   choice, 244
   continuous versus discrete, 427–428
   dependent versus independent, 24
   dummy, 653
   endogenous versus exogenous, 9
   slack versus surplus, 653
Vector, 62
   addition, 75
   geometric interpretation of, 73–76
   multiplication, 72–73
Vector space, 77–80

Venn diagram, 16

Walras, L., 53, 56n.
Waugh, F. V., 129n.
Weighted average, 641
Weighted sum of squares, 84

Young's theorem, 324

Zero matrix, 86
Zero-sum game, 745
Zero vector, 76

Euler's thm. total output = sum total paid

⟹ sum of partials × ea. factor = output

Marginal Productivity theory of income dist

$$Y = MPP_1 \cdot X_1 + MPP_2 \cdot X_2 + \ldots + MPP_n \cdot X_n$$

Homogeneous Production f'n

$$f(\lambda K, \lambda L) = \lambda^n f(K, L)$$ n = degree of homogeneity

  n > 1 ~ increasing rts.
  n = 1 ~ constant (linearly hom.)
  n < 1 ~ decreasing rts.

Generalized Cobb Douglas $Q = A K^\alpha L^\beta$

APP, MPP_L

TR

Q

AR = P = D

R.T.S.   TC MR

TVC

dim. P.T.S.

TFC

TR

π   MC

Q

AC
AVC

AFC

Factor MKT,

max π set $MRP_L = MFC$

Find optimal tax Rate 1st max $-\pi$ then max t
with $\bar{Q}$

Hessian > 0 max or min	concave $\cap$ $f''(x) < 0$
$= 0$ inflection pt.	convex $\cup$ $f''(x) > 0$
< 0 saddle pt.	

income elasticity $\varepsilon = \dfrac{MC}{AC}$

max $\Rightarrow$ negative definite $|H_2| > 0$ $H_1 < 0$

implicit f'n rule $\dfrac{\partial z}{\partial x} = \dfrac{-F_x}{F_z}$